FEARS, PHOBIAS, AND RITUALS

FEARS, PHOBIAS, AND RITUALS

Panic, Anxiety, and Their Disorders

ISAAC M. MARKS, M.D., F.R.C.Psych.

Professor of Experimental Psychopathology
Institute of Psychiatry
University of London

New York   Oxford
OXFORD UNIVERSITY PRESS
1987

Oxford University Press

Oxford New York Toronto
Delhi Bombay Calcutta Madras Karachi
Petaling Jaya Singapore Hong Kong Tokyo
Nairobi Dar es Salaam Cape Town
Melbourne Auckland

and associated companies in
Beirut Berlin Ibadan Nicosia

Library of Congress Cataloging-in-Publication Data
Marks, Isaac Meyer.
    Fears, phobias, and rituals.
    Bibliography: p.   Includes index.
    1. Fear.   2. Anxiety.   3. Obsessive-compulsive
neurosis.   4. Psychology, Comparative.   5. Psychiatry, Comparative.
I. Title. [DNLM: 1. Anxiety Disorders.   2. Fear.   WM 172 M346f]
RC535.M373   1987   616.85′223   86-23697
ISBN 0-19-503927-0

9 8 7 6 5 4

Printed in the United States of America
on acid-free paper

Acknowledgments

I am deeply indebted to innumerable friends and colleagues from diverse backgrounds with whom I have enjoyed working and talking over the years. Among the many psychologists, psychiatrists and biologists whose insights helped to shape this volume are David Barlow, Tom Borkovec, Edna Foa, Jeffrey Gray, Michael Gelder, John Greist, Robert Hinde, Ray Hodgson, Tom Insel, Eric Kandel, Malcolm Lader, Peter Lang, Andrew Mathews, Sue Mineka, Arne Öhman, Jack Rachman, Steve Suomi, Adolf Tobeña, Tom Uhde, and George Williams.

For their patient and penetrating comments on parts of the manuscript I wish to thank the following (numbers of the relevant chapters are in parentheses) Maria Avia (8), Christopher Coe (1–4), Robert Creek (16), Bernard Donovan (7), Edna Foa (1–4, 8–10, 13–16), John Greist (9, 10, 13), Irv Gottesman (6), Hugh Gurling (6), Robert Hinde (1–4), Tom Insel (13), Eric Kandel (7), Herb Leiderman (1), Paul Lelliott (9, 10, 13–16), Andrew Mathews (14, 15), Peter McGuffin (6), Sue Mineka (1–4, 8), Homa Noshirvani (9, 10, 13–16), Jackie Persons (1–4), Cliff Preston (8), Eugene Redmond (7), Dick Rodnight (7), Diyanath Samarasingne (9), Per-Olow Sjöden (2), Steve Suomi (1–4), Eric Taylor (5), Lila Tsaltas (8), Adolf Tobeña (1–8), George Williams (1–4), Jeffrey Wine (1–4) and Michael Woodruff (3). It goes without saying that any errors are mine.

The book was begun in 1982 during a year as Fellow at the Center for Advanced Study in the Behavioral Sciences at Stanford, made possible by a grant from the MacArthur Foundation. This facilitated stimulating discussion with leading scholars from varied disciplines. Most of the book was written while working at the Institute of Psychiatry and the Bethlem-Maudsley Hospital, London.

Preface

It was once said that there are three types of psychiatrists and psychologists—those who are brainless, those who are mindless, and those who are both. The first were said to be typified by psychotherapists, the second by biological determinists, and the third by those experimentalists who cling to the black box view of behavior. Such narrowness of discipline is less true today but it is still hard to cross boundaries, partly because the literatures are so separated. Nowhere is the need for better integration of the behavioral sciences more evident than in the study of fear.

This book brings together widely scattered literature on normal fear and phobic and obsessive-compulsive disorders. It supercedes *Fears and Phobias* which was published in 1969. Originally a new edition was intended, but it soon became clear that the field had been so transformed that only a new volume could meld knowledge from the many disciplines bearing on anxiety and panic.

As a result of the strides made over almost two decades, this book is more than twice longer than its predecessor, and even its 2000 references are but a sip of the flood of fine new work. Advances in biology, ethology, genetics, physiology, pharmacology, psychology, and psychiatry have deepened and widened what we know about normal and abnormal fears and rituals. The behavioral revolution has enabled formerly unrelenting phobic and obsessive-compulsive disorders to yield to treatment and—the final sophistication in therapy—has allowed many sufferers to help themselves. Even prevention is in sight.

Crossing interdisciplinary barriers may make it a bit easier for students, clinicians and behavioral scientists from different backgrounds to see what insights they might share. Dealing first with normal fear and then with the clinical syndromes, this book describes the phenomena and how they may be produced and modified. It tries to synthesize naturalistic and experimental work in animals and humans so that experimentalists, ethologists, and clinicians might better understand one another's work. Knowledge has grown about the many influences, from conception onward, on the development of normal and abnormal fear, the nature of fear-related syndromes, how clinicians can alleviate these, and some of the mechanisms involved.

In this book "fear" denotes any response that is usually defensive or protective, along with its bodily and (in humans) subjective concomitants. The subjective elements are a late evolutionary addition to a rich repertoire of protective behavior across phyla. In this broad sense fear includes both the defensive behaviors of invertebrates and the frightened fantasies of man. This general concept of fear contrasts with the way some researchers use the term to indicate purely physiological or subjective components of protective responses but not their accompanying motor behavior, such as avoidance or freezing.

Most of this book concerns fear and anxiety induced by identifiable cues. Because they are so phobialike, taste aversions, fainting at the sight of blood, and obsessive-compulsive syndromes are included even though they may be accompanied by the experience of nausea or distaste rather than of fear. The book excludes general stress and syndromes in which "free-floating" anxiety or spontaneous panic predominate despite their partial overlap with some forms of phobic and obsessive-compulsive disorders. Also omitted are forms of protective behavior like grooming which are unassociated with fear. Nor does the book deal with those types of avoidance, immobility, or attack that are unaccompanied by fear or allied emotions. We are not frightened when we avoid sitting on a pin, nor do we shun food, music, or painting that we dislike or move away from boring conversation at a party. The immobility of sleep or of intense concentration is not part of fear, nor is preattack immobility during hunting.

A broad perspective may make obvious what is hidden from a single viewpoint. Learning theorists took a long time to recognize what ethologists took for granted from the start—that according to their phylogenetic heritage, species differ greatly in their defensive responses and the situations that evoke them. The same stimulus may evoke terror in one species but be ignored by another, and species vary widely in the ease with which they learn to fear particular classes of stimuli. Such phenomena were ignored by learning theorists in their search for universal laws of learning, despite observations of interspecies differences in learning made by Thorndike as long ago as 1898.

The evolutionary background of a species can be critical in interpreting experimental results; for example, visual cues may rapidly induce food aversion in day feeders like quail but taste cues are more effective in the nocturnal rat. Few of the wide variety of natural fear behaviors and fear-evoking stimuli as well as the relevant environmental contexts and internal states of the organism have been studied experimentally. All too commonly a single response, stimulus, context and internal state are studied over a short period of time, with inevitable loss of perspective. Experimentalists can benefit from the insights of biologists, ethologists and clinicians working in the natural environment. Broader vision would bring faster advance.

Human beings are unique in some respects but not in others, and this has to be borne in mind when comparing emotions in man with those in other species. Creative links are possible if we remain aware of our evolutionary heritage of brain and learning mechanisms as well as sociocultural capacities. We should not only compare closely allied species but also remember that behavior can converge across different taxa in the face of common pressures and dangers. Similarly, there are important continuities and discontinuities between normal and clinical phenomena.

Resistance to studying the evolutionary background of human behavior carries a penalty, as Gould (1982) pointed out:

> The myth of ourselves as completely separate creations, divorced from our biological inheritance, has created an egotistical blindness to analogies which open the way to new and important discoveries about how we live and learn. . . . We cannot know where, during the course of evolution, our increasing mental capacities spawned the will that now battles with our genes for control of our behavior . . . [but] our genes still have a powerful hand in our affairs; . . . we should be treating ourselves as one of many interesting species. . . . The conviction that humans are infinitely plastic in all things at all times . . . is especially debilitating and open to ethological revision. . . . We must learn more about the behavioral programs specified in ourselves in order to circumvent those that, in our present social environment, predispose us to inhumane actions (Gould 1982 pp. 541).

And, I would add, to unwarranted fears.

Recent progress has strengthened links among such diverse behavioral sciences as genetics; biology; neuro- and psychophysiology; neurochemistry; psychopharmacology; ethology; developmental, experimental, and clinical psychology; psychiatry; and sociology. These links help us understand mechanisms behind normal fear and anxiety disorders. Clinical phobias have a nonrandom distribution that suggests our phylogenetic predisposition to fear special evolutionary dangers. Examples are infants' fear of strangers rooted in infanticide from the outgroup, toddlers' fears of heights and animals stemming from dangers faced by the young as they become mobile, and agoraphobia, which involves hazards met in venturing outside one's territory.

Other connections soften the distinction between "innate" and "learned" behavior. Many innate releasers of fear and "fixed" fear action patterns noted by early ethologists have been shown by psychologists to be modifiable by experience. Behavior with a genetic base thus need not be immutable in the way that was once thought. Conversely, not all effects of experience are reversible; early visual deprivation can lead to lasting structural changes in the optical system of kittens.

Interdisciplinary insights can thus connect apparently unrelated events. The tendency for sensitization to be associated with intermittent stimulation, and tolerance or habituation with continuous stimulation, is a widespread phenomenon seen in the acquisition and extinction not only of fear and rituals but also of epilepsy, drug addiction, and allergies. Understanding the influence of neuropeptides on fear may help us explain some mysteries about the onset and fluctuation of clinical phobias and rituals. Treatment research into these problems using antidepressant drugs and behavioral methods suggests better ways to classify those disorders and hints at biochemical substrates that may be involved. Knowing that withdrawal from noxious stimulation, habituation to repeated stimulation, and simple learning are all already present in unicellular protozoa has led to a search for similar cellular mechanisms across phyla that mediate withdrawal from danger. Cell biology is linking up with psychology and even psychotherapy in elucidating the molecular biology of defensive and other learning.

Some defensive mechanisms may be as fundamentally similar across phyla as the many metabolic reactions that we share with other taxa (Schopf 1978). Our ability to obtain energy by glycolysis—breaking down glucose into pyruvate—is shared with anaerobic bacteria and evolved more than 1.5 billion years ago. With more recently evolved aerobic organisms we share a newer more efficient way of obtaining energy by respiration utilizing oxygen. This still begins with the ancient anaerobic process of glycolysis but thereafter continues as the citric acid cycle of reactions that break down pyruvate and incorporate oxygen to produce carbon dioxide and water. Respiration became possible once plants evolved a capacity for photosynthesis, which released free oxygen that accumulated in the atmosphere and water. The same pattern of early anaerobic followed by later aerobic steps is seen in the reaction sequences used by our bodies to synthesize sterols and fatty acids.

A common metabolism leads to common dangers. Cyanide poisons protozoa as much as it does people because it inhibits similar respiratory processes. Oxygen is vital for respiration and therefore for protozoa and people, but it is a poison for anaerobes that do not respire.

Our layered evolutionary history might be read not only in our basic metabolism (and embryology—it has long been accepted that ontogeny partly recapitulates phylogeny) but also in our psychophysiology and behavior. Ancient neuronal processes of habituation and sensitization may be widespread across taxa (see Chapter 7) and superimposed on these in younger species like humans may be newer neural mechanisms of defensive learning.

In the area of fear behavior the move has hardly begun from natural history into quantitative evolutionary biology. Little is known about the extent to which fear repertoires have been shaped by strategies like selfishness, altruism, cooperation and nepotism, all of which affect reproductive success. A beginning is the demonstration that nepotism predicts the frequency of some alarm calls from mammals. Stranger fear in infants may have evolved as a protection against abuse and infanticide by conspecifics behaving selfishly.

The use of terms such as strategy, ploy, selfishness, and nepotism does not imply that animals make conscious choices. These terms are shorthand expressions to indicate mechanisms by which natural selection might work—animals behave *as if* they are selfish, altruistic, and so on. Strategies are programs, recipes or subroutines for action that animals carry out in the way a computer obeys its program (Dawkins 1982). Natural selection can be imagined as acting on a pool of alternative strategies of defensive behavior. Individual organisms are temporary executors and propagators of these strategies. Those strategies which win out when individuals compete with copies of themselves are evolutionary stable strategies (Maynard Smith 1978).

There is an interesting imbalance in the literature on defensive behavior. Textbooks of ethology usually devote little space to the subject and few ethologists review the area, despite their numerous articles on various aspects of fear. In contrast, for experimental psychologists and psychiatrists fear is a favorite topic, one that has been reviewed many times and forms a substantial proportion of the entire literature.

One point is neglected in most writings. Fear is traditionally seen as selected by pressure to escape predators of other species. This is, of course, vital, but an additional crucial selection pressure tends to be played down in the shaping of fear—that from conspecifics. Anyone watching groups of mice, monkeys or men interacting can see that in everyday life most fear reactions are shown to conspecifics rather than to other species. Social influences have probably been far more important in the evolution of fear than the attention devoted to it might suggest.

The literature relevant to fear has grown enormously since 1969, when the author published *Fears and Phobias* as an attempt at synthesizing what was then known. A computer search for articles from 1967 to 1984 with "phobia," "fear," "avoidance or escape behavior," or "obsessive-compulsive" in their titles yielded 11,000, and recently 1,000 articles a year have been appearing. In the last 7 years more than 46 books* have been published by professionals about fear and fear-related syndromes, if we exclude the many new volumes dealing solely with stress and nonsituational anxiety. Only the book edited by Sluckin (1979) united some of the work of ethologists, experimentalists, and clinicians, whose disciplines tend to stay separate instead of fertilizing one another. The area continues to need more integration.

No one has time to review 1000 articles a year. I have concentrated on the most careful observations and experiments I could find, trying to obtain a broad interdisciplinary perspective on fear. My training as an experimental and clinical psychiatrist working closely with psychologists influenced selection of the material, and most of the sources cited are regretfully in English. The venture into unfamiliar fields led not only to new insights but also to the inevitable pitfalls that await the innocent abroad.

Clinicians reading this book might wonder why on earth they should read about protozoa or antelope—what have these to do with patients? And for their part, ethologists or experimental psychologists might not bother to progress from the first two parts of the book to the clinical sections. With their antennae out, however, clinicians reading about the ethology, psychology, genetics, and physiology of normal fear may find echoes of problems described by their patients, while basic scientists who seek models of clinical syndromes will find salient clinical features that need to be incorporated into their models if those are to be at all realistic.

---

*For example, Agras 1985; Ballenger 1984; Bamber 1979; Beck & Emery 1985; Boudewyns & Shipley 1983; Boulougouris 1982; Boulougouris & Rabavilas 1977; Burrows et al. 1984; Chambless & Goldstein 1983; Clarke & Wardman 1985; Dupont 1982; Emmelkamp 1983; Eth & Pynoos 1985; Figley 1985; Gittelman 1986; Goodwin 1983; Gray 1982a & 1987; Hand and Wittchen 1986; Hersov & Berg 1980; Insel et al. 1984; Jenike et al. 1986; Jones et al. 1985; Kelly 1980; King & Hamilton 1986; Marks 1978 & 1981; Matthews et al. 1981; Mavissakalian & Barlow 1981; Mavissakalian et al. 1985; Mitchell 1982; Morris & Kratochwil 1983; Neuman 1985; Paolino 1984; Pasnau 1984; Rachman 1978; Rachman & Hodgson 1980; Scrignar 1983; Sheehan 1984; Sluckin 1979; Sonnenberg et al. 1985; Thorpe & Burns 1983; Trimble 1981a; Tuma & Maser 1985; Van der Kolk 1984; Yaryura-Tobias & Neziroglu 1983; Zane & Milt 1984.

Readers searching for fresh perspectives may see links between the habituation of protozoa to withdrawal from noxious media, quail escaping from a hawk, chaffinches mobbing an owl, and phobics and obsessive-compulsives responding to exposure treatment. Clinicians and neurophysiologists might consider potential connections between tonic immobility in seized animals, freezing panic in agoraphobics, and the fainting of blood-injury phobics. Ethologists, social psychologists, and clinicians could think about the diverse mechanisms behind birds' avoidance of eyespots on the wings of insects, staring as a threat in canids and primates, the widespread human use of magical defenses against the evil eye, and social phobics' panic on being stared at. Child psychiatrists, developmental psychologists, and sociobiologists may see a connection between the widespread fear of strangers in human infants and infant abuse and killing found in nonhuman primates and other species. Primatologists and behavioral psychotherapists might compare stereotypies in monkeys and rituals in humans.

A host of analogies present themselves when we see that humans are not only unique but also have features from a heritage shared with other species. Some analogies will be fruitful, others less so. Juxtaposing related fields can stimulate controlled speculation, testing of which will show what is productive. New ideas are emerging that may lead to better models uniting separate disciplines and explaining formerly obscure features of fears and rituals.

This book reports advances on a broad front, dealing with normal fear in the first half and clinical syndromes in the second. It describes (chapter numbers in parentheses) the natural features of everyday fear in animals and man and its evolutionary context (1), the cues that evoke fear (2), the varied forms of fear behavior in different species (3), and its adaptation to different environments (4). Following chapters trace how normal fear develops in the young (5), genetic influences on this process and on phobic and obsessive-compulsive disorders (6), and the physiology of fear and panic (7) and how they are learned (8). The second half reviews the classification of clinical syndromes of anxiety and panic disorder (9), and the main phenomena of agoraphobia (10), social and specific phobias and touch and taste aversions (11), illness phobias, traumatic phobias (post-traumatic stress disorder) and phobias and rituals in children (12), and obsessive-compulsive disorder (13). Finally there are 3 chapters on treatment. One concerns the principles of psychological treatment (14) and another their detailed application to particular syndromes both in adults and in children (15). The last chapter reviews the many controlled studies of drugs in these conditions, and psychosurgery and other physical treatments (16).

Contents

ABBREVIATIONS IN THE TEXT

bz	benzodiazepine
CS	conditioned stimulus
e	self-exposure homework between sessions
ê	anti-exposure homework between sessions
E	therapist-aided live exposure
ECG	electrocardiogram
ECT	electroconvulsive therapy (EST)
EEG	electroencephalogram
EMG	electromyogram
ER	evoked phobic or oc response
ES	evoking stimulus that brings on phobias and/or rituals
GAD	generalized anxiety disorder
GP	general practitioner
GSR	galvanic skin resistance (related to skin conductance)
HR	heart rate
MAOI	monoamine oxidase inhibitor
oc	obsessive-compulsive
OCD	obsessive-compulsive disorder
phobic-ocs	phobic and obsessive-compulsive patients
rp	response prevention
SC	skin conductance (related to GSR)
US	unconditioned stimulus

(Further abbreviations in Chapter 14 are explained in the text.)

I

NORMAL FEAR

1

Fear, Defense, and Evolution

NORMAL FEAR AND ALLIED EMOTIONS IN HUMANS

Function of Fear

> Men, during numberless generations, have endeavored to escape from their enemies or danger by headlong flight, or by violently struggling with them; and such great exertions will have caused the heart to beat rapidly, the breathing to be hurried, the chest to heave, and the nostrils to be dilated. As these exertions have often been prolonged to the last extremity, the final result will have been utter prostration, pallor, perspiration, trembling of all the muscles, or their complete relaxation. And now, whenever the emotion of fear is strongly felt, though it may not lead to any exertion, the same results tend to reappear, through the force of inheritance and association. . . . [T]he involuntary bristling of the hair (in animals) serves, together with certain involuntary movements, to make them appear terrible to their enemies; and as the same involuntary and voluntary actions are performed by animals nearly related to man, we are led to believe that man has retained through inheritance a relic of them, now become useless. . . . [T]he minute unstriped muscles, by which the hairs thinly scattered over man's almost naked body are erected, still contract under the same emotions, namely, terror and rage, which cause the hairs to stand on end in the lower members of the Order to which man belongs."
> (Darwin 1872 pp. 307–309)

Fear is a vital evolutionary legacy that leads an organism to avoid threat, and has obvious survival value. It is an emotion produced by the perception of present or impending danger and is normal in appropriate situations. Without fear few would survive long under natural conditions. Fear girds our loins for rapid action in the face of danger and alerts us to perform well under stress. It helps us fight the enemy, drive carefully, parachute safely, take exams, speak well to a critical audience, keep a foothold in climbing a mountain.

In its less extreme form fear can be not only useful but also enjoyable. Many people actively seek out and enjoy the fearful thrill of mastering danger. Racing car drivers, bull fighters, and mountaineers willingly expose themselves to extreme hazards. Thousands of spectators throng to take vicarious pleasure in the tension of dangerous sports. Millions of dollars are earned from enjoyment of the suspense of thriller films and books.

There seems to be an optimal amount of fear for good performance; too little and we risk being careless, too much and we react clumsily. Trainee parachutists perform poorly if they are overly frightened (Walk 1956), and even trained paratroopers may "lose their nerve" and become too afraid to jump (*The Times,* June 2 and 3, 1966). Soldiers under bombardment may vomit, defecate, and become so paralyzed with fear that they fail to take shelter or to move those people for whom they are responsible into safer areas. Actors and public speakers can be so terrified that they forget their lines.

Fear can follow rather than precede danger. In a sudden crisis quick action is needed to avert disaster, and we may become aware of fear only several hours after the worst danger has passed. This is well documented in cases of soldiers and air crew after combat and in civilians who have coped with bad accidents, fire, and earthquakes.

Features of Fear

Like other emotions, fear is a package of reactions that tend to occur together simultaneously or sequentially. These include visible behavioral expression, an inner feeling, and accompanying physiological changes (Landis 1964). In humans as well as in animals, two obvious behavioral expressions of fear present a striking contrast (Miller 1951). One is the tendency to freeze and become mute, which reaches its extreme form in death feigning. The opposite is to startle, scream, and run away from the source of danger. Behavior may shift rapidly from one pattern to the other when a frightened person first freezes and then suddenly scurries for shelter.

With strong fear there are unpleasant feelings of terror, an urge to run and hide, to cry, a pounding heart, tense muscles, trembling, liability to startle, dryness of the throat and mouth, a sinking feeling in the stomach, nausea, perspiration, an urge to urinate and defecate, irritability, anger, difficulty in breathing, tingling of the hands and feet, weakness or even paralysis of the limbs, a sense of faintness or falling, and a sense of unreality or of being distant from the event. Fear that continues for a long time leads to tiredness with difficulty in sleeping and bad dreams, restlessness, being easily startled, loss of appetite, aggression, and avoidance of further novel or tension-producing situations (Wickert 1947).

The many physiological counterparts to fear sensations and behavior have a sympathetic bias similar to that found in anger. These include a pale sweaty skin, hair standing on end, dilation of the pupils, rapid breathing and heart rate, rising blood pressure, increased blood flow through the muscles, and contractions of the bladder and rectum.

Like other emotions, fear produces biochemical changes that are detectable in a few minutes. Among these is secretion of adrenalin (epinephrine) by the adrenal glands and noradrenalin (norepinephrine) at peripheral nerve endings of the autonomic nervous system, and an increase in free fatty acids and corticosteroids in the plasma.

Emotional language reflects the way we experience fear with our bodies (Leff 1974):

> "My heart was in my mouth as I strode up the driveway. Although I hated his guts, my stomach turned over as I approached his house. I knocked on the door and my heart leapt as I heard his footsteps inside. Shivers went down my back as he fumbled with the catch; then as he flung open the door my skin crawled at the sight of him.
>
> "I speak from the heart when I say I can't stomach you," I blurted out. He laughed sneeringly and I felt my gorge rise.
>
> "You're a pain in the neck," he growled. His retort stuck in my throat.
>
> "I am here because of the woman whose heart you have broken," I asserted, and the thought of her brought a lump to my throat. He turned his back on me so suddenly that I almost jumped out of my skin. My brain reeled as I. . . ."

Terms and Definitions

A rich vocabulary for a phenomenon reflects its importance in everyday life, as we can see from the many words Eskimos have for snow. There is no shortage of expressions for fear and similar emotions. They convey subtle nuances of intensity, duration, surprise, pain, tremor, and diffuseness of the danger as well as past, present, and future loss. The reader can undoubtedly add more terms to a list like the following: solicitude, concern, misgiving, qualm, worry, disquiet, uneasiness, wariness, nervousness, edginess, jitteriness, apprehension, anxiety, trepidation, scare, alarm, fright, dread, agitation, anguish, panic, terror, horror, sensitivity; being pent up, troubled, unnerved, upset, distraught, aghast, or threatened; defensiveness, consternation, perturbation, disturbance, distress.

The interrelationships of emotions are evident in the associations such words prompt in normal individuals. In one study, 50 Americans had many associations common to both fear and to anxiety and others distinctive to each (Davitz 1970). Compared with anxiety, fear had rather more physiological associations and its cause was more obvious.

Definitions may clarify some of the ambiguities of terms used to describe fear and allied states, though many of the following labels are not mutually exclusive. *Fear* is the usually unpleasant feeling that arises as a normal response to realistic danger. *Anxiety* is an emotion similar to fear, but arising without any objective source of danger. A *phobia* is fear of a situation that is out of proportion to its danger, can neither be explained nor reasoned away, is largely beyond voluntary control, and leads to avoidance of the feared situation. *Phobic anxiety* is a subjective component of a phobia—the emotion that occurs in response to a phobic situation, object, or fantasy.

Panic denotes a sudden upsurge of acute intense fear, often associated with frantic attempts to escape (see Chapter 9). *Startle* is momentary fear of a sudden stimulus, and the *orienting reflex* is a brief physiological response to a novel stimulus. *Timidity* indicates a lasting tendency to show fearful behavior easily. In psychological writings *trait anxiety* resembles timidity and indicates a habitual tendency to be anxious over a long period of time in many situations—"I usually feel anxious"—whereas *state anxiety* refers to anxiety felt at a particular moment—"I'm anxious right now." Trait and state anxiety merge into one another at some point, as do the terms chronic and acute. *Stress* describes any condition likely to overload or strain an individual, and *threat* is the focused stress of immediate danger from an identifiable source.

Obsessions (ruminations) are the insistent recurrence of unwanted frightening thoughts despite active resistance against their intrusion; for instance, a mother may be plagued by terrifying urges to strangle her baby in its sleep. Obsessive[1] thoughts are often associated with *compulsive rituals*—repetitive actions that some individuals feel compelled to carry out against their better judgment, for example, a man might wash his hands a hundred times a day because he feels dirty, although he knows that his feeling and actions are irrational. Anxiety usually arises if the ritual is not completed, and situations that evoke the ritual are avoided when possible, as with phobias. Both obsessive thoughts and compulsive rituals tend to occur more in people who have always had *meticulous* and *perfectionist* personalities, otherwise known as *obsessive-compulsive traits;* these are normal behaviors (cleanliness, tidiness, or punctuality, for instance) carried out to unusual perfection.

Preoccupations are persistent ruminations without any sense of resistance: an adolescent may worry incessantly that he is sexually inadequate. *Superstitious fears and taboos* are collective beliefs shared by members of a culture about danger, such as the notion that bad luck follows walking under a ladder. *Sensitive ideas of reference* are beliefs that the actions and words of other people or forces refer to oneself when they do not; they can cause intense fear, and when held with tenacity become *paranoid delusions. Aversions* used to be synonymous with fears in the eighteenth century but today describe intense dislike (rather than fear) of touching, hearing, or tasting things that many of us are indifferent to—for example, the scraping of a knife against a plate, the screech of chalk against a blackboard; the feel of velvet, a peach, or a tennis ball; the taste of certain foods.

A *counterphobia* is the attraction some people have to a phobic situation or object so that they seek it out repeatedly, perhaps in an attempt to master fear. One example is that of a height-phobic woman who would not even ride on elevators and who subsequently became an air hostess (Frazier and Carr 1967).

A *soteria* (Laughlin 1956) is the opposite of a phobic stimulus and comes from the Greek word for a celebration of recovery from illness or escape from danger. It has also been called a Linus blanket, after the Schultz cartoon strip character, or, a transitional object. Soteria refers to objects that give people disproportionate comfort or pleasure; (for example the rags, bits of blanket, or stuffed animals that young children carry around with them). Their loss may

---

[1]As an adjective obsessive is used rather than obsessional in line with its accepted shorter form in the name of the syndrome obsessive-compulsive disorder (OCD)—and in light of the fact that compulsional is never used.

provoke a paroxysm of grief. Adults feel similarly about talismans and charms. Phobics may develop a soterial attachment to something that may reduce their fear even though it has never actually been used: they may keep sedative drugs or a bottle of smelling salts in their pocket in case they feel anxious or in danger of fainting.

The word fear comes from the Old English *faer* for sudden calamity or danger, and was later used to describe the ensuing emotion. (Oxford English Dictionary [OED 1956]). In Middle English the word continued to denote alarm or dread, as it still does today. Anxiety has its etymological origin in a Greek root meaning "to press tight" or "to strangle" (Lewis 1967). The Latin *anxius* and its derivatives all imply narrowness or construction, usually with discomfort. They denote distress, disquiet, and sadness rather than the uncertainty and fear denoted by the modern term. Relevant English terms include *ange* (trouble, affliction); *anger* (trouble, sorrow—now obsolete); *anguish* (excruciating or oppressive bodily pain or severe mental suffering); and *anxious* which has three definitions: (1) troubled in mind about some uncertain event, being in painful suspense; (2) full of desire and endeavor; solicitous, earnestly desirous; (3) (since at least 1661) agitation and depression, with a sensation of precordial tightness and distress (Lewis 1967; OED).

Panic was in use by 1603 (OED); it derived from the Greek rural deity Pan, who later personified nature. Pan presided over shepherds and flocks and delighted in rural music but was also said to produce abrupt and inexplicable terror. Phobia is from the Greek God Phobos, who provoked terror and flight in one's enemies; its derivative, phobia, acquired its present meaning about 1801 (OED).

FEAR AS AN EMOTIONAL RESPONSE SYNDROME

Emotions such as fear are response syndromes that are not defined by any single feeling or behavior but can be recognized from their typical evoking stimuli, response patterns (phenomenology), and courses (Averill et al. 1969; Lader & Marks 1971). Each emotion has its own varying bundle of features. The responses that make up an emotion tend to occur concurrently and/or sequentially but are often poorly correlated with one other. They can be conveniently grouped as *cognitive-subjective* (appraisal of danger with an accompanying sensation of fear), *motor-behavioral* (certain-action tendencies), and *physiological* (changes that mobilize the body for action).

Some aspects of what we fear and how we show it are biologically determined, while others are influenced by individual and group experience. Phylogenesis predisposes a species to respond to threat appropriately; socialization and individual experience build on that predisposition to shape fear responses especially typical for a particular group and individual. Biological facets predominate in fears such as that occurring with a sudden fall, while individual and cultural experience are more important in others, such as fear of a boss. According to Averill and coworkers (1969), "emotional reactions can be likened to a rope with one end anchored in the biological and the other in the cultural. No single strand (type of reaction) runs through the entire rope yet they are interwoven to form a single concept—emotional response."

Relationships Among Different Components of Fear

In an emergency we defend ourselves quickly before feeling any fear—for example, when jumping out of the path of a car rushing at us unexpectedly— and only worry and quake later, after completing our escape, when the import of what has happened has sunk in. Motor escape can occur immediately, but it takes somewhat longer for subjective feelings to arise. Different components of defense may be mediated by different neural pathways operating at different speeds, though triggered simultaneously by the same stimulus. Alternatively, it may be possible for some components to arise only after others precede them. In the crayfish even different motor components of escape are mediated by different neural mechanisms (see Chapter 7). In humans yet more varied neurophysiological pathways can be expected to mediate the many manifestations of fear.

Detection of threat involves a continual searching for, sifting through, and evaluation of cues, with fluctuation in fear reflecting continual appraisal and reappraisal. A given situation may be regarded as threatening for a variety of reasons. In soldiers undergoing paratroop training there was greater fear of failure than of physical injury, and the two fears were not closely linked (Basowitz et al. 1955).

Fear can start with the subjective perception of danger, followed quickly by physiological changes. The reverse can also happen, as after the injection of adrenaline. Tachycardia can lead to fear as well as cause it. In two patients increased beta-adrenergic activity led to severe tachycardia, palpitations, and anxiety (Frohlich et al. 1966). The physiological changes in turn can enhance the subjective sensation of fear.

Discordance Between Different Components of Fear

As we have seen, the different components of fear need not covary well. A woman may claim that she feels frightened yet look calm and show no physiological changes; she may appear agitated and show gross physiological signs of fear while maintaining that she is not fearful; or say she is frightened and look it, yet show no autonomic changes. Theoretically there are seven possible fear patterns (Table 1.1). The frequency of each of these patterns and the conditions that generate them remain to be determined experimentally. Pattern 1 is the commonest in marked fear. Here there is congruence (concordance, synchrony) between subjective, behavioral, and physiological features of fear. All the other patterns are discordant (desynchronous). Pattern 2 may occur when the patient is on beta-blockers that dampen down sympathetic responses, and presumably occurs after sympathectomy or cervical cord lesions. At times the absence of physiological indices of fear may seem inexplicable, although the

Table 1.1 Main possible patterns of fear

Component	1	2	3	4	5	6	7
Subjective-cognitive	+	+	+	−	−	−	+
Motor-behavioral	+	+	−	+	−	+	−
Physiological	+	−	−	+	+	−	+

Source: Lader & Marks 1971.

subject is in fact responding physiologically in ways that are not visible or being measured at the time (for instance, salivation and fast, shallow breathing rather than tachycardia and sweating). Fearful subjects might also show pattern 2 if they have a high threshold for autonomic responses to emotion in general or fear in particular. A related explanation would account for pattern 3, which is common in mild fear that is felt but not betrayed by motor or physiological signs.

The states labeled as stoicism or belle indifference can yield patterns 4, 5, and 6. Finally, patterns 3, 5, and 7 could result from self-control learned for cultural or personal reasons. A possible sequence is of a subject starting life with pattern 1, being taught to suppress outward signs of anxiety to show pattern 7, and later learning to suppress both physiological effects (pattern 3) and subjective sensations (pattern 5). According to Lazarus and coworkers (1968),

> [t]he precise pattern of agreement and disagreement between different components of anxiety contains within it information about the kind of transaction which a person is having within himself and with various aspects of his environment. A particular pattern might be the characteristic way for that person to respond physiologically or result from his attempt to disguise his anxiety, to simulate it, or to make his response conform to what is acceptable for him and his culture.

FEAR RESPONSES ACROSS SPECIES

Perspective on human fear comes from studying other animals. Evolutionary pressures have led to a large array of fear reactions across species without which they risk extinction. Fear behavior removes, protects, or defends the animal from present or anticipated threat. A fear repertoire comprises interrelated responses, each of which may be elicited by slightly different conditions and occur at the same time or in succession.

Fear responses in animals include expressive movements, odors, and sounds, which derive from intention movements and physiological changes such as increased respiration and heart rate (Archer 1979). Increased defecation and urination occurs in many species, including man. When in terror "a dog will throw himself down, howl, and void his excretions" (Darwin 1872). In vertebrates expressive movements of fear and of anger include erection of hair in mammals, feathers in birds, and fins in fish (Darwin 1872). In mammals the ears are often drawn back or erected, and in many primates the eyebrows may be raised and the eyes averted, lips retracted, teeth bared and chattering, and mouth opened widely in a fear grimace (see Chapter 3). The extent to which signal movements are adapted to convey information about the state of the signaler is a subject of much debate (Hinde 1981).

No single behavior is invariably a sign of fear in any species. We interpret the behavior functionally from its form and appropriateness for the situation, given the typical behavioral repertoire of that species in its natural habitat (Archer 1979). When several protective responses occur together, we can more confidently label them as fear behavior than we can any one response. When only one or two of these are present, their meaning is less clear. A baboon may move rapidly in anger as well as in fear, and a young chick may utter a distress call when it is cold or hungry as well as frightened. However, if an animal both gives an alarm call and rushes away from a stimulus then it is more probably frightened than in another mood; in other words, in this case the mediating mechanisms are more likely to be those involved in fear than in other patterns of behavior.

When several elements from fear or another mood repertoire are present, they seem to be recognized by other experienced conspecifics. Songbirds, for instance, have about 20 distinct innate calls to signal stress, alarm, hunger, threat, and so on (Gould 1982, p. 293). Many of these calls are accompanied by particular body postures—tail up, head feathers ruffled, wings quivering. These trigger appropriate responses in fellow birds.

We cannot assume that only one stimulus instigates a given behavior or that a single fear state leads to simultaneous activation of all forms of fear. Fear behavior describes a broad range of reactions to threatening stimuli by diverse forms of escape, immobility, or even attack, together with expressive responses and social signals, plus direct inhibition and facilitation of other behavior. Species and also individuals vary in the fear responses they show at different ages and in different contexts. A given animal will vary its behavior according to its environment and internal state. Many fear responses also occur at the same time as other emotional reactions. Such a variety of integrated fear responses available for different situations implies complex regulation by several control systems.

Explanations of biological phenomena such as fear need to distinguish between two levels of causation (Nesse 1984). Proximate (immediate) causes are those which induce an event in an individual organism—for example, those making an animal frightened at a particular time. Ultimate (evolutionary) causes are those which elicit the capacity for such fearful behavior in all members of the species; these causes are commonly discussed in terms of their survival value to individuals of that species in the face of specific forces of natural selection. This approach is inherent in Hinde's (1982) citation of Tinbergen's four questions about any behavior: its immediate and evolutionary causes and its ontogenetic and phylogenetic history.

Ultimately the selection and strength of a particular fear reaction shown at a given time depend upon the evolutionary history of the animal's species and its genetic endowment and historical background. More proximally they depend upon variables governing the ongoing stream of behavior such as the animal's long- and short-term internal state, the nature of the fear-evoking stimulus and its context, and the interval since that stimulus appeared. Such proximal features can be seen within the context of the overall flow of behavior.

Fear and the Stream of Behavior

Patterns of fear behavior arise within a broad stream of functional actions. Animals usually do one thing at a time in functional sequences if strongly activated, unless forced to change by other more powerful stimuli. The sequences tend to have characteristic durations of a few minutes or several hours. Over the course of a day an animal does various things depending upon its internal motivation. Spontaneous search and increased readiness to respond to different stimuli are functions of this motivation, and its variation with time results in a rich behavioral repertoire (Tinbergen 1952).

Functional sequences of behavior (or mood repertoires) are usually defined in terms of their apparent goals (feeding, aggression; grooming, defense). Each goal might be attained in a number of ways: hence defense might include withdrawal, immobility, appeasement, and even attack. We should distinguish here between (1) *goal,* the end state towards which an *individual's* behavior is directed and which, when achieved, switches that behavior off (for instance, the goal of a man running away from a fire is to reach a place where he will not be burned alive); and (2) *function,* the beneficial biological consequences through which natural selection acts to maintain that behavior in the repertoire of the *species* in question (Hinde, personal communication, 1982) (for instance, running away from overwhelming threat enhances the reproductive fitness of people who do so). The functional sequence engaged in can be stimulated by external or internal factors.

External stimuli for defense include morphological, behavioral, and other cues, some of which are frightening for all species and others for only a few (see Chapter 2). An example of a frightening species-specific morphological cue from a conspecific is the red breast of the male chaffinch. If the normally olive-brown breast of a female chaffinch is dyed red, undyed females and even some males avoid it; the red-breasted female then attacks and dominates them, even though it might otherwise have submitted without fighting. Hand-reared females that had never seen adult males avoided and were dominated by females with a red-dyed breast, showing that their respect for this morphological cue did not depend on social experience of males (Marler 1955). The chaffinch, like many other birds, is also frightened of morphological aspects of predators such as owls, which in this case evoke the aggressive defense of mobbing (see Chapter 3).

The longer and more frequently dangerous stimuli are present during a species' existence, the greater the pressure from natural selection for defenses against those stimuli to be built into that species as innate responses. A step short of this is for the stimuli to become prepotent cues for fear after only minimal experience; this seems to be the case in many human fears (see Chapter 8). Characteristic structural and behavioral releasers of defense responses have been called "sign stimuli," and these can be modified by experience. Even innate releasers of fear may soon be habituated to, while formerly neutral stimuli can become the signal for danger.

Internal factors can cause the same stimulus to evoke different fear responses at different times. Change in fear repertoires may be temporary and reversible; these are usually called motivational, provided they do not reflect changes in the sense organs or effector organs (Hinde 1982). Strong motivation is inferred from marked response to weak stimuli, and this is partly under hormonal control. When lasting change in behavior follows experience, this is usually called learning and is thought to reflect a more durable internal change than motivation.

The defensive and other functional sequences of movements evoked by external and internal cues are as characteristic for a species as are its structural features. Such action patterns are readily recognizable "melodies" within the stream of behavior and can be treated like morphological characters (Hinde 1982; Lorenz 1981). Fear patterns are more similar in related than in unrelated species, allowing a behavioral taxonomy that parallels the morphological one. The more behavioral resemblances there are between species, the closer they are likely to be in evolutionary terms, though convergent evolution from similar ecological pressures has to be excluded and is less likely if the shared features are numerous and diverse.

Species-characteristic repertoires of movement used to be called "fixed action patterns" (Lorenz 1937, cited by Hinde 1982) but are in fact quite flexible in "higher" species and in humans may be extremely complex, though still remaining recognizable as belonging to one or other of a large but finite number of behavioral repertoires. Recognition that there is some variability in even the most stereotyped movements led Barlow (1977) to suggest the alternative term "*modal* action pattern" to describe movements that are indivisible into meaningful smaller units and are typical of, but not invariably shown by all, members of the taxon in question.

The meshing of fear responses with other repertoires in the behavioral stream has been analyzed for the male chaffinch (Hinde 1982). At the start of courtship it has coexisting tendencies to attack and to flee from the female, along with a small inclination toward sexual behavior. As courtship proceeds, aggression decreases, and just before copulation sexual actions increase and the main conflict is between flight and sex. After dismounting the male chaffinch often gives an alarm call of the kind usually evoked by a bird of prey.

Another combination of repertoires is seen in the head-forward threat posture of chaffinches. This combines a component of flight (sleeking of the body feathers plus flexing of the legs) and of attack (sleeking of the head feathers plus slight raising of the wings). This threat posture is seen during encounters over food in winter and during territorial boundary disputes.

Escape and attack commonly alternate in quick succession, so together they have been termed *agonistic behavior* (Barlow 1981). This sequence is common in humans. In animals that grow in a social group, it emerges early. It can lead to dominance relations among nursing kittens, puppies, swine, and nestling birds, often while they are so young that their eyes are still shut. In chicks escape and attack appear separately and are subsequently integrated. In young cichlid fish some of the numerous modal action patterns of agonistic behavior emerge singly, others in clusters.

The type of fear behavior shown depends upon several factors. First is the type of functional sequence being disturbed. In voles and chicks, fleeing is more probable after disturbance during locomotion, but freezing is more likely after threat while the animals are still (Archer 1979). Another factor is distance of the animal from the frightening stimulus (Ratner 1967); certain animals freeze if the predator is some way off, escape if it is nearer, attack if cornered, and go into tonic immobility if actually caught. Sex of the animal may also be relevant: female rats, for example, are more prone to active escaping and male rats to immobility (Archer 1979).

Intensity of fear behavior varies with the phase of activity at which the interruption occurs and with previous experience of danger. Chicks startle more at the end of a bout of preening than at the beginning (Archer 1979). Although the "seet" alarm call of the adult great tit causes nestlings to cease begging, this effect is reduced just before feeding and after repeated exposure to artificial sounds resembling alarm calls, which presumably indicates that habituation has occurred; in contrast, the calls have great impact on the nestlings after simulated attack (Hinde 1982). Defensive behavior increases at times of greatest danger. After a raccoon's nightly raids, breeding colonies of the gull *Larus delawarensis* panicked on subsequent nights but not during the days (Curio 1976).

Weak fear-evoking stimuli can be generally arousing and facilitate nonfearful behavior, while strong fear-evoking stimuli may compete with it (Archer 1979). Mild fear can *enhance* eating, drinking, and sexual behavior in rats and can increase sexual stimulation in gulls, dogs, monkeys, and man (Archer 1979; Hinde 1970; see also Chapter 9). However, serious danger demands immediate priority action, so strong fear responses take precedence over and *suppress* other behavior such as exploration, eating, drinking, attack, or copulation.

Interruption of other behavior by fear responses may be intermittent (partial suppression, *alternation*). Animals feeding in an open space where they would be vulnerable to predators frequently stop feeding to look around. A novel environment similarly leads chicks and mice to break off feeding to look around. A novel environment similarly leads chicks and mice to break off feeding at intervals (Archer 1979).

Fear behavior may not only alternate with other responses but also *occur simultaneously*. A hungry bunting in flight toward a feeding dish at which a feared social superior is eating will flick its tail vigorously; tail flicking is an intention movement for taking off and thus common to approach and avoidance (Andrew 1956). A half-tame moorhen, when offered food, made incipient pecks and swallowing movements toward the food while also edging away from it (Hinde 1970, p. 401).

A punishing stimulus does not suppress fear responses that are reflexly evoked by the same stimulus, though it may inhibit other responses. In gerbils, sand-digging accompanies nesting, while alert-posturing occurs in response to sudden or aversive stimuli. Shocking gerbils while they were digging immediately suppressed digging permanently and increased alert-posturing; in contrast, shocking them during alert-posturing enhanced that, but not digging (Walters & Glazer 1971). This phenomenon is also seen in human infants, who will stop touching objects when spanked but are unlikely to stop crying.

When fear behavior occurs at the same time as behavior from another emotional repertoire, both may be *suppressed and replaced* by a third, functionally unrelated activity (*displacement*). Such behavior appears out of context and is usually incomplete unless the fear is strong and prolonged. Conflict between avoidance and approach during fighting or territorial disputes at the boundary may lead to sand-digging in the stickleback, preening or nest building in birds, and grooming in mammals (Tinbergen 1952). Primates such as orangutans and chimpanzees may scratch their fur when distressed (Tinbergen 1952). Humans under stress scratch their skin, bite their nails, or smooth their hair, all of these being comfort movements caring for the body surface; tense people might also rearrange their clothes, fidget, or talk hurriedly. Obsessive-compulsive rituals are somewhat like displacement activities. They are worse under stress, commonly concern grooming (excessive washing, cleaning, and tidying), and reduce anxiety (see Chapter 13).

Displacement activities are frequent during boundary disputes that evoke simultaneous flight and fight. Ambivalence during boundary disputes between two males may also lead to rapid alternation between retreat and attack in a "pendulum fight," such as occurs with sticklebacks, male snow buntings (where it can endure for an hour), and the prairie horned lark (Tinbergen 1952). In humans some repetitive marital disputes have this quality.

Away from the boundary more clear-cut escape or attack occurs. An intruder into a territory evokes attack from the owner, but if the same individual is met outside the territory it is ignored, and avoided if it is on its own ground. The likelihood of avoidance rises and that of aggression decreases with greater distance from the center of the territory. Human examples of this about—sports teams are happier playing on their home ground than away, and people tend to be less inhibited at home than outside. There are exceptions, as with people who lack restraint when on vacation in a new place where no one knows them.

EVOLUTION AND DEFENSIVE BEHAVIOR

Defensive responses arose as adaptations against threat from enemies and from other harsh realities in the environment. Throughout evolution there has been an arms race between defensive adaptations of prey and attempts by predators to overcome them (Dawkins & Krebs 1979). Enemies come from both inside and outside the species. The defensive repertoire of an animal forms a system as vital as its cardiovascular or reproductive system (Edmunds 1974).

A defensive system comprises sensory components that detect danger and motor components of fear behaviors, central and peripheral neural mediating processes; cellular, hormonal, and immunological responses to noxious stimuli and structural features such as armor plating, spines, shells, or unpleasant-tasting chemicals in the tissues. Fear refers to repertoires of protective behavior but not to built-in features such as shells or cellular, hormonal, and immunological responses uninvolved in behavior. In humans the articulation of fear adds a rich element to the many ways in which other animals display the emotion.

Constraints in the Evolutionary Arms Race

Adaptation is never perfect. There are many constraints to the perfection of design as prey and predator coevolve in the struggle to eat without being eaten, and such restrictions explain some anomalous fear behavior (Dawkins 1982, pp. 39–66). First are historical constraints. Evolution proceeds in tiny increments from one generation to the next. Adaptive organization is a "patchwork of makeshifts pieced together . . . from what was available when opportunity knocked, and accepted in the hindsight, not the foresight, of natural selection" (Pittendrigh 1958). Natural selection does not favor some useless mutation in the Cambrian simply because "it might come in handy in the Cretaceous" (Brenner, cited by Dawkins 1982). In the "adaptive landscape" (Wright 1932) selection favors local optima that might prevent evolution of ultimately superior, more global optima, although genetic drift is a brake on super-specialization.

A prey fish that sees the wriggly lure of an angler fish rushes into the jaws of death because usually wriggly things are not lures but worms. In William James's (1910) memorable phrase, "there are more worms unattached to hooks than impaled upon them; therefore, on the whole, says Nature to her fishy children, bite at every worm and take your chances." That advice is sound as long as there are few anglers around, but wariness is selected for if they increase. The converse also happens: maladaptive fear is fear of situations that are not currently dangerous, though they may have been in the past. (Many generals are continually fighting the previous war, not the present one.) In most countries human dread of snakes, spiders, and sharks is disproportionate to their danger, and toddlers' fear of strangers seems suited to a more brutish past. The panics of agoraphobics are like escape reactions triggered too readily when away from home territory. Our fear and dislike of others who are racially, religiously, or ideologically different is usually greater than the situation warrants, has killed tens of millions in this century alone, and now threatens our species. Humans' brain-extended physical prowess has outstripped their capacity to resolve fear and conflict. Because this problem may be an evolutionary hangover in our design need not mean that it is unmodifiable ("natural" phobias like those of snakes and spiders can be cured as quickly as social phobias which seem less natural—see Chapter 14).

Other constraints on adaptation are costs and materials (Dawkins 1982). Every defensive adaptation costs something in terms of lost opportunities to do other things. The mathematics of biological trade-offs, of the tangle of compromises, are extremely complex. Increased prey-vigilance time has to be offset against less time available for feeding or looking after offspring. Escape or threat have different advantages depending upon existing armory and the particular enemy and context involved. The problems of evolving a particular device may be too costly or beyond the biological capability of the species. Though many species have evolved to become unpalatable, this has not happened with birds' eggs, which are a favorite food of many species (Harvey & Greenwood 1978). Instead, selection has favored behaviors that minimize the detection of nests (distraction displays, concealment, short incubation periods) and the impact of predation (rapid replacement of lost clutches). Natural selection must act on the entire animal, and improvement of some defenses, including fear, may conflict with the efficiency of others or with other essential behaviors such as feeding or reproduction, so compromise has to be reached (Edmunds 1974). There can be no ultimate, fail-safe defense for prey, just as there is no effortless meal ticket for predators.

The interplay of prey-predator strategies and their costs is seen with the bombardier beetle (*Brachinus,* Eisner 1970); which is not only encased in heavy armor plating but also sprays boiling hot acid at attackers. To prevent this acid from destroying its insides, the bombardier stores the acid's precursors (hydrogen peroxide, quinones, and the enzymes that make them explosively active) in separate, plated tanks, ready to mix and expel at a moment's notice (Figure 1.1). The defense is effective; it hurts, disables, or even kills many predators. The bombardier pays the price of its armor plating, however, in its lumbering gait. Several species of beetle have evolved that mimic its defense without incurring the heavy cost (Gould 1982). They imitate the bombardier's awkward gait and odd, angular posture, but they lack the weaponry and, if attacked, will abandon their slow-paced act to run or fly rather than

Fig. 1.1 Bombardier beetles *(Brachinus)* defend themselves by heavy armor plating and by spraying a boiling, caustic acid at potential predators. To prevent the acid from destroying its insides, the bombardier stores the precursors in separate plated tanks, ready to mix in an outer vestibule and expel at a moment's notice. The price of the armor plating is the bombardier's lumbering gait. Several beetle species mimic this awkward gait and odd angular posture but lack the weaponry; if attacked they abandon their slow-paced act to run or fly away rather than fight. (From Gould 1982. Copyright © 1982 by Academic Press, NY. Reprinted by permission.)

stand and fight. In addition, the mimics lack the telltale odor that alerts the bombardier's most threatening predators to its presence.

Some animals have evolved effective strategies against the large, nourishing bombardier beetles (Gould 1982). Far from avoiding the beetles, all skunks, even ones that have never before encountered bombardiers, respond automatically to them and their mimics by closing their eyes tightly and rolling the beetles rapidly back and forth on the ground until they discharge their acid. Certain species of mice, too, actually prefer bombardiers as prey, holding their spraying apparatus firmly into the ground and eating from the head down.

The two defense strategies of the bombardiers, acid and armor, have become interwoven with two other evolutionary tracks. The acid-spraying reduced the threat from generalist predators, but some mammals developed specialized evasive tactics allowing them to exploit the bombardiers with little competition. Counterstrategies may evolve in turn against those mammals. Meanwhile the free-riding mimics moved in to take advantage of the bombardier's hard-won protection while retaining their agility.

Selection cannot perfect a defense system so that all individuals escape predation. In some studies about one in eight of potential ungulate prey have been consumed each year, leaving the healthier ones until they succumb in turn as they grow ill, old, or just plain unlucky (Gould 1982). Predator-prey systems usually evolve a balanced equilibrium, perhaps with some oscillation. The equilibrium can be simple in temperate, arctic, or island ecosystems where there are few species, but is very complex in the great diversity of the tropics.

A simple prey-predator equilibrium occurs with moose and wolves on the Isle Royale in Lake Superior (Mech 1970). Around 1900 some moose chanced to walk the 15 miles across the frozen lake to the previously mooseless island. In the absence of predators the moose population grew steadily to about 3,000 in 1935. This devastated the vegetation, and suddenly nearly 90% of the population starved. With fewer mouths to feed the grass and bushes soon recovered and the moose again increased to 3,000 by 1948, at which time the population crashed once more. These boom and bust cycles ended in 1949, when some lost timber wolves wandered across the ice onto the island and began to prey on the moose, whose defenses were good enough to protect the healthier adults. The island is now home to about 24 wolves, which cull out the unluckier young, the old, and the sick moose at the rate of about one every 3 days. They continually test the herds, but only about 10% of chases are successful. The result is a stable population of about 800 fit moose and equally healthy vegetation.

The type of predation pressure and habitat affects the typical fear responses shown by a species. The speed and efficiency of the predator and the availability of cover influence whether the initial response is immobility or escape, the speed and direction of flight, and whether there will be escape to another niche. Animals living on isolated islands free of predators, as in the Galapagos, tend to be unafraid of man and dogs. In most places predation pressure has led to prey being alert and vigilant, ready for action at the first sign of danger.

Fear behavior can be learned quickly and persist remarkably, and this is adaptive. Eight months after 2 of a troop of 80 baboons in a park were shot, the troop could still not be approached, even though the animals saw cars almost daily (Devore 1965). Phobias in humans can last even longer, over decades.

Selection pressures are asymmetric between predator and prey (Dawkins 1982). The rabbit on the whole runs faster than the fox because the rabbit is running for his life, the fox only for his dinner. Failure incurs greater penalty for the rabbit than for the fox, so the fox can afford to divert rather more resources to adaptations other than speed.

Man is the greatest predator on man. The ubiquity of our worry may come from the prime importance of adapting to complex, hierarchical social groups in constant interaction and possibility of imbalance.

Conspecific Pressures in Fear Evolution

Evolutionary pressures on fear behavior come not only from predators of other species but also from conspecifics, and fear reactions to predators and to dominant conspecifics can appear similar (Walther 1969). The more fearful animals are selected out during fights between sexual rivals. During each mating season male ungulates have fierce battles from which the more fainthearted and weaker retire and so do not pass on their genes that year.

During their daily life primates show fear far more often to conspecifics than to predators. Timid, low-status animals defer to those above, perhaps after an initial chastening skirmish. There is a balance in the selection of fear that allows immediate survival in the face of an aggressor but reduces reproductive success. In the dominance hierarchies of birds and mammals, high-ranking animals have easier access to food, territory, and mates, supply better parental care to their young, and rear more of them (Fuller & Thompson 1978, pp. 452–453). More fearful animals may be forced onto the periphery of the group or even to leave it, becoming vulnerable to predation. The most fearful animals often seem to survive less.

Timidity varies with age, however, and lifetime patterns are needed to assess reproductive success. There is inevitable variation in caution and courage both across individuals and within them from one moment to the next. Caution and courage are each adaptive in different situations. Fearful behavior is selected more often under some circumstances and brave responses under others. Over the generations a particular range of environmental pressures will yield a particular balance of prudence and valor in the population.

This process is at work in dominance hierarchies. If a leader in his prime is opposed the contender may be injured or killed. There comes a time when a challenge will win the day, and the first successful hero has the best opportunities to breed. In any population there are more timid animals biding their time, and changed circumstances may yet give them a chance. This was shown in territorial songbirds that hotly contest territories with the most abundant resources (Gould 1982, p. 361). Males arrive early in the season and contend for space, singing both to warn off neighbors and landless rivals, and to attract females. That timid but fit male songbirds are being excluded from the breeding population was found in a gruesome shootout experiment that few scientists would conduct today. When resident territorial breeders were killed, new "floater" males promptly took over. Indeed, floaters arrived nearly as fast as the experimenter could create vacancies with his shotgun, which suggests that the population of disenfranchised timid males was very large, very watchful, or both.

Killing of Conspecifics and the Evolution of Stranger Fear

Predation pressure from conspecifics is important for the evolution of fear and is a major cause of death under certain conditions. The abuse of animals by their fellows helps us understand a hitherto mysterious fear in humans—the fear of strangers so widespread in 8- to 24-month-old infants from both preindustrial and industrial countries (see Chapter 7). This fear is inexplicable from a contemporary Western perspective but adaptive from an evolutionary standpoint. The argument for this is made in detail to illustrate the value of an evolutionary perspective in understanding one human fear.

The case unfolds with mounting evidence that a host of species kill their fellows (Hrdy 1977). These include such diverse groups as crayfish, herring gulls, storks, European blackbirds, eagles, lemmings, rabbits, rats, hyenas, wild dogs, wolves, bears, hippos, lions, and at least 16 types of primates, man included. The killing is usually of strange, hence generally unrelated, conspecifics, especially young ones.

Among squirrels infanticide of conspecifics was found in 8 of 11 species (genus *Spermophilus*) (Sherman 1981). In Belding's ground squirrel at least 8% of all young born were murdered by conspecifics, who killed more juveniles than did any other predator species. Most slaying was by nomadic females and by 1-year-old males. Killings were never of cousins or closer kin and were unrelated to population density. Unlike the females, yearling males usually preyed on young near their burrows, killed only one juvenile per episode, fed on the carcass, and did not settle permanently near the victim's burrow. Yearling males and females might thus obtain different benefits from infanticide. Perhaps 1-year-old males get food while adult nomadic females remove potential rivals in acquiring safe nesting burrows.

Lactating female squirrels chase strangers out of areas around their burrows, perhaps to thwart infanticide, yet they share this area with their female relatives and offspring. The squirrels learn to recognize those with whom they grow up. Young introduced into the burrow of an unrelated female before she has learned to recognize her own offspring will later cooperate with her and her kin but attack their true relations. Daughters (but not sons) tend to settle near their birthplace, so normally any squirrel a youngster encounters regularly close to its mother is related.

The kin selection of related animals represented by the squirrel's cooperation with relatives and attack of unrelated strangers is mediated by the experience of normal socialization. Under normal conditions blood seems to be thicker than water because those with the same blood usually grow up together.

The rule seems to be "behave altruistically toward those reared in your own nest."

Cannibalism of adults as well as young is a feature of hyenas (Kruuk 1972), although infants are in greatest jeopardy because they are small and weak. The reproductive success of a mother depends partly on her ability to keep other hyenas of either sex from devouring her offspring, which may be one reason why female hyenas have come to outweigh and outrank males. Some conspecific killing of adults arises out of territoriality. Hyenas that intrude into the range of a neighbor may be attacked and killed even after submitting and trying to escape. So great is their respect for territory that a hyena clan will abandon a promising chase when the prey runs from their area into that of a rival clan.

In lions, males taking over a pride are liable to kill all cubs they find there (Bertram 1976, p. 297; Eaton 1974, p. 105). As such cubs are unrelated, this infanticide may reduce competition for the killer's genes. A male has but a brief ascendancy in the pride with only a short time to pass on its own genes. Its killing of the cubs helps the lactating bereaved mothers to conceive again and hastens the birth of its own offspring; and once these are born, the male allows them to feed first before the females. Females pregnant at the time of takeover abort spontaneously.

The fear of strangers seen so regularly in human infants may have evolved as protection against abuse by strange conspecifics earlier in the story of our own species or its predecessors. If such speculation is correct, it would predict frequent killing of infants by strangers in some primate species. In fact the same pattern of infanticide has come to light in many species of monkeys and great apes as well as in lions (Hrdy 1981, 1984). Among Hanuman langurs *(Presbytis entellus)* infanticide is not merely an aberrant response to over-crowding but a widespread feature of normal life (Hrdy 1984). Takeovers of monkey groups by strange males are frequently followed by attacks on infants, or missing infants:

> In thousands of hours of observation, normally tolerant male langurs have never been seen to attack an infant under any other circumstance. . . . [F]emales are at once hostile to the new male and intensely protective of infants. By contrast, females are nonchalant in the presence of an established troop leader, allowing their infants to play about him, to use his back as a trampoline, and to swing on his tail. At worst, a troop leader may grimace at a particularly obstreperous infant or threaten an infant interfering with him if he happens to be copulating. . . . [Males] attack only offspring accompanied by unfamiliar females. (Hrdy 1981, p. 85).

The same pattern of a usurping male killing the strange (and thus usually unre-lated) infants it finds in the troop it has taken over occurs in other monkeys in Africa, Asia, and South America. Supporting evidence was found in *Presbytis senex, cristata,* and *johnii, Cercopithecus ascanius, mitis,* and *campbelli lowei,* rhesus *(Macaca mulatta)*; howler monkeys *(Alouatta seniculus)*; and chacma baboons *(Papio ursinus)*, as well as in Hamadryas baboons *(Papio hamadryas)* during abnormal overcrowding.

Sobering evidence also comes from man's nearest relatives, chimpanzees and gorillas (Goodall 1977). Among 300 gorillas in Rwanda 3 cases of adult males killing infants were seen and 3 inferred. Infanticide appears most often when males have short tenure of access to females (Hrdy 1977), a feature also seen in lions. The average male langur dominates the females for about 27 months. Such rapid rates of male takeovers pressure the male to compress as much as possible of his females' reproductive output into his brief reign. By eliminating strange infants that are unlikely to be his own, a usurping male hastens the mother's return to sexual receptivity and reduces the time that will elapse before she bears his offspring. Females in turn are best off if they mate with the murderer as soon as they can to increase the chances of their offspring maturing before the next coup. In some species such as patas monkeys *(Erythrocebus patas)* the presence of male invaders may even stimulate a female to show estrous behavior and mate despite being pregnant (Hrdy 1977). After birth a monkey infant's survival is more likely if its mother associates with a male who tolerates it as a father does. Similarly, a male mouse introduced to another female and her litter is far less likely to attack the pups than a virgin male would be (Hrdy 1985).

Troop instability with frequent male takeovers increases the rate of infanticide. Over several years of such instability more than 80% of infants died among toque macaques and langurs. The situation worsens with overcrowding, as happened when large numbers of rhesus monkeys were released on a small island. In the first year while the colony formed and stabilized, more infants were killed by adult monkeys than died of any other cause (Carpenter 1942, cited by Goodall 1977).

Much infanticide may thus stem from males competing against other males and at the expense of females and their offspring. The practice is also maintained by competition among primate females themselves, who are quick to mate with the murderous male and may themselves kill the infants of other females, even though they also engage in communal child care. Female abuse of unrelated infants usually stops short of murder but nevertheless reduces the infants' chances of survival. Females often neglect, step, or sit on unrelated infants or drop them out of trees. On three occasions female chimpanzees belonging to a high-ranking lineage murdered and ate the offspring of low-ranking females who had physical disabilities (Goodall 1977). Among chimpanzees, females in a group are not usually close relatives, apart from mother-daughter clusters. Killing of strange infants gets rid of rivals to one's own infant. But under certain conditions it gets rid of potential helpmates, which is maladaptive.

Parents' killing of their own infants is generally counterproductive to survival of their line but does occur in certain instances, as in Hamadryas baboons (Rijksen 1981). Infanticide by parents may aid their inclusive fitness when greater survival of many more distantly related animals compensates for the loss of a few offspring (reviewed by Clutton-Brock & Harvey 1976, p. 208–209). Some birds preferentially feed older offspring so when food runs short the youngest survive less and may even be eaten by older siblings.

The killing of related infants, especially girls, has been widespread in many human societies, including modern China (Langer 1974). Reasons include poverty, low labor or reproductive value of offspring, and lack of confidence in paternity (Lenington 1981). Killing of one's own young has little to do with the evolution of fears of strangers as humans usually rear their own children and are not strangers to them.

There are some anecdotes of men murdering strange infants—for example, of American pioneer settlements raided by Indians who abducted the women but killed their small children (G. Williams, personal communication, 1982). Other evidence was cited by Hrdy (1977). In the Bible Herod "sent forth, and slew all the children that were in Bethlehem, and in all the coasts thereof, from two years and under" (Matthew 2:16), while Pharaoh commanded that all Hebrew sons should die at birth (Exodus 1:16). Occasionally a husband might kill an infant sired by some other male among Eskimos, Tikopia, and Mundurucu. In Brazil, invading males of the Yanamamo tribe rarely killed unrelated children but more typically kidnapped the mothers, leaving their infants behind, which is functionally equivalent to infanticide because the offspring probably starved. In Yanamamo society, males typically raided for women, and a few men are disproportionately represented in the gene pool of succeeding generations. As among lions and langurs, there is intense competition among males for females and a fast rate of political change. These shorten the opportunity for males to reproduce—2 to 3 years in the case of langurs, 2 to 10 among lions, and until the next raid among the Yanamamo.

Historically we read unending grisly stores of the victors in war either killing off all the vanquished or killing the men and taking the women as wives, but the fate of the children has not been carefully studied. Although offspring may have been more often killed than spared, sometimes they were regarded as assets to be socialized as future slaves or soldiers for the victor; this practice too would enhance fitness of the victor and his relatives.

Though there are notable exceptions in African and Amerindian societies, among whom fictive kin are common; an immense amount of human energy is spent ensuring that one's wife bears children carrying one's own genes, and providing for them and increasing their chances of survival. Female circumcision, insistence on bridal virginity, purdah, and numerous other customs testify to the widespread premium set on having biological progeny. Children are better cared for in general by their biological parents than by foster parents. Adopted and stepchildren are regarded as second best, and stepparents proverbially abuse their charges. It is natural to care for one's own child, noble to nurture someone else's. This could represent kin selection in those many societies where strangers, including children, are usually unrelated. In the United States stepchildren are more often severely abused than those living with both natural parents (Daly & Wilson 1982).

Human adults as well as children are more abused by unrelated than related relatives. Careful examination of their consanguinity showed that blood relatives were less likely to be slain in many twentieth-century societies and in thirteenth-century England (Daly and Wilson 1982). As in numerous primate species, murder may be exceptional in humans and disastrous for the human killer's inclusive fitness because of social sanctions when the deed is detected; when killing occurs, however, it more often involves those who are not blood related.

In the evolution of stranger fear, the strength of selection pressure from abuse by strangers needs to be calculated under varying conditions. Our behavior has altered over the last few thousand years through the imperatives of socialization, which override many earlier patterns of behavior. Behavioral traits that used to have survival value in the face of now largely defunct threats could take a long time to be selected out, however, and stranger fear might be an evolutionary hangover.

Could this gruesome fascination with murder and child abuse be misplaced? Some might feel that the evidence just reviewed oversells a "dog-eat-dog" view of nature. Yet animals are neither good nor bad. Conspecifics care, cooperate, court, and copulate, but they also fight and kill one another. On the one hand, stranger fear protects against strange conspecifics (who need not be unrelated), and appeasement inhibits attack when contact cannot be avoided. On the other hand, contact with one's fellows brings many advantages, including defense against predation, and these have led to the evolution of sociality. Species thus develop a balance between approach and avoidance of their fellows, which changes as circumstances do.

Does stranger fear merely reflect an infant's fear of separation from its caregiver? Stranger fear is undoubtedly greater in the absence of the caregiver and develops as the baby becomes able to toddle away from its caregiver to where it is likely to meet strangers. However, this does not explain why even when they are in their mother's arms, infants are afraid of strangers. Such fear of strangers even in the mother's presence strongly suggests it is more than just separation anxiety, even if the latter increases it. Two fears of any kind can summate.

Stranger fear in human infants is likely to be an evolutionary remnant reflecting widespread abuse and infanticide by strangers (both unrelated and related) during the evolution of hominids and their predecessors. Supportive evidence includes the number of primate species whose infants risk being killed as much as from interspecific predation and starvation, by conspecific males when they take over the group, and to a lesser extent by strange females (Hrdy 1981). Infanticide is not merely pathological but can be an adaptive strategy (Butynski 1982).

The argument would be further bolstered if we could show that increased infanticide within a species is associated with stronger fear of strangers. Both should be less frequent in unsociable primates such as orangutans. Data for this are worth studying, in order to separate infants' fear of nonthreatening strangers from their fear of threat displays. Though the two fears are connected (strangers may threaten), fear of threat displays would mainly aid survival in a dominance hierarchy: ignoring threats from dominant animals often leads to injury or even death. Because unsociable animals have less of a hierarchy, they should also show less fear of threat displays.

Among numerous species, many primates included, stranger fear is adaptive for adults as well as for infants. If a rhesus monkey encounters a strange group of conspecifics it is habitually attacked and may even be killed if escape is not feasible (Suomi et al. 1981). A strange adult male treeshrew meets the same fate when brought into the cage of another male (see Chapter 3); depending on the context, such attacks can reflect sexual rivalry, territoriality, or both.

In a way infanticide is an extreme manifestation of dominance. That it is usually committed by males reflects the rule among most primate species that females defer to males and can generally be displaced from access to commodities they both want. Why have females of most primate species not evolved to greater size or dominance, as female hyenas have, to compete better with males? The answer may lie in the energies needed to attain that strategy compared with those expended in competing with females by mating immediately with the usurper to produce a new infant (Hrdy 1981), but this fascinating issue takes us beyond the scope of the present book. Instead, the next chapter will survey the situations that most often evoke fear across species.

SUMMARY

Fear is the normal feeling and behavior that occurs in the presence of threat, is useful for survival, enhances performance if it is not extreme, and may even be sought for enjoyment. It consists of a variety of reactions that tend to occur together at the same time or over a period. There are many subtle variations in the spectrum of fearful emotions.

Fear is an emotional response syndrome with typical though varying patterns of evoking stimuli, responses, and course. Emotional responses are arbitrarily divided into cognitive-subjective, motor-behavioral, and physiological. Different facets may be mediated by different pathways and can be quite discordant, examples being stoicism and "overreaction." Some aspects of fear are biologically rooted and others depend on social and individual learning. Each species has its morphologically characteristic repertoire of fear behavior. The normal stream of actions may be enhanced or suppressed by, alternate with, or continue alongside, fear.

Fear develops in the course of evolution as an arms race between prey and aggressors from outside and inside its own species. Historical and cost constraints explain some of the many imperfections of design and anomalies of behavior. Evolutionary pressures help us understand some aspects of human fear, a good example being the origin of infants' fear of strangers in the higher risk of abuse and murder from strangers than from familiars.

2

Fear-Evoking Situations

Numerous hazards are general across taxa; others are not. Natural selection has led to corresponding similarities and differences across taxa in the situations that evoke fear. Variation by species is dealt with in this chapter, and human fears are located in an evolutionary context. Variation resulting from an individual's age, genetic makeup, and experience is discussed in chapters 5, 6, and 8.

The simplest but controversial model for fear evocation is that vertebrates have a biphasic approach-withdrawal system that first appears in the embryo, with approach to low-intensity stimuli and withdrawal from high-intensity stimuli (Schneirla 1965). This system might relate to the adaptive importance of such stimuli; that is, low-intensity stimuli are more likely to be followed by reward and high intensity ones by noxious consequences. The concept merely refers to an initial bias of the young nervous system, which subsequent experience can override, so that the low-intensity touch of a spider's web, for example, can eventually come to evoke strong fear ("prepotency" in Chapter 8).

Across sense modalities the stimuli producing withdrawal in neonatal vertebrates tend to be abrupt, intense, rapidly getting bigger and louder, and irregular in shape or timing (Schneirla 1965). Newly hatched chicks are disturbed by harsh sounds such as sneezing and chair scraping, and by bright light, sudden movement, or a black rectangle advanced rapidly toward them. Humans are often frightened by loud, abrupt claps of thunder or the sudden and unexpected appearance of someone close by.

We can conveniently divide fear-evoking stimuli into those from the physical environment and those from other animals. Both categories are discussed in the sections that follow.

PHYSICAL FEAR-EVOKING STIMULI

Survival requires an environment that satisfies an organism's basic needs for physical integrity, oxygen, food, water, the right temperature and humidity, a medium to dwell in, and shelter from predators. Stimuli that threaten these needs often lead to fearful withdrawal. Wholly terrestrial animals flee from fire and try to get out of water into which they have fallen. Abrupt, loud noise frightens many species (Russell 1979); thunder makes dogs cower in fright. On sudden loss of support, human infants catch their breath and clutch with their hands (Watson & Morgan 1917). Inflicting pain drives away animals; electric shock elicits running, jumping, hiding, or swimming away and is followed by decreased activity.

Heights

Height phobias in humans are an exaggeration of the normal healthy respect for heights seen in terrestrial animals. This is easily shown by a "visual cliff" simulated by a large sheet of transparent glass or plastic supported a foot or more above the floor (Gibson & Walk 1960; see also Figure 5.9). A sheet of patterned material is placed flush against the underside of half the glass, giving that half the appearance as well as the substance of solidity (the "shallow" side). The other half is clear, but the same patterned material is laid upon the floor a foot or more below the glass (the "deep" side). A subject placed at the divide between the shallow and deep sides can move onto either side. If it consistently chooses the shallow side it presumably detects visual depth and avoids receding edges.

When placed on the boundary between the deep and shallow sides many land-dwelling species, including land turtles, chicks, rats, goats, lambs, pigs, dogs, cats, monkeys, and human infants, initially move onto the shallow side and avoid the deep side (Gibson & Walk 1960). When placed on the deep side kittens and young goats tense and freeze, and neonatal monkeys show fear by crouching, calling, rocking, and self-clasping (Rosenblum & Cross 1963). With experience some animals eventually cease to avoid the deep side. Unlike their land-dwelling counterparts, aquatic species such as ducks and turtles venture onto the deep side from the start (Emlen 1963; Routtenberg & Glickman 1964; Walk, cited in Gibson 1969).

Avoidance is produced by vertical, not horizontal, depth cues (for instance, views through a doorway). Vertical depth is assessed from parallax at the edge and foot of the cliff arising when the head is moved, and from the patterns of the surfaces (Gibson 1969; Walk & Walters 1974). Some fears of heights may also involve proprioceptors in the neck and vestibular system: fear can be evoked by craning one's neck to look *up* at very high buildings as well as down from their top.

Adults fear the receding edge of a precipice, feel drawn over it, and have a protective reflex to withdraw from it, as do swimmers snorkeling on the surface of the sea looking down for the first time at the edge of a steeply receding reef. Fear may also appear in passengers when a low-flying helicopter skims the edge of a plateau or of a high building, producing a visual cliff. Trainee parachutists have to overcome their natural inhibition before they can jump comfortably from a plane.

Many people are uncomfortable in high-rise buildings, particularly if the exterior walls of glass run from floor to ceiling, and in glass-fronted elevators.

They feel a lack of privacy and dizziness on looking down outside through windows extending from the floor to the ceiling, and they feel their apartments are too brightly lit. These problems are eased a bit by curtaining the window to darken the room and make it seem smaller. At daytime gatherings in apartments of this kind, many people retreat from the well-lit side of the room to throng the darker interior. A woman who lived on the twenty-second floor described the discomfort resulting from a sense of too much space and light:

> When my husband first saw the view, he way lyrical. He said at night it was like fairyland. When we've company, they often spend the first half-hour looking out of the window. Some get dizzy though. We'd a fellow here, like a wrestler he is, short but muscular, and he wouldn't go near the windows at all. Just stood by the stove all evening. I felt like that at first. Now I only notice it when I'm cleaning the windows. The windows run right over for cleaning, but I have to get my husband to do it. My stomach just leaves me.
>
> To begin with, we put the children's bunks in the little bedroom. It's such a tiny room we had to put them up against the window, and my eldest daughter just refused to go to bed in the top bunk; she got in with the little one down below. . . .[O]ne day I got up myself to see what put her off. It was terrifying! Like lying on the edge of a cliff, just the glass between you and all that space. (*The Observer,* London, February 16, 1968, p. 21).

Another high-living tenant commented: "There's something about it which makes it feel unlike home. If you draw the curtains, you're cozy, but you're cut off from the world till next morning" (*The Observer,* London, February 16, 1968, p. 21).

Surrounding Space and Illumination

Animals are often disturbed if there is too much or too little space or light around them, the optimum amount depending upon their habits. Many species avoid open places that afford no cover. This partly depends on the level of light. Hamsters avoid bright light, though on a visual cliff they will stay on the shallow side even when it is bright if the deep side is dim (Lawlor M, personal communication, 1967). They avoid light less than they do heights, which makes good sense in terms of survival. Hamsters, rats, and mice tend to stay at the boundaries of an open space, rats even more so if the light is bright (Valle 1970). If the light is dimmed just above the human threshold of perception, hamsters use the open field much more. Rats choose to spend more time in a black than in a white area (Aitken 1974; Williams & Kuchta 1957). A lit open field or confinement in a transparent cylinder in the middle of a lit field produces stress in hamsters and rodents (Russell 1979).

Too much as well as too little cover can evoke fear. Small enclosed spaces such as elevators and tunnels frighten many people. Agoraphobics become anxious if they feel confined and unable to escape immediately from a frightening place. There has been little investigation of such claustrophobia. It can be measured by testing how close an enclosing screen can be brought toward people before they feel uncomfortable (R. Blumenthal, personal communication, 1975).

Darkness frightens many children and some adults. In 2 to 5 year-olds who were asked to enter a dark passage to retrieve a ball, 45% refused entirely or would not go unless accompanied (Jersild 1950; Jersild & Holmes 1935). The fear may be partly produced by the sense of being alone. In contrast, adult agoraphobics often feel easier in the dark than in the light (Marks & Herst 1970; and see also Chapter 10).

Everyday incidents show how the perception of space and light affect fear. A colleague went for a stroll on a vast tidal mud flat at low tide. At one point he was surrounded by an unbroken featureless surface of mud stretching from one horizon to the other. He became afraid until, as he continued walking, the sea-line finally broke the horizon again to provide a visual reference point, and the fear then abated. At a theater, this author sat high up at the side of the stage above the orchestra pit. As the performance began the lights in the auditorium dimmed, the curtain rose on a dark stage, and only the orchestra pit remained lit between the two dark expanses on either side. Immediately I felt drawn down into the orchestra pit below, had a sudden fear of the height, and withdrew from the edge of the balcony. As soon as the lights came on again in the auditorium the sensation disappeared.

Agoraphobics feel less anxious if they skirt the edge when crossing an open space. Visuospatial reflexes are disturbed in some elderly people who are too terrified even to cross an empty room in the absence of visual support, and they may have to cross the room on their hands and knees (Marks 1981a; see also Chapter 9). Such space phobics do not need to actually hold onto support, only to see it nearby. Many have various pathologies in the hindbrain, neck, or labyrinth, but the pathways involved are not yet clear.

Novel Places and Objects (Neophobia)

In a familiar environment an animal knows where to get its food, water, and shelter and how best to avoid predators. Novelty implies greater danger, and the strange and unfamiliar provoke fear in numerous species (Bronson 1968). Many frightening stimuli are novel, and this novelty may be more frightening than the stimuli themselves. By definition, the longer an organism is in contact with a novel stimulus, the less novel it becomes. Fear of novelty thus wanes as continued exposure leads to familiarity. Such exposure ameliorates clinical phobias (see Chapters 14 and 15).

Confinement to a novel area commonly evokes attempts to escape, or immobility, defecation, and distress calling, and these are greater the more novel the area (Archer 1976, Russell 1979). A new area at the boundary of the home range, or a novel object or localized stimulus in a familiar place, is initially avoided by rats, mice, baboons, macaques, chimpanzees, and young children. New foods, too, are often rejected at first by many species, including spiders, reptiles, birds, rats, and humans (Curio 1976; Russell 1979); food aversion can develop out of this phenomenon.

Rejection of novel prey may be mediated by fear; birds and mustelids give alarm calls or panic on seeing it (Curio 1976; pp. 103–106). Initial hesitation with new prey could stem from a fear of novelty, innate inhibition of response to particular stimuli, and/or generalization of noxious experiences with other prey. This lasts from 4 days in rainbow trout to a few seconds in songbirds and may be absent in many species. After a while the new prey is readily eaten. An interesting exception to the rule that prolonged exposure leads to more rapid habituation (see Chapter 14) was seen in captive pigmy owls, which were less ready to hunt their prey after having them permanently on view than after intermittent exposure to them (Scherzenberg 1970; p. 29, cited by Curio 1976). In humans the cultural evolution of national cuisine based on distinctive flavors enables us to overcome our neophobia by preparing new foods in familiar styles of cooking (Rozin 1977), though obviously such traditions are maintained by other factors too.

Fear of strange things is well documented in primates. Adult chimpanzees who saw a half-lifesize model of a chimpanzee's head screamed, erected their hair, and strongly avoided it; none would approach it even when separated from it by cage wire (Hebb & Thompson 1954). A young chimpanzee went into paroxysms of terror when given stuffed toys that faintly resembled animals with black buttons for eyes (Kohler 1925). Rhesus monkeys that had been reared by cloth-covered mother surrogates were placed in a new room full of novel objects but without the surrogate. They froze in a crouch or ran rapidly from object to object screaming and crying. Given the surrogate they clung to it. After a few trials the monkeys began to use the surrogate as a base from which to explore and handle the novel objects and then returned to it before venturing again into the strange new world (Harlow & Zimmermann 1959).

The fear of strangers seen so regularly in 8- to 18-month-old children (Chapters 1 and 5) is a fear of one kind of novelty. Fears of the uncanny occurred after age 1 year in children whose upbringing was monitored daily for years (Valentine 1930). Young children frequently fear unfamiliar masks. The elder sister of a 3-year-old girl brought home a wig from her school play and put it away in the toy cupboard. The little girl opened the cupboard and accidentally touched the wig. She screamed endlessly, and a fear of wigs began that lasted for many years even though fears of this sort in children are usually short-lived (BBC phone-in program 1974).

Though curiosity killed the proverbial cat, novelty can lead to new opportunities as well as danger. A healthy balance between fear of and approach to novelty is adaptive in a world where conservatism works well in an unchanging environment but initiative wins through in more tumultuous times when old formulas fail. It comes as no surprise that although novelty is apt to cause fear, it can also cause pleasure and be eagerly sought out. What decides which reaction will occur is obscure. Novelty may attract and repel in turn. Such approach-avoidance conflict is exemplified in the raven (Lorenz, cited by Berlyne 1960):

> A young raven, confronted with a new object, which may be a camera, an old bottle, a stuffed polecat, or anything else, first reacts with escape responses. He will fly up to an elevated perch and from this point of vantage, stare at the object . . . maintaining all the while a maximum of caution and the expressive attitude of intense fear. He will cover the last distance from the object hopping sideways with half-

raised wings, in the utmost readiness to flee. At last, he will deliver a single fearful blow with his powerful beak at the object and forthwith fly back to his safe perch. If nothing happens he will repeat the same procedure in much quicker sequence and with more confidence. If the object is an animal that flees, the raven loses all fear in the fraction of a second and will start in pursuit instantly. If it is an animal that charges, he will either try to get behind it or, if the charge is sufficiently unimpressive, lose interest in a very short time. With an inanimate object, the raven will proceed to apply a number of further instinctive movements. He will grab it with one foot, peck at it, try to tear off pieces, insert his bill into any existing cleft and then pry apart his mandibles with considerable force. Finally, if the object is not too big the raven will carry it away, push it into a convenient hole and cover it with some inconspicuous material.

Monkeys, apes, and human children show the same mixture of fear and curiosity with strange objects. Berlyne (1960) cited Russian researchers who watched the reaction of primates to tin boxes, toys, geometric figures, and smaller animals placed in their cages. At first the animals froze and stared at the strange object. After a while they would approach and look at it, sniff, touch, and eventually handle it. This exploration might last an hour, during which the animals would return to staring fixedly at the object. Inhibition was more prominent in certain animals, with living objects, and on the first day.

Whether a new situation will induce fear or exploration depends on many factors. What is novel depends on the individual's previous experience (though this is commonly not known to an observer); young chicks avoided a moving model less when it resembled their rearing pen (Bateson 1964). Novel stimuli may excite approach from curiosity, from fear, and from an attempt to reduce the danger of the unknown, as was found in rhesus monkeys (Symmes 1959). Individuals differ greatly in their traits of curiosity and timidity.

The degree of strangeness is also important. Extreme novelty more often induces avoidance and moderate novelty, approach. A mixture of old and new elements produces greater initial caution with increasing exploration as time goes on. Finally, fears of novelty attenuate in the presence of the mother (Bronson 1968; see also Chapter 5).

Food Aversion

This defensive response consists only of withdrawal, not immobility or attack. It is usually associated with nausea and vomiting, but human food aversions may be accompanied by fear as well: after mistakenly eating a taboo food, people may become terrified of imagined consequences.

Aversions to both plant and animal food start, generalize, and subside much like other avoidance behavior. Most aversions to food are taste aversions, but they may also be to its sight, smell, or symbolic aspects. Innate rejection of bitter substances occurs across phyla from protozoa to human newborn infants (reviewed by Garcia et al. 1977). New foods tend to be avoided; those whose ingestion is associated with nausea, for whatever reason, soon come to be avoided, even if the nausea occurs many hours after the food is eaten.

Food aversions can be extremely strong and enduring. Garcia's experiments on this topic arose from a story told to him by his mother (cited by Lorenz 1981). As a child she was given a big bar of chocolate just before the family boarded a boat that sailed on a very rough sea; she became very seasick and vomited, an episode that left her with a lasting horror of any sort of chocolate even though she had previously loved it.

The strength of food aversions probably accounts for the frequency with which nasty-tasting animals are vividly colored to advertize their noxiousness (see "aposematism," Chapter 3). A poisonous sting or bite produces the same food aversion as does nausea, and some mimics exploit this; for example, the dronefly *(Eristalis vinetorum)* imitates a honeybee *(Apis mellifera).* Southern toads *(Bufo terrestris)* ate both droneflies and honeybees when the prey were first presented, but after being stung by a bee the toads rejected both—the dronefly's mimicry was thus protective (Brower & Brower 1962).

From the predator's viewpoint, except where food avoidance becomes innate through a long process of natural selection, each hunter has to sample some aposematic prey before learning to avoid it (Figure 2.1; Edmunds 1974). Thereafter, only extremely hungry predators will try that prey again. Avoidance of noxious foods is crucial when small differences in expenditures of time and effort to obtain sustenance decide whether animals with limited budgets can survive under marginal conditions. That rapid learning to avoid toxic foods is widespread among vertebrates is thus scarcely surprising. It is very difficult to totally eliminate a population of wild rats by laying down poison,

Fig. 2.1 The start of food aversion in a bird. Monarch butterflies have a bright wing pattern that provides a cue that birds memorize after their first mistake. The distasteful chemicals of the monarch come from a milkweed plant that manufactures them for its own defense. Some other species of butterflies mimic the monarch's wing pattern and so share protection from educated birds. (From Gould 1982. Copyright © 1982 by Academic Press, Orlando. Reprinted by permission.)

as most steer clear of it after a few have become ill and died; weanling pups rapidly learn from adult rats which feeding sites, hence diet, to select (Galef 1977). This may be prepared learning such as that found with fear of snakes in rhesus monkeys (see Chapter 8).

Dramatic food aversions that rapidly reverse dominance between predator and prey were produced in wolves and coyotes (Garcia et al. 1977). The predators were first fed chopped mutton wrapped in raw sheep hide containing lithium chloride capsules, which induced vomiting. Thereafter, when presented with a lamb they would initially seize and then release it. Over half an hour the lamb became dominant once the predators gave way. As the lamb approached, the wolves gradually withdrew and responded like submissive pups, while the coyotes, a less social species, retreated and growled with ears laid back in a fighting stance. In the wolves and coyotes the food aversion was associated with 3 classes of response: (1) conditioned retching resembling the natural vomiting induced by lithium chloride; (2) conditioned disgust reflecting how the avoided food had become unattractive (coyotes urinated on, buried, or rolled the nauseating fresh meat as they do naturally to putrid offal), and (3) social responses to the former prey (wolves' submission to the sheep).

The learning of food aversion is similar among all vertebrates studied so far, be they fish, reptiles, or mammals, including man (Sjoden 1981; Archer et al. 1983). The similarity of central gustatory structures such as the neuropil in salamanders and the nucleus solitarius in man suggests that these learning resemblances stem from a common neurological source rather than from convergence resulting from common selection pressures (Garcia et al. 1977). Taste is a strong mediator of food-aversion learning in both mammals and birds, "as if the taste-visceral neuropil contains an 'and-gate' which allows other cues to become food cues when they are contiguous with taste" (Garcia 1981).

Food aversion is usually specific to the item associated with illness and to its taste rather than to its other features. The aversion is stronger when the nausea is paired with more intense tastes and when the CS (Taste)—US (nausea) intervals[1] are shorter, though strong food aversion can still occur with CS-US intervals of up to several hours. The effective CS-US interval can be much longer than with most other conditioned stimuli, but there are exceptions (Krane &Wagner 1975). Aversion learning is most marked with novel foods and generalizes readily to associated odors in different environments. In rats it can be blocked by preexposure either to the CS (Smotherman et al. 1980) or to the US (Revusky & Taukulis 1975) and can be abolished rapidly by exposure—for instance, by intraperitoneal injection of the fluid CS (Baum et al. 1974). Without exposure, food aversions tend to persist (Mineka et al. 1972).

There are some species and strain differences. Compared with albino rats, wild rats are more liable to avoid new foods and to develop conditioned taste aversion (Carroll et al. 1975). Concordant with their daytime feeding habits, quail and pigeons associate nausea more readily with visual stimuli than with taste. Food aversion develops more readily when stimuli are salient; in most

---

[1]CS = conditioned stimulus; US = unconditioned stimulus (see Chapter 8).

species salience is prominent in taste and tongue-tactile stimuli, and less so for olfactory, visual, and auditory stimuli. Salience and ease of learning is increased when the stimulus is intensified or novel (Garcia et al. 1977) or paired with taste and nausea (Sjoden & Archer 1983).

In humans, cultural and individual rearing patterns largely decide which foods are acceptable. Avoidance of unfamiliar foods is extremely common, especially in people who are not accustomed to a varied diet. Squirms and exclamations of disgust might be excited by the sight of others eating snails or insects. Conservatism of diet makes many immigrants unhappy when they cannot obtain their usual food in their usual surroundings, and even in times of famine there may be surprising reluctance to try out new diets.

Though frequent in normal people, food aversion was reported even more often in men rejected from the U.S. Navy on the grounds of neurosis (Wallen 1945). Both groups disliked similar foods, so neurotics may have a more general tendency to complain. Younger adults had more dislikes than older ones, which may reflect decrease in novelty of foods with experience and/or less intense taste stimulation with age as taste buds slowly atrophy. Experimentally, 2-year-old children prefer familiar to novel foods but come to accept new foods after they have been presented repeatedly (Birch & Marlin 1982).

Two questionnaire surveys examined the features of human food aversions. The first was in 696 Americans ranging in age from young children to the elderly (Garb & Stunkard 1974). Among respondents, a history of food aversion was reported in 38%, though only 24% had such an aversion currently. The aversion was usually to taste, but 6% also developed it to odors present at the time they ate the food, and 4% to associated aspects, including restaurants. Food aversions were present most commonly in children (30%) and least in those over 60 (6%). They usually began between ages 6 and 12 and disappeared after age 12. Avoidance was robustly persistent for up to 50 years in some subjects. Neither gender nor weight were relevant.

Fully 87% blamed their aversion on a gastrointestinal upset. Generally the aversion was acquired in merely one pairing of the taste and illness, but it could occur with a delay of up to 6 hours between the taste and the subsequent nausea. The aversion was specific to the food paired with illness and generalized to unpaired foods only in 6%. When both novel and familiar foods were eaten before the nausea, it was attributed to the new food in all but one instance, and 45% of the aversions involved new food. Aversion also developed disproportionately more to foods that had been previously disliked or eaten infrequently, and was more persistent with novel or previously disliked food.

The second questionnaire survey was of 517 American undergraduates (Logue et al. 1981). Food aversions were reported by 65%, a quarter being to alcoholic drinks. The most common age at which the food aversion began was 13 to 20, later than in the first survey, and aversions were slightly more common in women (70%) than in men (60%). Perhaps religious dietary taboos increase the acquisition of food aversions, which were more common in Catholics (76%) and Jews (67%) than in agnostics and atheists (35%).

As in the first survey, aversions often began after only a single pairing of food and subsequent upset and after long CS-US intervals. Aversions were also more likely to occur to unfamiliar foods and were usually to taste rather than to such other qualities as odor or appearance. Aversion started most often after forward than after backward or simultaneous conditioning. The learning was so strong that in 21% of those surveyed it overrode their certainty that they had been upset by something other than the now avoided food. In 29% the aversion generalized to other similar foods, and sometimes it had been initially acquired by observing others. The aversion could be overcome by eating the food without subsequent nausea (extinction).

A quasi-experimental model of food aversion is chemotherapy in cancer patients. The drugs cause the troublesome side effect of repeated nausea and vomiting, and this often conditions strong aversion of stimuli associated with chemotherapy, including food eaten beforehand (Redd & Andresen 1981). The illness is so potent a conditioner that eventually some patients begin to vomit before the drugs are injected and retch as they drive to the hospital, dress for the monthly clinic visit, or even merely think about the chemotherapy or receive a call from the oncology nurse.

The potency of illness conditioning was tested in children ages 2 to 16 who had chemotherapy for their neoplasia (Bernstein 1978). They were offered a novel ice cream 15 to 60 minutes before their chemotherapy. Children who had a gastrointestinal upset after the drugs were subsequently less likely to choose that ice cream again than controls who had the same drug-induced toxicity without the preceding ice cream. Most of the children were aware that the drugs caused their nausea and vomiting but nevertheless could not stop formation of a long-lasting food aversion. Adult chemotherapy patients, too, developed an aversion to a novel food presented prior to the nauseating drug (Bernstein & Webster 1980). A final quasi-experimental situation in which humans may develop aversion to food or drink is the treatment of alcoholism by chemical aversion or by covert sensitization, after both of which abstinence rates increase, sometimes with nausea as a response to the alcohol (Sjoden 1981).

FEAR-EVOKING STIMULI FROM ANIMALS

Fear is triggered by many stimuli generated by predators and conspecifics. Among these stimuli are abrupt movement nearby accompanied by sudden noise (like the pounding of feet or beating of wings), as well as stimuli more characteristic of only a few species.

Touch, Seizure, and Proximity

Animals, be they tubeworms or men, withdraw from sudden touch (see Chapter 7). Certain species escape from the touch of particular predators on the basis of chemical recognition: mollusks for instance, withdraw selectively from certain starfish (Chapter 3). If an animal is seized rather than merely touched, it struggles to free itself or may become still, perhaps after an initial tussle.

Escape is easier if dangerous stimuli are not allowed to come close, so distance receptors are used to avoid proximity to them. When danger comes close it threatens more, and fear is greater. The nearer a caged chaffinch is to a stuffed owl, the more likely it is to avoid the owl than to mob it (Hinde 1954). During treatment by exposure, phobic stimuli are more feared the nearer they are to the phobic patient.

Sudden Change and Movement

Sudden change startles many species, whether it is precipitate movement, noise, loss of support, or being plunged into darkness (Russell 1979; Scarr & Salapatek 1970). Stationary predators and prey often ignore one another, whereas movement catches the attention of and may frighten most animals if it is abrupt and nearby (Blanchard et al. 1975; Melzack 1952). Human toddlers may tolerate live or toy animals until they see the animal stalking or rushing toward them, which causes immediate fear (Haslerud 1938; Yerkes & Yerkes 1936). A 14-month-old girl showed great fear of a teddy bear when it was moved toward her; she turned away, trembling in every limb, yet when the teddy bear was still she would pick it up and kiss it (Valentine 1930).

Fear is more likely when another animal approaches rather than retreats (Russell 1979). Crabs, turtles, frogs, rhesus monkeys, and human infants are wary when a shadow projected on a screen in front steadily grows bigger, but not when it gets smaller or when the lit screen darkens. Objects approaching directly evoke flight from a shorter distance than do those coming obliquely on a miss path. An object rapidly coming closer looms as collision is imminent and begins to fill most of the visual field, subtending an increasingly large angle at the retina (Dill 1974); hence the saying "danger looms." Proximity may also be judged from other features, such as large size.

Being Looked At

Fear of two staring eyes is widespread throughout the animal kingdom. The more conspicuously eyelike the markings, the more they deter. Blest (1957) placed dead mealworms on a box and allowed birds (yellow buntings, chaffinches, and great tits) to approach and feed on them. As soon as a bird alighted on the box it completed an electric circuit that lit up a bulb below the mealworm, revealing one of several patterns on either side of the lure. The birds flew away more from circular patterns than from parallel lines or crosses of the same area or perimeter. The more similar the circle was to a vertebrate eye, the more effective it was in evoking escape (Figure 2.2). Conversely, removing the eyespots reduced the deterrent. When yellow buntings were presented with butterflies that had the eyespot scales rubbed off, they escaped less from these than from other butterflies with normal eye spots.

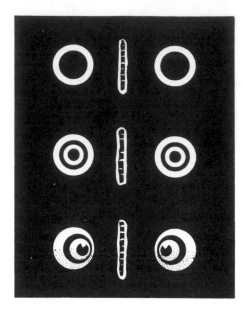

Fig. 2.2   Three of the models used by Blest (1957) to study birds' responses to the sudden appearance of different shapes. As soon as the bird approached the mealworm (center) a circle or eyespot was lit up on either side of it, and the bird's response was recorded. The single circle evoked the least escape and the eye with an eccentric pupil evoked the most. (From Edmunds 1974. Reprinted by permission.)

Other experiments also triggered fear by showing conspicuous eyes in the absence of other cues. Naive chickens strongly avoided a stuffed perched kestrel with pronounced glass eyes having a yellow iris and black pupil (Scaife 1976). Avoidance was reduced by covering the kestrel's eyes but not by altering its hawk-shaped beak. An equally novel stuffed kiwi with small eyes was approached rather than avoided, but replacing the small eyes with conspicuous ones changed this to strong avoidance. Tonic immobility was prolonged in chicks by the experimenter gazing directly at their eyes and when a stuffed hawk was present; covering its eyes reduced its effectiveness (Gallup & Maser 1977). A pair of brown glass eyes suspended above a chick also induced immobility.

Novelty cannot account for most of the frightening effects of prominent eyes. Yellow buntings avoided concentric circular eye patterns more than comparable crosses or parallel lines (Blest 1957), and eyes produced more avoidance if they were moved to "track" the chick's head rather than its feet (Scaife 1976). Immobility was precipitated in chickens only by eyes having a pupil-to-size ratio of 11:20; other ratios were ineffective (Gagliardi et al. 1976). It is interesting that in the one moth species *(Automeris io)* also studied, the eyespot pupil to size ratio was close to 11:20 (Figure 2.3)

Social phobics' fear of being watched is an exaggeration of the normal human sensitivity to eyes, which is evident from early infancy. Eyes are among the first figures visually perceived by the infant (Ambrose 1963), combining those features of the face which most attract fixation: a clearcut figure small enough to be perceived with a minimum of multiple fixation, color, movement, and light reflection. Two eyes are the minimal visual stimulus to elicit the first social response in an infant—its smile (Ahrens, cited by Ambrose 1961; Spitz & Wolff 1946), which gives such pleasure to its caretakers. Eyespots are part of the first figural entity expressed in the paintings of young children from all over the world (Jameson, personal communication, 1967). Out of the earliest scribbles the "big head" is the first to emerge between ages 3 and 4 (Kellogg 1959). This is a circle containing eyespots inside and sometimes outside, too. Legs are then added to the circle, followed by other parts of the body.

Being looked at means being the object of another's attention and intention. In normal individuals heart rate and skin conductance activity rose more when partners looked directly at rather than away from them (Ellsworth 1975); more pupillary dilation and brow movement was aroused by two horizontal eyespots than by three horizontal eyespots or two diagonal or vertical eyespots (Figure 2.4). Too frequent or prolonged gaze can produce such marked arousal that it is aversive, unless the context is nonthreatening or an explanation is provided. Direct gaze is socially salient and arousing, so the gaze of others triggers acute discomfort in self-conscious persons and is one of the most upsetting stimuli for social phobics. Autistic children tend not to look at other people's faces (Figure 2.5) (Hutt & Ounsted 1970).

Although staring is threatening for primates (see Chapter 3), it does not always frighten humans. Ordinarily staring arouses and engages the person being stared at, but the context decides what sort of engagement that is. Lovers enjoy looking into one another's eyes. In the right context looking increases another person's helpfulness. If a woman carrying a load of packages stands on a street corner and stares at a pedestrian who is waiting to cross, that pedestrian will cross faster than one who is not stared at. But if she drops a package and stares, the pedestrian is likely to approach, pick up the package, and hand it to her. The fallen package makes the engaging stare appealing rather than threatening (Ellsworth 1975).

Fig. 2.3 Eyespot patterns on an Io moth which deter bird predation. (From Gallup & Maser 1977. Copyright © 1977 by G. G. Gallup. Reprinted by permission.)

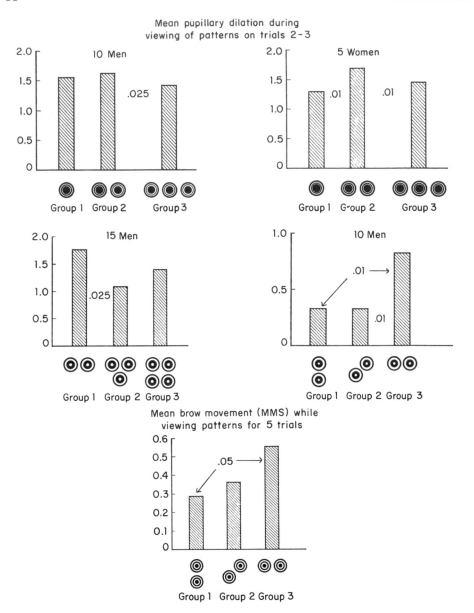

Fig. 2.4 Normal adults are aroused by eyelike patterns. Fifteen men and 15 women showed more pupillary dilation (indicating arousal) and brow movement (denoting negative interest) to slides of 2 horizontal eyespots compared with 2 diagonal or vertical eyespots or 3 eyespots. (Redrawn from Coss 1970.)

Where the context of a stare is neutral or ambiguous it can be unsettling and provoke escape. In an experiment a bystander either stared at drivers who stopped at a red light or gave them a quick glance of civil inattention. When the traffic light changed, drivers who had been stared at pulled away faster than those who had merely been glanced at. This result was replicated 11 times with the starer on a motor scooter or on the street corner, with subjects who were drivers or pedestrians, and with both sexes of experimenter and subject (Ellsworth 1975).

Snake-Like Cues

Fears of snakes may involve cues present only in certain species, or may be fear of more general features. Specific fears of poisonous coral snakes are seen in snake-eating birds (Smith 1975, 1977). The simple visual pattern that mediates this fear upsets hatchling birds that have never before seen a snake. Motmots *(Emomota superciliosa)* and great kiskadees *(Pitangus sulphuratus)* were presented with rods painted with various colored stripes running either lengthwise or in rings. The birds consistently avoided only rods with red and yellow rings.

More general snake-like cues are widely feared across many species, though the precise releasing features remain to be worked out. When snakes were

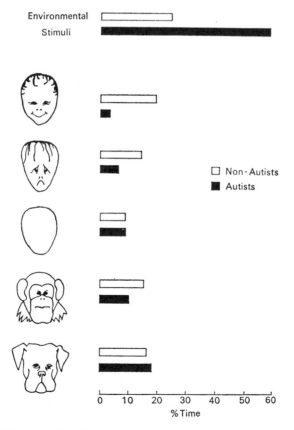

Fig. 2.5 Autistic children tend to show gaze aversion. During a 10-minute period, 8 autistic children inspected models of human faces less than did 6 normal children of the same age, and spent more time looking at environmental stimuli. (Data from Hutt & Ounsted 1970.)

taken into the monkey house in a zoo, "the monkeys at once fled back shriek-ing whilst the lemurs crowded to the front of the cage" (cited by Morris & Morris 1965). The many species of lemur are confined to Madagascar and nearby islands that have no poisonous snakes, though there are boa constric-tors. Snakes, snake skin, a crude snake model, or even large nematode worms in feces terrified young and adult chimpanzees and evoked strong avoidance (Kohler 1925; Lorenz 1971; Yerkes & Yerkes 1936).

Primates unafraid of snakes include not only lemurs but also the New World monkey *Callimico goeldii,* which may actually prey on them (Lorenz 1971). Snakes can produce alertness or aggressive defense rather than avoid-ance in rhesus monkeys (Butler 1964). The snake chutter alarm call of a vervet monkey spotting a snake causes other troop members to look toward the snake without immediately withdrawing, and is specific to that predator (Cheney & Sefarth 1981; Struhsaker 1967). California ground squirrels, too, may not with-draw but may on the contrary chatter, approach it, and touch its snout (Owings et al. 1977).

Contradictory findings can arise from differences in the snake's appearance and in the primates' age. Fear might be more likely if the snake is a certain color and pattern and is writhing, rearing, and hissing than if it is stationary or moving slowly. There was no snake fear in infant primates (Lorenz 1971) or in human infants up to 2 years old; in humans caution appeared by age 3½ and definite fear by age 4 (Jones & Jones 1928), while fear increased from age 4 to 6 (Morris & Morris 1965).

Terror of unfamiliar things, especially if they writhe, was seen dramatically in the author's son when he was 2½ years old. At that time he had never seen snakes, nor did he know the word for them. I had carried him over rocky ter-rain from a car to a beach at low tide. On the dried sand were exposed thou-sands of dried skeins of brown-black seaweed up to a foot long, looking like myriad dead eels or tiny snakes. Similar fronds of green seaweed waved in the shallow water nearby. As soon as the boy saw the dried seaweed on the sand he screamed in terror and clutched me tightly, trying to stop me from sitting on the sand. When I touched the seaweed he shrieked and refused to do the same. His panic increased when gentle waves rolled the seaweed nearby or when I held him over the water to show him the moving fronds. Slowly I tried to accustom him to the dried seaweed on the sand by playing with it myself and encouraging him to do the same. Only after a half-hour of this was he prepared even to sit on a patch of sand that had no seaweed. Then he became able to grab seaweed gingerly and quickly fling it away. He would not go near the water. The next day he touched the seaweed a bit more readily but was still obviously afraid. A week later he was able to throw the fronds away, but was still unhappy to leave them in his hand. He gradually lost his terror with con-tinuing exposure to the frightening situation.

It was noted earlier that naive snake-eating birds have a built-in fear of poisonous snakes that is independent of experience. In primates fear of snakes may develop a bit more flexibly, perhaps especially after snakes are briefly paired with fear. This can occur merely by seeing conspecifics display fear of snakes. Only wild-, not laboratory-reared, rhesus monkeys show snake fear; laboratory-reared animals evince it only if they have seen other rhesus displaying it (Cook et al. 1985; Mineka et al. 1980). Brief observation is enough to pass on snake fear (Figure 2.6A and B, p. 42) that can persist robustly, although the rhesus habituate to repeated nonthreatening presentations (Figure 2.7, p. 43). Snakes are prepotent stimuli for fear in rhesus, needing minimal learning for it to develop (see Chapter 8). In nature this learning would occur mainly through observation of frightened conspecifics, exemplifying cultural transmission. The same is likely to be true in humans. Despite the rarity of poisonous snakes in Britain, one-third of 6-year-old British children feared them.

Hawk Effect

More than a century ago Spalding (1873) vividly portrayed the instinctive defense of chicks against a deadly enemy.

> When 12 days old one of my little *proteges,* while running about beside me, gave the peculiar chirr whereby they announce the approach of danger. I looked up, and behold a sparrow-hawk was hovering at a great height overhead. Having subsequently procured a young hawk, able to take only a short flight, I made it fly over a hen with her first brood, then about a week old. In the twinkling of an eye most of the chickens were hid among grass and brushes. The hen pursued, and scarcely had the hawk touched the ground, about 12 yards from where she had been sitting, when she fell upon it with such fury that it was with difficulty that I was able to rescue it from immediate death. Equally striking was the effect of the hawk's voice when heard for the first time. A young turkey, which I had adopted when chirping within the uncracked shell, was on the morning of the 10th day of its life eating a comfortable breakfast from my hand, when the young hawk, in a cupboard just beside us, gave a shrill chip, chip, chip. Like an arrow the poor turkey shot to the other side of the room, and stood there motionless and dumb with fear, until the hawk gave a second cry, when it darted out at the open door right to the extreme end of the passage and there, silent and crouched in a corner, remained for 10 minutes. Several times during the course of that day it again heard these alarming sounds, and in every instance with similar manifestations of fear.

Experience can modify fear of hawks in birds (see Chapter 8, figures 8.10 and 8.11) but does not explain why it appears so readily at the right time. Experimenters have neglected Spalding's observations about the effect of the hawk's cry, concentrating only on the visual cues involved. Lorenz (Tinbergen 1951, p. 31) frightened newly hatched ducks and geese by moving a hawk/goose model (looking like a silhouette of a monoplane) about their heads to resemble a shortnecked bird of prey in flight. When moved in the opposite direction the model resembled a harmless long-necked waterfowl in flight and produced no escape reaction. Other workers also found greater activity evoked by hawk than by goose silhouettes in naive mallards (Green et al. 1966; Green & Carr 1968).

Cues other than the short neck also evoke fear. Wild turkeys of any age try to escape from anything appearing above them in dark silhouette against a lighter background and moving with a certain angular speed relative to the size of the object. Similar escape reactions occur from a fly creeping along the white

A. BEHAVIORAL AVOIDANCE

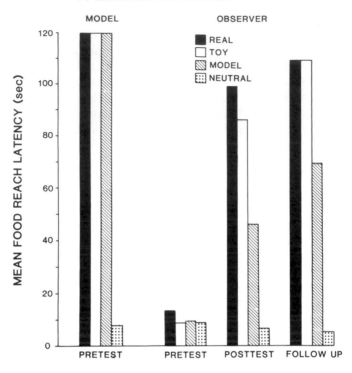

MODEL   OBSERVER

REAL
TOY
MODEL
NEUTRAL

MEAN FOOD REACH LATENCY (sec)

PRETEST   PRETEST   POSTTEST   FOLLOW UP

B. FEAR BEHAVIORS

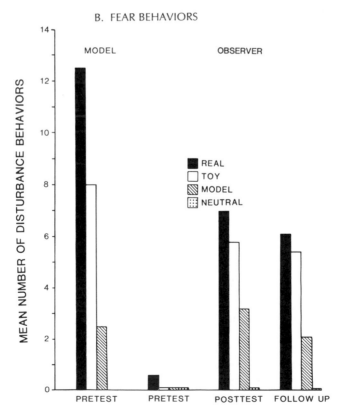

MODEL   OBSERVER

REAL
TOY
MODEL
NEUTRAL

MEAN NUMBER OF DISTURBANCE BEHAVIORS

PRETEST   PRETEST   POSTTEST   FOLLOW UP

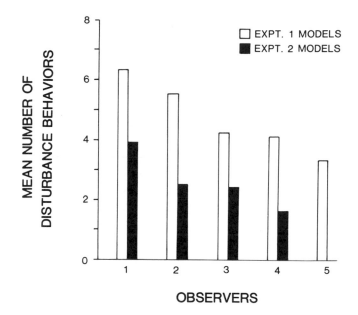

MODEL FEAR BEHAVIORS DURING CONDITIONING ACROSS OBSERVERS

Fig. 2.7 While serving as a model for successive rhesus observers (Figure 2.6 A and B), rhesus models showed steady decrease of snake fear with repeated exposure to snake stimuli over two experiments. Most of the reduction occurred in only one of the two models. (From Cook et al. 1985 unpublished.)

ceiling of the laboratory, a balloon floating across the sky, a helicopter, or a hawk *(Buteo buteo)* (Schleidt 1961, 1961a).

Additional cues may be involved. A live red-tailed hawk induced more freezing in naive bobwhite quail than did a life-sized silhouette with a similar neck (Martin & Melvin 1964). Naive mallard ducks were more wary of a hawk than of a goose silhouette even when the short neck had been deleted (Green & Carr 1968). Ducks living on a river escaped more from a stuffed hawk than from a hawk or goose silhouette (Rockett 1955). Finally, birds continued to fear a live hawk after having habituated to models of different shapes flown over them (Lorenz 1939, cited by Nash & Gallup 1976).

Fig. 2.6 Young rhesus monkeys rapidly acquire persistent fear of snakes by modeling. Ten laboratory-reared rhesus who were unafraid of snakes became markedly fearful and avoidant of them after 8 minutes spent observing two unrelated wild-reared rhesus (the models) showing fear of snakes; the fear and avoidance continued to 3-month follow-up. In (A) mean avoidance (delayed reaching for food across an open box containing snake and neutral stimuli) and in (B) disturbed behaviors are shown for the models at pretest and for the observers at pretest, post-test, and 3-month follow-up, separately for real, toy, and model snake stimuli, and for neutral objects (black and yellow cords and a block of wood). (From Cook et al. 1985 unpublished.)

The hawk model might evoke more escape because its blunt leading edge darkens the visual field more abruptly than the tapering front end of a goose, and sudden change is frightening. This does not explain why the hawk form was more effective than a triangle with the broad base leading, which causes equally sudden visual darkening (Green et al. 1966). Sudden massive increase in retinal stimulation enhances the hawk effect (Schneirla 1965). The hawk-goose model produced far more escape in chicks when it swooped than when it sailed toward them. Moreover, the same effect occurred in newly hatched gallinaceous chicks when objects as different as a stuffed bird, tea-tray, black rectangle, green box, and large black disc were swooped rapidly toward them.

Other studies found the hawk silhouette no more frightening than other shapes for ducks living on a river (Rockett 1955) and naive Leghorn chickens in a laboratory (Hirsch et al. 1955). In the latter the fear was greater when the stimulus was novel, fast, large, and cast a shadow; the fear extinguished in 10 to 12 trials and the chickens recovered spontaneously 2 to 3 hours later.

The novelty of shapes flying overhead can release disturbance (Schleidt 1961a, 1961b). Turkeys with no previous experience of flying objects were exposed to overhead circles, rectangles, or hawk silhouettes. They were first alarmed by all the shapes but habituated after repeated exposure. There appears to be a general responsiveness to objects of a certain apparent size and rate of movement. The hawk effect may result in part from habituation and may occur more in response to those shapes resembling long-necked geese that fly overhead frequently than rarer shapes such as those of hawks. Habituation is specific to stimulation that is repeated. Naive mallard ducks continued to fear models on the ground after having adapted to their flying overhead (Melzack et al. 1959).

Many hawks and other raptors have a habit of circling endlessly overhead, gliding effortlessly on thermal air currents. This suggests a nice dynamic. An animal would soon habituate to this recurrent stimulus in the sky and drop its guard if fear of hawks depended only on novelty, and perhaps the circling hawks are taking advantage of such habituation. For prey, however, it would be adaptive for hawk terror to be evoked by factors additional to novelty.

That this is so is suggested by several findings. Mallard ducks reared in social isolation without experience of objects flying overhead feared the silhouette of a hawk more than of a goose (Green & Carr 1968). In another study birds feared hawk and goose shapes equally on the first presentation and had habituated to both by the third presentation (Melzack et al. 1959). However, they habituated earlier—by the second presentation—to goose than to hawk shapes. Similarly, naive bobwhite quail escaped and froze strongly on first seeing a novel live *Buteo* hawk but only weakly to an equally novel modeled silhouette, and it took far more presentations of the live hawk before the escape and freezing had habituated to the same level as that of the model (see Figure 8.11) (Martin & Melvin 1964). Finally, the frequency with which three short-necked species of raptor overflew coots in the wild predicted the coots' regular disturbance to only two of the three species (Grubb 1977). Taking these experiments together it is obvious that although novelty makes a contribution, fear of hawks is more than mere neophobia, although the precise visual and auditory stimuli involved are not yet known.

Experience of actual predation is one factor mediating the fear of raptors (Grubb 1977). Wild American coots huddled protectively in a flock when overflown by bald eagles that prey on them, but not when overflown by two other short-necked raptors that do not usually attack them (osprey and red-shoulder hawk), nor by "short-necked" aircraft. Because the hawk and the aircraft flew over the coots as often as did bald eagles, novelty was not responsible. To the human eye the eagle and osprey seem to fly in the same way, so it is unclear how coots tell them apart (Grubb 1977).

Whatever the compound visual mechanisms behind the hawk effect, it is not present in humans. This is not surprising, given that raptors have rarely been dangerous for us as a species. Our fear of something swooping down could result from the effects of suddenness, movement, looming, and novelty, all of which are prepotent fear-evoking stimuli in humans.

Compound Releasers of Mobbing

The various factors making up the hawk effect show that the defensive response of some prey species to particular predators depends on more than novelty or movement unless the combined factors amount to a novel compound stimulus. Specific releasers of other defensive responses include compounds of plumage, eyes, and body shape and may also involve nonvisual cues, as occurs in the mobbing of owls and other predators by some small passerine birds (see Chapter 3). The mobbing defense involves alternate approach and retreat, visual fixation, and stereotyped movement and alarm calls (Curio 1975; Marler 1956). The optimal model stimulus of mobbing by chaffinches is a compound owl figure with a big head, short neck and tail, a solid contour, a patterned surface with spots, streaks or bars, brown or grey color, and, to a lesser extent, a beak and a pair of frontal eyes (Hartley 1950; Hinde 1954). The owl's call may also elicit mobbing in some small birds.

The pied flycatcher may have two distinct "channels" separately tuned to recognize each of its predators—the red-backed shrike and the Pygmy owl (Curio 1975). For the shrike the characteristic plumage of the male is crucial, and less mobbing occurs in response to movement, call, novelty, and the less striking female. Mobbing of the plumage is increased by large body size and correct orientation. For the owl the plumage texture seems critical, and the eyes and maybe the owl shape are important. Shrike and owl features do not potentiate one another.

The innate nature of the recognition is suggested by its presence in hand-raised birds that have never seen a predator. It also accords with the failure to condition mobbing, by five different methods, in both wild and captive birds to neutral and novel stimuli (Curio 1975).

Cues of Threat, Alarm, or Injury

Some prey escape from specific visual cues associated with attack by a predator. Though caribou may ignore wolves moving nearby, they will flee at the distant approach of a wolf with head lowered and pointing forward fixing its attention on the prey, making the neck and shoulder hair prominent (Pruitt 1965). Ungulates increase their flight distance from similar head lowering in African wild dogs and from bunched packs of hyenas and wild dogs, both being signs of greater danger (Schaller 1972; Walther 1969).

In primates, man included, fear occurs on seeing conspecifics who are threatening, frightened, or mutilated. Rhesus monkeys avoided photographs of threatening rhesus yet worked to obtain photographs of monkeys in other postures (Sackett 1966; see also Chapter 5 and figures 5.1 and 5.2). However, rhesus monkeys did not try to avoid the sight of a live, fearful conspecific (Butler 1964; Symmes 1959). Chimpanzees in a laboratory were terrified at the sight of a severed chimp head and of an anesthetized chimp (Hebb 1946), and in the wild showed fear grins to and avoidance of a physically disabled chimp (Goodall 1968); these reactions would have resulted partly from novelty.

Humans also have discomfort, skin conductance arousal, and heart rate changes on seeing someone who is physically disabled (Kleck 1966), pictures of mutilated human bodies (Hare 1972), accidents (Averill et al. 1972; Klorman et al. 1977), or blood (Connolly et al. 1976). At first sight of blood or surgery, fainting from slowed heart rate is not unusual in otherwise normal people, including medical students and nurses. Heart rate also slows in children seeing films of dental procedures for the first time (Melamed 1982).

On contact with their phobic stimulus, blood-injury phobics (unlike other phobics), are likely to show, after an initial rise, a dramatic drop in heart rate and a vasovagal faint (Marks 1981; see also Chapters 11 and 15). Though a slight slowing of heart rate may be part of the orienting reflex, the marked slowing with fainting that is typical of the response of blood-injury phobics is not, and cannot be attributed to novelty. This bradycardia to blood-injury stimuli may be an autonomic response of evolutionary significance that could conceivably be related to the tonic immobility reaction seen in so many species, a common feature of which is also bradycardia (Nash et al. 1976; see also Chapter 3). Grouse, for example, have an "emotional bradycardia" when they freeze on being approached (Gabrielsen et al. 1977).

Blood-injury phobics have unusually many family members with the same problem (see Chapter 6), and the problem starts quite early in childhood. They may be at the extreme end of a normal continuum of cardiovascular responsiveness to tissue-damage stimuli that is genetically influenced. It remains to be shown that the response of blood-injury phobics is an exaggeration of a normal human response to blood-injury stimuli, and that such phobics have tachycardia when in persistent contact with frightening stimuli unconcerned with tissue damage.

Smell

In humans smell is much less important than sound or sight, and there has been little experimental work on the effect of olfaction on fear. For other species, odors can be potent releasers of defensive behavior (Pfeiffer 1963, 1974).

Such odors can come from predators or from dead, injured, or frightened conspecifics. The latter are called alarm substances.

Odor of Predators

Many animals flee from the odor of their enemies. The mussel *Pecten,* the snail *Nassa mutabilis,* and limpets of the lower tidal zone escape from starfish and from extracts of starfish (see Chapter 3). Other limpets of the upper tidal zone, above the limit of the starfish, do not show this response. The Florida apple snail *(Pomacea paludosa)* falls off its support and burrows rapidly into sand on sensing the odor of its main turtle predators, *Sternotherus minor* and *Chelydra serpentina* (Curio 1976). *Paroctopus bimaculatus* gets very agitated when exposed to water coming from a tank in which its main enemy, the marine eel *(Gymnothorax mordax)* is living.

Numerous fish and reptiles respond to the odor of their predators. Coho and spring salmon swimming upstream may turn back on smelling mammalian skin. On smelling pike the European minnow, *Phoxinus laevis,* stops swimming and sinks slowly to remain immobile at the bottom. In minnows this reaction is not innate; it is absent in minnows with no previous experience of pike predation, but schools quickly learn to escape once they have smelt pike odor after natural predation or after its experimental pairing with the minnow's own alarm substance. Certain rattlesnakes recoil as though attacked when placed in the former habitat of their predator, the king snake; this reaction is unlearned, being present in rattlesnakes from areas where there are no king snakes.

Among mammals, golden hamsters posture defensively to the odor of dog and polecat, and some deer flee from the odor of man. Rats are disturbed during deep sleep on smelling a cat (Curio 1976) and freeze and urinate to the odor left behind by a cat, but not to another novel, distinctive odor such as trimethylpentane (Sieck et al. 1974), nor to a shrouded anesthetized cat (Blanchard et al. 1975). A tame hyena in a car was terrified at his first-ever whiff of lions 20 meters away that he could not see, and on another occasion one smell of an invisible caged leopard made him rush away far out of sight, not to return that day (Kruuk 1972). In contrast, many gazelle and other ungulates attend only occasionally to the odor of their predators and often ignore it, depending on other cues to detect prey (Schaller 1972; Walther 1969).

Odor of Injured or Frightened Conspecifics

Alarm substances signal danger to conspecifics (Pfeiffer 1963). The body juice of crushed conspecifics leads freshwater snails to escape out of the water or to burrow into the sand. Among insects alarm substances are common (Blum 1974). They release escape in several gregarious species of the bug order Hemiptera. The aphid *Myzus persicae* and species from four other genera discharge a secretion from their abdominal cornicles that is a powerful chemical stimulus to disperse nearby aphids, some species of which escape by dropping from the plant.

The aphid's alarm pheromone is trans-beta-farnesene, and wild potatoes containing this substance repel aphids (Gibson & Pickett 1983). It is present in the wild potato *Solomon berthaultii,* which is resistant to aphids, but absent in cultivated potatoes that are susceptible to aphids (*The Guardian,* May 12, 1983). Aphids *(Myzus persicae sulzer)* are disturbed by air coming from *S. berthaultii* but not from the cultivated potato *S. tuberosum* cv *Majestic;* moreover, aphids avoid leaves of the former but not of the latter, and also avoid plants experimentally contaminated with beta-farnesene.

Trans-beta-farnesene has been isolated from species in three different genera and evokes escape in three further species from two more genera, so the compound is not species specific. Another cross-species alarm substance is 2-hexenal, which is secreted from the third dorsal scent gland of the nymph of the red bug *Dysdercus intermedius* and is used for defense and releases alarm in adjacent individuals; it also evokes alarm in the ant *Crematogaster africana.* A concentration gradient is created that is centered on the alerted insects, thus providing directional information as well.

Hymenoptera, like ants and bees, often signal alarm with ketones, monoterpene aldehydes, formic acid, alkanes, alcohols, acetates, and sesquiterpenes. More than 40 compounds have been implicated in the alarm signals of ants. The alarm pheromones of social insects are identical to the defensive compounds of nonsocial arthropods and seem to be secondary adaptations of such chemicals.

Turning to vertebrates, newly hatched toad tadpoles and older schooling fish such as minnows flee rapidly from an injured conspecific and avoid the area for a long time. Minnows escape less from injured fish or other species (Manning 1978, p. 68). Blind fish also escape, but as individuals, not in a school. Removal of the olfactory nerve abolishes the response. For minnows the releaser is a chemical (probably a pterin) discharged into the water from club cells in the skin; these cells do not open onto the skin surface and release the alarm substance only when the epithelium is damaged (Pfeiffer 1963, 1974). Fish often cease to respond to the alarm substance after a few tests; tadpoles may take 20 minutes before slowly returning to the area after a test, and take much longer to habituate.

Other fish species have varied responses to alarm substances. The tench *Tinca vulgaris* and the crucian carp *Carassius carassius* swim excitedly with their heads against the bottom and their bodies at an angle of about 60° to the substrate, which disturbs the mud and conceals them. Some bottom fish, such as *Gobio fluviatilis* and *Nemacheilus barbatulus,* become motionless, especially as adults. Other fish, such as *Esmos lineatus,* crowd together at the surface and jump out of the water. Hatchet fish, *Carnegiela strigate,* which normally swim close to the surface, leave it and form a dense school in the middle of the tank.

Alarm substances may reduce cannibalism of young fish by their older fellows. An older minnow, after eating or injuring a very small conspecific so releasing its alarm substance, will take fright, swim away, and thereafter avoid the schools of small minnows. Immature northern squawfish *(Ptychocheilus oregonense)* were greatly alarmed after their eating of a smaller conspecific had released the alarm substance from it.

There are seasonal losses of fish alarm substance. Sometimes males in the breeding season do a lot of digging and fighting that injure the skin, and they need to turn off their alarm substance so as not to turn off the females (G. Williams, personal communication, 1982).

Fear of alarm substances among fish occurs regardless of habitat. It is restricted to the orders Ostariophysi and Gonorhynchiformes, which have common ancestors, suggesting that the fright reaction evolved before their divergence in the Cretaceous or Jurassic periods of the Oligocene (Pfeiffer 1963, 1974). The Ostariophysi order contains two-thirds of all species of fresh-water fish. Some of its members, such as the blind Mexican cave fish *Anoptichthys jordani,* have lost the fright reaction to alarm substances; there are no predators in the Mexican caves.

In tadpoles the alarm substance and fright reaction to it have been found only in the genus *Bufo* or in the family Bufonidae, which tend to swim in schools. Minnows and Bufo tadpoles do not respond to one another's alarm substances. Moreover, fish habituate rapidly and tadpoles very slowly to their respective fright substances. The similar defense by fish and by tadpoles of producing alarm substances and showing fright to them is thus convergent in origin.

Among mammals, mice avoid odorized airstreams from, and areas previously occupied by, a conspecific that had been stressed, despite having preferred its odor beforehand (Rottman & Snowdon 1972). The odor aversion was abolished by removal of the olfactory mucosa. Rats can discriminate between airstreams from shocked and unshocked conspecifics (Valenta & Rigby 1968).

Scent marking of territory is not found in humans but is common among other mammals, as anyone knows who has taken a dog for a walk. Conspecifics respect marked areas (Russell 1979). In the mouse the scent is a pheromone from the coagulating gland that is secreted in the urine under the influence of androgens; voided male rat urine also acts as a marker. Marker scent comes from glands in the flank of golden hamsters, near the eye in some deer, and under the tail in lemurs.

Sounds

Distress and alarm calls not only express mood but also alert and cause fear in other animals, especially conspecifics (see Chapter 3). An alarm call thus alarms and is a sign of alarm at the same time. When one animal in a group detects a predator and gives an alarm call, its fellows will become alert, freeze, or escape. Alarm calls release fear behavior in conspecifics independent of the intensity or suddenness of the cries. The effects of recorded alarm calls differ from those of nonalarm conspecific calls in herring gulls (Frings et al. 1955). In pheasant chicks, recorded adult alarm calls, unlike white noise of comparable intensity, evoked silent crouching (which in nature would lead to camouflage) (Heinz 1973). Unlike alarm calls, fright calls of the chick did not affect other chicks, being more like the flock calls that stimulate approach and brood-gathering calls from the hens.

Recordings of alarm calls have been successfully used to repel birds from areas where they are a nuisance to humans (Frings et al. 1955), such as farmlands and airports. Starlings *(Sturnus vulgaris)* can be driven away from roosts by broadcasting to them the recorded distress call of one of their fellows. Though herring gulls *(Larus argentatus)* have no distress call, they have a two-part alarm call. When the attention cry is broadcast the gulls rise into the air immediately, and after the alarm call they slowly circle away and leave. In contrast, food-finding calls of the same intensity are highly attractive. The alarm call of the herring gull also repels related species such as great black-backed gulls *(Larus marinus)* and laughing gulls *(Larus artricilla)*.

Many mammalian species have well-developed auditory alarm systems. A colony of marmots is alerted by the whistle of a member perceiving danger, and vizcachas respond to similar warnings (Bourliere 1955). The snort of an adult Thomson's gazelle alerts its fellows, and a fawn's distress cry will bring its mother rushing to it (Walther 1969). Vervet monkeys give at least four distinctive alarm calls to different types of predator, each releasing its appropriate form of defensive behavior; alarm calls are given most often to the most dangerous predators (Cheney & Sefarth 1981).

Fear is also shown to sounds that are part of the threat display of conspecifics (p. 11). Samurai warriors gave terrifying grunts as they cut down their opponents. Many other mammals give harsh, intense threat sounds like barks and roars. Nonvocal sounds are made by dominant male chimpanzees, which stamp on the ground or beat on tree trunks (Goodall 1968), while gorillas thump their chests and charge.

In contrast to the fear aroused by sounds from conspecifics, ungulates usually ignore the roars of lions and calls of hyenas unless the predators are very close (Walther 1969; Schaller 1972). This parallels their indifference to the odor, slow movement, and sight of distant predators (see Chapter 4). Rats, too, ignore recorded calls of a cat (Blanchard et al. 1975). Sensitivity to the calls of predators would be of little help to ungulate prey, since predators are especially quiet in their early stalking approach and make obvious sounds only when they rush for the final kill. At that stage of attack the pounding of rushing feet or beating of wings induce fear through the mechanisms of sudden, intense, and novel stimulation.

Birds may fear the cries of predators. Spalding long ago observed a turkey escaping from the cry of a hawk hidden from view. Some small birds give mobbing responses to the calls of the small owls that prey on them but not of the larger owls that do not (Miller 1952).

In humans, hearing and vision are the dominant channels influencing the stream of behavior. Human parents have an urge to rush to their baby's aid when it cries in fear or pain, and humans experience acute discomfort on hearing others screaming in agony or panic. The angry buzzing of bees instills panic in many people.

Selective attention to certain sounds starts early. Young infants attend more to particular durations of silence during speech regardless of the language spoken (Marler 1979), chunking the stream of sound, but whether there is a prepotent template of sounds that are preferentially learned as fear cues is unknown. There has been little experimental work on prepotent auditory triggers of fear, apart from loudness and abruptness. Some perceptual categorization of speech might reflect experience inside the uterus, where speech can be heard. Most frightening sounds, however, have presumably become so through experience after birth.

Being Alone

The dangers of being alone without our fellows are numerous (see Chapter 4). Although being alone helps some small, cryptic species to avoid predators, in many others isolated animals are more likely to be killed by predators and may have more difficulty in finding food or obtaining the warmth generated by group huddling or activity, not to mention problems in finding a mate. Important mechanisms have evolved to keep conspecifics attached to one another and to reestablish contact when it has been lost. Primate contact calls are often elaborate and frequent, especially in dense habitats (J. Caldecott, personal communication, 1984). An extensive literature documents the separation fear or anxiety that ensues when the crucial bond is disrupted between a young animal and its mother or other caretaker (see chapters 5 and 7), and the grief reaction that occurs in adult animals after other losses (Bowlby 1973). In general, fearful searching for the lost object is the dominant reaction soon after an attachment has been broken, and depression tends to occur later. Anxious clinging is prominent on reunion after separation (Figure 2.8).

Fig. 2.8 Juvenile rhesus regress to anxious mutual clinging on reunion after separation. Mother-reared infants cling to mother on reunion. (From Suomi et al. 1981. Copyright © 1981 by Raven Press.)

Primates reared in isolation grow less attached to companions and less distressed on separation from them, and may indeed be afraid of rather than comforted by conspecifics. For a socially reared organism, however, being alone is a novel experience that can itself be fear-evoking (Russell 1979). To what extent familiar conspecifics are more potent fear reducers than equally familiar inanimate situations remains to be determined.

Most humans prefer regular social contact with their fellows, hermits being notable exceptions. Fears are usually greater when we are alone than with a trusted companion. Agoraphobics commonly have no fear in public places except when they are unaccompanied (see Chapter 10). Although social phobics shun particular forms of social contact, such as meeting a stranger (see Chapter 11), they rarely like to be completely alone for most of the time.

SUMMARY

Species share similar fears as they do dangers. Fear is especially evoked by stimuli which are abrupt, intense, irregular, and rapidly increasing. Land-dwelling species fear heights and withdraw from the edge of a "visual cliff." They are afraid if there is too much or too little space or light around them. Novelty of objects, food, or situations is a widespread source of fear and of curiosity which die down as familiarity with them is gained. Food aversions are associated with nausea and vomiting more than with fear and can be very powerful and lasting if they are not habituated by exposure.

Fear is generated by many stimuli from conspecifics and other species. Sudden touch, proximity, approach, movement, or being looked at are potent elicitors of fear in humans and other species. Numerous birds and mammals, humans included, are alarmed by snake-like cues despite no or minimal traumatic experience of snakes. The terror that newly hatched birds have of hawk calls or shapes depends on several cues. The mobbing defense by passerine birds is elicited by compound predator features such as plumage, shape, size, orientation, and call.

When other animals are threatening, alarmed, or injured, fear is induced; the cues may be visual, auditory, or olfactory. The sight of blood can lead humans to faint in bradycardia. Alarm odors are found in two related orders of fish and one genus of tadpole; the alarm odors in fish and in tadpoles differ from one another, indicating convergent evolution. Ungulates seem unperturbed by the smells or calls from their predators, responding more to visual cues. Rodents avoid the smell of stressed conspecifics, and in many mammalian species animals respect the territorial marker scents of their fellows. In birds and mammals alarm calls from conspecifics are important triggers of fear; in monkeys different predators evoke contrasting calls. Humans feel discomfort on hearing other people cry out in distress. Separation from conspecifics is frightening for the young as well as for the adults of gregarious species.

3
Fear Behaviors: The Four Strategies

When danger threatens, an organism can ignore it and so court disaster. Survival is more likely if the animal tries to protect itself in some way. There are four main defensive strategies—to withdraw, become immobile, threaten or attack the enemy, or try to deflect or inhibit its attack. The two chief defensive strategies with predators are withdrawal or immobility, and a third, defensive attack, can alternate with them. Finally, if the enemy's attack cannot be prevented it might be deflected to become less damaging or, with conspecifics, to be inhibited by appeasement (submission). As we saw earlier, the behaviors that execute these four fear strategies may also appear in other behavioral repertoires. A lucid account of fear behavior from an evolutionary perspective appears in Barnard (1983).

The defensive strategies of humans are shared with distantly related taxa. Similar problems may induce similar solutions. In related species the solution is likely to be by a common mechanism (homologous), but across remotely related taxa apparently similar fear behavior can evolve by convergence utilizing very different causal mechanisms (analogous).

Relatively few differences are seen in fear behavior displayed inter- or intraspecifically. Aggressive defense may be one exception; the cheetah's interspecific threat display is not shown to its fellows (Eaton 1974). Another exception is appeasement, which is used frequently to avert attack from a conspecific but not from a predator of another species. A fear strategy works better if it is tailored to the degree and type of threat that has to averted.

WITHDRAWAL (FLIGHT, ESCAPE, AVOIDANCE)

Unicellular Organisms

Even one-celled organisms show the phenomena of withdrawal from danger, habituation to repeated stimulation, and simple learning, all of which occur throughout the animal kingdom and help the organism regulate its relationship to its environment. That protozoa without a nervous system show these features suggests potentially widespread similarities in cellular mechanisms of reaction to noxious stimulation since early in evolution. (Similarity in morphological or behavioral appearance does not, of course, prove identity of mechanism.)

If a bright pinpoint of light is focused on an advancing pseudopodium of a protozoan such as *Amoeba,* the pseudopodium withdraws. If the bright light is shone on the entire body of the amoeba it contracts suddenly and will extrude any half-eaten food. However, if it cannot escape from the light the amoeba, after a few moment's hesitation, shows habituation by ignoring the stimulus and resuming its normal activities (Curtis 1979, p. 900).

Protozoa with cilia, such as *Paramecium,* show slightly more complex behavior: avoidance by the whole organism. A paramecium continuously explores the environment ahead by shifting and sampling. Changes in its environment lead to avoidance. It turns away, always in the same direction, to its left from the cytostome, regardless of the side the stimulus comes from (Figure 3.1). This is achieved by relaxation of the beat of the body cilia. If a microscopist takes a blunt needle and jabs a paramecium on the aboral side, it still turns toward that side (Curtis 1979). If the negative stimulus is powerful, such as a solid object, hot or cold water or a noxious chemical, the paramecium will stop short, reverse its ciliary beat, back up, turn toward the aboral side about 30°, and then start forward again (Jennings 1906). Under strong stimulation it will turn a full 360° and continue to turn until an avenue of escape is found.

Paramecium also avoids neutral or alkaline areas. This property enhances survival because, like bacteria, which are its primary food, paramecium gives off carbon dioxide, creating a slightly acidic environment. By the simple mechanism of avoiding nonacidic areas, therefore, it tends to gather where there is food.

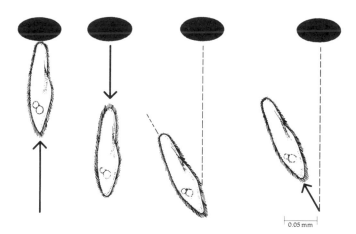

Fig. 3.1 Avoidance behavior in *Paramecium.* The dark oval at the top denotes a drop of a toxic substance, and the arrows indicate the direction of movement of the paramecium, which tests the substance, backs up, turns 30°, and starts forward again in a new direction. Many protists are capable of this sort of simple behavior. (From Curtis 1979. Copyright © 1979 by Worth Publishers, NY. Reprinted by permission.)

Additional features of learning and of blowing away a noxious stimulus are seen in the ciliate protozoan *Stentor* (Curtis 1979, p. 902). If poked with a needle, stentor avoids it by bending, always toward the aboral side. If poked repeatedly it contracts its body and then extends it again. After being jabbed several times it habituates and resumes feeding (which it cannot do when contracted) or detaches itself and swims away. It tolerates the noxious stimulus longer if its site of attachment had previously been a good feeding area, so some learning of reward is involved. It can also blow away noxious material by reversing its cilia.

We turn now from protozoa to their very distant relatives, the metazoa or multicellular animals.

Multicellular Organisms

Withdrawal from danger is usually rapid and can take many forms. Retreat from damaging stimuli into a protective enclosure occurs in sedentary animals; for example, if a sea anemone is touched it closes up quickly. The retreat can be behind anatomical defenses such as the spines of hedgehogs, armored plates of armadilloes, and shells of tortoises; such animals withdraw their soft, unprotected parts and then become immobile. Gravity-assisted withdrawal is seen in many spiders and some caterpillars and pulmonate mollusks that, when attacked, drop on a silken thread and later climb back up it.

More active escape from threat is seen in mobile animals. Their evolution of distance receptors and more sophisticated nervous systems gave them an early warning system that enabled them to perceive danger in advance and avoid it, rather than waiting for contact before escaping. This monitoring system requires central representations of environmental features, allowing detection of change from the discrepancy between observed and expected stimuli. Change then triggers appropriate action.

In active escape or avoidance the animal withdraws by running, jumping, swimming, flying, or suddenly dropping through the air. Escape may continue until a pursuing predator gives up the chase or the prey reaches safety. If escape is not possible and fear is extreme, there may be undirected attempts to escape in all directions (panic).

Avoidance can be merely passive: the animal ceases to approach a stimulus. Individuals become shy in places where they have been harrassed, for instance, pheasants roost in trees instead of on the ground after disturbance by ground predators (Curio 1976), and rape victims avoid the site of the attack and cues reminding them of it (see Chapter 11). Ever-present danger forces many animals to select safe habitats at a cost to feeding or mating opportunities. Lots of animals forage at a time of minimal danger; fish vulnerable to birds, for example, move into shallow water to feed at night (G. Williams, personal communication, 1982).

The precise type of escape varies with the species. Fish swim away from danger, sometimes to curious cover—like the pearl fish, *Carapus acus,* which retreats from predators into the anus of a sea cucumber (Edmunds 1974), or some African tilapias, whose young escape at time of danger into the mouth of either parent (Lagler et al. 1962, p. 289). Other fish will shelter among the spines of sea urchins or the stinging tentacles of sea anemones. Some species develop a life-style of routine concealment in holes they dig themselves or which are provided by other animals (hermit crabs live in mollusk shells). Other animals dive down a burrow or hole only when danger threatens; if predators follow, the entrance might be blocked or a second exit constructed. Species may use a mixture of flight and disguise; grasshoppers and some ground-dwelling birds flee a short distance and then rest motionless and cryptic. Humans withdraw from threat in a great variety of forms, from headlong rush in panic out of a burning building, to postponement of a meeting that is likely to turn nasty, to avoidance of even thinking about unpleasant things (see "dissociation," Chapter 14).

Erratic Escape (Protean Movements)

In Greek mythology Proteus frustrated his captors by constant transformation. Animals of many classes frequently flee from a predator not in a straight line but in an erratic irregular manner, with zigzags, spins, loops, bounces, tumbles, rolls, and dives (Humphries & Driver 1971). This unsystematic, protean behavior prevents the pursuer from predicting the detailed position of the prey and so decreases the probability of its being caught (Figure 3.2). A few predators, however, are more likely to attack an animal showing erratic, distressed, or panicky movements than one fleeing directly (Curio 1976).

PROTEAN DEFENCE BY PREY ANIMALS

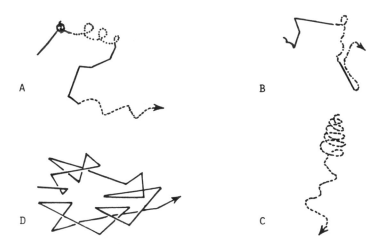

Fig. 3.2 Examples of a single erratic display. A = *Psychoda phalaenoides* disturbed by a touch; B = escape reaction of a duck flea *Ceratophyllus parei;* C = response of a chironomid disturbed from its resting place on a tree trunk. D = *Gasterosteus* chased by a merganser duckling. (From Humphries & Driver 1970. Copyright © Springer Verlag, Heidelberg. Reprinted by permission.)

Examples of erratic escape movements are the passive and power dives, loops, rolls, and tight turns of moths on perceiving strong ultrasonic pulses from a hunting bat; less strong pulses from a more distant bat leads the moth to fly in a straight line at top speed. Erratic escape is also seen in many other arthropods and fish and in the zigzag flight of snipe and ptarmigan, the European hare and Thomson's gazelle, and humans trying to avoid being shot.

Protean escape is prominent in groups of prey animals (see Chapter 4). A predator has to switch repeatedly among multiple choices from many simultaneous, individual erratic paths. The group may scatter, each individual using slightly different escape tactics. In a pheasant brood some flee in a straight line, others zigzag or double back, some may feign injury, and yet others freeze into immobility. This hinders anticipation by the predator, and, where there is cover, it produces more random dispersion of hidden individuals. Aggressive defense, too, may be erratic, as in mobbing, where many prey irregularly rush toward and away from the predator. A flock of birds might also fly in a united erratic pattern in which individuals' movements are coordinately bunched and zigzagging, with erratic shuffling of members' relative positions.

Changes in Appearance During Erratic Displays: Flash Colors and Sounds

In many species the confusing effect of alterations in movement and behavior is increased by rapid changes in appearance, particularly color and sound (Edmunds 1974; Humphries & Driver 1971). Animals often deceive predators by a flash of color as they move, which disappears when they come to rest. A striking example is the escaping cuttlefish *Sepia officinalis* (Holmes 1940): "While at one moment one's eyes are fixed on a white animal with two black spots, at the next it seems to have disappeared for its rapid movement is accompanied by total darkening of its body, by full expansion of all chromatophores [which is] ... most deceptive to a human observer." A conspicuous image is thus first presented to the predator and then suddenly switched off at the moment of escape. This disrupts a predator's searching image formed during initial contact with the prey. The predator may not only be deceived as to the whereabouts of the animal once the flash is over when the prey is still, but may also hesitate at this sudden movement and flash of color.

There are many examples of misleading stimulus patterns of escape. The small tortoiseshell butterfly *Aglais urticae* escapes in a fast, erratic zigzag ending in sudden concealment of the bright upper surfaces of the wings and a switch to cryptic immobility. Grasshoppers show flash colors and zigzag flight. The squid *Sepioteuthis* switches its brown color on and off rapidly when fleeing erratically after disturbance. An escaping school of sardines gives a brilliant silvery flash after which normal orientation is renewed and the school disappears. Further examples of flash colors abound in moths, mantids, frogs, and lizards. Flash noises may serve the same function of confusing the predator as do flash colors (for example, the buzz or click of grasshoppers when they fly, and the irregular bursts of ultrasound from arctiid moths, which deter attacking bats).

Flash colors are seen in many birds as they flap their wings and in the white rumps that ungulates and rabbits expose by lifting their tail when fleeing. These flashes vanish when the birds close their wings and when the animals stop and let their tails down. Such flashing white rumps may not only confuse the predator ("now you see me, now you don't") but also warn other prey that a predator is nearby. When fleeing from a predator it may be worthwhile warning other group members after they have been passed (Harvey & Greenwood 1980). The rump patch signal becomes a mutual alarm system within a species. It can also warn other species nearby; many species in the tropics that form mixed groups share the same colors on the rump or under the tail (Moynihan 1968). This evolution of a common sign-stimulus among unrelated species is an example of convergence facilitating protective interspecific communication; another example is alarm calls (see Chapter 4).

Yet another function of flashing white rumps might be pursuit invitations (Smythe 1970) that tempt a predator into fruitless and exhausting chase while there is still time to escape ("catch me if you can, but I know you're there and can easily escape, so let's get it over with right away, or you could chase less alert prey instead"). This ploy is of course only helpful if at that moment it is safer to flee than to freeze. The gain is less disruption of the prey's time and energy budget. At the end of an unsuccessful chase the prey is freed from keeping the exhausted predator under constant observation and can do other things instead.

IMMOBILITY

Withdrawal from danger is not always possible or helpful. The opposite strategy of keeping still may then come into play. Immobility reactions to fear-stimuli may be broadly divided into two forms, attentive and tonic.

Attentive Immobility (Freezing)

During attentive immobility an alerted individual remains motionless and monitors the source of danger, ready for fight or flight in an instant. Along with other species, we too "freeze in our tracks" and "prick up our ears" at sudden noise, trying to identify its source while scanning the visual field. The animal is very vigilant and responsive to external stimuli such as touch. Freezing may last seconds or hours and may cease gradually (by first moving the eyes, then the head, and finally the whole body) or end quickly in flight.

Attentive immobility can be more successful than flight. If a moose stands its ground when harried by wolves, it is less likely to be attacked and killed than if it runs away (Mech 1970, p. 219) (Figure 3.3). Such immobility may alternate with aggressive defense (p. 69), for instance, an alert moose at bay is belligerent and charges wolves at intervals. Freezing can also alternate with flight in quick succession and is more prominent in anoles if the threat is far away and if shelter is close by (Hennig et al. 1976).

Alternatively, attentive immobility may involve hiding quietly and still in camouflage or shelter (like King Charles in the hollow oak tree when the Roundheads were after him). Many ungulates, such as adult reedbuck and bushbuck and the young of gazelle, hartebeest, and eland escape predators by crouching motionlessly (Schaller 1972, p. 236). Very young animals may spend much of the day hidden in the grass with ears flattened and head close to the ground. Even when a predator stumbles on a fawn its startled flight is so precipitous that the predator often fails to react in time to catch it. Lions have passed repeatedly within 10 meters of crouched reedbuck, one of which lay hidden in tall grass within 5 meters of three lionesses for at least 3 hours.

When animals have their own protective structure they may become immobile after rapid withdrawal behind it (others, such as echidna, may retreat behind spines and burrow fast away). The cover might be a shell (mollusk, tortoise), armor (armadillo, pangolin), or sharp quills (hedgehog, porcupine,

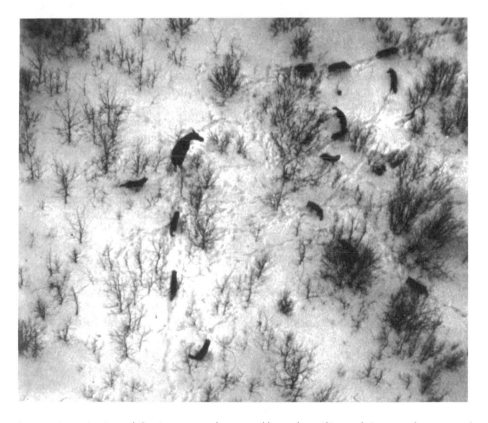

Fig. 3.3 Attentive immobility in a moose threatened by wolves. If it stands its ground upon attack it is usually able to fend them off. Here the moose stood for 5 min, and the wolves gave up and left. (From Mech 1970. Copyright © 1970 by Doubleday. Reprinted by permission.)

tenrec). Posture while immobile is appropriate to these structures (Bourliere 1964, p. 112), as is seen in three different genera of armadillo. *Tolypeutes* has a scapular shield shaped in sections like a horseshoe; it rolls itself into a ball if threatened, with the head and tail ends fitting closely together (Figure 3.4A), *Euphractus* has the shield more flattened in a low arc and presses itself against the ground when taken by surprise, whereas *Chlamyphorus* uses its posterior shield to close the burrow in which it takes refuge (Figure 3.4B). The Old World pangolins *Manidae* have armor made up of broad horny scales regularly overlapping like shingles on a roof; they roll themselves up into a ball (Figure 3.5), like *Tolypeutes.* The female of the Indian pangolin *Manis indica* also protects her young in case of danger by placing it on her belly and then curling her long protective tail around them both.

Tonic (Unresponsive) Immobility

Distinct from freezing, this reaction is the sudden onset of prolonged stillness and decreased responsivity in a previously active animal in the face of threatening stimulation. Tonic immobility is an extreme fear reaction in which the

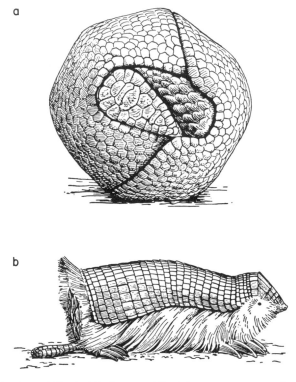

Fig. 3.4 Defensive immobility in (A) the armadillo *Tolypeutes conurus,* which rolls itself into a ball, and (B) *Chlamyphorus truncatus,* which takes refuge in a burrow and closes it with its posterior shield. (From Edmunds 1974.)

Fig. 3.5 Defensive immobility in the pangolin *Manis tricuspis,* which rolls itself into a ball. (From Edmunds 1974.)

animal or person is "scared stiff" and unresponsive to even painful or other intense stimulation. Although distinct from the freezing of attentive immobility, tonic immobility is not an entirely inattentive state. During it higher animals remain alert to changing conditions that might allow them to escape, and they often suddenly "come alive" and make their getaway at an opportune moment (Ewell et al. 1981; Sargeant & Eberhardt 1975). Until then the animal is "paralyzed with fear," and this inhibits attack from many predators.

In contrast to the limited writings about attentive immobility, there is a huge literature about this dramatic fear response, perhaps because it is so striking, discrete, and stereotyped (reviewed by Gallup 1974; Gallup & Maser 1977; Hofer 1970; Klemm 1971; Ratner 1967, 1976, 1977). Accounts of tonic immobility date back to ancient times (Klemm 1971). Homer's *Odyssey* refers to putting animals and men into trances with stroking movements. The Talmud notes immobilization of lizards, scorpions, and snakes, and that induction of such states was permitted on the Sabbath if done to protect oneself from those poisonous creatures. Uncertainty about the nature of tonic immobility is reflected in the numerous names given to it (Klemm 1971): death feint or shamming, thanatosis, playing possum, still reaction, akinesis, terror paralysis, paroxysmal inhibition, totstellung, animal hypnosis, mesmerism, entrancement, bewitchment, fascination, catalepsy, cataplexy, monoideism, rho, and letisimulation.

Tonic immobility is a robust defensive response documented in scores of invertebrate and vertebrate species ranging from arthropods and mollusks to fish, amphibians, reptiles, birds, and mammals, including humans. A few species seem resistant to the response, such as European wrens (Armstrong 1955, p. 249), kangaroo rats (Hofer 1970), and other species after being tamed, which may habituate them to being handled (Ratner 1967). The response may last from a mere 15 seconds to several hours, the average being 8 to 10 minutes in chickens; and it has endured for 8 hours or even, rarely, days in chickens and lizards (Prestrude 1977).

There are lots of ways to induce tonic immobility, as is seen from various folk practices, many of which use physical restraint (Ratner 1967). Japanese fishermen immobilize crabs by resting them on their backs, children "paralyze" frogs by turning them on their backs and stroking them on the stomach, and alligator wrestlers also induce tonic immobility. In laboratories rabbits are injected or have blood drawn after they have been immobilized by inverting them into a V-shaped trough and holding them briefly. Confinement during shipping or forceful manipulation of tired animals may lead to tonic immobilization for hours or even days. People who band birds observe that the bird may fight strongly and then become dead still in the bander's hand; the band is then very easy to apply, but if the bird is thrown into the air it recovers and flies away (Ratner 1976).

Experimentally, tonic immobility is reliably elicited by sudden, extremely threatening stimulation such as physical restraint, sudden noise, or being thrust into new surroundings (Hofer 1970). It can also be induced by sudden inversion (even in man). Death feigning can occur in opossums (Figure 3.6) and in hog-nosed snakes in the presence of a nearby predator even without being seized (Gallup, personal communication, 1982). Motionlessness is also induced by hooding birds, staring at chickens (Ratner 1967), and shining a light at fish. Artificial glass eyes suspended by themselves on wooden dowels markedly potentiate immobility in crabs and chickens, while covering the eyes shortens the reaction (Figure 3.7 and 3.8). There is disagreement about whether the tonic immobility induced by physical restraint is the same behavior as the motionlessness triggered by sudden noise, being thrust into new surroundings, being stared at, or the presence of a nearby predator even without being seized (M. Woodruff 1977 and personal communication, 1983).

Fig. 3.6 A Virginia opposum "playing dead." (From Bourliere 1955. Copyright © 1955 by Editions Payot. Reprinted by permission.)

Fig. 3.7 A chicken showing tonic immobility after brief physical restraint. (From Gallup & Maser 1977. Copyright © 1977 by Journal of Animal Learning and Behavior. Reprinted by permission.)

Onset can take from a fraction of a second to a few seconds. If restrained the animal first struggles frantically to escape but after a few seconds becomes silently still and unresponsive, even in the absence of further restraint. Some species, such as millipedes, certain snakes, and armadillos, also roll themselves into a ball. There will be no movement even to pinpricks, cutting, or electric shock. The animal seems to be dead or asleep, with waxy flexibility of

Fig. 3.8 Tonic immobility induced in a chicken by the staring eyes of a stuffed Cooper's hawk. Covering the hawk's eyes abolished the reaction. (From Gallup & Maser 1977. Copyright © 1971 by the Psychological Record. Reprinted by permission.)

limbs, hypertonicity of skeletal muscles, tremors of the limbs, occasional head turns and eye movements that may follow the predator, intermittent eye closure, and pupillary dilation. Defecation may occur in birds and guinea pigs (Ratner 1967), and occasional distress calls are given by chicks toward the end of the immobility (Gallup et al. 1971). Rarely the animal may also change color, as in the octopus and toadfish (Ratner 1977). Prolonged immobility is predicted in chickens by sustained eye closure and by defecation (Gallup et al. 1971).

Autonomic changes include pupillary dilatation (Boren et al. 1981), though pupillary reflexes seem intact in birds (Ratner 1967). Body temperature drops (Gallup & Maser 1977). Respiration is initially rapid and can be so fast and shallow in rodents that it looks like a fine, high frequency tremor of the whole body (Hofer 1970). Later the respiratory rate may drop below basal levels (Prestrude 1977). Heart rate may initially increase and then decrease, often markedly (Bourliere 1964, p. 116; Gallup & Maser 1977; Hofer 1970; Klemm 1971; Ratner 1967).

The neurophysiological and sensory-processing features of tonic immobility may change when it lasts a long time (M. Woodruff, personal communication, 1983). While the EEG during tonic immobility in rabbits and opossums is often first that of a normal awake, alert animal (Hofer 1970; Klemm 1971; Norton et al. 1964), if the state continues in rabbits for more than 2 to 3 minutes, slow waves appear in the neocortex and hippocampus (Harper 1971; Hatton et al. 1978). There are other complexities. When sleep patterns appeared in a rabbit, the normal EEG arousing reaction remained, which does not happen during central inhibition by narcosis (Svorad 1957). During tonic immobility in a frog and three guinea pigs the EEG slowed in frequency and the background rhythms disappeared (Schwartz & Bickford 1956).

Recovery often occurs with abrupt explosion into vigorous activity, commonly with lightning escape or attack (Hofer 1970; Wallnau & Gallup 1977). In birds it may be followed by injury feigning (Armstrong 1942, cited by Ratner 1967). Termination of tonic immobility may be heralded by vocalization, small movements, or return of color. Recovery is faster when the animal is near shelter and slower when close to the experimenter (Ewell et al. 1981; Hennig et al. 1976). Animals rarely die during the reaction, but parasympathetic cardiac arrythmias or fatal arrest are liable for up to a week after repeated reactions in newly trapped rodents (Hofer 1970).

The behavioral inhibition is efferent, not afferent. Immobile pigeons did not look in the direction of a loud noise made nearby six times, though their heart rate went up with each repetition, showing that they detected the sounds despite not reacting (Ratner 1967). During tonic immobility chickens are processing information; classically conditioned reactions acquired during it persist after it ends, while both retrieval and extinction of previously learned associations occur during it (Gallup & Maser 1977, Gallup et al. 1980). Contrary to its appearance of death the animal is extremely aroused, with rapid respiration (at least initially), intact EEG arousing reaction, and liability to explode into sudden activity. Tonic immobility, however, is more than mere high arousal. It is not increased by arousal resulting from hunger, from the frustration of withholding expected food, or from d-amphetamine (Gallup & Maser 1977).

An excellent account of tonic immobility is in chipmunks that showed prolonged splay-legged immobility upon forced emergence into an unfamiliar setting, and in 16- to 20-day old rat pups made immobile by sudden noise in unfamiliar surroundings for up to 5 minutes, with increased respiration rate and greatly reduced heart rate (Hofer 1970). Hofer also tested 31 wild rodents from 6 desert species in a standard open-field arena by exposing them to the noise of flat pieces of wood being slapped together, a cardboard silhouette of a hawk swooping down, and a 5-foot snake.

The rodents were taken alone in their nesting box into an open arena, where the top was removed, which allowed the sides to splay flat and thus suddenly exposed the animal to the open field. Immediately the ground squirrels and chipmunks struck awkward positions in the center of the arena as if stopped in midmovement in the single frame of a movie. Often their legs, tail, or head were stiffly stretched at an unusual angle to the body. Woodrats and a grasshopper mouse darted first to one side or the corner of the arena and crouched. Immobility lasting 2 to 60 minutes occured in 21 of the 31 animals and in 4 of the 6 species tested. Nocturnal species such as the kangaroo rat showed the least stillness. Tonic immobility was accompanied by very rapid, shallow, almost invisible respiratory flutter of the entire body. Heart rate went down, often greatly, but spinal EMG did not change from baseline level.

After activity was resumed, tonic immobility recurred on retest or if the hawk shape was swooped down, the snake was introduced, or the experimenter approached. Ten of the 25 animals remained immobile even with the snake curling around them. (Although food-deprived for 2 weeks, the snake ingested none of the rodents, moving away after a minute of close investigation). The remaining rodents were hyperalert and oriented to the head of the snake, with rapidly alternating approach and withdrawal.

Six members of 4 species were in unreactive torpor later when their cage was opened, felt cool to the touch, and had waxy flexibility of the limbs. Hours later they would again startle intensely to opening of the cage, with lightning escape reactions. Very low heart rate and arrhythmias were seen in two of these animals and in three others that became immobile on confinement by "cupping." Of the 31 animals, 26% died within a week, all the tested ones having shown cardiac arrhythmias of vagal origin. In captivity, tonic immobility no longer seems adaptive as the threat does not go away quickly, and repetition with incomplete recovery between episodes may end in fatal cardiac arrhythmias.

There are several similarities between tonic immobility and other fear reactions. First, it is induced by threatening stimuli, and procedures that increase fear also prolong immobility in chickens (Gallup & Maser 1977). Loud noise lengthens its duration. Shock prolongs it up to 20 times, and the more intense the shock, the longer the immobility. Conditioned stimuli that 2 days earlier had been paired with shock prolonged immobility 5 times, especially if the shock used during conditioning had been intense. Repeated, inescapable shock potentiated immobility more than 4 times compared to yoked controls that could escape shock. Suspension over a visual cliff lengthened immobility. Tonic immobility suppresses other responses that are made contingent upon it. Finally, adrenalin injections increase immobility.

Second, tonic immobility is reduced by methods that also diminish fear (Gallup & Maser 1977). Handling, taming, familiarity, and repetition of the stimulus reduce immobility, which might be why the reaction is rare in household pets. Safety signals that predict shock offset decrease immobility by 95%. Last, "tranquilizing" drugs such as meto-serpate for fowls, chlorpromazine at high doses, scopolamine, and imipramine all attenuate immobility; high doses of imipramine virtually abolish it.

Evolutionary Significance

The adaptive value of tonic immobility is based on the way that movement triggers attack by many predators. When the immobility follows the animal's rolling itself into a tight motionless ball, as in some snakes and armadilloes, it has the added advantage of protecting the vulnerable head in the center of the ball. Tonic immobility is a final defense reaction that comes into play when the animal is caught or about to be so, and improves its chances of escape. Numerous predators strike to kill only prey that move. Some predators, such as hawks, are loathe to eat dead meat and may actually starve to death unless fed moving prey.

If the prey remains still, predators often merely examine it, become distracted, and relax their attention, giving the prey a chance to escape (Curio 1976, p. 89; Darwin 1900; Gallup & Maser 1977; Ratner 1976; Thompson et al. 1981). Prey movement is a salient stimulus increasing the probability of attack from predators such as snakes, rodents, carnivores. It innately releases crouching, stalking, and catching actions in cats; an immobile prey animal is liable to attack only from cats highly experienced in hunting. Once a bird is still, a cat may leave it alone for a while. Of ducks induced into tonic immobility when sized by a fox, 58% survived the initial attack (Sargeant & Eberhardt 1975). Domestic cats stalked, attacked, and handled moving chickens and quail far more than they did birds induced into tonic immobility by the experimenter. There are anecdotes of an attacking lion and a polar bear respectively dropping the explorers Drs. Livingstone and Legault in order to attack another person who was moving.

Relationship of Tonic Immobility to Other Phenomena

The relationship of tonic immobility to attentive (freezing) immobility is problematic. Both are defensive reactions that begin abruptly in the face of danger and may last seconds or hours. In both states the animal is highly aroused, and the immobility may end with abrupt flight or attack. Freezing as well as tonic immobility can be associated with bradycardia, after initial tachycardia in rats (Malcuit et al. 1968). However, the autonomic patterns in the two states have yet to be worked out in detail across species.

The most striking distinction between the two states is motor reactivity, which is marked in freezing but almost absent in tonic immobility, though in the latter state, too, lightning escape is often tried when the predator relaxes its guard. Perhaps tonic immobility is freezing with superimposed motor inhibition when the fear is extreme, but there are other differences too. First, attentive immobility is more likely to occur when the danger is distant and tonic immobility as a terminal reaction to being caught. This might account for freezing being so much more common than tonic immobility. Second, during attentive immobility the animal is in the alert posture typical for that species, whereas tonic immobility can leave the animal in bizarre postures that may seem to sham death but often make no obvious sense. Third, the two forms of immobility differ neurophysiologically. Hippocampal, fornix, and septal lesions increase tonic immobility but decrease freezing in rabbits and rats, whereas cingulate lesions have the reverse effect (Woodruff et al. 1975, 1981; Woodruff & Lippincott 1976; Woodruff & Bailey 1979).

Tonic immobility may be an extreme variant of a general tendency to be still when in danger or before attacking another animal (Darwin 1900). Many view it as a last-ditch protective response induced when an animal is physically restrained on being caught by a predator (Thompson et al. 1981). However, though tonic immobility is reliably initiated by restraint, indistinguishable stillness is also produced by more distant stimulation, the common mechanism perhaps being extreme intensity of fear.

Several distinctions have been suggested between immobility produced by restraint and that brought about by other means (M. Woodruff 1977 and personal communication, 1981). Destruction of any of the sensory systems that bring distant stimuli to the brain has no effect on tonic immobility (Klemm 1976), nor does bilateral destruction for the labyrinth or olfactory bulbectomy. Moreover, transection of the brain stem does not abolish tonic immobility until made well below the neural level where all sensory input has been eliminated except for tactile sensation. In addition, destruction of the dorsal columns in rabbits reduces tonic immobility but not freezing, cued by sudden noise. Finally, the similar states of tonic immobility and rape-induced paralysis (pp. 68) are produced by rough handling from the attacker.

It could be argued that all sensory systems may stimulate an "immobility control center" so that all forms of stillness are similar in terms of central modulation and efferent outflow. There are several objections to this view (M. Woodruff 1977 and personal communication, 1983). It emphasizes only the efferent aspect of the response and errs in implying that the muscle responses in all forms of stillness are the same and that tonic immobility is an unitary state throughout its duration. This is not true in terms of postural adjustment, respiration, cardiovascular dynamics, or EEG (Carli 1974; Hatton et al. 1975; Klemm 1971). Furthermore, limbic lesions have effects on tonic immobility opposite to those they produce on immobility cued by novelty (Woodruff & Bailey 1979; Woodruff & Lippincott 1976). The various forms of stillness are thus not mediated by completely congruent neural nuclei and pathways.

As some of its synonyms suggest, many writers liken tonic immobility to hypnosis and catatonia. It has also been compared with sleep paralysis. Some male spiders induce immobility in the female during courtship (Savory 1928, pp. 207–208). When the male *Agelina labyrinthica* strokes the female she lapses into trance-like immobility. He carries her about by her leg grasped in his jaws, and she becomes mobile again only after mating is over. The male

Dysdera erythrina also induces "hypnotic" immobility in the female spider during courtship by caressing her.

Tonic immobility is unusual in that it is a defensive response often accompanied by slow heart rate, though species do vary in this. The slowing of heart rate indicates parasympathetic stimulation in mammals. It led to rapid death in diastole in wild Norwegian rats held tightly in the hand (Richter 1957). Wild rats have higher vagus tone than domesticated rats. If thrown into water wild rats swim for many hours, but they drown rapidly if they are briefly restrained in the hand beforehand, are given cholinergic drugs, or have their whiskers clipped. Conversely, drowning is delayed by atropine, which blocks parasympathetic stimulation.

Some slowing of heart rate is also found in cats during their brief immobility prior to attacking another animal (Adams et al. 1968; Zanchetti et al. 1972). Preattack immobility is accompanied by muscle vasoconstriction. During actual fighting heart rate and muscle blood flow both increase.

Immobility is seen in adult male tree shrews *(Tupaia belangeri)* that have lost a fight with another male (Von Holst 1972). If an adult male tree shrew is introduced into the cage of another that is an experienced fighter, it is immediately attacked, bitten, and subjugated within a few seconds. During the fight it will utter fear squeals. If not removed from the cage it will cower in a corner and is likely to die with vagal bradycardia in 1 to 4 minutes. The wounds are superficial and not a cause of death. A similar phenomenon is seen in wild rats that, if unable to escape from the territory of a dominant, resident male, may die after a few hours of intermittent attacks, even with no wounds (Barnett 1975).

If the defeated tree shrew is removed to the cage next door where it can see the victor but not be attacked, it will remain still in the corner but will follow the victor's movements with its head and show its sustained sympathetic arousal by the conspicuous fluffing of its tail. It will eat fairly normally. Daily brief reintroduction into the victor's cage leads to quickly renewed fighting and subjugation. Within 2 to 20 days the vanquished animals die of renal failure incurred from prolonged renal vasoconstriction. We are reminded here that during wartime many humans have died of "war nephritis" whose cause was unknown but could perhaps have stemmed from prolonged renal vasoconstriction during sustained intense fear (Von Holst 1972).

During extreme fear humans may become "scared stiff" or "frozen with fear." A paralyzed conscious state with abrupt onset and termination is reported by survivors of attacks by wild animals, by shell-shocked soldiers, and by more than 50% of rape victims (Suarez & Gallup 1979). Similarities between tonic immobility and rape-induced paralysis were listed by Suarez and Gallup (features noted by rape victims are in parentheses): (1) profound motor inhibition (inability to move); (2) Parkinsonian-like tremors (body shaking); (3) silence (inability to call out or scream); (4) no loss of consciousness testified by retention of conditioned reactions acquired during the immobility (recall of details of the attack); (5) apparent analgesia (numbness and insensitivity to pain); (6) reduced core temperature (sensation of feeling cold); (7) abrupt onset and termination (sudden onset and remission of paralysis); (8) aggressive reactions at termination (attack of the rapist after recovery); (9) frequent inhibition of attack by a predator (when rape victims cease to struggle and then freeze, many would be rapists lose their erection).

Another aversive situation associated with slowed heart rate—and fainting—occurs in humans seeing blood or injury (see chapters 11 and 15). Human fainting at the sight of blood shares with tonic immobility the slowing of heart rate in a dangerous situation. Perhaps this points to a common phylogenetic precursor and neurophysiological substrate (Hofer 1970).

Human heart rate also drops during the immobility induced by an unexpected loud noise, whereas expected loud noise leads to tachycardia (Hunt 1970). Twelve men were asked to blow up a balloon slowly and to control the air supply to prevent it bursting. However, the experimenter could bypass their control and burst the balloon. Bursting the balloon led to tachycardia, but if a loud horn was simultaneously sounded unexpectedly this led to bradycardia.

Though its physiology is unknown, prolonged motionlessness is seen in voodoo anxiety and death (Cannon 1942), and its mechanism might be related to those involved in tonic immobility. Brazilian Indians died of fright after being condemned and sentenced by a medicine man. Other cases recovered when the medicine man rescinded his sentence. A young black African unknowingly ate a taboo wild hen; on discovery of his "crime" several years later, he trembled, showed extreme fear, and died within 24 hours. A New Zealand Maori woman ate fruit that she learned later had come from a tabooed place, thus profaning her chief; she died the next day. Cannon surmised that death from fright occurred after prolonged sympathetic vasoconstriction leading to ischaemic damage of visceral capillaries with leakage of plasma into the extravascular space and dehydration and hypotension analogous to surgical shock. Another possible mechanism of delayed death is sympathetic renal vasoconstriction (like that postulated earlier in "war nephritis"). Vasovagal bradycardia could cause death soon after bewitchment.

AGGRESSIVE DEFENSE

A proverb has it that attack is the best form of defense; it can confer a selective advantage over escape to an inferior environment. Aggressive defense is associated more prominently with other fear behavior than is the aggression of hunting or fighting a rival male, and it differs from straight attack (Blanchard & Blanchard 1981). The defense usually comes into play in a mammal when an enemy is close to seizing it or actually does seize it.

Aggressive defense may begin from a distance, as in the mobbing attacks on predators from birds and some animals. When a predator appears, prey animals give a distinctive call and rush toward it. More prey join in the mobbing with a similar call, and soon the predator is surrounded and harried by calling birds that repeatedly dash toward and from it and sometimes defecate (Humphries & Driver; Ratner 1976). Some predators seem obviously harassed when mobbed, while others are not and may even kill a few of the mob. Very dangerous predators such as the sparrowhawk *Dendrocopus major* may be mobbed only at a distance, often for prolonged periods (Harvey & Greenwood 1978). Mobbing intensity increases during nesting periods, when parents take risks for the sake of the young, as they do when giving distraction displays or alarm calls.

Animals are more likely to retaliate when with young than at other times. It is unwise to disturb a she-bear with cubs. A wildebeest mare will attack wild dogs and hyenas if she is defending her foal but not when alone (Edmunds 1974). The wildebeest can ward off one hyena at a time by attack but not two or more, in which case it would be best for the wildebeest to run off; but this strategy is not always followed (Kruuk 1972; and see also Chapter 4). A Thomson's gazelle with a fawn will attack a threatening jackal but not larger predators.

In aggressive defense, animals use any available weapon. Resisting insects bite, scratch, sting, or eject noxious secretions; birds peck, stab, tear, scratch, or project stomach or cloacal contents; mammals bite, scratch, use horns or hooves, or, in the case of primates, throw objects such as branches and feces. Some structural defenses such as the spines of tenrecs may be first erected in a threat display and then used for attack (Eisenberg & Gould 1970). Weapons used in defense against predators may be structures used primarily for the capture of food—for example, the jaws and forelegs of mantids; the stings of scorpions, bees, and wasps; the beaks of birds; and the teeth of mammals and other small animals. Other weapons have evolved to enhance intraspecific defense as well as other behavior; the horns of deer, elk, musk oxen, and giraffe used against rival males; the secretions of anal sacs in the skunk and polecat; and the loud noise of cicada swarms. Cultural evolution of the human arms race has led to the ultimate in aggressive defense—nuclear weapons that might wipe us all out.

The discharge of noxious substances when danger threatens is a special form of aggressive defense. Spurts from stink glands occur in several families of mammals, such as the large striped-necked and crab-necked mongooses (herpestids) (Bourliere 1964). Among the civets (viverrids) the genera *Viverra* and *Vivericula* use the perineal gland to this end. Skunks (mustelids) are the champion stinkers, having very large anal glands from which they spray secretion for up to 12 feet. Before discharging their fetid odors animals may adopt a threatening attitude that varies with the species. Such threat displays are widespread and deserve more detailed description.

Threat Displays

When discovered by a predator many animals adopt a characteristic posture to intimidate, startle, warn, or bluff the enemy (Barnard 1983; Edmunds 1974). These are threat or "deimatic" displays (from the Greek meaning to frighten) that cause the predator to hesitate and increase the chance of escape. In threat displays the animal may enhance its apparent size by spreading its wings, fluffing its feathers or erecting its hair or spines, raising its head or appendages, rearing up, swirling its coils, or swallowing air or water to inflate its body. It may expose brilliant markings or display its weapons by baring its teeth, showing its horns, stamping its hooves, loudly beating its chest or wings, rattling its tail, snorting, hissing, or spitting.

A few mammalian threat displays appear in Figure 3.9. The tenrec raises its spines and bucks its head up and down repeatedly while stridulating. The porcupine erects and rattles its quills before charging backward to impale its enemy. Some skunks stamp on the ground with their hind feet. The spotted skunk gives a more complex display; it erects its tail, stamps it forefeet on the ground, and may even rear up on its forepaws and advance toward the predator presenting the full length of its black-and-white body to view, thus increasing its apparent size, and may finally squirt a nauseating fluid from its anal sacs. Cats rear themselves with arched back and tail and erect hair while hissing and spitting.

In human threat displays we threateningly rear ourselves to our full height while fear makes us feel "goosepimples" and our "hair stands on end." Even

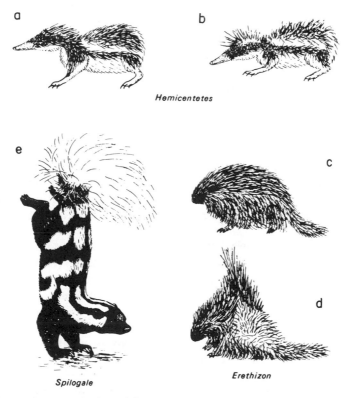

Fig. 3.9 Threat (deimatic) displays of three mammals. (a) The tenrec *Hemicentetes semispinosus* in normal posture with spines lowered, and (b) when facing a predator with spines raised and repeatedly bucking the head up and down. (c) The American porcupine *Erethizon* sp. in normal posture and (d) with quills erected when encountering a predator. (e) Spotted skunk *Spilogale putorius* displaying to a predator. Not drawn to same scale. (Adapted from Edmunds 1974).

more impressive is culturally evolved threat. Preindustrial man used terrifying masks and costume to frighten away his enemies; wonderful ritualized examples of these abound in the much-prized art of New Guinea and Central and West Africa. Bluff has always been a common human strategy to ward off attack, and disguise to elude capture.

Group-living animals may show group threat. When attacked by wolves, musk oxen form a defensive ring around the cows and calves, facing outward showing their sharp horns. Eland do the same against hyenas. Such group displays ward off attack and have clear survival value (Mech 1970).

Threat postures are often seen where there is a simultaneous tendency to attack and to flee (Baerends 1975; Manning 1979; see also Chapter 2). An excellent instance was noted in Canada geese (Blurton-Jones 1960, cited by Manning 1979). Tame geese ignored their keeper when he was dressed in old familiar clothes, attacked him if he wore a white coat, but fled if he appeared carrying a broom which he generally used to drive the geese into their house for the night. The geese threatened him (lowering their heads on outstretched necks and hissing) only if he came both wearing a white coat and carrying a broom (that is, bearing the cues for both attack and fleeing).

Some threat displays contain elements of both attack and escape. When rhesus monkeys threaten, their limbs reveal a compromise between advance and retreat, and they alternately lunge their head forward and pull it back. Detailed analysis of the threat posture of the lesser black-backed gull also shows a combination of escape and attack. The bird moves toward its rival with the neck stretched upward and slightly forward and the head and bill turned down. The wings' wrist joints are lifted clear of the body, and the plumage is slightly raised. All these are components of attack, but elements of escape are also seen as two rivals come close. The head moves back, the bill is lifted and the plumage sleeker, while the bird may turn sideways. The gull's movements during threat are the opposite of those seen during appeasement of a conspecific (Figure 3.10). This follows Darwin's principle of antithesis, originally derived from observations of dogs, that opposing emotions can often be recognized from their opposing patterns of movement. Antithesis is also seen in primates.

Threat postures indicate what the actor will probably, not definitely, do next—"I will stay, but may attack or flee if provoked" (Hinde 1981). This ambiguity allows the actor's next behavior, flight or attack, to depend in part on what the reactor does. The social releasers used in threat elicit both attack and flight from other individuals. Making the reactor uncertain of the actor's precise intentions often enables the actor to stay his ground without the expense of attack or defense. A games theory analysis might predict which conditions are likely to lead to the evolution of ambiguous or clear signals on each side during confrontation.

Not all threat postures can be regarded as a mixture of attack and escape, and certain species have several distinct threat postures. Some variation in threat posture may represent different intensities of motivation to attack and escape. Movements from the repertoires of feeding, preening, or nest building may also appear.

Threat displays are remarkably varied in some species, as we saw earlier in the cuttlefish *Sepia officinalis* (Holmes 1940). When attacked it suddenly displays two conspicuous black spots on the back by expanding black chromatophores (Figure 3.11a); then it may dart rapidly away, darkening as it moves, so that a pursuing predator is left attempting to follow a white object that no longer exists (flash behavior). With further irritation the cuttlefish changes color repeatedly as it swims, sometimes adopting a zebra pattern (crypsis), sometimes with two black spots (threat), and sometimes becoming pale with four black lines (threat) (Figure 3.11b). Finally it may eject a cloud of ink and come to rest motionless beneath the cloud, where it cannot be seen. At other times a disturbed cuttlefish may flatten itself, thus giving the illusion of increase in size, and become pale as a whole, with two black spots, two black rings around the eyes, and a black rim to its fins (Figure 3.11c).

Unlike their precopulatory displays, which are species-specific and diverse, many defensive displays of *Sepia* closely resemble those in other species of three orders of cephalopods (Sepiida, Teuthida, Octopida) (Moynihan 1975). These orders are thought to have diverged about 190 million years ago in the early Mesozoic. The similarities in both form and function between elaborate displays suggest that they evolved from a common origin. Such conservatism of evolution may be ascribed to two factors. Cryptic displays involving stripes and darkening of the arms match the relatively unchanging background of corals and seaweed, and other threat displays such as the eyespot patterns may

Fig. 3.10 Antithesis of threat and appeasement postures in the lesser black-blacked gull: (a) the upright display of threat; (b) appeasement, with the head held low on a shortened neck and the bill pointing upward, while the wings are pressed close into the flanks so that the wrist joints, which are very noticeable in threat, are completely hidden. (From Manning 1979. Copyright © 1979 by Arnold. Reprinted by permission. Photos by N. Tinbergen.)

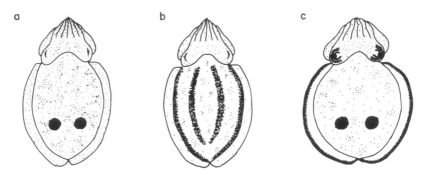

Fig. 3.11 Variation of threat display in the cuttlefish *Sepia officinalis*. When attacked it suddenly shows two conspicuous black spots on the back (a), then darts away and changes color repeatedly as it swims, sometimes with a zebra pattern, or becoming pale with four black lines (b). It may also flatten itself to seem larger and become pale with two black spots, two black rings around the eyes, and a black rim to its fins (c). (From Holmes 1940. Copyright © 1940 by The Zoological Society of London. Reprinted by permission.)

have remained stable to ward off conspecific and other predators. Signal patterns that are adapted to many kinds of receiver may change more slowly than those adapted to only one kind.

Behavioral Aposematism

Much threat behavior is bluff, but true ability to harm may also be openly displayed, and this is called aposematism. The harmful features may be a nasty taste, sting, or poisonous bite. Advertisement of such features may be by bright colors, as in some slugs, ladybird beetles, wasps, and coral snakes. Other aposematic advertisements may be behavioral, as in the acoustic warnings of rattlesnakes and the multimodal threat of cobras that hiss, rear up, and expand their neck. Aposematic displays help the advertising animal reduce the risk of injury that is likely to occur in even a successfully repelled attack.

Structural aposematism may reflect behavior indirectly—for instance, the bad taste of brightly colored monarch and queen butterflies. They acquire their bitter taste from cardiac glycosides ingested from certain milkweeks; the glycosides activate the vomiting center in vertebrate brains and so protect the plants. The butterflies' defense depends upon the proportions of bitter and nonbitter plants eaten by the larvae (Brower 1969). This reflects the availability of bitter plants and the eating choice of the larvae, which in turn may be influenced by metabolic costs traded for the protection afforded.

Some species protect themselves by mimicking the behavioral aposematism of other animals while not being nasty themselves; examples are beetles that mimic the gait of the acid-spraying bombardier (see Chapter 1), or harmless snakes that imitate the movements of poisonous ones. This imitation of the harmful by the harmless is Batesian mimicry, after Henry Bates, the nineteenth-century English naturalist. He originally described structural mimicry, but the concept applies equally to behavioral imitation. The mimic takes advantage of the predator's learning to avoid the noxious model. If the mimic became too common with respect to its model the system would break down because the predators would encounter palatable mimics too frequently.

Another form of mimicry is Mullerian, after Fritz Muller, a German zoologist of the late nineteenth-century. This is imitation of the harmful by the harmful and also referred initially to structural imitations. In addition it describes similar defensive behaviors among different noxious species, such as the hissing or buzzing among the 30 species of venomous rattlesnakes that belong to two genera. This type of mimicry benefits predators by reducing the number of color patterns they need to remember to avoid.

A final form of defensive imitation within species is automimicry (Brower 1969). Butterfly larvae that feed on poisonous plants serve as unpalatable models that protect conspecifics that have not fed on such plants. Automimicry affords even greater protection than Batesian mimicry because imitation is more perfect within than across species. If a bird stops eating the species after one experience of vomiting, then a butterfly population in which only 25% to 50% of individuals are unpalatable because the larvae fed on poisonous plants is almost as well protected as if all the butterflies were emetic. The population gets good protection even if only 10% of the larvae pay the metabolic costs that may be incurred by eating the poison (an intriguing issue for the evolution of altruism).

Threat Display of Eyespots and Eyes

Display of false and true eyes, such as that by cephalopods described earlier, is a widespread component of threat behavior in insects, amphibians, birds, and mammals (Cott 1940, pp. 387–398, 820; Hingston 1933, pp. 54–90, 142–145); this fits with eyes commonly being used in threat and hunting among animals. Eye displays may involve false eyes or genuine eyes displayed so as to make them conspicuous. The Brazilian toad *Physalaemus natereri* has a large eye mark on each side of the back of its abdomen and often presents its rump to predators (Edmunds 1974).

While smaller eyespots may be displayed on a less vulnerable part of the body, in order to actually invite attack, larger eyespots are chiefly concerned with intimidation. In careful experiments, displays of large eyespots deterred birds, usually temporarily (Blest 1957; see also Chapter 2). The butterfly *Nymphalis io* releases escape from yellow buntings by displaying four ocelli on the upper surface of its wings. Additional deterrents in other insects include a bright field of color surrounding the eyespots, rhythmic movements of the display, and the rustling noise that accompanies it.

Many birds rapidly learn to ignore eyespots, even though the initial avoidance is presumably innate because it occurs in birds that have been hand-reared in isolation and have never seen similar patterns before. Eyespot displays thus have more value if they are not displayed too frequently, and they are normally kept hidden unless the animal is alarmed. This concealment of the eyespots for most of the time also makes the bearer less conspicuous at rest, reducing the chance of attack from those predators that are not deterred by eyespots.

In primates the basic facial cue for threat is a fixed and direct stare (Redican 1975). At greater intensity the eyebrows are lowered and raised (eyebrow flash), thus exposing eyelid coloration in some species, with occasional blinking, ear flattening, and calling. When threatened a fearful primate gives rapid brief glances at its enemy, avoiding fixed eye contact. Many species grimace in a scared grin that may be given with avoiding eyes when fear is mixed with other emotional behaviors—for example, during submissive greeting and during copulation that is not initiated by the female, such as that during dominance-mounting and rape (J. Caldecott, personal communication, 1984).

The two expressions of threat and fear grin seem to follow Darwin's principle of antithesis. During threat the eyes stare, the teeth are covered, and the mouth is closed; with the fear grimace there is gaze aversion, the teeth are exposed, and the mouth is open (Redican 1975). Both staring and fear grimacing appear aversive; female juvenile rhesus monkeys avoid such stimuli (Redican 1975). Staring at a rhesus monkey changes both its behavior and the electrical activity in its brain stem (Wada 1961).

In humans, belief in the "evil eye" and power of the look seems universal independent of culture, as is the counteruse of large staring eyes in defensive magic (Tomkins 1963). Staring at people attracts their attention and becomes a threat if prolonged. Awareness of being looked at releases social action (Argyle & Kendon 1967; Kendon 1965). In keeping with this, attention to another's eyes is a basic feature of social behavior. When we look at other people or animals we scan mainly their eyes and their contour. Figure 3.12 is a record of eye movements while looking for one minute at a photograph of a girl's face (Yarbus 1967). These practically trace the eyes and outline of the face, half the fixations being on the eyes and the rest mainly on the contours. The avoidance of eye contact by many social phobics thus switches off a salient aversive stimulus.

DEFLECTION OF ATTACK AND APPEASEMENT (SUBMISSION)

During defensive behavior a prey animal may divert an attack away from itself, or to itself away from its young, or to some other less vulnerable parts of its own body where an attack is less likely to be fatal, and which may taste particularly nasty (reviewed by Barnard 1983; Edmunds 1974). The cuttlefish, as mentioned earlier, diverts a predator away from itself by ejecting a cloud of black ink that is rather viscous and diffuses slowly, giving the cuttlefish time to swim rapidly away (Holmes 1940). The sea hare *Aplysia* also ejects a cloud of purple fluid when attacked.

Some fish such as the largemouth bass *(Macropterus salmoides)* and bowfin *(Amia)*, create diversionary splashes in an opposite direction while the little school of young moves away (Lagler et al. 1962). Displays that distract a predator away from the young are also well known in birds such as waders and

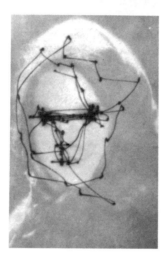

Fig. 3.12 Eye movements (bottom) during free examination of a photograph of a girl's face (top) with both eyes for one minute. The movements concentrate on the eyes and, less so, on the nose, mouth, and contour of the face. (From Yarbus 1967.)

ducks. When a large ground predator such as a dog or man approaches, the parent bird moves quietly away from its eggs or young and then gives an elaborate, conspicuous display that gradually takes it still further away from the young. Typically one wing is flapped prominently as though the bird is injured and unable to fly. When the predator is close the bird quickly flies off. When far away from the chicks the bird may give a static display, as if it is so badly injured that it cannot move (Simmons 1952). Others, such as the dunlin *(Calidris alpina)*, distract by creeping along the ground uttering squeaky notes like a small mammal. The loon *(Gavia)* and other water birds engage in antics that distract predators away from the young (Lagler et al. 1962, p. 289). Among mammals, the mother tiger may move prominently away from her cubs when a human is nearby (Schaller 1967, p. 269).

Diverting a predator to oneself away from one's young suggests kin selection such as that proposed for alarm calls (Harvey & Greenwood 1978). Parental distraction is most marked at the time of hatching in bird species with precocial young, and at the time of fledging in birds whose offspring are helpless at birth.

Deflection of attack *to* the young is seen at times in kangaroo mothers (Carrington 1963, p. 157). When danger threatens, a young joey scurries back to its mother who bends forward, opening her pouch for it to enter. When hard pressed by wild dogs, however, a kangaroo mother will sometimes unload her heavy baby. This increases her chance of escape and also deflects attack to the young. She usually has another tiny baby in her pouch as well as a fertilized embryo internally waiting to grow as soon as she is free of the older baby, so this extreme ploy may lead to more offspring surviving in the long run than would a dangerously slow escape.

Much as it goes against the grain, similar behavior is not unknown among humans. During the Assam massacres a "man described how he threw his daughter from his arms at the raiders chasing him, to save himself. There was no guilt or remorse in his voice—just relief that he had survived" (*The Guardian,* March 18, 1983, p. 7). A variant on this theme is the Greek legend of Agamemnon, who allowed his daughter Iphigenia to be sacrificed to appease the gods and so make the wind blow to enable the fleet to sail to Troy.

Behavioral and structural deflection of attack to a less vital part of the body is often seen. Snakes waggle the tip of the tail when disturbed (Wickler 1968, as cited by Edmunds 1974), and in the rattlesnake this also serves as a threat display. Unlike most butterflies, lycaenids usually rest on vertical surfaces with the head down rather than up, and if disturbed fly off unexpectedly downwards (Curio 1976, pp. 154–155). Some deceive predators even more effectively by thin, antennalike projections on the tips of hindwings, which are moved up and down for a few seconds after landing while the true antennae are kept still; the base of each false antenna is also marked to resemble a false small eye. One species even walks backward supporting the mimicry of the false head.

Attack may be deflected by small eyespots away from vital structures. The wings of many butterflies carry triangular beak marks implying escape after seizure by a bird. The beak marks on the wings are concentrated around the small eyespots, which are normally some distance away from the body, so the attack need not be fatal (Blest 1957). Swynnerton (1927, cited by Blest 1957) painted eyespots on the undersides of the wings of butterflies that were then released. Most of the butterflies were recaptured with beak marks or torn wings, and the injuries tended to be near the eyespots. That small spots invite attack was also shown in mealworms that were artificially adorned with such spots on their head or their tail. Yellow buntings pecked more at the spotted ends, as well as more at heads then at tails (Blest 1957).

Deflection of an attack is part of the human way of life. We defend ourselves from a blow with our arms or a shield, place ourselves between a threat and our children, lure the enemy away from our young or vital possessions, or create diversionary tactics in battle. In conversation we change the subject from potentially upsetting to more anodyne topics. We placate would-be critics with a joke or by criticizing ourselves first, which is less threatening.

Autotomy of a Non-essential Part of the Body

This form of deflection of attack is a last-minute defense. Not a few species can constrict and break off a part of their body when seized (autotomy) and often grow a replacement (Edmunds 1974). The sea slug *Discodoris fragilis* autotomizes part of its mantle, and this can grow again. Some bivalves that live buried in sand can break off and regenerate the projecting siphon if it is nibbled by a fish. Tail autotomy occurs in the sacoglossan mollusk *Oxynoe,* the lug-worm *Aricola,* and geckos and other lizards. In species such as *Ptychozoon* the tail is more highly colored than the rest of the body, increasing its power to divert. Long-tailed field mice also show tail autotomy (Bourliere 1964, p. 121). Limbs are often cast off by arthropods, and these regenerate at the next moult. Birds may moult their feathers and mammals shed their fur if they are grabbed, so a hawk that has struck a pigeon may be left merely with a talon full of feathers (Ratner 1976).

Lizard tails may continue to writhe for some time after being severed. If autotomized tails thrash vigorously, as they do in *Scincella latealis,* they divert predators to the tail away from the lizard, thus allowing it to escape; and they also prolong the time required for a snake to subdue the tail before swallowing it, thus increasing the lizard's escape time by 40% (Dial & Fitzpatrick 1983). Experimentally a cat pursued thrashing severed tails rather than lizards on 100% of trials but captured the lizards instead on every trial once the severed tails were exhausted. This species' tail is adapted to thrash vigorously after autotomy, having a higher lactate concentration for this anaerobic activity than the tail of *Anolis carolensis,* which when severed moves only moderately, too little to divert a cat's attack from the anole.

Autotomy of papillae, chelae, or stings all leave the predator with the most noxious part of its prey. Mollusks such as eolids and some dorids and sacoglossans break off their papillae when attacked (Edmunds 1974). The papillae are unpalatable and continue to writhe for some minutes after detachment, keeping the predator busy while the mollusk crawls away. Such papillae can regenerate later. The crab *Potamocarcinus* grabs a predator such as a sea otter with its chela and then severs it, leaving the otter to retreat in pain until it has removed the chela. Stings are cast off by some social hymenopterans (*Apis, Polybia,* and certain ants), but there is no regeneration and the loss often results in death of the insect.

Appeasement (Submission)

When humans deflect attack by a sop to Cerberus, such as breaking off a piece of our self-esteem to humble ourselves before we can be humbled, or when an animal gives up to a predator its young or a part of its own body, this becomes a form of appeasement.

Appeasement is mainly used by birds and mammals to inhibit attack when a conspecific threatens and escape is disadvantageous (Manning 1979, pp. 179–180). Appeasement often fails with a predator of another species and may not inhibit attack even from a conspecific. With dominant conspecifics appeasement is intimately linked with fear. Appeasement may stall attack from a conspecific and aid the animal to stay with its mate or group rather than disadvantageously to flee into isolation. Once dominance hierarchies are fixed, fights are rare and lower status animals frequently fend off trouble from their threatening fellows by gestures of appeasement. Submission need not always be associated with fear. We may appease small children to stop their discomfiting whining rather than from fear of them.

Postures of appeasement have been well described for wolves and dogs (Mech 1970), cheetahs (Eaton 1974), and primates (Redican 1975). Appeal to sexual behavior is often invoked in primates, where a subordinate of either sex often turns away from the dominant animal and crouches in the sexual presentation posture. It may be mounted briefly but is often simply allowed to move away from the aggressor.

The submissive posture of a chacma baboon is seen in Figure 3.13 (Bolwig 1959). It is the antithesis of threat and has some sexual components. The animal turns its side toward its opponent, presents its hindquarters and watches its superior with evasive glances toward the side. It never looks straight at its opponent; its mouth is opened, head and shoulders are lowered, eyebrows lifted, ears laid back, and hair kept smooth. This behavior, which may end with the animal taking flight or crouching on the ground if escape is impossible, seems to reduce its size. While crouching, the hindquarters are often held higher than head and shoulders and turned toward the opponent.

There are many other examples of antithesis of appeasement and threat in birds and mammals. When a black-headed gull alights on the territory of her mate, they may threaten each other briefly by displaying their dark face masks, but after a second or two both lift their heads and jerk them away from each other, hiding the face masks. In the kittiwake the appeasement posture turns the head away and down, hiding the yellow bill with its red mouth lining, which is used in threat. Like a tame dog being punished, an appeasing wolf lays

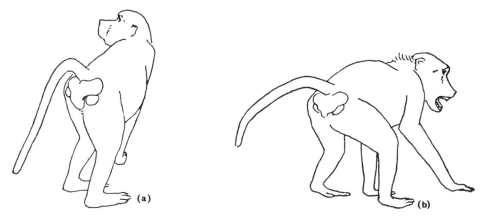

Fig. 3.13   The appeasement posture of a female chacma baboon to a threatening dominant animal (b), with a facial expression of fear. View (a) is a sexual presentation by an estrous female, looking back characteristically over her shoulder toward the male. (Adapted from Bolwig 1959.)

back its ears and turns away its head so as to present not its fangs but the nape of its neck, whereas a threatening wolf snarls with bared fangs and erect ears. A submitting cheetah averts its eyes and rolls onto its side, but when threatening it stares with open mouth at its opponent, growls, rises to its full height, rushes forward, and stamps both forepaws noisily on the ground. Finally, in humans we speak of a "disarming" smile, which is far removed from a threatening snarl, and the greetings of an upraised palm or a handshake are thought to indicate that no weapon is concealed in one's hand.

Submissive behavior may involve not only sexual behavior, as in monkeys, but also parenting repertoires. Infantile behavior is often seen in birds. The aggression of a male owl is reduced by the female's food begging as a preliminary to mating. In the lesser black-backed gull this appeasement gesture of food begging is also the antithesis of the threat posture. (Figure 3.10).

Appeasement is a normal feature of much human behavior. We give gifts to prevent anger or to placate people who are already cross. Religious sacrifice and prayer are on one level efforts to avert the wrath of God that descends in the shape of misfortune. Superstitious taboos are thought to fend off disaster and obsessive-compulsives often say that their ruminations and rituals stave off harm to themselves or other people.

SUMMARY

Fear behaviors are executed in one of 4 strategies—withdrawal, immobility, aggressive defense, or deflection of attack. Withdrawal is ubiquitous from protozoa to people and can be active or passive. Active escape may be not in a straight line but in an erratic, irregular path. The escaping animal may change its appearance or sound by means of flash colors and sounds. Some prey seem to invite being chased when they can get away easily.

The fear strategy of immobility may take two forms whose relationship to one another is problematic. In attentive immobility (freezing) the animal is obviously alert and ready for flight and may withdraw behind protective structures. In tonic immobility the animal seems unresponsive and dead but may suddenly escape when its captor relaxes attention, which might explain how the response evolved. It is especially easily induced by physical restraint, can last for seconds or hours, and is frequently accompanied by parasympathetic slowing of the heart rate. Similar slow heart rate with immobility is also seen in cats before they attack, in shrews that have lost a fight for dominance, and in humans seeing blood or unexpectedly hearing a loud noise. Tonic immobility has features in common with rape-induced paralysis in women and perhaps with voodoo death.

Aggressive defense is more likely when the animal is with young, and any weapon available may be used. It may start with a threat display by individuals or groups. Threat postures are often seen during simultaneous tendencies to attack and to escape. Much threat is bluff, but true ability to harm may be openly advertised (aposematism) in characteristic behavior. Display of false and true eyes is widely used as part of a threat display, and primates commonly stare threateningly.

Deflection of attack away from oneself or one's young is common. If a non-essential part is seized an animal may sever that part and grow a new one. Appeasement deflects attack from conspecifics. Individuals who are low in a social hierarchy frequently inhibit attack from their superiors by displaying submissively when threatened. Submissive behavior is often the antithesis of threat, and may draw on sexual and infantile repertoires.

4

Some Fear Adaptations

Given that each species has evolved ways of detecting signals of threat and of responding to those signals, what defensive adaptations ensue in their natural environment? A few of these form the substance of this chapter. We will examine how fear behavior manifests in groups and the various tradeoffs resulting from living together. Distress and alarm signals will be described. Finally, the rich defensive repertoires of some African plains animals will be set in the context of their particular life styles.

PROTECTION OF GROUPS

Many species bunch together when frightened. Examples of this behavior abound among aphids, fish, birds (Figure 4.1), and mammals such as ungulates, mongoose, and humans. Phobics and compulsive ritualizers typically feel easier when accompanied.

Groups afford protection in a variety of ways (Curio 1976; Bertram 1978; Edmunds 1974). Individuals in a group have an "early warning system," as their collective sense organs are more likely to detect the approach of an enemy than those of a single individual, and one alarm signal suffices for all. An individual can thus afford to be less wary in a group than when alone and is freed for more productive activities such as feeding.

This advantage was measured for starlings foraging alone or in groups of 5 to 10 (Powell 1974). Compared to single birds, starlings in groups spent more time feeding and less time in surveillance, and their reaction time to sudden display of a stuffed hawk was faster (Figure 4.2). Even a half-second lead may make the difference between life and death as a hawk swoops down. Up to a certain point the advantage increases with size of the group. Large colonies of bank swallows *(Riparia riparia)* detected a stuffed predator sooner than did small colonies (Hoogland & Sherman 1976, cited by Bertram 1978).

The task of guarding the group may be delegated to a lookout, as happens in many primates (man included) and in klipspringers *(Oreotragus oreotragus)* and dwarf mongooses *(Helogale undulata)* (Bertram 1978). Lookouts benefit

Fig. 4.1 A flock of starlings bunching together at the approach of a bird of prey. (From Tinbergen 1951. Copyright © 1951 by Oxford University Press. Reprinted by permission.)

less than other group members who are freed to do as they wish. Guards returning from patrol duty are not pleased to find that in their absence they were cuckolded or upstaged at work. In some species altruistic behavior reflects high relatedness among group members.

Groups can benefit several species together. A single starling foraging with 9 blackbirds showed the same increased feeding time and decreased vigilance time as did groups of 10 starlings (Powell 1974). This may partly explain why different species of birds and mammals frequently forage together. For example, baboons *(Papio anubis)* and impala combine color vision and high vantage point, respectively, with extremely sensitive smell and hearing.

Species often differ in what they eat. When they compete for food this disadvantage might be offset by a better mutual alarm system, so we would expect species to forage together more, the less they compete with one another in their feeding habits and the more they are exposed to predation. Species may also engage in a trade-off: one of them gains armed protection and the protector wins something else, such as being groomed by a cleaner fish.

A predator is less likely to encounter bunched than scattered animals in the same range. Moreover, when a group of prey is attacked only one or a few of its members are likely to be killed; the rest usually escape. The danger is diluted by numbers, the principle at work being the gain from maximizing competition for the bad things in life (G. Williams, personal communication, 1982). If an unprepared student is afraid that a teacher will call on her, she will be more secure in a large class than a small one, because she is then buffered by potential substitute victims. Protection by dilution is mathematically verifiable; it falls as the proportion of victims in the group increases and as the attack rate rises. (The latter is not linear: a herd of 100 antelopes does not get attacked 100 times more often than a lone animal.)

Especially vulnerable prey may escape detection by shielding behind stronger companions. In the presence of a spotted hyena (*Crocuta crocuta*), wildebeest (*Connochaetes taurinus*) calves escaped detection when they were led away by their mothers to the opposite side of the herd (Kruuk 1972; Figure 4.3). Even if detected, vulnerable animals in a group are protected by stronger companions. In times of danger men tend to guard women and children.

Lone animals succumb more easily. In the wild, watchful predators rapidly snap up fish or ungulates that are separated from their school or herd, especially if the individuals move abnormally (Neill & Cullen 1974; Schaller 1972). When ungulate herds run as a unit, a cheetah has barely 1 chance in 10 of making a kill; but if one individual hesitates a fraction of a second when the

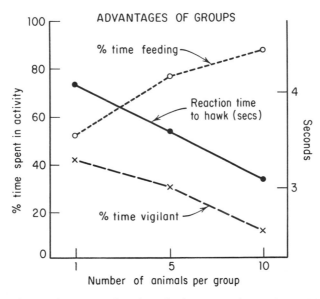

Fig. 4.2 Compared to singles, grouped starlings feeding more often and spend less time being vigilant, and they react faster to a flying hawk model. (Data from Powell 1974.)

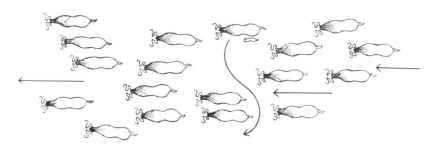

Fig. 4.3 When a herd of wildebeest pass a sleeping hyena (top left), a wildebeest cow with a calf (middle) leads its calf to the opposite side of the herd, and the remaining animals ignore the predator. (From Kruuk 1972. Copyright © 1972 by Univ. of Chicago Press. Reprinted by permission.)

rest run, thereby making itself an obvious target, its probability of being killed goes up threefold, and if it fails to rejoin the herd it has little hope of escape (Eaton 1974). He who hesitates, in other words, is lost. Similarly, in a violent revolution it is easier to survive when running with the mob than standing out alone.

Experimentally, too, individuals are caught more readily when alone than when in a group. When young coalfish were tipped into a tank containing cod, single fish were eaten in one-fifth of the time recorded for the first take of victims from a school of 25 to 30 (Radakov 1958, cited by Neill & Cullen). With larger schools, predators take longer to hunt and are less successful, showing more fear and hesitation in attacking, and more irrelevant and avoiding movements, as was found when 4 piscivores (pike, perch, squid, and cuttlefish) were tested with groups of 1, 6, or 20 prey fish (Figure 4.4). In another experiment, *Daphnia magna* were eaten less often by stickleback when in groups above a minimum size (Curio 1976). Pigeons, too, were most likely to be killed by a goshawk when alone, less so in groups of 2 to 10, and least of all in larger groups; escape began much farther away from the goshawk when the birds were in groups rather than alone (Kenward 1978).

Predators are deterred by a group of prey is several ways. They become more wary and are intimidated when the prey groups in a threat display. Against hyenas, for instance, eland *(Taurotragus oryx)* will face outward with the young inside the circle (Kruuk 1972). Moreover, defense is more effective by groups than by single animals. A leopard may kill single baboons but is no match for several adult males united against it. The same is true for ungulates with several species of predator and for humans in areas of big cities where robbers abound. Another gain from grouping is that hunters get confused when many individuals escape with irregular, protean movement (see Chapter 3), thus disrupting attempts to hunt and aim at one individual.

Both these gains occur in group mobbing whereby small birds harass raptors and small mammals. Axis deer *(Axis axis)* mob leopards, agoutis *(Dasyprocta punctata)* mob snakes (Simmons 1955; Smythe 1970), and hyenas mob lions (Kruuk 1972). The defense may be enhanced by erratic movements as a group. A good description is of Mexican Jays *(Aphelocoma coerulascens)* mobbing a Great Horned Owl *(Bubo virginianus)* for 40 minutes (Cully & Ligon 1976):

> When a Mexican Jay discovered the owl ... [it] would land on an exposed perch, bob its body, simultaneously flit its tail, and give a series of loud "weet" calls in rapid succession. This attracted the attention of others who then approached the owl and also began to mob it. Initially, flock members perched high in the trees. After about 3 min. they moved closer and onto more exposed perches. Several ... jays then typically began diving at the owl, some coming to within an inch ... of its head, which usually caused the owl to flinch. The jays appeared always to approach from behind or from the side and often two or more jays approached the owl at the same time. After 10–12 min. some flock members left, but returned periodically. For the next 10 min. 3–4 birds mobbed, but their approaches to the owl became less daring and less frequent. During the last 15 min. of mobbing only 1–2 birds remained at a time. Their calls became less frequent and they tended to perch at greater distances from the owl. Eventually the jays left.

When danger looms, individuals may retreat to a conspecific protector who may be a parent or more dominant in the hierarchy. Human phobics feel better in the presence of trusted companions or superiors. In many primate societies a female who is tolerated by the highest ranking male (indicated by his ignoring her presence or allowing her to groom him) benefits from his status (Gould

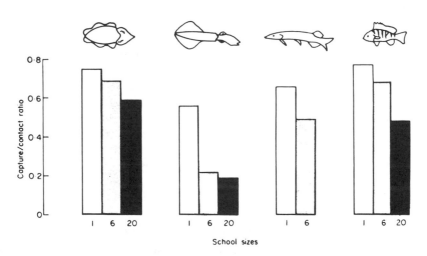

Fig. 4.4 Prey fish escape capture least when alone and best in larger groups. Results with four predators (from to right): cuttlefish, squid, pike, and perch. (From Neill & Cullen 1974. Copyright © 1974 by Academic Press (Inc) London. Reprinted by permission.)

1982). When she is attacked or threatened, she retreats toward his vicinity where she will not be pursued, and from this sanctuary will herself threaten the would-be attacker. Her offspring tend to be those of her overlord and are protected by him. When he dies she and her progeny fall in rank, though custom in the troop may continue to protect them even then. Following death of the alpha male a new network of alliances will develop with corresponding changes in the fearfulness shown by different animals. Such seemingly smooth workings of the primate hierarchy come from a continual sequence of subtle dominance interactions—passive displacements, averted glances, submissive postures, grooming ceremonies, and constant attention to the moods and movements of the higher ranking animals, especially of the boss.

Like everything else, group membership has its price. The costs and benefits alter with, among other things, the size of the group, the types of food, foe, and fear behavior, and their context. Some selection pressures in the course of evolution (such as cooperative breeding or hunting) make the species more social; others (such as competition for food) make it more solitary. Dozens of selection pressures compete in differing strengths and directions, and the optimal group size varies greatly with circumstance.

Defenses do not improve linearly as group size rises. Though the early warning system of prey gets better as individuals club together in small groups, the gain levels off beyond a certain group size. A thousand pairs of eyes see little more than a hundred. When a live trained goshawk *(Accipiter gentilis)* was used to attack feeding flocks of woodpigeons *(Columba palumbus)*, the detection distance rose from solitary pigeons to groups of 1 to 10 but not thereafter for groups of 11 to 50 or more (Kenward 1978). When in large herds, the calves of caribou *(Rangifer arcticus)* were more easily caught by wolves *(Canis lupus)* because they could not see the wolf stealing up on them (Crisler 1956, cited by Bertram 1978).

Safety in numbers disappears when the large size of a group impedes escape. We can easily get crushed to death in a dense human crowd rushing to escape from fire or attack. Panicking wildebeest stampeding in a herd to a river may drown their leading members, hundreds at a time so dying. Lion hunts are more successful with a large, unmaneuverable, milling mass of ungulates colliding into one another than are attacks on medium-sized herds (Schaller 1972, p. 235).

Gregariousness also invites wasteful predation (G. Williams, personal communication, 1982). Faced with a sudden abundance of prey, predators often kill much more than they need. They may kill several prey and eat only the easiest or choicest parts, whereas if only one prey were available they would consume most of it. Wasteful predation is seen with fish attacks on shoals (Williams 1966), hyena hunts of Thomson's gazelle (Kruuk 1972), and a fox getting into a hen coop.

Humans are the most wasteful predator of all. Nineteenth-century North American men annihilated huge flocks of passenger pigeons and nearly exterminated vast herds of bison. Bison were particularly easy prey as they failed to flee when their fellows were shot from a distance, allowing easy mass slaughter.

They had no time to evolve an appropriate signal for this new threat. These sad examples highlight the importance of distress and alarm calls.

DISTRESS AND ALARM SIGNALS

One advantage of group living is that fear responses evolve to become warning signals to which conspecifics can react quickly (Barnard 1983). The signals might be specific body movements in rabbits, the white rump or stotting (spronking) gait of fleeing ungulates, alarm pheromones in fish and ants, and sounds, which have been especially well adapted for group living. The role of distress and alarm calls as stimuli for fear was outlined in Chapter 2; here they are described as social responses to threat.

Distress calls may differ from alarm calls, and some species have one but not the other. The herring gull has an attention cry as well as an alarm call but not a distress call (Frings et al. 1955). Humans have many subtly different cries to express nuances of attention, distress, fear, and terror; their cries may be a summons for aid or a warning to get away.

The intensity of alarm calls can be graded. In the herring gull a weak disturbing stimulus such as a distant human releases a scarcely audible, high-pitched "hehe." As the intruder approaches the call gradually becomes louder. Its pitch may change a little, and the number of syllables increases from 2 to 4 or 5 (Tinbergen 1952). With increasing fear, alarm calls of several species (such as chicks or squirrel monkey) become longer and start at their top frequency without the initial rise commonly found in other calls (Figure 4.5). In Thomson's gazelle the soft snort of alarm becomes louder and deeper when it is in extreme peril.

Many alarm signals are similar across taxa, allowing animals to respond to alarm in other species as well as their own. This permits inter- as well as intraspecific communication, so mixed-species flocks of small birds may forage together, as do baboons and antelopes (Washburn & Devore 1961). White rumps are displayed by many types of ungulate and rabbit. Commonly, alarm calls are high-pitched whistles or squeaks on a single note with no phase or intensity differences, which makes the source more difficult to locate, unlike mobbing and courtship calls, which attract from a distance (Marler 1959).

Convergence during evolution has led to a common sign stimulus in different species of birds, which contrasts strikingly with their divergent territorial display songs. In blackbirds mobbing was elicited by a chorus of mobbing calls made up from four other bird species (Vieth et al., cited by Barnard 1983, p. 212). Figure 4.6 shows the similarity across bird species of two different types of call, one given to a perched owl, which elicits mobbing, and the other when a hawk flies over, which provokes a dash for cover (Marler 1959). The mobbing cry has a ticking or clucking quality that is easy to locate and summons groups to mob the predator. The alarm call, in contrast, must be difficult for prey as well as predators to locate; but this is no disadvantage, for the prey's imme-

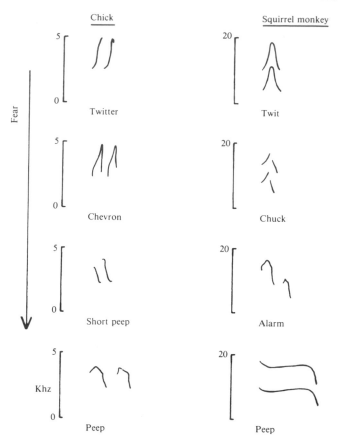

Fig. 4.5 As fear increases, the calls of chicks and squirrel monkeys become longer and start at their top frequency without the initial rise commonly found in other calls. (From Salzen 1979. Copyright © 1979 by Cambridge University Press. Reprinted by permission.)

diate response is to fly to the nearest cover, regardless of the direction of the call or of the hawk.

In monkeys as in birds, alarm calls are often similar among species (Marler 1975). Females and subadults of both the blue monkey *(Cercopithecus mitis)* and the red-tailed monkey *(C. ascanius)* give a "chip" alarm call at which both species alert, startle, and move into cover. They spend much time within earshot of one another, are active at the same time of day, and are vulnerable to the same predators (principally man, leopards, and eagles). The slow rate of divergence of the two species' "chip" calls during their evolution from a common ancestor may stem from the mutual benefit each gains from understanding the other's alarm call. In contrast, signal morphology has diverged for intraspecific action; for example, the two species differ in the calls they give to maintain distance between groups and to rally the troop prior to movement ("pyow" in the blue and "hak" in the red-tailed monkey).

Alarm cries increase the calling individual's own conspicuousness and risk.

Some species take this risk more often when their fellows are related—an example of kin selection. Black-tailed prairie dogs *(Cynomys ludovicianus)* of both sexes are more likely to give alarm calls during a predatory attack when they have close relatives in the home coterie than when nearby relatives are absent (Hoogland & Sherman 1981, p. 308). The same is true of Belding's ground squirrels *(Spermophilus beldingi)*, in whom alarm calls are rendered primarily by females with close relatives nearby (Sherman 1977), and of male but not female vervet monkeys *(Cercopithecus aethiops)* (Cheney & Sefarth 1981). However, alarm calls can obviously help unrelated as well as related individuals, and indeed other species. (The same is true for white rump alarm signals).

Different alarm calls may be given to different predators, allowing defensive action to be tailored to the type of predator that has been detected. The distinctive calls to terrestrial and to aerial predators, respectively, release upward flight into trees or downward flight into low cover in, for instance, the Burmese

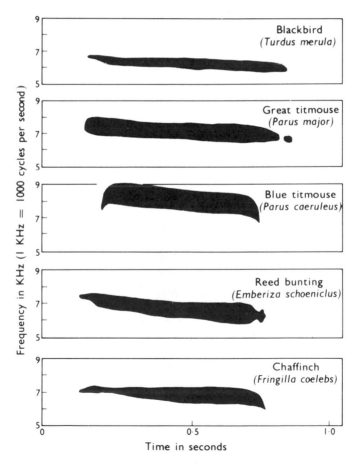

Fig. 4.6 Similarity of sound spectrographs of alarm calls from five species of passerine bird from four different families. They have similar form and pitch and are difficult to locate. (From Marler & Hamilton 1966. Copyright © 1966 by John Wiley & Sons, Inc.. Reprinted by permission.)

jungle fowl, some lemurs, and vervet monkeys (Owings et al. 1977; Russell 1979; Struhsaker 1967). House sparrows utter one kind of alarm call at the sight of fast-moving predators, which leads other sparrows to take refuge; another call is used in the presence of a slower-moving enemy and is the signal for mobbing assemblies (Daanje 1941, cited by Hartley 1950). California ground squirrels give a single loud whistle to low-flying hawks but chatter on detecting mammalian predators (Owings et al. 1977). Vervet monkeys on the ground respond to leopard-alarm and baboon-alarm calls by running into trees; to eagle alarms by looking up and running into bushes; and to snake alarms by standing on two legs and looking down and chuttering (Struhsaker 1967).

Alarm calls may have functions beyond that of alarm (Harvey & Greenwood 1980). Some might be given ventriloquially and divert the predator away from the caller. Sudden alarm calls can act as flash sounds by startling the predator and so aiding escape. They might also act as pursuit invitations (see Chapter 3). Finally, calls might promote prey aggregation, thus diluting the danger and improving cooperative defense.

ADJUSTMENT OF DEFENSES TO THE THREAT

Defense strategies need to be adjusted according to the context of the danger. Though animals higher in the phylogenetic scale show more flexibility in doing this, even lowly invertebrates may show quite varied and specific escape reactions and follow all four of the fear strategies described in the previous chapter.

What then is gained from vertebrate brains? The answer is that they enable animals to behave increasingly plastically with fewer constraints from built-in programs, more varied responses tuned to different sign stimuli (whether innate or learned), and more fine-tuned adaptation to a greater variety of present and future situations. Danger becomes more anticipated, and preventive action can be taken earlier. A crayfish escapes stereotypically mainly when touched, but a gazelle may keep a predator under observation from a distance, or retreat in a dignified walk, or run away in the stiff-legged jump of a pursuit invitation from a safe distance, or swiftly gallop away and dodge when pressed. In humans defensive behaviors take myriad forms of speech and action; some threats we anticipate and deal with decades ahead, though we are often shortsighted and threaten our own and many other species with extinction. We will examine some adjustments in invertebrates and then concentrate on mammals, especially ungulates, in which fear behavior in the natural environment has been most studied, particularly with regard to predators.

Some marine mollusks vary their escape reactions to predatory sea-stars and gastropods on the basis of chemical transmission (Edwards 1969). Herbivorous gastropods may escape when touched by carnivorous ones by fast movement away, sometimes swinging the shell about violently, and they may actually leap away. When the neogastropod *Olivella biplicata* contacts the starfish *Pisaster brevispinus* or one of its tube feet, it may turn sharply and crawl rapidly away. More often it flips over backward in a half-somersault and may swim away upside down, right itself, and crawl away fast (Edwards 1969). In a different reaction, after contact with a starfish the mollusk *Natica catena* will expand its foot to erect a fold of slimy tissue over its shell so that the starfish cannot get a grip while the mullusk crawls rapidly away. This response is elicited neither by other predators nor by mechanical stimuli (Purchon 1969).

A mollusk's response may be specific to the type of starfish (Edwards 1969). *O. biplicata* escapes from *P. brevispinus,* which lives in the same habitat, but does not flee from *P. ochraceus,* which inhabits a different area (Edwards 1969); it does not avoid another starfish that lives with and eats it *(Astropecten armatus),* but moves so quickly over the sand that the slow escape of *O. biplicata* would be futile and could not be selected for.

Mixed defenses are common among most animal classes, with different responses shown at different times. The degree and type of hazard decide whether an animal will freeze, withdraw, attack, deflect attack, or appease, as well as the speed of those responses. When disturbed, groups of animals may disperse rapidly and then hide in silent immobility. Camouflaged frogs, grasshoppers, and ground-dwelling birds may freeze during danger, perhaps after brief flight. If discovered they will escape again, or give an intimidating or startling display, or direct the predator away from vital areas. The sea cucumber discharges its internal organs as a distracting meal for its attacker (an unusual form of autotomy). If actually caught the prey can finally resort to tonic immobility, thus foiling those predators which kill only moving animals. Immobility may alternate with attack, as in a snake with a mongoose or a moose cornered by wolves.

Defenses vary with the threat even more among mammals than among mollusks. A mixture of alertness, differential alarm calls, threat, and aggressive defense is seen in the California ground squirrel (Owings et al. 1977). This species burrows near promontories such as logs and stones. When alert it will mount a promontory in order to see over the high grass, raise its head with wide-open eyes, and keep still. If it sees a mammalian predator it will chatter, but to a low-flying raptor it gives a single loud whistle. These differential alarm calls help its fellows take more appropriate defensive action. To a snake the squirrel may actually approach and even touch snouts, holding its bristled tail high while waving it from side to side, and kick sand into the snake's face with its forepaws, often causing the reptile to retreat.

Among ungulates, too, defenses depend upon the threat. A female gazelle with her fawn may attack a jackel and distract a hyena but retreat from a large carnivore (Walther 1969). A gazelle's erratic jumps help it avoid a lion or leopard but not a pack of hyenas or wild dogs. It may zigzag away from slower enemies, but if a cheetah bounds toward it at full speed it may gallop away without dodging (Schaller 1972, p. 317). Flight speed may be reduced when a herd contains young that run more slowly. A zebra herd with foals will flee only moderately rapidly with foals in the center, and if hyenas try to separate foals from the herd, stallions may fall back to defend them (Kruuk 1972, p. 184).

Precipitate flight might needlessly draw attention to the prey, so at times freezing or hiding is more appropriate. However, swift prey may actually taunt an enemy into chasing them under conditions most favorable to their own escape (Smythe 1970). Such a pursuit invitation might be given by the prey's flashing of its white rump or tail. It is useful for prey to detect a predator before being spotted and to flee before the predator's pursuit starts, provided the predator is about to give chase anyway. Once the predator gives up the hunt, prey animals are free to resume feeding. By inviting pursuit while they can detect the predator, prey reduce the chance that it will take them by surprise, shorten the duration of the threat, and lessen the disturbance to their normal activities. Pursuit invitations are found mainly in birds and mammals with young, so they can be regarded as a variant of the broken-wing trick by which parents distract predators from their offspring (G. Williams, personal communication, 1982).

Escape reactions may depend upon the angle at which an intruder approaches, as in *Dasyprocta patagonum,* an antelopelike rodent that lives in pairs on the Argentine pampas. If a man rides a horse directly at the animals they gallop directly away. If he approaches so as to be in clear sight but remaining well outside the flight distance of about 30 meters (m), they freeze and allow him to pass. If he rides obliquely toward them on a course that could eventually take him within 20 m of them, they wait until he is 30 to 40 m away and then flee with stiff-legged jumps for a short distance before sitting down and continuing to watch him. If he stops they get up and bound away again. They might repeat this pattern 4 times before walking away out of sight (Smythe 1970).

CASE STUDY OF AFRICAN PLAINS ANIMALS

Ungulate Defense Against Predators

The interplay of fear behaviors and their context is seen in rich detail in African plains animals such as hyenas (Kruuk 1972) and lions (Schaller (1972, pp. 234–236), and Thomson's gazelle has been especially well examined (Walther 1969). These three studies form the basis of the following account.

Most hoofed animals have bulging eyes to provide extreme wide-angle vision that spots slight movement, long mobile pinnae to localize sounds, and large nostrils and complex nasal passages to smell danger. Vision is the most important sense in open terrain; smell and hearing may help more in dense vegetation. Prey usually ignore calls of predators unless they are very near. While grazing they may keep an eye on a neighbor, and danger signals spread rapidly throughout the herd.

Vigilance varies among species and is less in individuals in large herds. The most alert are topi, hartebeest, waterbuck, and reedbuck, followed by impala and Grant's gazelle. Wildebeest, zebra, and eland may sleep so heavily that they fail to wake to a vehicle driving to within 5 m of them. Warthogs, too, are often incautious.

Some ungulates, such as reedbuck and bushbuck, avoid predators by hiding

motionless in thickets for much of the day, undetected even by nearby enemies. This and their alertness and sudden startled flight when detected make
it hard for lions to catch them. Avoidance of predators by remaining still is
limited to small and solitary species that are scattered under cover.

An alternative ploy used by most species is to form herds in the open and
run away if the predator gets too close or threatens from further away, but not
otherwise. A herd of ungulates is blasé about resting lions as long as they are
visible. A common sight in the African plains is that of lions resting encircled
by grazing gazelle, wildebeest, and zebra 25 to 100 m away.

When one or more lions merely walk along, ungulates raise their heads,
cock their ears, snort, and occasionally stamp a foreleg. These signals alert the
herd. Wildebeest may stop their incessant grunting when a lion approaches,
creating a pool of silence that is as effective a stimulus contrast as an alarm
snort, especially at night. Usually prey watch the predator until it moves on,
but at times they approach it and keep it under observation. This is called
curiosity or fascination (Kruuk 1972; Walther 1969). If a lion stops or turns
toward them the animals may wheel, flee a few meters, and look again, keeping
the distance between themselves and the lion at about 50 m. It helps to keep
sight of a predator that is mainly dangerous when it is hidden. In contrast, prey
do not usually follow wild dogs and hyenas, which hunt openly.

Unlike some other animals, ungulates do not avoid sites of previous
attacks, and they are vulnerable near drinking spots at rivers or gaps between
thickets. Hoofed animals tend to travel in single file, which decreases the likelihood of their stumbling on a hidden predator. During danger the young are
protected by being kept in the center of the herd.

Prey are often cautious about entering thickets. Herds may mill by a riv-
erine forest for more than an hour before going into or leaving it. At the slightest hint of danger they rush away from dense vegetation into the open, then
halt and look around. The same reluctance of ungulate herds to walk through
forests appears on the other side of the world among mountain sheep of the
Canadian Rockies (V. Geist, cited by Gould 1982, p. 448); this strategy may
protect against predators but slows their recolonization of areas from which
they have disappeared.

Most game animals flee only when an enemy has approached to a critical
distance that depends on how dangerous the predator is for the species. From
lions the flight distance of gazelle or zebra is greater than it is for larger prey;
it is perhaps 25 m for giraffe and buffalo, and none at all for hippopotami and
rhinoceri, which can defend themselves from attack. Many ungulates can out-
distance predators at full speed, and lions can capture an animal only if it can
be approached so closely that it can be grabbed or leapt upon before it attains
full running speed. If a lion walks toward prey they trot aside, and if it runs at
them they flee at a gallop. When attacked, gazelle and impala typically scatter,
thus confusing the predator; zebra and wildebeest bunch up unless the lions
actually run among them. Escape is rarely precipitous for more than a short
distance. Animals that have barely eluded a lion often stop within 50 m and
look back.

When actually pursued ungulates have special flight patterns. These include erratic dodging and zigzagging in most species; spectacular twisting leaps in impala and, to a lesser extent, Grant's gazelle and eland; bunching up in zebra; scattering in Thomson's gazelle; and sidestepping in wildebeest with the head lowered and twisted around to face the enemy. Warthogs dash for a burrow head first and at the last moment run abruptly to back into it while presenting their tusks to the pursuer.

Surprisingly little aggressive defense against predators is seen among African ungulates, the males' fearsome horns being used more against rival males of their own species. When caught, ungulates may cry out in distress, but most do little to prevent themselves being killed. Whether tonic immobility occurs is not known. Zebra only occasionally use their powerful hooves to kick smaller predators. Eland defend aggressively against hyenas and wild dogs; cows cooperate well in fighting even for unrelated calves in the herd. Antelope mothers defend their young against smaller predators, and among wildebeest the male may help, too. Wildebeest and especially buffalo may gore predators. North American moose lash out at wolves, while musk oxen form a defensive ring with their horns facing outward.

Defense is less successful when there are several predators at once. Even an exhausted wildebeest can fend off one hyena but may succumb to two, one on each side taking turns alternately to bite and dodge the horns. A wildebeest can prevent its calf from being taken in 85% of cases when there is only one hyena but in only 23% when there are two (Kruuk 1972).

It is instructive to examine separately the defenses of three species: wildebeest, zebra, and Thomson's gazelle. Brief descriptions of these defenses follow.

Wildebeest (Gnu, Connochaetes taurinus)

These live in three types of social unit—solitude (lone territorial bulls), bachelor (nonterritorial) herds, and cow-calf herds. Territorial bulls defend a small area against other bulls, while the herds of bachelors and of cows plus calves may contain up to several thousand animals that might be very scattered by day but concentrated in dense masses at night. Within the herd individuals' activities are highly synchronized.

The defenses of wildebeest are finely tuned to their predator's behavior, and they can gauge its hunting intentions from its posture, speed of movement, and grouping. They react with more curiosity and avoidance to stealthy cat carnivores than to hyenas. Wildebeest follow lion and cheetah for 100 m or more with their heads up, snorting occasionally. When a lion or cheetah walks through a herd an empty circle forms around them; the circle is larger with a lion (40 m) than with a cheetah (20 m). This reflects the danger—lions often kill both adult and calf wildebeest, whereas cheetah kill mainly calves. Wild hunting dogs (Lycaon pictus) rarely kill adult wildebeest, and herds keep about 20 m away from them, while territorial bulls allow the dogs within 3 m and sometimes even charge them; the flight distance soars to 200 m, however, if the dogs have recently hunted adult wildebeest in the area.

The variation of fear behavior with its intensity has been particularly well documented in wildebeest encountering hyenas. The response depends on the number of hyenas, minute details of their behavior, events immediately preceding their detection, and the wildebeest's social unit. Wildebeest start to react at a shorter distance from hyenas than from many other carnivores—they ignore a distant hyena but when it is nearer they may look at it, flee from it, attack it, or even move toward it without attacking. "Curious" wildebeest will walk or run toward a hyena or follow it with heads held high, and tightly bunched together if in a herd. In fleeing, the animals wheel and run, swishing their tails and closing up together in tight groups. Unlike flight, aggressive defense is much less communal: individual wildebeest run toward the hyenas with lowered heads trying to horn them. Wildebeest often snort when curious or just before fleeing, and grunt immediately after escaping.

If the hyena is not hunting, territorial wildebeest will largely ignore it beyond 8 m or just stand, head up, watching it; when closer the wildebeest will threaten it with lowered head and swishing tail. Large, dense herds may chase it away. Occasionally a territorial bull will snort at and avoid it. Single female wildebeest or nonterritorial males will avoid hyenas at 25 m but when in a herd react at 15 m and may graze or even lie down a mere 10 m from a recumbent hyena. Reaction distances are greater to a walking than a motionless hyena, and greater still when calves are present. When herds pass a resting hyena, mothers with calves move together to the side of the herd farthest away (Figure 4.3).

The greater the number of hyenas and their hunting intention, the more frightened the wildebeest become. The flight distance lengthens to 100 m if hyenas run toward them. If hyenas run into the center of a herd, it often splits into small groups that merge, split again, and merge once more in a huge melee. The wildebeest run silently, but as soon as the hyenas stop, they halt 20 to 80 m away in a chorus of grunts, and those closest to it will snort. A territorial male in the path of a running hyena will wheel around and flee, often in long stiff-legged stride that changes into a proper run if he is chased hard. As soon as the hyenas run after one particular animal, the others move out of the way and watch the show. If hyenas run straight toward a wildebeest in the process of pursuing another quarry, the former allows them to come closer before fleeing than when they run toward it with no other victim in sight. Successful escape from hyenas occurred in 57% of attacks by outrunning them, in 20% by disappearing into a herd, and in another 20% by entering the range of a neighboring hyena clan, on the boundary of which the hunting clan gave up (Kruuk 1972).

A wildebeest that has been singled out and chased will usually run in a straight line toward a herd, which may confuse the hyenas. Not infrequently it will run into water, which almost invariably leads to its being killed or drowned. The reason for this fatal aquatic habit is obscure. Once the wildebeest has been halted it makes faint attempts at dealing out blows and sways its head, moaning loudly as it is torn apart.

Calves are easily caught when less than half an hour old but thereafter run fairly fast and are soon able to keep up with the whole fleeing herd, though still slower than adults at full speed. A 4-day-old calf fleeing with its mother has outrun a hyena at 35 miles per hour (mph). While being chased and especially when separated from their mothers, calves call continuously with short single bleats, which leads the cow to attack predators when they get close, and nearby bull wildebeest and even zebra stallions may join in the defense. The mother's horns give the hyenas great trouble, and she goes on attacking as long as the calf is calling but stops when the calls cease with its death.

Wildebeest calves escaped from 68% of attacks by hyenas, usually by out-running them (49%) or by the mother's defense (29%). The latter was 100% successful if there was only one hyena, but totally unsuccessful against two or more (the calf would probably escape more often if it stayed close to its mother throughout the chase). The vulnerability of individual wildebeest calves to pre-dation is partly offset by synchronization of calving in a 3-week period in Jan-uary and February. This dilutes the danger by swamping the area with prey protected by the mothers and calves crowded together in defensive herds.

Zebra (Equus quagga)

Zebras have two forms of social unit: families (harems) consisting of 1 stallion, 1 to 6 mares, and an average of 5 to 8 foals; and bachelor groups of up to 15 stallions. These units may collect in large herds, especially at night, and are not territorial. Within the family units, one of the mares always leads the family while the others follow and the stallion walks behind, defending against other stallions and predators. Synchronization of calving is much less evident than in wildebeest.

As in wildebeest, the flight distance from prey increases with the danger. Zebra are the preferred prey of lions but are only rarely taken by cheetah, and they flee 50 m from lions but 25 m from cheetahs. Unlike wildebeest, which are nervous and curious, darting backward and forward, zebra are less curious and may just stand and stare at a passing carnivore, perhaps moving forward just a few steps.

A herd of zebra will ignore single hyenas barely 5 m away, merely looking at them and rarely snorting, but will flee from an alert hunting pack 100 m away, especially if the herd has been chased shortly before. Zebra walking past standing or recumbent hyenas may stop and look at them for several seconds with heads up, sometimes going several steps in their direction; they may fol-low walking hyenas for a few meters. Zebra have a shorter flight distance than wildebeest, but a mare with a young foal reacts from much farther away and is then followed by the rest of her family. Before fleeing from hyenas the family members bunch up, and several families may cluster into dense groups; foals run next to their mothers, both tending, as in wildebeest, to stay on the side farthest from the predator (Figure 4.7). Zebras usually flee at less than their full speed, barking excitedly in an impressive chorus during and after the run. Unlike wildebeest, they are reluctant to take to water when chased.

Zebras show aggressive defense when the stallion defends his family and the mare protects her foal. Only one zebra at a time will attack approaching hyenas, trying to bite and kick them with its forelegs, chasing them for up to 100 m with head near the ground, teeth bared, and ears flat. Rarely, a zebra may actually kill a hyena. Zebras are more likely to attack when the hyenas start to hunt, but as they continue the zebra stallion flees with his family. If the stallion has fallen behind while attacking, the family will halt until he has caught up and move off with him. Individuals from bachelor groups will also occasionally attack hyenas, but less strongly than a stallion defending his family. Stallions are better able to defend themselves than are mares and foals. Once caught by a predator, zebra show little aggression. Overall, zebras escape from 60% of hunts.

Thomson's Gazelle (Gazelle thomsonii)

Fear behavior has been well studied in Thomson's gazelle, a small, numerous species of the African plains which is easily hunted. Every carnivore from the size of a domestic cat upward may kill it, and fawns are especially vulnerable. Lions, leopards, cheetahs, wild dogs, hyenas, jackals, and baboons eat it regularly, eagles kill newborn fawns, and python also prey on them. Imperfect defense is compensated by a high reproductive rate from a relatively short gestation period of 5 to 6 months, mating and fawning throughout the year, early independence of the fawn with suckling ceasing after the third month, sexual maturity of the doe by the end of the first year, and readiness for conception a few weeks after the doe has given birth. Births are less synchronized than in wildebeest.

In the first 2 weeks of its life the fawn stays crouched motionless in one

Fig. 4.7 Before fleeing from hyenas zebra family members bunch up, and several families may cluster into a very tight group, foals running next to their mothers. The family is followed by the stallion, which repeatedly charges the hyenas running behind the family. (From Kruuk 1972. Copyright © 1972 by University of Chicago Press. Reprinted by permission.)

spot with its head on the ground and ears flat when there is danger. The mother wanders up to 500 m away, visiting the fawn now and then to feed it. She carefully licks its perineal area clean of urine and feces so that its smell will not betray its presence, and the fawn can remain undetected lying within a mere 2 m of predators. If disturbed the fawn will jump up and stot away, keeping its tail erect, thus exposing its white perineal area. This attracts the mother's attention, as does its bleating while chased, which can attract several female gazelles from over 200 m away. Up to four females might try to distract a hyena chasing a fawn by crossing just in front of the pursuer's nose or running alongside it just out of reach.

Like wildebeest, Thomson's gazelle has three social units—lone territorial males who defend their areas against other males, bachelor herds, and females in herds. Gazelle herds are more widely scattered than those of wildebeest or zebra, and the animals are better camouflaged from the human eye.

Despite its numerous enemies, Thomson's gazelle is not frightened all the time. After a gazelle has been caught the survivors soon resume grazing peacefully. Similar fear behavior is shown by the gazelle toward predators and to a very dominant conspecific. Some behaviors succeed well against both predators and conspecifics, while others work better with the latter.

To detect danger gazelles rely much more on sight than on hearing or smell. They often fail to react to alarm calls from other animals, and after dark rest quietly even though surrounded by the roaring of lions and howling of hyenas. Recognition depends on movement and on silhouette. Flight is quickly released by sudden change, strangeness, direct approach, large size, high visibility and speed, proximity, multiple enemies, and past dangerous experience.

The gazelle searches for predators by lifting its head and looking around occasionally, but may graze with its head down for up to 15 minutes before doing so. In a big herd at least one animal at a time has its head raised. As soon as it sees something unusual the gazelle erects its neck, puts its ears forward (Figure 4.8), lowers its croup, tenses its muscles, and sometimes stamps with a front leg. After watching something for a while an alert animal may suddenly move round in a small circle with hasty steps and then resume looking.

Gazelles may also approach to have a better look (curiosity, fascination). When male bustards make striking courtship displays in May, the birds are often surrounded by curious juvenile gazelles that come up with long necks from all directions, flee, and approach again. The gazelles come so close that the big bustard interrupts its display repeatedly to chase them away by beating its wings and hissing. Gazelles may also approach predators such as cheetah, leopards, and lions. On recognizing a predator up to 800 m away, a big and compact herd may approach to within 200 m and follow it if it moves, so reducing the chance of a surprise attack.

Flight occurs from predators and from very dominant conspecifics. Hyenas may chase adult or young gazelle 3 miles at 40 mph, and about a third of chases end in capture. Escape does not always involve galloping. When withdrawing from danger a gazelle may first walk, then stot and finally gallop and jump, or it may begin with a gallop and end with a walk (Figure 4.8). Jumps may be long and flat or, when pressed, arched and high. A fast, flat flight gallop may reach 50 mph.

Another jumping gallop is *stotting* (Figure 4.8, top right). This is a large bound, with the gazelle taking off from all legs almost simultaneously. The legs are held stiff and straight, and the feet are about a half-meter from the ground at the highest point of the jump. This gait is seen more in fawns and subadults than in adults and occurs during intraspecific play and fighting as well as flight. Stotting is contagious and alerts other animals. It occurs mainly at the start or end of flight, and is seen at the start only if the pursuer is not too close; oth-

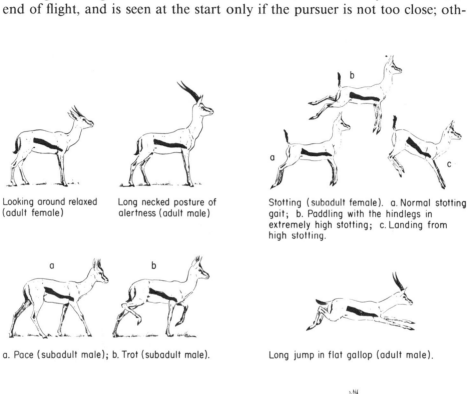

Looking around relaxed (adult female)

Long necked posture of alertness (adult male)

Stotting (subadult female). a. Normal stotting gait; b. Paddling with the hindlegs in extremely high stotting; c. Landing from high stotting.

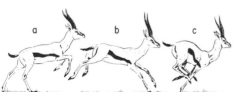

a. Pace (subadult male); b. Trot (subadult male).

Long jump in flat gallop (adult male).

Gallop (adult male). a. Initial jump; b. Becoming elongated; c. Becoming short.

Arched jump, predominantly in high grass areas (adult female). a. Coming up; b. Coming down.

Fig. 4.8 Various fear behaviors of Thomson's gazelle. Top left: looking around relaxed (adult female) and alert with body and neck erect and ears forward (adult male). Middle left: unhurried pace or trot (subadult male). Bottom left: hurried escape in a gallop in which the animal jumps, elongates, and then shortens (adult male). Bottom right: fast arched jump in high grass (adult female). Middle right: fast, flat flight gallop, which may reach 50 miles per hour (adult male). Top right: stotting, a large bound in which the gazelle takes off from all legs almost simultaneously, with the legs held stiff and straight; the hindlegs may paddle when the stot is extremely high (subadult female). (Redrawn from Walther 1969.)

erwise the gazelle starts in its fastest gait of a flat gallop. A gazelle never stots when hard chased but may at the end when the pursuer has given up. Stotting is common when fleeing from hyena and wild dogs but not from lion, cheetah, and leopard. When the herd flees stotting together, the flash color bobbing erratically on many rumps can prevent pursuers from concentrating on a single animal target.

During a hard chase the gazelle often zigzags sharply. If the predator catches up, the gazelle may double back, usually to no avail. More successful than doubling is crossing quickly just in front of the predator's nose, which diverts it momentarily. Flight gallops typically end with the gazelle stopping and looking back to check the enemy's position.

Flights by a large herd last longer if it is not split apart. Rarely, single animals may evade a predator by running into dense vegetation or into a herd of wildebeest. Flight is triggered more easily immediately after sundown, when many predators are active. Sudden heavy rain can start a false alarm.

Just when they begin to run, whether in attack or in flight, gazelles, especially females, snort and twitch their black-striped flank. The snort, and perhaps the flank twitch, serve as alarm signals. A snort (a soft "quiff") is given through the nose with the nostrils closed and pulled down. As soon as they hear it, neighboring gazelles look up and stare in the same direction as the snorter. The alert posture, warning signals, and flight of a conspecific are contagious. Alertness, alarm calls, and flight spread like a wave from the alerted animal throughout the vast scattered herd. Fawns in distress when pursued give a long cry with an open mouth ("aaa" or "uuu" with u as in murder). Attracted by this cry, the mother comes at full gallop and attacks the predator if it is not too big. When captured, adults and fawns give a loud, long-drawn-out guttural bleat until they die.

Gazelles will flee from cheetah and wild dogs (their main enemies) when they are still 350 m away, from lions (which prefer larger prey) when they come within 150 m, and from jackals (which normally only kill fawns) from a mere 5 to 50 m. As with wildebeest and zebra, gazelles react to tiny differences in the predators' behavior, especially if they are hunting. Gazelles will escape at distances of fully 2 kilometers (Km) from hunting wild dogs, but remain within 50 m when a pack is merely walking without interest in the game around them.

The reaction to hyenas depends upon their number and hunting intention, and the social category of the gazelle. When a single hyena walks toward a territorial male, from 35 m the gazelle will stop grazing and look at the hyena with head raised, watch it to within 15 m, then turn, snort softly, stamp its front feet, and run away a short distance at right angles to the direction of the hyena's walk. The gazelle then stops, turns, and watches the hyena again, and finally returns to its territory if the hyena has passed.

Female and bachelor herds react from farther away than territorial males. When a hyena walks through a herd, they quietly move out of the way as it nears and close up again behind it, retreating from farther away when they are in its path than alongside. An empty oval will extend 40 m around a single hyena and 100 m around two or more. If the approaching hyena runs up instead of walks, or if there are more than one, gazelle flee from up to 500 m away.

Escape and Other Selection Pressures

We have seen that all three species just described show most fear of those predators which are especially dangerous to their species, in a hunting posture, approaching directly and rapidly, with hunting companions, and have recently chased their prey. The type of fear behavior also depends upon competing selection pressures on the animal as a whole. Energy conservation might explain why gazelle and some other ungulates do not immediately gallop away from predators at top speed but instead usually stot first at medium speed and break into their fastest gallop only when the predator is about to catch up. Certain gaits conserve energy more than others at particular speeds and might be a way of gearing energy consumption to speed; stotting is more energy-saving than galloping at medium speeds. When predators lurk continually, prey have to save strength and would soon be exhausted if they constantly reacted beyond the minimum effort needed to get away. It is better to save energy-expensive flight such as a fast gallop for the rare occasions that call for it. This requires fine judgment, which is sometimes fatally wrong. A human observing might ask why an animal killed in a chase did not gallop away hard from the start, and the answer might come from the broader perspective of the animal's overall energy budget.

Similar considerations might explain why prey allow predators to approach so close before reacting. When surrounded by potential predators that attack only occasionally, prey cannot spend all their time in defense. Prey have a finite time-budget in which to graze, court, mate, and rear young, and time spent in fear behavior decreases the time available for all these other activities. An alert animal with head constantly up cannot graze, fight, or mate efficiently, so compromise must be reached. The animal looks around only occasionally, and companions improve its warning system and time budget. Other selection pressures may explain why smaller female zebra attack predators less than do the larger males, which are more likely to survive an attempt at driving away predators.

There are still many unexplained features of ungulate defense—for instance, why wildebeest often run fatally into water when chased, why wildebeest females cooperate so little in defense of themselves or their calves, why male Thomson's gazelle do not come to the rescue of their females or fawns, and why female Thomson's gazelle have lost the well-developed horns that were present in evolutionary predecessors as well as in other female gazellinea today, and would be so useful against jackals.

Fear Behavior in a Predator: Spotted Hyenas
(Crocuta crocuta)

Predators as well as prey have much to fear. This is well seen in one of the commonest hunters of the African plains, the spotted hyena (Kruuk 1972). Hyenas kill other species rapaciously but also have more to fear from their own kind than do most other carnivores. Yet cooperative group hunting demands social tolerance, and spotted hyena have to feed off larger prey while standing shoulder to shoulder with one another. When feeding, they compete more by eating very fast than by fighting and by running off alone with large pieces of meat.

Hyenas are cannibals. Adults killed in a clan fight or by lions are often eaten by their fellows, although hyenas clearly prefer the meat of their regular prey. It may take a whole day for hyenas to consume a hyena carcass completely, whereas in the same area they will totally devour a wildebeest within an hour and a gazelle within 7 minutes. Hyenas intruding into another clan's territory are fearful in posture (ears flat, mouth open, tail between legs, hindquarters down) and are viciously attacked and chased for up to 2 miles. As a hyena goes from its own range into a neighboring one it becomes more cautious and flees on recognizing other hyenas far away. So fearful are hyenas of a strange clan that they may abandon a hunt if their quarry runs into the territory of another clan. An intruder may slowly become accepted over several months if it persists in returning, hanging around the den, and joining in kills.

A mother hyena protects her offspring from cannibalism by marked aggressive defense, which is made easier by her being larger than males. She barely tolerates other females near her offspring until the young are about 2 weeks old, and invariably snaps at and chases males even from larger suckling cubs. Later she stands guard when her cubs are eating from the remains of a carcass in which other hyenas are also interested. In another defense against cannibalism, cubs creep out of reach of adults into small holes that they dig themselves.

As we would expect in an aggressive social animal, appeasement is well developed in spotted hyenas. They have elaborate greeting ceremonies in which they sniff and lick one another's genitals. The female's genitals externally are a replica of the male's and are used in appeasement (she has a clitoris as large as the male's penis and a false scrotum filled with fibrous tissue, and her androgen level is high). Both sexes have more obvious erections when greeting one another than during courtship. Such appeasement displays are less marked in the striped than in the spotted hyena; the female striped hyena has not evolved similar pseudomale genitals.

Hyenas fear not only their fellows but also larger carnivores. They retreat from lions stealing their kill, and Kruuk (1972) observed a young hyena being terrified at its first smell of lion and of leopard.

SUMMARY

Fear spurs individuals to seek the company of their fellows. The costs and benefits of group membership vary with the species and context. Up to a point more sensors yield a better early warning system, and a few lookouts suffice for all, allowing the rest of the group time to get on with other essential things. Erratic escape and aggressive defense can be more effective on a group rather than an individual basis. Uncoordinated large mobs may hamper efficient escape and are a temptation to wasteful predation.

Group living allows the evolution of warning signals from movement, odor, or sounds. Unlike signals for mating, which are species-specific, alarm signals like white rumps and calls are often similar enough among several prey species that forage together to allow mutual recognition. Different alarm calls may be given to different predators. Alarm calls may be more difficult to locate than other calls, unless they summon the group for aggressive defense like mobbing. Alarm calls put the caller at risk by drawing attention to him and may be given more often among related individuals, suggesting kin selection. Warning signals not only arouse one's fellows but also distract or startle the enemy and act as pursuit invitation.

Invertebrates have surprisingly varied defenses to threat. Species with more complex nervous systems vary their defense even more plastically according to context with better anticipation and prevention of threat. In mammals survival is promoted by many subtle combinations of different types of withdrawal, immobility, aggressive defense, and deflection.

Ungulates do a sophisticated dance of potential death with their predators, keeping them under observation or fleeing in a variety of ways according to the needs of the immediate moment and ultimate energy budgets and opportunity costs. They graze peacefully when surrounded by nonhunting predators, reacting when danger rises. Defenses also vary with the social organization of the species and the social unit of the individual. Predators also show fear, and hyenas carefully defend their young and themselves against their fellows.

II
MECHANISM

5

Development of Fear

The typical fears shown by a species vary with age, changing as the individual grows and matures. This chapter traces how fear develops through infancy and childhood, especially in humans, monkeys, and dogs. Fears of heights, strangers, and separation will illustrate this developmental process particularly clearly.

THE ONTOGENETIC PARADE AND ITS SUBSTRATE

In the course of development there is a predictable parade of normal fears that emerge, plateau, and decline. Human fears of separation and strange adults, for example, are common at age 8 to 22 months, of strange peers a bit later, and of animals and the dark later still. The first three fears start to decline from about age 2, and the latter two when the child is older. This ontogenetic sequence reflects maturation under genetic control during interaction with the environment.

Early neuronal connections result from genetic factors working within the embryonic environment; the persistence of many of these and of behavior dependent on them requires appropriate experience after and sometimes even before birth. Visual privation in kittens leads to marked changes in the visual cortex, and environmental impoverishment in infant rats is followed by altered brain chemistry and histology (Newton & Levine 1968; Rutter 1981). The fear of moving objects shown by very young chicks varies with their experience of illumination while in the egg (Dimond 1966; Salzen 1979). The more complex the animal, the larger the masses of nerve tissue that are less committed at birth, permitting experience to play an increasingly large role in neuronal connections during development (Jasper & Douane 1968).

Although disruption of the usual genetic or environmental influences can drastically change what happens, many developmental processes are sufficiently plastic with self-correcting features to allow the same steady state to be reached by a variety of routes (Bateson 1976). Despite widely varying patterns of child-rearing, fears of strangers and of separation are seen in children all over the world. Even children who are severely deprived of human contact become normal adults if they subsequently grow up in a secure home (Kagan 1979; Rutter 1981).

The stage at which disruption of genetic or environmental influences occurs can be critical. In the embryonic nervous system, trellis cells guide migrating neurons to their destination and then vanish, that particular template now being fixed. How differentiated a nervous system is at a given state limits how the environment can influence it. Rats, for instance, become able to condition taste aversion only gradually in the first few postnatal weeks (Schweitzer & Green 1982). Trellis behaviors that guide the young toward the actions required as adults can be much easier to perform and build on at certain sensitive stages of development than later on. Dogs that are not socialized before and during the first emergence of stranger fear remain scared of strangers thereafter. Monkeys reared in isolation display excessive fears that are hard to overcome when they are later placed with normal animals (Suomi et al. 1974).

We infer stages in growth from public events that flow from imperceptible preceding changes that have gradually been established (Kagan et al. 1978). The rise and fall of developmental phenomena depend upon intermeshing processes that are still largely unknown. These processes slowly consolidate to the point where they noticeably transform behavior. Largely hidden from view, they set the scene for suddenly visible shifts, just as the first winter frost on the window appears abruptly after a gradual cooling of the earth. Fear of strange events requires the prior learning of what is familiar, a process that starts in the womb. At first all is novel; only abrupt, big changes in stimulation startle the neonate. With development more subtle and complex discrepancies begin to arouse wariness, culminating in full-blown fear of strangers and of separation in human infants toward the end of their first year.

Universal developmental phenomena need not appear consistently at only one age and with merely one method of measurement. Some wariness of strangers is ubiquitous in children 8 to 12 months old, yet one observation of only their avoidance of a playful stranger keeping his distance may miss this. Its demonstration may require more longitudinal testing of several facets of the reaction to an insistently approaching stranger.

The Continuum of Control Between Genes and the Environment

Expression of the genetic program depends on the environment, and changing that environment will modify the resulting phenotype from fertilization onward. Even in utero the human fetal heart rate responds to the mother's distress (Talbert et al. 1982). Every species has to experience certain conditions in order to survive, and experience of these conditions rather than maturational changes within the young may determine a particular fear. Learning may also obscure maturation in two ways. First, early experience of a situation may prevent later fear of it from emerging at the age when such fear usually appears—that is, early familiarity can breed later contempt. Second, at the sensitive age at which a response matures, momentary experiences might greatly enhance the maturational reaction although at an earlier or later age they would have had little effect.

There are many gradations in the degree of learning needed for various fears to emerge. Some fears, such as those of examinations, occur only after special experience. Others, such as those of separation or of animals, arise in most children with no trigger beyond normal experience and are hard to suppress completely. The relevant cues are prepotent (latent or prepared) stimuli for fear, and the subject learns to fear them much more quickly than others (see Chapter 8). Such latent fears may appear as pseudoconditioning (Miller 1951). A stimulus may seem neutral at first, but after the subject has received a few electric shocks he or she shows strong fear of the stimulus even though it has never been paired with shock.

The delicate interaction of unlearned and learned elements in the development of children's fears was subtly traced by Valentine (1930): "The power of suggestion seems to be so much greater in certain ways, as in stimulating the fear of animals or of the dark, than it is in others on the many occasions that a parent uses it (as in suggesting that foods are [nasty], or that children will fall if they climb), that we can more reasonably believe that in the former cases suggestion is appealing to a latent impulse in the same direction, whereas in the latter cases there is no such innate tendency." Valentine posited a tendency to fear strange things, especially when closely associated with the familiar: "We must assume a further tendency to especially fear live, moving things, a faint tendency, so that it can easily be modified by repeated experience or even suggested away; yet sensitive, so that it can easily be stimulated by suggestion or by a supplementary stimulus causing a general disturbance."

Much resistance to the idea that our genes influence our behavior comes from the mistaken belief that "genetically controlled" implies "unmodifiable." In fact, even inbuilt fears can be modified. Phobias of animals as well as of examinations can be cured by exposure therapy. In order to prevent excessive fear we have to understand the relative contributions of internal and external factors to its origin. Chapter 6 describes the significant genetic contribution to timid temperament and to phobic and obsessive-compulsive disorders. Unraveling the developmental process by which this contribution is made will eventually help us to modify it.

Some of J. B. Watson's observations on infants were used to support Valentine's position (cited by Valentine): "Vincent showed no fear of the rabbit, even when it was pushed against his hands or face. His only response was to laugh and reach for the rabbit's fur. On the same day he was taken into the pen with Rosey, who cried at the sight of the rabbit. Vincent immediately developed a fear response; in the ordinary playroom situation he would pay no attention to her crying, but in connection with the rabbit, her distress had a marked suggestion value. The fear transferred in this way persisted for over two weeks."

The fear of the rabbit could not be entirely due to suggestion (modeling), because no fear was shown to other objects that were around when Rosey cried in Vincent's presence. Rather, when Vincent was disturbed he was more predisposed to fear the rabbit than the other stimuli. The observations of Vincent were borne out in work showing that rhesus monkeys quickly acquire a fear of snakes on watching another rhesus evince terror of a snake (Cook et al. 1985; see also Chapter 2).

Valentine's argument was that children are not born with a picture of furry animals or snakes labeled "danger" inside their cortex, but rather have a low threshold for showing fear to certain stimulus configurations, which automatically leads to fear of animals under certain conditions. This position accords with findings in rhesus monkeys reviewed below.

Unlearned Prepotent Fears and Rituals

With characteristic insight Charles Darwin suggested the idea of prepotent fears as long ago as 1877 when his son, 2 years and 3 months old, suddenly feared large caged animals at the zoo. Darwin asked, "May we not suspect that the . . . fears of children, which are quite independent of experience, are the inherited effects of real dangers . . . during ancient savage times? It is quite conformable with what we know for the transmission of formerly well-developed characters, that they should appear at an early period of life, and afterwards disappear."

Twenty years later Stanley Hall again suggested (1897, pp. 246–247) that our evolutionary inheritance makes our species more inclined to develop certain fears than others:

> The proportional strength of different fear elements and tendencies . . . fits past conditions far better than it does present ones . . . serpents are no longer among our most fatal foes and most of the animal fears do not fit the present conditions of civilized life; Yet again, the intensity of many fears, especially in youth, is out of all proportion to the exciting cause. The first experiences with water, the moderate noise of the wind, or distant thunder . . . might excite faint fear, but why does it sometimes make children on the instant frantic with panic? Must we not conclude that . . . human instinctual feelings . . . have been felted and macerated into their present form very gradually by social, telluric and cosmic influences, some of which still persist unchanged, but more of which have been either modified or are now extinct?

Subsequent work confirmed that species' perceptual systems are tuned to be especially sensitive to certain stimuli. Such perceptual biases may partly reflect "prewired" feature detectors and experience during sensitive periods (Suomi 1983c). Although humans and other animals may show fear of any situation at some time or other, certain situations are much more feared than others. Furthermore, fear appears at particular ages when the animal has had little or no experience of the situation concerned, though experience acts on the fear once it appears.

Two experiments in rhesus infants have demonstrated this. The first found selective sensitivity of rhesus infants to conspecific threat displays at age 2½ to 4 months (Sackett 1966). Eight infants were reared in isolation without ever seeing a monkey or a human after the first 9 days of life. In a daily test session, slides were projected onto a screen on one side of the cage. In some of these

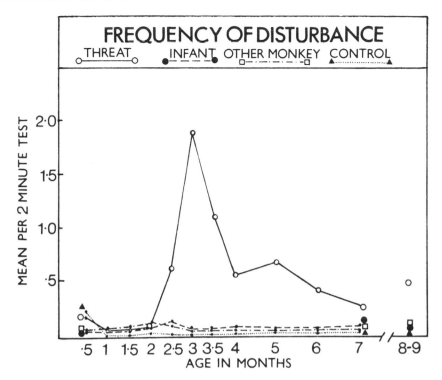

Fig. 5.1 Reactions of isolation-reared rhesus to experimenter-controlled slides shown daily. Disturbed behavior occurred only from age 2 months, peaked at 3 months, and waned thereafter. Disturbance occurred only in response to pictures of threatening adult rhesus; there was no disturbance to pictures of nonthreatening other infants or adult rhesus or of control inanimate objects. (From Sackett 1966. Copyright © 1966 by American Association for the Advancement of Science. Reprinted by permission.)

tests the infant could turn on the slides, which depicted monkeys in many poses, including threat, and inanimate objects.

Throughout the 9 months of testing there was little disturbance to any of the pictures except those of threat. However, starting at 2½ months and peaking at 3 months, all the monkeys were markedly disturbed (exhibiting fear, withdrawal, rocking, and huddling) whenever pictures of threatening monkeys appeared on the screen (Figure 5.1). From age 2½ to 4 months the monkeys rarely touched the lever to turn on the threat pictures (Figure 5.2). Pictures of rhesus infants aroused the most vocalization and play but did not produce the distress aroused by pictures of threat; control pictures of inanimate objects evoked the least interest.

Thus at least two socially meaningful pictures—monkey infants and monkey threat—were unlearned, prepotent activating stimuli for socially naive infant monkeys. From age 2 months they activated higher levels of all behaviors in all monkeys. Only threat pictures elicited fear, and then only in monkeys between 60 and 80 days old, not before. These fear responses waned about 110 days after birth. This could be because the aggression that would come

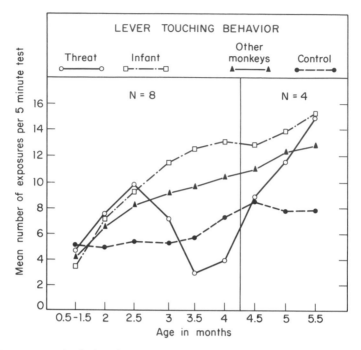

Fig. 5.2 Frequency with which isolation-reared rhesus touched a lever to show slides. Frequency dropped only from age 2½ to 4½ months, and only in response to pictures of threatening adult rhesus, not of nonthreatening other infants or adult rhesus or of control inanimate objects. (From Sackett 1966. Copyright ©1966 by American Association for the Advancement of Science. Reprinted by permission.)

from a real threatening monkey did not ensue after the threat pictures. When an isolated monkey was later brought into contact with conspecifics it did not show fear or withdrawal when attacked. The appropriate response to threat had atrophied, its development not having been reinforced at the time it first appeared.

The second experiment showed that rhesus fear appeared later than friendly responses, and that fear of conspecific and of human faces depends on age, stimulus configuration, and experience (Kenney et al. 1979). Twenty-six rhesus infants were reared under three conditions in which they could see (1) other monkeys and people, (2) one monkey neighbor, or (3) neither other monkeys nor people. From age 1 to 12 weeks they were tested for lipsmacking (friendly) or grimacing (fearful) responses to their own mirror image or to a human face.

There was an obvious age gradient in responses to the mirror and to the face. Monkeys younger than 20 days seldom lipsmacked or grimaced. Friendly lipsmacking occurred earlier than fearful grimacing and then declined, whereas grimacing rose progressively throughout testing (Figure 5.3).

Whether the initial response was friendly or fearful largely depended on the type of stimulus, regardless of rearing. Most often the mirror evoked a lipsmack and the human face a grimace (Figure 5.4). Eighty percent of infants responded first to the mirror—with a lipsmack—about 20 days before they first grimaced. First response to the human face came about a week later than to the mirror—and was a grimace in 76% of monkeys; 43% never lipsmacked to the human face, compared to only 4% that never lipsmacked to the mirror. Despite the first response to the human face appearing later than that to the mirror, the first grimace to the human face appeared earlier (45 days) than that to the mirror (55 days) and, unlike those to the mirror, grimaces to the human face increased progressively with age (Figure 5.5).

Individual experience produced neither the age gradient nor the differential influence of mirror versus face but could modify these effects. The most restricted infants, which had seen neither monkeys nor people, were the oldest before they responded for the first time; they also responded least overall and differentiated least between the two stimuli. Infants that had seen both monkeys and people responded earliest and most overall, and differentiated most between mirror and face.

Although rearing condition did not decide whether reactions to stimuli would be friendly or fearful, it did increase the first response to them. In rhesus

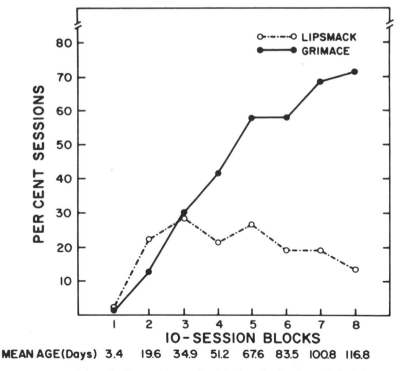

Fig. 5.3 Percentage of friendly lipsmacking or fearful grimacing by rhesus infants in response to a mirror and a human face. Regardless of rearing, lipsmacking occurred a bit earlier and declined somewhat after 3 months, whereas grimacing rose progressively to 4 months. Mean age shown is for the first session of each 10-session block. (From Kenney et al. 1979. Copyright © 1979 by John Wiley & Sons, Inc. Reprinted by permission.)

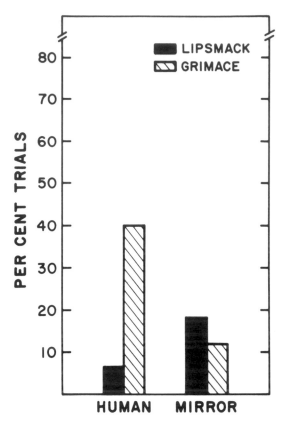

Fig. 5.4 Whether the response by rhesus infants was friendly or fearful varied with the stimulus regardless of rearing. A mirror reflecting the monkeys' own image evoked more friendly lipsmacks than a human face, which mainly evoked a fearful grimace. (From Kenney et al. 1979. Copyright © 1979 by John Wiley & Sons, Inc. Reprinted by permission.)

monkeys reared while seeing both other monkeys and people, the greatest initial response was to the human face, although for all rearing groups this reaction was usually a fearful grimace rather than a friendly lipsmack. Similarly, the greatest initial response in those who saw a neighboring monkey during rearing was to the mirror, although all rearing groups reacted to the mirror more with lipsmacks than with grimaces. Finally, infants reared with minimal yet equivalent exposure to other monkeys and people reacted least differently to mirror compared to face.

Rhesus fears of threat and of strange faces thus start as unlearned responses that soon become selective through social learning but develop abnormally if that is absent. The same is true for human smiling (Emde et al. 1976) and language. Unless he or she gets social feedback a deaf infant fails to develop spontaneous babbling into language and eventually becomes mute.

As with babbling in the deaf human infant, we saw that lack of social feedback in isolated rhesus infants leads to atrophy of their unlearned fear of threat, so they are attacked on later encountering conspecifics. In other isolated rhesus

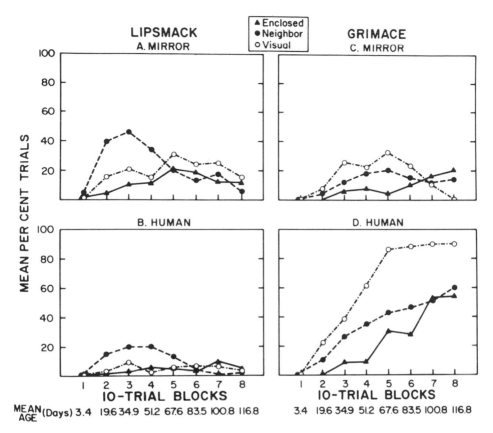

Fig. 5.5 Most rhesus infants responded first to a mirror—mainly by friendly lipsmacking—and then to a human face—usually by fearful grimacing. The first grimace to the human face appeared earlier than that to the mirror and rose progressively from age 19 days to 4 months, unlike grimacing to the mirror. Mean age shown is for the first session of each 10-session block. (From Kenney et al. 1979. Copyright © 1979 by John Wiley & Sons, Inc. Reprinted by permission.)

infants this problem was overcome by prolonged individual interaction with a slightly older conspecific. The latter persistently dragged the infants out of a self-clasping huddle into social play, eventually enabling the former isolates to become part of a group (Suomi et al. 1974). A similar sequence was seen with a female wolf cub reared in visual isolation from 3 weeks to 10 months; by being forced to interact with other, normal wolves, she gradually integrated with the group (Ginsburg 1975).

Intrinsic factors decide not only which stimuli evoke fear most readily in the young animal, but also which fear responses it gives to those stimuli. These fear reactions are its natural repertoire of species-specific defenses (Bolles 1970), which are learned more easily than others in frightening situations. In a new, frightening situation a species learns much more readily to perform its natural fear responses than to carry out behavior not usually shown when frightened.

Are There Prepotent Rituals?

Probably most normal children go through a transient phase of minor rituals not far removed from the counting and rhyming songs and games played endlessly by children all over the world, or the game of hopscotch. Normal rituals become apparent in children about 5 to 8 years old and might involve avoiding stepping on cracks in the sidewalk or touching alternate pickets in fences they are passing. Often, but not always, the children may feel that carrying out the ritual averts some awful disaster to others or to themselves.

This intriguing phenomenon has not attracted research, nor are there obvious animal parallels, so we know nothing about its age limits, origin, or possible connection with later obsessive-compulsive problems. While it is easy to see many children's fears as a response to special evolutionary dangers, this is less true for developmental rituals. Keeping to self-made rules seems to stave off imagined terrors and gives the child self-confidence. Could such rituals be species-specific defenses to reduce everyday anxieties? Are they aids to learning? Why do they appear at age 5 to 8? Only systematic study will tell.

A Maturational Fear Need Not Be Prepotent

A given fear emerging at a particular age need not imply concern with a special evolutionary danger but rather may indicate that perception has matured to a particular point. This was found in two cohorts of children studied for 10 months (Kagan 1981). Each child first played with toys on the floor while mother and examiner sat in the room. After 10 minutes they joined the child on the floor, and the mother held the child on her lap. With the child watching, the examiner slowly modeled three age-appropriate acts with the toys, such as feeding a bottle to a zebra or making a doll talk on the phone. Then the model said, "Now it's your turn to play," and allowed each child to play for 10 minutes.

From age 15 months onward, distress appeared during the minute after the model completed the three actions. The child fretted, cried, clung to the mother, and did not play. The distress peaked (Figure 5.6) just before age 2 in American children and at about 28 months in Fijian children, and in Vietnamese children in the United States. Distress was greater with unrealistic than with realistic toys, did not vary with the number of prior exposures to the model, and occurred whether the child was tested at home or in the laboratory.

It would be hard to argue that these children feared an evolutionary danger. Kagan thought this age-related anxiety came from the child's feeling that he ought to imitate the model but was unable to meet the standard just seen; it appeared that an awareness of standards for behavior and the child's own competence to meet them had grown in the months before age 2.

Fear After Initial Indiscriminate Approach

Fear follows an earlier phase of affiliation in birds and mammals (Salzen 1979; Smith 1969). On their first day newly hatched chicks approach most objects

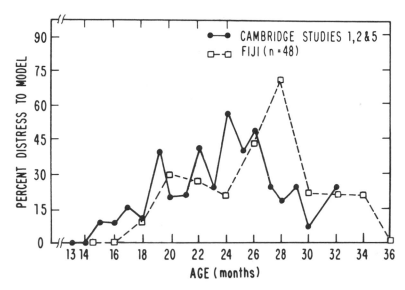

Fig. 5.6 A maturational fear need not be prepotent. Despite being on their mother's lap, from age 19 to 29 months children in Cambridge, Massachusetts, and in Fiji cried when an adult model, after demonstrating play, suggested that they follow suit. (From Kagan 1981. Copyright © 1981 by Harvard University Press. Reprinted by permission.)

and give distress calls to harsh sounds, bright light, or sudden movement, but avoid strange stimuli only from the second day. Tonic immobility is seen a bit later, in chickens at 8 days and in rats at 5 to 30 days (Halonen & Denny 1980). Initial friendliness without fear allows young animals to bond protectively to a nearby fellow, which in nature is usually the mother. Once fear of novelty has emerged, however, chicks imprint only if contact is enforced by preventing escape, upon which they gradually develop a new preference (Bateson 1981; Hoffman 1974). Such taming (bonding after fear has been overcome by arduous habituation) is not seen in the wild as older animals run away.

A longitudinal study of the way fear grows after initial approach and interferes with taming was made in dogs over 20 years ago (Scott & Fuller 1965). This excellent work has been neglected and deserves detailed account. In the first few weeks most of the puppies stayed with their mother and litter mates in their nursery rooms; at 16 weeks they were moved to large pens. (In guide dogs, kennel rearing beyond 14 weeks leads to timidity.) A broadly similar sequence was found in all five breeds examined (see Chapter 6).

Neonatal puppies are slow-moving and helpless—their brains are largely unmyelinated—and yelp to pain, cold, or hunger but not to loud noise. At about their third week the puppies' eyes opened. They began to eat, walk, and leave the nest area. Startle to sound and sudden movement appeared, and stable conditioning to shock became possible.

Before age 21 days there was no attachment to site or individuals (Gurski et al. 1980). From weeks 3 to 12 changes occurred that would lead a wild dog to limit its social contacts to conspecifics in the pack and run away from or attack all other animals; such changes had to be accommodated to produce tame animals. During this time social relationships developed easily to regular contacts. By 15 weeks the dominance order in the group was established, and the usual yelps of threat and subordination became much reduced. Response to strangers had changed from initial approach and play (including play-fight) to fear and, in older dogs, to potentially serious attack.

The period from age 3 to 12 weeks saw the appearance of social exploration with imitation, playful fighting, and sexual behavior, and, a bit later, fear of anything new in the puppies' environment, which led them to run away, startle, or freeze. If left alone in a strange place the puppies showed increasing distress, which peaked at 6 to 7 weeks and subsided in older dogs starting to explore their distant surroundings. Distress occurred more with separation from litter mates than from the mother (Davis et al. 1976). From age 5 weeks the reaction to a casual stranger changed from approach to fear and escape, and this grew stronger and more difficult to overcome, so that a casual stranger never made contact (Figure 5.7). It could be overcome with daily handling over 2 weeks, and puppies raised in a home from birth showed almost no fear of people at 5 weeks. In the absence of regular handling, however, stranger fear became progressively more extreme and increasingly prevented the formation of new relationships.

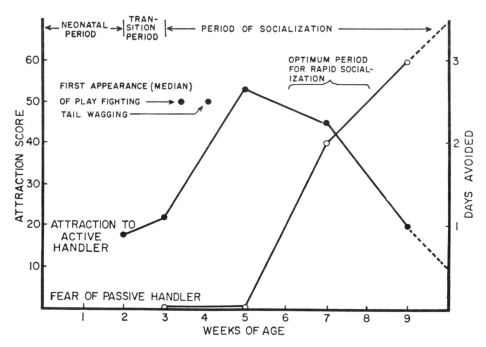

Fig. 5.7 If puppies are not handled they will, beginning about 5 weeks, develop increasing fear responses to humans which become almost impossible to reverse completely after 14 weeks or so. (From Scott & Fuller 1965. Copyright © 1965 by Oxford University Press, N.Y. Reprinted by permission.)

This growing fear of strangers was seen in puppies raised in large fields with few human contacts and then tested for 10 minutes daily with a passive observer. The puppies came to the observer almost at once at age 3 weeks, only after 2 days at 7 weeks, and at 14 weeks were so fearful that they never came close even after a week. Like wild animals, they were tamable only by enforcing human contact by keeping them confined and handfeeding them.

Avoidance of an active stranger declined to a low at 5 weeks and then rose steadily. Maximum habituation of avoidance after a week of human handling occurred at 3 weeks. The net result was rapid contact with a complete stranger only from age 3 to 5 weeks. The capacity for bonding rapidly reduced after 9 weeks. At 14 weeks, when these animals were for the first time restrained by a leash and led into strange places, they were more alarmed than were those which had been socialized, and the capacity for affiliation rapidly reduced after 9 weeks. Other puppies raised in isolation in small individual pens never escaped when brought from the pen for the first time at 16 weeks, but instead might crouch, adopt bizarre postures, or "fear bite."

Many species show the same sequence as do dogs of an early, critical period for affiliation followed by growing fear of the unfamiliar and later emergence of aggression, which hamper bonding if it has not already happened (Scott & Fuller 1965). In dogs the critical phase for bonding was at age 3 to 12 weeks, during which a small amount of experience had a great effect on later behavior. Whether bonding per se is especially great then is unclear (as is the role of the drop in heart rate about age 4 weeks); but the fear of strangers emerging from 5 weeks onward increasingly prevented the start of new relationships. The formation of a strong social bond needed only brief contact shortly at 3 to 4 weeks but hours or weeks of patient effort at older ages.

By adulthood fear of strangers is overcome only with extreme difficulty in the dog's close relative, the wolf (Ginsburg 1972; Mech 1970, p. 10). Taming an adult wild wolf took 7 months of exposure to persons sitting quietly in its cage for 15 minutes at a time every few days. (Perhaps longer periods of daily exposure might tame wolves more rapidly—prolonged durations of exposure are more therapeutic than shorter ones with human phobias and rituals—see Chapter 14.) At first the wolf tried desperately to escape by digging at the concrete floor, pawing at the door, and jumping into the air. It then retreated into the corner farthest from the experimenter in great fear, crouching, cowering, panting, trembling, salivating, defecating, and urinating. After a full month the wolf avoided by simply sitting relaxed as far away as possible in a corner, reverting to escape and fear if the person moved. Several months later it would allow approach and handling by, and even come toward, the experimenter, stopping if stared at by him. If dominated at this stage the wolf might either attack the person or regress to avoidance or escape and fear. Finally the wolf would wag its tail, approach without aggression, lick the experimenter and greet him mouth-to-mouth in wolf fashion.

As with other species, infant rhesus monkeys are also first friendly and later fearful (Kenney et al. 1979, Harlow & Zimmerman 1959). During their first 3 months, monkeys unhesitatingly approach almost all stimuli, and the larger, stronger, brighter, and more mobile the stimuli, the better. This would be lethal in the wild if it were not held in early abeyance by the mother monkey. At age 20 to 40 days a check-and-balance system of fear gradually develops. Large, mobile, strange stimuli now come to elicit avoidance. Aggression appears only late in the first year; the animal learns whom it may attack without painful retribution and whom it should defer to. The facial expressions of nonhuman primates emerge in a corresponding sequence starting with socially cohesive expressions (lipsmacking and play face) followed by fearful (grimace) and later still by aggressive (threat and yawn) expressions (Redican 1975).

Human infants progress through similar stages of smiling followed by fear. Normal human socialization prevents persistence of the extreme fear of strangers into adult life that is seen in wild wolves or dogs, but there are occasional anecdotes of such fear in wild children reared by animals.

Modifiers of Fear After It Emerges

Once fear has emerged it is triggered by dangerous experiences such as separation or strangers, and rhesus infants may remain jumpy for months later to minimal cues predicting further such events. Fear during development is increased by social deprivation, novel settings (and change in familiar ones), and rejecting, punishing mothers.

The particular pattern of fear behavior varies with age and mode of rearing (Suomi et al. 1981). Rhesus infants reared normally by their biological mother show facial grimacing and increased frequency and intensity of contact with mother and her nipple, and they stay close to her. Those reared by artificial surrogates or like-reared peers cling to their surrogate or peer partner and suck their own digits. Infant isolates instead clasp their own bodies, grimace, rock, and stop exploring. Socially competent juveniles and adolescents (age 2 to 5) may regress to earlier behavior, such as clinging to mother or peer; more commonly they are agitated, show stereotyped behavior, and cease their usual exploratory, play sex, or grooming activity. Their isolated counterparts regress to self-clasping and rocking. Adult rhesus older than 5 years will be agitated and pace up and down, while those with a history of social deprivation may mutilate themselves.

Age and rearing affect fear in other ways as well (Suomi 1983). As they grow older, rhesus infants prefer increasingly complex stimuli, but too novel or too complex cues quickly lead them to stop exploring and return to their mother. Infants interrupt most explorations by going briefly back to home base, after which they resume exploring. Peer-reared monkeys are overtimid with strangers in their first year but in the next year become overaggressive toward them. Isolates are excessively afraid of novelty until adulthood.

An observer of human infants discriminates more types of affects as the infants grow older (Johnson et al. 1982). In one study 597 mothers of infants 1 to 18 months old were asked to estimate when particular emotions began in their children. During the first 3 months most mothers reported the presence of distress, anger, interest, joy, and surprise; fear was reported in 58% of infants but shyness in only 9%. Shyness was judged to emerge more over age 3 to 9 months. Observers' judgments of infants' fear, surprise, and happiness are reliable even out of context in 10- to 12-month-old babies (Hiatt et al. 1979).

Gender also modifies fear behavior. When a rhesus was introduced into a protected inner cage inside the pen of an unfamiliar group, the group vigorously tried to attack the intruder as they would in the wild. For hours on end the newcomer, if male, would agitatedly pace up and down within the cage, but, if female, would hang upside down as far away as possible.

Influence of Social Referencing

Children search actively for emotional information from their caregiver (social referencing) and use this to appraise an uncertain situation (reviewed by Klinnert et al. 1983). When 2-year-olds were placed in the corner of a strange room containing toys and their mother was seated either facing them or with her back to them, half the children abandoned the toys in order to place themselves in front of the mother within "eyeshot" of her face. Inability to obtain emotional information causes unease. When a mother was asked to sit still-faced, not responding to her infant's overture during a 3-minute period, 1- to 4-month-olds reacted with distress and withdrawal, and the mothers also felt uncomfortable (Emde 1980). A mother's expression also alters her child's fears. In the presence of a new toy, children age 12 to 18 months moved close to her when she posed fear, toward the toy when she posed joy, and in between when she appeared neutral (Klinnert et al. 1983).

The more uncertain a child's situation the more it searches for emotional guidance and acts on it (Klinnert et al. 1983). One-year-old infants who were placed on a visual cliff 30 centimeters deep, with their mother across the deep side, would look down at the "depth" and then up at the mother's face. When mothers on the other side posed fearfully, the infants retreated from the cliff edge and showed distress, and none of them crossed the cliff—as compared to 74% who crossed when the mothers posed joy or interest, 33% who crossed with poses of sadness, and 11% with poses of anger. In contrast, if the deep side of the visual cliff was covered to make it shallow, the infants rarely looked at their mother; those who did were not affected by her expression and readily crossed to the other side.

A mother's expression seems to affect infants more after they start to crawl, but the effect of age on this remains to be determined (Bertenthal et al. 1983). Crawling infants were sober with a stranger if their mother expressed fear and smiled if she was smiling, whereas maternal expressions had few effects on infants not yet able to crawl.

The capacity for social referencing takes time to mature (Klinnert et al. 1983). From 2 to 5 months infants start to scan faces systematically and to discriminate among different facial expressions, including fear, but they still do not use this information meaningfully, smiling as happily in response to scowls or frowns as they do to smiles. From about age 5 months infants begin to resonate to the emotional expressions of others by reacting appropriately. By age 10 to 12 months the infant understands a mother's pointing gesture or direction of gaze. Much older children begin to understand that another person can have two emotions sequentially, and only at age 9 to 10 years do they realize that these may be simultaneous. In rhesus monkeys, too, appropriate responses to emotional expressions take time to mature, yet seem inborn. As we saw, even rhesus reared in isolation selectively fear threat displays at age 2½ months (Sackett 1966) and react negatively to a human stare and positively to their own mirror image (Kenney et al. 1979).

Effect of Early Experience on Later Emotionality

Events at all ages can modify fear, but if they take place at certain sensitive phases they have more permanent effects than at other times and may lastingly increase or decrease fear (reviewed by Immelman & Suomi 1981). Sensitive phases tend to occur when the young are with their family and last longer in species where the young leave it late. The outer age limits of sensitive phases are species-specific, and within those limits vary with genetic and environmental factors.

Some biological factors are associated with sensitive phases in birds. In ducks, increased corticosterone in the blood marks the end of the phase for filial imprinting. In domestic chicks the period of visual imprinting may coincide with increased protein synthesis in several brain regions, with the formation of new synapses and dendritic branches, and with the rearrangement of synapses enhancing the probability of contact for some neurons and disconnection of others and their death.

The effects of early learning can be hard to change. As we saw, if dog or wolf pups are not regularly handled by a human from their early critical period of socialization before fear of the unfamiliar has emerged, then that fear steadily rises in the next few weeks and seriously disrupts attempts to tame the animal. An isolated rhesus infant making first contact with normal monkeys may not recognize its fellows' threats yet be very fearful; if this initial contact is after age 8 months emerging aggression becomes an extra problem on both sides. Even at this stage the fear and aggression can be overcome to allow socialization, but only with difficulty over months of enforced encounter with insistently playful conspecifics or extremely patient tamers. The anxiety or aggression of isolated children, too, can be overcome if they are placed for years in good care.

Preference can be seen as a form of passive avoidance. If rhesus were reared for their first 6 months alone, with surrogates, with peers, or with women, and for the next 3½ years were allowed extensive normal interaction with conspecifics, then at the adult age of 4 years they still preferred their situation of early rearing—their young-boy rather than old-boy network.

How early experience influences later emotion also depends on the learning of contingency: that our actions may affect events. In humans and kittens self-mobility increases an emerging respect for heights. Human babies fear a moving clockwork toy less after learning to switch it on and off. Rhesus monkeys were more exploratory and less fearful even until adolescence if they grew up with mobile rather than immobile surrogates (Mason 1978). Other rhesus became more friendly and independent and less fearful if they were reared so that they could reward themselves (Mineka et al. 1985).

The opposite phenomenon is learned helplessness. Experience of uncontrollable, unpleasant events can increase fear and reduce ability to deal with disaster. Little is known about the factors that lead to helplessness rather than immunization, to sensitization rather than habituation (see Chapter 8).

"Stress immunization" implies that experience can enduringly reduce later emotionality. The concept underlay the harsh education of boys in ancient Sparta, and there is evidence for it in rats (Newton & Levine (1968). Until they were weaned at 21 days, infant rats were daily picked up and placed in a different environment for 3 minutes, or shaken violently, or given 3 minutes of mild shock. Compared to nonmanipulated controls, when these rats were placed as adults in a new environment they explored more freely, defecated less, learned adaptive avoidance more rapidly, and had less change in adrenal function. They had been "emotionally immunized." In acute experiments, manipulated (more experienced) animals detected changes in their environment better and responded less to novelty. Experience can also steel adults. In children brief, nonthreatening separations diminish later distress at more protracted separations (Stacey et al. 1970).

Even prenatal experience can affect offspring (Papousek & Papousek 1979). When pregnant rats were conditioned to uncontrollable anxiety-evoking signals, the offspring showed more open-field activity and defecation. Stressed human mothers have infants with more frequent colic, and illegitimate pregnancies are associated with increased fetal loss and perinatal mortality and morbidity. Conversely, greater handling of pregnant rats or of infant female rats decreased emotionality in subsequent offspring.

Class and Ethnic Factors

Social class can modify developmental fears through differential behavior of caregivers (reviewed by Kagan et al. 1978). In the United States middle-class mothers spend more time interacting with their 10-month-old babies than do working-class mothers; this may lead their children to develop cognitive skills and developmental fears slightly earlier. If presented with an old and a new toy, 10-month-old middle-class children looked more from one to the other than did working-class children and cried more when their mother left them alone in an unfamiliar room. In another study, 160 firstborn children were tested at 4, 8, 13, and 27 months. Fear of masks and of strangers occurred mainly at 8 months. Of these children, 39% of the upper-middle-class but only 17% of the working-class subjects cried on seeing the masks. If the mother left these children alone in an unfamiliar room with toys they had been handling earlier, crying occurred in 66% of the upper-middle-class but in only 28% of the working-class children.

Several studies found subtle ethnic differences in behavioral inhibition that could stem from genetic, dietary, cultural, and other factors (Freedman 1976; Kagan et al. 1978; Kagan 1979). Chinese-American neonates were calmer, less labile, and more easily placated than Caucasian-American newborns. The former were more impassive when a cloth was placed over the supine baby's face or when the baby was placed prone with its face against the bedding. Navajo infants, too, were more placid.

As they developed, Chinese-American infants continued to be a little less active, vocal, and irritable than Caucasian-Americans. At age 12 to 29 months, compared to Caucasian babies, Chinese children were more wary and inhibited with an unfamiliar peer, and smiled and vocalized less to human masks and visual patterns. In nursery schools, Chinese-American children reacted less to novelty.

Fearfulness as a Trait

Individual levels of fearfulness tend to be stable over time: genetic aspects of this are reviewed in Chapter 6. (Evidence in monkeys is reviewed later in this chapter, under "separation anxiety.") In humans, levels of fearfulness persisted from age 1 month to 8½ years, especially in boys (Bronson 1969). At age 1, extreme inhibition was related to earlier neonatal low orientation (attention to novel stimulus) and deviant reflexes (Kagan 1982). In 1-year-old infants, raised urinary cortisol on a control day predicted high urinary cortisol and fearfulness on later days when the mother left the house for an hour or a strange adult interacted with the infant at home (Tennes et al. 1977). From age 6 to 18 months the children showed stable timidity with novel toys over several months; timidity was somewhat less in boys than in girls and was related to their hormone levels at birth–positively for estradiol and negatively for progesterone and testosterone (Jacklin et al. 1983). Avoidant 12- to 18-month-old children later were highly dependent in preschool and even more so if they had been insecurely attached previously (Sroufe et al. 1983). In 21-month-old children inhibition to unfamiliar people or events was consistent over 2 sessions a month apart and remained so 10 months later (Kagan 1982). From age 2 to 2½ or 3 years, separation protest and stranger fear were moderately stable (Maccoby & Feldman 1972). At age 3½ social timidity was related to wariness in infancy and fearfulness in the second year (Kagan 1982).

Inhibition to the unfamiliar was the only one of 15 behaviors in the first 3 years of life that predicted behavior in adolescence and adulthood (Kagan & Moss 1962). Children who were extremely inhibited until age 3 were easily dominated by their peers, likely to withdraw from social interaction during the next 3 years, avoid dangerous activity, be less aggressive, conform with parents, be socially timid at age 6 to 10, and, in boys, avoid sports and other typically male activities as adolescents and masculine vocations as adults.

When change in inhibition occurred, it was almost always from an inhibited 21-month-old to a less inhibited 31-month-old. Rarely did an uninhibited child become more inhibited (Kagan 1982). Kagan suggested that this might reflect a tendency since World War II for American parents to encourage their children to become uninhibited.

INFANCY

Human neonates attend to visual contour and movement, and look less at three circles than at two that make an eyelike pattern (Kagan et al. 1978). Neonates usually show distress rather than fear, especially if the infant is tired, hungry, or fussy, or has Down's syndrome (reviewed by Smith 1979). Even 2-day-old neonates became distressed when conditioned sweet tastes were stopped during extinction (Blass et al. 1984). Very young infants are not wary of novelty but cry in response to hunger, cold, lack of contact with caretaker, pain, colic, and sudden or violent stimulation. Several cries may be differentiated: those of hunger from those of pain and, by week 3, the "fake" cry for attention. Within the first 2 weeks, infants cry when frustrated (as when a pacifier is taken away), when feeding is interrupted, or if a gratifying object is immediately removed; at 2 to 3 months a baby will tolerate feeding interruption but will cry if a toy such as a rattle is removed from its hands. By week 3 the infant may cry at a simple game if tired.

After the first few weeks infants attend to rapidly changing stimuli (such as swiftly moving, talking faces), especially those moderately different from previous ones; less attention is paid to very familiar stimuli, while extremely discrepant ones evoke sustained attention, wariness, or fear. Four- to six-month-olds attend more to slides of the face of a stranger than of the mother, and 1-year-olds prefer novel toys and rooms to familiar ones.

Before they are 6 months old, human infants show little fear. Thereafter they fear strangers, separation, and unfamiliar toys and objects (Scarr & Salapatek 1970); looming stimuli elicit crying and change in heart rate response from slowing to speeding (Hruska & Yonas 1972). These fears do not all develop at the same time (Scarr & Salapatek 1970; see also Figure 5.8), and they start long before shyness. In a longitudinal study of 25 Minneapolis children, about three-quarters showed not only timidity to strangers at age 6 months but also a later, different wave of shyness at about 18 months, which lasted 2 or 3 months; younger children were rarely coy or self-conscious (Shirley 1933).

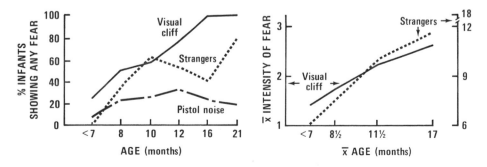

Fig. 5.8 Infants' fears do not all develop simultaneously. (Data from Scarr & Salapatek 1970.)

The early fears of five siblings growing up were observed closely by their psychologist father (Valentine 1930). One of the children was almost fearless, while the others were often frightened. Unlearned elements were prominent. Loud, novel sounds evoked fear from age 2 weeks to a few months. After a year the children feared uncanny objects, particularly if these were both familiar and strange, and animals—despite previous familiarity, ease, and no unpleasant experiences with animals. Between age 1 and 3 years they feared the sea even though four of the five children were with their father at their first encounter and were encouraged to go into the sea, and even though they had been delighted by their only past experience of being in water, in their baths. At age 5, two of the children were frightened of darkness. These five fears contrasted sharply with their courage after painful falls over obstacles, and with the way fearful thrills were sometimes eagerly sought in games that culminated in screams of terror.

A given stimulus did not invariably produce fear; minor changes influenced whether it would do so. (For example, a companion's presence could banish fear, and a teddy bear was frightening if it approached but not if it was still.) Others have also noted the effect of context as children grow old enough to evaluate it (Smith 1979). At age 10 months babies laughed at their mother wearing a mask at home but were more wary in a laboratory or if they had seen a stranger wearing the mask. A 15-month-old baby laughed when the mother picked him up by his heels but cried when a stranger appeared while the action was repeated.

Contingency and control become increasingly important with age. When babies saw a doctor preparing to repeat an injection first given a few weeks earlier, fear was rare before age 11 months but shown by a quarter thereafter (Levy 1951). Strangers are less frightening if the child is allowed to approach them in its own time. A child may fear a moving toy outside its control yet be happy on learning how to stop and start it.

Fear of Heights

By age 2 months human infants can perceive depth, and their heart rate slows—indicating attention—when placed on the deep as opposed to the shallow side of a visual cliff (Campos et al. 1978). The perception of depth is not accompanied by behavioral signs of fear and associated tachycardia until age 6 to 9 months, at which stage the heart rate response to the visual cliff shifts from slowing to speeding.

The developmental context from which this fear emerges was well reviewed by Bertenthal et al. (1983). From about their sixth month infants begin to crawl in exploration while using their caregiver as a secure base. This new ability to move around expands the infant's perspective by sharply increasing its encounters with new experiences, speeding the emergence of wariness of heights, spatial cognition, form extraction, and social communication.

That self-produced locomotion brings out a fear of heights was shown in the young kitten and monkey (Held and Hein 1963 and Hein 1972). From

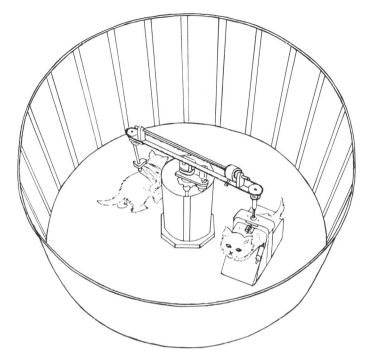

Fig. 5.9 A carousel in which one kitten could walk around as it wished while moving another kitten passively. Both kittens saw the same striped patterns inside the cylinder of the carousel; the first saw them moving as it walked, the second kitten did not. (Adapted from Held & Hein 1963.)

birth, kitten littermates were reared with their mother in complete darkness until selective visual exposure began at 8 to 12 weeks. This exposure took place in a "kitten carousel" (Figure 5.9) that gave each littermate the same amount of visual experience; but in half this was controlled by the kitten's movement and in half it was not. In the carousel one kitten was harnessed to an arm that it could rotate around the inside of a vertically striped cylinder, while a littermate was placed in a gondola on a second arm yoked to the first. One (active) kitten thus received visual feedback from its own movement and the other from passive movement.

As soon as testing showed that one kitten from each pair had visual placing and response to an approaching object, both were tested for avoidance of the deep side of a visual cliff. All actively reared kittens avoided the deep side, while none of the paired passive littermates did so, despite equal exposure to patterned visual stimulation. Even after 300 to 400 hours of exposure, passively reared kittens still did not show visual motor coordination.

That failure to avoid heights did not result from generalized response inhibition was shown in a further study. Each kitten had one eye open during active movement and the other during passive transport. Subsequent visual motor coordination was specific to the eye exposed during active movement. This and other studies by Hein indicated that visually guided behavior in kittens (and fear dependent on this) involves component systems that may be acquired separately during development.

Similar considerations apply to humans. Babies usually begin to be wary of heights some time after starting to crawl (Bertenthal et al. 1983). From 5 to 9 months the infant becomes reluctant to cross the deep side of a visual cliff to its mother calling from the other side, and its heart rate changes on being placed directly atop the deep side. Such fear is not seen as soon as the infant can crawl but only over the ensuing weeks as it gains experience in crawling (Campos et al. 1978). Infants who had crawled for less than a week crossed the deep side readily, while those who had crawled for more than 3 weeks had become hesitant, although previously they had gone straight across the deep side to reach their mother. At this stage, even after the infants were coaxed across by the mother, on subsequent testing a new upwelling of fear would be seen.

Fear of heights increases with crawling experience as well as with age. This was shown in infants aged 7.3 months, half of whom were already crawling and half not (Svejda & Schmid 1979, cited by Bertenthal et al. 1983). On testing with the visual cliff, heart rate increased in crawlers on the deep but not the shallow side and did not change on either side in noncrawlers.

Like crawling, walking also enhances fear of heights (Bertenthal et al. 1983). Infants were given "walkers" and were tested after 40 hours of such experience; at the start some had not yet crawled and others had spontaneously crawled for up to a week. Both groups were compared with age-matched controls without and with crawling experience. On the deep side of the visual cliff, heart rate increased significantly more in babies with walker experience than those without (Figure 5.10). Heart rate slowed consistently only in controls who had not yet crawled, and was lower in them than in noncrawlers with walker experience. Walking experience raised heart rate more among crawlers than among control noncrawlers.

Locomotor experience increased fear of heights measured by avoidance as well as by heart rate, regardless of age (Bertenthal et al. 1983). Only 25% of infants who had been crawling for 11 days avoided crossing over the deep side to the mother, compared with 80% of infants who had been crawling for 41 days; this was true whether they had begun to crawl at 6½, 7½ or 8½ months. Fear of heights emerges quickly soon after babies start to crawl (and to use invariant relations in coding spatial positions) and does not increase thereafter. The same was found in an older baby who had been born with two dislocated hips and after operation had been in a full body cast until age 8 months and did not crawl until a month later. On repeated testing from age 6 to 10 months, heart rate increase on the deep compared with the shallow side of the visual cliff became significant only at age 10 months. At the same time the child began to code correctly for spatial orientation.

Age as well as the start of crawling affects fear of heights (Scarr & Salapatek 1970). Before age 7½ months neither noncrawlers nor crawlers were afraid to cross the visual cliff in a study of 91 infants 2 to 23 months old. The most fearful had attained crawling or walking later. Height fear was unrelated to ability to crawl or walk, previous falls, or previous experience with vertical and

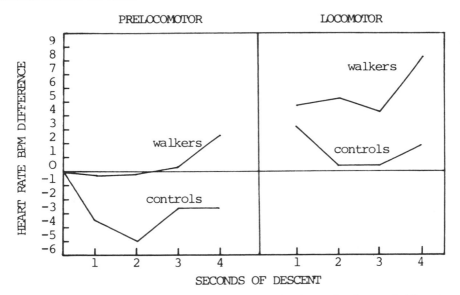

Fig. 5.10 Heart rate while infants were lowered toward the deep side of a visual cliff. Prelocomotor infants had not yet crawled, whereas locomotor infants had. Heart rate slowed mainly in noncrawling controls and rose with experience in a walker (walkers vs. controls) and with age (prelocomotor controls vs. locomotor controls). (Redrawn from Bertenthal et al. 1983. Copyright © 1983 by Plenum, NY. Reprinted by permission.)

horizontal glass surfaces. Fear was greater when infants initiated movement than when they were set passively on the cliff side. Babies younger than age 9 months would pat, lick, and feel their way across the cliff, while from 9 months onward they peered at it, touching it and showing distress. Some babies inched onto the deep side and "hung on" to the shallow side with a foot or hand.

Effect of Novelty

Novelty frightens yet fascinates many species, and both reactions may occur in quick succession (see Chapter 2). Depending on age, experience, and degree of novelty, among other factors, there may be strong approach or inhibition, crying, withdrawal, or freezing. The same stimulus may not affect younger animals but will frighten older ones until they get used to it.

Examples abound of fear growing with age. Rats did not avoid a new striped pattern from age 40 to 70 days but avoided it increasingly from 70 to 250 days; avoidance was prevented if other unfamiliar stimuli were introduced beforehand (Hudson 1940). Dogs avoided strange situations most at about age 6 weeks, while their fear of strange humans grew even beyond that; regular early handling reduced the fear (Scott & Fuller 1965). Rhesus monkeys' fear of a human face grew steadily from a few weeks of age (Kenney et al. 1979). When chimpanzees were shown a clay model of a chimpanzee's head, those 1 to 2 years old ignored it; 5- to 6-year-olds were fascinated by the model and came close to stare persistently and excitedly at it, while those 9 years or older avoided it strongly with screaming and hair erection even when separated from it by cage wire (Hebb & Thompson 1954). In children whose upbringing was monitored daily for years, fears of the uncanny occurred in nearly all children after age 1 (Valentine 1930).

Inhibition to the unfamiliar is a built-in response. Even newborns briefly stop moving and sucking when there is a sudden new sight or sound (Kagan 1979). As early as age 2 weeks an alert infant in a near upright position fears an approaching but not a receding object (Bower et al. 1977, cited by Kagan 1979). In 40 such infants, when a 20-centimeter cube approached to within 20 centimeters of a baby's face, the infant pulled his head backward, put its hands between his face and the object, and cried loudly, more so the closer the cube. Similar but less intense defense occurred against a shadow rapidly expanding on a screen.

Maturation and experience during development lead to important changes. The infant becomes capable of increasingly complex discriminations that change what it perceives as new, and this is modified by experience. Fear of strangers is minimal in dark-raised chimpanzees at their first encounter or in children who have always seen many people (Kenney et al. 1979).

The response to perceived unfamiliarity normally changes from approach to inhibition or distress. Yet unfamiliarity (incongruity) does not explain why at certain ages, independent of experience, some stimuli elicit more fear than do others, nor does it account for the appreciable lapse of time (up to several months in human infants) between the first perception of unfamiliarity and the first regular display of fear to it. Change from positive to negative reactions to strangers implies more than the mere ability to detect differences. A baby can distinguish the caregiver from strangers from 2 to 4 months onward and gradually ceases to bestow his radiant smile at all and sundry, reserving this for the caregiver and other familiars. To strangers the baby becomes sober and later wary, and by 8 months he may scream the house down. Over the next year this reaction slowly subsides, perhaps as a function of seeing many more strangers and habituating to them.

Developmental change in the response of young to strange stimuli follows the same course in species as disparate as humans, chimpanzees, rhesus monkeys, puppies, ducklings, and chicks. Initial positive reactions later change to ambivalence, wariness, and fear. Many human infants 8 to 12 months old go through a phase of inhibition to strange inanimate and animate stimuli (reviewed by Kagan 1979). To a novel object that is presented after a familiar one has been shown repeatedly, the infant reaches out almost at once prior to 8 months but only after a brief delay at age 12 months. Sighted or blind babies reach in the dark for an audible object more at 4 and 11 months than at 6 or 7 months. Infants from 3 to 30 months old often fixate least on a changing event when they are between the age of 7 and 9 months, and this is true whether they are American, rural Mexican, or Guatemalan. From age 6 to 12 months infants develop fears of sudden, unexpected, and looming objects; this fear declines in the second year.

The phase of inhibition can occur slightly later (Scarr & Salapatek 1970). When 91 babies from 2 to 23 months old were shown six stimuli—jack-in-the-box, strangers, heights, a mechanical dog, a loud noise (pistol shot), and friendly and horrifying masks—peak wariness usually occurred between 11 and 18 months, and infants younger than 7 months were rarely wary (Figure 5.8). Wariness of the various stimuli largely developed independently and did not correlate with tests of perceptual-cognitive ability. On retest 2 months later the babies showed a stable pattern of differences for fear and for temperament.

Change in the child's reactions with age due to learning has been touched on. Toward the end of the first year a baby uses current clues to anticipate something unpleasant. (The learning of fear is reviewed in Chapter 8).

Heart Rate and Behavioral Inhibition to Novelty

Alert, nonwary children have a slow heart rate that fluctuates in sinus arryth-mia (the normal increase in heart rate on taking a breath and decrease on exhaling). In wary infants heart rate rises and is less variable (less sinus arryth-mia), for example, during behavioral inhibition with new stimuli (Campos & Barrett 1984; Garcia-Coll et al. 1984; Kagan 1982). Extremely inhibited 21-month-olds had a higher and less variable heart rate when given novel visual and auditory cues; perhaps they had more sympathetic activity, which raises heart rate and blocks the vagal activity during expiration that normally slows the heart beat. When inhibited boys became adults, they had very little sinus arrhythmia.

Chinese-American children, who were more inhibited than Caucasian children, had less variable heart rates while processing visual and auditory information at age 9 to 29 months. Caucasian children with consistently high and stable heart rates showed more frequent separation protest than did matched counterparts who had lower and variable heart rates. Furthermore, those children who most reduced vocalizing to a new stimulus after habituating to familiar ones had the most stable heart rates while studying visual information. When 20 to 29 months old, these same children observed a peer playing. Of the eight with the most stable heart rates, five were inhibited with the peer, while none of the seven children with the least stable heart rates were inhibited. These differences continued to age 4. Compared with 21 formerly uninhibited children, the 22 formerly inhibited ones still had a higher and more stable heart rate, and more inhibition with a peer, reluctance to guess at difficult problems, and fixation on a passive rather than an active figure in various scenes (Kagan et al. 1984). Perhaps such early inhibition relates to later shyness and introversion.

Stranger Fear

Not all novel stimuli are equipotent in evoking fear. Strange humans are more frightening to human infants 6 to 24 months old than are other novel stimuli.

Evolutionary selection for this is suggested by the frequency of infanticide and child abuse in mammals, including monkeys and great apes (see Chapter 1). The fear is greater and emerges earlier with strange adults than with strange young peers, which fits with adults being more dangerous.

Reactions to novelty develop through the interplay of two evolving but opposing systems (Bronson 1972). On the one hand, there is curiosity about new situations and affiliation to people from very early on. On the other hand, from slightly later there is wariness of objects and recognition of people as being unfamiliar. With strangers the fear is of the stranger himself rather than his behavior; babies are not frightened when their mothers behave oddly by crawling on the floor, sucking a baby bottle, walking like a penguin, or putting on a mask (Sroufe 1977; Sroufe et al. 1974). The unpredictability and lack of control inherent in unfamiliar situations contribute to the wariness.

Strange Adults

Many have reviewed this topic.[1] Fear of strangers by human infants is a ubiquitous developmental phenomenon with similar form and age occurrence in the United States, United Kingdom, Guatemala, and Zambia, and among !Kung Bushmen, Hopi Indians, and Ganda (Smith 1979). It develops from age 4 to 9 months, the earliest sign being the infant's ceasing to smile at unfamiliar people (Figure 5.11). In other mammals and in birds, flight from strangers also follows a phase of indiscriminate approach (Freedman 1965). Stranger fear wanes toward the end of the second year, presumably because children start to get used to and learn how to deal with the diverse behaviors of strangers, who then cease to be strange. Elements may persist in childhood shyness or recur in social phobias later in life (see Chapter 12).

From age 4 to 24 months wariness of strangers is more likely to be seen if 12 conditions are satisfied:

1. The observation is (a) longitudinal, (b) in an unfamiliar setting, and (3) with the caregiver absent.
2. The approach is (a) by the stranger rather than by the child and (b) abrupt, and if (c) the child is touched by the stranger.
3. The stranger is (a) of normal height, (b) male, and (c) unresponsive to the child's signals.
4. The child has (a) experienced only one caregiver, (b) had few happy encounters with strangers, and (c) fewer secure attachments—children who are insecure at 12 to 18 months are less independent later as well.

Three additional modifiers are familial, ordinal, and gender factors. Stranger fear is more similar among identical than fraternal twins aged 22 months (Plomin & Rowe 1979). Firstborn react earlier. Girls respond a bit earlier, more often, and more intensely than do boys.

---

[1] For example, see Ainsworth et al. 1978; Brooks & Lewis 1976; Décarie 1974; Emde 1980; Horner 1980; Kagan et al. 1978; Morgan & Ricciuti 1966; Schaffer 1974; Sroufe 1977; Sroufe et al. 1983.

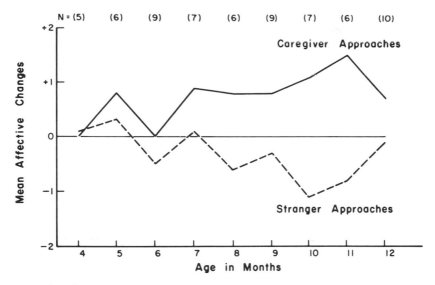

Fig. 5.11 The affective response to caregivers and to strangers differentiates from age 4 to 10 months, with positive responses appearing to caregivers and negative ones to strangers. (From Ricciuti 1974. Copyright © 1974 by M. Lewis & John Wiley & Sons. Reprinted by Permission.)

Without these conditions stranger fear may not be seen, but it is hard to eliminate. Experimenters on infant development expect an easy time when testing babies below 6 months and above 3 years of age, but some difficulty with ages in between. When Schwartz et al. (1975) studied twenty 5-month-olds and twenty 9-month-olds on the visual cliff they had to abandon testing of only four 5-month-olds, but fully sixteen 9-month-olds could not be tested because of inconsolable crying with the strange tester prior to being placed on the visual cliff.

Only some components of stranger fear will be present at any one time and age—for example, gaze aversion and heart rate acceleration (Smith 1979). Even as early as age 4 months, an infant may start to smile less at strangers than at its caretaker. At first the baby gives a fleeting smile, and with a sober face repeatedly looks from the face of the stranger to that of its caretaker, perhaps ending in crying. Older infants will stare less, turn their face away, crawl away and hide, and may scream. Stranger fear peaks in intensity at about age 12½ months and declines in the second year. In an operant situation, although the mother's face was rewarding for infants of 6 to 9 months, a stranger's face was neutral at 6 months and avoided at 9 months (Fouts & Atlas 1979).

Strangers can evoke interest as well as fear. Children may warily look and smile at, and even approach, strangers, but will quickly retreat if the stranger moves toward them, though its offer of a toy may reassure them. This balance between approach and avoidance is also seen in children and animals encountering other novel stimuli (see Chapter 2) and in the fascinated watch that ungulates keep on sufficiently distant predators (Chapter 4).

The various components of the stranger reaction can be better understood

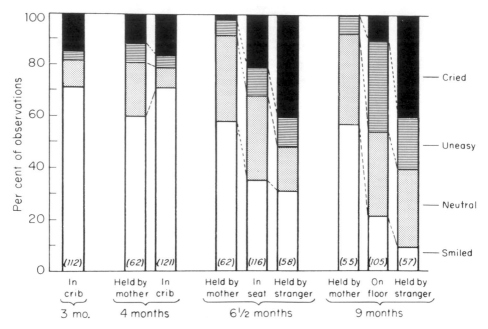

Fig. 5.12 Increase in various components of stranger fear with age and circumstances of the encounter (numbers of subjects in parentheses). (Bronson 1972. Copyright © 1972 by The Society for Research in Child Development. Reprinted by permission.)

by detailing an especially careful study (Bronson 1972), in which 32 infants at age 3, 4½, 6, and 9 months were observed reacting to unfamiliar objects and to the approach of a male stranger. Each age was assessed twice a few days apart. To strange inanimate objects, children showed mainly exploratory interest at all ages, with occasional wariness at 9 months. To strange persons, in contrast, wariness and avoidance emerged during the fourth month and became increasingly frequent as the infants grew older (Figures 5.12 and 5.13).

Most 2- to 3-month-old infants smile happily at all who approach. At 3 or 4 months, Bronson's infants still usually smiled at a female stranger, but some would after a brief smile stare fixedly at her for 12 to 30 seconds, frown, breathe heavily, and then cry. Nearly half the babies were wary in at least 1 of the 8 stranger presentations at this age, and repeating the trials at all ages increased the chances of wariness, not of habituation. Whether infants smiled or cried at 3 to 4 months depended partly on how easily they could identify the stranger as unfamiliar and partly on temperament—the few who at 4 months consistently cried at a stranger's hovering face had from birth been prone to distress during bathing or with a looming stimulus.

By 6½ months all infants seemed aware that a stranger was present; 78% were wary and about half were upset, the reaction depending upon the type of encounter. When in their mothers' arms the babies usually smiled and rarely cried, but they often cried when apart from their mother and when the stranger picked them up. In addition, male babies were less wary if their mother was

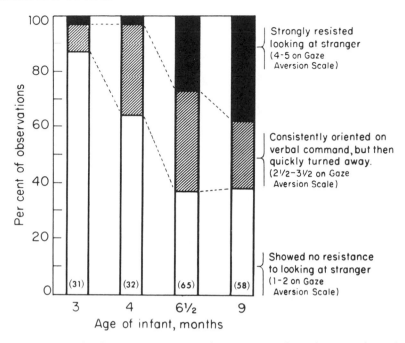

Fig. 5.13 Gaze aversion from strangers rose with age in nonsmiling infants (numbers of subjects in parentheses). (From Bronson 1972. Copyright © 1972 by The Society for Research in Child Development, Inc. Reprinted by permission.)

more attentive. This pattern continued at 9 months; on being held by a stranger, babies showed uneasiness even more frequently and seldom smiled (Figure 5.12).

As the children grew older, stranger fear increased and its form evolved. At first there was gaze aversion (Figure 5.13). A few 3-month-olds and many 4-month-olds were nonsmiling and turned away. By 6½ to 9 months, after firmly turning away from the stranger, infants would remain still, perhaps fingering a rug or toy. Nine-month-old babies, now mobile, often also crawled away from the stranger to the mother. Crying was common in younger infants but rare at age 9 months. Wary reactions rose in comparable situations from 20% at 3 to 4 months to 32% at 6½ months and 47% at 9 months. Similar steady growth of stranger fear with age, regardless of criterion, was found by Waters et al. (1975), the proportion showing fear depending on the criterion adopted (Figure 5.14; see also Figures 5.12, 5.13, and 5.17).

Factors other than age also modified the fear. Wariness rose considerably when the stranger picked up the infant. The mother's reassuring influence became evident from 6½ months onward. Infants often turning away from the stranger to look at their mother with neutral or troubled expressions; the mother's holding her infant reduced the wariness. Repeated exposure to many strangers from an early age did not reduce the fear, although an abundance of caretakers seemed to delay the ability to tell who was a stranger.

In sum, Bronson's infants were distressed at some situations even from the

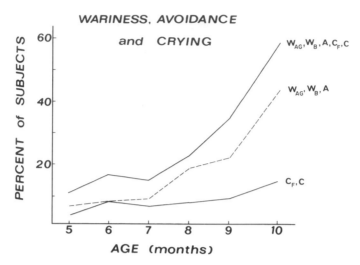

Fig. 5.14 Rise in stranger fear with age on different criteria (Waters et al. 1975, where C, C$_F$ are extreme distress reactions; W$_{AG}$, W$_B$, and A are wary reactions; and W$_{AG}$, W$_B$, A, C$_F$, C are negative reactions. More showed a mild negative reaction rather than intense distress. (From Waters et al. 1975. Copyright © 1975 by The Society for Research in Child Development, Inc.. Reprinted by permission.)

first weeks of life; wariness and avoidance of a stranger began to appear in the fourth month and were frequent at 6½ to 9 months. Infants who were often distressed during the first postnatal months were the first to become wary of strangers and remained more so as they grew older. New objects caused less wariness than did new people.

Fear of Strange Peers

Little work has been done on this subject. Despite wariness with a strange adult, 7- to 19-month-olds may still react neutrally or even positively to the approach of a strange child, though at 19 to 30 months children may retreat to their mother, inhibit play, and attend to the stranger (Smith 1979). Thereafter this apprehension begins to wane.

A phasic fear of strange peers was found in 62 working-class children 3½ to 30 months old in three pairs of play sessions—alone or with a strange peer plus its mother—at 13½, 20, and 29 months (Kagan et al. 1975). In the presence of a child's mother and of a strange peer plus its mother, play decreased most at 20 months (Figure 5.15) and distance from own mother at 29 months. This inhibition was probably induced more by the strange peer than the strange woman, because the child stared more at the peer than at the peer's mother. The inhibition was quickly overcome if the peer offered the child a toy. Inhibition was a bit less among day-care than home-reared children—the former had greater experience of strange peers. Inhibition to a peer peaked earlier in girls than in boys. Compatible data was found in another study; 11- to 18-month-old children stared more at a strange peer than did 6- to 10-month-olds

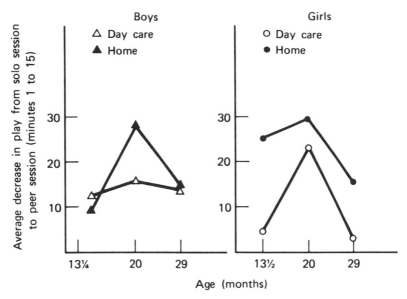

Fig. 5.15 Wariness of strange peers at age 20 months. Play was inhibited when a strange peer and its mother joined a child already playing in the presence of its own mother. The child stared more at the peer than at the peer's mother. (From Kagan et al. 1975. Copyright © 1975 M. Lewis & John Wiley & Sons. Reprinted by permission.)

in an experimental setting, although not in a home setting (Dragsten & Lee 1973).

Separation Anxiety

This anxiety reflects the special evolutionary danger of being alone, which is particularly great for the young (see Chapter 4). Unaccompanied children are more likely to have traffic accidents, sustain burns, or come to grief in other ways. Compared with controls, lone children are more often unwanted, unloved, or have a mother who is anxiously preoccupied with other problems (Bowlby 1973).

Humans

Infants are most likely to cry at their caretaker's departure from age 8- to 24 months, peaking at 9- to 13 months (Kagan et al. 1978; Smith 1979). Separation anxiety is similar among children all over the world—in the United States, barrios in urban Guatemala, subsistence-farming villages in the Guatemalan highlands, Israeli kibbutzim, and !Kung bands in the Kalahari (Figure 5.16)—and is also seen in children with Down's syndrome. It is the same if the caretaker is male or female, if there is one or many caretakers, and if the child is reared at home or in day care; and the anxiety is unrelated to the amount of

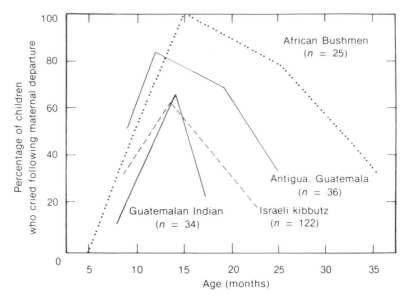

Fig. 5.16 Waxing and waning of separation anxiety across various cultures: percentage of children who cried following maternal departure. (From Kagan et al. 1978. Copyright © 1978 by Harvard University Press. Reprinted by permission.)

prior interaction with the caretaker and of past experience of unpleasantness during separation. The anxiety is greater if the child is in an unfamiliar setting or if no one familiar remains with it, if the caretaker leaves the child rather than vice versa or leaves by an unfamiliar exit, or if separation follows learned associations such as obvious preparations to go or closing of the door on temporary exit.

Like sighted infants, blind children have separation anxiety (Fraiberg 1975). They recognize their caretaker's presence from her or his voice, other sounds, and touch, and feel her or his face and compare it with that of a nearby stranger as a sighted child would do by visual scanning.

Disruption of an attachment bond can increase separation anxiety. Protest is greater on separation from people who are warm and playful with the child rather than merely giving it physical care (Smith 1979). However, the greatest distress is not always found after especially close interaction with the caretaker (Kagan et al. 1978).

Separation anxiety wanes from age 30 months onward. If the mother left her child in a strange room for 4 minutes, crying and decrease in play, speech, and movement was less frequent in 30- than in 14-month-olds (Cox & Campbell 1968). In a second study, children were placed in a strange room with their mother and then induced to leave her to go with someone to get some candy. When they returned to the room the mother had gone; at this point less distress and inhibition of play was seen in 38- than in 23-month-old children (Gershaw and Schwarz 1971).

Prolonged separation commonly leads to sequential reactions called protest, detachment, and despair (Bowlby 1973). First the child cries, screams, and struggles to find its caregiver, later seems oblivious of the separation, and finally is inactive and may seem depressed. Initial protest is the rule, but detachment and despair are more variable. The sequence echoes that seen in adult mourning after bereavement, except that grief tends to start with numbness.

On reunion after separation infants are often angry with their caregivers and avoid or even occasionally attack them (Main & Weston 1982). This is especially noticeable after long, stressful separations and in infants whose caretaker has previously been angry, inexpressive, or otherwise rejecting. Anger is more likely at first, particularly if there is no substitute caregiver, and avoidance comes later. Initial avoidance may merely be a blank look in the infant's eyes and, if the caregiver keeps looking at it, slow partial or total eye closure with gaze aversion, a reaction that may also occur with strangers. If picked up the infant is unresponsive. Avoidance may alternate with approach.

Like normal children, blind babies may also become disturbed when the caregiver returns. A blind boy of 14 months developed an acute reaction after his mother returned from an absence of 3 days, during which had had been cared for by friends and relations. During the first 2 weeks he screamed, shouted, and chanted loudly for hours, ceasing only when his mother held him, upon which he would crawl relentlessly all over her. When he was given pots and pans to bang together he did this with great gusto and the screaming ceased (Fraiberg 1971, cited by Bowlby 1973).

The acute distress sometimes seen during admission to hospital or to a residential nursery is probably due in part of separation from the caretaker to whom the child is attached and in part to the strange new environment (Rutter 1981). Distress is reduced by providing the child with a familiar caregiver (Ricciuti 1974) and by allowing the child its familiar routines, toys, and other comforts as much as possible to diminish the strangeness of its new situation. Where the child will eventually have to be left in new surroundings without its caretaker, prior accustoming of the child to its future environment (pre-exposure) reduces subsequent separation anxiety. Hospital admission is least upsetting for children who have experienced many normal, happy separations (Stacey et al. 1970). Preparation of the caregivers, too, reduces their anxiety and helps them cope better with the child's fears. On reunion the child's anger or detachment may subside sooner with an increase in mothering.

Single, isolated stresses in early life only rarely lead to prolonged disorder. Multiple, acute stresses more often do so, and long-term damage is most likely when these arise in the course of chronic adversity (Rutter 1981). Even prolonged separation from the caregiver generally has no adverse effects provided there are adequate substitute caregivers and a secure environment.

Echoes of the separation anxiety of infancy are brought out in adolescents and adults in times of disaster. People then search for one another and cling together, and companionship reduces fear. Bowlby (1973) relates the following incidents. In the first, a tornado struck a woman and her 15-year-old daughter:

"She [the daughter] said 'Mother, it's coming—a cyclone.' And I said, 'Mary, I'm afraid it is, but we're together.' And she said 'Mother, I love you and we're together.' . . . Our arms were around each other, and I said 'Whatever happens, Mary, let's cling together.'" In the second, after an explosion, two injured men tried to crawl out of a burning factory. One of them had a broken leg, and recounted, "Then Johnny . . . came alone. I said 'Johnny, help us—we can't walk.' His arms were broken and he said 'I can't help you, but I'll stay with you. If you can crawl, I'll guide you.' Talk about cheer! That helped me more than anything—just when he said 'I'll stay with you.'"

Members of a family or other social group cohere not only when disaster looms or strikes but for days or weeks after it is over, the children and parents eagerly stick together (Bowlby 1973). In the weeks after a tornado hit a Mississippi cinema, one-third of 185 children aged 2 to 12 who had been present remained anxious, typically clinging to parents and wishing to sleep with them. Boys were as much affected as girls. Anxiety was greater in children who had been in the impact zone or had been injured, if another family member had died or been injured, or a parent was markedly anxious. The children were also uneasy with noise and in places associated with the tornado.

Other remnants of the separation anxiety of childhood are seen in adult phobics, whose fears are often greatly reduced by the presence of companions. Because this is true for agoraphobia as for other phobias, some have suggested that agoraphobia is rooted in earlier separation anxiety, but this goes beyond the evidence (see Chapter 10). A few agoraphobics actually feel better when alone.

Relation of Stranger Fear to Separation Anxiety

Fear of strangers differs from distress at separation from the caretaker. Even while in the arms of its mother a child at the right age fears strangers, albeit at reduced intensity (Figure 5.12). Conversely, separation anxiety occurs even when there are not strangers around. The two fears summate if the child is separated from its caretaker in the presence of a stranger, and correlate slightly (Sroufe et al. 1974). Many tests for one of the two fears have compounded both situations.

The emergence of both fears might depend upon similar cognitive growth. Infants only a few weeks old begin to tell their mother from strangers (Smith 1979). Three-week-old infants sucked a teat more if this allowed them to hear the voice of their mother rather than of a strange woman. In the fifth week a baby may cry briefly on being left. Two- to seven-week-old babies looked more at their mothers than at a stranger and might turn away (though other workers found that face-voice expectations developed later, being absent at 5 months but present at 8 months; 4- to 6-month-old infants preferred slides of an adult female stranger most, of the mother next, and of a 5-month-old infant least). More obvious reactions to strangers are seen from 4 months on.

Fears of strangers and of separation might arise from the infant's growing ability to retrieve past events from memory and hold them to allow comparison with present events, and from the infant's uncertainty at what to do when separated (Kagan et al. 1978) or with strangers. Stranger fear correlates not with object permanence but with person permanence (Smith 1979), but relates less to it than does separation protest (Fraiberg 1975).

Nonhuman Primates

Not only human but also monkey infants are disturbed on separation from their mothers. Nonhuman primates have been investigated more fully (Kraemer 1985; McKinney 1985; Mineka 1982; Mineka & Suomi 1976; Suomi & Harlow 1976; Suomi et al. 1981; Suomi 1982–1984). Separations lasting from a few minutes to months have been studied in macaques, langurs, and chimpanzees in the laboratory and in the wild. Distress is produced by denial of tactile contact even if the mother remains within sight, sound, and smell. The reaction consists of immediate panic, followed sometimes by later depression, and on reunion with mother there is anxious attachment and fearfulness that may last for years. Separation reactions are not limited to young monkeys. They occur at all ages, including adults.

Premature separation of a rhesus infant from its mother can lead to extreme pathology (Kraemer 1985). In the acute phase, although they are capable of eating or drinking without maternal aid, a few die if they are not helped. Social isolation for various periods during the first year of life has led to failure to produce offspring, and if females are artificially impregnated they may mutilate and kill their babies.

Separation from peers leads to similar protest followed by despair, as does separation from mother, especially in peer-reared infants (Suomi & Harlow 1976). Normally the mother-infant bond wanes from 3 to 6 months, whereas peer bonds begin by 3 months, strengthen until 1 year, and continue at least through adolescence until age 5.

In nearly all primate species and laboratories, single forced separation leads at once to dramatic panic (protest), which may last for hours to a week. The infant becomes agitated, screams in a thousandfold increase in vocalization, frantically seeks contact with his or her mother, ceases exploration and play, and shows many physiological changes. Mothers protest like their offspring, but less intensely or persistently. Protest increases if the separated infant is removed to a strange environment or if the mother can still be seen or heard (Hinde & McGinnis 1977; Young et al. 1975).

In some species and contexts protest is followed by despair (called depression if severe); the infant looks sad and clasps itself in a withdrawn, motionless huddle. This is reduced by post-separation access to other monkeys. Proneness to delayed depression varies among individuals, being more common among those who in their first month of life had already shown the greatest heart rate and cortisol responses to stress; this variation is at least partly genetic in origin. The amount of depression also differs greatly among primate species; it is minimal in patas *(Erythrocebus patas)* and squirrel *(Saimiri sciureus)* monkeys (Suomi & Harlow 1976).

Separation panic and depression seem to involve different systems (S. Suomi 1982 and personal communication, 1982). Monkeys that protest most at separation hardly ever show subsequent depression. Very low doses of alpha-methyl-paratyrosine (AMPT), which blocks dopamine and noradrenalin synthesis, increase post-separation despair (Kraemer & McKinney 1979) but not protest or reactions on reunion. Fusaric acid, which reduces noradrenalin, reduces despair (McKinney 1985). "Normal" doses of the antidepressant drug imipramine reduce protest immediately but, as in humans, decrease depression only after 10 to 14 days (and relapse is likely on stopping the drug, while ECT also reduces post-separation depression in monkeys).

On reunion mother and infant immediately cling to one another far more than they did prior to separation. Over ensuing weeks and months this "anxious attachment" may subside and infants may resume interacting with peers, but often clasp themselves; sometimes the anxiety increases (Mineka et al. 1981a). The more similar the reunion environment is to that prior to separation, the more rapid and complete is the infant's return to its previous social behavior. If the separation lasts for 6 days, reunion may be followed for up to 2 years by less exploration and more fear of novelty even when near the mother. After 7 months' separation, on reunion rhesus monkeys that have previously been repeatedly separated avoid the mother, whereas controls prefer her (Suomi et al. 1983).

The infant's response to separation varies with its genetic endowment, age, type of attachment, duration of the separation, and care during that period (Suomi & Harlow 1976; Suomi et al. 1981). Reactions are more similar among related than among unrelated infants. Disturbance after separation occurs in rhesus between 2 to 12 months old and peaks at 3 months, by which age the fear response has matured. Older monkeys reared in the nuclear family and separated for the first time at age 5 years became disturbed only if the post-separation environment did not socially compensate for the loss incurred on separation.

Repeated separation from lifelong partners alters the immediate and long-term effects as it does in humans, and age also modifies outcome. Mother- or peer-reared rhesus 2 to 8 months old showed less protest with only mild despair, and on reunion clung more than controls. Seven months later, mother-reared infants still tended to avoid their mothers (Suomi et al. 1983) as children do. Unlike their infant counterparts, on repeated separation from lifelong partners, juvenile or adolescent rhesus (whether peer- or nuclear-family-reared) became increasingly agitated and depressed over successive separations, and social activity decreased on each reunion (Mineka et al. 1981). During intermittent separation those rhesus which had low cerebrospinal fluid (CSF) noradrenalin drank more alcohol than when with their peers (McKinney et al. 1984).

Post-separation disturbance is greatest in infants with rejecting, punishing mothers or who remain closest to their mothers and explore least. The offspring of permissive mothers who allow their infants to explore freely show the least post-separation depression if they have access to other monkeys—findings similar to those in humans. This partly accounts for species differences in separation reactions (Young et al. 1975). Pigtail macaques spend more time in close contact with their mothers than do bonnet macaques *(Macaca radiata)* and show more severe post-separation protest and despair. These responses appear at similar ages but with different intensities in pigtail, rhesus, and patas monkeys.

The demand on bonnet mothers' time and energy to obtain food prior to separation affects the reaction to separation (Plimpton et al. 1981). Bonnet infants growing up with hard-working mothers on prolonged high-foraging demand increased in social precocity, spent more time off their mothers, and interacted earlier and more with other group members. The crunch came, however, when they had to cope with the stress of their mothers being removed from their social group. The supposedly independent infants then became more depressed and were more disturbed on reunion.

Physiological Responses to Separation

In young macaques and squirrel monkeys, maternal separation leads to marked rise in cortisol within 5 to 8 minutes, which lasts for several hours if separation continues (for days in squirrel monkeys, which have much higher cortisol output than most other primates). Rises in plasma cortisol, heart rate, and body temperature occur even if the infant remains motionless and is adopted by a substitute mother (Coe & Levine 1981; Levine 1982 & 1983; McKinney 1985; Reite et al. 1981; Suomi 1983–1984).

On reunion with the mother, if separation lasted less than an hour cortisol returns to baseline within 5 to 8 minutes, but it takes 2 to 4 hours to start to drop and days to return to baseline after prolonged separation. Cortisol rises are soon blunted if separations are repeated over a short time, but behavioral reactions habituate more slowly. Rhesus monkeys reared with live rather than inanimate surrogates develop greater post-separation lability of both behavioral and cortisol responses; these also return to baseline more quickly.

Dexamethasone failed to suppress cortisol in rhesus who showed marked stereotyped behavior 4 days after they were separated from their peers and placed in a new cage (Kalin et al. 1984). Such cortisol nonsuppression is seen in some humans who have severe depression. The rhesus displayed little of the huddling that is an index of their depression.

Noradrenalin in the CSF is low in rhesus who huddle often. It is lowered by AMPT, which increases despair, and raised by fusaric acid, which ameliorates despair (McKinney 1985).

Heart rate and body temperature rise immediately in young pigtail and bonnet macaques separated from their mothers; such rises persist into the first night of separation. Thereafter these measures vary greatly among different infants: they return to baseline in some, actually decrease in others, and in a few fluctuate markedly with frequent arrhythmias if separation is prolonged.

Separation in these infants also changes the EEG power spectrum during the day and disrupts sleep patterns at night. On the first night of separation, sleep latency and number of arousals rise dramatically, and there is less total sleep time, deep sleep, and frequency and duration of rapid eye movement (REM) periods. On subsequent nights of separation the sleep patterns begin to return to normal, though the infants continue to wake up frequently and to have disturbed REM cycles. Individual differences in EEG patterns increase the longer that separation is maintained.

On reunion there is a rebound with rises above pre-separation baseline levels of total sleep time, frequency and duration of REM periods, and body temperature. Most measures return to normal within a week of reunion, but periodic heart rate arrhythmia can persist for several weeks or more.

Physiological and behavioral changes concur immediately after separation, but beyond the first night they diverge and seem almost independent of one another. Cortisol returns to baseline more rapidly than do most behaviors, while heart rate, body temperature, and EEG changes may persist up to a week after reunion, long after behavior returns to normal, and may remain evident during sleep. Immune-system responses continue to be deficient for several weeks after reunion with the mother, and periodic heart rate arrhythmia may persist for several weeks or more in some subjects.

Two points emerge. First, as we saw in Chapter 1 and figures 5.12 through 5.14, there is no ideal measure of fear—the criteria adopted strongly affect whether abnormal emotion is detected. Second, social separation may have long-term deleterious consequences even after behavior has become normal, consistent with the higher morbidity and mortality risks in humans for a year after they lose a spouse (Brown et al. 1977).

Predicting High-Risk Individuals

Some rhesus infants who in unstressed settings are behaviorally and physiologically indistinguishable from their fellows are, when stressed, at lastingly high risk for anxiety and depression, at least to adolescence, at age 3 years. This risk manifests only during stress: the infants are unusually timid in the face of novelty, and react to separation with more extreme initial protest and rise in cortisol and with greater later depression. High risk is predicted by reactions to mild challenges—heart-rate and cortisol reactions in the first month of life, behavioral responses, and proportion of REM sleep (Suomi 1982, 1983).

Measures even before age 1 month can predict fear years later. At age 28 days, rhesus infants were started on a 10-day series of 8 daily conditioning trials to a tone followed by white noise, and thereafter were reared for a year either alone with an inanimate surrogate, or with peer groups. Heart rate decrease during the interval between onsets of tone and of noise predicted fear and depression over the next 2½ years. In peer-reared infants increased plasma cortisol 2 hours after stressful removal from an incubator at age 22 days predicted a similar rise 18 months later after stressful separation from peers for 2 hours. In contrast, baseline cortisol on days 1, 7, 14, and 21 before removal from the incubator, or later on days 28 and 35, did not predict individual differences in later stress reactivity (S. Suomi, personal communication, 1982).

Genetic factors contributing to high risk are suggested by the greater variability of heart rate, cortisol, and behavioral responses to frightening situations among unrelated monkeys than among siblings and half-siblings. All were separated from their mothers at birth and reared in identical laboratory environments. The heritability index (h_s^2) was a high .73 (Suomi et al. 1981).

Whether the genetic risk is actually expressed depends on the environment (Suomi 1983, 1984). Individuals at high risk (early heart-rate slowing) for later responses to novelty of extreme fear and, to social separation, of marked depression and marked and prolonged rise in plasma cortisol, may grow up normally in socially rich and stable environments lacking such stressors. Yet they will become disturbed in socially impoverished settings (such as surrogate-only rearing) or with severe or repeated stress (such as prolonged or recurrent social separation); later, 80% of the females who become mothers will neglect or abuse their first offspring. As we know in humans, too, emotional development is a product of both genetic makeup and rearing history.

Repairing the Harm

Even in adult rhesus isolates, social housing may be beneficial, and in separated infants the damage is reduced by providing adult female caretakers ("aunts") who take an interest in them. A playful young rhesus can also be an excellent therapist (Suomi et al. 1974; Suomi 1982). Normal human children, too, have helped blind peers to overcome social deficits (Sisson et al. 1985). Rhesus reared in total isolation for the first 6 months of life were exposed to a socially normal "therapist" 3 months old, which was still clinging often but was too young to be aggressive or to have complex social play. The isolates had contact with these therapists for five 2-hour periods weekly over 6 months. Initially the isolates ran to a corner and rolled into a ball while the therapist approached and clung to it. Within 2 weeks the isolates reciprocated the social contact, and as the maturing therapist clung less and played more the isolate gradually responded with play, too. By the end of 6 months the former isolates were initiating play, and over the next 2 years into adolescence they became almost normal socially. In contrast, infants remaining alone continued to self-clasp and to move and explore little. The earlier that therapy was begun, the better. Compared with the 6-month-old isolates, rhesus infants isolated for the first year of life showed less complete long-term recovery after such therapy.

Although much of the harm from isolation can be remedied, the appearance of recovery can mask latent deficits (Kraemer 1985). These appear when previously isolated rhesus are faced with social demands, upon which they may regress to earlier withdrawal, aggression, or stereotyped behavior. Sexual behavior may remain defective despite improvement in other respects. Rhesus that seemed normal 2 or 3 years after social deprivation in infancy were hypersensitive to d-amphetamine; it produced clinging, submission, and short bouts of severe aggression and wounding of other monkeys (Kraemer et al. 1984).

CHILDHOOD

Young children have many more fears than adults, starting with no apparent cause and subsiding again with as little reason. Like most childhood emotions, these fears are more volatile and intense than in adults, and they change as the child grows. According to Thompson (1962, p. 289):

> [A]lmost every parent has observed the sudden onset of a fearful response as the child moves forward in perceptual growth. Yesterday the 2-year-old child was not afraid of the roar of the vacuum cleaner, today he is terrified—and he has had no

intervening experience with either the vacuum cleaner or other loud noises. This type of fear often disappears just as suddenly. We can only infer that the child's perceptual response to the vacuum cleaner is undergoing change as a result of the joint interaction of maturation and learning.

What a child fears as it grows alters through development and through exposure to fresh situations. When a child suddenly becomes afraid of things it has long experienced without fear or trauma, such as small animals and birds, then its fear of such prepotent stimuli is developmental. In contrast, fear may stem from exposure to a new situation, such as school, which is also unpredictable—another prepotent stimulus. Not only novelty but also sudden changes in physical stimulation evoke fear. Moreover, children can, through social learning, develop fears of objects or situations they have never encountered, many of these being cultural stereotypes. Another factor is illness or stress, during which children often regress, as do monkeys; forgotten fears may recur until the children are well, after which the fears disappear once more.

Childhood fears are not impressively related to other problems such as nightmares or bedwetting (Lapouse & Monk 1959) or other pathology (Graziano et al. 1979). A few workers found some weak relationships. At age 3 fears were significantly but lowly correlated with physical timidity and, in girls, temper tantrums (MacFarlane et al. 1954), and were inversely correlated with over-activity. By age 5 fears in both sexes correlated with irritability, tantrums, and timidity and, in girls, overdependence, mood swings, poor appetite, and timidity. Fear during air raids correlated significantly with other signs of maladjustment (John 1941), and after a tornado was greater in children who had earlier experienced marked separation anxiety or had a markedly anxious parent (Bowlby 1973). Most phobic children develop into normal adults; if they do have problems later these are usually emotional but need not include phobias (Zeitlin 1982, cited by Rutter & Garmezy 1983).

The Objects Feared

Children fear quite varied situations, and what these are partly depends on age, as we have seen (Graziano et al. 1979; Johnson & Melamed 1977; Rutter & Garmezy 1983). Fears characteristic of infancy decline rapidly during the preschool years except that stranger fear may persist as shyness. Some fears (such as that of animals) rise rapidly from the preschool years onward only to fall again later. Others (such as that of darkness), as well as shyness, show a less consistent age trend. A few arise mainly from adolescence onward—fears of sex, of failure, and agoraphobia.

There are two fears that when found in adults are usually reported to have persisted since childhood. The first is of blood and injury (see Chapter 11); the second is of animals, which in the great majority of cases begins before age 7 (Marks & Gelder 1966). Older people appear to be resistant to acquiring fears of animals. The rare animal phobias that start for the first time in adolescence or adult life are usually associated with trauma such as a dog bite, whereas such fears in young children generally appear unexpectedly for no obvious reason. Like fears of other animals, those of snakes usually start in childhood (Agras et al. 1969). Animal fears diminish rapidly from age 9 to 11 in both sexes (Angelino et al. 1956).

Many fears are common. All but 9% of fears were shared by other children among rural schoolgoers aged 4 to 16 (Pratt 1945). Certain fears are more frequent than others, especially those of animals, darkness, storms, thunder, and strange events. The most frequent at age 2 to 4 are of animals, and at 4 to 6, darkness and imaginary creatures (MacFarlane et al. 1954, Jersild 1950). Among children 2 to 6 years old the most common fears were of doctors, dogs, storms, and darkness (Hagman 1932). At age 6 to 12 children gave their most frequent dread as mysterious events and the next most common as animals— often beasts they had never encountered (Jersild et al. 1933); bodily injuries, which they had all had to some extent, did not frighten them.

The wariness of strange peers that begins in the second year of life continues thereafter. Even at age 6 to 7 there is more initial gaze avoidance, immobility, and automanipulation among unacquainted than acquainted peers (Jormakka 1976, cited by Smith 1979). Fear of strange peers and of other novelty induces anxiety in most children when they first attend a nursery school or playgroup. However, they usually adapt rapidly, as Slater (1939) found in 40 children aged 2 to 3½ years (Figure 5.17). They attended nursery school for 4

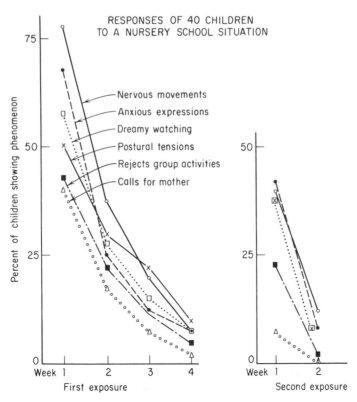

Fig. 5.17 Of 40 normal children attending nursery school for the first time, most had initial anxiety that waned rapidly over a few weeks. (From Slater 1939. Copyright © 1939 by The Society for Research in Child Development, Inc. Reprinted by permission.)

to 6 weeks and then returned every 6 months for further observation over 2 weeks until they reached kindergarten age. During the first period most of the children were uneasy, but this declined steadily and disappeared in the great majority by the fourth week. By the second period of observation far fewer children showed anxiety, and they adapted much more quickly to the now familiar situation.

Not surprisingly, fear of school appears only when children start going to it—at age 3 to 6 in various countries; it resurges when they change from primary to high school, which in many countries is at age 11. Older schoolgoers worry about social relations (Angelino et al. 1956; Croake 1969), shyness not having diminished by age 15 (Shepherd et al. 1971), and are concerned about injury (Bauer 1976, Miller et al. 1974). Adolescents aged 15 to 18 are more anxious about death than are younger children or older adults (Koocher et al. 1976), and among 12- to 18-year-olds the most common fear was of nuclear war (Solantaus et al. 1984).

Incidence

It is perfectly normal for children to have specific fears. Frequencies vary widely according to the age, criteria adopted, and method of ascertainment. Parents report fewer fears in their children than do the children themselves— 41% fewer with 482 children 6 to 12 years old selected from the telephone directory of Buffalo, New York (Lapouse & Monk 1959). Of that sample 43% (36% boys, 50% girls) had 7 or more fears out of the 30 about which mothers were questioned; blacks had more fears than whites. In younger 4-year-olds in Great Britain (Newson & Newson 1968), mothers reported definite recurrent fears to be present in two-thirds.

Fears of animals increase at age 2 to 4 and of darkness and imaginary creatures at age 4 to 6 (Angelino et al. 1956; Jersild 1950; MacFarlane et al. 1954). Beyond that age most specific fears decline, as was found in 1,096 children over a 14-year period (MacFarlane et al. 1954). Mothers' reports were obtained for a sample of every child born over an 18-month period in Berkeley, California, in 1928–1929; highly educated families were overrepresented. Of the children 90% had at least one specific fear between the ages of 2 to 14. Incidence peaked at age 3 (56% of boys, 67% of girls—figures similar to those in the study of British 4-year-olds) and declined slowly with age; further peaks appeared at age 9 for boys and age 11 for both sexes.

The same decrease in fears with age was found from teachers' reports of 142 schoolchildren age 2 to 7 in Leicester, England (Cummings 1944, 1946). Specific fears were reported for 23% of boys and 38% of girls. Decline with age was from 33% before age 4 to 22% at age 4 to 6 and to only 13% at age 6 to 8. The fears were transitory, 72% having decreased 6 months later and 17% disappearing by 18 months' follow-up. Unlike specific fears, generalized anxiety did not decrease with age. In another English sample, fears of animals did not (Shepherd et al. 1971).

Similar decline of most fears as children grew older was found in 50 who were actually confronted with various situations (Holmes 1936). In 2-, 3-, 4-, and 5-year-olds, the percentages for fears of a strange person were 31, 22, 7, and 0, respectively, and for dogs 69, 43, 43, and 12 (for snakes, however, they did not decline: 34, 55, 43, and 30). Fears of being left alone, darkness, and loud noise also diminished from age 2 to 4 and disappeared by age 5.

Gender

Commonly there are few differences among boys and girls (Maccoby & Jacklin 1974; Maurer 1965; Miller et al. 1971; Nalven 1970 [cited by Graziano et al. 1979]). Many, however, have found more fearfulness among girls.[2] MacFarlane et al. (1954) found no gender difference until age 11, after which boys showed a more rapid loss of most fears, leaving teenage girls on average with more fears than teenage boys. In adults gender incidence varies with the type of situation feared (see Chapter 9).

Influence of Social Factors

Fears of animals might be more common in rural children age 4 to 11 (75%, Pratt 1945; 50%, Wallis 1954) than in urban children (15%, Jersild & Holmes 1935). Many of the fears, however, are of beasts never seen in the region.

Modeling by others plays a part. At the moment a fear stimulus was presented youngsters would look at the adult who was with them (Hagman 1932). Preschool children were more afraid of air raids if their mothers were fearful (correlation [r] = .59, John 1941). Children are more likely to be afraid when alone than when with a trusted, fearless companion (Jones 1924). Their kind and number of fears are similar to those in their mothers (r in number = .67 in Hagman 1932) and siblings (r = .65 to .74, May 1950). In contrast, another study found no relation between the number of fears in children and their mothers' worries (not fears) Lapouse & Monk 1959).

SUMMARY

Normal young have fears that rise and fall in a predictable sequence at particular phases of development. This parade is driven by genetic expression in a normal environment whose disruption at sensitive stages can alter the brain and fearful behavior, despite great plasticity in the face of adversity. Some fears emerge without any experience of the relevant situation (innate), others arise after a tiny trigger (prepotent), and yet others need more obvious learning. The first two types are of special evolutionary dangers such as heights, strangeness and separation, but they can be modified by experience. Rituals as well as fears may be prepotent.

[2]Angelino et al. 1956; Bamber 1974; Croake & Knox 1973; Cummings 1944; Dunsworth 1961; Grant 1958; Hall 1897; Lapouse & Monk 1959; Pratt 1945; Scherer & Nakamura 1968; Spiegler & Liebert 1970.

Very young birds and mammals are first friendly and then fearful. From then on, new bonds can be formed only after arduous habituation has overcome the fear and, in older young, emerging aggression as well. From age 5 months the fears of children are markedly influenced by social referencing to the caregiver. Early and even prenatal experiences can lastingly alter subsequent fear, but little is known about the interacting factors that predict whether an experience will sensitize or steel. Fear increases with social deprivation and in novel settings. Minor class and ethnic differences are present whose origins are still unclear. Over time, fearfulness tends to be stable but its mode of expression alters with age.

Neonates are distressed by abrupt or discomfiting stimuli. Obvious fears emerge in babies all over the world from 6 months onwards—of heights, strange objects and persons, and separation. Fear of heights depends upon both age and the start of locomotion in kittens and humans. Novelty fascinates as well as frightens, but fear of it grows with age, and what is novel depends on cognitive growth and experience. Heart rate is slow and fluctuating in children who are alert yet unafraid but rapid and stable if they are wary.

Strange people are more frightening than strange objects, and at least 15 modifying factors are known. In their absence the stranger reaction is easily missed. It dies down by 20 to 24 months but may persist as shyness. Unfamiliar peers evoke fear later than do strange adults, peaking at about 20 to 29 months. Fear of separation, like that of strange adults, peaks at 9 to 13 months and wanes from 30 months onward; the two fears are different but can summate, and blind children also have them. Prolonged separation leads to protest, detachment, and then despair. On reunion there may be anger and avoidance. Echoes of earlier separation anxiety are seen in frightened adults.

In nonhuman primates the features of separation anxiety are like those in humans. Some species differences result from their varying patterns of attachment. Separation protest and despair seem to be mediated by different systems. Repeated and more prolonged separations lead to more severe and lasting reactions. Physiological responses subside quicker than do behavioral ones, yet heart rate and plasma cortisol responses in the first month of life may predict fearfulness over the next few years. Severe consequences may ensue because of both genetic and experiential factors. Harm may be prevented by appropriate therapy, both in humans and in other primates.

Normal young children have intense specific fears that come and go for no obvious reason and have little relation to other pathology. The objects feared vary with development and with exposure. Two frequent fears—animals and blood-injury—if found in adults have usually persisted since childhood. Other common fears include shyness, darkness, storms, and thunder. Fears decline with age, especially in boys, who have slightly fewer fears than girls.

6

Genetics of Fear

Defensiveness varies greatly among species (rabbits are more timid than tigers) and among individuals within species (some rabbits are more timid than other rabbits). The range of stimuli that a species fears and its defensive responses to those stimuli reflect natural selection of genotypes over the generations and cultural transmission among members of that species. If a category of predators drops out, so do its prey's defenses against them. For example, on the Galapagos Islands, where predatory mammals are lacking, hawks, marine iguanas, and penguins (*Buteo galapagoensis, Amblyrhynchus cristatus,* and *Sphenis cristatus*) allow themselves to be touched by humans when they are on land, but in the water the iguanas and penguins are threatened by sharks and flee from a swimming person (Eible-Eibesfeldt 1970). Decades of contact with humans have not greatly increased these species' defensive behavior, which presumably derives mainly from genetic makeup. Where predators have long been present, animals have been selected for their ability to show and learn defensive behavior and to transmit it to one another.

Individuals within a species vary in their degree of fear of particular stimuli as a function of their individual genetic makeup and the environment in which it is expressed. The product is a phenotype that describes what is, not what could be (Plomin & Rowe 1979): "Even if most of the extant phenotypic differences for a particular trait were determined by genetic differences, that does not mean that the trait is immutable environmentally."

Other sources of variation within individuals are due to age (fear being greater at certain phases of development—[see Chapter 5]), natural selection of particular fear stimuli in a species's repertoire (prepotent stimuli and prepared associations), and cultural transmission and individual learning (see Chapter 8). This chapter will examine how genetic predispositions cause variation of fear among individuals within species. These predispositions form the raw material on which natural selection acts.

Fear and anxiety are not unitary characteristics but assemblies of numerous features that relate variably to one another. They have many different meanings for the behavioral geneticist. In animals fear and anxiety have been called emotionality (defined as scores for exploration or defecation), avoidance conditioning, freezing, or startle. In humans they have referred to changes in skin conductance or heart rate; to self- or observer ratings of fear, worry, or autonomic symptoms in the present (state) or over some enduring period (trait); or to criteria of one or other anxiety syndrome.

There is much specificity of different aspects of defensive behavior in animals and in humans. The various tests of fear and anxiety (for instance, the numerous measures of neuroticism) are grouped together here only to give a broad perspective on the many indicators of negative emotional states that have been found. Their grouping does not denote a unitary phenomenon, less still that there must be continuity between normal fear and syndromes of morbid anxiety.

Whatever the criteria for fear or anxiety, numerous studies have found genetic influences on emotion in animals. Each species has characteristic patterns of fear behaviors that vary slightly among individual members of that species. It is not yet known whether the genetic control acts via more basic behavioral units of which those action patterns are composed, or if it is continuous, although the former seems more probable. The marvelous plasticity of our gestures need not be continuous but could depend on a finite number of discrete behavioral units produced by genes. Whichever the case, there must be "many pathways, each with its own set of detours, from a locus on a strand of DNA to behavior" (Carey & Gottesman 1982). The pathways are especially confusing because (1) many genes are pleiotropic—each gene affects more than one trait, (2) trait variation is affected by many genes interacting within the genotypic system, and (3) gene expression is variable, thereby leading to more than one phenotypic manifestation of any trait. The final and as yet unrealized goal is to link a gene and its biochemical product with its consequences for the ontogeny of the nervous system and resultant defensiveness.

Defensive behavior develops out of a complex interaction of multiple genes that takes place in embryonic and subsequent environments. A hint of a strand in that interaction comes from work on the human pro-opio-melanocortin (POMC) gene, which codes for several polypeptide hormones (Whitfeld et al. 1982). POMC is processed in the pituitary into adrenocorticotrophic hormone (ACTH) and other hormones that affect defensive behavior, among other things. The pattern of similarity of POMC protein among different species is reflected in the nucleotide sequence of the coding regions of the gene.

GENETIC CONTROL OF AVOIDANCE IN INVERTEBRATES

Genetic variation in mammalian fear is produced mostly by combinations of genes interacting with each other, for the most part in non-additive fashion. Nevertheless, some understanding of components in these interactions may be obtained from single-gene analysis of defensive reactions in unicellular organisms and invertebrates (reviewed by Fuller & Thompson 1978, p. 463; Gould 1982, pp. 316–319, 329).

At least 20 single-gene mutations are known in pathways mediating avoidance in the bacterium *E. coli*. This is haploid—that is, it has only one copy of each gene—so that functionally important mutations must be directly expressed. Its behavioral repertoire consists of movement toward some substances and away from others. This occurs in response to sampling of the environment using about 24 kinds of receptor molecules (one for each of six different sugars, for example). The bacterium integrates the input from hundreds of thousands of these receptors, compares the sum with the result from a few seconds previously, and then "decides" (if things are getting worse) to try another direction. Each receptor seems to be a binding protein, and the eight receptors that signal the cell that it has encountered something noxious appear to be aromatics, fatty acids, $H+$, hydrophobic amino acids, indole, leucine, acetate, and benzoate. The transduced responses are averaged in three groups (the integration system) through an enzyme, MCP, which is specific to each group. The three MCPs are averaged by a tumble generator, which decides whether things are getting worse or better. The tumble generator then passes its message to the flagellar motors.

Studies in *paramecium* have used chemicals to alter some of the DNA bases that affect its membrane potential and resultant avoidance behavior. Normally a paramecium backs away when things get worse and then sets out in a new direction. The direction in which the propeling cilia beat is controlled by the voltage across the cell membrane, which is in turn controlled by sensory receptors. Mutants have been produced that go only forward *(pawn)*, or avoid spontaneously *(paranoiac)*, or swim too fast *(fast)*. Each mutant's behavioral problem is produced by particular genetic effects on its membrane potential. Pawns lack the voltage-dependent ion gates that yield positive feedback for action potentials; paranoiacs have a deficit in membrane repolarization; and fasts have a raised membrane potential.

Avoidance learning is affected by different types of mutation in the fruitfly *Drosophila*. One mutant, *amnesiac*, remembers what odor to avoid for a few minutes but then forgets, seeming unable to retrieve from long-term memory. Another, *turnip*, never learns to avoid odor and seems to have no short-term memory, but when a heterozygote is created with one normal and one turnip gene, it remembers for a very short time. Finally, dunce cannot learn and also fails to habituate; that is, avoidance does not wane when a stimulus is presented repeatedly. The twin failures of dunce to learn to avoid and to habituate result from a single genetic defect—it lacks an enzyme that also affects habituation in the sea snail *Aplysia* (see Chapter 7).

Genes can modify escape by preventing the normal stimulation required during sensitive phases for the neural substrate of escape to develop. If that stimulation is not experienced at the appropriate time, then the brain fails to respond to it when it occurs later, and this can affect escape. Predominance of one class of stimuli during a sensitive period can permanently destroy or attenuate responses to others. This may stem from competition among incoming cells for synaptic space on target cells in the cortex (Gould 1982, pp. 111, 324).

Such an effect was found for escape responses in mutant crickets (Bentley 1975). A puff of compressed air directed onto the crickets sorted them into jumpers that were caught by a vacuum cleaner and nonjumpers that were left behind. Nonjumpers included a single-gene mutant lacking sensory hairs on its vibration-sensitive cercus in the tail. The nerve from this cercus converges with that from another tail cercus, which is sensitive to touch. The hairless cercus was electrically normal, but the interneuron that integrates the information from both cells to send an escape message higher up the nervous system was abnormal. The interneuron was affected only secondarily. If the cercus of a normal cricket is waxed during development, the cercus remains functional but the higher-level interneuron ceases responding to it, as in the mutant with the hairless cercus (Murphey, cited by Gould 1982).

NORMAL FEAR

Normal Fear in Animals

Most forms of behavior can be enhanced or reduced over the generations by appropriate selective breeding. The number of generations needed to produce a strain with the desired features depends upon their degree of heritability. In such experiments humans replace nature as the architect by choosing individuals with particular characteristics and mating them together to the exclusion of other members of the species who show these characteristics less. Animals have thus been bred for tonic immobility (Gallup & Maser 1977), for emotionality, and for conditioning of active and passive avoidance, escape, and heart rate (Fuller & Thompson 1978; Plomin et al. 1980).

One well-known experiment bred for the tendency of rats, like other mammals, to defecate and urinate when frightened. Rats were reared together in a cage and were then exposed to noise and an unaccustomedly wide illuminated arena (open field) upon which they defecated, urinated, and explored. These behaviors indicated "emotionality" or "reactivity," and high and low scorers could each be selectively inbred (Hall 1951). Selection soon yielded two strains, reactive and nonreactive, and these were maintained to the sixtieth generation of selection (Broadhurst 1981). Figure 6.1 shows the rats' defecation scores to the twentieth generation. The differences were shown to relate to genetic factors rather than to the pre- or post-natal environment.

Selection carries a price, and the nonreactive (but not the reactive) strain became difficult to breed (Broadhurst 1981). Rats that were bold and did not defecate or urinate in the open-field arena declined in fertility. The only way to maintain the strain was to allow selection of rats with slightly increased defecation scores closer to those of the original parent population. Nonreactive rats were also more liable to seizures (Gray 1979) and had more benzodiazepine receptor binding sites in the brain (Robertson et al. 1978).

The two strains differ in emotional behavior and learning on hundreds of measures in laboratories in many countries (Broadhurst 1975). One example is the contrast in incubation of avoidance during the day after they had merely one shock (Figure 6.2, based on data from Morley 1977) (incubation here denotes learning without further relevant experience). There were 17 reactive and 17 nonreactive rats. During the first three unshocked trials no rats avoided

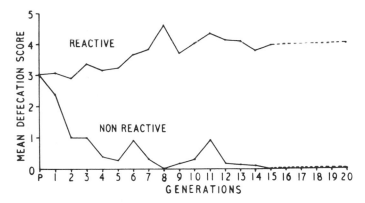

Fig. 6.1 Defecation scores for parent rats (P) and for successive generations (S_1 to S_{20}) bred selectively for high (reactive) or low (nonreactive) emotional elimination in the open-field test. Selection was suspended after S_{14}; at S_{20} there was no reversion to parental values. (From Broadhurst 1981a. Copyright © 1981 by Pergamon Press, Oxford. Reprinted by permission.)

stepping down from a platform onto the grid floor of a cage. On the fourth trial the rats were mildly shocked (0.25 mA) the moment they stepped down and were then removed immediately to a retaining bucket. On trial 5, a minute later, no shock was delivered. Already 8 of the reactive and 4 of the nonreactive rats avoided stepping down during this 5-minute trial; at the end of the 5 min-

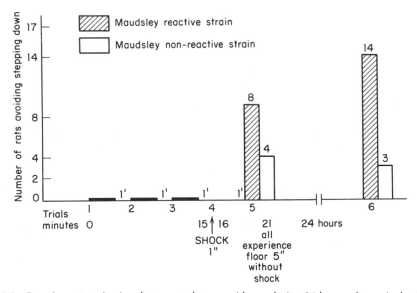

Fig. 6.2 Reactive rat strains incubate step-down avoidance during 24 hours after a single shock; nonreactive strains do not. (Data from Morley 1977.)

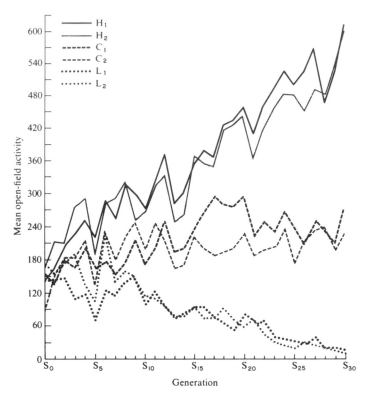

Fig. 6.3 Mean open-field activity scores of six lines of mice: two selected for high (H_1 & H_2) and two for low (L_1 & L_2) open-field activity, with two randomly mated within line to serve as controls (C_1 and C_2). (From DeFries et al. 1978. Copyright © 1978 by Plenum. Reprinted by permission.)

utes these avoiding rats were lifted from the platform and placed on the grid floor and allowed to remain there for 5 seconds before being returned to their home cage. All the rats had thus experienced the cage floor for at least 5 seconds without shock. Trial 6 was 24 hours later; now incubation of fear became evident but only in the genetically susceptible animals. This time, 14 reactive but only 3 nonreactive rats avoided stepping down. During the 24-hour interval fear incubation had occurred in 7 reactive but no nonreactive rats; fear had been lost by 1 reactive and 1 nonreactive rat. Fear incubation was thus a feature of genetically reactive but not of genetically nonreactive rats.

Another experiment selected for open-field activity in mice (DeFries et al. 1978, reviewed by Plomin et al. 1980 and Barlow 1981). Over 30 generations a 30-fold difference developed between the high and low lines, the low-active strain nearly reaching the bottom limit and the high line running the distance of a football field during two 3-minute test periods (Figure 6.3). Although the mice were selected for open-field activity, defecation rates in the open field also diverged: average defecation scores became 7 times greater in the low-active than the high-active strain (Figure 6.4). Open-field inactivity and defecation

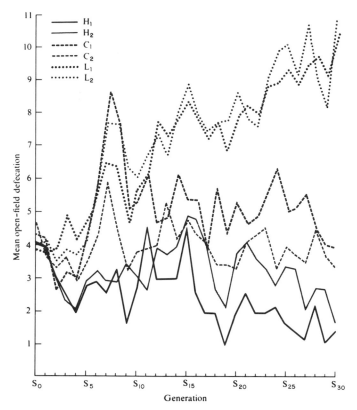

Fig. 6.4 Mean open-field defecation scores of six lines of mice: two were selected for high (H₁ & H₂) and two for low (L₁ & L₂) open-field activity, with two randomly mated within line to serve as controls (C₁ and C₂). (From DeFries, et al. 1978. Copyright © 1978 by Plenum. Reprinted by permission.)

correlated .80, indicating that individual differences in activity and defecation are influenced by many of the same genes. Heritability was moderately low, about .25 and .10 for activity and defecation, respectively. The minimum mean number of loci responsible for the strain differences was about 3.2 for activity and 7.4 for defecation. The genes producing differences in the open field and in defecation had mainly additive effects (Halcomb et al. 1975).

Mice have also been selectively bred for active avoidance. Such inbred lines yield less variable experimental results than do random-bred heterogeneous stock (reviewed by Plomin et al. 1980). An example comes from active avoidance conditioning. This is often studied in a "shuttle box," which has two sections and an electrifiable grid floor. An animal is placed in one section; a light is flashed on and is followed by a shock via the grid floor, which continues until the animal moves to the other compartment. Animals learn to avoid the shock by moving to the other section as soon as the light comes on. In genetically heterogeneous Swiss mice, scores for shuttlebox avoidance learning

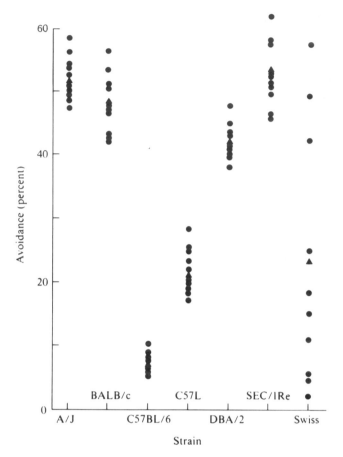

Fig. 6.5 Shuttlebox avoidance learning in six strains of inbred mice and a random-bred (Swiss) strain. Each point is the avoidance (expressed as a percentage) of a mouse over five sessions; triangles denote the strain mean. (From Oliverio 1977. Copyright © 1977 by Elsevier/North Holland Press. Reprinted by permission.)

range from near zero to more than 50% (far right of Figure 6.5). In contrast, six inbred strains have less variable avoidance: scores were low or high depending on the strain, ranging from about 8% to 53% (strains C57BL/6 vs. SEC/1Re in Figure 6.5).

Various mouse strains differ greatly in rates of learning avoidance (reviewed by Plomin et al. 1980). Figure 6.6 shows this for three strains. Strain C57BL/6 shows practically no avoidance, whereas strain DBA/2J rapidly learns to avoid by the third day of training. These strain differences were not peculiar to avoidance; they were also found for mice learning to run through a maze to get food.

Rat strains, too, have been bred for avoidance (Broadhurst 1981). Some were first selected in Rome for rapid or slow escape-avoidance conditioning. Later a third, unselected control strain was added. After 13 generations the Roman high-avoidance strain avoided 70% of the time compared with 30% in

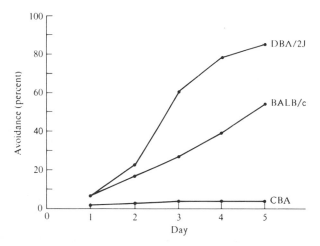

Fig. 6.6 Avoidance learning over 5 days (100 trials daily) for three inbred mouse strains. (From Bovet et al. 1969. Copyright © 1969 by the American Association for the Advancement of Science. Reprinted by permission.)

controls and less than 5% in Roman low avoiders (Figure 6.7). These rats differed in open-field activity as well as avoidance. Other rat lines were bred differing only for avoidance, not for activity (Brush 1977; Brush et al. 1979).

The difference in avoidance between the two Roman rat strains is accompanied by other behavioral and biochemical differences (Driscoll et al. 1985). Compared with low avoiders, high avoiders defecate more during novel stimulation and afterward have lower plasma corticosterone, ACTH, and prolactin

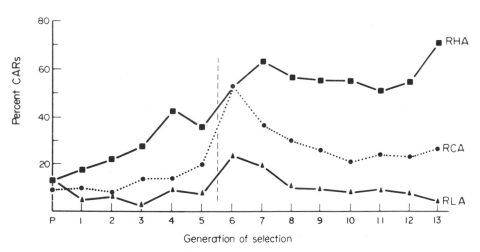

Fig. 6.7 Percentage of successful conditioned avoidance responses (CAR) in a shuttlebox of parent rats (P) and of successive generations (S_1 to S_{13}) bred selectively for high (RHA) or for low (RLA) avoidance, or left unselected as controls. Between S_5 and S_6 the experiment was transferred from Rome to Birmingham. (From Broadhurst 1981. Copyright © 1981 by Pergamon Press, Oxford. Reprinted by permission.)

responses. High avoiders also have raised 3H-diazepam binding to benzodi-azepine receptors in the cortex, hippocampus, striatum, thalamus, and pons-medulla, much the same as with Maudsley reactive rats, and differ in the regional distribution of those binding sites. Finally, the two strains diverge in their serotonergic and dopaminergic activity in several brain regions; the ser-otonergic discrepancy appears after inescapable shock and avoidance acquisition.

Dogs have been bred for all sorts of characteristics over thousands of years. Pointers were selectively bred into two separate strains, one fearful, the other not (Dykman et al. 1965, 1969; Murphree et al. 1966, reviewed by Fuller & Thompson 1978). Breeding began with a few pairs of dogs that were either timid or confident (stable). By the F2 generation 90% of the offspring of the originally timid dogs were fearful, and 80% of the progeny of the originally stable pointers were stable. A visitor would cause the timid ones to hide and freeze, and the others to approach wagging their tails. Timid dogs were less active in a strange room, froze during a loud sound, learned poorly in operant and other free-moving situations, and reacted more to positive and negative conditioned stimuli. Given the association of freezing with bradycardia (see Chapter 3), it is noteworthy that in timid dogs, which froze often, the heart rate was low from birth onward, averaging 80 beats per minute (bpm) and not vary-ing with petting nor declining much even after extensive handling; in stable dogs it averaged 120 bpm and declined during petting.

Hippocampal theta activity (trains of high-voltage waves at 4 to 8 Hz) was absent in alert timid dogs (Lucas et al. 1974), which is interesting because in normal dogs hippocampal theta activity reduces with orienting and avoiding and returns as they habituate to the situation. Nervous pointers were also hyperresponsive to dopaminergic stimulation and had increased L-dopa in the blood (Angel et al. 1982).

Since the pointers' environments were constant, their differences were best accounted for by genetic factors, probably polygenic in nature. In the timid strain freezing was inversely related to friendliness and exploratory activity, while in the stable strain these were independent. Behavior of the two strains did not differ when they were in their home cages and in the absence of human or novel stimuli. Maturation was important: activity scores and freezing time to noise became typical by age 3 to 4 months.

The development of pure and hybrid varieties of five dog breeds (basenjis, beagles, cocker spaniels, Shetland sheep dogs, and wire-haired fox terriers) was studied over two decades by Scott and Fuller (1965) and reviewed by Fuller and Thompson (1978). Dogs within a breed did vary greatly genetically, but across breeds there were also marked genetic differences that varied with age (Figure 6.8) and seemed to increase rather than to decrease with experience. Basenjis seldom barked and were very fearful of people; at 2 months old they could be rapidly tamed. Breed differences accounted for 22% to 41% of the variance of heart rate change during a handlers' friendly approach, and 26% of the variance of 13 pooled variables. Most of the emotional reactions seemed situation-specific: basenjis, for instance, were afraid of strange apparatus but not of other dogs. Selection for confidence in one situation did not necessarily

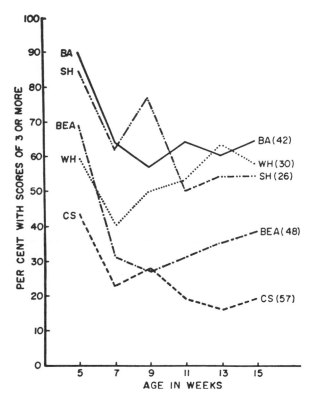

Fig. 6.8 Differences in defensive behavior (avoidance and vocalization in five dog breeds over time. (From Scott & Fuller 1965. Copyright © 1965 by University of Chicago Press. Reprinted by permission.)

affect timidity in another. Unwanted timidity occurred in almost every breed, its very universality suggesting that it is necessary for existence.

Other differences among dog breeds were noted in passive-defensiveness, which was greater in German shepherds than in Airedales; both were more passive-defensive when reared in a kennel than in a home (Krushinskii 1962). When "low-adaptation" breeds such as collies were placed in a room where they had learned classical motor defenses, they developed persistently raised heart and respiration rate, salivation, high energy metabolism, and urinary catecholamine and vasopressin release (Corson 1977; Corson & Corson 1983). These reactions diminished if avoidance was allowed and did not occur in "high-adaptation" breeds such as beagles and hounds. Finally, from age 3 to 8 weeks Shetland sheep dogs were timid and kept away from an experimenter; beagles and wirehaired terriers were social and continuously sought contact with him; and basenjis were curious and approached both him and inanimate objects (Freedman 1958). The effect of breed interacted with age and mode of rearing. When older, of all the breeds, beagles, which had been previously indulged rather than disciplined, became the most shy of humans.

Tonic immobility is another defensive behavior under genetic influence

(Gallup & Maser 1977). Even after rearing under identical conditions, White Leghorns remain immobile 4 times longer than do Production Reds, and hybrid offspring from these two strains are immobile for durations in between. In selective breeding experiments, within one generation the progeny of parents that had long reactions remained immobile 4 times longer than chicks from parents that exhibited brief responses. Similar breed differences in tonic immobility are found in rats (McGraw & Klemm 1973).

Very little research has examined the genetics of fear in primates. Work is beginning in rhesus monkeys. Heart-rate slowing and cortisol response to challenge in the first month of life, which predict fearfulness, separation anxiety, and depression over the next 3 years, are more similar among siblings and half-siblings than among unrelated monkeys even though they were reared together under similar conditions (Suomi 1983c).

Though our theme is within-species genetic variation, we might mention that defensive action patterns of hybrids among species can reflect contributions from each of the parent species (McGrath et al. 1972). The duration of distress calls of hybrids from a chicken/pheasant mating is intermediate to those of the two parent species, though closer to that of pheasants. The upward inflection of frequencies, however, is patterned as in the pheasant. This suggests that dominance deviation might be involved.

Normal Fear in Humans

Siblings differ from birth onward in the intensity of their startle response and fears (Valentine 1930). Over their first year of life both smiling and fear of strangers developed more similarly among monozygotic (MZ) than dizygotic (DZ) twins (Freedman 1965). At age 22 months apprehension during interaction with a stranger, but not with the mother, was more similar among identical than fraternal twins (Plomin & Rowe 1979). Slightly older twins (3 to 4 years old) showed substantial genetic influence on their emotionality (Plomin & Rowe 1977). In 7- to 8-year-old twins, emotionality, tension, and shyness were more similar among MZ than DZ twins (O'Connor et al. 1980). At age 7 years MZ twins were more concordant than DZ twins for separation distress, emotional reactivity, and being fearful/inhibited, but not for fearfulness (Goldsmith & Gottesman 1981).

In adults emotionality, nervousness, and shyness were more similar among MZ than DZ twins; moreover, MZ twins reared apart resembled one another more than did DZ twins reared together (Shields 1962). Furthermore, in this and in two other studies (Juel-Nielsen 1965; Newman et al. 1937), MZ twins reared apart were almost as similar as were those reared together. In contrast, nearly 5,000 Finnish twins who had a lower heritability for neuroticism when reared apart than together, environmental factors explained at least 60% of the variance in the former (Koskenvuo et al. 1983).

Additive genetic effects outweighed environmental ones in explaining the covariation of neuroticism and symptoms of anxiety and depression in 3,810 pairs of adult MZ and DZ twins (Jardine et al. 1984). There was also genetic variation specific to depression. Neuroticism and introversion were genetically independent. The common family environment and social influences shared by cotwins were not important.

Other studies, too, found substantial genetic contributions to personality traits related to timidity (reviewed by McGuffin & Reich 1984). This was the case for social introversion in normal adolescent twins (Gottesman 1963) and for neuroticism in adults (Eysenck & Prell 1951). Genetic factors contributed about half the variance of all dimensions of the California Psychological Inventory in 850 sets of twins (Loehlin & Nichols 1976). Further twin data with normals have found significant heritability for (1) being highly-strung, easily upset, and a worrier, whether measured by the Minnesota Multiphasic Personality Inventory (MMPI), the Eysenck Personality Inventory, or the Differential Personality Questionnaire; and (2) the specific form of this anxiety, such as rapid change in mood versus constant worrying (reviewed by Carey & Gottesman 1981).

Physiological responses associated with emotionality are also more alike in MZ than in DZ twins. Examples include habituation of skin conductance responses and their number of spontaneous flunctuations, pulse and respiration rate, blood pressure changes, and EEG variables (Carey & Gottesman 1981; Hume 1973; Lader & Wing 1966; Vandenberg et al. 1965; Young 1971).

Four studies examined genetic effects in responses to fear survey schedules given to normals and their relatives. In the first, "consistent evidence of heritable variation" was noted in responses from 91 MZ and 60 DZ twin pairs and 66 pairs of parents and their twin offspring (Rose et al. 1981). In the second, similar evidence was found in 354 pairs of like-gender twins age 14 to 34 (Rose & Ditto 1983). A twin's fearfulness on all fear factors could be predicted from the cotwin's score and the interaction of cotwin's score with pair zygosity, but prediction was twice better for fear of misfortune for a loved one than for fears of dangerous places. Fear of death was equally similar among MZ and DZ twins during development but more similar among MZs by the time they reached maturity.

From the foregoing two studies, two fear factors (social criticism and leadership) were subjected to critical path analysis in order to separate correlated genetic and cultural effects (Neale & Fulker 1984). Both fear factors had about equal environmental and additive genetic components, with only a small amount of negative genetic-environmental covariance induced by parental phenotypic influences on their offspring.

The third investigation (Torgersen 1979), of 99 same-sex twin pairs (11 of the pairs having one twin as an inpatient for neurosis). interviewed them and gave them a fear questionnaire. The MZ were more similar than DZ twins in terms of strength and type of fear, except for separation fears (agoraphobia).

The fourth study (Carey & Gottesman 1982) was of 654 family members of 151 psychology students. Compared to first-degree relatives of the entire sample, those of the 10 agoraphobia-like probands out of the 151 had more phobias (any phobia—animal phobia, nonanimal phobia, multiple phobias, agoraphobia, and obsessions), fears (of nasty animals such as snakes, rats, spiders, and bats, and health, agora- and social fears), and orderliness. No difference was found for fears of "normal" animals (dogs, cats, horses, birds, fish) and of physical situations (heights, storms, water and swimming, doctors, hospitals, and enclosed places). There was thus a familial aggregation of many phobias and fears, although obviously this need not be genetic in origin.

ANXIETY SYNDROMES

Undifferentiated Anxiety Disorders and Neuroses

Varying diagnostic labels and methods of study over the years and in different countries make it hard to compare investigations and to work out the heritability of each anxiety syndrome recognized today. Data will therefore be included not only on phobic and obsessive-compulsive disorders but also on panic disorder, generalized anxiety, and neurosis. The topic has been well reviewed by Carey (1982), Carey and Gottesman (1981, 1982), and Murray and Reveley (1981).

Familial prevalence has been investigated by asking probands or another family member about illness in the family (family history studies) or by interviewing all relatives (family studies). The latter miss fewer cases and so yield a higher prevalence rate. Heritable problems must run in families, but familial prevalence clearly need not imply heritability. Adoption and twin studies are more conclusive, but only twin studies have been done for neuroses.

Family and Family History Studies

As early as 1879 Beard wrote that "hereditary descent terribly predisposes to neurasthenia." From then until 1948 at least 19 separate reports noted a familial predisposition to anxiety disorder (Cohen et al. 1951). For example, a family history of nervousness was found among 45% of World War I soldiers with Da Costa's syndrome (Oppenheimer & Rothschild 1918), and of cardiac neurosis among 25% of World War II soldiers (Wood 1941).

Studies of anxiety disorder were reviewed by Carey (1982) and are seen in Table 6.1. Except for the most recent ones, samples with "anxiety neurosis" include an unknown number of cases with agoraphobia and panic disorder. Most of the earlier reports were of family history (FH) studies in which the proband with anxiety neurosis was interviewed about the presence of the disorder in family members. Fewer cases were likely to be missed by the family studies (FS), in which all relatives were interviewed directly.

About twice as many cases of anxiety neurosis are found among female as among male relatives (Table 6.1). A similar ratio is found in the study by Cloninger et al. (1981) if one adds to the definite cases included in Table 6.1 the questionable anxiety neurotics blindly diagnosed (19% of females, 8% of males) (Carey 1982). This preponderance of females among relatives reflects that seen

Table 6.1 Prevalence of anxiety neurosis among relatives of anxiety neurotics

Study	Degree of relationship	Type of study	Prevalence in relatives (%)			
			Males	Females	Total	(Controls)
Brown 1942	Second	FH			3	
Pauls et al. 1979	Second	FH	5	14	10	
McInnes 1937	First	FH			15	
Brown 1942	First	FH			16	
Cohen et al. 1951	First	FH	12	20	16	
Noyes et al. 1978	First	FH	13	24	18	(3)
Wheeler et al. 1948	First	FS			49	(6)
Alanen 1966	First	FS			41	
Crowe et al. 1983[a]	First	FS	17	33	25	(2)
Cloninger et al. 1981	First	FS	2	13	8	
Slater & Shields 1969	DZ twins	FS			4	
Torgensen 1979	DZ twins	FS			9	
Schepank 1976[b]	DZ twins	FS			17	
Slater & Shields 1969	MZ twins	FS			41	
Torgensen 1979	MZ twins	FS			30	
Schepank 1976[b]	MZ twins	FS			33	

Source: Adapted from Carey (1982).
Note: Blank cells represent zero.
[a]Panic disorder only.
[b]Neurotic symptoms.

for anxiety neurosis in the general population and in general medical practice but is greater than that in psychiatric practice (Lader & Marks 1971).

Table 6.1 shows that the prevalence of anxiety disorder among 1° (first-degree) relatives in family history studies is 15% to 18%—that is, 2 or 3 times more than that in two of the three nontwin family studies. (An exception is the study of Cloninger et al. [1981], in which low prevalence may have stemmed from their selecting only cases that fit a strict definition [Carey 1982]). Relatives of anxiety neurotics have a far higher prevalence of the disorder than the available controls. The lifetime risk of anxiety neurosis was 6% among the controls of Wheeler et al. (1948)—only an eighth of the prevalence found in the children of their probands diagnosed as having "neurocirculatory asthenia" 20 years earlier. Among the relatives of the surgical controls of Noyes et al. (1978), the risk of anxiety neurosis was 3%—merely a sixth of that among the relatives of their probands with anxiety neurosis. In a subset of the sample of Noyes et al. (1978), the 1° relatives of 41 probands with panic disorder had an age-corrected risk of anxiety disorder of 25% compared with 2% in 1° relatives of controls (Crowe et al. 1983). In the general population the prevalence of anxiety disorder is about 4% (Helgason 1978; Lader & Marks 1971; Weissman et al. 1983).

Of a proband's genes, half are shared with 1° relatives and a quarter with 2° (second-degree) relatives. Genetic effects might predict that the risk would be double in 1° compared with 2° relatives, and this is roughly the case in Table 6.1. The pooled risk of anxiety disorder is 15% for 1° relatives and 6% for 2° relatives. However, the correlations in liability based on a population preva-

Table 6.2 Increase in prevalence of anxiety neurosis among siblings of anxiety neurotics as the number of affected parents rises

| | Number of parents with anxiety neurosis | | |
Study	Neither	One	Both
McInnes 1937	8	27	—
Cohen et al. 1951	16	22	35
Noyes et al. 1978	9	23	44
Crowe et al. 1983[a]	18	42	

Source: Adapted from Carey & Gottesman 1981.
[a]Panic disorder only.

lence[1] (K_p) of .04 suggest that the data could reflect the common environment shared by 1° relatives (P. McGuffin, personal communication, 1984).

The risk to 1° relatives should be greater when both parents have anxiety disorder and least when neither have it; this turns out to be the case (Table 6.2). Prevalence was also higher in relatives of probands with chronic as opposed to acute anxiety neurosis—22% versus 5% (Cohen et al. 1951). Such findings make polygenic-multifactorial inheritance plausible (McGuffin & Reich 1984). Here liability to the disorder within the population is normally distributed, but only those whose vulnerability is above a certain threshold acquire the disorder. Ill probands have relatives with a shift of mean liability toward and beyond the threshold, and thus more of their kin are affected than those of normals. However, more than genetic factors alone are involved, as most studies find that parents of probands have higher rates of illness than do siblings (McGuffin & Reich 1984).

Are other disorders overrepresented in the families of anxiety neurotics? Alcoholism may be more common (Noyes et al. 1978; Weissman et al. 1983). Children have a greater risk or major depression or phobia if their parent proband has both major depression and either agoraphobia or panic disorder (Weissman et al. 1983). The minor congenital cardiac anomaly of mitral valve prolapse (MVP) may be more common among anxiety neurotics than among controls, hinting that the older terminologies for anxiety neurosis ("irritable heart," "neurocirculatory asthenia") may be more than just figuratively true (Crowe et al. 1981). However, the familial incidence of panic attacks is no higher among probands with MVP than among controls (Crowe et al. 1982). A higher familial incidence of panic attacks in the 12 MVP probands who also had panic attacks than in the 38 without them suggests independent segregation of MVP and panics.

Twin Studies

Four twin studies of neurosis suggest that there is a genetic predisposition to anxiety both as a symptom and as a syndrome (reviewed by Fuller & Thomp-

---

[1]K_p is the degree to which combined genetic and environmental factors are producing the disorder in the relatives of probands when compared to the population prevalence.

son 1978; see their Table 17-4). The concordance rate for the syndrome was 56% for MZ and 40% for DZ twins, excluding the twins of Slater and Shields. Much greater MZ–DZ differences were found in two more series of twins with anxiety neurosis where probands were ascertained more systematically, one from the Maudsley Twin Register in London (Slater & Shields 1953) and the other from the Norwegian Twin Register (Torgersen 1978). Starting with one affected twin, the two studies found concordance rates of 41% and 30%, respectively, for MZ twins but only 4% and 9% for DZ twins (Table 6.1), MZ–DZ differences being significant in both studies. Slater and Shields (1969) reexamined their series for marked anxiety rather than a diagnosis of anxiety state. The concordance rate for MZ twins rose from 41% to 65% and for DZ twins from 9% to 13%.

The DZ twin data yield a much lower risk for anxiety disorder (4% to 9%) than the other studies (15% to 49%) of 1° relatives. This may partly reflect differing diagnostic criteria. High rates in 1° relatives were found when probands had severe *DSM-III* type panic disorder (Crowe et al. 1983), and lower familial rates were obtained when probands came from an unselected series of psychiatric outpatients (Cloninger et al. 1981).

More familial effects are seen in men than in women. Among same-gender neurotic twins who had had psychiatric treatment, greater MZ than DZ concordance for neurosis was absent in females and present only in twins who were male or had been psychiatric in-patients (Torgersen 1983). Greater familial tendencies among males than among females was also found for phobic fears among same-gender twins (Torgersen 1983) and for neuroticism scores on the MPI rated by neurotic inpatients (Coppen et al. 1965).

Such sex differences might be explained by cultural variables such as sex-role stereotypes affecting women more than men. Men may be less subject to such social pressures and show the disorder only when the genetic loading is high. The issue is related to one raised by Reich et al. (1972). A sex difference might reflect a multifactorial-threshold inheritance in which male phobics and neurotics have the less common "narrow" form of the disorder and therefore more severely affected relatives in larger numbers, while women have a more frequent "broad" form with fewer and less severely affected kin.

Defined Anxiety Syndromes

Many of the studies reviewed so far have employed broad diagnostic labels such as neurosis or anxiety. We turn now to reports that used more detailed diagnostic categories.

Panic Disorder

Familial effects emerged from a pedigree analysis of the relatives of 19 probands with panic disorder (Pauls et al. 1980). The same was found in a larger family study, from the same center, of relatives of 41 probands with panic disorder, 11 of whom also had agoraphobia as a diagnosis and a further 11 as a symptom (Crowe et al. 1983). Controls were hospital personnel matched for age and gender. Diagnosis were blind, and morbidity risks were age corrected. The lifetime morbidity risk of definite plus probable panic disorder for 1° relatives of panic-disorder probands was 25% (33% for women, 17% for men), compared with merely 2% for relatives of controls; corresponding figures for definite panic disorder alone were 17% versus 2%. Of the panic-disorder probands, 61% had either definite or probable panic disorder in at least one 1° relative, compared with only 10% in control families. Compared to controls, there was no excess of generalized anxiety disorder or primary depression, and only a small trend to more alcoholism; however, secondary depression was increased (16% versus 7%). Of interviewed relatives of panic-disorder probands, 55% had received treatment for their anxiety—psychiatric in 14%.

One report compared the relatives of 77 probands who had major depression plus panic disorder with the relatives of probands who had major depression without any anxiety disorder (Leckman et al. 1983). The presence of panic disorder in depressed probands more than twice increased the risk to their relatives of major depression, panic disorder, phobia, and/or alcoholism.

Phobic Disorders

Of the various forms of phobic disorder, most family data has concerned agoraphobia and one type of specific phobia—that of blood and injury. Very little has been reported on other specific phobias, social phobia, or illness phobia.

Agoraphobia. It is important to separate this phobia from other cases of panic disorder because agoraphobics are more often female, handicapped by phobic avoidance, and eminently treatable by exposure. In agoraphobia a high familial prevalence of anxiety, phobic and depressive disorders, and sometimes alcoholism has usually been found, rates being at least twice as high among female than among male relatives (Table 6.3). An exception was the study of Buglass and coworkers (1977); among the relatives of agoraphobic women they found little familial prevalence compared to normal controls, apart from an increase in other psychiatric disorders among brothers (17%). Most other workers reported increased familial morbidity. A high rate of phobic disorders was found among mothers (31%) and in increase in other neuroses among both parents (55% of mothers, 24% of fathers) (Solyom et al. 1974); and a higher-than-expected rate of school phobia was found among children (14% for ages 11 to 15) (Berg 1976). More neurosis was noted in the families of agoraphobics (33%) than of temporal lobe epileptics (Harper & Roth 1962). More family histories of depression and alcoholism were found among the relatives of agoraphobics than of social and simple phobics (Munjack & Moss 1981).

In a family study of agoraphobia, panic disorder, and nonanxious controls (20 probands per group), the morbidity risk for all anxiety disorders among 1° relatives was 32%, 33%, and 15%, respectively, the risk for relatives of controls being lower (Harris et al. 1983). Risk of anxiety disorder was more than twice greater among female relatives of ill probands, and male relatives of agoraphobics were also at higher risk for alcoholism. Relatives of agoraphobics were at

Table 6.3 Anxiety disorder in first-degree relatives of agoraphobic patients

	Parents		Siblings	Children	All relatives		
Buglass et al. 1977	N		17[m]				
Solyom et al. 1974	55[f]	31[f]		14			
	24[m]						
Munjack & Moss 1981					I[ad]		
Harris et al. 1983	20[f]		55[f]	40	45[f]	9[z]	4[af]
	15[m]		20[m]		17[m]		30[am]
Moran & Andrews 1985	**20[fz]**		**17[fz]**		**19[fz]**		
	10[mz]		**3[mz]**		**7[mz]**		

Note: Percentage of relatives with any anxiety disorder are in ordinary type; any phobias are in bold type, and agoraphobia is in bold type+[z].

N = not increased.
I   = Increased.
[a]   = Alcoholism.
[d]   = Depression.
[f]   = Female relatives in that category.
[m]   = Male relatives in that category.
[z]   = Agoraphobia.

increased risk not only for agoraphobia but also for panic disorder and for other phobias. Major depression and other psychiatric disorders were not increased in the relatives of ill probands. The increased rate of alcoholism in relatives of agoraphobics was consistent with the findings above of Munjack and Moss (1981) and in anxiety neurotics (Cohen et al. 1951; Crowe et al. 1980; Noyes et al. 1978).

An Australian study of 60 agoraphobic probands (52 women and 8 men) ascertained the familial risk of agoraphobia by questionnaire and interview data (Moran & Andrews 1985). Among all parents and siblings of probands the risk of current or past agoraphobia was 12.5%; the risk was twice greater among female relatives (Table 6.3) but was similar among the relatives of female and of male probands. Parents had no less risk than children. Direct transmission through three generations, which is usually regarded as a feature of dominant inheritance, was reported in only two families. The overall risk was greater than the 4.1% estimate of population incidence of agoraphobia (see Chapter 9).

Within another family study of anxiety disorders (Cloninger et al. 1981), the greatest familial prevalence of anxiety neurosis was in kindreds of six probands who had severe chronic agoraphobia. Among twins with panic disorder or agoraphobia with panic attacks, anxiety disorders were more than 5 times as frequent in MZ than in DZ cotwins (Torgersen 1983a). Whether the similarity of the twins' childhood environment was high or low did not affect the degree of concordance within the MZ or DZ groups.

Why agoraphobia runs in families, and especially among female relatives, remains unclear. Some of the higher risk for females could reflect cultural effects. Males might experience similar panic but avoid less and drink alcohol more—consistent with the increased risk of alcoholism among the male relatives of agoraphobics. An additional source of difference might be that males avoid less than females, accounting for the lower female preponderance in anxiety states (including panic disorder without agoraphobia) and in those forms of obsessive-compulsive disorder where avoidance is not prominent (see Chapter 9).

The familial prevalence of agoraphobia is unlikely to result solely from modeling within the family (Moran & Andrews 1985). Many of the Australian agoraphobic probands had never heard of agoraphobia, let alone met a sufferer, and 85% came from a family in which neither parent was agoraphobic. Nine years after developing agoraphobia one female proband met her biological mother for the first time; the mother told the proband that she, her sister (the patient's aunt), and son (the patient's half-brother) were also agoraphobic. There were no agoraphobics in the patient's adoptive family.

Blood-Injury-Phobias. These particular specific phobics have the strongest family history of all the various forms of anxiety disorder. Unlike most other phobics, the majority of blood-injury phobics report other family members with a similar problem (Connolly et al. 1976; Marks 1981; Yule & Fernando 1981). Among blood-injury phobics fully 68% had biological relatives who were blood phobic, a rate 3 to 6 times higher than the frequency of corresponding phobias among the relatives of agora-, social, dental, or animal phobics (Marks 1969; Marks & Herst 1979; Öst et al. 1984a, 1984b). The concordance of blood-injury-illness phobias was higher among MZ than among DZ twins.

This strong family history suggests that blood-injury phobias may originate in a genetically determined, extreme autonomic response. Unlike the tachycardia that is the usual response of most phobics on encountering their phobic stimuli, the cardiovascular response of blood-injury phobics to their phobic stimuli is biphasic, consisting of initial tachycardia followed by profound bradycardia even to the point of asystole and fainting (Chapter 11). The degree of bradycardic response to blood-injury may be normally distributed in the general population for genetic reasons (just as are height, intelligence, and many other features that are under partial polygenetic control). Presumably only those who have an extreme bradycardic response faint readily and are thus liable to develop the phobia. This would yield a blood-phobic population with a strong family history, as is found. The bradycardic response is probably present from an early age, as blood-injury phobias start selectively in childhood rather than later. It remains to be demonstrated that relatives not only faint frequently but also have an extreme bradycardic response to blood-injury.

Perhaps other phobias, too, may be partly initiated on the basis of other autonomic specificities under genetic and/or environmental influence. For example, when anxious, those with labile blood flow in the cheeks might blush more readily than others and so be liable to become phobic about blushing; those with undue gastric motility might when anxious vomit easily after eating and thus be prone to develop a phobia about that. In addition, blushing may be an autonomic response specifically tied to social cues in the same way that bradycardia with fainting seems linked to blood-injury stimuli, so causing blushers to become phobic of social rather than of other situations (see "preparedness," Chapter 8).

Phobic Disorders As a Whole. Twenty-one twin probands with phobic disorders were meticulously investigated by Carey (1982). Of these, 88% of the 8

MZ cotwins had either a phobic disorder or phobic features, compared with only 38% of the 13 DZ cotwins. One MZ and one DZ cotwin had had psychiatric treatment for phobias. Several observations argued for a genetic rather than a modeling effect. First, even twins raised apart were concordant. Second, in at least two of the concordant MZ pairs, the type of phobia present in the one twin was unknown to the other. Third, in one pair of female identical twins, both twins broke down while they were apart in different countries. Fourth, several pairs were concordant in having fears from the agoraphobic cluster but discordant in which particular fears these were (darkness and enclosed places versus leaving the house alone).

The MMPI on these twins also suggested genetic effects (Carey & Gottesman 1981). Obsessives and phobics had almost identical mean MMPI profiles, so the two diagnoses were pooled. The mean profile reflected a dysthymic personality with much tension, obsessive-compulsive worry, feelings of personal inadequacy, and autonomic symptoms of anxiety. Low hypomania and high social introversion scales suggested someone quiet, seclusive, conventional, anergic, sensitive, and socially submissive. Profiles from MZ cotwins paralleled those for probands but were less extreme. A similar but less marked profile was seen in DZ cotwins but lacked a peak on the psychasthenia scale. Probands were higher than DZ cotwins on the depression and psychasthenia scales. There was further evidence of the heritability of phobias from the MMPI of 26 other twins reared apart on average from 4 months to 24 years old, (Gottesman et al. 1982).

Obsessive-Compulsive Disorder (OCD)

This topic was reviewed by Murray and Reveley (1981) and McGuffin and Reich (1984). Excluding the atypical report of Lewis (1935), some noteworthy psychiatric abnormality was found in a high proportion of relatives— 40% to 50% of parents, 19% to 39% of siblings (Table 6.4), and 16% of children (Carey 1978). Again excluding Lewis (1935), OCD was found in 2% to 10% of parents and siblings (Table 6.4), and in a lower proportion, but still 8 times more than in the general population, by Rosenberg (1967). However, among 174 relatives of 10 cases of severe OCD, not one case of OCD was found, although three

Table 6.4 Percentage of disorder in first-degree relatives of obsessive-compulsive (O-C) patients

	O-C disorder		O-C personality		Any noteworthy psychiatric condition	
	Parents	Siblings	Parents	Siblings	Parents	Siblings
Lewis (1935)	37	20	18	10		76
Brown (1942)	7	7	33	20	50	36
Rudin (1953)	5	2	3	3	40	19
Kringlen (1965)	10					
Carey (1978)	5		14		48	39

Source: McGuffin & Reich (1984).

cases had high obsessive-compulsive symptom scores on the Leyton Obsessional Inventory, and 12% of 1° relatives had past other psychiatric illness (Hoover & Insel 1984; Insel et al. 1983). Responses of 404 normal twin pairs to the Leyton Inventory indicated that the hereditary proportion of the variance was 44% for obsessive traits and 47% for obsessive symptoms (Murray et al. 1981).

Among obsessive twins, Carey (1978) found reports of 30 concordant and 13 discordant MZ pairs, and of no concordant but 14 discordant DZ pairs; 2 more concordant DZ pairs were described by McGuffin & Mawson (1980). This MZ–DZ difference could reflect a tendency to report concordant pairs more often. In the largest twin series (15 MZ, 15 DZ), obsessive symptoms or features were found in 87% of MZ and 47% of DZ twin pairs (Carey 1982). Interesting discordance was present in identical triplets (McGuffin et al. 1982) who all became psychotic, but only one of whom developed obsessive-compulsive disorder as well (subsequent to the report).

Major Depression Plus Anxiety Disorders

We saw earlier that family studies suggest links between depressive disorder and anxiety disorders (including agoraphobia and panic disorder), and that

Table 6.5 Percentage of illness among first-degree relatives by proband group

	Diagnosis of Relative		
		Anxiety Disorders	
Proband group	Major depression	Concurrent with depression	Separate from depression
Normal	6	1	4
Major depression − anxiety disorder	10	1	8
Major depression + anxiety disorder	18	4	10

	Alcohol abuse	Major depression	Total anxiety	Any phobia	Separate anxiety	Panic
Normal	8	6(7) **0**	5(7)	**1**	**0**	**0**
Major depression, no anxiety	9	11 **11**	9	**0**	**0**	**0**
Major depression + agoraphobia[1]	10	12 **22**	8	**11**	**11**	**6**
Major depression + panic	21	20 **26**	16	**12**	**37**	**5**
Major depression + gen anx dis.	11	20 **3**	14	**0**	**6**	**0**
Panic alone	(6)	(4)	(25)			(25)

Source: Adapted from Weissman et al. 1983.
[a]Any phobia for children of probands
Note: Bold figures indicate percentage of illness among children of probands.
Parentheses indicate data from Crowe et al. (1983).

alcoholism is increased among the male relatives of agoraphobics. More evidence of such links comes from a family history study in which the risk of anxiety disorder was greater among 1° relatives of probands who had both major depression and anxiety disorder (rather than major depression alone), or than among normals (Table 6.5 and Weissman et al. 1983). This risk was raised whether the anxiety disorder occurred separately from or concurrently with major depression. If the parent proband also had either agoraphobia or panic disorder (but not of generalized anxiety disorder), this greatly increased the risk in the children of major depression, any phobia, or separation anxiety (Table 6.5). Separation anxiety and alcohol abuse was greatest of all in the children of probands who had additional panic disorder. Perhaps anxiety and depression are part of a shared diathesis, with anxiety disorders being heterogeneous and separate disorders, and panic disorder being the most severe form in terms of familial transmission.

SUMMARY

Genotypic variation contributes to differences in defensive patterns among individuals within a species. Its phenotypic expression depends on the environment in which the individual develops, and describes what is, not what could be. Genetic influences on a trait need not mean that it is immutable environmentally. Potential paths from genes to defensive behavior are hinted at by single-gene analysis of avoidance behavior in invertebrates, but the details are still largely unknown.

Animals have been selectively bred for many types of defensive behavior—emotionality ("reactivity"), tonic immobility, conditioning of active and passive avoidance, escape, and heart rate. Genetic differences in defensive behavior have been accompanied by differences in the number of benzodiazepine receptors in the brain, hippocampal theta activity, in heart, respiration and salivation rates, and in energy metabolism, cortisol response to challenge, urinary catecholamines, and vasopressin release. Inbred lines yield less variable experimental results than do random-bred heterogeneous stocks. Selection can carry a price in fostering other deleterious characteristics.

Normal human fear is partly under genetic control from infancy onward. Compared with fraternal (DZ) twins, identical (MZ) twins are more similar as infants in their fear of strangers and as children and adults on measures of emotionality, emotional lability, neuroticism, shyness, social introversion, worry, tension, and fears and on physiological variables like pulse and respiration rate, blood pressure, EEG, and skin conductance.

Among the relatives of probands with anxiety disorders such problems are far more common than in control families. Twice more cases are present among female than among male relatives, and among first- than among second-degree relatives. The more parents that have anxiety disorder, the greater the risk to first-degree relatives. Alcoholism and secondary depression may also be overrepresented among relatives. Parents of probands have higher rates of anxiety disorder than do siblings, suggesting that more than genetic risk is involved. Twin studies also suggest a genetic predisposition to anxiety both as a symptom and as a syndrome; this may be less evident in women than in men as sex-role stereotyping may lead women to display fear and anxiety more readily.

Using finer diagnositc categories, the highest familial incidence of all is in blood-injury phobia, which may originate in a genetically influenced autonomic predisposition from childhood onwards to have bradycardia and faint to blood-injury stimuli. Familial and genetic influences are also evident in panic disorder, agoraphobia, and phobic disorders as a whole. The presence of panic disorder in depressed probands increases the risk to their relatives of major depression, panic disorder, phobia, and/or alcoholism. MZ are more concordant than DZ twins for phobias and MMPI profile, internal evidence on phobias arguing for a genetic rather than a modelling effect. Most authors have found more obsessive-compulsive problems among the relatives of oc probands than in the general population, and more concordant MZ than DZ twin pairs.

7

Physiology of Fear

Nervous systems evolved to produce behavior under the full blare of nature's physical forces (Camhi 1983). In order to survive, species require mechanisms that efficiently avert threat without impairing other functions also essential to survival and reproduction. The potential to elude threat is built into the brain under genetic and developmental control. The strength of built-in pathways is altered by the environment through learning, so leading to new patterns of defensive behavior. Threat might be eluded by a simple reflex like that involved in quickly jumping out of the path of an oncoming car before any emotion can be experienced, or by prolonged execution of a phased plan of escape from persecution, during which time the refugee might feel constant fear.

There is no precise point at which we can say that fear enters, as complexity increases from the reflex jump of a cricket or a human to the harassed exodus of a refugee. The former hardly involves fear but the latter obviously does. Nor is there a clear divide between fear, anxiety, and other responses to stress. Relevant neural pathways range from simple reflex arcs, which are fairly well understood, to processes that are still totally obscure. This chapter, like the rest of the book, includes defensive reflexes in which emotion is not obvious and which we share with invertebrates, as well as fearful responses that may have evolved from them or separately.

Recent advances in this area have brought together the unlikely bedfellows of cell biology and psychology and psychotherapy. Treatment of phobias and rituals by exposure involves repeated contact with the phobia- or ritual-evoking stimuli until fear subsides (see Chapter 14). This parallels the ubiquitous process of *habituation* found in organisms from protists to man (see Chapter 8). Habituation is the response decrement that occurs on repeated presentation of a noxious stimulus.

Phobias and rituals may relapse after trauma or a depressive episode. This, too, resembles a process widespread throughout phylogeny—*sensitization,* which is the increase in defense evoked by strong or noxious stimuli. Whereas habituation allows an animal to ignore repeated innocuous events, sensitization leads it to attend to potentially dangerous ones.

In some people phobias or rituals can be induced for the first time by trauma and are subsequently evoked repeatedly by formerly neutral stimuli that have become associated with the traumatic stimulus. This process is *classical conditioning,* which again is present in both invertebrates and vertebrates.

Habituation, sensitization, and classical conditioning occur in similar form in mammals and invertebrates. Moreover, in structure, chemistry, and function, human neurons and synapses are very much like those of a squid or a snail. The properties of any nervous system depend in part on such components, just as operation of a computer reflects the features of its microchips. Understanding the learning of invertebrates may thus reveal mechanisms of general import. In addition, the ways that neurons or microchips are assembled and programmed produce further dimensions of complexity that have to be understood in learning how brains or computers work. The size and architecture of invertebrate and human brains differ hugely, so we have to study ourselves directly if we are to develop reasonably complete explanations of human behavior.

We will first review defensive learning in invertebrates. Inquiry into their cellular mechanisms of defensive behavior is bringing cell biology and psychology together in a fertile synthesis. Among the foremost workers in this field are Kandel and his associates, on whom the following account largely depends (Carew et al. 1983; Hawkins et al. 1983; Hawkins & Kandel 1984; Kandel 1983, 1984; Kandel & Schwartz 1981, 1982).

INVERTEBRATES

Cell Biology of Defensive Learning

The marine snail *Aplysia californica,* whose nervous system contains only 20,000 central neurons, can develop conditioned association of a mild and a traumatic stimulus and show a defensive state resembling conditioned fear in mammals. *Limax maximus,* a land snail, can show higher-order associative learning (including blocking, second-order conditioning, and preconditioning). Other invertebrates capable of associative learning include *pleurobranchaea, Hermissenda,* locusts, and leeches.

The search for cellular mechanisms of defensive behavior is easier in higher invertebrates, whose central nervous systems contain larger (up to 1,000 micrometers) and fewer (10^4–10^5) neurons than are found in vertebrates (10–100 micrometers; 10^{12}) (Kandel & Schwartz 1982). The brain of man has between 1 and 10 million times more components. Moreover, invertebrates have many "identified neurons" that are unique and invariant across all members of the species, being distinctive in location and at times in color.

Cellular substrates of defensive learning have been studied extensively by Kandel and his associates for reflex withdrawal of the external organs of the mantle cavity of the marine snail. In mollusks the mantle cavity, a respiratory chamber housing the gill, is covered by a protective sheet, the mantle shelf, which terminates in a fleshy spout, the siphon. When the siphon or mantle shelf is lightly touched, the siphon, mantle shelf, and gill all contract vigorously and withdraw into the mantle cavity.

This response can habituate, sensitize, and be conditioned. During a single training session of 10 to 15 light touches *Aplysia* reduces its withdrawal by two-thirds, the short-term habituation lasting for hours. Four or more such training sessions lead to long-term habituation for up to 3 weeks.

If after habituation the tail (or head) is then shocked, the gill and siphon will withdraw more vigorously from the next touch on the siphon. This sensitization persists for minutes to weeks depending on the intensity and number of shocks. It lasts several hours after a single severe shock, 1 day after 4 consecutive shocks, several days after 16 successive stimuli, and several weeks after 16 spaced stimuli given 4 per day for 4 days. Sensitization not only dishabituates previously habituated reactions but also enhances normal (naive) responses.

Habituation is specific to the sensory pathway that has been stimulated, whereas sensitization spreads more widely. There are two independent sensory pathways that originate in the skin of the siphon and of the mantle shelf. Repeatedly touching either skin or shelf habituates withdrawal of the gill only to the stimulated, not the unstimulated, pathway (skin OR shelf). In contrast, a subsequent shock to the tail will sensitize both the habituated and the non-habituated pathway (skin AND shelf). Sensitization may generalize to a range of responses. This can also happen with anxiety in humans. For days after extremely stressful stimulation has stopped, the snails are restless and try again and again to escape from their cages, which normally they do not do (Kandel 1976, p. 656).

Neuronal Locus of Defensive Learning

Habituation and Sensitization. Defensive learning in *Aplysia* seems to be mediated by changes at a common locus—the synaptic connections made by sensory neurons onto motor neurons and via interneurons. The presence but not the strength of these connections stems from developmental processes. Gill and siphon- withdrawal depend on motor neurons fired by two groups of sensory neurons, one of which innervates the siphon skin, the other the mantle shelf. Of the several interneurons, at least one inhibits and others excite. The sensory neurons synapse both directly onto motor neurons and indirectly via interneurons; the motor neurons synapse directly onto the muscles that effect the behavior.

In response to a novel stimulus the sensory neurons produce large, excitatory postsynaptic potentials (EPSPs) in the motor neurons, which discharge strongly, producing brisk withdrawal of the gill and siphon. If the stimulus is repeated 10 times, the sensory neurons trigger progressively smaller EPSPs in the motor cells, leading to steadily fewer discharges and less withdrawal until there is none. Habituation has occurred.

To understand such neuronal changes with defensive (and other) learning we need to know some basic aspects of neuronal function (summarized by

Alkon 1983 and Kandel 1984). When a neuron is stimulated it fires on all-or-none signal called the action potential, which travels to the axon terminal region, there triggering release of a chemical transmitter. The transmitter in turn interacts with the membrane of the follower neuron to give rise to an excitatory signal—the EPSP (neurons also give inhibitory signals, which we can ignore here).

The action potential is a wave of depolarization of the neuronal cell membrane traveling along its length. The depolarization describes reduction and ultimately reversal of the membrane potential from its resting value of -50 mV to $+50$ mV. At rest a neuron (cell body and processes) is polarized, its inside being negative with respect to the outside. This difference in potential across the membrane reflects a much higher concentration of potassium (K^+) inside the cell and of sodium (Na^+) outside it. These concentrations are regulated by ionic currents through pores (channels) that stud the membrane. The channels are specific to particular ions and are closed at rest, opening when the membrane potential changes.

There are two major ionic currents—Na^+ and K^+. Each flows through its separate gated protein channels in the cell membrane. At rest the membrane is much more permeable to K^+ than to Na^+; the K^+ ions tend to leak out, leaving the inside of the resting neuron negative. Na^+ channels open in response to a sensory stimulus (in the case of a receptor cell), or to a chemical transmitter on the postsynaptic membrane, or to a change in membrane potential, allowing Na^+ ions to flow in, thus making the inside of the cell positive. This is the rising or depolarizing phase of the action potential. In turn K^+ flows out of the cell through its channels; this gives the declining or repolarizing phase of the action potential (the K^+ outflow restores the negative resting potential of the cell). If these changes in membrane potential spread along the entire length of the axon, they constitute the action potential or nerve impulse.

A third minor current is especially important at the axon terminal (presynaptic part of the synapse)—that of calcium (Ca^{++}). This Ca^{++} current is small, about 1% the size of the Na^+ or K^+ current, and contributes little to the action potential. Rather, it acts as a messenger for the cell to release chemical transmitter at the axon terminal.

The transmitter is released from the terminal not as single molecules but in packets containing about 5,000 molecules. Enclosed in small subcellular organelles called synaptic vesicles, these packets are released from varicose expansions of the axon (synaptic) terminals. A given vesicle fuses with the external membrane of the terminal, extruding its contents into the synaptic cleft between the nerve cells; this occurs only at certain points within the axon terminal, called active zones. At these active zones dense projections serve as docking sites for the vesicles. Apparently Ca^{++} must be present for the vesicles to bind at these docking sites, fuse with the external membrane, and release their packet of transmitter.

When the nerve impulse (action potential) nears the axon terminals it depolarizes them slightly and opens up the Na^+ channels. Na^+ moves into the terminals, there generating the ascending limb of the action potential. The depolarization of the action potential also opens up the Ca^{++} channels in the terminal, allowing some Ca^{++} to enter it. The action potential in turn opens the K^+ channels, the K^+ inflow leading to the descending limb of the action potential and turning off the Ca^{++} current that regulates release of transmitter from the terminal.

Habituation and sensitization involve reversible decrease or increase, respectively, in the amount of transmitter released at preexisting synaptic connections made by sensory neurons onto motor and interneurons. Change in the amount of transmitter released at these connections (terminals) alters the size of synaptic potentials—the strength of the excitatory connections—between sensory neurons and their follower cells.

The memory for short- and long-term habituation in *Aplysia* is a reversible decrease in the strength of these connections. This results from each successive action potential progressively reducing the flow of Ca^{++} into the presynaptic terminal, leading there to reduced release of transmitter and reduced effectiveness of that synapse. (The sensitivity of the receptor molecules in the postsynaptic cells is not altered). After habituation training, the proportion of sensory neurons with detectable connections to motor neurons was only 30% a day and a week later and 58% 3 to 4 weeks later, compared to 90% of sensory neurons in control unhabituated snails. Duration of the habituation depends on the number of stimulations. Relatively little repeated stimulation (40 trials over 4 days) leads to long-term memory over several weeks.

At the same site—the terminals of the sensory neurons—changes opposite to those of habituation occur with sensitization. There is a progressive increase in the amount of transmitter released by each impulse; this enhances both the functional synaptic connections and the behavior. Sensitization is thought to be mediated by cells that use serotonin as their transmitter and by other cells using a related aminergic transmitter. These cells contact the terminals of the sensory neurons and increase Ca^{++} influx and thus transmitter release. A sensitizing shock to the head not only reverses previous habituation behaviorally but also restores, within an hour, synapses that had been functionally disconnected and would have remained so for weeks.

Defensive learning produces morphologic as well as functional changes. Release of transmitter from the presynaptic vesicles occurs at varicose expansions of the axon terminal. These varicosities contain active zones where the vesicles dock before releasing transmitter. In naive snails active zones are found in 40% of varicosities of sensory neurons. The percentage reduces to 10% in habituated animals, and the few remaining active zones are smaller than in control varicosities. In contrast, with sensitization 70% of varicosities have active zones, and these zones are larger than in control snails.

Sensitization is thought to result from a biochemical cascade at the membrane of the presynaptic terminal of the sensory neuron (Kandel 1984). It could start with the transmitter serotonin or a related substance activating a receptor (Figure 7.1). The receptor engages a coupling (G) protein, which activates an adenylate cyclase that increases free cyclic adenosine 3', 5'-monophosphate (cAMP) within the terminal. Free cAMP then detaches a catalytic subunit from a protein kinase enzyme. This catalytic subunit phosphorylates a particular type of K^+ channel protein or an associated regulatory protein, thereby chang-

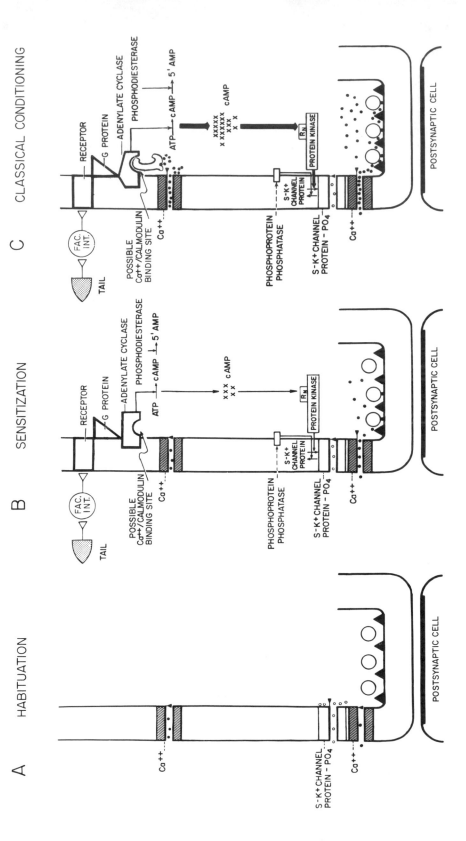

A HABITUATION B SENSITIZATION C CLASSICAL CONDITIONING

ing its charge and thus its shape. This closes K^+ channels, reducing the number open during the action potential. Decrease in K^+ current slows repolarization of the action potential. In turn this allows more Ca^{++} to flow into the terminal, more binding of synaptic vesicles to release sites, and more release of transmitter. After some time the action of the protein kinase is reversed by a protein phosphatase removing the phosphate groups from the K^+ channel.

The memory for short-term sensitization may lie either in the continued synthesis of cAMP by adenylate cyclase or in diminished degradation of the cAMP by phosphodiesterase. Short-term grades into long-term sensitization and may have a common cellular locus and mechanism. For long-term memory an alteration of gene expression is suggested, involving a new regulatory unit for the protein kinase being synthesized which prolongs phosphorylation of the K^+ channel.

Conditioning. Defensive responses may be learned nonassociatively (through habituation and sensitization) or associatively (through classical and operant conditioning). For associative learning to occur, two stimuli or a stimulus and a response must be associated in time. In classical conditioning an initially weak or ineffective to-be-conditioned stimulus (CS) affects behavior only after it has been paired with a strong unconditioned stimulus (US). After conditioning, but not after nonassociative learning, the animal behaves as if the CS predicts the US. Frequently a reflex shows both sensitization and classical conditioning to the same CS and US. In such cases the behavioral change produced by paired presentations of CS and US is greater or more lasting than that produced by unpaired presentations.

The siphon- and gill-withdrawal reflexes of *Aplysia* can be classically conditioned. If a mild touch to the siphon (CS) that evokes feeble withdrawal is followed immediately by a strong shock to the tail (US), powerful withdrawal occurs. Even a single such trial produces some learning, which becomes progressively more robust with more training trials. If the sequence is repeated 30 times, then for up to 4 days later conditioned snails withdraw more from the CS than do sensitized animals that had the US alone or controls that had the CS and US in an unpaired or random manner. Moreover, the siphon or the mantle shelf can each be differentially conditioned to pairing of a weak CS to

---

Fig. 7.1 Cellular mechanisms of habituation, sensitization, and classical conditioning of the *Aplysia* gill and siphon withdrawal reflex. (A) With habituation, repeated stimulation of a siphon sensory neuron (the presynaptic cell) produces prolonged inactivation of Ca^{++} channels in that neuron (denoted by closed gates) leading to decreased Ca^{++} influx during each action potential and decreased transmitter release. (B) With sensitization, strong stimulation of the tail stimulates facilitatory interneurons, which leads to prolonged inactivation of K^+ channels in the siphon sensory neuron through a sequence involving cAMP and protein phosphorylation. Closing these K^+ channels broadens subsequent action potentials; this in turn increases Ca^{++} influx and transmitter release. (C) With classical conditioning, strong tail stimulation amplifies facilitation of transmitter release from the siphon sensory neuron if the tail stimulation is preceded by action potentials in the sensory neuron. This may result from "priming" of the adenyl cyclase by Ca^{++}, which enters the sensory neuron during the action potentials, so that the cyclase produces more cAMP when it is activated by the tail stimulation. (From Hawkins & Kandel 1984. Copyright © 1984 by American Psychological Association. Reprinted by permission.)

either with a strong shock US to the tail. As we saw earlier, the siphon and the mantle shelf each has its own sensory neurons whose activation can independently act as a CS, just as they can independently mediate habituation.

As in vertebrates, classical conditioning in *Aplysia* is specific not only to the stimulated pathways but also temporally. It is maximum when the CS precedes the US by about 0.5 seconds. If the CS precedes the US by 0.5 seconds, the sensory neurons of the CS pathway will be firing action potentials just before the facilitator neurons from the US pathway act on the terminals of the CS neurons. The facilitators then enhance presynaptic facilitation more than if the sensory neurons either had not been recently active or had been active after the US is presented. This "activity-dependent enhancement of presynaptic facilitation" requires impulse activity from the CS and the US neurons to converge and coincide in the terminals of the CS sensory neurons (Hawkins et al. 1983; Kandel & Schwartz 1982; Walters & Byrne 1983). Transmitter release and duration of action potential from the CS sensory neuron rises more after a series of pairing trials in which its action potentials immediately precede the US than when they are unpaired.

The amplified response of classical conditioning may be mediated by activity-dependent enhancement of the same cAMP cascade that underlies sensitization. Sensory neurons exposed to serotonin just after a train of action potentials has been generated in them show a much greater rise in cAMP than those exposed to serotonin alone. The signal for the sensory neuron that activity has occurred, which triggers the cAMP cascade, seems to be the influx of Ca^{++}. This perhaps binds briefly to the protein calmodulin. Involvement of the cAMP cascade in learning is further supported by the fact that single-gene *dunce* mutants of *Drosophila,* which cannot sensitize or associatively condition, lack cAMP phosphodiesterase and have abnormally high concentrations of cAMP (Duerr & Quinn 1982).

Avoidance conditioning may involve changes in cell bodies and axons as well as synapses (Alkon 1983; Hawkins et al. 1983). The marine snail *Hermissenda crassicornis* learns to avoid light, which is associated with rotation (simulating sea turbulence). Such learning lasts for days and is accompanied by changes in the long-term regulation of ion flow across the cell membrane. There is a steady rise in intracellular Ca^{++} that activates calcium-dependent enzymes. These allow the phosphorylation of membrane proteins, which regulate the flow of Ca^{++} and K^+ ions. After avoidance training ends, the intracellular Ca^{++} subsides to normal, but the phosphorylation of proteins persists for days while the conditioning lasts. This could cause long-lasting activation of protein kinases, which might then maintain membrane changes leading to persistent increase in neuronal excitability.

A protein kinase whose injection into *Hermissenda* neurones simulates conditioning effects also produces similar changes in the membrane of neurones in the cat (Alkon 1983). Mammals are vastly more able than mollusks to resolve sensory information and to associate stimuli and, in the case of humans, to invest these associations with meaning in a rich emotional context, or to repress them. Differences in aversive learning across taxa may result more from differences in circuitry than in cell biology. Perhaps the diffusely projecting aminergic systems of the mammalian brain play the same role in sensitization and conditioning as do the facilitating neurons in the abdominal ganglion of *Aplysia* (Kandel 1984).

In a landmark paper, Hawkins and Kandel (1984) suggest that learning is a family of related processes that range from habituation to conditioning to insight learning. Higher forms of learning may have evolved from lower forms. As an example, conditioning could have evolved from sensitization by a small change in adenyl cyclase, making it sensitive to the Ca^{++} that enters the cell during an action potential, thus giving rise to the activity dependence of facilitation. Yet higher types of learning may have similarly evolved from the mechanism of conditioning. Single neurons with limited plasticity could, when combined in large numbers in particular circuits, produce advanced forms of learning. In theory, several higher-order features of conditioning, including generalization, extinction, second-order conditioning, blocking, and the effect of contingency, could be accounted for by combinations of the cellular processes that underlie habituation, sensitization, and classical conditioning.

We turn now from cell biology to some neurophysiological mechanisms mediating defensive behavior in invertebrates.

Neural Pathways for Defensive Behavior

The escape reactions of invertebrates are like the withdrawal reflexes of vertebrates. Habituation, sensitization, and conditioning resemble defensive behavior, in which the emotion of fear is obvious. Invertebrates have receptors to detect the approach of enemies, some of them extremely sensitive. The receptors are linked to small neurons to mediate slower elements of escape, and, in many species, giant fast-conducting neurons to start the first lightning escape response. Larger fibers conduct impulses faster than small ones, but this quick-acting system leads to more stereotyped responses because fewer fibers can be packed into the same space; thus, the detailed information needed for more varied reactions is sacrificed. Simultaneous stimulation of large and small neurons can activate fast and slow escape systems in parallel, the first quick act resulting from the fast giant system and subsequent slower responses from the slower smaller system. Often neurons are coupled together so that stimulation of one produces positive escalating feedback in several neurons that discharge together in an all-or-none response. Let us see some permutations of these mechanisms in several species.

We start with the sea slug *Tritonia*. Within 2 to 6 seconds of being touched anywhere on its body by a starfish enemy, starfish extract, saline, or soap, it reacts with a stereotyped sequence of escape movements lasting 10 to 90 seconds (Ewert 1980; Willows 1971). The slug contracts dorsally to pull its extremities back from danger and extends its paddlelike organs; these actions are followed by alternate bending of the dorsal and ventral surfaces in 1 to 8 cycles. These rhythmic swimming movements carry the slug up off the bottom into the water current and away. The response can be initiated by a single, giant command neuron near the central commissure joining the two halves of the brain. Stimulating that cell for less than a quarter-second may elicit a playing out of *Tritonia's* normal swimming escape response in all its details. The stimulated neuron fires for only about 3 seconds, after which other neurons drive the escape sequence. These are interconnected and can fire almost synchronously. The excitation can be fed back within the group to allow a cascade of impulses that drives escape by swimming. A simple oscillating switch powering the dorsal and ventral muscles could alone control the alternating swimming movements.

A switchlike mechanism is seen in the defensive release of ink from the ink gland in the mollusk *Aplysia* (Camhi 1983; Kandel 1976). Three motor neurons innervate this gland, and an intense barrage of action potentials in these three cells leads to the release of ink. Activity in these cells is virtually all-or-none in character; the cells are generally either quiescent or, when excited by presynaptic neurons, very active, and intermediate levels of activity are rare. This all-or-none property partly derives from the electrical coupling of the three cells to each other, each synapsing onto the other two, so that if any one is stimulated there is positive feedback with rapid escalation into a marked train of action potentials.

Like *Tritonia,* the crayfish *Procambarus clarkii* also has giant command interneurons triggering rapid escape via fast-conducting giant fibers (Ewert 1980). If one stimulates the posterior third of a crayfish by tapping on or directing a jet of water at its abdomen, this triggers pit-hair receptors in the carapace. These fire sensory interneurons that in turn fire the lateral giant interneuron (LGI), which starts a fast escape routine (Camhi 1983). The crayfish immediately cancels other ongoing behavior and flexes its abdomen downward, which pitches the animal upward and forward. This tail flip is fast (it begins within 10 to 20 milliseconds and is completed within 60 milliseconds of the stimulus) and all-or-none in character (Wine & Krasne 1972). The LGI, which mediates the tail flip, is not a single neuron but rather a bilateral segmented chain of neurons; these are tightly coupled electrically to form a single functional unit that inhibits other neuronal circuits that might compete with escape behavior. Immediately after the initial fast single tail flip, the crayfish swims away from the threat more slowly (latency 240 milliseconds) under the control of small slow-acting neurons, moving its swimmerets and alternately extending and flexing its abdomen.

The first fast flexing tailflip is the power stroke of escape produced by central action of the giant cells. The return stroke of rapid abdominal reextension with minimal counterthrust is a chain reflex triggered by sensory feedback from the flexion. Serial ordering of the two escape responses of fast flip followed by slow swimming results from parallel activation by the same sensory stimulus of two separate behavioral units with different intrinsic reaction times, the first being rapid (giant cells) and the second slow (smaller cells) (Reichert & Wine 1982; Wine & Krasne 1981, 1982). Abdominal extension and flexion can be stimulated by octopamine and serotonin, respectively, so that chemical coding of specific behaviors may be possible (Camhi 1983).

If the crayfish is stimulated suddenly visually or by touch on the anterior part of its body, it escapes backward with a fast tail flip that is more curled than that evoked by posterior stimulation and is mediated by a different circuit via a medial giant interneuron (MGI). (In earthworms one MGI and two LGIs mediate forward and backward escape, respectively [Drewes 1982, cited by Camhi 1983].) Sudden stimuli thus produce rapid stereotypes forward or backward flips triggered by the lateral or medial giant interneurons, respectively. In contrast, gradual stimuli such as slowly looming objects lead to more varied delayed tail flips and trajectories mediated by smaller slower neurons that are thought to be phylogeneticaly older.

Similar giant cell neurons mediating rapid escape from touch and nongiant neurons involved in slower escape are found in sabellid worms such as *Branchioma vesiculosum;* repeated touch leads to habituation of the giant system first and only later of the nongiant system (Krasne 1965). Other species with giant-cell systems for rapid withdrawal into burrows or tubes are *Lumbricus terrestris, Nereis virens,* and *Myxicola infundibulum.* Cockroaches, too, have giant cell neurons for rapid escape. In all these species repeated stimulation leads to habituation of transmission from sensory nerves to intersegmental giant axons.

Restraint of the crayfish strongly inhibits escape in a form of tonic immobility. This inhibition originates in the supra- and subesophageal ganglia and, to a lesser extent, in the thoracic ganglia. Inhibition is unilateral, even though most pathways in the escape systems are tightly coupled bilaterally (Wine & Krasne 1982).

Noctuid moths, a favorite food of bats, have simple ears to increase their chances of getting away (Roeder 1965). Each ear (one on each side of the thorax) has merely two receptors that allow surprisingly sophisticated avoidance of bats. One receptor (A1) is sensitive to soft interrupted sounds, the other (A2) to loud ones. The A1 receptor begins firing to cries from a bat that is 100 feet away, long before the bat could detect the moth. Since the rate of A1 firing is proportional to the loudness of the sound, the insect can decide whether the bat is getting closer. If the bat is above the moth the A1 firing rate fluctuates with every up-and-down movement of the moth's wings, and if the bat is below there is no such fluctuation. The moth locates the bat's horizontal position from the intensity of stimulation of the ear on each side.

The moth's antidetection strategy is to present a low profile and fly directly away from a bat sound, orienting so that the stimulation of each A1 receptor is equalized. Discrepancies between the activity of the two A1 receptors cause the brain to stimulate the thoracic ganglion to steer the moth away from the side that is more strongly stimulated until there is synchrony between the two sides, at which point the insect will be flying away from the bat. Provided the moth can stay out of range for a few seconds, the odds are that it will escape, as the bat rarely flies for long in a straight line.

Escaping in a straight line is effective only outside the bat's 8-foot detection range. Within this range the bat could easily overtake a moth flying away directly; instead, the moth flees erratically with wild loops and power dives, which make it harder to catch and may enable it to fall onto masking plants. A bat about to strike a moth makes a loud noise, stimulating the A2 receptor to fire. This is relayed to the brain, which may shut off central steering mechanisms regulating the motor neurons in the thoracic ganglion. leading to erratic movements.

Like moths, lacewings also have simple ears whose neurons can detect bat cries; however, lacewings fly slowly, and their only response is a power dive. When fired by high-frequency calls, the ears send signals that shut down the wing muscles.

The cockroach has an elegantly simple means of escaping from predators, which are detected from the air movement caused by their approach (Alcock 1979; Roeder 1965). The air puff stimulates a host of tiny hairs that cover the cerci, two small thin projections gracing the end of the abdomen. Each hair is delicately poised in a socket and attached to a sensory neuron. Hair movement generates a receptor potential that travels to the axon hillock, where it may trigger an action potential. This races down the axon of the cercal nerve to a giant interneuron (GI) whose giant axons are 30 microns (about 1/10,000 inch) in diameter, compared to 3 microns for a typical fiber in the nerve cord, and conduction to the metathoracic ganglion is correspondingly faster—3 milliseconds as opposed to 30. This enables the insect to react in 50 milliseconds rather than in 75. The cost of this emergency warning system is cruder information, since only one large fiber, instead of 10 small ones, can be packed into the available space. A 50% increase in reaction speed entails a 90% reduction in information. The GI receives input from many sensory neurons and fires only if it receives action potentials from many neurons at the same time or in quick succession, indicating a biologically significant event. Firing by the GI starts a motor program for the cockroach to scurry away immediately. If many input fibers are stimulated repeatedly, however, the GI quickly stops responding after an initial burst of activity—that is, it habituates.

VERTEBRATES

Inframmalian Issues

Compared to invertebrate brains, vertebrate ones are far larger and have a more complex and different structure, although not only their cell biology but also certain components may be similar. Fish and larval amphibians, for example, have in their hindbrain a pair of giant cells (Mauthner cells) that control the local spinal-cord reflexes responsible for their swimming undulations. One of these two giant cells serves as a command neurone that initiates the startle response (Figure 7.2) (Ewert 1980).

If one taps the side of an aquarium, the fish turn in a flash and swim in the opposite direction, their reaction time being about 10 milliseconds; a comparable natural stimulus might come from suddenly approaching predators. The vibration triggers hair cells, which synapse on neurons in the eighth cranial nerve ganglion. The latter in turn synapse on a Mauthner cell whose axon leads after decussation to the spinal cord. Escape begins within 2 milliseconds of the action potential in the Mauthner cell, which activates, via chemical synapses,

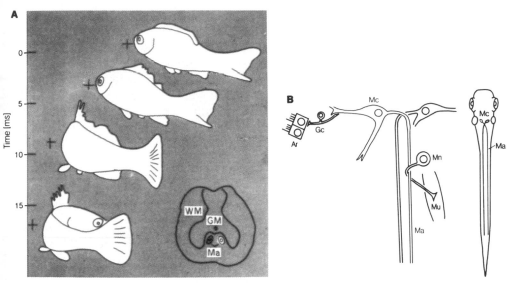

Fig. 7.2 The giant Mauthner cell prompts the startle response in teleost fish *Paralabrax clathratus* (kelp bass). (A) A vibratory stimulus occurs at 0, and the fish responds with fast-body-bend. The crosses are a fixed reference point. Section (bottom right) through spinal cord shows grey matter (GM), white matter (WM), and Mauthner axons (Ma). (B) Simplified neuronal circuit mediating startle response (Ar, auditory receptors; Gc, eighth ganglion cell; Ma, Mauthner axon; Mc, Mauthner cell; Mn, spinal motor neuron; Mu, muscle). (From Ewert 1980. Copyright © 1980 by Springer Verlag, N.Y.. Reprinted by permission.)

a pool of contralateral spinal neurons. Only the first phase of escape, the fast body bend, is commanded by the Mauthner cell spike; the subsequent return flip and swimming are controlled by other neuronal systems (this dual-control system, one fast and the other slow, is reminiscent of that in the crayfish and in *Branchioma).* By 100 milliseconds after the startle response begins, the fish has moved away about a body length. The response habituates to repeated sensory stimulation. In the absence of Mauthner cells the fast body bend is triggered less reliably. Mauthner cells disappear in amphibians when they metamorphose to lead a terrestrial life.

Giant cell systems mediating escape have not been identified in mammals, and the pathways for startle are unclear. The giant Betz cells in the mammalian motor cortex have not been identified as elements in such a pathway.

Defensive response in vertebrates depend upon interactions of several brain regions. In the common toad *Bufo bufo,* for example, recognition of prey and enemy stimuli depends on interactions of the tectum, thalamo-pretectal region (TP), and forebrain (Ewert 1980). Visual recognition depends on a system in the optic tectum of the midbrain, and the toad will try to eat small objects moving like worms and will avoid large, tall ones moving in unwormlike fashion, especially in the upper visual field. Electrical stimulation of particular brain regions triggers prey catching or enemy avoidance. Avoidance is particularly stimulated from the pretectal and tegmental regions of the midbrain. According to the precise site stimulated, the toad will turn away from an invisible enemy or duck or jump away in panic. If in contrast the TP region is destroyed while preserving the optic tectum, escape ceases, and the toad tries to catch anything that moves, even apparent enemies. If the lesion is only in one hemisphere, the toad tries to capture an enemy shown to the eye whose optic nerve leads to the lesioned hemisphere, yet it avoids the same object shown to the other eye. If the whole telencephalon is removed or the lesion is rostral to the TP region, then avoidance increases, even of small moving visual stimuli. Removing the TP region as well eliminates escape irreversibly, and the toad tries to capture anything that moves.

The search for brain regions mediating defensive behavior is confused by the fact that stimulating a given area may have varied effects at different times (Ewert 1980). A chicken standing next to a stuffed polecat virtually ignores it. However, if the diencephalon is stimulated electrically the chicken adopts a fighting stance, threatens the polecat, and lunges at it. When stimulation ceases the chicken remains standing and threatens only mildly. If stimulation continues the chicken may instead fly away screaming.

Central Pathways in Mammals

Just how the mammalian brain mediates fear and related behavior is still far from clear. It represents a vast expansion of the invertebrate interneurons that mediate defensive behavior. Various theories or models of anxiety involve particular sets or subsets of brain structures but have not been adequately mapped onto the rich complexity of normal and clinical phenomena. A convincing theory or model should explain in detail what mediates withdrawal, immobility, aggressive defense, or deflection of attack. It should trace the different substrates of the features that distinguish various phobias and rituals, including their motoric, subjective, and physiological aspects (see chapters 9 through 13). We have a long way to go before realizing this ambition.

Two important points have emerged so far. The first is that the specificity with which the many components of the emotional bundle called "fear behaviors" are acquired and extinguished seems to have a corresponding specificity of physiology mediating their expression and learning, though little of it has been unraveled. There is similar specificity in the neural pathways mediating different components of the escape responses of invertebrates.

The second point is that normal and abnormal emotions seem to involve certain deep brain structures more than they do the cerebral cortex. Among the relevant deep structures are (Figures 7.3 and 7.4): (1) the limbic system, including the hypothalamus, septum, hippocampus, amygdala, and cingulum; (2) other bodies, such as the thalamus, locus ceruleus, median raphe nuclei, and dental/interposital nuclei of the cerebellum; and (3) connections among these. Destruction or electrical or chemical stimulation of these areas cause greatly varying disturbances in aspects of defensive behavior. The particular pattern that ensues depends on precisely which points and connections are involved. Permutations include excess or deficit in the acquisition, expression, or extinction of passive or active avoidance or classical conditioning; conflict; condi-

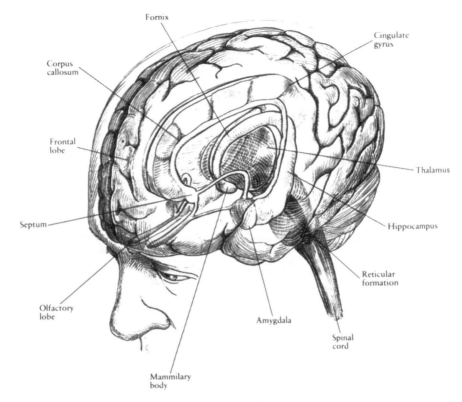

Fig. 7.3 Central pathways known to be involved in defensive reactions. (From Blum 1985. Copyright © 1985 by W. H. Freeman, S. F. Reprinted by permission).

tioned suppression; freezing or tonic immobility; autonomic concomitants of fear, such as changes in heart rate or hair bristling; and the subjective experience of fear. In the literature many of these have been employed as measures of fear or anxiety.

Deep Structures: Humans

That emotional expression involves deep brain structures was noted in nine patients who had post-encephalitic hyperkinesia (Smirnov 1966). Three hundred electrodes were inserted for therapeutic reasons into different parts of the cortex and deep brain. Different areas were then electrically stimulated or coagulated. This yielded emotional reactions in less than 10% of the regions studied, none in the cortex. Regions yielding emotion were the ventrolateral and ventroposterior thalamic nuclei, the subthalamic region, hippocampus, amygdala, and tegmentum. Stimulation of these areas made patients feel sudden emotion unconnected with their current thoughts or environment, yet the emotion was not felt as alien. The subjective emotion was accompanied by corresponding motor and autonomic changes.

In a handful of human cases, stimulation of deep structures has lead to fear (Delgado 1969). Medial thalamic stimulation gave a feeling "rather like having

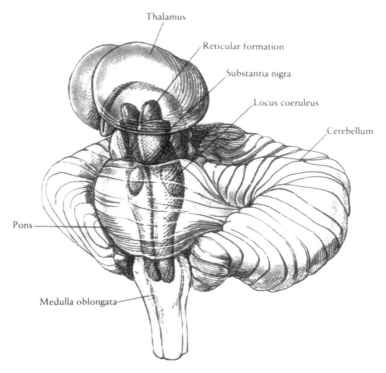

Fig. 7.4   Central pathways known to be involved in defensive reactions. (From Blum 1985. Copyright © 1985 by W. H. Freeman, S. F. Reprinted by permission).

just been missed by a car and leaped back to the curb and went B-rr" and a very unpleasant sensation in the guts. Stimulation of the dorsolateral thalamic nucleus evoked the same anxiety usually felt by another female patient who had periodic severe anxiety, suicidal tendencies, and depression. In yet another case, stimulation of that nucleus made the patient appear fearful and look around, saying that she felt threatened and something horrible would happen; the response was stereotyped on different days, began with a delay of less than a second, lasted only as long as the stimulation, and was remembered without upset. Pallidal stimulation evoked anxiety and restlessness in some patients, with anxious screaming if the stimulation was repeated. Amygdaloid stimulation also led to fear, and temporal lobe stimulation to the "illusion of fear."

Deep Structures: Animals

Impressive work links the cerebellum and brain stem to the learning of classically conditioned defensive reflexes such as closure of rabbits' nictitating membrane (NM) and eyelid to a tone CS with a corneal airpuff US (Thompson 1983). This requires at least two components: (1) a conditioned-fear circuit involving an opiate-sensitive system that is partly in the brain stem, and (2) a learned, discrete, adaptive response circuit including the medial dentate and lateral interposital nuclei of the cerebellum linked to the pons through the superior cerebellar peduncle.

Systemic morphine abolishes a just-learned NM/eyelid conditioned response (CR) but has no effect on the UR. Abolition is obtainable solely by applying opiates to the rostral region of the fourth ventricle and by affecting the *mu* receptor. Opiates also abolish classically conditioned heart-rate slowing to periorbital shock in the rabbit. Overtraining protects against opiate abolition; perhaps the cerebellar circuit becomes more autonomous when the motor response is well learned, with conditioned fear then becoming less critical.

The standard NM/eyelid CR can be learned without any brain tissue above the thalamus, although the hippocampus is required when the task calls for more memory. The CR is preceded by a neuronal template appearing in part of the ipsilateral medial dentate/lateral interpositus nuclei of the cerebellum. This precession is up to 50 milliseconds, consistent with the minimum onset latency of 80 milliseconds for CRs in well-trained rabbits and with the short CS-US onset interval needed to learn the CR (less than 70 milliseconds between the corneal airpuff US and the tone CS). The lateral ipsilateral cerebellum is also essential for classical conditioning of the hindlimb-flexion reflex in rabbits, and in dogs ablating the cerebellum abolishes well-trained leg-flexion conditioning. Although in rabbits bilateral lesions of the dentate/interpositral nuclei abolish the NM/eyelid CR, they leave intact conditioned heart-rate slowing to periorbital shock (a CR which partly depends on circuits in the amygdala and hypothalamus).

We saw that aminergic transmitters are involved in defensive sensitization and conditioning in invertebrates. In primates some aspects of fear are mediated by the noradrenergic locus coeruleus (LC)—a tiny blue (cerulear) streak in the dorsolateral tegmentum of the pons comprising only about 400 neurons—and associated alpha$_2$-adrenergic receptors (Ballenger et al. 1984; Insel et al. 1984; Redmond 1983; Redmond & Huang 1979, 1982). In monkeys mild stimulation of the LC alerts them with wide-open eyes and increased body movements. As intensity of stimulation increases they chew, move their tongues, grind their teeth, grasp the chair, scratch, self-mouth, yawn, pull their hair, wring their hands, struggle to escape, and jerk their bodies. Such fearful behavior is also seen when they are threatened by humans or are given the alpha$_2$-adrenergic blockers piperoxane or yohimbine, which activate the LC and raise plasma levels of the noradrenergic metabolite 3-methoxy 4-hydroxy phenylethylene glycol (MHPG). The fear is reduced by bilateral lesions of the LC and by the alpha$_2$-adrenergic drug clonidine and other drugs such as diazepam, morphine, and propranolol, which reduce both LC activity in animals and human anxiety. However, the anxiolytic buspirone increases LC firing.

Some work in humans is relevant. Yohimbine makes some psychiatric patients and normal volunteers tense (Charney et al. 1983), but it is not a good model of anxiety (Henauer et al. 1984). It raises pulse rate, systolic blood pressure, and MHPG. Pretreatment of normals with clonidine or diazepam blocked the tension, but diazepam did not block the rise in MHPG, blood pressure, and autonomic symptoms. When given alone, only clonidine, not diazepam, reduced MHPG and blood pressure. Diazepam was thus anxiolytic without decreasing noradrenergic turnover, which is consistent with the low density of benzodiazepine receptors in the LC (Insel et al. 1984).

The locus ceruleus is thought to be part of an "alarm system" (Redmond 1977). It gives rise to the dorsal ascending noradrenergic bundle, which innervates much of the forebrain, including the septal area and hippocampus. When this bundle is destroyed, animals learn to perform a rewarded response normally but are slow to stop it when the reward is withdrawn (Gray 1979).

Several deep structures and substructures coordinate to mediate different forms of defensive-aggressive behavior. Some areas are excitatory and others inhibitory, with reciprocal connections between them (Fonberg 1966). Stimulation of different hypothalamic points led to flight, defense, attack, and eating (Hess 1954, cited by Ewert 1980). It induced fear at certain points and at others fear and rage, with accompanying hair bristling, pupillary dilation, sweating, and raised blood pressure (Figure 7.5). In the posterior hypothalamus, stimulation elicits sympathetic reactions, raised somatic tone, cortical desynchronization, behavior arousal, and, if continued, flight or fight, whereas anterior hypothalamic stimulation produces opposite effects (Mayes 1979). Perhaps the hypothalamus changes the probability that specific patterns such as fear will occur; that is, it may affect motivation (Jurgens 1974).

The sensitivity of reciprocally innervated structures determines the intensity of reactions ensuing from their stimulation (Mayes 1979). Increased muscle activity like that in fear increases posterior and decreases anterior hypothalamic sensitivity. The limbic system, too, may alter such sensitivity, and hippocampal lesions lead to perseveration of passive avoidance.

The dependence of different aspects of fear reactions on different brain areas was seen with flight and defense in dogs (Fonberg 1966). Flight and avoidance conditioned rapidly when a sound was paired with stimulation of

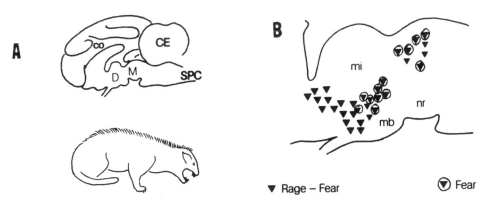

▼ Rage – Fear   ⊙ Fear

Fig. 7.5   Points in the cat hypothalamus at which stimulation by a chronically implanted electrode elicited rage-fear and fear: (A) sagittal section; (B) enlarged section. CO, cerebral cortex; D, diencephalon; M, mesencephalon; CE, cerebellum; SPC, spinal cord; mb, mamillary body; mi, massa intermedia thalami; nr, red nucleus (From Alcock; redrawn from Hess, W. R. (1954), Das Zwischenhirn, 2. Aufl. Schwabe, Basel. Copyright © 1980 by Sinauer Associates. Reprinted with permission.)

brain points associated with flight but only slowly when the sound was paired with stimulation of areas associated with defense, although with the latter, rapid classical conditioning still occurred. Similarly, in the goldfish conditioned avoidance but not conditioned escape was extinguished by removing the forebrain, which contains precursors of the mammalian limbic system (Snowdon et al. 1966). In rats the cortex was needed for complex motor but not emotional and cue aspects of response to an aversive situation (Carlson 1966), whereas septal lesions impaired learning of two-way but not of free-choice avoidance (Dalby 1970).

Lesions of the mammillothalamic tract speeded the extinction of conditioned avoidance in cats and rats (Krieckhaus 1966), and, in rats and hamsters, had more effect when it had been learned with high rather than low emotional arousal (Bunnell 1966). Lesions in the pallidus, adjacent internal capsule, and mesencephalic gray lead to taming of wild Norwegian rats (Blanchard 1981, 1981a).

In the amygdala, stimulation of its dorsomedial part evokes fear and flight, which motivate avoidance learning, whereas stimulation of its basolateral part inhibits fear and other behaviors such as attack, feeding, and conditioned alimentary reactions (Isaacson 1974). Raising the intensity of amygdaloid stimulation changes the response from attention to fear and finally to rage (Gloor 1960). This corresponds somewhat to the way an increasingly arousing stimulus leads to an orienting and then defensive response. Similar effects are produced more rapidly by stimulating the ventromedial hypothalamus and the central gray of the midbrain, and these seem to be the downstream path for such effects from the amygdala (Mayes 1979). The amygdala and hippocampus have high densities of benzodiazepine (bz) receptors, and injection of bzs into discrete amygdaloid nuclei reduces conflict (Insel et al. 1984). In humans fear is the most common emotion during stimulation of the amygdala or overlying temporal cortex and also in temporal lobe epilepsy (see Chapter 12).

Repeated subconvulsive electrical stimulation of the amygdala in dogs leads to a form of sensitization called kindling, which brings to mind the step-wise onset of many panics, phobias, and obsessive-compulsive rituals. Over days and weeks as each amygdaloid stimulation is repeated, mild motor automatisms appear which gradually evolve into complete epileptic fits (Goddard et al. 1969). The motor after-discharge threshold progressively decreases to the point at which previously subthreshold levels now reliably elicit an after-discharge. Kindling is fairly specific to the brain region being stimulated and does not reflect a general increase in brain reactivity, although there is some inter-facilitation between kindling in the amygdala and in the septum. The development of kindling requires a spacing of at least several hours between each stimulation—about 24 hours is optimal—and massing the periods of stimulation together prevents it. We are reminded here that phobias and rituals are extinguished more quickly by prolonged than intermittent exposure therapy (chapters 8 and 14).

Repeated daily subconvulsive doses of lidocaine also cause kindling of limbic seizures and increased apomorphine-induced stereotyped chewing in the rat (Csernansky et al. 1985). Dopamine D2 receptor density rose in the amyg-dala and nucleus accumbens of kindled rats but not in nonkindled rats that also had lidocaine.

Destruction of the amygdala markedly "pacifies" humans and reduces their feelings of fear (Mark & Ervin 1970), and in animals impairs the acquisition of taste aversion, active and passive avoidance, and conditioned suppression (Mayes 1979). These impairments may result from insufficient fear developing. Rats with small basolateral amygdala lesions are slower than normals in learn-ing active avoidance and have lower plasma corticosterone during their first avoidance sessions but not beforehand (Ursin et al. 1975).

The amygdala may act as a comparator mediating the association of stimuli with threat (Mayes 1979). Innately frightening stimuli may be processed with-out it, perhaps in the hypothalamus, but whether unlearned fear remains after amygdalectomy is not yet known. Learning of active and passive avoidance is affected by different parts of the amygdala. The amygdala is the hub of a net-work linked to the rest of the limbic system and to many other parts of the brain. It is strongly connected with the septum and hippocampus, which them-selves interlink and connect with the orbital frontal cortex.

The septum and hippocampus may inhibit the activation of fear behavior by the amygdala and seem critical for habituation to orienting and frightening stimuli, although whether they mediate subjective fear is not known (Mayes 1979). Hippocampal theta activity is reduced when normal animals orient and avoid, and returns after they habituate; it is nearly absent in pointer dogs selected for emotionality, including freezing (Fuller & Thompson 1978). The reduction of conflict and of learned helplessness by diazepam is related to its action on the hippocampus (Campbell et al. 1980).

Gray (1982, 1982a) suggested that anxiety consists of overactivity in a behavioral inhibition system, which includes the septum and hippocampus; the Papez circuit running from the subicular area in the hippocampus to the mammillary bodies, anterior thalamus, cingulate cortex, and back to the subic-ular area; the inputs to the septo-hippocampal system from the entorhinal area and prefrontal cortex and from ascending noraminergic, serotonergic, and cho-linergic pathways; and the noradrenergic inflow into the hypothalamus and perhaps down to the locus ceruleus providing autonomic outflow. This system is said to be activated by novel, punishing, or nonrewarding stimuli, and is muted by anti-anxiety drugs. It is thought to compare predicted to actual sen-sory events and to be activated when there is a mismatch or when the predicted event is aversive. The septo-hippocampal system, in particular, has been called "an organ of hesitation and doubt" (Simonov, cited by Gray 1979).

Hippocampal memory traces seem important for more complex forms of defensive learning such as latent inhibition, discrimination reversal, and trace conditioning (Thompson 1983). In rabbits the NM/eyelid CR is predicted by a neuronal template in pyramidal neurons of the CA3-CA1 region of the dorsal hippocampus, even though rabbits can learn a simpler CR without a hippo-campus. Perhaps simple classical conditioning is a form of "procedural" mem-ory (learning how) that can function purely with lower structures, including the cerebellum as noted earlier, while more taxing tasks that require "declarative" memory (learning what) may call on the hippocampus. Humans with diencephalic or hippocampal/temporal lesions can perform tasks such as mirror reading (procedural) yet report verbally no memory of having done so (declarative). The hippocampus may become engaged in all forms of defensive learning even if it is essential only for those forms which require complex memory.

The cingulate gyrus in cats appears more important for the acquisition of new avoidance and defensive behavior than for the performance of such responses after they have been well learned (Ursin 1969). It may inhibit physiological reactions to fear once avoidance has occurred (whereas habenular lesions, which disrupt septal projections, impair one-way avoidance) (Mayes 1979). Lesions of the cingulum in rats do not impair avoidance learning but rather prevent the normal decrease in fear (Coover et al. 1974) and in plasma corticosterone (Ursin et al. 1975), which occurs when an avoidance response is overtrained.

Neocortex

Although deep structures seem more concerned with emotion, the neocortex has some role. Frontal (orbitomedial) leucotomy reduces anxiety, agoraphobia, and obsessive-compulsive problems (Marks et al. 1966; Tan et al. 1971; Chapter 16). This could act by interrupting pathways going directly from the frontal lobe to the amygdala and dorsomedial nucleus of the thalamus rather than to the septum and hippocampus. (Dorsomedial thalamic lesions in humans also reduce anxiety [Orchinik et al. 1950, cited by Mayes 1979].)

Evidence about the laterality of cortical involvement is conflicting (Leventhal & Tomarken 1985). Some work suggests that the right side is more involved with unpleasant emotions such as fear and the left one with pleasant affects (Fox & Davidson 1986, 1986a; Mayes 1979). When humans saw neutral, amusing, or unpleasant films while wearing contact lenses directing input to only one or the other hemisphere, heart rate increased most to unpleasant films with input directed to the right side, and to pleasant films with input directed to the left side (Dimond & Farrington 1977). Left-sided damage is more associated with anxiety, crying, hostility, and boasting, whereas right-sided lesions are more often accompanied by apathy, underplaying, and anosognosia. In contrast, however, patients with left temporal epilepsy had more trait anxiety and dysphoria (Perini & Mendius 1984), and normals showed greater left parietal EEG activity during affective arousal (Ketterer 1982) and located emotional imagery in their left hemispace (Koff et al. 1983).

A clear cortical connection with fear is in the anterior temporal lobe, which contains part of the amygdala and links with other parts of the limbic system. Clinical observations that the experience of fear during epilepsy is associated with anterior temporal lobe disturbances on either side (see Chapter 9) accord with findings reviewed earlier that amygdaloid stimulation in animals commonly produces fear. Epileptic fear may involve experiential, cognitive, and/or autonomic components indicating the separate ingredients that make up fear. Temporal lobe seizures may also start with stereotyped repetitive behaviors, and there may be marked obsessive-compulsive features interictally (Bear & Fedio 1977). Obsessive-compulsive phenomena have also been described with temporal lobe tumors, post-encephalitic parkinsonism involving deep structures, and left frontal lobe dysfunction (see Chapter 13).

Neurotransmitter Systems

Neuroanatomical structures induce fear by synaptic transmission. This involves multiple chemical signals, some of which stimulate presynaptic and others postsynaptic neurons. At least 30 different neurotransmitter substances are known so far, produced in systems that link various parts of the brain. More than one neurotransmitter may be produced by the same neuron. A few of these neurotransmitter systems relate to facets of fear and anxiety, and some of these—aminergic and serotonergic—are implicated in defensive learning in invertebrates.

Noradrenergic (NA) System

Less than 1% of receptors in the brain are noradrenergic. They seem to mediate some forms of anxiety (Hoehn-Saric 1982). Part of the noradrenergic system was referred to earlier—the locus ceruleus (LC) and the dorsal ascending noradrenergic bundle, activation of which produces some fear behaviors. The tiny LC contains nearly half the noradrenergic neurons and produces over 70% of the total noradrenalin found in the brain. It innervates the cerebral and cerebellar cortices, limbic system, brain stem, and spinal cord, and has wide afferent connections. These links make the LC a likely center for mediating "alarm reactions."

Links between noradrenalin and anxiety were reviewed by Ballenger et al. (1984). In animals, turnover of central noradrenalin rises after shock or exposure to strangers or cold and occurs at different rates in different regions; urinary adrenalin and noradrenalin also rise after stress. In humans, peripheral noradrenalin was raised in chronically anxious patients, dental phobics, and normals in frightening situations—pilots in a tight spot, parachutists, and students during exams. In depressed people, anxiety was related to raised plasma noradrenalin and adrenalin, cerebrospinal fluid (CSF) noradrenalin, and urinary MHPG.

Several anxiolytic effects of drugs are reflected in reduced noradrenergic activity (Ko et al. 1983). Clonidine binds preferentially to alpha-adrenergic receptors and modulates how much noradrenalin nerve impulses release at central and peripheral noradrenergic terminals; in animals it also inhibits the spontaneous firing of noradrenergic neurons in the LC, reduces noradrenergic turnover in the brain, and decreases MHPG in the brain and plasma. Although clonidine inhibits anxiety in anxiety disorders and opiate withdrawal, tolerance to it quickly develops, so the drug is not of great clinical value.

Suppression of central noradrenergic neurons is seen with benzodiazepines (bzs) and monoamine oxidase inhibitor (MAOI) and tricyclic antidepressants that may also reduce phobic anxiety (Ko et al. 1983). Bzs interact with GABA receptors on noradrenergic and other neurons, whereas the tricyclics act on different receptors. However, even though LC activity decreases with antidepressants, their anxiolytic and antidepressant effects usually take weeks to develop and are not explained by such short-term changes.

The noradrenergic metabolite MHPG reflects noradrenergic activity in the brain (Elsworth et al. 1982) and peripherally. MHPG increased from baseline shortly after six agoraphobics were exposed to their phobic situations, and correlated highly ($r = .76$) with anxiety both at rest and during physical activity (Ko et al. 1983). After clonidine or imipramine was given, MHPG diminished if phobic anxiety fell but not if it continued. In contrast, however, neuroticism in normals related to lower plasma MHPG (Ballenger et al. 1983).

Although coffee and tea consumption is not correlated with anxiety in most people (Eaton & McLeod 1984), caffeine makes agoraphobics and normals tense and intensifies stress-induced effects in animals (Boulenger et al. 1984; Charney et al. 1984, Rapoport et al. 1984; Uhde et al. 1984; see also Chapter 10). Acute doses of caffeine can stimulate central noradrenalin secretion and sensitize central catecholaminergic receptors, while other methyl-xanthines raise unit activity in the LC. In addition, caffeine affects adenosine function and competes for binding at bz receptors.

Serotonergic (5-HT—5 Hydroxytryptamine) System and Tonic Immobility

Serotonin levels vary with various kinds of stress, but findings are inconsistent (Ballenger et al 1984; Hoehn-Saric 1982.) Serotonergic neurons are located in the raphe nuclei and the brainstem reticular system. The more caudal ones send descending pathways to the spinal cord, and the more rostral ones project to three major ascending pathways reaching the hypothalamus, the preoptic and septal areas, hippocampus and all cortical areas, and the corpus striatum.

Tonic immobility in chickens is linked to serotonin and its precursor tryptophan (Gallup et al. 1977). The reaction was abolished after 10 days on a low tryptophan diet of corn (maize) and returned within a week of restoring normal diet. In birds and mammals, tonic immobility is altered by serotonin-reduced activity in the midbrain raphe nuclei and their postsynaptic serotonergic receptors (Wallnau & Gallup 1977), and is abolished by brain transection at that level.

Tonic immobility is prolonged by the following:

1. Injections of tryptophan.
2. Monoamine oxidase inhibitors such as pargyline and iproniazid, which prevent breakdown of serotonin in the synaptic cleft and so allow its accumulation.
3. LSD-25, which may compete with serotonin for postsynaptic receptor sites and reduce activity of serotonergic neurons.
4. Intraventricular injections of serotonin.

5. Intraventricular injections of imipramine, which blocks serotonin uptake in the presynaptic neuron (peripheral injections of imipramine and serotonin reduce immobility).
6. Morphia.
7. Electric shock, which has morphinelike effects (Wallnau & Gallup 1978). The morphinelike effect is not blocked by naloxone, but it is by parachlorophenyl-alanine (PCPA), which depletes brain serotonin by preventing the hydroxylation of tryptophan into serotonin. However, PCPA also blocks d-amphetamine-induced reduction of immobility.

Tonic immobility is not a simple function of raised serotonergic activity alone (Gallup & Maser 1977). PCPA blocks d-amphetamine-induced reduction of immobility, and d-amphetamine increases electrical activity of raphe nuclei. Moreover, electrical activity of the raphe nuclei is suppressed by many of those compounds which prolong tonic immobility.

Bird-mammal reversals further complicate the picture; drugs that produce a serotonergic behavioral syndrome in rats reduce the duration of tonic immobility in chickens (Boren et al. 1981). Perhaps immobility is prolonged by action on presynaptic "autoreceptors," which would decrease serotonergic stimulation of postsynaptic neurons in other areas. However, increased postsynaptic receptor stimulation is found with drugs that on the one hand produce the serotonergic behavioral syndrome and on the other shorten tonic immobility.

Some unifying ideas are possible (J. Csernansky, personal communication), 1982). Serotonin can be both an inhibitory and an excitatory neurotransmitter. Inhibitory effects could be mediated via serotonin-1 sites (perhaps adenylate cyclase-linked), and excitatory influences might act through serotonin-2 sites. LSD-25 is an antagonist at serotonin-2 sites but an agonist at serotonin-1 sites. The prolongation of tonic immobility by both LSD-25 and by serotonin might be mediated by inhibitory, serotonin-1 type synapses. Such synapses inhibit firing in the raphe nuclei, suppression of which is linked to tonic immobility.

Benzodiazepine Receptors and the Gamma-Aminobutyric Acid (GABA) System

Antianxiety drugs such as benzodiazepines (bzs) may act via particular subtypes of stereospecific bz receptor, which in turn affect GABA-ergic transmission (Costa 1985; Insel et al. 1984). Bz receptors are more widespread than noradrenergic or serotonergic ones. They are found all over the central nervous system and not especially in areas relaying emotion, even though the limbic system is very sensitive to bzs (Hoehn-Saric 1982). Bz receptors are most dense in the cerebral cortex, cerebellum, and amygdala, and less so in the hippocampus, striatum, and spinal cord.

Evidence that bz receptors mediate the anxiolytic actions of bzs includes (1) a high correlation between in vitro affinity for bz receptors and (a) clinical potency as an anxiolytic and (b) anticonvulsant and anticonflict effects in mice, (2) altered bz binding of "anxious" rats; and (3) lower density of bz receptors in the brain and spinal cord of Maudsley reactive than nonreactive strains of rats (Gray 1979). However, the reactive rats are not only more fearful but also less susceptible to seizures than are nonreactive rats. Low density of bz receptors is thus associated as much with liability to fits as to fear.

In addition to being anxiolytic, bzs are also sedative, anticonvulsant, and muscle relaxant. Less sedating but still anxiolytic and anticonvulsant are the non-bz triazolopyridazines; they, too, bind to bz receptors, but mainly to a type 1 variety (several kinds of bz receptor are coming to light). Some pyrazolopyridines are also anxiolytic and less sedating, and modulate bz binding.

Compounds that bind to a receptor are ligands. No endogenous bz ligand has yet been found, though several substances have been suggested for this role, including the purines inosine and hypoxanthine, nicotinamide, beta-carbolines, and an unknown peptide factor (Paul et al. 1982). Three types of exogenous bz ligands are recognized. *Agonists* facilitate its actions and are anxiolytic, such as bz drugs. *Antagonists* block the receptor and thus the action of an agonist but have no intrinsic activity of their own (for instance, the imidazo-diazepine RO-15-1788). *Active antagonists* block the receptor but are also anxiogenic, such as beta-carboline-3-carboxylic acid ethyl ester (BCCE). (They are also called inverse agonists because they evoke anxiety yet decrease GABAergic transmission.) The bz receptor may thus mediate not only the reduction but also the genesis of anxiety.

BCCE causes agitation when injected into chair-adapted male rhesus monkeys (Crawley et al. 1985; Insel et al. 1984; Skolnick et al, 1984). Injected animals display distress calls, increased head and body turning, immobility for more than 5 seconds, defecation and urination, and raised plasma cortisol, adrenalin and noradrenalin, heart rate, and blood pressure. The behavioral effects of BCCE occur even at rest with high doses but at low doses are seen mainly with the mild "challenge" of the investigator approaching. BCCE effects are blocked by prior administration of the bz agonist diazepam or antagonist RO 15-1788, or the GABA agonist THIP. They are only partly attenuated by clonidine (an alpha$_2$-adrenergic agonist) or by propanolol (a beta-adrenergic blocker). Although some BCCE anxiogenesis resembles that of locus ceruleus stimulation, which is noradrenergic, BCCE does not increase MHPG, the major central noradrenalin metabolite. Rises in heart rate, blood pressure, and plasma catecholamine after BCCE were not prevented by the serotonergic antagonist cyproheptadine, although it did inhibit most of the behavioral effects of BCCE as well as the rise in cortisol and ACTH. The complete syndrome evoked by BCCE may thus depend upon the activity of several neurotransmitter systems.

Although humans have not yet taken BCCE, a closely related bz active antagonist, FG-7142 (beta-carboline monomethylamide), has been given to two healthy volunteers (cited by Insel et al. 1984). Both subjects developed intense "motor unrest and a strong feeling of inner tension . . . of impending doom"; in one case this was so intense that lormetazepam was given, which improved the discomfort in minutes. FG-7142 has also been given to two monkeys, causing effects similar to those of BCCE—head and body turning, hyperresponsiveness to approach, and robust increase in plasma cortisol.

GABA-RECEPTOR, BENZODIAZEPINE BINDING SITE, ANION CHANNEL COMPLEX

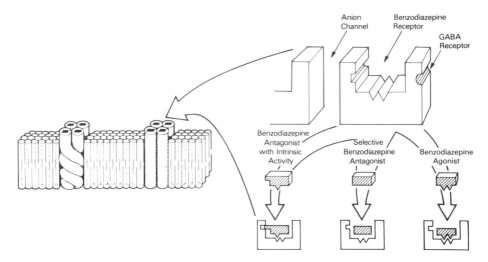

Fig. 7.6 Model for the GABA-receptor benzodiazepine binding site, anion channel complex. (From Insel et al. 1984. Reprinted by permission of Dr. T. Insel.)

BZ anxiolysis may be mediated in parts of the limbic system (Insel et al. 1984). The hippocampus and amygdala have high densities of bz receptors; bz injection into discrete nuclei of the amygdala reduces conflict; and stimulation of part of the amygdala is anxiogenic. Insel and associates speculate that bz receptors concern fear or conflict and that noradrenergic receptors are involved with alarm or panic.

The bz receptor is thought to consist of four proteins and to include several binding sites for agonist, antagonist, and active antagonist (Figure 7.6) (Hoehn-Saric 1982, Insel et al. 1984). This receptor is in turn part of a larger complex, being functionally (and perhaps structurally) coupled to both a receptor protein for gamma-amino-butyric acid (GABA) and a chloride (Cl) channel. Bzs enhance the action of GABA, whereas GABA raises affinity for the bz receptor of ^{3}H-diazepam, barbiturates, and permeable anions such as Cl. Binding to the bz receptor in the presence of GABA may increase permeability to Cl and thus to a cascade of intracellular events resulting either in membrane hyperpolarization or in reduced release of neurotransmitter with depolarization.

GABA is an inhibitory transmitter that is widespread in the nervous system. It decreases neuronal activity by opening Cl channels directly linked to GABA receptors, thereby causing an influx of Cl into the neuron, hyperpolarizing it on postsynaptic sites and making it less responsive to other stimuli; at presynaptic sites GABA reduces incoming signals by afferent depolarization. GABA may prevent neurones that are usually paroxysmally active from so responding to normal or excessive stimulation (Haefely 1985). Most GABA-ergic neurons are interneurons, exerting presynaptic effects near their cell bodies and postsynaptic inhibition more distantly. Their terminals innervate the locus ceruleus and the raphe nuclei but are not dense in the brainstem. Although the rise and fall in GABA-ergic function can reduce and augment anxiety, respectively (Costa 1985), some drugs that promote GABA activity, such as picrotoxin and amino-oxyacetic acid, do not reduce anxiety (Gray 1979).

Neuropeptides Including Endogenous Opioid Peptides

Neuropeptides affect many behaviors, including avoidance (de Wied 1983; Krieger & Martin 1982). Some neuropeptides have overlapping behavioral profiles yet retain certain specificity. They are also present outside the nervous system, where they have other effects.

One group of workers found that vasopressin enhances acquisition and retards extinction of avoidance, whereas oxytocin has the reverse effect (de Wied 1983; Gispen et al. 1976). Others had difficulty replicating this (Gash & Thomas 1983). The effects of such peptides might be mediated less by direct action on the brain than by indirect autonomic effects.

Opiates can suppress the acquisition of conditioned fear and defensive reflexes, an example of which we saw earlier with the NM/eyelid reflex (Thompson 1983). Conversely, fear and anxiety can inhibit pain in animals and humans, presumably through opiate activity (Bolles & Fanselow 1980; Malow 1981; Ward et al. 1983). In monkeys the noradrenergic locus coeruleus system is inhibited by endogenous opioids and by opiates, and this may account for the anxiety seen during opiate withdrawal (Redmond & Huang 1982).

Stress leads to simultaneous release into the circulation of both ACTH and beta-endorphin, and pituitary cells contain both peptides, which share the common precursor pro-opiocortin (Miller 1983). Plasma levels of beta endorphin (ir) and ACTH are closely related (Lim & Funder 1983). Alpha-endorphin speeds the acquisition of avoidance and delays extinction, whereas gamma-endorphin quickens extinction, and des-tyrosine gamma-endorphin is even more active. As the latter does not bind opiate receptors, the behavioral effect may be dissociated from them.

Stress changes opioid levels in the brain (McGivern et al. 1983). Single shock sessions reduced enkephalin in the hypothalamus and striatum. Twenty-one days of shock (6 hours on/6 hours off) in rats reduced MET and LEU enkephalin in the brain but not adrenals, markedly decreased pain threshold, and enhanced the analgesic effect of morphine; although core body temperature was raised, the hyperthermic response to morphine was unchanged. Conditioned fear reduces binding of ^{3}H-N-LEU enkephalin in rat brains. There appear to be enkephalin-sensitive receptors in the hypothalamus that regulate ACTH, and, in turn, steroids seem to regulate brain opioids. Enkephalins may modulate the negative feedback loop of the pituitary adrenal axis during stress.

Endorphins may mediate learned helplessness—the phenomenon of exposure to inescapable shock in one situation retarding learning to escape from shock in a new one 24 hours later (Whitehouse et al. 1983). Helplessness does not occur in animals that have previously had either no shock or only escapable shocks. Forcing a helpless animal to carry out the escape routine, thus exposing it to the experience of escape switching off the shock, leads to normal escape learning; that is, it abolishes the helplessness. Such abolition is prevented if the opiate antagonists naloxone or naltrexone are injected 15 minutes prior to the shock-escape sequence, though they impair escape learning in other rats that were pretrained with escapable shocks or had no previous experience of shocks (Whitehouse et al. 1983). Inescapable or repeated shocks appear to induce a short-term rise in endogenous opioids, as the pain threshold rises after such shocks but not after escapable shock or simple restraint. This analgesia is reversed if the opiate antagonist naltrexone is injected before the shocks are given.

Repeated swimming stress seems to produce endogenous opioids in mice, as they developed a tolerance of having their tail immersed in hot water similar to that induced by morphine (Christie et al. 1982). Both in intact and adrenalectomized rats, such stress was followed by changed beta-endorphin (ir-immunoreactive) levels (Lim & Funder 1983). In intact rats, levels rose fourfold in plasma, diminished in the anterior and neurointermediate lobes of the pituitary, and were unchanged in the hypothalamus; adrenalectomized rats showed similar but even more marked changes. Levels were unchanged by morphine, but naloxone prevented the lowering of neurointermediate lobe levels otherwise found following the swimming stress. Both acute and chronic dexamethasone, but not deoxycorticosterone, attenuated the stress-induced changes in plasma and anterior pituitary, and none of these compounds affected levels in the neurointermediate lobe. The post-stress changes in plasma and anterior pituitary levels thus seem to be sensitive to glucocorticoids but not to involve pathways including opiate receptors; in contrast, neurointermediate lobe changes are steroid independent and involve endogenous opioids.

Severely anxious patients often have respiratory symptoms that might be related to stress-induced activation or release of endogenous opioids and ensuing feedback mechanisms. In animals, endorphins appear to inhibit central respiration by desensitizing the central chemoreceptors to CO_2 and directly inhibiting respiratory neurons (Isom & Elshowihy 1982). Inescapable foot shock over 30 minutes in rats increased respiratory ventilation (which was potentiated by naloxone or the inhalation of carbon dioxide) and to analgesia. These effects were reduced if the foot shock was continued daily for 11 days, suggesting that levels of endogenous opioids vary with duration of stress and that tolerance developed to their respiratory effects after they were repeatedly released following each stress session. Naloxone-induced stimulation of respiration increased as the CO_2 concentration was raised.

The release of endogenous opiates in healthy human volunteers during a cold pressor test (putting a foot into ice water as long as they could stand it) was suggested by their enhanced tolerance of subsequent electric shock, which was reversed by injection of naloxone but not of placebo (Jungkunz et al. 1983). Performing mental arithmetic, which raises noradrenalin and heart rate, had no effect.

Other relationships of opiates to anxiety and stress were noted by Post et al. (1984). Cerebrospinal fluid (CSF) opiate binding was higher in normals who were less anxious at the time of lumbar puncture and in less neurotic females. After surgery, plasma beta-endorphin rose; the highest levels of that compound and of CSF opiate binding was in patients needing the least analgesic drug. High anxiety and urinary cortisol both correlated with raised CSF opioid binding (though not ir beta-endorphin) in depressed patients but not in normals. In a snake phobic, live exposure therapy led to an initial rise in plasma beta-beta-endorphin that fell within 30 minutes as anxiety diminished (Thyer & Matthews 1985).

Opiates may partly mediate chronic obsessive doubts. Such doubts increased in two patients after double-blind injection of naloxone but not of placebo (Insel & Pickar 1983). Replication is needed—others found little effect of naloxone on anxiety in normals and in anxious patients (Ballenger et al. 1984).

We saw earlier that in rats naloxone partly prevents acute stress from raising central opioid peptides and reducing pain sensitivity. Both these responses habituate with repeated exposure to stress (Akil et al. 1976). Perhaps neuropeptides partly mediate the improvement of phobics and ritualizers during exposure treatment (during which they habituate to continuing contact with phobia- and ritual-evoking stimuli). Neuropeptides may also explain why during the stress of athletic activity or of combat, athletes or soldiers may not notice injuries yet later will require large doses of analgesics, and how some blood phobics and epileptics briefly defer their faint or fit until it is less dangerous to fall down. In addition, opiates could underly the Kamin effect in rats, whereby conditioned avoidance is weaker just after shocks have ceased at the end of the acquisition phase than it is a few hours later (see Chapter 8).

Interaction of Central and Peripheral Mechanisms

Long ago James and Lange suggested that emotion was the perception of its peripheral concomitants, while others maintained that affect was purely central in origin. Cannon's (1929) lucid critique of a purely bodily view of emotion still holds. First, artificially inducing visceral changes typical of strong emotions does not produce them. Injecting adrenalin rarely produces emotions experienced as genuine; people so injected may label the resultant mild feeling to fit prevailing circumstances (Schachter & Singer 1962), but this effect is not large and many workers could not replicate it (Leventhal & Tomarken 1985). Moreover, although catecholamine-secreting phaeochromocytomas are classically cited in textbooks as a cause of anxiety, none of 17 patients with a secreting tumor of this kind had panic or agoraphobia, and only 2 met criteria for generalized anxiety disorder and 2 for major depression; the tumors secreted noradrenalin in 6 of the cases and adrenalin plus noradrenalin in the remaining 11 (Starkman et al. 1985).

Second, we cannot as yet match our many nuances of emotional feeling with correspondingly different patterns of bodily change, although we might eventually get a better fit as our methods improve. There are some differences between fear and anger (for instance, we flush when angry but go white when frightened), and other differences have been noted experimentally (Ax 1953; Schacter 1957); but at the moment there are more impressive similarities than differences in the peripheral changes occurring in contrasting emotional states.

A third objection by Cannon (1929) was that emotions may occur without any visceral activity, as in sympathectomized animals and people and after lesions of the cervical spinal cord. Experimental work suggests that the peripheral components of fear enhance but are not essential for the acquisition of fear and are not necessary for its expression. Sympathectomized dogs acquired an avoidance response far more slowly than control dogs and were quick to extinguish it; however, two of the dogs which were deprived of visceral innervation only after acquisition failed, like normal dogs, to extinguish avoidance quickly (Wynne & Solomon 1955). We might still nevertheless ask, "Did they *feel* frightened as well as avoid?"

This problem was studied in 25 paraplegics and tetraplegics (Hohmann 1962, cited by Schachter 1964). They were divided into five groups according to the level of their spinal cord lesion. The groups fell along a continuum of visceral innervation and sensation from minimal impairment at the sacral level to maximal disruption in the neck. If visceral activity was important for the experience of emotion, then the higher the lesion, the less the emotion that the subjects should feel. Each subject was asked how he felt in situations of fear, anger, grief, sexual excitement, and sentimentality; to recall an emotional incident prior to his injury and a comparable event following it; and to compare the intensity of his emotional experiences before and after injury.

The comparison on fear and anger is seen in Figure 7.7 (Hohmann's data, plotted by Schachter 1964). Clearly the higher the lesion and the less the visceral sensation, the greater the loss of emotionality. The same applied to sexual excitement and grief, the only exception to the trend being sentimentality. Typically subjects reported acting emotionally without feeling it, in order not to be taken advantage of by others. Emotion without feeling was repeatedly described by subjects with cervical lesions: "I say I am afraid, like when I'm going into a real stiff exam at school, but I don't really feel afraid, not all tense and shaky, with that hollow feeling in my stomach, like I used to." These descriptions contrast with the feelings lacking emotion in other subjects after an injection of adrenalin ("I feel as if I were very frightened; however, I am calm") (Maranon 1924, cited by Schachter 1964).

The two sets of introspections are opposite sides of the same coin (Schachter 1964). Both central and peripheral components are needed for the full experience of emotion. Emotion is attenuated when bodily comcomitants are present without the central state (as in subjects injected with adrenalin) or when a situation induces central feeling without a peripheral component (as in tetraplegics).

A dissenting study found that anxiety and depression scores were similar in tetraplegics and paraplegics and were unaffected by the level of the spinal cord lesion, most scores being within the normal range (Nestoros et al. 1982).

The interaction of central and peripheral emotional mechanisms is implied by the fact that unconsciousness and anaesthesia eliminate the adrenal effects of psychological stress (reviewed by Mayes 1979). At autopsy adrenocortical

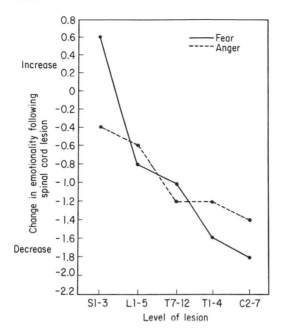

Fig. 7.7   The less intense the fear and anger felt, the higher the spinal cord lesion (From Hohmann 1962, cited by Schachter 1964. Copyright © 1962 by Stanford University Press. Reprinted by permission.)

changes were present in patients who had died while conscious but were not seen in those who had died after continuous coma.

Unity of peripheral and central mechanisms is also suggested by the absence of habituation of the orienting reflex in sleep (Johnson & Lubin 1967). When people heard repeated tones while awake, their orienting reflex habituated, as measured by EEG, heart and respiration rate, galvanic skin response (GSR), and finger plethysmography. With sleep onset the orienting reflex returned on all measures and habituated very little.

Peripheral Mechanisms

So far we have reviewed experiments that altered central neural states and examined the consequences for defensive behavior. Few studies have altered peripheral systems to see how that changes fear—most studied the patterning of reactions to emotion. Relevant peripheral domains include the autonomic, neuroendocrine, and immune systems, and blood and lipids.

Autonomic Profile of Fear Compared with Other Emotions

Both fear and anger spark much autonomic activity but with different patterns. In an adult whose gastric mucosa was visible through a gastric fistula opening on the surface of the abdominal wall, the mucosa would blanch when he was

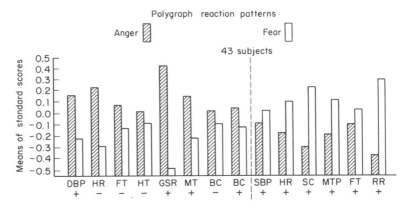

Fig. 7.8 Differential autonomic responses for fear and anger. (From Ax 1953. Copyright © 1953 by The American Psychosomatic Society Inc. Reprinted by permission of Elsevier Science Publishing Co., Inc.

frightened but redden and secrete acid when he became angry (Wolff & Wolff 1947).

The most successful physiological differentiation of fear from anger was in 43 volunteers who were made by ingenious stratagems to feel alternately frightened or angry (Ax 1953). Of 14 measures taken during these periods, 7 discriminated between fear and anger (Figure 7.8). Three measures increased with fear (skin conductance—SC+; number of muscle tension peaks—MTP+; and respiration rate—RR+), and four changed with anger (rises in diastolic blood pressure—DBP+; falls in heart rate—HR−; number of galvanic skin responses—GSR; and rises in muscle tension—MT+). No discrimination was found for six measures (face and hand temperature—FT−, FT+, HT−; ballistocardiogram—BC−, BC+; and rises in systolic blood pressure—SBP+).The physiological profile separated fear from anger in all but one subject. Intercorrelations of measures were very low. The physiological pattern of fear was similar to that from injecting adrenalin alone, and of anger to that of injecting adrenalin and noradrenalin together.

Using a method similar to that of Ax, Schachter (1957) differentiated physiological responses to fear, anger, and pain in 48 subjects, 15 of whom had also been included in Ax's report. Some subjects were hypertensive and others normotensive. Regardless of blood pressure, the effect of fear was adrenalinlike, of pain noradrenalinlike, and of anger either or both. Criteria for a noradrenalinlike effect were (1) marked rise in peripheral resistance; (2) drop in at least two of the following three measures: cardiac output, stroke-volume, and heart rate; and (3) rise in diastolic pressure. For an adrenalinlike effect, opposite criteria were taken, but systolic rather than diastolic pressure was used.

Although the physiological profiles for fear, anger, and pain showed some differences, these were not large. None are known to separate fear from nonsituational anxiety. Another study examined cardiovascular patterns after fear and other emotional states in 32 subjects. Compared to anger, fear produced less rise in cardiovascular measures (Schwartz et al. 1981).

Autonomic Aspects of Fear

Four types of measure are mainly used (Lader 1976): (1) the immediate response to frightening versus neutral stimuli, (2) the baseline level in chronically anxious versus normal people, (3) the time it takes for the response to a single discrete stimulus to return to prestimulation level (adaptation), and (4) the time that responses to repeated discrete stimuli take to return to prestimulation level (habituation).

A single frightening stimulus in relaxed people produces many brief autonomic responses. Loud sounds and electric shocks usually increase heart rate, skin conductance, and muscle tone, constrict skin blood vessels, and dilate pupils (Lader & Marks 1971). Subjective fear, if present, follows the stimulus, often after a delay. If shock is expected, then there is sweating with rises in and further fluctuations of skin conductance, while heart rate rises in the preceding 30 seconds and slows just before the shock is due. The increase in rate is greater after previous experience of the shock and occurs whether the shock is mild or strong and whether or not subjects are usually anxious.

Patients with anxiety states may show increased sweating to drugs as well as to frightening stimuli. Compared to normal women, anxious ones showed more spontaneous sweat gland activity and greater response to carbachol and to phenylephrine (Maple et al. 1982).

Prolonged experience of war and terrorist activities greatly increased both the systolic and diastolic blood pressure of pregnant women (Rofé & Goldberg 1983). Ordeals such as stressful films, examinations, and parachute jumps increase sympathetic activity. There is sweating and rise in heart rate and systolic blood pressure, and vasoconstriction in skin and splanchnic regions but dilatation in muscle. Total peripheral resistance drops so that stroke volume and cardiac output rises. The pupil dilates and salivation diminishes.

Physiological Responses to Parachuting

That physiological responses to stress alter with successful experience was shown in sport parachutists (Epstein 1962; Fenz 1975; Fenz & Epstein 1967). In a novice, GSR activity rises toward the moment of the jump and to words associated with parachuting. The peak appears earlier with successful experience and with cues more remote from the jump. Figure 7.9 shows this change in a single parachutist after 2, 5, and 19 jumps; the same pattern was found in in all 7 subjects tested. Earlier appearance of the peak seems a function of mastery. It does not occur on repeated testing in the absence of experience, is reversed after a mishap, and speeds up in better jumpers, who have greater emotional control when jumping.

Like GSR, subjective fear also peaks increasingly early with competence (Figure 7.10). Reported fear is greatest not at the time of the jump, which is the point of maximum danger, but at decision points, which advance with experience. For novices, the critical decision is at the ready signal, when they can delay or cancel the jump. For experienced jumpers it is on waking in the morning, as the decision largely hangs on the weather—once they have made

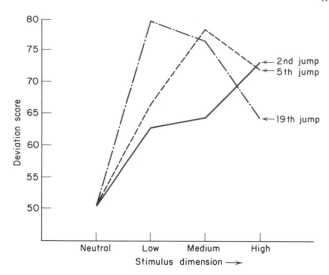

Fig. 7.9 Galvanic skin response (GSR) reactions in a word association test by a single parachutist appear earlier in the stimulus dimension as experience is gained. Six other parachutists showed the same pattern. Deviation score represents corrected differences on GSR lability and mean reaction to neutral stimuli (From Epstein 1962. Copyright © 1962 by University of Nebraska Press. Reprinted by permission.)

up their minds, they know they will jump; other anxiety peaks occur when opening the parachute and at landing.

In another study 10 novice and 10 experienced parachutists were compared. Skin conductance and heart and respiration rates were recorded continuously during ascent in the aircraft and at selected points before and after the jump. The curves of novices and veterans were similar to begin with but then diverged. Just before the jump, heart rate rose sharply in novices to a mean of 145 beats per minute (bpm) but fell in veterans. The peaks for subjective fear were earliest, followed in turn by skin conductance and heart and respiration rates.

Among experienced parachutists the pattern differed according to their mastery of the art. In capable veterans, heart rate rose early in the jump sequence and then fell steadily until it was nearly normal at the time of the jump. In poor veterans, however, heart rate rose from 92 bpm at the start to 122 bpm at the point of exit. Novices had unreliable control of fear and were less aware of their state ("I was not afraid at all until I looked down and saw my knees trembling. Then I realized how scared I really was").

In combat flying, too, fear lessens once dangers have been mastered (Bond 1952). The same event that profoundly influences a cadet on his first flight means less later and is hardly noticed by a seasoned flyer: "Every dangerous event, as it comes up, is broken off and isolated to become the subject of rumination and repetitive conversation. Every possibility is explored, every potential outcome considered, and all defensive action carefully rehearsed. Once

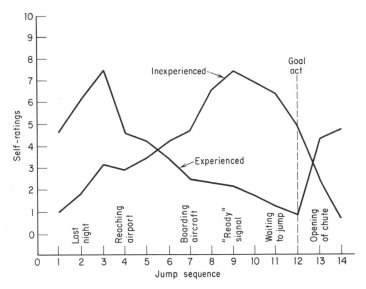

Fig. 7.10   Along a dimension of events leading up to and following a parachute jump, self-rated fear of experienced parachutists appeared earlier than in novice jumpers (*n* = 33 per group). (From Fenz & Epstein 1967. Copyright © 1967 by University of Nebraska Press. Reprinted by permission.)

mastered, the event drops into the preconscious, and attention is then turned to a new one. . . . ''

The last sentence corresponds to the way that peaks came earlier in the parachutists as experience was gained. These could reflect habituation to the worst (latest) dangers that have been repeatedly encountered and overcome. More attention can then be paid to mild earlier problems that were previously unnoticed while fear was at its height. That inhibition of fear by habituation is incomplete is suggested by the after-discharge found in veteran parachutists after the jump; this was found in other parachutists as well (Basowitz et al. 1955). Sometimes inhibitory control breaks down, for example, when experienced parachutists become afraid after unexpected trivial changes in the normal jumping routine (Epstein 1967).

It is not yet clear how far these findings in parachutists can be generalized to other frightening situations. In other experiments with noxious stimulation Epstein did not find fear peaks displacing earlier with experience, or he found this for heart rate but not for skin conductance. Among bomb-disposal operators the most competent and experienced subjects had the lowest heart rate in the most stressful period awaiting electric shocks (Cox et al. 1983).

Reactions to Phobic Situations

Phobic stimuli cause autonomic responses similar to those induced by normal fear and greater than those to neutral stimuli (Mathews 1971). Compared with nonphobics, spider phobic students had skin conductance changes that were greater and longer while watching pictures of spiders than of neutral stimuli (Geer 1966) and were also more persistent (Wilson 1967). Although persistent, GSR responses to phobic stimuli do eventually habituate with repeated and/ or prolonged exposure, which is the basis of treatment (Wilson 1966).

Phobic patients, too, respond more autonomically to phobic than to neutral stimuli. This was found in 77 cases in 6 different studies (Marks & Huson 1973). Figure 7.11 summarizes the patients' responses to phobic and neutral imagery and to hearing talk about phobic situations. Before therapy, phobic could be discriminated from neutral imagery on heart rate in four of six studies, on skin conductance in two of six studies, and on subjective anxiety in all six studies. After exposure therapy, clinical improvement was reflected on autonomic measures and, after a while longer, on subjective anxiety.

It is not surprising that subjective reports of fear more consistently separate phobic from neutral stimuli than do autonomic measures. Subjective report of what someone avoids and fears is, after all, the initial criterion for deciding what constitutes his or her phobic or neutral stimuli. In contrast, autonomic changes are only a peripheral reflection of the central state he or she is reporting.

In the above studies heart rate, skin conductance, and subjective fear correlated poorly with one another. It is well known that various autonomic measures correlate poorly with one another and with feelings and behavior. Fear, like other emotions, is an emotional response syndrome whose components are imperfectly coupled (Mathews 1971). Autonomic measures reflect many processes quite apart from emotional arousal, are subject to physiological restraints giving ceiling and floor effects, and are orchestrated together in widely differing ways in emotional situations. Furthermore, a correlation expresses a relationship between phenomena at only one point. More subtle statistics are needed to demonstrate coherence among different events that fluctuate over time.

Another measure, forearm blood flow, also rises more during images of intense than of mild phobias or of neutral topics (Gelder & Mathews 1968). However, as in other studies (Kelly 1966; Kelly & Walter 1968), forearm blood flow rose most of all while subjects did mental arithmetic at speed, and subjective fear was greatest during phobic imagery. Forearm blood flow rose 10 to 20 times with exercise as compared to 2 to 3 times with anxiety. The correlation of forearm blood flow with anxiety is low: .24 to .28. Finger pulse volume is another measure sensitive to physical or social threat (Smith et al. 1984).

We saw that in normal people a frightening stimulus causes several brief autonomic responses. Chronically anxious patients may have a rise in the basal level of many functions, such as the rate of spontaneous fluctuations in skin conductance; with frightening stimulation such already raised measures may not increase much further (Lader 1976), perhaps because of a ceiling effect. The responses of anxious patients are also slow to return to prestimulation levels (that is, to adapt)—this is true for skin conductance, blood pressure, electromyogram (EMG), forearm blood flow, and pupil size (Lader 1976).

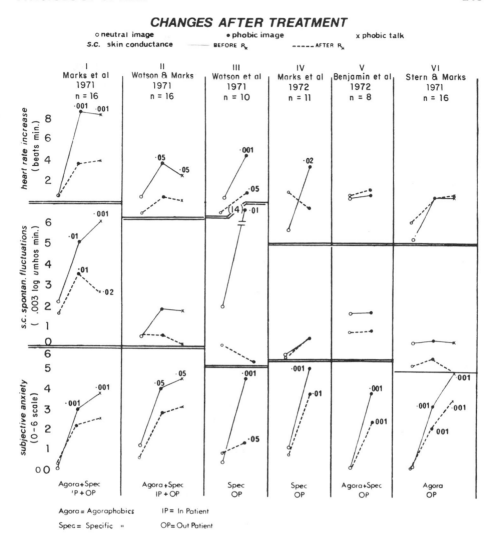

Fig. 7.11 Psychophysiological reactions to neutral and phobic imagery and to hearing talk about phobic situations in 77 phobic patients treated by exposure in 6 different studies. Before treatment, responses to phobic stimuli were significantly greater on heart rate in 4 of 6 studies, on skin conductance in 2 of 6 studies, and on subjective anxiety in all 6 studies. After treatment, autonomic responses decreased rather more than did subjective anxiety. (From Marks & Huson 1973. Copyright © 1973 by the British Journal of Psychiatry. Reprinted by permission.)

Habituation refers to the decrement in response as discrete stimuli are repeated. In normal awake subjects exposed to a series of identical stimuli, reactions usually diminish rapidly. During sleep, habituation of autonomic orienting reflexes may decrease or disappear (Johnson 1970; Johnson & Lubin 1967). Response decrement may be quicker when the pathways involve more relays (Davis et al. 1982). In rats, startlelike responses first sensitized and then habituated to repeated electrical stimulation of the cochlear nucleus, but only sensitized and did not habituate to similar stimulation of the caudal reticulo-pontine nucleus (Davis et al. 1982). After repeated stimulation of the corneal reflex in humans, a later component of the EMG mediated by a longer poly-synaptic circuit habituated, while an early component dependent on a short paucisynaptic pathway only sensitized (Sanes et al. 1978).

Anxiety seems to slow habituation. In normal students habituation of the orienting reflex (on GSR and pulse width) to tones and slides was slower when the second test session preceded an oral examination than when it did not (Maltzman et al. 1971). Compared to normals, anxious patients continued to respond for longer when stimulation was repeated; that is, they had impaired habituation. Skin conductance responses to repeated tones habituated more slowly in anxious agoraphobics than in specific phobics who were not anxious in the absence of their phobic stimuli (Lader et al. 1967). This difference, how-ever, was between diagnostic groups; within patients, habituation rate did not correlate with subjective level of anxiety. In another study, after repeated bursts of white noise the EMG decreased more in normals than in anxious patients (Davis et al. 1954). Similarly, when seeing a terrifying film twice within a week, at the second showing autonomic activity (skin conductance, heart rate and variability, finger pulse volume, and respiration) decreased in nonanxious patients but rose in anxious subjects (Clemens & Selesnick 1967).

Responsivity and habituation are, of course, unlikely to be uniform over all stimuli, times, situations, and systems. There may be individual response specificity, one person reacting more in one modality than in another (Lacey 1967). Anxious patients with cardiovascular complaints had more heart rate rise and variability than EMG changes, whereas the converse was found for those with head and neck pains (Malmo & Shagass 1949). There was even spec-ificity within muscles; anxious patients with headaches had high frontalis EMG, whereas those with aches in the limbs had raised forearm EMGs (Sains-bury & Gibson 1954).

Responses in Obsessive-Compulsive Disorder

Obsessive-compulsive patients were similar to normal controls at rest (Bou-lougouris 1977). However, they showed more tachycardia to shock and more skin conductance responses to either shock or to ritual-evoking stimuli. Their skin conductance responses over several trials also habituated more slowly than those of controls. The latter was also found by Lelliott and coworkers (1986); good outcome was predicted by marked responsivity before treatment but not by habituation rate, which failed to correlate with anxiety and depression.

The responses of obsessive-compulsives to 6 weeks of clomipramine or of clorgyline were compared with placebo (Zahn et al. 1984). Only clomipramine produced clinical improvement. Both drugs reduced skin conductance indices at rest, but only clomipramine reduced skin conductance and heart rate res-ponses to loud tones and tonic and phasic skin conductance responses in a two-flash discrimination task. A larger heart rate increase to loud tones predicted more improvement. Responses to ritual-evoking stimuli were not reported.

Cardiac Arrhythmias and Sudden Death from Fright and Stress

The heart rate slows in humans hearing unexpected (but not expected) loud noise or seeing blood or injury; the slowing can end in vasovagal fainting (see Chapters 11 and 15). During tonic immobility there often is bradycardia and parasympathetic arrhythmia, and, rarely, death in diastole, as occurred in wild Norwegian rats held tightly in the hand (Richter 1957; see also Chapter 3).

In animals, high neural input to the heart during stress may trigger sudden death (reviewed by Lown 1982). After dogs had a single shock while in a sling over 3 days, each time they were subsequently placed in the sling without shocks the ventricular fibrillation threshold was 70% less than in dogs in a tranquil cage. The dogs then had the descending coronary artery occluded and were allowed to recover from the acute myocardial infarction and to become free of arrhythmia. Being placed in the sling and other nasty stimuli now evoked ventricular tachycardia and extrasystoles, which disappeared when the dogs were returned to the tranquil cage. Similarly, pigs allowed to adapt over 4 to 8 days to a laboratory had less ventricular fibrillation after coronary occlusion.

The evidence in man is circumstantial (Lown 1982). Ventricular premature beats have increased during emotional stress testing and diminished during sleep and relaxation. In a young girl, ventricular fibrillation started when she was awakened by a thunderclap and recurred whenever she was roused by an alarm clock. In a middle-aged man with no heart disease, malignant ventricular arrhythmias began while roughhousing with his teenage daughters and thereafter occurred during psychiatric interviews, stressful emotions, and REM sleep; the arrhythmias reduced during non-REM sleep, meditation, and with beta-adrenergic drugs and diphenylhydantoin. Cardiac arrhythmias might be involved in voodoo anxiety and death, but cardiac data are not available.

Among 117 patients malignant ventricular arrythmias involved three factors (Lown 1982): (1) mycardial electrical instability, (2) intense daily psychological burden such as depression or emotional entrapment, and (3) a charged psychological event, which was present in 21% of patients, usually less than an hour before an arrhythmia—these "trigger" patients had less coronary artery disease.

The situations in which sudden cardiac death or potentially lethal arrhythmias occur range from overwhelming catastrophes, to relatively ordinary everyday upsets, to trivial circumstances having the features of conditioning stimuli, or nothing of note (Engel 1978). The emotions include startle, fright, anger, helplessness, excitement, and even joy. Sometimes there is a preceding buildup for weeks or months of life changes causing disappointment, dissatisfaction, and depression. Type A behavior was associated with postoperative ventricular (but not atrial) arrythmia shortly after coronary bypass surgery (Freeman et al. 1984).

Perhaps in extensive ischemic myocardial disease, even minimal unrecognized psychological events precipitate arrhythmia. Neural stimulation of the myocardium is the product of complex interactions of immediate perception, recall of past emotional events, conditioned reflexes, and concentrations of neurotransmitters and their precursors at various brain sites. Even diet can affect brain neurotransmitter synthesis (Lown 1982). The amino acids L-tryptophan and tyrosine, precursors for serotonin and noradrenalin, respectively, protect animals against ventricular fibrillation. However, in chickens a low-tryptophan diet reduces tonic immobility, which returns when a normal diet is restored (see Chapter 3).

NEUROENDOCRINOLOGICAL ISSUES

Fear is accompanied by widespread changes in the neuroendocrine system, which can be thought of as a third effector system of the central nervous system along with the motor and autonomic systems. Many of the changes are in the hypothalamic-pituitary-adrenal axis (HYPAC) (well reviewed by Rose 1980 and Stokes 1985). HYPAC changes may be modulated by enkephalins (McGivern et al. 1983). Changes start with the transport of corticotropin-releasing hormone (CRH) from hypothalamic neurons along portal capillaries leading from the hypothalamus to the anterior pituitary. This releases adrenocorticotropic hormone (corticotropin, ACTH) into the blood, leading the adrenal cortex to secrete corticoids such as corticosterone and cortisol (hydrocortisone). The adrenocortical response is part of a broader neuroendocrine reaction to stress, including rise in growth hormone, prolactin, catecholamines (adrenalin and noradrenalin), and testosterone. Melatonin, too, is raised in anxiety neurosis and becomes normal after therapy (Singh et al. 1980).

Human cortisol responses to stress are seen even in infants less than a month old. In normal adults, HYPAC function is activated by arousing stimuli such as stressful interviews, dramatic war movies, anticipation of surgery or examinations, novelty such as the first day of hospital admission as a volunteer or inexperienced flight as aircrew, and, in men only, anxiety induced during a hypnotic trance. Not all normal subjects show a neuroendocrine response to potentially frightening situations, and it is often absent during chronic stress (for example, in helicopter ambulance medics in combat, or in parents over 2 years after losing a child to fatal illness). HYPAC activity falls during relaxing activities such as viewing nature films or resting, or during a hypnotic trance.

Corticosteroids increase in animals if there is rapid rise or fall in external or internal stimulation (Levine et al. 1973) and is evoked by novelty, uncertainty, and conflict (reviewed by Hennessy & Levine 1979). The hormonal response varies widely with differing intervals between trials, durations of stimulation, and the gender and species. Early experience of handling in infant rats leads to enduring decrease in corticosterone response to handling or novelty when they become adults, and a faster return to baseline after shock. Conversely, previous experience with shock sensitizes the corticosterone response to novelty or to passive avoidance training.

Plasma cortisol rose in rhesus monkeys under stress, such as exposure to aggression from strangers or novel training to avoid shocks in a shuttlebox (Scallet et al. 1983). Inescapable shock enhanced the rise. Both plasma cortisol and beta-endorphin were lower in animals previously exposed to the shuttlebox without being shocked. Plasma cortisol rose more with greater aggression of the strangers toward the newcomer. The suppression of cortisol by dexamethasone is lessened if behavioral stress immediately precedes the blood sampling (Kalin & Shelton 1984).

Separation anxiety is a much-studied trigger for cortisol production in monkeys (reviewed by Coe 1983 and Levine & Coe 1981; see also Chapter 5). In rhesus the response is limited. Squirrel monkey, like all New World monkeys, have much higher adrenal output and response to stress than Old World monkeys such as rhesus. Whereas the response of ACTH is very quick and transient, that of cortisol peaks 2 hours later. The cortisol response is buffered if the infant remains in the home cage after the mother is removed, or if it is immediately reunited with her after momentary separation—another familiar female does not suffice. On reunion after longer separation infants still show a cortisol response, although behavior is no longer disturbed. The mother's cortisol level returns to resting levels quicker than that of the infant.

No biochemical markers specific to fear have yet been found, although many regard catecholamine or cortisol levels as indicators of distress. Catecholamine excretion is raised as much by playing bingo or watching comic films as it is by distressing experiences (Frankenhaeuser 1975; Levi 1972) and did not rise during treatment of specific phobics by live exposure (Gaind 1976). But urinary adrenalin and noradrenalin correlated with anxiety in normal men (Faucheux et al. 1983) and was raised in panic-anxiety patients (Nesse et al. 1985a). The ability to rapidly mobilize and demobilize adrenalin correlates with good adjustment (Frankenhaeuser 1975) and parallels the more rapid return to baseline of autonomic responses to fear in normals than in the anxious patients seen earlier. The HYPAC system may be activated more if the task is uncontrollable and distressing rather than challenging yet controllable (Frankenhaeuser 1983).

Individual variability among normals often cannot be explained by individual differences in fear. As with autonomic responses, there is frequent discordance among different biological systems that subserve emotion. There are exceptions (Stokes 1985). In 1-year-old infants whose mother left them for an hour, urinary cortisol was higher in infants who were fearful or fussy rather than happy or indifferent to the separation. Among young adults who had intravenous catheterization twice, the plasma growth hormone and cortisol responses on the first occasion were greater in those reporting more symptoms to the experience; these responses reduced the second time round. Compared to more easygoing (type B) people, hard-driving (type A, coronary-prone) subjects had cardiovascular and neuroendocrine hyperresponse to mental arithmetic and to a reaction-time task; during mental arithmetic they had more blood cortisol, noradrenalin, and adrenalin, and during the reaction-time task they had more testosterone and, for subjects with hypertensive relatives, more cortisol.

Specific phobics have a variable neuroendocrine response to phobic stimuli. In 12 phobics (6 of blood and mutilation, 6 of snakes or spiders) greater distress, skin conductance level, and cortisol excretion occurred with phobic than with neutral slides, responses of blood and of animal phobics being similar (Fredrikson et al. 1983). However, when 11 specific animal phobics had 2 hours of live exposure treatment, they looked and acted extremely frightened; this fear gradually subsided as the session progressed, yet plasma cortisol did not rise, and plasma growth hormone rose only slightly and variably (Curtis et al. 1976, 1978). During two previous orienting sessions these subjects had shown an initial orienting response of increased plasma cortisol that soon decreased, while growth hormone had remained largely unchanged.

In a subsequent experiment on 10 animal phobics by the same group, similar exposure raised not only subjective anxiety, heart rate, and blood pressure but also plasma cortisol, noradrenalin, adrenalin, insulin, and growth hormone, though it did not change plasma glucagon or pancreatic polypeptide (Nesse et al. 1984 and Figure 7.12). Rises in cortisol and blood pressure were greater with exposure therapy carried out in the evening than in the morning. Although the subjective and behavioral signs of anxiety were consistently intense, the size, consistency, timing, and concordance of endocrine and cardiovascular responses varied considerably.

Other examples of discordance come from rats. Repeated preexposure to a novel milk solution led to more rapid waning of cortisol than of avoidance of the solution during extinction after conditioned taste aversion (Smotherman et al. 1980). The converse sequence occurred during open-field testing over 5 days, during which the usual response of hyperactivity followed by freezing habituated while hormonal rises continued (Ader 1969, cited by Hennessy & Levine 1979).

In patients with major depression in whom anxiety is commonly prominent, the HYPAC system is overreactive. About 45% have raised plasma and CSF cortisol and 24-hour urinary free cortisol excretion, abnormally flattened and raised circadian rhythm of plasma cortisol, and resistance to dexamethasone suppression (DST). However, the DST is usually normal in anxiety syndromes such as panic disorder (agoraphobia) (Curtis et al. 1982; Lieberman et al. 1983; Sheehan et al. 1983) and uncomplicated obsessive-compulsive disorder (Monteiro et al. 1985).

Additional changes may be seen with challenging events, though the pattern is by no means clear (Stokes 1985). In 14 young healthy men making their first parachute jump, plasma prolactin, growth hormone, and thyroid stimulating hormone (TSH) were unchanged in the days and immediately before the jump; just afterward the hormones rose, but in only 5 of the 14 men. Prolactin also rose in other subjects after 40 minutes of meditation but not in matched resting controls. After a stressful session there was a rise in prolactin and cortisol, but lower anxiety, in physically trained rather than in untrained subjects. In contrast, neither prolactin nor TSH rose in phobics during frightening exposure (Curtis et al. 1979; Nesse et al. 1982). Although the TSH response to TRH is blunted in some euthyroid-depressed patients, this has not been reported for anxiety. Other disturbances are of dopamine beta hydroxylase and monoamine

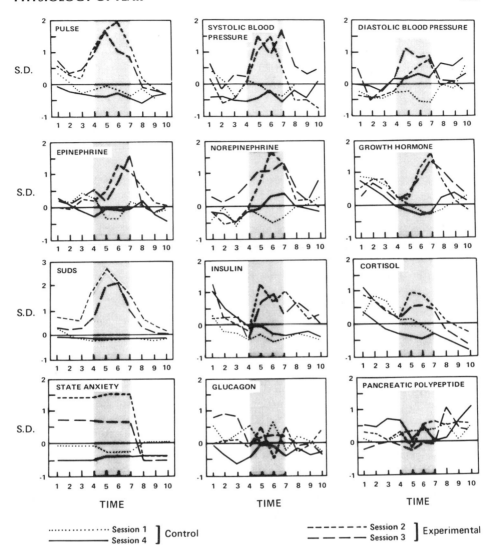

Fig. 7.12 Plasma hormonal changes during exposure in vivo. Ten animal phobics had exposure treatment during sessions 2 to 3 from times 4 to 7; each of the 9 time intervals denotes 20 minutes, and the total time per session is 3 hours. With exposure there were rises in subjective anxiety (SUDS), pulse rate, blood pressure, plasma cortisol, adrenalin, noradrenalin, insulin, and growth hormone, but not in plasma glucagon or pancreatic polypeptide. (From Nesse et al. 1984. Copyright © 1984 by Elsevier Science Publishing Co., N.Y. Reprinted by permission.)

oxidase inhibitor (MAO) activity of blood platelets in affective disorders with marked anxiety (Coursey & Buchsbaum 1981). Hyperprolactinaemia is associated with raised anxiety (Fava et al. 1982, 1983).

Testosterone is reduced in men after stress and in rhesus monkeys after becoming subordinate. Conversely, young men who rise in status through their own efforts and have associated elation show raised testosterone over the next couple of days. This is paralleled by rhesus showing a similar rise after winning a fight. In olive baboons *(Papio anubis)* social rank again affected endocrinal state, this time adrenocortical function (Sapolsky 1984). High-ranking males had lower basal levels but more rapid post-stress rise in cortisol than subordinates, and showed faster and greater suppression of circulating cortisol in response to dexamethasone.

Although neuroendocrinal response varies slightly for fear compared to anger, no unique pattern for fear is yet known, and the mechanisms are obscure. When rhesus monkeys acquired a conditioned emotional response by disruption of their lever-pressing for food, both 17-hydroxycorticosteroids and noradrenalin rose, yet adrenalin did not even though it rose with other emotional behaviors (Brady 1966). After 72 hours of conditioned avoidance of shock in monkeys, thyroid, gonadal, and adrenal hormone changes endured long after avoidance behavior had stopped (Brady 1966).

Our discussion until now has been of endogenous compounds that are produced in response to fear, anxiety, or stress. In addition, giving certain substances, such as caffeine, yohimbine, BCCE, sodium lactate, and carbon dioxide (see Chapter 10), can induce tension.

Immunity, Blood, and Lipids

Immunity, blood, and lipids change with stress, but their implications for fear are unclear. In mice, being handled or rapidly spun leads not only to rise in coricosterone within 5 minutes but also to many changes in the immune system at varying speeds. Within 1 to 2 hours there is lymphocytopenia and fall in T cells; within 24 hours, thymic involution and smaller mass of spleen and peripheral lymph nodes; and subsequently there is reduced resistance to tumor implants (Riley 1981).

Immune responses can be suppressed by conditioning, just like fear (Ader 1982; Ader et al. 1983). Rats were given a novel fluid (saccharin) paired with the immunosuppressive drug cyclophosphamide (CY) and were then injected with sheep red blood cells. Some of these conditioned rats were then reexposed to the saccharin; their antibody response to the sheep cells was less than that of conditioned rats not reexposed to saccharin or of nonconditioned rats exposed to the saccharin. In mice the development of autoimmune disease (systemic lupus erythematosis) was prevented by similar conditioned immunosuppression (Ader & Cohen 1982).

Stress may increase proneness to infectious diseases and cancer, presumably through suppressing immune mechanisms; in contrast, some stressed people release beta-endorphins that stimulate lymphocyte production and may protect against cancer (A. Mayes, personal communication, 1984). Six weeks after bereavement, spouses showed less response to phytohaemagglutinin than did controls, although other immune and hormonal measures were normal (Bartrop et al. 1977). Volunteers with obsessional symptoms were more susceptible to infection with rhinovirus and with influenza virus (Broadbent et al. 1984).

Folklore speaks of a "blood-curdling scream." In animals Cannon noted in 1915 that blood coagulation was hastened by injecting adrenalin, though this was not a direct effect on the blood. Blood clotting was also speeded by splanchnic stimulation if the adrenals were present but not if they were absent, and by painful stimulation and emotional excitement. The latter also increased the red cell count, but only if upper abdominal sympathetic innervation was intact, and the effect was irregular if the spleen was denervated. Cannon reported a finding by Menkin that white blood cells also increased, by an average of 13%, after brief emotional disturbance, gradually subsiding to baseline, as did the red cell increase, in half an hour.

In humans, stress may alter some coagulation factors, but the changes were inconsistent in a review by Steptoe (1981). In a study since then, students under stress and agoraphobics had raised platelet factor 4 and beta-thromboglobulin (Levine 1983). In the agoraphobics these compounds diminished while on alprazolam or ibuprofen and increased after the drugs were stopped; however, clinical improvement occurred only to the alprazolam, so it is unclear how the blood changes related to anxiety. We are reminded that patients with panic disorder or "neurocirculatory asthenia" had excess cardiovascular deaths 12 to 35 years later (Coryell 1983; Coryell et al. 1982, 1983; see also Chapter 10).

Lipids, too, rose with short-term emotional arousal from viewing disturbing films, taking examinations, or military training (reviewed by Dimsdale & Herd 1982). Free fatty acids rose almost invariably, and cholesterol increased 8% to 65% but could be highly labile. Triglyceride response was inconsistent. Recurrence of myocardial infarction was lower in post-coronary subjects, whose Type A time-pressured behavior lessened more in a behavior modification than a control program, but lipid levels were not given (Thoresen et al. 1982).

Free fatty acids rose within 15 minutes during anxious but not hostile remarks made by 48 subjects as their blood was drawn for assay (Cleghorn et al. 1967). Their changes in free fatty acids during REM sleep also correlated with anxiety in dream reports. Mobilization of free fatty acids seemed to depend on the secretion of catecholamines in the short-term.

SUMMARY

In sea snails defensive learning is associated with changes in the activity of sensory and facilitatory neurons. Via the Ca^{++} channels learning alters the membrane of sensory neurons and modulates the amount of chemical transmitter released at their presynaptic terminals. At such terminals habituation decreases the Ca^{++} influx and thus reduces the release of transmitter; this leads to synaptic depression. Conversely, greater release of transmitter and thus synaptic facilitation occurs with sensitization and classical conditioning; this may stem from indirect rise in Ca^{++} from depression of the K^+ channel. Classical conditioning may involve a Ca^{++} sensitivity of the cAMP cascade in the sensory neurons. This augments cAMP-dependent phosphorylation, which closes K^+ channels and prolongs the action potential. The general phylogenetic aspects of associative learning are most likely to be at such molecular and biophysical levels. Complex learning may follow a biological grammar that combines elements from the cellular alphabet of simpler forms of learning.

Invertebrates have sensitive receptors linked to small neurons to mediate slower elements of escape and, in many species, giant fast-conducting (command) neurons for the first quick but stereotyped escape response. Simultaneous stimulation of large and small neurons respectively activate fast and slow escape responses in parallel. Several neurons may be coupled together to allow escalating feedback leading to an all-or-none response. Moths have 2 receptors responsive to different sounds, which operate together to steer them away from the direction of an approaching bat. Cockroaches detect the air movement from approaching predators as they stimulate cercal hairs linked to giant interneurons.

Fish and laval amphibians have giant (Mauthner) cells in their hindbrain to mediate startle. Mammalian equivalents are not known. Vertebrate defensive responses depend upon interactions among several brain regions. The outcome of stimulating a particular area may vary from one occasion to the next.

Mammalian deep structures that mediate certain components of fear and other defensive behaviors include the dentate and interposital nuclei of the cerebellum, locus ceruleus and median raphe nuclei, hypothalamus, septum, hippocampus, amygdala, cingulum, and thalamus. In humans stimulation of thalamus, subthalamus, pallidum, hippocampus, amygdala, and tegmentum causes sudden emotion, whereas cortical stimulation does not. Fear and obsessive-compulsive phenomena occurring during epilepsy suggest temporal lobe involvement. Surgical lesions to fronto-amygdaloid and fronto-thalamic pathways reduce anxiety.

Several subcortical areas seem linked together in subsystems mediating different aspects of defensive behavior. The locus ceruleus and dorsal ascending noradrenergic bundle is thought to be part of an alarm system; drug or direct stimulation of this system causes anxiety, while blocking it reduces fear. Septhippocampal, amygdaloid, and other limbic elements may be part of an inhibitory system that compares present input with past experience and mediates hesitation and doubt. In dogs, repeated intermittent stimulation of the amygdala leads to the kindling of limbic epilepsy, whereas massed stimulation produces tolerance; these two points also apply to the onset and habituation of phobias and rituals in humans.

Several neurotransmitters are involved with fear and anxiety. From the brainstem the locus ceruleus and its ascending noradrenergic pathway may constitute an alarm system, and serotonergic pathways are involved in tonic immobility. Some antianxiety drugs may act on benzodiazepine (bz) receptors, which affect GABA-ergic inhibition via a chloride channel in the neuronal membrane. Bz receptors are widespread throughout the nervous system, including limbic areas. The affinity of bz drugs for bz receptors correlates with their clinical potency as anxiolytics, and reactive rats have fewer bz receptors. Three types of ligands bind to the bz receptor: agonists that facilitate it, antagonists that block it but are intrinsically inactive, and active antagonists (inverse agonists) that not only block it but are also anxiogenic. Anxiolytic drugs may also suppress central noradrenergic activity that is reflected in reduced noradrenergic metabolites like plasma MHPG.

Among the neuropeptides, vasopressin enhances acquisition and retards extinction of avoidance, while oxytocin has the reverse effect; both effects might be mediated by peripheral rather than central actions. Beta-endorphin and ACTH levels are closely related. With acute stress and anxiety central opioid peptides increase and pain sensitivity lessens, both effects being reversed by naloxone and habituating with repeated exposure to the stress. Perhaps such mechanisms relate to the habituation of phobics and of obsessive-compulsives during exposure therapy. Endogenous opioids may mediate learned helplessness. Their release and ensuing feedback mechanisms might also explain some respiratory symptoms of severely anxious patients. Naloxone has worsened obsessions in 2 patients.

Autonomic activity aids the acquisition of emotional behavior but is not needed for its maintenance once it has been acquired. In the absence of autonomic arousal during emotional behavior less emotion is experienced. If a subject is mildly aroused physiologically for no obvious reason, he may label this arousal in terms of how he sees the prevailing circumstances. Finally, unconsciousness seems to prevent the endocrine response to stress and habituation of the orienting reflex.

The physiological patterns of fear differ a bit from those of anger or pain, but are like those of phobia and non-situational anxiety. Different indices of fear correlate poorly with one another. In normals a frightening stimulus leads to many brief autonomic responses—raised heart rate, skin conductance and muscle tone and blood flow, vasoconstriction of skin blood vessels, and pupillary dilatation, which may endure in chronically anxious patients. Subjective fear and accompanying physiological changes in parachutists are greatest at choice points that occur progressively earlier with experience. Responses to repeated discrete stimuli tend to diminish. This habituation may disappear during sleep. Obsessive-compulsives respond like phobics. Fear and stress can trigger parasympathetic and sympathetic arrhythmias and, in animals, death in diastole or in ventricular fibrillation. The threshold for such fibrillation drops during stress.

Fear and stress are accompanied by widespread endocrine changes, including activation of the hypothalamic-pituitary-adrenal axis. There is release of CRH, ACTH, corticosterone and cortisol, adrenalin and noradrenalin, growth hormone, prolactin and perhaps melatonin, and decreased testosterone in men and monkeys. Endocrine responses are more prominent during acute than chronic stress and soon habituate, individual variability increasing as the stress continues. There is frequent discordance among hormonal and other biological systems subserving emotion. Corticoid response occurs especially with rapid rise or fall in external or internal stimulation, and with novelty, uncertainty and conflict; it varies greatly according to intervals between stress, durations of stimulation, sex, species, and social rank. Ability to quickly mobilize and demobilize adrenalin may relate to good adjustment and parallels the more rapid return to baseline of autonomic responses to fear in normals than in anxious patients.

Many stressors lead to various changes in the immune system at differing speeds, and these changes can be suppressed by conditioning. Stress can raise proneness to infectious diseases and cancer, presumably through such immune mechanisms. Fear in dogs increases the red and white cell count and the coagulability of the blood, and human agoraphobics have increased platelet factor 4 and betathromboglobulin. Lipids rise with short-term emotional arousal, and mycardial infarction recurs less if patients reduce their time-pressured behavior. Free fatty acids may rise more with anxiety than with hostility.

TOWARD INTEGRATION[1]

Is there some order in the numerous circuits and neuroregulators that we have seen implicated in the acquisition and expression of many different defensive behaviors across phyla, and in the human clinical syndromes in which they appear? Despite the complexity of the issues, the task of integration no longer seems altogether hopeless. The same four basic strategies of defensive behavior—withdrawal, immobility, aggressive defense, and deflection of attack—identified in Chapter 3 are found in both invertebrates and vertebrates, although only the first two strategies seem to be involved in phobic and obsessive-compulsive disorders. Also common across phyla are the basic forms of learning such as habituation, sensitization, and classical and operant conditioning.

It is, of course, a cliché that similar behaviors have repeatedly evolved across taxa independently of one another by different mechanisms (that is, convergence). Yet, conservation of evolutionary mechanisms has been found repeatedly. Is there any reason to believe that some of the shared defensive strategies and ways in which they are modified by learning are mediated by common physiological mechanisms? Are there enough points in common among invertebrates and vertebrates to make this likely?

Some organizing principles are emerging. First, in vertebrates 50 years of research have produced convincing evidence that several deep structures in the brain are involved in fearful withdrawal and immobility. Withdrawal in both aplysia and mammals is modified by changes not at the peripheral sensory receptor in skin or muscle, but central to the body of the sensory neuron—at the synapse of the sensory neuron with an interneuron and/or a motor neuron in aplysia, such synapses being in the spinal cord and brain in mammals. The deep mammalian structures related to fear behavior include the limbic system, basal ganglia, hypothalamus, and brain stem and cerebellar nuclei. We do not yet understand the role of the neocortex—it may contribute to cognitive aspects of fear that are finally expressed through the deep structures.

Tentative circuits have been sketched that are involved in some varieties

[1]This section was coauthored by Dr. Adolf Tobeña.

of withdrawal and immobility, some being known in more detail than others (Gray 1982). We will oversimplify. Escape is partly mediated by circuits through the peri-aqueductal grey matter, some hypothalamic nuclei, and amygdala. The substrate for active avoidance is obscure but may relate to activity in the cingulate cortex. Passive avoidance is controlled by the septo-hippocampal system and afferents to it from the locus ceruleus and rostral raphe nuclei in the brain stem; the amygdala may also be relevant. Tonic immobility is affected by the median raphe nuclei in the brain stem and their efferents. Circuits for freezing and for startle remain to be worked out.

Second, in the last 15 years knowledge about neurotransmitters and neuromodulators has refined our understanding of the relevant circuits. Impressive correspondence have been found among distributions of particular compounds (noradrenalin, serotonin, GABA, and neuropeptides), pathways, and structures mediating defensive behaviors. Study of such compounds in simpler invertebrate nervous systems has produced data relevant to elementary forms of learning that modify normal and abnormal defensive behavior.

As we saw earlier, in aplysia gill withdrawal followed by immobility is sensitized by serotonergic stimulation. Related effects of serotonin are seen in vertebrates, including mammals. It increases tonic immobility, probably facilitates freezing in rats (Driscoll and Bittig 1982), and definitely enhances the suppression by punishment of behavior during approach in conflict situations (Graeff 1981; Sepinwall 1983). The same neurotransmitter, serotonin, consistently augments immobility and suppression of behavior across phyla. Such evidence thus supports Kandel's (1984) suggestion that serotonergic systems sensitize those forms of defensive responses, which involve cessation of ongoing activity. However, there is no good evidence that clinical forms of anxiety are increased by serotonergic agonists or reduced by serotonergic antagonists.

In mammals, noradrenergic systems can play a parallel activating role, but more for alarm with increased motor and autonomic activity than for immobility and freezing. We saw mammalian evidence of this for the locus coeruleus and fibers ascending from it, but data about such systems in invertebrates are lacking. In normals and in anxious patients, noradrenergic agonists increase anxiety and antagonists reduce it (Charney et al. 1984).

An intriguing feature of the two best-known defense-activating systems (serotonergic and noradrenergic) is that their nuclei of origin are in an area as old as the brainstem (locus ceruleus and raphe), with their long projections spreading up and down for a considerable distance. The nuclei are in a region where they could easily be activated by sensory inputs and then, depending on the type of input, activate relevant forebrain structures that regulate defensive outputs. This might be part of the function of the reticular activating system. Recent evidence suggests that there are complex but still obscure interactions between the serotonergic and noradrenergic systems.

There may be additional defense-activating systems. One could be dopaminergic from the ventral tegmentum to frontal cortex (Gray 1982; Iversen 1985). In recent work the anxiolytic drug buspirone involved dopaminergic mechanisms (Taylor et al. 1983); dopaminergic turnover in frontal cortex rises during the immobility of rats that can be conditioned to unavoidable footshock and blocked by benzodiazepines (Reinhard et al. 1982). There might perhaps also be endogenous anxiogenic compounds acting on bz receptors, such as some beta-carbolines and purines (Haefely 1983; Sepinwall 1983).

In contrast to the focal fear-activating systems with their long projections are the diffuse, inhibiting, short GABA-ergic circuits and associated bz receptors present throughout the brain and spinal cord. These appear to modulate the ascending activating systems (serotonergic, noradrenergic, and maybe dopaminergic) rather than to directly inhibit the deep structures that express fear. Certain anxiolytic drugs such as bzs seem to act in this indirect fashion by potentiating the GABA-ergic and bz complex.

Another mechanism for attenuating defensive behavior appears to involve neuropeptides, including endogenous opiates, which are mainly known as inhibitors of pain. Noxious stimuli can decrease pain, apparently by producing opiates acting on pain pathways. Fear probably does the same, fear taking priority over pain (Bolles & Fanselow 1980). Conversely, long-continued production of endogenous opiates could inhibit ascending fear pathways, thus reducing fear. Opiates could act like the other (GABA-ergic) inhibiting system through short circuits present diffusely in the nervous system.

Habituation is the attenuation of responses by repeated stimulation. It is found across phyla and has been carefully studied in defensive behavior. The main treatment to reduce phobias and rituals—exposure—can be regarded as a form of habituation. Could fear habituation be mediated by the two known inhibiting systems—GABA-bz complexes and opiates? The GABA-bz complex is not a good candidate, as the reduction of fear in animals and in humans by bz drugs or alcohol does not last, and large doses may actually impair habituation from exposure (Gray 1982; see also Chapter 9). As stress continues, both opiate production and fearful responses diminish: perhaps these reflect the same process?

Another possibility stems from the fact that repeated stress in rodents can lead to widespread down-regulation of central noradrenergic postsynaptic receptors (Stone 1983); this correlates closely with reduction in behavioral responses to repeated stress. The same receptors are down-regulated by most known antidepressants (Charney et al. 1981; Snyder & Peroutka 1984), which are anxiolytic for some phobics and obsessive-compulsives (Marks 1983). The possibility thus arises that both a psychological treatment (exposure) and drug treatment may act on the same receptors. It would be interesting to test this notion in simpler organisms, such as invertebrates, in which habituation of withdrawal and of threat to repeated stimulation has been well described.

Pathological anxiety might result from malfunction of the mechanisms involved in sensitization and/or habituation of fear-anxiety and other defensive responses. Anxiety could arise through direct or indirect increase in sensitizing mechanisms, and the converse should apply with habituating mechanisms. Sensitizing and habituating mechanisms interact.

Sensitization is relatively nonspecific. Perhaps we could equate generalized anxiety with pathological sensitization. Is it merely facile to compare the enduring agitation of sensitized snails to the motor equivalents seen in an anxiety state (GAD and panic disorder) and in many agoraphobics?

Unlike sensitization, habituation is specific, and this is mirrored by the specificity of exposure. Response decrement during habituation is found only in those pathways which have been repeatedly stimulated, just as specific reduction in fear of particular phobia- and ritual-evoking situations is seen as exposure is directed at them. Little generalization is seen either with habituation or with exposure. We cannot argue automatically from therapy to etiology, but it is tempting to suppose on the one hand that phobias and compulsive rituals were acquired and/or maintained with the same specificity that is needed for their reduction by exposure, and further, that they might be linked to specific failures of habituation. On the other hand, we saw that known fear-attenuating mechanisms (GABA-bz, opiate, and maybe others) are widely distributed in the brain.

If we mapped out the overlapping and distinctive clinical features and treatment requirements of various forms of anxiety disorder, we would get a series of interlocking Venn diagrams. Despite the considerable overlap, there seems to be some specificity of mechanism for each disorder. Some of these specificities may derive from the differing behavioral components (freezing, startle, escape, passive and active avoidance) that appear in various anxiety disorders. Attempts to match such behavior with clinical features yield some plausible analogies for anxiety reduction by behavioral treatment but shed less light on the origins and maintenance of anxiety (See Chapter 8).

Is the study of brain mechanisms more illuminating? Some forms of anxiety disorder might in theory be triggered at specific points of the various circuits mediating different aspects of anxiety. Could obsessive-compulsive disorder originate in failure of a normal "checking" function of a comparator in the septo-hippocampal system (Gray 1982)? Are the spontaneous panics of agoraphobia and anxiety states massed (perhaps epileptic) discharges of the central noradrenergic neurons in the locus ceruleus and maybe serotonergic neurons nearby, triggered perhaps by unknown metabolic changes (Haefely 1983)? The stuttering onset of anxiety/panic is reminiscent of how intermittent stimulation of the amygdala kindles epilepsy. Perhaps such malfunctions could produce the types of withdrawal and of immobility seen in anxiety syndromes.

More precise links need to be traced between such potential malfunctions with resultant defensive responses of the kinds found with phobias and rituals, and the ways in which they can be sensitized, conditioned, and habituated. The attenuation of fear and anxiety by exposure treatment and by drugs may not operate by direct correction of such malfunctions; they could act via more indirect processes. If so, better knowledge of those malfunctions might lead to the development of more direct and even more potent treatments. Whatever physiological dysfunctions are eventually found, however, they are not likely to be simple panic buttons. More probably they are complex disturbances meshing with genetic, developmental, and traumatic and vicarious learning effects.

8

Learning of Fear

Defensive behavior is not only under genetic, developmental, and physiological control, but also waxes and wanes with experience. It is this topic to which we now turn. Through learning, organisms select defensive behaviors that permit survival of environmental changes occurring within a lifetime, allowing exploitation of a far broader range of conditions than would be possible on the basis of information stored in the gene pool alone. A genetic program controls behavior by translation into a neural program that is more open to experiential modification in vertebrates than in invertebrates, allowing more individual tailoring of behavior to an animal's habitat. Within individuals, the neural programs governing learning may be more open for some kinds of behavior than for others. Even the most flexible neural programs and learning, however, depend ultimately on genetic programs. The next section reviews how phylogeny affects the rise and fall of fear.

EVOLUTION AND DEFENSIVE LEARNING

The within-organism selection that we call learning is rooted in evolutionary biology (elegantly reviewed by Öhman & Dimberg 1984 and Ohman et al. 1984). Individuals seem to have been selected for their readiness to associate events that have a high chance of being causally related in the natural habitat. Most of the significant sequences of events likely to occur during an animal's lifetime have already been experienced by its ancestors, who were selected for their ability to detect and respond to those sequences. Though gene pools are produced by the experience of the species as a whole, they result in organisms that can benefit from personal experience, too, by learning. Natural selection has led to genes that allow individual experience to change behavior so as to enhance survival in a hostile environment.

Natural selection changes the relative frequency of alleles in the gene pools. The unit of selection is not behavior but the genes of an individual and its relatives, to whose inclusive fitness it contributes. An individual that can modify its behavior to benefit from experience is more likely to survive and pass on its genes. But this process has limits. As Alexander (1975, p. 83) stated, "Because an organism is a bundle of selective compromises, no single one of its attributes is likely to be maximized." From these compromises come biological constraints that shape defensive behavior in predetermined directions, as we will see shortly.

Evolution and learning both generate variation among which successful units are selected and retained with higher frequency than in the original set. Although evolutionary selection changes the gene pool for future generations, learning dies with the individual unless that individual passes on its learning to others and also continues to affect subsequent generations. This is *culture*— a set of shared experiences based on the spread of information within a group, which thus transcends the generations. It saves each individual from having to start from scratch.

Just as the gene pool is the sum of all genes within all organisms within a group, so cultural information resides not in any one individual but in the total pool of group members. Like genetic programs, culture is manifested by the behavior of those members. And, like genes, cultural items can be viewed as replicators that can propagate themselves (Williams 1981). Examples include methods of childrearing, cooking, religious practice, and political organization, all of which evolve in a matrix of stable social institutions. Cultural items are propagated with less generational lag than are genes, and are acquired by observational learning. Culture is Lamarckian in the sense that acquired cultural characteristics can be transferred to new generations. Culture depends on learning, which in turn depends on the gene pool, and vice versa. All are in a state of continual evolution (Dobzhansky 1972, p. 528).

Prepotency and Preparedness

A common fallacy is the notion that demonstration of the learning of a given behavior precludes its having a biological base. In fact, this base may produce a universal grammar of individual and social learning whose deep structure constrains its surface expressions. All species learn some things far more easily than they do others, a facility shaped by natural selection in particular environments. For each species a nonrandom range of situations triggers a limited repertoire of defensive behavior. Fear of snakes is widespread in primates, whereas fear of leaves is not. Snake fear mainly begins in rhesus monkeys after they see conspecifics displaying such fear (Mineka 1984b; see also Chapter 2). But why do rhesus acquire it so quickly (after 2 sessions—12 trials over 8 minutes)? Does its speed of acquisition reflect a species propensity for fear to stick to snakelike (and a few other) cues rather than to leaves or flowers? And why are conspecifics such powerful models? The same questions apply to blackbirds' learning of mobbing.

Rhesus monkeys learn more pliably than do blackbirds. Human flexibility is the greatest of all, but it is not infinite. Even in humans some forms of learning seem to be constrained (prepotent, prepared) and others far more general.

We are ridden by a mass of prejudices that obstruct rational decision and cause extreme misery. (Nazis fighting a desperate war assigned scarce resources to genocide instead of to the war effort.) Salience of a situation governs our decision more than do calculations of probability. Fears of sharks and of rabies are widespread, although most people's chances of succumbing to either are minuscule. In contrast, few have more rational fears of cars or cigarettes, despite knowledge that these kill hundreds of thousands more people than do sharks or mad dogs. The new perils of modern life have not been present long enough to materially alter our genetic endowment. Whether constrained or not, no learning can "ultimately evade being evaluated by natural selection. We can only hope that, for our own species, this evaluation shall not take place in the holocaust of a nuclear war" (Öhman & Dimberg 1984).

Resistance to the overwhelming evidence of prejudice in the way we learn partly stems from the mistaken belief that constrained means immutable. Even if a twig is bent from the start, however, we may be able to straighten it. Learning can override genes to some extent. Prepotent fears, such as those of spiders or blood, are readily overcome by prolonged exposure. The question is not whether a given fear depends on genes *or* learning, but how much it depends on each and exactly which interacting factors lead to its rise and fall.

The situations that evoke fears, phobias, and rituals are nonrandom. In the nineteenth and early twentieth centuries Darwin, Hall, and Valentine suggested that some children's fears are innate and reflect past evolutionary dangers (see chapter 5). It is easy to think of fears that enhanced survival in the past (say, of animals) or continue to do so in the present (fears of heights, separation, and perhaps strangers). This idea is intrinsic to more recent and related concepts of prepotency (Marks 1969) and preparedness (Seligman 1970). Prepotency indicates that particular stimuli are salient for a given species, which attends selectively to them rather than to others even at their first encounter. Preparedness is the idea that certain stimuli associate selectively with one another and with particular responses, some connections being more available than others. There seems to be greater and lesser affinities of association analogous to chemical bonds (some atoms and molecules bond together more than do others). To change the metaphor, preparedness is the lightning conductor that directs learning along certain paths rather than others. In addition, whatever the signal of danger, each species learns certain defensive responses more easily than it does others, and learning is quickest when these responses are part of the species' innate defensive repertoire (Bolles 1970).

Such biological priming is efficient and makes evolutionary sense. Few survive if they wait to be bitten before trying to escape. Animals have evolved to learn from minimal cues about danger. As with imprinting, where it is left to experience to inscribe the precise parental features that the offspring recognizes, so the specifics of danger are better left to the environment than to the gene pool to convey. Such learning avoids wasteful defense against safe stimuli. In Chapter 4, for example, we saw how African plains animals are fine-tuned to react not to predators so much as to their distance, hunting intent, and other signs of immediate danger. Species propensities may apply to all learning, whether defensive, sexual (Marks 1972a), or other.

Birds and mammals seem predisposed not only to learn important things quickly but also to do this at the right time, at a developmental age when it will be especially helpful to begin. Chapter 5 illustrated an interaction between maturation and learning: mobility speeds the emergence of height fear in babies at the age when they are about to start crawling, but the fear is a function of age as well. How much rapid learning contributes to maturation in the emergence of fears of separation, strangers, and animals is not yet clear. It is striking that those fears start at about the age when they would be adaptive—as the baby starts to move away on its own in the case of separation and stranger fears, and as the child explores further afield in the case of animal fears.

Difficulty in Conditioning Human Phobias

Evolutionary aspects of learning were long ignored by psychologists. For several generations it was assumed that laws of learning are universal across species, that all stimuli and responses are equipotential, and that phobias are simply conditioned fear responses. Substantial negative evidence was ignored. That this was so beautifully highlights the power of fashion in science (Samelson 1980). Learning theorists endlessly cited a single case of a little boy, Albert (Watson & Rayner 1920), as an exemplar of their paradigm, just as psychoanalysts cited Freud's case of another little boy, Hans, in support of their theory that phobias were symbolic representations of a conflict. Albert was an 11-month-old toddler who became frightened of a white rat after a steel bar was struck making a loud noise behind his head whenever he reached for the rat, causing him to cry. Samelson pointed out that Albert was not frightened as long as he sucked his thumb—fear started only when his thumb was yanked out of his mouth—and that Watson and Rayner never reported a replication, although they had probably tried to produce one.

Nor was this result replicated when English (1929) made a similar noise whenever a 14-month-old girl grasped a wooden painted toy duck. Despite 50 trials no conditioned fear was established to the duck because the noise itself failed to evoke fear. In English's words, "The writer must confess his surprise—and admiration—at the child's iron nerves. In the later trials the metal bar was struck a tremendous blow with a two-pound hammer. Professors in remote parts of the building, students, and other children able to make a verbal report, all spoke of the distasteful and alarming nature of the sound." Yet a month later this same child feared new patent leather boots when she saw them for the first time, which fear generalized to objects next to it. And fear conditioned easily to a stuffed black cat but not to a wooden duck.

Another failure to replicate, in 15 babies about the same age as Albert, was noted by Bregman, a student of Thorndike's (Thorndike 1935). The conditioned stimulus (CS) was not a white rat but six other objects, and the unconditioned stimulus (US) was not the clang of hammer on steel bar but an electric bell rung behind the baby's back, which caused fear or startle. Little fear ensued. Thorndike (1935) concluded that Albert

was a special case and was definitely misleading concerning the probability of "leaving on the infant's plastic nature a reaction pattern . . . " by any such quick

and easy process of "conditioning." On the contrary, the influence of joint stimulation is so slight that we cannot demonstrate even its existence. . . . (These results)
are like what parents usually get who try to shift attitudes (of children) toward fear
of matches, knives, bottles, dangerous spots, and the like or toward tolerance and
affection for uncles, aunts, physicians, cod-liver oil, green vegetables, keeping on
mittens and the like. Progress is slow.

There are occasional sudden and dramatic shifts from a few associations (often
only one), as when a child who is frightened and hurt shortly after being seated
with a stranger in a railway car seat is extremely averse to being seated with any
stranger in such a seat for months thereafter (but these are rare).

This last example in fact suggests prepared learning (see Chapter 5 on stranger
fear).

Despite Thorndike's strictures and his 1898 doctoral dissertation data on
constraints in learning (for instance, of self-licking and other grooming responses), he formulated a universal law of effect (instrumental conditioning) across
situations and species. Until 1970 learning theorists largely ignored the importance of learning what comes naturally, though ethologists had recognized this
principle all along. The case of Albert hardly qualifies as a pilot study, let alone
as the weighty exemplar of a conditioning paradigm cited by many textbooks
despite their insistence on the need for replication, controlled experimental
design, and appropriate statistics. Presumably their quest for universal laws of
learning led them to clutch at straws. A few writers from the learning tradition
did point out that the case of Albert was overstated (Kimble 1961; Valentine
1930). It took no account of the type of CS—fear might condition much more
easily to furry objects than to opera glasses.

Concordant data come from aversion therapy for sexual fetishism and for
alcoholism. It is very hard to produce phobias of fetish objects or alcohol by
repeatedly pairing them with shocks or vomiting (Bancroft & Marks 1968).
Although aversion may neutralize sexual attraction to women's clothes, phobias rarely result.

Some difficulties in obtaining human conditioning might have stemmed
from the use of paradigms that ignored issues of prepotency and preparedness,
as well as sensitive ages for learning. In the last decade aspects of this topic
have been seriously studied, and this work will now be reviewed.

Inanimate and Interspecific Situations

That we perceive, learn, and do what comes naturally has not been easy to
demonstrate conclusively in the laboratory. A pioneer step in this regard is the
"differential conditioning" paradigm of Öhman and his coworkers for interspecific (Öhman et al. 1984) and social defensive learning (Öhman & Dimberg
1984) in humans.

In the Öhman paradigm, one group of subjects is shown slides of commonly frightening ("fear-relevant") stimuli such as snakes or spiders, while
other subjects see slides of rarely frightening ("neutral") objects such as flowers, mushrooms, or boxes. The slides appear in three phases. First, to establish
a baseline, subjects see the slides alone (unpaired, "habituation"). Next is a

conditioning (pairing, "acquisition") phase during which half the slides (CS+) are quickly followed by an unpleasant unconditioned stimulus (US) such as mild shock or white noise, while the other half are not (CS−); usually snakes (or spiders) serve as CS+, and spiders (or snakes) as CS−. Finally, subjects again see the slides without a US (unpaired, "extinction"). Responses of skin conductance (SC), finger pulse volume, and/or heart rate are measured.

Prepotency (stimulus salience) is indicated by differential orienting responses to fear-relevant versus neutral slides prior to pairing. Subsequent conditioning is shown by differential response to CS+ versus CS− slides during pairing and extinction, and preparedness by superior differential conditioning (faster acquisition and/or slower extinction) to fear-relevant versus neutral slides. Although fragile, both prepotency and preparedness are commonly found in these experiments.

As evidence of prepotency, even in nonfearful subjects SC responses to snakes and spiders are often greater than to neutral stimuli during initial unpaired habituation and at the first paired conditioning trial. (For examples, see Cook et al. 1986; Fredrikson et al. 1976, p. 309; Fredrikson & Öhman 1979; Fredrikson 1980; McNally & Reiss 1984; Öhman et al. 1976, p. 321; Öhman et al. 1978). For heart rate, prepotent deceleration (indicating orienting) is only occasionally present (see, for instance, Fredrikson & Öhman 1979).

Öhman and his coworkers found differential conditioning suggesting preparedness whether the US was direct experience of a shock, mere threat of a shock, or seeing a model display fear. Conditioning of SC and of finger pulse volume was more obvious with fear-relevant than with neutral slides and was accompanied by more unpleasant feelings in the rare instances where this was examined. The effect was not seen if the US was not aversive. Preparedness was found less in the second (paired acquisition) than the third (unpaired extinction) phase; SC responses took longer to return to baseline for CS+ fear-relevant slides.

During extinction, responses usually declined in parallel regardless of slide content. Extinction of responses to paired stimuli and habituation of responses to unpaired stimuli also proceeded at a similar speed. Often responses to CS+ fear-relevant slides declined at the same rate as to other slides but did not reach baseline level by the end of 10 to 12 unpaired extinction trials; perhaps this simply reflected the fact that those responses had been higher at the start of extinction and so needed more time or a longer series of unpaired trials to fall to baseline. After all, most clinical phobics and ritualizers require hours of exposure before their fear declines to near zero.

Another feature of phobics and ritualizers is that they feel no better on being told that their worries are groundless. In keeping with this, Öhman and his coworkers often found that telling subjects at the start of their extinction phase that shocks would cease would immediately abolish responses to neutral but not to fear-relevant stimuli. This, however, could not be replicated in all experiments by the Öhman group nor by several other workers, (McNally & Foa 1986; Öhman et al. 1984).

To separate out cultural from phyletic influences, differential conditioning was compared to slides showing evolutionary old versus recent dangers. Phyletically old fear-relevant stimuli such as snakes and spiders yielded slower extinction of SC responses than did phyletically new fear-relevant stimuli such as firearms pointing sideways away from the observer (Cook et al. 1986) and broken electric cords and electric plugs (Hugdahl & Kärker 1981). The first study also found that the highest conditioned heart rate acceleration during acquisition was to snakes and spiders. (A caveat about that study is that perhaps the firearms should have pointed *at* the observer to be fear-relevant.)

Could prepotency (salience) alone account for the subsequent preparedness found frequently in these studies, and for the greater response of subjects seeing snake/spider slides when these were paired (conditioned) rather than unpaired? This explanation is unlikely for four reasons (M. Fredrikson and also A. Öhman, personal communications, 1980). First, prepotency is not found with finger pulse volume even when preparedness occurs on this measure (responses during extinction take longer to reach baseline with fear-relevant than neutral slides). Second, preparedness was found only for an aversive US (shock) but not for a neutral US (tone), although prepotency was present initially for both US groups (Öhman et al. 1978). Third, although complex stimuli (abstract paintings) were more prepotent than simple stimuli (color only), they did not condition more. Fourth, salience is more obvious for dorsal than for palmar SC responses, yet the reverse is true for differential conditioning (Fredrikson 1980). Fear-relevant stimuli are thus probably both prepotent and prepared, but prepotency is not essential for preparedness.

The demonstration of preparedness may partly depend on the types of CS and US and the response being measured, as Lang and his colleagues found in careful work in Wisconsin and Florida (reviewed by Cook et al. 1986). In four experiments with the US as noxious noise rather than the shock used by the Öhman group, there was little evidence of preparedness of SC responses to fear-relevant stimuli, despite reliable overall conditioning and the unconditioned response (UR) from noise being as large as that from shock. Nevertheless, more cardiac acceleration occurred to fear-relevant than to neutral stimuli.

Perhaps snakes and spiders condition less when the aversive US is auditory rather than tactile (both taxa bite)? The Lang group tested whether preparedness would be greater if the US was noxious noise compounded with vibration to the hand rather than the same noise alone (Cook et al. 1986). Adding the tactile to the auditory US gave prepared SC conditioning more consistent with that of Öhman. Furthermore, during acquisition, conditioned rise in heart rate developed to slides of snakes and spiders but not to neutral slides, and this preparedness measure, too, was enhanced by adding the vibration.

Greater preparedness of snake and spider stimuli to associate to tactile than to auditory USs was confirmed by Cook and his colleagues in two further studies using shock rather than vibration as the tactile stimulus. In the first, a shock US had effects like those of a compound vibration-plus-noise US, giving preparedness of snakes and spiders for SC during extinction, and for rise in heart rate during acquisition. Next, Cook and coworkers compared a shock US with a noise US. Half the subjects in each group were told at the start of extinction that they would get no more shocks. As before, preparedness was found with the shock US for SC during extinction and heart rate during acquisition; only heart rate showed preparedness with the noise US as well. A pooled analysis was then undertaken of all the Wisconsin and Florida studies. This found preparedness of the conditioned rise in heart rate during acquisition, especially when the US was tactile (vibration or shock) rather than auditory (noise).

Although reliable preparedness was found using tactile USs, SC signs of it in the extinction phase disappeared when subjects were told that there would be no more shocks. Moreover, preparedness SC effects could be induced by instructions alone—that is, when subjects saw slides while expecting a shock or noise but not actually receiving it (Cook et al. 1986). As the authors comment, "it is just as likely that the information processing patterns of the brain are shaped by evolutionary considerations as are the response patterns of the visceral nervous system."

In brief, the Lang group, like the Öhman group, found support for the idea that phobia-relevant stimuli prompt a special conditioned response, and found preparedness even more for heart rate than for SC. Across experiments the preparedness of heart rate acquisition was more reliable than preparedness of SC extinction and showed less influence of CS-US "belongingness"; in other words, phobia-relevant stimuli induced conditioned heart rate acceleration whether they were paired with a tactile or an auditory US.

In the absence of prior fear, snakes can become safety signals as well as flowers can (McNally & Reiss 1984). Preparedness is not negated by this finding, nor by the fact that exposure treatment improves phobias of spiders at least as quickly as it does phobias of less obviously relevant stimuli, such as feathers (Watson et al. 1972).

Social Situations

Throughout evolution other people have been vital for our survival, so it is natural that we are so responsive to their emotions and intentions. Our fellows' facial expressions are powerful stimuli that evoke similar feelings in us (reviewed by Öhman & Dimberg 1984). When a model looks angry, pained, or happy, EMG activity rises in the observer's corrugator muscles that frown the eyebrow, orbicularis oculi that narrow the eye, or zygomatic muscles that lift the corners of the mouth in a smile. Being looked at is especially frightening for social phobics.

Angry or frightened human expressions are prepotent stimuli that produce conditioned activation more readily than do happy expressions. Three groups of students were conditioned to pictures of angry, happy, or neutral faces. Each subject saw repeated random presentations of pictures of two different faces displaying the same emotions. During initial unreinforced presentations of the faces (habituation phase) there was no difference in skin conductance (SC) response between groups of students or pictures. In a subsequent acquisition phase, one of the two different faces (CS+) was followed by a shock US, whereas the other (CS−) was not; the CS+ quickly came to evoke reliably larger SC responses than did the CS−, regardless of whether the facial expressions were angry, happy, or neutral. In the next phase (extinction), the faces were shown without shock; greater SC response to CS+ versus CS− continued with angry faces but disappeared with happy or neutral faces. The students had readily associated all faces with shocks but lost this association more slowly when the faces signaled the threat of anger.

Similar results were found using the threat of fearful rather than angry expressions (Orr & Lanzetta 1980, reviewed by Öhman & Dimberg 1984). Fearful, neutral, or happy faces were presented in compound with a neutral stimulus (a tone) as signals for an aversive US. During extinction the two components of each CS were tested separately to see which had associated more to the aversive US. Fearful faces overshadowed tone, tone overshadowed happy faces, and tone and neutral faces did not differ.

Angry faces were effective CSs only when looking at the subject as though he or she was the target of attention (Öhman & Dimberg 1984). Extinction of SC responses to angry faces looking away was as rapid as to happy faces. The critical issue was the direction in which the faces looked during extinction. Subjects who had been conditioned to an angry face looking away continued to respond if it faced them during extinction. In contrast, subjects who had been conditioned to an angry face looking at them promptly ceased to respond if it looked away during extinction. The subjects associated an angry display with a US regardless of its direction, but showed that learning during extinction only when the angry face looked at them. Conversely, a SC response to an angry person's face without shock diminished more if the subject had previously been conditioned to that person looking happily at rather than away from him.

An intriguing question is whether direction affects the response to frightened as well as to angry expressions. Danger is higher on seeing an angry person look at us rather than away, but this is less true when we see someone afraid. Learned responses to fearful faces might be less sensitive to the direction they face. However, we can gauge their expression better when they face us, so the effect of more information may override other considerations.

Are learned responses to anger specific to the angry person? This is so if acquisition involves only one person's angry face and extinction involves another; the resistance to extinction of the CS+ then disappears. We do not yet know whether person-specificity would remain if more than one person's angry face was shown during acquisition.

Issues To Be Resolved

Differential conditioning is fragile and elusive. Although it was obtained repeatedly in Öhman's original laboratory in Uppsala, Sweden, and often in Lang's group in Wisconsin and Florida, it was weak in Chicago (McNally 1986) and could not be found in Belgium (Eelen, personal communication, 1983), in Philadelphia (McNally & Foa 1986), or even by Öhman himself in Bergen, Norway. For preparedness to occur, the US may have to be in a particular sensory modality, as we saw, and its intensity can affect outcome (A. Öhman, personal communication, 1980). A more aversive US (loud noise) was used in Wisconsin (Cook et al. 1985) than in Uppsala (mild shock), producing much larger URs. This conditioned neutral stimuli more, which, by a ceiling effect, might obscure any greater conditioning of fear-relevant stimuli. When in a later trial Lang's group used a less aversive and shorter US, their SC results approached those of Uppsala.

Other differences among laboratories are less well understood. Compared with neutral slides, snake slides gave differential conditioning both in Uppsala and in Bergen, whereas spider slides did so only in Uppsala. In Belgium and in Florida, telling subjects at the start of extinction that no more shocks would be given abolished responses to fear-relevant as well as to neutral stimuli.

SC responses subsided more slowly with intense stimuli, whether they were very unpleasant *or* pleasant (have prior "significance"—Maltzman & Boyd 1984). But this fails to explain why fear-relevant stimuli were more "significant" (prepotent) in some studies than in others.

The conditions essential for preparedness effects are not clear and need to be elucidated over a broader range of stimuli and responses. Very few fear-relevant stimuli have been studied to date—snakes and spiders, and guns and electric sockets. Experimenters failed to measure subjective anxiety, and none examined avoidance, both of which are critical for models of phobias. Nor has anyone tested the prepotency of those stimuli and responses which are commonly involved in obsessive-compulsive disorder (see Chapter 13) and whether they associate together selectively. It would also be worth testing preparedness effects with (1) other evolutionary important stimuli, such as heights in babies aged 6 months, strangers in babies aged 8 months, and darkness and thunderstorms at later ages; (2) the same stimulus-response link across differently aged children, (3) differing durations of the phase between acquisition and extinction, which may illuminate the incubation of fear; (4) MZ twins reared apart versus DZ twins, and (5) more evolutionary new versus old dangers.

Support for the preparedness notion comes not only from the Öhman paradigm but also from an "overshadowing" study of Mineka and coworkers (1984b) which deserves replication in humans with careful control for salience of stimuli. When rhesus monkeys watched models show fear of a combined flower/snake stimulus, they acquired a fear only of snakes, not of flowers. We are reminded that taste aversion conditions more readily to recent new taste CSs than to even more recent but less "relevant" events such as tones or light flashes.

The concepts of relevance and preparedness are not far apart, and exploring one might illuminate the other. It makes good evolutionary sense that functionally related events such as taste and vomiting seem more linked than others that rarely occur together under natural conditions. Preparedness studies have to take into account the usual adaptation and ecology of the species being studied, hard as that might be to guess for humans prior to civilization.

It is intriguing that preparedness for SC appeared more during extinction than during preceding acquisition, whereas for heart rate it appeared more during acquisition. Perhaps very rapid SC conditioning masked a difference between phobia-relevant versus neutral stimuli. The finding of preparedness of SC during extinction ties nicely with the idea (Marks 1981) that many phobias and rituals may result as much from failed extinction as from enhanced acquisition, just as the progress of some cancers seems due as much to failure of immune mechanisms as to the production of cancer cells. All of us have lots of minor fears and rituals (and cancer cells), but these do not generally grow into a problem because they are quickly extinguished (habituated) by deliberate exposure (and immune processes). This view suggests that efforts at prevention should promote exposure without avoidance (Chapter 14).

In light of the possibility that acquisition might result as much from failed extinction as from new learning, the rest of this chapter will review some salient issues in the rise and fall of fear.

FEAR ACQUISITION

Paradigms of Defensive Learning

In chapters 1, 3, 5, and 6 we noted the many forms of defensive response that have been regarded as expressions of fear. How experience affects their acquisition, maintenance, and decline has been examined in a vast number of studies in animals and to a lesser extent in humans. Habituation is described later, and sensitization is noted in Chapter 7. Here we will deal with defensive learning involving conditioning and social learning. The topic has been extensively reviewed by McIntosh (1983) and Mineka (1985), to whom much of the following is indebted.

Classical Conditioning

The usual paradigm for learned fear is classical (Pavlovian) association of a neutral stimulus (the to-be-conditioned CS), such as a light or tone, with an aversive stimulus (the unconditioned US), such as shock. A neutral stimulus becomes an aversive CS (CS+) if it signals an aversive US, and conversely becomes a conditioned safety signal (CS−) if it heralds relief from that US or a long period without a US.

Conditioning develops not from CS-US pairings as such but from the probability that a CS predicts the US or gives new information about it. First, 10 CS-US pairings lead to conditioning only if additional USs are not presented at other random points in time as well; that is, the CS must predict the US, CS-US contiguity alone being insufficient (Rescorla 1967). Second, if a CS that has already been established as a conditioned stimulus (CS_1) is compounded with a second CS that has not been so conditioned (CS_2), then conditioning to CS_2 will be blocked if $CS_1 + CS_2$ is paired with the US (Kamin 1968). Conditioning occurs selectively to good predictors of reinforcement at the expense of worse predictors.

Although temporal contiguity is neither necessary nor sufficient, fear conditioning is often most rapid when the US follows the CS at an interval of up to a minute or so, although there may be different effective CS-US intervals for various CS-US combinations. Conditioned taste aversion can occur despite hours elapsing between a food CS and the subsequent US of nausea and vomiting. Another exception is backward fear conditioning, evidence for which is mounting (Spetch et al. 1981). Classical conditioning is faster if the CS and US are along similar dimensions and spatially contiguous.

The associability of stimuli may decrease after *preexposure* to a CS, which procedure is indistinguishable from that used to obtain habituation or extinction—repeated presentation of an unpaired stimulus in a stable context. Gradually it ceases to evoke the responses it produced the first time and becomes difficult to condition to a US (latent inhibition). The effect may be context-specific and can be enduring; recovery between sessions is incomplete, and responding declines more rapidly in the second session than in the first. Vicarious and direct preexposure have similar effects in rhesus monkeys (Mineka et al. 1984b). Somewhat related to preexposure is *learned irrelevance*—retarded conditioning of a CS to a US after prior experience of their independence.

Avoidance Conditioning

The usual paradigm for phobias is passive or active conditioned avoidance. This occurs when an animal is allowed to avoid an aversive US (such as a shock) either by doing something that switches it off (jumping or running away from the site where a shock is experienced) or by inhibiting approach to its locus. Avoidance is learned if it reduces the probability, frequency, or intensity of aversive stimulation.

In unsignaled (free-operant, Sidman) avoidance there is no signal (though usually time serves as one). The animal is able to postpone or cancel the shocks by making the avoidance response. In signaled avoidance a discrete warning CS (a tone or a light, for example) is given just before the US, and the US is withheld if the animal performs the required avoidance response or terminated if avoidance occurs during it (escape). Most of these experiments arrange that the avoidance response turns off the warning signal. Early in avoidance training the warning CS becomes frightening because it has been paired with the US. However, once the animals have learned to make the avoidance response as soon as the CS comes on, thus avoiding the US, they no longer appear frightened of the CS, which has ceased to predict the US. Whether the US is signaled or unsignaled, an animal that learns to avoid it quickly may never experience the US again after the first few trials.

Laboratory animals have been trained to avoid only the US, not the CS (Mineka 1985). It is often said that the stimuli avoided by phobics and ritualizers are CSs, not USs, but this is hard to decide. Some think that such stimuli are the direct source of a US (for instance, a bite from dogs), implying that prepotency is embedded in them. This could just conceivably apply to stimuli such as animals and heights, but not to feathers, chocolate, or the host of other unnatural targets for rarer phobias and rituals. Most phobics and ritualizers know that their fears are absurd and not the source of a US.

Whether a stimulus is a CS or a US may be relevant only to the readiness of an organism to attend and attach fear to it. Once the association has occurred, it may be immaterial whether that stimulus had originally been a US or a CS. Whatever ways stimuli became frightening, from then on they can all be regarded as CSs with the same rules of generalization, maintenance, and extinction. In the clinic, established phobias and rituals cannot be talked away, and all seem to subside in a similar manner with exposure. Habituation is no respector of origins, causing even the most innate defensive reponses to die down just like learned ones (see Chapter 7 and below). Moreover, for both innate and learned defense responses, different facets of the response may decline at varying rates. Avoidance may subside well before physiological or subjective signs of emotion do (discordance, desynchrony).

A common operant paradigm of fear is punishment of an appetitive response, which produces conflict between approach and avoidance. An animal may first learn to run to a certain point or press a lever to get food and is then shocked while doing those things; fear is measured by the ensuing reduction in approach or in lever pressing. The behavior may be suppressed more if punished before the consummatory point than after it. Although punishing a conditioned response usually suppresses it, punishing avoidance sometimes actually increases it, a paradox called vicious-circle behavior. Another paradigm is frustration, where a reward is withheld after the animal has learned to expect it.

An operant situation reminiscent both of preexposure to the CS and of learned irrelevance is the learned helplessness that follows preexposure to many inescapable shocks (USs). Animals that first have inescapable shocks and then have the chance to learn an avoidance response to switch off the shocks often fail to do so or are slow to learn it. Prior experience of an inescapable US interferes with their learning to do something that will now terminate an aversive US. Such learned helplessness can be abolished by forcing the animals to carry out the avoidance response—that is, by dragging them to the other side of a shuttlebox when such movement is required to stop the shock. The animals then learn that they can control the shock. Another way to abolish learned helplessness, in rhesus monkeys, is to show a different fear stimulus (a net previously used to restrain them) at shock onset, and to remove it immediately after the monkey completes the avoidance response (Rush et al. 1983).

Social Learning

Groups of animals learn by observing one another and develop a culture distinctive for their group. Recognition and fear of enemies can be culturally transmitted very readily in birds. This was ingeniously shown for the aggressive defense response of mobbing in five experiments with blackbirds *(Turdus merula)* (Curio 1978). Two cages were placed on opposite sides of a hallway in sight of each other. One contained an "observer" blackbird, and the other cage contained a second blackbird serving as "teacher." Between these two was a four-chambered box that could be rotated so that each bird could see opposite chambers. The remaining two chambers were empty. A stuffed Australian honeyeater *(Philemon corniculatus)* was chosen as the to-be-conditioned object

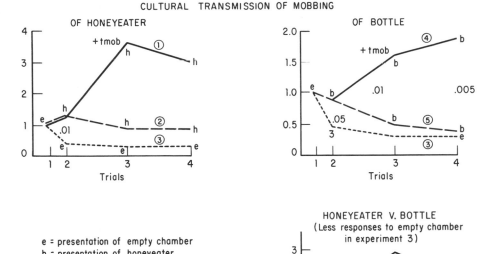

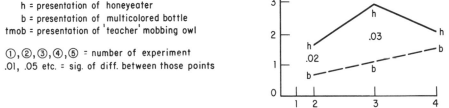

Fig. 8.1 Cultural transmission of mobbing in blackbirds in a single trial. (Data from Curio 1978.)

placed in the chamber shown to the observer blackbird, as it is novel, resembles no predator of blackbirds, yet is of a size similar to some of their predators. A stuffed little owl *(Athene noctua)* was shown to the teacher in the opposite chamber at the moment that rotation of the box exposed only the honeyeater to the observer. Between trials the box was rotated so that both observer and teacher saw only the empty chamber. Except for the third trial the teacher was visually shielded from the observer.

Strong single-trial vicarious conditioning resulted (Figure 8.1). On trial 1, the observer blackbird saw only the empty chamber, with little effect. On trial 2 the observer saw only the novel honeyeater, which evoked a small mobbing response that subsided when the observer saw the honeyeater again alone on trial 3. However, the response on trial 3 was very different if the observer saw not only the honeyeater for the second time but also simultaneous mobbing by the teacher blackbird of the owl (tmob in Figure 8.1); the teacher furiously tried to mob the owl through the cage, giving nearly 60 "tix" calls per minute, and the observer would now try to mob the honeyeater far more than on the previous trial when it had seen the honeyeater alone. At trial 4 the observer saw the honeyeater for a third time, again alone. Marked mobbing occurred once more—the observer had been strongly conditioned to the novel bird in merely one trial. Though strong, the observer's mobbing of the honeyeater on trials 3 and 4 was less marked than the teacher's mobbing of the owl; no "tix" calls were given.

This single-trial cultural transmission was remarkably persistent. It was passed on through a chain of six blackbirds where each observer in turn became the teacher for the next. Mobbing remained as strong in the sixth bird at the end of the chain as it had been in the first, and was even stronger when the honeyeater was presented alone in the test subsequent to vicarious conditioning.

There were several pointers to the honeyeater's being a prepotent and prepared stimulus for conditioning. First, even on first presentations as novel stimuli the honeyeater was more salient (evoked more mobbing) than a multi-colored plastic bottle of similar length to the honeyeater (trial 2 in the lower right quadrant of Figure 8.1). Second, habitation to repeated stimulation was more rapid with the empty chamber than with the honeyeater on its own (top left quadrant of Figure 8.1). The greater preparedness of the honeyeater than of the bottle as a conditioning target was seen when each was presented at the same time that the observer could see a teacher blackbird mobbing an owl hidden from the observer. Both on the conditioning (third) trial and on the subsequent (fourth) trial, when the honeyeater or bottle were again shown alone, mobbing was greater to the honeyeater, although there was also a rise in mobbing to the bottle (lower right quadrant of Figure 8.1).

Mobbing of predators is an innate aggressive-defensive response obtainable from birds raised in isolation, and the mobbing call is similar across several species who share mutual enemies (see Chapter 3). The response is widespread in birds and mammals despite being time-consuming and potentially dangerous for the mobber. Cultural transmission of enemy recognition in merely one conditioning trial recruits allies from the flock who benefit the teacher directly by joining attack on the predator and driving it away more easily. Social transmission might also benefit the teacher through kin selection in the way that alarm calls do in squirrels (see Chapter 4), but this remains to be demonstrated.

Humans are more flexible than blackbirds, yet some of our fears and prejudices might be transmitted as quickly and enduringly by observational learning of prepotent cues and reactions, especially during childhood and adolescence. Fears of snakes, spiders, and various human races and ethnic groups are transmitted unchangingly across the generations. It is an uphill struggle to reduce our destructive fear and hatred of outgroups, which has killed tens of millions across the millenia to the present day. Rapid observational learning may lead to such persistent fears unless they are subsequently habituated by repeated corrective (habituating) experiences. These two principles alone— quick learning by observation and absence of later habituation—might explain many cultural fears. Such fears might be prevented by carefully applying those two principles to education and the media.

Absence of cultural as well as innate fears probably accounts for the tameness of animals living on islands that are relatively free of predators (see Chapter 6), and the speed with which predation leads to rapid acquisition of fear and its cultural transmission to succeeding generations. This was seen in 1914 in what is now the Addo Park in South Africa (Gould 1982, p. 285). A hunter was asked to exterminate a herd of 140 elephants. By a year later he had shot all but 20 but could not kill the rest, and the area became a preserve in 1930. Although they have not been shot at since, and practically all the elephants who were originally hunted have died of old age, this fourth-generation herd remains shy and strangely nocturnal, and very dangerous.

What is true for birds and elephants is also true for primates. Persistent snake fear was readily transmitted by modeling from wild-reared rhesus parents to their adolescent offspring and among unrelated rhesus who barely knew one another. Disturbance in the models correlated fully .96 with subsequent disturbance in the observers (Mineka et al. 1984b, 1985; see also Chapter 2). There is no doubt that human fear can begin by observational learning (modeling) (Bandura 1969), as anyone who has seen panic spreading in a crowd will realize. Equally, watching someone behave courageously can inspire others to emulate that example. But though modeling affects the rise and fall of fear, its importance for persistent phobias and rituals is less well established.

Aversive Learning as a Model for Phobics and Obsessive-Compulsives

Despite early hopes that conditioning paradigms would match clinical states, no learning model completely fits phobic or obsessive-compulsive (oc) syndromes as a whole. Nevertheless, there are some interesting minimodels—parallels between certain laboratory and clinical features (well summarized by Mineka 1985, on whom much of this section is based).

Phobic and OC Fear and Avoidance

One parallel is the way that an extinguished fear or avoidance CR can be *reinstated* by reexposure to the US alone in the original context (Rescorla & Heth 1975). The US need not be the one originally involved in conditioning (in one study, a horn reinstated a fear conditioned response (CR) established with shock. Long ago Pavlov observed that when his dogs nearly drowned in a chance flooding of his laboratory, conditioned reflexes that had previously been extinguished became reinstated. Similarly, phobics and ocs who improve after exposure may relapse years later after depression or a trauma unrelated to the onset of their disorder; these setbacks can be overcome by further exposure (see Chapter 15). Like dishabituation, reinstatement and relapse are forms of response increment after previous response decrement.

Another parallel is how, even long after conditioning with a moderately intense US, a subsequent US of greater intensity can *inflate* the CR (Rescorla & Heth 1974). This is a bit reminiscent of the stuttering growth of phobias and rituals; in agoraphobics, spontaneous panics could serve as USs, but in other cases the US, if any, is often obscure.

When avoidance responses are trained with *serial CSs* (such as a tone, then light, then a vibration followed by a shock), subsequent extinction takes much longer. The early part of a CS rapidly elicits enough fear to produce escape/ avoidance so that in the extinction phase, when the US is discontinued, it is hard for the animal to learn that the later parts of the CS are no longer followed by a shock. Some argue that many phobic and oc stimuli can be thought of as serial CSs that are similarly hard to extinguish, with performance of the earliest responses in the series avoiding occurrence of later ones (Levis & Boyd 1979). Suggested examples of serial CSs are fear of fear in agoraphobics, obsessive thoughts, and compulsive rituals.

After acquiring a conditioned fear animals tend to remain afraid but to forget quite what they are afraid of—the specificity of the fear diminishes (Hendersen 1978). In contrast, conditioned inhibitors of fear in animals tend to fade over a few months. Both processes might lead to loss of discrimination between fearful and safe places or events, and so to the generalization of fear; however, it is unclear how important they are in humans. Such factors might partly explain why so few phobics and ocs give a history of trauma.

In animals more fear is produced and conditioned by uncontrollable rather than controllable aversive events. In rats, uncontrollable shock was followed by prolonged estrus cycles in females and more fear and less learning of escape from shock through bar press in subsequent offspring, particularly males; the latter could have ensued from uterine or rearing factors (Seligman 1975). Human phobics often feel they might lose control, though it is hard to judge how much this feeling causes or results from fear. Perhaps both effects interact. Similarly, phobics who feel in control of their own destiny may be more likely to engage in the exposure that will diminish their phobia, and fear reduction itself can lead to a sense of mastery. The extent to which such processes operate clinically is unclear. Even controllable events are more aversive if they are unpredictable (novel) rather than predictable. In the absence of control, predictable aversive events still cause fear.

Compulsive Rituals

Four animal parallels to rituals have been proposed (Mineka 1985). The first two are repetitive behaviors induced by training.

1. *Well-trained avoidance:* As dogs learn to avoid a traumatic US their avoidance becomes increasingly stereotyped, occurs with decreasing latencies and steadily fewer signs of anxiety, and persists for hundreds of trials without any further US unless the avoidance is blocked while the CS continues (Solomon et al. 1953).
2. *Abnormal fixations:* Rats that were repeatedly forced to jump from a stand to solve an insoluble discrimination problem continued to make the fixated response even after the problem had been made soluble and they seemed to know the correct response; for example, they might orient to the left and now correct side, but still jump off to the right side (Maier 1949). Punishing the fixated response strengthened it.

The third and fourth types of repetitive behavior seem to be unlearned responses to stress.

3. *Primate stereotypies:* Primates under stress often engage in repetitive stereotypic locomotion or ritualistic movements such as picking teeth or strumming the mesh of the cage. These happen especially in monkeys reared in isolation or repeatedly separated.
4. *Displacement activities:* These are seen in many species during conflict or high arousal—examples are repetitive grooming or nesting (see Chapter 3), which might be analogous to compulsive washing or tidying.

Rituals have some features of unsignaled Sidman avoidance (Teasdale 1974), which lessens the chance of shocks and is under poor stimulus control; and ocs find it similarly hard to tell safe from unsafe cues. Many rituals of ocs are attempts to avoid future danger, which task can never be finished. Noncontingent safety signals decrease and noncontingent fear stimuli increase Sidman avoidance; ocs seem to have few safe thoughts and many frightening ones.

Most compulsive rituals and some obsessive thoughts reduce anxiety. Sufferers are more likely to ritualize when they feel tense and usually feel better after ritualizing (see Chapter 13). In animals, occasional free shocks increase conditioned avoidance. Shocking avoidance also sometimes increases it (vicious-circle behavior), perhaps because that raises anxiety, which is then decreased by avoidance.

Are there animal counterparts to the way that oc rituals (and agoraphobia) generalize widely? In animals, new established fear CSs can immediately acquire control over avoidance responses previously established in the same context. Moreover, responses that reduce fear of frustration in one situation often recur when the animal is frightened or frustrated in different contexts where those responses are of no help. Similarly, oc rituals (and agoraphobia) often spread when the patient is miserable for some reason.

Mineka (1985) cites three examples of inappropriate, regressive "rituals" appearing during frustration in new situations.

1. Dogs were trained first to lift their leg to avoid shock and/or airpuffs and then to make an increasingly hard appetitive discrimination (Fonberg 1956). The latter induced progressive disturbance in the dogs, during which leg lifting rose without any further cues for it. Additional shaking-off movements appeared in dogs previously conditioned to avoid airpuffs into the ear.
2. Hungry rats were trained to jump hurdles or climb for occasional reward by food in a short, black-sided box (Ross 1964). Thereafter the rats were made thirsty but could drink water each time they ran down a long, narrow, white runway. Finally the water was withheld despite such running (extinction schedule); the jumping and climbing now re-emerged despite there being no hurdles to jump or appropriate box to climb out of; that is, those instrumental responses had became conditioned to frustration.
3. Animals were frustrated in one situation, and idiosyncratic rituals

emerged as the instrumentally learned response. When they were later frustrated for the first time in a different context, idiosyncratic rituals re-emerged (Amsel & Rashotte 1969).

Obsessive-compulsives manifest both passive and active avoidance and also escape. Cleaners or checkers will passively avoid evoking cues such as dirt or doorlocking and, if this is not possible, actively avoid and escape from those cues and their expected consequences by ritualistic cleaning and checking. It is not known whether ocs have a high childhood background of parental criticism, punishment, or overprotection (forms of avoidance training) (see Chapter 13).

In some ocs and phobics, avoidance (and rituals in ocs) seems to be partly independent of fear, being either present while fear is absent before therapy or remaining after fear has declined during exposure therapy in another instance of discordance (Marks et al. 1969; Walton & Mather 1963). In an animal parallel, a small amount of exposure reduced fear but not associated stereotyped jump-up avoidance (Mineka et al. 1981).

In animals as in man, oc (and phobic) fear and avoidance are reduced if avoidance and the rituals are prevented, especially if CS exposure is long and is not terminated by escape or avoidance—ritualistic or escape/avoidance behavior no longer signal the start of a safe period. There are close parallels between anxiety-reduction across phyla.

Generalized (Freefloating) Anxiety and Spontaneous Panic

These conditions are present in most agoraphobics at some stage (see chapters 9 and 10) and in generalized anxiety disorder and panic disorder without phobias. Such anxiety and panic were mimicked by animals with experimental neurosis that were described long ago by Pavlov, Gantt, and Liddell (reviewed by Mineka & Kihlstrom 1978). They were restless, hypersensitive, apprehensive, distractible, autonomically hyperactive (rapid respiration and heart rate, muscle tension, piloerection, mydriasis), and had difficulty in learning.

In the studies that produced experimental neurosis, vital events (food for a hungry animal, shock for a restrained one) became uncontrollable, unpredictable, or both. Lack of control, uncertainty, and helplessness may contribute to anxiety and depression in animals (Mineka & Hendersen 1985). Much recent animal work found that exposure to uncontrollable or unpredictable (as opposed to controllable or predictable) aversive events led, among others, to impaired learning of control in subsequent tasks, passivity, reduced aggression, ulcers, analgesia, raised cortisol, and changes in neurotransmitters. A few of these features appear in human panic as well. Uncontrollability seems more important than unpredictability, though the two often go together.

Experimental neurosis may have some similarities to the long-term sensitization seen in mollusks after unsignalled, unpredictable, and uncontrollable aversive stimuli (Kandel 1983; see also Chapter 7). Such sensitization was proposed as a model for chronic anxiety and generalized anxiety disorder. Certain aspects of experimental neurosis are also seen when primate offspring protest at being separated from their parents (see Chapter 5), and with classical conditioning in mammals of interoceptive CSs and/or USs that are outside awareness (Razran 1961). Such interoceptive CS are part of daily life and theoretically could play a role in freefloating anxiety and psychosomatic disorders, but little is known about this. Evidence is similarly lacking for the equating of generalized anxiety with classical conditioning to external stimuli that are ubiquitous in the environment (Wolpe 1958).

Another explanation for generalized anxiety might be instrumental interoceptive conditioning; this has been shown in animals and humans for responses of heart rate, blood pressure, or skin conductance, using rewarding brain stimulation or shock avoidance as reinforcers. Such experiments seem unlikely models because the conditioned effects are so small and specific and require more tightly controlled feedback and reinforcement than would occur naturally (Mineka 1985).

Shortcomings of Animal Models of Anxiety Syndromes

Despite the parallels, animal models incompletely simulate the anxiety syndromes they try to mimic. The following sections discuss some of these shortcomings in detail.

Few Cases Start after Direct or Indirect Trauma

In Chapter 5 we saw conclusive evidence that young subhuman and human primates develop certain fears without any traumatic experience. Moreover, phobic and oc patients and volunteers rarely remember a traumatic onset (Marks 1977; Murray & Foote 1979, Rachman 1978; Rimm et al. 1977). Öst & Hugdahl (1981) put the figure at over 50%, but they called initial panic in the phobic situation a "trauma," which is a tautology; one should include only an independent US in otherwise unchanged circumstances. (The same authors later noted "that it is only a minority of the cases for which the UCS to the *first* anxiety attack can be identified" [Öst & Hugdahl 1983]). The same confound was also present in another report (McNally & Steketee 1985).

One could, of course, postulate an interoceptive US triggering the first panic, but that has to be demonstrated, not merely speculated. Spontaneous panic might act as a US in some agoraphobics but is uncommon in other phobics and ritualizers. Most cases have unaccountable discomfort as the primary event that is secondarily attached to other stimuli or feelings that then lead to avoidance and rituals. Only the latter process could truly be called conditioning, not the initial discomfort.

Some phobic and oc problems begin after aversive life events not obviously related to the subsequent problem (see chapters 10 through 13). Examples are bereavement, marital separation, accident, or physical illness. This is hardly specific to phobic or oc syndromes. Many disorders such as depression, schizophrenia, asthma, and myocardial infarction, to name but a few, follow major upheavals of a similar kind that are more frequent than in unaffected individuals. Massive physical and psychological disturbance render people susceptible to a large variety of disorders, and organic and psychiatric disorders often begin at related times within an individual (Hinkle & Wolff 1957). In addition, phobic and oc problems frequently begin during a depressive spell and remain after it clears. Of equal interest are those many cases which start without any preceding depression or major change in the sufferer's environment.

Modeling. Are traumatic conditioning histories so infrequent because phobics and ocs acquire their worries vicariously by seeing other people being frightened? Though we saw earlier that such modeling can powerfully transmit normal fear, there is little to suggest that it accounts for more than a small proportion of all phobics and ocs. Few say that they saw relatives or others with similar problems. Only among blood phobics do more than half the cases give a history of a family member with a similar problem, and that may well reflect genetic transmission of a liability to heart-rate slowing with blood-injury stimuli. For other phobics and ocs, although familial incidence is indeed above chance expectations, this still leaves only exceptional cases with an affected family member. Even then, the pattern of the problem in the relative commonly differs from that in the patient; furthermore, each may be ignorant of its presence in the other. Thus, modeling of that pattern is unlikely to explain its coexistence.

The rarity of vicarious phobic conditioning might be due to immunization against it by frequent encounters in the presence of nonphobic models (vicarious courage). Perhaps fear modeling has a lasting effect only if the individual encounters a new situation together with a phobic model either repeatedly or the first time. Such encounters might be rare. Modeling could also be of traits such as timidity or meticulousness that might predispose to the development of particular phobias and rituals. This would not preclude a possible genetic contribution as well. Learning does not occur in a genetic vacuum.

Forgetting and Recall of Initiating Trauma. Could patients simply have forgotten their original trauma? In animals, once second-order conditioning has occurred, the first-order CR is sometimes extinguished without decreasing the second-order one (Rizley & Rescorla 1972). Perhaps human phobics and their relatives forget the initial CRs, remembering only more recent higher-order ones. Other cases may have forgotten initial depression, conflict, or frustration that are less memorable than sharply defined traumatic events. The frustration of withholding expected rewards can bring on emotionality in animals (Mineka 1985). If forgetting is part of the answer, then memories of first-order traumatic conditioning, depression, conflict, and frustration might be more frequent, the more recent the onset of the problem. This has not been tested.

It is hard to study in animals whether the inclination to forget unpleasant things itself maintains phobias. Early Freudian treatments held that neurosis came from repression of traumatic memories, relief depending on recovering those memories. This is unlikely to be a general rule. When trauma is known to have precipitated the phobic or oc problem, sufferers can usually discuss it fairly openly; yet this does not lead to relief.

Exceptionally, during treatment or chance events the patient will recall a long-forgotten trigger, and recall may herald remission of the phobia in the manner predicted by early analysts. Such cases of phobia were reviewed by Marks (1969). Most remembered a trauma from childhood rather than adult life, except for dramatic cases of war neurosis in which subjects were relieved by abreaction (see Chapter 14). The histories are well documented and leave little doubt that occasionally recall of forgotten traumas is followed by relief from phobias connected with them.

We must be cautious, however, about the role played by forgotten traumas in the genesis of phobias. The recall was decades after the original events, and it is unclear when they were forgotten or whether there were other important traumas that were never recalled although the phobia improved. The forgetting could have occurred long after the problem had begun and included events unrelated to the trauma. Some of the forgotten traumas were recalled during hypnotic and abreactive sessions, which can relieve anxiety despite the fact that their content is irrelevant to the cause. Most phobics clearly remember the onset of their phobias, whether traumatic or not, and obtain no relief from talking about them. Memories can return because of improvement rather than the reverse, as we see sometimes in grief and post-traumatic stress disorder. Finally, patients can become able to talk about embarrassing things for the first time as they gain confidence on improvement during exposure (Lamontagne & Marks 1973).

Incubation—Delay Between Trauma and Problem Onset

Studies of aversive learning in animals have found little evidence of the incubating lag period that is so common clinically between the sudden trauma or events causing anxiety, guilt, or impotent resentment and subsequent phobias or rituals. The clinical problem often starts not straight after the trauma but only after a delay of a few days, and may take years to reach full intensity. What is happening during the incubating phase after the trauma? The process may be a form of sensitization.

Some patients rehearse the trauma in their mind, building up emotion to the point of kindling avoidance of the painful situation; avoidance lessens tension, strengthening the tendency to further avoidance in an addictive cycle. For example, a shy woman of 42 had long felt sensitive to the stares of people. She was given the wrong change in a shop and was too uneasy to claim her proper change back. After a few weeks she gradually became uncomfortable in the shop, then could not go into it, and later could not even pass it in the street lest she saw the man who had shortchanged her. She was always able to remember the trigger, and talking about it did not relieve her phobia.

Other patients are adamant that there was no mental rehearsal during the delay. A young man had his leg fractured in a motorcycle accident and was immobilized in plaster for 6 months, during which time he looked forward to riding again. On removal of the plaster and getting back on his motorcycle he felt fine, but a few minutes later fear began as he entered situations reminiscent of his accident, forcing him to return home and stop riding permanently.

In war neurosis, Kardiner & Spiegel (1947) saw the acute phase as the time when it became organized. To prevent this they recommended early therapy of the shell-shocked soldier as near as possible to the front lines and the sounds and smells of battle. (The same principle lies behind the adage "if you fall off a horse or a bicycle, get back on immediately.") A rat study found a critical period of about 3 days after shocks during which reexposure to the traumatic situation enhanced extinction of the newly conditioned fear (Willmuth & Peters 1964).

Immunizing exposure need not even be to the relevant trauma if it is done quickly enough. Stressful swimming for 5 minutes extinguished newly conditioned jump-up avoidance in rats as much as did 5 minutes of preventing such avoidance (flooding) if extinction was tried straight after the swimming stress. However, if 2 hours elapsed before trying to extinguish avoidance, the stress-immunizing effect of swimming had gone, though it remained for flooding (Baum et al. 1985a & 1985b). Perhaps neuropeptides mediate such effects (see Chapter 7).

Like other aspects of defensive responses, incubation is under genetic influence in rats; after a single shock of a step-down response, emotionally reactive rats incubated avoidance more than did nonreactive rats (Morley 1977; see also Figure 6.2). Genes apart, potentiating factors include very intense USs and very brief CSs. The processes governing incubation are ill-understood and deserve more study than they have had so far. The topic has been discussed by Eysenck and peer reviewers (1979). Relevant factors may include those which lead to sensitization, conditioning without incubation, and slowed extinction. Animal experimenters have had difficulty in replicating a study by Rohrbaugh & Riccio (1970) that found incubation of aversive conditioning to a CR (A. Tobeña, personal communication, 1985). If incubation resembles sensitization (that is, results from repetition of noxious USs), then it should be studied using unpaired USs. A related phenomenon is vicious-circle behavior (paradoxical enhancement of fear).

Incubation effects are related to the paradoxical enhancement of fear and may be seen with brief CS exposure following shock (Woods 1974). It was studied in rats by Rohrbaugh & Riccio (1970). Approach along an alley to food and/or water was shocked; the rats were then allowed to remain in the alley unshocked during the interval between shock conditioning and subsequent testing—being in the alley was the CS. After having been only 5 minutes in the alley, the rats took longer to eat in subsequent testing, but after 50 minutes of such CS exposure they ate more quickly.

In a second study, rats were shocked on one (black) side of a shuttlebox and were then placed in the other (white) compartment, where they were not shocked. For 8 to 12 days after completion of shock training, the rats had varying durations of unshocked CS exposure by being placed first on the black and then on the white side for 0, ½, 1, or 5 minutes. Fourteen days after shock training the rats were tested for time spent on the safe white side. More fear was retained with CS exposures of ½ and 1 minute than with 0 or 5 minutes. The authors noted a similar finding by Greenfield that three 1-minute exposures to an apparatus during a 14-day interval between conditioning and testing also enhanced fear.

Rats in a third experiment (Rohrbaugh et al. 1972) were repeatedly shocked after hearing a tone and then, unshocked, heard the tone CS in the same cham-

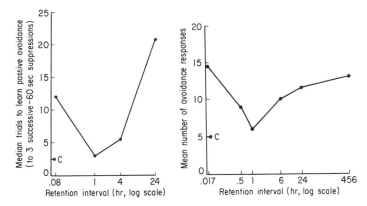

Fig. 8.2   The Kamin effect. Avoidance learning is less manifest at ½ to 6 hours after completion of avoidance training than immediately after the end of training or 24 or more hours later. (From Klein & Spear 1970 and Kamin 1957.)

ber for 0, ¼, or 5 minutes. Subsequent drinking in another test situation was suppressed by the tone, especially in rats that had had unshocked exposure to the tone for ¼ minute between acquisition and testing.

Unlike prolonged exposure or no exposure at all, brief exposure in these three different studies—¼, ½, or 1 minute—could sensitize. Might this relate to the Kamin effect (Brush 1971), wherein after acquisition, conditioned avoidance is found to weaken if tested 3 to 5 hours later but to strengthen again if tested subsequently (Figure 8.2)? Both phenomena could result from unknown hormonal and/or memory factors.

Vicious-Circle Behavior

Increase of avoidance after punishment has been noted in rats and gerbils (Melvin 1971). Such vicious-circle behavior can occur whether the punishing stimulus is the same or different from that used in escape training. If punishment takes place at the completion of a response sequence and this contingency is marked by spatial or other cues, then the vicious-circle effect is reduced. Once stable vicious-circle behavior is established, its vigor rises with gradually increasing punishment. Marked increase in punishment from training to extinction may diminish the effect. More vicious-circle behavior is produced by punishment after avoidance training than after escape training. Chlorpromazine injected between the period of escape training and of extinction prevented vicious-circle behavior in punished groups and speeded the extinction of unpunished controls—this phenomenon was not state dependent.

Melvin cites two naturalistic examples of vicious-circle behavior. A quail imprinted on a hawk was severely shaken by it, yet continued to follow it. One of Harlow's monkeys was shocked for clinging to a mother surrogate; this resulted in the infant's clinging even more tightly to its pain-inflicting surrogate. Similar self-defeating behavior in humans is all too familiar.

Lack of a Realistic Paradigm for Agoraphobia

Research is hampered by lack of a convincing model of agoraphobia in animals. Could an animal that is afraid to leave its home base be regarded as agoraphobic? Experimenters might try to produce that picture with profit. They might also test which external stimuli are associable with endogenously generated fear. Perhaps the alarm from stimulation of the locus ceruleus or other areas conditions differentially with varying surroundings, metabolic and motivational states, and genetic makeup. Perhaps a monkey given locus ceruleus stimulation both in its home cage and in equally familiar places outside that cage would subsequently avoid its surroundings more readily than its cage, just as an agoraphobic who panics both outside and inside the home comes to avoid outside places more than the home (although some agoraphobics avoid even sleeping in their beds if they experienced panic there—J. Greist, personal communication, 1986). If such differentially conditioned alarm can be obtained, will the threshold for its evocation be reduced by avoiding relevant surroundings or by altering the metabolic or motivational state of the animal? Work of this kind might lead to worthwhile animal models for agoraphobia.

Inappropriateness of Laboratory Terminology for Human Patients

A problem is encountered in applying laboratory language to human patients (Marks 1977). To illustrate this, let us try to use conditioning labels for the typical features of a female agoraphobic. She complains that each time she waits for a bus she has a wave of panic, breaks into a cold sweat, and wants to rush back home. Soon just thinking about the bus stop or her panic evokes further anxiety-panic in a rising spiral of anticipatory anxiety and fear of fear.

The operant (instrumental or Skinnerian) model labels the bus stop as a discriminative stimulus (S^d) for panic, though the reinforcer that stamped in the panic response is obscure. Turning to Pavlovian (classical) conditioning terms, in our frightened woman at the bus stop, what is the US, UR, CS, or CR? Because there is usually no clearcut traumatic onset to human phobias or rituals, we cannot assume that they have been "conditioned," only acquired—there may have been no pairing of a CS with a US. In a typical Pavlovian experiment a single CS-US sequence is arranged to produce defensive conditioning, with a CS-like tone or light and a US of shock or noise. Most phobias and rituals, however, are evoked by situations that are seldom linked convincingly to traumatic experiences other than inexplicable anxiety itself. No one knows the human equivalent of the unconditioned shock given to the rat. The phobia or ritual simply appears, and external candidates for the US are unconvincing. Had our frightened woman once been attacked while waiting at the bus stop we would construe that attack as a US that produced a UR of fear and covert escape. But such trauma is exceptional at the first onset of anxiety or panic in agoraphobics or ocs. Discomfort generally starts out of the blue without any external unpleasant event. Thereafter sufferers blame subsequent anxiety or discomfort on the initial surrounding chance events.

If we regard the initial spontaneous unease or panic as a US that is prepared to become conditioned to surrounding events and so become a CS, then laboratory terminology is a bit more applicable to phobics (or ocs), but still confusing. Perhaps the sequence is a form of interoceptive conditioning—the discomfort originating in a discharge (the US) from the locus ceruleus or some other neural system, for whatever reason, and then linking to surrounding events along prepared pathways. After the panic has begun it serves as a CS that is rapidly associated with the bus stop as a higher order CS (and perhaps preparedness may explain why the panic associates with public places rather than with flowers or trees, the former being more dangerous). Although the panic arose for unknown reasons that had nothing to do with the bus stop, once panic has become associated with it (making a higher order compound CS), then escaping from that bus stop somehow reduces the panic. We do not know why panic gets linked to public places only in some people, remaining unattached (freefloating, spontaneous, unpredictable) in others who have anxiety states (panic disorder without agoraphobia). In agoraphobics the bus stop becomes a CS that evokes a CR of panic.

The initial panic could be seen as a US, but if it was secondary to other events it becomes a UR; later panic to the bus stop is a CR. When fear of fear comes into play, a fear CS triggers a CR of more fear. The initial act of phobic avoidance becomes a UR and subsequent ones, CRs. Similar ambiguity is found in trying to extend laboratory labels to oc phenomena. In someone who has repeated obsessions or overchecks the locks on his house for an hour, what is the US, CS, UR, or CR? Operationally, what are "unreinforced CS presentations" for an agoraphobic, a ruminator, or a compulsive ritualizer? Such questions are hard to answer.

An Easier Clinical Terminology

A "C" before stimulus and response denotes that they are conditioned, a "U" that they are unconditioned or endogenous. Usually we have no idea which is correct, and in truth by the time we see the patient it hardly matters how the train of events began. Whether the spark was endogenous or external, or a combustible combination of both, does not affect clinical management of the developed syndrome, though it is important for ultimate prevention of the syndrome in the community as a whole. Conditioning terms describe events in laboratory animals where initial and subsequent events are known from the start; the labels are hard to apply to patients. Clinicians need a better terminology to make sense of what their patients describe.

An easier language can be evolved for clinical problems, one that guides us straight to treatment. It is unnecessary to initiate a fruitless search for an unknowable US. Instead we can simply speak of the ES, the evoking stimuli that currently trigger the ER (evoked response) of phobias, obsessions, and rituals. Neither ES nor ER make assumptions about antecedent USs and URs. The ES is close to the operant notion of S^d and the Pavlovian idea of CS but makes no assumptions about etiology.

Without making untestable guesses about origin, the terms ES and ER tell us what a patient should do to lose his or her fears and rituals—confront the ESs until the ERs subside. Why prolonged exposure to the ESs reduces rather than sensitizes the ERs is a vital but unsolved question; however, the easier ES-ER language points the clinician to a successful treatment strategy. The task is to search for those ESs (usually avoided situations or feelings) which evoke the ERs (fear, avoidance, obsession, rituals) and then persuade the sufferer to maintain contact with the ESs until he or she gets used to them. The avoidance profile (ESs) that the patient details at assessment—and these include feelings as well as external cues—is the key to what he or she should do to get better. Cure comes from the patient's initiating and maintaining exposure to hitherto avoided ESs without avoidance (that is, to block that part of the ER) until the urge to avoid dies down, after which other aspects of the ER (autonomic reactions and subjective discomfort) will decline similarly.

Stimulus Generalization and Symbolism

The powerful human capacity for abstract representation creates special problems in translating the rules of stimulus generalization worked out in animals. Fear and avoidance spread in animals from one context to another based on simple sensory cues. In humans, the spread may be on the basis of complex feelings. As an example, a woman went to church unusually early one Sunday morning in order to visit her sick husband in the hospital afterward. She surprised him there holding the hand of a strange woman, so discovering their longstanding relationship. Thereafter the patient became anxious on Sunday mornings, avoided the church, hospital, and dress she wore that Sunday, and made wide detours of the store where her rival had worked and places where she and her husband had been together—motels, restaurants, and certain streets and highways. The fears abated quickly 2 years later when these connections were unraveled in therapy (Lief 1955).

Similar sensory generalization of anxiety was noted in Freud himself (Jones 1953), although it did not amount to a phobia. Several times over some years he felt faint at meetings in the same room in the Park Hotel in Munich where he had had earlier arguments with Fliess, Jung, and Riklin. (In his thirties Freud also had some fears of traveling by train, though without avoidance).

In a laboratory hierarchy of stimulus generalization, the responses to stimuli diminish in proportion to the dissimilarity of those stimuli from the initial CS. With humans this can sometimes be shown clearly (Gelder & Marks 1970). But the rule can be difficult to apply when meaningful connections spread from one stimulus to another along complex dimensions. Among the tangled networks of meaning, links may appear along unexpected lines. Fear of harm could subsume hurting people by running them over in a car; bumping, shooting, stabbing, strangling, poisoning, or infecting them; merely thinking badly of them; or even doing things previously done while having a bad thought about them. In someone who first fears poisoning people and so avoids giving them tea, and later gets equally frightened of running them over and so stops driving cars, are these manifestations of stimulus generalization along one dimension of harm, or do they represent two hierarchies? If the two fears are equally strong, do they represent separate hierarchies (poisoning versus running over, rather than the common theme of harm)? The decision is arbitrary.

Similar difficulties face therapists trying to decide whether a fear of crowded supermarkets in an agoraphobic is separate from his or her dread of leaving home alone. Both may be equally frightening and both come from a well-defined clinical cluster (see chapters 9 and 10), although their common theme, apart from being away from home, is hard to discern. That both trigger panic merely means that both are phobic situations. The question is why panic occurs more in those particular places rather than in others.

Can we test the separateness of hierarchies by seeing whether exposure therapy to one apparent theme reduces others to which the patient has not been exposed? Sometimes this works well. Often, however, it does not. Despite the fact that a patient's fears of a given situation melted away after exposure to it, apparently very similar hierarchies may obstinately fail to lessen in intensity until they, too, are exposed in turn. To consolidate their gains, patients with multiple fears usually need to work hard at exposing themselves to every situation they fear. Habituation does not usually generalize much, tending to be specific to the stimulus that was exposed repeatedly, whereas sensitization tends to be wider (see Chapter 7 and below).

On hearing a phobic/oc patient start to describe his or her problem, experienced clinicians can make good guesses as to what will follow. Phobic/oc symptoms spread along apparently preformed paths that therapists learn to predict quite well. While some of the fault lines are understandable in terms of sensory context, relevance, prepotency, and preparedness, others are obscure. The explanations that ocs give for their beliefs and behavior may have a certain crazy logic, but why *that* particular logic is selected rather than the many alternative possibilities is intriguing. We can understand the worry of an oc woman who feared harming people, but not why it focused on an anti-coagulant never seen in daily life that she thought might get into their tea (in which case it would do no real harm anyway), rather than knives seen at every mealtime that could readily be used to stab. In the case of agoraphobia Freud wrote (1895, p. 136): "We often find the recollection of a state of *panic;* and what the patient actually fears is a repetition of such an attack under those special conditions in which he believes he cannot escape it." But why should the agoraphobic find panic more inescapable in some conditions than in others? Freud (1892, p. 26) had earlier suggested with Breuer the possibility in hysteria of "a symbolic relation between the cause and the pathological phenomenon."

Symbolism is a broad form of stimulus generalization. Pavlov described long chains of conditioned events as "higher-order conditioning," and speech and thought as the "second signaling system," while Osgood (1953) wrote of them as "representational mediational processes." If the spread of phobic and oc fears does not strictly conform to simple laboratory examples of stimulus generalization because the "stimulus" in humans can be compound complexes of ideas, is it more appropriate to call the spread "higher-order conditioning"? That requires pairing of the first-order CS with a second-order CS, the second-order cue with a third, and so on. Such pairing could in theory occur merely in thought, not necessarily in real life. Indeed the mere ascription of new meanings might constitute S-S pairings of that kind. If so, there may be no way to detect a difference between stimulus generalization and higher-order conditioning when dealing with thoughts and images.

We all have anecdotes of mediational processes generating fear. A 3½-year-old girl was happily going through a deserted courtyard until her parents said it was part of a palace. Immediately she wanted to leave and asked fearfully whether the king's soldiers would hurt her. For her, "palace" at that moment connoted frightening armed men, although at other times she enjoyed passing palaces where soldiers with weapons could in fact be seen. Words are symbols that can terrify. A swastika inspired dread in Nazi-occupied communities, and a shout of "Fire!" may cause violent panic in a crowded theatre. The response to hierarchies of phobic stimuli can be discontinuous at points of special significance. For instance, in a rabies phobic imagining himself at various periods after potential exposure to infection, his skin conductance response suddenly rose at the imagined period of 10 days—the incubation time for rabies (Agras 1966).

Undoubtedly mediational or symbolic cues can become linked to anxiety. A serious problem is that anything can in theory be a symbol for anything else. Given inspiration we could juxtapose almost any two things in our minds and find a link between them, although some links will seem more plausible than others. Strict criteria are therefore needed to exclude the chance that the symbolism or attribution ascribed to a given phobic or oc worry is not merely a Rorschach test of the investigator. Such criteria for distinguishing causal association from post-hoc rationalization are very hard to establish (Marks 1972). Lack of a reliable way to tell chicken from egg hinders progress, which requires careful work on symbolism and meaning in groups of subjects. A step in this direction is Lang's (1983, 1985) demonstration that two aspects of representations of fear cues—"stimulus propositions" (descriptive cues) and "response propositions" (sensations)—are to some extent separately encoded and retrieved in phobics. Further delineation of how fear cues are encoded in networks and then retrieved from them may solve some of the mysteries.

FEAR REDUCTION (HABITUATION AND EXTINCTION)

The waning of a defensive responsive on repeated stimulation seems to follow the same rules regardless of whether it was originally learned (in which case the decline is called extinction) or innate (when the decline is termed habituation). "Habituation" will therefore be used here to cover both.

Habituation and Other Types of Response Decrement

Decline in defensive responses may result not only from habituation but also from sensory adaptation, neuromuscular fatigue, motivational changes, biorhythms, aging, and tissue damage (Leibrecht & Askew 1980). Habituation is easily distinguished from adaptation or fatigue, which are probably peripheral phenomena. Adaptation or fatigue disappear after a short rest or on changing the site of stimulation. After habituation, however, a slight change in the nature of the stimulus may allow the response to reappear (dishabituate), although the same sense organs are involved. As an example, a *Branchioma* tubeworm requires several hundred successive contractions evoked by electrical stimulation of its giant fibers before fatigue sets in, yet far fewer touches of its crown of tentacles will reduce withdrawal, and touching any other part of the crown will yield no response either; this indicates that the response is choked off between the sense organs and the giant fiber system (Wells 1968). The situation is similar for a phobic patient early in exposure therapy: after fear of a particular stimulus has declined, minor changes in that stimulus may rekindle the fear, showing that the earlier decline was not due to fatigue.

Decrement in response resulting from changes in motivation (such as hunger) or in biorhythms (such as remission of severe premenstrual tension) can be detected because it varies more with those states than with experience. This is complicated by the possibility of state-dependent learning (what occurs in one mood state may not transfer to another). Habituation is a waning of response largely independent of motivational states or biological cycles, and also of age and tissue damage.

Similarity Across Taxa and Defensive Responses

Although there may be differences not yet discovered, the habituation of simple and of complex defensive responses is very similar across species, be they mollusks, mantids, or men (Kandel & Schwartz 1981; Thompson & Spencer 1966; and Figure 8.3). In general, a defensive response declines more rapidly

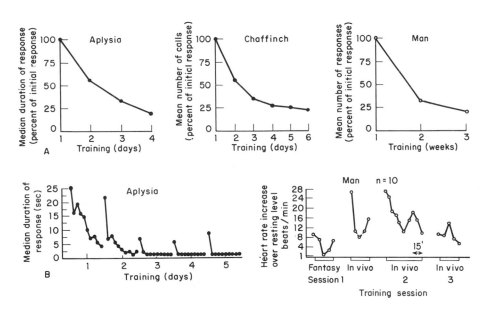

Fig. 8.3 Across species there is similar habituation to repeated stimulation of various defensive responses (redrawn from Kandel & Schwartz 1981). On the left is the duration of siphon withdrawal in *Aplysia*. Top middle shows the number of calls given by the chaffinch while mobbing a live owl presented 3 times daily. Top right depicts habituation of the galvanic skin response (GSR) of man to a tone; each data point is the mean result of a weekly session of up to 50 tone presentations. Lower right shows the reduction in heart rate during 3 sessions of exposure in vivo treatment of a cat phobic. Lower right shows buildup of habituation in *Aplysia* during four days of training. (From Watson et al. 1972.)

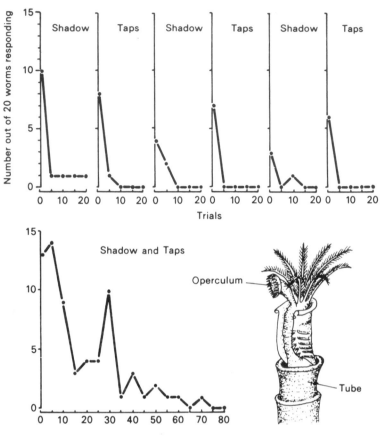

Fig. 8.4 Habituation is specific to the pathway that has been stimulated, as is seen with two stimuli, a moving shadow and a sharp tap on the aquarium, in the serpulid polychaete *Mercierella enigmatica*. Top shows the number of animals responding to each stimulus on its own with stimuli alternating after every 20 trials. Bottom shows the number of animals responding to both stimuli together during 80 trials. (From Wells 1968, fig 8.10, & Day 1967, fig 38.5.)

with frequent stimulus presentations within sessions, and with more frequent sessions. Habituation is quicker with weak than with strong stimuli and generalizes from one stimulus to another related one. Early in habituation, the response recovers after stimulation has ceased but dies down with yet further stimulation. The response also returns (dishabituates) on stimulation of a fresh pathway (Figure 8.4) or on strong stimulation of the same pathway. Dishabituation may itself habituate if it occurs frequently. Previous experience of the stimulus (preexposure) usually hastens habituation; why the converse of sensitization sometimes occurs is ill-understood. In complex sequences of defensive behavior, the early orienting components generally habituate more slowly than do terminal, consummatory ones. Finally, and especially importantly from the clinician's viewpont, habituation can last a long time—at least 17 hours in polychaete worms (Clark 1960), days in mantids, weeks in mollusks, and years or indefinitely in humans.

To highlight similarities across taxa, let us juxtapose the habituation of several types of defensive response in invertebrates and in birds with that of phobics and ocs to their evoking stimuli (ES) during exposure therapy.

Invertebrates

To bird predators a mantid gives an innate aggressive defense—a threat display with many components. The mantid directs the antennae obliquely backward, opens the mouth widely to show the colored mandibles, raises the prothorax and extends the forelegs laterally to reveal a big black spot on each femur, raises the wings to display two eyelike stigmas on the forewings, twists and tilts the abdomen to the side, makes a rustling noise by rubbing the abdomen against the wings, and sways violently from side to side. This defensive response was carefully measured in a balanced design (Balderrama & Maldonado 1971).

Three groups of 24 mantids *(Stagmatoptera biocellata)* were daily shown either canaries, Java sparrows, or shiny cowbirds 30 times, 3 minutes at a time, every quarter of an hour. Sessions ceased when the mantids responded less than 3 times during 15 consecutive trials. At the end of this habituation phase the three groups were each subdivided, half resting for 2 days and half for 6 days, followed by a second ("dishabituating") phase similar to the first except that each mantid saw a bird different from that seen previously. (Of mantids that saw canaries during the first phase, half now saw Java sparrows and half saw shiny cowbirds, and so on.)

Repeatedly presenting birds led to clear decrease in the mantids' frequency of threat display and number of components in the display, as well as in the response duration (Figure 8.5). Some bird movements evoked more displays than did others. After a rest the displays returned to some extent, more so after a 6-day than after a 2-day rest period. Given that the mantid's adult life span is only about 5 months, habituation lasting 6 days is like 3 years on a human time span. Shiny cowbirds—natural predators of the mantid—released stronger threat displays than did Java sparrows or canaries, both of which are seed eaters that only occasionally peck insects. The more dangerous stimulus (cowbird) produced a slower and lesser decline (Figure 8.6) (as prepared stimuli did in the extinction phase of Öhman-type experiments in humans), and they also dishabituated the habituation that had already occurred to a weaker stimulus such as a Java sparrow or a canary. Dishabituation sets the habituation process apart from fatigue, which should affect *all* responses. Dishabituated threat was less than that evoked by the same bird in naive mantids, indicating some generalization of habituation. Finally, dishabituation declined on repetition.

Now to the human parallel. During exposure treatment, when phobics or ritualizers repeatedly encounter their ES, the evoked response (ER) steadily reduces. ER components include avoidance, rituals, subjective anxiety, tachycardia (except for blood-injury phobics, who respond with bradycardia—see chapters 11 and 15), and sweating. The speed with which each component declines varies, but all tend to diminish with continuing stimulation, just as

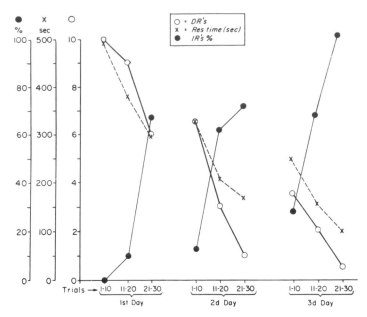

Fig. 8.5 Habituation of threat responses from mantids *(Stagmatoptera biocellata)* to birds presented 30 times 3 minutes at a time every 45 minutes. After a rest the responses returned somewhat. Deimatic (threat) responses (DR) and incomplete responses (IR) both decreased steadily. Response time (res time) steadily took longer. (From Balderrama & Maldonado 1971. Copyright © 1971 by American Psychological Association. Reprinted by permission.)

they do in the mantid. Also as in the mantid, in the early phase of treatment when habituation is incomplete, phobic and oc ERs tend to return somewhat after a rest from exposure. This is seen in Figure 8.7, which shows the mean heart rate for nine patients with specific phobias who were treated by exposure to imagined and real phobic stimuli (Watson et al. 1972). Tachycardia decreased markedly during exposure sessions, returning a fair amount from the end of the first to the start of the second session, but only slightly from the end of the second to the start of the third practice sessions. Phobic attitude (for instance, whether "spider" was rated as good or bad, pleasant or unpleasant) improved more slowly than heart rate, a phenomenon we might call "cognitive lag."

Again as in mantids, after exposure treatment habituation may generalize from weaker to stronger phobia-evoking stimuli, even though the stronger stimulus can dishabituate some of the decline that has occurred in responses to weaker stimuli. Figure 8.8 shows one of the nine phobics seen in Figure 8.7. This was a cat-phobic woman for whom ginger-colored (red) cats were her worst phobia and black cats her second worst. When a live ginger cat was first presented 6 feet away, her heart rate rose to 130, compared to 120 to a black cat 6 feet away (the first G and B, respectively, on the top left in Figure 8.8). With continuing exposure to the black cat, her heart rate fell to normal (habituation), after which presenting the ginger cat now evoked less tachycardia than

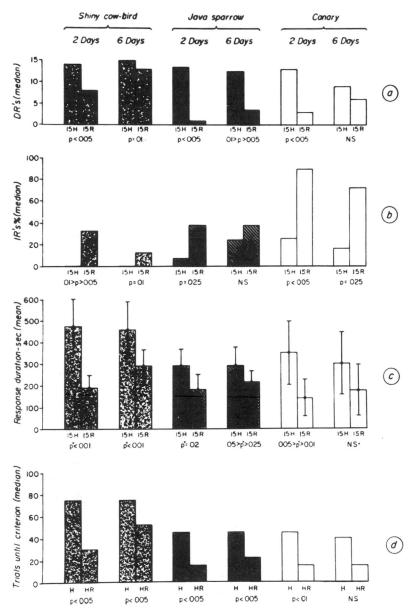

Fig. 8.6 In mantids, threat responses to more dangerous predators (shiny cowbirds) are more prolonged and take longer to habituate than those to less dangerous ones (Java sparrows and canaries). DR, deimatic (threat) responses; IR, incomplete responses; H, first 15 habituation trials; R, first 15 trials of recovery period. (From Balderrama & Maldonado 1971. Copyright © 1971 by American Psychological Association. Reprinted by permission.)

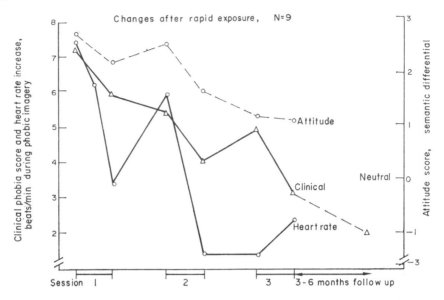

Fig. 8.7 Habituation of heart rate, phobic behavior (clinical scale), and phobic attitude (semantic differential ratings) in nine specific phobics during exposure in vivo treatment. Fear returned a bit between sessions, less so after the second than after the last session. (From Watson et al. 1972. Copyright © 1972 by Pergamon Press. Reprinted by permission.)

previously (dishabituation, but with stimulus generalization of habituation from the black to the ginger cat).

The mantid's threat displays had been stronger and slower to habituate to certain bird movements than to others, and in human phobics habituation is similarly slow to particular stimulus configurations. For example, spider phobics take especially long to get used to spiders' movements, social phobics to being looked at, agoraphobics to being alone in crowded public places. As mentioned, humans also share with mantids the long duration of habituation after this has been intensively trained; in phobics and ocs it lasts for at least 4 to 7 years after exposure treatment.

Another feature shared by human and invertebrate habituation is the longer time it takes to obtain habituation to complex as opposed to simpler stimuli. In the polychaete worm *Mercierella enigmatica,* which inhabits a tortuous calcareous tube into which it withdraws when danger threatens, habituation takes longer to occur to a moving stimulus plus a sharp tap on the aquarium than to either stimulus separately (Figure 8.4). During exposure therapy in humans, habituation occurs to the particular features of the ES that have been confronted, with only limited spread to related stimuli; and the more numerous the phobic features that patients have needing to be habituated, the longer the exposure required to obtain useful improvement. As an example, specific animal phobics usually fear few stimuli and require less exposure than do most agoraphobics and ocs, who worry about a wider range of stimuli.

Not reported in humans is the impairment of generalization noted in the

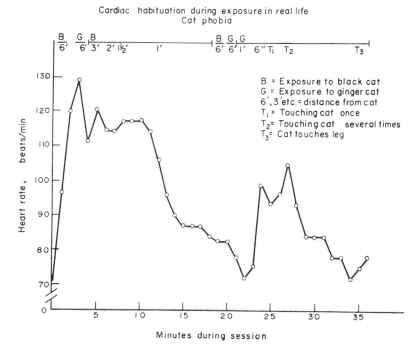

Cardiac habituation during exposure in real life
Cat phobia

B = Exposure to black cat
G = Exposure to ginger cat
6', 3' etc. = distance from cat
T_1 = Touching cat once
T_2 = Touching cat several times
T_3 = Cat touches leg

Fig. 8.8 Habituation of heart rate in a cat phobic during 36-minute exposure to a ginger-colored (red) and a black cat; ginger cats were the most feared stimulus, and black cats the second most frightening. Continuing exposure to the second most feared stimulus led to habituation, with some dishabituation as the worst stimulus was reintroduced, but not to its original level (instancing some stimulus generalization of habituation). Heart rate to the worst stimulus also reduced as exposure to it continued. (From Watson et al. 1972. Copyright © 1972 by Pergamon Press. Reprinted by permission).

polychaete worm *Nereis pelagica:* habituation of withdrawal from one stimulus, such as sudden vibration, slowed habituation to another, such as movement (Clark 1960).

Birds

Escape and Freezing of Quail with a Hawk. Bobwhite quail *(Colinus virgianus)* were hatched and raised in outdoor pens with opaque roofs to prevent prior experience of raptors (Martin and Melvin 1964). They were then tested individually twice daily over 11 days with each of two stimuli swooping over their pen: a live red-tailed hawk *(Buteo jamaicensis)* and a model of its silhouette (Figure 8.9). In a balanced crossover design 18 quail were shown the live hawk or its model for 5 days and the alternative stimulus over the subsequent 6 days.

When either hawk stimulus was first presented, the quail usually ran or flew for up to 5 seconds and then stopped and crouched, immobile, for about 12 minutes while vibrating the neck intensely. Between trials there was incom-

Fig. 8.9 Two stimuli used to test fear-habituation in bobwhite quail *(Colinus virgianus).* On the left is a red-tailed hawk *(Buteo jamaicensis)* and on the right, a life-sized silhouette of it. (From Martin & Melvin 1964. Copyright © 1964 by Springer Verlag, N.Y. Reprinted by permission.)

plete displacement pecking with the beak not touching the ground or anything else. The quail showed more fear to the live hawk (running, flying, crouching) and more orienting to the model (turning or raising the head); over successive days fear fell and orienting responses rose (Figure 8.10).

Fear responses lasted fully 21 times longer to the first presentation of the live hawk than of the model (Figure 8.11). Fear decreased steadily with repeated experience of both stimuli, but it took 5 days before fear of the hawk shortened to the same brief duration as that evoked by the model. Prior habituation to the model before crossover generalized to reduce fear of the live hawk at its first presentation after crossover, and to greater habituation to it on subsequent crossover trials.

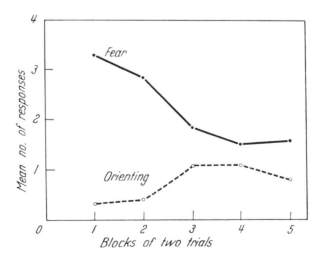

Fig. 8.10 Over 5 days of daily testing in bobwhite quail, fear reduced and orienting responses increased. (From Martin & Melvin 1964. Copyright © 1964 by Springer Verlag, N.Y. Reprinted by permission.)

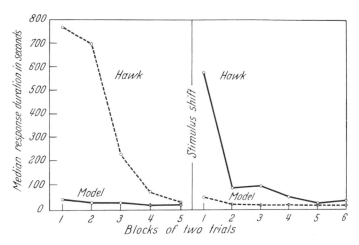

Fig. 8.11 In bobwhite quail, fear responses lasted far longer to a live hawk than to its modeled silhouette, decreased with repeated presentations of the stimuli, and reduced more quickly to the model than to the live hawk; prior experience of the model (left of the figure) speeded subsequent habituation to the live hawk (right of the figure). (From Martin & Melvin 1964. Copyright © 1964 by Springer Verlag, N.Y. Reprinted by permission.)

Parallels are seen in the clinic. As exposure progresses and phobics and ocs lose their fear, they cease avoiding their ES and orient more toward it. They show more fear of the real stimulus than of an imperfect model; in Figure 8.8, for example, the patient's tachycardia to live cats on their first presentation occurred despite her having already habituated to imagined cats.

Mobbing by Chaffinch. Even hand-reared chaffinches *(Fringilla coelebs)* give defensive mobbing calls ("chink-chink") on seeing an owl or other predators for the first time, plus intention movements of flight (see Chapter 3). Calls start almost immediately, rise to a peak frequency, and wane gradually over about 30 minutes. Careful study was made of the decline in wild-caught chaffinches of mobbing calls to presentations of a stuffed owl and a toy dog for 6 minutes at a time (Hinde 1960). Results had clinical parallels (within parentheses below) beyond those of habituation and dishabituation already described.

The more dangerous natural threat—owl—evoked more mobbing than did dog. Calls declined more when the same stimulus was repeated than when the second stimulus differed from the first, especially after long initial presentations (habituation was specific), but rose when the stimulus was changed (dishabituation). Calls lessened more after short than long rest intervals (phobic and oc fears decline less with interrupted than continuous exposure), but this effect was not stimulus-specific. Calling was quicker on second presentations after a long rest, and rose to long first presentations of dog 24 hours after owl (early in exposure treatment, anxiety returns somewhat between sessions, but such resurgence wanes as habituation strengthens with further exposure). With the relatively weak habituation employed, waning in one response was some-

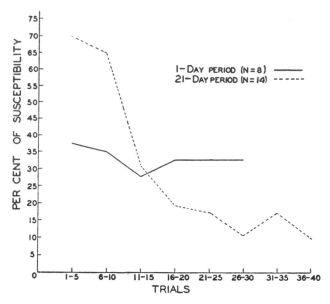

Fig. 8.12 Chickens habituated to repeated induction of tonic immobility when 40 trials were given over 21 days, but not when 30 trials were given over 1 day. (From Gilman et al. 1950.)

times accompanied by increase in another; this might have disappeared with longer exposure.

Tonic Immobility in Chickens. Like other defensive responses, tonic immobility habituates persistently to repeated stimulation. Habituation is specific to the method used to induce immobility and may dishabituate following further aversive stimuli. As an example of habituation, when chickens were immobilized twice daily over 20 days to a total of 40 trials, on successive days there was steady decline in (1) susceptibility, (2) duration, (3) frightened movements when the experimenter approached to start the trial, and (4) attempts to escape when immobility ceased (Gilman et al. 1950) (Figure 8.12, broken line). In another study (Nash & Gallup 1976), after tonic immobility had been induced only 5 times daily over 4 consecutive days, habituation continued for at least 2.5 months.

Typically, the stronger the initial response to a stimulus, the longer it will take to habituate (Nash & Gallup 1976). This may mediate strain variations in speeds of habituation of tonic immobility; White Leghorns, for instance, take nearly twice longer to habituate than do Production Reds. Habituation takes longer to achieve if birds are disturbed while immobile. When tonic immobility was induced 5 times daily over 3 days, by day 4 it lasted fully 9 times longer in chickens that had been prodded every 60 seconds after the stillness began than in those whose response had been allowed to run its course. Allowing the reaction to continue during training also speeded habituation of another, nondefensive, response—nystagmus (Holsopple 1924, cited by Nash & Gallup 1976).

Surprisingly, massed practice within sessions did not habituate tonic immobility, whereas it speeds habituation during exposure therapy and prevents the kindling of epilepsy that occurs with spaced stimulation (see Chapter 7). Tonic immobility did not decline when chickens had 30 successive trials with intertrial intervals (ITIs) of about 15 seconds (Figure 8.12, solid line). Massed practice may in fact sensitize it (Prestrude 1977, Nash & Gallup 1976). In 3-week-old chickens immobility was induced once and allowed to run its course, followed by 5 trials that were terminated by prodding the birds 15 seconds after induction. The ITI between these 5 trials was either 0, 5, 15, 30, or 60 seconds. Following these the birds had another test induction, which was allowed to run its course. Results resembled a "delay of punishment" gradient. Chickens that were immediately reinduced (0-second ITI) were actually sensitized, while the others habituated more as the ITI lengthened.

Perhaps with a 0-second ITI the reinductions of tonic immobility resembled punishment of an avoidance response, which is likely to increase avoidance (vicious-circle effect). Study of this type of phenomenon may give some clue as to why phobic and oc fears sensitize during exposures to ESs when the disorder is developing but habituate with exposure during therapy. Shorter ITIs may make it more likely that fear is rising than falling at the start of prolonged offset of the ES. Phobics usually try to switch off rising anxiety by immediate escape or avoidance until they learn during therapy to continue exposure to the point where their anxiety has started to fall before stopping exposure. Whether more persistent habituation ensues from exposure sessions ended on a "good note" of falling rather than of rising fear will be discussed further.

Extinction of Conditioned Avoidance

The reduction of phobias and rituals by exposure is intriguingly similar not only to the habituation of innate defensive responses but also to the extinction of conditioned avoidance. In the usual paradigm, avoidance is conditioned by first presenting a CS followed by a noxious US unless the animal makes the appropriate avoidance response. Extinction is achieved by subsequent unpaired exposure to the now aversive CS without the US, but while blocking the avoidance response or by prolonging the CS beyond the start of avoidance.

If either of the latter two conditions are not added to mere unpaired presentation of the CS, then extinction may be hard to attain because avoidance is likely to occur before the animal can discover that the US has been switched off and would not follow the CS even if there were no avoidance response. In the same way, before exposure treatment phobias and rituals continue for years partly because sufferers escape from their ES too quickly to learn that ensuing discomfort would subside eventually anyway, even if they continued to face the ES without switching the discomfort off immediately by running away or by ritualizing.

Extinction of defensive responses is slower when they are stronger—for instance, if they had originally been paired with an intense US. The unpaired

CS can first be presented weakly to elicit only minimal fear and then gradually increased in strength (desensitization), or the CS can be presented in full strength from the start (flooding) (see Chapter 14). Various forms of flooding in animals have been called forced exposure or reality testing, environmental press, response prevention, and detainment (reviewed by Baum 1976 and Mineka 1985). All force the animal to experience the feared situation. In patients the exposure is voluntary, though encouragement and social pressure constitute indirect restraint.

A common way to extinguish conditioned avoidance in animals is preventing their avoidance, so forcing them to experience the CS. Baum studied this systematically in rats (reviewed by Marks 1981). Avoidance was trained by dropping a rat on the grid floor of a cage (the to-be-conditioned CS) and a few seconds later shocking its feet via the grid (US) unless it jumped or climbed (CR) onto a safety ledge provided halfway up the side of the cage. The rat was allowed to remain on the ledge for 30 seconds (the intertrial interval), after which the ledge was retracted for a moment, causing the rat to fall to the grid floor and thus initiating the next training trial. As rats naturally jump in response to shock, they quickly learned to jump onto the ledge before receiving shocks.

When shock was turned off to start the extinction phase, the rats could not know this and simply continued to jump to safety on the ledge each time they were placed on the grid floor. However, if shock was turned off and in addition the safety ledge was removed, rats placed on the grid first tried strenuously to jump onto a now nonexistent ledge and were forced into contact with the CS (grid floor). The jumps now declined rapidly, after which the rats remained placidly on the grid.

Many of Baum's findings have clinical counterparts. Response prevention (rp)—and therefore CS exposure—had to last beyond a certain critical period if it was to produce extinction. This period was longer if the US had been more intense during and before avoidance training. Clinically, more intense phobias and rituals seem to need more exposure than do mild ones.

Extinction of rat avoidance was hastened if rp trials were massed by shortening the intervals between trials and between sessions. As mentioned, this is true, too, for habituation of unlearned defensive responses and also of phobias and rituals (see Chapter 14). Rat avoidance also became steadily weaker with repeated reacquisition and extinction testing, so that by the fifth time it had declined to the same extent as with rp; similar findings were noted by Akiyama (1968, 1969). After relapse phobics and ocs usually seem to remit more quickly with reexposure than they do the first time.

The avoidance responses reduced more quickly if Baum's rats were accompanied by fearless rats or had the chance to see other rats having rp, too. However, modeling alone extinguished avoidance less than did rp alone, which was highly effective. We are reminded that most phobics, especially agoraphobics, feel better while in company, although this does not lead to extinction of the fear.

Avoidance also declined faster if the rats were forced to move around and explore the cage by direct handling or by using a loud buzzer, which raised

exploratory activity (Baum et al. 1985); this led rats to come into more intimate contact with the grid CS. Conversely, extinction was slowed by confinement, which could be construed as preventing the rat from being exposed to
many facets of the grid CS. This again accords with clinical experience that it
is important to persuade phobics and ocs to expose themselves to as many
facets of the ES complex as is possible.

Four of Baum's rat findings have no human counterparts. First, extinction
was speeded if rp was accompanied by positive intracranial stimulation to the
right lateral hypothalamus (Gordon & Baum 1971), but was not influenced by
aversive stimulation of the reticularis pontis caudalis. Second, a peripheral
muscle relaxant, suxamethonium bromide, did not affect extinction (Baum et
al. 1985a). Third, rp was more successful if it began 30 minutes after acquisition rather than immediately (Baum 1972a). Finally, rp was impaired if it took
place in the light rather than in the dark.

The reduction of avoidance from flooding can generalize to responses different from the one that was flooded. In rats, preventing jump-up avoidance
of light speeded extinction of shuttlebox avoidance of tone, and giving tone
unpaired that used to lead to jump-up avoidance hastened reduction in shuttlebox avoidance of light; however, preventing shuttlebox avoidance of light
did not speed extinction of jump-up avoidance of tone (Mincka 1976). Similar
generalization but with asymmetry was found in the flooding of phobics. When
for 2 hours at a stretch patients imagined normally frightening scenes irrelevant to their phobia, their phobias improved as much as after imagining phobic scenes, although generalization of gains was more consistent after relevant
than irrelevant flooding, and only gains with the latter correlated with anxiety
experienced during flooding (Watson & Marks 1971). We also saw earlier that
immediately after acquisition, irrelevant swimming stress in rats speeded
extinction of conditioned avoidance as much as did rp; but this effect wore off
after 2 hours, at which time only rp was effective (Baum & Leclerc 1974). More
work is needed to tell us how stress immunization (see chapters 5 and 14)
relates to the generalization of fear reduction.

SOME THEORETICAL PROBLEMS IN FEAR REDUCTION

Although flooding can reliably extinguish both conditioned avoidance and
fear, their rates of decline overall and relation to one another vary with different flooding procedures (Miller et al. 1982; Mineka 1979). This is to be
expected, as the various components of defensive responses are only imperfectly coupled and may be differentially learned and expressed through several
interacting cueing and neurophysiological mechanisms whose precise natures
are still unclear. Among the critical variables are (1) long enough CS exposure
without the US, (2) allowing the unpaired CS to continue despite avoidance
responding, and (3) preventing the avoidance response in the presence of the
unpaired CS. These variables are interconnected and hard to disentangle;
response prevention often increases exposure to the CS.

Habituation Versus Sensitization

Various forms of response decrement to repeated stimulation are called habituation, extinction, inhibition (conditioned, reciprocal, or external), adaptation, fatigue, exhaustion, getting used to it, satiation, and boredom. Adaptation generally means that the sensory receptor has stopped responding, and fatigue that the neuromuscular junction has become inactive. Habituation is a more central process, from the efferent path of the sensory neuron upward in invertebrates, and in an unknown site in mammals.

Varieties of response increment to repeated stimulation are called sensitization, conditioning, or recruitment. Their neural locus overlaps with that of habituation in mollusks but is obscure in mammals.

What is the difference between exposure that habituates and exposure that sensitizes? This vital question seeks to define the conditions and mechanisms behind the difference. Part of the answer may be that systematic, regular exposure usually habituates, whereas brief or irregular exposure may not and might perhaps sensitize. Such an arrangement makes sense in evolutionary terms. In nature an animal has to respond rapidly to sudden threat if it is to survive, but if it is still safe after a frightening stimulus has come again and again, that stimulus is less likely to signal danger, and the animal must get on with all the other things it has to do in life.

Duration of Exposure

Whatever the reason, the evidence is overwhelming that defensive responses decline more, the longer that noxious stimulation continues beyond a certain point. This is true whether the responses were unlearned in invertebrates and birds, learned in three differing studies by Rohrbaugh and Riccio (1970), or in clinical phobias (see Chapter 14). Much other work heavily supports this conclusion.

Within-Sessions Exposure

That longer exposure enhances extinction was shown in rats having response prevention (rp) and CS exposure (Figure 8.13). Where rat avoidance had been conditioned with mild shock, 1 minute of rp did not reduce avoidance, but 3-minute and 5-minute periods were highly effective (Baum 1969a). Even longer exposures—30 minutes—were needed where avoidance had been learned with strong shocks (Siegeltuch & Baum 1971), or if random shocks had preceded avoidance training. Another study (Boyd 1981) also found that conditioned avoidance learned with more intense shock required longer exposure to obtain extinction. Massing rp by shortening the intertrial intervals speeded extinction of avoidance (ITIs of 0 versus 6, 30, and 54 seconds) (Baum 1973b; Oler & Baum 1968). One study found repeated short CS exposures to be no better than one long one (40 at 5 seconds versus 1 at 200 seconds) (Berman & Katzev 1972), but these times were shorter than the most effective times used by Baum

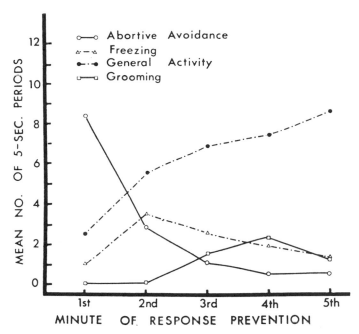

Fig. 8.13 In rats the reduction of conditioned avoidance and resumption of general activity is greater, the longer that response prevention continues (From Baum 1969. Copyright © 1969 by Canadian Psychological Association. Reprinted by permission.)

in his studies reviewed earlier (300 to 1800 seconds), Reynierse and Wiff (1923) (300 to 900 seconds), and Uno and coworkers (1973) (300 seconds). The speed of extinction steadily increased as CS duration rose from 0 to 400 seconds (Katzev & Berman 1974) (Figure 8.14). In rats, briefly preventing avoidance plus a limited exposure reduced fear but not avoidance, but longer rp reduced both (Mineka et al. 1981). The robustness of the enhancement of extinction by prolonging CS exposure is impressive given the different types of rats, avoidance responses, and shock intensities used in the various experiments where this was found.

An exception to the rule that longer within-session stimulation reduces fear more in animals is the work noted earlier on tonic immobility in chickens.

Nearly all human studies of the topic attest that prolonging exposure reduces fear more than does shorter exposure, but the limits of this process remain an enigma. (The conditions at ES offset and during the interstimulus and intersessions intervals may be as important as the duration of exposure itself.)

Is It Necessary to Prevent CS Avoidance or Its Termination?

The problem was studied in three flooding variants in rats, the first two involving total and the third incomplete response prevention (Miller et al. 1982). The

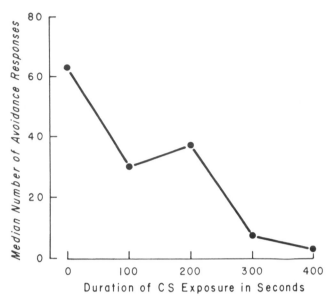

Fig. 8.14 In rats conditioned avoidance reduces more, the longer that response prevention continues. (From Katzev & Berman 1974. Copyright © 1974 by American Psychological Association. Reprinted by permission.)

first moved a cage wall to make a safety ledge inaccessible. The second had a cage wall moving back and forth every 30 seconds to reveal the ledge intermittently, but the rat was prevented by a transparent barrier from jumping onto it. The third was the same as the second except that there was no barrier, so the rats could jump onto the ledge intermittently but, if they did so, were soon dumped back onto the grid floor by movement of the wall. Each variant lasted 5 minutes.

All three flooding variants abolished both avoidance and fear more than did simply leaving the rats in their home cage for 5 minutes. The third, however, was the best of all; its incomplete response prevention included exposure to two additional facets of the CS that were absent from the first two groups. These were repeated dumping on the grid floor, and the failure of jumping onto the ledge to terminate the CS so that it ceased to be a safety signal (in the first and second groups, only abortive jumps were possible that did not end on the ledge).

There is some clinical evidence that preventing avoidance from becoming a safety signal seems more important than stopping the response itself (see Chapter 14). Perhaps avoidance prevents habituation more if it terminates the ES for a long time. Avoidance seems to be reinforced if discomfort reduces lastingly when sufferers escape from or avoid the ES (rituals involve both actions) to remain in a "safe" area. Improvement during exposure treatment is enhanced by enduringly blocking escape and avoidance of the ES in overt behavior and in covert thought. Prolonged relief from avoidance may be more reinforcing than just a temporary respite would be. Briefly deferring completion of an exposure task with the intention of merely "having a breather" and finishing that task later may be less pathogenic than prolonged avoidance. Prolonged exposure could be more habituating than brief exposure because it is less likely to lead to prolonged relief ensuing from avoidance of the ES. Compatible with this idea is a study in rats (Mineka et al. 1981). Briefly preventing avoidance plus a limited exposure reduced fear but not avoidance, although longer response prevention reduced both. But agoraphobic patients did improve even when allowed prolonged escape if anxiety became too high (de Silva & Rachman 1984).

Most work suggests that dissociating the avoidance response from the CS and US is important for the response to decline. In accord are the results of Miller and coworkers (1982) in rats and Lipsedge (1974) in ocs. Also in agreement is a human Baum-type study finding that extinction was hastened by preventing avoidance in a way that dissociated it from the CS and US (Carasa et al. 1978). On hearing a tone (CS), students had to press three buttons in a certain order (avoidance CR) to avoid shock to the calf (US) from following. During subsequent flooding the tones were sounded without shock while half the subjects continued to be able to press the buttons (CS exposure, no response prevention, no CS termination by the response), and the other half were prevented from so doing by having their hand pulled by a rope (CS exposure with response prevention analogous to that of Baum). Finally, all subjects had an extinction test (CS exposure, CS termination by the response). Skin conductance responses were greater when the students were allowed to make the avoidance response throughout flooding (though it did not terminate the tone), but declined at the same rate in both groups during subsequent extinction trials. Avoidance CRs during those extinction trials declined faster in students who had had CS exposure with avoidance allowed but not terminating the CS, than in those who had been prevented from making the response.

Discriminating Between Acquisition and Extinction, and Other Variables

Many animal studies have found that extinction of avoidance is hastened if the animal is given clues that it has passed from an acquisition to an extinction phase, much as instructing humans that acquisition has ended can rapidly abolish aversive conditioning. Such clues include response prevention, delayed CS termination, and delayed US termination (Reynierse & Wiff 1973). Other clues are removing a feedback stimulus during extinction if it had been a source of information during acquisition, and withholding the US if the animal fails to avoid (Katzev & Hendersen 1971).

Allowing the CS to continue while the animal makes the avoidance response achieves the same end whether the CS is intermittent or continuous (Shearman 1970). The longer the CS continued after rats jumped away, the more rapidly they ceased to avoid it (Delprato 1974; Katzev 1967). However, continuing the CS beyond the moment that the avoidance starts is not essential for extinction (Berman & Katzev 1972; Delprato 1974). More important is exposure to the CS without the US a few seconds after the avoidance response (Delprato 1974).

Although giving positive intracranial stimulation together with response prevention speeded extinction (Gordon & Baum 1971), adding a positive stimulus such as eating to CS exposure did not (Delprato 1973a, 1973b; Delprato & Jackson 1974); Delprato and Jackson concluded that unreinforced exposure, not counterconditioning, was the critical factor.

Habituation to Aversive Versus Other Stimuli

Habituation occurs not only to unpleasant stimuli but also to neutral or pleasant ones. If we repeat any word to ourselves hundreds of times, it gradually becomes meaningless—a phenomenon called semantic satiation. If we play the same piece of music over and over again, it will soon lose its appeal; if it goes on even longer it will become aversive. We can have too much of a good thing. What happens with repeated stimulation in art, friendship, affection, and love? Why is it that the deeper the symbolism and meaning associated with a poem, sculpture, or painting, the more satisfying it becomes and the longer it takes to induce boredom? Yet simplicity of line in a work of art can prolong its attraction if it is done well (whatever that means)?

How does habituation relate to satiation and to boredom? The rules for habituation to unpleasant stimuli may not be quite the same as those for getting used to pleasant ones or for the loss of meaning of neutral stimuli. Work on such questions could help us better understand the conditions and mechanisms that lead to habituation as opposed to sensitization.

Fear Reduction Without Exposure

We noted earlier that defensive responses decrease not only with adaptation, fatigue, and habituation from repeated stimulation, but also with changes in motivation, biorhythms, aging, and tissue damage. Phobic and oc responses also diminish, albeit not enduringly, with anxiolytic and antidepressant drugs (see Chapter 16). When antidepressants work through reducing the dysphoric mood that often accompanies phobias and rituals, that could exemplify motivational change, but it might not account for all drug effects.

Occasionally psychological treatments that contain no exposure also improve phobias and rituals (see Chapter 14). Their effects are more fragile and less predictable than those of exposure but are theoretically crucial. They suggest that exposure might to some extent be seen as one of several methods that teach broad coping skills, some of which reduce phobias and rituals. Conversely, the specific effects of exposure can generalize into wider coping skills. Some phobics gain enough confidence from having conquered their phobias to deal with fresh problems as well. As an example, after a dog phobic lost her fear in merely two afternoons of exposure in vivo, she went on unaided to become more assertive with her parents also. Exposure thus teaches some people how to cope with unpleasant feelings in general, not merely with their phobias. We met this issue before when discussing relevant versus irrelevant flooding.

Courage and Fear Habituation

The qualities that produce courage need not be the reverse of those predicting anxiety, and they deserve examination. Some have been studied in jobs calling for unusual confidence. Among 105 superior jet pilots aged 20 to 40 most (67) were firstborn children with unusually close father-son relationships (Reinhardt 1970). They were candid, self-confident, desired challenge and success, were not introspective, tended to keep interpersonal and emotional distance and dreamed often of mastery of difficult situations and happy outcomes. They had very low neuroticism and very rarely consulted physicians. They were not risk-takers or counterphobic. Their cool personalities were similar to those found in astronauts, British and American aircrew (Goorney 1970), and successful bomb disposal workers.

Compared with 20 unsuccessful bomb disposal operators, 20 successful ones had fewer close personal ties, a wish to work on their own and with things as opposed to people, and a tendency to nonconformity, relying less on conventional values and judgments (Cooper 1982). They seemed able to keep psychological and social distance from others and to be flexible in their approach to work.

Congruent results were obtained by Hallam (1983). Bomb disposal operators who were rated as above average by their superiors were especially calm, confident, and psychologically fit. Those who had been decorated for their bravery were even more so, and scored zero for hypochondriasis. During an increasingly difficult auditory discrimination task under threat of shock for making errors, decorated operators had the lowest heart rate, although their subjective and behavioral responses were the same as for undecorated operators who had similar training (Rachman 1984). Overall heart rate was even higher in young soldiers with no bomb disposal experience and was highest of all in civilians (Figure 8.15).

A handful of people are almost fearless from the start. Most of the rest of us who are normally fearful can be trained to become more courageous. Bomb disposal operators increased in skill and confidence after training. Completing one bomb disposal task helped considerably, whereas dealing with hoaxes or false alarms did not (Rachman 1984). Parachutists gain in skill and confidence as training proceeds (see Chapter 7). And exposure therapy trains patients to become courageous in the face of pathological fear. In general, the more realistic the training, the greater the ensuing skill and confidence under fire. Courageous leadership, group cohesion, and keeping busy all help as well.

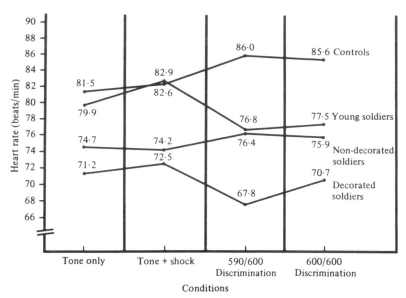

Fig. 8.15 Bomb-disposal operators who had been decorated for bravery showed lower heart rates than did their nondecorated counterparts, young soldiers, or control civilians. (From Rachman 1984. Copyright © 1984 by Pergamon Press, Oxford. Reprinted by permission.)

SUMMARY

Learning depends on genetic programs that have survived natural selection for inclusive fitness. It is Lamarckian in that an individual's information is modified by his environment. Like genetic information, however, learning dies with the individual unless it has been passed on to others—social learning leading to culture. Both individual and social learning may have a biologically rooted grammar. There are probably phyletic predispositions to tune in to certain stimuli, to respond in particular ways, and to associate certain things rather than others.

Studies have found that we condition heart rate more and extinguish skin conductance responses less when an unpleasant US is associated with snakes and spiders than with neutral stimuli, but this preparedness effect is fragile. Responses depend on the quality of the US and the associated CSs and the manner of CS-US pairing. Preparedness to fear snakes and spiders is greater when the US is tactile (shock or vibration) rather than auditory (noise), occurs even if the subject expects such USs without actually experiencing them, and may vanish if subjects are told at the start of extinction that there will be no more USs. We readily mirror other people's emotions and are prepared to associate aversion with angry and frightened expressions on other people's faces, but not with happy faces. This association is greater if the angry person faces us rather than looks away, and is specific to the person who is angry.

More study is needed of a much wider range of ages, stimuli and responses (including subjective experience and avoidance), incubation and genetic effects, and of an overshadowing paradigm while controlling for salience.

Fear can be learned by classical, operant, or vicarious conditioning. For a stimulus to be conditioned it must convey new information. Conditioning is decreased by preexposure to a future CS. Paradigms for experimental fear are conditioned avoidance (which is learned if it reduces the probability, frequency, or intensity of aversive stimulation), conditioned suppression of an appetitive response, and frustration by withholding an expected reward. Learned helplessness follows inescapable punishment and can be abolished by forcing the animal to carry out the required response. Conditioned avoidance is seen of the US, not the CS. The generalization, maintenance, and habituation (extinction) of fear seem similar whether the aversive stimulus is a CS or a US. Persistently strong normal fear can be learned in a single trial at the appropriate age, but social learning seems less frequent in the acquisition of phobias and rituals.

Aversive learning has parallels and shortcomings as a model of clinical events. Parallels to phobic and oc fear and avoidance may include the reinstatement (relapse) of fear and avoidance after reexperience of an unpleasant stimulus, the prolonging of extinction where avoidance responses have been trained with serial CSs, the fading in specificity and of conditioned inhibition of fear over time, the greater fear produced by uncontrollable than controllable aversive events, the generalization of fear both to similar cues and when the subject is frustrated or miserable, the occasional persistence of avoidance after fear has diminished, and the reduction of fear and avoidance by prolonged exposure and blocking of avoidance (including rituals). Additional parallels to oc rituals are well-trained avoidance and abnormal fixation in rats, and unlearned primate stereotypies under stress, and displacement activities in many species during conflict or high arousal. Animal counterparts to generalized anxiety and spontaneous panic may include experimental neurosis, learned helplessness, and interoceptive conditioning.

A problem for the aversive learning model is that few phobias start after a trauma, and that in such cases the phobia may begin not immediately after the trauma, but only after a lag period of incubation lasting a few days. However, most anxiety disorders do not usually originate in a single or even a few trials of fear conditioning or avoidance learning occurring in a vacuum. The paucity of a convincing history of direct or vicarious trauma at the onset of phobic and oc syndromes could partly result from forgetting of 1st-order CRs after 2nd-order CRs were established. In addition, many experiential (Mineka 1985) and biological variables prior to, during, and following a conditioning experience affect how much fear is experienced, conditioned, and subsequently maintained. Early experience of control and mastery can reduce fear in frightening situations later in an infant monkey's life. Control or predictability of US termination during conditioning reduces the amount of fear that is conditioned. Conditioned fear can be inflated by postconditioning trauma (whether related to the original US or not) and can spread to new situations through forgetting of US specificity. Potential biological influences on defensive learning include neuroendocrine and immunological factors at the time of the threat (Chapter 7).

The aversive learning model does not explain why it is so difficult to condition new human phobias—perhaps the stimuli and responses were not prepotent or prepared. How vicious circle behavior in animals relates to human sensitization is obscure. Nor does animal work tell us when human fears spread as stimulus generalization or as higher-order conditioning, or illuminate the role of symbolic (mediational) processes. A final problem is the difficulty in applying laboratory concepts (US, UR, CS, CR) accurately in the clinic. Clinicians do not need them, because whether the phobias or rituals were originally conditioned or not is irrelevant for treatment; therapists need simply delineate the evoking stimuli (the ES) and promote contact with them while discouraging avoidance (part of the ER).

When a defensive response declines with repeated evocation by stimulation, the decline due to habituation can be distinguished from that due to sensory adaptation, neuromuscular fatigue, motivational changes, biorhythms, aging, and tissue damage. It is specific to the stimuli presented, with only limited generalization. Habituation of unlearned responses and extinction of learned ones are similar to one another and follow similar rules across taxa. Response decrement is usually quicker to frequent and prolonged stimulus presentations within sessions, frequent and prolonged sessions, and weaker and simpler stimuli and tends to disappear (dishabituate) unless it has been well learned, in which case it may persist for many years. Dishabituation may occur with fresh strong stimulation of the same or a different pathway. These principles apply whether the habituation is of withdrawal of a polychaete worm to movement, an aggressive threat display of a mantid to a bird, escape and freezing of quail with a hawk, mobbing of an owl by a chaffinch, tonic immobility in chickens, conditioned avoidance in rats, or phobias and rituals in humans.

A theoretical snag is definition of those conditions that differentiate habituating from sensitizing exposure. Habituation is more likely when exposure is more regular, prolonged, and systematic. With briefer periods many unknown factors may decide whether a given duration of exposure at a particular time flips a switch from habituating to sensitizing mode. What happens during the intertrial and intersession intervals and at the end of the session may be as important as the duration of exposure. Habituation is most likely to be produced by prolonging the periods during which the avoidance response is prevented and there is exposure to the CS (ES). It also seems important that the subject should continue to experience the CS (ES) despite having completing the avoidance response, so that the avoidance response is dissociated from the CS.

Whether the rules for habituation are the same for neutral and pleasant stimuli as for unpleasant ones is unclear. Some phobias and rituals decline by non-exposure treatments, but these results are much less predictable and are less understood. Normal people can learn to keep up their courage in the face of unusually frightening situations—to some extent exposure is a treatment that promotes courage. How courage in the face of specific dangers can promote more general stress immunization, and vice versa, is a subject for future study.

III
CLINICAL SYNDROMES

9

Phobic and Obsessive-Compulsive Phenomena: Classification, Prevalence, and Relationship to Other Problems

From Hippocrates to the nineteenth century, phobic and obsessive-compulsive (oc) problems were occasionally described but not clearly distinguished as disorders in their own right until late in the last century. As a term "phobia" was used on its own only from the start of that century. Thereafter it gradually gained acceptance in its current sense: an intense fear that is out of proportion to the apparent stimulus, cannot be explained or reasoned away, and leads to avoidance of the feared stimulus.

After 1870 many careful descriptions of phobic and oc disorders appeared, starting with Westphal's classic accounts of agoraphobia in 1871 and of oc disorder in 1878. In 1895 Freud separated common phobias of things most people fear to some extent (such as death, illness, and snakes) from specific phobias of things or situations that inspire no fear in the average person, such as agoraphobia. That same year Henry Maudsley in the *Pathology of Mind* approved Westphal's agoraphobia as a separate syndrome; in the 1895 edition, however, he included all phobias under melancholia and derided the big-sounding names given to each type of phobic situation, since many phobias were often found together or successively in the same case. In 1913 Kraepelin included in his textbook a brief chapter on irrepressible ideas and irresistible fears, but did not separate phobic from oc phenomena. About that time Janet (1925) lucidly detailed the features of oc disorder and its treatment by exposure.

Phobias achieved a separate diagnostic label in the *International Classification of Diseases (ICD)* only in 1947, and in the American Psychiatric Association classification (now called *DSM*, for *Diagnostic and Statistical Manual*) as late as 1952. Even by 1959 only three out of nine classifications used in different countries listed phobic disorder as a diagnosis on its own (Stengel 1959). In the last two decades subdivision began of phobic and oc disorders (Marks & Gelder 1965; Marks 1969, 1970), and *DSM-III* (1980) extended this. Anxiety and related disorders appeared in the *ICD* for the first time in the seventh revision (1955) and came under 18 rubrics in the ninth revision (1983). European nosology for these disorders implies less hard-and-fast dividing lines than the *DSM-III* (Jablensky 1985). Some of the problems created by the original hierarchical classification of the *DSM-III* may be eased if it is revised so that multiple anxiety disorder categories may coexist in individuals, with severity as the only determinant of primary versus secondary status (Spitzer & Williams 1985).

PROBLEMS OF CLASSIFICATION

To classify means to arrange phenomena into classes possessing common attributes. Any set of features can be classified in endless ways, the utility of which depends on their purpose. The most useful are those classifications which "carve nature at the joints," so that several types of attribute are present in all members of one class but absent in members of other classes. In clinical science the attributes of a class may be shared symptoms and signs, etiology, pathophysiology, prognosis, or response to treatment.

Ideally, in a given class all these subsets of common attributes should coincide, but few classifications approach this ideal. At the other extreme are nosologies whose assignment to classes tells us only about one subset of features and no other. There would be little point to dividing phobics into those with and without a squint, as this predicts nothing more about other attributes shared by the two classes. Fortunately we can pick out types of phobic and oc problems that are less arbitrary because they have clinical correlates to support their usefulness. Much current research is examining relevant issues, and present classes may need revision as knowledge advances.

Special Difficulties in Classifying Phobic and OC Problems

Three problems must be resolved in classifying phobic and oc symptoms. First, such symptoms can involve almost any situation. Second, they may occur together with almost any other psychiatric symptom. Third, they may be found to a minor degree in almost anybody, and we can hardly call everybody disordered.

Such problems are not insuperable. To take the first one, since phobic and oc symptoms may involve virtually any stimulus, a taxonomy dependent on the stimulus would result in an endless terminology. Such a classification was prominent until this century, and numerous Greek and Latin prefixes were attached to -phobia according to the object or situation that was feared (a long table of such phobias appears in Tuma and Maser 1985) A taxonomy of this kind is unhelpful. It is true, however, that certain phobic and oc symptoms tend to involve particular clusters of situations, each cluster having its own correlates (for example, a fear of crowds tends to be associated with other agoraphobic attributes, and a fear of dirt with oc rituals). These clusters naturally overlap but are useful for purposes of description, etiology, treatment, and prognosis. The phobic or oc situation is therefore of some importance and cannot be entirely ignored.

The second problem is that phobic and oc phenomena can occur either on their own or as part of an entire range of psychiatric disorders. Phobias include such contrasting states as children's ephemeral fears of darkness or animals to the vague phobias found in some personality disorders and the multiple panics of a housebound agoraphobic. Obsessive-compulsive problems range from an isolated, recurrent, unpleasant thought to repetitive rituals of a wide variety that cripple the sufferer and his or her family. It is not surprising that some regard these disorders as maladaptive "habits" that themselves constitute the problem without any underlying cause, while for others they are but the visible aspect of deeper pathology. Each view may be correct in different cases, and the varying significance of phobic and oc phenomena is difficult to formulate only if we assume a unitary origin for all of them instead of recognizing that multiple factors play a role in their genesis.

The third issue—that most people have minor fears and rituals—is again shared with other mental health problems. Only in relatively few people do such minor fears and rituals become serious depressive disorders or fixed delusions. Normal troubles that do not require treatment and abnormal worries that do are at opposite ends of a continuum and shade into one another at some point. In threatening situations it is abnormal *not* to feel fear. (When in the fifteenth century Erasmus fled from the plague as people died from it in swarms, he wrote to a fellow fugitive: "Really, I consider total absence of fear, in situations such as mine, to be the mark not of a valiant fellow but of a dolt.")

Most people are wary at the top of a cliff or when meeting strangers in a new country. This anxiety is protective, common, and normal. But very few stay away from work for fear of the bus ride to get there. Such severe fears are uncommon, a handicap, and abnormal. Many quirks are as adaptive as minor fears. Being precise, orderly, and perfectionist helps our work, but is indicated if most of the day is spent plagued by indecision, resisting intrusive thoughts, endlessly washing hands, spending hours rechecking locks on doors and windows, hoarding mountains of trivia until there is no room left to move at home, and driving others crazy with such odd ways.

Phobic and OC Symptoms Versus Disorders

Phobic and oc symptoms are often seen as minor complaints in many disorders. They may occur as part of a depressive disorder, waxing and waning at the same time as the more prominent depressive symptoms. They may be a feature of generalized anxiety disorder, abnormal personality, and schizophrenia. In these conditions treatment largely depends on management of the major condition in which the phobic or oc symptom occurs, although the latter may sometimes be amenable to behavioral treatment despite persistence of the major condition. It is not always easy to separate symptom from disorder.

We are here mainly concerned with problems in which phobic and oc complaints predominate and are not merely a minor accompaniment to another major condition. When phobic and oc difficulties dominate the clinical picture and are handicapping, we call them phobic or oc *disorders*. These disorders assume many forms ranging from an isolated phobia, obsession, or ritual in an otherwise well person to diffuse, extensive problems in the context of other psychiatric problems. Many sufferers never ask for help.

This chapter focuses on patterns of such disorders in adults. Patterns in children are discussed in Chapter 12.

PHOBIC AND OBSESSIVE-COMPULSIVE DISORDERS IN ADULTS

Table 9.1 shows the main groupings of phobic disorder and obsessive-compulsive disorder (OCD) in adults. The most common are the normal minor fears and rituals that most of us have. Problems sufficiently intense to be called disorders occur in only a small proportion of adults. Among students, for example, most might feel mildly squeamish in the presence of nonpoisonous snakes, but only 20% reported intense fear, while merely 1% to 2% actively avoided a snake enough to be labeled as phobics (Lang 1966).

Both phobic and oc disorders are syndromes of anxious avoidance that respond well to exposure therapy. They are classified as "neurotic disorders" in the *ICD-10* and as "anxiety disorders" in *DSM-IIIR*. Phobic disorders fall conveniently into four groups—agoraphobia (fear of public places), social phobia, specific phobia (fears of animals, heights, thunderstorms, etc.), and illness phobia. A fifth type of phobia—obsessive-compulsive—is accompanied by compulsive rituals and is thus a form of OCD, although its phobic component has much in common with other phobic disorders. OCD can be broadly grouped into obsessions (repetitive thoughts, ruminations) and compulsive rituals. Rituals can be further subdivided into overlapping variants.

All these groups overlap, as do their subgroups. Agoraphobics often have social phobias and occasionally also complain of specific phobias and rituals. Many illness phobics have some checking rituals. Ritualizers usually have obsessions as well. Despite the overlap, subjects within the subgroups have more in common with one another than with sufferers in other subgroups.

There are interesting differences in gender incidence among the various subgroups. Women preponderate among agoraphobics, specific phobics, and compulsive cleaners, but men more often have compulsive checking; social phobias occur equally among men and women.

Other Potential Dimensions of a Taxonomy of Phobic and OC Disorders

At least four other dimensions could form a basis for classifying these problems, but they are a less comprehensive guide to phenomenology and treat-

Table 9.1 Main phobic and obsessive-compulsive disorders in adults

	Sex incidence	Diffuse or focal	Avoidance of cues	Spontaneous panics	Percent of Maudsley phobics[a] or oc	Related disorders
Agoraphobia (*DSM-IIIR* subset of panic disorder)	F > M	diffuse	++	++	60	Anxiety states
Social phobias	F = M	varies	++	±	8	Shyness, avoidant or sensitive personality, social dysfunction
Specific (simple) phobias	F > M	focal	++	−	17	Simple phobia
Illness phobias	?	varies	+	±	15	Hypochondriasis
Obsessive-compulsive Rituals: cleaning, repeating, checking, hoarding, orderliness	F > M[1] M < F[2]	varies diffuse	++ +	±	84	
Thoughts without rituals	?	varies	+	±	16	Worry, ruminations

[a]Data from Marks (1969).
[1]For cleaners.
[2]For checkers.

ment. They include avoidance, multiple versus focal problems, panic, and subjective experience. Each is discussed below.

Avoidance

The value of behavioral treatment has been most proven in sufferers who regularly avoid the situations that evoke their phobias or rituals. In fact, delineation of the avoidance profile is the first step in an exposure program of treatment. For nonavoiders the value of behavioral treatment is still uncertain. Nonavoiders include some illness phobics, some compulsive checkers, and those obsessives whose intrusive thoughts are unaccompanied by rituals.

The feared stimuli that are avoided are commonly external—for example, crowded supermarkets for agoraphobics or touching the ground for compulsive handwashers. Fear may also be of internal stimuli (palpitations thought to indicate heart disease, for example, or murderous obsessions); sufferers try to avoid thinking about them or external cues that may bring them on. Exposure therapy is usually easy to devise when the avoidance is of external cues but is less straightforward when avoidance is solely of internal stimuli. Certain cases fear both internal and external stimuli: agoraphobics who not only avoid public places but also fear heart palpitations, thoughts of going mad, and many other symptoms of fear cued by such places; or ocs who worry about harming their children and thus hide any knives at home far from temptation.

Multiple Versus Focal Problems

Phobic/ocs with multiple problems tend to have more generalized anxiety and depression and to need longer behavioral treatment. Multiple phobias are usually from the agoraphobic cluster rather than a random assortment of, say, fears of snakes, storms, and dirt. Among phobics, most agoraphobics have multiple fears; specific phobics are focal, and social phobics are in between. Among ocs, a single hierarchy of ritual-evoking fears is more often found in washers than in checkers, who frequently have many different cues evoking checking rituals.

Panic

Panic or panic attack are imprecise terms covering a wide range of discomforts. In the main they denote an abrupt surge of intense anxiety rising rapidly to a peak that either (1) is cued by particular stimuli (phobic or situational panic/anxiety) or by thinking about them (anticipatory phobic panic/anxiety—a subset of phobic panic), and/or (2) occurs without obvious cues (spontaneous, unpredictable, nonsituational, uncued, or generalized panic/anxiety)—this is on a continuum with less phasic tonic anxiety that is constantly in the background.

By definition nearly all severe phobics (apart from some blood and food phobics) have phobic panic, including anticipatory panic, so that classifying phobias according to its presence is tautologous. During phobic panic, autonomic symptoms and thoughts vary little across different types of phobia—all phobics feel heart changes, tense muscles, and sweaty palms (Hugdahl & Öst 1985). Spontaneous panics are most common in agoraphobia and in panic disorder without agoraphobia (anxiety states), but between 33% and 70% of agoraphobics have none (Angst & Dobler-Mikola 1983; Weissman et al. 1985). Spontaneous panics may also result from taking caffeine or amphetamine and during withdrawal from opiates and barbiturates.

Panic (combining spontaneous and phobic) is found in nearly all phobics of any kind, OCD, panic disorder, generalized anxiety disorder (GAD), and most cases with major depression (Table 9.2). One-third of cases of "manic depressive disease" had "anxiety attacks" (Cassidy et al. 1957). Most agoraphobics who do not seek treatment report never having had panic (sudden fear, anxiety, or uneasiness), unlike treated patients (Boyd et al. 1985). Data were not given for spontaneous versus phobic panic or anxiety, nor for mild anxiety or for avoidance; anxiety may be construed as panic mainly when it rises above a certain level, so subjects seeking treatment may have had more severe anxiety than those who did not. As panic and anxiety shade into one another, their distinction becomes rather arbitrary.

Panic thus does not separate out different anxiety disorders or indeed many depressives. It is also common in normal young adults (more than a third reported it in the past year), especially those with high trait anxiety, somatic and cognitive anxiety, agoraphobic fears, and depression (Norton et al. 1985). There appears to be no discontinuity between panic in normals and in patients—more occurs in people who have anxiety and depression or a family history of the same.

The association of panic with anxiety and depression is largely with regard to spontaneous panic, which is rare in specific phobics, who have little general anxiety (Table 9.3) yet do have intense phobic panic on encountering their phobic stimulus. Spontaneous panic correlates highly with general anxiety and depression in agoraphobics (Marks et al. 1983). In keeping with this, more and stronger panics occur in patients with a history of spontaneous (unpredictable) panics than in those who had had only predictable (phobic) panics (Barlow et al. 1985). The former are more likely to report loss of control—understandable when the source of the discomfort is obscure—and dizziness. No comparison is available for the symptom profile of spontaneous as opposed to phobic panics within the same patients.

In spontaneous panics the cue for panic is obscure. Sometimes careful interviews or daily recording may reveal triggering cues such as arguments with relatives (Freedman et al. 1985) or other concerns, but often the search is in vain; the attribution of cues becomes a projection test of the observer.

Europeans have paid less attention to the difference between tonic tension and surges of panic than has the American *DSM-III*. The *DSM-III* assumes that panic is central to the origin and treatment of panic disorder (a label that includes most agoraphobics) but does not emphasize the vital distinction of phobic from spontaneous panic, which affects both handicap and treatment. Phobic panic is (1) associated with avoidance of the triggering situations and (2) effectively treated by exposure; neither point is true for spontaneous panic (though it might improve with prolonged exposure to fantasies of panic—sys-

Table 9.2 Anxiety, depression, and panic across diagnostic groups

	Major depression n = (6)	GAD[2] (12)	Panic disorder[3] (17)	Agoraphobia (41)	Social phobia (19)	Specific phobia (7)	Obsessive-compulsive (6)
Anxiety[1] (mean)	30	23	22	26	21	17	25
Depression[1] (mean)	27	13	14	16	13	14	24
% with "panic"[4]	83	83	100	98	89	100	83
"Panic"[4] frequency	83	75	100	98	84	85	83
% diagnosis on DSM-III panic criteria	100	29	82	74	50	33	100
% diagnosis met except for panic frequency	100	75	100	98	84	85	83
% reports of panic	83	83	100	98	89	100	83

Source: Data from Barlow et al. 1985.

[1]Scores on Hamilton scales (anxiety—35 items; depression—24 items).

[2]Generalized anxiety disorder.

[3]Without regular avoidance.

[4]Spontaneous or phobic (situational).

Table 9.3 Summary of clinical and psychophysiological data (updated from Marks 1969)

	OCD	Anxiety states	Agoraphobias	Social phobias	Animal phobias	Normals
Percent women	55	50	75	60	**95	50
Onset age	22	25	24	19	*6	—
Treatment age	34	36	32	27	30	—
Overt anxiety (0–6)		2.6	2.0	2.0	*0.4	**0
Hamilton anxiety	25[+]	22[a]	26	21	17[b]	
Hamilton depression	24[+]	14[a]	16	13	14[b]	
FQ anxiety-depression	22		20	18		**8
FQ agoraphobia	14		*27	11		*5
FQ social phobia	17		15	*23		*7
FQ blood-injury phobia	12		17	10		8
Modified Cornell		—	34	21	13	10
Neuroticism		**37	30	29	*21	20
Extroversion		**14	19	19	24	25
GSR: spontaneous fluctuations		36	32	33	*2	6
GSR: habituation rate		29	39	39	*68	64
Forearm blood flow		**4.8	2.9	2.6	2.2	2.0
Eyeblink CR acquisition		11	15	19	***21	14

Sources: Data are composite from several studies, some unpublished. Main sources:
Sex incidence, onset and treatment age, and overt anxiety: Marks & Gelder 1967; Lader 1966; Kelly 1966.
Cornell and neuroticism scores: Gelder et al. 1967; Kelly 1966.
Hamilton anxiety and depression: Barlow 1985.
FQ = Fear Questionnaire (Marks & Mathews 1979); data from Cottraux, personal communication, 1985.
Psychophysiological data: GSR; Lader et al. 1967; Lader 1966.
Forearm blood flow at rest: Kelly (unpublished).
Eyeblink CR acquisition: Martin et al. (1969); Martin (unpublished).
n = 18 to 84 in different cells (except [+], where n = 6).
*Differs significantly from other psychiatric groups
**Differs significantly from all groups
***Differs significantly from all groups except social phobias
[a]Panic disorder.
[b]Simple phobia.

tematic clinical research on this issue remains to be done). Avoidance is the most crippling aspect of phobias and, to a lesser extent, of OCD; as mentioned, working out the avoidance profile is the first stage of exposure therapy. In contrast, spontaneous panic is certainly unpleasant but does not change life-styles unless it becomes linked to environmental cues, in which case it changes to phobic panic with avoidance. This happens in many agoraphobics but not in panic disorder without agoraphobia.

The mere presence of panic predicts far less about the nature of the clinical syndrome and its treatment than does the type of situation that cues the panic. Simply knowing that someone has panic tells one very little about its diagnosis or treatment. However, certain types of situation tell us a great deal. Knowing that someone fears crowds predicts that he or she is likely to have other fears from the agoraphobic cluster too, plus associated nonphobic symptoms, and that exposure therapy may be indicated. Hearing that someone fears thunderstorms predicts that the fear is probably specific and treatable by exposure. Learning that someone fears dirt predicts that obsessions and rituals are probably present and that exposure and response prevention may be needed. Knowing that panics are *not* cued by any situation predicts the absence of phobias and rituals and that live exposure is impractical, although fantasy exposure might conceivably help.

The Subjective Experience of the Evoking Stimulus

The *ICD-9* classifies anxiety disorders according to whether anxiety is a major or minor defining feature. It groups together states of anxiety, fear, dread, panic, phobias, apprehension, and worry. As mentioned, when in contact with their phobic stimuli, phobic/ocs usually report fear or anxiety, or panic when this is intense. During such phobic anxiety/panic most phobics experience similar autonomic sensations and negative thoughts (Hugdahl & Öst 1984).

There are some exceptions. Agoraphobics tend to feel more dizzy, blood phobics more faint, and social phobics more worried about others' opinion of them (Hugdahl & Öst 1984). Further exceptions are those ocs who on contact with their ritual-evoking stimulus deny feeling afraid or anxious, insisting that they feel only disgust or discomfort. Some blood-injury phobics report no fear on seeing blood, merely nausea before fainting. Food aversions are associated with nausea and touch aversions with tingling in the fingers and shivers down the spine. How much such selective associations of particular feelings with different forms of avoidance reflect our species' inbuilt "wiring" or shared experiences is not yet known.

Some argue that agoraphobics have unique cognitions such as fear of fear and of losing control (Foa et al. 1985). These may not be restricted to agoraphobia. "Anxiety sensitivity" also occurs in other anxiety disorders (Reiss et al. 1986), and similar internal fears are found in most phobic syndromes (Hugdahl & Öst 1984). Only further careful controlled comparison of agoraphobics with other anxiety disorders can settle the issue.

PHOBIC DISORDERS

The Agoraphobic Syndrome (Panic Disorder with Agoraphobia)

The agoraphobic syndrome—agoraphobia with or without panic disorder—is the most distressing and also the most common variety seen in mental health care. It accounts for about 60% of all phobic disorders at the Maudsley Hospital, London. Agoraphobia (Westpahl 1871) derives from the Greek *agora* meaning an assembly or market place (not open spaces, as is commonly believed). The term describes varying combinations of fears of going into stores, crowds, and public places; traveling alone in trains, buses, planes, and (less often) cars; entering closed spaces such as elevators, tunnels, theaters, and churches; crossing bridges; having haircuts; and leaving or remaining at home alone. Some cases simply have a mild travel phobia or fear of enclosed spaces. At the other extreme are agoraphobics with multiple phobias plus generalized anxiety, depression, and other difficulties. Although mild fear of open spaces is often seen in agoraphobia, it is not a central feature.

Agoraphobia comprises a group of problems whose protean manifestations have led to many labels since 1870, each highlighting some aspect of the condition; none, however, is all embracing. The current *DSM-III* term is panic disorder with agoraphobia (Spitzer & Williams 1985). Past labels have included platzangst or platzschwindel (Benedikt 1870), panphobia (Clevenger 1890), anxiety hysteria (Freud 1919), phobic anxiety state (Klein 1964), anxiety state, anxiety neurosis (Lancet 1952, p. 79), severe mixed psychoneurosis (Klein 1964), endogenous anxiety (Claycomb 1983; Sheehan et al. 1980), phobic-anxiety-depersonalization syndrome (Roth 1959), calamity syndrome (King 1962), nonspecific security fears (Snaith 1968), locomotor anxiety (Abraham 1913b), street fear (Miller 1953), topophobia (Beard 1879), kenophobia (Weiss 1964), barber-shop fear (Erwin 1963), homebound housewife syndrome (Kraft 1967), and prostitution fear. Many terms for agoraphobia with generalized anxiety emphasize its cardiovascular aspects (Skerritt 1983): nervous palpitation or irritable heart (Da Costa 1871; Oppenheimer et al. 1918), soldier's heart, aviator's syndrome, hyperesthesia of cardiac nerve centers, effort syndrome (Lewis 1917), neurocirculatory asthenia and cardiac neurosis (Cohen & White 1950), beta-hyperresponsiveness, and mitral valve prolapse syndrome.

At least two-thirds of agoraphobics are women, and most develop their symptoms after puberty, usually between age 15 and 35 (see Chapter 10). The syndrome is rare in childhood (Rutter et al. 1970). Multiple phobias occur that center around going out alone but generalize rapidly to many other situations. Numerous other nonphobic (nonsituational) anxiety symptoms are often present, including spontaneous panics and chronic tension even at rest, dizziness, depression, depersonalization, and oc phenomena. Once the syndrome has persisted more than a year it runs a fluctuating course with minor (not complete) remissions and relapse over many years. Social phobias are usually present in agoraphobia but are not the main handicap; public speaking was the most common fear in 1,000 agoraphobic club members (Marks & Herst 1970).

The diffuse symptomatology is reflected by high scores on the Fear Questionnaire (Marks & Mathews 1979), Hamilton Anxiety scale (Barlow et al. 1985), SCL-90 (Sheehan et al. 1980), and Cornell Symptom Checklist and Neuroticism on the MPI (Tables 9.3 and 9.4; Solyom et al. 1974). In keeping with this, 50% of agoraphobics feared poor health and fatal illness as well as public places, more than normal volunteers did, even though the agoraphobics had no more actual physical illness than the volunteers (Buglass et al. 1977). Alleviation of the diffuse anxiety by medication or psychosurgery has been accompanied by improvement in the phobias (see Chapter 14).

Again reflecting their diffuse anxiety, agoraphobics show increased spontaneous fluctuations in skin conductance and slowed habituation of skin conductance responses to repeated auditory stimuli (Table 9.4 and Lader et al. 1967). Surprisingly, forearm blood flow is only slightly raised (Table 9.4). Agoraphobics acquire and extinguish eyeblink conditioned responses at a normal rate, unlike animal phobics (Martin et al. 1969); the significance of this is not known.

Evidence for Agoraphobia as a Distinct Syndrome

There is abundant evidence for the unity of the protean features of agoraphobia as a syndrome distinct from other phobias and anxiety disorders. Very similar clinical features are reported from America, Europe, Australia, and Asia. Compared with other phobias, agoraphobia runs a more fluctuating course (Buglass et al. 1977), involves a different cluster of phobias, and is associated with more nonphobic anxiety-depression. No other anxiety disorder has its characteristic pattern of agoraphobic avoidance. It tends to remain distinct when followed up over 4 to 9 years, although it might be punctuated by minor affective episodes (Burns et al. 1983; Emmelkamp & Kuipers 1979; Lelliott et al. 1986; Marks 1971; McPherson et al. 1980; Munby & Johnston 1980).

Multivariate analyses in nine clinical studies yielded very similar agoraphobic and anxiety/depression factors in more than 3,400 subjects in England, Holland, and America. These included 275 neurotic patients (Roth et al. 1965), 250 mixed psychiatric outpatients (Dixon et al. 1957), 111 psychiatric inpatients (Schapira et al. 1970), 500 psychiatric inpatients (Fliess et al. 1971), 72 phobic patients (Marks 1967), 300 phobic patients plus 1,000 phobic club members (Marks & Mathews 1979), 171 phobic patients (Hallam & Hafner 1978; Hallam 1985), another 703 phobic club members (Arrindell 1980), and community samples and psychiatric hospital patients (Derogatis & Cleary 1977; Lipman et al. 1979) (see Table 9.4, A–I). All these studies point to a certain subset of phobias often accompanied by particular symptoms of anxious-depressed mood.

Agoraphobic and anxiety with or without depression items came out as one factor in two studies (Roth et al. 1965, who labeled their first factor as phobic-anxiety-depersonalization; Fliess et al. 1971). A separate agoraphobic factor concerning the usual fears of such patients was found by Dixon and coworkers (1957), Marks (1967), Schapira and coworkers (1970), Marks and Mathews (1979), Hallam and Hafner (1978) and Arrindell (1980) (Table 9.5 B–E, I). It correlated well with the clinical diagnosis made independently (Marks 1967). (The sample reported by Hallam and by Hallam and Hafner included some patients studied by Marks and Mathews). Psychiatric patients with miscellaneous diagnoses or with specific or social phobias did not yield such a factor (reviewed by Hallam 1978), nor did volunteers with specific fears (Meikl & Mitchell 1974).

In short, multivariate analyses of phobic or other psychiatric subjects yield a particular group of *agora*phobic fears and of nonphobic anxiety with or with-

Table 9.4 Agoraphobic and anxiety-depression factors from nine studies

A. Clinical data: 275 neurotic patients (Roth et al. 1965)

Phobic-anxiety-depersonalization

Situational phobias (agoraphobic)
Panic attacks
Depersonalization and derealization
Temporal lobe features
Marked precipitant
Sudden onset
Dizzy attacks

Anxiety-depression

Chronic neurotic personality
Anxiety personality features
Marked depression
Mood instability
Sensitivity, paranoid
Social maladjustment
Childhood anxiety and neurotic traits

B. Questionnaire replies: 72 phobic patients (Marks 1967)

Phobias

(Diagnosis of agoraphobia)
Fainting in public
Train journey
Being left alone
Crowded place
Alone in large open space
Surgical operation
Crossing a bridge or street

Anxiety-depression

Factor not reported, but agoraphobics
  scored higher than social phobics on:
  Cornell Symptom Checklist
  Tavistock Inventory
  paranoid irritability

C. Questionnaire replies: 300 phobic patients and 1,000 phobic club members (Marks & Mathews 1979)

Phobias

Traveling alone by bus or coach
Walking alone in busy streets
Going into crowded shops
Going alone far from home
Large open spaces

Anxiety-depression

Feeling miserable or depressed
Feeling irritable or angry
Feeling tense or panicky
Upsetting thoughts coming into your mind
Feeling you or your surroundings are
  strange or unreal

D. Questionnaire replies: 171 phobic patients (Hallam & Hafner 1978; Hallam 1985)

Phobias

Travel by train or bus
Football
Going into street or open place
Shopping
Travel by ship
Tunnels
Cinema, theatre or church
Travel by plane
Elevators
Hairdresser

Anxiety-depression: 1

Depressed, don't want to live
Feel strange, unreal, in dream
Feel irritable or angry
Generally tense, anxious, nervous
Lonely
Unwanted intrusive thoughts
Exhaustion or tiredness
Sudden panic for no reason

Anxiety-depression: 2

Breathing difficulty
Giddiness or dizziness

E. Questionnaire replies: 250 neurotic patients (Dixon et al. 1957)

Phobias

Being left alone
Large open space
Water and drowning
Crossing a bridge or street
Train journeys

F. Interview of 111 psychiatric inpatients with affective illness (Schapira et al. 1970)

Phobias

Crowds
Travel
Leaving home
Social

G. Psychiatric ratings: 500 consecutive psychiatric inpatients (Fliess, Gurland, & Cooper 1971)

Phobic anxiety

Situations evoking anxiety/avoidance
Trembling, hand shaking, weak at knees
Sweating, clammy hands
Hot and cold feelings, blushing, pallor
Fear of staying home alone
Fear of going out alone

(*Continued on next page.*)

Table 9.4 *Continued*

Fear of being in enclosed place	Enclosed places
Fear of being in crowds	Being in a strange place
Butterflies/sinking feelings in stomach	High places
Heart pounds or flutters	Crowded places like shops, cinema, church
Mouth dry, coated	Travel on buses, subways or trains
Dizziness, faintness, giddiness	Being in an elevator
Heart flutters	Crossing streets
Mouth dry, coated	Eating or drinking in public
Can't breathe, choking, chest tightness	Being alone
	Fainting or collapsing in public

H. Community samples and hospital patients (adapted from Derogatis & Cleary (1977) and Lipman et al. 1979 (cited by Hallam 1985)

Phobic-anxiety

Afraid to travel in buses, subways, trains
Afraid to go out of the house alone
Uneasy in crowds, such as shopping
Spells of terror or panic
Suddenly scared for no reason
Afraid you will faint in public
Having to avoid certain things, places or
activities because they frighten you

I. Questionnaire replies: 703 members of a phobic club (Arrindel 1980)

Phobias

Being in open spaces or on the street
Going out of the house alone

Somatic anxiety

Headaches
Faintness or dizziness
Pains in heart, chest, lower back
Nausea or upset stomach
Soreness of muscles
Trouble getting breath
Hot or cold spells
Numbness or tingling in part of the body
Heavy feelings in arms or legs
Lump in throat
Heart pounding or racing
Trouble falling asleep
Feeling weak in part of the body
Restless or disturbed sleep
Thinks something serious is wrong with
body

---

out depression symptoms, either as one factor together or as two separate factors. The cluster occurs slightly even in normal students (Arrindell et al. 1984).

Clinical and statistical evidence thus confirm that agoraphobia is a coherent clinical syndrome with well-defined though varying phobic features that, once established, persist together over many years. Although the core syndrome is clear, some cases overlap with other conditions. When agoraphobic avoidance and nonsituational panic-anxiety are both marked, then the labels either of agoraphobia or of anxiety state (*ICD-9,* or its *DSM-III* equivalent of panic disorder) become equally appropriate, hence the frequent term phobic-anxiety state. How agoraphobia relates to the *DSM-III* category of generalized anxiety disorder is unclear.

The intimate relationship of agoraphobia with anxiety states is seen in the history of past spontaneous (nonphobic) panics in 76% to 98% of agoraphobics (Marks et al. 1983; Roth et al. 1972; Zitrin et al. 1980). The proportion with spontaneous panic in the weeks before interview is much lower—only a third in the sample of Angst and Dobler-Mikola (1983). We saw earlier that practically all subjects with anxiety and even depressive disorder had panic if this was defined as spontaneous or phobic (Barlow 1985). Many agoraphobics seem to have anxiety states with superimposed agoraphobia. Cues for anxiety can occur in anxiety neurosis; these are often thoughts of dying or of social rejection (Beck et al. 1974). Among anxiety neurotics 10% had marked phobic avoidance and 53% had less disruptive fears (Woodruff et al. 1972). It is a mystery why only some cases with marked anxiety or spontaneous panics rapidly develop phobic avoidance with consequent severe handicap, while others never become phobic.

Anxiety states differ from agoraphobics in having less female preponderance (Hare 1965), fewer phobias, more diffuse tension, and corresponding skin conductance and forearm blood flow activity. They also condition eyeblinking marginally less and are more introverted and neurotic (Table 9.4 and Solyom et al. 1974).

Agoraphobia can be accompanied by habitual hyperventilation and resemble the syndrome of that name (Bonn 1984; Lum 1981; Magarian 1982). If the depressive component becomes as prominent as the agoraphobic avoidance, then the terms neurotic depression *(ICD-9)*, major depressive disorder, or dysthymic disorder *(DSM-III)* might be used. Burton's comment in 1621 remains valid: some are sad, others fearful, yet others both. During periods of depression preexisting phobias are likely to intensify; when the depression remits, the phobias often abate.

The scope for multiple labels was highlighted in 100 consecutive patients who presented with spontaneous panic attacks and polyphobias (Sheehan & Sheehan 1982). All these cases met the criteria for *DSM-III* agoraphobia, panic disorder, generalized anxiety disorder, conversion disorder, and atypical somatoform disorder, as well as for *ICD-9* phobic neurosis. The great majority also earned the terms anxiety neurosis (95%), atypical depression, or hysteria (92%), and 81% had obsessive-compulsive and 68% hypochondriacal symptoms.

Fluctuations in the clinical state of a given patient over a period can earn her or him a variety of diagnoses at different times: agoraphobia, panic disorder with or without agoraphobia, minor depression, hyperventilation syndrome, and so on. Whether these are all variants of the same disorder is not known, but each term emphasizes a feature requiring treatment in its own right (such as exposure for agoraphobic avoidance, perhaps with the addition of anxiety-management training for spontaneous panics, antidepressants for depression, and breathing exercises for hyperventilation).

Despite such fluctuations over time, there is impressive agreement among many studies about the long-term stability of the clinical features of agoraphobics over 4 to 8 years' follow-up (see Chapter 10). They usually remain agoraphobic unless they have remitted with treatment, and do not generally evolve into other syndromes such as specific phobia, OCD, anxiety state, manic-depressive disorder, or schizophrenia.

Deficiences of DSM-IIIR Concerning Agoraphobia

A central weakness is that DSM-IIIR fails to specify the *type* of situation that evokes panic and avoidance, and simply mentions phobic avoidance. But it is the *agora*phobic cluster—not fears of blood, spiders, illness, thunderstorms, or dirt—which is mainly associated with spontaneous panics and multiple phobias. Having a phobia from within that cluster predicts that (1) it will usually be associated with multiple other phobias, (2) these other phobias will usually be from within rather than outside that cluster, and (3) there are also likely to be many other nonphobic symptoms, including spontaneous panics. In contrast, a phobia from outside that cluster is much more likely to be focal) specific, simple) and with fewer nonphobic symptoms.

Another defect is that DSM-IIIR does not sufficiently clearly separate "panic attacks" cued by thinking about or entering agoraphobic situations (phobic panics) from those which are not (spontaneous, nonsituational, unpredictable).

Social Phobia

Social phobia involves fear of scrutiny from other people and leads to gaze aversion and avoidance of eating, drinking, blushing, speaking, writing, or eliminating in their presence. Social phobics often fear that they might act or look stupid. The gaze aversion was long ago emphasized by Beard (1879, p. 306): "This form of morbid fear is often accompanied with turning away of the eyes and hanging down of the head. . . . In some cases I hold the head of the patient between my hands, so as to bring his face opposite mine, and even then he will involuntarily turn away his eyes."

Social phobics constitute about a quarter of phobics in London and Canada (Chapter 11). Unlike all other adult phobic disorders, social phobias are almost as common in men as in women. The onset age is usually after puberty with a peak in the late teens; it largely overlaps with that of agoraphobia, except that few social phobias begin after age 30. Many report excessive shyness since early childhood, a feature that is genetically influenced (see Chapter 6). Compared with agoraphobics, social phobics presenting for treatment in England and Canada are more often single, male, a few years younger, and of higher socioeconomic class and education (Amies et al. 1983; Solyom et al. 1985). Other features are given in Table 9.3 and Chapter 11.

In number of phobias and amount of nonphobic anxiety, social phobics are intermediate to agoraphobia and specific phobia. They are as introverted as agoraphobics, though less so than cases of anxiety states. They acquire eyeblink conditioned responses quite rapidly. Skin conductance and forearm blood flow are indistinguishable from that of agoraphobics. The more diffuse examples of social phobia may have minor agoraphobic symptoms, but many have very specific phobias.

Specific Phobias

Specific (*DSM-IIIR* simple) phobias are focal phobias restricted to specific situations such as animals, heights, thunder, darkness, travel, closed spaces, or driving. Although agoraphobics frequently have fears of closed spaces such as elevators, subways, or planes, the reverse is not always found, as some claustrophobics have isolated focal fears without the anxiety-depression found in agoraphobia. Specific phobics have few other psychiatric problems and form about 17% of all Maudsley Hospital phobics. Their gender incidence as a group is unknown, apart from animal phobics, of whom the vast majority are women. The onset age varies widely from early childhood to old age, with the important exceptions of animal and blood phobics, who usually start in early childhood.

Animal phobics have been been studied in more detail than most other specific phobias. In cases presenting for treatment as adults the animal phobia usually began in early childhood before age 8 and persisted fairly continuously thereafter. Before puberty, animal phobias are common in boys and girls (MacFarlane et al. 1954), so these adults are probably the residuum of the earlier, much larger group. Although before puberty animal phobias occur often in both sexes, the few remaining after puberty are usually in women; these involve a monosymptomatic phobia of a single animal species with little generalization despite persistence of the phobia over decades. In the absence of the phobic stimulus there is usually no tension, panic, or other problem. Along with this, skin conductance responses show few spontaneous fluctuations and habituate normally to successive auditory stimuli (Lader et al. 1967), and forearm blood flow is normal (Table 9.3).

Specific phobics are usually especially easy to treat by exposure, needing less time to complete treatment than other phobics and obsessive-compulsives.

Illness Phobias

This little-studied group includes cases with intense fears of dying and of illnesses such as cancer, heart disease, and venereal disease. Such phobics ruminate without end that they might have any one of a host of diseases. They may avoid anything reminding them of that disease, including media articles or broadcasts on the subject, and they have checking rituals, such as endless palpation of the breasts in a search for cancer until those are bruised, or interminable requests for examination and reassurance from doctors and relatives. Illness phobias are intermediate between phobic and oc disorders. The rumination resembles an obsession except that there is no subjective sense of resistance, and the rituals may be as troublesome as in any OCD. Although illness phobias are often prominent in depressive disorders and fluctuate with the depression, in a few patients the illness phobia occurs and persists independent of any other symptom.

Illness phobia can be regarded as a form of focused hypochondriasis (*DSM IIIR* somatization disorder). In hypochondriasis the fears are diffuse and not of any particular malady. The phobias occur in both sexes, and the particular illness feared varies with what is fashionable in the culture.

OBSESSIVE-COMPULSIVE DISORDERS

These involve repeated obsessions (thoughts, ruminations) or rituals (actions) that intrude against the sufferer's will and are usually known to be senseless.

Most patients resist the obsessive thought or the urge to ritualize, but resistance may be absent, especially in very chronic ritualizers, after psychosurgery, and in children. If prevented from carrying out their rituals sufferers generally become uncomfortable or anxious.

Some obsessions occur without being followed by compulsive rituals. Most rituals, however, are preceded by obsessions—they are the thoughts executed in action. As an example, a mother ruminating about contaminating her child might repeatedly clean herself and her house to remove all conceivable dirt and sources of infection.

Like phobia, OCD is also a syndrome of anxious avoidance. It shades into phobia to the extent that an oc feels anxious during the obsessions or rituals, frequently avoids situations that evoke them (compulsive washers avoid dirt), and improves with exposure treatment. OCDs also differ from phobic disorders in several ways. (See Chapter 13, which fleshes out the following brief discussion of the main forms of OCD).

OCD presents problems in taxonomy similar to those regarding phobias. The best guide to the phenomenology and treatment of OCDs is a division of these disorders into two overlapping forms—rituals with obsessions, and obsessions alone.

Compulsive Rituals with Obsessions

Avoidance of ritual-evoking cues is usual among ritualizers, especially among women, and related obsessions are usually also present. Compulsive cleaners shun anything remotely connected with dirt or infection. The avoidance can be bizarre, as in a woman who shunned anything colored brown, which reminded her of chocolate; she also avoided cues connected with her deceased mother, including other family members and certain places.

There are many overlapping forms of rituals, and they have been subdivided into the following variants (based on 45 of the author's cases—Stern & Cobb 1978). Some patients had more than one type of ritual (so that the percentages below add up to more than 100%), and some rituals fall outside these categories.

Cleaning (51%): This occurs more in women than in men, usually with fears of dirt and avoidance of imagined foci. Sufferers might feel contaminated each time they urinate, defecate, masturbate, touch the floor or a pet, or pass a hospital, with ensuing hours of washing and bathing, followed by disinfection of all objects in the house that they touched while feeling dirty.

Repeating (40%): Number rituals are a prime example of repeating, as in a woman who, every time a certain thought came into her mind, had to repeat either 5 times or in multiples of 5 whatever action she was carrying out at the time—whether this was touching a coffee cup or stirring it with a spoon. Eleven percent of cases studied had to repeat the action until it had been completed "correctly."

Checking (38%): This is more common in men than in women. Subjects may spend hours checking that the windows and doors of the house are locked on leaving their home in the morning or retiring to bed in the evening, or hunt throughout the house for invisible fragments of broken glass, needles, or pins for fear they will be lethally swallowed by the entire family, or search for knives and put them away lest they stab others, or check for hairs they may have shed, or constantly retrace the route over which they have driven their car looking for the corpses of people they think they may have knocked down.

Hoarding (category added by author—2%): Sufferers find it terribly hard to throw rubbish away, spend hours sorting out kitchen scraps, store valueless papers for decades, and buy vast quantities of canned foods and objects that they never use. Removal of the accumulated hoard evokes great anxiety, and it may become impossible to move in a hoarder's house where rooms and passages are cluttered with thousands of unused items.

Orderliness (9%): This concerns compulsions to arrange objects in a particular way. One patient could not study because he spent so much time arranging pencils, pens, and erasers on his desk in an idiosyncratic manner.

Slowness without Visible Rituals

Slowness in completing an activity is usually due to repetition of the whole sequence or of its components. In some cases there are no visible rituals. Most of the latter cases seem lost in thought and later say that they were carrying out mental checks or executing the activity in a precise sequence. A few cases can give no reason for the slowness. Extreme slowness without overt rituals is uncommon, seen much more among men than women, and especially hard to treat. The patient can take hours to dress, have breakfast, or carry out everyday actions. The slowness is selective, so that a patient might take seven hours to bathe and an hour to cross the road, yet talk, walk, drive, and play tennis at normal speed.

Obsessions

Obsessive thoughts or ruminations are stereotyped thoughts that insistently intrude upon the patient's mind against his or her will and recur despite all attempts to banish them. Many obsessions concern worries about contaminating or harming other people or going against some social taboo such as swearing or making inappropriate sexual advances in public. Most ritualizers have some obsessions preceding their compulsive actions, but a small minority of ocs have obsessions without rituals. For the latter, behavioral treatment is less successful than for ritualizers.

PREVALENCE OF PHOBIC AND OC DISORDERS AND SYMPTOMS

Although we have long known that anxiety and mixed anxiety-depression are frequent, it has only recently become apparent quite how common phobic and obsessive-compulsive disorders are. This was found in several community surveys in the United States, Germany, and Switzerland, such incidence being highest in the most recent studies (summarized in Table 9.5). Prevalence of anxiety disorders was stable when it was ascertained twice in the same way at an interval of over 25 years in a Canadian county (Murphy et al. 1984).

The prevalence of anxiety disorders found across studies varies with many factors. One is the setting of the study—whether the sample comes from the community as a whole, GP surgery, general hospital, or psychiatric outpatients or inpatients. Another is its age and sex composition; prevalence is greater in middle life than in the very young or old, and, for most types of anxiety disorder, in women than in men. Prevalence rates rise the longer the period of risk, for example, lifetime rather than 1-year, 6-month, or one point in time.

Rates are also higher if the criterion for "caseness" (case definition) is broad for diagnosis and mild for severity, symptoms being more frequent than disorders. The thresholds at which particular anxiety symptoms are taken to amount to a disorder vary widely across different diagnostic systems. Prevalence rates were more than twice as common when diagnosed as ICD phobic state than as PSE/CATEGO or Feighner phobic neurosis or as RDC phobic disorder (Sireling et al. 1987). Given the common admixture of anxiety and depression, nonexclusive diagnostic systems which allow more than one diagnosis may yield a clearer picture than exclusive ones which make depressed mood exceed anxiety hierarchically as with CATEGO.

That prevalence increases, the milder the criterion of severity is seen from a community survey of 800 people in Camberwell, London (Bebbington et al. 1982). One-month prevalence of all anxiety disorders was 2.9% (4.5 female, 1.0 male) but of generalized anxiety symptoms was 7.6% (11.8 female, 2.9 male). Similarly, they found severe agoraphobia with avoidance in only 0.2% (both cases women) but agoraphobic symptoms in 17.4% (25.3 female, 8.6 male); no case of severe social phobia with avoidance but social unease in 16.3% (18.9 female, 13.3 male); and no case of severe OCD with avoidance but oc symptoms in 10.8% (14.4 female, 6.8 male).

Equally, in an interview survey of a community sample in Vermont ($n = 325$, Agras et al. 1969) current prevalence of phobias as a whole was 7.7%; of illness/injury phobias, 3.1%; of agoraphobia, 0.6%; and of severe phobias, only 0.2%. The frequency of a condition in psychiatric practice is thus not a good guide to its prevalence in the general population. In Vermont agoraphobics constituted only 8% of all phobics but fully 50% of treated phobics (60% of Maudsley phobics were agoraphobic [Marks 1969]). Although illness/injury phobics were 5 times more frequent than agoraphobics in the community, they were less common among treated phobics (34%).

Only a quarter of severe phobics in Vermont were in treatment. Fewer than 1 per 1,000 (including only a quarter of severe phobics) were currently in psychiatric treatment for phobias, although 9 per 1,000 had been treated for phobias at some time. In line with this, only a sixth of 19–20 year olds in a Zurich community were being treated, while among general practice attenders in London none of the handicapped phobics had been treated for their phobias (Sireling 1986).

Table 9.5 Community prevalence of anxiety disorders and symptoms (%)

Period of prevalence	Weissman[a]	Uhlenhuth[b]	ECA[c]	Wittchen[d]	Angst[e]	Agras[f]	Bebbington[g]	Väisänen[h]	Orley[i]	Costello[j]	Schwab[k]	Marks[l]	Surtees[m]
	point	1 year	6 mths.	6 mths.	1 year	point	1 month						
n =	511	3161	11506	1504	600	325	800	991	206	444	1645		576
All anxiety disorders	4.3			8.1	8.4		2.9	18.7[n]				3.4	7.6[j]
General anxiety disorder	2.5	6.4			2.3								
Anxiety state							7.6[o]						
Panic disorder	0.4		0.8	1.1	3.1	0.2							
Phobic disorders	1.4									0.7			
Agoraphobia ± panic		1.2	3.8	3.6	1.8	0.6	0.2						
Social phobia			1.7										
Specific phobia			7.0	4.1									
Other phobias		2.3			1.2								
Phobic symptoms						7.7	17.4[n]		15	19	16		
Obsessive-compulsive Disorder	0		1.6	1.8			0						
Symptoms							11	2.5	2.4		14		

a = Weissman et al. 1978.
b = Uhlenhuth et al. 1978.
c = epidemiological catchment area survey (Weissman 1985; Myers et al. 1984).
d = Wittchen 1986.
e = rates with social impairment and avoidance (Angst & Dobler-Mikola 1983).
f = Agras et al. 1969.
g = Bebbington et al. 1982.

h = Väisänen 1975.
i = Orley & Wing 1979.
j = women only (Costello 1982).
k = Schwab et al. 1979.
l = mean of 5 different surveys in US, UK & Sweden (Marks & Lader 1973).
m = Surtees et al. 1986.
n = agoraphobic symptoms.
o = including mild symptoms.

From the Vermont survey 26 untreated phobics were followed up 5 years later, none having been treated by a doctor or clergyman in the meantime (Agras et al. 1972). Over the 5 years, improvement was marked in subjects who were first seen when younger than 20 but was only slight in those 20 or over. Initial severity of the main phobia did not correlate with outcome, and improvement was greater in focal than in diffuse phobias. These findings agreed with others that during childhood and adolescence, phobias tend to diminish over time (Marks 1969), whereas in adults in primary care, chronic phobias remained largely unchanged over a year without exposure therapy (Marks 1985a).

Prevalence rates in later United States community surveys were reviewed by Weissman (1985). Using RDC criteria, in a structured interview of 511 people in New Haven, Connecticut, the current prevalence was 4.3% for any anxiety disorder (Research Diagnostic Criteria) (similar to that of anxiety disorder as reviewed by Marks & Lader [1973]; 2.5% for generalized anxiety disorder (GAD); 1.4% for phobic disorder (type not specified); and 0.4% for panic disorder; no cases of OCD were found (Weissman et al. 1978). There was overlap within the anxiety disorders and of the anxiety disorders with major or minor depression. Over 80% of persons with GAD, 17% with panic disorder, and 19% with phobia had at least one of the other anxiety disorders in their lifetime; 30% of phobics had had panic disorder at some time previously. Over 7% of persons with GAD, 2% with panic disorder, and 4% with phobia had major depression at some time. Only a quarter of persons with any current anxiety disorder had received treatment for these problems in the past year, although they were high users of health care facilities for nonpsychiatric reasons and of minor tranquilizers; people with panic disorder were the highest users of psychotropic drugs.

In a large United States general population survey by interviewers who gave a symptom checklist, (n = 3,161, Uhlenhuth et al. 1983), 1-year prevalence (the proportion of people who had the disorder at any time during a year) was, for GAD, 6.4% (8 female, 4.3 male); for agoraphobia/panic, 1.2% (1.8 female, 0.5 male); for other phobias, 2.3% (3.1 female, 1.3 male); for major depression, 5.1% (6.9 female, 2.8 male); and for other high psychic distress, fully 10.5% (12.6 female, 8.4 male). Surprisingly, agoraphobia/panic was most common at ages 50 to 79. Other phobias were by far the most prevalent under age 35; major depression and GAD did not differ much among age groups; and other psychic distress declined steadily with age. The last category confirmed clinical impressions that mixed anxiety-depressive disorders are very prevalent. As noted by Weismann and co-workers (1978), use of antianxiety drugs was highest in agoraphobia/panic subjects.

In much the biggest study, the ECA survey in three communities in New Haven, Baltimore, and St. Louis (total n = 11,506), the pooled 6-month prevalence rate was 0.8% for panic (60% more in women), 3.8% for agoraphobia (300% more in women), 1.7% for social phobia (50% more in women), 7.0% for specific phobias (100% more in women), and 1.6% for OCD (50% more in women) (Myers et al. 1984; Weissman 1985). Again there was overlap within the anxiety disorders and between them and depression. Rates were highest at ages 25 to 44 and lowest above age 64 (Weissman 1983).

Table 9.6 Four-week prevalence of anxiety syndromes

	Panic disorder	General anxiety	Agoraphobia	Social phobia	Simple phobia
Men	1.8	2.4	0.4	0.5	0.5
Women	3.8	5.1	1.5	1.5	2.9
Men and women	2.8	3.8	1.0	1.0	1.7

Source: Angst & Dobler-Mikola 1983.

In a Munich community sample (n = 1504) the 6-month prevalence of all anxiety disorders was 8.1%, of panic disorder 1.1%, of agoraphobia 3.6%, specific phobia 4.1%, and of OCD 1.8% (Wittchen 1986). As in the ECA survey, panic disorder without agoraphobia was the least common anxiety disorder, though panic symptoms were nearly three times more frequent than panic disorder. Women had a higher rate for all anxiety disorders than did men, and especially for agoraphobia—2½ times more frequent.

A Swiss study sampled 600 of all 19- to 20-year-olds in Zurich (Angst & Dobler-Mikola 1983). The 4-week prevalence of anxiety syndromes is seen in Table 9.6. The 4-week, 3-month, and 1-year prevalence rates of impairing phobic disorders were of a similar order of magnitude. For agoraphobia and agoraphobia with panic pooled together, these rates were 2.8% for women and less than a third of that for men; for other phobias, 2.0% for women and 0.3% for men. For anxiety and panic the female preponderance was less marked; with the sexes combined, 4-week, 3-month, and 1-year prevalence of disorder with social impairment were 3.5%, 4.3%, and 5.4%, respectively. For all anxiety disorders, total 1-year prevalence was 8.4%, and total 1-year treatment prevalence was 1.4%.

In primary care settings it is now well established that about a sixth or more of attenders have impaired mental health and that the bulk of those so affected have anxiety-depression (Shepherd et al. 1966, Surtees et al. 1986). This is true not only in Western countries but also in developing countries (Colombia, India, Sudan, Philippines [Harding et al. 1980]; Turkey [Ozturk 1980; Kenya [Dhadphale et al. 1983]). Few have examined the prevalence of particular anxiety disorders in primary care. Of 1,241 adult GP attenders in London (Sireling 1987), 6.6% reported phobias at interview, half of which caused substantial impairment, though *none* had been treated. This figure resembled that in two U.S. primary care studies, where the prevalence of phobic disorder was 5.8% (Hoeper et al. 1979) and 6.8% (Schulberg et al. 1985) using the RDC and DSM-III respectively. Two-fifths of the London phobics were agoraphobic and a third had specific phobias. Of patients treated by their GP for depression, 36% reported phobias. Put another way, substantial impairment from a phobic condition was found in one-thirtieth of GP attenders and in one-seventh of cases being treated by the GP for depression.

That agoraphobia was the most frequent phobic problem among GP attenders fits with its being the commonest phobic disorder in psychiatric practice (Agras et al. 1969, Marks 1969). In community surveys, however, specific phobias are the most common (ECA and Munich); they are probably less likely to cause handicap and thus urgency in seeking treatment. The 10% rate of agoraphobia among depressives being treated by their GPs in London (Sireling 1987) compared with 22% among Newcastle inpatient depressives (Schapira et al. 1970). Of the London GPs' phobics, 28% were agoraphobic. The rarity of social phobia among GP attenders was compatible with Burns's (1980) and Costello's (1982) findings that mild social fears are very common but severe social phobias are not.

Phobic symptoms are more frequent than phobic disorder in the community, as we saw in the American study of Agras (1969). In another American sample, phobic symptoms were found in 16% and were commonest among black women, the poor, aged, widowed, or separated (Schwab et al. 1979). Among 444 normal Canadian women aged 18 to 65 who were interviewed with the Psychiatric Status Examination-9, only 0.7% had incapacitating phobias (all had social phobia according to *DSM-III* criteria); but fully 19% were phobic in the sense of having "intense fear plus avoidance" (Costello 1982). Surprisingly few of the women (26%) were completely free of the fears studied. Twenty-three percent had intense fears, and 82% of these (19% of the total sample) avoided the feared situation to some degree. Disregarding intensity, the prevalences of different fears were 43% for animals; 41% for "nature" (heights, tunnels, enclosed spaces, etc.); 29% for social situations; 21% for "mutilation" (injections, hospitals, doctors, blood); and 13% for "separation" (such as agoraphobic fears of taking journeys and of large open spaces). The prevalence of fears and phobias declined with age but was not associated with social class, education, employment, or number of children at home. Similarly frequent phobic symptoms were found among German medical and surgical inpatients, 25% of whom had severe social anxiety (Kunsebeck et al. 1984).

The frequency of phobic symptoms in the West is matched in rural Africa. In two Ugandan villages phobic symptoms were found in 16% of women and 13% of men; corresponding figures for obsessions were 2.0% and 2.8% (Orley & Wing 1979).

Among psychiatric patients in the United States and United Kingdom, about 2% to 3% have phobic disorders (Errera & Coleman 1963; Hare 1975; Terhune 1961). Of these about half are agoraphobic (Agras et al. 1969; Marks 1970). Phobic symptoms are naturally far commoner than phobic disorders and are present in 20% of United States psychiatric patients (Errera & Coleman 1963; Frazier & Carr 1967).

Turning to OCD, in the three American community surveys reported by Weissman (1985), the pooled 6-month prevalence rate for OCD was 1.6% (58% higher in women than in men), with no strong relationship to age. This compares with a 2.5% prevalence in Finland (Väisänen 1975) but is far higher than the rates of less than 0.1% in studies before 1970 (reviewed by Carey et al. 1984) and in the surveys of Weissman and coworkers (1978) and of Bebbington and coworkers (1982). The syndrome was rare among children 10 to 11 years old in the Isle of Wight (Rutter et al. 1970). Among psychiatric patients OCD is found in 1% to 3% of adults (Black 1974; Hare 1965: Ingram 1961a; Michaels & Porter 1949; Pollitt 1960), and in 0.2% to 1.2% of children (reviewed by Flament & Rapoport 1984). Obsessive-compulsive symptoms are much more common than the disorder. Prevalence in the community is 14% in the United

States (Schwab et al. 1979) and 11% in the United Kingdom (Bebbington et al. 1982); the low figure of 2.4% was obtained in Uganda (Orley & Wing 1979).

Anxiety disorders thus turn out to be common psychiatric problems, community prevalence in most studies being, for all anxiety disorders 2.9–8.4%, and for particular syndromes, 1.2–3.8% for agoraphobia, 1.7% for social phobia, 4.1–7.0% for specific phobias, and 1.8–2.5% for OCD (one London survey found much lower rates for agoraphobia and for OCD). The syndromes overlap with one another and with depression. Phobic and oc symptoms are even more frequent than the corresponding disorders. Female preponderance is greatest for agoraphobia and least with social phobias and OCD.

Epidemiological findings can have important implications. One is that anxiety disorders are not a privileged product of Western stress. The cross-cultural similarities in the prevalence of anxiety disorders as a whole across the globe are more impressive than the differences, though more detailed study may yet reveal fine-grain cross-cultural variations in the prevalence of particular anxiety syndromes. Meanwhile, mixed anxiety-depression is the most common presenting problem in primary care wherever this has been examined in the Americas, Europe, Asia and Africa, accounting for a sixth to a third of *all* attenders whether in industrial or developing countries.

Another conclusion from the epidemiological work is that anxiety disorders impose a heavy demand on health care services, which would be swamped if all sufferers asked for help. How to meet the demand is a major challenge. For anxiety without avoidance an economic and effective approach remains to be demonstrated. There is more hope for the large proportion who have phobic and oc disorders (the twin syndromes of anxious avoidance). Both these syndromes can be effectively treated by the behavioral method of live exposure. Yet the great majority of disabled phobic cases are untreated, figures for OCD being unavailable. Recently exposure therapy has been given successfully and economically with minimal professional input by means of systematic self-help (Chapter 14). Dissemination of this self-exposure approach applied early to phobic and oc problems before they become chronic might reduce their prevalence and even help to prevent some of them.

RELATIONSHIP OF PHOBIC AND OC PROBLEMS TO OTHER CONDITIONS

Nonsituational Anxiety/Panic and Depression

Obsessive-compulsives and phobics (especially agoraphobics) frequently have problems such as generalized tension/anxiety, spontaneous panic, worry (a stream of persistent unpleasant thoughts about unsolved problems [Borkovec 1985]), and depressed mood (tables 9.3 and 9.4). These phenomena overlap with one another. Though perplexing, the association between anxiety and depression is well recognized (Klerman 1980; McNair & Fisher 1978; Sptizer & Williams 1985) and is seen across cultures. At the height of their disorder, anxiety and tension were among the most frequent symptoms of 575 depressive patients in Canada, Iran, Japan, and Switzerland (Jablensky et al. 1981). The puzzling relationship of anxiety and depression needs review in its own right. Extensive study of this complex issue in many centers suggests that there are several interacting systems. Several points have been established about phobic-oc phenomena.

1. The various phobic and oc subgroups remain distinct when followed up over several years. In the minority of phobic patients in a London sample who remained unimproved 4 years after exposure therapy, their symptoms remained mainly phobic in nature despite many depressive episodes requiring treatment (Marks 1971). The same was true for Dutch agoraphobics (Emmelkamp & Kuipers 1979) and ocs (Emmelkamp & Rabbie 1983) followed up over 4 years.

2. Except for specific and perhaps social phobics, the course of phobics and ocs is often punctuated by episodes of depressed mood during which freefloating anxiety, panic, phobia, and oc symptoms may worsen. Among Canadian agoraphobics presenting to a general hospital, 91% had prominent affective symptoms at some time (Bowen & Kohout 1979). In the series of Barlow (1985) a clinical diagnosis of depressive disorder was made in 39% of agoraphobics, 21% of social phobics, 35% of panic disorder, and 17% of GAD. Depression scores were high in many samples of agoraphobics (Marks 1983; Sheehan et al. 1980; Telch et al. 1985) and of ocs (Barlow 1985; Marks et al. 1980). Depressive items load high in factors obtained in studies of agoraphobics (Table 9.5).

3. Despite point (2), many phobics and ocs have no freefloating anxiety, spontaneous panic, or depression. Perhaps the association of anxiety disorders with depression is overemphasized in psychiatric practice, as sufferers in the community without depression may be less likely to seek psychiatric help.

4. Patients with depressive syndromes usually have freefloating anxiety and panic (Barlow 1985) but have phobic and oc symptoms less often.

5. Regardless of syndrome, freefloating anxiety, spontaneous panic, and depressed mood are closely associated.

The vexing distinction of depression from anxiety and panic is the hardest of all to tease out, especially in cases with no phobic or oc symptoms. Some overlap merely reflects the same items having been used to measure both anxiety and depression in different measures (Foa & Foa 1982). Even excluding this, however, at the levels of both symptom and syndrome, anxiety and depression overlap so much that some have despaired of separating them; others have been satisfied with the distinctions they found. Both lumpers and splitters can call on supporting data whether the glass is called half full or half empty often seems to depend on arbitrary interpretations of statistical data. In a discriminant function analysis, is a two-thirds discrimination of anxiety and depression clear? In a multivariate analysis, are the two poles of a component proof of separateness or merely two sides of the same coin?

Another problem is that the literature often includes phobic and oc problems under "anxiety," so we are unclear how much it bears on those problems rather than on more generalized forms of anxiety. The following review omits studies that specifically exclude phobic and oc problems.

Evidence for Communality of Anxiety and Depression

In a community sample 67% of subjects with psychiatric disorder had anxiety plus depression that could not be differentiated, most of these running a brief course (Tennant et al. 1981). In another primary-care population 96% of those with psychiatric disorder had an anxiety-depression syndrome that could not be reliably subdivided; it was termed "minor affective illness" (Cooper & Sylph 1973). Nor could 240 neurotic outpatients be reliably subdivided into anxious and depressed syndromes (Johnstone et al. 1980). Of inpatients with anxiety states, 24% were rediagnosed as depressive illness when readmitted 5 years later (the reverse occurred in only 2%). According to Kendell (1974), "the magnitude of the diagnostic change creates obvious difficulties for those who maintain that there is a fundamental difference between anxiety states and depression."

Among anxiety states, brief depressive episodes occurred in 44% over 6 years (Noyes et al. 1980) and in 60% over 5 to 12 years (Cloninger et al. 1981). Among 62 anxiety neurotics from a psychiatric clinic, 10% of whom had severe phobias, half had "secondary affective disorder" (Woodruff et al. 1972). On a depression scale, anxiety states scored like depressive neuroses and were distinguished only by higher anxiety; depression and anxiety correlated .47 (Fleiss et al. 1971). In cases of generalized anxiety or panic disorder, one-third described a major affective disorder at some time (Dealy et al. 1981). Compared to the rest, the depressed subsample included more women, depression, and panic disorder but a similar family history of anxiety neurosis or depression; in the entire sample, panic disorder and depression correlated highly— the "evidence does not appear to support the notion of two diseases." Finally, several factor-analytic studies of ratings had difficulty in extracting separate anxiety and depression factors (Cohen et al. 1966; Endicott et al. 1975, Table 4; Lorr et al. 1963; Spitzer et al. 1967; Wittenborn & Holzberg 1951).

In cases with agoraphobia or panic disorder, 68% had a past or current episode of major depression (Breier et al. 1984). When panic disorder with secondary depression and depression with secondary panics were compared, the similarities were more impressive than the differences, and the outcome was worse when both depression and panics were present than when either occurred alone (Van Valkenburg et al. 1984).

Lumpers (those finding communality of anxiety and depression) are also supported by the raised frequency of depression in the relatives of patients who have agoraphobia (Munjack & Moss 1981) or panic disorder (Crowe et al. 1983). Consistent with this, if cases of major depression also had agoraphobia or panic disorder, this greatly raised the risk of major depression or anxiety disorder in the children (Weissman et al. 1984).

Many found an intimate relationship of anxiety and depression among symptoms as well as syndromes. In a normal community sample 8 scales reflected a single dimension of nonspecific distress that was likened to demoralization (Dohrenwend et al. 1980); components involved anxiety and dread as well as sadness and poor self-esteem, and were "so strongly related to each other that they are almost certainly measures of the same thing." Among healthy volunteers the Zung anxiety scale correlated .67 with the Zung depression scale (Merz & Ballmer 1983). SCL-90 scores for anxiety and depression correlated .6 among emergency-room patients and .7 in psychiatric outpatients (L. Beutler, personal communication, 1982). Among psychiatric in- and outpatients, anxious thoughts correlated even more strongly with depressed than with anxious feelings (Thorpe et al. 1983).

Symptoms of anxiety and depression were also associated in specific disorders. In post-traumatic stress disorder, Symptom Checklist-90 subscores of anxiety and depression correlated .88 with each other and .93 and .94 with the total pathology score (Horowitz et al. 1981). Of these patients 97% complained of feeling blue, 97% of worrying, 95% of feeling tense and keyed up, and 94% of nervousness and shakiness inside (Horowitz et al. 1980). In agoraphobics, freefloating anxiety and depression correlated .4 ($p < .001$) (Williams & Rappoport 1981) and .6 (Marks et al. 1983). In OCD, depression and anxiety correlated .7 and freefloating anxiety was almost as good a predictor of the response of ritualizers to an antidepressant as was depression (Marks et al. 1980; Mawson et al. 1982). Depression scores were raised in agoraphobics and OCDs, the latter not differing from major affective disorder (Barlow 1985).

Evidence Separating Anxiety from Depression

The two syndromes were separated by Downing & Rickels (1974). A discriminant function analysis split anxious from depressed neurotic female outpatients (Prusoff & Klerman 1978), but 35% could not be assigned correctly, and anxiety correlated .5 to .6 with depression; anxious subjects had anxiety similar to that of depressed patients but higher depression and somatization. A rare separation of antecedents of anxiety states from those of depressive illness was made among 164 young women in primary care (Finlay-Jones & Brown 1981), of whom 78 (45%) had psychiatric morbidity on the General Health Questionnaire, but it is sobering how many cases had a mixed diagnosis. In these women unpleasant life events in the previous year (rated without knowledge of the psychiatric state) associated with psychiatric disorder; loss events related to depression, danger events to anxiety, and both loss and danger events to mixed anxiety-depression. In a comparison of major depression with *DSM-III* anxiety disorders, although the latter often earned the diagnosis of depressive disorder, major depressives scored higher on retardation, helplessness, and suicidal thoughts (Barlow 1985).

A family history study suggested separation—the families of probands with agoraphobia and panic disorder has raised frequencies of anxiety disorder and alcoholism but not of affective disorder (Noyes et al. 1982). A twin study separated anxiety disorder from neurotic depression. Concordance rates of MZ twins exceeded those of DZ twins only for the former (Torgersen 1985); 84% of the "anxiety disorder" patients also had phobias, presumably agoraphobia.

Extensive studies concluding that anxiety and depression are distinct are those of Roth and coworkers (Guerney et al. 1970, 1972; Kerr et al. 1974; Roth et al. 1972; Roth & Mountjoy 1982; Schapira et al. 1972). They first examined and followed up 145 patients with either "anxiety state" or "depressive illness." Although the two groups overlapped, anxiety states had more panics, vasomotor signs, emotional liability, dizziness, agoraphobia, depersonalization, and derealization. Depressives had more depression, which was worse in the morning and more labile; early waking; suicidal acts; and retardation. Although depressive mood and tension were equally frequent with both diagnoses, anxiety states had more persistent tension with episodic depression, and depressive disorders had the reverse. Principal component analysis yielded a bipolar component with depression at one pole and anxiety at the other, and discriminant function analysis yielded a bimodal distribution of items that correlated with the diagnosis of anxiety state, among which panics were prominent. Anxiety states also had more family history of neurotic illness and personality disorders, more premorbid social anxiety and maladjustment, and responded better to tricyclics and to electroconvulsive therapy (ECT). At 4-year follow-up, chronic anxiety states had more persistent symptoms and acquired depression over the years, although diagnostic crossover between the two groups was exceptional.

In a second study (Caetano & Roth 1983), of 117 patients with phobias and depressive anxiety (not endogenous depression), anxiety was again largely separable from depression by multivariate analysis. Finally, among 152 inpatients with primary depression and/or anxiety, principal components and discriminant function analysis distinguished between depressed and anxious patients.

Contrasting outcomes of anxiety and of depression were also found among inpatients with panic disorder ($n = 116$) or unipolar depression ($n = 123$) (Coryell et al. 1983). Over a 5-year follow-up, recovery at some time was seen in 60% and 16% of patients who had depression or panic disorder, respectively; this difference increased with time and was no less if those who had received antidepressants or ECT were excluded. Unlike most, the authors specify the proportion who had agoraphobia—only 7% (and merely 38% of the whole group were female); so the results of this study do not apply to that syndrome.

In a review of three early-factor analytic studies not mentioned so far, of depressives in general practice, in- and outpatients, Mullaney (1984) claimed that anxiety and depression factors could be separated orthogonally. Children's emotions of anxiety and depression could be differentiated on the basis of self- and teachers' reports (Blumberg & Izard 1985).

Physiological studies could distinguish anxiety from depression "only if particular care with subgrouping of patients is exercised" (Lader 1975, p. 129);

activity was raised in anxious and suppressed in retarded (but not agitated) depressives. The problem, however, is precisely the distinction between anxiety disorders and anxious, not retarded, depressives. Features of REM sleep differentiated GAD from primary nondelusional depression (Reynolds et al. 1983). Although both anxious and depressed patients often have raised 3-methoxy-4-hydroxyphenylglycol (MHPG) and free urinary cortisol, the two measures correlated significantly only in depressives (Schatzberg et al. 1983). Finally, anxiety disorders and manic-depressive disorder could be separated on EEG variables (Sitaram et al. 1984).

After decades of research in many centers we are still uncertain how to relate anxiety to depression at the level of both syndrome and symptom. (The debate is like that between the lumpers and splitters of endogenous and reactive depression.) Two follow-up studies found that depression runs a more fluctuating course than anxiety. We also know now that although phobic and oc disorders often have episodes of general anxiety and depression, they remain distinct as syndromes over the years and respond to exposure treatment that is less helpful for depression. In contrast, antidepressant drugs have a broad-spectrum effect in many different syndromes when anxiety-depression is present (see Chapter 16). The patterns of overlap and separation suggest that there are several forms of anxiety and depression of differing origins, the presence of one predisposing to the development of others as well. The predispositions are not symmetrical. Depression is nearly always associated with anxiety, but anxiety often occurs without depression. And phobic and oc disorders commonly exist without general anxiety or depression.

Alcoholism and Drug Dependence

Long ago Westphal (1871) noticed that "the use of beer or wine allowed the [agoraphobic] patient to pass through the feared locality with comfort." Alcohol is a ubiquitous anxiolytic whose effects are variable and to some extent dose dependent. The latter was nicely captured in a passage about workers constructing a R100 airship, who had to clamber up 90-foot ladders that were secured only at the base and so swayed alarmingly (Shute 1956, pp. 68–69). Once a rigger applying for a job at the plant was sent up one of these ladders to see if he could cope. "The rigger got up halfway, and stuck; . . . We couldn't take him on unless he could climb, but the men were sorry for him, and Jimmie took him into the canteen and stood him a beer before sending him away. After his beer the rigger asked if he could have another shot at that bloody escape [ladder]. So they sent him up again, and that time he got three-quarters of the way up before he stuck. So they had him down and gave him another beer, and so strengthened he got right up to the top, and got his job. Within a week . . . [he was] able to climb anything, without the beer." Jimmie's lasting improvement presumably resulted from exposure.

There are occasional reports of phobics and ocs who are dependent on alcohol and anxiolytic drugs (Marks et al. 1966; Quitkin et al. 1972; Smail et al. 1984) and of successful outcome by withdrawal from alcohol plus treatment of the agoraphobia by exposure (Marks et al. 1977; Samarasinghe et al. 1984) or imipramine (Hudson & Perkins 1984). However, 106 adult outpatient neurotics (including 30 agoraphobics, 20 social phobics, 12 specific phobics, and 21 ocs), did not drink more than the general population (Samarasinghe et al. 1984), the small proportions of drinkers being similar among each of the diagnostic subgroups. Although a third of the patients took minor tranquillizers in a dose equivalent to 10 milligrams of diazepam or more per day, alcohol and other drugs were neither reliable anxiolytics nor used regularly as such. Consistent with the latter, in specific animal phobics confronted by their phobic animal, fear, avoidance, and tachycardia did not reduce more with alcohol than with placebo (Thyer & Curtis 1984).

Among other agoraphobic outpatients 10% to 20% were alcoholic on various criteria (Bibb & Chambless 1986). Compared to nonalcoholic ones, drinking agoraphobics had more intense panic, depression, social phobia, fear of somatic symptoms, and catastrophic thoughts. They used alcohol more to reduce dysphoria and had originally started drinking to reduce anxiety. Alcoholic agoraphobics also reported more abusive upbringings and disordered childhoods. Neither the drinking nor the phobias consistently began earlier; this was also true for one sample of inpatient alcoholics with phobias (Bowen et al. 1984) but not for another in which the phobias were said to have preceded the drinking (Mullaney & Trippett 1979). Among 60 further agoraphobics, alcoholism began before the agoraphobia in 14% and after it in only 4% (Breier & Charney 1985).

Alcoholism was found among 15% of 500 anxiety neurotics, of whom only 10% had severe phobias (Woodruff et al. 1972). Gender incidence was not mentioned in that study, but combined anxiety neurosis plus alcoholism was much more common among men than women in a community sample in Iceland (Helgason 1964) and in psychiatric outpatients in the United States (Cloninger et al. 1981). However, anxiety did not relate to drinking among unreferred male social drinkers (Rohsenow 1982a, 1982b; Schwarz et al. 1982).

A family history of alcoholism is more frequent among agoraphobics than among social and specific phobics (Munjack & Moss 1981) or nonanxious controls (Harris et al. 1983); more frequent drinking was found only in male relatives. Anxiety neurotics, too, have a raised family rate of alcoholism (Cohen et al. 1951; Noyes et al. 1978), again especially in male relatives (Cloninger et al. 1981; Crowe et al. 1980).

Among alcoholics, probands have more neuroses and higher neuroticism scores than do their nonalcoholic cotwins (Mullan et al. 1985). Agora- and social phobias are common among alcoholic inpatients (Bowen et al. 1984). Of 102 alcoholic inpatients, 32% had such disabling phobias, and another 35% had "borderline" phobias (Mullaney & Trippett 1979). (Interestingly, the men had twice more social phobia than agoraphobia, and the reverse was true for women.) The drinking began earlier in those with disabling rather than borderline phobias.

Using more stringent criteria among 60 alcoholic inpatients and members of Alcoholics Anonymous, fewer but still common phobias were found (Smail et al. 1984). When last drinking, over half had phobias (40% of these agoraphobia, 40% social phobia, 20% both); the phobias were severe in 18% and mild in 35% of subjects, and the most severely phobic men were also the most alcohol dependent. Again, the agoraphobia and social phobia often preceded the drinking problem. The lowest figures came from a study of 84 alcoholic inpatients, of whom 14% had phobic disorders; one-sixth had social phobias (Weiss & Rosenberg 1985).

Some caveats are needed. First, retrospective reports may distort the frequency of fears starting before excessive drinking began. Second, phobic frequency among alcoholic inpatients may be no guide to phobic frequency in alcoholics outside the hospital; a double handicap may lead to admission more readily than a single one. Conversely, alcoholism could be more frequent among phobics and ocs as a whole than among those referred as outpatients for behavioral treatment because (1) alcoholic phobics and ocs may be more likely to be referred elsewhere to a unit specializing in alcoholism, and (2) alcohol may aid some phobics and ocs to tolerate their fears without seeking treatment.

All the phobic alcoholics of Smail et al. (1984) reported that alcohol had helped them cope with fear, and almost all had used it to that end. Similarly, of 18 outpatients referred for phobias rather than for alcoholism, most had found alcohol helpful in coping with fears, but more men than women had used it for this purpose; in this respect these phobics differed from the neurotics of Samarasinghe and coworkers (1984). Perhaps those phobics and ocs who find alcohol especially helpful are more likely to develop alcohol dependence, which then fuels their worries.

Although the vignette from Neville Shute cited earlier illustrates that alcohol can lower avoidance, in other cases alcohol may reduce fear but not avoidance; such discordance was found, for example, in snake-fearful students and was not due to expectancy (Rimm et al. 1981). Moreover, alcohol may paradoxically lessen fear briefly but thereafter actually raise anxiety and depression both among nonalcoholics (Logue et al. 1978) and alcoholics (Stockwell et al. 1984). Among 24 inpatient alcoholics, phases of heavy drinking were associated with increased agora- and social phobia, which improved during subsequent periods of abstinence. Most subjects thought that although their fears predated the alcoholism, the fears worsened after drinking became a problem. Alcohol seems to have a biphasic effect. People feel better for the first couple of hours after a drink, which makes them more likely to drink again, but the delayed dysphoria that follows can build up to make them feel ultimately worse (Stockwell 1980). Dysphoria induced by heavy drinking may well "fuel" or even create a phobia. In keeping with this view, some phobias disappear after alcohol is withdrawn.

An additional interesting possibility is that "dry shakes" and "panic" may describe the same experience (Stockwell et al. 1984). Subjects who reported "dry shakes" were not only the most alcohol dependent but also the most agora- and social phobic. Equally, the symptoms of panic and of opiate withdrawal may be similar. There are links between the physiological pathways involved in pain, on the one hand, and fear-anxiety, on the other (see Chapter 7).

Fears, Phobias, and Epilepsy

Only rarely does epilepsy complicate phobic or oc disorders, though quite often fears and rituals can accompany epilepsy. As early as 1879 Jackson described fear with an epigastric aura as part of the epileptic attack. Like depression and anxiety, fear can occur before, during, or after other epileptic phenomena (Betts 1981). Rarely, fear can occur on its own as the sole ictal experience, and it has been mistaken for the spontaneous panic common in agoraphobia. The fear can be accompanied by terrifying visual (occasionally auditory) hallucinations or by visceral sensations (tachycardia, palpitations, tachypnea, "gooseflesh," pallor, flushing, sweating, borborygmi, belching, flatus, vomiting, diarrhea, and micturition). Fear in epilepsy often arises during a state of clouded consciousness, and the behavioral accompaniments of fear (such as pallor, sweating, gooseflesh, cowering and shouting "no, no," or running with a look of terror from the room) are then seen in an amnesic state after which the experience of fear itself cannot be recalled.

Ictal fear often feels unnatural, inexplicable, and contentless, without relation to environmental factors (Weil 1959; Williams 1956). Its unnatural quality may result from its being out of context, a hallucination induced by the local epileptic discharge, which, having arisen, is without previous causal percept or cognition. The fear can attach itself to otherwise neutral stimuli. In two patients, when their attack began, any object at which they were looking (such as a telephone or a chair) suddenly seemed threatening, which they recognized as inappropriate (Daly 1975). Shifting their gaze elsewhere reduced the fear, while looking again at the original object increased it, followed by loss of consciousness and automatism.

Epileptic fear may be like an expectant thrill rather than unpleasant. One patient had, from age 3 to 12, fleeting feelings of pleasant anticipation ("like before going to the circus"), and thereafter of fearful anticipation ("like going to the dentist"); accompanying some of those feelings was clouded consciousness, tachypnea, and a right anterior temporal spike wave discharge on EEG (Betts 1981).

Ictal fear usually occurs only at the start of a fit and lasts but a few seconds, whereas anxiety, irritability, and depression may endure for days before and after a fit (Betts 1981). Interictally, too, patients with limbic epilepsy may have fear and other disturbances as stable, enduring problems rather than simply as paroxysmal events (Bear 1985). Autonomic responses to neutral and emotional stimuli may increase even if baseline activity does not (Bear et al. 1981), and carbamazepine may improve not only the fits but also the interictal EEG and fear (Hermann & Melyn 1984). Anxiety itself can trigger a fit, especially if there is overbreathing.

After a seizure epileptics may become phobic of entering places where they had a fit lest another attack is precipitated, and they may then need treatment for the phobia independent of the epilepsy. Where phobias and epilepsy coexist, treatment of the phobia by exposure may improve both the phobia and the fits. Examples include a 31-year-old man with movement epilepsy from the age of 7 in whom agoraphobia began at 16 (Pinto 1972), and a 36-year-old man with sudden, bizarre, and violent movements triggered by social phobic stimuli (Parrino 1971). Self-control methods can reduce generalized anxiety and fit frequency (Betts 1981).

Williams (1956) wrote an excellent review of ictal emotions. He saw 2,000 epileptics living normal home lives, of whom 165 had complex feelings during the fit. Of these, 100 (5% of all cases) felt an emotion as part of the epileptic experience itself and not simply as a response to ictal events. Williams was not concerned with other emotional disturbances surrounding the epileptic fit, such as apprehension that an attack may occur, fear evoked by the knowledge of an impending fit, alarm, dismay, or distress caused by the ictal events, or subsequent malaise with depression and distress in the postictal period. Of the 100 patients who experienced emotion as part of the epileptic experience, the great majority (61%) felt fear, 21% felt depression, and the rest experienced pleasure or displeasure.

The focus causing ictal emotions was localized by finding the lesion at operation, angiography, encephalography, or inference when emotion occurred as part of a march of several ictal events. Most had left-sided or bilateral discharges, although in another series, temporal lobe epileptics with neurotic symptoms usually had a right-sided focus (Shukla & Katiyar 1980). Of 61 cases who felt fear as part of the ictus, 35 had an anterior and 17 a middle temporal lesion (Figure 9.1). Fear was experienced in 70% of patients when the epileptic discharge involved the anterior half of either temporal lobe, both with distur-

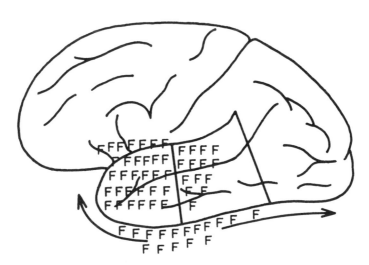

Fig. 9.1 Site of the lesion in 61 cases of epilepsy who felt fear as part of the ictal experience. In the great majority the lesion was in the anterior and middle temporal lobe. (From Williams 1956. Copyright © 1956 by Oxford University Press, Oxford. Reprinted by permission.)

bance of the outer and other surfaces of the lobe. In contrast, when depression was felt, lesions were diffusely distributed over the temporal lobe. Pleasure and displeasure were chiefly associated with posterior temporal lesions. When lesions or foci were above the Sylvian fissure, ictal emotions were unlikely to arise. The evidence from Williams's series of patients agrees with Macrae's account (1954) of seven cases of epileptic fear arising with organic lesions of the medial surface of the temporal lobe.

Williams's observations were largely borne out by Weil (1959). He found temporal lobe epilepsy in 132 out of 388 subjects with "symptomatic" epilepsy. Of these, 28 patients (7% of all cases and 21% of those with temporal lobe epilepsy) experienced ictal emotions; in half of these the emotion was fear, and in the other half, depression. Like Williams, Weil noted that ictal fear was associated with cortical temporal lobe pathology, whereas ictal depression was associated with diffuse temporal lobe lesions.

The emotional experience of epileptic fear may be distinguished from its somatic, visceral, and cognitive accompaniments, just as the various components of fear may appear separately experimentally and in therapy. The following case illustrates separation of emotional and cognitive elements.

Ictal Fear with Secondary Cognition (Williams, Case 1)

A woman 45 years old had had brief stereotyped attacks for 16 years without cause. She suddenly felt "terribly frightened" and "horrible all over." This fear was intense and unnatural, and with it she always had the thought, "Now I'll know what I am frightened about"—but never did. She felt stone cold, sweated profusely, and had visceral activity ("my inside feels like a washing machine"), and her body felt light. She went very pale. There was no loss of consciousness, and the whole attack, which began and ended abruptly, was over in a few seconds.

Fear during an ictal experience varies from slight unease to stark terror, and may be brief or more prolonged. The patient may say, "I feel afraid *as if* something may happen," rather than "I am afraid that (a definite event) will occur." What thought exists is secondary to the emotion.

Fear may occur anywhere in the march of an epileptic experience, early in the attack, in the middle, at the end, or alone. Ictal fear can be provoked by natural fear, as in the following case, where the attack began with vertigo and visceral changes (pallor and sighing) accompanying the emotion of fear.

"Unnatural" Ictal Fear Provoked by Natural Fear (Williams, Case 3)

A girl 11 years old had had frequent brief attacks for 5 years. They happened in the morning particularly and were induced by a sudden fright or surprise. She would stare and go pale, then for a few seconds would go quiet or say a few confused words. Then she would sigh deeply and say, "I was so frightened." She felt as if she were spinning around, then afraid, "as if someone is going to be knocked over, or as if someone has gone away." It felt unnatural, not caused by the attack; it "is something inside me"; "then I turn natural and am all right." There was a sharp spike focus in the left temporal lobe. She was physically, intellectually, and emotionally normal.

Commonly, epileptic fear is associated with other experiences during the attack related to the site of the disturbance and its march over the cortex. In

12 cases seen by Williams a visual or auditory hallucination was closely related to the fear. In other cases ictal fear was linked to a disturbed body concept or to other emotions. One case showed mixed ictal fear and ictal pleasure; the discharge arose in the anterior half of the temporal lobe.

All of Weil's and half of Williams's cases of ictal fear also had some accompanying visceral changes, such as holding of breath, nausea, retching, belching, flatus, epigastric sensations, palpitations, tachycardia, gooseskin, or sweating. Visceral changes immediately preceded or followed the affect as commonly as all other ictal disturbances together; each of these changes is an element of the normal emotional response syndrome of fear. Cortical mediation of autonomic and visceral activity appears to be through the inferior part of the frontal cortex, the insular cortex, and the adjacent limbic temporal cortex. Since the emotion of fear may be subserved in the anterior temporal cortex, Williams suggested that the cortices subserving fear-motor and fear-sensory events are contiguous. Although ictal fear does not usually involve all components of fear, sometimes they are integrated, and surgical removal of the abnormal focus can abolish the fear attacks.

Total Fear Response during Epilepsy (Williams, Case 19)

A 7-year-old epileptic boy experienced very frequent attacks of pure fear, many of which were witnessed in the hospital. When in bed he would often suddenly look frightened and rapidly burrow under the bedclothes, emerging in a few seconds, flushed and sweating, saying he had had a terrible fear. When up he might impulsively rush to the nearest nurse (or, failing a nurse, a male patient), clasp that person around the legs and bury his face in them, and cease in a moment, flushed, with the same explanation. He later became an aggressive delinquent. At age 14 he had an extensive right temporal lobotomy on the basis of electrocorticographic changes, with cessation of the fear attacks.

In some cases a moment-to-moment correlation can be demonstrated between the experience of emotion and temporal lobe abnormalities, as in the following example in which, as in the previous case, surgical removal of the lesion abolished both the seizures and the accompanying anxiety.

Ictal Fear During Abnormal Temporal Lobe Activity (Weil, Case B; Figure 9.2)

A housewife 29 years old had had seizures from age 17. At first these had lasted a few seconds and consisted of a few dyskinetic movements followed by brief confusion with automatisms. After age 22 her mood became labile and she had episodes of "strangeness and fear." An EEG administered when she was on anticonvulsant drugs was normal (Figure 9.2, left). After drugs were discontinued a second EEG after hyperventilation showed left temporal focal spikes and delta waves (Figure 9.2, right), during which she felt inexplicable "anxiety" and "terrible fear." Shortly afterward she had a left temporal lobe seizure with masticatory movements, contralateral head turning, and confusion.

A left carotid arteriogram revealed a large racemose angioma in the entire left temporal lobe and part of the left frontal lobe. After the angioma was removed by surgery, the temporal lobe seizures and anxiety episodes ceased.

In another study (Brodsky et al. 1983), 10 cases of episodic anxiety, often with impulsive behavior and refractory to anxiolytic drugs, showed, after 24-

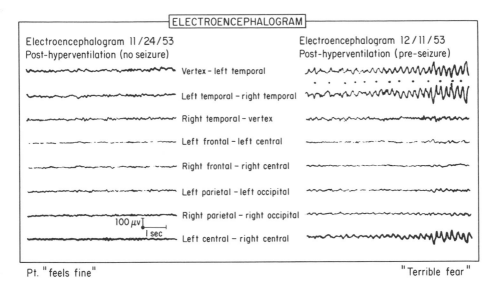

Fig. 9.2 Left-sided EEG after hyperventilation in a 29-year-old woman with an angioma of the left temporal lobe, temporal lobe seizures, and ictal fear. The left of the figure shows the normal EEG while the woman was on anticonvulsant drugs. On the right of the figure is the EEG after drugs were stopped, showing left temporal focal spikes and delta waves during which the patient said she felt "terrible fear" (From Weil 1959. Copyright © 1959 by Mrs. Berry Weil in the name of her late husband, Dr. Andre A. Weil. Reprinted by permission.)

hour sleep deprivation, a temporal focus of high-voltage, slow-frequency activity that was absent on routine EEG; these symptoms and EEG activity were relieved by anticonvulsant drugs.

Selective Postictal Phobias

Very rarely, a phobia may manifest in the postictal phase without being present in the interictal phase. W. A. Lishman has drawn attention to the following case. A 51-year-old telephonist had had temporal lobe epilepsy since age 29. At first she had had an uncinate olfactory aura. Of late she felt bilateral numbness of the face before a seizure. During attacks she had brief unconsciousness with incontinence. Seizures came in bouts of 5 to 6 daily at intervals of several months. Until age 43 mild depression would ensue postictally for 1 to 2 days. At that time a few hours after an attack, her husband made sexual demands of her, and she fled in terror from the bedroom. Thereafter each ictus was followed for 7 to 10 days by marked depression, retardation, and a severe phobia of men and of darkness. In the interictal phase there was no fear at all.

EEG showed spiking in the right anterior temporal region. Spikes continued in serial EEGs during the postictal mood change, accompanied by a rise in skin conductance fluctuations during the visualization of phobic but not of neutral fantasies that disappeared during the interictal phase (Figure 9.3). Physiological measures thus confirmed the patient's self-report that phobic anxiety was present postictally but absent interictally.

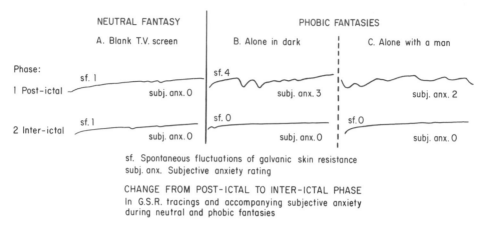

Fig. 9.3   Change from postictal to interictal phase in spontaneous fluctuations of the galvanic skin response and in subjective anxiety during phobic and neutral fantasies. (From Marks 1969. Copyright © 1969 by Heinemann Medical. Reprinted by permission.)

The patient had been afraid of the dark until age 16. Between ages 37 and 43 she had 4 bouts of depression and 3 suicidal attempts related to marital disharmony. Her depression cleared after she separated from her husband at age 43. It seems that psychologically significant events became linked to the neurological mechanism of her epilepsy and were reactivated as a phobia whenever seizures occurred.

In contrast to fear, *obsessive-compulsive phenomena* are rarely associated with epilepsy (reviewed by Hymas 1986 and Kettl & Marks 1986). Temporal lobe seizures have been compared with OCD as they may present with stereotyped repetitive behaviors, and the interictal characteristics include oc features (Bear & Fedio 1977). The occasional EEG and other abnormalities are discussed in Chapter 13.

Epileptic attacks of fear point to both temporal lobes, especially the anterior portions, as part of the neurophysiological substrate for the experience of fear. They highlight the various components of which fear is composed (experiential, cognitive, and autonomic), as these arise separately in some cases. Very rarely, a phobia may occur selectively postictally even though it is absent at other times. Obsessive-compulsive phenomena seldom occur with epilepsy. Given the frequency of anxiety and depression before and after fits and their common association with phobic and oc disorders, it is surprising that more cases have not been described of phobic and OCD together with temporal lobe epilepsy. Perhaps the epilepsy or antiepileptic drugs disrupt learning.

Space Phobia

The hallmark of this pseudo-agoraphobic syndrome is a fear of falling in the absence of visuospatial support (Marks & Bebbington 1976). The features of

13 space phobics were summarized by Marks (1981). Most were elderly women.

In space phobics the perception of open unsupported space leads to a fear of falling and inappropriate rescue reactions. The fear is triggered by visuospatial rather than kinaesthetic or height cues. This feature is a gross exaggeration of phenomena often found to a mild degree in agoraphobia. Sufferers may be unable even to cross a small room except by going on their hands and knees, unless they skirt the walls without having to actually touch them. At least in the early stages, actual physical support was unnecessary, only visual evidence that such support was a few inches nearby. As one patient said, "I need to be closed in while I'm walking. The fear is the space around me." One patient abolished the unsteadiness by closing her eyes. Patients commonly crawled on the floor to cross a room, or walked close to walls or hedges in streets. All but one were afraid of falling—the exception felt pulled to the driver's side while driving and had found herself on the wrong side of the road. One patient could hardly walk yet rode a bicycle normally, another could dance on a crowded dance floor but had to leave if the crowd left, another felt all right only if his eyes were absolutely still, and yet another who fell repeatedly did not learn to protect her face by stretching out her arms.

Disability from space phobia is often crippling. Both male patients in the series had lost their jobs; others gave up driving. Exacerbations often began after falls superimposed on earlier disability, when one patient's car overturned, and in three others during a time of family illness. The disorder progressed in several patients until they were confined to a wheelchair, even indoors.

Six features distinguished the space phobics from agoraphobics.

1. Space phobia started far later—the mean onset was 31 years later (55 years compared with 24 years), and none began before age 40.
2. When present, agoraphobic features usually began long before the space phobia did and were disproportionately much milder than the space phobia. Fears of public places, which are so salient in agoraphobia (for example, of public transportation, crowds, heights, or elevators) were noted in 5 of the 13 patients, but only 2 consistently avoided such situations.
3. Intense fears both of falling and of open space without visual support were the central feature of space phobia but are usually mild or absent in agoraphobia.
4. Unlike agoraphobics, space phobics rarely had accompanying depression, nonsituational anxiety or panic, or personality difficulties.
5. Unlike agoraphobics, space phobics frequently had diverse neurological and/or cardiovascular disorders that could have caused neurological problems. These progressed in some patients until they were confined to a wheelchair. The abundant organic signs seemed excessive even given the elderly age of these patients. Space phobia may indicate disturbed integration of vestibulo-ocular reflexes as a result of diverse lesions in the neck or more centrally.

6. Last, but not least, agoraphobics respond well to treatment by exposure in vivo, whereas space phobics respond poorly. Exposure was tried in nine space phobics, but their improvement was fragile, with liability to rapid relapse.

Neurological and/or cardiovascular symptoms or signs occurred in 10 of the 13 patients, although none complained of vertigo. Three had tinnitus, five had cervical spondylosis, and one had a history of neck injury. One case had X-ray signs of cervical spondylosis and also head titubation, central nystagmus to the left, caloric responses showing directional preponderance to the left, and diffuse nonfocal abnormality on the EEG (a neurologist thought the patient had a lesion at or above the vestibular nucleus). Another patient had mild spastic hemiparesis attributed to cervical spondylosis. Two cases had tinnitus alone, and another had hypertension. One patient had giddiness on looking right, a bruit over the right carotid, bilateral extensor plantar reflexes and increased knee jerks, X-ray signs of cervical spondylosis, and a right canal paresis; a neurologist thought she had vertebrobasilar artery insufficiency. One case had tinnitus, cervical spondylosis, and autonomic, extrapyramidal, and cerebellar deficits; the patient died of the Shy-Drager syndrome. Another had a history of neck injury, ataxia, sensory neuropathy of the legs, CT-scan signs of cerebral atrophy, and an EEG suggesting diffuse brain dysfunction. One patient had atrial fibrillation and blockage of both femoral arteries. Another had left-right nystagmus, cervical spondylosis with osteoarthritis, kyphoscoliosis, spina bifida occulta, signs of ischaemia of cochlear and vestibular neurones, dilation of the lateral ventricles, and minimal cerebral atrophy on the CT scan.

Five of the 13 cases began or greatly worsened after a fall. Space phobia might be related to a condition often seen after falls in old age (Isaacs 1978), after which elderly people become frightened of further falls, clutch at any object without regard to its value as a source of support, and often walk on their heels rather than their forefeet. Occasional patients fail to make corrective movements of their upper limbs when falling and go on rapidly to become immobile, as happened with one of the space phobics. Why is extreme anxiety on walking after a fall so common in old age but not in younger age groups? Young children fall regularly without becoming anxious. Contributory factors to anxiety in the elderly may be poorer agility and greater risk of fractures, loss of righting reflexes as a result of neuronal fallout, and focal neurological damage. Anxiety then becomes realistic.

Should space phobia instead be called falling phobia? The term "falling phobia" would not include the two cases from the series whose main fear was of space and depth cues while driving. All who are afraid of falling are not space phobic, and not all phobics fear falling. In some cases, space phobia is a transient phase in a developing disorder of balance that progresses to the point where the patient finds it almost impossible to stand unaided even in the presence of visuospatial cues.

Although space phobia is clearly separate from agoraphobia, it may involve some overlapping physiological mechanisms. With agoraphobia, fear of open space is an inconstant minor feature, and falls are very rare; but fear of public places is a central feature, and dizziness (but not vertigo) is common. Agoraphobia was long ago called "platzschwindel" and attributed to labryinthine disorder (Benedikt 1870), and other patients have been described with anxiety and vestibular type symptoms (Pratt & McKenzie 1958). The author has seen a woman of 60 with agoraphobia plus a tendency to veer to the right while walking out of doors, but without any space phobia. Investigation of the pathogenesis of space phobia might indicate mechanisms by which many anxiety symptoms are expressed—for instance, dizziness, fears of falling, and the normal fears generated by specific visuospatial and kinaesthetic cues such as fears of a visual cliff, looking up at a skyscraper, or the total absence of spatial cues (see Chapter 2).

SUMMARY

Phobic and oc symptoms can involve almost any situation, coexist with most psychiatric symptoms, and be found in minor form in most people. When phobic and oc symptoms dominate the clinical picture and are a handicap then they amount to a phobic or oc disorder. Such symptoms tend to fall into six overlapping clusters (syndromes), four phobic and two oc (see below). Each syndrome has distinctive correlates, forming different disorders that are heuristically useful for phenomenology (which situations evoke the phobic and oc symptoms, associated symptoms, onset age, sex incidence), etiology, treatment, and prognosis.

Although at least 4 other dimensions could form a basis for classification, they would be less useful guides to such aspects. These are whether sufferers regularly avoid situations that evoke phobic or oc symptoms (which makes them suitable for exposure therapy), whether the problem is multiple or focal (the former take longer to treat by exposure and more often need antidepressants as well), whether spontaneous panics are present, and whether the subjective experience when confronted with the evoking stimulus is fear, discomfort, or nausea.

Phobic and oc disorders together constitute the syndromes of anxious avoidance that respond well to exposure therapy. The four main phobic syndromes are agora-, social, specific, and illness phobias. All avoid external cues that trigger anxiety. In clinical practice the most common and distressing phobic syndrome is agoraphobia, a cluster of fears of going into various public places, especially if alone, plus multiple other symptoms of anxiety-depression; the protean forms of agoraphobia have earned it many different names. Social phobics are particularly sensitive to scrutiny, usually show gaze aversion, and have less anxiety-depression than agoraphobics. Specific phobics generally have isolated fears with few other problems. Illness phobics have had little systematic study.

Overlapping with, yet different from, phobias is OCD. Compulsive rituals with obsessive thoughts are the commonest form. Various types of rituals often occur together, including cleaning, avoiding, repeating, checking, orderliness, and hoarding. Obsessions are intrusive repetitive thoughts, generally stereo-typed and unpleasant. Slowness is usually the result of overt or covert rituals. Behavioral treatment is most successful for rituals, and least reliable for obsessions or slowness without visible rituals.

Most forms of phobic and oc disorder are more common in women than in men, except that social phobics are as frequently men as women, and men preponderate with checking and slowness without visible rituals. Onset age for most forms is between ages 18 to 45, except that animal and blood-injury phobias start before age 8, shyness may be lifelong, and some compulsive rituals start in childhood.

The prevalence of syndromes of anxious avoidance is far higher than used to be thought. Community prevalence in recent studies was 1.2 to 3.8% for agoraphobia, 1.7% for social phobia, 7.0% for specific phobias, and 0.1 to 2.5% for OCD. Phobic and oc symptoms are much more common than the corresponding disorders. Female preponderance is least with social phobias and OCD. The syndromes overlap with one another and with depression.

Nonphobic anxiety and panic, worry, and depression are common among agoraphobics and ocs, and to a lesser degree in social phobics. These 4 symptoms are obviously related to one another and to phobic and oc syndromes in ways that are not yet understood. Agoraphobics are most liable to spontaneous panics. In hospital samples, phobias are very common among alcoholics, but alcoholism is less frequent among phobics or ocs. Though one drink may reduce fear in the short term, continued drinking may increase it. Fear can occur as part of a temporal lobe seizure, especially that emanating from the anterior portion, yet phobic and oc syndromes are seldom associated with epilepsy.

Space phobia is a pseudoagoraphobic fear of falling when perceiving space without nearby support. Sufferers need visual boundaries rather than physical support to walk or drive across open spaces. Most are women. Unlike agoraphobia, space phobia starts after age 40 and rarely has accompanying depression or nonphobic anxiety or panic, but is associated with diverse signs of neurological and/or cardiovascular disorder. Space phobics seem to have disturbed visuospatial reflexes. Their problem may progress to crippling disability, and, again unlike agoraphobia, it does not respond lastingly to exposure treatment.

10

The Agoraphobic Syndrome
(Panic Disorder with Agoraphobia)

The agoraphobic syndrome (panic disorder with agoraphobia) is the most common and most distressing phobic disorder seen in adult patients. It was named by Westphal (1871) to describe the "impossibility of walking through certain streets or squares, or possibility of so doing only with resultant dread of anxiety." Today it still denotes fears of public areas such as streets, shops, or vehicles.

Around this common theme the clinical picture varies widely. At one extreme, some travel phobias or claustrophobias can be isolated fears; in such cases the label of agoraphobia is overinclusive and actually misleading if taken in the strictly literal sense. At the other extreme, severe cases often have not only agoraphobia and other phobias but also spontaneous panics, depression, depersonalization, obsessive-compulsive, and other symptoms; for these patients the term agoraphobia is underinclusive and indicates only part of their entire clinical picture. As we would expect, this syndrome of protean symptoms has had many labels (see Chapter 9). Fresh interest in the phenomenology has led to a surge of recent studies and reviews of agoraphobia (Foa et al. 1985; Franklin 1985; Hallam 1985; Hugdahl & Ost 1984; Persson & Nordlund 1985; Roth 1984; Tearnan et al. 1984; Williams 1984).

WHY IS THE CONDITION CALLED AGORAPHOBIA?

A frequent misconception is that agoraphobia is a fear of open spaces. In fact, the Greek *agora* refers not to open spaces but to public places of assembly, as befits the frequency of fears of streets and crowded places found in this condition. The exact cluster of phobias varies slightly from one patient to the next; "agoraphobia" is a fuzzy set whose most usual and constricting elements are fears of public places of various kinds. The similarities are more impressive than the differences. The characteristic features of agoraphobia is *not* fear of cats, thunder, sex, or cancer but rather fear of public places, which is pathognomonic and predictive of other typical features (See Chapter 9 and Table 9.4). Simply knowing that someone fears going into the street and crowded places predicts that person's liability to show many other aspects of the syndrome such as other typical external fears, including those of enclosed places; internal fears (for instance, that of fear itself and its somatic aspects—fear of palpitations, dizziness, or harmful fates such as being ill, fainting, dying, losing control, or going mad) (Chambless et al. 1984; Foa et al. 1985); and spontaneous panics and depressive spells. Although frequent in agoraphobics, rather similar internal fears also occur in other phobics (Hugdahl & Ost 1984) and so are not central to agoraphobia. It is the agoraphobic avoidance that leads to crippling housebondage; fear of fear or of going mad is very unpleasant but causes less handicap to daily life.

Conditions other than agoraphobia may lead a sufferer to become housebound. Obsessive-compulsives stay home to avoid "contamination," dog phobics to avoid dogs, social phobics or paranoid schizophrenics to avoid people. These problems are distinct from agoraphobia not because of their internal fears but because of other typical phenomena. The diagnosis of obsessive-compulsive disorder (OCD) requires the presence of repetitive thoughts or rituals as well as a fear of being contaminated; that of dog phobia requires fear when near dogs; of social phobia, unease when in particular social situations; and of paranoid schizophrenia, the presence of paranoid delusions and ideas of reference as well as other schizophrenic features. To diagnose agoraphobia, some fear of and tendency to avoid public places is a *sine qua non;* the fear of fear or of harmful consequences to oneself are frequent concomitants but not essential features. A woman who avoids public places because they frighten her is agoraphobic even if she is not afraid of fear itself or of going mad. Similarly, someone who fears panic but goes out freely into public places is not agoraphobic but rather has an anxiety state (panic disorder without agoraphobia).

The label of agoraphobia does not merely denote a fear of leaving home, just as "depressive disorder" does not simply mean depressed mood. Indeed, a person may have that disorder without ever admitting to depression, but if he or she expresses suicidal ideas, self-blame, or forebodings of disaster, has lost his or her appetite, and cannot sleep, then most clinicians would regard that cluster of features as a depressive disorder. The term "depressive disorder" is helpful because depressive mood is the commonest aspect of the syndrome, even though on occasion depressive mood is overshadowed by other features. Similarly, with the agoraphobic syndrome the most constant feature is a coherent cluster of phobias centering on public places; these phobias run a fluctuating course together through episodic exacerbations and partial remissions. The core symptoms appear so constantly together as to require unitary consideration. Atypical cases could of course be classified differently.

There are alternative terms with the same literal sense as agoraphobia—kenophobia, *platzangst* in German, and *peur des espaces* or *horreur du vide* in French (Weiss 1964). Agoraphobia, however, is now the accepted label for fear of public places. Some writers correctly point out that agoraphobia describes such fears inadequately; Prince (1912) and Klein (1964) regard the crux of this condition as the fear of suddenly being rendered helpless during panics, whereas Weiss (1964) singles out the sense of internal danger, "an unbearable feeling of illbeing to which they react with severe anxiety." Such features are indeed found in many agoraphobics, being commonly linked to the core cluster of characteristic phobias.

Labels for any protean syndrome are bound to be underinclusive, and agoraphobia seems the least unsatisfactory of those proposed so far. Phobic anxiety state, panphobic syndrome, or phobic-anxiety-depersonalization fail to draw attention to the most frequent phobias found in the syndrome. The *DSM-III* term "panic disorder with agoraphobia" (Spitzer & Williams 1985) is also unsatisfactory (see Chapter 9). *Any* phobic, whether frightened of heights, cats, cancer, or social scrutiny, panics either on contact with the phobic situation (phobic or situational panic) or on thinking about it (anticipatory panic—a subset of phobic panic). Moreover, spontaneous (nonphobic, nonsituational) panic is absent in up to two-thirds of agoraphobics (Angst & Dobler-Mikola 1983; Weissman et al. 1985) yet is present in many people who have no agoraphobia, including other phobic, depressed, or panic-disordered patients (Fawcett & Kravitz 1983; Roth & Argyle 1985; and Chapter 9). In contrast, all agoraphobics have agoraphobia. Mild agoraphobics may have fears too mild to be called panic, but the fears must be of public places to earn the label.

Autobiographical Accounts

Autobiographies vividly illustrate the features giving rise to the various labels for the enduring distress of agoraphobia. (Although the condition is more common among women, early autobiographies are from men, just like the cases of Westphal in 1871 and most referred cases in India today [Raguram & Bide 1985]; referral patterns change as services become available). An early account comes from an American whose agoraphobia began when he married at age 22 (Clevenger 1890).

> The first noticeable symptoms . . . were extreme nervous irritability, sleeplessness and loss of appetite. Any little excitement would throw me into a state of almost frenzy . . . Palpitation, spasmodic breathing, dilation of the eyes and nostrils, convulsive movements of the muscles, difficulty in articulation, etc., were the more prominent features. A sense of impending danger seemed to descend, spoiling every pleasure, thwarting every ambition. The dread of sudden death which was at first marked, gradually subsided, giving way more to a feeling of dread—not of dying suddenly—but of doing so under peculiar circumstances or away from home. I became morbidly sensitive about being brought into close contact with any large number of people. Finding myself in the midst of a large gathering would inspire a feeling of terror (which) . . . could be relieved in but one way—by getting away from the spot as soon as possible. Acting on this impulse I have left churches, theatres, even funerals, simply because of an utter inability to control myself to stay. For 10 years I have not been to church, to the theatre, to political gatherings or any form of popular meeting, except where I could remain in the background, with means of egress convenient. Even at my mother's funeral . . . I was utterly unable to bring myself to sit with the other members of the family in the front of the Church. Not only has this unfortunate trait deprived me of an immense amount of pleasure and

benefit, but it has also been a matter of considerable expense. More than once I have got off a crowded train halfway to the station for which I was bound, merely from my inability to stand the jostling and confusion incident to the occasion. Times more than I can recall I have gone into restaurants or dining rooms, ordered a meal and left it untouched, impelled by my desire to escape the crowd . . . (or) have bought tickets to theatres, concerts, fairs or whatnot, merely to give them away when the critical moment arrived and I realised the impossibility of my facing the throng with composure. To illustrate: I remember once going from Chicago to Omaha with my little boy. On entering the sleeper I found it crowded. I at once became ill-at-ease. As the train moved on I became more and more desperate, and finally . . . procure(d) a section by myself . . . (in) a stateroom . . ., paying $10 extra for it. Had it been $100 and I had the money, I should have bought it without once counting the cost.

[A fear of open spaces] has been at times very pronounced. Many a time I have slunk in alleys instead of keeping on the broad streets, and often have walked long distances—perhaps a mile—to avoid crossing some pasture or open square, even when it was a matter of moment to me to save all the time possible. The dominating impulse is to always have something within reach to steady myself by in case of giddiness. This feeling is at times so strong that even when on a steamboat or a vessel, I cannot bear to look across any wide expanse of water, feeling almost impelled to jump in out of sheer desperation. . . . This malady . . . has throttled all ambition, and killed all personal pride, spoiled every pleasure . . . over this the will seems to have no control. At times buoyed up by stimulants or temporary excitement, I have faced situations which would ordinarily have filled me with extreme trepidation; but as a rule I have to yield or suffer the consequences. What those consequences would be, I do not know.

Other autobiographies depicted anxiety that gradually became attached to agoraphobic situations (Vincent 1919, pp. 295–299), spasmodic increase in agoraphobia starting at age 30 after several years of intermittent anxiety unrelated to any particular situation, and fear of fear and of doing something silly (Leonard 1928, pp. 238, 278, 302, 309) (for both, see Marks 1969).

In these accounts there was no hint of precipitants at onset, but once developed, the agoraphobia was intensified by traumatic events—with Vincent after a boy was murdered in his village, with Leonard after his wife's suicide. The first anxiety occurred out of the blue, after which the original situations in which they occurred became increasingly capable of kindling the same anxiety. The constant background anxiety was present even at rest, and secondary aggravating situations were gradually avoided to stave off sudden surges of this anxiety. The difficulties in these well-developed cases were thus of two kinds— background general anxiety not related to any special situation, and the particular phobic situations that exacerbated it. Escape from the fear-evoking situation bred further escape—a crucial point for exposure therapy, which emphasizes the importance of remaining in that situation until the anxiety subsides somewhat (see Chapter 14).

Most agoraphobias fluctuate considerably, often for no obvious reason. Vincent described common ploys to alleviate his phobias—darkness, storms, landscapes with a limited view, riding a bicycle, gripping a suitcase.

At times my phobias are much more pronounced. . . . Sometimes, after a strenuous day, on the following morning I find myself almost dreading to walk across a room;

at other times I can cross the street without any pronounced discomfort. . . . Usually I feel better in the evening than in the morning, partly because the darkness
seems to have a quieting effect on me. I love a snowstorm, a regular blizzard, and
feel much less discomfort going about the town or riding on the train on such days,
probably because one's view is obstructed. In fact, I welcome stormy days . . . on
such days I make it a point to be out and about the town. I dread going on water
in a boat, especially if the surface is smooth; I much prefer to have the waves rolling
high. The most restful place in all the world for me is in a wood, where there is
much variety with here and there little hills and valleys, and especially along a
winding brook. . . . I love quiet, restful landscapes . . . let the landscape be bold and
rugged and bleak, and it strikes terror [into me]. . . . I ride a bicycle along the streets
with comparative comfort where I should suffer agony [if] I had to walk. In walking
I feel least uncomfortable in passing along the street if I carry a suitcase or travelling
bag—something to grip. . . . I have such a dread of crossing a long bridge on foot.
(Vincent 1919, pp. 295–299)

Much of the suffering in this condition is hidden, since agoraphobics can
conceal their disorder for long periods if they manage to work. Leonard's
account was published when he had been agoraphobic for 48 years. Only his
closest relatives and friends knew of his problem, and he continued as a professor of English at the University of Wisconsin during this time, living very
near the campus. Vincent never sought medical aid for his agoraphobia and
led an active public life while concealing his fears.

Sigmund Freud occasionally mentioned his agoraphobia. From age 31 to
43 he was anxious about traveling by train but did not avoid it, and would
hesitate while crossing a wide street (Clark 1980; Jones 1953). In the last 20
years innumerable other self-descriptions have appeared. They show good
agreement about the features of agoraphobia, as do observation from clinicians, to which we now pass.

DEMOGRAPHIC ASPECTS

Gender

In nearly all European or American series of agoraphobics, at least two-thirds
are women, whether in clinical samples (Hafner & Marks 1976; Hand et al.
1974; Marks 1969), in the community (Angst & Dobler-Mikola 1983; Weissman 1985), or in mixed samples (Marks & Herst 1970; Thorpe & Burns 1983).
In India, 79% of agoraphobics attending a psychiatric clinic were men, but this
may well reflect referral patterns, since many of the patients were university
educated (their illiterate counterparts tend to consult native healers first).
Moreover, in India a fear of public places is more culturally accepted among
women, fewer of whom are major wage earners, so the agoraphobia causes less
financial hardship to the family (Chambers et al. 1982).

The marked female preponderance in agoraphobia is noteworthy, as it is
less obvious in three overlapping conditions: (1) anxiety states (panic disorder
without agoraphobia) (Angst & Dobler-Mikola 1983; Hare 1965; Weissman
1985), which have similar spontaneous panics but no avoidance; (2) social

phobia (Amies et al. 1983; Marks 1969; Stravynski et al. 1983), even though social anxieties are common in agoraphobia; and (3) OCD (see Chapter 13), in which phobic avoidance can be prominent.

Age of Onset, of Handicap and at Treatment

Agoraphobia usually begins in young adults 18 to 35 years old reviewed by Marks 1969; Thorpe & Burns 1983). Mean onset age was 28 in two large series, each of nearly 1,000 agoraphobics (Marks & Herst 1970; Thorpe & Burns 1983). In the latter series the problem began before age 16 in 9% and after age 40 in 13%. If agoraphobia starts in middle age or later, then one should exclude depression or space phobia—see Chapter 9.

Handicap began on average 15 months after onset of the agoraphobia in members of a correspondence club called the Open Door (Marks & Herst 1970). Once the phobias started, 80% were never again completely free of them. The mean time elapsing before agoraphobics sought help was 17 months from a general practitioner (GP), 34 months from a psychiatrist, and 57 months from a "spiritual healer" (in most Western countries medical, psychological, and other health care providers are probably consulted before spiritual ones; the reverse is true in pre-industrial societies). On average a GP had last been visited 18 months earlier and a psychiatrist 32 months earlier; 41% had seen the GP for "nerves" in the previous year. For their phobias, only 5% had never seen a doctor; 95% had seen a GP and 67% a psychiatrist; 17% had been a psychiatric inpatient; and 15% had seen a religious or spiritual healer. In psychiatric series the mean age at treatment is usually in the 30s, and a mean symptom duration of 8 to 12 years is common (Hafner & Marks 1976; Marks et al. 1983; Sheehan et al. 1980).

Agoraphobia began earlier in cases with past separation anxiety as children (Breier & Charney 1985), and treatment was sought 6 to 12 years earlier in those with a history of school phobia (Berg et al. 1974), fears of the dark or leaving parents, or night terrors (Klein 1964; Marks 1969). Two compatible explanations are that such childhood anxieties sensitize someone to later agoraphobia, or that both problems reflect a generally fearful predisposition.

Marital Status, Religion, Education, Class, and Work Status

At the time they come for treatment most agoraphobics are married, as we would expect in young to middle-aged adults. Their spouses are of average age (Marks 1969; Thorpe & Burns 1983) and not especially neurotic. British agoraphobics resembled the general population in intelligence, religious affiliation, and social class (Marks & Herst 1970; Thorpe & Burns 1983). However, the prevalence of agoraphobia in United States communities was higher among people who were low in socioeconomic status, or separated or divorced (Boyd 1985).

Although agoraphobics are average with respect to occupational status and income, the disorder may prevent sufferers from working or handicap their work. Fewer female agoraphobics from The Open Door correspondence club were at work (23%) than were women in the general population of comparable age and marital status (38%) (Marks & Herst 1970). Of Open Door subjects with a job, most felt that their fears interfered with it. Similarly, in the sample of Thorpe and Burns (1983), 76% thought their agoraphobia hindered their work appreciably, while 48% said they would change their jobs but for their phobias, often feeling trapped and unable to apply for new jobs.

Although some Open Door agoraphobics may have gone to work to avoid being alone, the usual factors associated with a job also operated. Compared to nonworking agoraphobics, those at work had more fears of being alone, a later onset age of fears, a more independent and outgoing past personality, and were currently younger and more educated, had fewer young children, and resided in larger towns.

Only 17% of Open Door women who had no outside job were content to remain as housewives; the rest said they would take outside work were it not for the agoraphobia (this percentage was even higher among unemployed men). Desire to work seemed due to both the added frustration that phobic restrictions caused in a lively personality, and increased severity of illness; compared to contented housewives, those wanting outside work had more severe and disabling phobias, fears of being alone, depression, exhaustion, irritability, and physical illness; had had more sociable and independent personalities in the past; and currently were younger and had a lower family income, but formerly had been of higher occupational status.

PRECIPITATING FACTORS, MODE OF ONSET, AND COURSE

Factors Precipitating Onset

Traumatic events at the onset are rare and were reported by only 3% to 8% of agoraphobics (Franklin 1985; Goldstein & Chambless 1978). Figures for the frequency of more general precipitating factors range widely from 10% (Friedman 1950) to 83% (Roth 1959), presumably reflecting disparate interpretations of which events are relevant. In a small series precipitants were no more frequent among women with agoraphobia than those with anxiety states (Buglass et al. 1977). By contrast, other agoraphobics reported twice the number of adverse life events in the year prior to onset than did controls over the same period, especially events concerning personal illness, injury, or operation; breakup of a relationship; and financial problems (Franklin 1985). Similar increase in adverse life events precedes the onset of many other conditions, including depression, schizophrenia, and myocardial infarction.

Studies of the frequency of direct and indirect (vicarious) conditioning of human phobias have not always separated events that clearly preceded the onset from those which were already the first signs of the disorder itself (see Chapter 9). Panic, for example, is often cited as a precipitant of phobias (Munjack 1984) but in fact is an early sign of phobia. The same applies to an analysis of nearly 1,000 agoraphobics by Thorpe and Burns (1983); 70% noted at least one triggering event and 26% noted two. Such events included trauma to self (32%) or witnessed in others (6%) and death or illness of a relative or friend (27%). However, many "precipitants" may merely have been the first sign of agoraphobic anxiety—citations of direct trauma included "I felt faint and nearly collapsed while queueing in the supermarket" and of indirect trauma included such minor events as "the lady in front of me in the supermarket collapsed" and "when downtown I saw a friend have a bad epileptic fit." The presence and nature of a precipitant does not seem to affect the subsequent course of agoraphobia.

Agoraphobics often regard trivial events at the time of their first anxiety as the trigger to their disorder, even though identical ones may have occurred previously without mishap. If they start taking an antidepressant drug they may blame it for agoraphobic symptoms that may have been present for many years previously. In Chapter 8 we saw that panic of any kind may condition someone to certain concurrent external stimuli (taste aversions may start by attributing nausea and vomiting to the most novel recently ingested substance, and superstitious oc behavior may reflect similar conditioning), and that such associations are hard to overcome even if the sufferer knows them to be irrational. Some events merely draw attention to the problem after it has begun, just as a newly-discovered breast cancer may be attributed to a trivial recent bump. But other events may act as nonspecific stressors in people already liable to the disorder. In controlled studies of panic disorder, including agoraphobia, life events (but not those involving loss or death) had increased shortly before onset; perception of the events might have been critical (Roy-Byrne et al 1985).

An intriguing finding is an Australian report that agoraphobia began much more often in summer (57%) and hot weather (59%) than in winter (11%) or cold weather (0%) (Franklin 1985). This accords with 35% of the British Open Door sample noting that hot weather aggravated agoraphobia once it had begun. This link with hot seasons and ambient temperature might result from partial overlap of the physiological sensations of heat and of anxiety, to which agoraphobics seem peculiarly sensitive, and from the greater light usually prevailing in hot weather. However, the prevalence of agoraphobia is not obviously greater in hot than in cold countries, although careful cross-country comparisons are not yet available.

Factors Precipitating Request for Treatment

Help is more likely to be sought not only as the agoraphobia or nonphobic aspects become increasingly severe but also as the ability of the sufferers to confide problems in others increases, and as caring practices in the community improve. Untreated were compared with treated agoraphobics in 1,200 members of The Open Door, most of whom rated their agoraphobia as "a nuisance, but I can cope" (Marks & Herst 1970). Agoraphobics who had never had any treatment at all were especially socially timid and could not confide easily in intimates and other people. Surprisingly, their phobias and other problems were as severe as in members who had seen GPs. Psychiatric treatment was associated with more severe and incapacitating phobias and nonphobic symptoms. Those who had been psychiatric inpatients had the most (and more severe) phobias and other neurotic symptoms such as tension, depression, obsessions, and exhaustion. Their fears hampered them more in their daily activities; they needed more help, and most could not get it when necessary. Despite the greater social timidity and anxiety of those who had been inpatients as compared to outpatients, they could nevertheless confide in other people.

Mode of Onset and Course

The onset can be sudden within a few hours, more gradual over a few weeks, or develop slowly over several years after a prodromal stage of vague intermittent anxiety. Cases of sudden onset may start with acute, sustained panic that is followed by phobias causing disability, relentlessly increasing to housebondage within a few weeks; others begin with vague intermittent anxiety that merges into fluctuating agoraphobia over many years. The period elapsing between the first symptoms and maximum disability varies correspondingly, as does the duration of symptoms before treatment is sought. Many patients may be uneasy about going out alone for decades, yet manage to conceal or cope with their fears until the anxiety increases further or new situations arise that make them or their family unable to cope any longer, thus leading to referral for treatment. The types of course possible between the two extremes are legion, and their import for treatment or outcome is not known.

Two case histories of agoraphobia starting in teenagers will show the extremes possible in mode of onset and, incidentally, of premorbid personality. Both cases had their problem before live exposure therapy became available.

Sudden Onset of Agoraphobia in a Sociable Person

A girl of 19 suddenly went home from her work as a shop assistant and screamed that she was going to die. She spent the next two weeks in bed and thereafter refused to walk beyond her front gate. She failed to improve after four months as an inpatient and after discharge left her home only twice in the next seven years. She spent her time gossiping with neighbors, listening to the radio, and with a boyfriend who fathered her child when she was 27, though she continued to live with her mother. At ages 20, 25, and 31 she was readmitted to the hospital for depression and worsening of her phobias and anxiety. From age 32 until last seen at 36 she made a gradual, partial recovery and became able to go on short bus rides and shopping.

As a child she had had a good relationship with her parents, although her mother had been hospitalized for depression. One sister was agoraphobic. The patient had encopresis and enuresis until age 12; before her phobias began she was sociable, had many friends, and often went dancing. Until age 32 she was anorgasmic but thereafter achieved normal sexual satisfaction with her boyfriend.

Slow Onset of Agoraphobia in a Dependent Personality

A girl of 17 gradually developed fears of leaving home; these eased at 20 when she attended a psychiatric clinic but became more marked after her son was born at 26, when she became afraid of meeting people and getting lost in a crowd. For the next two years she was limited to traveling by bike or car to her mother's home a mile away; thereafter she could not go beyond her own home and stopped shopping. She improved again after psychiatric admission at 29, became pregnant after discharge, and made further small gains after her second child was born. For the next six years until last seen, she was able to do only local shopping, fetch her child from school, go out with her husband.

She was dominated all her life by her mother, had enuresis and fears of the dark until 9, and was always a shy and dependent person. The marriage was unremarkable except for her sexual frigidity.

The overall pattern of fears at the onset tends to persist as the disorder progresses, though severity may alter. Patients asking for help noted that their profile of fears had remained very similar since they began 7 years earlier, except that fears of public places, such as buses, trains, crowded shops and places far from home, had worsened (Franklin 1985 and Table 10.1).

Table 10.1 Ranking of 20 worst fears of 76 agoraphobics "if entirely alone in these situations" a) at time of onset and b) currently

At time of onset		At time of presenting for treatment	
Rank	Fear	Rank	Fear
1	Feelings of panic	1	Feelings of panic
2	Fainting or collapsing	2	Traveling by bus or train
3	Losing control	2	Going far from home
4	Causing a scene or public disturbance	4	Fainting or collapsing
5	Going mad	5	Losing control
6	Traveling by bus or train	6	Causing a scene or public disturbance
7	Dying	7	Going into crowded shops
8	Going far from home	8	Dying
9	Having a heart attack	9	Walking in busy streets
10	Walking in busy streets	10	Going mad
11	Being left alone	11	Having a heart attack
12	Going into crowded shops	12	Being left alone
13	Standing in line	13	Standing in line
14	Large open spaces	14	Large open spaces
15	Feeling anxious, nervous, or agitated	15	Waiting at traffic lights
16	Palpitations	16	Feeling anxious, nervous, or agitated
17	Confusion; being unable to think clearly	17	Palpitations
18	Feeling that self and surroundings were strange or unreal	18	Weakness in legs
19	Trembling, shaking	19	Crossing bridges
20	Weakness in the legs	20	Confused, unable to think clearly

Source: Franklin 1985.

Transient partial forms of agoraphobia may come and go without the subject's ever receiving treatment, but once the problem has continued for a year it tends to go on, and such cases frequent psychiatric clinics. The course is typically punctuated by remissions and relapses of varying duration. In the earlier stages a brief episode may clear up completely after a few days or weeks, but in chronic cases seen in psychiatric clinics, partial rather than total remissions seem to be the usual outcome in the absence of treatment (Buglass et al. 1977) until later life is reached. In the Open Door sample (Marks & Herst 1970), only 20% reported periods of complete remission after their phobias began. Complete recovery was described in autobiographical accounts of phobic states (Landis 1964). The course after treatment is noted in Chapter 15.

CLINICAL PICTURE

The typical symptoms of agoraphobia have not changed in autobiographical and clinical accounts of the condition since Westphal's description a century ago. Clinical features can be conveniently divided into phobic aspects evoked by particular situations, and nonphobic (nonsituational) aspects.

Phobic Features (Situational Fear/Panic and Avoidance)

The main fears are of leaving home and going into streets, crowds, enclosed public places such as shops, theatres, cinemas, restaurants, church, elevators, or tunnels; travel by underground or surface trains, buses, ships, and planes (less often cars, except on freeways); standing in lines, going on bridges, or sitting in the chair at the dentist or hairdresser. These fears occur in variable combinations over the years and are associated with nonphobic, neurotic symptoms (see Chapter 9 and below). Social fears are also common in agoraphobia—fears of talking, trembling, blushing, eating, or writing in front of other people, or of being stared at.

The central cluster of phobias in agoraphobia is impressively similar in most cases despite the variation from one case to another, a point already noted by Prince in 1912. In Tables 9.3 through 9.5 in Chapter 9 and above, we saw abundant evidence for the unity of the syndrome from autobiographies, clinicians' accounts, and questionnaire, prognostic, and physiological studies. The most prominent features in 900 agoraphobic women from The Open Door (Marks & Herst 1970) appear in Table 10.2, and the fears of 477 other agoraphobics (from Doctor 1982) are seen in Table 10.3.

Typically, agoraphobia starts with discrete episodes of anxiety outside the home that might be mild at first and slowly intensify over successive episodes, or amount to severe panic from the start. The sufferer suddenly feels anxious, ill or weak; has palpitations, lightness, and dizziness in the head (as opposed to true vertigo); feels a lump in the throat and weakness in the legs; and has an

Table 10.2   Main phobias and other problems of 900 agoraphobic women from The Open Door

Phobias	Percent scoring 3 or 4	Mean for all patients	Other problems	Percent scoring 3 or 4	Mean for all patients
Speaking to audiences	60	2.4	Exhaustion	42	2.2
Underground trains	50	2.2	Tension	38	2.2
Trains	47	2.1	Obsessive thoughts	37	1.9
Crowds	28	2.0	Loneliness	32	1.7
Buses	38	1.9	Depression	29	1.7
Heights	36	1.9	Fears of fainting	31	1.5
Theaters	39	1.8	Giddiness	26	1.5
Hairdressers	31	1.8	Panic	24	1.5
Street, open spaces	23	1.8	Irritability	19	1.5
Tunnels	36	1.7	Headaches	22	1.4
Elevators	30	1.7	Depersonalization	22	1.3
Dentist	28	1.6	Fears of dying	22	1.3
Parties	21	1.5	Overchecking, tidiness	22	1.3
			Palpitations	20	1.2
			Suicidal ideas	15	0.8
			Fears of disease	9	0.7

Anchoring points on rating scale for:		
Score	Fears	Other problems
0	Almost no fear at all	Very little
1	Makes me uneasy but I don't avoid it	Occasionally
2	Makes me particularly uneasy—I avoid it when possible	Often
3	Frightens me even to think of it—I always avoid it	Very often
4	Terrifies me so much that every moment of my life is miserable	Nearly all the time

Source: Marks & Herst 1970.

Note: For fears of open spaces and streets, percentage breakdown for each score was 0–12%; 1–32%; 2–33%; 3–14%; 4–9%.

illusion of walking on shifting ground. Sufferers feel unable to breathe, or breathe too rapidly or deeply; they fear they may faint, die, scream out loud, "lose control," or "go mad." Very intense panic may root the sufferer to the same spot for some minutes until it lessens, after which she or he may run to a haven of safety—a friend or the home.

The Lancet (1952) provides the following self-description of an agoraphobic panic:

At the height of a panic I just wanted to run—anywhere. I usually made towards reliable friends ... from wherever I happened to be. I felt, however, that I must resist this running away, so I did not allow myself to reach safety unless I was in extremity. One of my devices to keep a hold on myself at this time was to avoid using my last chance, for I did not dare to think what would happen if it failed me. So I would merely go nearer my bolt-hole and imagine the friendly welcome I

Table 10.3   Degree to which 477 agoraphobics feared 14 situations

Situations	Panic-provoking (%)	No problem (%)
Driving on freeways	43	29
Airplanes	39	18
Closed-in places	25	17
Heights	23	18
Audiences	22	20
Department stores	20	27
Crowds	18	15
Bridges	15	39
Supermarket lines	11	35
Parties	11	35
Being alone	11	51
Elevators	10	37
Restaurants	10	36
Unfamiliar places	8	21

Source: Doctor 1982

should get. This would often quieten the panic enough for me to start out again, or at least not to be a nuisance or use up any good will. Sometimes I was beaten and had to feel the acute shame and despair of asking for company. I felt the shame even when I hadn't to confess to my need.

The episode usually lasts for a few minutes but in rare cases may continue for several hours. Once it is over the sufferer may avoid returning to the scene of the original panic for some time. The attack can pass, leaving the subject feeling as fit as before, and many months may go by before it recurs. Normal activities may continue until, after a succession of such episodes over years, the agoraphobic begins to restrict her or his movements. Panic may lead to medical consultation for symptoms suggesting cardiovascular or vestibular disorder, but physical examination shows no abnormality beyond the signs of anxiety. The problem is indistinguishable from an anxiety state (panic disorder) except that agoraphobic panic occurs mainly in public places (rather than, say, at home or in the presence of cats or thunderstorms) and leads to avoidance of those situations. Why the panic is particularly associated with those situations is a mystery. The physiological and cognitive symptoms during agoraphobic panic are very similar to those reported by other phobics in the presence of their phobic stimuli (social, dental, claustro-, and animal phobics) (Hugdahl & Ost 1984).

Another mystery is why some sufferers go on to develop a crippling avoidance, whereas others endure their anxiety-panic repeatedly without ever avoiding concomitant cues. Perhaps the former have more intense and frequent panic. In contrast, some agoraphobics develop avoidance without major spontaneous or even phobic panic.

Agoraphobic avoidance begins especially after an intermittent anxiety or panic in public situations. The sufferer starts to avoid places where panic was first experienced and then gradually avoids new situations for fear that those too might precipitate further panic. Once she cannot get off an express train, as soon as anxiety starts she will restrict herself to local trains; when these, too, become the setting for anxiety she retreats to buses, then to walking, then to going only a few yards from home, until finally she becomes unable to proceed beyond the front gate without a companion. In rare instances the sufferer becomes bedridden for a while if bed is the only place where she finds the panic bearable. Some may panic even in bed and may thereafter avoid sleeping in bed. Agoraphobics with marked avoidance are usually tense all the time wherever they may be, and acute panics punctuate this backdrop.

Agoraphobics tend to be panphobic. Fear of enclosed places is usual (Johnston et al. 1984); it was present in nearly two-thirds of agoraphobic women, starting before the agoraphobia in just under half of these (M. Dwarka, personal communication 1980). Agoraphobics also score higher than specific phobics or normals on almost every item of fear questionnaires, including blood-injury and social situations (Belfer & Glass 1982; Buglass et al. 1977; Martin et al. 1969; Solyom et al. 1974). Two-thirds have social fears, such as fear of looking silly or causing a scene during their panic, and speaking to audiences was the most common fear in Open Door agoraphobics (Table 10.2).

Short-Term Fluctuations with External and Internal Events

Agoraphobia fluctuates rapidly with minor changes in the subject's external and internal environment, fluctuating from day to day in 90% of the nearly 1,000 agoraphobics of Thorpe and Burns (1983). Already Westphal (1871) had noted that the

> agony was much increased at those hours when the particular streets dreaded were deserted and shops closed. The subjects experienced great comfort from the companionship of men or even an inanimate object, such as a vehicle or a cane. The use of beer or wine [helped]. . . . One man even sought, without immoral motives, the companionship of a prostitute as far as his own door. . . . [S]ome localities are more difficult of access than others, the patient walking far in order not to traverse them. . . . [I]n one instance, the open country was less feared than sparsely housed streets in town. One case also had a dislike for crossing a certain bridge. He feared he would fall into the water. In this case, there also was apprehension of impending insanity.

Westphal's observations in three men apply equally to cases of both sexes seen in this century.

Anxiety peaked in midafternoon in panic disorder with or without agoraphobia (Cameron et al. 1985); this could reflect circadian and/or environmental factors. The anxiety of agoraphobics usually worsens if they are alone, far from home, in strange surroundings, and anticipating having to stay long in the feared situation (Sinnott et al. 1981). Most feel easier near a trusted person, pet, or object and become dependent on them and afraid of being left alone. In more severe cases, requests for constant company places a strain on relatives and friends. Rarely, subjects find it easier to travel alone. Of nearly 1,000 Open

Door agoraphobics, 65% felt better accompanied and only 5% felt easier going out alone. Distraction, too, can help.

Agoraphobics are more frightened where they cannot reach "safety" or a trusted person with speed and dignity. They try to achieve a balance between not feeling trapped or embarrassed and having help available. In a cinema, theater, church, or restaurant they feel easier near an aisle or exit so they can make a quick dash away if seized by sudden panic. A ground-floor apartment near the main entrance to a building is preferred to one many floors up to which access is more difficult. A telephone nearby may reassure. Some cannot tolerate confinement in a hairdresser's or dentist's chair, hence the label "barber's chair syndrome" (Erwin 1963); experimental neurosis is produced in animals by restraining them either mechanically or by previous training to be quiet (Cook 1939). Again because it is hard to exit immediately, some cases will not bathe in the nude—this fear is separate from the obsessive sexual thoughts such situations may cue.

Trains are less frightening if they often stop at stations and have a corridor and toilet. Journeys are easier that pass the home of a potentially helpful friend, doctor, or police station; knowing the friend or doctor is at home makes the journey less difficult—the *possibility* of aid is the important point. One woman would go on a particular bus route because it passed a police station outside which she would sit if she became too tense. Even when agoraphobics cannot stay on a bus or train for one stop, they may still be able to travel by car and may comfortably drive alone many miles.

Other useful ruses include the grip of walking sticks, umbrellas, suitcases, shopping carts, baby carriages, newspapers folded under the arm, or a bicycle to push rather than to ride to work, and strong sucking candies in the mouth. One man removed his belt whenever he felt anxious, and a woman had the urge to rid herself of all clothing when she panicked and could wear only garments that could be closed in front by zippers—she carried a pair of scissors and a bottle of beer in her purse when she left home (Weiss 1964). An army officer felt anxious crossing a square in civilian clothes but not when he wore his uniform with his sabre at his side (Legrand du Saulle 1895). A man afraid of crowds would sometimes face them clutching a bottle of ammonia in his hands in case he felt faint (Errera & Coleman 1963).

Aggravation of agoraphobia by strong light is intriguing, given the links between melatonin and the noradrenergic system (see Chapter 7). The association of agoraphobia with hot weather (and thus usually more light) was noted earlier. Agoraphobics often feel easier in the dark, going out more freely at night than in the daytime; even wearing dark glasses helps—just over a third of the Thorpe and Burns agoraphobics wore sunglasses outdoors for this reason. Among Open Door agoraphobics the phobias were said to be better in the dark in 34% and worse by day in 23%. Of another 175 agoraphobic women in the United Kingdom, 74% said they were sensitive to sunlight, and many were troubled by fluorescent light in shops (M. Dwarka, personal communication, 1980). During the stress of mental arithmetic or the cold pressor test, agoraphobics became more tense and emotional in fluorescent than in incandescent light, whereas lighting did not affect controls having the same tests (Hobbs et al. 1984). Some agoraphobics say their fears abate during rain or storms (26% of the Open Door sample), when it is darker.

A preference for less light explains some topographic features that intensify agoraphobia. Usually the fear is greater the wider and higher the space, and less if the vista is interrupted by trees, rain, or irregularities in the landscape. A clergyman felt dizzy as soon as he went into the open but obtained relief by creeping around hedges and trees, or, as a last resort, by putting up his umbrella (Westphal 1871). In contrast, another person felt anxious during a party on a private lawn and wanted to break down the surrounding fence (Weiss 1964). Ugly architecture worsened agoraphobia in one case (Vincent 1919).

Claire Weekes, an Australian doctor, conjured up many of these features in the archetypal figure of "Aggie Phobie": a woman walking at night up a dark alley in the rain while wearing dark glasses, sucking candies vigorously in her mouth, with one hand holding a dog on a leash, with the other trundling a shopping cart.

When standing in the street or on a train platform, agoraphobics may feel drawn to jump beneath an approaching bus or train and so have to look away from the ongoing vehicle. This fear is related to the impulse normal people often feel to jump when looking down from a great height. Fear of heights is found in some agoraphobics and is countered by withdrawal from the edge of such heights or by avoiding them completely. Bridges evoke similar fear, especially long, narrow bridges with open sides high above a river. If there is a waist-high parapet between the subject and the edge of the cliff or bridge, the fear is diminished.

The anticipation of pleasure can be better than its fulfillment, and the converse applies in agoraphobia. For weeks before a planned journey an agoraphobic dies a thousand deaths from anticipatory anxiety; if the same journey is sudden and unexpected, however, she or he can do what was impossible if forewarned. Sufferers can board a bus if they do not have to wait for it at the stop, but should there by any delay, panic rapidly builds up and may prevent them from boarding the vehicle when it finally arrives.

Agoraphobia that has been stable for some time can be exacerbated suddenly by as many factors as those which might have precipitated the original episode. Remissions, too, may coincide with similar sudden life events. The second case cited earlier (on p. 322) felt worse after the birth of her first child and better after her second child was born.

Any stressful situation might intensify agoraphobia. Depression often aggravates agoraphobia to the point of major disability; after the depression clears, the handicap reverts to its previous lower level. Sometimes agoraphobia starts for the first time during severe depression and remains as residual fears when the depression lifts. Fatigue and physical illness intensify agoraphobia. So does confinement of the patient to bed, as she or he ceases to practice going out, thereby making it harder to resume former activities when once again ambulant.

Alcohol and anxiolytic drugs palliate agoraphobia for the few hours that the substance is in the blood stream (see chapters 9 and 16). With their help many phobics (not only agoraphobics) can temporarily break new ground, but with some exceptions this effect does not usually last after the dose wears off. Certain agoraphobics carry a stock of tablets that they take shortly before a journey or some other anticipated stress, or merely keep a bottle of tablets in their pocket as a talisman, never actually ingesting them. A small minority of agoraphobics become addicted to anxiolytics or alcohol, but most cases can stop taking these substances once the anxiety subsides (see Chapter 9).

Any event that heightens motivation allows agoraphobics to extend their activities for a while. A patient of mine became able to go out again for a while after expressing intense rage on identifying me with her dominating husband; at other times, however, she quivered with resentment against another patient in the ward but could not express it—on such occasions she was less venturesome (Shapiro et al 1963).

Nonphobic Features of Agoraphobia

An important aspect of agoraphobia is its frequent complication by other symptoms such as general anxiety, spontaneous surges of panic, depression, obsessive-compulsive features, depersonalization, and sexual disorders. Agoraphobics score higher than nonphobics on most subscales of the MMPI (Solyom et al. 1974).

General Anxiety and Spontaneous Panic

General (freefloating, tonic, background, nonsituational) anxiety is common in agoraphobics wherever they are, forming a pervasive backdrop of tension that might be constant or fluctuate considerably for no obvious reason. Such tension was the second most common nonphobic symptom in the Open Door sample (Table 10.2). Lasting general anxiety merges into the more acute, abrupt phasic disturbance of spontaneous panics.

Spontaneous panics ranked only eighth in order of frequency of nonphobic problems among Open Door agoraphobics (Table 10.3), and in other series 33% to 70% did not complain of much general anxiety or spontaneous panics (Angst & Dobler-Mikola 1983; Harper & Roth 1962; Weissman et al. 1985). Spontaneous panics correlate highly with general anxiety and depressed mood (Chambless 1985; Marks et al. 1983) but can start quite out of the blue. They tend to diminish over the years (Breier & Charney 1985).

Spontaneous panics may strike at any time of day or night, but stressful tasks may trigger panics in those prone to them. They may be few and far between or repeated in an intense staccato over a variable time. Some begin abruptly and reach a peak within a few seconds. They commonly last a few seconds or minutes and (rarely) may go on for an hour or more. Panics can be very distressing and leave the sufferer apprehensive, weak, or washed out for hours after they have subsided. When panics are pronounced, patients may urge their doctors for relief by drugs or any other means available; some are admitted as emergencies and investigated for cardiovascular, epileptic, or other disorder. Many feel impelled to rush out of the place where panic occurs to gain quick relief, after which fear of that situation rapidly worsens. A vital aspect of exposure treatment is that the patient stands her or his ground and remains in the situation until the panic subsides, which may take half an hour or longer; patients thus learn that there is no need to run away in order to feel better—the panic will die down anyway if they simply remain long enough where they are.

For many cases the first panic in a public place prompts avoidance of that place, which may spread to situations where they have never panicked. Avoidance may start after mild unease not amounting to panic. Agoraphobics may deny having had any initiating panic (S. Brandon, personal communication, 1985) or any spontaneous panics at all, as we saw above, and agoraphobia is as likely to remit before as after cessation of panics (A. Rifkin, personal communication, 1985). Spontaneous panics are thus an important but by no means the only factor causing agoraphobic avoidance.

The symptoms and worst fears (cognitions) experienced by 100 agoraphobics during panic are seen in Table 10.4. Other features of panic may be tingling sensations, waves of warmth, and hyperventilation, as well as fears of catastrophe such as death, heart attack, stroke, fainting or collapse, urination or defecation, insanity, screaming, creating a scene in public, or appearing ridiculous to others. Unlike obsessive-compulsives, agoraphobics do not seem to worry about harm befalling other people (Foa et al. 1985). The fears of catastrophe concern the agoraphobics themselves and have also been called fear of fear or the "cognitions" of agoraphobia. Except that no external stimulus is apparent, such cognitions and also the autonomic feelings resemble those occurring during the phobic panic that surges in any phobics (not only agoraphobics) confronted with their phobic situation (Hugdahl & Ost 1984). More detailed research is needed to tell if there are fine differences.

The features of spontaneous panics are also like the diffuse autonomic reaction experienced by normal people during an acute, unexpected fright ("I thought I would die of fright" is a common phrase). Two agoraphobics who were also phobic of animals indicated to this author that their agoraphobic panic felt internal in origin even when precipitated by being in public, whereas their panic with animals felt more external. Some have in fact labeled agoraphobia an "endogenous anxiety" (Sheehan et al. 1980). (An animal conditioning model for this was suggested in Chapter 8.)

The role of internal (interoceptive) stimuli is problematic. Some writers trace the panic to unconscious feelings of diverse kinds. The exercise is as much a projection test of the observer as of the sufferer, and it is hard to judge when interoceptive cues are indeed precipitants or merely post-hoc rationalizations.

Agoraphobics seem to be oversensitive to internal bodily sensations such as those evoked by feared public situations, hot weather, strenuous exercise, hunger, or disturbing thoughts. Compared with specific phobics and with normals, agoraphobics score higher for awareness of their bodies and autonomic sensations and for belief in the catastrophic consequences of anxiety (Belfer & Glass 1982); anxiety-sensitivity is higher in agoraphobia than in other anxiety

Table 10.4   Agoraphobics' panic symptoms, fears, and main restrictions

A. During a panic attack ($n = 100$)				
Symptoms	Percentage	Worst fears	First (%)	Second (%)
Nervous and tense	93	Death	13	20
Dizzy or faint	83	Fainting/collapsing	38	16
Agitated	80	Heart attack	4	4
Palpitations	74	Becoming mentally ill	6	1
Weak legs	73	Causing a scene	6	7
Trembling/shaking	72	Inability to get home/	6	26
Feeling totally unable to cope	66	to place of safety		
Stomach churning	65	Losing control	7	9
Sweating/perspiring	65	(becoming hysterical)		
Shortness of breath	59	Other personal illness	10	7
Confused	58			
Things not quite real	57			
Loss of control	52			
Tightness/pressure in head	43			
Difficulty with eyes (blurred vision, etc.)	36			
Feeling of becoming paralyzed	19			

B. Main effect of agoraphobia on subjects' lives			
Men ($n = 112$)	Percentage	Women ($n = 818$)	Percentage
Unable to work	42	Social restrictions	29
Lack of social contacts	29	Personal psychological effect	23
Personal psychological effect	11	Marital disharmony	14
Marital disharmony	9	Unable to work	14
Travel restrictions	4	Travel restrictions	11
Guilt *re* children	2	Guilt *re* children	6

Source: Adapted from Thorpe & Burns 1983.

disorders (Reiss et al. 1985). Agoraphobics may simply be sensitized from the experience of more intense fear than most other people have, rather than having a qualitative difference in their type of fear. It is worth trying to demonstrate that for a given increase in heart rate or sweating, say, agoraphobics react with more subjective anxiety than do others. Perhaps their reactions to lactate, isoproterenol, caffeine, and hyperventilation, all of which produce autonomic effects and anxiety in agoraphobics more than in controls, indicate such a propensity.

General anxiety and panics in agoraphobia are like those in anxiety states (panic disorder without agoraphobia). In agoraphobia they occur together with the typical fears of going out, traveling, or remaining alone, and the major handicap is not spontaneous panic but avoidance of such activities. Someone who suffers only from spontaneous panics but does not avoid public places can lead a normal life between episodes, but if those spontaneous panics lead to agoraphobic avoidance, then the handicap becomes obvious and the sufferer needs exposure therapy. Anxiety states and agoraphobia merge in some cases so that both labels would apply; at the extremes of divergence, however, only one or the other label would be appropriate. At present, exposure can be recommended with confidence only for agoraphobia with regular avoidance, and it still needs to be tried systematically for anxiety states (see Chapter 9).

Depersonalization

This is dealt with in some detail, as certain writers have stressed its relationship to agoraphobia. During depersonalization one feels temporarily strange, unreal, disembodied, cut off or far away from immediate surroundings, and one's voice sounds strange and distant; during derealization similar changes seem to occur in the environment, as if the world is behind a veil and the surroundings are vague. Both phenomena are equivalent, and "depersonalization" here will cover both. Like panic, it is a temporary phasic event that lasts a few seconds or minutes and rarely lasts several hours or even longer. Onset and termination are generally abrupt. In mild cases the symptoms may not be easy to distinguish from anxiety feelings such as floating, dizziness, or "cotton wool" in the head.

Depersonalization may arise from changes in normal sensory experience due to hyperventilation, fever, drugs, emotional shock, extreme fatigue, or sensory isolation (Hallam 1985). It may occur in up to 50% of normal men and women (Nemiah 1975) and need not be accompanied by any other psychiatric complaints (Davison 1964). Normal students' descriptions of their own depersonalization "differed in no obvious way from those encountered clinically and were every bit as striking" (Meyers & Grant 1972).

The detached quality of depersonalization is shared with normal peak (oceanic, transcendental) experiences, but the latter are regarded as pleasant and desirable, unlike depersonalization. Also resembling depersonalization is the detached aspect of "break-off," which occurs in up to 35% of jet pilots when flying solo at high altitude with little to do and which can be abolished by re-engaging in flying maneuvers (Sours 1965). During break-off the pilots have vivid fantasies that are mostly pleasurable, but those reporting break-off described it as highly unpleasant with anxiety, loneliness, and giddiness; these symptoms were more evident in "unstable" individuals.

Like depression, depersonalization is found with or without anxiety or agoraphobia. It correlates with neuroticism (Hallam 1985) and with anxiety and panic in psychiatric inpatients and accident victims (Noyes et al. 1977). Anxiety in public places was found in 33% of female but only 6% of male students with depersonalization (Meyers & Grant 1972). Depersonalization was present in 56% of the agoraphobics of Harper and Roth (1962) but in only 22% of those of Marks and Herst (1970). In other agoraphobics (Buglass et al. 1977) 37% had current depersonalization as compared with only 13% of normal controls, in whom it was less severe; it seemed "unwarranted to elevate depersonalization to the status of a cardinal symptom of the agoraphobic syndrome." In the phobic-anxiety-depersonalization syndrome, 80% of cases had phobias—they closely resembled agoraphobics with prominent depersonalization (Roth 1959), and their features were thought to indicate temporal lobe dysfunction. This conclusion is premature: although depersonalization can occur in temporal lobe disturbances, many agoraphobics do not experience it.

Extreme anxiety may trigger depersonalization. An agoraphobic woman had repeated arguments with her boyfriend during which he threatened to leave her; each time, these precipitated acute anxiety followed by severe depersonalization. Another case felt severe anxiety for some minutes while skin conductance was being recorded and then suddenly complained of feeling strange and unreal; at that point skin conductance activity diminished (Lader 1966). Perhaps depersonalization can be a cut-off mechanism triggered by anxiety reaching a given level. At other times detachment precedes anxiety, as in three pilots in whom anxiety and phobia of flying appeared after the break-off phenomenon (Sours 1965, cited by Hallam).

Depression

Agoraphobics often have repeated depressive episodes (see Chapter 9), the first episode usually being before or within a few weeks or months of the first panics (Uhde et al. 1985). Patients feel blue, hopeless, or irritable; cry; are more anxious and panicky; lack interest in their work; sleep badly; and have raised scores on depression questionnaires (Marks 1983). Severe retardation, nihilism, bizarre delusions, and serious suicidal ideas seldom feature. During periods of depression agoraphobia tends to worsen—increased panics may sensitize patients to formerly comfortable situations, and lack of interest may lower motivation to cope with tasks hitherto managed with difficulty. As depression clears, so might the agoraphobia. Such concurrent agoraphobia is merely a "masked" or "latent" depression; however, it is better formulated as agoraphobia aggravated during a depressive episode. Agoraphobia and depression interact but are separate disorders that run largely distinct courses.

Obsessive-Compulsive (OC) Phenomena

Many oc phenomena involve fears that are disproportionate to their apparent stimulus and could thus strictly be called phobias, but usually more subjective resistance is felt. Obsessive-compulsive features are minor in most agoraphobics and fluctuate largely independently of the phobias. The most common are minor checking compulsions and rituals, or thoughts of harming others with knives, by strangling, or by other means. Agoraphobics may fear that they will strangle their infants and so avoid being alone with them. Others have obsessions about exposing their bodies in public, or soliciting men; Deutsch (1929) regarded these as important causes of agoraphobia, but such obsessions are in fact usually absent. Earlier we saw that some agoraphobics have obsessionlike fears of jumping from heights or in front of an oncoming train or bus, or feeling drawn down against their will; such fears are more closely stimulus bound than most obsessions.

Respiratory Changes

Normal people breathe faster on becoming anxious. Hyperventilation itself produces faintness, dizziness, anxiety, tingling, tachycardia, and finger vasoconstriction, and these changes are greater in those with higher neuroticism (Clark & Hemsley 1982; Thyer et al. 1984). The symptoms of hyperventilation are similar to those of panic and in some agoraphobics seem to precede anxiety (Ley 1985). Severely anxious agoraphobics also complain that "I can't take deep enough breaths" or "I can't catch my breath." Sighing was common in neurocirculatory asthenia (Cohen & White 1950). In keeping with their high general anxiety, agoraphobics have increased breathing, sighing, and yawning as well as skin conductance activity and heart rate (Franklin 1985). Elective hyperventilation led to more distress than in controls—80% reported it as similar to panic, and in a minority it evoked frequent respiration that was hard to control. Others also reported that agoraphobics became anxious on hyperventilation (Bonn et al. 1984; Clark et al. 1985; Ehlers & Margraf 1985). Adding 5% CO_2 to the air being hyperventilated raised the proportion of agoraphobics who panicked (Gorman et al. 1984). We will see later that many other procedures also induce anxiety in agoraphobics.

An unknown proportion of agoraphobics may get into a vicious circle by overbreathing when they become anxious, thus aggravating their anxiety—they breathe themselves into a lather, so to speak. This can be controlled by breathing exercises (Franklin 1985). However, most descriptions of the hyperventilation syndrome do not mention agoraphobia as a feature (Lum 1981; Magarian 1982), and there has been no careful assay of the proportions of agoraphobics who hyperventilate before, during, or after their fear.

Willpower and Impact of the Disorder

Role of Willpower

In the early stages of agoraphobia, sufferers often try to master their fears by briefly venturing into their dreaded situations, but then retreat, after which the next foray in that direction becomes more difficult. Escape breeds subsequent avoidance unless prevented by remaining for the half-hour or so that elapses before the panic dissipates. Learning to stay put is a key exercise in exposure treatment.

The limits of tolerance fluctuate with many circumstances. In emergencies (a house on fire or an accident), sufferers will temporarily overcome their phobias and venture forth. Once the emergency subsides the phobia reappears in pristine form. A Viennese Jewess could walk only a few blocks from her home in Vienna. When the Nazis came to power her choice was flight or a concentration camp; she fled, and for the next two years traveled halfway around the world until arriving in the United States. On settling in New York she developed the same travel phobia that she had had in Vienna (Laughlin, 1956). Why she had not habituated is unclear.

The fluctuating nature of agoraphobia makes it difficult for family and friends to accept that the disorder is not the result of mere laziness, lack of willpower, or a way of getting out of awkward situations—"if she can master her phobias in an emergency, then surely she just needs to be forced to go out?" But it is very hard for agoraphobics to muster their energies in such a way that every minor shopping trip is treated like a house on fire. Not only agoraphobics but everybody performs unexpected feats in an acute crisis, but it would be unrealistic to demand such feats of everybody as a routine; for a very anxious agoraphobic, a small sally outside the house requires great effort, trivial though this is for a normal person. Encouragement and forbearance are needed to complete an exposure program of treatment.

When there is repeated spontaneous panic or marked depression, agoraphobics find it particularly difficult to exercise their willpower, as a 31-year-old woman said (Lancet 1952, p. 74):

> I could barely get myself to the office or stay in it until it was time to go. I was always exhausted, always cold; my hands were clammy with sweat; I cried weakly and easily. I was afraid to go to sleep; but I did sleep, to wake with a constricting headache, dizziness and tachycardia. To these now familiar symptoms were added waves of panic fear followed by depression. The panics almost overwhelmed me. I felt very much more frightened when I was alone and but little less frightened with other people. There were only three with whom I felt at all safe and able to relax, though even with them I was behind the screen of my fear.

Once agoraphobics have few spontaneous panics and are comfortable away from their phobic situations, it becomes easier to go out repeatedly to try and conquer their fears. Sometimes they discover by accident that they can in fact go out again. One woman had a lobotomy for severe agoraphobia; she felt more relaxed thereafter but remained housebound for a year, until one afternoon a friend who had just visited left a handkerchief behind; the patient rushed into the street to return the handkerchief and to her surprise felt quite relaxed in a place she had previously dreaded. She proceeded systematically to do more and more, and remained relatively well when last seen four years later.

The same sequence is described by a professional writer. After decades of unsuccessful treatment she tried systematic exposure and found that it worked. Her first panics began at age 25 and increased until she was housebound by day through "fears which continually kept me in a state of anxiety so severe as often to practically paralyse me for hours as I lay wracked and tortured on my couch. . . . [T]he core of [my phobias] was an abject fear of light . . . so overpowering that I darted out into the daylight only to be driven back as if by an unseen force into the darkened room where I could find the comparative peace and feeling of safety, although even there I had to fight off periods of intense fear" (Mrs. F. H. 1952, p. 162). Over the next 22 years her treatment included Christian Science, a stay in two sanatoria and two psychiatric clinics, 6 months of psychoanalysis with Sandor Ferenczi, and visits to another five psychiatrists. At age 47 she slowly began to widen her activities: "I had reached farther and farther in my wanderings. . . . I decided to get on a bus. . . . I boarded the dread thing. . . . I realised I had to go over and over the same trail again in order to do a good job" (p. 163). She managed to take up her life again without crippling fears and commented: "Shrouded in mystery [is] why . . . I was able to look at all my fears unaided and at the particular time I did" (p. 176).

Indirect evidence that improving generalized anxiety makes exposure easier comes from events after severe agoraphobics had a modified lobotomy (Marks et al. 1966). The operation was followed by an immediate sustained drop in general anxiety; phobias improved more gradually. There was greater improvement in subjects with sociable and outgoing personalities rather than shy, solitary personalities; this suggests that the greater efforts of the former contributed to their more rapid rehabilitation. Similarly, in mixed phobics improvement after desensitization was less in patients with traits of depression, hopelessness, and self-consciousness, apparently because they did not fully utilize opportunities for rehabilitation (Gelder et al. 1967). The same applies to agoraphobics, whose improvement from self-exposure generalized less when mood and motivation had been low before treatment (Lelliott et al. 1986a). Such findings are not surprising, given the persistent effort needed to complete exposure therapy.

The effort is best described by the same woman who portrayed her acute state years before (Lancet 1982, pp. 81–83):

> For three years I had been unable to make a train journey alone. I now felt it was essential to my self-esteem to do so successfully. I arranged the journey carefully from one place of safety to another, had all my terrors beforehand, and traveled as if under light anaesthesia. . . . I realised I could do what I had been unable to do. Soon after this I had to learn to drive. I passed the driving test without difficulty. . . . Waiting in traffic blocks brought at first a return of panics—and there was no running away.
>
> The essentials are my few safety depots—people or places. The safety radius from them grows longer and longer. I am still claustrophobic; that rules out underground trains for me, and I use the District Railway. I find it difficult to meet relations and childhood friends, and to visit places where I lived or worked when I was very ill. But I have learnt to make short visits to give me a sense of achievement and to follow them when I am ready for it by a longer visit. Both people and places are shrinking to their normal size. Depression usually returns about a week before menstruation, and I have learned to remind myself that life will look different when my period begins. . . . I am also learning that it is permissible to admit to anxiety about things I have always sternly told myself are trifles to be ignored. Many of them, I find, are common fears.
>
> If I am fearful of going anywhere strange to meet my friends I invite them home instead, or meet them at a familiar restaurant. . . . Strangers, too, can be more helpful than they know, and I have used them deliberately: a cheerful bus conductor, a kindly shop assistant, can help me to calm a mounting panic and bring the world into focus again. If I have something difficult to do—to make a journey alone, to sit trapped under the drier in a hairdresser's, or to make a public speech—I know I shall be depressed and acutely afraid beforehand. I avoid trying myself too high meanwhile. When the time comes I fortify myself by recalling my past victories, remind myself that I can only die once and that it probably won't be so bad as this. The actual experience now is not much worse than severe stage fright, and if someone sees me to the wings I totter on. Surprisingly, no-one seems to notice.
>
> I dare not accept my sickness—fear—because it never stays arrested. My very safety devices become distorted and grow into symptoms themselves. I must therefore, as I go along, break down the aids I build up; otherwise the habits of response to fear, or avoidance of occasions of fear, can be as inhibiting as the fear itself.

The value of motivation in the treatment of agoraphobia needs no further comment.

Impact on the Patient and Family

Mild cases such as Freud (who feared train travel) might experience only fleeting anxiety that causes barely a ripple in the life pattern and is not noticed by others. In severe cases the agoraphobic becomes housebound for decades and places a considerable burden on other family members. The involvement of family members grows as the sufferer's activities become curtailed. She may require an escort to and from work, or give up her work; her spouse has to do the shopping and ferry children to and from school out of necessity rather than choice; social activities are curtailed or abandoned. She might insist on a constant companion because she feels unable to remain alone at home without anxiety, and her spouse may lose time from work (Buglass et al. 1977) or his actual job. Family holidays are forgone. Driving a car may hide the problem for a long time, as even severe agoraphobics can feel safe in a car despite distress with other modes of travel. If the sufferer's work can be done at home and there is help at home, again the agoraphobia can be concealed for years.

The main effects of agoraphobia on the lives of subjects reported by Thorpe and Burns (1983) appear in Table 10.4. Disturbed work was at the top of the list for men, and social restriction was named by 29% of both sexes. Travel restrictions were noted by comparatively few, suggesting that subjects were less handicapped than agoraphobics who seek treatment at hospital.

How the sufferer and her family respond to the problem depends largely on their personality and circumstances. In a well-adjusted and affluent patient and family, restrictions may be coped with by providing increasing help with a minimum of friction, and the agoraphobic will accept limitations only after battling unsuccessfully to extend the range of her activities. Where she has few personality or economic resources and comes from a family with preexisting friction, the agoraphobia becomes a new source of argument and is used by each party in their own interests, as any symptom would be; the patient may confine herself more than the anxiety warrants (see Chapter 15).

CHILDHOOD BACKGROUND, SEX, AND MARRIAGE

Parental Family

Most uncontrolled work finds that agoraphobics come from stable homes (Marks & Gelder 1965; Roth 1959; Terhune 1949; Thorpe & Burns 1983), with two exceptions (Snaith 1968; Webster 1953). In a well-controlled study the family backgrounds of agoraphobic housewives from psychiatric outpatient clinics were largely like those of matched normal controls (Buglass et al. 1977). The agoraphobics had similar family size, birth order, and parental age, as well as deprivation and psychological disorder; they did, however, have more non-biological relatives at home and more brothers with psychological disorder (chiefly nonphobic). Others, too, have noted that the birth order of agoraphobics is unremarkable (Marks & Gelder 1965; Terhune 1949). There is, however, much evidence of increased anxiety and depression, and perhaps alcoholism in the relatives of agoraphobics (see Chapter 6).

Do agoraphobics come from overprotective parents? On the basis of uncontrolled impression early writers thought that agoraphobics' mothers had been overprotective (Terhune 1949; Tucker 1956; Webster 1953). This was not confirmed in five later studies that compared agoraphobics with other neurotics or normal controls. Three of the studies were in the United Kingdom. English agoraphobics recalled no more overprotection by their parents than did other phobics (Snaith 1968). Other English agoraphobics did not rate their parents as having been more overprotective than controls, and indeed scored mothers as having been *less* caring (Parker 1979, 1983). Compared with normal controls' descriptions of their mothers, Scottish agoraphobics and controls recalled similar past and current type and frequency of contact with and affection and liking for their mothers, but more past and current ambivalence toward them (Buglass et al. 1977). These Scottish agoraphobics had not been more dependent on mother premorbidly, although currently they did feel more dependent on her and resented this. Their current dependency probably resulted from rather than caused their agoraphobia.

Dutch agoraphobics reported their parents as similar to those of social and height phobics (Arrindell et al. 1983). Finally, compared with normal nonphobic controls. Canadian agoraphobics did not rate their mothers as overprotective, although they rated higher than all controls together (Solyom et al. 1974, 1976). The balance of evidence thus strongly suggests that agoraphobics' parents had not been overprotective before onset of the syndrome.

Early Years and Personality

The idea that agoraphobia is rooted in separation anxiety in childhood (Chambless & Goldstein 1981; Liebowitz & Klein 1979) is not borne out by most research. Anxious children do not complain of panics (Hershberg et al. 1982). No more childhood separation anxiety was reported in agoraphobia or panic disorder than in generalized anxiety disorder (Raskin et al. 1982), simple phobia (Thyer et al. 1985), or normal controls (Buglass et al. 1977), although one study found more school phobia among agoraphobic than simple phobic women (Gittelman & Stein 1985).

Except for the last-named study, school phobia seems more related to adult neurosis in general rather than to agoraphobia in particular—it is as common in other anxiety disorders as it is in agoraphobia (22%) and is more frequent in both groups than among nonpsychiatric controls (Berg et al. 1974; Tyrer & Tyrer 1974). Nor does early separation (as opposed to separation anxiety) relate specifically to later anxiety. Separations resulting from parental or childhood illness, parental marital discord, and wartime evacuation all related more to adult depression than anxiety (Tennant et al. 1982). But a history of childhood fears of any kind does predict earlier onset of agoraphobia and seeking help for it.

Childhood fears were reported more often among agoraphobics (60%) than among temporal lobe epileptics (Harper & Roth 1962). Such early fears were common in a survey of nearly 1,000 agoraphobics (Thorpe & Burns 1983)— fears of school (32%), the dark (46%), being easily hurt (70%), and other situations (47%); however, the proportion noting childhood nightmares, bedwetting, nailbiting, thumbsucking, and stammering was similar to that in normal children (Lapouse & Monk 1959). There are no reports of excessive aggressiveness or truancy during the childhood of agoraphobics.

Premorbid personality has been described as "soft," passive, anxious, shy, and dependent (Roberts 1964; Roth 1958; Terhune 1949; Tucker 1956). These descriptions, however, were based on uncontrolled work. Compared with normal controls, 30 agoraphobic women reported no excessive dependence on their mothers prior to onset of the agoraphobia (Buglass et al. 1977), and premorbid relationships had been similar. The same agoraphobic women had lowered self-esteem, which was related not to their premorbid functioning but to their current illness (A. Presley, personal communication from N. Kreitman, 1983). On semantic differential scales, compared with controls the agoraphobic women devalued themselves (less fair, understanding, good, kind) and viewed themselves as less dynamic (less independent, fast, active, hard). The husbands of the agoraphobics shared this perception. It seemed to result from the illness, because when the agoraphobics rated themselves (or their husbands rated them) as they had been prior to the illness, they scored normally. Current handicap seems to lower self-esteem, and many other types of psychiatric patient also have a poor self-image, including neurotics, ocs, and aggressive psychopaths (Marks 1965).

Compared with controls agoraphobic women are neurotic and "sensitizers" (Arrindell & Emmelkamp 1985; Turner et al. 1983). Sensitizers are anxious/neurotic (Slough et al. 1984), which is more true for agora- than most other phobics (see Tables 9.2 and 9.3). The agoraphobics were also "defensive" on "deny-bad" and "general desirability" scales. As the sufferers' morbid versus premorbid states were not distinguished, such findings might well reflect their disorder rather than premorbid personality.

Some agoraphobics are undoubtedly active, sociable, and outgoing before their problem begins. Agoraphobia occurs "in people of all types and characteristics, amongst the normally self-reliant as well as amongst the timid" (Prince & Putnam 1912).

Sexual and Marital Function

Sexual Adjustment

Sexual dysfunction is common among normal people, so the question is whether it is more so among agoraphobics. One sample found more "total frigidity" among agoraphobic women (Roth 1959), but the prevalence of sexual disorder in them is of the same order as that in women with anxiety neurosis

(Winokur & Holeman 1963), oc inpatients (Marks 1965), and hysterics (Winokur & Leonard 1963). Sexual disorder is less common in agoraphobic men than women. In the Open Door sample, regular sexual enjoyment and orgasm was reported in 83% of the agoraphobic men but in only 60% of the agoraphobic women. When present, sexual complaints in the agoraphobic men were mainly of impotence or premature ejaculation, which are the commonest sexual problems in other men as well.

In a detailed controlled study, premorbid sexual adjustment was virtually the same among agoraphobic as normal women (Buglass et al. 1977). The two groups reported similar parental attitudes to sex; discussion of sexual matters during childhood and adolescence was mostly taboo. Menarche occurred at the same mean age (13), and the durations of both menstrual bleeding and cycle length were also comparable. More agoraphobics than controls reported at least one boyfriend other than their husbands; similar proportions of both groups found sex pleasurable in the first year of marriage and satisfactory prior to the illness (or the equivalent period in the controls). About 25% had never had orgasm.

The picture changed markedly with onset of the agoraphobia. Two-thirds of the female patients who married before becoming agoraphobic reported a marked loss of libido as compared to only one control; many agoraphobics continued intercourse primarily to please their husbands. Agoraphobics also complained more often of dysmenorrhea and had received more treatment for gynecological problems, but whether these antedated onset of the agoraphobia was not noted. Another sample of agoraphobics reported more sexual problems than did social phobics (Solyom et al. 1986).

Marital Adjustment

The marriages of agoraphobics are like those in the general population. Marital adjustment seemed normal in 95% of 158 agoraphobics (Sim & Houghton 1966) and unrelated to the wife's agoraphobia (Torpy & Measey 1974). Such impressions are borne out by many careful controlled comparisons.

The marriages of agoraphobic and normal women were very similar on most measures of attitude, behavior, domestic organization, marital interaction, husbands' and children's psychiatric symptoms, and social interaction (Buglass et al. 1977). Compared to normals, the agoraphobic women (but not their husbands) had fewer activities in larger social groups and did less of the shopping, but did not differ in overall contacts with family and friends. The agoraphobics' husbands had worked fewer hours since the onset of the problem, attributing this to the need to spend more time with their wives. Although these husbands felt they had become more sympathetic in time, their wives did not confirm this: only about half said that their husbands were concerned or sympathetic at any stage. A second controlled study of agoraphobic women also found that the husbands were no more defensive or disturbed than those of nonphobic psychiatric patients or normal controls, and that marital adjustment was similar to that of happily married controls (Arrindell et al. 1985; Arrindell & Emmelkamp 1985a & 1986).

Two further studies found that pretreatment marital adjustment scores of agoraphobics were similar to those of normal controls (Cobb et al. 1984; Monteiro et al. 1985). Another found similar reported marital satisfaction among agoraphobics and nonagoraphobics (Fisher & Wilson 1985). In addition, two other reports noted that agoraphobics' spouses were not neurotic and that their scores did not increase with length of marriage or severity of the phobia (Agulnik 1970; Hafner 1977a)—Agulnik studied both men and women patients. The risk of a spouse's becoming neurotic seems greater when the neurotic patient is a husband rather than a wife and rises the longer the neurosis has been present, suggesting that it is a consequence, not a cause, of the condition (Hagnell & Kreitman 1974).

From uncontrolled data certain writers argue that agoraphobia is somehow manufactured in order to meet the needs of a disordered marriage and keeps the couple together, improvement in the agoraphobia jeopardizing the marriage (Hafner 1976, 1977, 1977a, 1977b; Hand & Lamontagne 1976). As Mathews et al. (1981, p. 42) note, this "idea seems unnecessary and implausible. On the other hand, it is entirely possible that once phobic anxiety has started, its course will be influenced for better or worse by people close to the patient. Thus, if the husband of an agoraphobic woman is quite content that his wife should be housebound, he may be uninterested in or even obstructive to attempts at treatment that threaten to disturb his domestic calm. [We believe such situations to be] unusual and atypical." Conclusions about the relationship of marital adjustment and outcome of treatment need to be based on controlled research rather than anecdote. In such research agoraphobics' marriages remained stable after their phobias improved (see Chapter 15).

BIOLOGICAL ISSUES

Occasional cases of agoraphobia begin after organic problems such as subarachnoid hemorrhage, encephalitis, brain tumor, multiple sclerosis, hyper- or hypothyroidism, miscarriages, major operations, or amphetamine withdrawal. Menstruation worsens generalized anxiety and panics in agoraphobics (Breier & Charney 1985). Such factors are not peculiar to agoraphobia. They have a role like that of other stressful life events such as bereavement, separation from home, family illness, or emotional crises. Identical factors can trigger the onset or aggravate the course of a wide variety of physical and psychiatric illnesses.

A recent intense surge of biological studies of agoraphobia has yielded little of substance so far. There have been a great many reports of biological changes in the syndrome. However, none of those changes have yet been shown to be either (1) specific to agoraphobic as opposed to other types of anxiety, or (2) the cause rather than the product of anxiety. Until these two crucial points are settled by adequate controls, the search for biological markers is likely to be in vain. Those points remain open in most of the work reviewed below.

Scanning by positron-emission tomography (PET) revealed abnormal left-right asymmetry of cerebral blood flow in part of the parahippocampal gyrus in seven panic disorder patients who panicked with lactate infusion (how many were agoraphobic was not specified), but not in three more patients who failed to panic with lactate, nor in six normal controls (Raichle et al. 1983; Reiman et al. 1984). Unfortunately all the patients but only two of the controls knew that lactate would be infused at an undisclosed time and that this could precipitate panic. The patients thus had more anxiety-evoking expectation about the procedure than the controls, and the PET findings might easily reflect this rather than their panic disorder per se. (Expectancy has more effect on panic disorder than normal subjects.)

During sleep, panic disorder patients had a normal EEG (unlike depressives) but were restless, consistent with their hyperarousal (Roy-Byrne et al. 1985). One study claimed that EEG in panic disorder to be like that in narcolepsy (Adams et al. 1985). Agoraphobics have also been said to have defective muscle coordination and balance and visual-perceptual and oculomotor function (Blythe & McGlown 1982), but ratings were not blind, nor was there a nonagoraphobic control.

Mitral Valve Prolapse (MVP)

MVP occurs in 4% of normal adults (Devereux et al. 1985). Some cases have palpitations, fatigue, and dyspnea resembling that of anxiety. When compared to controls such cases had increased plasma adrenalin and noradrenalin at rest, and raised urinary creatinine and 24-hour adrenalin and noradrenalin; isoproterenol infusions reproduced the symptoms in dose-related fashion (Boudoulas et al. 1983). High resting adrenergic tone and overreaction to isoproterenol could be a sign and product of anxiety rather than its cause, and so further illustrate that any anxious people, not merely those with MVP or panic disorder, may have biological signs of anxiety. Other workers concluded that MVP and neurosis are independent conditions. One hundred and three MVP cases confirmed by echocardiography had no more neuroticism or neurotic symptoms than 67 cases with other cardiac diseases or than patients in primary care (Hickey et al. 1983). Women who had an auscultatory click, murmur, or both had no more palpitations, dizziness, weakness, and chest pains than women without auscultatory abnormalities (Procacci et al. 1976).

A flurry of interest was stirred by reports of up to 50% of panic-disordered and 44% agoraphobic women having MVP, compared with a 4% to 17% prevalence in normals (reviewed by Gorman et al. 1981a; Kantor et al. 1980; Liberthson 1983; Mavissakalian et al. 1983). However, only 15% of a later sample of agoraphobic women had MVP, and those with and without MVP did not differ on demographic, clinical, and psychological variables (Mavissakalian et al. 1983). (In contrast, another sample of panic-disordered cases with MVP [versus those without MVP] had higher resting plasma noradrenalin, prolonged EKG interval QT_c, higher pCO_2, and more respiratory complaints [Fyer et al. 1985].) There was no case of MVP among 50 agoraphobics screened by echocardiography (Hickey et al. 1983), and little MVP among the agoraphobics of Ballenger and colleagues (1984) or panic disorder patients of Shear and coworkers (1984).

Earlier high rates may have reflected excess referral of MVP subjects who had anxiety (Hartman et al. 1982), as the 16% prevalence of panic disorders in physician-referred patients with MVP is similar to the 10% to 14% prevalence of severe anxiety states found among all patients in cardiological practice, but much higher than the 2% to 5% prevalence of anxiety states in the natural population and the 3% prevalence of panic in family members with or without MVP—a less selected population. Other research found that MVP was unrelated to familial morbidity risk for anxiety neurosis (Crowe et al. 1980) and segregated independently from panic (Crowe 1982), and in panic disorder did not affect the outcome of treatment with imipramine (Gorman et al. 1981a) or the induction of panic by the infusion of sodium lactate (Gorman et al. 1981b).

Recent studies thus "argue against the notion that MVP might be a major factor in the etiology or prognosis of agoraphobia" (Mavissakalian et al. 1983). For a minority of agoraphobics the palpitations, fatigue, and chest pain of MVP might be a focus of concern, just as agoraphobics with epilepsy may avoid situations in which they had a fit and with Meniere's syndrome may focus on the vertigo; similarly, agoraphobics overreact to the symptoms produced by hyperventilation (Franklin 1985), CO_2-inhalation, and perhaps lactate infusion.

Autonomic and Biochemical Changes

Many autonomic and biochemical changes can be detected during agoraphobic and other forms of tension. These changes may not be specific to agoraphobia. They might occur with panic/anxiety of many origins, including agitated (as opposed to retarded) depression and sudden fright.

Spontaneous and phobic panics in agoraphobics, as in other phobics, are accompanied by raised heart rate, skin conductance and EMG activity, and skin temperature (Freedman et al. 1985; Lader & Mathews 1970; Marks & Huson 1973; Taylor et al. 1985). During spontaneous panics there are also small increases in blood pressure, plasma cortisol, noradrenalin, and MHPG, and decreased oral temperature (Cameron et al. 1985). MHPG was higher in panic disorder patients who had frequent panics than in depressives or normals (Charney et al. 1985). In agoraphobics MHPG rose after they entered their phobic situation; this rise was reduced by clonidine or imipramine (Ko et al. 1983; see also Chapter 7).

At rest, panic disorder patients also have tachycardia and heart rates that are more variable than in controls (Taylor et al. 1985). Other baseline changes in noradrenergic function have been inconsistent. At rest, plasma adrenalin and noradrenalin (and heart rate) were high in agoraphobics, but plasma MHPG and urinary catecholamine metabolites (MHPG, VMA, metanephrine, normetanephrine) were normal (Ballenger et al. 1984; Cameron et al. 1984). Normality of the peripheral sympathetic system in agoraphobics was suggested by the fact that plasma adrenalin and noradrenalin, although already high, rose further and normally on standing.

Plasma adrenalin and noradrenalin did not relate to phobia or depression, nor did they change with imipramine; however, plasma MHPG and urinary catecholamine metabolites did fall (Ballenger et al. 1984). MHPG was higher in agoraphobics who were improved one year after desimipramine than in those who were not, and did not relate to clinical response (Sweeney 1983).

Monoamine oxidase activity in platelets was increased in agoraphobics relative to controls, and plasma p- and m-HPA were lower (Yu et al. 1983).

Alpha-adrenergic function was normal in a few patients with panic disorder and agoraphobia; they did not secrete increased prolactin (Grunhaus et al. 1983). However, in other panic disorder patients (how many had agoraphobia was not noted), the number of platelet alpha$_2$ adrenoreceptors was low as measured by yohimbine but not clonidine (Cameron et al. 1983). Further data from the same group suggested that panic features were not due to beta-adrenergic hyperresponsiveness but could be from downregulation of beta-receptors because of increased adrenergic stimulation (Nesse et al. 1984).

Concerning hypothalamic-adrenocortical function, the dexamethasone suppression test (DST) was normal in most patients with panic disorder (Faludi et al. 1985, Lieberman et al. 1983, Sheehan et al. 1983, Williams et al. 1983; Uhde et al. 1985), panic disorder plus agoraphobia (Curtis et al. 1982), agoraphobia (Ballenger et al. 1984a; Cottraux & Claustrat 1984), or both (Bridges et al. 1986). Cottraux and Claustrat found a trend to an abnormal DST in agoraphobics who also had major depression or depression in first-degree relatives. Among other agoraphobics the DST was normal in those who were not depressed; it was abnormal only in the depressed subsample (Dackis et al. 1985). Platelet ^{3}H-imipramine binding was also normal in panic disorder (Uhde et al. 1985).

Administering clonidine, TRH, and CRH, blunted the responses of growth hormone, thyroid-stimulating hormone, and ACTH, respectively, for both panic disorder and major depression, as compared to normal controls (Uhde et al. 1985).

Raised urinary output of tribulin (a MAOI inhibitor and central benzodiazepine [bz] receptor ligand) has been found in chronic generalized anxiety disorder and after lactate-induced panic in panic disorder patients (whether any had agoraphobia is not specified) (Sandler et al. 1983). Tribulin could be another of the many biological products rather than causes of anxiety. The same applies to carcinoids, which rise in acute or chronic stress and return to normal thereafter (Peterson 1983).

Turning to hematological aspects, platelet factor 4 (PF4) and beta-thromboglobulin (BTG) were raised in agoraphobics with panics and in medical students under stress (Levine 1983; Sheehan et al. 1984). When the agoraphobics were given either alprazolam or ibuprofen, PF4 and BTG fell to a similar extent even though clinical improvement occurred only with alprazolam. After the drugs were stopped, PF4 and BTG returned to their previously high levels. High plasma levels of either of these platelet release products suggest platelet activity, being found in patients with in vivo platelet aggregation and increased platelet turnover (such as myocardial infarction or prosthetic cardiac valves), and with transient cerebral ischemia and completed stroke (reviewed by Sheehan et al. 1984). Perhaps raised PF4 and BTG in agoraphobia relate to a finding that nailfold capillaries were twisted in neurocirculatory asthenia, unlike the nontwisted hairpin loops of normals (Cohen & White 1950). As with hypertension, such results indicate potential links between agoraphobia and future cardiovascular disease, but replication is needed. (Other relevant changes in lipids and immunity during stress were reviewed in Chapter 7.)

Anxiogenic Procedures

Agoraphobics by definition panic on entering agoraphobic situations, and they also often panic spontaneously. We saw the biological effects of such anxiogenesis above, and of biochemical anxiogenesis in normals in Chapter 7. Here we will review other anxiogenic methods in agoraphobics. In panic disorder with or without agoraphobia, anxiety has been raised by caffeine, yohimbine, sodium lactate, or isoproterenol infusion, CO_2 inhalation, hyperventilation, exercise, pain, and discomfort. As mentioned, such effects need not point to specific pathophysiology. They could reflect a liability of any anxious person to overreact to certain autonomic symptoms produced in various ways. Many of the reports fail to specify how many cases were agoraphobic.

Caffeine worsened the generalized anxiety and panics of agoraphobics interviewed by Breier and Charney (1985). In a controlled study of other agoraphobics, caffeine was dose-related to anxiety and depression but not to phobia (Boulenger et al. 1984). Compared to controls, agoraphobics more often stopped taking coffee because of untoward side effects and were also more aroused (anxiety, alertness, and insomnia) after one cup of coffee, although this did not relate to their higher state- or trait anxiety at baseline. These workers then gave oral caffeine and placebo to patients with panic disorder and to normals. Caffeine was more anxiogenic in patients and led to a dose-related rise in anxiety, plasma control, and lactate and noradrenalin; the anxiety was lowered by alprazolam (Bierer et al. 1985). Caffeine may act on bz and adenosine systems, and can trigger cardiac arrhythmias. It can induce anxiety in normals without raising the noradrenergic metabolite MHPG (Charney et al. 1984).

The alpha$_2$-antagonist *yohimbine* has produced anxiety, panic, and raised MHPG in panic disorder and agoraphobic patients more than in normals, whereas placebo did not (Charney et al. 1984; Uhde et al. 1984, 1984a). The two agoraphobics who had most anxiety after yohimbine were those who later responded best to clonidine, which was the opposite effect to yohimbine on firing of the locus ceruleus (Uhde et al. 1984a). The anxiogenic effect of yohimbine could be mediated via bz receptors or via adrenergic, dopaminergic, or other systems.

Isoproterenol infusion produced more frequent panic but not more tachycardia in panic disorder patients than in normal controls, to the same extent as did sodium lactate (Rainey et al. 1984b; Youssef et al. 1985). Another controlled study, however, failed to find panic with isoproterenol infusion, and found less heart rate rise than in controls (Cameron et al. 1984; Nesse et al. 1984), despite higher baseline levels of heart rate, higher plasma adrenalin and noradrenalin throughout rest, exercise, and infusions, and raised plasma growth hormone and cortisol. Moreover, response to intramuscular adrenalin in anxious patients was like that in controls, with rise in plasma adrenalin, noradrenalin, and heart rate; post-injection anxiety was also similar and correlated with post-injection heart rate in anxious subjects (Mathews et al. 1981).

Hyperventilation can produce panic in panic patients (Gorman et al. 1984), and in agoraphobics it did so more than in normals (Franklin 1985). At rest, such patients also had lower pCO_2 than normals, which rose to normal after learning to control their breathing (Bonn et al. 1984; Salkovskis et al. 1986). We do not yet know, however, what proportion of agoraphobics (1) have rapid breathing and low pCO_2, and (2) have this as a cause rather than a result of their anxiety.

CO_2 inhalation has led to panic in panic disorder (Gorman et al. 1984) and in agoraphobic and panic disorder patients using 35% CO_2/65% O_2 single inhalations (Griez & Vandenhout 1983; van den Hout et al. 1986). Rebreathing until $FiCO_2$ rose to between 7% and 10% could be tolerated less by agoraphobics than by controls, but ventilatory and panic response did not differ; nearly all subjects developed panic (Woods et al. 1985). In neurocirculatory asthenia, rebreathing air until CO_2 accumulated to 4% led patients to sigh far more than controls and to symptoms that most believed were identical to or like their anxiety attacks (Cohen et al. 1951).

In accord with these findings are changes found in another carefully controlled study—changes resulting less from the disorder itself than from higher levels of baseline anxiety and higher expectancy effects (Ehlers et al. 1985). Similar rise in anxiety (subjective, heart rate, systolic and diastolic blood pressure) occurred in normal controls as in patients with panic disorder with or without agoraphobia to three types of challenge: (1) 5½% CO_2/94.5% air inhalation for 20 minutes, (2) cold pressor test, and (3) mental arithmetic. Rises in response to CO_2 were to higher levels in patients, but from higher baseline levels to start with. The three patients and single control who asked to stop the CO_2 inhalations prematurely had had higher baseline levels of subjective anxiety and cardiovascular arousal than their counterparts, who continued to the end of the 20 minutes, with correspondingly higher responses to the three challenges. Controls and patients rated all three challenges as similarly unpleasant and like their usual panic/extreme anxiety.

In the foregoing study, apart from their higher baseline anxiety, patients differed from controls in having a greater expectancy effect from wearing the gas mask used to inhale CO_2. On the first day, when subjects knew that no CO_2 would be given, wearing the mask did not alter cardiovascular arousal; on the second day, when subjects were expecting CO_2, wearing the mask produced greater rises in patients. Expectancy led to less rise than did CO_2 inhalation itself. The total effect seemed a function of both initial anxiety and expectancy. These workers concluded that CO_2 inhalation was a nonspecific stressor in these patients (Margraf et al. 1985a).

Infusion of sodium lactate produces a picture like that from inhaling CO_2. Numerous reports suggest that infusion of sodium lactate (but not of dextrose or saline) leads to intense anxiety more in panic disorder and/or agoraphobia than in normal controls (Appleby et al. 1981; Grosz & Farmer 1972; Kelly et al. 1971; Liebowitz et al. 1984, Pitts & McLure 1967; Rainey et al. 1984). A lucid critique of 13 such studies (Margraf et al. 1985) noted that many were only single-blind, gave inadequate information about sample features, matching procedures, settings, instructions, and measures, and had inadequate control strategies. Lactate infusions could indeed induce anxiety resembling natural panic but not necessarily identical to it, and did so in only a mean of 56% of panic patients and also in other patients; baseline levels and the cognitive-emotional state of the patient also affected whether panic would result. Controls and patients with GAD and panic differed quantitatively, not qualitatively. Margraf and coworkers concluded that "lactate effects can be entirely explained by the interaction of perceived physiological changes, past experience, environmental cues, and their appraisal as threatening or dangerous."

In a well-controlled study by the same group (Ehlers et al. 1986), similar increased anxiety and heart rate response occurred to lactate (but not to saline infusion or the experimental setting alone) in patients with panic disorder with or without agoraphobia as in normal controls. Patients were not more reactive to lactate than were controls except on systolic and diastolic blood pressure. Lactate-induced anxiety was rated as similar to natural panic/anxiety but not to depression; patients gave more extreme ratings ("very similar" or "dissimilar") (just as patients with OCD or aggressive psychopathy both gave more extreme semantic differential ratings than did controls [Marks 1965]). Panic patients differed from controls less in their reactivity to lactate than in having continuously higher anxiety and heart rate from the start of baseline until the end of the session.

Consonant with the conclusion of Margraf and coworkers is the fact that panic from lactate infusion occurred in 62% of patients with depression plus panic (McGrath et al. 1985). Moreover, lactate panic occurred at the same rate in other patients with major depression as in those with panic disorder or agoraphobia (Cowley et al. 1985). Lactate-induced panic is clearly not syndrome specific.

Lactate-induced panic is reduced by prior medication with MAOI or tricyclic antidepressants (Kelly et al. 1971; Rifkin et al. 1981) or alprazolam (Carr et al. 1984). Such "blocking" might reflect the damping down of general anxiety by antidepressants as long as they are given, and would probably disappear on stopping the drugs, given the high relapse rate on doing so (see Chapter 16). This view predicts that the nondrug treatment of exposure would also lower lactate- (and other) induced anxiety because it, too, reduces spontaneous panic and general anxiety when phobias diminish (Marks 1983); this was found by Guttmacher and Nelles (1984).

Exercise intolerance on a treadmill is indicated by the heart rate rising more quickly in panic disorder patients than in normal controls; the difference is due to a subsample with MVP (Crowe et al. 1985). Many reports earlier this century (reviewed by Cohen et al. 1951) noted that neurocirculatory asthenics could not do hard work, as it induced their symptoms (hence the term "effort syndrome"). Patients had abnormally high pulse and blood pressure after swinging dumbbells and performed and responded abnormally to a 100-meter run wearing a gas mask, compared with normals. At rest patients had slightly raised pulse and respiration rates but normal oxygen consumption and blood lactate. During exercise on a treadmill and stepping up and down, abnormalities appeared—less oxygen intake, higher rise in pulse rate, blood lactate, and pulmonary ventilation, and ability to continue the task for only half to two-thirds of the time that normals could. Effort on a bicycle led neurotic patients to ventilate more per 100 milliliters of oxygen assimilated and to have a greater rise in blood lactate (Jones 1948). A similar picture is seen in people who seldom exercise; the role of this factor is not known.

Intolerance of discomfort was found in neurocirculatory asthenia (reviewed by Cohen et al. 1951). Patients perceived a beam from a hot lamp as painful at a level similar to that in controls, but winced at a lower level and pulled away far more; likewise, they ceased to sustain a tight hand grip more quickly, and a tight sphygmomanometer cuff produced more increase in respiratory volume but not in blood pressure. Neurotic patients stopped exercising earlier than controls, before a "physiological end-point" had been reached (Jones 1948). Duration of panic disorder patients enduring a gas mask while expecting CO_2 was not reported in a test finding that it aroused them more than controls (Ehlers et al. 1985), nor was it noted in a cold pressor test. Blood pressure rose as in controls from a similar baseline, whereas anxiety and heart rate rose more than in controls but from higher baseline levels (response to mental arithmetic was as to the cold pressor test). On blood pressure and prolactin, the reaction to a cold pressor test in panic disorder and agoraphobia was the same as in controls (Grunhaus et al. 1983). Cohen and colleagues (1951) reviewed earlier cold pressor studies of neurocirculatory asthenia that found increased rise in pulse rate and pulmonary ventilation, but again not in blood pressure; patients also overreacted to sudden, intense light or sound. In another study, tones, touch, and startle led to more tension in panic disorder than in controls (Moreau 1985). One study found no difference in pain sensitivity between panic disorder and controls (Roy-Byrne et al. 1985a).

Hypoglycemia produced anxiety but not panic in panic disorder. It is thought unlikely to be responsible for spontaneous panics (Uhde et al. 1984; Vittone 1985).

Causation of Anxiogenic Effects

As mentioned, many anxiogenic effects might reflect a tendency for anyone anxious to overreact to certain autonomic symptoms, especially when they expect to panic, rather than a dysfunction peculiar to agoraphobia (Insel et al. 1984). In anxiety (panic) disorders with or without agoraphobia, panic/anxiety and corresponding autonomic changes are induced not only by several biochemical agents and hyperventilation but also by the expectation of discomfort, by pain, and by exercise.

We are little closer to a biological marker specific to agoraphobia than were enquirers into the effort syndrome earlier in this century. Progress would be faster if there were more controlled comparisons of anxiety responses to anxiogenic procedures not only in agoraphobia but also in other syndromes with prominent anxiety, and in anxious normals. Moreover, biochemical anxiogenesis should be carefully compared with psychological anxiogenesis (including exposure therapy) in the same patients to check which reactions are biochemical and which psychological in origin. (In an agoraphobic patient, for instance, lactate-induced panic was subsequently abolished after live exposure treatment [Guttmacher & Nelles 1984].) A common end path could transmit all forms of anxiety and their reduction, however they are caused.

The autonomic and biochemical changes of panic in panic disorder have a profile like that found in extreme normal anxiety. Panic can occur despite normal blood pH, lactate, pyruvate, ionized calcium and adrenalin (Levin et al. 1984; Rainey et al. 1984), and glucose (Gorman et al. 1984b). The panic induced by lactate and CO_2 could result partly from hypercarbic activation of central chemoceptors, perhaps at the medullary area postrema or ventral surface (Carr & Sheehan 1984). The anxiogenic effect of hyperventilation, too, could result from lowering of neuronal pH in such chemoceptors, and might improve by nondrug means. Adding breathing exercises plus isometric relaxation to live exposure enhanced the improvement of agoraphobia in a controlled study, but respiratory changes were not measured (Franklin 1985). Behavior can produce biochemical abnormalities, but changing that behavior might also improve them. To the adage "for every twisted thought a twisted molecule" we might add, "for every straightened thought a straightened molecule."

Excess Long-Term Mortality

The possibility of excess long-term mortality comes from two long-term follow-ups of anxiety-disordered patients in Iowa. Two caveats are needed. First, the proportion who were agoraphobic was tiny; most agoraphobics are women, but they formed only 38% of the first cohort (Coryell 1983; Coryell et al. 1982) and 57% of the second (Coryell et al. 1983). Second, excess cardiovascular deaths may have resulted indirectly from smoking and hypertension rather than from anxiety itself.

The first study examined mortality in former panic-disordered inpatients (mostly men), 35 years after index admission and compared them with oc or depressive disorder patients. There was no excess mortality in OCD. Men with panic disorder and their depressed controls had an excess of unnatural deaths, these being later and more cardiovascular (atherosclerotic) in panic disorder; women showed a supporting trend. Suicide accounted for a surprisingly high 20% of the deaths in panic disorder and for 16% in depression. The findings are contrary to those of Wheeler and coworkers (1950), who included no psychiatrically ill reference group. The second follow-up was 12 years after index contact of outpatients who had anxiety neurosis compared with matched surgical patients. Men showed a trend to excess mortality from cardiovascular disease and from suicide (Coryell et al. 1985).

SUMMARY

In adult psychiatric clinics agoraphobia is the most frequent and handicapping phobic disorder. It is a coherent though protean syndrome. The central feature is a variable combination of characteristic fears and avoidance of public places like streets, shops, public transport, crowds, assemblies, and tunnels. Fear/panic and associated autonomic sensations and thoughts are triggered by entering or thinking about such places, especially when alone. Though multiple, the fears have a pathognomonic pattern and do *not* usually concern non-public situations like cats, darkness, blood, water, glass, dirt, or cancer, though cases may fear being alone at home. Fears with avoidance often restrict ability to work and to leave the home, and can lead to housebondage. Panic is not pathognomic of agoraphobia, as it is also found in many other conditions. Autobiographies testify to many features of the syndrome.

Two-thirds or more of agoraphobics are women. Socioeconomic and marital status, parental background, and premorbid personality are usually unremarkable. Agoraphobia often prevents normal work. There is no increased frequency of past separation anxiety or dependence, though onset is earlier in agoraphobics who give a childhood history of school phobia.

Agoraphobia usually begins between age 18 to 35—later onset suggests possible depression or space phobia. More start during hot than cold weather. The onset is often preceded by excessive adverse life events, but not by obvious trauma. Initial panic in a public situation is already a sign of the problem, not its cause. The onset can be sudden, gradual, or stuttering, and the course may fluctuate somewhat, but once present for a year the condition may persist for decades without total remission if untreated.

Agoraphobics have a characteristic cluster of fears of public places, and also many other fears, including social ones. In addition, many cases also have nonphobic (nonsituational) symptoms like spontaneous panics and tension, hyperventilation, dizziness, thoughts of fainting, dying or losing control, exhaustion, depression, obsessions, depersonalization, and loss of libido. None of these are pathognomonic.

The fears of agoraphobics usually increase when sufferers are alone, far from home, in unfamiliar or confined surroundings, exposed to bright or fluorescent light, when there is no easy exit with speed and dignity, and during depressive episodes. It is temporarily eased by opposite conditions like the presence of a trusted companion or talisman, or by sedative drugs.

On confronting or expecting a phobic situation the panic of agoraphobics is like that of any other phobic, and their general tension, spontaneous panic and depersonalization are indistinguishable from those occurring in anxiety states (panic disorder without agoraphobia) or indeed with a normal intense fright. Agoraphobia often worsens during the depressive episodes that commonly punctuate its course, and may also be aggravated by hyperventilation.

Short sallies into agoraphobic situations from brief efforts of willpower lead to only temporary gains unless pressed to the point of habituation as is done in a concerted program of exposure treatment. Response of the sufferer and her family to the disability depends on their personality and circumstances.

Agoraphobics tend to come from stable homes with parents who were not overprotective before onset of the problem. Premorbid personality did not differ from that of controls; low self-esteem may date to after onset of the disability.

The only controlled data for premorbid sexual adjustment found this to be normal in agoraphobic women. Subsequent to its onset agoraphobics develop more sexual dysfunction; the same may be equally true of other conditions with prominent anxiety, which reduces capacity for sexual enjoyment.

Marital adjustment of agoraphobics was consistently similar to that of controls in several careful studies.

Various biological changes reported in agoraphobia may not differ from those found with any form of intense anxiety/panic. Changes include left-right asymmetry of cerebral blood flow in the parahippocampal gyrus on PET scan, raised MHPG in the phobic situation, and raised platelet factor 4 and beta-thromboglobulin. Temporary aggravation of fear is caused by caffeine, yohimbine, inhalation of CO_2, infusion of sodium lactate or isoproterenol, hyperventilation, heat, and physical and mental effort; this could reflect a general tendency of anxious people to overreact to certain autonomic symptoms produced in various ways. The dexamethasone suppression test is normal and mitral valve prolapse is probably not especially frequent.

11

Social and Specific Phobias

This chapter will examine the features of social and specific phobias. Social phobias are about halfway between agoraphobia and specific phobia in terms of the number of fears and the degree of nonphobic anxiety and depression. Within the specific phobias, several subgroups will be defined.

SOCIAL PHOBIAS

Up to a certain point social anxiety is normal and indeed may facilitate function. Over the millenia, fear has been recognized that "amazeth many men that are to speak, or show themselves in publick assemblies, or before some great personages, as Tully confessed of himself, that he trembled still at the beginning of his speech; and Demosthenes that great orator of Greece, before Phillipus" (Burton 1621, p. 143). Prominent public figures commonly have qualms before major appearances. Throughout her career Maria Callas would shake with fear while in the wings awaiting to sing (*The Guardian,* September 17, 1977), and Harold MacMillan, the British Prime Minister, felt nauseous before question-time in Parliament.

When moderate, social anxiety may be but an inconvenience, as Thomas Hardy wrote in *Far From the Madding Crowd:* "'Why, ye've hardly had strength of eye enough to look in our young mis'esse's face, so I hear, Joseph?'... 'Yes,' continued Joseph Poorgrass—his shyness, which was so painful a defect filling him with a mild complacency now that it was regarded as an interesting study. 'Twere blush, blush, blush with me every minute of the time, when she was speaking to me.'"

Marked social anxiety can gravely disrupt activity, as in a case of Hippocrates who "through bashfulness, suspicion, and timorousness, will not be seen abroad; loves darkness as life, and cannot endure the light, or to sit in lightsome places; his hat still in his eyes, he will neither see, nor be seen by his good will. He dare not come in company, for fear he should be misused, disgraced, overshoot himself in gesture or speeches, or be sick; he thinks every man observes him" (Burton 1621, p. 272).

Social phobics are afraid of a variety of situations in which other people may look at or form an opinion of them; the fear is not of a crowd per se. This distinguishes them from agoraphobics, who usually avoid crowds but say that this results from a fear of being enclosed or suffocated by the crowd rather than of being watched by people in it. Agoraphobics are often afraid of causing a scene or appearing silly when they go out, but they have no difficulty looking an interviewer in the eye. In contrast, social phobics are fearful of being observed, can engage in certain activities only as long as nobody is looking at them, and often avert their gaze during interview. This is a pathological intensification of a normal phenomenon that is widespread among many species, its counterpart being the evolution of eyespots as a protective device (see chapters 2 and 3). Many cultures build on this biological base by teaching children not to look into other people's eyes.

Many features of social phobia were among a factor extracted from questionnaire responses of 250 psychiatric outpatients (Dixon et al. 1957); other factors concerned agoraphobia (see Table 9.5) and injury. The following were elements of the social phobia factor:

1. I am afraid I may look ridiculous or make a fool of myself, or make a foolish mistake, or seem unintelligent or ignorant.
2. I hate walking past a crowd of people.
3. I am uncomfortable with people I don't know or when I am the center of attention (for instance, when crossing a dance floor).
4. I am uncomfortable when I don't know what's expected of me.
5. I become nervous speaking to someone in authority.

Social phobias overlap with social dysfunction (*DSM-III* avoidant personality disorder), and treatment for both problems is sought in young adult life; they often occur together (Greenberg & Stravynski 1985). We do not know whether social phobias relate to the fear of strangers of infancy, subsequent shyness, or introversion. Stranger fear is a normal developmental phenomenon in the first two years of life, (Chapter 7). This and subsequent shyness are under genetic influence, (Chapter 5), and shyness seems to vary continuously in the general population. How socialization modifies this remains to be worked out in detail. Blind adolescents lack certain social skills but are not especially anxious (Van Hasselt et al. 1985).

Demographic Aspects of Social Phobias

Prevalence

In a United States community survey the 6-month prevalence of social phobia in 2 urban populations was 1.3% for men and 2.0% for women (Myers et al. 1984), but these figures were inflated by cases with social anxiety as part of another syndrome, such as agoraphobia. In a British questionnaire survey, between 3% and 10% of first-year students had typical social phobias (Bryant & Trower 1974).

In psychiatric clinics social phobia is the second most common phobic disorder (agoraphobia being the most common), both in the author's unit in London and in the United States (Liebowitz et al. 1985). Social phobics formed about 25% of all the author's phobics in this decade and of a series in a Canadian clinic (Solyom et al. 1986) and in India (Raguram & Bhide 1985).

Gender

In psychiatric clinics women are less preponderant among social phobics than among other phobics; their proportion among various series is between 52% and 60% (Amies et al. 1983; Marks 1969; Nichols 1974; Öhman et al. 1985; Shafar 1976; Thyer et al. 1985). Men were in the majority (77%) among cases with social dysfunction and associated anxiety who were selected for social skills training (Stravynski et al. 1982), as well as among subjects with social inadequacy (Bryant et al. 1976).

Age of Onset and at Treatment

Onset age is most often in the teens or early adult life, the mean being 15 to 21 in British, Swedish, and American series (Amies et al. 1983; Marks & Gelder 1966; Öhman et al. 1984; Persson & Nordlund 1985; Shafar 1976; Thyer et al. 1985). Onset before puberty is rare—no social phobics were found in a large survey of children 10 to 11 years old (Rutter et al. 1970). When the sample included subjects with social dysfunction and anxiety, the onset was usually in adolescence (Stravynski et al. 1982).

Subjects came to psychiatric clinics about 6 to 20 years after the problem began. Mean age at presentation was 27 to 34 (Amies et al. 1983; Marks & Gelder 1966; Öhman et al. 1985; Persson & Nordlund 1985; Shafar 1976); it was 34 in social dysfunction and anxiety (Stravynski et al. 1982).

Marital Status, Social Class, and Education

Rather fewer social than other phobics are married or cohabiting, which might partly reflect their relative youth as well as their social phobia. The proportion of single status was 50% in Marks (1969) and 38% in Amies and coworkers (1983). In those with both social dysfunction and social phobia the proportion who were single rose to fully 95% (Stravynski et al. 1982); 60% were virgin, and most of the remainder had difficulties in sexual performance (Greenberg & Stravynski 1985).

In clinical series that examined the point, social phobics came from a higher social class than the general population (Amies et al. 1983; Persson & Nordlund 1985), and the same was true for cases of social dysfunction with anxiety (Greenberg & Stravynski 1985). In addition, social phobics were upwardly mobile through education or marriage, and were more often in the upper social classes than were their parents, unlike agoraphobics from the same clinic (Amies et al. 1983). Social phobics were also superior to agoraphobics in education and verbal intelligence (Persson & Nordlund 1985).

The overrepresentation of social phobics in clinical samples could reflect referral patterns. More literate and influential people may take advantage earlier of increased medical interest in social phobia and press harder for its treatment, as they do with other conditions. Subjects may also ask for help more if they are keen to remedy a problem involving sensitivity to social criticism, a point suggested by the upward mobility of the sample where this issue was studied.

If community surveys show that social phobias are indeed more prevalent among upper-class or more educated people, this might be explained in terms of differing socialization patterns among classes. Whether wider cultural influences contribute much to the community prevalence of social phobias deserves study, as many cultures teach children and especially girls to avoid looking directly at people and not to speak until spoken to.

Clinical Features

The features of social phobias were described by Beard (1879), Kraupl Taylor (1966), Marks (1969), and, in a recent upwelling of interest, by Amies and colleagues (1983), Liebowitz and coworkers (1985c), Persson and Nordlund (1985), and Solyom and coworkers (1986).

Onset of most social phobias among 25 cases of the author's was over some months or years, usually with no clear precipitant, although emotional situations might sensitize the patient. For example, fears of shaking in public began for the first time in a young woman at her wedding service as she was walking up the church aisle with her father and wondering if her future husband was really good enough for her. The fears worsened shortly afterward when she ate in a restaurant after visiting her husband in the hospital. A small number of social phobias began suddenly after trigger incidents. For example, a young man at a dance felt sick at a bar and vomited before reaching the toilet, making an embarrassing mess; thereafter he became afraid of going to dances, bars, or parties. In a few cases there had been social sensitivity since early childhood, which gradually increased after puberty.

Patients with social phobias may be afraid of eating or drinking in front of other people; they fear that their hands will tremble as they hold their fork or cup, or that they will feel nauseous or have a lump in their throat and be unable to swallow as long as they are watched. One patient said; "When I go out to eat in strange places I cannot eat, my throat feels a quarter of an inch wide, and I sweat." The fear is usually worst in elegant, crowded restaurants and least in the safety of the home, but a few patients even find it impossible to eat even in the presence of their spouses. Such patients become unable to go out to dinner or to invite friends home, for fear that their hands will tremble when drinking tea or handing a cup to a friend. Social life thus becomes very restricted.

For fear of shaking, blushing, sweating, or looking ridiculous, patients will not sit facing another passenger in a bus or train, nor walk past a line of people. They are terrified of attracting attention by behaving awkwardly or fainting. Some may leave their house only when it is so dark or foggy that they cannot be seen. Some avoid talking to superiors, and stage fright will stop them from performing to an audience. They may cease swimming lest their bodies be exposed to the gaze of strangers. They might avoid parties and be too embarrassed to talk to people. "I can't have normal conversation with people. I break out in a sweat, that is my whole problem even with the missus," said a man who nonetheless had enjoyable sex with his wife. Some patients are afraid only when with the opposite sex.

Patients of this kind are often afraid to write in public and will not visit a bank or shop because they are terrified their hand will tremble when writing a check or handling money in front of someone else. Fear of shaking may prevent a secretary from taking shorthand or typing, a teacher from writing on a blackboard in front of a class and from reading dictation, a seamstress from sewing in the factory, and an assembly-line worker from assembling a package. Harmless activities such as knitting or buttoning a coat can induce agonizing panic when done in front of other people.

Nearly always in such phobics the fear is that their hands or heads *might* shake; yet it is rare for such patients to actually tremble or shake so that their writing becomes a scrawl, their teacup rattles against the saucer, their soup is spilled when they raise the spoon to their lips, or their head nods visibly when talking. This is in striking contrast to patients with organic tremor such as that of Parkinsonism, who shake vigorously but unself-consciously and have no fear of doing anything in public despite their disability.

Some sufferers fear that they might vomit in public or see other people vomiting. Normally this should cause little incapacity, but these phobics also avoid any situation where there is a remote chance that they or others will vomit; each pale face is viewed as a potential vomitor. They may shun teaching children, traveling on a bumpy bus or coach, going on a boat or to parties, walking outside a bar, or eating onions. Vomiting phobias include a specific phobic component when the sufferer is even afraid of vomiting when alone.

Typically social phobics fear criticism, scrutiny by others, and blushing, and they have low self-esteem. They usually seek treatment for discomfort or handicap socially, at work, or in college. Some come for complications such as increasing alcohol consumption or depression. Alcohol dependence was present in about 20% of social phobics at Maudsley and Oxford hospitals, compared with 7% of agoraphobics (Amies et al. 1983), and social phobias are common among alcoholics (see Chapter 9). Some history of depression was present in nearly half the social phobics at Maudsley and Oxford, as well as in New York (Liebowitz et al. 1985c). Suicidal attempts had been made by 14% of social phobics but only 2% of agoraphobics (Amies et al. 1983). General anxiety at rest was present in 22% of Maudsley cases. In social situations, socially anxious versus nonanxious people had fewer positive and more negative thoughts, attributed awkwardness more to themselves than to the situation, had more rise in heart rate and blood pressure, and were rated as being less skillful (Beidel et al. 1985).

Many social phobias are fairly focussed, as in the following case:

Social Phobia as an Isolated Complaint

A 34-year-old unmarried secretary presented with a fear of vomiting of 13 years' duration. As a child her mother would not assist the children when they vomited and instead would ask the father to help. Although the patient had been concerned about other children vomiting at age 5, she did not develop a phobia until age 21, when she became afraid that other people or she herself would vomit on the train, and she began to avoid travel. This fear became fluctuatingly worse in the last 5 years. She woke at 5:15 A.M. daily in order to travel to her office in the city before rush hour but could, under duress, return during rush hour. For two years she had drunk a bottle of brandy a week to calm her fear of traveling, in addition to taking intermittent chlordiazepoxide. She feared increasing dependence on the brandy. For 5 years she had avoided eating in public places, restaurants, or strangers' homes. She also avoided going to theaters with friends if she could help it because it was easier to leave the theater if she was alone, should her fear of vomiting develop. In fact she had never vomited in public nor seen anybody else vomit for many years.

Away from the phobic situation she was neither anxious nor depressed. Her work was satisfactory. Her sexual experience was almost nonexistent. After four years of group psychotherapy she felt more comfortable in the company of men and got on better with people generally, but her phobia did not improve. Later, after 12 sessions of fantasy exposure, she became able to eat in restaurants alone and in company without undue anxiety, to travel in crowded subways, and to enjoy social situations more.

When social phobics also have generalized anxiety and depression they resemble severe agoraphobics and could justifiably be included under the common rubric of "phobic anxiety state," as the following case illustrates:

Social Phobia with Diffuse Anxiety

A 30-year-old single typist had social phobias of 3 years' duration which restricted her social life. In the previous year she had not been out alone except to travel to work, had stopped that 2 months previously, and had come to the hospital with her mother. She feared people looking at her, shaking while drinking in public, and any social situation. In addition, even when resting at home she was continually on edge, shaky, and restless, and panicked occasionally, without any obvious cues for this. She was calm only when she had alcohol or sedative drugs. In addition she had been intermittently depressed and wanting to cry for 2 years, and especially in the week before attending the hospital.

The more diffuse varieties of social phobia and social dysfunction (Greenberg & Stravynski 1985) resemble Japanese cases of "shinkeishitsu" (Caudill & Doi 1963), of whom those seeking treatment are predominantly male (Good & Kleinman 1985). Shinkeishitsu is characterized by tense interpersonal relations, anthropophobia, and fears of light and sound (Caudill & Schooler 1969). "Anthropophobia" denotes fears of blushing, meeting the gaze of others, or having one's facial expression be displeasing to others. Anthropophobics experience inability to find topics of conversation and awkwardness when appearing before others, uneasiness when people are nearby, and reluctance to meet them because of the belief that their looks are ugly (Kora 1968). The latter resembles the Western category of dysmorphophobia.

An example of shinkeishitsu is a 33-year-old man who since age 26 had anthropophobia, insomnia, headache, and a feeling that feces remained even after evacuation (Kora 1968). He found it very painful to talk to people and would often droop his head in the middle of a conversation and avoid looking into the eyes of the other party. Gradually it became painful for him even to talk to his children. Work in his office became extremely unpleasant, and he sought treatment when he virtually ceased leaving home except to go to work.

Family, Personality, and Background

Parents are rated by social phobics as having been overprotective yet uncaring (Arrindell et al. 1983; Parker 1979). Close relatives with phobias were reported in 9% to 20% of cases (Amies et al. 1983; Marks 1969). Although uncommon, this is probably still more than in the general population.

Half the 25 Maudsley cases had been fearful, timid, or shy as children. After puberty 45% were relative isolates and 26% had been sociable. Most patients were living with their immediate families. In those who were married, the marriages seemed fairly happy. Sexuality was normal in most of the men but in only 23% of the women. Only one case had had previous psychiatric treatment.

Differentiation from Other Syndromes

Agoraphobia

Social phobia can be regarded as a separate syndrome from agoraphobia. Despite some overlap, in three countries social phobics from psychiatric clinics differed from agoraphobics in many respects (Amies et al. 1983 in Great Britain; Persson & Nordlund 1985 in Sweden; Solyom et al. 1986 in Canada). Social phobics were younger when their problem began and when they sought treatment; were more often male, single, and of higher social class, education, and intelligence; and were more upwardly mobile. Their mothers worked outside the home less often. They had more dominant fathers and a more unsatisfactory relationship with them. Social phobics were also more "aggressively nonconforming" (which correlates with intelligence), and onset was more gradual and less often after a bereavement. Of Canadian social phobics, 48% cited precipitants, of which fewer were domestic and more were school and work problems than among agoraphobics. (More social phobics than agoraphobics also cited "fright" as a trigger, but this was not distinguished from the first sign of a phobia and thus could be tautologous). Both syndromes were equally fluctuant.

Although agoraphobics had quite a few social fears, social phobics had more fears of being introduced, meeting people in authority, visitors to the home, being watched doing something, being teased, eating at home with acquaintances or family, writing in front of others, and using the telephone. Social phobics scored higher on the Willoughby Personality Schedule of social anxieties (Turner et al. 1983). They also complained much more of blushing, used more alcohol, and had attempted suicide more.

Compared to agoraphobics, social phobics had fewer fears in general, especially those from the agoraphobic cluster (including less fear of leaving home, streets, buses, shops and supermarkets, crowds, cinemas, elevators, and heights). In addition, they has fewer specific phobias of some animals, deep water, and blood. Social phobics also had less sleep disturbance, weakness in limbs, breathing difficulty, dizziness or faintness, actual fainting, buzzing in the ears, depersonalization, or obsessive-compulsive (oc) ruminations or rituals.

General anxiety was as high in social phobics as agoraphobics in the Canadian sample (Solyom et al. 1986), but a bit less so in the British and Swedish studies (all found it higher than in specific phobics) (see Table 9.4). Canadian group differences on depression and social maladjustment were the same as for anxiety, although levels were low, and fewer social phobics than agoraphobics had sexual dysfunction.

Both syndromes had similar intensities of target phobias and fears of enclosed spaces, eating in restaurants, and drinking in coffee shops. They did not differ on panics, palpitations, vegetative and muscular tension and other somatic symptoms of anxiety, fatigue, irritability, emotional lability, introversion, defense of status, passive dependency, and neuroticism—the last two also being similar to those in anxious neurotics. Palpitations were as frequent as in other types of phobia (Hugdahl & Ost 1984). Unlike agoraphobics, Australian social phobics did not respond to hyperventilation or auditory tones by increased anxiety, skin conductance activity, or heart rate (Franklin 1985).

Social Dysfunction

Synonyms for social dysfunction are avoidant personality disorder (*DSM-III*), social inadequacy (Bryant et al. 1976; Curran et al. 1980), deficient social skills, and extreme shyness. Subjects have anxiety and difficulty in forming superficial or intimate relationships, although these are sought and desired (Greenberg & Stravynski 1985). Social phobias merge imperceptibly with social dysfunction; no formal comparison between them has been published, but it is worth examining features of the latter.

Forty-six subjects with social dysfunction and associated anxiety were compared with other anxiety disordered outpatients referred for behavioral psychotherapy at the Maudsley Hospital (Greenberg & Stravynski 1985). Their social dysfunction was "lifelong"; most (61%) had had no friends at school and had recognized their problem in their teens. They had difficulty in initiating and maintaining social interaction and friendships, especially with strange peers and the opposite sex; had few social activities apart from going to a bar; and found it hard to go to parties or dances. When with people, they feared ridicule or criticism, looking silly, losing control, or panicking, and they did not easily reveal their feelings. When subjects did talk, their talking tended to be at rather than with people, for too long, too much about themselves, unexpressive, monotonous, inappropriate, and with averted gaze (Bryant et al. 1976). Most of the latter's cases were depressed, and more were unemployed than in the general population. Over 60% of Maudsley cases had had past psychiatric treatment, especially for depression (35%) and for the social dysfunction (22%). In another sample, (of students), lack of assertion correlated with depression, low self-esteem, interpersonal anxiety, and fear of disapproval (Lefevre & West 1981).

Referrals for social dysfunction are largely single men. This may reflect

Western values that expect men to take the initiative, especially in courtship, and women to be more compliant. Compared with other outpatients, Maudsley cases of social dysfunction had a similar mean presenting age (34), but, like social phobics, superior social class and education. Three-quarters were living either alone or with their parents. Fifty-seven percent were virgin and most of the remainder had sexual difficulties—these may have contributed to referral. Many of the patients asked for sex therapy after social skills training made intimate relationships more likely.

Interestingly, more socially dysfunctional men (but not women) were only children or first-born. This was also found by Bryant and Trower (1974). Perhaps it is disadvantageous for males to have no older sibling as a social role model. Among ocs, too, first-born males predominate (Snowdon 1979).

Dysmorphophobia

The fear and avoidance shown by social phobics is largely distinct from that of dysmorphophobics, whose problem may also drive them to avoid social situations and live as a recluse. Dysmorphophobia is a persistent complaint of a specific bodily defect that is not noticeable to others (Morselli 1886); occasionally several parts of the body are involved. The fixity of the idea can amount to a delusion, and some cases have additional schizophrenic or organic features (Connolly & Gipson 1978; Hay 1970, 1983; Thomas 1984); others develop no other psychotic phenomena even after prolonged observation. Unlike anorexics, who are convinced that they are too fat, or transsexuals, who feel that their entire body is of the wrong sex, dysmorphophobics have no disturbance of the body image as a whole. In contrast to social phobics, dysmorphophobics do not think that their anxiety is silly, nor do they feel much better when away from social situations that they avoid; they are more preoccupied with a specific aspect of their body. Some cases are intermediate.

The gender ratio in the community is unclear. General practitioners in Britain tend to refer dysmorphophobic women to a surgeon and men to a psychiatrist (Hay 1970a). Minor worries about one's appearance are common in adolescence, and the morbid intensification called dysmorphophobia is usually seen in adolescence or young adult life; many cases have always been shy.

The following features of dysmorphophobia are based on reported cases and a series referred to the author's unit. Their complaint may be of the face, penis, breasts, or hips; of body or limbs being wrinkled, misshapen, or too large or small; or of bad odors coming from sweat in the axilla or from the breath, genitals, or rectum. Talking about the problem can evoke great anxiety. Sufferers may worry that others comment adversely about their appearance or smell and so avoid their company. They may be unable to look others in the eye and try to conceal the body part of which they are self-conscious, growing their hair or wearing a hat to conceal imagined baldness or misshapen ears, wearing dark glasses to hide the shape of their eyes, or avoiding swimming so that others will not see their body or genitals. Some will not look in mirrors because their reflection upsets them, or wash zealously to remove odor imperceptible to anyone else.

Many cases importune plastic surgeons to correct the supposed stigma, but cosmetic surgery is usually to no avail unless there is a visible minor deformity, in which case great benefit may result (Hay 1983; Thomas 1984). Problems other than the specific bodily preoccupation also persist afterward. Among patients who had rhinoplasty 15 years earlier, more of the 86 who had been operated on for aesthetic reasons were severely neurotic (32) or schizophrenic (6) than among the 101 who had been operated on for disease or injury (Connolly & Gipson 1978). Depression, too, is frequent; in a dermatology clinic it was more common among dysmorphophobics complaining of too little or too much hair or of skin blemishes than it was among cases of psoriasis or among normal controls (Hardy & Cotterill 1982). Occasional cases improve after antidepressants (Jenike 1985). Although exposure treatment is applicable to dysmorphophobics who avoid social situations, they often refuse it; if they accept, improvement tends to be slower than in social phobics.

The following case illustrates body odor as a central preoccupation leading to extreme social avoidance. The patient's personality was normal.

Dysmorphophobic Fear of Body Odor

A woman of 35 had for 16 years been worried that her sweat smelled terrible. The fear began just before her marriage when she was sharing a bed with a close friend who said that someone at work smelled badly, and the patient felt that the remark was directed at her. For fear that she smelled, for 5 years she had not gone out anywhere except when accompanied by her husband or mother. She had not spoken to her neighbors for 3 years because she thought she had overheard them speak about her to some friends. She avoided cinemas, dances, shops, cafes, and private homes. Occasionally she visited her in-laws, but she always sat at a distance from them. Her husband was not allowed to invite any friends home; she constantly sought reassurance from him about her smell; and strangers who rang the doorbell were not answered. Television commercials about deodorants made her very anxious. She refused to attend the local church because it was small and the local congregants might comment on her. The family had to travel to a church 8 miles away in which the congregants were strangers; there they sat or stood apart from the others. Her husband bought all her new clothes as she was afraid to try on clothes in front of shop assistants. She used vast quantities of deodorant and always bathed and changed her clothes before going out, up to 4 times daily.

At assessment she was timid, blushed often, and averted her gaze. She had prolonged exposure therapy involving gradually resuming social contact and ceasing to use deodorants or wash excessively. After 6 sessions of therapist-aided exposure and many months of self-exposure with the husband acting as cotherapist, she stopped avoiding social situations or averting her gaze, and the fear of body odor slowly faded. Gains were maintained to 1-year follow-up.

Other Conditions

Paranoid delusions may lead schizophrenics to shun company as much as social phobics do, but other psychotic features usually indicate the problem. Similarly, obsessive-compulsives can become housebound for fear that contact with situations outside will trigger rituals. The rituals make obvious what the trouble is.

SPECIFIC PHOBIAS

Specific (simple, focal) phobias are restricted to discrete situations and are not usually accompanied by the generalized anxiety, spontaneous panic, and depression that commonly trouble agoraphobics and, to a lesser degree, social phobics, nor do they have the psychophysiological concomitants (see Table 9.4). The term specific phobia is preferable to the *DSM-III* label of "simple phobia" because it draws attention to the focal nature of the problem without the misleading sense of mildness that "simple" implies. Particular specific phobic stimuli may generate extremely intense panic indistinguishable from that of agoraphobia, and the handicap may be extreme.

These focal phobias can involve virtually any situation, but in clinical practice the most common are fears of specific types of animals or insects, blood or injury, dental or medical procedures, urination or defecation in public toilets, heights, noise, thunder, storms or wind, darkness, flying, driving, enclosed places, eating particular foods, or sexual activity. Most kinds of specific phobia are more common in women, start at any age, and may endure for several decades. Animal phobias tend to start in early childhood, and blood, dental, and thunderstorm phobias before adolescence (Liddell & Lyons 1978; Öst 1986a). Some specific phobias have special features of interest that merit separate consideration, even though treatment of all of them follows common principles.

Animal Phobias

Animal phobias are isolated fears of animals or insects such as birds (or feathers), cats, dogs, frogs, spiders, moths, bees, and wasps. The most common in the clinic is fear of birds and spiders. Such phobias involve fear and avoidance of animals in their own right rather than a fear of contamination by them. (Contamination fears have different clinical correlates and are better regarded as an obsessive-compulsive disorder.)

As we saw in Chapter 7, fears of animals are a normal developmental feature of childhood, which arise between ages 2 and 4 and then subside. Few actual phobias of animals persist beyond puberty, but a residuum of fear may continue. Mild fears of snakes, spiders, mice, dogs, and other species are extremely common in the general population, with some variation in the species feared in different countries. Rarely are the fears strong enough to be called a phobia and to drive the subject to ask for help—they are uncommon in adult clinics. Many single case reports of animal phobia were noted by Marks (1969). A series of 23 cases from the Maudsley Hospital form the substance of this section.

Onset Age and Gender

In the great majority of adults who present with an animal phobia, the phobia dates back prior to ages 8 to 10 (Hugdahl & Öst 1985; Marks & Gelder 1966;

McNally & Steketee 1985). These phobics are the remnant of most of their generation who, as children, had been frightened of animals. The selective age at which animal phobias begin suggests a sensitive phase for their acquisition (see Chapter 8), and once this is safely passed, the mechanism that allowed them to develop seems to become dormant. Of the four patients in the Maudsley series with bird phobias, two also had agoraphobia and two had social anxieties. In each of these four patients, the bird phobias started in early childhood, whereas their other fears began after puberty. Similarly, two other patients who feared contamination from animals and so had handwashing rituals developed their fears and rituals in adult life. Maturation clearly affects when fears start, what is feared, and the form the fear takes.

Gender incidence is heavily female. Single case reports nearly all concern women, and the 23 Maudsley cases included only one man. Although in young children animal phobias are common in both sexes, by age 10 to 11 they are already much rarer in boys (Rutter et al. 1970).

Reasons for Seeking Treatment

Animal phobias in adults have generally been continuously present for decades since childhood. Why do these phobics come for treatment when they do? Intensity apart, several factors affect how disabling a phobia will be. First is the frequency of the relevant animals in the patient's neighborhood. Someone may cope easily where the animals are rare until he or she moves to another environment where they are plentiful. A spider-phobic woman managed well in a town flat, became anxious and sought help after she moved to a country cottage infested with spiders, and felt better again on moving to yet another home that was free of spiders. Another woman began treatment when she could not take up a residential art scholarship in an old, spider-infested hostel, and her career became jeopardized. A young woman moved from one town with few pigeons to another where they were ubiquitous; she had to ask for help when she became unable to walk to work through streets abounding with pigeons.

Other animal phobics attended on hearing for the first time that treatment had become available. Some came for fear of transmitting their phobia to their young children. A few brought different problems such as depression to the doctor, who then spotted the phobia and suggested that it be treated. Depression often magnifies pre-existing trouble and drives people to seek aid for it despite having previously tolerated it well. Finally, certain cases ask for treatment of a phobia in the silent hope that other problems they find hard to talk about will also be dealt with. An example is loneliness—social contact with a hospital might be as important in an empty life as relief of an isolated symptom. Given the same disability, lonely people seek medical aid more than do other patients (Mechanic 1962).

Mode of Onset

In adults the origins of animal phobias are usually lost in the mist of early childhood memories, but a few can be dated to specific incidents. A cat phobia began when one little girl watched her father drown some kittens, a dog phobia started after a dog bite, a bird phobia began after a child posing for a photograph in Trafalgar Square took fright as a bird alighted on her shoulder and she couldn't move—the resultant photograph preserved the record of the origin of her phobia. A feather phobia began when an infant strapped in a baby carriage was startled by a strange woman with a large feather in her hat bending down to look at the baby. (Why the ensuing phobia was of feathers, rather than of the prepotent stimulus of strangers, remains a mystery.)

Most animal phobias start in childhood with no convincing traumatic origin. Only 23% of a series ascribed the onset to "a frightening encounter with the animal," and the animal never inflicted pain (McNally & Steketee 1985). The authors did not specify whether such fear at the first encounter was of real threat or rather the first sign of a phobia's development. Young children appear prepared to acquire intense fears of animals with little or no cause (see Chapter 8). In contrast, the few animal phobias that start in adult life are usually precipitated by a relevant trauma such as a dog bite (Friedman 1966); adults seem to need the extra push of a nasty incident before a lasting fear can develop.

In most cases we know little more than did Freud (1913) about the onset:

> The child suddenly begins to fear a certain animal species and to protect itself against seeing or touching any individual of this species. . . . The phobia is as a rule expressed towards animals for which the child has until then shown the liveliest interest, and has nothing to do with the individual animal. In cities, the choice of animals which can become the object of phobia is not great. They are horses, dogs, cats, more seldom birds, and strikingly often very small animals like bugs and butterflies. Sometimes animals which are known to the child only from picture books and fairy stories become objects of the senseless and inordinate anxiety which is manifest in these phobias. It is seldom possible to learn the manner in which such an unusual choice of anxiety has been brought about.

In children, fears of animals remit quickly without any apparent reason or because everyday activities expose them to the animals long enough for habituation to set in. The fears may be stamped in through repeated, brief, teasing exposures of the feared object by other children. We do not know why a small proportion continues after puberty.

Clinical Picture

The subject complains of a long-standing, stable phobia of an animal or insect, and usually there are few other problems such as depression or generalized anxiety (see Chapter 9 and Table 9.4). Practically any animal or insect may be involved. Maudsley cases included 10 phobias of birds and feathers—pigeons were especially feared, whereas smaller birds such as canaries could be tolerated more easily. Six phobias were of spiders, two of dogs, and one each of cats, worms, and frogs. A Philadelphia series included 10 snake, 4 cat, 4 bird, 2 dog, and 2 spider phobics (McNally & Steketee 1985).

Sudden movement of the species evokes particularly intense fear—the fluttering of birds' wings, scurrying of spiders, or jumping up of dogs or cats.

(Along with other species, humans are programmed to perceive and react to movement very sensitively [see Chapter 2]). Patients with fears of one kind of animal rarely feared other dissimilar species. Seven patients had additional minor fears—two of these patients had social fears sufficiently intense to prevent them from eating in restaurants, and two had agoraphobia.

The degree of handicap caused by the phobia varies with its intensity and the prevalence of the species involved. In mild cases the phobia is a nuisance rather than a disability. A woman living in the country could not go near ponds containing frogs or look at pictures of frogs in books, and phobia of locusts prevented an archaeologist from going on digs in countries where locusts were common. With intense phobias of ubiquitous animals the distress can be great and sustained, as in a bird-phobic woman who could not go to work through the streets of London and so gave up her job and remained indoors all day, only venturing out at night when pigeons no longer flew about.

Although a focal phobia might seem a trivial problem, contact with the phobic object may induce striking distress, panic, sweating, trembling, and terror that may wake a patient from a deep hypnotic trance. The panic subsides when the phobic stimulus is removed. A spider-phobic woman screamed when she found a spider at home, ran away to find a neighbor to remove it, trembled in fear, and had to keep the neighbor at her side for two hours before she could remain alone at home again; another spider-phobic found herself on top of the refrigerator in the kitchen with no recollection of getting there. A third threw herself off a galloping horse when an arachnid fell on her off a tree branch. Yet another, who could not swim, jumped out of a boat into the sea to escape a spider.

The disproportion between the real danger and the intensity of a phobia is highlighted when the stimuli are as innocuous as butterflies or moths. A woman who was phobic of them had to keep her windows tightly shut at home in summer and several times had to leave buses and trains on discovering butterflies or moths in them. Her phobia caused several accidents. When riding a bicycle she saw a butterfly and fell off, bringing down her friends riding behind her. Twice she fell backward into a stream when avoiding large butterflies flying across her path. Another time she stood on a chair to clean a wardrobe, by mistake picked up a large dead moth, fell off the chair in surprised fear and sprained her ankle. She could never enter a room containing butterflies or moths and always checked for their absence before entering. The fear did not extend to earwigs, stag beetles, furry caterpillars, or spiders—"I'd rather deal with a boxful of black widow spiders than one large English moth," she insisted.

By far the majority of animal phobics expect on encountering their feared animal to panic or to experience dire consequences of panic such as going insane, having a heart attack, acute embarrassment, or accidental injury while fleeing (McNally & Steketee 1985). Only a minority believe that the animal will hurt them.

Patients search for the feared animal wherever they go. The slightest hint of its presence will disturb them where the average person would not notice it. Some are plagued by recurrent nightmares of the animals they fear. They dream that they are surrounded by large spiders or swooping birds from which they cannot escape. Signs of improvement during treatment are diminished awareness of the creatures in the environment and disappearance of nightmares about them.

Dog Phobia with Depression of Independent Cause

A married woman 24 years old had at age 18 months been bitten and dragged from the room by a German shepherd; since then she had always run away from dogs. If a dog was loose in the street she had to cross the road to go the other way, and this would make her late for appointments. She could not go alone on walks for fear of meeting dogs. She came in for treatment of the phobia, as she was afraid of passing it on to her young infant. She felt neglected by her husband and when referred was having an affair. Shortly after she began treatment by exposure in fantasy, her lover broke off the relationship. She became severely depressed and made a suicidal gesture. The dog phobia continued through these events.

Family, Personality, and Background

Animal phobics tend to come from stable families with few relatives fearing animals (Marks 1969). Only three (15%) had first-degree relatives with the same phobia as the patient. One of these three transmitted the fear to her daughter, who then reinforced her own fear; they both came in for treatment. Twenty percent had nervous mothers.

Half the cases had been fearful or shy, or had cried often as children. Their school and work history was unremarkable. There was wide variation in personality and sexual adjustment. Most were married and living with their families. Twenty-eight percent had had previous psychiatric treatment for their phobias before coming in for treatment, for depression, anorgasmia, aggressive outbursts, phobias, and blepharospasm, and one patient had had hysterical paraplegia without psychiatric treatment.

Blood-Injury Phobias

Humans tend to be squeamish at the sight of blood, injury, or gross deformity—a natural propensity similar to the alarm of many species when conspecifics are hurt (see Chapter 2), and which contributes to the stigma borne by deformed and ill people. As an example, a kidney patient who had to spend 2 days a week in bed attached to a dialysis machine was told by his Municipal Council to draw the curtains of his sick room or to fit frosted glass to the window to spare the distress felt by neighbors on witnessing the dialysis scene (*The Guardian,* February 23, 1983). This queasiness can be unlearned. Medical students steel themselves to overcome unease at the sight of autopsies, wounds, and surgery, and soldiers are taught to ignore the horrors of war.

Mild fear of blood is common in children (44% of 6- to 8-year-olds and 27% of 9- to 12-year-olds—Lapouse & Monk 1959) and in adults. Intense fear is less frequent, amounting to a phobia in 2% to 3% of children and adults, and constituting one of the most common phobias in adults in the community (Agras et al. 1969; Miller et al. 1974; Yule & Fernando 1980). Both the mild fear and severe phobias are seen more often in females than in males (Öst et al. 1984; Yule & Fernando 1980). Most blood phobics are married, and work status is unremarkable. General anxiety is infrequent (Öst & Hugdahl 1985).

Like phobias of animals, those of blood and injury in adults usually date back to early childhood in most published cases. In a large series, mean onset age was 7 years even though mean age at presentation for treatment was 31 (Öst et al. 1984). This may be another instance of selective learning at a particular age (see Chapter 8), although it is hard to guess why late acquisition is so rare.

When the natural mild fear of blood or injury is magnified to phobic severity, it can lead to substantial handicap. Sufferers may avoid essential medical procedures, preferring to endure remediable disease even if it threatens life. They avoid otherwise attractive careers as doctors or nurses. Women may also avoid becoming pregnant because it and childbirth are associated with blood and medical examinations and procedures.

Several features are peculiar to blood-injury phobics: diphasic cardiovascular response with fainting, nausea without fear, and a strong family history. These are discussed in turn below.

Diphasic Cardiovascular Response with Fainting

In most phobics, heart rate goes up on encountering the dreaded object and stays up persistently until gradual habituation sets in, if exposure continues over the next 20 to 60 minutes; actual fainting is rare even though feelings of faintness are common, especially in agoraphobics. Blood-injury stimuli, however, set a different and diphasic sequence in train; initial sympathetic activity is soon overtaken by vagal inhibition.

At first there may be a transient, slight rise in heart rate and blood pressure. Within a few seconds or minutes this is followed by marked vasovagal slowing of heart rate (Öst et al. 1984a), perhaps to the point of brief asystole. Blood pressure drops; there is nausea, sweating, and pallor; and the subject may faint. Vasovagal bradycardia may not occur if the blood-injury stimuli are seen for only 10 seconds or less (Prigatano & Johnston 1974)—the slowing takes up to 4 minutes to develop (Öst 1986). In contrast to their diphasic reaction to blood-injury stimuli, these phobics have a normal tachycardia in response to stress such as mental arithmetic or the Stroop color-word test (Öst 1986b). Like blood-injury phobics, normals also show vagal inhibition to blood-injury stimuli despite sympathetic activation such as raised adrenalin, noradrenalin, and free fatty acids, and a fall in triglycerides; a concurrent drop in glucagon was attributed to parasympathetic activity (Carruthers & Taggart 1973). Blood-injury phobics differ from normals in degree, not type, of cardiovascular reaction to blood or injury (Öst 1986).

The vasovagal response often leads to fainting. Unlike other phobics, those who fear blood, injury, or injections actually faint, often repeatedly, at the sight or mention of their phobic stimulus (Cohn et al. 1976; Connolly et al. 1976;

Curtis & Thyer 1983; Horne & McCormack 1984; Marks et al. 1977; Marks 1978, 1981; Nimmer & Kapp 1974; Öst et al. 1984a; Wardle & Jarvis 1981). Some can defer the faint slightly until it is safer to fall down (certain epileptics, too, can delay their fit). Other phobics seem to lack this autonomic specificity of blood phobics (Connolly et al. 1976); they may faint in hot, overcrowded situations but are not prone to faint at the sight of blood.

In blood-injury phobics, fainting may precipitate focal or generalized seizures (Schraeder et al. 1983). A 21-year-old student fainted in church while listening to a reading of suffering from Fox's *Book of Martyrs;* rhythmic contractions of his right arm were followed by generalized tonic-clonic activity and urinary incontinence. Several prior episodes of unconsciousness were related to the sight of blood or description of cardiac catheterization. His parents and sister reported frequent syncope induced by pain or the sight of blood, but without seizures. While again listening to the offending passage during EEG and ECG monitoring, he had 25 seconds of asystole ending in EEG silence and another fit. Ambulatory monitoring revealed episodes of progressive sinus bradycardia with PR-interval prolongation and Wenckebach atrioventricular block. A ventricular pacemaker was implanted, and there were no further symptoms over a 1-year follow-up.

The fainting of blood-injury phobics echoes that of blood donors, dental patients, and audiences of violent films, whose heart rate may briefly rise and then drop persistently (Averill et al. 1972; Melamed 1982; Öst et el. 1984a). In a series of blood donors 15% either fainted or looked faint (Graham 1961). Even medical audiences had a modest bradycardia when viewing violent films (Carruthers & Taggart 1973). Twelve percent of blood donors who fainted also had some type of convulsive movement, usually a brief spasm; generalized tonic-clonic activity was rare (Lin et al. 1982). Whether needle phobics usually faint is unclear.

Perhaps reflex fainting to blood-injury cues is related in evolution to the "emotional bradycardia" of grouse on freezing when approached (Gabrielsen et al. 1977) and during tonic immobility in many species (see Chapter 3). It could be an adaptive response evolved in circumstances where immobility produced less risk of further injury than did flight. However, if vasovagal stimulation induces asystole that is too prolonged, the subject may die. This could be one mechanism of sudden death from voodoo spells and under other emotional circumstances (reviewed by Comfort 1981; Lown 1982; Schraeder et al. 1983; see also Chapter 3). Dropping dead from startle or fright can be familial and associated with syncope (Engel 1978), as is the fainting of blood-injury phobics. Severe asystole and EEG silence can even be induced voluntarily (Kothari et al. 1973).

A consequence of the cardiovascular response of blood-injury phobics is that during treatment by prolonged exposure, their heart rate is normalized by increasing, not decreasing, to baseline (Figure 11.1). Early in exposure, heart rate often drops to 30 to 40 beats per minute or even zero. Figure 11.2 shows asystole over 20 seconds in one case. Fainting from a drop in blood pressure may be prevented by lying down (Connolly et al. 1976; Lloyd & Deakin 1975; Marks et al. 1972), tensing the muscles (Kozak & Montgomery 1981; Öst et al.

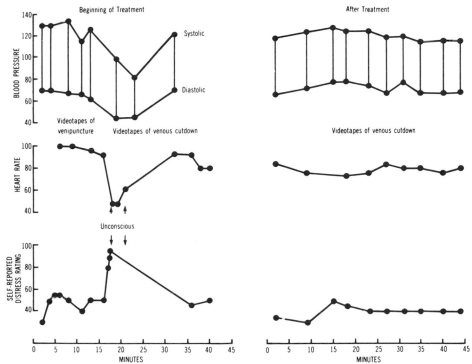

Physiologic and Subjective Recordings for Mr. A

Fig. 11.1 Heart rate, blood pressure, and subjective distress at the start of exposure treatment of a blood phobic. After initial tachycardia, heart rate slowing and hypotension began about 7 minutes after starting to watch a videotape of a venepuncture, with subjective distress and fainting about 5 minutes later; within 20 minutes heart rate and blood pressure had returned to normal. After 11 hours of exposure plus additional self-exposure homework over 2½ months, blood-injury stimuli ceased to evoke fainting. The patient was a 37-year-old biological research worker. His anxiety and faintness at the sight or description of blood and medical procedures dated to age 12 and threatened his work. His father and son had a similar problem. (From Curtis & Thyer 1983. Copyright © 1983 by the American Psychiatric Association. Reprinted by permission.)

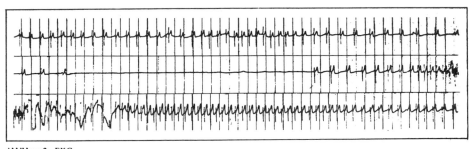

Abbildung 3 EKG

Fig. 11.2 ECG of a blood phobic during exposure shows asystole for about 25 seconds, followed by compensatory tachycardia and then normal heart rate. The patient was a 25-year-old man who since age 7 had fainted regularly during injections or venepuncture. Fainting ceased after he was treated by exposure in vivo in 4 sessions over 2 weeks during which 24 blood samples were taken. (From Hand & Schröder 1976. Copyright © 1976 by G. Braun Verlag. Reprinted by permission.)

1984a), or inducing other feelings, such as anger (Figure 11.3). Relaxation may actually increase fainting by reducing the blood pressure still further.

Nausea Without Fear

A second feature of blood-injury phobics is that contact with their phobic stimuli may trigger more nausea and faintness than fear or anxiety. They may avoid blood-injury stimuli more to avert fainting than fear, although anticipation of a faint can cause anxiety. Sufferers have an exaggerated physiological reflex that literally makes them "sick at heart" on seeing blood. Although nausea is usual from vasovagal stimulation, vomiting is exceptional. One patient of the author's distinguished his nausea on seeing blood from that felt with vomiting.

Strong Family History

A third difference between blood-injury and other phobics is that the former have more relatives with a similar problem (Connolly et al. 1976; Marks 1981;

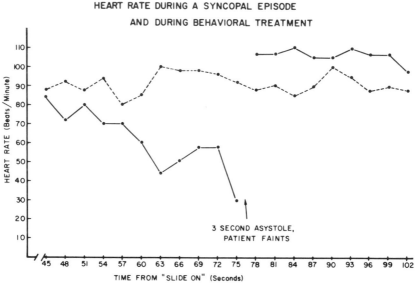

Fig. 11.3 Fainting and its subsequent prevention during the first exposure session in a blood-phobic man. After initial exposure to a slide of a mutilated body, heart rate slowed at 54 seconds, with 3 seconds of asystole at 75 seconds, when the patient fainted; heart rate resumed at 100 beats per minute (----). Further bradycardia or syncope during the continuing exposure session were prevented by the patient's being deliberately angered in role-play with the therapist role-playing his father and criticizing him. The subject was a 28-year-old premedical student with blood-injury phobia and repeated fainting since age 4. He improved much less during exposure while relaxed than while having concurrent self-induced angry feelings about various situations that were role-played with the therapist. Over 4 weeks of self-exposure the angry feelings were faded out, followed by work as a volunteer in a hospital emergency room. At 6-month follow-up he was free of symptoms. (From Cohn et al. 1976. Copyright © 1976 by the Williams & Wilkin's Co. Baltimore. Reprinted by permission.)

Yule & Fernando 1980). Among blood-injury phobics 68% had biological relatives who were blood phobic (Öst et al. 1984b), a rate 3 to 6 times higher than the frequency of corresponding phobias in the families of agora-, social, dental, or animal phobics (Marks 1969; Marks & Herst 1970; Öst & Hugdahl 1984; see also Chapter 5). The concordance of blood-injury-illness phobias was higher among MZ than among DZ twins (Torgersen 1979).

This strong family history suggests that blood-injury phobias may originate in a genetically determined, extreme autonomic response. The degree of bradycardic response to blood or injury may be normally distributed in the population for genetic reasons (just as are height, intelligence, and many other features under partial polygenetic control). Presumably only those few who have an extreme bradycardic response faint readily and are thus liable to develop the phobia. This would yield a blood-phobic population with a strong family history, as is found. The bradycardic response is probably present from an early age, as most blood-injury phobias start in childhood. It remains to be shown that relatives not only faint frequently but also have an extreme bradycardic response to blood or injury.

Perhaps other phobias, too, may be partly initiated on the basis of other autonomic specificities under genetic and/or environmental influence. For example, when anxious, those with labile blood flow in the cheeks might blush more readily than others and so be liable to become phobic about blushing; those with undue gastric motility might when anxious vomit easily after eating and thus be prone to develop a phobia about that. It is also possible that blushing is an autonomic response specifically tied to social cues in the same way that bradycardia with fainting seems linked to blood-injury stimuli, so that blushers would become phobic of social rather than of other situations.

Case History of Blood Phobia

A 29-year-old woman had since age 4 fainted at the sight of blood or injury, or even when hearing the subject discussed. She was unable to fulfill her ambition to become a teacher lest she fainted while dealing with children's cuts as part of her work, and she avoided violent films and plays. She became ashamed of her problem and determined to overcome it after she fainted in a hospital emergency room with her son sitting on her lap while his scalded foot was being dressed. Treatment was by exposure to scenes of blood and injury; her fainting was prevented by her lying down during the first few sessions. She became able to deal with injuries to her children and to have her varicose veins injected; by 1-year follow-up she had enrolled in a first-aid class, begun a teacher-training course, and been to films and plays depicting blood and injury.

Phobias of Dentistry

Fears of Having Dental Work

Fear of dental procedures has an honorable history, as has its treatment by the modeling of exposure:

It was in the Month of December 1578, when she was excessively tormented with that Distemper [toothache] that she [Queen Elizabeth] had no Intermission day nor

Night, and it forced her to pass whole Nights without taking any Rest; and came to that Extremity, that her Physicians were called in and consulted. . . . The pulling it out was esteemed by all as the safest way; to which, however, the Queen, as was said, was very averse, as afraid of the acute Pain that accompanied it. And now it seems it was that the Bishop of London being present, a Man of high Courage, persuaded her that the pain was not so much, and not at all to be dreaded; and to convince her thereof told her, she should have a sensible Experiment of it in himself, though he were an old Man, and had not many Teeth to spare; and immediately had the Surgeon come and pull out one of his Teeth, perhaps a decayed one, in her Majestie's Presence. Which accordingly was don: and She was hereby encouraged to submit to the Operation herself. (John Strype's *Life of Bishop Aylmer*, cited by Wilson 1954)

Such drastic measures are fortunately not usually needed to help dental fear, a subject well reviewed by Lindsay (1983). The problem is pervasive. In a representative sample of 900 adults in a small Dutch town, extreme anxiety about dentistry was noted by 20% of regular attenders and 32% of irregular attenders (Schuurs et al. cited by Lindsay 1983). In a representative sample of 784 women in Gothenburg, Sweden, from 38 to 54 years old, point prevalence of dentistry phobia was 13% (intense phobias in 4%); prevalence was higher in women with less education and from a lower social class (Hallstrom & Halling 1984). Most people have at least mild dental fear, and about 40% of adults delay or avoid visits to the dentist unless they are in trouble, but only some 5% have dental phobia (Gale & Ayer 1969; Kleinknecht et al. 1973). Onset age tends to be in childhood and adolescence (Mathews & Rezin 1976); mean age was 12 in a Swedish series (Hugdahl & Öst 1984). Females present with the problem rather more than do males (Kleinknecht et al. 1973; Lautch 1971; Sermet 1974; Wardle 1982).

Fear in children leads to disruptive behavior in a dental surgery, and adults may shun dentists totally, allowing mild caries to progress to severe pathology. Avoidance of dental treatment through fear has led men to refuse army service and to enlisted men being court-martialed (Borland 1962). Dental phobics especially fear the injection needle and the drill, and respond to them with muscle tension rather than nausea (Kleinknecht et al. 1973); this is somewhat surprising for discomfort of oral origin and distinguishes dental fear from the separate problem of hypersensitivity of the gag reflex. Most people are slightly uncomfortable during dental treatment, but much less so than they expect to be (Lindsay 1983).

Anxiety may increase sensitivity to pain. Those fearful of dentistry expect more pain beforehand than they actually experience during it (Kent 1984; Wardle 1984). They anticipate more pain from dental procedures than do nonphobics (Wardle 1982) but have similar pain tolerance during them. Nevertheless, they have a lower pain threshold (Lautch 1971) or a similar threshold but more pain (Klepac et al. 1980) with an electric current applied to an incisor but not to an arm. Pain habituates with continual tolerable stimulation of the tooth pulp; but the episodic, infrequent, and brief nature of the discomfort that is usual during dental procedures probably minimizes habituation (Lindsay 1983). Continual mild electrical stimulation enabled two severely nervous dental patients to accept dental treatment (Klepac 1975).

The fear can depend on particular cues. One young woman fainted every time a session began in the chair as long as her dentist wore a white coat; when once he wore a business suit instead, this did not happen, although she fainted again at the next session, which he conducted in a white coat. From then on the dentist wore a sports shirt during her treatment, and the fainting stopped. The patient then disclosed nightmares concerning a childhood tonsillectomy and memories of the white uniforms of doctors and nurses (Borland 1962).

Although dental phobia frequently occurs on its own, it is often associated with fears of blood, injury, and hospitals. Compared with controls, dental phobics have more unfavorable attitudes to doctors, out- and inpatient treatment, emotional disorders and tranquillizers; more neurotic and introverted scores on the EPI; and as children had more dislike of and poorer progress at school. Not surprisingly, they also have more dental pathology (Sermet 1974, Shaw 1975, Lautch 1971). In addition, dental phobics give a history of more past dental trauma (but this may be a phobic interpretation of experiences that to others might seem unremarkable, and many were anxious during dentistry from the start), and of more parents who dislike dentistry and had extractions under general anesthesia (Lindsay 1983; Shoben & Borland 1954).

Few physiological features have been reported. As occurs also at the sight of blood, heart rate may drop during dental procedures in naive subjects (Melamed 1982), and fainting is not rare; its frequency diminishes when the dentist is reassuring and gradual in his approach (C. Wilks, personal communication, 1985). Plasma adrenalin is higher in dental phobics than in controls before and during dentistry (Edmondson et al. 1972).

Dental phobics present special problems in treatment because it takes time, empathy, and good communication to arrange acceptable grading of exposure that allows patients to get used to the procedures without rushing out of the surgery in terror. If the fee is for each item of service, then a gradual approach means loss of income for the dentist. Treatment is easier if the dentist regards the fear as part of the professional problem he or she has to deal with rather than as an annoying obstacle standing in his or her way (Borland 1962). It can be helpful for the patient to have some control over stopping the dental drill by prearranged hand signals to the dentist or by pressing a cut-off switch on the armrest of the dental chair. When a switch was available nearly every patient used it to stop the drilling once or twice during the first few minutes of drilling, but hardly ever thereafter.

Suitable education can reduce normal dental fears (see Chapter 15). Children are helped by preexposure—playing in a dental office and meeting the dentist first without having treatment (Lindsay & Busch 1981). Peer modeling can be useful and is economically achieved with videos. Compared with controls, young children had less fear and disruptive behavior during dentistry if they had just seen a 10-to-13 minute video of a peer coping with anxiety during dentistry and being rewarded for cooperation (Melamed et al. 1975a, 1975b). There was some sensitization on seeing a brief (4-minute) demonstration of injection and examination without a child in the chair (Melamed et al. 1978). Cooperation rose with clear instructions and feedback, and fell if the dentist criticized a child's appropriate behavior but ignored it if the child cooperated (Melamed et al. 1983).

Hypersensitivity of the Gag Reflex

Dentists meet the problem of gagging often. It does not involve fear of dentistry or pain. Rather, it is an exaggeration of the normal protective gag reflex of the oropharynx, which we all experience on sticking a finger inside our mouth sufficiently far back near the soft palate. When this reflex becomes hypersensitive the stimuli triggering it widen to include foreign objects in the mouth so that dentistry cannot be tolerated, nor can very minor pressure on the neck. Severe cases may gag, retch, and get tears even on feeling, hearing, smelling, or thinking about dentistry or related stimuli. The subject may be unable to brush his teeth, button his collar, or have his mouth, face, neck, or shoulder touched without provoking gagging, and the triggers may spread to smells or sights vaguely associated with unpleasant oral experiences. Oral pain or irritants such as a post-nasal drip may worsen the problem.

An example of such intense gagging was seen by the author in a man of 20 who had the problem since age 6. He became unable to wear high-necked sweaters, which restricted his job opportunities. He would gag even while dictating letters on the phone, especially to strangers; on gagging he couldn't open his mouth or speak. Sucking candies helped but rotted his teeth. He was on the waiting list for dental treatment under an anesthetic. He couldn't say "aaahh" during a medical examination, would gag if he had injections in the upper arm but not elsewhere, and might suddenly clam up when ordering a meal or movie tickets. He had dreams of being choked and could not stand being under bedclothes. At interview he looked relaxed but took a candy to suck before speaking. He could not stick his tongue out beyond his teeth nor open his mouth widely. He wore an open-necked shirt, and on trying to close his collar at my request he had to stop speaking. If he or I touched his neck his eyes watered and he gagged intensely.

Many of the cases are male and date back to childhood, as in two of the three cases described by Wilks & Marks (1983). In later life oral trauma can trigger gagging, as in a middle-aged truck driver seen by the author in the Middle East. His problem began immediately after he was severely beaten in the face by soldiers, losing most of his teeth. His gagging was so intense that he could not eat solid foods, only liquids, and so he lost much weight.

Both hypersensitive gagging and vasovagal fainting at the sight of blood are exaggerations of normal reflexes that are mediated through the medulla, and fear may be absent in either problem. Both can be treated successfully by exposure. Hypersensitive gaggers learn to tolerate foreign objects in their mouth by keeping marbles or buttons in the mouth for extended periods every day, starting with single small ones and increasing their size and number as tolerance develops, and by prolonged brushing of the teeth. Because gagging is worsened by the habit that gaggers have of swallowing tensely with pursed lips, clenched teeth, and the tongue thrust forward against them, they are taught to swallow with the teeth slightly apart and the tongue relaxed on the floor of the mouth. Dental procedures begin with the therapist gently and repeatedly stroking the front of the tongue until there is habituation, which may take up to half an hour or longer, and then doing the same further back. Slowly the patient will become able to tolerate simple dental procedures such as examination, cleaning and scaling, after which the dentist may progress as needed to drilling, filling, or extraction of teeth, or taking impressions to construct dentures. At every point the patient is in control of what is done and tells the dentist when to stop by raising a hand. As treatment progresses, patients may become more aware of the precise triggers of their gagging, and the enlarged trigger area steadily shrinks to normal.

A Case of Gagging

A 31-year-old man was referred for inability to accept dental treatment because of gagging, which had begun 10 years earlier on starting conservative dental treatment (Wilks & Marks 1983). It worsened progressively so that he could not tolerate fillings or the construction of partial dentures, and eventually not even a dental examination. He became unable to button up the top of his shirt or to wear a tie. Heat, heavy perfumes, and the smell of frying fish made him retch and want to vomit. He could not clean his teeth in the morning when he had smoker's catarrh, only later in the day when the drip ceased.

Treatment included cutting down his smoking to reduce the drip, and prolonged graded exposure. His tongue was stroked repeatedly and lengthily, first at the tip and then further back, and between sessions he had to daily hold beads and buttons in his mouth for several minutes, to brush his teeth with a toothbrush gradually progressing to the back teeth, to button the top buttons of his shirt, and to wear his tie first loosely and then more tightly. Over 9 sessions the patient became able to tolerate dental procedures and dentures, and was wearing these without discomfort at 12 months' follow-up.

Phobias of Doing Dental Work

Not only dental patients but dentists too can become phobic of dentistry, in this case of carrying it out, and may give up their profession because of this fear. Exposure of the dentist to progressively more difficult activities is not easy to arrange. The following case shows how this was achieved over 17 sessions with the help of another dentist and of the patient's wife as cotherapist (Marks & Wilks 1979).

Dental Phobia of a Dentist

A general dental practitioner 43 years old had a 4-year phobia of dentistry and associated depression, and had stopped working 10 months previously. He had become a dentist because it was expected of him, but he did not resent this. In 1968, 2 years after the death of his father (who had also been a dentist), the patient came under heavy work and financial pressure. In 1973 he was put on methyldopa for hypertension and became dizzy when bending over patients. The next year he sold his practice, ceased working for 3 months, and then held several dental posts carrying out limited procedures. Each time he resumed dentistry he felt anxious and depressed and had headaches, yet he still wished to practice and continued to read dental journals.

At interview in 1977 he was mildly depressed, and twice when speaking about his father's death cried and changed the subject. Over two sessions of guided mourning in which he was encouraged to speak and write about his father's death

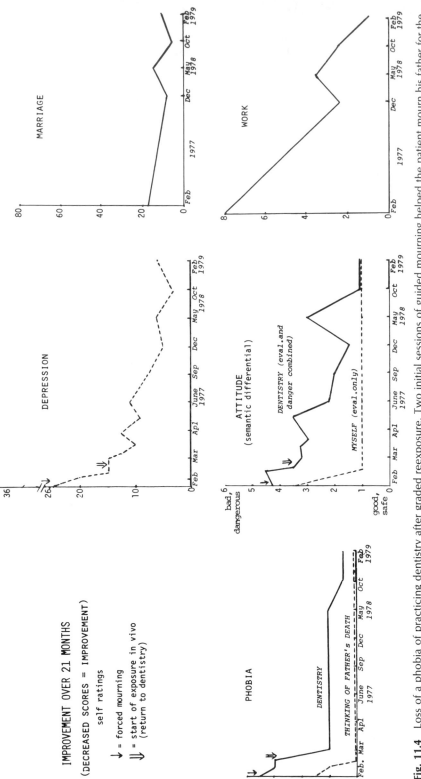

Fig. 11.4 Loss of a phobia of practicing dentistry after graded reexposure. Two initial sessions of guided mourning helped the patient mourn his father for the first time after his death 9 years previously, and to lessen his depression, but did not change his phobia. Subsequent graded reexposure to dentistry with careful pacing of the workload improved the phobia, and the patient resumed dentistry, continuing to work full-time at 4 years' follow-up. (Adapted from Marks & Wilks 1979.)

at length, he became comfortable talking about it, but his fear of practicing dentistry hardly changed (Figure 11.4). Treatment now focused on his gradually returning to dentistry for slowly increasing lengths of time. First he worked as a locum while carefully pacing his workload so that it did not incur undue stress; his wife monitored the load by working as his receptionist and became his financial manager to reduce his concern about money. Gradually the length and number of sessions were increased and frequency of consultation was faded out. He began to work full-time after 7 months' treatment and was maintaining this without undue stress at 8-year follow-up. Mood was normal and the marriage remained stable (Figure 11.4).

Eating Phobias

Eating phobias assume two distinct forms. One overlaps with hypersensitivity of the gag reflex, which was described earlier. This is a phobia of swallowing due to a fear of choking. The problem is precipitated by any food, not a particular taste or odor. It may be greater for solids than for liquids, so that sufferers might be able to swallow only liquids or, at best, only mushlike baby food. Severe weight loss may occur. The difficulty is a gross exaggeration of the dry mouth and lump in the throat that occur normally with everyday fear. (A test of witchcraft in many cultures was to ask the suspect to put a pebble in the mouth; if it was dry on being taken out, this signified fear and thus guilt of the suspect.) Fear of choking may occur on its own or be associated with agoraphobia and severe generalized anxiety, in which case it has been called "globus hystericus." Treatment is by graded exposure to increasingly solid foods, progressing from liquids to mush to solids and ending with dry toast.

The problem was described by a woman of 49: "Since I've been a child I've had this stupid phobia of swallowing. Whenever I drink or eat the muscles of my throat go into spasm and I make this crowing noise, my eyes water, and I get a terrible panic." This happened whether she was eating alone or with other people, and it so embarrassed her that she often would not eat out, which hampered her job in public relations. She thought she had acquired the problem after watching her mother, whose stridulous noises while eating in front of others had often embarrassed her.

The second type of eating phobia is very different. This is food aversion; some of its features across species were reviewed in Chapter 2. Minor forms are called food fads. Religious taboos proscribe meat for Hindus and pork for Muslims and Jews. If religious people eat their forbidden food by mistake or coercion, they may vomit or feel nauseous for days. (In his autobiography Mahatma Gandhi, a vegetarian, described this reaction after eating meat.)

Unlike phobias of swallowing, food aversions involve restricted types of food. The nausea, retching, and perhaps vomiting that occurs on contact with the avoided food contrasts with the experience of anxiety that is triggered by most phobic stimuli. Food aversions usually start in childhood or adolescence (Garb & Stunkard 1974; Logue et al. 1981) unless there is a clear-cut conditioning experience, as occurs commonly in cancer clinics, many of whose patients develop a conditioned aversion to odors preceding or accompanying chemotherapy. Its development might be reduced by minimizing the presence of distinctive odors in chemotherapy clinics (Nesse et al. 1980). The problem rarely presents in mental health care. In the author's clinic, food aversions have usually concerned meat or greasy foods. The problem is overcome by using the exposure approach. If the hitherto avoided food is eaten repeatedly, the nausea gradually disappears just as does the anxiety with other phobias on prolonged exposure to the relevant stimulus.

Sphincteric Phobias

Some people are afraid or unable to urinate (urinary retention) when others are nearby so that they waste much time at work and socially waiting for everyone else to leave the toilet before they can perform, and may totally avoid urinating in toilets outside the home. The difficulty disappears if they are certain that no one else is around or likely to come, and in that respect is like a social phobia. They worry that someone might knock on the toilet door or see or hear them urinating or be waiting impatiently outside.

Other phobics have the opposite problem of too frequent urination or defecation outside their home, so they run to the lavatory dozens of times a day and avoid places where a toilet is not within easy reach for fear of wetting or soiling themselves. Fears about urination are more frequent than those about defecation; concern may be about only one or the other, or both, and may not involve sexual function. Sphincteric phobias can greatly limit social activity, prevent people from going away on vacations, and even determine their choice of job or career according to the ease of access it allows to a toilet, which has to be a private one in cases of retention.

Although such problems are not uncommon in the clinic, the literature about them is limited to case reports. Those of urinary retention reported treatment by psychotherapy (Chapman 1959; Wahl & Golden 1963; Williams & Johnson 1956), carbachol (Cooper 1965), aversion and assertive training (Barnard et al. 1966), hypnosis (Knowles 1964), and variants of exposure (Elliott 1967; Glasgow 1975; Lamontagne & Marks 1973; Poole & Yates 1975; Ray & Morphy 1975; Wilson 1973). Those of urinary frequency used forms of exposure (Jones 1956; Poole & Yates 1975), including paradox (Timms 1985).

Phobia of Urinating Away from Home

A woman of 50 had for 30 years not been able to pass urine outside her own home, retaining urine for up to 48 hours if necessary. She avoided visiting friends on weekends. Nevertheless she could defecate in a public toilet and had normal sexual relations. Before attending exposure treatment sessions, which were held in midafternoon, she was asked not to urinate at all beforehand that day, and to drink 5 cups of coffee. Exposure consisted of sending her thus primed into the hospital toilet and telling her that she could not leave until she had passed urine, no matter how long it took. In the first sessions the therapist waited far away, and as she got used to this he gradually moved nearer and spoke to somebody outside. At first she took fully two hours to pass a few dribbles, but gradually she voided larger amounts more quickly, until by session 12 she passed two liters almost immediately, showing the tremendous storage capacity her bladder had developed over the years. At first she had no desire to urinate outside her home even when her bladder was greatly distended, but as treatment went on the urge to void appeared; she became able to do so in public toilets and in the home of a friend. After this she confessed her problem to her friend for the first time. At a year's follow-up she continued to void in public toilets without trouble but still had problems in one near her work that had not been involved in treatment. Figure 11.5 shows her (Miss A's) increasing ability to void quickly and in larger amounts, with steady reduction in the amount of residual urine. It also shows similar improvement in another patient (Mr. B) treated in the same way (Lamontagne & Marks 1973).

A variant of exposure was described in a man who was unable to urinate or defecate in toilets outside his home (Wilson 1973). Desensitization in fantasy produced no real-life improvement. He was then asked to urinate in "safe" conditions alone, but just at the moment when urination became inevitable, to imagine someone walking in. He then had to imagine the scene progressively earlier, and after two weeks he was able to imagine urinating next to another man, after which he was required to do this in real life. His urination improved but he remained unable to defecate in a public toilet. This addition of fading fantasies to exposure is similar to that used in orgasmic reconditioning for sexual deviation (paraphilia).

Urinary frequency, too, can be treated successfully by exposure. In the author's unit this problem is helped by asking patients to refrain from urinating for steadily longer periods of time while carefully charting the time periods. Figure 11.6 shows the outcome with this method in a 34-year-old school teacher whose urinary worries and frequency prevented her from visiting friends, going on vacation, or attending conferences. Decreased urinary frequency and increased social activities continued to 6 months' follow-up. A variant of this approach was described in a 24-year-old man with frequent urination for 7 years (Poole & Yates 1975). He was asked to refrain from urinating for progressively longer periods during a daily, fixed 12-hour period, but was then allowed to urinate freely during the remaining 12 hours. Over 31 weeks, urinary frequency gradually declined to normal during both the fixed and free periods. Improvement continued to 3-year follow-up.

Frequency of defecation (functional diarrhea) can be treated in the same way as urinary frequency and has also been successfully treated by fantasy desensitization (Cohen & Reed 1968).

Flying Phobias

Flying Phobia in Passengers

The growing dependence of life styles on air travel drives ever more people to seek help for flying phobia. The fear may prevent them from accepting jobs or promotions to positions that require much flying, and may restrict where they can go on vacation or to visit family or friends. Perhaps 10% of people who do not fly avoid it because of fear; about 20% of those who do fly have substantial anxiety during the flight and many manage it only with the aid of alcohol or

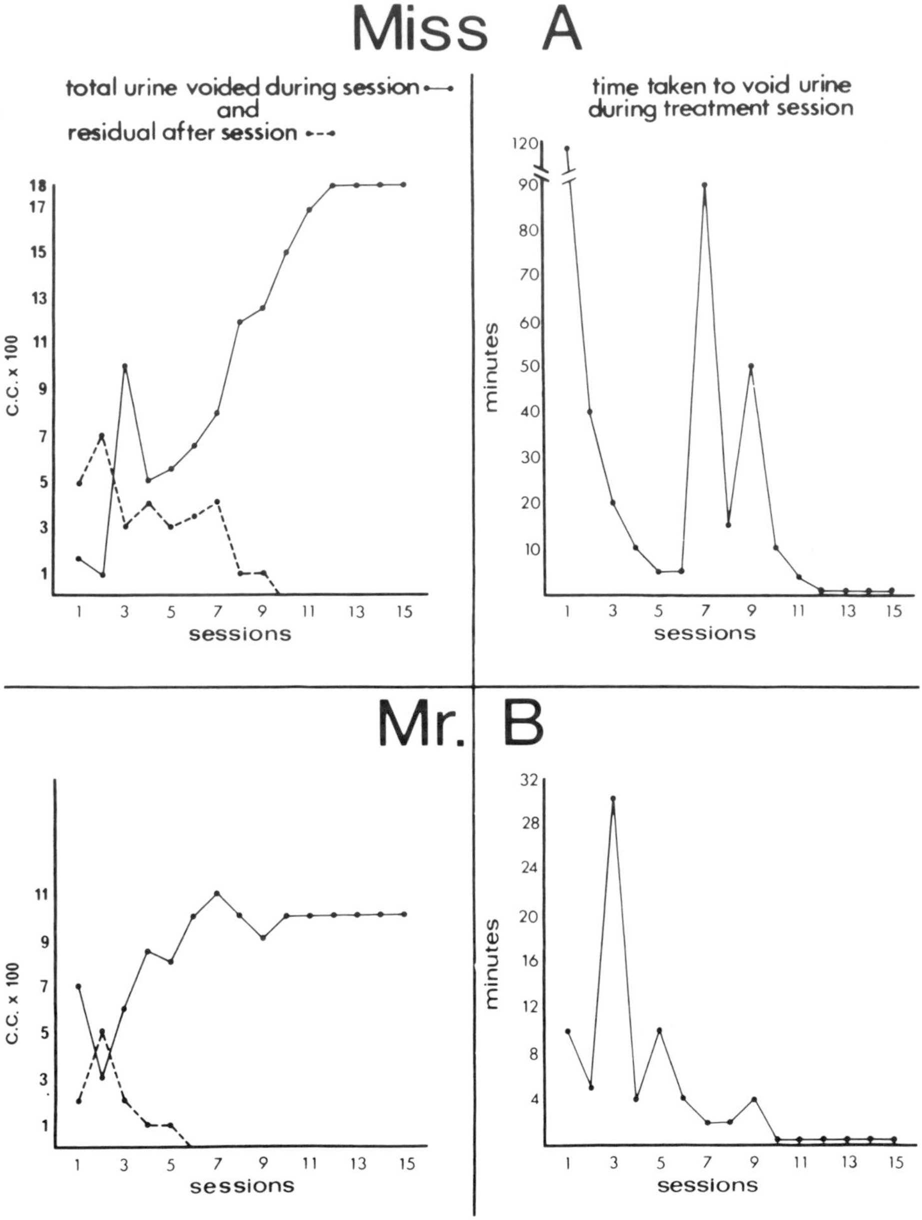

Fig. 11.5 Improvement during treatment by exposure of chronic phobias to urinating in toilets outside the home. The patients were asked to come to treatment sessions with full bladders and then to sit on a hospital toilet until they voided, which took ½ to 2 hours at first, gradually dropping to a few seconds by the end of treatment. Exposure homework consisted of doing the same in public toilets outside the home and hospital. The amount of urine voided gradually increased, and residual urine decreased to zero. After discharge, both subjects continued to void twice daily outside the home up to 6 months' follow-up. (From Lamontagne & Marks 1972. Copyright © 1972 by Academic Press, Orlando. Reprinted by permission.)

DECREASE IN URINARY FREQUENCY BY INTERPOSING INCREASING DELAYS

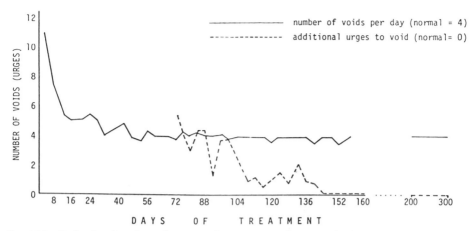

Fig. 11.6 Reduction in urinary frequency in a woman who was asked to steadily increase the times between urination and to record these in a diary. Decreased urinary frequency and increased social activities continued to 6-month follow-up. (Case of the author's treated together with Dr. Paul Cameron.)

sedatives (Greist & Greist 1981). Women present with flying fear more often than do men (Denholtz & Mann 1975). Four aspects of flying that are especially feared are the possibility of a crash (although flying in large commercial planes is statistically safer than driving a car), confinement, instability, and heights (Howard et al. 1983). Flying phobia can be an isolated problem on its own or one of the many fears of agoraphobics.

Treatment by appropriate and graded exposure carries practical difficulties as great as those with dental phobics. Controlled treatment studies of exposure variants in flying phobics were reported by Solyom and coworkers (1973) and Howard and coworkers (1983). Organizations such as Fraidycats have helped groups of frightened would-be passengers by arranging training flights under the auspices of reassuring aircrew who explain the meaning of every noise. Where flight simulators are available, sufferers may be taken into them to get used to the cues. Flying phobics may be asked to imagine themselves buying an airplane ticket, going to the airport, boarding a plane, and going on a flight, and thereafter do this themselves in real life.

Unexpected setbacks are bound to happen in treatment. One phobic woman was put on her test flight from Tel Aviv to Paris only to find that it was hijacked to Entebbe. A woman patient of the author's reached the point of being escorted to the London airport for a flight to Athens. While she was waiting in the plane ready for takeoff, the pilot announced an hour's delay because of mechanical failure. She felt that her worst fears had been confirmed and ran out of the plane back into the terminal. Fortunately, a flight attendant eventually persuaded her to return into the plane; she flew off, and her fears eased.

Aircrew

Phobias of flying in experienced aircrew have been studied mainly in military rather than civilian personnel. The following refers to flying phobias in peacetime. (Those originating in combat are discussed with traumatic phobias—(see Chapter 12).

Although flying phobia is a major cause of personnel being grounded in peacetime (O'Connor 1970), it affects only a tiny minority of aircrew. It usually comes on gradually together with irritability and insomnia (Armstrong 1936). Compared with normal aircrew, 20 who became phobic of flying reported more childhood and other adulthood phobias preceding the fears of flying and more flying accidents in their families but not for themselves (Aitken et al. 1981) (This contrasts with uncontrolled accounts of frequent accidents before the onset of flying phobias [Armstrong 1936; Goorney & O'Connor 1971].) In the controlled study, phobics also had more marital or sexual problems. In addition, they had more spontaneous fluctuations in skin conductance and greater skin conductance responses to the first 3 of a series of 20 tones, but habituation soon set in, unlike the reaction of agoraphobics (see Chapter 9). The two groups did not differ on heart rate or forearm blood flow, or on the EPI, Taylor Manifest Anxiety Scale, or 16 Personality Factor Scale. Another study of only six phobic aircrew found them more neurotic and introverted than normal aircrew (Goorney 1970).

Unlike aircrew who are phobic, those who are fatigued after long spells of flying duty and have no other psychiatric problems readily return to flying after temporary grounding (Goorney & O'Connor 1971). Nor is flying phobia noted as a problem in the 80% of aircrew who survive ejection from an aircraft, despite the fact that many of them sustained wedge compression vertebral fractures needing months of treatment, and 40% had continuing emotional reactions of some fear, anxiety, anger, disgust, or altered motivation (Fowlie & Aveline 1985). Flying phobics usually require some form of graded exposure ("flying rehabilitation"), the response to which is favorable (Aitken et al. 1971; Goorney & O'Connor 1971).

Recurrent Nightmares

Recurrent nightmares resemble specific phobias in that stereotyped cues trigger anxiety plus avoidance without other problems necessarily being present, and in their treatability by exposure methods. Sufferers avoid recounting details of the content, which can relate to trauma years before (see Chapter 12).

Practically everybody has occasional nightmares as a child and as an adult. These are to be distinguished from night terrors, which occur in normal young children and may last from 1 to 15 minutes (reviewed by Hersen 1972). The child will be inconsolable at the time but will not remember this afterward. In contrast, sleepers who wake from nightmares often remember the content. Nightmares amount to a distressing problem in 6% of the population, their frequency being related to other forms of sleep disturbance and to scores on the Taylor Manifest Anxiety Scale.

The literature on persistent nightmares consists mainly of case reports (reviewed by Marks 1981) of treatment by forms of exposure such as desensitization (Cavior & Deutsch 1975; Geer & Silverman 1967; Ross et al. 1971; Silverman & Geer 1968; Shorkey & Himley 1974), implosion (Haynes & Mooney 1975), self-regulation (Garfield 1976), and varieties of repeated rehearsal with or without mastery (Bishay 1985; Cutting 1979; Handler 1972; Marks 1978). A controlled study of students found that desensitization decreased nightmare frequency and intensity more than did discussion of the nightmares or mere recording of their frequency; follow-up was incomplete (Cellucci & Lawrence 1979). Several of these reports used not only exposure but also abreaction and mastery, and the respective contribution of each component is unclear. Intriguing anecdotes tell of adults and children learning to control their own dreams without abreaction (Garfield 1976; Stewart 1969); for instance, children who mentioned a frightening dream of falling were told, "That's a wonderful dream—next time you feel yourself falling in your dream, spread out your hands and start to fly, and soon you'll find yourself soaring." With practice over weeks or months, formerly terrifying dreams were said to gradually become transformed into pleasant ones.

A case history illustrates that despite the presence of other complex pathology, a recurrent nightmare of 14 years' duration rapidly disappeared after it was rehearsed a few times with great effect and given a triumphant ending, and remained absent at 3-year follow-up (Marks 1981). The nightmare was independent of coexisting compulsive rituals, sexual problems, and fluctuating depression.

Rehearsal Relief of a Nightmare

A woman of 45 had repeated bouts of depression from 1964 onward for which she had repeated psychiatric admission, antidepressants, and ECT. In 1966 she had several fugues diagnosed as temporal lobe epilepsy, and an EEG in 1976 suggested chronic nonprogressive temporal lobe pathology. She then revealed extensive compulsive checking rituals that had been present since 1968. She was also virgin and masturbated to masochistic fantasies.

Her father had been alcoholic and died from cirrhosis of the liver after developing dementia. Her mother had been dominant and possessive and never got along with her. The mother died in 1962, after which the patient discovered her own illegitimacy; this upset her greatly. Three maternal relatives had depression, suicided, or attempted suicide.

In 1977 the patient was admitted for treatment of her recently disclosed rituals, and these improved rapidly with live exposure and response prevention. Just before discharge she had a disturbing nightmare that she revealed (for the first time to anyone) had recurred in stereotyped form about every 3 months since 1963, starting a year after her mother's death. The dream would wake her about 1 A.M., after which she would lie awake the rest of the night, remaining so tense the next morning that she would not go to work until the afternoon. She was encouraged to recount the nightmare's content in detail. This she did under great tension. It concerned herself killing her mother, whose dead eyes then bored into her terrifyingly.

The patient was persuaded to relate the nightmare immediately twice more; all three accounts were virtually identical, and their account together totaled no more than 20 minutes. Each time the recounting evoked intense crying, ending with a shout: "My bloody mother. She always wins." Affect was least the third time around. The patient was asked to write down detailed descriptions of the nightmare including victorious endings in which she, not her mother, won, and she was discharged the next day. When seen the next week she produced three vivid written accounts of the nightmare, each with a different gruesome ending in which she bloodily disposed of her mother once and for all. She was also briefly encouraged to rehearse defiance of authority. Soon she returned to work and over the next six years had no further nightmares or rituals and was active socially, but remained a virgin. Intermittent depression continued as previously and needed ECT at one point.

In two more patients of the author's and three of Bishay's (1985), recurrent nightmares were again treated successfully by a similar approach. In Bishay's cases, altering the ending of the nightmare to become triumphant, happy, or neutral led to marked improvement; trauma had preceded onset of the nightmares in two of his three cases.

Other Specific Phobias

Natural phenomena such as darkness, wind, storms, and especially thunderstorms and lightning frequently inspire fear to the point of its becoming a handicap. In the summer, thunderstorm phobics listen intently to weather forecasts and besiege many a metereological bureau with a stream of anxious inquiries about the weather. When thunder is forecast in a few hours' time, they avoid venturing out of doors. They long for winter with its rarity of thunderstorms. During a thunderstorm they may cower under the bedclothes or in a closet until it is well over (perhaps joined by their pet, which may be very disturbed by loud thunderclaps and firework explosions); and they may become incontinent.

One woman of 48 had had a thunderstorm phobia for 28 years. In her words, "I just can't carry on with my housework during a thunderstorm. I sit and wait for it to happen. When and if it does I sit in a darkened cupboard until it's over—all night if necessary. I also clamp right up as regards talking and get aggressive. I listen to every weather forecast, which I know is silly. I wish to God I could cure myself. I make my husband and daughter fed up with me."

The fear of noise other than thunder may intensify to phobic proportions. Some people are so terrified of balloons popping that they will not attend parties where this may happen. One woman was afraid of whistling; although she was not afraid of birds and could hold them, certain frequencies of birdsong frightened her, a high soprano voice made her tense, and she was sent into a frenzy of terror if a human whistled. This fear hampered her work in filmmaking because anyone whistling at work made her so frightened and angry that she could not face returning to the studio for the next few days.

Enclosed spaces can engender severe fear (claustrophobia) on their own, but this fear is also commonly found with agoraphobia. Sufferers are afraid of being shut in tunnels, elevators, or underground trains. One claustrophobic man worked as a roof expert and had to complete a job on the roof of a 600-

foot-high tower. He walked to the top twice a day rather than go up in the elevator.

Fear of heights is common enough in mild form and is normal across many species (see Chapter 2), but only rarely does it become incapacitating. Mean onset age in 38 adult height phobics was 12 years (Williams et al. 1985). Occasionally children might climb up a tree and then freeze in fright on looking down and have to be rescued. Minor features of the visual cliff are critical. Severe phobics may not be able to get down a flight of stairs if they can see the open stairwell but manage if it is closed. They will be frightened looking out of a high window stretching from floor to ceiling but not if the window is obscured to waist level or higher. They may have difficulty crossing bridges on foot because the edge is near, yet be able to do so in a car. Anxiety may be evoked not only by looking down but also by looking up (for example, when peering at the top of skyscrapers from street level).

Flying phobias were discussed earlier. These and phobias of travel by bus, train, or boat can occur on their own or as part of the agoraphobic syndrome. (In contrast, phobias of fainting, collapse, having a fit, dying, or going insane are generally not seen on their own but are part of the cluster of symptoms seen in anxiety states or the agoraphobic syndrome). Driving can become the focus of a phobia, especially after an accident.

Autonomic equivalents of phobias are focal disturbances cued by particular triggers. The sphincteric phobias described earlier are examples of these. Other instances are the blushing, nausea, vomiting, or excessive sweating (hyperhydrosis) that some social phobics experience only in the presence of other people. Yet others are the minority of asthmatics whose bronchospasm occurs only in particular psychological situations; desensitization can be useful for them (Moore 1965).

Sexual anxiety may result from severe generalized anxiety of any cause, with resultant poor sexual performance, or it may be a specific fear. Failure of erection, premature ejaculation, anorgasmia, and vaginismus may be associated with anxiety in the presence of the opposite sex, especially in potentially sexual situations. In women the fear may generalize to avoiding being touched even by small children. Sexual dysfunction is outside the scope of this book, although some of its features and treatment are shared with those of phobias (Bancroft 1983; Marks 1978, 1981). The same applies to morbid grief, one aspect of which is avoidance by the bereaved of thinking or talking about anything connected with the lost loved one; this avoidance can be helped by guided mourning, although other aspects of the problem may not be (Cohen et al. 1986; Mawson et al. 1981).

The most unlikely situations come to evoke dread. One woman was so terrified of wigs and false hair that she could visit her hairdresser only after he had hidden all wigs. She could not go near anybody wearing a wig in a store and would rush past false hair and be unable to have a meal opposite anybody wearing one. Once she nearly rushed out of a room through a glass window when a stranger walked in wearing a wig. She felt ashamed and embarrassed by her fear. Another woman became phobic of firemen's helmets, yet another of leaves. Other phobias may be of going through a door if voices can be heard on the other side, of running water, of being grasped from behind (Bagby 1922), of reading books or even letters (Timpano 1904), of dolls (Rangell 1952), and of outer space or cosmic disaster (Ashem 1963; Kerry 1960). The list of specific phobias is endless, and every behavioral clinic has its collection of curiosities.

AVERSIONS

Quite a few people are not actually afraid of certain situations but have a strong dislike of touching, tasting, or hearing things that most people are indifferent to or may even enjoy (J. Price & Kasriel 1973, unpublished). Aversions are like specific phobias but differ from them in that aversions are (1) associated with discomfort that is not fear or anxiety and (2) evoked by stimuli different from those which evoke phobias, obsessions, or rituals. We do not know whether aversions can be habituated by prolonged exposure to the evoking stimuli, as happens with phobias and rituals.

The horrible feeling accompanying aversions is clearly not fear, although the components overlap. Aversions send shivers down the spine, set the teeth on edge, and make sufferers suck their teeth, go cold and pale, and take a deep breath. Their hair stands on end, and they feel unpleasant and sometimes nauseated but not frightened. With touch aversions there may be a desire to wet the fingers, wash them, or cover them with cream; some are made worse when the skin is rough or the nails are unevenly clipped so that the fingertips catch as they pass over a surface.

One man had an intense dislike of fuzzy textures such as those of the skins of peaches, new tennis balls, or certain carpets, and could not enter a room containing a new carpet of such a texture. When playing tennis he would wear a glove to handle the ball until the fuzz wore off. Other people find it difficult to handle old pearly buttons, cotton wool, velvet, and similar articles. Some may like the sight of velvet in shops even though they dislike its touch. Similar discomfort can be produced by the squeak of chalk on a blackboard or the scrape of a knife on a plate.

These aversions may sound trivial but can be disabling. One woman disliked the sound of chalk scraping on a blackboard so much that she gave up a cherished ambition to be a teacher. Another found velvet so unbearable that she could not bring herself to go to children's parties. A third said, "All kinds of buttons make me squeamish. I've been like this since I was a young baby and my uncle had the same thing. I can only wear clothes with zip fasteners and hooks, not buttons."

A variety of aversions are common. In a British radio broadcast, Price and Kasriel (1973), invited listeners to write in about any aversions they might have. The letters poured in. Most described more than one touch aversion. The most common revulsion was of touching cotton wool, wire or steel wool, or velvet; several people were fascinated by the surface they could not touch, especially shiny buttons. Also frequent were taste or smell aversions that caused people to avoid certain foods, especially onions. Common auditory aversions are to scraping sounds, as noted.

Many people who wrote in had hated wearing velvet party clothes as children as in the following confession:

> Ever since I have been able to remember, I have been quite unable to touch velvet. [When I was aged 3] it was all the rage to have a velvet party frock with a white lace collar and cuffs. When the time for the party arrived I was duly dressed in this creation and I just stood with my arms six inches from my sides, with fists clenched, and would only say "it's nasty," and my opinion has never altered (I am in my late forties now). Last summer, when shopping for some dress material, I made my way to the velvet display (I have always liked the look of it), telling myself "this is ridiculous; you are a big girl now; be brave; handle it—it won't bite." I think I stood there for quite two minutes, persuading myself that it really was lovely stuff. I stretched out my hands and grabbed a handful—but the effect was the same! Teeth all on edge! Sheer horror! Isn't it just ridiculous? I have now given up hope of ever being able to sail into a party or theatre in the lovely velvet dress. If I visit anyone with velvet scatter cushions, I make sure it comes nowhere near my bare hand or arm!

Another man wrote of his problem with suede. "I have had an aversion all my life to touching suede, or items of a similar texture. If I accidentally brush against a suede coat I instantly become covered in goosepimples, my hair tingles, cold shivers run up my spine and I recoil as if I have been burnt! Even the thought of it causes a skin prickling! I have never enjoyed tennis because of the texture of the ball. Card tables mean brushing the tips of my fingers over the nap of the cloth—I do not play cards as a result. Having to clean a carpet with shampoo is an exercise that makes me grit my teeth and sweat, not from effort but physical abhorrence of the feel of the wet rug tufts. I cannot wipe a wet wooden spoon—a standing joke with my wife."

Yet another wrote, "I cannot bear the feel of wet wool or synthetic woollens such as Acrilan or Orlon, and after handling them in the wash cannot even stand the touch of my own fingers against each other until my hands are thoroughly dry. I have the sensation of my teeth being 'on edge' and have to put my tongue between my teeth to cushion the feeling."

Aversions to peach skin can prevent people from peeling peaches, and they may have to ask others to do the job. The aversion can become extreme: "I have a very acute and pronounced aversion to the skin of peaches, and to a lesser degree apricots. To see anyone bite the skin of a peach produces immediate revulsion, and even after several hours the recollection of such an act can make me shudder violently."

Rubber can also provoke extreme responses: "As a child I used to dread having to play games with balloons at birthday parties, and often I tearfully tried to convince my mother not to make me put on Wellington boots. I did not mind wearing them as long as somebody else put them on for me. . . . At the touch of balloons or Wellingtons I get goosepimples and shivers down my back, my teeth begin to chatter and I get short of breath . . . as if I had been plummeted into cold water. Admittedly I *can* bear to touch these things when it is necessary for my own children, and my reaction is not quite so violent as when I was a child, but I still have to take a deep breath in order to overcome the shivery feeling."

As Price and Kasriel point out, these aversions are more the pinpricks than the burdens of life, but they may in a few cases affect choice of career (such as nursing or teaching), and work in the home (washing up after meals because of the touch of plates and pans). Rarely, they can be quite severe, as the following account testifies.

> We have a son aged 8 who has a vast and ever-increasing list of tactile and oral aversions. . . . This only started at about age 6 and grows all the time. It would be almost easier to list the things that don't give him "the shivers." . . . He is averse to all synthetic materials, many kinds of wool, and brushes, paper tissues, the sound of skipping, floor scrubbing, sand on the beach! I never know when purchasing a garment whether it can be worn or not. He manifests his aversion by going pale, sucking in his lips, shivering, and in extreme cases his hair stands up . . . if it increases much more he will be going to school stark naked! He is the elder child of two [the second being a girl showing no such aversions]. My husband and I have one or two aversions to a minor degree. He is still very attached to a soft toy, a smelly tattered dog who gives him enormous pleasure both to touch and smell.

An adolescent disliked not only velvet but also suede, cotton wool, and fluffy ties: "Immediately I touch any of these fibers my body tingles from top to bottom. I am only 15 and when I was a young child my mother had no idea what I felt like when she put me in ghastly velvet dresses or gave me fluffy ties. I cannot bear the velvety tip of a cigarette and it stopped me smoking."

Some of the letters described aversions running in families: "My father would not allow my mother to wear velvet as he could not bear to touch it [when dancing]. This applied to anything like velvet—plush, brushed nylon, etc. I have inherited this phobia now. Also my daughter (age 27) follows with this dislike, even as a baby, of plush type toys with furry sides, so that it is a case of three generations [I am 54] hating the same materials, for no reason."

Interestingly, the sensation of one's teeth being set on edge does not depend on actually having teeth: "Most of my family "suffered" from this kind of torture. My mother hated saucepans being scraped by a spoon and referred to her "teeth going on edge" when, in fact, she was completely toothless and wore dentures top and bottom. A brother hated those blocks of cooking salt being cut up, also fingernails scraping down a wall. My dislike is children making balloons squeak with fingers, or squeaking and polished floors—the thought makes me feel horrible as I write. I cannot bear to touch cotton wool, which sort of makes a scroopy feeling in my fingers. Neither can I bear the feel of wire wool or Brillo pads. My eldest daughter cannot stand me filing my fingernails for one thing, and the youngest daughter hates touching velvet."

Another woman felt so shivery when touching cotton wool that she decided not to study nursing because of it. Then, "as modern methods use forceps for most dressings, I applied to do nursing. I found at first the irritation was quite severe but as the cotton wool was placed in a cold solution such as methylated spirits or cleaning solution this awkwardness of touching the wool disappeared.

Today, although I do not like touching it, it does not send the shivers up me quite so much."

The dislike seemed to run in one family. "My husband cannot stand cotton wool anywhere near him, our son is the same, our daughter likewise when small. For her I left pieces of it around the house and so cured her but the other day she told me that the fear is returning. She is 27 years old."

SUMMARY

Minor social anxiety is normal and even helpful, but severe social phobias can be crippling. Social phobias usually start in adolescence or early adult life. Compared to other phobics social phobics are less preponderantly female or married and have higher social class and education. Onset is usually gradual. Social phobics fear and avoid social activities that may lead them to be scrutinized or criticized—eating, drinking, writing, speaking, acting, swimming, sewing, or knitting. Gaze aversion is frequent. Many fear they will shake or blush, a few that they will vomit or see others vomit. Associated depression, general anxiety, and alcohol dependence are not uncommon.

Overlapping conditions are social dysfunction (avoidant personality disorder), shyness, and shinkeishitsu. The fears of social phobics are more limited to particular situations and more discrete in onset than the anxiety of social dysfunction; the latter is more like a trait of extreme shyness. Social skills deficits are less obvious in social phobia than in social dysfunction. The two groups overlap; they fear some similar situations, and have more males and higher social class and education than do other phobics. Males are even more common among referrals for social dysfunction than for social phobia.

Though social phobia shares some features with agoraphobia it is a separate syndrome; social phobics have more social and far fewer agoraphobic fears, felt that they blush more, have rather less nonphobic anxiety, are less often female, have superior social class and education, and mean onset age is about 6 years earlier. Somewhat related to social phobia is dysmorphophobia. This is a persistent complaint of a specific bodily defect in appearance or smell that is not noticeable to others and may lead to marked social avoidance and anxiety.

Specific phobias of animals or insects are common in boys and girls aged 2-4 years but usually subside rapidly. A few continue into adult life. In adults phobias of animals are rare, found mainly in women, and usually date back to early childhood without obvious reason for the onset; the course is steady thereafter. Late onset is usually associated with trauma. Treatment is often sought when changes in life style or the environment increase contact with the relevant species. Severe cases show striking panic and escape on contact with the phobic stimulus, but away from it there is little more anxiety, depression or other problems than in normal people.

The natural unease of humans at the sight of blood, injury, or deformity is associated with initial tachycardia followed by vasovagal bradycardia and drop in blood pressure that may end in fainting. In extreme cases avoidance of blood-injury stimuli may lead to serious disability. Blood-injury phobias usually start in childhood. They differ from other phobics in their diphasic cardiovascular response leading to fainting as opposed to persistent tachycardia, their experience of nausea and faintness rather than fear, and their much more frequent history of relatives with the same problem. They become literally "sick at heart" through exaggeration of a normal reflex that may have evolved in a defensive mechanism widespread among many species.

Mild fear of dental procedures is usual while phobias of them affect up to 5% of the population, leading children to be disruptive in the examination room and adults to avoid dentistry altogether, with dire results for their teeth. Dental phobia is more common in females, starts in childhood or adolescence, and is associated with similar fears in parents and some increase in other emotional problems. Dental phobics expect more pain but may not experience it more during dentistry. Hypersensitive gagging is another problem that leads to avoidance of dentistry; fear need not be present. Fear and gagging can be relieved by graded exposure and allowing the patient to signal pain and to stop the procedure temporarily seems helpful; the dentist needs extra time to treat fearful patients. Videos of modeled exposure help children. Like patients, dentists, too, may fear dentistry and so give up their profession, and again exposure can help this problem. Careful attention is needed to overcome the practical difficulties involved in devising appropriately graded exposure for dental fears and gagging.

In one type of eating phobia there is a fear of choking, which may be very specific or may be associated with agoraphobia or generalized anxiety. Another eating phobia is food aversion, in which only certain foods induce nausea and vomiting. Some sphincteric phobias concern fear of urinating or defecating too frequently when outside their home and sufferers insist on being near a toilet at all times; other sphincteric phobias involve a fear of urinating when people are nearby, leading to urinary retention. Flying phobias prevent many people from traveling and occasionally disable aircrew, too.

Recurrent stereotyped nightmares plague some individuals, who then try to avoid thinking or talking about the content. Specific phobias may concern natural phenomena such as darkness, wind, thunder, lightning, enclosed spaces, heights, or sexual situations. Touch and sound aversions produce avoidance with subjective discomfort rather different from that found in phobias. Sufferers will avoid touching certain textures (for instance velvet, wool, suede, peaches, or rubber), or hearing the scrape of a knife on a plate or chalk on a blackboard. Little is known about these aversions.

12

Traumatic Phobias, Illness Phobias, and Children's Phobias

Three unrelated types of problem are grouped here for convenience—phobias of trauma and illness, and children's phobias. Traumatic phobias are broad-spectrum disturbances after extremely traumatizing experiences such as concentration camps, combat, torture, or rape. Natural disasters—fire, flood, tornadoes, earthquakes, air and train crashes—produce a milder form of a similar clinical state that becomes severe in a minority of survivors.

Fears of illness flit though the minds of most people at one time or another. Who has not looked at a spot on his hand and wondered if it were a form of cancer or other dread disease? Many a medical student thinks he harbors the disorders he happens to be studying at the time, and suffers a succession of illness fears as he ploughs through his medical curriculum (Bianchi 1971; Hunter et al. 1964). These fears soon pass, however, as medical students habituate with repeated exposure to the diseases in question, just as they get used to the sight of blood and injury that initially make many of them squirm.

Fears and minor rituals are normal and ubiquitous in children. They usually subside by puberty and rarely become enduring disorders (Abe 1972; Agras et al. 1972). Among the few phobic and obsessive-compulsive (oc) children referred for psychiatric treatment, there are many types of fear and rituals.

TRAUMATIC PHOBIAS (PTSD)

The normal reaction to disaster is immediate stunned immobility, apathy, and depression, followed later by aggressive irritability (Janis 1954), and often grief from the losses inherent in such events. This picture is intensified in post-traumatic stress disorder (PTSD). The disorder is characterized by irritability, tension, startle, depression, insomnia, nightmares, and flashbacks as well as fear and avoidance of cues reminding the sufferer of the original situation (Hocking 1977; Horowitz 1976; Van der Kolk 1984). No clear divide separates the normal response to ghastly events from a definite disorder—they shade into one another.

Distress usually manifests immediately after the trauma and may intensify over the years—time does not heal all wounds. There can be a lag period between the trauma and onset of the pathology. Examples are cited where combat did not produce problems obvious at the time, yet years later intrusive thoughts, nightmares, and flashbacks relating to the experience appeared (Belenky 1985; Van der Kolk et al. 1982; Van Putten & Emory 1973).

The more intense the trauma, the worse the PTSD, whether immediately or long afterward. Especially bad experiences in concentration camps and in combat led to both acute and chronic distress. Within days of a sniper attack at school, those children who had been most traumatized were the most disturbed (Pynoos et al. 1985). Later disturbance after a severe burn was already foreshadowed by distress during delirium while in hospital (Blank & Perry 1984).

More intense and prolonged trauma not only intensifies distress in certain individuals but also raises the number of people who become anxious. American aircrew in World War II were more likely to break down as combat danger increased (Bond 1952).

Trauma especially knocks people already reeling from previous losses and who lack support. Three months post-rape, the most severe reactions were in women who had had more preceding bereavement and fewer loving relationships with men (Kilpatrick et al. 1984).

Post-traumatic distress can be the norm in the traumatized population, and it can also be persistent. Only 35% of deputy sheriffs involved in shooting incidents in Los Angeles said they were not affected by it (Stratton et al. 1984). Some psychiatric symptoms were present in nearly everyone seen 5 months after a hotel skywalk collapsed (Wilkinson 1983) and in all children 4 years after they had been in a kidnapped schoolbus (Terr 1983). A sizeable proportion of rape victims continue to have some distress for years. Six months after the Great Fire of London, Samuel Pepys wrote in his diary (1667, p. 87), "to this very day I cannot sleep a-night without great terrors of the fire."

Such observations contradict others we will see presently that suggest that most people are resilient in the face of recurring danger. This discrepancy may partly reflect the fact that different studies employ different criteria for symptoms and breakdown, and that they concern widely varying circumstances regarding the duration, intensity, and meaning of the trauma and whether support was at hand. Disagreements across studies will be easier to resolve when more standardized criteria are adopted that define the degrees of (1) trauma, (2) support to cope with the trauma, and (3) the post-traumatic symptoms and syndromes. We have to remember, too that anxiety and courage are not mutually exclusive. People can be courageous and resilient and yet be anxious at the same time.

The literature noting that most people cope with adversity points to how few soldiers break down in wartime and afterward. Only a minority of Vietnam veterans had symptoms amounting to a disorder (Van Putten & Yager 1984). The same is true for civilians. In Britain in World War II most people endured air raids well without mass panic, and psychiatric disorder did not increase; although transient fear was common, persistent phobias rarely developed (Rachman 1978). Little anxiety was noted in Israel in wartime (cited by Rachman 1985). Israeli children living under almost constant shelling were, like control children, not anxious, and psychological disorders on collective farms were no more frequent in the 2 years after the Yom Kippur war than in the 2 calm years before it. If fear does rise, it soon falls when peace returns. Fear in Israeli students in wartime fell within a few months when the situation calmed down, but it rose again when war recurred (Goldberg et al. 1977). The same was noted in Arab students. Shortly after acute hostilities had ended in Lebanon, students who had been besieged reported no more anxiety than those who had evacuated to safe environs, and both samples scored lower on war-related stimuli than they had prior to the invasion (Saigh 1984).

Relationship of PTSD to Other Phobic Syndromes

PTSD overlaps with those specific (focal) phobias that start after a trauma such as a car accident or dog bite. (Most focal phobics do not remember a trauma at onset but in other respects are indistinguishable from focal phobics who do—see Chapter 11). Beyond their both being post-traumatic anxiety syndromes, PTSD and post-traumatic focal phobias share two further important features. First, both involve fears of specific cues. This feature is part of the definition of PTSD and has been shown experimentally. Mild combat stimuli evoked fear in Vietnam veterans with chronic PTSD more than in veterans who had combat experience but no PTSD, and in psychiatric inpatients without PTSD (Malloy et al. 1983). Second, both are mitigated by exposure treatment, though for PTSD this point rests mainly on case reports (see chapters 14 and 15).

The chief difference between PTSD and focal phobias is that PTSD involves more striking trauma at the onset and more generalized distress apart from the phobias. These differences can be rather arbitrary, and many cases fit either diagnosis equally well. If focal refers only to the phobias rather than to the entire clinical picture, then PTSD can be regarded as a focal phobia that tends to focus on the harrowing initiating experience and does not usually spread to agoraphobic, social, illness, or obsessive-compulsive cues. But PTSD entails an additional, wider nonphobic disturbance that is usually absent in a focal phobia. PTSD is thus a focal phobia of traumatic onset, with generalized distress.

PTSD resembles agoraphobia in that both entail rather similar nonphobic symptoms as well as phobias—general anxiety, irritability, depression, and depersonalization. The phobias differ, however: phobias from the agoraphobic cluster are not a feature of PTSD, and those from PTSD concern the trauma.

The features of traumatic phobias have been especially well described in the severe form that follows intense trauma from concentration camps, combat, and rape. Each of these situations will be dealt with separately.

Concentration Camp Syndrome

A sobering guide to the picture of concentration camp syndrome is that of Eitinger (1969). He studied 227 survivors of Nazi camps 12 years or more after liberation, by interview, psychological tests, and, in most, air encephalogram. Anxiety was still troublesome in 43%, often with nightmares and other sleep disturbances. The remainder had other problems. Horrible associations with past events would recur repeatedly and could not be discussed with closest friends or relatives. They would be stirred up by the most harmless stimuli. Seeing a person stretching his arms would revive memories of fellow prisoners hung up by their arms during torture; seeing an avenue of trees would bring memories of rows of gallows with swinging corpses; children playing peacefully might suddenly call to mind others who had been emaciated, tortured, and murdered.

Two-thirds of the survivors had been disturbed while in the camps—suffering severe chronic anxiety, tension, turmoil, despair, and severe depression. Anxiety was particularly prominent in those who had been in death cells for long periods or who had taken part in illegal organizations that had been uncovered, leading to execution of other members. The more serious the cause of the arrest, the greater the likelihood of anxiety. Bombing attacks had terrified those locked in their cells while bombs and buildings fell around them.

In patients seen up to a quarter-century after liberation, anxiety continued to be distressing and incapacitating. It correlated with higher anxiety during imprisonment and with chronic brain damage, which in turn was related to severe psychological or physical torture, head injury, and loss of weight. Current anxiety was greatest of all in survivors who had been very young when arrested and in those few who had suffered serious mental disorder prior to imprisonment. Anxiety was not related to post-war circumstances.

A similar picture was seen in a small series of 13 Cambodian refugees 3 years after a 2-to 4-year concentration camp experience (Kinzie et al. 1984). They, too, avoided thinking or talking of what they had gone through, startled easily, felt numb, and had intrusive thoughts and nightmares.

Combat Phobia (Battle or War Neurosis)

War's grim visage frightens most combatants, and it is surprising that persistently crippling fear is the exception rather than the rule. It might seem scarcely appropriate to call such fear a "phobia," given the chances of dying in battle. However, overwhelming fear may prevent people from taking elementary safety measures, and those who panic are more liable to die. The literature tends to describe combat reactions in the air and on the ground separately.

Reactions in the Air

Nearly all aircrew have strong fear during combat, according to 4,500 American airmen at interview (Wickert 1947). They felt their fear in the entire body, not just in the mind. Less than one-third thought fear impaired their efficiency; more stated that fear increased it. Breakdown to the point of becoming flying phobic occurred in only about 1% (Bond 1952).

In American aircrew during World War II the prime cause of breakdown during air combat was danger itself (Bond 1952). The number of emotional casualties among heavy bomber crews correlated .7 with the number of aircraft lost. Phobias rose sharply when losses exceeded 8% and the chances of witnessing a disaster were much higher. Men repeatedly traced their initial difficulties to a mission that had suffered heavy losses. In contrast, breakdown was not related to fatigue or to overall activity in the air. Even a personal or family history of neurosis played little part.

Chance factors largely determined whether a trauma was followed by a phobia. Position in a flying formation influenced visibility of harrowing events and attention at these moments. It mattered much whether the parachute of an escaping friend opened safely or caught fire or blew into another aircraft. According to Bond (1952, pp. 131–132), "it makes a difference, too, whether a flak burst hits directly in the bomb bay so that all pieces of the ship and its occupants are blown beyond the field of vision, or whether the expression on a wounded or a parachuting man's face is immediately discernible. The physical appearance of the man in jeopardy, how well he is known to the spectator or how well liked, the details of his character and of his circumstances in life— all combine [to affect outcome]. . . . The unevenness of individual exposure to the details of danger was so widespread that it would be erroneous to regard combat as a uniform test."

A phobia of flying was heralded by airsickness, pseudobends, headaches, vertigo, and cautiousness in the air to the exclusion of other safety measures. Phobias often began with something reminding the man of his precarious position—a trivial accident, an unexpected gust of wind, a momentary sticking of the controls. Onset tended to be at the start of a fresh step in training—the first flight at night, on instruments, or in formation, or in a more complicated or new type of aircraft. The phobia commonly spread in ripples to related circumstances but always remained centered around flying, which emphasizes the focal phobic element in PTSD.

The phobia made little practical sense in that it often developed for safe maneuvers but not for dangerous ones. One outstanding fighter pilot delighted in combat yet was unwilling to fly over water. Several men refused to fly higher than 8,000 feet, although they risked with ease danger below that level. Some pilots were so afraid of parachuting that they rode severely damaged planes into a crash landing and were decorated for choosing the more hazardous course. A navigator who was terrified of flying was shot down and soon afterward came upon a small group of dispirited infantrymen hemmed in by a large number of the enemy; his joy at being on the ground enabled him to lead the men out of a very dangerous position. Flying phobias increased the danger to the phobic, for they led to uncertainty and inefficiency in the air. Seized with a nameless fear before landing, a few men crashed their planes as a result; not a few bailed out needlessly or made serious navigational errors.

After 3 to 6 weeks' rest almost all the men with flying phobias were fit for noncombatant duty, although many had persistent nightmares. Practically none returned to combat flying (Bond 1952). The severity of the symptoms is illustrated by a man whose problems began on a mission during which his plane was twice damaged badly and two men aboard were killed. At a rest home he spent the first two weeks lying on the grass with his face down, deeply depressed, speaking to no one, preoccupied with guilt and whether he was alive. At first he was unable to eat, sleep, or mingle with others, to talk about flying or listen to others speak about it, or to have contact with his air base. He was extremely sensitive to noise of any kind. He improved slowly initially and then rapidly. At the end of 6 weeks he could do ground duty.

The fear had surprisingly little contagiousness in an experiment during which 110 emotionally disabled airmen lived for a week with 550 healthy airmen on leave in a rest home (Bond 1952). Conversation was virtually confined to aviation and combat, and no therapy was given to the ill air crew. Nevertheless, at follow-up only 1% of the healthy airmen had become disturbed, even though many of them had been sent to the rest home to recover after a bad crash or a ditching.

Reactions on the Ground

Normal fear in ground combat has been absorbingly reviewed by Corsellis (1980). Most soldiers are fearful at some stage of fighting, between 5% and 20% to the point of involuntary urination and defecation. Of veterans returning from the Spanish Civil War, only 9% said that they never experienced fear in action, and 26% had no fear going into their first action. The chief fear at first was of being a coward (36%) or of being crippled or killed (each 25%). With experience both the fear of being a coward and overall fear diminish.

As in airmen, although mild fear can enhance performance in soldiers, intense fear seriously interferes with it, as occurred at least once in 65% and several or many times in 23% of 277 wounded American combat veterans in Europe (Stouffer et al. 1949). These proportions might be so much higher than the 1% of aircrew mentioned above who became disturbed because "interference" with performance may not qualify as a breakdown unless it happens much of the time.

It is remarkable that in World War II only a small minority of American riflemen fired their weapons at available targets even when they were under intensive attack and about to be overrun (Marshall 1947). Many did not defend themselves but simply stood their ground facing the enemy without fighting until they were killed. This was found in a survey of hundreds of different actions in the Pacific and in Europe. Even in crack units only about 25% of American soldiers who were in a position to fire weapons at the enemy did in fact fire, let alone aim properly. In the average unit in action the figure was only about 15%. Men equipped with heavier or more specialized weapons were more likely to use them, and weapons manned by more than one man were nearly always fired.

When a man imagines death at hand he may have "a fierce desire to rivet impressions even of the commonplace like the curve of a roof, the turn of a road, or a mere milestone. What a strange emotion all objects stir when we look upon them wondering whether we do so for the last time in this life" (Fussell 1975, p. 327). The focusing on the inessential and tunnel vision produced by extreme fear degrade speed and accuracy of performance (Berkun 1962).

Extreme panic stopping function accounts for a substantial proportion of total war casualties from any cause, which varies from one war to the next. During two world wars 12% of all casualties in the British army were psychiatric (6% of all battle casualties) (Ahrenfeldt (1958). In Middle East wars the percentage of all casualties that were psychiatric was 50% among Arabs in 1967, 30% among Israelis in 1973, and 23% among Israelis in 1982 (Belenky & Jones 1983).

Performance under extreme stress is unpredictable, and there are many stories of timid introverts performing great feats of valor in battle while the extroverts were ineffective, although the frequency of such events is not known (Grinker & Spiegel 1945), and isolated incidents are no guide to the general pattern. Severe combat reactions were far more frequent among Israeli soldiers in Lebanon who had premorbid personality disorder (Margalit & Segal 1983). Familial prevalence of psychopathology has been little studied; one series of veterans with chronic PTSD noted this among 66%, chiefly in the form of alcoholism, depression, and anxiety disorders (Davidson et al. 1985).

The number breaking down rises when cohesion is lacking and when combat is intense and sustained (Figure 12.1). As conflicts dragged on, breakdowns mounted in the Iran–Iraq and other wars (Mahajer & Mottaghi 1985). Although it is hard to know how much weight to place on distant memories, chronic PTSD in veterans was related to more stressors, joining in atrocities, separation from the unit, and the killing of a buddy in action (Davis et al. 1985), and more PTSD symptoms were recorded among veterans who remembered war-related traumatic events than among those who did not (Pearce et al. 1985). Fear of combat is aggravated by witnessing mental collapse in a fellow soldier, which 49% of American soldiers said made them jittery (Stouffer 1949). (The lack of contagion among airmen cited earlier was during contact in a rest home away from the battle zone—this could make a crucial difference.) How much exhaustion predisposes to panic is not clear.

Although avoidance of combat cues is a classic feature of war neurosis, counterphobic behavior leading to further problems has also been observed, in Iranian soldiers who had PTSD (Majaher & Mottaghi 1985). Such cases might feel an urge to watch TV reports from the battlefield, participate in noisy and crowded religious ceremonies, or even sneak onto the battlefield. Catastrophic reactions might then ensue. Perhaps such behavior is more likely when strong morale and ideological commitment to war inhibits avoidance and fear. Fear was infrequent as a symptom of PTSD in the Iranian series.

Prevention

Abolishing war would do away with combat phobia but is not likely in the foreseeable future. Based on his review Corsellis (1980) made several recom-

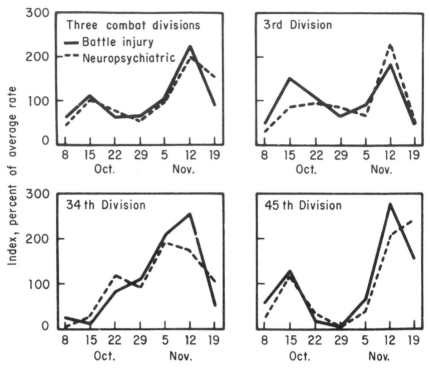

Fig. 12.1 In World War II the number of neuropsychiatric admissions of soldiers was closely related to the number of battle injuries. (From Glass & Bernucci 1966.)

mendations to decrease fear and breakdown and to increase combat efficiency. Marked fear degrades performance, and military equipment is more likely to be used reliably if its operation is simple. Soldiers should be picked for the absence of "psychological weakness." In training and battle some measures likely to be useful can be gauged from comments of Spanish Civil War veterans that their fear in battle was helped by belief in war aims (77%), good leadership (49%), military training (45%), information on the military situation (38%), esprit de corps (28%), hatred of the enemy (21%), and distraction and keeping busy (17%) (Dollard 1944).

From time immemorial soldiers have been toughened up to conquer fear by rigorous training and discipline and by other means, including the exposure principle. Training conditions closely simulating real battles are essential. As part of their training, British soldiers in two world wars were sent to slaughterhouses to get used to carnage and were taught to hate the enemy by viewing photographs of atrocities (Ahrenfeldt 1958). After an air accident airmen were advised to "wipe the blood off the cockpit and climb back in" (Armstrong 1936). The fear of loss of reputation becomes stronger if the soldier identifies closely with his immediate colleagues, and the same compatible group needs to be kept together in training and in battle. It is helpful for them to be reassured that feeling frightened is normal. Maintenance of morale is obviously critical.

Seeing soldiers breaking down is particularly unsettling for their fellows, so that rapid evacuation and treatment of such casualties is important. Those who become unable to cope with mental strain should not go into battle; officers need to learn to recognize the signs.

Rape

This all-too-common trauma affects hundreds of thousands of women in the United States every year. Rape causes a stress syndrome whether the victim is a woman (Steketee & Foa 1986; Kilpatrick et al. 1982, 1984) or a man (Goyer & Eddleman 1984). During the rape there is great fear and helplessness. Afterward distress continues, with depression, self-blame, poor self-esteem, numbing, restrictions in activity, insomnia, anxiety, hyperalertness, difficulty in concentrating, fatigue, hostility, and suspiciousness. Victims have flashbacks and nightmares as well as fear and avoidance of cues concerning the rape or vulnerability to further attack (fears of darkness, strangers, being alone). Up to half of victims develop sexual dysfunction. Suicidal attempts are nearly 9 times more frequent in victims of rape or robbery than in nonvictims—most of these attempts being after the rape; 55% of all suicide attempts in a sample of community women were by crime victims (Kilpatrick et al. 1984a).

Distress gradually subsides in the days and weeks after rape, but only about 20% of victims are free of symptoms a year later; depression and reduced sexual frequency and arousal remained more troublesome than among controls, with 12% of victims having flashbacks during sex. At 1- and 2-year follow-up victims still had more anxiety and lower self-esteem than nonvictims. More than half still felt restricted and ventured out only with friends 15 to 30 months post-rape, and up to 41% continued to be more depressed than controls even at 3 years' follow-up (Ellis et al. 1981; Nadelson et al. 1982).

More short-term impact is associated with a prior psychiatric history. The amount of disturbance up to 4 years later was predicted from the early level of distress 6 to 21 days post-rape. Women with the highest distress at 3 months post-rape had the initially greatest distress and lowest self-esteem, and more family bereavement in the previous year (and thus perhaps depression); 44% had no loving, intimate relationship with a man (presumably being more often alone). The latter two factors may reduce a woman's ability to cope. Most studies suggest that there is less immediate and long-term impact of rape where there is good social support. Socioeconomic status and unemployment, and previous experience of victimization, were associated with more symptoms 4 to 6 years later.

Some women are vulnerable to rape (Steketee & Foa 1986; Kilpatrick et al. 1984). Compared with matched nonvictims, before the rape victims were more likely to have been nonassertive, physically abused as children and adults, and sexually abused as children; to have had professional help for psychological problems; and to have been depressed or attempted suicide. Victims were also less likely to drive cars or to own weapons or protective devices, thus making them easier prey. Vulnerability to being raped does not mean that the woman provokes it, any more than a deer provokes a wolf to seize it. It does mean that assertive behavior and other precautions may deter some would-be rapists.

ILLNESS PHOBIAS

In some people unfounded fears of illness are so insistent that they seek medical advice repeatedly despite reassurance that all is well on examination and investigation. Commonly these people approach a general physician. A substantial proportion of outpatients in general hospitals require reassurance that their complaint is not serious. Where the fears concern multiple bodily symptoms and a variety of illnesses, we speak of hypochondriasis. When the fear persistently focuses on a single symptom or illness in the absence of another psychiatric disorder, the term illness phobia (or nosophobia—Ryle [1948]) is appropriate; it is a focal form of hypochondriasis.

Diffuse hypochondriasis is a feature of many different conditions (Ladee 1966). It can be a lasting personality trait, a response to anxiety and stress, or part of a depressive or schizophrenic illness. Hypochondriasis was well recognized by the seventeenth century. Burton (1621, p. 272) wrote that "some are afraid that they shall have every fearful disease they see others have, hear of, or read, and dare not therefore hear or read of any such subject, not of melancholy itself, lest, by applying it to themselves that which they hear or read, they should aggravate and increase it." In the vast literature on hypochondriasis, most writers do not classify it on its own but regard it as part of some other disturbance.

General forms of hypochondriasis overlap with illness phobias. Undoubtedly many people present with a single fear of disease that is part of a depressive disorder; such fear waxes and wanes with the depression and is thus a depressive concomitant. Yet others may be part of an abnormal personality or obsessive-compulsive or other psychiatric disorder. Nor do we know how small the residue is of patients who have illness phobias as the main complaint without other complicating factors. Phobias of illness should be distinguished from the alarming sense of dying that accompanies organic problems, including the constricting chest pain of angina pectoris, labyrinthine vertigo, anaphylactic shock, too large a dose of adrenalin, and vasovagal attacks (Ryle 1948). This sensation of dying is very distressing while it lasts, but once it has passed most people are not left with a persistent fear of death.

Systematic studies of illness phobia are surprisingly rare given its frequency. Among phobics in psychiatric outpatients, illness phobics formed 15% of the total in London (Marks 1969), 24% in Bangalore, India (Raguram & Bhide 1985), and 34% in Vermont (Agras et al. 1969). In addition, of the most common group of phobics in London—agoraphobics—9% also had fears of illness and 22% of dying. Among healthy university students accorded the chance of a free health examination, 6% had fears of disease, although these were not severe enough to lead to psychiatric treatment (Ryle 1948). Fears of illness were found in 8% of children 4 to 11 years old (Pratt 1945); however, actual phobias were present in less than 1% of 10-to 11-year-olds (Rutter et al. 1970). Brief epidemics of acute anxiety and illness behavior can sweep through a school or other community to involve a sizeable proportion of its members (reviewed by Mohr 1980), but such short-lived "epidemic hysteria" is very different from the chronic complaint of an illness phobic not shared by those around him or her.

Etiology

The causes of illness phobias are probably multiple (reviewed by Bianchi 1971; Ryle 1948; Straker 1951). The previous health history in the patient or his or her family may have sensitized him or her to a particular disease or body system, say, to cancer or the heart, where there has been a corresponding history of such disorder. Identification with a close relative or friend in pain might lead an illness phobic to feel similar pain in a similar site. Specific traumatic events during maturation may have significance for certain bodily symptoms. Fear of a given illness can reflect relevant psychological problems; for instance, someone who is guilty about sexual adventures may worry about venereal disease. A patient may mistakenly misinterpret the silence of a taciturn doctor as an ominous sign that frightening information is being concealed from him or her. The threshold of uneasiness that leads someone to ask for help lowers with generalized anxiety, depression, or loneliness, leading to increased "illness behavior" (Mechanic 1962).

All these factors may be potentiated by an upbringing in surroundings where undue attention is paid to physical disease. Response to pain and disease takes place within an elaborate cultural context in which the patient, the family, and the community respond in socially patterned ways. In a study of this, Jewish and Italian Americans responded emotionally and exaggerated their pain experience in contrast to Irish and "old" Americans (Zborowski 1952).

Awareness of a given disorder rises further when there is a public campaign to disseminate information about it, and illness phobias reflect to some extent those worries which are fashionable either in the culture at large or in the family subculture. Early this century a campaign to educate the public about tuberculosis, for example, caused many to present with fears of that disease (Pope 1911); today it is fashionable to worry about cancer and heart disease. Fear of venereal disease used to be in strong vogue, and quite recently anxiety about it was present in one-third of Ugandan students (German & Arya 1969). Current venereal fears in the West are no longer of syphilis but of herpes and AIDS (Oates & Gomez 1984). Many homosexuals fear AIDS, interestingly apparently more among the less promiscuous who are at less risk (Miller et al. 1984); the latter might have both greater temperamental timidity and less opportunity to habituate to the risky situation. Koro, the fear of the penis retracting into the abdomen, is endemic among Chinese in Southeast Asia (Ngui 1969) and is rare in India, Canada, and Great Britain (Shukla & Mishra 1981); Chinese women may fear retraction of the nipple or clitoris.

Although physical disorder can trigger an illness phobia and there is many a case of unnecessary cardiac invalidism after a coronary, usually there is no history of disease to explain it. Indeed, cases are recorded where development of the feared disease in fact led to resolution of the fear. One man was beside himself with venereophobia and soon required admission to a mental hospital. After discharge he contracted primary syphilis with a typical chancre large enough to see himself. From that moment his mental symptoms disappeared and he happily attended for antisyphilitic treatment (Rogerson 1951).

Clinical Picture

Illness phobics worry excessively that they might have one or other disease, despite being perfectly healthy; or their fear may be far greater than is warranted by a disorder that they actually have. The fear is constant and distracts them from everyday activities more than might be the case, had the disease feared really been present. (In the words of Sir Philip Sidney, "fear is more pain than is the pain it fears.") These phobics constantly search for signs of disease. No skin lesion or bodily sensation is too trivial for their keen senses. Women who are afraid of breast cancer may palpate their breasts so hard and often that they are bruised all the time. Illness phobics may misinterpret genuine physiological sensations and jump at every normal quiver of the body, palpitation of the heart, or contraction of the gut. The anxiety itself may produce fresh symptoms such as abdominal pain and discomfort resulting from pylorospasm, and this will reinforce the gloomy prognostications.

With illness phobias the patient cannot escape the triggering events, as they are largely internal, although he or she may avoid media programs or articles about cancer or give hospitals and other potential sources of infection a wide berth. Specific phobics can switch off their fear by the simple expedient of avoiding the external stimulus. This is less easy for illness phobics to do, as avoidable external stimuli are only part of the range of triggers, and they cannot switch off the usual noise made by a body; the slightest change in its pitch becomes a potential cause for alarm.

Few series of patients with fear of a given disease have been reported. Ryle (1948) described 31 cases of cancer phobia, 21 of whom were women. The mean age was 50 (ranging from 33 to 75). Many had other psychiatric problems; 13 patients were "nervous or had a breakdown previously." Physical anxiety symptoms were common—colonic spasm, flatulence, globus hystericus. Twelve cases had lost a near relative or acquaintance from cancer or had intimate knowledge of such a case.

MacAlpine (1957) studied 24 syphilophobics seen in a dermatology department of a general hospital and in a mental hospital. All except one patient were male—this reflecting a male preponderance similar to that in another series described by Schuermann. The excess of men might be due to cultural and anatomical factors: men are more promiscuous than women, know more about venereal disease, and can more freely observe their genitals for minute changes. Mean age at treatment was 38 (ranging from 17 to 55); the highest actual incidence of syphilis is in the third decade. There was a high proportion of bachelors—52% of the men. Forty-two percent had been psychiatric inpatients previously, and another 16% were severely disturbed. Twelve of the patients were seen only once. All 10 who were seen repeatedly improved somewhat after 3 to 6 interviews.

All the patients had been investigated repeatedly for syphilis, having had a mean of 6 negative Wasserman tests without being reassured; one patient had 22 negative tests in a year. The fear had usually been present for years. Although all patients gave a history of risk, close questioning revealed this idea to be misconceived or even delusional in more than half. "Risk" was conceived in terms of "strange looks, drinking or eating from utensils that may previously have been used by a syphilitic, the inevitable lavatory seat, and sleeping in strange beds." Four patients who gave lurid accounts of sexual experiences were later found to have been impotent at the relevant times.

A rare controlled study compared 30 disease-phobic and 30 matched non-disease-phobic inpatients from a general hospital psychiatric unit (Bianchi 1971). Fully 50% of both groups were diagnosed as depressive, and duration of the fear was short—less than one year in 60%; hence the findings may not apply to chronic nondepressed illness phobics. Sixty-seven percent were women, and the mean age was 40. The main diseases feared were cancer (47%), heart disease (30%), and infection (7%). The principal symptom was pain (60%). Identification with relatives' illnesses was evident in 53%. Compared with the controls, the disease phobics were currently more anxious and self-pitying, and previously had been more prone to inhibition of anger, bodily concern, and low self-esteem. As children they had more often been the youngest siblings, and more described themselves as having been weak, sickly, and overprotected. They reported more frequent family illness and more maternal deaths. Experimentally they felt and stopped a 1-second electric current to the fingers at lower voltages; they felt the sensation more readily and tolerated pain less. Whether such augmentation was true for other sensations and was an enduring trait is not known.

Syphilophobia has been regarded as analogous to two complaints in which women predominate—delusions of parasitosis or of growing or losing hair (MacAlpine 1957). In cases such as these, where almost invisible blemishes are seen as augurs of doom that others would dismiss, the illness phobia does resemble dysmorphophobia (see Chapter 11) but lacks its social avoidance.

Search for Reassurance

This is the most incapacitating feature of severe illness phobia. For most of us, minor worries about illness are dismissed after brief reassurance. However, illness phobics may be ruled by the search for security and reassurance to the exclusion of all else. In addition, they may have obsessive-compulsive rituals to avoid dirt or infection. A case in point was the billionaire Howard Hughes, who took extraordinary precautions to protect himself. He became a recluse, went on a strange diet, and refused to see doctors. In fact his fear seemed to hasten his death. When he became really ill and emaciated, a doctor could be brought to him only when he was unconscious and on the point of death. By then it was too late to rescue him, although elementary medical attention could have helped him earlier.

Illness phobics may make hundreds of phone calls and visits to doctors throughout the area in a vain attempt to seek reassurance. Telling the illness phobic that all is well allays his worries only for a short time, and the search for reassurance soon starts again. Two extreme cases of the author's will illustrate this.

A woman of 32 had been to 43 emergency departments in hospitals over the previous 3 years and had had X-rays in every part of her body. Sometimes she was scared she was going to die of cancer of the stomach, other times of thrombosis, yet other times of a tumor in the brain. Examinations never revealed any abnormality, and each time she emerged from the hospital "rejuvenated—it's like having been condemned to death and given a reprieve." But within a week she would seek out a new hospital "where they won't know I'm a fraud. I am terrified of the idea of dying, it's the end, the complete end, and the thought of rotting in the ground obsesses me—I can see the worms and maggots." She was petrified of having sex with her husband for fear of rupturing herself and bursting a blood vessel, and afterward would get up at 2 A.M. and stand for hours outside a hospital to be in reach of help.

The second case was a man of 53 with illness phobia for 28 years. He had consulted doctors hundreds of times to seek reassurance about his health, and quizzed factory inspectors and water supply officials about the purity of substances he had touched or ingested. He had been off work for nearly half his working life. He made his wife telephone endless doctors and other authorities to reassure him. Having had more than a hundred X-rays, he developed fresh worries about their having caused leukemia. He also had compulsive rituals.

An addiction to reassurance can be broken by teaching long-suffering relatives to apply exposure by response prevention. When patients ask for reassurance they hope to receive a reply that they are not ill or infected. Such a reply assuages their fear briefly, but it soon surges back. What the illness phobic avoids is a thought that all of us have to endure: that we might be ill and die. Illness phobics avoid this idea instead of facing it realistically. If their worry about illness is not switched off immediately by reassurance, they then must learn to tolerate it like the rest of us. Their repeated requests for reassurance are like an alcoholic waking up with the shakes. A nip of alcohol settles him for a while but soon the shakes recur, more alcohol is needed, and so the vicious circle continues. Only stopping all alcohol breaks the addiction in the long run. In the same way addiction to reassurance is broken by consistently withholding reassurance.

If an illness phobic frequently pesters his or her spouse with "do I look pale, am I ill?," the spouse is taught to reply not "no, you seem OK to me" but instead "hospital instructions are that I don't answer such questions." In the therapist's presence the couple repeatedly rehearse a scene in which the phobic asks the spouse for reassurance and she or he gives the standard reply that she or he may not answer the request. This simple transaction can be surprisingly difficult to learn, and the couple may have to rehearse it 10 times or more before they can undertake it correctly. The patient's doctor, too, may need to be taught to withhold unnecessary examinations and tests. If reassurance is withheld consistently the frequent requests for it may increase briefly as an "extinction burst" but thereafter will usually drop out. The couple may need to be in regular touch with the therapist to support this treatment approach, as it is naturally against one's instincts to withhold comfort from loved ones even if it is in their interests in the long run.

PHOBIC AND OBSESSIVE-COMPULSIVE DISORDERS IN CHILDREN

School Phobia (School Refusal)

A disabling form of phobic disorder among children is school phobia with its educational and social consequences. This phobia is a well-known but uncommon problem (reviewed by Berg 1984; Berg & Jackson 1985; Hersov & Berg 1980).

Frequency, Sex and Age Incidence

Although most children show anxiety about school at one time or another, especially in the first few years, this is generally short-lived and clears up with minimum or no treatment (see Figure 7.1). Among 1,034 Venezuelan children 3 to 14 years old, 18% had intense fears of school, but only rarely were such fears combined with frequent absences (Granell de Aldaz 1984). Among other children these fears were found in 1% (Miller et al. 1972) or less—0.7% (Rutter et al. 1970). In the sample of Rutter et al., school phobias formed in 3% of the total 5% who were identified as being psychiatrically disturbed among all 10- to 11-year-olds. Of another random sample, 5% of schoolchildren disliked and tended to avoid secondary school, but how many were phobic is unclear (Mitchell & Shepherd 1967). School phobics form only about 1% to 5% of child referrals to clinics and psychiatrists (Chazan 1962; Graham 1964; Kahn & Nursten 1962; Smith 1970). Among all phobic referrals the proportion of school phobics ranges widely from 9% (Windheuser 1977 and personal communication, 1980) to 68% (Miller et al. 1972).

In most studies about 60% of school phobics are boys (Baker & Wills 1979; Berg & Collins 1974; Hersov 1960b; Rodriguez et al. 1959; Smith 1970)—a male excess less than in most childhood behavior disorders (Rutter et al. 1970). An exceptional series in which two-thirds of the school phobics were girls is that of Palmer (1966). Peak onset age of school refusal in England is 11 to 12, the age when most children move from a primary to a higher school.

Mode of Onset and Precipitants

In most cases school refusal develops gradually; increasing reluctance eventually culminates in outright refusal (Hersov 1960b). Actual refusal might be preceded by physical symptoms and signs of anxiety that are increased by pressure to get the child to school. A few cases begin suddenly after a break in school-going on the Monday morning following a weekend, on the first day of a new term, or on the day of return to school following illness. A common precipitant is change to a new school or class. Less often it begins after the death, departure, or illness of a parent.

Clinical Features

Usually the child simply refuses to go to school (Hersov 1960a). Young children may give no reason at all, whereas older ones will attribute it to various aspects of school life. Complaint may be made of being bullied or teased, or self-consciousness of appearance. Children may be afraid of a teacher, poor performance at games or school work, undressing in front of other children, taking a public bath or shower after games, or vomiting or fainting during school assembly. There may be anxiety about menstruation, puberty, or masturbation. Many worry that their mother might come to some harm while they are at school. Often they cling to their mother, following her around the house like a 2-year-old. Others are willful and aggressive, and yet others both (Berg 1984).

School refusers may not only express fear but also have physical symptoms and signs of anxiety, particularly in the morning when they are encouraged to leave the house for school. Anxiety may be obvious although the child denies that he or she is frightened of anything. Typically school refusers say at breakfast that they are nauseous and may vomit, and complain of headache, diarrhea, abdominal pain, sore throat, leg pains, difficulties in eating and sleeping, and other fears. They may be tearful or irritable, look pale, tremble, and urinate frequently. Depending on the dominant picture some children are treated for one of a range of possible illnesses. The symptoms and signs usually subside once the child is allowed to stay at home and resume only when attendance at school is expected (Waldfogel et al. 1957); the child usually then goes out to play without difficulty. A period away from school because of actual physical illness can be followed by superimposed school refusal.

Depression is common among school phobics and is associated with recent life events, organic factors in early life, and a parental history of depression (Kolvin et al. 1984). Compared with normals, school phobics' self-esteem is low, which is true also for other disturbed children (Nichols & Berg 1970).

How much the child tries to overcome the fear of school varies (Berg 1984). Some get up early and put on their school clothes, and they may even leave the house but turn back on the way. Others adamantly refuse to get out of bed, wash, and dress, and may even barricade themselves in their room or run off until it seems safe to return. There can be threats of suicide, perhaps overdoses, and (rarely) suicide attempts.

Adolescents and young adults may have a fear of college or work, resembling the school phobia of younger children, and similar family pathology is frequent (Coolidge et al. 1960; Levenson 1961). These adolescents have a history of school phobia when younger.

Family Setting

Compared with controls, school phobics came from families of average size (Hersov 1960b), less often in the middle of sibships and more frequently as the youngest child (Baker & Wills 1978; Berg et al. 1972; Smith 1970). Families were unusually stable with few parental absences before age 5, but an excess of parents had a history of psychiatric disturbance, mainly of depression or anxiety (Baker & Wills 1978; Hersov 1960b). Similar increased psychiatric illness was found in the mothers of children with disturbances other than school phobia (Berg et al. 1974a).

The parents of school refusers have problems suggesting that they fail to help their progeny overcome the normal transient fear of school that most children have at some time, thereby contributing to its becoming an enduring school phobia. Most of the fathers were inadequate and passive in child management. Half the mothers were overindulgent and dominated by their children, whereas a quarter were at the opposite extreme of being demanding, severe, and controlling (Hersov 1960b). Some mothers were overanxious and clung to their children (Eisenberg 1958); such relationships were mutually constricting and tinged with hostility. Mothers of school refusers encouraged displays of affection and condoned undue dependence and staying at home more than did mothers of other children (Berg & McGuire 1974), were more neurotic on the EPI scale (Berg 1969), and often had been unhappy with their own parents (Hersov 1960b). The mothers of children with separation anxiety had more of that same problem themselves than did the mothers of children with behavior disorders or with no psychiatric contact, as judged by TAT themes for separation concerns (Breit 1982).

School Refusal Versus Truancy

School refusal is clearly different from truancy (Hersov 1960a). Truants do not refuse to go to school but use many wily stratagems to stay away, pretending to go to school but instead wandering about alone or in the company of other truants, their whereabouts unknown to their parents, who first learn of the problem from the school or other sources. Truancy is often associated with other delinquent behavior, less emotional distress, frequent change of school, a history of parental absence in childhood, and inconsistent discipline at home. On the Junior EPI scale, truants are average on introversion and low on neuroticism (Aldridge-Smith 1974). Truants are particularly common in socially disadvantaged areas.

In contrast to truancy, school phobia is an anxiety disorder in offspring from stable families. School-phobic children bluntly refuse to go to school, show no other delinquent behavior, and often have worked and behaved well at school (Hersov 1960a). School phobics also have more somatic symptoms of anxiety than truants, including disturbed eating and sleeping, abdominal pain, nausea, and vomiting. On the Junior EPI scale they are introverted (Alldridge 1974; Blagg 1979).

Separation Anxiety or Fear of School?

Some writers have held that school phobia is a misnomer for school refusal on the grounds that the problem is a fear of leaving the mother (Johnson et al. 1941; Waldfogel et al. 1957). This is too one-sided a view, however. Even though separation anxiety was evident in 36% of the cases of Hersov (1960b), 22% of that series had fears focused clearly on the school, not on the mother (Hersov 1960b). Both factors are often present in the same case. Separation anxiety cannot be inferred simply from the fact that the child will go to school only if his or her mother comes with him or her. Any phobia is partly improved in the presence of a trusted companion, and school phobia is no exception. Separation anxiety can be inferred with greater confidence when overt fears are expressed of leaving the mother or of harm befalling her when she is out of sight.

Relationship to Agoraphobia

This topic is reviewed in Chapter 10. About 10% of adult agoraphobia starts before age 16, one manifestation of which could be school refusal. Only about one-fifth of agoraphobics report past school phobia—a proportion similar to that found in women with other psychiatric problems—and its presence does not predict any particular symptom (Berg et al. 1974). A history of school phobia is more common in adult neurotics than in controls (Tyrer & Tyrer 1974), although one study found more school phobia among agoraphobic than specific phobic women (Gittelman & Klein 1985).

It is sometimes thought that school phobia and agoraphobia reflect the same problem of separation anxiety, but this is an oversimplification. School phobia and agoraphobia share the features of anxiety when away from home and a preference for staying at home. Both conditions are associated with a strong family history of anxiety and depression. They differ in that at least as many school phobics are boys as girls and they do not have spontaneous panics, whereas agoraphobics are more often female and many have spontaneous panics.

Although school phobia and agoraphobia do not seem to be directly connected, follow-up into adult life suggests an indirect link. First, people prone to fear develop it in different forms in response to the different stressors of child and adult life. Second, regardless of individual proclivity, having one type of anxiety disorder may predispose an individual to acquire another later in life. Agoraphobics with past school phobia do present for treatment earlier than those without such a history (see Chapter 10—no data are available for other types of phobia or for obsessive-compulsives, and this point deserves study). The former may be more severe, and knowing the ropes of referral from earlier experience may make it easier to ask for treatment the next time a problem crops up.

Follow-Up

When school refusers grow up they develop neurotic and affective disorders more than might be expected (reviewed by Berg 1984). When 16 school pho-

bics were seen 6 years later, 10 remained disturbed with phobias or other neuroses (Warren 1965). At 10-year follow-up of subjects who had been school
phobic, 12%s of 145 were agoraphobic (as many males as females), and 30%
had been treated for psychiatric disturbance (Berg 1984); 33% of 46 were said
to be severely disturbed (Coolidge et al. 1964), and 75% of 24 had at least mild
psychiatric disturbance compared to about 14% of the controls (Waldron
1976). At a 21-year follow-up, subjects had a "lifelong pattern of fear of separation" (Eisenberg 1958).

The large series of Berg (1984) deserves further mention. He traced 85% of
168 subjects (54% male) who had received inpatient treatment for school
refusal a decade earlier at a mean age of 14. Bright children treated when quite
young had done best. During the 10 years since discharge, subjects as a whole
had been well or markedly improved for 75% of the time, although there had
been much morbidity. The females had raised phobic and general anxiety, and
were more likely than the males to have had psychiatric treatment. Males and
females who had had psychiatric treatment had more limited social relationships, poorer work records, and depression. Of the whole sample, 15% had had
psychiatric treatment as outpatients and 6% as inpatients—rates that were far
higher, especially for outpatient treatment, than in the general population of
similar comparable age. (This excess rate might again reflect not only increased
psychopathology but also the fact that having broken the initial referral barrier
once might make it easier for cases to get help next time).

Other Children's Phobias

Fear of sleeping alone is common at some stage of normal development. When
severe it may lead to the child's sharing the parental bed and the disruption
that entails. Like other phobias it can be treated by graded exposure (Howlin
1984). The little that has been written on children's phobias other than those
of school and of sleeping alone has usually been from the standpoint of treatment and is dealt with in Chapter 15.

Obsessive-Compulsive Disorder

Obsessive-compulsive disorder (OCD) is rare in children. Not one case was
found among more than 2,000 10- to 11-year-olds (Rutter et al. 1970), and
frequency among psychiatric referrals of children and adolescents ranged from
0.2% (Hollingsworth et al. 1980) to 1.2% Adams (1973). Although OCD is rare
in children, among adults more obsessive-compulsives (ocs) than agoraphobics
report that their problem began before age 15 (see chapters 10 and 13).

Referred cases are more common in boys and may start at any age, and
intelligence is about average or marginally above (Adams 1973; Bolton et al.
1983; Flament et al. 1985; Hollingsworth et al. 1980). Until onset of the disorder peer relationships are variable, and in most cases school difficulties seem
to result from the problem rather than cause it (Bolton et al. 1983).

Onset is usually gradual (Adams 1973). The oc features in children are similar to those in adults and may take up most of the waking hours; these and their organic associations are detailed in Chapter 13. Both obsessive ruminations and compulsive rituals often occur together, but the child may have only one or the other. Obsessive-compulsive adolescents are anxious, and about one-half resist their rituals (Bolton et al. 1973). Most cases recognize that their worries are senseless and also go through major depression at some stage (Flament & Rapoport 1984).

Nearly all affected children involve their parents and sometimes siblings in their rituals (Adams 1973; Bolton et al. 1983). There might be repeated requests for reassurance, daily demands for cooperation in rituals for hours, and domination of practically every action in the home, with shouting of instructions and violent tempers if family members hesitate to obey. Such behavior naturally causes much misery and anger in the family and conflict in the parents on how to manage the child (Bolton 1983).

Association with Autism and Mental Handicap

For some reason fears and rituals are common in subnormal and especially autistic children (Wing 1976). Autistic children are disturbed by changes in their familiar routine, but it is difficult to predict just which changes will upset them and which they will ignore. One child accepted the move from one house to another but became frantic because he was given a new bed cover. Another child refused to wear any new clothes without a series of temper tantrums. There may be dramatic scenes if a new route is followed for the daily walk, if someone sits in a different place at table, or if the household chores are done in a different order from usual. The children may be fascinated with regular patterns of objects or sounds, and make long lines or patterns of household objects. Some play the same record over and over again, or collect objects— such as dead holly leaves, plastic bottles, ashtrays from restaurants, bits of paper, bicycle chains, or specially shaped lumps of concrete—for no obvious reason. Older children who have a good vocabulary may be absorbed with certain topics such as electricity or species of birds, ask repeated questions on these subjects, and demand standard answers; the interest is not creative but is repetitive and stereotyped.

The rituals may persist into adulthood, and they can respond to exposure treatment. An example is a boy of 18 with a history of childhood autism and severe deficits in social skills, who at 9 was rigid, pedantic, and remote, at 13 slow and excessively tidy, and thereafter increasingly slow in dressing, eating, or going to bed. He varnished wood excessively and found it difficult to stop anything he was doing (Lindley et al. 1977). He had intensive treatment by exposure in vivo with modeling, response prevention, prompting, pacing, tricyclic drugs, and social skills training. During 3-year follow-up the rituals and slowness remained improved, but most of the social skills problems persisted, and the patient did not maintain regular employment. This result was comparable to that obtained in another ritualizer with a history of autism from the series of Marks and colleagues (1980). His rituals, too, improved lastingly after exposure treatment, but his lack of social skills was much more difficult to alter with training. That the former was more easily modified in these two cases suggests that different mechanisms may underlie autists' rituals as opposed to their social skills deficits.

An example of phobia with mental handicap is a boy of 17 with brain damage since age 4 after post-measles encephalitis. Thereafter he became so terrified of dogs that he could not even go into the garden of his own home alone. The problem was overcome with a few sessions of exposure in vivo in the author's unit.

SUMMARY

Unusual intense stress is followed in most people by mild transient disturbance. In a minority this reaction may mount to a traumatic phobia (post-traumatic stress disorder—PTSD) if the trauma has been very severe and prolonged and if the sufferer has been brain damaged and had previous breakdowns and a vulnerable personality without social support. PTSD can be regarded as a focal phobia originating in severe trauma, with the addition of marked nonphobic distress. The features of PTSD are irritability, tension, startle, depression, insomnia, nightmares and flashbacks, and fear and avoidance of cues reminiscent of the original trauma. The syndrome tends to start straight after the trauma, but onset may be delayed, and its course may be very chronic. Concentration camp survivors showed PTSD even 25 years after the experience.

During combat even marked fear is normal and may improve fighting ability up to a point beyond which performance drops. Surprisingly few riflemen actually shoot even when about to be overrun by attackers. Fear is aggravated by seeing others break down during danger. It is reduced by rigorous training and discipline under conditions similar to the later scene of battle, and if the same group of compatible soldiers stay together throughout. Breakdown occurs in only a minority of combatants who form a tangible proportion of all casualties. Combat phobia is more likely with low cohesion, intense and sustained combat, and heavy and visible losses.

Rape is one of the most common causes of PTSD, causing the typical picture, plus frequent sexual dysfunction and suicidal attempts. Chronic reactions are predicted by marked early distress. Women especially vulnerable to rape are those who previously were nonassertive, abused as children, and had psychological problems.

Mild fears of illness occur in most people, including medical students, but are usually transient. Rarely they become persistent with repeated requests for reassurance and avoidance of cues concerning the feared disease. Specific illness fears shade into more general hypochondriasis that can be part of a depressive or other disorder. Though common among phobic psychiatric patients, illness phobias have been little studied, apart from forms seen in brief epidemics of anxiety. Cultural, familial, and individual backgrounds can sensitize illness behavior and the type of illness feared. Most illness phobics have no discernible physical disease; some overreact to detectable disease. Their addiction to reassurance subsides if reassurance is consistently withheld by relatives, friends, and physicians.

Most children have mild fears and rituals at some stage that subside by puberty and rarely become a persistent problem. School refusal is one of the most common and handicapping of the phobias, but affects only a tiny minority of children. More school refusers are boys than girls, and they tend to be youngest children. Peak onset age is about 11 to 12. Onset is usually gradual, anxiety and its physical manifestations rising as schooltime looms in the morning, and disappearing if the child is allowed to stay at home. Depression and also separation anxiety may be present. Relatives have an increased incidence of depression and anxiety, and parents tend to be poor at child management and to encourage dependency in the child. Unlike school phobics, truants do not refuse to go to school; conceal their absence from school; are not anxious, neurotic, or introverted; show other delinquent behavior; and tend to be poorly disciplined at home and to come from unstable families. School phobia is associated with later anxiety and depression in adult life, and with an earlier onset age of agoraphobia.

Obsessive-compulsive disorder is rare in childhood, although not a few adult cases say that it began in childhood. It is seen more often in boys than girls, and onset tends to be gradual. Most recognize the absurdity of their worries yet involve their families in their rituals, sometimes tyrannizing relatives and causing much conflict. The majority are anxious and have depressive spells. Rituals and fears are unusually common in autism and in mental handicap, but seem more treatable by exposure than the social skills deficits also found in autists.

13

Obsessive-Compulsive Disorder

One of the earliest portrayals of obsessive-compulsive disorder (OCD) is that of Esquirol (1838) concerning a "monomanic" woman plagued by absurd irresistible ideas, hesitation, indecision, and slowness, together with compulsive rituals before eating, rising in the morning, and retiring to bed at night. A classic description of the syndrome was made by Westphal in 1878.

"Obsession" derives from the Latin "obsidere," meaning to besiege. Obsessions[1] denote repetitive thoughts, whereas compulsions or rituals are their counterpart as repeated actions. Most OCD cases have both obsessions and compulsions. Details of the genetics of OCD appeared in Chapter 6, of causation in chapters 5 and 8, and of childhood cases in Chapter 12; its definition, taxonomy, phenomenology, and prevalence were outlined in Chapter 9. This chapter fleshes out that information and integrates the burgeoning literature on the subject, which includes at least 11 books[2] and hundreds of articles over the past 12 years.

DEMOGRAPHIC ASPECTS

Gender

Although most phobias have a marked female preponderance, this is not true for OCD despite its phobic features. The gender ratio was nearly 1:1 among 2,244 cases from 18 series, although there was some variation. Females constituted 50% of 628 patients from 6 series reviewed by Yaryura-Tobias & Neziroglu (1983),[3] 51% of 1,336 obsessive-compulsives (ocs) from 11 other

---

[1]As an adjective we will use "obsessive" rather than "obsessional" in light of its accepted shorter form in the name of the syndrome "obsessive-compulsive disorder" and the fact that "compulsional" is never used.
[2]See, for instance, Beech 1974 & Vaughan 1978; Cammer 1976; Emmelkamp 1983; Insel 1984; Jenike et al 1986; Marks 1978, 1981; Mavissakalian et al. 1985; Rachman & Hodgson 1980; Yaryura-Tobias & Neziroglu 1983.
[3]Adams 1973; Costa Molinari et al. 1971; Kayton & Borge 1967; Pujol & Savy 1968; Yaryura-Tobias & Neziroglu 1983.

series reviewed by Black (1974),[4] and 55% of 307 ocs from the author's unit (Noshirvani et al. 1986).

The proportions of women and men are roughly equal in OCD as a whole, but they differ in some oc subtypes (Noshirvani et al. 1986). Among 307 of the author's cases, women more often had compulsive washing (66% versus 54%) and avoidance (47% versus 40%), and men more often had compulsive slowness (26% versus 6%). In addition, more women had a past history of anorexia nervosa (9% versus 0%) and of treated depression (51% versus 32%); their OCD began about 3 years later (mean age of 24). Maudsley Hospital ocs showed no significant gender difference for checking. The excess of females among oc washers in the Maudsley series fits with the excess of women with cleaning rituals and contamination fears among ocs in Edinburgh (Dowson 1977). This finding was not replicated in Toronto (Roy 1979); in that sample, male ocs more often had obsessions with a sexual content.

Age of Onset and at Treatment

Like most anxiety disorders and minor depression, OCD usually starts in adolescence and young adult life. In 8 series of OCD (Black 1974) 81% of cases began between ages 10 and 40 (including 21% between ages 10 and 15); mean age was 20 to 25 with 10% starting before age 10 and 9% after age 40. Most ocs began between age 10 and 30 in other series cited by Yaryura-Tobias and Neziroglu (1983). The mean onset age was 22 in the author's 307 patients, 92% starting from age 10 to 40 (Noshirvani et al. 1986).

More males began young at between age 5 and 15 among the author's 307 cases, whereas more females started later at age 26 to 35. Similar early onset age for male ocs was found in Noshirvani's analysis of a sample from Foa, and in childhood OCD (Rapoport & Flament 1985).

Sufferers usually present for treatment some years after onset of the OCD, as young or in early-middle-age adults at the time. Mean oc symptom duration was 8 years in the series of Pollitt (1957); in that of Noshirvani and coworkers (1986) it was 12 years, and the mean age at presentation was 34. Similar figures for six other series were cited by Yaryura-Tobias and Neziroglu (1983). The age of ocs at treatment is comparable to that for agoraphobia, anxiety states, and "reactive" ("neurotic") depression (Schuyler 1974).

Single Status and Infertility

About half of adult oc patients are single, which is more than would be expected for age-related controls, and contrasts with agoraphobics, most of whom are married (Black 1974; Roy 1979; Yaryura-Tobias & Neziroglu 1983). Single status is more common among male than female ocs; among 307 cases

---

[4]Blacker & Gore 1955; Greer & Cawley 1966; Ingram 1961b; Kringlen 1965; Lo 1967; Müller 1953; Noreik 1970; Pollitt 1957; Ray 1964; Registrar-General 1953; Rüdin 1953.

of the author's, 46% of the men and 68% of the women were married at a mean age of 34 (Noshirvani et al. 1986). Obsessive-compulsives marry later on average than do depressive psychotics, schizophrenics, or other neurotics (Hare et al. 1972).

Later age at marriage may contribute to the low fertility of oc unions, which produce even fewer children than do those of schizophrenics. In two oc series, marriages were childless in 29% and 23%, respectively (Hare et al. 1972; Rachman & Hodgson 1980). In the United Kingdom 19% of all oc marriages are childless. Once it develops, OCD, like many other syndromes, can seriously disrupt a household. Premorbid marital adjustment in ocs awaits systematic study.

Sociocultural Factors

Social class of ocs varies greatly in different studies, although several suggest that ocs are of above-average social class and intelligence, which is a related variable (Black 1974; Rachman & Hodgson 1980; Yaryura-Tobias & Neziroglu 1983). These findings are from hospital rather than community samples, so slightly raised social class and intelligence may be features less of OCD as a whole than of those subsamples seeking care. Only careful sampling in the community can settle the issue. The author has seen several subnormal patients with OCD.

OCD occurs widely in China, India, and Egypt as well as in Western countries. Whether there are fine-grain differences between cultures in its prevalence, form, or intensity is not known. Accident cases in orthopedic wards had more oc symptoms and traits (not OCD) in Ireland than in England (Kelleher 1972) or in Scotland (Scott et al. 1982); oc scores were especially high in bachelor Irish men and rural Irish women. Although there were far more Catholic Irish than English subjects, religion was unlikely to explain the cross-national differences, because English non-Catholics scored higher than English Catholics. We do not know the reasons for the cross-country differences in oc symptoms and traits, nor whether there were differences for OCD as well. Obsessive-compulsive symptoms and traits in twins are more affected by environment than by heredity (Clifford et al. 1984), but how this occurs is still obscure.

There is little information on parental characteristics of ocs. One retrospective study found that, compared to washers, checkers perceive their mothers as having been more meticulous and demanding (Steketee et al. 1985).

Season of Birth and Birth Order

One study examined the season of birth for all oc inpatients in the United Kingdom and found this to resemble that for the general population (Greenberg 1981).

An excess of first-born or only children among male ocs was found in some studies (Kayton & Borge 1967; Snowdon 1979), but not in another (Insel et al.

1983c). Male oc relatives of oc patients also tend to be first-born (Carey 1978), and first-born male relatives have more oc symptoms than those born later (McKeon 1983). This might result from parental inexperience or higher expectations, and lack of siblings. The last is supported by a finding that, compared to controls, the children of houseproud compulsive mothers had more intense interaction with adults, more time alone, and were physically restricted, and their days were more structured, less easy-going, and less peer-oriented (Cooper & McNeil 1968).

CLINICAL PICTURE

Precipitants, Mode of Onset, and Course

Precipitants of OCD were found in 30% to 69% of cases in different studies reviewed by Black (1974), but were also found in 55% to 58% of other neurotics and controls. Among 83 cases in the author's unit, ocs had more life events in the year prior to onset of the OCD than did matched normal controls (McKeon et al. 1984b). Obsessive-compulsives with obsessive, anxious, and self-conscious personalities had experienced fewer life events than ocs without such traits; that is, their threshold for breakdown was lower.

Onset can be insidious over years or, less often, sudden within a few hours, or there may be an acute exacerbation of a slowly gathering problem. Some patients have episodes of varying length that clear up completely before their disorder becomes chronic. In one analysis the onset of compulsive cleaning was usually sudden and of compulsive checking was usually gradual (Rachman & Hodgson 1980), but this needs replication. In three studies summarized by Black (1974), the initial course was static or steadily worsening in 57%, phasic in 13%, and fluctuating in 30%. In such hospital samples ocs who fail to remain in remission will inevitably be overrepresented, and there are no figures for the course of community cases. Remissions have been induced by religious or military discipline (Janet 1908; Ray 1964). Relapses may follow fatigue, depression, any cause of anxiety, and recurrence of conditions that initially triggered the problem.

Outcome 1 to 20 years later in 309 cases from 16 studies showed marked improvement in 23% and mild improvement in a further 23% (Black 1974); this was without psychosurgery and before the introduction of live exposure therapy, which has transformed the outlook for the majority who are ritualizers (see Chapter 15).

Forms of OCD

The main forms of OCD (briefly outlined in Chapter 9 and Table 9.2) will now be detailed. Their classic features of repeated, intrusive, and senseless ideas and/or acts were described more than a century ago (Westphal 1878). The most common form is repetitive rituals (compulsive acts) combined with obsessions (thoughts, ruminations)—these make up between 69% and 94% of clinical cases (Akhtar et al. 1975; Dowson 1977; Noshirvani et al. 1986; Welner et al. 1976). Far less frequent are rituals alone, obsessions alone, and slowness alone. In an alternative breakdown, a cluster analysis of responses on the Leighton Obsessional Inventory from 69 cases yielded 32 doubters (hesitancy and indecision), 30 contaminaters (body and clothing), and 7 checkers, but mixed forms were usual (Murray et al. 1979).

Most cases have about 1 to 3 central themes of concern accompanying the rituals or obsessions. Among washers and cleaners the themes usually concern contamination from bodily secretions such as feces, urine, or sperm; from germs, dirt, or chemicals; or (exceptionally) from bizarre items such as chicken soup or chocolate. The themes may be very specific: fear of contamination from urine but not from feces, sperm, or menstrual blood; fear of rabies but nothing else; of Weil's disease but no other; of dirt solely from dogs or from rats; of fire or broken glass but no other hazard; or of being blasphemous or obscene. Other worries concern broader themes such as "dirt," "germs," "cancer," harming others, or making mistakes, without specifying any particular type of dirt, germs, cancer, harm, or mistake. Occasionally over the years there may be some change of theme and of rituals. In rare cases patients ritualize or are slow with no worrying themes accompanying the behavior.

Worry that their fear might be realized leads many ocs to ritualistically and addictively request reassurance from relatives and friends ("did I wash properly?," "did I run over somebody?," "did I put glass in the food?"). Reassurance comforts transiently after which the cycle starts all over again unless reassurance is consistently and firmly withheld (see Chapter 15).

Like phobics, ocs attend selectively to cues associated with their worries. When cases with OCD simultaneously heard a neutral tape through one ear and an oc-relevant tape through another, they attended and had SC responses more to oc words such as "urine," "feces," and "radiation" than to the neutral word "pick" (Foa & McNally 1985). This selective vigilance was abolished once their OCD improved from 3 weeks of treatment by exposure with response prevention.

Compulsive Rituals with Obsessions

This is the most common form of OCD. About half the cases mainly wash and clean and the rest chiefly check; washing and checking coexist as often as they are found alone, and the same patient may be predominantly a checker at one time and a washer at another (Noshirvani et al. 1986). Washing as a dominant form occurs more among women, but checking is found about equally in both sexes. Washers have more overall fears and avoidance of external cues, whereas checkers are more concerned about future harm (Steketee et al. 1985).

Ritualistic washers and cleaners usually worry about and avoid "contaminants" and anything remotely connected with them, and sometimes even avoid places where the worries happened to occur. Contact with contaminants leads to prolonged washing and cleaning. This may consist of hundreds of brief washes or cleanings each lasting only a few seconds, or a few thorough washing/cleaning spells each continuing an hour or more.

A typical washer was a single woman of 23, a bank clerk, who for 5 years had been worried that she might become pregnant during petting even though she was a virgin. She became afraid to visit the bathroom after her boyfriend had been there lest she catch "pregnancy" from it. In addition, for 18 months she had feared that a small wart of her finger was cancerous. She avoided any objects that might contaminate her with "cancer germs," fearing that she would pass such germs from her wart onto her family, and began to wash too much. She washed her hands 125 times a day, used 3 bars of soap a day, took 3-hour showers, and washed her hair repeatedly for fear of contamination with a cancer-causing germ. Because cancer can take so long to emerge she felt that she could never be proved completely safe. She also checked electrical switches repeatedly because they seemed dangerous, and often looked back over her shoulder anticipating some nameless threat. She dreaded being the last to leave the office at night and so have to lock up.

Ritualistic checkers usually worry that death, disease, or disaster may befall other people or themselves, and they check to avert such harm, usually repeatedly. Anxiety may lead them to dress and undress in a set order 20 times lest a husband have a car accident, or retrace their route in a car many times to search for the corpses of people they may have knocked down and repeatedly phone the police asking for reports of these, or repeat the behavior that occurred during the thought "God is ugly" several times until that thought disappeared and was thus undone. Fear of fire leads to checks of electrical appliances, wires, and stoves; fear of burglary to checking of windows and doorlocks; fear of making mistakes to checking of letters and envelopes.

Typical of such checkers was a truck driver who became afraid that he might have caused an accident, and so repeatedly checked his route and notified the police. He also checked that taps were turned off, razor blades were put away, mats were not ruffled, and numerous other situations, making normal life impossible and interfering with his previously happy marriage.

Other checkers may be concerned not with disaster but with orderliness, hair, or hoarding. A man of 29 spent up to 5 hours a day washing and combing his hair, checking for head (not pubic and animal) hairs in his bed and on the floor around it. If hairs came on his clothes he felt uncomfortable and was impelled to remove them. Another young man, among his many rituals, spent up to 4 hours a morning vacuuming and polishing his room at home, searching for hair, and worrying that it might have penetrated electrical equipment. Checkers concerned with orderliness will insist on doing things in a set order that has to be completed without interruption, otherwise the whole sequence has to be started again, or they will arrange everything at home in a specific tidy pattern, disturbance of which evokes great unease. Hoarders fear throwing away something valuable and may check for hours before discarding rubbish, accumulating a weird collection of old newspapers, appliances, food scraps, tins, soap, and clothes.

Rituals repeated by number are common in many washers and checkers. The washing/checking sequences may have to be repeated a total of, say, 3, 4, or 7 times, or multiples of these, and the entire sequence may be restarted from the beginning if interrupted before its completion. Two cases were described by Cammer (1976). The first used numbers to avert harm: "I have to touch the venetian blinds 4 times, then all the *objets d'art* in the vestibule 5 times. That prevents harm to my older brother. He comes home safely, and proves that my ritual works. . . . If I don't go through with it, I start to suffer."

The second case, a successful detective, shows that even extensive counting rituals may not be very handicapping nor be designed to avert harm or discomfort. "I count the number of letters in the words spoken to me in any conversation, and I can tell you instantaneously the exact total of letters up to 350 or so. When you say 'Good morning, John' I make an immediate mental note that this has 15 letters. When you asked me 'does your counting obsession interfere with your conversation with people' I answered 'not really,' but before I answered I noticed that your question contained 64 letters. I also must count the number of letters on every street sign. That does interfere sometimes, especially when I am in a hurry to get somewhere in the car and there are lots of signs in the streets. If there are 3 numbers in a house or store window I must multiply them. For example, I see 275 on a building. I multiply $2 \times 7 \times 5$ very rapidly. It equals 70."

Exceptional rituals may involve the strangest situations. A young woman had intense and inexplicable urges to watch her lovers' bowel action, though this did not excite her sexually. When her lover went to the toilet, she could not bear to be shut out and shouted at him if she could not watch him. When allowed to watch, she would stare at the feces for several minutes. This compulsion rather dampened the enthusiasm of her boyfriends.

Occasionally compulsive rituals and avoidance are linked to morbid jealousy, which can afflict either sex. Jealousy may cause repeated searching of the partner's clothes and other possessions for signs of infidelity and endless cross-examination of the partner about his or her movements. Alcoholism is not uncommon. The jealous rituals may be reduced by response prevention, thus making life easier for the couple, even though the jealous ruminations continue (Cobb & Marks 1979). As an instance of morbid jealousy, a woman aged 19 was afraid of her boyfriend looking at other women, sought constant ritualistic reassurance from him about it, and insisted that he call her from work to confirm that he had not looked at women. Her worry prevented either of them from visiting places where there might be attractive women (bars, discos, parties, cinemas), from looking at certain friends, or from watching certain TV programs or looking at pictures of women in newspapers or magazines. Her father was jealous of her mother after she had affairs.

Compulsive Slowness Without Visible Rituals

Repeated obsessions and rituals and the need for orderliness slow sufferers in the time they take to complete everyday activities such as dressing or undressing. Occasionally slowness is the most visible problem (well reviewed by Hymas 1986). Eighty percent of such cases are men (Noshirvani et al. 1986). Careful inquiry usually reveals that even when no visible rituals are present to explain the slowness, there are nevertheless mental checks or obsessions that do so, or the need to follow a meticulous preset order without repetition (H. Ratnasuriya, personal communication, 1986). Such cases may take hours to do things most of us can accomplish in a minute or two. Although they may be surprised when told how many hours they have taken to get dressed or to cross the road, their estimation of objective time is normal (Rachman 1974).

Compulsive slowness does not affect automatic behavior such as driving a car or playing fast games in which one is continually responding to ongoing cues. Patients who take hours to finish dressing or undressing are nevertheless able to play a splendid game of badminton, squash, or table tennis. They promptly execute commands to get up, sit down, or cross the room.

Extreme slowness without visible rituals seems to affect self-initiated actions that are not externally prompted. When prompted and paced, sufferers speed up considerably without showing much anxiety, only to slow down once more when prompting and pacing is withdrawn, even if it has been given for months over hundreds of hours and faded out very gradually over further months; tape-recorded prompts from the therapist that the patient plays when alone have not been a great help. This makes extreme slowness without visible rituals very difficult to treat, and the case whose improvement was documented by Rachman (1974), Marks and colleagues (1975), and Rachman and Hodgson (1980) did not retain many gains at long term follow-up. The poor final outcome of these cases separates them from the average ritualizer, who not only improves rapidly to treatment by exposure with response prevention but also maintains his or her gains after the therapist withdraws from the scene.

A typical example is a man who had been out of work for 8 years because of slowness. He would take several hours to dress and have breakfast in the mornings. To be in time for his afternoon appointment with me, he had to shave the previous day. When asked how long it took him to have a bath he replied "Do you mean from the time I actually get into the bath, or from the time I start *thinking* of having a bath?" Bathing took 5 hours. To cross a road would take another few hours, because he not only had to check that no cars were coming but he also had to look at every car parked along the road nearby in case they were about to move off. By the time he had finished looking inside the parked cars, he would have to start looking up and down the street several times once more, by which time he felt he had to look inside the parked cars again. To switch off a light, he first checked that his shoes were insulated and would look many times at his soles before he dared to risk electrocution by putting his hand on the light switch. This slowness affected many of his actions, yet he drove his car well above the speed limit. He would speed up in self-initiated actions if supervised but lapsed as soon as he was left on his own, and taped prompts did not help. After hundreds of hours of treatment by prompting, pacing, and coaching, he was no better than at the start. He believed his behavior was normal given the risks involved, and that other people were taking unreasonable risks. (Such delusional fixity of belief excludes cases from a *DSM-III* diagnosis of OCD, but no other feature separates them, and other typical oc cases with fixed beliefs have responded to treatment by response prevention, with the belief disappearing as their behavior changes [Lelliott & Marks 1987]).

Does compulsive slowness overlap with the basal gangliar disorder of Parkinsonism, which often entails slowness (especially in initiating movement) as a feature, and is also more common in men? Unlike Parkinsonism, compulsive slowness has no tremor or rigidity, is much more selective in affecting only particular actions, and starts in younger rather than elderly men. The author has had no success in trying to help two cases of compulsive slowness with anti-Parkinsonian drugs such as L-dopa and amantidine.

Obsessions Without Rituals (Ruminations)

Most people have unpleasant thoughts from time to time that can usually be banished fairly easily unless they become dysphoric (Rachman 1985). In a few people the thoughts become persistent obsessions—repetitive, intrusive ideas that may be fleeting or last an hour. They usually concern unacceptable ideas about violence, sex, obscenity, or minor peccadillos. The thoughts may be evoked by external cues or come out of the blue. Although experienced as absurd, obsessions are hard to drive away, impair concentration, and cause considerable distress. Pure obsessions without rituals are unusual (16% of all ocs in the series of Noshirvani et al. 1986); however, most ritualizers have obsessions that they try to switch off by engaging in rituals.

Obsessions lead to avoidance of evoking cues. Sufferers worried that they may harm others may go to great lengths to shun potential weapons or defenseless babies. A housewife may hide sharp knives in her kitchen far out of reach to remove temptation, and mothers may request constant company for fear of strangling their baby if left alone. The concern may be about harming oneself rather than others. Obsessives can be afraid of swallowing pins, broken glass, or other sharp objects, and go to ridiculous extremes to guard against the remotest chance of this happening. Preventive rituals are common, as in a man who held bad thoughts at bay by keeping his hands in his pockets when approaching other people.

The risk of translating obsessive ideas into terrible actions is in fact very small. It is rare for oc patients to actually swear, stab, or strangle in the manner they fear. Out of 300 oc patients of the author's, only 3 yielded to their antisocial impulse. One was a young woman who felt compelled to pick scabs off her young son's skin when they formed after he scratched himself; after treatment, this problem disappeared. A less happy outcome ensued in another woman who felt impulses to kill her 2-year-old child and sacrificed a pet tortoise instead; eventually she had to be separated from her daughter.

Obsessive ideas that induce anxiety can usually be distinguished from thoughts that sufferers deliberately think to reduce anxiety—so-called cognitive rituals. One form of cognitive ritual is mental checking, the covert counterpart of visible acts of checking.

Two of the four following cases from the Maudsley Hospital had both obsessions and cognitive rituals. A man had violent and sexual thoughts about people that were precipitated by letters from or talk about them; the thoughts were kept at bay by stopping what he was doing when they came on and striving to achieve a good thought (a cognitive ritual), after which he could resume the interrupted activity. To reduce the obsessions he would also wash briefly about 80 times a day to symbolically clean the bad or unwanted thought, violently shake his head or other parts of his body, change the names of places or characters, or concentrate intensely on a distracting thought or activity.

Another case was a 35-year-old mother who since age 18 had worries of blinding her children or of harming their ears by shouting at them. Her obsessions might arise without external cues or if she saw knives or was alone with her children. Her three children had to be taken care of by her parents. She threw away many sharp instruments and stored others where she could not reach them. At age 24 she briefly cleaned her first baby's diapers compulsively. Her worries fluctuated over the years and were accompanied by much depression. She had had much psychiatric treatment.

A third case obsessed for hours whether she had murdered a solitary old lady who had died shortly after visits from her; she made repeated phone calls and visits to the local police station to check that death had been due to natural causes, but these failed to reassure her, and she also had recurrent depression. A fourth patient had intrusive distressing images of four people lying dead in open coffins in an open grave; the images could occur spontaneously or in response to violent or aggressive material in a book or on television, and once they intruded she had to stop ongoing activity until she could imagine the same four people standing and walking about healthily (a cognitive ritual).

Nature of Obsessive-Compulsive Symptoms

Nearly everyone has occasionally experienced brief runs of repetitive thoughts or actions, but these can usually be dispelled easily and so cause minimal discomfort. By definition these become a clinical problem only when they persist intrusively for reasons that are unclear. In 1891 William James drew attention to the "fiat" that we normally give ourselves to mark the end of a sequence of thoughts or actions and which seems to be missing in ocs. It is a mystery how an oc decides that 4 hours rather than 4 minutes or 4 seconds of washing are enough to dispel contamination, or why 20 rather than 2 checks will avert disaster. Number rituals may be shortened by jumping in multiples (for example, from 6 to 3); the sequence may be lengthened in the reverse order.

Obsessions and rituals are generally experienced as intrusive, forcing themselves on the patient against his or her will ("ego-alien" or "ego-dystonic"). Resistance to the oc thoughts or urges is usual, but some cases yield to their impulse without a sense of compulsion. When the obsession or urge to ritualize comes on, most sufferers feel discomfort—frequently anxiety, but some call it disgust or unpleasantness. The urge to ritualize and the execution of the sequence can cause great distress when the patient knows that these herald hours of pointless toil. Actually completing the ritual usually reduces the anxiety (see Chapter 14), but what signal triggers a sense of completion is obscure.

Most ocs experience anxiety/fear on contact with their evoking stimuli (Grayson et al. 1982), and this is reduced (cancelled, undone, or neutralized) by certain thoughts and rituals (Rachman & Hodgson 1980; Van den Hout & Hessels 1984). Some thoughts might raise anxiety; others reduce it. One patient felt bad at the thought of chicken soup and better at that of Palmolive soap; in another the number 3 caused anxiety while 7 cancelled it (Foa & Steketee 1979). Another case neutralized the thought "drop dead" by repeating 5 times the thought "long may he live" (Hoogduin 1986). Neutralizing thoughts have been called cognitive rituals (Rachman & Hodgson 1980). Cancelling or anxiety-reducing features ("undoing") and indecision can spawn long sequences of undoing the undoing. In the course of treatment, oc ideas or acts that increase anxiety require exposure to the evoking stimulus, whereas those that cancel it need response prevention.

Foa et al. (1985) suggested labeling both ideas or acts that evoke anxiety as obsessions, and those which reduce it as compulsions. Before such usage is adopted, it needs to be shown in a series of patients that the same obsession or ritual does not at one time relieve anxiety and at another evoke it. Moreover, such usage would exclude occasional oc ideas and acts that are unassociated with discomfort, although their features are otherwise the same. It seems easier for therapists to continue the traditional labels of ideas as obsessions and acts as compulsions, but to note whether they evoke anxiety (in which case exposure should be encouraged) or reduce it (in which case such ideas or acts should be prevented).

Obsessions tend to increase with anxiety and decrease with relaxation (Leger 1978) or with increased EEG alpha waves, which some construe as a relaxed state (Mills & Solyom 1974). There was a steep rise in unwanted, intrusive, and distressing thoughts in mothers whose children were being hospitalized for elective surgery, and these thoughts reduced quickly to normal after surgery was successfully completed (Rachman 1985). Normals have a rise in intrusive ideas not only after seeing a stressful film but also after seeing an erotic one, more than after a neutral film (Horowitz 1976). Haunting thoughts thus seem to result from *any* intensely emotional experience, be it unpleasant or pleasant, whether it is related to disaster or to exciting sex.

Most patients know that their oc thoughts and behavior are senseless, but a few link these to beliefs held with an intensity amounting to a delusion and may even have related hallucinations, such as a voice commanding them to "repeat that action," yet show no other psychotic features (Lelliott et al. 1986b). They usually fail to comply with exposure plus response prevention, as they see no reason to adhere to a therapeutic program. In a case whose beliefs were delusional but who nevertheless carried out the treatment instructions, his rituals improved greatly and lastingly, and the delusion disappeared; his preexisting depression continued to fluctuate (Lelliott & Marks 1987).

Distress from Obsessive-Compulsive Problems

Personal Distress

Although traits such as neatness and cleanliness are virtues that help people in their jobs and everyday life, when the behavior governs every action it is not a trait but part of an oc disorder. This can cause great suffering and handicap.

A 25-year-old married woman vividly portrayed her problem (Marks 1965) in the following description.

> This obsession spoils everything I do. If I had the courage I'd kill myself and get rid of the whole lot—it goes on and on, day after day. The obsession governs everything I do from the minute I open my eyes in the morning until I close them at night. It governs what I can and can't touch, where I can and can't walk. I can touch the ground but I can't touch shoes or hems of coats, can't use the toilet without washing my hands and arms half a dozen times—and they must be washed right up the arms. If anybody touches their shoes I can't let them touch me—because then I would feel unclean and have to wash. It all started from the toilet—first human dirt, then dog dirt. I can't bear dogs—when I go out on the street I must be careful where I walk. I'm always afraid that I might have stepped in some dirt.
>
> [And if you actually get contaminated?] That's the funny thing about it—it's not all that bad. My first feeling is panic and I want to die—but I know you can't die just by wishing it, so then I've got to wash with a special procedure which never seems to come to an end—have to wash the tap and round the tap before washing my hands. I know it's all in the mind and ridiculous but can't accept it. I don't know why I'm so afraid of dirt all the time, but I am.
>
> [Do you fight the feeling?] Yes, I do all the time, and usually succeed in the end after an hour or two, but the fear is still there. It frightens me because I don't know how to handle it, or what to think. Nothing in life interests me, I don't care what I look like, or what I eat. I do get flashes where I care very much, but for just a minute. I used to spend an hour washing every bit of me in the bath—washing all the time, but I only take half an hour, and now I can go and use a public toilet if it's clean. But the fear is more outside now—watching where I can walk. Things seem to change, and the fear slides over onto something else. What the fear started off with is still there, but it enlarges, and spreads to things I could have touched alright before. Once a long time ago I tried stopping washing for a week—but it was terrible, I got awful nightmares, and was ready to scream all the time. After that I never tried stopping it again. But I can't go on like this, I want to care, I don't want to go on feeling life's useless.

The handicap caused by OCD can be at least as great as that of chronic schizophrenia and last as long, for several decades. Many of the author's cases lost their jobs because rituals made them arrive late or work far too slowly, and they might stop all social life and become reclusive. Sufferers can spend much of the day and night in repetitive washing, checking, or counting, and so never get to bed before 4 A.M. Even then they may drop exhausted to sleep in their clothes on a couch in the lounge rather than go through interminable bedtime rituals. Some sit still in a chair most of their waking hours to avoid becoming "dirty," which would start endless hours of washing themselves and their surroundings. A young man had for months not used a toilet because it triggered a washing routine, so instead he urinated and defecated in his pants without removing them afterward, and he reeked accordingly. A woman who washed her hands a 100 times a day until they were raw and bleeding ran out of money to buy the vast amount of soap she used and so stole it from a store; when the police arrested her they could not record her fingerprints because she had washed them away. She, too, smelled awful, as she washed her hands only up to the elbows and left the rest of herself unwashed.

Many patients' surroundings become off-limits areas for fear of contamination or harm, and patients restrict themselves to a few safe places. Only one or two rooms of the home may be used; the rest are shut off for decades because they seem contaminated. Patients may move from one house to another every few months as each one in turn seems to become dirty, and these moves cause disruption and financial hardship. A judge would never use the toilet at home because it was contaminated, and instead would get in his car to drive into a safe area where he could defecate or urinate. He could not endure sex because it seemed dirty. He gave up his job and dressed in a shabby stained suit bulging from the wads of tissues he kept in his inside pocket to wrap around door handles before touching them. He never shook hands with anyone. Other patients discard clothes after wearing them only once or twice because the garments seem to feel dirty.

Effect on the Family

In some cases the family seems unaffected, but in others it is severely disrupted by the patient's loss of job, money, and social life. When rituals prevent patients from contributing normally to running the home then relatives may have to take over completely. Patients may also ask relatives to join in rituals and avoidance behavior.

The families of many of the author's cases lead grotesque lives. A woman fearing "contamination" of her home forced her family to move 5 times in 3 years and totally avoided a "dirty" town in the area. Visitors might be forbidden to enter the house, leading to social isolation for all. Obsessive-compulsives may insist that family members strip naked of the clothes and shoes that they wore out of doors before allowing them into the house. In the home, relatives may be forbidden from entering certain rooms or touching particular objects, the bathroom may be occupied for hours, and they may be allowed to go to bed only after the rituals have ended. A girl of 18 forced her parents to watch her lengthy bedtime rituals to ensure that she did them properly, to hold her toothbrush and tumbler of water, and finally to submit to repeated, ritualistic goodnight kisses.

Relatives may be pressured by patients too tired to continue with their rituals to wash or disinfect clothes, or to get up in the middle of the night to check for the tenth time that the baby is still breathing or the burners on the stove are switched off. A 17-year-old forced his mother to clean his cutlery and crockery repeatedly and then wait on him to put sugar, salt, and pepper in his food because he would not touch their containers. Another young patient forbade her parents to read newspapers for fear of their spreading contamination from the dirty newsprint. Still another did not allow his mother to clean the house when he was home (which was most of the time), lest she dirty him with dust. A middle-aged woman who feared contamination from chocolate forbade her husband to eat chocolate anywhere at any time, whether she was present or not; on returning home each night he had to recount precisely what he had eaten that day. Often relatives have to answer interminable ritualistic requests for reassurance: "Am I clean?" "Did I knock somebody down?" "Is the stove switched off?" "Are the children safe?"

Even if the family can firmly resist such demands—and that is no easy matter—their homes may look strange. The toilet may be brightly clean and strongly disinfected while parts of the kitchen are caked with month-old remains of food (the counterpart of some patients having hands raw from hours of washing while the rest of them is filthy). Dedicated cleaners will stock the kitchen, bathroom, and toilet with piles of soap bars, rubber gloves, boxes of washing powder, tissue paper, rolls of paper towels, toilet paper, and bottles of disinfectant. Compulsive checkers put long checklists at strategic points. Tidiers will have spotless homes with everything in place, but it may be almost impossible to move in a hoarder's home, whose passages and rooms become cluttered with old newspapers, cans of food, broken equipment, bits of string, nails, and screws. One man stored an old car rusting on blocks in the garage while his new car was left exposed to the elements in the street.

Effect on Children. Children may be markedly affected by oc behavior. Their oc parent may cease to look after them and increase their emotional deprivation by bizarre physical restrictions. For fear of contracting cancer an oc mother who was almost immobilized refused to touch her children or their belongings, and forbade them from touching her body, clothes, or toiletries; they were prohibited from walking near pharmacies or hospitals, playing with children living in "suspect" households or bringing friends home, and on returning from school had to take off their clothing and carry out cleaning rituals. Another woman had checking and cleaning rituals that dominated her family's home life; her young children were obliged to undress at specific times and places and only when she was seated in a particular chair downstairs; their rooms were dirty and disorganized, as she could not touch most of their contents. In other families schooling was disrupted by frequent moves of home dictated by oc fears.

A woman with a fear of tuberculosis restricted her husband and 2-year-old son to one of the four rooms available at home, and the boy was cooped up in a playpen all day lest he crawl into "infected" areas; the unused rooms were locked and became covered in dust over the years. Her lengthy rituals led to meals being skimpy and late, and she could not feed her son for fear of giving him tuberculosis, which she had suffered decades earlier. She opened doors only with her elbows or feet to avoid germs on the doorknobs, had long ago ceased working as a secretary, and stopped all visitors to the home, including the grandmother. She spent much of her day washing her hands dozens of times until they bled.

It is a tribute to their resilience that most children of ocs who grow up in such abnormal environments have no obvious problems themselves. Concern with passing the problem onto their child leads some patients to ask for help. Some children develop oc features during the parent's illness or much later, and these may resemble those of the parent or be very different. In one family the mother and two daughters slept together in the same bed, and all three developed similar handwashing rituals based on fears of dirt; the father and brother slept together in another bed, and neither developed rituals.

Sex. Coitus can be surprisingly normal despite severe contamination fears. A man whose life was governed by washing away imaginary dog dirt nevertheless contracted gonorrhea from a prostitute. Sometimes sexual activity is part of a broader worry about cleanliness, prolonged washing rituals being mandatory for both partners before and after intercourse, so that coitus may tail off and cease completely. In other cases, vigorous and enjoyable sex may continue in the face of all these obstacles.

In other cases sex or its products are the chief focus of concern. Either sex may fear pregnancy from distant contact and go to extreme lengths to avoid their bodies or clothing touching other people. A capable engineer rearranged his working day to avoid sections of his home town for fear of sexual contamination, and engaged in coitus solely in a sterile room at home that contained only a bed and was kept locked at all other times. He and his partner had to carry out elaborate cleaning rituals before entering the room, both naked, and the cleaning rituals were repeated immediately upon leaving it. Clothing or other items that became inadvertently contaminated were cleaned and disinfected or, if that failed, discarded. His partner insisted that he obtain treatment, and he improved dramatically with exposure therapy. Another man would spend hours after ejaculation immobile with his arms outstretched in front of an open window "drying" because semen made him feel wet.

Response of Relatives. Some relatives will simply not comply with the patient's requests to join in the rituals. Others comply thinking it will help him or her. Yet others may protest but be tyrannized into grudging submission by the tantrums, screams, and physical abuse from the patient that may follow refusal. In many households the battle continues to rage over the years. Some relatives get fed up and leave. A few come to share the patient's oc beliefs and happily collude in all he or she does, rarely even to the point of *folie à deux.*

Relatives are in a quandary in the face of extraordinary oc demands. Yielding to them leads to escalation and to hamstringing of normal activity by anyone at home. The dilemma is particularly painful if the family's refusal to participate in rituals leads the oc to leave home to escape contamination and ritualize to his satisfaction. Should they settle for a quiet life and just comply with the patient's weird requests to avoid upsetting him or her, or should they refuse and risk a flood of abuse pouring over them, not to mention the handicap to their own lives that will ensue? Gentle but firm refusal to comply is in fact kinder in the long run, despite the initial upset that this may cause. Unless the relatives do only what they consider normal without being bludgeoned into submission to unreasonable demands, the patient's rituals may spread still further into any social space that is made available. By applying the therapeutic principle of exposure and response prevention, relatives can become effective therapists, but they need support in this exacting role (see Chapter 15).

RELATION OF OCD TO OTHER CONDITIONS

"Obsessive" (Anancastic) Personality and "Cognitive Style"

Both obsessive thoughts and compulsive rituals tend to occur more in people who have always had meticulous and perfectionist personalities, although such problems can occur in the most slipshod of people. Meticulous habits can take many forms. One person might be uneasy unless he uses up the last tiny sliver of soap, another cannot bear to see a picture on the wall hang slightly askew, yet another hates being untidy or having the merest speck of dirt on himself or his clothes or in his home. People vary enormously in this regard, and such differences cause many a squabble between people who live together. Dr. Elizabeth Fenwick caught this variation beautifully:

> I once met a woman who ironed diapers. When I asked her why she did it she said because it made them square. Aesthetically I can appreciate square diapers as well as anyone, but there are some things I am not prepared to make a good many sacrifices for. On a 0–5 Ironing Rating Scale I would probably score around 2, in front of the people who don't iron sheets and only do the bits of their husband's shirts which are going to show, but way behind the pyjama and towel and vest and diaper ironers. . . .
>
> [My grandmother] used to make ginger biscuits. Each biscuit was 3 inches in diameter and weighed ½ oz. It weighed ½ oz. because she cut off a piece of dough and trimmed it and weighed it on her scales until that was what it weighed, and there was no cheating by weighing a 2 oz. lump and cutting it into 4 either. All this sort of thing takes time, of course, which is one reason why I am not as obsessional as I might be. My grandmother never cut a piece of string in her life, no matter how enticing the contents of the parcel. She undid every knot and wound it into a neat little ball, and put it away in a chocolate box labelled String (Oddments), and in the left hand front corner of the drawer next to the one marked Candles, which contained candles. Whenever there was a fuse or power cut at home it was always quicker to nip round to grandmother's and borrow a candle rather than hunt around in the dark for our own.

The characteristic personality traits include orderliness, cleanliness, fastidiousness, meticulousness, parsimony, pedantry, persistence, endurance, and unemotionality. Most read like a list of Victorian virtues and are indeed helpful in everyday life, becoming a handicap only when they are present to an extreme degree. The dividing line can be hard to draw. "We" are of course always careful, conscientious, and firm, while "they" are rigid, pedantic, and obstinate. In psychoanalytic accounts traits are called "obsessive" or "ego-syntonic" when perseverance leads to success, orderliness brings clarity, and limited checking avoids error (Ingram 1961b; Sandler & Hazari 1960). When they hamper adjustment, with orderliness and discipline becoming ends in themselves, indecision and fear of error making any task endless, and rigidity cramping originality and invention, then such features are called "anal-erotic," "ego-dystonic," or "anancastic" symptoms.

A retrospective history of premorbid markedly obsessive traits is common in OCD (an average of 71% in 7 series reviewed by Black 1974), and is given more often by oc than by other neurotics (Ingram 1961a; Kringlen 1965; Tyrer et al. 1983). To put this in perspective, although such traits are common in OCD they are also frequent in other neuroses and in normals. The frequency of the traits in normals is not known. However, obsessive personality traits were reported in 53% of patients with anxiety, hysterical, and depressive neuroses as well as in 72% of OCD patients (Kringlen 1965). Moreover, the reported excess in OCD may be weighted by retrospective distortion.

One study claimed that two subtypes of obsessive personality traits were each related to a subtype of OCD (Rachman & Hodgson 1980). The personalities of cases of compulsive cleaning were frequently "morose, obstinate, irritable," whereas those of compulsive checkers were more "submissive, vacillating, uncertain." In a previous study less than half of OCD cases fell into either of these two categories of traits (Ingram 1961a).

A substantial minority of patients with OCD did not have an obsessive personality premorbidly (16% to 36% in 5 series reviewed by Black 1974), and some may even have been untidy slobs. Contrary to the stereotype of a restrained personality, there may be emotional outbursts unrelated to the thwarting of rituals. The patient in the classic description of OCD (see p. 434) was liable to repeated sudden outbursts of temper and physical violence. Obsessive-compulsive symptoms were similar in 10 ocs who had been impulsive since childhood compared with another 10 who had not (Hoehn-Saric & Barksdale 1983).

Obsessive-compulsives are often said to be hostile and defending against unconscious anger, a prominent theme in psychoanalytic writings. Marks (1965) found no evidence that ocs were excessively afraid of or defending against aggression; they scored like actively aggressive psychopaths. Nor did ocs differ from depressives on anger and hostility (Millar 1983), although the two groups had different patterns of correlations among various measures, and other ocs found some situations more annoying than did other neurotics.

Neuroticism is raised in ocs (Rabavilas et al. 1977) as it is in any group with raised generalized anxiety (see Table 9.3). Similarly, fear of criticism is raised in OCD but not specific to that syndrome, as it is also raised in agoraphobics and social phobics but not in specific phobics (Thyer et al. 1984; Turner et al. 1979).

Numerous "cognitive" features have been found that could be as much a sign of OCD as its cause, hence will not be discussed in detail (reviewed by Rachman & Hodgson 1980, pp. 56–57; Foa 1985b). Obsessive-compulsives cannot tolerate uncertainty or ambiguity, tend to form underinclusive concepts (Turner et al. 1983), and use personal constructs that cluster into isolated groups with no linking construct. Among volunteer students, compared to noncheckers, checkers had poorer logical memory for meaningful sequences of tasks carried out at a computer terminal, although their scores were within the normal range (Sher et al. 1984). Among oc and non-oc outpatients sorting cards according to two neutral principles (cleanliness and important mistake) and two oc principles (size, heat), ocs sorted the cards into more piles with fewer cards per pile, especially for the oc principles (Persons & Foa 1984). They made finer distinctions among items that non-ocs viewed as similar and also took more time to do so; however, the ocs were also more depressed, which might explain both differences.

It is not clear whether neuroticism, fear of criticism, and the various cognitive differences that have been found were present premorbidly or whether they are a manifestation of the disorder itself after it develops.

Many beliefs (rationales, thoughts) that accompany oc rituals are like everyday magical or superstitious beliefs that have become fixed and carried to extremes. Greek patients with OCD were more superstitious than were matched normal controls, with similar but less marked differences among the relatives of the two groups (Rabavilas et al. 1977). The superstitions of ocs and their relatives deserve more attention, given the magical nature of much oc thinking.

In brief, most cases of OCD had "obsessive" personalities premorbidly, but such traits are also common (if somewhat less so) in other anxiety disorders and in normals. Most people with such traits never develop OCD, and up to one-third of patients with OCD never had an "obsessive" personality. It is not known whether cognitive features that have been described were present before the oc syndrome developed.

Normal Religious Ritual

Freud (1907) ventured to describe oc neurosis as "an individual religiosity, and religion as a universal obsessional neurosis." However, religious writings and clerics clearly distinguish normal religious ritual from pathological scrupulosity. The clergy are more permissive than are patients with OCD. Obsessive-compulsives do not follow the usual conventions and instead use their own idiosyncratic rules. A Jewish patient of the author's had endless rituals to separate "milk" from "meat" food and utensils. He refused treatment by exposure with response prevention, but agreed to discuss his worries with a rabbi. When the rabbi pointed out that the rituals were far in excess of normal religious observance, the patient retorted, "He's not a proper rabbi"—his belief was fixed to a delusional degree.

Other religious ocs were detailed by Greenberg (1984). All were observant Jews, and the onset of their OCD occurred at the time of religious commitment in all cases except one who had an orthodox upbringing. They had repetitive actions with a religious rationale (to prevent meat and milk from mixing, bread from being introduced into the Passover home, or prayers being said without adequate preparation and devotion).

Five distinctions of compulsive rituals from religious rites emerged. First, the zealousness of all the cases was limited to particular topics without excessive concern for all areas of religious practice. Second, the topic might be of minimal religious significance. Third, the oc ritual could actually interfere with full religious practice, making one patient arrive late for services and shorten his prayers, while another violated observance of the Sabbath in order to clean herself. Fourth, unlike religious rites, the rituals were in most of the cases associated with distress and resistance and interfered with normal social function—that is, they were ego-dystonic rather than syntonic. Last but not least, the patients all had additional nonreligious rituals.

Half the ocs in a psychiatric clinic in an Orthodox Jewish area of Jerusalem had oc problems concerning religion at some time in their disorder, according to Greenberg (1984), who wrote that "religious patients thus have religious compulsions just as religious psychotics have religious delusions." Their religious commitment is likely to be pathoplastic rather than pathogenetic.

The exposure treatment of religious ocs works within the limits of religious practice, and these limits are discussed among the patient, therapist, and cleric. A Jewish patient cannot be asked to eat bread on Passover or to omit prayers completely. However, understanding rabbis have agreed with the therapist in banning pre-prayer ablutions and repetitions of prayers, and allowing the carrying of sealed nonkosher meat.

OCD and Phobic Disorders

Similarities

Obsessive-compulsive and phobic problems resemble one another in three ways.

1. As with phobics, the relevant evoking stimuli (ES) often induce anxiety, which in ocs leads to obsessions and rituals. In both syndromes sufferers may fear harm from contact with the ES. Anxiety or discomfort may be minimal in ocs who are very chronic, have had psychosurgery, or are children.
2. Both phobics and ocs avoid or escape from their ES, and oc avoidance can be extensive. This may lead to handicap as great as that from the inordinate time wasted on senseless and repeated rituals and thoughts. Exceptional patients have no obvious cues bringing on the obsessions or rituals, but most have a clear avoidance profile that is very complex in severe cases.
3. Both phobic and oc syndromes respond well to exposure treatment. It persuades patients to reenter hitherto avoided situations and to remain in them until the ensuing discomfort subsides (see Chapter 14).

In brief, taken together phobic and oc disorders form the *syndromes of anxious avoidance*. Most phobics and ocs experience discomfort with and avoid particular external cues, and both these features can be relieved by exposure.

Differences

OCD differs from phobias in at least seven ways, the last four of which are related. These differences are ones of emphasis rather than clearcut distinctions, and they are not easily defined.

1. Phobics have persistent worries around a central theme, whereas ocs have more stereotyped repetitive thoughts and actions that need treatment by self-imposed response prevention as well as exposure.
2. The evoking stimuli are different. Untidiness, dirt, contagion, or harm to others are common oc worries but cause few phobics much difficulty. Knowing that someone is afraid of dirt predicts that he or she probably has related oc rituals without avoidance of buses or dogs per se. Equally,

knowing that people are afraid of buses or dogs predicts that they will probably not have rituals. Some ocs do avoid buses or dogs that seem dirty or have certain associations, but it is the latter, not the buses or dogs as such, that they avoid. In contrast, buses or dogs cause panic and avoidance in agoraphobics and dog phobics without any other associations.

3. On contact with the ES the emotional experience in OCD may not be intense anxiety. Although ocs are usually tense in the presence of their ES, they look less panic-stricken than do phobics. Many ocs experience discomfort other than anxiety, and washers sometimes report disgust. Obsessive-compulsives differ from agoraphobics but not from specific phobics in having fewer spontaneous panics, although ocs may have spontaneous obsessions. But blood or food phobics, too, may not feel anxious with their ES.

4. Oc discomfort is less stimulus-bound and spreads more than in phobics. Both phobics and ocs are uncomfortable on encountering their evoking stimuli, but ocs may take longer to feel better after they avoid or escape from it, and may ruminate and ritualize for hours afterward about remote consequences of contact with their ES. This remoteness is in time, place, and logical connection. Obsessive-compulsives who worry about getting rabies, or cancer, or becoming pregnant, may avoid very distantly related situations that to the average person's mind could not possibly be harmful. A patient with oc worries about rabies may avoid not only touching dogs but even contact with objects that a dog may have last touched weeks or months before or places where it may have been, or people who could have been there. Similarly, a woman terrified about possible injury from glass splinters was more afraid about fragments she suspected but could not find at home than of glass splinters she actually found and removed with her bare hands.

5. The evoking stimuli that trigger oc problems may be more abstract than those which evoke phobias. Cats and thunderstorms are discrete phobic stimuli and public situations somewhat less so; in contrast, "untidiness," "dirt," or "danger" seem less tangible. A man fearing contamination from dogs disliked touching a single dog hair as much as live dogs, and touching it would initiate handwashing for hours. Obsessive-compulsive fear is less of the ES itself than of the vague consequences of contact; this leads to widespread ripples of avoidance and protective rituals. Moreover, compulsive rituals can be present that are unconnected with the professed fear.

6. Another point, related to the two preceding ones, is that oc worry about remote consequences of contact with an ES more than about the ES itself makes such worry more oriented to the remote future than is the anticipatory anxiety of phobics. Contact with the ES may trigger fears of contamination or disaster that have to be averted by washing or checking for hours afterward. Compulsive washers may touch a "contaminated" object quite easily if they anticipate reducing the ensuing discomfort by washing repeatedly.

7. The abnormal beliefs associated with avoidance are more elaborate in ocs than in phobics. The cognitions associated with phobias are quite simple. Agoraphobics commonly fear that they will faint, die, or lose control if they go out and also fear fear itself and its autonomic symptoms, but they do not elaborate such fear into a wider net of beliefs. In contrast, oc rituals are often accompanied by complex ideas about how infection spreads, harm comes to people, or magic numbers influence events.

In brief, unlike phobics, ocs have repetitive thoughts or actions evoked by stimuli that are different, more abstract and future oriented, and linked to more elaborate abnormal beliefs. Compared with the panic of phobics, oc panic is less obvious and their discomfort less stimulus-bound.

Depression

Obsessive-Compulsive Symptoms in Depressive Disorders

Obsessive-compulsive features are common in depressive problems. Obsessive-compulsive symptoms and traits were present in about 22% of inpatients with psychotic or neurotic depression (Kendell & Discipio 1970; Lewis 1934) and were increased in depressed outpatients (Stonehill & Crisp 1976). Of 398 inpatients with depressive psychosis, 25% had obsessions excluding suicidal ruminations (Gittleson 1966); 13% showed obsessions before the onset of depression, and their depression began at a younger age than in the remaining depressives. Of these 13% a quarter lost their obsessions during subsequent depression, and a quarter developed them; samples of OCD in treatment trials obviously exclude the former type of patient and include the latter, and may thus overemphasize the association of depression with obsessions. Pre-existing obsessions were associated with a lower rate of suicide or suicidal attempts, more obsessions with the depression, and worsened obsessions persisting after the depression improved.

Both latter points were also noted by Kendell and Discipio (1970), whose depressives' oc symptoms were raised during episodes of depression, but not to the intensity of patients with OCD. A high proportion of those who developed new oc symptoms when they became depressed had not had premorbid obsessive traits. On recovery from depression the oc symptoms reduced to a lower but still abnormal level. Obsessive traits may persist after the depression improves (Paykel et al. 1976). However, in another study, recovered depressives showed no more oc features than did controls (Wooster 1963).

Only in 5% of obsessions coexisting with the depression did the obsessions amount to a delusion (Gittleson 1966). In another 208 "endogenous" depressives, preexisting oc symptoms were again associated with the absence of delusions as well as with the absence of hypomania and of retardation; oc symptoms were associated rather with the presence of anxiety and agitation and a previous anancastic personality (Videbech 1975). There was a similar conjunction of oc features with less retardation but with more anxiety and agitation in depressives between 20 and 29 years old (Vaughan 1976).

Depressed Mood in OCD

In OCD as in agora-, social, and traumatic phobias and in anxiety states, depressed mood is frequent (Goodwin et al. 1969, Foa & Foa 1982). Thirty-five percent of patients with typical OCD also met the criteria for primary affective disorder (Coryell 1981). Past treated depression had occurred in 42% of 145 cases of the author's (Noshirvani et al. 1986), and within 10 years of onset of the OCD, 34% of another 144 cases had received treatment for moderately severe depression (Rosenberg 1968). In four controlled studies initial depressed mood was prominent in OCD and improved after treatment with antidepressants, but was liable to recur subsequently once the drug was withdrawn (Marks 1983). Depression is more marked among female than male ocs (Mawson et al. 1982) and is associated with more severe rituals and anxiety (Marks et al. 1980).

The vast majority of the many ocs who develop depression show it in the anxious "neurotic" form that has not yet been satisfactorily separated from anxiety disorders (see Chapter 9); other labels for the mood disturbance are dysthymia, dysphoria, reactive or minor depression, and demoralization. Anxiety is prominent with the depressed mood, so that anxiety-depression is a more appropriate label (Marks 1983). Irritability, too, is common, especially with prolonged rituals (Farid 1983). Psychotic depression is rare and occurred in only one of the author's cases.

Many ocs seek help only when depression supervenes, and this may exaggerate its prevalence in clinical samples of ocs. Among ocs depressive symptoms were present in 17% at the time the OCD began but in fully 42% at the time of admission (Kringlen 1965). As with phobics, untreated ocs may have less mood disturbance than treated cases, and if so, OCD and depression may be less linked than they sometimes appear to be. In addition, as mentioned earlier, series of OCD would naturally omit cases who lose their oc symptoms when they become depressed (Gittleson 1966). Ideas about the etiology of OCD that are based on samples with much depression may be misleading.

Many label depression with OCD as primary or secondary, according to its timing or its relative severity. This distinction is often arbitrary and very difficult to make. Depression may develop before, during, or after the OCD (Marks et al. 1975). The two covary in some cases and are independent in others. Depression, rituals, and anxiety can correlate highly and form part of the same component in principal component analyses repeated over time (Marks et al. 1980). Nevertheless, depression that covaries with OCD can be uncoupled by exposure treatment, which reduces rituals more than the tendency to recurrent depression (Boersma et al. 1976; Marks et al. 1980). Severe depression may halt progress with exposure therapy because it lowers both motivation (Lelliott et al. 1986) and habituation (Foa 1985). Current depression predicts the liability of ocs to take antidepressants over the next 2 years (Mawson et al 1982). (The role of antidepressants in OCD is detailed in Chapter 16.)

The suicide rate of depressed ocs is less than in other depressives (Templer 1972). There are no strong familial links between manic-depressive and oc disorder. Although the relatives of ocs have a slightly raised prevalence of depression and of manic-depressive psychosis (Brown 1942; Rüdin 1953; Sakai 1967), this increase is far less in the families of patients with OCD rather than primary affective disorder (5% versus 21%, Coryell 1981). Among 145 ocs of the author's, 46 had a family history of treated depression, 8 of treated OCD, and only 3 of both; this overlap is less than one would expect if familial factors were important (Noshirvani et al. 1986).

Biological Markers of Depression in OCD

The dexamethasone suppression test (DST) was normal in all 18 ocs in a series of Lieberman and coworkers (1985) series. The DST was also normal in 96% of another 50 patients with uncomplicated OCD and normal mood (Monteiro et al. 1986); abnormal DSTs (failures to suppress cortisol) were found in ocs complicated by alcoholism, depression, cancer, a history of anorexia, or a reversed diurnal rhythm.

More frequently abnormal DSTs were reported in other series of OCD (25%—Insel et al. 1984; 30%—Cottraux et al. 1984; 37%—Insel et al. 1982a; 50%—Asberg 1983). Such figures might have been swelled by slightly more mood disturbance. The Hamilton Depression (17-item) score was 17 in the series of Cottraux and 14 in the suppressors of Insel and colleagues (1984), but among nonsuppressors was 10 (Insel et al. 1984; Monteiro et al. 1986). Abnormal DSTs might also have resulted from unreported complications such as past anorexia that had been found in 16% of the female ocs of Monteiro and coworkers (1986).

Disturbances that are found during depression also occur in OCD complicated by depressed mood and have been reported in tiny numbers of ocs with normal mood, but these findings need replication (Insel et al. 1982b, 1984b; Weizman et al. 1985). Perturbations include blunting of the plasma growth hormone response to clonidine, decreased ^{3}H-imipramine-binding and sleep disturbances—sleep was shallow (decreased delta sleep), fragmented (increased awake-movement time), and short (decreased total sleep time), and REM latency was reduced. (The notion that ocs may have a serotonergic disturbance is discussed below.)

In conclusion, oc symptoms are common in depressive disorder, especially the anxious neurotic form and in cases where personality had previously been obsessive. In the latter the oc symptoms are greater and more liable to persist after the depression remits. In OCD episodes of neurotic depression are frequent before, during, and after the OCD, especially in women. Depression and OCD can covary or be independent. When depression is severe it can interfere with exposure therapy. Some depressed ocs have biological disturbances that are also found in depression. Depression is probably overrepresented in samples seeking treatment for OCD because (1) such samples would exclude ocs who lose their oc symptoms on getting depressed, and (2) ocs are probably more likely to seek help on becoming depressed than at other times.

Delusions and Psychoses

Like phobics, ocs usually recognize that their worries and actions are probably senseless, and as we saw earlier, it is rare for oc beliefs to become fixed to a delusional degree.

The bizarre nature of many oc rituals and beliefs sometimes misleads clinicians into diagnosing schizophrenia. Although it is true that a tiny number of cases do flower into full-blown schizophrenia, the frequency of this sequence was a mere 0% to 3% in 9 series reviewed by Black (1974), and was less than 1% among cases in the author's unit. Schizophrenia is thus no more common in OCD than it is in the general population.

Other psychoses are also rare in OCD. Two of 56 of the author's cases on clomipramine developed marked mania virtually overnight within weeks of starting the drug; the rituals faded away dramatically for the duration of the manic episodes. The mania cleared after a few weeks, and the rituals gradually returned thereafter. Similar remission of rituals as mania began was described by Kendell and Discipio (1970). Depressive psychoses are rare, as we saw.

Anorexia Nervosa

Links between oc phenomena and anorexia have long been recognized. The association of anorexia with meticulous orderliness led Palmer and Jones (1939) to regard anorexia as a form of "compulsion neurosis," a label also approved by DuBois (1949). The frequency with which oc personality traits and symptoms are said to be associated with anorexia nervosa varies over so great a range (3% to 83% in the review by Steinhausen & Glanville 1983; see also Kasvikis et al. 1986) as to be meaningless and to suggest that widely differing criteria were employed in various studies. Anorexia tends to be more severe in anorexics who have oc symptoms (Hecht 1983). In a few cases of anorexia with oc symptoms, after the weight returns to normal, aggressive self-mutilation emerges to be added to the continuing oc features (Yaryura-Tobias & Neziroglu 1983).

There is a clearly raised incidence of past anorexia nervosa in women with OCD (Kasvikis et al. 1986); it is reported by 12% of 151 females but by none of 129 males. In contrast, not a single case from 100 agoraphobics from the same unit (83 women, 17 men) gave a history of anorexia. Past anorexia is thus selectively associated with women (not men) who have OCD rather than with anxiety disorder of any kind.

Among the 16 oc women who had a past history of anorexia the eating problem began before the OCD in 9, after it in 5, and in the same year in 1; the mean onset age of the anorexia and of the OCD was almost the same. The OCD began earlier among those with a history of anorexia (18 versus 24), and they were less often married, as would be expected from their youth. By the time the 16 women came for treatment of their OCD the anorexia had usually cleared up. The rituals were similar in form in ocs with and without a past history of anorexia. This association could point to overlap in some of the neural mechanisms involved—oc phenomena were a feature of encephalitis lethargica, and hypothalamic disturbances can lead to anorexia—but this is very speculative.

In brief, oc traits and symptoms are commonly reported among anorexics, and women with OCD have a markedly increased past history of anorexia. The significance of this is unclear.

Tics and Gilles de la Tourette Syndrome

Obsessive-compulsive symptoms are often reported together with tics and with the Gilles de la Tourette syndrome, whose features are multiple vocal and motor tics (reviewed by Hymas 1986). The reported frequency of oc symptoms independent of the tics varies from 0% to fully 90% (Fernando 1967; Montgomery et al. 1982; Nee et al. 1982; Shapiro et al. 1972; Yaryura-Tobias & Neziroglu 1983), indicating the need for much tighter criteria. Rather more oc symptoms are present among child tiqueurs (13%) than controls (7%) (Corbett 1969). The families of Tourette patients may have a raised incidence not only of tics but also of compulsive rituals and agoraphobia (Comings & Comings 1985; Montgomery et al. 1982; Nee et al. 1982). Despite a possible excess of rituals in Tourette sufferers, the great majority of patients with OCD do not have the Tourette syndrome.

The Tourette syndrome can be precipitated by L-dopa (Turner et al. 1983), while haloperidol (and clomipramine) are said to improve the swearing and tics, although their effect on associated rituals is unclear. Stereotyped movements sometimes also occur in the dopamine-depleted syndrome of Parkinsonism and in schizophrenia, which is improved by drugs that reduce dopamine. Perhaps, therefore, dopamine dysfunction can lead to stereotyped acts. Whether this is true for OCD remains to be seen.

Organic Associations

"Organic" features are occasionally detected in cases of OCD, but there is marked disagreement about their frequency. Since the mind is the brain in action, psychopathology must at some level reflect dysfunction of brain activity. Our division of "organic" from "functional" reflects our ignorance, as the two are at the ends of a continuum along which neurology and psychiatry merge into one another. Present tests of brain function are fairly crude. As more fine-grain indicators of brain activities are developed, dysfunctions will become more reliably evident. Better attention to controls and to sampling would also reduce the current discrepancies of opinion. The subject was reviewed by Turner and coworkers (1983), Kettl and Marks (1986), and Hymas (1986).

Neurological Correlates

There were many reports of oc symptoms starting after encephalitis lethargica in the wake of the pandemic in the years following World War I (see Bender 1935; Brickner 1940; Laplane et al. 1984; McCowan 1928; Schilder 1938). The oc phenomena included counting and other rituals and obsessive thoughts, but not prolonged oc washing and cleaning. They often occurred in short crises lasting some minutes and could be accompanied by oculocephalogyric fits, anxiety, and aggression.

Many of the cases had Parkinsonism from lesions of the basal ganglia and substantia nigra. Unfortunately no neuropathological difference was observed between post-encephalitic cases that did and did not develop oc features. Parkinsonian patients often find it hard to perform two voluntary motor acts at the same time, so they are forced to carry out one after another the many separate motor movements in getting dressed, for example; completion of the sequence is slow compared with the normal concurrent approach (Schwab et al. 1954). Compulsive counting, checking, and orderliness without anxiety but with psychic akinesia was noted in three cases of encephalopathy with globus pallidus lesions following a wasp sting or carbon monoxide poisoning (Ali-Cherif et al. 1984; Laplane et al. 1984). Other compulsive head movements and shouting were noted in a man with basal gangliar and cortical lesions from carbon monoxide poisoning (Pulst et al. 1983). Although oc phenomena may accompany basal ganglion pathology, severe OCD very rarely does, and Parkinsonism is usually a disorder of the elderly whereas OCD mainly affects young adults. Morbid and premorbid "obsessional" traits (not symptoms) are said to be frequent in Parkinsonism (Trimble 1981). Perhaps paradoxically, oral levadopa for the syndrome may produce oc symptoms as a side effect (Yaryura-Tobias & Neziroglu 1983).

Another rare association of OCD is with diabetes insipidus. Five of nine cases described by Barton (1965) had obvious OCD quite apart from water drinking; one of the five had a pinealoma, and another was post-encephalitic. Either the diabetes insipidus or the OCD could start long before the other began. Vasopressin did not relieve the oc problem (Barton 1976). One study found more history of neurological disorder in OCD than in other neuroses (Grimshaw 1964).

Head injury was followed by oc features in 3% of 415 cases (Hillbom 1960) but in only 2 of another series of 670 sustained penetrating head injuries, forming a mere 1% of the subsample who developed severe psychiatric disorder (Lishman 1968). In 4 other cases, 2 of them from the author's unit, OCD developed shortly after head trauma, even within 24 hours (McKeon et al. 1984b); one of these patients had an identical twin who had neither suffered brain injury nor developed OCD.

In contrast, a third of 33 ocs had a history of birth injury, more than did other psychiatric patients, and the rituals in this third tended to be more "bizarre or magical" (Capstick & Seldrup 1977); however, only one case had physical signs of brain damage. This work needs replication.

Links between OCD and epilepsy were noted in a trickle of case reports (see Chapter 9). Different studies report great discrepancy in the proportion of

OCD cases who have abnormal EEGs and neuropsychological tests; some of these changes could have resulted from the oc symptoms as well as caused them, a logical problem noted earlier in "organic" signs found in agoraphobia (see Chapter 10).

Some found disturbed EEGs in 48% to 65% of ocs (Inouye 1973; Pacella et al. 1944; Rockwell & Simons 1947; Sugiyama 1974). Others put the figures far lower at 11% to 20% (Bingley & Persson 1978; Ingram & McAdam 1960; Insel et al. 1983). Occasionally the EEG is abnormal over the temporal lobes, as was found in 33% in one series (Jenike & Brotman 1984), whereas in three other ocs, theta waves and spiking that were present when awake became more localized and appeared over temporal areas during sleep (Epstein & Bailine 1971). Other EEG anomalies were noted in ocs but not in controls (McCarthy & Foa 1985).

Abnormal EEG variability and neuropsychological tests in 11 ocs were said to suggest left frontal lobe dysfunction (Flor-Henry et al. 1979), and abnormal neuropsychological tests were claimed to point to fronto-temporal dysfunction in another 23 cases (Flor-Henry & Schopflocher 1985). This conclusion was not shared by Insel (1984) in a study of the EEG and neuropsychological tests in a further 18 cases of OCD.

The sleep EEGs of patients with OCD differed from those of controls but were similar to the EEGs of age-matched depressives (Insel et al. 1982a, 1984). Among adolescents who had OCD plus a history of major depression, the sleep EEG again resembled that of young adults with primary depression (Rapoport et al. 1981).

In children with OCD, EEG abnormalities were uncommon, mild, and nonspecific (Flament & Rapoport 1984). These children nevertheless had deficits on neuropsychological tests similar to those in frontal lobe lesions and had increased ventricular/brain ratios on CT scan, a finding also reported in schizophrenic but not in oc adults.

Visual evoked potentials of ocs were said to be abnormal, especially with more complex visual tasks (Beech et al. 1983; Ciesielski et al. 1981). Different components of evoked potentials in 14 ocs were distinguishable from those of matched nonpatients, other neurotics, and schizophrenics (Shagass et al. 1984). Obsessive thoughts, like ideas of reference and verbal hallucinations, correlated with longer post-imperative negative variation (Bachneff & Engelsmann (1983).

CT scans of ocs are usually normal (Insel et al. 1983; Rapoport et al. 1981), although a series of 16 adolescents with OCD had higher mean ventricular-brain ratios and more spatial perceptual deficits of frontal type than did matched controls (Behar et al. 1984). Changes in cerebral blood flow were noted during exposure of oc washers (Zohar et al. 1985); as usual, the question is whether such changes are the product rather than the cause of anxiety.

Psychosurgery

Relief of OCD after psychosurgery indicates some of the pathways that can partly mediate the problem, although they may well be downstream from its origin. Benefit has followed surgical variants lesioning the orbital frontal cortex, anterior cingulum, or related areas (here we will not consider the unwanted side effects that can detract from the outcome). In 334 ocs from 12 series (reviewed by Yaryura-Tobias & Neziroglu 1983, p. 197), 54% improved markedly and a further 24% improved moderately after a variety of psychosurgical operations.

Other reports also noted gains after frontal lobe surgery. Following bifrontal stereotactic tractotomy of the posterior orbital cortex, about 50% were markedly improved in the series of Strom-Olsen & Carlisle (1971) and of Goktepe et al. (1975). The latter noted these gains at 2- to 4½-year follow-up; at 3-year follow-up there was marked improvement in 67% of another 24 cases that were among the 334 noted above (Bridges et al. 1973). At 5-year follow-up after bimedial frontal leucotomy there was marked relief of oc symptoms in 50% of cases but in only 23% of matched controls, and post-surgery cases were also better in work and social adjustment (Tan et al. 1971). Fewer marked gains were reported in two series—only 30% after restricted orbital undercutting (Sykes & Tredgold 1964) and 38% after frontal leucotomy in OCD plus depression and 0% in cases without depression (Post et al. 1968).

Some success has been reported from capsulotomy, which disrupts the anterior limb of the internal capsule and adjacent mediobasal white matter. The proportion of ocs who were much improved after capsulotomy was 71% of ocs 3 years later in a series among the 334 cases mentioned earlier (Bingley et al. 1977). In another series 58% of 8 cases were at least moderately better after capsulotomy, but none of 3 cases improved after cingulotomy (Kullberg 1977).

Cingulotomy was followed by benefit in several series. Forty-two percent of 16 cases of OCD were greatly improved and another 42% had some benefit after bilateral anterior cingulotomy (Lewin 1961); 92% of another 12 cases showed worthwhile gains after cingulotomy (Meyer et al. 1973). Of a large series of 49 ocs, 77% were substantially or markedly improved after multifocal leucocoagulation of the anterior cingulate gyrus (Crowe 1973); 27% had previously attempted suicide, suggesting that a high proportion had also been depressive. Seventy percent of 24 ocs were much improved after cingulotractotomy (Bailey et al. 1977). In two more oc cases who also had depression, in one patient orbital leucotomy helped the depression but only later cingulectomy helped the oc symptoms, whereas in the second case cingulectomy was done first and reduced the oc symptoms, but the depression lifted only after later orbital leucotomy (Lewin 1973). Perhaps, then, OCD is helped more by cingulate than by frontal lesions.

Electrical Stimulation of the Brain

Electrical stimulation of non-oc patients has yielded information relevant to oc phenomena. In one woman, area 6 on the mesial side of the left hemisphere was stimulated repeatedly while she recited the alphabet; at each stimulus onset and throughout the period of stimulation the patient said the same letter over and over again (Brickner 1940). This perseveration ceased instantly when the stimulation was stopped; the area was excised, but pathological examination detected no abnormality. Different movements such as sucking, palpation, or nibbling were evoked in 52 epileptics during electrical stimulation of certain sites in the anterior cingulum (Talairach et al. 1973). The patients experienced these movements as involuntary and forced on them, as occurs with compulsive rituals. Unlike rituals, however, the movements were associated with euphoria, not anxiety, were not repetitive, and were less complex.

The frequency of rituals in autism is discussed in Chapter 12. Repeated stereotyped self-mutilation may be found in mental handicap as a result of the DeLange and the Lesch-Nyhan syndromes in children (reviewed by Yaryura-Tobias & Neziroglu 1983). Self-mutilation, however, differs in form from the rituals and obsessions of OCD, so its relevance is questionable.

Metabolic Correlates

So far no biological markers have been found for OCD that are unambiguously separate from depressed mood. Earlier we noted a suggestion that dopamine dysfunction may be involved in the Tourette syndrome, Parkinsonism, and schizophrenia, in all of which stereotyped acts may occur, and that we are ignorant of dopamine function in OCD.

Another suggestion is that (1) serotonin is relatively unavailable in OCD and (2) clomipramine's effect on the syndrome is due to its inhibition of serotonin reuptake (reviewed by Turner et al. 1983; Yaryura-Tobias & Neziroglu 1983). Compared with controls, oc patients had lower levels of blood serotonin but not of its urinary metabolite 5-HIAA; after 2 weeks on 100 milligrams daily of clomipramine, blood serotonin diminished further, while 5-HIAA was unchanged. Plasma clomipramine correlated with improvement of ocs in one study (Stern et al. 1980) but not in another (Marks et al. 1986); it also correlated with decrease in cerebrospinal fluid 5-HIAA (Åsberg et al. 1982), but in that study plasma clomipramine correlated negatively with decrease in oc symptoms (Thorén et al. 1980).

Chapter 16 shows that in all these studies, depression as well as oc features improved and to a related extent, and that serotonin and clomipramine effects can often be accounted for by the concomitant depression so common in OCD; moreover, the evidence for serotonin's being superior to less serotonergic antidepressants is at best marginal. Additionally, clomipramine, like other antidepressants, affects noradrenergic as well as serotonergic function. The support for a specific serotonergic dysfunction in OCD without depressed mood is thus rather slender.

Turning to a different system, one study found that ocs more often have A and less often O blood groups than do normals, whereas phobics are the reverse (Rinieris et al. 1983). Another controlled study, however, found a normal distribution of ABO blood groups in ocs (McKeon 1983).

Autonomic Function

Some hyperarousal of ocs has been found. They had more skin conductance (SC) and heart rate response to anticipated physical and psychological stress than did normals (Rabavilas et al. 1977b), and their SC was hyperreactive to loud, unpleasant tones but not to decision-making tasks (Beech & Liddell 1974). Their SC responses to loud tones resembled those of agoraphobics and of individuals in anxiety states; all are slow to habituate (Lelliott et al. 1986). Finally, in ocs compared to placebo, both clomipramine and clorgyline reduced SC activity, but only clomipramine produced clinical improvement and diminished SC and heart responses to loud tones and tonic and phasic SC responses in a two-flash discrimination task (Zahn et al. 1984).

SUMMARY

OCD occurs almost as often in men as in women, though more females are washers and have a past history of anorexia, while males show more slowness without visible rituals. Onset is usually in adolescence or young adult life, with presentation some years later. Ocs marry later and less and have fewer children than the general population. Treated cases have a slightly raised mean social class and intelligence. There may be a trend for male ocs to be first-born or only children, and first-born male relatives have an excess of oc symptoms. Season of birth is normal.

There is a surfeit of life events prior to onset of OCD, especially in those with normal personalities. Onset is usually insidious with stuttering exacerbations. Much the most common form of OCD is repetitive rituals plus obsessions rather than either alone. The usual rituals are washing and checking, and emphasis may be on one rather than the other. Most rituals and obsessions involve 1 to 3 central themes of concern about contamination or other harm befalling oneself and others, orderliness—including doing things by number, making mistakes, or some other gaffe; themes may be specific or broad. Like phobics, ocs are on the lookout for ESs and try to avoid them. Addiction to ritualistic requests for reassurance is common. Rituals can feature in morbid jealousy. Delay in completing everyday activities is a frequent result of repeated rituals or mental checks, or of doing things in a set sequence that may not be interrupted. Extreme slowness affects self-initiated acts more than those that are externally prompted.

Oc rituals and ideas differ from their normal counterpart in being persistent and intrusive, and sufferers usually resist them and regard them as absurd. In exceptional cases they are linked to fixed delusions. Oc phenomena may increase or decrease (cancel, undo, neutralize) anxiety, the former needing exposure and the latter response prevention. Dysphoria tends to increase obsessions. Severe OCD is among the most crippling of all psychiatric disorders for the patient, spouse, and children and may prevent any semblance of normal social, sexual, or family life. If untreated it can continue for decades with loss of job, frequent moves of home, defective child-rearing, social isolation, and pressure on relatives to join in rituals and to take over parental and homemaking roles that the patient cannot fulfil. Relatives may comply willingly, be bludgeoned into submission, or successfully resist involvement. The damage spreads less if relatives calmly and firmly resist when the patient tries to tyrranize or implore them to participate in the rituals.

People with an "obsessive" personality are not handicapped by it, and the great majority develop no OCD, but they are slightly overrepresented in the clinical syndrome. Neuroticism, fear of criticism, and cognitive aberrations may be found in several anxiety disorders, not only in OCD, and may be as much features of the syndromes as etiological. Religious oc rituals are common among ocs in orthodox communities and differ from normal religious practices.

Obsessive-compulsive and phobic disorders have important similarities and differences. Both are syndromes of anxious avoidance that improve with treatment by exposure. Compared with phobics, ocs have more stereotyped, repetitive thoughts and actions, which need the additional treatment maneuver of response prevention; the stimuli evoking anxiety in ocs are different, and may be more abstract and more oriented to the remote than the immediate future. Moreover, the unpleasant affect is sometimes discomfort rather than anxiety, and oc phenomena are less stimulus-bound and spread more. The abnormal beliefs of ocs are also more elaborate.

Clinical samples of ocs may show more disturbed mood than do untreated ocs because (1) depression may raise the chances that an oc will seek help and (2) OCD series would exclude cases who lose their oc symptoms on becoming depressed. In those presenting with depressive disorder, oc symptoms are frequent; preexisting oc symptoms may worsen during the depression and persist after it remits. In cases asking for help with OCD, fluctuating depression is common. The depression associated with oc symptoms is usually of the neurotic, anxious variety with few biological or psychotic features. "Biological markers" of depression may be found in ocs who also have depressed mood. Evidence of a dopaminergic or serotonergic dysfunction in ocs is still tenuous.

Obsessive-compulsive beliefs rarely amount to a delusion, and schizophrenia is found no more often in OCD than in the general population. Very rarely, oc patients may develop mania, upon which the oc symptoms will disappear only to return when the mania subsides.

Obsessive-compulsive symptoms occur rarely after "organic" features such as lesions of the hypothalamus, third ventricle, and basal ganglia (for example, after encephalitis and encephalopathy). A handful of ocs have diabetes insipidus, and a marked excess of women with OCD give a history of anorexia— again pointing perhaps to hypothalamic and third-ventricle dysfunction. There is no agreement on how much abnormality there is on EEGs, evoked potentials, and neuropsychological tests. OCD rarely coexists with epilepsy; oc phenomena may appear during the fit, and stimulation of area 6 on the mesial side of the left hemisphere has led to concurrent repetitive speech. Surgical lesioning of anterior cingulate and medial frontal areas can improve severe and intractable OCD. Such data indicate pathways that can mediate occasional oc symptoms but could be well downstream from the usual mechanisms that start and maintain OCD, and precise understanding of them is still a long way off. Most cases of OCD have no organic pathology detectable by present methods; there is great disagreement about the proportion who have abnormal EEGs or psychological tests, or a history of brain injury.

IV
TREATMENT

14

Principles of Psychological Treatment

The outlook for most sufferers from phobic and oc disorders has been transformed over the last 20 years to the extent that we might speak of a behavioral revolution. We will briefly trace the emergence of the concept of exposure and criticisms of the idea. The results of live and fantasy exposure will be documented. Exposure will be shown to be most valuable when it is prolonged. We will see that so far no optimal level of arousal during exposure has been demonstrated, though clinicians agree that patients do best when actively engaged in the exposure task so that the emotional experience can be centrally processed to allow habituation to proceed. The relevance of abreaction is discussed and whether exposure is related to more general issues of problem solving. Finally we will examine ways of facilitating exposure and review the relative failure of cognitive approaches to help the syndromes of anxious avoidance.

THE EXPOSURE PRINCIPLE

Since the 1970s it has been increasingly realized (Marks 1973) that the many behavioral treatments that reduce morbid anxiety share a common procedure—continued exposure to the stimulus that evokes anxiety until discomfort subsides. Exposure therapy resembles the way in which repeated presentations of the relevant stimuli habituate and extinguish normal innate and acquired fear (see chapters 7 and 8, which also define the various types of response decrement). Although exposure became an accepted treatment only recently, its diverse roots reach back through the centuries. The exposure principle appears in Zen meditation, Senoi dream interpretation, the writings of John Locke, and early psychoanalysis (reviewed by Marks 1972b, 1978).

A lovely historical example of self-exposure comes from Goethe (1770, pp. 326–327). He had phobias of heights, diseased bodies, loud noises, and dark, lonely places, and decided to remedy these infirmities when he was a 20-year-old law student at Strasbourg University.

I ascended quite alone the highest pinnacle of the cathedral spire, and sat in the so-called neck under the knob or crown, as it is called, for a quarter of an hour, before I ventured to step out again into the open air, where, on standing on a platform scarcely an ell square, without anything particular to hold on to, one sees before one the boundless land, while the nearest objects and ornaments conceal the church and everything on which and above which one stands. It is exactly as if one saw oneself carried up into the air in a balloon. Such anxiety and pain I repeated so often until the impression became quite different to me, and I have therefore derived great advantage from these practices in mountain travels and on geological studies, and on great buildings, where I have vied with the carpenters in running over the freelying beams and the cornices of the building, and even in Rome, where one must run similar risks in order to obtain a nearer view of important works of art.

Goethe went on to treat his other fears in the same way.

Examples also abound of inadvertent exposure that is therapeutic. In World War II a Normandy woman was phobic of thunder and lightning until the Allied invasion. She was then bombed for 20 consecutive days while in a shelter; on emerging from it she was no longer phobic (Solyom et al. 1974). But inadvertent exposure does not always lead to habituation. An agora- and claus-trophobic man was imprisoned alone in a cell for 3 months—unjustly, he claimed—and remained claustrophobic afterward. Which of these two out-comes would be the more usual with unwilling exposure is almost impossible to study because of ethical constraints: exposure therapy can of course be given only to sufferers who are willing to carry it out.

Emergence of Exposure as a Key Factor

Exposure did not even appear in the index of this book's predecessor, *Fears and Phobias* (1969). At that time behavioral treatments were still fairly weak in their effects. Three developments since then strikingly increased their value for phobic and obsessive-compulsive (oc) disorders. The first was a gradual appreciation that reliable methods to reduce fear involve an element of expo-sure (Marks 1973; the plethora of labels for those methods is detailed in Marks 1975). This appreciation led to concentration on that element and the elimi-nation of redundant components such as relaxation. Second was the move from fantasy to live exposure, which needed a therapist's presence less. This paved the way for the third development. Clinicians began to see that what clients did themselves between therapy sessions could be as important as or more important than the actual sessions in the clinic. It turns out that most sufferers can complete live self-exposure successfully without a therapist hav-ing to be present, especially if it is systematized with the aid of an appropriate manual and diary.

In growth areas of science, issues change as experiments eliminate those which are peripheral. This is well shown in the healthy evolution of behavioral treatment. In 1969 its dominant mode for phobic-oc disorders was systematic desensitization, and there was some interest in flooding/implosion, both given in fantasy. Even though the two approaches were contrasting forms of exposure, little attention was paid to that ingredient. Thereafter, studies showed that neither low nor high arousal were critical for improvement, nor were intermittent approach up a hierarchy, modeling, or reward (reviewed by Marks 1978). As its potency was recognized, live exposure began to replace fantasy exposure. Desensitization versus flooding ceased to be a central issue. Modeling was found to work only when it contained the element of exposure—fear fell only on observing a therapist doing exposure, not on observing him or her carrying out relaxation without exposure. Relaxation failed to reduce fear unless it was combined with exposure, and it rarely enhanced exposure. High anxiety evocation was not essential. Shaping was seen to be of approach to the feared stimulus; in no experiment was the subject shaped away from it. Even some avoidance was compatible with improvement provided exposure followed at some point. What the subject thought during exposure was not crucial as long as he or she was not dissociating but rather engaging in the task and letting the frightening stimuli in to allow habituation to occur with continuing stimulation. The optimal treatment rule at present is to elicit the subject's avoidance profile—all the situations he or she avoids because they evoke phobic-oc features—and to persuade him or her to confront those evoking stimuli (ESs) repeatedly until the ensuing unease dies down.

The mechanisms by which exposure reduces fear are not yet clear, but it is nonetheless an important fact that treatments which fail to include exposure as an ingredient fail to achieve reliable effects. It is certainly true that individual phobics and ocs sometimes improve while on a waiting list or having relaxation, dynamic psychotherapy, or hypnosis. But exposure seems necessary for reproducible outcomes. For groups of patients, little fear reduction occurred with treatments that contained no exposure, such as relaxation (Marks et al. 1975, 1980), dynamic psychotherapy (Gelder et al. 1967), hypnosis (Marks et al. 1968), assertion training (Emmelkamp et al. 1983), or cognitive therapy. After one of two therapists obtained good results with problem solving (Jannoun et al. 1980), these could not be replicated by two subsequent therapists (Cullington et al. 1984). Deliberately omitting the element of exposure by giving anti-exposure instructions virtually wiped out the benefit from self-help instructions (Greist et al. 1980), clomipramine (Marks et al. 1986), and imipramine (Telch et al. 1985).

To say that exposure is a necessary therapeutic component for reliable group effects does not mean that it is sufficient. Motivation, dedication, and other factors help to make it successful. And it is of great theoretical interest why individuals sometimes lose their phobic and oc problems without any exposure at all. Understanding such exceptional cases would illuminate some mechanisms that can reduce fear, but the phenomenon of fear reduction by nonexposure methods has to be made reliable before it can be examined systematically.

Criticisms of Exposure

It has been objected that all treatments contain exposure, but a moment's thought shows this to be wrong. We can relax subjects without any exposure, or model all kinds of things for them without exposure, praise them without exposure, provide psychotherapy without exposure, or hypnotize patients without exposure. None of these procedures are great fear reducers.

Another objection is that exposure is "merely" a procedure, not a principle with any explanatory power, so that exposure tells us nothing about the mechanism of fear. This is misleading, as there is no clear divide between procedures, principles, and mechanisms. One could hardly criticize a chemist for carrying out a "mere" procedure when he or she searches for essential ingredients in a potent chemical mixture by distilling out its various fractions until its potency disappears. That search is an essential aspect of fundamental science. Impure mixtures are poor investigatory tools. We have to eliminate redundant impurities while recognizing that there may be no single key factor acting alone, but rather several components acting together as critical compounds, and that the use to which those compounds is put may determine their optimal composition.

The discovery of insulin was a great advance in learning about diabetes, although over the next 60 years it was found to act on several sets of interacting mechanisms whose complexity seemed to grow as research proceeds. When we have refined our therapeutic mixture to the point of obtaining a pure, potent crystal, then we are much better placed to unravel the processes by which it affects an organism. We are reaching that point concerning the crystal of exposure and the mechanisms by which it reduces fear, now that we know that it does this reliably without any need to relax, provoke terror in, praise, or model for subjects, or to wrestle with their cognitions, although these procedures are occasionally slightly adjuvant. The best way to help is to promote exposure in some way. The next stage is to find out precisely which mechanisms underlie response decrement during exposure. That phase has in fact begun (see Chapter 8).

A third objection to exposure is that it is not essential for fear reduction in every single case. This is true. However, although nonexposure methods sometimes lessen fear in individuals, unlike exposure they fail to reduce fear reliably in groups. And in any case, insulin is no less valuable a discovery because other compounds also lower the blood sugar to some extent.

In the rest of this chapter we will examine critical aspects of exposure for phobic disorder and obsessive-compulsive disorder (OCD). They will be dealt with together, as most treatment principles apply equally to both these syndromes of anxious avoidance. The chief difference is that response prevention is added to exposure for OCD; this will be discussed. Here, *E* is therapist-aided live (in vivo) exposure, and *e* is self-exposure outside the clinic.

MODALITIES OF EXPOSURE

Live Versus Fantasy Exposure

The closer practice is to the real thing, the better the results one would expect. Live exposure (also called in vivo or real exposure, behavior rehearsal, or performance) should therefore be better than fantasy exposure. The overall trend of results suggests that this is probably so, although many comparisons of live with fantasy exposure had confounding influences such as differing durations and pace of exposure or other adjuvants (reviewed by Marks 1978). In phobics powerful outcomes of live exposure were found in controlled studies in volunteers (Bandura et al. 1969; LoPiccolo 1969; Sherman 1972) and uncontrolled work in patients (Marks et al. 1977; Watson et al. 1972).

A few controlled clinical studies also showed the value of live exposure. In specific phobics, graded live exposure (shaping) was better than graded fantasy desensitization (Crowe et al. 1972). For social anxiety, social skills training, which includes live exposure, was better than fantasy desensitization at follow-up, and both were better than a control group (Marzillier et al. 1976). In agoraphobics, live was better than fantasy exposure, but the latter was by tape recorder and there was a time confound, with live always following fantasy exposure (Stern & Marks 1973). Even without a time confound, however, in ocs 80 minutes of live exposure was better than 80 minutes of fantasy exposure, although there was no follow-up (Rabavilas et al. 1976).

In a study of agoraphobics (Emmelkamp & Wessels 1975) 23 cases had twelve 90-minute flooding sessions 3 times weekly. The first four sessions were either live or in fantasy, or sessions in which the first half was fantasy and the second half live exposure. Thereafter all patients had eight 90-minute self-exposure sessions. Live was clearly superior to fantasy exposure, the combined method was next best, and fantasy exposure the least effective. Subsequent self-exposure added little to the two live flooding conditions but did enhance gains from fantasy flooding alone.

In another trial in agoraphobics (Johnston et al. 1976; Mathews et al. 1976), 36 cases had 16 weekly 90-minute flooding sessions given as 16 in fantasy, 16 live, or 8 in fantasy followed by 8 live; all patients had self-exposure between sessions (e) with diaries but no manual. There was more change from live than fantasy exposure at the end of each session, but all three treatments were equally effective at the end of treatment and at 6 months follow-up. Weekly exposure sessions in the clinic seemed to help less than daily e at home.

In the above study e might have reduced differences between live and fantasy clinic sessions; live was better than fantasy exposure only at the end of the sessions, not later once patients had practiced e. The gap of a week between clinic sessions allowed more time for e practice, and diaries were given, which may have systematized e more. In contrast, less e might explain the greater superiority of live over fantasy exposure in the study of Emmelkamp and Wessels (1975); its thrice-weekly clinic sessions allowed less time for e between sessions and no diaries were kept, so e may have been less systematic.

Three studies by Foa and coworkers found no clear superiority of live over fantasy exposure, but confounds restrict conclusions. In ocs 10 sessions of 90-minute fantasy and 30-minute live exposure were better than 120 minutes of live exposure at follow-up, but both groups had response prevention (rp), and there were no data on fantasy exposure alone (Foa et al. 1980b). Among oc checkers, 19 cases had 15 daily 2-hour sessions of fantasy or live exposure, neither with rp. However, during week 4 all cases had 8 hours of domiciliary treatment, presumably with live exposure. This might have obscured differences between fantasy and live exposure, both of which were equally helpful up to a mean of 10 months' follow-up. Neither group did as well as other ocs who had both fantasy and live exposure with rp (Foa & Goldstein 1978). Finally, the outcome of agoraphobics was no better after 8 biweekly sessions of live than of fantasy exposure, but they were not conducted over the same experimental period (Chambless et al. 1982); subjects had been asked to avoid *e* between sessions.

Another comparison of live with fantasy exposure was in 30 social phobics (Shaw 1979). Up to 6 months' follow-up they improved equally with 10 sessions of fantasy flooding, desensitization, or social skills training (which contains live exposure). As in previous studies, differences may have been obscured by all cases having *e,* although it was without a manual. No difference between live and fantasy exposure was also found in six agoraphobics (James et al. 1983), but here the order of condition was unbalanced and numbers were tiny.

Live was superior to fantasy exposure in 24 children 5 to 10 years old who feared swimming. They had graded exposure either as (1) four sessions in fantasy and then four sessions live, or (2) eight sessions live, or (3) they acted as controls (Ultee et al. 1982).

Exposure to filmed fear cues can reduce fear and prepare children for dental and medical procedures (see Chapter 15). But exposure to fear cues on film was less powerful than live exposure within the same study (Bandura et al. 1969) or across studies. (Outcome with filmed cues in agoraphobics [Lee et al. 1983; Tyrer et al. 1983] was weaker than with systematic live self-exposure with a manual and diaries [Ghosh & Marks 1986; Jannoun et al. 1980].)

Fantasy exposure is worth considering when the real stimuli evoking fear are not readily accessible for live exposure and when films of the same do not evoke fear. Examples are some thunder and lightning phobias, social phobias (such as worries about speaking at infrequent board meetings), or the cognitive rituals, harming fantasies, or obsessions without rituals of certain ocs. The patient can actively tell his or her fantasied exposure scenes to the therapist rather than merely hear them told. Another active kind of fantasy exposure is role play, which may help social phobics progress to live exposure.

In conclusion, live exposure is probably more potent despite experimental confounds in most studies of this issue. The issue has become rather academic since the discovery that self-exposure is so powerful. It is carried out live in the natural environment and allows the sufferer to arrange for habituation to the precise situations that are troublesome. In theory, self-exposure could be carried out in fantasy, by listening to tapes; however, fantasy exposure leaves a transfer gap: live stimuli still evoke fear even after the subject has habituated to them in fantasy (Barlow et al. 1969; Watson et al. 1972). Live exposure is thus still needed even after there has been complete habituation to fantasy exposure. In light of this problem, it is more efficient for the sufferer to perform live exposure from the beginning.

Self-Exposure

The value of self-exposure is now affirmed by a wealth of data from several types of design in most forms of phobic-oc disorder. Fantasy desensitization was of some help when self-administered by tape recorder (Denholtz & Mann 1975, reviewed by Marks 1975). Graded live exposure in the form of successive approximation led to some gains in phobic volunteers and patients in many single case studies (reviewed by Emmelkamp 1982; Marks 1978). In group designs, compared with therapist-aided exposure in fantasy and/or in vivo, such self-exposure yielded similar gains in phobic patients (Crowe et al. 1972; Emmelkamp 1974; Everaerd et al. 1973) and in ocs (Boersma et al. 1976; Emmelkamp & Kraanen 1978) and was even superior in snake-phobic volunteers (Hepner & Cauthen 1975). Praise for progress did not enhance self-exposure in agoraphobics (Emmelkamp & Ultee 1974), but feedback of attainment did, in rat-phobic volunteers (Rutner 1973). Uncontrolled work found good results of home-based self-exposure (*e*) in 25 ocs (Hoogduin 1985; Hoogduin & Hoogduin 1983). For dental phobics, too, *e* was useful (Klepac et al. 1984).

Self-exposure in the clinic was as or almost as helpful as therapist-aided exposure (*E*) in two more controlled studies in volunteers. One was in 50 acrophobics who had one of four variants of *E* or self-exposure (Bourque & Ladouceur 1980). Across the five exposure conditions, subjects improved similarly in anxiety and heart rate and took a comparable time to complete the hierarchy; the mean time was 115 minutes. The second study was in 48 snake-phobic students (O'Brien & Kelley 1980). They had one or two clinic sessions of (1) self-exposure only, (2) self-exposure mainly, (3) *E* mainly, and (4) *E* only; no group had self-exposure between sessions. The mean exposure time was 79 minutes. On nearly all measures the four groups improved comparably and at similar speeds.

Home-based self-exposure initiated by the patient was helpful and did not result merely from homework or self-help instructions. In 18 agoraphobics who had 45 minutes of clinician contact over 10 weeks, recording *e* in a diary was better than recording a diary of emotional events (McDonald et al. 1978). Moreover, removing exposure as a self-help ingredient destroyed the effect (Greist et al. 1980). In a 2-week balanced crossover design with 20 minutes of clinician contact a week, 13 phobics and 4 ocs had a week of *e* and another of *ê* (anti-exposure—"give yourself a total rest from anxiety and avoid whatever brings on your fears or rituals; if by chance you encounter something upsetting, escape or ritalize as you wish"); relevant activities were noted in a diary. Despite initially similar expectancies, patients improved more during *e* than *ê*, actually worsening a bit during *ê*.

Adding an instruction manual and spouse involvement to *e* with a diary yielded impressive gains in uncontrolled work; mean clinician time per patient was 7 hours (Mathews et al. 1977). This good result was replicated in a controlled study (Jannoun et al. 1980). Twenty-eight agoraphobics had either *e* or problem solving of life stresses, each involving the spouse and with a mean of 3½ hours of therapist contact; *e* again had a strong effect and was superior to problem solving.

The potency of *e* in the two foregoing studies seemed to result from adding a manual rather than spouse involvement. The same group found that *e* plus a manual carried out alone was as good as *e* plus a manual completed with the aid of a spouse (Mathews et al. 1981); both conditions were better than a wait-list control up to 6 months' follow-up. In four more controlled studies of spouse involvement, the inclusion of a partner as exposure cotherapist again failed to enhance outcome lastingly in three (Cobb et al. 1984; Emmelkamp & DeLange 1983; Mathews et al. 1981) but did in two others (Arnow et al. 1985; Barlow et al. 1984). Thus only two of six studies found an advantage in adding spouse involvement to *e*.

Marked gains from *e* required no interaction with a clinician beyond initial screening in the largest controlled study of *e* (Ghosh et al. 1986). Seventy-one phobic patients were randomized to receive *e* instructions over 10 weeks from a self-help book (*Living With Fear,* Marks 1978a), a psychiatrist, or a computer. Apart from a 1½-hour initial assessment, mean clinician time per patient in the three groups was only 0, 1.6, and 1.5 hours, respectively. All three groups improved markedly and equally up to 6 months' follow-up in both the agoraphobic (*n* = 40, Ghosh & Marks 1986; see also Figure 14.1) and social/specific phobic subgroups. Neither the clinician nor the computer had any advantage over the manual.

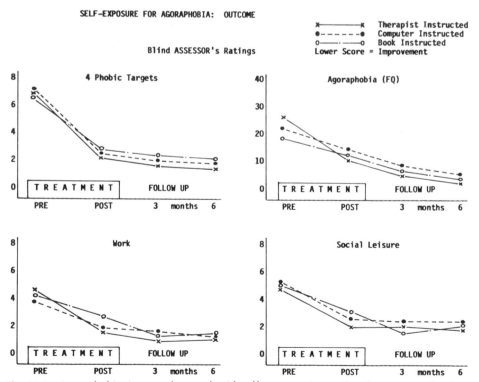

Fig. 14.1 Agoraphobics improved as much with self-exposure instructions from a manual as from a computer or a psychiatrist. (From Ghosh & Marks 1986. Copyright © 1986 by Academic Press. Reprinted by permission.)

Among agoraphobics seven more controlled studies found *e* helpful. Gains after *e* persisted to 5-year follow-up in 40 cases (Cohen et al. 1984; Lelliott et al. 1986a; see also Chapter 16). Improvement was similar whether *e* had been added to 45-minute sessions of therapist-aided exposure (*E*) or relaxation (*R*), or to imipramine or placebo; *E* plus *e* had only a temporary advantage over *R* plus *e*. In 74 other agoraphobics, progress to 9 months' follow-up after *e* was similar whether it had been given alone, with *E*, with dynamic psychotherapy, or with relaxation (Alström et al. 1984). Two further studies found *e* helpful in agoraphobics (Mavissakalian et al. 1983a; Pollard & Jensen 1984). Yet other cases improved similarly whether *e* was instructed from a clinic or from home (Gournay & Howells 1985), or by phone or in face-to-face interview (Johnson 1986, unpublished), but these cases gained more when they were in a neighborhood group and used each other as exposure destinations (Sinnott et al. 1981). A note of dissent is of poor results in six cases who had *e* with a manual, perhaps because of their severity and lack of motivation—most failed to practice *e* for longer than a week (Holden et al. 1983; D. Barlow, personal communication, 1985).

Social-phobic patients improved with *e* up to 6 months' follow-up (Butler et al. 1984). Dating anxiety fell in volunteer students who had *e* with no therapist contact (Arkowitz et al. 1975). They had a program of six weekly practice dates, each with a different matched opposite-sex partner who had similar anxiety. Subjects were told that the aim was not to find an ideal partner but to increase dating comfort and frequency. Each week the student was sent the name and phone number of the partner to be dated that week. Practice dating increased the frequency of dates with partners outside the study until 3 months' follow-up, and this continued in the 60% who could be followed up for 15 months; less social avoidance and distress and more social skill also resulted. Improvement was greater after *e* than after a wait-list control (Christensen et al. 1975; Kramer 1975) or reading and discussing a manual (Royce 1975). Gains in women were related to the number of practice dates they had (Thomander 1975). The effect of practice dating was not enhanced by (1) post-date feedback from partners about what they liked and disliked in the subject; (2) weekly group social skills training, including modeling and behavior rehearsal; or (3) cognitive restructuring (Kramer 1975; Royce 1975).

The subjects in these studies had all engaged in at least one date a month before starting practice dating. Compared with those who dated often, they were less attractive, and the women were less socially skilled. Caution is needed before extrapolating from such students to people with severe social skills deficits, but the principle is worth trying to adapt for them.

A rare report of *e* giving no benefit is in social phobics (Alström et al. 1984a). Forty-two cases had 3 months of *e* (no manual or diaries) plus anxiolytics, and (1) nothing else, (2) 2 to 4 hours of *E* live and sometimes in fantasy, (3) dynamic support plus some cognitive therapy for a half-hour weekly, or (4) relaxation. Up to 9 months' follow-up *e* alone did not improve, *E* plus *e* did best, and the other two groups did less well. Perhaps *e* alone failed to help because it was not systematic—patients had no manual and were not asked to keep *e* diaries.

Self-exposure is helpful not only for agora-, social, and specific phobia but also for OCD. This was noted earlier in three Dutch studies (Boersma et al. 1976; Emmelkamp & Kraanen 1978; Hoogduin 1985). It was found again in chronic ritualizers (Marks et al. 1986; see also Chapter 16). Thirty-seven of the ritualizers had clomipramine and were randomized to (1) *e* for 23 weeks, (2) *e* for 8 weeks followed by *E* until week 23, or (3) *ê* (anti-exposure); all cases had 45 minutes of weekly contact with a therapist and recorded *e* or *ê* in a diary. Outcome was far better in *e* than in *ê*; 9 of the 12 *ê* patients complained at not improving despite therapy, so after week 12 they were crossed over to receive *e* plus *E,* after which most improved. Yet again, omitting exposure almost eliminated therapeutic effects, as had been found previously in comparisons with *e* (Greist et al. 1980) and with imipramine (Telch et al. 1985; also see Chapter 16). Adding 2-hour *E* sessions to *e* from week 8 enhanced outcome only slightly, mainly on social adjustment at 9 months (Marks et al. 1986).

Role of Self-Exposure in Clinical Practice

Controlled studies agree on the value of self-exposure for most types of phobic-oc disorder, especially with a manual and diary recording *e* tasks for regular review. Still to be tested is the value of reading an *e* manual without any prompting from a clinician. Two patients in the book-instructed condition of Ghosh and Marks (1986) had in fact previously bought the book but did not follow its directions until they were asked to do so in the trial; hence initial contact with a clinician is an important motivator for some people. This raises critical theoretical issues that affect many fields. Why should certain people who know exactly what to do need a helper before they can do it? Some can learn a language, tennis, or carpentry by self-practice with the aid of books and tapes without any coaching; others, even if highly intelligent, find such tasks a losing battle despite intensive skilled teaching. Many ill-understood variables affect this process.

The need for therapist-aided exposure for phobic-ocs has diminished as self-exposure manuals have been refined. This is welcome, as *E* is boring, time-consuming, and expensive. Patients on the author's long waiting list are asked to first try treating themselves with *e* using *Living With Fear* as a manual, and they not infrequently improve enough therewith without needing a therapist. For most of the remaining phobic-ocs, the clinician's role is to assess the problem and teach people to help themselves better.

Some people do it all by themselves, devising and completing their self-exposure program without ever seeing a clinician. Others need a bit of prompting and therapist-aided exposure to get started and then take off on their own. Many require a clinician to instruct them and monitor their progress at intervals without actually doing exposure with them. A few want therapists to continue helping them indefinitely with exposure despite having repeatedly improved during sessions; the long-term outcome in such cases is dubious, as eventually the therapist must fade out of the scene. Clinicians need to teach patients to expect setbacks and rehearse dealing with them alone, but should be available for the odd booster session that some people require.

DURATION OF EXPOSURE, INTERVALS BETWEEN EXPOSURE, AND AVOIDANCE

Duration of Exposure Sessions

Chapter 8 reviewed evidence that with animals, long is better than short exposure; it also alluded to similar findings in humans, which will follow in detail shortly. This well-established fact conforms with a broader principle. Continuous is more likely than intermittent stimulation to produce tolerance (habituation) in a wide variety of physiological, biochemical, and behavioral phenomena in animals (Post 1980). Examples include the kindling of epilepsy by electrical stimulation of the amygdala or by giving cocaine or flurothyl, behavioral response to amphetamine or apomorphine or to alcohol withdrawal, serotonergic response to ECT, endocrine response to immobilization stress, allergic response to antigens, and the pituitary response to luteinising hormone releasing hormone (*MRC News,* Feb. 1984). The effect of intervals between stimulations seems to interact with the intensity and duration of stimulation and with the output measure chosen.

This is not the place to discuss how this wide-ranging principle might reflect mechanisms of molecular memory. Because of its clear implications for clinical practice, however, we will present the weighty work showing that fear is reduced more by long than by short exposure in humans.

Sessions of Fifty Minutes or Longer

Marks (1972b) noted that in human volunteers, longer durations of fantasy exposure were in general more helpful than shorter ones; the mean duration of fantasy flooding was 56 minutes in 9 effective studies compared with 32 minutes in 8 ineffective ones. Work since then largely confirmed that longer sessions are better, although even short sessions can be of some help.

A within-session advantage for longer fantasy exposure was found in 48 speech-anxious volunteers (Chaplin & Levine 1980). They had audiotaped fantasy exposure sessions either for 50 minutes or for two 25-minute periods with a 10-minute interval between sessions. The sessions were repeated weekly 2 to 4 times to yield a total exposure duration of 100, 150, or 200 minutes. More sessions led to more gains. Fall in anxiety within sessions was greater with continuous than with interrupted exposure, but between sessions was similar in both conditions (Figure 14.2). In the continuous condition, anxiety rose during the first 25 minutes and fell thereafter. In contrast, anxiety was still rising at the end of each of the two 25-minute periods within the interrupted condition; despite this, the overall anxiety curves were lower in the second than in the first 25-minute periods and in later than in earlier sessions. Ending exposure before anxiety had begun to fall had thus not impeded either within- or between-session habituation.

Within-session anxiety ran a similar course during 90 minutes of fantasy exposure in agoraphobics and ocs (Foa & Chambless 1978). Anxiety first rose and then leveled off, and started to fall only after 50 minutes of exposure had

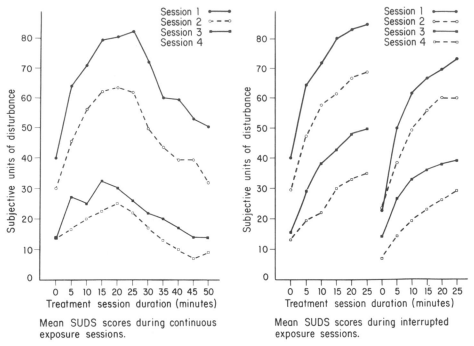

Fig. 14.2   Fall in anxiety within sessions was greater when exposure was continuous rather than interrupted, but between sessions was similar in both conditions. (From Chaplin & Levine 1981. Copyright © 1981 by Academic Press. Reprinted by permission.)

gone by. Similarly, in another study of fantasy exposure, anxiety rose and then plateaued, and had not fallen by the end of 50-minute sessions (Watson & Marks 1971).

There were similar findings in 16 other agoraphobics (Stern & Marks 1973). They had two fantasy exposure sessions either continuously for 80 minutes or for eight 10-minute periods interspersed with eight 5-minute periods of neutral material, followed by two live exposure sessions either continuously for 120 minutes or for four 30-minute periods with 30-minute intervals between. The total duration of exposure was the same in both groups but was continuous in long and interrupted in short exposure. Fantasy always preceded live exposure. Outcome 3 days after sessions was similar in short versus long fantasy exposure, which had limited effects; but outcome was clearly superior in long versus short live exposure. Within sessions, heart rate fell only in the second hour of live exposure; this fall was greater during long than short exposure (Figure 14.3. However, subjective fear diminished equally in both groups. Initial expectancy of improvement did not correlate with outcome.

The Stern and Marks findings were replicated in 12 ocs (Rabavilas et al. 1976), this time balancing for the order not only of short versus long duration but also of fantasy versus live exposure. Patients had four biweekly exposure sessions, one each of fantasy exposure for 80 minutes or for eight 10-minute periods interspersed with eight 5-minute themes, and live exposure with response prevention for 80 minutes or for four 20-minute periods with four 10-minute neutral periods between them. As in the previous study, outcome 3 days after each session was similar for long versus short fantasy exposure and superior for long versus short live exposure both for oc and depressive symptoms.

An exception to the rule that longer exposure is better was a finding from a crossover study that 16 agoraphobics showed only a nonsignificant trend to improve more with 1 hour of live exposure than with 2½ hours separated by a quarter-hour (McFadyen & Presly 1977).

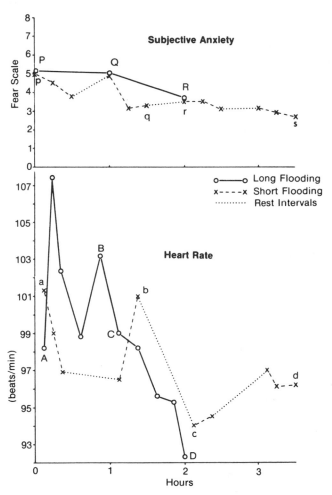

Fig. 14.3 Reduction of subjective fear and tachycardia in agoraphobics was greater in the second than in the first hour of live exposure given for 2 continuous hours (long flooding). Short exposure (flooding) was for 4½ hr with half-hour rest periods in between. (From Stern & Marks 1973a. Copyright © 1973 by Archives General Psychiatry. Reprinted by permission.)

One- to Fifty-Minute Sessions

In the six volunteer studies below, 1 to 20 minutes (′) of exposure were less effective by the end of the session than either 0′ or 30 to 50′ (the first four studies were in snake fear, the fifth in spider fear, and the sixth in surgery fear). Less reduction in avoidance of the phobic stimulus was found in the following instances:

1. Live exposure of 15′ as opposed to 0′, 30′, or 45′ (Miller & Levis 1971).
2. Live exposure of 15′ versus 0′ or 45′ (Stone & Borkovec 1975).
3. Live exposure of three 10′ exposure sequences with 5′ intervals between versus 30′ continuously (Girodo & Henry 1976).
4. Live exposure given 20′ continuously or in sequences of 1′ exposure alternating with 1′ rest to a total of 10′ or 20′ versus 40′ continuously (Kotila 1969).
5. Six 8′ imaginal exposure sequences at 4′ intervals versus 48′ (but only when arousal level was low rather than high) (Mathews & Shaw 1973).
6. Habituation to fear cues occurred only after 60′, not 20′, of fantasy exposure (McCutcheon & Adams 1975).

The foregoing data do not suggest that brief exposure actually sensitizes in the sense of increasing response to above baseline levels, just that brief exposure is less effective than long exposure. In a balanced study of this point, insect-fearful students had 0 or 30 seconds (″) exposure to cockroaches or a frog. Five minutes later, after 2′ exposure to one of the two stimuli, there was no rise in fear, avoidance, heart rate, or skin conductance to either stimulus (Markus & Canavan 1985).

Brief exposure was neither sensitizing nor therapeutic in two thoughtful experiments by Marshall (1985). In his first study, Marshall exposed 60 chronic height phobics in one of six conditions (mean duration of exposure [in minutes] for each condition are in parentheses):

1. No exposure (0).
2. Exposure until fear had just started to reduce (8′).
3. Exposure until fear had fallen by 75% (13′).
4. Exposure until there was no fear for 1′ (23′).
5. Exposure until there was no fear and then continuing for a third of that time further (32′).
6. Exposure as in condition 5, except that during the added third of exposure, subjects made coping self-statements (31′).

Brief exposure did not affect fear for worse or better. Prolonging exposure until fear had all but dissipated was therapeutic, but prolonging exposure beyond that point (overlearning) was not helpful. Adding coping self-statements did not increase improvement at the end of treatment but did at 4-week follow-up.

Marshall's second study exposed 30 height phobics in conditions 2, 3, and 4 above, except that now similar total exposure time was reached across conditions by giving repeated but interrupted exposure to subjects in groups 2 and 3 according to their respective conditions until they had received the same total exposure time as yoked counterparts in group 4 who received continuous exposure (the intertrial intervals were not reported). Continuous exposure (condition 4) did best to 4-week follow-up, whereas brief interrupted exposure (2 and 3) did not improve.

In summary, in Marshall's studies brief exposure did not sensitize. Exposure of 23' to 32' was better than 0', 8', to 13' exposures and was better given continuously than in brief interrupted spurts, thus replicating the findings of Stern and Marks (1973) and of Rabavilas and colleagues (1976). Prolonging exposure beyond the point where fear had fallen to baseline did not enhance outcome; this finding deserves to be replicated.

Exposure of Less Than a Minute

Again, longer exposure was better, in three studies. The first two were in snake-fearful students and the third in mixed agoraphobic patients and insect-phobic volunteers. More fear reduction was obtained by 30" versus 12" or 3" of exposure (Ross & Proctor 1973), by 30" versus 5" (Sue 1975), and by 30" and 45" versus 5" (for high hierarchy items, both during and some days after treatment) (Watts 1971, 1973, 1974). In the last population, interstimulus intervals of 40" versus 15" were better for high hierarchy items immediately, but this superiority did not last over a week; strong items thus desensitized faster if long imaginal presentations were used with longer interstimulus intervals.

In line with these results is work on the galvanic skin response (GSR) in students. The decrease in response to noise was speeded by shorter interstimulus intervals (mean of 51" versus 96") (Glass & Singer 1972). GSR habituation to tones or shock was speeded with interstimulus intervals of 30" but delayed when they were 60" or 90", and declined more rapidly with interstimulus intervals of 15" versus 30" (Winokur 1962).

Duration of Intersession Intervals

The duration of intersession intervals did not affect outcome in volunteer studies (Hall & Hinkle 1972; Marshitz et al. 1973) but did in the only controlled clinical study, which was in agoraphobics (Foa et al. 1980). Ten daily 2-hour sessions of live exposure were superior, especially on avoidance, to 10 such sessions given weekly, although the latter was also beneficial; patients had no self-exposure between sessions. That massed sessions are better than spaced sessions supports results from within-session studies that concentrating exposure beyond some unknown point enhances fear reduction.

Prevention of Escape/Avoidance or Its Termination
of the Evoking Stimulus

Animal evidence on this issue was discussed in Chapter 8. Here we will deal with human data. They pose an important puzzle: although escape or avoidance are often thought of as antitherapeutic, this seems to be true only outside a program of exposure therapy.

Studies show that phobics and ocs who were asked to practice anti-exposure—to avoid the ES for a week or more did not improve with therapist contact even if they were given antidepressants (Greist et al. 1980; Marks et al. 1986; Telch et al. 1985). Yet escape or avoidance immediately after exposure need not hinder therapeutic gains. Phobias still improved in agoraphobics and other phobics when they were asked to face their ES until they felt anxious and then to escape and report to the therapist, upon which they were asked to return to the ES immediately (Boersma et al. 1976; Crowe et al. 1972; Emmelkamp 1974; Emmelkamp & Kraanen 1978; Emmelkamp & Ultee 1974; Everaerd et al. 1973). Escape had not lastingly switched off the ES.

Even more prolonged escape after therapist-aided live exposure (E) did not stop agoraphobics from improving (de Silva & Rachman 1984). Twelve cases had eight weekly sessions of (1) E ceasing as soon as fear reached a preset level (escape)—unlike the foregoing studies, patients were not asked to reenter the phobic situation immediately but only to return the next week; or (2) E continuing until fear dropped by 50% (endurance). There was no self-exposure. Both E groups improved more than did six controls on a waiting list; E ending in prolonged escape did not sensitize and was only marginally inferior to more enduring E, in which condition cases had longer exposure.

It is unclear whether the preset level of fear that triggered escape in group 1 was as high as that previously experienced by patients encountering their natural ES; perhaps the level of fear from which escape occurs modifies the probability that this will strengthen future escape. The above study needs to be replicated, examining this point and controlling for the total duration of E. It is still possible that prolonged avoidance retards habituation more if it terminates the ES for a long rather than a short time, and this problem requires further examination. In the clinic, improvement during exposure treatment seems to be enhanced by enduringly blocking escape and avoidance of the ES in both overt behavior and covert thought.

Preventing avoidance from becoming a safety signal heralding the start of an anxiety-free period may be more important than stopping the avoidance response itself. In a pilot study oc washers were exposed to their ES and then allowed to wash provided that they reexposed themselves during washing (so that it ceased to be a safety signal); improvement proceeded at the same rate as in cases who were exposed and asked not to wash (Lipsedge 1974). This experiment dissociated the avoidance response from the conditioned stimulus (CS) and unconditioned stimulus (US), which feature seems important if the response is to decline. In Chapter 8 we saw evidence that extinction in humans was hastened by preventing avoidance in a way that dissociated it from the CS and US (Carasa et al. 1978), a result according with others in rats (Miller et al. 1982).

Prevention of Rituals

Obsessive-compulsive rituals usually switch off or avoid discomfort that is part of the ES; preventing the rituals thus usually raises anxiety at first. (Habituation will eventually occur if response prevention goes on for some hours.) Response prevention (rp) thus inevitably involves exposure to the ES, although the reverse need not be true. In one study rp reduced rituals more than anxiety (Foa et al. 1980a), but this could not be replicated (Foa et al. 1984). In both studies, exposure without rp decreased anxiety more than it did rituals, so rituals seem to be maintained not only by anxiety but also by other factors.

Foa and coworkers thought their results indicated that rituals are cued not only by contaminants and discomfort but also by bathrooms, water faucets, sinks, and the like—that is, the compound ES contains more than just contaminants. One wonders what the outcome might be if exposure-alone cases were systematically exposed not just to contaminants but also to bathrooms, water faucets, and sinks. Would rp still retain its superiority in reducing rituals? Whatever the precise mechanisms by which the various components of oc problems improve, results argue that both exposure and response prevention should be part of treatment, which in the long run works almost as well when self- as when therapist-administered.

Response prevention need not be supervised around the clock. Twenty-four-hour supervised rp reduced the frequency of rituals (but not of anxiety) more than did 1-hour supervised rp followed by self-imposed rp; within 2 weeks, however, this superiority had disappeared (Robertson 1979). At 2 to 4 years' follow-up the two groups had maintained similar improvement. In fact rp does not even need to be supervised. Good results were obtained with instructions for rp given to outpatients treating themselves (Hoogduin 1985; Marks et al. 1986).

GRADIENT OF AND AROUSAL DURING EXPOSURE

Gradient (Slow Versus Fast Exposure)

We can wade into cold water bit by bit or just dive in. Or, to change the metaphor, when removing a band-aid from our skin, we can peel it slowly or rip it off. Similarly, exposure to fear cues can be gradual, starting with slightly frightening cues and slowly moving to terrifying ones (that is, desensitization), or it can begin at the top of the hierarchy, with the most alarming first (that is, flooding). The speed of approach depends on the patient, the time available, and the rate of habituation. A too-rapid approach may lead to noncompliance and dropping out; whether it produces a lasting increase in fear (sensitization) is not known, nor whether there is an optimal speed for low or high anxiety-evoking stimuli.

Both slow and rapid exposure work in the end, but rapid seems to work faster. In volunteers, habituation was greatest to the most frightening slides in a series (Eberle et al. 1975), and approach to a snake was terminated later in the sequence when approaching fast over 2 minutes than when approaching slowly over up to 8 minutes (Hastings & Walker 1975). In 28 phobic patients, improvement to a preset criterion was attained in fewer sessions and less time, and without increasing peak anxiety within sessions, with rapid than with slow exposure, although the amount of final improvement was similar in both groups (Yuksel et al. 1984). The criteria for moving up the hierarchy during E had been, in rapid E, once fear of a situation had dropped by 2 on a 0 to 8 scale, and in slow E, once it had dropped by 4. All patients also had e but with no control of its pace. (The study needs replication without this masking effect.)

In line with results favoring rapid exposure are those of Williams and coworkers (1985). Thirty-eight chronic height-phobic volunteers had one or two 1½-hour sessions of (1) rapid E as fast as possible together with exposure aids (mastery), or (2) slow E keeping anxiety low (desensitization), or (3) no treatment control. Self-exposure was discouraged. Therapist-aided exposure was terminated before the 3-hour limit if the criterion was reached, which occurred earlier in rapid E (153 minutes) than in slow E (178 minutes). Up to 1 month follow-up, rapid E was better than slow E in improving avoidance, anticipated anxiety, fearful thoughts, and self-efficacy; both groups were better than the untreated controls. The superiority of the rapid E group could have resulted not only from faster exposure but also because they were the only group to have exposure aids (performance- or response-induction aids).

If rapid exposure resembles starting at the top rather than the bottom of the phobic-oc hierarchy, then the in vivo findings of Yuksel and coworkers (1984) are similar to those from studies of this issue with fantasy exposure. All showed that whether exposure starts at the top or the bottom of the hierarchy either made no difference (Cohen & Dean 1968; Guilani 1972; Krapfl & Nawas 1970; Mathews & Shaw 1973; Suinn et al. 1970; Welch & Krapfl 1970), or favored starting at the top (Cohen & Dean 1968).

A relevant issue is that of systematic desensitization as opposed to flooding (implosion). In two studies there were short-term advantages of fantasy flooding when it was administered without drugs (Marks et al. 1971) or with thiopental (Husain 1971). However, fantasy flooding was no better than fantasy desensitization in three other studies (Crowe et al. 1972; Gelder et al. 1973; Shaw 1979). Apparently conflicting results in two of those studies were found on analysis to be potentially due to differences in the type of live exposure given to patients after they completed the fantasy sessions. Marks and colleagues (1971), who found flooding to be better, had maintained the difference between the gentle (desensitization) and forceful (flooding) approaches not only during fantasy but also during live exposure. In contrast, Gelder and coworkers (1973) found desensitization and flooding to be nearly equally effective but had added four sessions of rather similar live exposure to both fantasy desensitization and fantasy flooding, which may have obscured differences between the two conditions.

The comparison of desensitization with flooding contains some confounds. Fantasy desensitization involves not only starting with less frightening cues and keeping fear low throughout, but also very brief exposures and relaxation between exposure periods. In contrast, fantasy flooding begins near the top of the hierarchy and aims to maximize fear during exposure, which is continuous and without relaxation. Continuous long exposure sessions are better than interrupted short ones, but the point on the hierarchy at which exposure starts seems unimportant. It is also unimportant whether there is marked relaxation or high anxiety during exposure, a point to which we now turn.

Arousal Level During Exposure

Low Arousal

Arousal is reduced by relaxation, which also enhances the vividness of phobic imagery (Levin & Gross 1985). However, in the absence of exposure, relaxation is not therapeutic (Marks et al. 1980, 1975), nor does relaxation training enhance exposure (Harris & Johnson 1983, reviewed by Marks 1975). This conclusion is reinforced by the results of four Swedish studies with "applied relaxation" (AR) or "applied tension" (AT). Subjects first learned to relax and tense their muscles and then to practice this while confronting fantasied and real phobic cues. Despite the labels, therefore, AR and AT included exposure (*e* with or without *E*).

Two AR studies were with agoraphobics. In the first (Öst et al. 1984b), 36 cases had 12 weekly sessions. Patients were divided into those responding to a behavioral test mainly by tachycardia or mainly by avoidance; each group was subdivided into half having AR with some *E* plus *e* and the other half having *E* plus *e* with coping instructions but no diaries. Up to 15 months' follow-up both treatments did equally well, unlike two previous studies (Öst et al. 1981, 1982) in which claustrophobics and social phobics who were mainly tachycardic improved more from AR while avoiders gained more from *E* with skills training. Thus, AR did not enhance *E* plus *e*. Treatment matched to the patient's phobic response pattern yielded no better results than a nonmatched method (this was also found in dental phobics—Jerremalm et al. 1985).

In the second agoraphobic study (Jansson et al. 1986), 36 cases had 12 sessions of AR or *E*, after which all had *e* with a diary and monthly phone calls for 5 months. Improvement in both groups was similar and further increased over 15 months' follow-up. Gains correlated with the percentage of *e* goals attained on the diary in the first 5 months, although high and low goal attainers had comparable final outcome.

A further two AR studies were with blood-injury phobics. In the first (Öst et al. 1984), 16 cases had 9 weekly 50-minute sessions of *E* or of AR with *E* only in sessions 7 and 8, plus corresponding *e* with diaries throughout. Therapist-assisted exposure was better than AR plus *E* after treatment, but both had improved similarly by 6 months' follow-up; 10 of the 16 cases became blood donors. In a replication study comparable results were obtained from AT (1 session AT and 4 with *E* plus *e*), AR (8 sessions AR and 2 with *E* plus *e*), and AT plus AR (7 sessions AR, 1 of AT, 2 of *E* plus *e*) (Öst, L. G., personal communication, 1986).

High Arousal

This is aimed at by flooding, which tries to frighten the subject as much as possible during exposure until he or she can no longer feel fear. The form of fantasy flooding called implosion presents not only phobic-oc-cues but also cues concerning conflicts such as guilt and aggression not directly related to the phobic-oc problem. Such irrelevant anxiety cues do not enhance outcome; nor does extreme fear. High is no better than moderate fear during exposure, and within-session fear does not predict outcome (Foa et al. 1977; Hafner & Marks 1976, reviewed by Marks 1975, 1978). In one study of fantasy exposure in dental phobics, high anxiety had less good short-term effect than did low anxiety (Mathews & Shaw 1973).

Paradoxical intention or logotherapy (Frankl 1955) is related to flooding. It tries to persuade the phobic-oc to aggravate the clinical problem (for example, for agoraphobia, the patient is told to go outside and bring on a heart attack; for obsessions, to try to increase them; for erectile impotence, to have foreplay without an erection). The paradoxical instructions may be given with humor and their absurdity emphasized. Paradox may help some patients when they are stuck at certain points during exposure, although there is no convincing evidence that it is needed as a routine. Claims that paradox helps agoraphobia and fears of urinating outside the home (Ascher 1979, 1981; Michelson & Ascher 1984; Strong 1984) cannot be evaluated because of confounds regarding the duration and speed of exposure. Another form of high arousal occurs in abreaction (catharsis), whose therapeutic value is erratic (pp. 497–481).

Engagement Versus Dissociation

Given that neither very low nor very high arousal enhances exposure, is there an optimal level? This has not been well documented. What does seem important is maintenance of attention to the fear cues (engagement) until discomfort dies down. Attention or engagement can be regarded as a minimum level of arousal necessary for exposure to work.

Contact with fear cues during exposure has to be emotional as well as physical. Most clinicians agree that patients improve more if they engage in the exposure experience, attending to and feeling it in all its aspects; conversely, subjects do less well if they block, dissociate, discount, ignore, or covertly avoid or escape from the fear (Marks 1981, p. 56). In other words, the exposure should be functional, letting the emotional information access central representations of fear so that they can be activated, processed, and habituated (Borkovec 1982; Foa & Kozak 1986; Lang 1979). Habituation can start only when the signal arrives centrally, at which point we become aware of it.

The mechanisms by which central activation leads to habituation are being explored in simple organisms (see Chapter 7). That habituation is so specific to the stimuli that are repeated during exposure suggests that it involves a matching of incoming stimuli with central representations of the fear. The better the fit, the better their activation and habituation; the converse is true if the stimulus input is degraded. This might explain why exposure is usually better when given live rather than in fantasy and with engagement rather than dissociation, so that the input can access more facets of the emotional memory. (The emotion itself can be viewed, in Lang's words, as a differentiated action set, often context bound, based on a specific information structure in memory.)

Everyday life is often made easier by denial or detachment. It helped Moshe Dayan, for example, weather criticism when the opposition screamed abuse at him while he was speaking in the Israeli Knesset: "Though it was not at all pleasant, I went on with my speech, and felt no psychological stress. I withdrew myself, a sensation familiar to me from the battlefield, when I would cut myself off emotionally from reality. What was happening in the Knesset was happening in a fog and was unreal to me, like the burst of shells when crossing a field of fire" (*Newsweek*, 1981).

We have many gates that bar unpleasant experience from reaching consciousness. Those gates protect us from being overwhelmed so that we can go on functioning. They allow us to maintain activation at a level that energizes rather than paralyzes, a point implicit in the Yerkes-Dodson curve of long ago. For exposure to work, most of those gates need to be open. The experience of fear must pass all our defenses, which try to stop it from reaching our awareness so that the emotion can be processed to the point of becoming habituated.

Blocking can be hard to spot in therapy. In an oc who felt contaminated when urine was placed on his arm during exposure, anxiety would be very high for a few minutes and then fall sharply, but return the next day. It turned out that he imagined "freezing" the contaminated area to prevent its spread and then ceased attending to it (Foa & Kozak 1986). Dissociation may be involuntary, as in a spider phobic who said when she imagined a spider: "*It* suddenly jumped away from me out of the open window." We know little about the parameters governing dissociation, and it may be extremely hard to prevent. The best we can do is ask the patient to make the exposure situation feel as real as possible and attend to all its aspects.

Psychotherapists distinguish between intellectual and emotional insight; only the latter is linked to progress. We can know things with our head but not with our heart: we can know at many levels. Ideas and feelings have to penetrate and sink in, their implications digested, if they are to exert their full effect. This process takes time for both painful and pleasant events. Grief takes weeks, months, or even years to be resolved and worked through. Fortunately, habituation in exposure therapy may start in half an hour and be complete within days or weeks. But it can start only when the message gets to our brain; we learn nothing if it goes in one ear and out the other, so to speak.

There is thus a consensus that phobic-ocs do not do well if their exposure experience does not seem real, if they feel depersonalized or derealized and say they are not really there, or if their mind continually wanders from the task in hand. Experimental evidence is beginning to uphold the idea that engaging exposure is better than dissociative exposure. To the extent that physiological activation reflects increased attention, the engagement hypothesis is supported by findings that exposure works better if subjects have raised heart rate or skin conductance activity during early contact with phobic-oc or neutral stimuli.[1] In more direct experiments, fear reduction lasted longer in oc patients (Grayson et al. 1982) and in snake-phobic volunteers (Sartory et al. 1982) if subjects

---

[1]See, for instance, Borkovec & Sides 1979; Foa et al. 1986; Lang et al. 1970; Lelliott et al. 1986; Marks et al. 1971; Vermilyea et al. 1984; Watson & Marks 1971; Zahn et al. 1984.

attended to the exposure task than if they were distracted during exposure by a videogame or reading a magazine. Engagement was also more valuable than distraction or neutral involvement in children who were treated for severe burns (Kavanagh 1983) or underwent dentistry (Klinger et al. 1984, cited by Foa & Kozak 1986).

FEAR REDUCTION: SPECIFIC HABITUATION VERSUS GENERAL COPING ABILITY

Habituation tends to be specific to the fear cues that have been repeatedly present (see chapters 7 and 8). In multiply phobic subjects, exposure tends to reduce only those phobias which have been treated, with little generalization to unexposed cues (Williams & Kleifield 1985). Exposure therapy seems more a process of specific habituation/extinction than of acquiring a general ability to cope with unpleasantness (stress immunization).

Courage is often regarded as a general readiness to face a wide variety of noxious situations, and to some extent it can be trained. How habituation relates to courage is an intriguing issue. To what extent does gaining confidence in one situation make one more courageous in others, and does teaching courage in a normally frightening context generalize to reduce phobic-oc problems? In other words, can we teach stress immunization, and would it help phobic-ocs? Conversely, how much does habituation to particular phobic-oc evoking stimuli generalize to other fear cues, and does it help subjects deal with anger and with sexual arousal? Is exposure therapy itself partly a form of stress immunization? And does exposure have to be relevant to the patient's phobic or oc complaints, or can one reduce them by teaching courage more broadly?

Relevant and Irrelevant Fear Cues

The last question has been addressed by three controlled studies comparing exposure to phobia-relevant versus irrelevant fear cues. The first was a crossover design in 6 specific phobics and 10 agoraphobics (Watson & Marks 1971). All patients had sixteen 50-minute sessions of fantasy flooding over 6 weeks. Half the cases had 8 relevant and then 8 irrelevant sessions, and half had them in the reverse order. By 3 or 4 days after each block of treatment, patients in both conditions had improved equally on clinical and attitudinal measures and on heart rate (HR) and skin conductance (SC) responses to neutral and phobic imagery.

Less anxiety occurred in irrelevant fear sessions that followed relevant ones, but the converse did not apply (Figure 14.4) (in both conditions, cases remained anxious at the end of the 50-minute sessions). The two treatments also had different predictors of outcome. Outcome to relevant flooding correlated with more pretreatment SC and HR activity to phobic and normal fear scenes and SC activity to neutral scenes but with less HR activity to neutral scenes, and did not relate to anxiety during sessions. In contrast, outcome to irrelevant flooding correlated with more anxiety during relevant or irrelevant

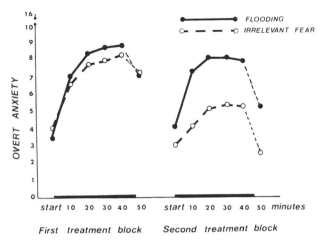

Fig. 14.4 Less anxiety occurred in irrelevant fantasy flooding sessions that followed relevant fantasy flooding sessions, but the converse did not apply (in both conditions, cases remained anxious at the end of the 50-minute sessions). (From Watson & Marks 1971. Copyright © 1971 by Academic Press. Reprinted by permission.)

flooding sessions but was *worse* with more pretreatment HR and anxiety during neutral scenes.

Unlike Watson and Marks, two other studies found that relevant was slightly superior to irrelevant fantasy exposure. One was in a small crossover study of 6 cases with obsessions who had 6 hour-long sessions 3 times a week (Emmelkamp & Giesselbach 1981). Relevant exposure was a bit better after treatment, but the analysis did not exclude a possible order effect, and the sample was tiny.

The other study favoring relevant fear cues was in volunteers fearful of viewing surgery (McCutcheon & Adams 1975). Relevant fantasy exposure reduced the fear more than did irrelevant frightening scenes (of snakes), provided these were given for 60 minutes. When scenes lasted only 20 minutes, SC fluctuations rose post-test in both fear imagery groups and fell in resting controls.

In volunteers, snake phobias reduced after listening to irrelevant fear cues, especially if this was followed immediately by relevant phobic cues (Hodgson & Rachman 1970). There are anecdotes of war neuroses improving after abreaction of disturbing material unrelated to the precipitating trauma (Sargant 1957), and of other intense emotions (sexual arousal or anger) reducing anxiety in animals (Liddell 1956) and humans (Marks 1965), at least temporarily. Relief from abreaction is relevant to the question how much fear reduction occurs through specific habituation and how much through other mechanisms. The problem deserves further exploration.

Role of Abreaction

Abreaction (catharsis) originally denoted the intense emotion that may accompany a revival of traumatic memories under hypnosis. More recently it has come to mean any intense emotional experience during treatment. The emotion can be of many kinds, not only fear, and may involve problems unrelated to the trauma that precipitated the distress (Wilde 1942). Much was published about abreaction for traumatic phobias (post-traumatic stress disorder [PTSD]) during and after the two world wars. Since then relevant reports have mainly appeared in the literature on flooding.

The clinical features and consequences of abreaction appear similar whichever way the emotion is induced. Inductive methods include psychodrama, films, hypnosis, suggestion, or drugs given by inhalation (chloroform, ether, or nitrous oxide) or intravenously (barbiturates such as hexo-, pento-, or amylobarbitone, or methylamphetamine or diazepam). Catharsis can also occur spontaneously or can be triggered by sudden noises, alcohol, discussion about combat, or psychotherapy.

Some therapists used abreaction as their prime therapeutic instrument (Sargant 1948, 1957) in a manner resembling implosion or other fantasy flooding. Others used it as but one aspect of clinical management including live exposure (Bond 1952; Edkins 1949; Schwartz 1945). For example, Edkins (1948) abreacted 44 cases of chronic PTSD in a mean of 12 sessions, most under chloroform and a few with ether. The patients were encouraged to relive past events and to keep an abreaction diary of their symptoms, dreams, and external events. Sedatives were withdrawn and exposure homework was set; for example, an ex-prisoner of war saw a film of camp life, and a fireman was asked to drive again after a crash. Most cases improved, some after initial setbacks.

Intense emotion was more easily induced in shell-shocked soldiers in the field shortly after their disturbance began than later after transfer away from battle (Brown 1920). Acutely ill patients with amnesia, confusion, and hallucinations and dissociative symptoms such as paralysis were easier to abreact and relieve than were chronic patients (Garmany 1953; Rosen & Myers 1947; Shorvon 1953). The longer the symptoms persisted, the more difficult they were to remove (McDougall 1920).

During abreaction patients might be oblivious of the therapist's presence or remain in contact with him throughout (Bond 1952): "In almost every case the patient could be roused from his apparently deep reverie simply by being told that the interview was over. [When a doctor tried to hurry a man to the traumatic part of his flying mission] the patient stopped his detailed description and rebuked the physician by saying, "No, no, not yet Doc, we're only over the Channel." In a few minutes he said, "Now, Doc, there it is, there's the flak!" and abreacted violently. Patients would slip back and forth from direct to indirect discourse . . . demonstrating the great difficulty they were having in deciding whether the incident was past, present, or possibly future."

It is not known whether abreacted emotion has to be unpleasant for relief to occur. Perhaps intense sexual arousal or joy is similarly therapeutic. The lasting behavioral change of religious conversion may be ushered in by a period of religious ecstasy (James 1902).

The literature suggests that abreaction needs to continue for some time if relief is to follow, and that longer may be better, as in exposure therapy. Some have posited a critical end point of emotional collapse (Sargant 1957; Shorvon 1953) or transmarginal inhibition, as in Pavlov's dogs, who lost their conditioned reflexes after nearly drowning in the floods in Leningrad (Epstein 1970). Unfortunately for this concept, the dogs later gradually recovered the reflexes in question.

While abreaction is often followed by relief of distress, this sequence is by no means invariable (Bond 1952). The intensity of the abreacted feeling was not obviously related to outcome. Often intense emotion would appear repeatedly without improvement. This was true for both spontaneous and induced abreactions (McDougall 1920). In at least a few men with PSTD the abreaction itself acted like a new trauma, and anxiety increased each time a trauma was relived without subsequent relief. Sometimes transient relief failed to recur after subsequent abreaction (Kennedy 1960). Other pilots with flying phobias relived their stressful experiences without anxiety and without benefit.

A rare physiological study of abreaction was in a normal female volunteer of 25 (Lifshitz & Blair 1960). On seven occasions under hypnosis she relived nearly drowning at age 10. During successive abreactions there was a reduction in facial expression, HR, SC, respiration rate, frontalis EMG, cheek temperature, and body movement. The woman continued to show anxiety to unrelated traumatic incidents, showing that the habituation had been specific.

Early writers such as Freud ascribed symptom relief to the discharge of affect linked to the revived memory. But memories may be revived without emotion. Some writers regarded the production of affect per se, not the memory, as crucial for improvement (Brown 1920; Sargant 1957; Shorvon 1953). Others stressed the therapeutic value of the return of the memory itself (McDougall 1920) and strove to help the patient remember his or her experiences after the abreaction had subsided and to relate these to other aspects of his or her personality (Grinker & Spiegel 1945; Rosen & Myers 1947).

If the revival of lost memories were the sole mechanism of improvement, then the abreaction of experiences that the patient has never undergone should not be therapeutic. But the experience of fear that is irrelevant to a phobia can improve it, and abreaction may be followed by relief even though the "relived" events are fictitious (Wilde 1942) and might simply have been suggested. A soldier in a tank regiment could be excited to the point of "emotional collapse" only after being persuaded that he was trapped in a burning tank, which had never really happened (Sargant 1957, p. 61). In religious ceremonies a subject may feel better after abreacting possession by spirits that might be more relevant to his religious beliefs than to the problems that are relieved. It is likely that abreaction acts through a variety of mechanisms that might be additive rather than mutually exclusive.

"Organic Memories" During Abreaction

Intense abreaction may be accompanied by "organic memories" or "somatizations." A hand blanched at the time a memory of past injury to it recurred (Edkins 1949). When a man relived the experience of being tied up 12 years previously, rope marks appeared on his forearm (Moody 1946); a few minutes later weals appeared on both forearms and gradually became indented, and finally fresh petechiae were seen along their course. These marks lasted for several hours after the abreaction had ended. In a woman, skin lesions appeared during her abreaction of trauma from many years before (Moody 1948); hyperemia began minutes after the abreaction started, followed by edema, petechiae, and then slight flaking of the epidermis. The changes lasted up to a day after abreaction. Trained observers witnessed them several times during repeated abreactions of different traumata, and each time the area affected was the bodily part involved in the abreacted memory.

The phenomenon is reminiscent of religious stigmata (Jacobi 1923). It also resembles other psychogenic skin lesions (Moody 1946):

> Skin blisters, for instance, have been produced hypnotically at *specified points* on the body surface, with the exclusion of all possible sources of error. Localised urticaria of *specified areas* of the body has been produced by similar means; so also have oedema and cutaneous gangrene. Many cases of spontaneous haemorrhage of a psychogenic nature have been described. . . . Neural pathways undoubtedly exist by which psychic contents may be projected on to the body *in a highly specific manner;* and it is reasonable to suppose that, in such cases, the psychic content or image, with its emotional charge, acts as the afferent side of a reflex arc the efferent counterpart of which is [autonomic]. . . . Such traumatic experiences are not restricted to adult life or to the battlefield. They may occur also in the formative years of early childhood and may involve regions of the body other than the skin and subcutaneous tissue.

Organic memories raise questions about the nature of physiological changes during exposure as well as abreaction. How are the skin changes mediated? To what extent are they a response to current stimuli or to the evocation of earlier memories? As patients improve during exposure, the cues they are confronting for the first time in years may bring back long-forgotten experiences. This point warrants expansion.

Revival of Memories During Exposure

In chronic phobics, forgotten memories linked to a long-avoided fear cue may surface when that cue is encountered again either deliberately or by chance. One of the author's patients with a phobia, of all things, of firemen's helmets, suddenly remembered during exposure that her fear had begun many years previously soon after she saw a fireman falling to his death during an exercise.

Two intriguing examples during exposure therapy were described by Segraves and Smith (1975). In the first, during fantasy desensitization a clergyman who was anxious about leading religious services had trouble imagining performance of a service with an older colleague and a female church custodian. Suddenly he remarked, "I keep remembering that slut custodian wandering about the church in a loose housecoat, and also her face kept resembling my mother's. You know, I just remembered that my mother used to always do that at home." Thereafter he could imagine the scene without trouble and improved with continuing treatment.

The second example was in a bird-phobic woman during live exposure.

Prior to touching a duck she said, "I want to touch the duck, but somehow feel that it's wrong. It reminds me of dating in high school when I desired intercourse but always said no." Then she touched the duck and cried with relief. That night she had a dream with sexual connotations. Both cases felt easier after revival of the memories; the therapist had merely persuaded the patients to maintain exposure without discussing the symbolic significance of their fear cues.

A final example is a snake-phobic woman who after 40 minutes of live exposure panicked and ran out of the room (Hafner 1978). On her return 15 minutes later she wept for 10 minutes and felt strong guilt. On stopping crying she recalled a long-forgotten episode. At age 13 while on a country walk she had seen a snake and had run away in panic, shouting "I'd rather see my mother dead than see another snake." Her guilt rose transiently and then fell, and she continued the exposure calmly. In her second session she felt mounting anger with the snake and after 10 minutes suddenly screamed obscenities at it, jerking her whole body with rage and banging her fists on the chair. This frenzy lasted 3 minutes; then she sobbed unrestrainedly and finally felt calm. Her improvement after 4 hours of exposure remained at 6 months' follow-up.

Relief of phobias has also occurred after chance encounters prompted the return of long-forgotten worries related to the onset of the fear. We cannot jump to conclusions concerning the potential significance of such memories for the onset and maintenance of the fear (Marks 1969 and Chapter 8). A related issue is that some people become able to talk about their fears only after, not before, relief from exposure (Lamontagne & Marks 1973). The important procedural point is that to help the problem the therapist need not spend much time probing for meaning, which in any case may emerge as exposure goes on.

Problem Solving and Assertion Training

Is habituation from exposure really necessary for fear reduction? Could anxiety diminish merely from learning coping skills, from realizing how to deal with life problems? Training such problem solving (PS) without exposure is an unreliable treatment for agoraphobia. In one study agoraphobics did better with e than with PS, but one of the two therapists also got good results with PS (Jannoun et al. 1980). Cases in both conditions had graded treatment at home with the spouse, a manual, self-monitoring, and homework; in PS patients spent 1 hour daily identifying stressful life problems, discussing ways of solving them, and setting targets to do this. However, the good effect of PS by one therapist could not be replicated by two other therapists in a second trial of PS without exposure in 14 agoraphobics, even though patients rated PS as important in treatment (Cullington et al. 1984). The therapist saw the patient and spouse at home 5 times in 4 weeks for a total of 3¼ hours; follow-up was to 6 months.

Assertion training (AT) is another approach to teaching a fairly broad coping skill. Like problem solving, AT without systematic exposure is not much

help for agoraphobia, although it can increase assertion. Twenty-one unassertive agoraphobics had ten three-hour sessions biweekly of E plus e, or AT, or
both; no diaries were kept (Emmelkamp et al. 1983). Each treatment improved
its target problem. Up to 1 month follow-up, E plus e was superior on phobias
and AT on assertion; some cases became more assertive after E alone.

Similar findings were obtained by Thorpe et al. (1985). In a crossover study,
8 agoraphobics had E plus e or AT, each for four 1½-hour sessions. Phobias
and anxiety-depression improved only with exposure. Assertiveness improved
only with AT, but this was transient and no longer present at 6 months' follow-
up. No between-groups effects were noted.

Results from these two studies accord with others that assertive and unassertive agoraphobics benefitted equally from exposure (Emmelkamp 1980a)
and that success of exposure was unrelated to assertiveness (Emmelkamp &
van der Hout 1983). Unassertiveness is not a special problem in agoraphobic
women, who are as assertive as nonagoraphobic women (Buglass et al. 1977).

ADJUVANTS TO EXPOSURE

Response-Induction Aids

A complex task is easier to learn if we undertand exactly what has to be done,
can break it down into easy stages, and have a detailed guide to carrying out
each stage. The tough task of exposure is no exception to this rule. It is simple
enough to learn the exposure principle, but quite another matter to apply it in
a flexible strategy that can be adapted to changing and often unexpected circumstances. Patients often remember little of even quite easy instructions from
their doctors, so a good practical guide is of great value, as we saw in the discussion of self-exposure.

Helpful tips on how to proceed in detail can be called response-induction
aids (Bandura et al. 1974) or performance or exposure aids. The aids might
emanate from the therapist, the client, or both. Which aids are appropriate
varies with the cues that evoke fear. In general, however, the aids involve carrying out exposure in manageable bits, doing difficult things briefly at first and
then for gradually longer periods, engaging in the task rather than dissociating
from it, discouraging avoidance, varying the tasks undertaken until fear has
subsided to all relevant cues, fading out the aids as the subject acquires confidence and competence, and modeling by the therapist of what needs to be done
if that is not clear. One common "aid" is undesirable—large doses of benzodiazepine drugs or alcohol during exposure (see Chapter 16).

The value of exposure aids from the therapist was affirmed in snake-phobic
volunteers (Bandura et al. 1974). All clients had E with modeling, together with
either high, moderate, or low amounts of exposure aids that were faded when
no longer needed. Aids included touching the snake together with the therapist,
doing this for brief but increasing durations, and starting with gloves, with a
baby snake, and with the snake held fast. Improvement was greatest in subjects
who had E with moderate or high exposure aids. There was no follow-up.

Exposure aids may also have been beneficial in height phobics (Williams et al. 1985). Apart from some already mentioned, the aids consisted of holding the subject, encouragement of looking down the visual cliff, and ceasing defensive, tight gripping of one's clothes. In this study exposure aids were confounded with more rapid exposure, but in a second study without such a confound (Williams et al. 1984) exposure aids again enhanced the outcome of exposure. Thirty-two volunteers with height or driving phobias had (1) rapid E together with exposure aids (mastery), (2) rapid E without exposure aids, or (3) no treatment; e was discouraged. Therapist-aided exposure was given in from one to three 1- to 1½-hour sessions and ceased before a 3-hour limit if criterion was reached, which occurred within 146 minutes in E with exposure aids and 155 minutes in E without them—a nonsignificant difference. But E with exposure aids was superior to E without them for avoidance, self-efficacy, and anticipatory and performance anxiety. Both treatments were better than no treatment. No follow-up was noted.

In acrophobic volunteers a controlled study found no enhancement of exposure from exposure aids (Bourque and Ladouceur 1980).

Routine modeling of exposure by a therapist often fails to enhance exposure (Bourque & Ladouceur 1980, reviewed by Marks 1978) or has only a slight effect (Boersma et al. 1975; Coburn 1983). The point is of some importance, given that self-exposure without a therapist is now a dominant mode of therapy. It is redundant to demonstrate what to do to people who already know it well, but for those who really do not know how to carry out exposure, modeling the skill may be worthwhile. Filmed modeling of exposure was helpful only in young children who had no experience of dentistry, not in those who did have such experience (Klorman et al. 1980). Exposure aids that included a component of modeling have been useful, but they did not dissect out the contribution of modeling per se.

Praise of progress is a natural part of most therapies, and exposure is no exception. There does not seem to be a large contribution from systematic reinforcement added to exposure (reviewed by Marks 1975, p. 106), but encouraging clients' efforts assists motivation.

Biofeedback of heart rate, skin conductance, or other indicators of anxiety is a less natural addition to exposure. In controlled studies biofeedback did not enhance gains from exposure (Nunes & Marks 1976, reviewed by Emmelkamp 1982; Marks 1978). The popularity of biofeedback may stem in part from its promotion of therapist income rather than client outcome.

Other attempts to promote exposure have been by aversion relief, in which fantasy exposure terminated a series of shocks (Solyom et al. 1971, 1972b) and by respiratory relief, in which exposure coincided with the end of prolonged breathholding (Orwin et al. 1973, 1975). Results of aversion relief were negative and of respiratory relief were difficult to interpret because of problems in experimental design (Marks 1981).

Respiratory control has recently become popular for panic (Bonn et al. 1984; Clark et al. 1985; Franklin 1985; Salkovskis et al. 1986). Proper evaluation of this procedure requires better controlled factorial designs with long-term follow-up, plus measures of respiratory rate. The approach assumes that hyperventilation is a common problem aggravating agoraphobia, which is correctable by teaching proper breathing. However, we do not yet know what proportion of agoraphobics hyperventilate at rest and in the phobic situation, and how many of each would benefit lastingly from breathing exercises. Some patients may find it useful to have very brief instruction in deep breathing, but it is premature to recommend prolonged respiratory training as a routine in exposure therapy.

Hypnosis has been unimpressive in two controlled studies. In one, 28 phobics improved with 12 weekly sessions of either fantasy desensitization or hypnosis, but the former was rather better, and overall effects were weak (Marks et al. 1968). The second study, in 32 agoraphobics, found that hypnosis plus *e* was no better than *e* alone over 4 weeks (Van Dyck et al. 1984).

Group exposure can save therapist time if many cases present at the same time with problems triggered by similar cues. Numerous analog studies have used group exposure for convenience. Clinically, much controlled work with groups has concerned agoraphobics, and group and individual exposure have had comparable outcomes (Emmelkamp & Emmelkamp-Benner 1975; Hafner & Marks 1976). Cohesive groups improved more than noncohesive ones in one study (Hand et al. 1974), but this could not be replicated (Teasdale et al. 1974). Improvement from group exposure was also noted by other workers (Boisvert et al. 1983; Watson et al. 1973). Self-help clubs for agoraphobics exist in several countries, but few promote group exposure; most are engaged mainly in publishing a newsletter.

Social skills training is usually done in groups. Although it affords opportunities for multiple role modeling, it has not been shown to be superior to individual social skills training. A pilot study of this point found no difference in outcome (Stravynski et al. 1982).

Finally, drugs have been extensively used to help exposure relieve phobic-oc disorders. This topic is reviewed in Chapter 16.

Cognitive Approaches

Whereas exposure therapy tries to alter avoidance in the hope that cognitive and physiological gains will also follow, cognitive methods try first to alter thoughts to pave the way toward change in behavior. Unlike exposure, which encourages a direct approach to the stimulus that evokes fear in real life and fantasy until there is habituation of behavior, physiology, and thoughts, cognitive therapies attempt to change false beliefs in the hope that this will change behavior. Most cognitive methods have a component of exposure, in that at some point subjects are asked to practice cognitive maneuvers in the presence of fear cues, thus becoming adjuvants to exposure.

Cognitive methods come in several overlapping forms. Some identify irrational ideas and challenge them; examples are rational emotive therapy (Ellis 1962) and cognitive or rational restructuring (Goldfried et al. 1974). Others try to change the client's internal dialogue through, for instance, self-instruction or self-statement training (Meichenbaum 1977). These techniques and others are seen in cognitive therapy (Beck & Emery 1985), anxiety management training (Suinn & Richardson 1971), and coping exercises (Klepac et al. 1984).

Controlled Results

The recent vogue for cognitive approaches has led to a spate of controlled tests of their value for phobic-oc problems (Öst & Jannsson 1986), mostly as an adjuvant to exposure and occasionally without it. These are summarized in Table 14.1. Most of the investigations the table presents are randomized controlled studies that included a treatment package with a cognitive method as a major component while excluding it from a comparison group. Which designs actually achieved this contrast is not always easy to decide, and some designs did not avowedly test cognitive methods yet in fact constituted such a test. Some authors' conclusions that cognitive therapy was valuable rest on outcomes that were significant only within, not between, groups, or were present in only a few of many relevant measures.

In referring to Table 14.1 we should remember that a wide variety of names have been given to various cognitive and exposure approaches. The many therapy labels used by authors are reduced to a few basic modes given in the table. Even these are rather complex, but less so than the babel of terms that has proliferated in the literature.

The abundance of cognitive research seen in Table 14.1 has yielded a lean therapeutic harvest in comparison with that of exposure alone, which is a better way to improve most phobic-ocs. In the great majority of studies, cognitive methods alone had little effect and combined with exposure failed to enhance the amount or speed of improvement. The exposure yardstick is crucial in view of the reliability of exposure even when it is self- rather than therapist-administered.

Table 14.1 shows that in six studies of agoraphobics, cognitive therapy (CT) either did not enhance improvement with exposure or did not do as well as E or e with distraction instructions. In social anxiety marginally more hope for CT emerged, although different studies had conflicting results. Two found CT to enhance exposure and social skills training (SST), six had equivocal results or found some improvement from CT alone, and 12 found that CT did not enhance exposure/SST or failed to improve problems without it. In specific phobics one study was positive at follow-up, one was slightly and transiently positive, and four were negative. The only study in OCD was negative. Across all phobic-oc syndromes, of 33 controlled studies of CT, 4 were positive, 6 equivocal, and 23 negative. Whether the type of CT was mainly rational emotive, self-instructional, or other did not make a difference.

Six studies explicitly examined CT without any component of exposure. Of these one in agoraphobia yielded very little change (Emmelkamp et al. 1978), and five noted improvement, usually modest, in social anxiety. Of these five finding benefit, the approach was rational emotive in two (Emmelkamp et al. 1985a; Thorpe et al. 1976), self-instructional in two (Glass et al. 1976; Thorpe 1975), and cognitive restructuring in one (Linehan et al. 1979). (The study of Thorpe and coworkers is not in Table 14.1, as it had no group without CT;

Table 14.1 I: Controlled studies of cognitive methods

Cognitive Therapies
RE = rational emotive therapy
CR = cognitive or rational restructuring
 SI = self-instruction or self-statement training
CT = cognitive therapy
AM = anxiety management training

Exposure Therapies
E = therapist-aided exposure in vivo
e = instructed self-exposure, live homework between sessions (programmed practice)

Design Details
   n = no. of completing subjects, sess = sessions, ′ = minutes, h = hour(s), d = daily,
   w = weeks/weekly, m = months/monthly, y = year, fu = followup.
Diary = record of relevant homework (e.g., of CR or of *e*).
Designs used parallel groups without crossover unless otherwise noted.

Agoraphobia

A. *No positive studies* in agoraphobics.

B. *Six negative studies* (CT did not enhance *E* or produced little change without *E*):
1. Mavissakalian et al. 1983a: 26 patients. 12 w 90′ self-exposure within sess, (a) with SI or (b) with paradoxical intention; patients complied only in using SI, not paradoxical intention. No diaries. Self-defeating thoughts decreased late in both groups between weeks 6–12 without a rise in coping statements. Up to 6-m fu, both groups improved equally in phobias and reduction in anxiolytics; SI improved less on depression.
2. Emmelkamp et al. 1978: *n* = 21, crossover study, five 2-h sess d of (a) CR or (b) *E*, or *e*. CR produced little improvement and was inferior to *E*.
3. Emmelkamp & Mersch 1982: *n* = 27, 8 2-h sess over 4 w of (a) CR, (b) *E*, or (c) CR + *E*. CR included fantasy exposure with SI. No *e*, no diary. At post-test, *E* and CR + *E* were better than CR alone for phobias. At 1-m fu the three groups were similar as CR subjects had improved further, which was attributed to self-exposure; CR subjects were superior on assertiveness. Addition of CR + SI did not enhance effect of *E* alone on any phobic variable.
4. Emmelkamp et al. 1985b: 43 patients had six 2½-h group sess over 3 w of (a) group *E* + *e* with a diary, (b) SI with fantasy exposure but no *e*, or (c) RE with a manual but no *e*. *E* + *e* was consistently superior to SI and RE up to 1-m fu. Subsequent *E* + *e* given to all groups led to further improvement.
5. Williams & Rappoport 1983: 20 agoraphobics with driving fears had 11 h of (a) *E* or (b) *E* + CT; *e* prohibited. Despite compliance *E* + CT was no better than *E* up to 5-m fu; gains were similar for both groups even for decline in phobic thoughts.
6. Pollard & Jensen 1984: preliminary report. *n* = 28, 1 w of *e* with diaries (a) alone; (b) with added audiotaped; or (c) written coping instructions (controlled breathing, reassurance, attending to the present and not to fearful thoughts, relabeling, and anger evocation); or (d) with distraction. The two coping groups were no better than the distraction group, all three being better than *e* alone.

Social Anxiety

Notation as above, plus:
  des = fantasy desensitization
  SST = social skills training (coaching, modeling, role play, feedback, *E* and often *e* as well; variants of assertion training, behavior rehearsal, response acquisition)

A. *Two positive studies* (CT consistently better than exposure alone or other methods):
1. Butler et al. 1984: 45 patients, 7-w instruction sess, total of 7½ h (AM took less than 2½ h), two booster sess at 2- and 6-w fu, detailed treatment manuals, and 1-h *e*/d (patients practiced a mean total of 8.6 h/w). Had (a) *e* + AM (relaxation, distraction and rational SI); (b) *e* +

free association to socially phobic events (e − AM); or (c) wait-list control. Up to 6-m fu both e groups improved more than controls, who did not improve; e + AM was superior to e − AM especially at 6-m fu; during 1-y fu no patient asked for further help after e + AM but 40% did so after e − AM. Pretreatment about 50% of each group had already been using some form of AM, and about 25% had found this helpful. After treatment 93% used AM in e + AM and 79% in e − AM, with 86% and 14%, respectively, saying this was effective. Use of AM thus rose after exposure whether or not patients had been trained in AM, although adding AM training to exposure increased such use slightly. Which components of AM enhanced e needs identification.

2. Kendrick et al. 1982: 53 pianists with performance anxiety had 3 w 1½- to 2-h sess of (a) CT, (b) SST, or (c) wait-list control; groups (a) and (b) also had E + e. Both improved more than controls, with a fall in negative and rise in positive thoughts. CT + e was more effective than SST at 1-m fu on signs of anxiety and on self-efficacy, but not on subjective anxiety.

B. *Six equivocal studies* (CT had slight effect alone, or in comparisons was only better on a few measures and inferior on others):
1. Thorpe 1975: 32 unassertive students had six group sess of (a) SI, (b) SST, (c) des, or (d) discussion control. No homework between sessions. No between-group difference of SI versus SST, although SI had more within-group effects. Improvement was limited, SI and SST being similar and better than control with des in between. SI improved without exposure.
2. Kanter & Goldfried 1979: 68 volunteers with interpersonal anxiety, 7 1½-h/w group sess + e with diaries. Had (a) CR, (b) CR + des, (c) des, or (d) wait-list control. Pretreatment expectancy was similar in the four groups. The two CR + e groups were slightly superior to des + e alone on self-report but not behavioral measures. The three treated groups improved more than wait-list, which did not improve, and consolidated their gains at 2-m fu.
3-4. CT was comparable to exposure in reducing social phobias, both in 34 patients (Emmelkamp et al. 1985a) and in volunteers—17 from newspaper ads and 18 via the classroom (Emmelkamp et al. 1985). Had six 2½-h group sess of (a) E + e, (b) RE, or (c) SI with fantasy exposure. All groups kept diaries of relevant homework done. No group had SST. Up to 1-m fu the three treatments yielded similar gains both in patients and in volunteers. In patients there was slight superiority of E + e over RE and SI only on HR during a behavioral test, and for RE over SI on only one phobia scale. In volunteers E + e tended to be best only on HR, and RE was better than SI only on social anxiety and irrational beliefs. RE patients improved without any exposure.
5. Glass et al. 1976: 81 women-shy male students had four or five 1- 1½-h sess of (a) SST, (b) SST + SI, (c) SI, or (d) wait-list control. Both SST groups did best on role play; SI subjects made more subsequent phone calls. SI alone group improved without exposure. Only 74% of subjects were rated at 6-m fu.
6. Schelver & Gutsch 1983: 35 student volunteers had 5 w of self-treatment based on reading (a) RE therapy (Ellis's *Guide to rational living*), or (b) logotherapy (by Frankl, describing paradoxical intention), or (c) control (reading own material). Only the RE reading material was a manual with structured exercises. No diaries. RE reading led to significantly more gains than control but not logotherapy reading. No fu.

C. *Twelve negative studies* (failure of CT to enhance exposure/SST or to help without it):
1. Stravynski et al. 1982: 22 outpatients (77% male) with both social phobia and skills deficits had 8 w 1½-h sess plus 4 boosters over the next 6 m, of (a) SST alone or (b) SST + CT. Up to 6-m fu both groups improved comparably and at same speed, with SST and SST + CT on behavioral and cognitive measures, including irrational beliefs, and on mood. There had been no gains during up to 9 w of pretreatment multiple-baseline monitoring. As SST involved each social target in turn, so their performance increased and anxiety fell during it; untrained social tasks improved much less and more slowly. At 6-m fu there was a rise in social activity and skills, which usually stopped short of intimate heterosexuality, although this may have developed over a longer period, as happened over 16 m in another study (Falloon et al. 1977).

Table 14.1 *(Continued)*

2. Frisch et al. 1982: 32 male outpatients with interpersonal impairments or social avoidance had (a) SST, (b) SST + stress management including relaxation and CR, or (c) minimal treatment control. Both active treatment groups improved in social skills after treatment, with no differences between them.

3. Wolfe & Fodor 1980: 64 unassertive women outpatients had two weekly 2-h sess of (a) SST, (b) SST plus RE, (c) discussion, or (d) wait-list control. Both SST groups did equally well (no between-group differences) whether or not RE had been added, and both were better than discussion or controls.

4. Alström et al. 1984: 42 social phobics (see p. 465).

5. Linehan et al. 1979: 79 unassertive women volunteers had 8 w sess of (a) SST, (b) SST + CR, (c) CR, (d) discussion, or (e) wait-list control. Groups (a)–(c) had relevant homework with diaries. Expectancy was similar in groups (a)–(d). After treatment, on between-group analyses SST and SST + CR yielded similar gains (SST + CR was a bit better than SST alone on a few within-group analyses), both being better than discussion or control; the CR alone group improved somewhat despite having had no exposure. Results were unimpressive; at 2-m fu the four treatment groups did not differ.

6. Hayes & Marshall 1984: A series of three studies of public-speaking anxiety:
   Study I: 56 volunteers had eight 2-h biweekly sess of (a) SI, including brief 3′ exposure; (b) SI + E until they habituated (giving speeches that were videotaped); (c) SI + habituating E + SST; or (d) discussion + relaxation. Up to 6-m fu (n = only 31), the combined group (c) did best; SI + exposure was less effective, and SI alone was ineffective.
   Study II: 42 volunteers had (a) SST, (b) exposure, or (c) both. Up to 6-m fu (n = 35) the two SST groups did best, exposure alone doing less well.
   Study III: 14 patients had 6 w 2-h sess of (a) SST plus E plus e (30′ speeches at home without an audience, 3 times/w), or (b) as (a), but without e. After treatment both SST groups improved greatly with a trend for (a) to do best. No fu—in some studies e effects increased during fu.
   Taking the three experiments together, SI alone had little or no effect and did not enhance SST, which was the best, E being next best, with e adding some value (a floor effect and absence of fu may have obscured some of its value). The program helped both volunteers and patients. Improvement was accompanied by a fall in negative thoughts but no rise in positive ones.

7. Thorpe et al. 1984, Study I: 27 unassertive student volunteers had two 1½-h group sess of (a) SST/behavioral rehearsal (e.g., "No, I'm unable to help today, why not check with so-and-so?"), (b) emotional rehearsal (e.g., "Remember, it's my right to say 'no'"), or (c) cognitive rehearsal (e.g., "Practice reducing your anxiety as you imagine the situation") with SI. SST was best, but there was no fu.

8. Thorpe et al. 1984, Study II: 28 unassertive student volunteers had two 1½-h group sess of (a) SST, (b) RE imagery (emotional and cognitive rehearsal + SI to increase assertion), (c) as (a) and (b) combined, or (d) as (a) and (c) combined. SST cases improved most on an avoidance test but not on other measures; no fu.

9. Hammen et al. 1980: 55 unassertive volunteers had 8-w sess of (a) SST, (b) SST + CR + SI, or (c) wait-list control; no group had homework. Both treatments improved equally and more than controls. Up to 4-w fu, SST + CR + SI failed to enhance SST alone, even in unassertive people with many dysfunctional thoughts; such thoughts predicted poor outcome with each treatment.

10. Kramer 1975, Royce 1975: CR did not enhance the effects of practice-dating (a form of e) in date-anxious students. No further details available.

11. Sharp & Forman 1985: To reduce anxiety during teaching, 60 teachers had one of two training packages, both including SST + e but only one containing CT. 60 teachers had eight biweekly 2-h group sess of training in (a) stress inoculation (education, relaxation, CR, SI); (b) classroom management (discussion, training in behavior modification); or (c) wait-list control. Up to 4-w fu controls were unchanged but both training conditions improved comparably in anxiety and behavior. CR + SI had not enhanced outcome of SST + e.

12. Hausman 1984: 29 lonely students had 5 weekly 2-h group SST sess ± CR + SI training. Neither condition had much effect up to 3-w fu.

13. Dawson 82: For speech-anxious Ss, SI was superior to socratic dialogue.

(14. Biran et al. 1981: Pilot report of only two cases phobic of writing in public; after baseline assessment they had five sessions of CR followed by 5 of E. E was superior to CR. Too few cases to draw conclusions from.)

Specific Phobias

A. *One positive study:* Marshall 1985: 20 height phobics had 32' of live exposure with or without coping self-statements. The latter did best at 4-w fu.

B. *One slightly positive study:* Emmelkamp & Felten 1985: 19 height phobic volunteers had one 60' sess of (a) E alone or (b) E + CT. At post-test both groups improved equally on heart rate and avoidance, and E + CT had less anxiety than E alone. Negative thoughts fell and positive ones rose with E + CT, but did not change with E alone. Heart rate and anxiety fell at the same time. No fu.

C. *Four negative studies:*
1. Biran & Wilson 1981. 22 volunteers phobic of heights, elevators, or darkness had five 50' sess over 2–3 w of (a) E or (b) CR + brief fantasy exposure. Up to 1-m fu CR was inferior to E in yielding less improvement in avoidance, fear, and self-efficacy. At 1-m fu unimproved CR subjects had E and then improved as much as those who had E from the start. Gains from E increased further at 6-m fu.
2. Ladouceur 1983: 36 animal phobic volunteers had up to 8 biweekly 1-h sess of (a) E with modeling, (b) as (a) + SI, (c) as (a) + thinking aloud, or (d) discussion. On avoidance and self-efficacy, at post-treatment the discussion group had not changed whereas all three E groups improved equally. At 1-m fu E plus SI was inferior to E alone—adding SI to E had actually impaired improvement. Anxiety declined similarly in all four groups.
3. Girodo & Roehl 1978: 52 flying-phobic volunteers had (a) information giving, (b) SI training, or (c) both. Anxiety during a normal flight was similar with or without SI.
4. If coping exercises are a cognitive method, then there is a preliminary report of a fourth negative study (Klepac et al. 1984). Dental phobics had (a) six 2-h sess practicing three coping strategies during increasing pain from electrical tooth pulp stimulation; (b) practice of the same coping strategies, but self-administered with a manual and with fantasy exposure; (c) graded E viewing videotaped dental restoration and then exploring a dentist's office; or (d) wait-list control. Adding coping exercises to exposure was of dubious value. All three treated groups improved equally, but more than controls, on dental pain tolerance and self-efficacy. Dental visits tended to rise most with self-treatment (coping and imaginal exposure) and with exposure without coping.

Obsessive Compulsive-Disorder

A. *One negative study:* Emmelkamp et al. 1980b: 15 ocs had 10 sessions of graded E with response prevention. In 7 of the 15 patients the sessions began with a ½-h sess of SI; up to 6-m fu they did no better than the 8 who had E without preceding SI.

public-speaking fears in volunteers fell more with a rational emotive than a self-instruction approach up to 3 months' follow-up.) There is thus no evidence for the superiority of any one of the various cognitive approaches.

Perhaps cognitive methods can play a small role in helping some social phobics, unlike agoraphobics or specific phobics, but as yet that role remains to be defined. In OCD uncontrolled case reports claimed that cognitive restructuring improved compliance with response prevention (Jaremko 1982; Salkovskis & Warwick 1985) and reduced obsessions and cognitive rituals (Robertson et al. 1983), but these claims await controlled study.

The unreliability of cognitive methods for these problems contrasts sharply with the big strides made by self-exposure approaches, but not for lack of trying. Why have cognitive therapies had such discouraging outcomes? At first sight it seems obvious that attitudes and thoughts affect behavior, and that modifying them should change behavior. But it is hard to conquer race prejudice, for instance, by extended rational discussion. It seems to yield more readily when bigots come into prolonged, intimate contact on an equal footing with many people from the race they dislike, so allowing the development of close interracial relations. That strategy is performance-based exposure.

There is an additional point. Piano teachers often teach their pupils that before playing a piece of music, they should think carefully about its structure, work out exactly what they want to achieve, and only then start playing. Similarly, many pole vaulters, shotputters, and other athletes think a long time about what they are aiming at before carrying out their actions. This type of action-oriented thought, of behavior rehearsal, is not a feature of cognitive therapy, except insofar as it involves exposure.

Perhaps existing cognitive therapies are on the wrong track. They may be like the efforts of those who try to modify race prejudice by reasoning. These therapies try to change thoughts that seem more the product than the cause of phobic-oc problems. In the same way, feedback of heart rate could lower heart rate during exposure, but this did not reduce anxiety more than did exposure without such feedback (Nunes & Marks 1976); tachycardia is only one of many signs of a phobia and not necessarily its key feature. There is no evidence that a decrease in negative thoughts precedes the reduction of fear, although this should be seen if cognitive methods worked in the way they are often assumed to do. Negative thoughts and attitudes improved as fear fell after exposure without cognitive therapy (Stravynski et al. 1983; Watson & Marks 1971), and in the only study to report on the detailed timing of change, loss of negative thoughts occurred later than the reduction in some other signs of fear (Mavissakalian et al. 1983a).

For cognitive therapy to break down the prejudice that is a phobia, it needs to become action oriented. It needs to help clients work out what they are striving for and the detailed steps needed to attain that end, and then to practice those steps covertly as well as overtly. But that would be behavior therapy—problem definition, breaking down the solution into manageable pieces, and rehearsing those steps covertly and overtly, first in the training situation and then in the natural environment. Such skills training (of which SST is one type) and programmed practice (of which e is an example) are helpful. But challenging irrational beliefs, cognitive or rational restructuring, and current types of self-statement rehearsal are largely redundant for the relief of phobic/oc problems.

SUMMARY

The behavioral revolution in treating phobic-oc disorders came with the realization that most methods that reliably help them persuade the subject to maintain exposure to fear cues until discomfort subsides. This exposure principle has been recognized for centuries but was only systematized recently in behavioral treatment. Redundant nonexposure elements in treatment have gradually been eliminated. Though nonexposure approaches occasionally reduce fear, they are too erratic to investigate properly, let alone to use routinely in clinical practice. Objections that all treatments contain exposure overlook the many procedures that exclude it. Criticisms that exposure is a mere procedure miss the point that an essential procedure in fact constitutes a principle and starts us on the road to unravelling mechanism.

Exposure is probably better when carried out with real rather than fantasied fear cues. The latter can be resorted to when live exposure is difficult to arrange. Filmed cues and role play are useful steps towards live exposure for some problems.

Live self-exposure is the most cost-effective mode as it greatly reduces demands on therapist time. Much controlled work has shown its value for agora-, social, and specific phobics and for ocs. Detailed exposure manuals and diaries to record self-exposure homework help sufferers to execute their program properly. Some people can treat themselves without any help from a clinician, while others need variable amounts of coaching, pacing, and therapist-aided exposure before the therapist can fade out.

In planning a self-exposure program it should be remembered that long exposure periods reduce fear more than do shorter ones. In nearly all studies over a wide range of time periods longer exposure produced more habituation. The optimal duration may interact with the intensity and pervasiveness of the fear, with the intervals between stimuli and sessions, and with the characteristics of ES offset, all of which points have been insufficiently explored. In several studies fear-reduction occurred even if the subject escaped from the ES and then immediately reexposed to it, and in pilot work, if escape was followed by reexposure even a few days later. The latter point needs further examination.

In ocs outcome to exposure was not impaired if the ritual was allowed to continue in a manner that no longer terminated the ES (the ritual ceased to act as a safety signal). Fear-reduction was enhanced if oc rituals were prevented in addition to the exposure being carried out. Like exposure, response prevention works well when self-imposed, and imposing external constraints achieves little in the long run.

Rapid exposure seems to yield clinical gains a bit more quickly than does slow exposure, but ultimately the pace of exposure is governed by what the sufferer is able to do. Fear does not necessarily habituate more quickly to fast firm exposure than to slower graded exposure with fear kept to a minimum. During exposure neither low nor high arousal facilitates outcome, nor has an optimum level of arousal been demonstrated. There is no need to add relaxation training to exposure or to deliberately make the patient feel extremely anxious rather than simply engaged.

Phobias improve somewhat with irrelevant fear exposure, but this may be through a different mechanism than with relevant exposure and data is conflicting on whether it is as efficient. Neither problem-solving nor assertion training reliably reduced phobias in the absence of exposure. Clinically habituation is usually fairly specific to the fear cues to which the patient has been exposed, marked generalization being unusual. There is no clear divide where specific habituation ends and general coping ability starts, and we know very little about their interaction.

Abreaction and exposure are overlapping phenomena. They share theoretical conundrums, though fear-reduction from abreaction appears to be more erratic. The effects of abreaction seem similar whether the emotion is induced by drugs or psychological means or occurs spontaneously. Symptom relief may result from several mechanisms. Under certain yet-to-be-defined conditions acute and chronic distress may reduce after intense emotional experiences involving negative feelings like fear, anger, guilt, or aggression (and perhaps intense positive feelings might achieve the same). Improvement might be lasting or transient or not occur at all, and a few people may sensitize. Even the abreaction of emotion about events that are fictitious or otherwise unrelated to the distress has been followed by relief, though for how long is not known.

Rarely, transient skin lesions may appear within minutes on parts of the body which correspond to abreacted incidents about being tied or beaten in the past. During exposure therapy unexpected affect may be abreacted concerning forgotten incidents, memory of which is cued by the long-avoided phobic situation; in such cases habituation continues as exposure proceeds.

Though exposure seems an apparently simple task, in fact it can be quite complicated. Response-induction aids assist sufferers to initiate and complete an exposure program. Such aids include grading and varying the tasks, attending to all the fear cues, modeling where need be, fading out aids as fear subsides, and other individually tailored aids for specific problems. Modeling can help those who are not sure what they have to do, but is not necessary as a routine. Praise for progress motivates the patient to work hard. Whether breathing exercises are helpful for some patients needs further study. Hypnosis has had indifferent results. Group exposure might save time if there are too many cases of the same kind to allow treatment on an individual basis.

A major research effort in many centers has produced disappointing results from cognitive therapies for phobic-oc problems, both in patients and in volunteers. Cognitive approaches added almost nothing to the value of exposure for agora- and specific phobics, and had limited effects alone. For social anxiety certain cognitive methods combined with exposure may be of marginal utility; even here the evidence is not strong. None of the various cognitive approaches were consistently better than one another. Whether cognitive methods can increase compliance with exposure in unwilling subjects remains to be seen. A handful of studies found some improvement, generally slight, from cognitive methods without any exposure. These are theoretically important in showing that exposure is not the only route to anxiety-reduction even if it is the best one.

15

Psychological Treatment: Clinical Issues

In this chapter we move from the principles of psychological treatment for phobic and obsessive-compulsive (oc) problems to more applied aspects. These include what happens at follow-up, prognostic factors, marital issues, and problems specific to particular clinical syndromes.

FOLLOW-UP AND PROGNOSTIC ISSUES

Long-Term Follow-Up

It has been argued that once a controlled treatment ends, more and more extraneous factors come to operate on the patient, so that prolonged follow-up ceases to cast a useful light on the value of that therapy. This is too strong a view, especially for chronic conditions that usually fail to remit without treatment. Although external factors do mount as time goes on, no one would seriously question the importance of a 10-year survival figure after treatment for cancer. By the time most phobic/ocs come for therapy, they have had their problem for many years, often for a decade or more. Were treatment to help them only for a few months, it would be mainly of academic interest.

The issue is not important merely to the patient but also to health care planners. In both a pilot and a controlled study the cost of nurse therapists treating phobic/oc patients behaviorally was more than offset by subsequent tangible benefits, provided these continued for longer than 2 years after treatment ended (Ginsberg & Marks 1977; Ginsberg et al. 1984). The tangible benefits consisted of decreased use of health care resources after patients completed the index treatment; calculations ignored the substantial intangible benefits from behavioral treatment, such as reduced fear and depression. From the community's viewpoint it seemed less expensive to offer such patients nurse therapy than to let them languish untreated. The point has even more force now that so many phobics and ocs can be treated by self-exposure with minimal monitoring by a clinician.

We will presently see an impressive array of long-term studies showing that most chronic phobics and ocs retained their gains during the 2 to 9 years of follow-up after exposure therapy. The outcome is all the more impressive because it holds up across treatment centers in Europe, the United States and Australia. Indeed, it is one of the better documented stories in mental health care (reviewed by Jannson et al. 1985). Most phobic/oc patients feel much better and lose their main handicaps after live exposure, although they may retain slight anxiety without avoidance.

That the improvement of phobic/oc cohorts remained stable at follow-up does not mean, of course, that people never relapse after exposure therapy. Some undoubtedly do, mainly for two reasons. The first is occurrence of an affective episode. This is more likely in cases who were previously depressed— for instance, in the agoraphobics of Lelliott and coworkers (1986a). When depression occurs it is often relieved by antidepressants, after which exposure therapy may be needed. The second trigger for relapse is the occurrence of events resembling those during the original problem. (For example, a mother's past ritual of picking scabs off her young son's skin returned when he developed chicken pox, and a driving phobia may recur after an accident.) In this connection, extinguished shuttlebox avoidance returned in rats when they had further CS-US pairings (Katzev & Balch 1974).

When relapse occurs and mood is normal, a few booster sessions along the same lines as previously usually restores patients to their previously improved state, although the author has had a few exceptions where this could not be achieved. Such exceptions are outweighed by the many other cases who consolidated their gains during follow-up. The stability of or further improvement in group means of cohorts that have been followed up reflects a balance between those two types of sequence. Most commonly the patient's condition seems to improve somewhat further in the early months of follow-up and to remain stable thereafter.

Phobic Disorders

Most long-term follow-up studies have been of agoraphobics. The longest near-complete follow-up was in 65 of 66 agoraphobics 5 to 9 years after fantasy or live exposure treatment (Munby & Johnston 1980, Oxford). In terms of agoraphobia they were much better than they had been before treatment 5 to 9 years earlier, with little change since 6 months' follow-up. Anxiety and depression also improved. Patients who had self-exposure sought much less retreatment during temporary setbacks than those who had fantasy exposure (desensitization or flooding). No symptom substitution was found. Another long follow-up was of agoraphobics 5 to 8 years after exposure therapy; again gains continued (Hand 1986).

A 5-year follow-up after self-exposure was made in 40 of 45 agoraphobics (Lelliott et al. 1986a, London). At 2 years gains had continued (Cohen et al. 1984). At 5 years, improvement remained on self- and assessor ratings of agoraphobia, mood, spontaneous panics, anxiety, and marital adjustment. On the global phobia score, 30% were much better, 52% improved, and 18% unchanged. There was no difference between cases who had previously had, in addition to self-exposure, either imipramine or placebo, or brief therapist-aided exposure or relaxation. Phobic gains generalized more in those who had begun with very low rather than moderate depression, and was greatest in cases who started with the least anxiety and the best motivation and marital, work, and social adjustment. Spontaneous panics did not predict outcome.

Three series were followed up for a mean of 4 years after exposure. The first was after fantasy desensitization or psychotherapy; 65 of 70 phobics (36 agoraphobics, the rest social or specific phobics) were followed up. The cohort retained its gains in phobias, anxiety, and depression on self- and assessor ratings, and no new problems developed (Marks 1971, London). The second was after live exposure; among 70 of 81 agoraphobics followed up by mail, 75% remained improved in phobias and depression and some even extended their gains, with no new neurotic disturbances (Emmelkamp & Kuipers 1979, Holland). Outcome did not correlate with initial depression, problem duration, or social anxiety. The third 4-year follow-up was also by mail, in 56 agoraphobics (69% of the original sample); once more, improvement continued in phobias and work adjustment (McPherson et al. 1980, Scotland).

An 8-year follow-up after exposure was made in merely 18 of 32 agoraphobics; these 18 did not differ from the rest on pretreatment scores (Burns et al. 1986, Lancashire). At 8-year follow-up, gains continued and often extended on self- and assessor ratings, although as usual few cases were free of symptoms. Shorter follow-up with stable improvement was noted in three series of agoraphobics 1 to 2 years after controlled studies of exposure (Hafner 1976, London; Jansson et al. 1986, Sweden; Mavissakalian & Michelson 1986, Pittsburgh).

In contrast to the continuing gains in chronic phobics for many years after exposure therapy is the lack of improvement in adult phobics who had no such treatment while seeing a general practitioner for a year (Marks 1985) or saw no doctor or other helper for 5 years (Agras et al. 1972).

Obsessive-Compulsive Disorder

There are fewer long-term follow-ups after exposure of OCD than of phobias. The longest was a Dutch 3½- to 4½-year follow-up of 42 ocs, 85% of the original sample (Emmelkamp & Rabbie 1983). These ocs retained their improvement on self-ratings of oc symptoms, anxiety and depression; 57% were much better, 23% improved, and 20% unchanged.

The next longest follow-up was a mean of 2.8 years in 15 ocs after an uncontrolled study in Greece (Boulougouris 1977). Once more, improvement was stable; it compared well with that found 2 years after exposure in 20 ocs in London (Marks et al. 1975), in whom 75% were much better, 5% improved, and 20% unchanged. Very similar gains were maintained in a second London sample seen 2 years after a controlled study of exposure; 37 of the original 40 ritualizers were followed up (Mawson et al. 1982). In a third London sample,

20 ocs remained well 2 to 4 years after exposure (Robertson 1979). Further stability of gains at 1- to 2-year follow-up was reported in 21 ocs in the United States (Foa & Goldstein 1978) and six cases in Australia (Catts & McConaghy 1975).

Comparisons between behavioral and nonbehavioral series are especially difficult because they might differ in their clinical features. The above-detailed outcomes after exposure therapy seemed superior to those among 16 samples of ocs 1 to 26 years after nonbehavioral treatment (reviewed by Black 1974). Among 190 outpatients, 381 out- and inpatients, and 309 inpatients, 60%, 57%, and 46%, respectively, were better, and 40%, 43%, and 54% were unchanged. The exposure cases of Marks and coworkers (1975) and Mawson and coworkers (1982) had been inpatients, and their improvement rate of 80% exceeded that of 46% in the nonbehavioral inpatient samples. The Dutch sample after exposure, which had an 80% improvement rate, had largely comprised outpatients.

Prognostic Factors

Whatever predicts subsequent events is a prognostic variable. The most valuable predictors are those present before treatment starts. They aid the selection of clients likely to benefit from a given treatment and so maximize the good use of the client's and therapist's energy. There are many inconsistencies in the prognostic factors found across behavioral (Steketee et al. 1985a) and nonbehavioral (Black 1974) studies. In general, however, good outcome to exposure occurs in most phobic/ocs who regularly avoid phobia- or ritual-evoking stimuli, have normal mood, comply with therapy, and do not take high doses of sedatives or alcohol. Less improvement occurs in patients who begin depressed and anxious or with poorer work, social, or marital adjustment (Foa et al. 1982; Klosko et al. 1984; Lelliott et al. 1986a; Mawson et al. 1982). If there is concomitant depression, behavioral treatment helps once mood has lifted with drug treatment (Baer et al. 1985). Obsessions without rituals do indifferently well. Failure because of noncompliance with behavioral treatment occurred in about a quarter of patients in the author's clinic.

Chronicity is not a major prognostic factor for phobic/oc disorders after exposure. With occasional exceptions (such as Foa et al. 1982; Hoogduin & Hoogduin 1983), it does not augur poorer outcome. Successful behavioral treatment in phobic/ocs has generally been in samples with mean problem durations of a decade or more. It is remarkable how crippling phobic and oc handicaps that have been present for many years can melt within a few weeks or even days of exposure therapy. Perhaps cases of very brief duration take even less time to treat, but they rarely feature in controlled trials.

Predictors during treatment are process variables that suggest how treatment works and help clinicians modulate it to improve outcome. Dissociation during exposure seems to retard fear reduction, so the therapist instead tries to promote attention to the task. Engagement represents a certain minimum level of arousal during therapy; we saw earlier that neither very high nor very low arousal during treatment predict outcome. Progress in the first few sessions can be a good guide to long-term outcome.

Predictors at the end of treatment are too late to help the therapist do anything to make therapy more effective up to that point, but may indicate how to prevent relapse during follow-up. For example, socially isolated and unemployed ocs may start ritualizing again simply to pass the time. To forestall this, it is probably worth encouraging them to do interesting things to fill their time, and, if they lack social skills, to train them in these so as to reduce their isolation.

Expectancy

Expectancy is measured at the start of therapy. A review of the relation between volunteers' initial expectation of outcome to exposure with their subsequent actual outcome came to no clear conclusions (Emmelkamp 1982). In phobic/oc patients, results are conflicting. A positive correlation was found in some studies (Emmelkamp & Wessels 1975; Emmelkamp & Emmelkamp-Benner 1975; Marks et al. 1986; Mathews et al. 1976) but not in others (Greist et al. 1980; Stern & Marks 1973). Even where expectancy has an effect, it is generally weak and accounts for only a small part of the variance. Patients find most therapeutic approaches surprisingly credible and expect them to work, yet independent of this, exposure is the most consistently potent therapy.

High expectations are a mixed blessing. On the one hand, they may improve outcome by raising compliance (Marks et al. 1986): the patient is more willing to work hard if the work seems likely to be worthwhile than if there is no hope. On the other hand, if hopes are too high and the cure does not materialize at once, hopes may be dashed and treatment terminated before it has been properly tried.

Therapist Variables

On the whole, therapist variance explains relatively little about outcome with exposure. We would expect warm, friendly therapists to get better results by motivating patients to work harder in exposure programs. This was shown in volunteers with snake fears (Morris & Suckerman 1974) and test anxiety (Ryan & Moses 1979) and in post hoc analyses of phobic/oc patients (Emmelkamp 1983; Rabavilas et al. 1979). But it was not found in acrophobic volunteers (Morris & Magrath 1979) or in agoraphobics (Gustavsson et al. 1985). The evidence on therapist warmth is thus conflicting.

To keep the matter in perspective from the point of view of delivery of services, therapist variance is in practice far less important than treatment variance. Most professional therapists can get good results, with one proviso: they have to give the right patient the right treatment, systematically. This skill can be taught to most therapists, and it is easier to teach with a detailed training manual (Marks et al. 1986a). In the author's unit over the last 12 years, 60 nurses trained to become autonomous-behavior therapists had results that were as good as those of psychologists or doctors (Marks et al. 1977, 1978;

Marks 1985a). By now such nurses have treated about a thousand patients, of whom most were phobic/ocs. Repeated comparisons showed that the similarities of patient outcomes from various trainees were far more striking than their differences. Only exceptional nurse therapists got consistently poor results. Exposure therapy was rapidly learned by other nurses, too (Benjamin & Kincey 1981) and by medical students (Stern 1975). And, as we saw earlier, numerous sufferers can now treat themselves by self-exposure without a clinician; therapist variance is even less important for them.

Self-Efficacy

Much has been written about ratings of self-efficacy (SE) as a predictor of behavior immediately after those ratings. SE measures how likely one would be to succeed if one attempted a task—that is, one's self-confidence. It can be rated before, during, or after treatment, and it correlates highly with performance in a behavioral test just after the rating. In phobics asked to rate SE concerning a phobic task, SE is low before treatment and rises after subjects improve with exposure treatment.

SE at the end of treatment was said by Bandura (1983) to be the major mediator of fear reduction, and he recommended that therapy should aim at raising SE. But the best way to increase SE is by exposure, the same procedure that reduces fear. Moreover, SE correlates highly not only with performance of a frightening task but also with the fear expected during it, as was shown in ingenious work with 50 snake-fearful students (Kirsch 1982, 1985). Most refused to try to hold a snake because it would frighten them, not because they felt inept. They were certain that they could hold the snake if they really "had to." If a task is frightening, SE reflects a subject's willingness (rather than ability) to do it. This willingness rises, the less the anticipated fear; correlations between SE and expected fear range from .69 to .90. Willingness (SE) also rises in proportion to the reward offered. Snake-fearful students said they would be more likely to approach a live snake if offered incentives—38% for a mere $5, and most for $20 or less. The higher the anticipated fear, the greater the incentive needed to change SE ($r = .49$).

By contrast, SE about a nonfrightening task indicates belief in one's ability rather than willingness to do it (Kirsch 1982, 1985) and does not reflect expected fear. For most subjects SE about a neutral task is unaltered by offering incentives. Of 50 snake-phobic students, 54% did not change their SE about being able to toss a wad of paper into a wastebasket for any hypothetical incentive, even for $1 million or to save their own or someone else's life; 76% did not change their SE for the hardest paper-toss—all said they lacked the necessary skills ("holding a snake doesn't take any skill, but throwing paper does"). Eighty-four percent of the students were willing to try the hardest paper-toss without any incentives, despite their certainty that they would not succeed (low SE) and none expected to be frightened while doing so, despite low SE.

Two other samples showed similarly high correlations between SE, expected anxiety, behavior, and subjective fear pre- and post-treatment: snake-phobic volunteers (Kirsch et al. 1983) and height and driving phobics (Williams et al. 1984). Often the correlations of approach are higher with preceding SE than with other preceding ratings, and these high correlations fuel claims for SE as a critical mediating variable. Much better understanding would come from directly examining the timing and sequence of reductions in various fear components during exposure. Only when x always falls before y is x a strong candidate as a mediating variable. An argument based on correlations, even partial ones, is much weaker.

MARITAL ISSUES IN THE TREATMENT OF PHOBIC/OC DISORDERS

The key questions in this area are whether (1) phobic/oc improvement impairs subsequent marital function, (2) preexisting marital maladjustment worsens phobic/oc outcome with therapy, (3) having a spouse as exposure cotherapist improves phobic/oc outcome, and (4) the optimal therapeutic strategy in the presence of both phobic/oc and severe marital problems is marital therapy or exposure therapy. These issues have been studied mainly in agoraphobics; few data are available in ocs. Concerning a fifth issue—initial adjustment of spouse and of the marriage—careful research found these to be similar in agoraphobics and the general population (see Chapter 10). The area was reviewed by Vandereycken (1983) and Monteiro and coworkers (1985).

Does Agoraphobic Improvement Impair Marital Function?

A hoary symptom-substitution myth is that a reduction in agoraphobia jeopardizes marital adjustment. This idea is disconfirmed by impressive data from eight studies. Those data consistently indicate that as their phobias ease, most agoraphobics' marriages do not worsen but rather remain unchanged or improved to the end of follow-up.

Up to 3 months' follow-up of 12 agoraphobics after exposure, initially dissatisfied spouses remained so, and satisfied spouses became even more content as patients' phobias reduced (Bland & Hallam 1981, 1981a). In two further studies (Cobb et al. 1980; O'Brien et al. 1982) marital adjustment in most cases either improved or remained stable after exposure eased their phobias. Up to 6 months' follow-up of 19 agoraphobics after exposure, marital and sexual adjustment improved as well as phobias, without symptom substitution (Cobb et al. 1984). At 2- and 5-year follow-up of 27 agoraphobics after exposure, reduction in agoraphobia was accompanied by stable or improved marital, sexual, social, and work adjustment (Lelliott et al. 1986a; Monteiro et al. 1985).

There is thus excellent evidence that after agoraphobia improves, marital adjustment usually does not worsen but on the contrary tends to remain stable or take a turn for the better. This is not to deny that wide variations in individual reactions can be found, as is true after *any* problem is overcome, be it arthritis, blindness, or illiteracy. Reactions range from one delighted husband's "It's marvelous, my wife can do the shopping on her own now and I can go with the lads to football on Saturday afternoons" to another's sad comment, "I don't know what we are going to talk about, now that we can't talk about her problem" (Cobb 1983).

Exceptional cases can of course always be found whose marriages worsen as phobias ease (Barlow et al. 1981; Cobb et al. 1984; Hafner 1976). An agoraphobic who improved after exposure with her husband as cotherapist said: "Treatment made us talk more and go out together. That's when I realized we had very little in common. So we have agreed to split up" (Cobb 1983). Most agoraphobics in treatment are in an age band that has a high rate for separation and divorce, so it is hardly surprising that occasional agoraphobic marriages go wrong, given that about one in three of all marriages end in divorce. Conversely, and also as expected, some single patients marry in the course of a study (Monteiro et al. 1985). There is no evidence in any of the literature that such events happened more often than would be expected by chance. Substantial drop in marital satisfaction after exposure treatment was found in only 2 of the 19 agoraphobics of Cobb and coworkers (1984), and in only 1 of the 6 cases of Barlow and colleagues (1981)—and that patient had *not* improved in her phobias.

Two widely cited claims contradicted even by the claimants' own uncontrolled data are that (a) agoraphobics who began dissatisfied with their marriage became even more so after treatment (Milton & Hafner 1979; in their Table 1, after treatment initially unsatisfactory marriages actually improved slightly rather than worsened), and (b) husbands of initially hostile agoraphobics were adversely affected by their wives' improvement (Hafner 1977a, contradicted by his Tables 1 and 2).

A third claim, of a danger of symptom emergence as phobias improve (Hafner 1976), is again not borne out by the claimant's data (see Marks 1981, p. 239, and critiques by Stern 1977 and Emmelkamp 1982). Hafner's patients, who began with the best marital adjustment, improved most on all measures; conversely, those starting with the poorest marriages improved least in all areas, although they still improved significantly in phobias; only one measure (satisfaction with spouse) worsened in any way, and that not significantly so.

Does Marital Dysfunction Impair Phobic Outcome?

Most evidence suggests that patients who are best off to start with do best in the long run, although findings are not unanimous. Data from six studies followed the biblical adage that "unto every one that hath shall be given, and he shall have abundance," showing greater improvement in agoraphobic and other neurotic symptoms in cases who had better pre-existing marital adjustment.[1] In a seventh study, patients who complained less about their partners

[1]See, for example, Bland & Hallam 1981; Hafner 1976; Hudson 1974; Lelliott et al. 1986a; Mathews et al. 1977, Milton & Hafner 1979; Monteiro et al. 1985.

during treatment improved more (Emmelkamp & van der Hout 1983). However, in two studies initial marital adjustment did not relate to agoraphobic outcome at 1 to 6 months' follow-up (Cobb et al. 1984; Emmelkamp 1980). A tentative finding that spouse's mood related to agoraphobic outcome at follow-up (Hafner & Ross 1983) needs to be replicated and tested in more detail.

Good initial marital adjustment as well as better initial work and social adjustment predicted the best long-term outcome (Lelliot et al. 1986; Monteiro et al. 1985). In many health care problems, those who start better off are those who gain most from any therapy. These results could be explained in terms of the problem-solving capacity of the relevant social field (Marks 1981). That is, people and their families are likely to accommodate to change (whether improvement or deterioration) more easily if they already have sound problem-solving capacity (indicators might be good initial marital, social, and work adjustment), and more poorly if that capacity is faulty.

Does poorer initial marital, sexual, work and social adjustment denote greater severity or chronicity of phobias at the start? Evidence from Monteiro and coworkers (1985) suggests not. Compared with initially maritally adjusted cases, those with less good marriages began with similar phobia scores; however, they did start with more depression, which difference was no longer significant at follow-up. Such low mood could cause or result from marital trouble, or both may interact; once present, low mood could reduce the benefits of exposure by decreasing motivation and compliance and perhaps by slowing habituation.

Impact of Partner as Exposure Cotherapist When Marital Discord Is Not a Complaint

Most couples are willing to work together on an exposure homework program (Mathews et al. 1981), but evidence is inconsistent on the value of such joint effort. There have been six controlled studies of this issue, all but one in agoraphobics. Four found that home-based self-exposure *(e)* carried out alone by patients led to substantial improvement but was not lastingly enhanced by adding a partner as exposure cotherapist. In two of these four negative studies, partner involvement conferred a temporary advantage at the end of treatment but not later as the patient-alone condition improved further during 6 months' follow-up (Emmelkamp & DeLange 1983 with 12 ocs; Mathews et al. 1981 with agoraphobics). In the remaining two negative studies there was no advantage to spouse exposure cotherapy at the end of treatment or at 3 to 6 months' follow-up (Boisvert et al. 1983 with 24 agoraphobics; Cobb et al. 1984 with 19 agoraphobics).

In one positive study, 28 agoraphobic women had cognitive restructuring plus *e* either with or without their spouses. There were 12 weekly 1- to 1½-hour group sessions discussing the need for *e* and assigning it with cognitive help; *e* was recorded in a diary (Barlow et al. 1984). Agoraphobia improved more in patients who had been helped by spouses. The number of recorded *e* practice sessions related to outcome only as a trend. Follow-up was not reported. On comparable clinical phobia scales, improvement was less than that in Maudsley Hospital agoraphobics who had *e* (Ghosh & Marks 1986).

The second positive study was in volunteer agoraphobics (Arnow et al. 1985). Twenty-four phobic women had 12 hours of group therapist-aided exposure (*E*) without spouses over 3 successive days, followed by *e* with diaries and 3 weekly 90-minute meetings of phobics and spouses in small groups with the therapist to aid completion of *e*. Thereafter the couples had eight weekly meetings in similar groups to train in either relaxation or communication skills to modify phobic avoidance (for instance, persuading a husband to stop mentioning his worry that it was unsafe for his wife to go out alone, have him show more interest in her progress and be less accommodating to her fears). After 3 weeks of group *E* plus *e*, phobias improved markedly. After 8 subsequent weeks of couples training, there was further slight improvement in phobias in the communication but not relaxation condition that was retained somewhat better up to 8 months' follow-up; couples also showed more positive and fewer negative behaviors in the communication condition, but no gains in dyadic adjustment.

Most of the gains took place during the first 3 weeks of exposure. In the subsequent 8 weeks the small superiority of communication over relaxation training could have been due to the discussion of issues retarding exposure, which was present in communication but not relaxation training; going out alone rose after the former but fell after the latter. Perhaps changing spouse responses to the phobic's panic and avoidance prevents relapse. If so, this could be tested by comparing (1) training in communication without an exposure component with (2) training in solving problems in implementing exposure but not in other communication.

Involvement in exposure of significant others apart from spouses did not convincingly augment gains in agoraphobics at 3 months' follow-up (Jones et al. 1980), but too few details were reported for adequate evaluation.

Unrelated partners can assist as self-exposure cotherapists. Nonprofessional former phobics who had successfully completed their own self-exposure were also helpful for some agoraphobics (Ross 1980).

Marital Versus Exposure Therapy When Phobic/OC and Marital Problems Coexist

In a single case study of an oc with a bad marriage, the rituals failed to reduce with *E* plus *e* but then fell rapidly with contract marital therapy (Stern & Marks 1973a). When the idea of marital therapy as the optimal approach was tested in a larger controlled study, however, it was not confirmed; the single case turned out to have been an exception. In a crossover design 11 phobic/ocs who also wanted help for marital discord had either *E* plus *e* or contract marital therapy without exposure, in both treatments with spouse involvement (Cobb et al. 1980). *E* plus *e* improved both phobic/oc and marital targets, whereas marital therapy improved only marital targets; improvement was maintained to a 13-month follow-up. A second study found that reciprocity counseling was ineffective for patients who have both phobias and marital discord (Emmel-kamp 1982).

PARTICULAR SYNDROMES

The clinical features of phobic and oc syndromes were described in chapters 9 through 13. Here we will review evidence that behavioral treatment helps each of those syndromes and discuss the application of the exposure principle to each of them in practice.

Phobic Disorders

Agoraphobia

Fantasy exposure is of limited value for agoraphobia (Gelder & Marks 1966; Klein et al. 1983). In contrast, marked reduction of agoraphobia by live expo-sure has been documented in dozens of controlled studies (chapters 14 and 16 and Thorpe & Burns 1983). Many of these obtained good outcome with live self-exposure using an appropriate manual (such as Marks 1978 and Mathews et al. 1981) and a diary. Persistent improvement was made not only in agora-phobic avoidance but also in agoraphobic panic, spontaneous panic and mood, and marital and work adjustment. The MMPI also improved (Mollard et al. (1984), and tachycardia and skin conductance activity lessened. Moreover, in the only report of this point, lactate-induced panic disappeared once an ago-raphobic improved from self-exposure (Guttmacher & Nelles 1984).

Not everybody gets better, and the search for how to help the minority of failures has had little success (Emmelkamp & van der Hout 1983). The major-ity of those who do not benefit are noncompliant, and there is not much cli-nicians can do to assist them. Involving a partner as an exposure cotherapist has had mixed outcomes in controlled studies. A few agoraphobics fail to habituate despite good compliance, normal mood, and not being on anxiolytics (Marks 1981). Perhaps some do not attend enough to concomitant hyperven-tilation and might benefit from breathing exercises, but this needs further con-trolled experiments.

Aids for exposure in agoraphobics include the general advice noted earlier to grade exposure in stages that can be handled and engaged in fully for as long as possible (best for hours at a time until fear is falling), to continue the pro-gram until the subject is comfortable with all formerly frightening cues, and to fade out supports as confidence is gained. Detailed ways of mapping out the exposure program in detail appear in Marks (1978) and Mathews and cowork-ers (1981).

Useful tips also abound in the newsletters of agoraphobic correspondence clubs. To condense them:

> Use no pills or alcohol. Give yourself time to work on your goals one by one, be persistent, and practice, practice, practice. It may be easier to practice returning

home by yourself than to leave home alone. Let your feelings come, don't run away from them, expect and accept the panic—don't fight it or run away but instead just stay your ground. Do anything that helps you remain in the phobic situation and concentrate on it until your fear is easier. Only use distraction if it is essential to remain where you are—for instance, feel the coolness of coins in your hands, look at your reflection, study a design on your dress or a leaf on the ground, pretend a stranger on the bus is traveling with you. Expect many setbacks and use them as cues for further exposure.

Social Phobia

Exposure treatment for social phobics is similar to that for most phobics. Management takes on an additional dimension, however, when the social phobic has the extra disability of social dysfunction. Such cases require not only an exposure program but also training in the requisite social skills (SST). As mentioned, SST involves, in addition to fear reduction by exposure, the modeling of new skills, coaching, prompting, role rehearsal, and role reversal. The extent to which fear reduction and skill acquisition generalize to one another remains to be determined.

There is much evidence for the value of exposure alone and of SST for social fears with and without social dysfunction. Controlled studies in the area were reviewed by Marks (1985b). The early form of exposure called systematic desensitization produced only limited improvement in mixed social phobia with dysfunction. In three of five studies, desensitization was inferior to SST, and in two it was no better than control, although in another study (Kanter & Goldfried 1979—see Table 14.1) it was better than a wait-list control. Desensitization was not better than psychotherapy.

In a search for types of patients helped by SST and self-exposure homework (e), 51 patients with a variety of problems had 10 weekly 75-minute group sessions of (1) SST plus e, or (2) SST plus nonexposure homework, or (3) discussion and nonexposure homework (Falloon et al. 1977). In up to 16 months' followup SST was superior to discussion. Patients who completed daily e did better than those who finished nonexposure homework, so improvement resulted not merely from compliance but from the actual tasks that patients complied with. The 30 subjects who had social phobia and social dysfunction improved lastingly; gains were in social behavior, getting jobs at a time of rising unemployment, and forming heterosexual relationships. In contrast, the few trial cases who had schizophrenia or alcohol or drug dependence did badly.

Chapter 14 described many controlled studies in which SST helped samples with varying mixtures of social phobia and dysfunction both in patients and volunteers.[2] Also noted earlier was the reduction of social phobias by exposure (Alström et al. 1984a; Butler et al. 1984) and by self-exposure in the form of practice dating (Christensen et al. 1975).

Turning to uncontrolled series, exposure benefited social anxiety (Marks et

[2]For patients, see Falloon et al. 1981; Frisch et al. 1982; Stravynski et al. 1982; Wolfe & Fodor 1977. For volunteers, see Glass et al. 1976; Hammen et al. 1980; Hayes & Marshall 1984; Haynes-Clements & Avery 1984; Kendrick et al. 1982; Thorpe 1975; Sharp & Forman 1985; Thorpe et al. 1984.

al. 1977, 1978) and fear of vomiting (Philips 1985), and SST helped social skills problems (Kindness & Newton 1984). In children who were socially isolated, conversational skills improved with training, although up to 2 months' follow-up they had not yet produced greater peer acceptance (Whitehill & Hersen 1980). The social behavior of blind children (which is often defective) improved up to 4 months' follow-up after they were taught appropriate skills by normal peers (Sisson et al. 1985).

A realistic self-exposure program can usually be arranged for people who fear eating or blushing in public, or going to parties. But it is less easy to arrange prolonged, graded live exposure when the fear is of infrequent situations such as asking for a raise or acting brief parts on stage. With such fear cues, role playing and also fantasy exposure may help.

It takes time to reduce the extreme shyness of social phobics who have social dysfunction as well. Although SST helps them initiate social approach fairly quickly, much longer is needed to develop intimate relationships. To help this process along, after starting with SST over some weeks added benefit may come from a few extra coaching sessions spaced over a year or more.

Helpful hints for patients for exposure during social interaction are detailed by Butler (1985). They include the following:

1. Respond to anxiety symptoms by approach rather than withdrawal.
2. Remember where you are and don't pretend to be elsewhere.
3. Greet people properly with eye contact.
4. Listen carefully to people and make a mental list of possible topics of conversation.
5. Show that you want to speak; initiate conversation (asking questions is easier, as it switches attention to the person expected to reply).
6. Speak up without mumbling.
7. Try to produce the symptoms of anxiety (if you sweat in company, move away from an open window, wear an extra sweater, and accept hot food and drink).
8. Tolerate some silences.
9. Wait for cues from others in deciding where to sit, when to pick up a drink, and what to talk about.
10. Learn to tolerate criticism by introducing controversy deliberately at an appropriate point.

Subjects may learn ingenious ways to break down the social task into manageable bits. The husband of an oc patient of the author's was reluctant to praise his wife for her progress during her exposure therapy ("no one ever praised me as a child, so why should I praise others now?"). But he then hit on the idea of taping his voice praising her and playing the tape to her a few times, after which he became able to praise her directly without the tape.

Specific Phobias

Specific (simple) phobias are especially responsive to behavioral treatment, although there may be problems, in arranging live exposure for less accessible stimuli such as thunder and lightning. Some creativity may be needed in exactly matching the exposure situation to what is feared. Case histories illustrating how to tailor the exposure strategy to various types of specific phobia abound in the literature. Examples regarding phobias of animals, blood, passing or retaining urine in public toilets, having or practicing dentistry, and nightmares appear in Marks (1977, 1981; Marks et al. 1986a; see also Chapter 11). Other descriptions concern therapy for phobias of thunder and lightning (Öst 1978), firearms (Naud et al. 1973), noise (Yule et al. 1974), eyepatches (Thomas & Rapp 1977), getting angry (Blanchard 1975), and, again, urinary retention (Espie 1985). Although this is not the place to document them all, a compilation for therapists confronted with the diverse varieties of specific phobia would be useful.

Blood-Injury Phobia

This type of specific phobia deserves special mention because it can be life-threatening and requires special precautions during exposure therapy. Treatment for blood-injury phobia is mandatory when it endangers life by preventing essential medical procedures, such as urgent surgery, blood transfusion, or insulin injections for diabetes. Such an emergency is a not uncommon reason for referral, although even then some sufferers would rather literally die than have a venepuncture or operation. In some cases the fear may not involve blood but only needles, injections, or medical or dental procedures. Whether these should all be lumped into a single category is unclear.

Exposure therapy follows the same lines as in other phobics, with one exception. Of all phobics, blood-injury phobics are unique in developing bradycardia and actual fainting on contact with their fear cues (Chapter 11). To reduce the chances of fainting from hypotension during exposure, it is desirable to begin exposure with the subject lying down, inducing feelings such as anger (see Figure 11.3), or tensing the muscles (relaxation may actually provoke a faint). Whereas fear reduction in other phobics is accompanied by the heart rate dropping to normal, in blood-injury phobics the heart rate shows a corresponding rise to baseline.

There are only two controlled reports of series of blood-injury phobics treated by exposure (McCutcheon & Adams 1975; Öst et al, 1984a). Öst and his colleagues had follow-up to 6 months; marked improvement had continued, and most cases became blood donors. Many single cases benefited from exposure treatment, nearly all up to several months' follow-up.[3]

One single-case report concerned treatment of a double phobia (Wardle & Jarvis 1981). A man of 25 had for 10 years avoided public places for fear of fainting to blood-injury cues. Such fainting had begun at age 10. Live exposure to public places improved the fear of going into them but not of blood or injury; fear of the latter fell only when the patient was exposed to them over three 1-hour sessions by having a venepuncture and watching blood.

[3]Babcock & Powell 1982; Cohn et al. 1976; Connolly et al. 1976; Elmore et al. 1980; Fryrear & Werner 1970; Hsu 1978; Kozak & Montgomery 1981; Leitenberg et al. 1970; Lloyd & Deakin 1975; Marks et al. 1977; Nimmer & Kapp 1974; Yule & Fernando 1980.

Reducing Distress from Dental, Medical, and Surgical Procedures

This topic was reviewed by Horne & King (1986). Most people are not phobic of such procedures but find them distressing. This distress seems to lessen when the situation is openly confronted and accepted. Although providing information sometimes fails to help postsurgical pain (Scott & Clum 1984), a review of 25 studies from the United States concluded that patients who are carefully informed about what to expect and do before, during, and after medical procedures probably have less subsequent stress and morbidity (Havik 1980). Preparation of the average patient need not be time consuming—less than a half-hour providing information was as effective as longer periods. Individual caretakers had more effect than audio-visual aids, which in turn were better than no preparation at all. Among the caretakers, nurses were as effective as doctors and psychologists and yielded a far higher cost-benefit ratio.

In keeping with the value of openly but gently informing acute patients is the care given to the terminally ill in hospices. Helping patients accept the inevitable and enhancing their comfort is the hallmark of hospices, and informal observation suggests that they reduce distress for the dying person and his or her family. In healthy people, too, openly facing fears of death reduced fear more than did nonexposure approaches (Vargo & Batsel 1984), although that study had an invariant order of treatment and no follow-up.

Much experimental work has been done in children. Preexposure is of value before elective procedures. For example, the child is allowed to play in the dental surgery room and with some of the equipment before finally undergoing dental procedures, or gets to know a ward and its staff for a while before admission and also gets used to separating from its parents.

At least 16 studies have used exposure to filmed fear cues in preparation for hospital and surgery (reviewed by King & Hamilton 1986). Age and previous experience affect the type of preparation that is best. Compared with irrelevant information or a film, a relevant slide-tape show the night before elective surgery improved feelings and recovery for children 8 to 17 years old but led to more anxiety, disruption, and medical concerns in younger ones 4 to 7 years old who had had previous surgical experience (Melamed & Hermecz 1983). Young, experienced children may need alternative preparation.

Children can learn how to cope from a model (Melamed & Hermecz 1983). Those without prior experience of dentistry were actually sensitized on seeing an anesthetic injection and oral examination in the absence of a model showing them what to do. In contrast, patients having their first operation were more cooperative with anesthesia induction and recovery from surgery after viewing a peer model coping with the procedures. Fear also decreased and cooperation improved in 8- to 14-year-old children who had participant modeling of controlled breathing and distraction imagery prior to injection. But modeling helped only those children who did not know what to expect from dentistry; it was redundant in those who already had prior experience of it (Klorman et al. 1980).

Active participation (engagement) enhances preparation (Klingman et al. 1984). When dentally phobic children aged 8 to 13 saw a film of peers practicing controlled respiration and imagery during dentistry, those who were encouraged to practice the same maneuvers while watching the film did better than children who were just told that the film might help them. Engaged children gained more information from the film, had lower breathing rates and dental anxiety while watching it, and were less disruptive during subsequent actual dentistry. In another study, nine severely burned children showed less maladaptive behavior, depression, and anxiety when staff cared for them in the hospital with emphasis on patient control and focus on the procedure rather than with staff control and patient distraction (Kavanagh 1983).

Especially active preparation may be useful for painful medical procedures such as those undergone by some cancer patients. Five children aged 3 to 7 had less distress during such procedures after being taught breathing exercises and emotive imagery and practicing these in role play and with filmed modeling (Jay et al 1985).

Adult dental phobics were helped by behavioral treatment in controlled studies. Dentistry was completed more often, and with less anxiety, in subjects having behavior therapy than in those who had dental procedures under general anaesthesia (Berggren & Linde 1984). The effect is lasting. Ninety-six percent of dental phobics had finished their course of dentistry a year after group treatment (Jerremalm 1985), and most had regular dental care in the 2 years after other exposure treatment. (Exposure therapy for hypersensitivity of the gag reflex during dentistry is described in Chapter 11.)

Severely subnormal patients may need clear rewards with exposure if their fears are to be overcome. In 17 severely subnormal cases 8 to 20 years old with dental fears, dental behavior improved more in those who had two 45-minute sessions of steady reward for good dental-chair behavior rather than merely getting juice and food (Kohlenberg et al. 1972, cited by King & Hamilton 1986).

Traumatic Phobias (PTSD)

The recent surge of interest in post-traumatic stress disorder (PTSD) is not matched by much controlled research, so we can get only a vague impression of what is helpful. Most of the following are case reports of varying sophistication.

Exposure in several guises was of some use in PTSD, even in chronic cases. After fantasy exposure, two cases who had chronic PTSD after helicopter and car accidents improved in anxiety, nightmares, insomnia, and guilt up to 1 year after two sessions of relaxation, 7 to 8 of fantasy exposure, and exposure homework (McCaffrey & Fairbank 1985). Chronic problems in three Vietnam veterans were relieved by fantasy exposure; the reduction in fear as one scene was imagined generalized to similar untreated scenes but not to dissimilar ones until those were imagined repeatedly as well (Figures 15.1 and 15.2; Keane & Kaloupek 1982). A veteran with PTSD of 36 years' duration improved to 2 years' follow-up after only three-1 hour sessions of implosion (Black & Keane 1982). A woman who had had forced incest 10 to 13 years previously improved up to 1-year follow-up after five 90-minute sessions of implosion over 9 days (Rychtarik et al. 1984). Another woman raped 7 years previously benefited

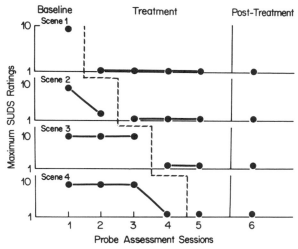

Fig. 15.1 Exposure to fantasies of combat cues reduced combat phobia of 5 years' duration in a 32-year-old Vietnam veteran. A multiple baseline design found that subjective distress to each of various scenes decreased as each was dealt with in treatment. (From Fairbank & Keane 1982. Copyright © 1982 by Academic Press. Reprinted by permission.)

from fantasy desensitization (Wolff 1977). The effect of abreaction was noted in Chapter 14.

Fantasy flooding helped Vietnam veterans (Miniszek 1984) and four other physical and sexual assault victims (Haynes & Mooney 1975). Other cases of PTSD improved with fantasy desensitization (Kipper 1977; Schinder 1980).

Treatments of rape victims have so far been uncontrolled (reviewed by Steketee & Foa 1986). Counseling is usual in the early phase. Improvement was noted in 17 cases after fantasy desensitization in the first 3 months, and in 21 cases after 14 sessions of cognitive therapy including self-exposure (such as going out alone) (Frank & Stewart 1983, 1983a). Persistent post-rape problems were helped by stress inoculation, which included exposure (Kilpatrick et al. 1982). Rape and incest victims who had sex dysfunction at least 2 months later improved with sex therapy or stress inoculation training, but there were many dropouts, and comparisons were not possible (Becker & Abel, cited by Foa 1986).

Grief is a reaction to the trauma of loss, but it is not classified as PTSD. The exposure approach of guided mourning has a limited role to play in reducing one deficit within the syndrome of morbid grief—avoidance of cues reminding the bereaved of the deceased (Cohen et al. 1986; Mawson et al. 1981).

Combat Phobias

If breakdown occurs, it should be treated early (Kardiner & Spiegel 1947). To this end the Israeli army recently treated cases in a setting that was close to the sight and sound of battle and had a military rather than a hospital character.

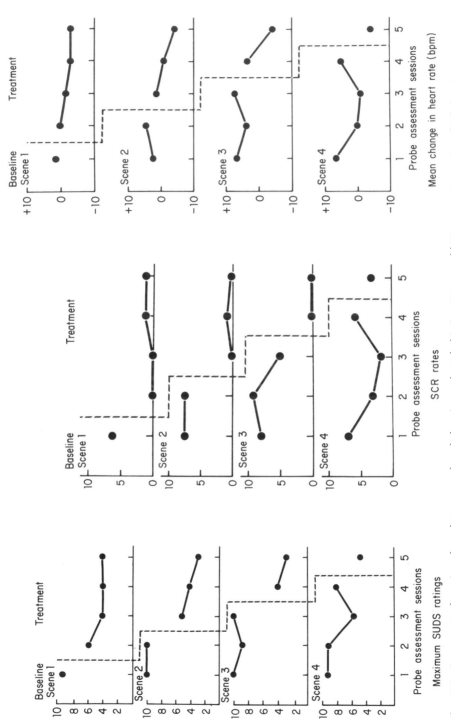

Fig. 15.2 Exposure to fantasies of combat cues reduced chronic combat phobia in a 31-year-old Vietnam veteran. A multiple baseline design found that subjective distress (SUDS), skin conductance responses (SCR), and heart rate tended to decrease to each scene in turn as it was introduced into treatment. (From Fairbank & Keane 1982. Copyright © 1982 by Academic Press. Reprinted by permission.)

Others deliberately delayed exposure until the patient had been in the hospital for at least a few days, as in 14 American soldiers who startled severely to noise and even to music (Saul et al. 1946). The soldiers saw twelve 15-minute showings of increasingly loud war films. Reactions to the films gradually changed from terror to boredom, and all but one of the soldiers improved. The therapy was likened to the accustoming of police horses to the din of traffic by repeated exposure to startling sounds. Similar noise therapy given in a hospital setting was described by McLaughlin and Millar (1941).

Repeated reliving of the experience does not always help combat phobias. In American aircrew in World War II, "often the abreaction would occur with great intensity over and over again, but with very little or no benefit to the patient. . . . In at least a few men the abreaction itself acted like a new trauma" (Bond 1952, p. 115). In a case cited in this instance the exposure was under thiopentone, which may have retarded habituation (see Chapter 16). Other causes of failure to habituate may be too-brief exposure and also exhaustion. Exposure has not been studied sufficiently systematically in combat phobias to delimit the conditions essential for it to be habituating.

Obsessive-Compulsive Disorder

Compulsive Ritualizers

Long ago Janet (1925) observed that ocs joining the army or the church often improved with the discipline (response prevention or rp) imposed by authority, and that a husband was able to check his wife's crises of overscrupulousness. Since then careful research has repeatedly shown that compulsive ritualizers improve well with live exposure and response prevention, and gains tend to persist over several years' follow-up (reviewed by Foa et al. 1985; Marks 1981; see also Chapter 14). Improvement generalizes from reduction in rituals to less anxiety and depression and better work, leisure, and family adjustment. This conclusion is supported by extensive controlled work[4] in Europe and the United States, uncontrolled series, and single case reports too numerous to mention. A round-the-clock imposed rp is no better in the long run than that which is shorter or self-imposed. Indeed, good results flow even when the clinician does no more than act as coach to the patient's own homework program of self-administered exposure plus rp (Hoogduin & Hoogduin 1983; Marks et al. 1986).

It would not be an exaggeration to say that behavioral treatment has transformed the outlook for most phobics, and this is even more true for most oc ritualizers. This is no mean feat in a syndrome that can be every bit as handicapping as chronic schizophrenia. Few improvements are more satisfying for clinicians to see. Treatment can restore normal family life in patients who for

---

[4]Controlled trials include Boersma et al. 1976; Emmelkamp & Kraanen 1977; Emmelkamp et al. 1980; Foa et al. 1980, 1980a, 1986; Marks et al. 1975, 1980, 1986; Robertson 1975. Uncontrolled series include Anderson 1977; Catts & McConaghy 1975; Foa & Goldstein 1978; Hand & Tichatzky 1979; Hoogduin 1985; Julien et al. 1980; Kirk 1983; Meyer et al. 1974; Marks et al. 1977, 1978; Rabavilas et al. 1976; Robertson 1979: Less impressive results came from Heyse 1975.

a decade or more had hands raw and bleeding from washing all day, would never touch any family member, crippled the family with incessant demands that they wash as well, prevented them from having visitors in the house for years, vetoed family holidays, and caused them to move repeatedly for fear of dirt. There are, of course, some treatment failures, mainly in the important minority (about 25%) who do not comply with exposure and rp instructions. But most sufferers cooperate fairly well despite the dedication required for real benefit.

The success of live exposure and rp contrasts with the poor results obtained in OCD with fantasy desensitization (Beech & Vaughan 1978; Cooper et al. 1965; Furst & Cooper 1970; Marks et al. 1969; Walton & Mather 1963). Anxiety might diminish yet compulsive behavior persist—this is less likely after live exposure and response prevention.

A problem peculiar to a tiny proportion of ocs is slowness without overt or cognitive rituals. Behavioral treatment has helped a handful by use of prompting and pacing but is far less reliable than it is in ritualizers. In the author's unit the hundreds of treatment hours given to such patients did not yield corresponding therapeutic benefits. The author's adult cases of slowness usually relapsed soon after supervision was withdrawn, no matter how carefully, and the same occurred in a 13-year-old boy (Clark et al. 1982).

As in phobics, the emphasis in ocs is on promoting approach to fear cues and discouraging avoidance. In addition, the rituals used to escape from or avoid discomfort are prevented. This response prevention is itself a form of exposure, as it brings on the type of discomfort that triggered the ritual; the discomfort slowly subsides while the patient continues to abstain from engaging in rituals. Such response prevention is carried out by asking patients to do whatever brings on their urge to ritualize (for instance, touching dirt for a washer, untidying a room for a tidier, leaving the house for a checker) and then to refrain for steadily longer periods from washing, checking, or tidying—say, first for half an hour, then an hour, and so on. Only persuasion, not force, is used to stop the rituals—ocs have to learn to stop themselves.

The need for such response prevention is carefully explained. The patient is told that although the ritual quickly brings relief from the anxiety that prompts it Rachman & Hodgson 1980), performing it is like a drug addict's getting rapid relief from withdrawal symptoms by taking the drug, only to have the symptoms return a few hours later. This vicious circle has to be aborted by ceasing to ritualize for increasing periods until these last several hours. In this way the sufferer can discover that the discomfort and urge to ritualize will slowly die down even without ritualizing (Figure 15.3). Although the ritual would switch the urge off quickly, that would help only temporarily. The urge soon returns unless the ritual is aborted, which will weaken the discomfort and urge the next time.

Modeling of exposure has not enhanced outcome when used as a routine (Rachman et al. 1973), and the modeling of relaxation without exposure had no effect (Roper et al. 1975). But for a few patients who no longer remember what normal behavior is in a given context, it can be helpful to show them. (For example, in a man with compulsive slowness who took hours to shower,

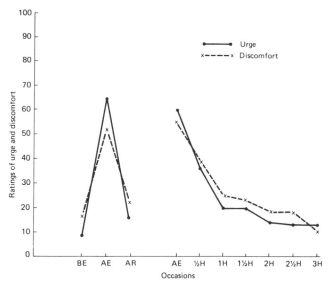

Fig. 15.3 Left side of figure: Before 11 compulsive washers touched dirt they had no discomfort or urge to wash (BE), but on touching dirt they felt uncomfortable and wished to wash (AE); completing their washing ritual abolished discomfort and the urge to wash further. Right side of figure: The same 11 patients were now asked to refrain from washing. After touching dirt (AE) washers again felt uncomfortable and had an urge to wash, but this discomfort and urge subsided to baseline over the next 3 hours, most rapidly within the first hour. (From Rachman, de Silva & Roper 1976. Copyright © 1980 by Pergamon Press Ltd., Oxford. Reprinted by permission.)

a male nurse modeled taking a shower at normal speed; the patient said this helped a lot, as he had literally forgotten how to shower properly.) And occasional patients use the therapist's example to give them courage; in one instance, an oc afraid of dirt had the confidence to touch garbage cans between sessions when she thought of the therapist putting a garbage can cover on his head.

A handful of cases need some inpatient treatment prior to the outpatient phase. Sometimes this leads to transient relief in the absence of the evoking cues, during which time treatment cannot be applied. This period is shortened by asking the patient to do things that evoke rituals—a washer should bring in contaminated clothing, and a checker might mail letters without checking them first. Generalization of improvement requires that the patient test himself or herself out in the natural environment where the oc problem occurs, which is usually at home. Occasionally it is helpful for a therapist to accompany the patient home for a few hours to boost the self-exposure program in that setting.

It is not rare for OCD to complicate mental subnormality and autism, especially in males. Among the author's cases, some were helped by exposure and response prevention (as in Lindley et al. 1977), but treatment is time consuming, and there were several failures when patients or their relatives adhered poorly to instructions. Success up to 3 months' follow-up was obtained in three subnormal men by reward of behavior incompatible with checking and overcorrection of inappropriate responses (Matson 1982).

Family Members as Exposure Cotherapists. Relatives need to be involved in the treatment only if the rituals concern them. If a mother will not hug her children for fear of germs, insists that the family strip, bathe, and put on fresh clothes before entering the house, or asks her husband to check several times a night that the lights are off, then it is desirable for those family members to become exposure cotherapists. But this has to be with the patient's agreement. Given such consent a few brief meetings with the relevant family members and the patient allows the exposure program to be coordinated and progress to be monitored. The children can be asked to hug their mother daily, the family to keep their outside clothes on when entering the inner sanctum of the house, the husband to gently but firmly refuse to check the lights. These actions can be prefaced by saying "the hospital has told me to . . . ," thus deflecting responsibility onto the therapist and lessening the chance of a big argument. For difficult cases the author's ward has a special apartment in which the family can stay with the patient for a couple of days to begin the exposure program together before completing it at home.

Having family members as cotherapists helps to extinguish a ritual peculiar to ocs and illness phobics—repeated requests for reassurance. The cycle of "Am I still dirty? Did I tidy properly? Do I look ill? Did I kill that child?" followed by the relative's increasingly exasperated "No, dear, you're all right" is often repeated dozens of times or more and needs to be broken. This goes against the grain of many relatives who naturally want to reassure loved ones and not withhold immediate comfort; that, however, simply strengthens the patient's addiction to reassurance.

If, instead, the relatives persistently answer ritualistic questions with "the hospital told me not to answer," spoken in a deadpan, unemotional voice, the endless cycle will come to an end. But the relative's deadpan reply has to be given over and over again, like a broken record, until the patient gives up asking for reassurance. Relatives have to persist unemotionally despite the patient's anger that often flares up at first, and to continue to do the same if the patient slyly changes from ritualistic questions to statements equally designed to get reassurance. Some families need repeated role rehearsal of the appropriate response together with the patient before they consistently achieve a therapeutic rather than an addictive reply. Their reward is the gradual fading of the patient's endless requests for reassurance.

At one time the author ran group meetings for several ocs and their families together to swap helpful ideas. Although the gatherings generated much mutual good will and information, they did not seem to save therapist time or enhance outcome more than meetings with single families.

Obsessions without Rituals

Although obsessions sometimes remit with nonbehavioral approaches, such as a high-protein diet (Rippere 1983), there is no sustained research to commend these approaches. More work supports the use of behavioral methods, but even they are less reliable for pure obsessions (reviewed by de Silva 1984; Marks 1981) than they are for rituals. Often ritualizers report that their obsessions remain despite reduction in the rituals after live exposure and response prevention. Pure ruminators are much rarer than are ritualizers (see Chapter 13), which partly accounts for the paucity of controlled studies with reasonable cell sizes.

Behavioral treatments for obsessions can be broadly divided into two contrasting types, exposure and thought-stopping.

Exposure. Exposure methods for obsessions have also been called habituation training, satiation, flooding, or implosion. They are carried out in fantasy or by subjects speaking out their thoughts at length; to initiate exposure the obsession may be brought on not only by deliberately thinking about it but also by contact with external triggering cues (live or audiotaped), and some workers add aversion relief. In self-exposure, patients are asked to set aside a daily period (say, 15 to 30 minutes) to ruminate deliberately as much as possible (resembling the deliberate "worry" period that Borkovec prescribed for worriers); whenever the obsession comes at other times, the patient is asked to sit down and think it through until it can be pursued no longer (Hoogduin 1985). In a variant of this method, relatives were taught to ask the patient whenever he or she seemed preoccupied, "Are you thinking of . . . (the obsession)?" and then "Tell me all about what you were thinking"; they were then to listen attentively and uncritically as long as the patient wished to speak (Vogel et al. 1982).

Prolonged exposure has helped obsessions in uncontrolled series and single case reports. Fantasy exposure had a limited effect on each of two series of six patients (Emmelkamp & Giesselbach 1981; Stern 1978). In other small series of five cases each, self-exposure was useful (Hoogduin 1985), as was help from the therapist that allowed patients to speak out their obsessions at length (Vogel et al. 1982). One woman improved on reciting her obsessions for a long time into a tape recorder whenever they came (Crook & Charney 1982). Listening to his own voice endlessly describing the obsessions on a tape recorder helped one man (Salkovskis 1983). Paradoxical instructions to intensify flatus emissions lastingly reduced obsessions about them (Milan & Kolko 1982). Exposure led to short-term reduction in discomfort associated with obsessions in nonpsychiatric patients (Parkinson & Rachman 1980). In contrast, in five cases fantasy exposure had little effect (Gurnani & Vaughan 1981).

Thought Stopping. This approach is also termed blocking or response interruption. The patient repeatedly brings on the obsession and then tries to drive it away each time by shouting, making a loud noise, switching attention, thinking of another nasty thought, or self-inflicting a brief aversive stimulus— for example, snapping an elastic band on or giving a short shock to the wrist.

Thought stopping was unimpressive in a controlled trial; 4 of 11 patients gained more by learning to stop neutral than obsessive thoughts, arguing that they acquired a coping set rather than specific habituation (Stern et al. 1975). In three series, each of six patients, thought stopping was helpful carried out by faradic aversion (Kenny et al. 1978), or had variable results (Stern 1978), or was inferior to assertive training (Emmelkamp & van der Heyden 1980). A single case was enduringly helped by switching attention (Gordon 1983). Imaginal thought stopping also reduced rituals that did not occur in the therapy session (Turner et al. 1983).

Comparison of Exposure and Thought Stopping. Both exposure and thought stopping share a common element: persuading the patient to bring on rather than avoid the obsessions. The subject continues obsessing for a long period in exposure but for only a few seconds at a time in thought stopping, so exposure should be superior if the results in ritualizers and phobics are anything to go by. This, however, has not been the case. Comparisons of exposure and thought stopping have been inconclusive. In small series of patients both approaches had similar effects (Emmelkamp & Kwee 1977), or exposure was only minimally better (Hackman & McLean 1975; Likierman & Rachman 1982). In 51 volunteers there were similar results from five sessions of desensitization, dismissal (a type of thought stopping), or both; all three groups were better than two control groups (Kazarian & Evans 1977).

One man improved lastingly with both approaches together (Headland & McDonald 1986). After reciting his obsessions into a walkman tape recorder he carried it around with him and switched it on whenever they began. This would stop the thoughts.

Theoretically it is remarkable that exposure, which works well with overt motor rituals, should be so much less predictable with covert obsessions that seem rather similar. Both obsessions and rituals are repeated intrusive events that may be cued by external stimuli or occur without an obvious trigger. Both may either reduce or induce anxiety (the former have been called cognitive rituals), although anxiety is more often reduced by rituals and induced by obsessions. Perhaps anxiety-reducing thoughts should be treated by thought stopping (response-prevention) and anxiety-inducing ones by exposure, but it might be difficult to separate out the two types of thought. Pilot reports described above (Hoogduin 1985; Vogel et al. 1982) suggest two points that deserve more study for anxiety-inducing obsessions: (1) setting aside daily periods in which to obsess all the time, (2) seeking out external or internal cues that bring on the obsession and then letting it run its course until it habituates. In addition, if anxiety-reducing thoughts (cognitive rituals, mental checks) are also present, these should be prevented by thought-stopping, distraction or other means.

Disorders in Children

Phobic Disorders

Live exposure therapy was outlined by Locke in 1693: "If your child shrieks and runs away at the sight of a frog, let another catch it, and lay it down at a good distance from him: at first accustom him to look upon it, when he can do that, then to come nearer to it, and see it leap without emotion, then to touch it lightly, when it is held fast in another's hand, and so on, till he can come to handle it as confidently as a butterfly or a sparrow."

The abundance of careful, controlled studies of phobic disorders in adults contrasts with their rarity in children with severe chronic phobias presenting in a clinic as opposed to fears for which help was not sought. Only cautious conclusions can thus be drawn about clinical populations, particularly as children's fears are so volatile (see Chapter 12). What evidence there is suggests that the exposure principle works as well as in adults: "The most effective techniques in overcoming fears are those that *help the child to become more competent and skillful and that encourage him to undertake active dealings with the thing that he fears*" (Jersild & Holmes 1935a, p. 102, authors' italics). That conclusion came from an interview survey of parents' ways of dealing with their children's fears. In a later questionnaire survey of parents and an assessment of their children, the children had lower anxiety when parents had encouraged them to deal with the fearful situation by means of reward, modeling, and persuasion rather than punishment, force, or reinforcement of dependency (Zabin & Melamed 1980).

Two controlled clinical studies deserve mention. The first was in 33 children 6 to 12 years old with severe chronic fears at night leading to disruptive behavior. These reduced more among children who attended with parents for 3 weeks' instruction in nightly "self-control" by relaxation, pleasant images, and self-statements, than among controls (Graziano & Mooney 1980). Gains continued to 1-year follow-up. Controls who were crossed over to have similar treatment then improved similarly. Therapeutic ingredients of the package included exposure, reward, relaxation, pleasant fantasies, and self-statements.

The second study was in 30 neurologically impaired children who feared buses or dogs. They had either 10 weekly 5-hour sessions looking at pictures or models of buses or dogs, then touching them, and finally live exposure, or served as controls (Obler & Terwilliger 1970). Treated children improved and controls did not. Generous rewards had been given for progress.

Since the work of Jersild and Holmes (1935) and the even earlier single case of Jones (1924), numerous reports of single cases and uncontrolled series continued to suggest the value of exposure (reviewed by Graziano et al. 1979; Johnson & Melamed 1977; King & Hamilton 1986; Morris & Kratochwil 1983). Similar exposure variants were utilized as in adult phobics—given live, on film or in fantasy, with rapid or slow approach, for brief or prolonged periods, and with or without modeling, systematic reward, or reciprocal inhibition. Again as in adults, treatment should not begin until it has been established that the salient problem is indeed a phobic/oc disorder and does not merely reflect a wider dysfunction in the child and/or family.

It goes without saying that application of the exposure principle has to be tailored to the special circumstances of childhood. Treatment can be presented as a game in young children, and parents or other carers are enlisted as cotherapists. All need to clearly understand what is required. Detailed presentation of the exposure approach in children has been most clearly given for school phobia and follows below. (Work with children's fears of dental and medical procedures and with social skills deficits was described earlier.)

School Phobia

To keep a school refuser away from school cuts him or her off from normal experience and puts his or her psychological development at risk. Early return of the child to school is therefore a central feature of management. There have been many single case reports of behavioral methods of doing this (reviewed by Graziano et al. 1979; Hatzenbuehler & Schroeder 1978). Attempts to achieve this mainly by fantasy desensitization had unimpressive results (Miller et al. 1972), but an approach also including live exposure had better outcome, although there were few details and no follow-up (Lowenstein 1983).

Focus on return to school was described long ago in other series (Davison 1961; Kennedy 1965; Talbot 1951). More recently, that approach yielded impressive results in an uncontrolled study of chronic cases mainly aged 11 to 16 (Blagg & Yule 1984). After live exposure therapy, 30 children attended school more (28 improved) and had less separation anxiety than 16 after hospitalization and than 20 after home tuition and psychotherapy. The latter did badly; they were older than the group having behavioral treatment. Improvement continued to follow-up, which was 1 to 3 years in most cases. Exposure treatment was vastly more economic, lasting a mean of only 2½ weeks compared with 9 months for hospitalization and 1½ years for home tuition. A good randomized controlled study is overdue.

Blagg & Yule (1984) gave a splendid account of the art of applying the exposure principle in practice. That principle is firm but careful return of the child to school in a way that is finely tuned to individual factors in the child, the family, and the school. At the start he or she is assessed for potential physical problems, appropriateness of the school, whether the fears are realistic, separation anxiety, and reward by parents for nonattendance. Both parents and teachers need to be involved and to agree that the child will return to school and how to achieve this. If parents are very anxious or cannot exercise control, then other close relatives might be involved.

On the way to school the escort should be able to handle the child's temper tantrum without distress and have enough time to take him or her to school for long enough to allow the fears and protests to subside; this usually takes a few days but may take much longer. If very vigorous protests are expected, then two escorts could be provided. Teachers should welcome the child back with praise; they should not be sarcastic, quiz the child about his or her absence, set too much work, or send the child home if he or she makes physical complaints. The child has to know exactly where to go in school at any time, and to role rehearse what he or she will say when friends ask why he or she has been absent. If the child complains of bullying or if testing reveals a learning problem, then appropriate remedies are needed. Parents should praise the child for remaining at school and ignore physical complaints.

At follow-up the therapist needs to be in frequent contact with the school until the child has attended full-time without trouble for at least 6 weeks. Special care is needed after long absences from genuine illness, a long weekend or a holiday, or when the child's timetable is reorganized.

Antidepressants have also been used in school phobics. There is one controlled trial of imipramine and another of clomipramine; only the former had an effect (see Chapter 16). Great caution is needed before using medication in children when cost-effective psychological alternatives are probably available.

Children with Obsessive-Compulsive Disorder

Unlike the plenitude of controlled studies of behavioral treatment in adult ocs, there are none in children with OCD. Encouraging and enduring success was reported in most cases from an uncontrolled series of 15 adolescents (Bolton et al. 1983). The oc problem had been present for a mean of 2 years. Treatment was mainly by self-imposed response prevention together with the help of the family. Some cases were admitted, upon which the problem might transiently remit and then relapse a few days later (as happens with adults as well) until more lasting gains occurred with behavioral treatment. Thirteen of the 15 patients were followed up at a mean of 2 years after treatment, at which time 77% were much improved and 15% improved. One of the 15 cases had compulsive slowness and did badly (Clark et al. 1982).

Only one hour of therapist time was needed to supervise live exposure and response prevention in a girl of 11. Her rituals and tics improved to 1 year follow-up (Zikis 1983).

SUMMARY

In phobic disorders gains after exposure therapy were stable or improved further in at least 6 studies at 4 or more years follow-up (all but one were in purely agoraphobic samples). The same was true for ocs at 4 year follow-up in 1 study and at 2 years follow-up or longer in 3 studies. Improvement in fears and rituals generalized to work and leisure activities and to marital adjustment.

The outlook with exposure is good in chronic phobic/ocs who consistently avoid certain cues, have normal mood, are compliant, and are off sedatives and alcohol. Within such samples gains are fewer if patients start with much free floating anxiety or depression and poor work, social, or marital adjustment. Dissociation during treatment augurs less progress. Expectancy has at most a small effect, presumably as a motivator of compliance. Prediction of outcome depends much more on the method of treatment than on the therapist.

Self-efficacy is similar to self-confidence and explains little as a prognostic factor. SE is like avoidance and tachycardia in being a sign of phobia; it rises with expected fear and falls with incentives to perform and as fear reduces during exposure. For SE to be a potent predictor it should rise *before* fear drops during therapy; that remains to be demonstrated.

Though there will always be exceptions, most marriages remain stable or improve a bit after agoraphobia is ameliorated. Evidence is conflicting on whether agoraphobics with poor marriages do less well on phobias than do those with happy marriages. Studies also disagree on whether phobic/oc outcome is enhanced by routine use of a partner as an exposure cotherapist. The added bother of such involvement may be justified when the partner impedes the exposure program in some way. The optimum therapeutic strategy to help phobics and ocs who have bad marriages seems to be to offer exposure therapy first. Marital therapy can be offered as an option afterwards, though few accept it (Emmelkamp 1979, Hand et al. 1974, 1977).

Agoraphobics improved enduringly in many well-controlled studies, in phobias, spontaneous panic and mood, marital and work adjustment. Self-exposure had good results when given with a manual and a diary to record exposure homework. Most of these impressive results were obtained without medication. Having a partner as exposure cotherapist has not reliably improved outcome. Whether controlled breathing enhances exposure needs further study.

The few controlled studies in patients with social phobia noted lasting improvement after live exposure; though self-exposure has been useful it needs more research in social phobics. When social dysfunction is also present then social skills training is worthwhile. SST includes exposure through role play and homework; controlled work found it helpful both in patients and in numerous studies of volunteers. After intensive SST infrequent booster sessions may help socially dysfunctional patients during the year or more it may take to develop intimate relationships.

Specific phobias respond well to exposure approaches. Blood-injury phobics may faint in the early stages of therapy unless precautions are taken to maintain blood pressure by lying flat or other methods. Preexposure before surgical procedures reduces children's anxiety about them, and good preparation seems to lessen postsurgical distress and morbidity both in children and in adults. Active engagement in the process helps further. Dental phobics are lastingly helped by exposure therapy.

Traumatic phobias (PTSD) have not yet been subjected to controlled group studies, though there are numerous case reports of even chronic cases showing long-term benefit after prolonged exposure. Anecdotes tell of subjects failing to improve or getting more anxious with repeated abreaction, a point that deserves further study.

Numerous fine, controlled trials in ritualizers found long-term benefit from live exposure with response prevention. It teaches ocs that the quick fix of transient anxiety reduction by ritualizing is similar to that of an addict's taking of heroin—the discomfort soon returns. Lasting relief requires the slower decline of discomfort (habituation) which occurs with persistent live exposure plus response prevention.

Modeling of exposure is sometimes a helpful adjuvant. Self-imposed exposure and response prevention is sufficient in most cases. A few may need a therapist-aided exposure and even an inpatient phase beforehand. Family members who are drawn into the rituals need to assist management as cotherapists, with the patient's agreement. They promote exposure, refuse to ritualize when asked to do so, and withhold reassurance.

Behavioral treatments are less trustworthy for obsessions without rituals. Exposure and, to a lesser extent, thought stopping have been of some help in small studies and case reports, but their effects are variable. More research is needed into systematic self-exposure for anxiety-inducing obsessions plus response prevention for anxiety-reducing thoughts.

Controlled group trials in children are almost absent and are long overdue. Uncontrolled single cases and series suggest that exposure relieves both phobic and oc problems. Management has to be tailored to the special needs of children. Parents and teachers are enlisted as cotherapists, and treatment can be presented as a game for young children. With school phobics firm but careful return of the child to school seems to have rapid and lasting results.

16

Physical Treatments of Phobic and Obsessive-Compulsive Disorders

The usual physical treatment for phobias and obsessive-compulsive disorder (OCD) is by drugs. Pharmacotherapy is the central theme of this chapter, but we will also survey other physical agents, including psychosurgery. For brevity, the drug review will deal mainly with controlled, random-assignment, double-blind studies in which at least five patients of homogeneous diagnosis completed each drug and comparison cell. Much less can be concluded from small or heterogeneous samples or from unblind, single-blind, or uncontrolled studies without random assignment (such as Kelly et al. 1970; Solyom & Sookman 1977). In addition, to be detailed here the study sample had to have a phobic disorder or OCD as the main problem, not merely phobic or oc symptoms with depression or some other problem as the dominant one (see, for instance, Cassano et al. 1981; Karabanow 1977).

Several controlled drug studies were rigorous and others less so. Common problems include tiny cell size and too-brief or no follow-up. Most trials had a controlled phase lasting 2 to 12 weeks and no systematic, long-term, drug-free follow-up. Once the controlled phase is over, many patients seek further help elsewhere, but detailed follow-up can nevertheless yield crucial information about duration of benefits. Given that most phobic and oc cases have had their worries for nearly a decade by the time they enter the trials, improvement is of limited interest if it occurs mainly during medication and perhaps a month or two after stopping it; more important is what happens thereafter. If a drug must be continued for years lest relapse ensues, then its utility is reduced by the added expense, side effects, and hazards, which are not negligible, as we will see. This point has even more force now that a lastingly effective nondrug treatment is available—live exposure, which has no drug side effects and can often be self-administered (see chapters 14 and 15).

Another common problem is scanty reporting of sample characteristics, raw pre-post scores, and drug side effects. Statistics are sometimes questionable because of inattention to the overall pattern of outcome; conclusions are sometimes drawn from within-group rather than between-group differences and may ignore improvement in mood, absence of sufficient cases with normal mood to test whether it is a predictor, and floor effects distorting correlations with outcome. Also occasionally neglected are interactions of drug with accompanying exposure instructions. Few reported plasma levels of drug. A final problem comes when preliminary outcome reports of subsamples alter with a later, larger sample, in which case the latter was regarded as definitive.

Tables 16.1 and 16.2 summarize most of the controlled drug studies of agoraphobia/panic disorder and of OCD. Trials are included that (1) gave the drug orally, (2) randomly assigned cases to contrasting cells, (3) were double-blind, (4) had at least five cases completing each of the contrasted groups, and (5) excluded cases with a diagnosis of primary depression (although initial mood was depressed in most of the studies reporting this variable). The complexity of the tables reflects the fact that simple "x was better than ( ) y" conclusions can mislead unless set in the context of the various designs, comparison groups, and measures used across studies. Several studies had drug plus psychological treatment cells. Another source of variation not depicted in the tables is the clinical nature of the samples: some had more depressed mood than others. Agoraphobics might include a few social phobics. OCD sometimes included a few cases of obsessions without rituals, whereas others only included ritualizers.

Despite the pitfalls in comparing such different studies, a fairly consistent picture will emerge as we go through each study in detail. Numbers of patients refer to completers, where these could be determined; to save lengthy repetition, henceforth E refers to therapist-aided live exposure, e to self-exposure instructions, and $\hat{e}$ to no-exposure instructions.

DRUGS IN AGORAPHOBIA/PANIC DISORDER

There have been 21 qualifying controlled studies of oral drugs in this condition, two-thirds of them with tricyclic or monoamine oxidase inhibitor (MAOI) antidepressants. Four of the investigations appear twice in Table 16.1, as they examined more than one class of drug. Four studies of intravenous barbiturates are not shown.

Antidepressants

Most studies were of imipramine (11) or phenelzine (6). One study was of iproniazid, and one of clomipramine with and without tryptophan.

Tricyclics

All but one of these studies was of imipramine. Three came from the Klein group in New York. In the first (Klein 1967), 9 agoraphobics had imipramine 150 to 300 milligrams per day (mg/d) and 10 had placebo, for 6 weeks. Exposure instructions seemed implicit in the comment that "phobic manipulations

Table 16.1 Controlled studies of oral drugs for agoraphobia/panic disorder

Author	Weeks on drug	Drug completers (n)	Drug effect[a] on: ag (A)	pa (B)	dep (C)	Initial dep: high vs. low dep (D)	corr. with ag improvemt. (E)	Relapse after drug ceased	Comparison groups: effect on agoraphobia
Antidepressants									
Klein 1967	6	9	+						imip > placebo[b]
Zitrin et al. 1983 }	26	42	+	+	-			26%	imip > placebo
Klein et al. 1983 }									desensitiz = support
Zitrin et al. 1980	26	29	+	+	-		—	27%	IEe > PEe
Mavissakalian & Michelson 1982, 1986	12	62	+	-	-				imip > placebo, IEe = IDe > PDe, Ee = De
Mavissakalian et al. 1983	12	15	(+)	(+)	(+)				eI > I
Marks et al. 1983 }	26	23	-	-	-		no drug effect		imip = placebo, IEe = PEe, Ee > Re
Cohen et al. 1984 }									
McNair & Kahn 1981	8	13, 13	-	+	+	+			imip = chlordiazepoxide for ag[c]
Telch et al. 1985	26	20	±	±	+	#			imip > placebo, eI > eĪ
Sheehan et al. 1980	12	18, 19	+	anx		#	—	yes	imip = phen > placebo
Sheehan 1984								yes	imip = phen = alprazolam > placebo
Liebowitz 1984	6	10	-		-		no drug effect		imip = alprazolam > placebo
Solyom et al. 1981									phen Ee = placebo Ee, Ee > no Ee
Tyrer et al. 1973	8	16	+	anx	-			yes	phen > placebo
Mountjoy et al. 1974	4	13	-				no drug effect		phen + bz = placebo + bz for ag[d]
Lipsedge et al. 1973	8	32	-	anx				yes	iproniazid + e = placebo + e for avoidance
Pecknold et al. 1982	8	16	(+)		(+)	+			clomipramine ± tryptophan equal

									Results
Benzodiazepines										
Ballenger et al. 1985 a & b						+				alprazolam > placebo
Liebowitz 1984					+	+				alprazolam = imip > placebo
Sheehan 1984					+	+			yes	alprazolam = imip = phen > placebo
Noyes et al. 1984	2	XO	21, 21	+	+					diazepam > propanolol
Hafner & Marks 1976		sd	20	+	—	+	anx		no drug effect	sd diazepam + E = placebo + E
McNair & Kahn 1981	8		13, 13	—	—	—	—		—	imip > chlordiazepoxide[c]
Beta-Blockers										
Noyes et al. 1984	2	XO	21, 21	—	—					diazepam > propanolol
Ullrich et al. 1975	2		16	+	+	anx				aprenolol + e > placebo + e
Hafner & Milton 1977		sd	11	—	—					sd propanolol + E = placebo + E

Notes:

ag = agoraphobia
pa = spontaneous panic
dep = depression
anx = anxiety
E = therapist-aided exposure
e = exposure homework
ē = no exposure homework
> = better than

I, imip = imipramine
phen = phenelzine
XO = crossover design
D = discussion
R = relaxation
sd = single dose
# = too few initially undepressed to test

[a] + = significant between groups, (+) = significant within groups, — = not significant
[b] On global outcome; no report on ag, pa, or dep
[c] Imip better for panic and depression
[d] Phen plus bz better for social phobia

. . . respond[ed] positively to firm direction and support" (p. 124). Imipramine improved more than placebo cases on global outcome. No measures of phobia, panic, or depression were reported.

The second Klein study included not only imipramine but also desensitization in fantasy, which is of little value for agoraphobia (Klein et al. 1983; Zitrin et al. 1983). Sixty-three chronic agoraphobics had placebo plus desensitization ($n = 21$) or about 180 mg/d of imipramine with either desensitization ($n = 18$) or support ($n = 24$). Medication was for 26 weeks. Psychological treatment was given individually in 26 weekly 45-minute sessions; support was dynamically oriented and nondirective. Imipramine was superior to placebo for reducing phobias and panic. Initial depression was fairly low and did not correlate with outcome, nor did mood improve. Desensitization was no better than support.

In a third study these workers gave 26 weeks of imipramine (I) 150 to 300 mg/d or placebo (P) plus therapist-aided live exposure (E) and exposure-homework (e) (Zitrin et al. 1980); comparison groups were thus IEe ($n = 29$) and PEe ($n = 25$). All patients had Ee from weeks 5 to 15, consisting of 10 sessions of about 2 hours of group E plus e but without an instruction manual or diary records of e. Both groups improved, as would be predicted given that both had exposure (see Chapter 14). Imipramine was superior to placebo at weeks 14 and 26 for phobia, spontaneous panic, and global improvement. Initial depression scores were fairly low and did not correlate with outcome. At 6-month follow-up, 27% of imipramine and 6% of placebo patients had relapsed.

By 5-year follow-up (C. Zitrin, personal communication, 1984), there was no difference between imipramine and placebo cases from the two studies of Zitrin and coworkers (1983, 1980). The overall relapse rate was 25%. Per group, the rate for imipramine plus desensitization was 18%; for imipramine plus support, 19%; for placebo plus desensitization, 21%; for imipramine plus Ee, 45%; and for placebo plus Ee, 32%.

In brief, the three studies by the Klein group all found imipramine helpful for agoraphobia. Two of the studies showed an effect on phobia and panic but not depression, and also that initial depression did not correlate with fall in phobias. Fantasy desensitization was no better than support; short-term gains from Ee were enhanced by imipramine.

Two studies were by the Mavissakalian group in Pittsburgh. In the first, 62 chronic agoraphobics had a mean of imipramine 130 mg/d or placebo 170 mg/ d for 12 weeks (Mavissakalian & Michelson 1982, 1983, 1983a, 1985; Michelson & Mavissakalian 1985). Each of the two drug groups was divided into two subgroups having 11 weekly 90-minute group sessions of either E or discussion (D). All cases had e without a manual and had to record e in a diary. The four groups were thus IEe ($n = 14$), IDe ($n = 17$), PEe (17), and PDe (14).

All four groups improved to 1-month follow-up—all complied with e, carrying out about four 90-minute e outings weekly; nearly a third of placebo cases were much improved at post-treatment after e alone (group PDe). For the entire sample, phobias reduced steadily until 1-month follow-up. Anxiety and depression improved early from the first 4 weeks onward. Imipramine improved phobias (IEe and IDe did better than PDe) but not anxiety, panic, or depression. Phobias but not panic reduced more with imipramine at a

higher dose (mean of 187 versus 67 mg/d). Side effects of imipramine prevented optimal dose being given in 43% of cases. Imipramine plus therapist-
aided exposure (IEe) did no better than either alone (IDe or PEe) except on 1
of 13 measures, which could have occurred by chance. E had no effect in the
total sample of 62, although in an earlier subsample of 49 cases E and imipramine had equal effects (Mavissakalian 1984). At follow-up, heart rate had risen
in imipramine and fallen in E patients (imipramine often causes tachycardia).
Outcome was best in cases who improved concordantly on several measures,
including heart rate.

In the second study by this group (Mavissakalian et al. 1983b), 15 agoraphobics had imipramine 125 mg/d either alone (I, n = 7) or with e (Ie, n =
8) for 12 weeks. I cases had no homework, and Ie patients saw a psychologist
individually for eight 1-hour instruction sessions in how to carry out e and
keep a diary of e tasks. Both I and Ie improved in phobias, panic, anxiety, and
depression; Ie was consistently superior for all of these (Figure 16.1). The effect
of e could not be separated from that of merely seeing a psychologist for eight
sessions, but e without such contact in other work (Ghosh & Marks 1986) was
as therapeutic as in the Pittsburgh study. As in the first Pittsburgh study, panic
did not improve before other symptoms, again suggesting it did not play a primary role.

In brief, a Pittsburgh study found that imipramine was better than placebo
but not than therapist-aided exposure; the latter enhanced self-exposure,
improving agoraphobia and panic even without imipramine. In a second Pittsburgh study, self-exposure enhanced the value of imipramine. In both studies,
imipramine improved depression and anxiety early and panic a bit later.

In research from the Maudsley Hospital, 45 chronic agoraphobics had
about 150 mg/d of imipramine or placebo for 26 weeks (Cohen et al. 1984;
Lelliott et al. 1986a; Marks et al. 1983). In addition, the two drug conditions
had either individual E or relaxation (R) for three to six 60-minute sessions
over 12 weeks, during which time all cases also had e plus an instruction manual and had to record e in a diary. The four comparison groups were thus IEe,
IRe, PEe, and PRe.

Imipramine had virtually no therapeutic value at any point up to 5 years'
follow-up, despite the fact that it caused side effects and that there had been
satisfactory plasma levels of imipramine and metabolite (at week 12 there had
been a slight drug effect on two of the many scales used—no more than might
have been obtained by chance). Initial mood of patients had been normal. Brief
Ee was better than Re for phobias until week 36, after which Re caught up. All
groups improved, presumably largely because of e, and maintained their gains
in phobias and in spontaneous panic over 5 years. Panic began to improve
after phobias did (Figure 16.2). Pretreatment depression and poor motivation
(but not panics) predicted a less good outcome 5 years later not on target phobias but on generalization of gains—perhaps depression reduced motivation to
carry out enough self-exposure to consolidate improvement.

In summary, the Maudsley Hospital study found no imipramine effect, a
short-lived E effect, and improvement of all groups, all of whom had e. Initial
depression predicted fewer long-term gains.

Two drugs were tested in another study (Sheehan et al. 1980). Fifty-seven

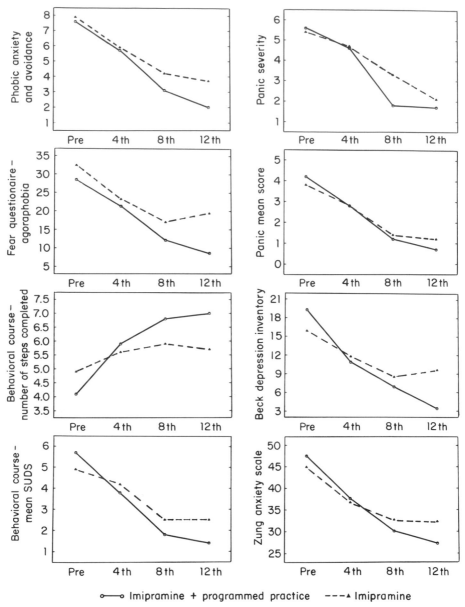

Fig. 16.1 Imipramine plus exposure homework was superior to imipramine alone for reducing phobias, panic, anxiety, and depression (el versus I). In the illustration, "programmed practice" = e.) (From Mavissakalian et al. 1983b. Copyright © 1983 by British Journal of Psychiatry. Reprinted by permission.)

chronic agoraphobics with panics had 12 weeks of imipramine 150 mg/d, phenelzine 45 mg/d, or placebo; cell sizes were 18, 19, and 22, respectively. Each drug was better than placebo by week 6 and yet more so by week 12. Phenelzine was superior to imipramine on only 3 of 17 scales, none of them concerning phobias. Both drugs were widely patholytic, reducing not only phobias but also depression, anxiety, hostility, oc symptoms, and even psychoticism (Figure 16.3). Phobic outcome did not correlate with initial depression, but there were too few initially undepressed cases to test this adequately. Relapse was common on stopping either drug.

A second study by Sheehan (1984) again found imipramine and phenelzine to be equally effective and superior to placebo for reducing agoraphobia, panic, and depression; compared to alprazolam, the antidepressants took longer to improve phobias and improved depression more. Eighty-three percent of cases relapsed on stopping drug.

Another study by Liebowitz (1984) found imipramine and alprazolam to be more effective than placebo. Further details of this and the Sheehan study await publication.

There were two imipramine studies in volunteer agoraphobics. In the first, 26 chronic phobics (mainly agoraphobic) had about 8 weeks of imipramine 130 mg/d or chlordiazepoxide 55 mg/d, plus seven 30 to 45-minute supportive interviews (McNair & Kahn 1981). Imipramine was superior to chlordiazepoxide in improving panic, depression, anxiety, and anger but not agoraphobia. Imipramine most reduced agoraphobia but not panic in cases who had initially been most depressed, which was "not entirely congruent with Klein's views that relief of the agoraphobic component is also independent of depression" (p. 78). As in the two Pittsburgh and the Maudsley studies, improvement in panic did not precede that of agoraphobia, which suggests that panic was not primary in the process.

The second volunteer study examined the interaction of imipramine and exposure in 29 agoraphobics (Telch et al. 1985). There were three cells—I$\hat{e}$, IEe, and PEe; completers per cell were 10, 10, and 9, respectively. Subjects had

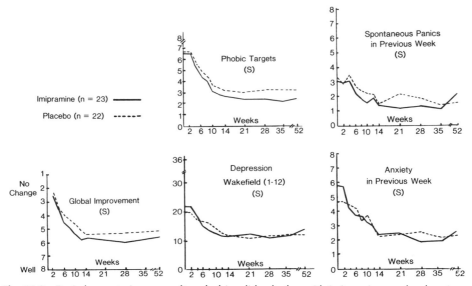

Fig. 16.2 Panic began to improve after phobias did, whether with imipramine or placebo given together with exposure. Imipramine had no effect. (Adapted from Marks et al. 1983.)

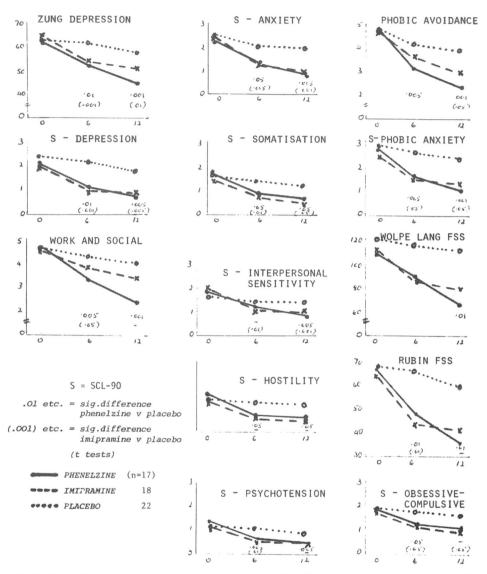

Fig. 16.3 Both imipramine and phenelzine were broadly patholytic in reducing not only phobias but also depression, anxiety, and hostility, among others. (Drawn from data in Sheehan et al. 1980.)

about 180 mg/d of imipramine or placebo for 26 weeks. During weeks 6 to 8 half the imipramine and all placebo cases also had *Ee*—three 3-hour sessions of group *E* during week 5, plus a treatment manual and *e* helped by spouses and recorded in a diary; this was monitored in weekly 90-minute sessions. The remaining imipramine cases repeatedly had anti-exposure instructions (*ê*) for the first 8 weeks.

By 8 weeks the two exposure groups (*IEe* and *PEe*) had improved more than *Iê* on phobias, the behavioral test, and excursions, but the three groups improved equally on depression. Imipramine did not enhance exposure (IEe versus PEe) except in reducing depression; imipramine with anti-exposure (I$\hat{e}$) improved all three depression measures but only one of eight phobia measures. Improvement in depression and in phobias correlated on several measures. At week 26 IEe was still the best, and better than PEe, with little difference between I$\hat{e}$ and PEe. In particular, I$\hat{e}$ had not reduced panic. Initial depression levels had been fairly high—a mean of 23 on the 21-item Beck scale and 66 on the Zung scale, with too few undepressed cases to test whether they too benefited from drug. No drug-free follow-up was reported.

To conclude, in the absence of exposure, imipramine had only weak effects and was not antipanic. Exposure alone was only weakly antipanic and antidepressant unless imipramine was given as well. Best results were with imipramine plus exposure in this moderately depressed sample.

A pilot comparison of imipramine with diclofensine (an isoquinoline) in 25 cases with panic or phobic disorder found that the two drugs produced similar improvement in anxiety, panic, and depression (Dajas et al. 1985). Another trial not qualifying for Table 16.1, as it was not double-blind, compared imipramine with propanolol in 23 cases of panic disorder, 17 of whom were agoraphobic; 15 more cases dropped out (Munjack et al. 1985). The study used a crossover design; each drug was given for 6 weeks followed by 1 week taper and 1 week off drug. Imipramine dose was up to 150 mg/d and propanolol up to 160 mg/d. Patient preference was split equally between imipramine and propanolol. Both drugs produced similar gains in panics and fear.

Tryptophan did not enhance the value of clomipramine in 24 agoraphobics and 16 social phobics (Pecknold et al. 1982). Patients had clomipramine either with tryptophan or with placebo for 8 weeks. The clomipramine dose was up to 200 mg/d; that of tryptophan, up to 8 mg/d. From weeks 8 to 10 patients had clomipramine alone. By week 10 agoraphobics and social phobics in both groups improved in phobias, depression, and social adjustment, with few differences between them. Depression improved as well as phobias.

A general practice comparison of clomipramine with diazepam did not qualify for Table 16.1, as agoraphobics and social phobics were not separated; symptom duration was a minimum of merely a month (Allsopp et al. 1984). Thirty-three patients had 12 weeks of clomipramine 25 to 150 mg/d or diazepam 10 to 30 mgs/d. Clomipramine was superior in improving phobic anxiety and lifestyle. Depression was present initially in 22 of the 33 cases and then improved with both drugs.

Monoamine Oxidase Inhibitors

Of the seven controlled studies of MAOIs, six examined phenelzine. The positive results of Sheehan and coworkers (1980), Sheehan (1984), and Liebowitz (1984) were mentioned above. A fourth study gave 32 agoraphobics and social phobics phenelzine 45 mg/d or placebo for 8 weeks (Tyrer et al. 1973; Tyrer & Steinberg 1975). By week 8 phenelzine produced superior improvement in phobias (secondary not main), anxiety, and work, but not mood, which was normal to start with. This was the only study apart from the two by Zitrin and coworkers to find an antidepressant effect on agoraphobia but not on depression. Response correlated with phenelzine dose. Relapse was frequent on stopping drug. At 1-year follow-up, drug was no better than placebo.

The fifth phenelzine (phen) study was of 40 phobics—the great majority were agoraphobic and a few were social phobic (Solyom et al. 1981). Cases had phenelzine 45 mg/d or placebo for 6 weeks. Half of each drug condition also had graded *E* plus *e* with diaries monitored by three phone calls a week; the other half had no exposure. The four drug groups were thus phen*Ee*, phen, P*Ee*, and P. Phenelzine did not improve phobias or depression. Initial depression level had been low (L. Solyom, personal communication, 1981). Exposure was superior to no exposure for phobias up to 2 months' follow-up.

A sixth study gave 13 agoraphobics 4 weeks of 60 mg/d of phenelzine or placebo, both groups also having diazepam 15 mg/d plus nitrazepam 10 mg/d (Mountjoy et al. 1977). Patients receiving phenelzine plus benzodiazepines (bzs) improved more on social phobia but not agoraphobia. Panic and depression were not reported.

A phenelzine study not qualifying for Table 16.1 was in 30 agora-, social, and specific phobics; the cell size for agoraphobics was probably less than five, and their contribution to results was unspecified (Solyom et al. 1973). Patients had 1 of 3 conditions over 3 months: phenelzine 45 mgs/d, placebo with brief psychotherapy, or fantasy flooding. Psychotherapy was in six sessions biweekly. Flooding was in 12 hour-long sessions. Phobias reduced more with phenelzine and with flooding than with placebo. Depression improved only with flooding. At 2-year follow-up all 6 cases who stopped taking phenelzine relapsed compared with only 10% of flooding patients.

One MAOI study was of iproniazid (Lipsedge et al. 1973). Sixty agoraphobics were randomly assigned to one of six groups in a 2×3 factorial design. The comparison groups relevant here are iproniazid plus *e* versus placebo plus *e*. Thirty-two cases had 150 mg/d of drug or placebo for 8 weeks plus *e* with diaries recording this. By the end of treatment iproniazid did not improve phobic avoidance but did improve anxiety, and that tended to relapse soon after drug withdrawal. During 2-year follow-up all patients had iproniazid, so follow-up is hard to interpret.

In summary, in four of six qualifying studies, phenelzine helped agoraphobia (and depression too in three of these four); a negative study had a sample with initially normal depressed mood, and one study helped social but not agoraphobia. A study of iproniazid found no effect on phobic avoidance, only on anxiety. Phenelzine and fantasy flooding reduced phobias comparably where this was studied, and live exposure was superior to no exposure.

"Anxiolytics": Barbiturates, Benzodiazepines and Beta-blockers

Although we saw that antidepressants are usually anxiolytic as well as antidepressant, only barbiturates and benzodiazepines (bzs) are customarily referred to as "anxiolytics" or "sedatives." Their therapeutic action is much faster than that of antidepressants, within hours or days rather than weeks.

Barbiturates

These have largely been superseded by bzs, which are safer in case of overdose. The only controlled studies have been by intravenous injection; five of these six trials used barbiturates as an adjuvant to some form of exposure.

Two of the studies were of thiopental. In the first, agoraphobics who had intravenous thiopental improved more than controls up to 3 months' follow-up, but the controls included cases who had not had an injection, and too few details were reported for adequate assessment (King & Little 1959). The second study injected intravenous thiopental or saline in agoraphobics or social phobics during flooding or desensitization in fantasy (Husain 1971). Thiopental facilitated flooding but made no difference for desensitization. The crossover design precluded conclusions about persistence of effects during follow-up.

Intravenous methohexitone was used as an adjuvant to fantasy exposure in five studies with some kind of control, but none included an injection control. Among severe agoraphobics discouraging results were reported in one study of fantasy desensitization (Yorkston et al. 1968), but three other studies noted more improvement with fantasy desensitization given with methohexitone than with muscular relaxation (Lipsedge et al. 1973; Mawson 1970; Razani 1974). Finally, among 27 agoraphobics, of those who had eight sessions of fantasy flooding with or without methohexitone, improvement was greater in the nondrug group up to 4 months' follow-up, and gains were fewest of all in attention-control (nonexposed) cases; methohexitone seemed to retard improvement, and poor response was predicted by poor across-session habituation (Chambless et al. 1979).

In brief, one of two studies of thiopental was positive but did not allow conclusions about follow-up. With methohexitone two studies were negative and three were positive but had no injection control; hence follow-up was inconclusive. Given that intravenous drugs can be dangerous and usually require a medical presence beyond the act of prescribing, only more major and lasting gains from better controlled studies would justify such injections. At present there is little to commend intravenous barbiturates for agoraphobia, and in one study they actually impeded improvement from fantasy exposure.

Regular Administration of Benzodiazepines

Alprazolam has had four studies and diazepam, one. In a multicenter 8-week study of panic with or without agoraphobia, alprazolam was superior to placebo by week 1 and continued so to week 8 for spontaneous and phobic panic; 50% to 60% of drug improvement had occurred by week 1 (Ballenger et al. 1985a, 1985b); the report on outcome during drug-free follow-up is awaited with interest. Other studies also found alprazolam to be superior to placebo but no different from imipramine or phenelzine (Liebowitz 1984; Sheehan 1984) or from equivalent doses of diazepam (D. Dunner, personal communication, 1985). Alprazolam reduced panic (but not avoidance) more rapidly than did antidepressants. Relapse is usual on stopping alprazolam (Sheehan 1984). Further details await final publication. Special attention is needed to the problem of dependence that is so common with long-term bzs (Petursson & Lader 1981).

A 2-week study gave diazepam 30 mg/d or propanolol 240 mg/d to 42 cases with agoraphobia, panic disorder, or generalized anxiety disorder; the number of agoraphobics was unspecified (Noyes et al. 1984). There was no placebo control. By 2 weeks diazepam was superior to propanolol for phobias, panics, anxiety, global improvement, and heart rate even in cases with predominantly somatic rather than psychological anxiety. Troublesome side effects were present with both drugs. Follow-up was not reported.

A critical question currently under study is how outcome to regular bzs compares with that to exposure and endures at drug-free follow-up.

Single-Dose Studies

Two studies examined diazepam plus exposure in agoraphobics. In a study too small to appear in Table 16.1, four agoraphobic inpatients had 20 mg of diazepam or placebo shortly before each of 12 exposure sessions in a crossover design (Johnston & Gath 1973). Exposure was 45 minutes of fantasy flooding followed by 60 minutes of therapist-aided live exposure (E) on 3 consecutive days of each of 4 weeks. Outcome the day after each treatment block was better with diazepam. No follow-up conclusions are possible.

In a larger study, 30 agoraphobic outpatients had four 3½-hour E sessions over 2 weeks, live exposure starting after a single 7.5 mg dose of diazepam or placebo (Hafner & Marks 1976). Diazepam or placebo was given either a half-hour or 3½ hours before E sessions began, yielding three cells: peak diazepam (starting a half-hour after the dose), waning diazepam (starting 3½ hours after the dose), or placebo ($n = 10$ per cell). Exposure was in groups of six patients, each group containing two patients from each cell. There was no crossover, and there were no dropouts. Up to 6 months' follow-up all groups improved substantially and equally with no drug effect on any measure, although diazepam patients had a bit less discomfort during group exposure. Improvement was presumably due to the live exposure given to all patients.

Small doses of bzs do not seem to retard learning during exposure therapy. A pilot study of intravenous diazepam during exposure suggested, however, that high doses might impair outcome (McCormick 1972). Several of this author's agoraphobics failed to habituate to adequate exposure and were then found to be taking moderate to high doses of bzs or alcohol; after such substances were withdrawn, the patients improved with further exposure. Since the author's unit introduced a policy of allowing no more than low doses of bzs or alcohol before starting exposure, failures of habituation have become very exceptional. This clinical impression needs controlled testing.

To conclude, bzs reduce fear and anxiety more rapidly than do antidepressants, but the effect usually wears off soon after stopping bzs. There is a risk of drug dependence and no evidence of lasting value from bzs after drug withdrawal, whether they had been given alone or as an adjunct to exposure. The final verdict awaits results from research now in progress.

Beta-Blockers

There have been four studies of these drugs in agoraphobics: one of alprenolol (A), two of propanolol, and a small study of oxprenolol.

In the alprenolol study (Ullrich et al. 1975) 24 chronic agoraphobics were randomized into one of three 2-week groups: 200 mg/d of alprenolol or placebo together with exposure homework (*e*) or *e* without placebo; *e* was monitored daily. The three groups were thus A*e*, P*e*, and *e* (each *n* = 8). By the end of week 2, alprenolol plus *e* was superior to the other two *e* groups on autonomic symptoms and agoraphobia. Follow-up was not reported.

In the first propanolol study 23 agoraphobics had a single 40-mg dose of propanolol or placebo shortly before the start of each of three 5-hour sessions of group therapist-aided exposure in vivo (*E*) given on alternate days (Hafner & Milton 1977). Eleven cases completed propanolol-*E* and 12 placebo-*E*, two cases having dropped out of the propanolol and none out of the placebo condition. Propanolol plus *E* was slightly *less* effective than placebo plus *E* up to 3 months' follow-up.

The second propanolol study was the 2-week comparison with diazepam described earlier (Noyes et al. 1984). Propanolol was inferior to diazepam.

A fourth beta-blocker study, of oxprenolol, had too few cases to appear in Table 16.1 (T. Silverstone and M. Bernadt, personal communication, 1978). Agoraphobics had oxprenolol 240 mg/d or placebo for 8 weeks, after which they had live exposure. Oxprenolol did no better than placebo.

In summary, propanolol was inferior to diazepam or placebo when regularly administered without exposure or when given as a single dose just prior to exposure. Regular oxprenolol was no better than placebo. Regular alprenolol enhanced the value of exposure.

General Issues

Role of Mood and Panic in Agoraphobic Outcome with Drugs

The role of these features is a controversial topic. With respect to mood, an obvious issue is whether antidepressants act on agoraphobia via the concomitant depression that is so common (see chapters 9 and 10, and figures 16.1 and 16.3). This can be examined in several ways.

First, does initial depression correlate with phobic outcome to drug? Only two studies looked at this (Table 16.1, column E); neither found a correlation (Sheehan et al 1980; Zitrin et al. 1980). Elementary statistics teach us that correlation is hardly a final criterion of causal relation. Closely linked phenomena may fail to correlate. The same emotional state of fear is reflected by changes in subjective anxiety, avoidance, skin conductance, and heart rate, yet in phobics who improve after treatment, changes in these variables rarely intercorrelate (chapters 1 & 7). It would be a serious mistake to conclude that they are therefore unrelated. The same caution is needed concerning the absence of correlations of initial mood with phobic outcome in the only two studies of this point. Other criteria also need attention.

A second criterion is categorical: does agoraphobia improve more in initially most depressed versus least depressed patients? This was examined by two studies, and both found such a relationship. Agoraphobia (but not panic) improved only in cases who were initially depressed (McNair & Kahn 1981), and improvement on a phobia questionnaire was greater in those with a higher initial Hamilton Depression score (Pecknold et al. 1982).

Third, does drug improve depression as well as agoraphobia? Often it does—in four of the eight reports of a drug effect on phobias and/or panic, which also gave data on depression (Table 16.1, column C: Mavissakalian & Michelson 1982; Mavissakalian et al. 1983; McNair & Kahn 1981; Pecknold et al. 1982; Telch et al. 1985). In the remaining three studies depression did not improve, although phobias did (Tyrer et al. 1973; Zitrin et al. 1980, 1983).

A fourth criterion is whether phobia or depression improve first. Most studies report too few data points to judge this. In two studies this could be gauged (Mavissakalian & Michelson 1982; Mavissakalian et al. 1983)—mood returned to normal somewhat earlier than did phobias (Figure 16.1).

No study with a positive drug effect reported analysis of a fifth possible criterion—whether gains in depression and gains in phobia correlate. Finally, a sixth criterion is feasible: how drug effect in the various samples relates to their levels of depressed mood at the start. In both negative studies of antidepressants, initial mood was normal (Marks et al. 1983; Solyom et al. 1981). In the nine studies that found an antidepressant effect on agoraphobia and also reported initial mood, mood was normal in two (Zitrin et al. 1980, 1983) and at least moderately depressed in seven (Liebowitz 1984; Mavissakalian & Michelson 1982; Mavissakalian et al. 1983; Pecknold et al. 1982; Sheehan et al. 1980; Sheehan 1984; Telch et al. 1985).

Turning from depression to spontaneous panic, *DSM-III* regards panic as the node of action by antidepressants. However, no study has reported panic improving before phobias. In the four studies examining this point, panics improved slightly after the phobias did (Marks et al. 1983; Mavissakalian & Michelson 1982, 1983a; McNair & Kahn 1981). Panic did not improve when imipramine was given with anti-exposure (Telch et al. 1985). It is thus unlikely that panic is the prime focus of drug action.

A wider issue becomes evident on looking at measures other than mood and phobia/panic. This is that antidepressants are fairly widely patholytic—they improve not only phobia/panic and depression but also hostility, anger, and other problems where this was measured (Figure 16.3 and McNair & Kahn 1981). Reduction in phobia, panic, and depression occur as part of a broad field of problems improving with medication. It might be misleading to think that antidepressants directly affect panic, phobia, or depression. Such drugs may well act indirectly on antecedent factors whose nature is still obscure. In contrast, exposure produces more and earlier reduction in phobias than in other problems, as it is less globally patholytic. Exposure acts more specifically on phobias than do drugs.

In brief, whether the changes in phobia and mood with antidepressants are related partly depends on the criterion of relationship. Each of two studies found no correlation of initial depression with phobic outcome. However, in another two studies phobias improved more in those who had been initially depressed; in five of eight studies depression as well as phobia improved; and in each of two studies depression improved a shade earlier than phobia. Both negative studies had normal initial mood, and seven of nine positive studies had depressed mood at the start. Often there is some relationship between depression and phobic outcome with antidepressants; occasionally there is not. Panic improves somewhat after phobias, if anything. It may be fruitful to explore a wider field of change from antidepressants than simply depression, phobias, and panic.

Interaction of Drugs with Exposure

Antidepressants have been studied with fantasy desensitization, fantasy flooding, E, e, and Ee. Ee and e were enhanced by imipramine in two studies (Mavissakalian & Michelson 1983a; Zitrin et al. 1980), but Ee was not in a third (Marks et al. 1983), nor was Ee or fantasy flooding enhanced by phenelzine (Solyom et al. 1971, 1973). Anti-exposure abolished the antiphobic but not the antidepressant effect of imipramine (Telch et al. 1983). Desensitization was no better than support (Zitrin et al. 1983). E enhanced e in two studies (Marks et al. 1983, temporarily; Mavissakalian & Michelson 1982), and Ee was superior to no Ee (Solyom et al. 1981). Live exposure has a consistent effect (Table 16.1, far right: $eI > I$ [Mavissakalian & Michelson 1983a], $eI > êI$ [Telch et al. 1985], $Ee > De$ [Mavissakalian & Michelson 1982], $Ee > Re$ [Marks et al. 1983], $Ee >$ no Ee [Solyom et al. 1981]). No study found that antidepressants reduced the effect of exposure.

Single doses of diazepam or of propanolol did not enhance E (Hafner & Marks 1976; Hafner & Milton 1977). Alprenolol enhanced e (Ullrich et al. 1975).

Thus, antidepressants are compatible with exposure and occasionally enhance it, especially if mood is dysphoric to start with. Imipramine had no antiphobic action when patients had anti-exposure instructions. Exposure in vivo is regularly effective ($eI > I$, $eI > êI$, $Ee > De$, $Ee > Re$, $Ee >$ no Ee). More work is needed to judge whether bzs and beta-blockers are useful adjuncts to exposure.

Problems of Drugs

The attraction of oral drugs if they achieve their intended purpose is the ease with which they can be prescribed by the doctor and taken by the patient. For the doctor it is simpler to say "take these pills" and check their effects than to outline and monitor an exposure program. For the patient it is easier to swallow the pills than to make the consistent effort of carrying out adequate exposure.

Like all treatments, however, drugs bear a price tag. This includes their cost, the time it takes for them to act, their side effects, the dropout rate, and relapse on stopping drugs. Each of these problems is detailed below.

Cost varies greatly with the type and brand of drug used. Drug costs mount the longer the drug has to be taken, which often seems indefinitely given the problem of relapse. The cost of exposure therapy has diminished sharply with the advent of self-exposure; the amount of therapist time needed for most patients has fallen to a few hours or less needed to monitor progress.

The *time elapsing before a drug becomes therapeutic* varies with the drug. With antidepressants, side effects start immediately but benefits take time to develop, starting within 2 to 3 weeks and rising up to 12 weeks where this issue was studied. It is often difficult to persuade patients to wait that long for help. Unlike antidepressants, bzs produce both benefits and side effects within minutes or hours, and these may mount over weeks. With exposure most cases begin to habituate within the first session but may take weeks or months to complete the full program.

Drug *side effects* are rarely reported in detail (Marks et al. 1983; Noyes et al. 1984). They are easily forgotten by clinicians and make drugs intolerable for many patients. Drugs cause "minor" discomforts such as drowsiness, dizziness, dry mouth, sweating, unsteady hands, constipation, and blurred vision, depending on the type of compound; and it would be interesting to know how many patients cannot drive a car or have car accidents because of their drugs.

It is hard to ignore the rarer serious problems—hypertension from not sticking to a low tryptamine diet for MAOIs, cardiac and motor complications of tricyclics, poor concentration from bzs, fits following rapid cessation of bzs, dependence on bzs, rare blood dyscrasias, and the unknown dangers that may manifest decades after a drug has come into common use.

Exposure therapy also has side effects—mainly the effort and discomfort involved in executing an exposure program. Usually these are acceptable, and some patients who reject exposure also reject drugs.

Dropouts from placebo groups are rather fewer than from antidepressants (Marks 1983). A third to a fifth dropped out from imipramine or from MAOIs.[1] Fewer data are available for dropouts from other psychotropics; the rate was 22% with chlordiazepoxide (McNair & Kahn 1981) but only 8% with 3 doses of propanolol (Hafner & Milton 1977) and 0% with 4 doses of diazepam (Hafner & Marks 1976).

The dropout rate from exposure therapy is rather similar to that from imipramine or MAOIs—about a quarter of suitable patients either refuse to start or fail to complete an adequate trial (Marks 1981).

Relapse after stopping drugs is a frequent problem, even after they have been taken regularly for 6 months. Almost all studies finding a drug effect on agoraphobia and commenting on events after drug withdrawal mentioned relapse as a problem (Table 16.1). This is true for both antidepressants and for bzs (83% after a year, according to Sheehan 1984), although definitive comment on the bzs must await the publication of studies recently completed and in progress. Return of agoraphobia on ceasing drugs that may have been taken

---

[1]The dropout rates reported by some researchers are, for imipramine, 36%, Marks et al. 1983; 33%, McNair & Kahn 1981; 31% Mavissakalian & Michelson 1982, 1983; 29%, Zitrin et al. 1980; 24%, Sheehan et al. 1980; 21%, Zitrin et al. 1983; 20%, Telch et al. 1985; 16%, Mavissakalian et al. 1983. For MAOIs, reported dropout rates are 27% (Tyrer et al. 1973), 23% (Lipsedge et al. 1973), and 18% (Pecknold 1982).

for 6 months or more is a major snag in a chronic disorder. It is hard to justify years of pharmacotherapy when alternative, enduringly helpful methods such as exposure are available. Of course, occasional relapse also occurs after completing exposure therapy, but this usually responds lastingly to brief booster treatment.

To sum up, the price tag attached to drugs makes them undesirable as the first line of treatment for agoraphobia when there is an effective nondrug alternative. If agoraphobics refuse exposure therapy, drugs might be refused too but are worth offering. Antidepressants are certainly indicated where the agoraphobic also has depressed mood.

DRUGS IN OTHER PHOBIAS

Social Phobia

Several of the agoraphobic studies included some social phobics but did not analyze them separately. We lack controlled studies of psychotropic drugs in clinical social phobics. One report noted that socially phobic outpatients did no better with 4 weeks of propanolol 160 to 320 mg/d than with placebo, but gave no further details (Falloon et al. 1981).

In musicians who were not unduly anxious, several trials found some benefit from giving single doses of beta-blockers in advance of the performance. One study gave 22 string players atenolol (100 mg) or placebo 6½ hours before they performed (Neftel et al. 1982). Atenolol did not improve performance but did reduce stage fright and heart rate; urinary catecholamines rose more with atenolol.

Another study gave 33 string players nadolol (40 mg), diazepam (2 mg), or placebo, in a crossover design (James & Savage 1984). Nadolol reduced tachycardia and improved string playing but did not lower anxiety. Diazepam slightly impaired performance. Other studies in musicians found some improved performance from oxprenolol (40 mg) (James et al. 1977), pindolol (5 mg) (James et al. 1983), and propanolol (Brantigan et al. 1982). Beta-blockers still need to be compared with exposure in musicians.

Specific Phobias

The largest study of specific phobics was of imipramine and desensitization in fantasy (Zitrin et al. 1983). Patients were randomized to have 26 weeks of placebo with desensitization ($n = 23$) or imipramine 180 mg/d plus either desensitization ($n = 22$) or support ($n = 17$). Psychological treatment was given individually in 26 weekly 45-minute sessions; support was dynamically oriented and nondirective. There was no superiority of imipramine over placebo or of desensitization over support. (Fantasy desensitization is an outdated form of behavior therapy that has been superseded by live exposure—see Chapter 14.)

The effect of a single dose of diazepam on exposure was examined in chronic specific phobics (Marks et al. 1972). In a crossover design with an incomplete Latin square yielding 12 cases per cell, 18 patients were assigned at random to two 2-hour sessions of live exposure, each session being in one of three conditions, starting 1 hour after oral diazepam 0.1 mg/kg (peak diazepam), or 4 hours after the same dose (waning diazepam), or 1 to 4 hours after oral placebo. By 2 or 3 days after sessions, phobias had improved under all three conditions but more so with waning diazepam than with placebo; peak diazepam was in between. Gains were unrelated to levels of serum diazepam. The crossover design precluded conclusions about long-term drug effects.

How single doses of diazepam or the beta-blocker tolamol affected specific phobics during an exposure test was studied in a crossover design (Bernadt et al. 1980). Twenty-two animal-phobic volunteers were exposed to their feared stimulus for 10 minutes 1½ hours after a single dose of tolamolol (200 mg), diazepam (10 mg), or placebo. This was done 3 times at intervals of at least a week. During the exposure test, tolamolol abolished the fear-induced tachycardia but not avoidance or anxiety, whereas diazepam reduced avoidance but not tachycardia. Medication had little effect on subjective fear.

School Phobia

Two controlled drug trials are available, one each of imipramine and clomipramine. Imipramine was given to children who had been out of school for 2 weeks or more; mean age was 11 (Gittelman-Klein & Klein 1971). They were seen weekly with family who were instructed to be firm about school attendance. Sixteen children completed imipramine and 19 placebo. Dose was 150 mg/d for 6 weeks. At 3 weeks there was no difference, but by 6 weeks imipramine children were superior at being back at school, had fewer physical complaints, and were less depressed (12 of the 35 completers had been rated as depressed by the psychiatrist). The imipramine group also had more side effects and more dropouts (five versus two with placebo).

The other study was of school phobics who had been out of school for a mean of 6 months. Twenty-seven had clomipramine and 19 placebo in a dose of 40 to 75 mg/d over 12 weeks (Berney et al. 1981). All children were encouraged in due course to attend school. Clomipramine had no effect on phobias, although depression improved in the girls (44% of all the children had been depressed, a rate not very different from that in the imipramine sample above).

DRUGS IN OBSESSIVE-COMPULSIVE DISORDER

The main results of drug use for OCD are summarized in Table 16.2. Twenty controlled studies of OCD met the criteria for discussion here. Of the studies of tricyclic antidepressants, 12 were of clomipramine, 2 of desimipramine (Insel et al. 1985; Rapoport et al. 1980), 1 each of nortriptyline (Thorén et al. 1980), amitryptiline (Ananth et al. 1981), and imipramine (Volavka et al.

1985). One study was of imipramine versus placebo (Foa et al. 1986). Nontricyclic antidepressant studies were one each of nisoxetine (Yaryura-Tobias & Neziroglu 1983), clorgyline (Insel et al. 1983), and zimelidine (Insel et al. 1985). Of nonantidepressant drugs, two were of lithium (Geisler & Schou 1969; Hesso & Thorell 1969), one of clonidine (Lipsedge & Prothero 1986), and one of a single dose of amphetamine (Insel et al. 1983c). Two studies appear twice in Table 16.2 because they concern both tricyclics and nontricyclics (Insel et al. 1983b, 1985). Only two studies systematically controlled for exposure (Marks et al. 1980, 1986); a third had exposure without a nonexposure control (Foa et al. 1986).

Antidepressants

Tricyclics:

Clomipramine. Nine of the 10 tricyclic studies were of clomipramine because of speculation that it is specifically anti-oc linked to its inhibition of serotonin reuptake at the presynaptic terminal (see Chapter 13). This belief dies hard even though in 7 of 10 studies clomipramine reduced not only oc symptoms but also depression (see Table 16.2, columns 3 and 4; see also below).

Tricyclics: Parallel Designs

The largest and longest studies are two from the Maudsley Hospital. The first (Marks et al. 1980; Mawson et al. 1982; Stern et al. 1980) was of 40 chronic oc ritualizers. They had either clomipramine (C) or placebo (P) for 36 weeks (mean dose was 183 mg/d from weeks 4 to 10 and 145 mg/d at week 18); all were inpatients during weeks 4 through 10. From weeks 4 to 7 the C and P groups were subdivided to have fifteen 45-minute sessions of relaxation (R) or E plus corresponding homework (r or e), yielding 4 randomized cells of 10 cases each—CRr, CEe, PRr, and PEe. From weeks 7 to 10 all patients had 15 sessions of 45 minutes of E plus e. Ee included self-imposed response prevention (rp), and where necessary cases were also treated at home with relatives as cotherapists.

Clomipramine improved rituals, depression, anxiety, and social adjustment. Gains were evident by week 4 and maximum from weeks 10 to 18 but reduced by week 36 just before medication was phased out; were no longer significant by 1-year follow-up; and had disappeared by 2-year follow-up. Clomipramine helped only those patients with initially depressed or anxious mood (Figures 16.4 and 16.5). Several cases relapsed on stopping clomipramine and improved once more on restarting it. Relapse was greater for depression than for rituals; exposure seemed to prevent full reemergence of rituals during subsequent affective episodes.

Within a "therapeutic window," plasma levels of clomipramine and its metabolite desmethylclomipramine (DMC) correlated with outcome. Plasma levels correlated with dose but not with side effects, and side effects were unrelated to outcome.

Table 16.2 Controlled studies of oral drugs in obsessive-compulsive disorder

Author	Weeks on drug		Drug completers (n)	Drug effect[a] on: oc (A)	Drug effect[a] on: dep (B)	Depression effect: initial score w/imp: oc imp (C)	Depression effect: initial score w/imp: r with oc imp (D)	Depression effect: initial score w/imp: r with oc imp (E)	Relapse after drug ceased	Comparison groups: effect on oc symptoms
Antidepressants: **Tricyclics**										
Marks et al. 1980 } Mawson et al. 1982 }	36		20	+	+	+			yes	clo > placebo clo = exposure (weeks 4–7)
Marks et al. 1986 } Monteiro et al. 1986 }	27		36	+	+	−	+	+	?	clo > placebo[e] exposure > clo
Thorén et al. 1980 } Thorén et al. 1980a }	5		8, 8	+	+	+	−		yes	clo = nortriptyline clo > placebo, nortrip = plac
Ananth et al. 1981	4		10,10	(+)	+	−	−			clo = amitriptyline
Mavissak. et al. 1985	12	XO	7	+	(+)	−	−	+ −*		clo > placebo
Rapoport et al. 1980	5	XO	8	−	−					clo = desimip = placebo
Flament et al. 1985[b]	5	XO	22	+	−	−		+	yes	clo > placebo
Insel et al. 1983b } Zahn et al. 1984 }	6	XO	12	+	+	−	−		yes	clo > clorgyline clorgyline, no effect
Montgomery et al. 1980, 1981	4	XO	14	+[d]	−	−	−			clo > placebo (obs, not rituals)
Yaryura-Tobias et al. 1976	13[b]	XO	3	+	+				yes	relapse on stopping clo > placebo (obs, not rituals)

Reference	n	design/week			notes	comparison
Volavka et al. 1985	12	7,8	(+)	(+)	—	clo = imip for oc symptoms
Insel et al. 1985	5	XO 6,8,5	+	+		clo > desipramine or zimelidine
Foa et al. 1986	22	19	—	+		imipramine = placebo for oc symptoms
Antidepressants: **Nontricyclics**						
Yaryura-Tobias & Nez. 1983	20	XO 8	—	—		nisoxetine = placebo
Insel et al. 1983b	6	XO 12	—	—	no clorgyline effect	clo > clorgyline
Insel et al. 1985	5	XO 5	—	—	no zimelidine effect	clo > zimelidine
Other drugs						
Geisler & Schou 1969	6	XO 6	—	—		lithium = placebo
Hesso & Thorell 1969	10	XO 10	—	—		lithium = placebo
Insel et al. 1983c	sd	XO 12	(+)	—		sd amphetamine, placebo
Lipsedge & Proth. 1986	4	XO 16	—	—	no clonidine effect	clonidine = placebo

Notes: imp = improvement   XO = crossover design
clo = clomipramine   r = correlates
sd = single dose   *+ = for week 4; — = for week 12
> = better than

[a]+ = significant between groups,   (+) = significant within groups,   — = not significant
[b]Children and adolescents
[c]Comparison with placebo only over 2 weeks
[d]For obsessions, not rituals
[e]Only when exposure homework was present

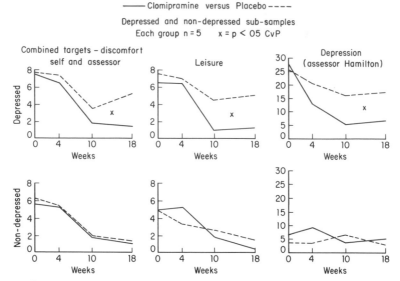

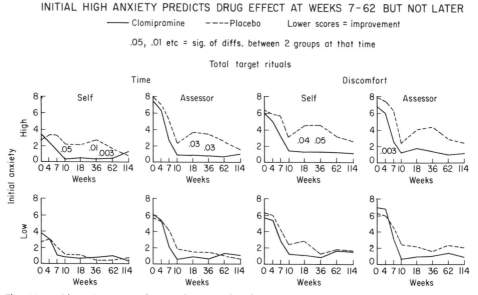

Fig. 16.4 Obsessive-compulsives who started with depressed mood improved on clomipramine, whereas those who started undepressed did not; change scores of the two subgroups differ significantly (denoted by x). Between weeks 4 and 10 all cases also had exposure treatment. — = depressed mood pretreatment (n=5); --- = normal mood pretreatment (n=5). (Adapted From Marks et al. 1980, Mawson et al. 1982.)

Fig. 16.5 Obsessive-compulsives who started with anxious mood also improved on clomipramine; those who started calm did not improve. See Fig. 16.4.

During weeks 4 through 7 exposure was superior to relaxation for reducing rituals; relaxation had little effect. Reduction in rituals tended to be greatest in the clomipramine plus exposure (*CEe*) group. Compliance with both exposure and relaxation rose with clomipramine.

At 2-year follow-up gains were retained, and rituals decreased most in cases who had had 6 rather than 3 weeks of *Ee*. With regard to rituals 67% of patients were much better and 16% improved—an outcome very similar to that in a previous study of ritualizers 2 years after exposure without drugs (Marks et al. 1975). During the follow-up after week 36, cases who had begun the study with greater anxiety or depression were prescribed more tricyclics.

The second Maudsley study had 12 or 13 patients per cell and no obligatory inpatient phase (Marks et al. 1986). Forty-nine chronic ritualizers were randomized, in a ratio of 3:1, to clomipramine 200 mg/d or placebo for 31 weeks. Clomipramine cases were further randomized into three subgroups from week 0—one had antiexposure homework (group *Cê*—"avoid ritual-evoking cues; if avoidance is not feasible, then you can ritualize"), and two subgroups had *e* (*Ce₁* and *Ce₂*). From week 8, *Ce₁* continued with *e*, and *Ce₂* now had *E* as well (becoming *CeE*). Placebo cases had *e* from weeks 0 to 8 (*Pe*) and *E* thereafter (becoming *PeE*). The comparison groups were, for weeks 0 through 8, *Cê*, *Ce* (*Ce₁* + *Ce₂*), and *Pe*; thereafter they were *Ce₁*, *CeE*, and *PeE*. *E* and *e* followed the lines of the first study.

Patients began this second study with normal mood—mean Hamilton Depression score was only 8 compared to 18 in the first study, which may explain why clomipramine had much less effect this time. The limited drug effect was only for weeks 0 through 8 (*Ce* versus *Pe*) and not subsequently (*CeE* versus *PeE*). Anti-exposure homework almost abolished gains from clomipramine (*Ce* versus *Cê*). The greatest gains were from *e*; by week 17 all but 3 of the 12 anti-exposure cases (*Cê*) had to be crossed over to receive *e* and then *Ee*, as they complained at not improving despite treatment (which included clomipramine). *E* had a relatively limited advantage over *e* (*CeE* versus *Ce₁*). At week 52 there continued to be no gains from clomipramine and few gains from *E*; patients maintained the improvement that had begun earlier.

Better early outcome of rituals with clomipramine related slightly to plasma levels of drug and its metabolite, but there was no "therapeutic window." Drug effect was unrelated to initial depression but did relate to improvement in depression. Of patients who had some initial depression, those who did not improve in depression did not improve in oc symptoms. At 9 months, a month after all medication had ceased and by when all but three cases had received exposure, outcome was better in those who had initially normal mood and resisted their rituals.

The limited drug effect was at a price. The usual side effects developed, including dry mouth, sweating, unsteady hands, constipation, difficulty in focusing eyes, dizziness, and drowsiness. In the second study anorgasmia began and persisted in all but one of the clomipramine (but in none of the placebo) cases who were engaging in regular coitus; it was discovered only in a structured interview—a self-rated questionnaire in both studies did not pick up the anorgasmia (Monteiro et al. 1986). Hypomania developed in 2 of the

59 cases who began clomipramine in both studies, so they had to be withdrawn.

In brief, in both Maudsley studies, (1) clomipramine improved rituals and mood; (2) drug effect on rituals was linked to initial depressed/anxious mood or to improvement in mood; (3) drug effect tended to wane with time, although some cases relapsed on stopping the drug and improved on resuming it; (4) there were troublesome drug side effects; and (5) exposure was better than relaxation or anti-exposure for rituals (gains from it persisted and were greater in those who had initially normal mood). The clomipramine effect almost vanished if patients concurrently had anti-exposure rather than exposure instructions.

Four other clomipramine studies employed parallel designs. Twenty-four chronic ritualizing inpatients had 5 weeks of clomipramine 150 mg/d, nortriptyline, or placebo (n = 8 per group) (Thorén et al. 1980). Cases were mildly encouraged to resist compulsions. By week 5 clomipramine was superior to placebo for rituals and depression, and nortriptyline had effects in between those of clomipramine and placebo, differing significantly from neither. After the 5-week controlled phase all patients were offered clomipramine plus "behaviorally oriented therapy according to the principles laid down by Marks"; half the cases responded and retained their gains for 1 to 4 years, but others relapsed within weeks of reducing or stopping the drug. Anorgasmia was a pronounced side effect of clomipramine.

Initial depression related to poor outcome with clomipramine at the end of 5 controlled weeks. In Table 1 of Thorén and coworkers, obsessions improved 3 times more in the three clomipramine patients who had been the most depressed pretreatment than in the remaining five nondepressed cases. Figure 16.6 shows the same effect for the four most and four least depressed at the start. Initial depression was unrelated to outcome in the later open phase, by

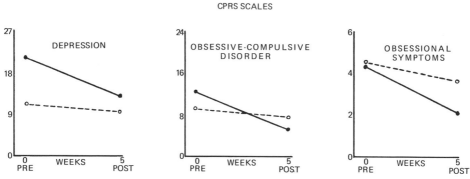

Fig. 16.6. Obsessive-compulsives who started with depressed mood improved on clomipramine, whereas those who started undepressed or calm did not. Change scores of the initially depressed and nondepressed subgroups differed significantly to the end of the 5-week controlled phase even though they did not differ in a subsequent uncontrolled phase, when all patients had clomipramine plus "behaviorally oriented therapy according to the principles laid down by Marks." — denotes score 18+ on CPRS pretreatment, n=4; --- denotes score 17- on CPRS pretreatment, n=4. (Data drawn from Thorén et al. 1980.)

when the study was unblind and uncontrolled, and all cases had clomipramine plus behavior therapy. Initially depressed cases who did badly with clomipramine also had low pretreatment levels of 5-hydroxy indolacetic acid (5HIAA— a serotonin metabolite) and homovanilic acid (HVA—a dopamine metabolite) in the cerebrospinal fluid (Thorén et al. 1980a), which levels also predicted poor outcome in depression.

In a 4-week study, 20 chronic ocs had 150 mg/d of clomipramine or amitriptyline (Ananth et al. 1981). There was no placebo control. Compared with amitriptyline, clomipramine produced more improvement in depression and anxiety, but not in oc symptoms.

In a 12-week study of 12 ocs, 7 had clomipramine 300 mg/d and 5 had placebo (Mavissakalian et al. 1985). Clomipramine improved more than placebo cases on oc symptoms, and on depression *both* groups improved equally (Figure 16.7). Among clomipramine cases, depression had returned to normal by week 4, but oc symptoms continued to fall until week 12. The 7 clomipramine cases were pooled with 3 others from a previous study plus 5 who had imipramine. Among these 15 cases, the 5 initially most and 5 initially least depressed improved equally on oc symptoms, the former also losing their depression (the number on clomipramine in each subgroup was unspecified). Improvement in depressive and oc symptoms correlated at week 4 but not at week 12, depression having dropped to normal by week 4 before oc symptoms did.

In the fourth parallel design, ocs had 12 weeks of clomipramine or imipramine (each $n = 8$) in a mean dose of about 280 mg/d (Volavka et al. 1985). Imipramine cases began with worse oc traits and symptoms. Up to week 12 both drugs improved oc and depression symptoms; clomipramine was better for depression and obsessions (but not for oc symptoms, behavior, or interference) up to week 12. Initial depression did not relate to outcome. Side effects were comparable with the two drugs—nausea, dizziness, dry mouth, constipation, blurred vision, and ejaculatory disturbance.

Crossover Designs

Six clomipramine studies used crossover designs. Two of these were in children and adolescents. The first was in eight severe chronic adolescent inpatients who had little initial depression (Rapoport et al. 1980). Up to 150 mg/d of clomipramine, desimipramine, or placebo were given for 5 weeks. Neither drug was superior to placebo.

The second crossover design compared clomipramine with placebo in 19 child and adolescent in- and outpatients with OCD, mainly male, whose mean age was 14 (Flament et al. 1985). Medication was given for 5 weeks to a dose of 3 mg/kg/d (maximum 200 mg/d) as tolerated. Patients were encouraged to resist their compulsions but had no systematic exposure-homework.

Clomipramine was superior for oc symptoms, not mood. Relapse was likely on withdrawal of drug. Improvement in oc symptoms did not correlate with initial depression but correlated highly with improvement in depression, despite the fact that initial mood had been fairly normal (findings like those of

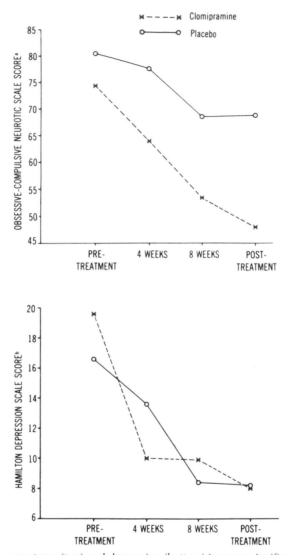

Fig. 16.7 Both oc symptoms (top) and depression (bottom) improve significantly with clomipramine, although drug effect was significant only for the former, as depression also improved with placebo. Depression returned to normal (score 10) before oc symptoms did (Mavisakkalian et al. 1985.) Copyright © 1985 by American Psychiatric Association. Reprinted by permission.

Marks et al. 1986 and Mavissakalian et al. 1985 at week 4). Plasma levels of clomipramine and DMC were unrelated to dose or outcome but did relate to side effects, which also were unrelated to outcome. Two clomipramine cases had acute dyskinesia, and one had a grand mal seizure.

A third crossover design in adult ocs (in- and outpatients) compared 6 weeks of clomipramine 236 mg/d with clorgyline (a MAOI) and had no full placebo control (Insel et al. 1983). Five of the 12 cases who completed at least one drug phase had obsessions without rituals. Clomipramine was superior in reducing oc symptoms and also reduced depressed mood (Figure 16.8). The course of depression and oc symptoms were closely related in one case (Figure 1 of Insel et al. 1982c), but for the whole group, decrease in oc symptoms was no greater in those who had more initial depression, nor did it correlate with decrease in depression. Clomipramine also reduced heart rate (HR) and skin conductance (SC) responses to loud tones and tonic and phasic SC responses in a 2-flash discrimination task, whereas clorgyline did not (Zahn et al. 1984). Relapse was common within weeks of stopping medication. Fall in oc symptoms correlated with plasma clomipramine. Side effects included anorgasmia and tremor.

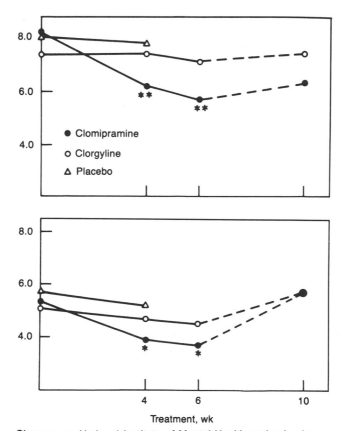

Changes on National Institute of Mental Health scales in obsessions (top) and depression (bottom) in patients receiving clomipramine (n = 12), clorgyline (n = 11), and placebo (n = 13). Dashed lines denote changes during postdrug placebo periods. Significant changes from baseline ratings (asterisk, *P*<.05; double asterisk, *P*<.01; two-tailed *t* test for paired data) are evident only with clomipramine.

Fig. 16.8 Both oc systems (top) and depression (bottom) improve significantly with clomipramine even though there was no correlation between initial level of depression and improvement in oc symptoms, or between oc and depressive improvement. (From Insel et al. 1983. Copyright © 1983 by American Medical Association. Reprinted by permission.)

A fourth crossover study was in 14 chronic adult ocs with acute relapse but no depression (Montgomery 1980; Mongomery et al. 1981). They had 4 weeks on clomipramine 75 mg/d or placebo, plus fantasy desensitization (which is ineffective for OCD). Clomipramine was superior to placebo for improving obsessions and tension but not rituals. Patients began with Hamilton Depression scores of less than 16, and gains were unrelated to these scores (which did not improve) or to plasma level of drug or desmethylclomipramine.

Finally, one crossover study employed a relapse design (Yaryura-Tobias et al. 1976). Over 4 months 13 ocs had clomipramine 300 mg/d except during weeks 4 through 6 or 6 through 8, when double-blind placebo was given. Ruminations and depression increased during the placebo weeks.

In the fifth crossover design, ocs had 5 weeks on either zimelidine ($n = 5$) or desimipramine ($n = 8$), followed by 4 weeks on placebo and then 5 weeks on clomipramine ($n = 9$, of whom 3 were from an earlier trial, which destroyed the randomization) (Insel et al. 1985). Dose for each drug was up to 300 mg/d. Zimelidine lead to no gains, whereas desimipramine improved one oc subscale, but the two drugs did not differ from one another. Clomipramine improved oc and depressive symptoms, but this was not a completely randomized group.

The lack of response to zimelidine was noteworthy, given its potency as a serotinin uptake inhibitor. The ocs had normal platelet ^{3}-H-imipramine binding and serotonin uptake but raised 5-HIAAA in the cerebrospinal fluid; the latter was reduced by zimelidine despite the fact that the drug had no clinical effect. The ocs appeared to have normal serotonin uptake and raised serotonin turnover (Insel et al. 1985).

Other Tricyclics

One study was of imipramine and exposure in 31 chronic ritualizers (Foa et al. 1986). The sample was divided into highly and nondepressed subgroups, half of each getting imipramine 233 mg/d or placebo for 22 weeks. From weeks 6 to 10 all cases also had fifteen 90′ sessions of therapist-aided exposure—each 45′ in fantasy and 45′ live—plus continuous response prevention, and all cases were given 4 hours of exposure homework daily, which was monitored weekly from weeks 10 to 22. Exposure diaries were not obligatory.

Until week 6 imipramine was superior to placebo for depression but not for oc symptoms or anxiety, the drug effect on depression being present only in the initially depressed subsample. By week 10 after the entire sample had exposure treatment, oc symptoms improved as well. Gains were maintained to week 22. Greater peak heart rate during early exposure predicted better outcome at week 22. Drug-free follow-up is in progress.

We saw earlier that three other tricyclics were ineffective for oc symptoms—nortriptyline (Thorén et al. 1980), amitriptyline (Ananth et al. 1981), and desimipramine (Rapoport et al. 1980). Desimipramine had a weak effect (Insel et al. 1985). We also saw above that both clorgyline and zimelidine (which are nontricyclic antidepressants) were ineffective for OCD (Insel et al.

1983b, 1985). Two studies of fluvoxamine (a potent serotonin reuptake inhibitor) are in progress.

Other Drugs

There has been one study of clonidine in ocs with obsessions rather than rituals (Lipsedge & Prothero 1986). In a crossover design 16 patients completed 1 month of clonidine 300 mg/d or placebo. Outcome with clonidine was no better than with placebo.

Two crossover studies of lithium noted no superiority over placebo (Geisler & Schou 1969; Hesso & Thorell 1969). A single dose of d-amphetamine (30 mg) but not of placebo improved oc symptoms up to 6 hours later in a crossover study of 12 ocs, but no between-group effects were noted (Insel et al. 1983c).

Finally, in a crossover design in three ocs and five agoraphobics, a single dose of 60 micrograms of intranasal DDAVP (1 desamino-D-arginine[8] vasopressin) prior to a session of E did not enhance e between sessions or outcome after a week, but using e may have swamped possible effects, and within-session effects were not measured (Greenberg & Belmaker 1985).

Is Clomipramine Superior to Other Drugs for OCD?

It is difficult to compare clomipramine adequately with other drugs, as only the former has been studied extensively. No study has yet found clomipramine to be significantly better than other tricyclics; its apparent superiority over desimipramine and zimelidine depended on including nonrandomized patients in the clomipramine group (Insel et al. 1985). Other reported superiority, over imipramine, was for depression and obsessions only, not for oc symptoms, behavior, or interference (Volavka et al. 1985). Nonsignificant trends to superiority were found over nortriptyline (Thorén et al. 1980) and amitriptyline (Ananth et al. 1981) but not over desimipramine (Rapoport et al. 1980); in the last-named study neither drug had an effect. Clomipramine was superior to the MAOI clorgyline, but the latter was ineffective (Insel et al. 1983).

Looking at weaker evidence from within-group effects, all but 1 of the 12 clomipramine studies found that it reduced oc symptoms. Imipramine reduced both oc and depressive symptoms in one study (Volavka et al. 1985) but only depression in another (Foa et al. 1986). Desimipramine had a weak effect (Insel et al. 1985). Clorgyline, nisoxetine, clonidine, and lithium had no effect.

The data supporting the superiority in OCD of clomipramine over other antidepressants, in particular tricyclics, are thus tenuous at best. Other antidepressants need more study before definitive conclusions can be drawn. Clomipramine has a remarkable ability to induce anorgasmia, and when taken as an overdose is especially lethal. The original speculation that clomipramine was specially valuable because it inhibited serotonin uptake is negated by the fact that zimelidine, another serotonin uptake inhibitor, has no effect.

Relation of Mood and OC Outcome with Antidepressants

It is commonly held that "high depression ratings are not a prerequisite for an antiobsessional response to clomipramine" (Zohar & Insel 1986). This is too simple a view, however. As with agoraphobic outcome to antidepressants, whether oc improvement to such drugs seems related to mood depends on the criterion adopted. Among controlled studies this is evident in Table 16.2, columns B–E. Depression as well as oc symptoms improved with antidepressants in 10 of 12 studies (column B). On a second criterion, initially most depressed cases had more oc reduction than those who were least depressed initially in only two of seven studies of this issue (column C) (when only depression, not oc symptoms, reduced with imipramine, this gain too was solely in cases with high initial depression [Foa et al. 1986]). A third criterion is whether initial depression correlated with oc reduction; only one of seven studies of this point found such a relationship (column D). Finally, decrease in depression correlated with that in oc symptoms in all three studies examining this (column E)—in one there was a correlation at week 4 but not week 12, perhaps because of a floor effect from mood falling to normal by week 4 before oc symptoms did (Figure 16.7) (Mavissakalian et al. 1985).

At least four uncontrolled studies reported improvement in both depressive and oc symptoms. In 12 ocs given clomipramine for 16 weeks, both oc and depressive symptoms improved (Singh 1983). Among 8 ocs of whom 3 had clomipramine and 5 imipramine for 12 weeks, depression, anxiety, and oc symptoms fell in parallel (Mavissakalian & Michelson 1983b). Among 8 ocs given fluoxetine for 12 weeks followed by 10 days of exposure, both depression and oc symptoms fell, and initial depression correlated with reduction in distress (Turner et al. 1986). Finally, Capstick and Seldrup (1973) noted better outcome in depressed ocs than in "true" ocs.

Taking all the studies together, there is strong evidence for some link between mood and oc outcome with antidepressants. The link, however, is complex. Obsessive-compulsive outcome did not usually correlate with initial depression scores but did correlate with reduction in depression; depressive and oc symptoms usually fell in parallel. Antidepressants nearly always improved oc symptoms in ocs who also had dysphoria, and rarely also did when mood was normal. Such coupling of oc outcome with depressive outcome is less obvious with exposure.

Earlier we saw the broad-spectrum action of antidepressants in agoraphobia. The same is true in OCD, and again it may be a mistake to focus purely on the link between oc outcome to drug and mood. Clomipramine reduced not only oc and depressive symptoms but also anxiety where it was studied (see, for instance, Ananth et al. 1981; Marks et al. 1980, 1986). The reduction in oc, depressive, and anxiety symptoms by antidepressants could reflect actions on common underlying factors whose nature is still obscure.

Comparison of Antidepressants in Agoraphobia and OCD

There are impressive similarities of antidepressant drug action in both syndromes of anxious avoidance. Drug effect took weeks to start and months to rise to a maximum, and relapse was usual on stopping the drugs. In both agoraphobia and OCD the drug effect was usually on mood as well as on target problems, although correlations of target problem outcome with initial mood were usually insignificant. In both conditions, where this could be judged drug action was broad-spectrum, improving not only target problems and depression but also background anxiety and other problems. Both in agoraphobia and OCD the value of tricyclics for target problems almost disappeared when anti-exposure instructions were given with the drugs. Exposure had a more specific effect on target problems than did drugs in both syndromes and seemed to protect against full reemergence of target problems during later affective episodes, but not against depression itself. In neither syndrome are antidepressants incompatible with exposure; if anything, the two approaches are complentary in the presence of dysphoria, but when mood is normal the value of antidepressants is more moot.

The trade-offs of drugs versus exposure are similar for both agoraphobia and OCD. Most drugs are easy to prescribe, take, and monitor but have side effects and potentially worse hazards; relapse is a problem once medication stops. Exposure needs dedication in the face of discomfort and informed monitoring but causes more lasting gains in target problems.

Drug dropouts were fewer in OCD than in agoraphobia, but this may be because of different drugs being tested. Most studies of clomipramine had 11% to 14% dropouts (Flament et al. 1985; Insel et al. 1983b; Marks et al. 1980; Mavissakalian et al. 1985; Rapoport et al. 1980; Thorén et al. 1980), although Volvaka and coworkers (1985) had a 36% rate from clomipramine and 33% from imipramine, and 22% of imipramine cases of Foa and colleagues (1986) dropped out.

OTHER PHYSICAL TREATMENTS

Exposure to Chemically Induced Anxiety

Inhalations of carbon dioxide can be anxiogenic (see Chapter 7) but have also been tried for agoraphobia in an exposure paradigm that encourages confrontation with chemically induced anxiety rather than contact with the usual evoking stimulus (ES). Unencouraging results were obtained in an agoraphobic patient (Griez & Vandenhout 1983). Fifty sessions of repeated 35% CO_2/65% O_2 inhalations over 5 days (a total of 25 hours) reduced phobic anxiety somewhat, but not avoidance; after live exposure, avoidance dropped markedly and anxiety fell further.

Rather better results came from the same workers with a randomized but nonblind 2-week crossover study of 11 patients with panic disorder and 3 with agoraphobia (Griez & Vandenhout 1984). Six 90-minute sessions of similar CO_2 inhalations were compared with 120 mg/d of propanolol. Over 2 weeks CO_2 was superior to propanolol for reducing fear of autonomic sensations and agoraphobic avoidance. Although improvement was noted to 6-month follow-up, details were not supplied, and the crossover design precludes conclusions about long-term gains.

Lactate-induced anxiety was also tried in an exposure paradigm in uncontrolled work from which conclusions are hard to draw (Bonn et al. 1973).

Exposure to the ES with Physical Adjuvants

The effect of respiratory relief at the onset of very brief live exposure was studied in 15 specific phobics, all but 2 of animals (Orwin et al. 1975). In a randomized crossover design, patients had up to 8 exposure trials per session, each trial lasting up to 15 seconds, in 1 of 3 conditions—exposure alone, respiratory relief, or augmented respiratory relief. In respiratory relief the patient took a deep breath, exhaled maximally, held her breath while pinching her nostrils for as long as possible, and, on restarting breathing, pressed a button to bring the ES nearer. In augmented respiratory relief, after maximum exhalation, instead of breath holding, patients maximally inhaled a CO_2/O_2 mixture and then pinched their nostrils, and so on.

By the end of treatment both respiratory relief groups were better than those with brief exposure alone, which did not improve; differences between the two respiratory relief groups were not reported. However, ratings were not blind, exposure homework was uncontrolled, and all cases had respiratory relief at follow-up, so conclusions from follow-up are not possible.

A related paradigm is aversion relief at the onset of exposure (Solyom et al. 1973a). Forty airplane phobics had one of four treatments: (1) fantasy desensitization and viewing films of flying; (2) aversion relief (subjects wrote their own phobic narrative, which was taped, and then had relief from finger shocks while listening to this narrative and while watching flight films); (3) same as (2) but without shocks; and (4) group discussion of flying fears and other experiences. Before ending their sessions all patients met a pilot and discussed air travel at an airport, and then had a 15-minute practice flight as a group with the therapist. All four conditions thus had some exposure in vivo, and all groups improved. In another aversion relief study of agora-, social, and specific phobics, outcome was very similar for aversion relief with taped exposure versus fantasy desensitization (Solyom et al. 1973).

Psychosurgery

The effect of psychosurgery in OCD was reviewed in Chapter 13. Further uncontrolled reports noted that a few ocs were improved after gamma capsulotomy at 3- and 7-year follow-up (Hindus et al. 1985), and that 78% of 49 ocs were improved up to 20 months after limbic leucotomy (Kelly & Cobb 1985).

In agoraphobia a controlled study examined the issue (Marks et al. 1966). That was a retrospective comparison 5 years after treatment, of 22 severe chronic agoraphobics who had had a modified frontal leucotomy with matched cases who had had other treatment. Leucotomy patients did better than controls on phobias and general anxiety, and work adjustment improved markedly. Personality changes were mild and unrelated to outcome. Maximum improvement of background anxiety occurred within the first 3 months, whereas phobias continued to improve after the first year. The findings were like those of another retrospective controlled study, of bimedial leucotomy in severe chronic ocs (Tan et al. 1971).

These studies were done before effective behavioral treatment had become available for phobic and oc disorders. Today psychosurgery would never be recommended for these conditions except for a tiny minority of chronic cases in whom adequate systematic exposure and drug treatment had been repeatedly tried and failed. Detailed studies are needed of the long-term outcome of psychosurgery in chronic phobics and ocs who had previously failed to improve with exposure treatment.

SUMMARY

All but 2 studies of antidepressants in agoraphobia were of imipramine or phenelzine, most finding an effect on phobias. In 11 imipramine studies the drug effect on agoraphobia was positive in 8, absent in 2, and in one it was positive for global improvement without a measure of phobias. Of 6 phenelzine studies 4 found a drug effect on agoraphobia. Therapeutic drug action is slow to start, within 4 weeks, and rises to a maximum in 12 weeks or more. Relapse is usual on stopping antidepressants even after they have been taken for many months.

Initial depression did not correlate with agoraphobic outcome to antidepressants in the only 2 studies of this point. Nevertheless, where other criteria of a relation between mood and phobic outcome were studied, (i) phobias improved more in those who had been depressed at the start, (ii) depression as well as phobia improved more often than not, (iii) depression improved a bit earlier than phobia, and (iv) mood at the start had been normal in both negative studies and depressed in 7 of the 9 positive studies. When they had an effect, antidepressants were widely patholytic, reducing hostility and anger as well as phobias, panic, and depression. Where this could be examined with imipramine, panic improved a bit later than depression or anxiety and did not improve if antiexposure was added to the drug, indicating that panic was not the main target of drug action. Antidepressants seem fairly nonspecific relievers of distress on a broad front in anxiety disorders as a whole.

Antidepressants made no difference to outcome of live exposure in 3 studies and enhanced it in 2. The effect of imipramine was virtually abolished by anti-exposure instructions in the one study of this issue. Live exposure was effective in the 5 studies testing this.

Barbiturates have only been studied intravenously, with unpromising outcome. Oral benzodiazepines reduce fear rapidly, but relapse is usual soon after stopping them and there is a risk of drug dependence. Only 1 of 4 studies of beta-blockers was encouraging, and that was to enhance exposure.

Drugs have the attraction of being easy to prescribe and to take. Antidepressants have the disadvantage of taking several weeks to start acting though side effects start straight away and may contribute to the high dropout rate. All phobia-reducing drugs have undesirable side effects and potential hazards, as well as a high relapse rate when drugs cease. Exposure therapy has the disadvantage of needing more effort from the patient than mere swallowing of pills, but has no drug side effects and relapse is not a major problem.

Serious study of drugs for clinical social phobics has not yet begun. Single doses of beta-blockers have helped musicians perform a bit better, but have not been compared with exposure.

Imipramine had no effect on specific phobias. Of single-dose studies, waning diazepam facilitated exposure therapy in the short-term, while peak diazepam reduced avoidance and tolamolol reduced tachycardia during a brief exposure test. No drugs have been examined for long term effects in specific phobias, a vital point given how effective unmedicated exposure is for them.

In school phobia, high dose imipramine in a sample including cases of short duration helped both the phobia and associated depression, but moderate doses of clomipramine in chronic cases did not help either problem.

In 9 of 10 controlled studies of OCD, clomipramine reduced oc symptoms (Table 16.2, Column A) and usually depression and anxiety as well. The link of mood with oc outcome to drugs was complex. Clomipramine improved mood as well as oc symptoms in 8 of 10 studies and fall in depression correlated with that in oc symptoms in 3 of 3 studies. On the other hand, initially most versus least depressed cases had more oc reduction in only 2 of 7 studies, and initial mood correlated with oc reduction in only 1 of 7 studies.

Clomipramine could take up to 10 weeks to have maximum effect which waned by the 9th month on drug, despite frequent relapse on ceasing medication, and there was no effect over 1–5-year followup. Clomipramine produced a fair number of side effects, especially persistent anorgasmia. In contrast, exposure causes rituals to start reducing within hours (though it needs to continue for weeks or months) and usually confers lasting benefit, without drug side effects.

Two studies compared clomipramine and exposure. In one, drug and exposure reduced rituals similarly in the short-term, though drug improved mood more. In the other study a clomipramine effect on oc symptoms was virtually abolished by antiexposure instructions; and again, drug improved mood more. In OCD, clomipramine can only be recommended with confidence as an adjunct to exposure and in the presence of dysphoric mood; even then, it was not significantly superior to other tricyclics such as amitriptyline, nortriptyline, and desimipramine. Design problems preclude conclusions from one study finding that clomipramine was better than desimipramine and zimelidine. No drug effect on oc symptoms was found in 2 studies of desimipramine, in one study each of imipramine, zimelidine, clorgyline, nisoxetine, and clonidine, and in 2 studies of lithium. In one study imipramine failed to help oc symptoms but did reduce depression.

Pilot studies in agoraphobics have tried exposure paradigms using anxiety induced by CO_2 inhalation or lactate infusion, but their results seem no better than straightforward exposure to the ES. The same holds for attempts to combine exposure with the relief of inhaling after prolonged breathholding or of stopping a series of shocks. Systematic studies are needed of the value of psychosurgery for chronic agoraphobics and ocs who failed to improve with adequate exposure and drug treatment.

References

Abbreviations

APA   American Psychiatric Association
WPA   World Psychiatric Association
AABT   Association for Advancement of Behavior Therapy
EABT   European Association of Behavior Therapy
Am   American
Br   British
Can   Canadian
bz   benzodiazepine
oc   obsessive-compulsive
OCD   obsessive-compulsive disorder

Abe K (1972). Phobias and nervous symptoms in childhood and maturity: Persistence and associations. *Brit J Psychiat, 120,* 275–283.

Abraham K (1913b). A constitutional basis of locomotor anxiety. In *Selected papers* (1948) Hogarth, London (cited by Edward Weiss, 1964).

Adams DB, Baccelli G, Mancia G et al. (1968). Cardiovascular changes during preparation for fighting behaviour in the cat. *Nature, 220,* 1239–1240.

Adams JR, Wahby VS, & Giller EL (1985). EEG of panic disorder and narcolepsy. Paper to APA. Dallas, May.

Adams PL (1973). *Obsessive children. A sociopsychiatric study.* Brunner/Mazel, New York. Butterworths, London.

Ader R (1982). Conditioned immunopharmacologic effects. In *Abstracts of APA* (p. 111). Toronto, May.

Ader R & Cohen N (1982). Behaviorally conditioned immunosuppression and murine systemic Lupus erythematosus. *Science, 215,* 1534–1536.

Ader R, Cohen N, & Bovbjerg D (1983). Immunoregulation by behavioral conditioning. *Trends in pharma Sci, 4,* 78–80.

Agras S (1966). Stimulus-response relationships in phobia. Paper to IV World Psychiatry Congress. Madrid, September.

Agras WS (1985). *Panic: Facing fears, phobias and anxiety.* Freeman, NY.

Agras S, Sylvester D, & Oliveau D (1969). The epidemiology of common fears and phobias. *Compr Psychiat, 10,* 151–156.

Agras WS, Chapin N, & Oliveau DC (1972). The natural history of phobia: Course and prognosis. *Arch Gen Psychiat, 26,* 315–317.

Agulnik PL (1970). The spouse of the phobic patient. *Br J Psychiat, 117,* 59–67.

Ahrenfeldt RH (1958). *Psychiatry in the British Army in the Second World War.* Columbia University Press, NY

Ainsworth M, Blehar M, Waters E, & Wall S (1978). *Patterns of attachment. A psychological study of the stranger situation.* Erlbaum, Hillsdale, NJ.

Aitken PP (1974). Aversive stimulation and rat's preference for areas differing in novelty value and brightness. *Animal Behaviour, 22,* 731–764.

Aitken RCB et al. (1971). Treatment of flying phobia in aircrew. *Am J Psychother, 25,* (4) 530–542.

Aitken RCB, Lister JA, & Main CJ (1981). Identification of features associated with flying phobias in aircrew. *Br J Psychiat, 139,* 38–42.

Akhtar S, Wig NN, Varma VK, Pershad D, & Verma SK (1975). Phenomenological analysis of symptoms in obsessive-compulsive neurosis. *Br J Psychiat, 127,* 342–348.

Akil H, Madden J, Patrick RL et al. (1976). Opiates and endogenous opioid peptides. In *Pain & Society,* Kosterlitz HW & Terenius LY (Ed.) Elsevier, NY.

Akiyama M (1968). Effects of extinction techniques on avoidance response. *Bulletin of the Faculty of Education, Hiroshima University, 17,* 173.

Akiyama M (1969). Relation between extinction techniques and extinction of avoidance response in albino rats. *Jap Ann Animal Psychol, 19,* 15.

Alanen YO (1966). The family in the pathogenesis of schizophrenia and neurotic disorders. *Act Psychiat Scand, 42,* (Supp. 189), 1.

Alcock J (1979). *Animal Behaviour: An evolutionary approach.* Sinauer Associates, Sunderland, MA.

Aldridge-Smith J (1974). Personality in school non-attenders. Unpublished MSc thesis, University of Glasgow.

Alexander RD (1975). The search for a general theory of behavior. *Beh Sci, 20,* 77–100.

Ali-Cherif A, Royere ML, Gosset A, Poncet M, Salomon G, & Khalil R (1984). Troubles du comportement et de l'activité mentale aprés intoxication oxycarbonée. *Revue Neurologique, 140,* 401–405.

Alkon DL (1983). Learning in a marine snail. *Sci Am, 249,* 64–74.

Allsopp LF, Cooper GL, & Poole PH (1984). Clomipramine and diazepam for agoraphobia and social phobia in general practice. *Current Med Res Opinion, 9,* 64–70.

Alström JE, Nordlund CL, Persson G et al. (1984). Four treatment methods in agoraphobic women. *Act Psychiat Scand, 70,* 1–17.

Alström JE, Nordlund CL, Persson G et al. (1984a). Four treatment methods in social phobic patients. *Act Psychiat Scand, 70,* 97–110.

Ambrose JA (1961). Development of the smiling response in early infancy. In BM Foss (Ed.), *Determinants of infant behaviour* (vol. I, p. 181). Methuen, London.

Ambrose JA (1963). The concept of a critical period for the development of social responsiveness in early human infancy. In BM Foss (Ed.), *Determinants of infant behaviour* (vol. II, pp. 208–9). Methuen, London.

Amies PL, Gelder MG, & Shaw PM (1983). Social phobia: A comparative clinical study. *Br J Psychiat, 142,* 174–179.

Amsel A & Rashotte ME (1969). Transfer of experimenter-imposed slow-response patterns to extinction of a continuously rewarded response. *J Comp Physiol Psychol, 69,* 185–189.

Ananth J, Pecknold JC, Van den Steen N, & Engelsmann F (1981). Double-blind study of clomipramine and amitriptyline in obsessive neurosis. *Progress in Neuropsychopharm 5*, 257–262.

Anderson J (1977). Treatment of obsessive-compulsive disorder. Unpublished manuscript.

Andrew RJ (1956). Behaviour in conflict-situations, with special relevance to *Emberiza* spp. *Br J Animal Beh, 4*, 41–45.

Andrew RJ (1962). *Annals of New York Academy of Science 102*, 296–315.

Angel C, DeLuca DC, Newton JEO, & Reese WG (1982). Assessment of pointer dog behaviour. Drug effects and neurochemical correlates. *Pavlov J Biol Sci, 17*, 84–88.

Angelino H, Dollins J, & Mech EV (1956). Trends in the "fears and worries" of school children. *J Genet Psychol, 89*, 263–267.

Angst J & Dobler-Mikola A (1983). Anxiety states, panic and phobia in a young general population. In *World Psychiatry Congress Proceedings, Vienna.* Plenum, NY.

Appleby IL, Klein DF, Sachar EJ, & Levitt M (1981). Biomedical indices of lactate-induced panic. In Klein DF & Rabkin JJ (Eds.), *Anxiety: New research and changing concepts* (pp. 411–425). Raven, NY.

Archer J (1976). Organization of aggression and fear in vertebrates. In *Perspectives in Ethology,* Vol. 2, Bateson PPG & Klopfer P (Eds.), Plenum, NY.

Archer J (1979). Behavioural aspects of fear. In Sluckin W (Ed.), *Fear in animals and man* (ch. 3, pp. 56–85). Van Nostrand, NY.

Archer T, Sjoden P, & Nilsson L (1983). Contextural control of taste-aversion conditioning and extinction. In Balsam P & Tonie A (Eds.), *Context and learning.* Erlbaum, Hillsdale, NJ.

Argyle M & Kendon A (1967). The experimental analysis of social performance. In Berkowitz L (Ed.), *Advances in experimental social performance* (vol. 3). Academic Press, NY.

Arkowitz H, Christensen A, & Royce S (1975). Treatment of social inhibition by real-life practice. Paper to Amer Assoc of Beh Ther.

Armstrong EA (1955). *The wren.* Collins, London.

Armstrong HG (1936). A special form of functional psychoneuroses appearing in airplane pilots. *JAMA, 16*, 1347–1354.

Arnow BA, Taylor CB, Agras WS, & Telch MJ (1985). Enhancing agoraphobia treatment outcome by changing couple communication patterns. *Behav Ther* (in press).

Arrindell WA (1980). A factorial definition of agoraphobia. *Beh Res Ther, 18*, 229–242.

Arrindell WA & Emmelkamp PMG (1985). A test of the repression hypothesis in agoraphobics. *Psychol Med, 15*, 125–129.

Arrindell WA & Emmelkamp PMG (1985a). Psychological profile of the spouse of the female agoraphobic patient. *Br J Psychiat, 146*, 405–414.

Arrindell WA & Emmelkamp PMG (1986). Marital adjustment, intimacy and needs in female agoraphobics and their partners. *Br J Psychiat, 149*, 592–602.

Arrindell WA, Emmelkamp PMG, Brilman E, & Monsma A (1983). An inventory to assess parental rearing practices. *Act Psychiat Scand, 67*, 163–177.

Arrindell WA, Emmelkamp PMG, Monsma A, & Brilman E (1983a). Perceived Parental rearing practices in phobic disorders. *Br J Psychiat, 143*, 183–187.

Arrindell WA, Emmelkamp PMG, & Van der Ende J (1984). Phobic dimensions across samples, gender and nations. *Adv Beh Res Ther, 6*, 207–254.

Asberg M (1983). Biology and drug treatment of obsessive-compulsive disorders. Paper to World Psychiatric Assoc. Vienna, July.

Asberg M, Thorén P, & Bertilsson L (1982). Clomipramine treatment of obsessive-compulsive disorder: Biochemical and clinical aspects. *Psychopharm Bull, 18*, 13–21.

Ascher M (1979). Paradoxical intention in the treatment of urinary retention. *Beh Res Ther, 17,* 267–270.

Ascher M (1981). Paradoxical intention for agoraphobia. *Beh Res Ther, 19,* 533–542.

Ashem B (1963). The treatment of disaster phobia by systematic desensitisation. *Beh Res Ther, 1,* 81–84.

Averill JR, Opton EM, Lazarus RS (1969). Cross-cultural studies of psychophysiological responses during stress and emotion. *Internat J Psychol, 4,* 83–102.

Averill JR, Malmstrom EJ, Koriat A, & Lazarus RS (1972). Habituation to complex emotional stimuli. *J Abn Psychol, 80,* 20–28.

Ax AF (1953). The physiological differentiation between fear and anger. *Psychosom Med, 15,* 433–442.

Babcock HH & Powell DH (1982). Vasovagal fainting: Deconditioning an autonomic syndrome. *Psychosomatics, 23,* 969–973.

Bachneff SA & Engelsmann F (1983). Correlates of cerebral event-related slow potentials and psychopathology. *Can Psychol Med, 13,* 763–770.

Baer BL, Minichiello WE, & Jenike MA (1985). Behavioral treatment in 2 cases of OCD with concomitant bipolar affective disorder. *Am J Psychiat, 142,* 358–360.

Baerends GP (1975). An evaluation of the conflict hypothesis as an explanatory principle for the evolution of displays. In Baerends GP, Beer C, & Manning A (Eds.), *Function and evolution in behaviour.* Oxford University Press, NY.

Bagby E (1922). The etiology of phobias. *J Abnorm Psychol, 17,* 16–18.

Bailey HR, Dowling JL, & Davies E (1977). Cingulotractotomy for severe depression. In WH Sweet, S Obrador, & JG Martin-Rodriguez (Eds.), *Neurosurgical treatment in Psychiatry,* (pp. 229–251). University Park Press, Baltimore.

Baker H & Wills U (1978). School phobia: Classification and treatment. *Br J Psychiat, 132,* 492–499.

Baker H & Wills U (1979). School phobia children at work. *Br J Psychiat, 135,* 561–564.

Balderrama N & Maldonado H (1971). Habituation of the deimatic response in the mantid (*Stagmatoptera biocellata*). *J Comp Physiol Psychol, 75,* 98–106.

Ballenger J (Ed.) (1984). *Biological aspects of agoraphobia.* American Psychiatric Press, Washington, DC.

Ballenger JC, Post RM, Jimerson DC et al. (1983). Biochemical correlates of personality traits in normals. *Pers Indiv Diff, 4,* 615–625.

Ballenger JC, Post RM, Jimerson DC et al. (1984). Neurobiological correlates of depression and anxiety in normals. In Post RM & Ballenger JC (Eds.), *Neurobiology of mood disorders.* Williams & Wilkins, London.

Ballenger JC, Peterson GA, Cox DJ et al. (1984a). Norepinephrine and epinephrine in agoraphobia.In *Abstracts of the APA Annual Meeting* (Paper 30D, p. 82).

Ballenger J, Burrows G, & Swinson R (1985a). Alprazolam for panic disorder. In *Abstracts of the APA Annual Conference* (Abstract NP83). Dallas, May.

Ballenger JC, Burrows GD, Rubin RT et al. (1985b). Alprazolam treatment of agoraphobia/panic attacks. In *Abstracts of the World Congress of Biological Psychiatry* (Abstract 302.6, p. 227). Philadelphia, September.

Bamber JH (1974). The fears of adolescents. *J Genet Psychol, 125,* 127–140.

Bamber JH (1979). *The fears of adolescents.* Academic Press, London.

Bancroft JHJ (1983). *Human sexuality and its problems.* Churchill Livingstone, NY.

Bancroft JHJ & Marks IM (1968). Electric aversion therapy of sexual deviations. *Proc Roy Soc Med, 61,* 796–798.

Bandura A (1969). Principles of behavior modification. Holt, Rinehart & Winston, NY.

Bandura A (1977). Self-efficacy: Toward a unifying theory of behavioral change. *Psychol Rev, 84,* 191–215.

Bandura A (1983). Self-efficacy determinants of anticipated fears and calamities. *J Pers Soc Psychol, 45,* 464–469.

Bandura A, Blanchard E, & Ritter B (1969). Desensitization and modeling to induce behavioural, affective and attitudinal change. *J Pers Soc Psychol, 13,* 173.

Bandura A, Jeffery RW, & Wright CL (1974). Efficacy of participant modeling as a function of response induction aids. *J Abn Psychol, 83,* 56–64.

Barlow DH, Leitenberg H, Agras WS, & Wincze JP (1969). The transfer gap in systematic desensitization: An analogue study. *Beh Res Ther, 7,* 191–196.

Barlow DH (1985). The dimensions of anxiety disorders. In Tuma H & Maser J (Eds.) *Anxiety and anxiety disorders* (ch. 26, p. 479–500). Erlbaum, Hillsdale, NJ.

Barlow DH, Mavissakalian M, & Hay LR (1981). Couples treatment of agoraphobia: Changes in marital satisfaction. *Beh Res Ther, 19,* 245–255.

Barlow DH, O'Brien GT, & Last CG (1984). Couples treatment of agoraphobia. *Beh Ther, 15,* 41–58.

Barlow DH, Vermilyea J, Blanchard EB, Vermilyea BB, Di Nardo PA & Cerny JA (1985). The phenomenon of panic. *J Abn Psychol, 94,* 320–328.

Barlow GW (1977). *Modal action patterns.* In Sebeok TA (Ed.), *How animals communicate* (pp. 98–134). Indiana University Press, Indianapolis.

Barlow GW (1981). Genetics & development of behavior. In Immelmann K, Barlow GW, Petrinovich L, & Main M, *Behavioral development: The Bielefeld Interdisciplinary Project* (chap. 8, pp. 191–251). Cambridge University Press, NY.

Barnard CJ (1983). *Animal behaviour: Ecology and evolution.* Croom Helm, London.

Barnard GW, Flesher GK, & Steinbrook RM (1966). Treatment of urinary retention by aversive stimulus cessation and assertive training. *Beh Res Ther, 4,* 232–236.

Barnett SA (1975). *The rat: A study in behaviour.* University of Chicago Press, Chicago.

Barton R (1965). Diabetes insipidus and obsessional neurosis. *Lancet, 1,* 133–135.

Barton R (1976). Diabetes insipidus and obsessional neurosis. *Am J Psychiat, 133,* 235–236.

Bartrop RW, Lazarus L et al. (1977). Depressed lymphocyte function after bereavement. *Lancet, 1,* 834–836.

Basoglu M et al. (1986). Predictors of outcome with clomipramine and exposure in obsessive-compulsive ritualizers. (In preparation).

Basowitz H, Persky H, Korchin SJ, & Grinker RR (1955). *Anxiety and stress. An interdisciplinary study of a life situation.* McGraw-Hill, NY.

Bateson PPG (1964). Effect of similarity between rearing and testing conditions on chicks following an avoidance response. *J Comp Physiol Psychol, 57,* 100–103.

Bateson PPG (1976). Rules and reciprocity in development. In Bateson PPG & Hinde RA (Eds.), *Growing points in ethology.* Cambridge University Press, Cambridge.

Bateson PPG (1981). Control of sensitivity to the environment. In Immelmann K, Barlow GW, Petrinovich L, & Main M (Eds.), *Behavioral development: The Bielefeld Interdisciplinary Project.* Cambridge University Press, NY.

Bauer DH (1976). An exploratory study of developmental changes in children's fears. *J Child Psychol Psychiat, 17,* 69–74.

Baum M (1969a). Extinction of an avoidance response following response prevention: Some parametric investigations. *Can J Psychol, 23,* 1–10.

Baum M (1969b). Socially facilitated extinction of an avoidance response during response prevention (flooding) in rats. *Beh Res Ther, 7,* 57–62.

Baum M (1972a). Flooding (response prevention) in rats: Effect of immediate vs. delayed flooding and of changed illuminations during flooding. *Can J Psychol, 26,* 100.

Baum M (1973b). Extinction of avoidance in rats: The effects of chlorpromazine and methylphenidate administered in conjunction with flooding (response prevention). *Beh Res Ther,11,* 165.

Baum M (1976). Instrumental learning. In Feldman MP & Broadhurst A (Eds.), *Theoretical and experimental bases of the behaviour therapist.* Wiley, NY.

Baum M & Leclerc R (1974). Irrelevant stress experience vs. response prevention (flooding) interpolated between avoidance acquisition and extinction in rats. *J Psychiat Res, 10,* 307–314.

Baum M, Foidart DS, & Lapointe A (1974). Rapid extinction of a conditioned tasted aversion following unreinforced intraperitoneal infection of the fluid CS. *Physiol Beh, 12,* 871–873.

Baum M, Pereira J, & Leclerc R (1985). Extinction of avoidance responding in rats is facilitated by noise. *Can J Psychol, 39,* 529–535.

Baum M, Roy S, & Leclerc R (1985a). Failure of a peripheral muscle relaxant (suxomethonium bromide) to increase the efficacy of flooding (response prevention) in rats. *Beh Res Ther, 23,* 361–364.

Bear DM (1985). Interictal behavior in temporal lobe epilepsy. Paper to APA. Dallas, May.

Bear DM & Fedio P (1977). Quantitative analysis of interictal behavior in temporal lobe epilepsy. *Arch Neurol, 34,* 454–467.

Bear D, Schenk L, & Benson H (1981). Increased autonomic responses to neutral and emotional stimuli in patients with temporal lobe epilepsy. *Am J Psychiat, 138,* 843–845.

Beard GM (1879). Morbid fear as a symptom of nervous disease. *Hos Gaz, 6,* 305–308.

Bebbington P, Contractor N, Hurry J, & Tennant C (1982). Prevalence of anxiety and obsessional symptoms in the Camberwell Community. (Unpublished data).

Beck AT & Emery G (1985). *Anxiety disorders and phobias: A cognitive perspective.* Basic, NY.

Beck AT, Laude R, & Bohnert M (1974). Ideational components of anxiety neurosis. *Arch Gen Psychiat, 31,* 319–325.

Beech HR (Ed.) (1974). *Obsessional states.* Methuen, London.

Beech HR & Liddell A (1974). Decision making, mood states, and ritualistic behaviour among obsessional patients. In Beech HR (Ed.), *Obsessional states* (ch. 6, pp. 161–174). Methuen, London.

Beech HR & Vaughan M (1978). *Behavioural treatment of obsessional states.* Wiley, NY.

Beech HR, Ciesielski KT, & Gordon PK (1983). Further observations of evoked potentials in obsessional patients. *Br J Psychiat, 142,* 605–609.

Behar D, Rapoport J, Berg C, Denkla M, Mann L, Cox C, Fedio P, Zahn T, & Wolfman M (1984). Computerized tomography and neuropsychological test measures in adolescents with OCD. Am J Psychiat, 141, 363–368.

Beidel DC, Turner SM, & Dancu CV (1985). Physiological, cognitive and behavioral aspects of social anxiety. *Beh Res Ther, 23,* 109–117.

Belenky GL & Jones FD (1983). Implications of Arab-Israeli wars for psychiatric casualties. In *WPA Abstracts* (Abstract 5250, p. 71). Vienna, July.

Belenky GL & Taube SL (1985). Combat reaction spectrum disorder. Paper to APA. Dallas, May.

Belfer PL & Glass CR (1982). Agoraphobic anxiety and fear of fear: A cognitive-attentional model. Paper to AABT. Los Angeles, November.

Bender L (1935). Anatomopathological data on personality. *Am J Psychiat, 92,* 325–351.

Benedikt M (1870). Uber Platschwindel. *Allg Wien Med Ztg, 15,* 488.

Benjamin S & Kincey J (1981). Standardized behavioural treatment for agoraphobic inpatients by untrained therapists. *Br J Psychiat, 138,* 423–428.

Bentley DR (1975). Single gene cricket mutations: Effects on behaviour, sensilla, sensory neurons and identified interneurons. *Science, 187,* 760–764.

Berg I (1969). School phobia—its classification and relationship to dependency. *J Child Psychol Psychiat, 10,* 123–141.

Berg I (1976). School phobia in the children of agoraphobic women. *Br J Psychiat, 128,* 86–89.

Berg I (1984). School refusal. *Br J Hosp Med,* January, 59–60.

Berg I (1985). Teenage school refusers grow up: A 10-year followup of 168 inpatients. *Br J Psychiat, 147,* 366–370.

Berg I & Collins T (1974). Wilfulness in school-phobic adolescents. *Br J Psychiat, 125,* 468–469.

Berg I & Jackson A (1985). Teenage school refusers grow up: Followup of 168 subjects 10 years after inpatient treatment. *Br J Psychiat, 147,* 366–371.

Berg I & McGuire R (1971). Are school phobic adolescents overdependent? *Br J Psychiat, 119,* 167–168.

Berg I, Butler A, McGuire R (1972). Birth order and family size of school-phobic adolescents. *Br J Psychiat, 121,* 509–514.

Berg I, Marks IM, McGuire R, & Lipsedge M (1972). School phobia and agoraphobia. *Psychol Med, 4,* 428–434.

Berg I, Butler A, Pritchard J (1974a). Psychiatric illness in the mothers of school-phobic adolescents. *Br J Psychiat, 125,* 466–467.

Berggren U & Linde A (1984). Dental fear and avoidance: Two modes of treatment. *J Dent Res, 63,* 1223–1227.

Berkun MM (1962). Performance decrement under psychological stress. Human Resources Office, Presidio of Monterey, CA.

Berlyne DE (1960). *Conflict, arousal and curiosity* (pp. 122–127). McGraw-Hill, London.

Berman L (1942). The obsessive-compulsive neurosis in children. *J Nerv Ment Dis, 95,* 26–39.

Berman JS & Katzev RD (1972). Factors involved in the rapid elimination of avoidance behaviour. *Beh Res Ther, 10,* 247.

Bernadt MW, Silverstone T, & Singleton W (1980). Beta-adrenergic blockade in phobic subjects. *Br J Psychiat, 137,* 452–457.

Berney T, Kolvin I, Bhate SR et al. (1981). School phobia: clomipramine and short-term outcome. *Br J Psychiat, 138,* 110–118.

Bernstein IL & Webster MM (1980). Learned taste aversions in humans. *Physiol Beh, 25,* 363–366.

Bernstein K (1978). Learned taste aversions in children receiving chemotherapy. *Science, 200,* 1302–1303.

Bertenthal BI, Campos JJ, & Caplovitz KS (1983). Self-produced locomotion: An organizer of emotional, cognitive, and social development in infancy. In Emde RN & Harmon R (Eds.), *Continuities and discontinuities in development.* Plenum, NY.

Bertram BCR (1976). Kin selection in lions and evolution. In Bateson PPG & Hinde RA (Eds.). *Growing points in ethology.* Cambridge University Press, London.

Bertram BCR (1978). Living in groups: predators and prey. In Krebs JR & Davies NB (Eds.), *Behavioural ecology* (ch. 3, pp. 64–96). Blackwell, London.

Betts TA (1981). Depression, anxiety and epilepsy. In Reynolds EH & Trimble MR (Eds.), *Epilepsy and psychiatry* (ch. 6). Churchill Livingstone, London.

Bianchi GN (1971). Origins of disease phobia. *Aust NZ J Psychiat, 5,* 241–257.

Bibb JL & Chambless DL (1986). Alcohol use and abuse among diagnosed agoraphobics. *Beh Res Ther, 24,* 49–58.

Bierer LM, Uhde TW, Boulenger J-P, Jimerson DC, Linnoila M, & Post RM (1985). Caffeine: Anxiogenic and neuroendocrine effects. Paper to APA. Dallas, May.

Binder J, Dobler-Mikola A, & Angst J (1982). Prospective epidemiological study of psychiatric syndromes in young adults. *Psychother Psychosom, 38,* 128–140.

Bingley T & Persson A (1978). EEG in chronic OCD before and after bilateral anterior capsulotomy. *Electroenceph Clin Neurophysiol, 44,* 691–696.

Bingley T, Leksell L, Meyerson BA, & Rylander G (1977). Long term results of anterior capsulotomy in chronic OCD. In W Sweet, S Obrador & JG Martin-Rodriquez (Eds.), *Neurosurgical treatment in psychiatry.* University Park Press, Baltimore.

Biran M & Wilson GT (1981). Cognitive vs behavioral methods in the treatment of phobic disorders. *J Consult Clin Psychol, 49,* 886–899.

Biran M, Augusto F, & Wilson G (1981). In vivo exposure vs cognitive restructuring in the treatment of scriptophobia. *Beh Res Ther, 19,* 525–532.

Birch LL & Marlin DW (1982). "I don't like it, I've never tried it": The effects of familiarity on 2-year olds' food preferences. *Appetite, 4,* 353–360.

Bishay N (1985). Therapeutic manipulation of nightmares and the management of neurosis. *Br J Psychiat, 147,* 67–70.

Black A (1974). The natural history of obsessional neurosis. In HR Beech (Ed.), *Obsessional states* (ch. 2, pp. 19–54). Methuen, London.

Black JL & Keane TM (1982). Implosive therapy in the treatment of combat-related fears in a World War II veteran. *J Beh Ther Exp Psychiat, 13,* 163–165.

Blacker CP & Gore AT (1955). *Triennial statistical report.* Bethlem Royal and Maudsley Hospitals, London.

Blagg NR & Yule W (1984). Behavioural treatment of school refusal. *Beh Res Ther, 22,* 119–127.

Blagg N (1977). A detailed strategy for the rapid treatment of school phobics. *Bull Br Assoc Behav Psychother, 5,* 70–75.

Blagg N (1979). The behavioural treatment of school refusal. Unpublished doctoral dissertation, University of London.

Blanchard EB (1975). Brief flooding treatment for a debilitating revulsion. *Beh Res Ther, 13,* 193–195.

Blanchard RJ & Blanchard DC (1981). The organization and modeling of animal aggression. In Brain PF & Benton D (Eds.), *The biology of aggression.* Sythoff & Noordhoff, Amsterdam.

Blanchard RJ, Mast M, & Blanchard DC (1975). Stimulus control of defensive reactions in the albino rat. *J Comp Physiol Psychol, 88,* 81–88.

Blanchard DC, Blanchard RJ, Lee EMC, & Williams G (1981). Taming in the wild Norway rat after lesions in the basal ganglia. *Physiol Beh, 27,* 995–1000.

Blanchard DC, Williams G, Lee EMC, & Blanchard RJ (1981a). Taming of wild *Rattus norvegicus* by lesions of the mesencephalic central gray. *Physiol Psychol, 9,* 157–163.

Bland K & Hallam RS (1981a). Relationship between graded exposure and marital satisfaction in agoraphobics. *Per Indiv Diff, 1,* 282–287.

Bland K & Hallam RS (1981). Relationship between response to graded exposure and marital satisfaction in agoraphobics. *Beh Res Ther, 19,* 335–338.

Blank K & Perry S (1984). Relationship of psychological processes during delirium to outcome. *Am J Psychiat, 141,* 843–847.

Blass EM, Ganchrow JR, & Steiner JE (1984). Classical conditioning in newborn humans 2–48 hours of age. *Infant Beh Dev, 7,* 223–235.

Blest AD (1957). Function of eyespot patterns in the Lepidoptera. *Behaviour, 11,* 210–254.

Bloom FE (1984). *Brain, mind and behavior.* Freeman, San Francisco.

Blum MS (1974). Pheromonal sociability in the hymenoptera. In Birch MD (Ed.), *Pheromones* (pp. 222–245). North Holland, London.

Blumberg SH & Izard CE (1985). Patterns of emotion in anxious and depressed children. In Tuma H & Maser J (Eds.), *Anxiety and anxiety-related disorders.* Erlbaum, Hillsdale, NJ.

Blurton-Jones NG (1959). Experiments on the causation of the threat postures of Canada geese. *Rep. Severn Wildfowl Inst 1960,* 46–52.

Blythe P & McGlown D (1982). Agoraphobia. *World Medicine,* London, July.

Boersma K, Den Hengst S, Dekker J, & Emmelkamp PMG (1976). Exposure vs response prevention in oc patients. *Beh Res Ther, 14,* 19–24.

Boisvert JM, Marchand A, & Gaudette G (1983). Group treatment of agoraphobia with or without partners. Paper to AABT. Washington, DC, December.

Bolles RC (1970). Species-specific defense reactions and avoidance learning. *Psychol Rev, 77,* 32–48.

Bolles RC & Fanselow MS (1980). A perceptual-defensive-recuperative model of fear and pain. *Beh Brain Sci, 3,* 291–323.

Bolton D & Turner T (1984). Obsessive-compulsive neurosis with conduct disorder in adolescence: Two cases. *J Child Psychol Psychiat, 25,* 133–139.

Bolton D, Collins S, & Steinberg D (1983). The treatment of obsessive-compulsive disorder in adolescence. *Br J Psychiat, 142,* 456–464.

Bolwig N (1959). Study of the behaviour of the chacma baboon *Papio ursinus. Behaviour, 14,* 136–163.

Bond DD (1952). *The love and fear of flying.* International Universities Press, NY.

Bonn JA, Harrison J, & Rees WL (1971). Lactate induced anxiety: Therapeutic applications. *Br J Psychiat, 119,* 468–471.

Bonn JA, Harrison J, & Rees L (1973). Lactate infusion in the treatment of "free-floating" anxiety. *J Can Psychiat Assoc, 18,* 41–46.

Bonn JA, Readhead CP, & Timmons BH (1984). Enhanced adaptive behavioural response in agoraphobics pretreated with breathing retraining. *Lancet, 2,* 665–669.

Boren JL, Suarez SD, & Gallup GG (1981). P-chloroamphentamine: Effects on tonic immobility, activity and temperature in chickens. *J Comp Physiol Psychol, 95,* 991–1002.

Borkovec T (1982). Functional CS exposure in the treatment of phobias. In Boulougouris J (Ed.,) *Learning theory approaches to psychiatry* (pp. 95–102). Wiley, NY.

Borkovec TD (1985). Cognitive avoidance, anticipated frustrative nonreward, and issues of control in human anxiety. In Tuma H & Maser J (Eds.), *Anxiety and anxiety disorders* (ch. 25, p. 463–478). Erlbaum, Hillsdale, NJ.

Borkovec T & Sides J (1979). Relaxation and expectance in fear reduction via graded imaginal exposure to feared stimuli. *Beh Res Ther, 17,* 529–540.

Borland LR (1962). Odontophobia–inordinate fear of dental treatment. *Proceedings of the Dental Clinics of North America* (pp. 683–695), November.

Boudewyns PA & Shipley RH (1983). *Flooding and implosive therapy.* Plenum, NY.

Boudoulas H, King B, & Wooley CF (1983). Mitral valve prolapse: A marker for anxiety? In *Abstracts of the WPA Conference,* (Abstract S779, p. 176). Vienna, July.

Boulenger JP, Udhe TW, Wolff EA, & Post RM (1984). Increased sensitivity to caffeine in panic disorders. *Arch Gen Psychiat, 41*, 1067–1071.

Boulougouris JC (1977). Variables affecting outcome in obsessive-compulsive patients treated by flooding. In Boulougouris JC & Rabavilas AD (Eds.), *Treatment of phobic and obsessive-compulsive disorders* (ch. 9, pp. 73–84). Pergamon, Oxford.

Boulougouris JC (1982). *Learning theory applications to psychiatry.* Wiley, Chichester.

Boulougouris JC & Rabavilas A (1977). *The treatment of phobic and obsessive-compulsive disorders.* Pergamon, NY.

Bourliere F (1955). *The natural history of mammals.* Harrap, London.

Bourque P & Ladouceur R (1980). An investigation of various performance-based treatments with acrophobics. *Beh Res Ther, 18*, 161–170.

Bovet D (1977). Strain differences and learning in the mouse. In Oliverio A (Ed.), *Genetics, environment and intelligence* (pp. 79–92). Elsevier/North Holland Biomedical Press, NY.

Bovet D, Bovet-Nitti F, & Oliverio A (1969). Genetic aspects of learning and memory in mice. *Science, 163*, 139–149.

Bowen RC & Kohout J (1979). The relationship between agoraphobia and primary affective disorders. *Can J Psychiat, 24*, 317–321.

Bowen RC, Cipywnyk D, D'Arcy C, Keegan D (1984). Alcoholism, anxiety disorders, and agoraphobia. *Alcoholism: Clinical and Experimental Research, 8*, 48–50.

Bowlby J (1973). *Attachment and loss* (vol. II: *Separation*). Basic Books, NY.

Boyd JH (1985). Panic: Prevalence risk factors and treatment rates. Paper to APA. Dallas, May.

Boyd TL (1981). The effects of shock intensity on fear incubation (enhancement). *Beh Res Ther, 19*, 413–418.

Brady JV (1966). Autonomic and endocrine correlates of emotional conditioning in rhesus monkeys. In *Abstracts of XVIII International Congress of Psychology,* (vol. I, p. 224). Moscow, August.

Brantigan CO, Brantigan TA, & Joseph W (1982). Beta blockers and beta stimulation in stage fright. *J Med, 72*, 88–94.

Breier A & Charney DS (1985). The natural course of agoraphobia-panic disorders. Paper to APA. Dallas, May.

Breier A, Charney DS, & Heninger GR (1984). Major depression in patients with agoraphobia and panic disorder. *Arch Gen Psychiat, 41*, 1129–1135.

Breit M (1982). Separation anxiety in mothers of latency-age fearful children. *J Abn Child Psychol, 10*, 135–144.

Brickner RM, Rosner A, & Munro R (1940). Physiological aspects of the obsessive state. *Psychosom Med, 11*, 369–383.

Bridges M, Yeragani VK, Rainey JM & Pohl R (1986). DST in panic attacks. *J Biolo Psychiat.*

Bridges PK, Goktepe EO, & Maratos J (1973). Obsessional neurosis and depression after psychosurgery. *Br J Psychiat, 123*, 663–674.

Broadbent DE & MHP, Phillpotts RG, & Wallace J (1984). Prediction of experimental colds in volunteers by psychological factors. *J Psychosom Res, 28*, 511–523.

Broadhurst PL (1975). The Maudsley reactive and nonreactive strains of rats: A survey. *Beh Gene, 5*, 299–319.

Broadhurst PL (1981). The making and unmaking of behaviour. In Richard Lynn (Ed.) *Dimensions of personality* (ch. 3, pp. 39–51). Pergamon, NY.

Brodsky L, Zuniga JS, Casenas ER et al. (1983). Refractory anxiety: A masked epileptiform disorder? *Psychiat J Univ Ottawa, 8*, 42–45.

Bronson GW (1968). The fear of novelty. *Psychol Bull, 69,* 350–358.

Bronson GW (1969). Fear of visual novelty: Developmental patterns in males and females. *Dev Psychol, 2,* 33–40.

Bronson GW (1972). Infants' reactions to unfamiliar persons and novel objects. *Monographs of the Society for Research in Child Development, 37,* (3).

Brooks J & Lewis M (1976). Infants' responses to strangers: Midget, adult and child. *Child Dev, 47,* 323–332.

Brower J & Brower LP (1962). Experimental studies of mimicry 6: The reaction of toads (*Bufo terrestris*) to honeybees (*Apis mellifera*) and their dronefly mimics (*Eristalis vinetorum*).

Brower LP (1969). Ecological chemistry. *Science, 220,* 22–29.

Brown FW (1942). Heredity in the psychoneuroses. *Proc Roy Soc Med, 35,* 785–788.

Brown GW, Harris T, & Copeland JR (1977). Depression and loss. *Br J Psychiat, 130,* 1–18.

Brown W (1920). In *Symposium on the revival of emotional memories and its therapeutic significance. Br J Med Psychol, 1,* 30.

Brush FR (1971). Retention of aversively motivated behaviour. In Brush FR (Ed.), *Aversive conditioning and learning.* Academic, NY.

Brush FR (1977). Behavioral and endocrine characteristics of rats bred for good and poor avoidance behavior. *Act Nerv Super, 19,* 254.

Brush FR, Froehlich JC, & Sakellaris PC (1979). Genetic selection for avoidance behaviour in the rat. *Beh Genet, 9,* 309–316.

Bryant B, Trower P, Yardley K, Urbieta H, & Letemendia FJJ (1976). Social inadequacy among psychiatric outpatients. *Psychol Med, 6,* 101–112.

Bryant B & Trower PE (1974). Social difficulty in a student sample. *Br J Educ Psychol, 44,* 13–21.

Buglass D, Clarke J, Henderson AS, Kreitman N, & Presley AS (1977). A study of agoraphobic housewives. *Psychol Med, 7,* 73–86.

Bunnell BN (1966). Lesions of the amygdala and septal nuclei: Effects upon aggressiveness and social dominance in rodents. In *Abstracts of the XVIII International Congress of Psychology* (vol. I, pp. 314–315). Moscow, August.

Burns LE, Thorpe GL, Cavallaro A, & Gosling J (1986). Agoraphobia 8 years after behavioral treatment. *Beh ther, 17,* 580–591.

Burrows GD, Newman TR, & Davis B (Eds.). (1984). *Anti-anxiety agents.* Elsevier, NY.

Burton R (1621). *The Anatomy of Melancholy* (11th ed. 1813, vol. 1). London.

Butler G (1985). Exposure as a treatment for social phobia: Some instructive difficulties. *Beh Res Ther (in press).*

Butler G, Cullington A, Munby et al. (1984). Exposure and anxiety management in the treatment of social phobia. *J Consult Clin Psychol, 52,* 642–650.

Butler RA (1964). Reactions of rhesus monkeys to fear-provoking stimuli. *J Genet Psychol, 104,* 321–330.

Butynski TM (1982). Harem-male replacement and infanticide in the Blue Monkey (*Cercopithecus mitus stuhlmanni*) in the Kibale Forest, Uganda. *Am J Primatol, 3,* 1–22.

Bygott D (1972). Cannibalism among wild chimpanzees. *Nature, 238,* 410–411.

Caetano D & Roth M (1983). Separation between depressive disorders and anxiety state. In *WPA Proceedings* (Abstract S611, p. 144). Vienna, July.

Cameron O, Hollingsworth P, Nesse R, Curtis G, & Smith CB (1983). Platelet alpha$_2$ adrenoreceptors in panic anxiety. In *WPA Proceedings* (Abstract). Vienna, July.

Cameron OG et al. (1984). Response to adrenergic stimulation in panic disorder. Paper to APA Annual Meeting. Los Angeles, May.

Cameron OG, Kotun J, Lee MA, & Murphy S (1985). Diurnal variation of abnormal anxiety. Paper to APA. Dallas, May.

Cameron OG, Lee MA, Curtis GC, & McCann DS (1985a). Psychobiologic changes during spontaneous panic. Paper to APA. Dallas, May.

Camhi JM (1983). *Neuroethology: Nerve Cells and the natural behaviour of animals.* Sinauer Associates, Sunderland, MA.

Cammer L (1976). *Freedom from compulsion.* Simon & Schuster, NY.

Campbell JL, Sherman AD, & Petty F (1980). Diazepam anxiolytic activity in hippocampus. *Commun Psychopharm, 4,* 387–392.

Campos JJ (1976). Heart rate during infant emotional development in the infant. In Lipsitt LP (Ed.), *Developmental psychobiology.* Wiley, NY.

Campos JJ & Barrett KC (1984). New understanding of biological and cognitive influences on emotional development. In Izard C, Kagan J, & Zajonc R (Eds.), *Emotion, cognition and behavior.* Cambridge University Press, NY.

Campos JJ, Emde RN, Gaensbauer T, & Henderson C (1975). Cardiac and behavioral responses in infants' reactions to strangers. *Dev Psychol, 11,* 589–601.

Campos JJ, Hiatt S, Ramsay D, Henderson C, & Svejda M (1978). The emergence of fear on the visual cliff. In Lewis M & Rosenblum LA (Eds.), *The development of affect* (ch. 5, pp. 149–181). Plenum, NY.

Cannon WB (1915, 1929). *Bodily changes in pain, hunger, fear and rage. Researches into the function of emotional excitement.* Harper & Row, NY.

Cannon WB (1942). "Voodoo death." *Am Anthr, 44,* 169.

Capstick N & Seldrup J (1977). Birth abnormalities and subsequent development of obsessional symptoms. *Act Psychiat Scand, 56,* 427–431.

Capstick N & Seldrup J (1973). Phenomenological aspects of obsessional patients treated with clomipramine. *Br J Psychiat, 122,* 719–720.

Carasa P, Fernández J, Torrubia R, & Tobeña A (1978). Activaded electrodermal durante la adquisición y extinción, mediante dos procedimientos de inundación, de un condicionamiento de evitación en humanos. In *Proceedings of the Second World Congress of Biological Psychiatry, 800,* 175.

Carew TJ, Hawkins RD, & Kandel ER (1983). Differential classical conditioning of a defensive withdrawal reflex in *Aplysia Californica. Science, 219,* 397–400.

Carey G (1978). A clinical-genetic study of obsessional and phobic states. Doctoral dissertation, University of Minnesota.

Carey G (1982). Genetic influences on anxiety neurosis and agoraphobia. In Mathew RJ (Ed.), *The biology of anxiety* (ch. 4, pp. 37–50). Brunner/Mazel, NY.

Carey G & Gottesman I (1981). Twin and family studies of anxiety, phobic and obsessive disorders. In Klein DF & Rabkin J (Eds.), *Anxiety: new research and changing concepts.* (pp. 117–136). Raven, NY.

Carey G & Gottesman I (1982). Defining cases by genetic criteria. In Wing JK, Bebbington P, & Robins LN (Eds.), *What is a case? The problem of definition in psychiatric community surveys* (ch. 5, pp. 29–41). Grant McIntyre.

Carey G, Gottesman II, & Robins E (1984). Prevalence rates for the neuroses: Misguides to evaluating familiality. *Psychol Med,* (in press).

Carli G (1974). Blood pressure and heart-rate in the rabbit during animal hypnosis. *Electroenceph Clin Neurophysiol, 37,* 231–237.

Carlson K (1966). Aspects of avoidance learning stored subcortically. Paper presented to Eastern Psychological Association. New York, April.

Carr DB & Sheehan DV (1984). Panic anxiety: A new biological model. *J Clin Psychiat,* *45,* 323–330.

Carr DB, Sheehan DV, Surman OS et al. (1984). Lactate induced anxiety. In *Abstracts of the Annual Meeting of APA* (Abstract no. 30B). Los Angeles, May.

Carrington R (1963). *The mammals.* Time, NY.

Carroll ME, Dine HI, Levy CJ, & Smith JC (1975). Neophobia and enhanced neophobia in the albino rat. *Compar Physiol Psychol, 89,* 457–467.

Carruthers M & Taggart P (1973). Vagotonicity of violence: Biochemical and cardiac responses to violent films and TV programs. *Br Med J, 3,* 384–389.

Cassano GG, Castrogiovanni P, & Mauri M (1981). Chlorimipramine ± haloperidol and diazepam in phobic-oc neurosis. *Prog Neuropsychopharm, 5,* 129–138.

Cassidy WL, Flanagan NB, Spellman M, & Cohen ME (1957). 100 manic-depressive patients and 50 medically sick controls. *J Am Med Assoc, 164,* 1535–1546.

Catts S & McConaghy N (1975). Ritual prevention in the treatment of obsessive-compulsives. *Austr NZ J Psychiat, 9,* 37–41.

Caudill W & Doi LT (1963). Interrelations of psychiatry, culture and emotion in Japan. In Goldstein I (Ed.). Man's image in medicine and anthropology. Internat Univ Press, NY.

Caudill W & Schooler C (1969). Symptom patterns and background characteristics of Japanese psychiatric patients. In Caudill W & Lin T (Eds.). Mental health research in Asia and the Pacific. East-West Center Press, Honolulu.

Cavior N & Deutsch A (1975). Systematic desensitisation to reduce dream-induced anxiety. *J Nerv Ment Dis, 161,* 433–435.

Cellucci AJ & Lawrence PS (1979). The efficacy of systematic desensitisation in reducing nightmares. *J Beh Ther Exp Psychiat, 9,* 109–114.

Chambers I et al. (1982). Agoraphobia in India and Britain. Unpublished manuscript.

Chambless et al. (1982). Exposure and communications training in the treatment of agoraphobia. *Beh Res Ther, 20,* 219–231.

Chambless DL (1985). The relationship of severity of agoraphobia to associated psychopathology. *Beh Res Ther, 23,* 305–310.

Chambless DL & Goldstein AJ (1981). Clinical treatment of agoraphobia. In Mavissakalian M & Barlow DH (Eds.), *Phobia: psychological and pharmacological treatment.* Guildford, NY.

Chambless DL & Goldstein AJ (Eds.) (1983). *Agoraphobia: Multiple perspectives on theory and treatment.* Wiley, NY.

Chambless DL, Foa EB, Groves G, & Goldstein AJ (1979). Flooding with methohexitone in the treatment of agoraphobia. *Beh Res Ther, 17,* 243–251.

Chambless DL, Caputo GC, Bright P, & Gallagher R (1984). Fear of fear in agoraphobics. *J Cons Clin Psychol, 52,* 1090–1097.

Chaplin EW & Levine BA (1980). Total exposure duration and interrupted versus continous exposure in flooding. *Beh Ther, 12,* 360–368.

Chapman AH (1959). Psychogenic urinary retention in women: Report of a case. *Psychosom Med, 21,* 119–122.

Charney DS, Galloway MP, & Heninger GR (1984). Caffeine effects in healthy humans. *Life Sci, 35,* 135–144.

Charney DC, Menkes DB, & Heninger GR (1981). Receptor sensitivity and action of antidepressant treatment. *Arch Gen Psychiat, 38,* 1160–80

Charney DS, Heninger GR, & Redmond DE (1983). Yohimbine-induced anxiety and increased noradrenergic function in humans: Effects of diazepam and clonidine. *Life Sci, 33,* 19–29.

Charney DS, Heninger GR, & Breier A (1984). Noradrenergic function in panic anxiety:

Effects of yohimbine in healthy subjects and patients with agoraphobia and panic disorder. *Arch Gen Psychiat, 41,* 751–63.

Charney DS, Heninger GR, & Redmond ED (1984a). Neurobiological mechanism. In *Abstracts of the APA Annual Meeting* (Abstract 30C, p. 82). Los Angeles, May.

Charney DS, Heninger GR, & Price LH (1985). Noradrenergic function in anxiety and depression. Paper to APA. Dallas, May.

Chazan M (1962). School phobia. *Br J Educ Psychol, 32,* 209–217.

Cheney & Sefarth (1981). Selective forces affecting the predator alarm cells of vervet monkeys. *Behaviour, 76,* 25–61.

Christensen A, Arkowitz H, & Anderson J (1975). Practice dating as treatment of college dating inhibitions. *Beh Res Ther, 13,* 321.

Christie MJ, Trisdikoon P, & Chesher GB (1982). Tolerance and cross tolerance with morphine resulting from physiological release of endogenous opiates. *Life Sci, 31,* 839–845.

Ciesielski KT, Beech HR, & Gordon PK (1981). Some electrophysiological observations in obsessional states. *Brit J Psychiat, 138,* 479–484.

Clark DA, Sugrim I, & Bolton D (1982). Treatment of primary obsessional slowness in a 13-year-old male. *Beh Res Ther, 20,* 289–292.

Clark DM & Hemsley DR (1982). Hyperventilation; Individual variability and its relation to personality. *J Beh Ther Exp Psychiat, 13,* 41–47.

Clark DM, Salkovskis PM, & Chalkley AJ (1985). Respiratory control as a treatment for panic attacks. *J Beh Ther Exp Psychiat, 16,* 23–30.

Clark RB (1960). Habituation of the polychaete nereis to sudden stimuli. *Animal Beh, 8,* 82–103.

Clark RW (1980). *Freud: The man and the cause.* Cape, London.

Clarke JC & Wardman W (1985). *Agoraphobia: A clinical and personal account.* Pergamon, Sydney, Australia.

Claycomb JB (1983). Endogenous anxiety: Implications for nosology and treatment. *J Clin Psychiat, 44,* 19–22.

Cleghorn JM, Peterfy EJ, Pinter EJ, & Pattee CJ (1967). Effect of stress on levels of free fatty acid. *J Can Psychiat Assoc, 12,* 539–548.

Clemens TL & Selesnick ST (1967). Psychological evaluation of medication for repeated exposure to a stressor film. *Dis Nerv Sys, 28,* 98–104.

Clevenger SW (1890). Heart disease in insanity and a case of panphobia. *Alien Neurolo, 7,* 535–543.

Clifford CA, Murray RM, & Fulker DW (1984). Genetic and environmental influences on obsessional traits and symptoms. *Psychol Med, 14,* 791–800.

Cloninger CR, Martin RL, Clayton P, & Guze SB (1981). Followup and family study of anxiety neurosis. In Klein DF & Rabkin J (Eds.), *Anxiety: New research and changing concepts* (pp. 137–150). Raven, NY.

Clutton-Brock TH & Harvey PH (1976). Evolutionary roles and primate societies. In Bateson PPG & Hinde RA (Eds.), *Growing points in ethology* (pp. 195–238). Cambridge University Press, London.

Cobb JP (1983). Interaction between neurotic problems and marriage—implications for the therapist. *Irish J Psychother, 2,* 65–68.

Cobb JP & Marks IM (1979). Morbid jealousy featuring as obsessive-compulsive neurosis: treatment by behavioural psychotherapy. *Br J Psychiat, 134,* 301–305.

Cobb JP, McDonald R, Marks IM, & Stern RS (1980). Psychological treatments of coexisting marital and phobic-obsessive problems. *Beh Anal Mod, 4,* 3–16.

Cobb JP, Mathews AM, Childs-Clark A, & Blowers CM (1984). The spouse as co-therapist in the treatment of agoraphobia. *Br J Psychiat, 144,* 282–287.

Coburn M (1983). Effects of participant modeling on in vivo exposure in the treatment of agoraphobia. Doctoral dissertation, University of Denver, Colorado.

Coe CL & Levine S (1981). Normal responses to mother-infant separation in nonhuman primates. In Klein D & Rabkin J (Eds.), *Anxiety: New research and changing concepts* (p. 155–178). Raven, NY.

Coe CL, Wiener SG, & Levine S (1983). Psychoendocrine responses of mother and infant monkeys to disturbance and separation. In Moltz H & Rosenblum LA (Eds.) *Symbiosis in parent-young interactions* (in press).

Cohen F & Dean SJ (1968). Group desensitization of test anxiety. In *Proceedings of the 76th Annual Convention of the American Psychological Association, 3,* 615–616.

Cohen J, Gurel L, & Stumpt JC (1966). Psychiatric symptoms at 13 timepoints from hospital admission. *J Con Clin Psychol, 30,* 39–44.

Cohen M (1983). High familial prevalence of neurocirculatory asthenia and panic disorder at the Mass General Hospital. Paper to the Upjohn Conference on Biological Considerations in the Etiology and Treatment of Panic Disorders. Boston, November.

Cohen ME & White PD (1950). Life situations, emotions and neurocirculatory asthemia (anxiety neurosis, neurasthenia, effort syndrome). *Tr Assoc Res Nerv Ment Dis, 29,* 832–869.

Cohen ME & White PD (1951). Life situations, emotions and neurocirculatory asthenia (anxiety neurosis, neurasthenia, effort syndrome). *Psychosom Med, 13,* 335–357.

Cohen ME, Badal DW, Kilpatrick A, Reed EW, & White PD (1951). The high familial prevalance of neuro-circulatory asthenia. *Am J Human Genet, 3,* 126–158.

Cohen R (1966). Effects of group interaction and progressive hierarchy presentation on desensitization of test anxiety. *Beh Res Ther, 4,* 17–24.

Cohen SD, Monteiro W, & Marks IM (1984). Two-year follow-up of agoraphobics after exposure and imipramine. *Br J Psychiat, 144,* 276–281.

Cohen SD, Sireling L, & Marks IM (1986). Guided mourning for morbid grief: a replication (in press).

Cohen SI & Reed J (1968). Treatment of "nervous diarrhoea" and other conditioned autonomic disorders by desensitization. *Br J Psychiat, 114,* 1275–1280.

Cohn CF, Kron RE, & Brady JP (1976). A case of blood-illness-injury phobia treated behaviourally. *J Nerv Ment Dis, 162,* 65–68.

Comfort A (1981). Sorcery and sudden death. Letter to *J Roy Soc Med, 74,* 332.

Comings DE and Comings BG (1985). Hereditary agoraphobia with panic attacks and hereditary obsessive-compulsive behaviour in relatives of patients with tourette syndrome. *Brit J Psychiat* (in press).

Connolly FH & Gipson M (1978). Dysmorphophobia—a long-term study. *Brit J Psychiat, 132,* 568–570.

Connolly JC, Hallam RS, & Marks IM (1976). Selective association of fainting with blood-injury-illness fear. *Beh Ther, 7,* 8–13.

Cook E, Hodes R & Lang PJ (1986). Preparedness and phobia: Effects of stimulus content on human visceral conditioning. (Unpublished manuscript).

Cook M, Mineka S, Wolkenstein B, & Laitsch K (1985). Observational conditioning of snake fear in unrelated rhesus monkeys. *J Abn Psychol, 94,* 591–610.

Cook SW (1939). A survey of methods used to produce "experimental neurosis." *Am J Psychiat, 95,* 1259–1276.

Coolidge JE, Willen M, Tissman E, & Waldfogel S (1960). School phobias in adolescence. *Am J Orthopsychiat, 30,* 599.

Coolidge J, Brodie R, & Feeney B (1964). A ten-year follow-up study of 66 school-phobic children. *Am J. Orthopsychiat, 34,* 675.

Cooper AJ (1965). Conditioning therapy in hysterical retention of urine. *Br J Psychiat, 111*, 575–577.

Cooper B & Sylph J (1973). Life events in the onset of neurotic illness: An investigation in general practice. *Psychol Med, 3*, 421–435.

Cooper CL (1982). Personality characteristics of successful bomb disposal experts. *J Occ Med, 24*, 653–655.

Cooper JE, Gelder MG, & Marks IM (1965). Results of behaviour therapy in 77 psychiatric patients. *Br Med J, 1*, 1222–1225.

Cooper JE & McNeil J (1968). A study of houseproud housewives and their interaction with their children. *J Child Psychol Psychiat, 9*, 173–88.

Coover G, Ursin H, & Levine S (1974). Corticosterone levels during avoidance learning in rats with cingulate lesions suggest an instrumental reinforcement deficit. *J Comp Physiol Psychol, 87*, 970–977.

Coppen JA, Cowie V, & Slater E (1965). Familial aspects of "neuroticism" and "extraversion." *Brit J Psychiat, 111*, 70–83.

Corbett J (1969). Tics and Gilles de la Tourette Syndrome—a follow-up study and critical review. *Brit J Psychiat, 115*, 1229–1241.

Corsellis DHG (1980). Fear as a military factor. (Unpublished manuscript.)

Corson SA (1977). Psychophysiologic aspects of stress and distress. In *WPA Abstracts* (Abstract 462), Honolulu, September.

Corson SA & EO (1983). Conditioning of autonomic functions. In *Abstracts of the World Congress of Psychiatry* (Abstracts S201, 203, pp. 62–63). Vienna, July.

Coryell W, Noyes R, & House D (1985). Excess mortality in panic disorder. Paper to APA. Dallas, May.

Coryell W (1981). Obsessive-compulsive disorder and primary unipolar depression. *J Nerv Ment Dis, 169*, 220–224.

Coryell W (1983). Mortality after 30–40 years: Panic disorder v other discrete psychiatric illnesses. *Psychiatry Update, APA Annual Review* (vol. II).

Coryell W, Noyes R, & Clancy J (1982). Excess mortality in panic disorder: A comparison with primary unipolar depression. *Arch Gen Psych, 39*, 701–703.

Coryell W, Noyes R, & House D (1983). Mortality and morbidity associated with panic related forms of anxiety. Paper to Upjohn Conference on Biological Considerations in the Etiology and Treatment of Anxiety Disorders. Boston, November.

Coryell W, Noyes R, & Clancy J (1983). Panic disorder and primary unipolar depression: Background and outcome. *J Affect Dis, 5*, 311–317.

Coss RG (1970). The perceptual aspects of eye-spot patterns and their relevance to gaze behaviour. In Hutt SJ & Hutt C (Eds.), *Behaviour studies in psychiatry* (ch. 7, p. 121). Pergamon, Oxford.

Costa E (1985). BZ/GABA interactions: The neurobiology of anxiety. In Tuma H & Maser J (Eds.), Anxiety and anxiety disorders (ch. 2, p. 27–52). Erlbaum, Hillsdale, NJ.

Costa Molinari JM, Equillor M, Romeu J, & Tizon J (1971). In S Monserrat-Esteve, JM Costa Molinari, & C Ballus (Eds.), *Patologia obsesiva* (ch. 11, p. 253). Graficasa, Màlaga.

Costello CG (1982). Fears and phobias in women: A community study. *J Abn Psychol, 91*, 280–286.

Cott HB (1940). *Adaptive Coloration in Animals* (pp. 82, 387–389). Methuen, London.

Cottraux J & Claustrat B (1984). Le test à la dexaméthasone dans l'agoraphobie avec attaques de panique. *L'Encéphale, X*, 267–272.

Cottraux JA, Bouvard M, Claustrat B, & Juenet C (1984). Abnormal dexamethasone suppression test in primary obsessive-compulsive patients: A confirmatory report. *Psychiat Res, 13,* 157–165.

Coursey RD & Buchsbaum MS (1981). Biological high-risk research strategy: A review of recent studies. In Regier DA & Allen G (Eds.), *Risk factor research in the major mental disorders.* DHHS Publication No. (ADM) 81–1068. US Govt. Printing Office. Washington, DC.

Cowley DS, Dager SR, & Dunner DL (1985). Lactate panic in primary depression. In *Abstracts of the World Congress of Biological Psychiatry* (Abstract 242.1). Philadelphia, September.

Cox D, Hallam R, O'Connor K & Rachman S (1983). An experimental analysis of fearlessness and courage. *Br J Psychol, 74,* 107–117.

Cox FM & Campbell D (1968). Young children in a new situation with and without their mothers. *Child Dev, 39,* 123–131

Crawley JN, Ninan PT, Pickar D, Chrousos GP, Linnoila M, Skolnick P, & Paul SM (1985). *J Neurosci* (in press).

Croake JW (1969). Fears of children. *Human Dev, 12, 239–247.*

Croake JW & Knox FH (1973). The changing nature of children's fears. *Child Study J, 3,* 91–105.

Crook JO & Charney DL (1982). Treating obsessions by paradoxical practice with a cassette recorder. In DuPont RL (Ed.), *Phobias* (ch. 19, p. 178–181). Brunner/Mazel, NY.

Crowe HJ (1973). Intracerebral polarization and multifocal leucoagulation in psychiatric illness. *Psychiat Neurolog Neurochir* (Amsterdam), *76,* 365–381.

Crowe MJ, Marks IM, Agras WS, & Leitenberg H (1972). Time-limited desensitization, implosion and shaping for phobic patients. *Beh Res Ther, 10,* 319.

Crowe RR (1982). Panic attacks in family members of patients with mitral valve prolapse. In *Abstracts of APA Annual Conference* (p. 70). Toronto, May.

Crowe RR, Pauls DL, Slymen DJ, & Noyes R (1980). Morbidity risk in families of anxiety neurotics ± mitral valve prolapse. *Arch Gen Psychiat, 37,* 77–79.

Crowe RR, Pauls DL, Kerber RE, & Noyes R (1981). Panic disorders and mitral valve prolapse. In Klein DF & Rabkin J (Eds.), *Anxiety: New research and changing concepts* (pp. 103–116). Raven, NY.

Crowe RR, Gaffney G, & Kerber R (1982). Panic attacks in families of patients with mitral valve prolapse. *J Affect Dis, 4,* 121–125.

Crowe RR, Noyes R, Pauls DL, & Slymen D (1983). A family study of panic disorder. *Arch Gen Psychiat, 40,* 1065–1069.

Crowe RR, Pauls DL, Venkatesh MR, Van Valkenburg C, Noyes R, Martins JB, & Kerber R (1985). Exercise stress testing in panic disorder. Paper to APA. Dallas, May.

Csernansky JG & A, Glick SA, & Hollister LE (1985). Lidocaine kindling with increased apomorphine stereotypy and mesolimbic dopamine D2 receptor density. *Psychopharm Bull, 21,* 707–711.

Cullington A, Butler G, Hibbert G, & Gelder MG (1984). Problem solving: Not a treatment for agoraphobia. *Beh Ther, 15,* 280–286.

Cully JF & Ligon JD (1976). Comparative mobbing behaviour of scrub and Mexican Jays. *The Ark, 93,* 116–125.

Cummings JD (1944). The incidence of emotional symptoms in school children. *Br J Educ Psychol, 14,* 151–161.

Cummings JD (1946). A followup study of emotional symptoms in school children. *Br J Educ Psychol, 16,* 163–177.

Curio E (1975). Functional organization of antipredator behaviour in the red flycatcher: A study of avian visual perception. *Animal Beh, 23*, 1–115.

Curio E (1976). *The ethology of predation.* Springer, NY.

Curio E (1978). Cultural transmission of enemy recognition. *Science, 202*, 899–901.

Curran JP, Miller IW, Zwick WR, Monti PM, & Stout RL (1980). The socially inadequate patient. *J Consult Clin Psychol, 48*, 375–382.

Curtis GC & Thyer B (1983). Fainting on exposure to phobic stimuli. *Am J Psychiat, 140*, 771–774.

Curtis GC, Nesse R, Buxton M, Wright J, & Lippman D (1976). Flooding in vivo during the Circadian phase of minimal cortisol secretion. *Compr Psychiat,17*, 153–160.

Curtis GC, Nesse R, Buxton M, & Lippman D (1978). Anxiety and plasma cortisol at the crest of the circadian cycle. *Psychosom Med, 40*, 368–378.

Curtis GC, Nesse R, Buxton M, & Lippman D (1979). Plasma growth hormone: Effect of anxiety during flooding in vivo. *Am J Psychiat, 136*, 410–414.

Curtis GC, Cameron OG, & Nesse RM (1982). The dexamethasone suppression test in panic disorder and agoraphobia. *Am J Psychiat, 139*, 1043–1046.

Curtis Helena (1979). *Biology.* Worth, NY.

Cutting D (1979). Relief of nightmares. *Br J Psychiat, 134*, 647.

Da Costa JM (1871). On irritable heart: A clinical study of a functional cardiac disorder and its consequences. *Am J Med Sci, 61*, 17–52.

Dackis CA, Pottash ALC, & Gold MS (1985). DST testing of depressed agoraphobics. In *Abstracts of the World Congress of Biological Psychiatry* (no. 148.3). Philadelphia, September.

Dajas F, Lista A, Nin A et al. (1985). Clinical and neurochemical effects of imipramine and diclofensine in panic and phobic disorders. In *Abstracts of the World Congress of Biological Psychiatry* (Abstract 129.3). Philadelphia, September.

Dalby DA (1970). Effects of septal lesions on the acquisition of 2 types of active avoidance behaviour in rats. *J Comp Physiol Psychol, 73*, 278–83.

Daly DD (1975). Ictal clinical manifestations. In Penry JK & Daly DD (Eds.), *Complex partial seizures and their treatment. Advances in neurology* (vol. II). Raven, NY.

Daly M & Wilson M (1982). Homicide and kinship. *Am Anthropol, 84*, 372–378.

Darwin C (1872). *The expression of emotion in men and animals.* Murray, London.

Darwin C (1877). A biographical sketch of an infant. *Mind, 2*, 285–294.

Darwin C (1900). A posthumous essay on instinct. In Romanes GS (Ed.), *Mental evolution in animals* (n.d.). Appleton, NY.

Davidson J, Swartz M, Storck M et al. (1985). A diagnostic and family study of post-traumatic stress disorder. *Am J Psychiat, 142*, 90–93.

Davis G, Breslau N, Brooks E et al. (1985). PTSD: The quantity and quality of wartime stressors. In *Abstracts of the World Congress of Biological Psychiatry* (no. 129.4). Philadelphia, September.

Davis JF, Malmo RB, & Shagass C (1954). Electromyographic reaction to strong auditory stimulation in psychiatric patients. *Can J Psychol, 8*, 177–186.

Davis KL, Gurski JC, & Scott JP (1976). Interaction of separation distress with fear in infant dogs. *Dev Psychobiol, 10*, 203–212.

Davis M, Parisi T, Gendelman DS et al. (1982). Habituation and sensitization of startle elicited electrically from the brain stem. *Science, 218*, 688–689.

Davison K (1964). Episodic depersonalisation. *Br J Psychiat, 110*, 505–513.

Davison S (1961). School phobia as a manifestation of family disturbance. *J Child Psychol Psychiat, 1*, 270–287.

Davitz JR (1970). *The language of emotion.* Academic, NY.

Dawkins R (1982). *The extended phenotype: The gene as the unit of selection.* Freeman, Oxford.

Dawkins R & Krebs JR (1979). Arms race between and within species. In *Proceedings of the Royal Society* (Series B, 205, pp. 489–511).

Dawson RW (1982). Comparative contributions of cognitive behaviour therapy strategies in the treatment of speech anxiety. *Austral J Psychol, 34,* 297–308.

Day JH (1967). Monograph on Polychaeta of Southern Africa (Part 3, Sedentaria, Figure 38.5, p. 811). Trustees of British Museum (Natural History), London.

Dealy RS, Ishiki DM, Avery DH, Wilson LG, & Dunner DL (1981). Secondary depression in anxiety disorders. *Comp Psychiat, 22,* 612–618.

Decarie T (1974). *The infant's reaction to strangers.* International University Press, NY.

DeFries JC, Gervais MC, & Thomas EA (1978). 30 generations of selection for openfield activity in laboratory mice. *Beh Genet, 8,* 3–13.

Delgado JMR (1969). *Physical control of the mind.* Reprinted in Karbias EM & Andrews LM (Eds.), *Man controlled: Readings in the psychology of behaviour control* (1972, pp. 40–68). Free Press, Collier-MacMillan, London.

Delprato DJ (1973a). An animal analogue to systematic desensitization and elimination of avoidance. *Beh Res Ther, 11,* 49.

Delprato DJ (1973b). Exposure to the aversive stimulus in an animal analogue to systematic desensitization. *Beh Res Ther, 11,* 187.

Delprato DJ (1974). Post-response exposure to warning signal in avoidance extinction. *Animal Learning Beh, 2,* 59–62.

Delprato DJ & Jackson DE (1974). Counterconditioning and exposure only in the treatment of specific conditioned suppression. *Beh Res Ther, 11,* 453.

Denholtz MS & Mann ET (1975). An automated audiovisual treatment of phobias by non-professionals. *J Beh Ther Exp Psychiat, 6,* 111–115.

Derogatis LR & Cleary PA (1977). Factorial invariance across gender in the SCL-90. *Br J Soc Clin Psychol, 16,* 347–356.

De Silva P (1984). Speech to Institute of Psychiatry, London, June.

De Silva P & Rachman S (1984). Does escape behaviour strengthen agoraphobic avoidance? A preliminary study. *Beh Res Ther, 22,* 87–91.

de Wied D (1983). Endocrinology in Reproduction. In *Proceedings of the Third International Symposium on Psychoneuroendocrinology.*

Deutsch H (1929). The genesis of agoraphobia. *Internat J Psychoan, 10,* 51–69.

Devereux RB, Shear MK, Kramer-Fox R, Hartman N, Lutas E, & Brown WT (1985). Mitral valve prolapse: An overview. Paper to APA. Dallas, May.

Devore I (Ed.) (1965). *Primate behavior.* Holt, Rinehart, NY.

Dhadphale M, Ellison RH, Griffin L (1983). Frequency of psychiatric disorders among patients attending semi-urban and rural general out-patient clinics in Kenya. *Br J Psychiat, 142,* 379–383.

Dial BE & Fitzpatrick LC (1983). Lizard tail autotomy: Function and energetics of postautotomy tail movement in Sciacella lateralis. *Science, 219,* 391–393.

Dill LM (1974). Escape response of zebra danio (*Brachydanio rerio*): I. The stimulus for escape. *Animal Beh, 22,* 711–722.

Dimond S (1966). Imprinting and fear—a system governed by visual experience during the development of the embryo. *Bull Br Psychol Soc, 19,* 63–4.

Dimond SJ & Farrington L (1977). Heart rate responses to films shown to the right or left hemisphere of the brain. *Act Psychol, 41,* 255–261.

Dimsdale JE & Herd JA (1982). Variability of plasma lipids in response to emotional arousal. *Psychosom Med, 44,* 413.

Dixon JJ, De Monchaux C, & Sandler J (1957). Patterns of anxiety. *Br J Med Psychol, 30,* 34–40, 107–112.

Dobzhansky T (1972). Genetics and the diversity of behavior. *Am Psychol, 27,* 523–530.

Doctor RM (1982). Pretreatment survey of agoraphobics. In RL DuPont (Ed.), *Phobia: Summary of modern treatments* (pp. 203–214). Brunner/Mazel, NY.

Dohrenwend BP, Shrovt PE, Egri G, & Mendelsohn FS (1980). Non-specific distress and other dimensions of psychopathology. *Arch Gen Psychiat, 37,* 1229–1236.

Dollard J (1944). Fear in battle. *The Infantry Journal* (n.p., Washington, DC).

Downing RW & Rickels K (1974). Mixed anxiety-depression. Fact or myth? *Arch Gen Psychiat, 30,* 312.

Dowson JH (1977). The phenomenology of severe obsessive-compulsive neurosis. *Br J Psychiat, 131,* 75–78.

Dragsten SS & Lee LC (1973). Infants' social behaviour in a naturalistic versus experimental setting. *Am Psychol Assoc,* 65–66.

Driscoll P & Battig K (1982). Behavioural, emotional and neurochemical profiles of rats with high and low, two-way avoidance. In Lieblich I (Ed.), *Genetics of the brain* (pp. 95–123). Elsevier, Amsterdam.

Driscoll P, Gentsch C, Lichtsteiner M, & Feer H (1985). Selection for extreme differences in two-way avoidance. In *Abstracts of the World Congress of Biological Psychiatry* (Abstract 2042). Philadelphia, September.

DuPont RL (Ed.) (1982). *Phobia: Comprehensive summary of modern treatment.* Brunner-Mazel, NY.

du Saulle L (1895). De l'agoraphobie. *Practicien, 8,* 208–210.

DuBois FS (1949). Compulsion neurosis with cachexia (anorexia nervosa). *Am J Psychiat, 106,* 107–115.

Duerr JS & Quinn WG (1982). Three *Drosophila* mutations that block associative learning also affect habituation and sensitization. *Proc Nat Acad Sci USA, 79,* 3646–3650.

Dunsworth FA (1961). Phobias in children. *J Can Psychiat Assoc, 6,* 191–294.

Dykman RA, Murphree OD, & Peters JE (1969). Like begets like: Behavioural tests, classical autonomic and motor conditioning and operant conditioning in 2 strains of pointer dogs. *Ann NY Acad Sci, 159,* 976–1007.

Dykman RA, Murphree OD, & Ackerman PT (1965). Litter patterns in the offspring of nervous and stable dogs: II. Autonomic and motor conditioning. *J Nerv Ment Dis, 141,* 419–431.

Eaton RC (1974). *The cheetah: The biology, ecology and behaviour of an endangered species.* Van Nostrand, NY.

Eaton WW & McLeod J (1984). Consumption of coffee and tea and symptoms of anxiety. *Am J Pub Health, 74,* 66–68.

Eberle TM, Rehm LP, & McBurney DH (1975). Fear decrement to anxiety hierarchy items effects of stimulus intensity. *Beh Res Ther, 13,* 255.

Edkins JRP (1949). Further developments in abreaction. In Harris NG (Ed.), *Modern trends in psychological medicine* (pp. 165–288). Hoeber, NY.

Edmondson HD, Roscoe B, & Vickers MD (1972). Biochemical evidence of anxiety in dental patients. *Br Med J, 4,* 7–9.

Edmunds M (1974). *Defence in Animals.* Longman, NY.

Edwards DC (1969). Predators in *Olivella biplicata,* including a species-specific predator avoidance response. *The Veliger, 11,* 326–333.

Ehlers A & Margraf J (1985). Perceived heart rate changes and hyperventilation as anxiety triggers in panic patients. Paper to EABT. Munich, August.

Ehlers A, Margraf J, Roth WT, Taylor CB, Maddock RJ, & Kopell BS (1985). CO_2 as a trigger for panic in panic patients. Paper to APA. Dallas, May.

Ehlers A, Margraf J, Roth WT et al. (1986). Lactate infusions and panics in patients and controls. *Psychiat Res, 17,* 295–308.

Eible-Eibesfeldt I (1970). *Ethology: The biology of behavior.* Holt, Rinehart, NY.

Eisenberg L (1958). School phobia. A study in the communication of anxiety. *Am J Psychiat, 114,* 712–718.

Eisenberg L (1981). The physician as interpreter: Ascribing meaning to the illness experience. *Compr Psychiat, 22,* 239–248.

Eisenberg JF & Gould E (1970). The tenrecs: A study in mammalian behaviour and evolution. *Smithson Contr Zool, 27,* 1–137.

Eisner T (1970). Chemical defense against predation in arthropods. In Sondheimer E & Simeon JB (Eds.), *Chemical ecology.* Academic Press, NY.

Eitinger L (1969). Anxiety in concentration camp survivors. *Aust NZ J Psychiat, 3,* 348–351.

Elliott R (1967). A case of inhibition of micturition: Unsystematic desensitization. *Psychol Rec, 17,* 525–530.

Ellis A (1962). *Reason and emotion in psychotherapy.* Lyle-Stuart, NY.

Ellis EM, Atkeson BM, & Calhoun KS (1981). An assessment of long-term reaction to rape. *J Abn Psychol, 90,* 263–266.

Ellsworth DC (1975). Direct gaze as a stimulus for aggression. In Pliner P, Kramer L, & Alloway T (Eds.), *Nonverbal communication of aggression* (pp. 53–76). Plenum, NY.

Elmore RT, Wildman RW, & Westefeld JS (1980). Systematic desensitization for blood phobia. *J Beh Ther Exp Psychiat, 11,* 277–279.

Elsworth JD, Redmond DE, & Roth RH (1982). Plama and cerebrospinal fluid 3-methoxy-4-hydroxyphenylethylene glycol (MHPG) as indices of brain norepinephrine metabolism in primates. *Brain Res, 235,* 115–124.

Emde RN (1980). Levels of meaning for infant emotions. In Collins WA (Ed.), *Development of cognition, affect and social relations.* In *Minnesota Symposia on Child Psychology* (vol. 13, pp. 1–37). Erlbaum, Hillsdale, NJ.

Emde RN, Gaensbauer TJ, & Harmon RJ (1976). Emotional expression in infancy. In *Psychological Issues Monograph 37.* International Universities Press, NY.

Emlen JT (1963). Determinants of cliff-edge and escape responses in herring gull chicks. *Behaviour 22,* 1–15.

Emmelkamp PMG (1974). Self-observation vs flooding in the treatment of agoraphobia. *Beh Res Ther, 12,* 229.

Emmelkamp PMG (1979). Behavioral study of clinical phobias. In Hersen M, Eisler RM, & Miller PM (Eds.), *Progress in behaviour modification* (vol. 8). Academic, NY.

Emmelkamp PMG (1986). Behaviour therapy with adults. In Garfield S & Bergin A (Eds.), *Handbook of psychotherapy and behaviour change* (3rd ed.). Wiley, NY.

Emmelkamp PMG (1980). Behavioural treatment of obsessive-compulsive patients. Paper to Learning Theory Symposium. Crete, April.

Emmelkamp PMG (1980a). Agoraphobics' interpersonal problems: Their role in the effects of exposure in vivo therapy. *Arch Gen Psychiat, 37,* 1303–1306.

Emmelkamp PMG (1982). *Phobic and obsessive-compulsive disorders.* Plenum, NY.

Emmelkamp PMG (1983). Long-term followup of obsessive-compulsives. Paper to WPA Annual Meeting. Vienna, July.

Emmelkamp PMG & DeLange (1983). Spouse involvement in the treatment of obsessive-compulsive patients. *Beh Res Ther, 21,* 341–346.

Emmelkamp PMG & Emmelkamp-Benner A (1975). Modeling and group treatment with self-observation in agoraphobics. *Beh Res Ther, 13,* 135–139.

Emmelkamp PMG & Felten M (1985). Cognitive and physiological changes during exposure in vivo treatment of acrophobia. *Beh Res Ther, 23,* 219–223.

Emmelkamp PMG & Giesselbach P (1981). Relevant vs irrelevant exposure for obsessions. *Beh Psychother, 9,* 322–329.

Emmelkamp PMG & Kraanen J (1978). Therapist-controlled v self controlled exposure in vivo in obsessive-compulsive patients. *Beh Res Ther, 15,* 491–495.

Emmelkamp PMG & Kuipers ACM (1979). Agoraphobia: A followup study 4 years after treatment. *Br J Psychiat, 134,* 352–355.

Emmelkamp PMG & Kwee KG (1977). Thought-stopping v prolonged exposure in imagination for obsessional ruminations. *Beh Res Ther, 15,* 441–444.

Emmelkamp PMG & Mersch PP (1982). Cognition and exposure in vivo in agoraphobia: Short-term and delayed effects. *Cog Ther Res, 6,* 77–88.

Emmelkamp PMG & Rabbie DM (1983). 4-year followup of OCD after psychological treatment. Paper to WPA. Vienna, July.

Emmelkamp PMG & Ultee KAA (1974). Successive approximation vs self-observation in the treatment of agoraphobia. *Beh Ther, 5, 605–613.*

Emmelkamp PMG & van der Heyden H (1980). Treatment of harming obsessions. *Beh Anal Mod, 4,* 28–35.

Emmelkamp PMG & van der Hout A (1983). Failure in treating agoraphobia. In Foa EB & Emmelkamp PMG (Eds.), *Failures in behaviour therapy* (ch. 4, pp. 58–81). Wiley, NY.

Emmelkamp PMG & Wessels H (1975). Flooding in imagination v flooding in vivo in agoraphobics. *Beh Res Ther, 13,* 7.

Emmelkamp PMG, Van der Helm M, Van Zanten BL, & Plochg I (1980). O-c patients: Self-instructional training in exposure. *Beh Res Ther, 18,* 61–66.

Emmelkamp PMG, Van der Hout A, & De Vries K (1983). Assertive training for agoraphobics. *Beh Res Ther, 21,* 63–68.

Emmelkamp PMG, Mersch PP, & Vissia E (1985). Analogue outcome research with cognitive and behavioral interventions. *Beh Res Ther, 23,* 83–86.

Emmelkamp PMG, Kuipers ACM, & Eggeraat JB (1978). Cognitive modification versus prolonged exposure in vivo in agoraphobics. *Beh Res Ther, 16,* 33–41.

Emmelkamp PMG, Mersch PP, Vissia E, & Van der Helm M (1985a). Social phobia: Cognitive and behavioral interventions. *Beh Res Ther, 23,* 365–369.

Emmelkamp PMG, Brilman E, Kuiper H, & Mersch PP (1985b). Self-instruction, rational emotive therapy and exposure in vivo for agoraphobia. *Beh Mod* (in press).

Endicott JE et al. (1975). Mental status examination record (MSER). Reliability and validity. *Comp Psychiat, 16,* 285–301.

Engel GL (1978). Psychologic stress, vasodepressor (vasovagal) syncope, and sudden death. *Ann Intern Med, 89,* 403–412.

English HB (1929). Three cases of the "conditioned fear response." *J Abn Soc Psychol, 34,* 221–225.

Epstein AW & Bailine SH (1971). Sleep and dream studies in obsessional neurosis with particular reference to epileptic states. *Biol Psychiat, 3,* 149.

Epstein S (1962). Measurement of drive and conflict in humans. In Jones MR (Ed.), *Nebraska Symposium on Motivation* (pp. 127–206). University of Nebraska Press, Lincoln.

Epstein S (1967). Toward a unified theory of anxiety. In Maher BA (Ed.), *Progress in experimental personality research* (vol. 4, pp. 1–89). Academic, NY.

Epstein S (1970). Anxiety, reality and schizophrenia. *Schizophrenia, 2,* 11–35.

Errera P & Coleman JV (1963). A long-term followup study of neurotic phobic patients in a psychiatric clinic. *J Nerv Ment Dis, 136,* 267–271.

Erwin WJ (1963). Confinement in the production of human neuroses: The barber's chair syndrome. *Beh Res Ther, 1,* 175–183.

Espie CA (1985). Treatment of excessive urinary urgency and frequency by retention control training and desensitization. *Beh Res Ther, 23,* 205–210.

Esquirol E (1838). De la monomanie. In *Des Maladies Mentales* (vol. 1, ch. 11). Bruxelles.

Eth S & Pyrnoos RS (1985). *PTSD in children.* Am Psychiat Press, Washington, DC.

Everaerd WT, Rijken HM, & Emmelkamp PMG (1973). Successive approximation and self-observation in the treatment of agoraphobia. *Beh Res Ther, 11,* 105–117.

Ewell AH, Cullen JM, & Woodruff ML (1981). Tonic immobility as a predator-defense in the rabbit. *Beh Neur Biol, 31,* 483–489.

Ewert JP (1980). *Neuroethology.* Springer, NY.

Eysenck HJ & Prell DB (1951). The inheritance of neuroticism: An experimental study. *J Ment Sci, 97,* 441–465.

Eysenck HJ (1979). The conditioning model of neurosis. *Beh Brain Sci, 2,* 155–199.

Fairbank JA & Keane TM (1982). Flooding for combat-related stress disorders. *Beh Ther, 13,* 499–510.

Falloon I, Lindley P, McDonald R et al. (1977). Social skills training of outpatient groups. *Br J Psychiat, 131,* 59–609.

Falloon I, Lloyd GG, Harpin RE (1981). Treatment of social phobia: Real life rehearsal and non-professional therapist. *J Nerv Ment Dis, 169,* 180–184.

Faludi G, Kaskó M, Böszörményi Z, & Perényi A (1985). DST in panic disorder and major depression. In *Abstracts of the World Congress of Biological Psychiatry* (Abstract 148.2). Philadelphia, September.

Farid BT (1983). Adverse mood states and oc phenomenology. Longitudinal study of 11 obsessional neurotics. Master's dissertation, University of Leeds.

Faucheux BA, Baulon A, Poitrenaud J et al. (1983). Heart rate, urinary catecholamines and anxiety during mental stress in men. *Age Ageing, 12,* 144–150.

Fava M & GA, Kellner R et al. (1982). Psychological correlates of hyperprolactinemia in males. *Psychother Psychosom, 37,* 214–217.

Fava M & GA, Kellner R et al. (1983). Psychosomatic aspects of hyperprolactinemia. *Psychother Psychosom, 40,* 257–262.

Fawcett J & Kravitz HM (1983). Anxiety syndromes and their relationship to depressive illness. *J Clin Psychiat, 44,* 8–11.

Fenz WD (1975). Strategies for coping with stress.

Fenz WD & Epstein S (1967). Gradients of physiological arousal in parachutists. *Psychosom Med, 29,* 33–51.

Fernando SJM (1967). Gilles de la Tourette syndrome: A report of four cases. *Br J Psychiat, 113,* 607–617.

Figley CR (1986). *Trauma and its wake: Study and treatment of PTSD.* Grunner-Mazel, NY.

Finlay-Jones R & Brown GW (1981). Types of stressful life event and the onset of anxiety-depressive disorder. *Psychol Med, 11,* 803–815.

Fisher LM & Wilson TG (1985). Psychology of agoraphobia. *Beh Res Ther, 23,* 97–107.

Flament M & Rapoport JL (1984). Childhood OCD. In Insel TR (Ed.), New Findings in OCD (ch. 2, pp. 23–43). American Psychiatric Press, NY.

Flament MF, Rapoport JL, Berg CJ et al. (1985). Clomipramine treatment of childhood OCD. A double-blind controlled study. *Arch Gen Psychiat, 42,* 977–983.

Fliess JL, Gurland BG, & Cooper JE (1971). Some contributions to the measurement of psychopathology. *Br J Psychiat, 119,* 647–656.

Flor-Henry P (1985). Paper to World Congress of Biolog Psychiatry. Philadelphia, September.

Flor-Henry P & Schopflocher D (1985). Further neuropsychological studies of obsessions. In *Abstracts of the World Congress of Biological Psychiatry* (Abstract 214.3). Philadelphia, September.

Flor-Henry P, Yeudall LT, Koles ZJ, & Howarth BG (1979). Neuropsychological and power spectral EEG investigations of OCD. *Biol Psychiat, 14,* 119–130.

Foa EB (1985b). Cognitive dysfunction and treatment in obsessive-compulsive disorder. Unpublished manuscript.

Foa EB & Chambless DL (1978). Habituation of subjective anxiety during flooding in imagery. *Beh Res Ther, 16,* 391–399.

Foa EB & Foa UG (1982). Differentiating depression and anxiety: Is it possible? Is it useful? *Psychopharm Bull, 18,* 62–68.

Foa EB & Goldstein A (1978). Continous exposure and complete response prevention in obsessive-compulsive neurosis. *Beh Ther, 9,* 821–829.

Foa EB & Kozak MJ (1985). Treatment of anxiety disorders: Implications for psychopathology. In Tuma AH, Maser JD (Eds.), *Anxiety and anxiety disorders* (ch. 23, pp. 421–452). Erlbaum, Hillsdale, NJ.

Foa EB & Kozak M (1986). Emotional processing of fear. *Psychol Bull, 99,* 20–35.

Foa EB & McNally R (1985). Sensitivity to feared stimuli in obsessive-compulsives: A dichotic listening analysis. Cogntive Ther & Res (in press).

Foa EB & Steketee GS (1979). Obsessive-compulsives: Conceptual issues and treatment interventions. In Hersen RM et al. (Eds.), *Progress in behaviour modification* (pp. 1–53). Academic, NY.

Foa EB, Blau JS, Prout M, & Latimer P (1977). Is horrow a necessary component of flooding (implosion)? *Beh Res Ther, 15,* 397–402.

Foa EB, Jameson JS, Turner RM, & Payne LL (1980). Massed vs spaced exposure sessions in the treatment of agoraphobia. *Beh Res Ther, 18,* 333–338.

Foa EB, Steketee GS, & Milby JB (1980a). Exposure vs response prevention in obsessive-compulsive washers. *J Consult Clin Psychol, 48,* 419–420.

Foa EB, Steketee G, Turner RM, & Fischer SC (1980b). Imaginal exposure to feared disasters in obsessive-compulsive checkers. *Beh Res Ther, 18,* 449–455.

Foa EB, Grayson J, & Steketee G (1982). Depression, habituation and treatment outcome in obsessive-compulsives. In Boulougouris J (Ed.), *Learning theory approaches to psychiatry* (ch. 12, pp. 129–142). Wiley, Chichester.

Foa EB, Steketee G, Grayson JB et al. (1984). Deliberate exposure and blocking of obsessive-compulsive rituals. *Beh Ther, 15,* 450–472.

Foa EB, Steketee G, & Young MC (1984a). Agoraphobia. *Clin Psychol Rev, 4,* 431–457.

Foa EB, Steketee GS, & Ozarow BJ (1985). Behavior therapy with OCD. In Mavisakalian M, Turner SM, & Michelson L (Eds.), *OCD* (ch. 2). Plenum, NY.

Foa EB et al. (1986). Imipramine in OCD: Effect on depression and obsessive-compulsive symptoms. Unpublished manuscript.

Fonberg E (1956). On the manifestation of conditioned defensive reactions in stress. In *Bulletin of the Society of Science and Letters of Fodz.* Class III. *Science, Mathematics and Nature, 7,* 1.

Fonberg E (1966). Emotional reactions evoked by electrical stimulation of subcortical structures and their role in the conditioning of alimentary and defensive reactions. In *Symposium no. 3: Integrative forms of conditioned reflexes* (pp. 125–129). Presented to *XVIII International Conference of Psychology.* Moscow, August.

Fouts G & Atlas P (1979). Stranger distress: Mother and stranger as reinforcers. *Infant Beh Dev 2,* 309–317.

Fowlie DG & Aveline MO (1985). The emotional consequences of ejection, rescue and rehabilitation in Royal Air Force Aircrew. *Br J. Psychiat, 146,* 609–613.

Fox NA & Davidson RJ (1986). EEG asymmetry in response to the approach of a stranger and maternal separation in 10 month old infants (in press).

Fraiberg S (1975). Development of human attachments in infants blind from birth. *Merrill-Palmer Quarterly 21,* 315–334.

Frank E & Stewart BD (1983). Treating depression in victims of rape. *Clin Psychol, 36,* 95–98.

Frank E & Stewart BD (1983a). Treatment of depressed rape victims. In Clayton PJ & Barrett JE (Eds.), *Treatment of Depression.* Raven, NY.

Frankenhauser M (1975) Catecholamines and emotion. In Levi L (Ed.): *Emotions— their parameters and measurement.* Raven, NY.

Frankenhauser M (1983). Sympathetic-adrenal and pituitary-adrenal response to challenge. In Dembroski TM, Schmidt TH, & Blümchen G (Eds.), Karger, Basel.

Frankl V (1955). *The doctor and the soul: From psychotherapy to logotherapy.* Knopf, NY.

Franklin JA (1985). Agoraphobia: Its nature, aetiology, maintenance and treatment. Unpublished manuscript, Sydney.

Frazier SH & Carr AC (1967). Phobic reaction. In Freedman AM & Kaplan HI (Eds.), *Comprehensive textbook of psychiatry.* Williams & Williams, Baltimore.

Fredrikson M & Öhman A (1979). Cardiovascular and electrodermal responses conditioned to fear-relevant stimuli. *Psychophysiology, 16,* 1–7.

Fredrikson M (1980). Orienting and defensive reactions to phobic and conditioned fear stimuli in phobics and normals. Doctoral dissertation, University of Uppsala.

Fredrikson M, Sundin O, & Frankenhauser M (1983). Cortisol excretion to affective stimulation. *SPR Abstracts, 20,* 440.

Fredrikson M, Hugdahl K. & Öhman A (1976). Electrodermal conditioning to potentially phobic stimuli. *Biol Psychol, 4,* 305–314.

Freedman D (1958). Constitutional and environmental interactions in rearing of 4 breeds of dogs. *Science, 127,* 585–586.

Freedman D (1965). Hereditary control of early social behavior. In Foss BM (Ed.), *Determinants of infant behavior III* (pp. 149–155). Methuen, London.

Freedman DG (1976). Infancy, biology and culture. In Lipsitt LP (Ed.), *Developmental psychobiology* (pp. 35–54). Wiley, NY.

Freedman RR, Ianni P, Ettedgui E, & Puthezhath N (1985). Ambulatory monitoring of panic disorder. *Arch Gen Psychiat, 42,* 244–248.

Freeman AM, Fleece L, Folks DG et al. (1984). Psychiatric symptoms, type A behavior and arrhythmias following coronary bypass. *Psychosom, 25,* 586–589.

Freud S (1892). On the psychical mechanism of hysterical phenomena. In *Collected Works* (Vol. I, pp. 24–26). Hogarth, London.

Freud S (1895). A reply to criticisms on the anxiety neurosis, In *Collected Works* (Vol. I, pp.107–127). Hogarth and Institute of Psychoanalysis, London.

Freud S (1907). Obsessive actions and religious practices. In *Standard Edition of the Complete Psychological Works of Sigmund Freud* (vol. IX, pp. 115–127). Hogarth, London.

Freud S (1913). *Totem and taboo,* p. 127. Hogarth, London, 1955.

Freud S (1919). Turnings in the world of psychoanalytic therapy. In *Collected Papers, 2,* 399–400. Hogarth and Institute of Psychoanalysis, London.

Friedman D (1966). Treatment of a case of dog phobia in a deaf mute by behaviour therapy. *Beh Res Ther, 4,* 141.

Friedman JH (1950). Short-term psychotherapy of "Phobia of Travel." *American J Psychother, 4,* 259–278.

Frings H & M, Cox B, & Peissner L (1955). Recorded calls of herring gulls *(Larus argentatus)* as repellents and attractants. *Science, 121,* 340–341.

Frisch MB, Elliott CH, Atsaides JP et al. (1982). Social skills and stress management to enhance patients' interpersonal competencies. *Psychother: Theory Res Practice, 19,* 349–358.

Frohlich ED, Dustan HP, Page IH (1966). Hyperdynamic beta adrenergic state. *Arch Int Med, 177,* 614–619.

Fryrear JL & Werner S (1970). Treatment of a phobia by videotaped modeling. *Beh Ther, 1,* 391–394.

Fuller JL & Thompson WR (1978). *Foundations of behavior genetics.* Mosby, St. Louis, MO.

Furst JB & Cooper A (1970). Failure of systematic desensitization in two cases of obsessive-compulsive neurosis with fears of insecticide. *Beh Res Ther, 8,* 203–206.

Fussell P (1975). *The great war and modern memory.* Oxford University Press, London.

Fyer MR, Gorman J, Goetz R, Liebowitz M, Fyer AJ, & Klein DF (1985). Mitral valve prolapse and panic disorder. Paper to APA. Dallas, May.

Gabrielsen G, Kanwisher J, & Steen JB (1977). Emotional bradycardia: a telemetry study in incubating willow grouse. *Act Physiol Scand, 100,* 255–257.

Gagliardi GJ, Gallup GG, & Boren JL (1976). Effect of different pupil to eye-size ratios on tonic immobility in chickens. *Bull Psychonom Soc, 8,* 58–60.

Gaind R (1976). The role of beta blockers as an adjunct in behavior therapy. Paper to EABT. Greece, September.

Gale EN & Ayer WA (1969). Treatment of dental phobias. *J Am Dent Assoc, 78,* 1304–1307.

Galef BR (1977). Social transmission of food preferences: An adaptation for weaning in rats. *J Comp Physiol Psychol, 91,* 1136–1140.

Gallup GG (1974). Animal hypnosis: Factual status of a fictional concept. *Psychol Bull, 81,* 836–853.

Gallup GG & Maser JD (1977). Tonic immobility. In Maser J & Seligman M (Eds.), *Psychopathology: Experimental models* (ch. 10, pp. 334–357). Freeman, San Francisco.

Gallup GG, Nash RF, & Wagner AM (1971). Tonic immobility in chickens: Response characteristics and methodology. *Beh Res Meth Instr, 3,* 237–239.

Gallup GG Jr et al. (1977). Tryptophan and tonic immobility in chickens: Effects of dietary and systemic manipulations. *J Comp Physiol Psychol, 91,* 642–648.

Gallup GG, Boren JL, Suarez SD et al. (1980). Evidence for the integrity of central processing during tonic immobility. *Physiol Beh 25,* 189–194.

Garb JL & Stunkard AJ (1974). Taste aversions in man. *Am J Psychiat, 131,* 11, 1204–1207.

Garcia J (1981). Commentary on Johnston TD (1981). Contrasting approaches to a theory of learning. *Beh Brain Sci, 4,* 125–173.

Garcia J, Rusiniak KW, & Brett LP (1977). Conditioning food-illness aversions in wild animals. In Davis H & Hurwitz HMB (Eds.), *Operant pavlovian interactions.* Wiley, NY.

Garcia-Coll C, Kagan J, & Reznick JS (1984). Behavioral inhibition in young children. *Child Dev, 55,* 1005–1019.

Garfield P (1976). *Creative dreaming.* Futura, London.

Garmany G (1953). Discussion on abreaction. *Proc Roy Soc Med, 43,* 155–157.

Gash DM & Thomas GJ (1983). What is the importance of vasopression in memory processes? *Trends in Neurosciences, 6,* 197–198.

Geer JH (1966). Fear and autonomic arousal. *J Abn Psychol, 71,* 253–255.

Geer JH & Silverman I (1967). Treatment of a recurrent nightmare by behaviour modification procedures. *J Abn Psychol, 72,* 188–190.

Geisler A & Schou M (1969). Lithium treatment for obsessive-compulsive neurosis. *Nord Psykiat, 23,* 493–495.

Gelder MG & Marks IM (1966). Severe agoraphobia: A controlled prospective trial of behaviour therapy. *Br J Psychiat, 112,* 309–319.

Gelder MG & Marks IM (1970). Transsexualism and faradic aversion. In Green R (Ed.), *Transsexualism and sex reassignment.* Johns Hopkins University Press, Baltimore.

Gelder MG & Mathews AM (1968). Forearm blood flow and phobic anxiety. *Br J Psychiat, 114,* 1371–1376.

Gelder MG, Marks IM, & Wolff HH (1967). Desensitisation and psychotherapy in the treatment of phobic states. *Br J. Psychiat, 113,* 53–73.

Gelder MG, Bancroft JHJ, Gath DH et al. (1973). Specific and non-specific factors in behavior therapy. *Br J Psychiat, 123,* 445–462.

German GA & Arya OP (1969). Psychiatric morbidity amongst a Uganda student population. *Br J Psychiat, 115,* 1323.

Gershaw NJ & Schwartz JC (1971). The effects of a familiar toy and mother's presence on exploratory and attachment behaviors in young children. *Child Dev, 42,* 1662–1666.

Ghosh A & Marks IM (1986). Self-directed exposure for agoraphobia: A controlled trial. *Behav Ther* (in press).

Ghosh A, Marks IM & Carr AC (1986). Self-exposure for phobias. *Br J Psychiat* (in press).

Gibson EJ (1969). *Principles of perceptual learning and development.* Appleton, NY.

Gibson EJ & Walk RD (1960). The "visual cliff." *Sci Am, 202,* 64–71.

Gibson RW & Pickett JA (1983). Wild potato repels aphids by release of aphid alarm pheromone. *Nature, 302,* 608–609.

Gibson W (1970). Effect of a predator on the sleep of a prey. *Psychology, 6,* 231.

Gilman TT, Marcuse FL, & Moore AV (1950). The induction of tonic immobility in animals. *J Comp Physiol Psychol, 43,* 99–111.

Ginsberg G & Marks IM (1977). Costs and benefits of behavioural psychotherapy: A pilot study. *Psychol Med, 7,* 685–700.

Ginsberg G, Marks IM, & Waters H (1984). Controlled cost-benefit analysis of nurse therapy for neuroses in primary care. *Psychol Med, 14,* 683–690.

Ginsburg BE (1975). Nonverbal communication: Effect of affect on individual and group behavior. In Pliner P, Kramer L, & Alloway T (Eds.), *Nonverbal communication of aggression.* Plenum, NY.

Ginsburg BE (1972). Anxiety: A behavioural legacy. In *Ciba Symposium No. 8: Physiology, Emotions and Psychosomatic Illness* (pp. 163–172). Elsevier, NY.

Girodo M & Henry DR (1976). Cognitive, physiological and behavioural components of anxiety in flooding. *Can J Beh Sci, 8,* 224–231.

Girodo M & Roehl J (1978). Coping preparation and coping self-talk during the stress of flying. *J Consult Clin Psychol, 46,* 978–989.

Gispen WH, Reith MEA, Schotman P, Wiegant VM, Zwiers H, Bohus B, & De Wied D (1976). Neuropeptides, brain and behavior. In van Praag HM (Ed.) *Research in neurosis* (pp. 192–202). Bohn, Scheltema, Utrecht.

Gittelman R & Klein DF (1985) Childhood separation anxiety and adult agoraphobia. In Tuna H & Maser J (Eds.), *Anxiety and anxiety-related disorders* (ch. 20, pp. 389–402). Erlbaum, Hillsdale, NJ.

Gittelman-Klein R & Klein DF (1971). Controlled imipramine treatment of school phobia. *Arch Gen Psychiat, 25,* 204–207.

Gittleson NL (1966). The effect of obsessions on depressive psychosis. *Br J Psychiat, 112,* 253–9, 261, 705, 883, 889.

Glasgow RE (1975). In vivo prolonged exposure in the treatment of urinary retention. *Beh Ther, 6,* 701–702.

Glass AS & Bernucci RS (1966). *Neuropsychiatry in World War II.* Office of the Surgeon-General, Department of the Army, Washington, DC.

Glass CR, Gottman HM, Shmurak SH (1976). Response-acquisition and self-statement modification for dating-skills training. *J Consult Clin Psychol, 23,* 520–526.

Glass D & Singer JE (1972). *Stress and adaptation: Experimental studies of behaviour effects of exposure to aversive events.* Academic, NY.

Gloor P (1960) Amygdala. In Field J (Ed.), *Handbook of Neurophysiology* (Vol II): (Section I chap. LVIII) American Physiological Society.

Goddard GV, McIntyre DC, & Leech CK (1969). A permanent change in brain function resulting from daily electrical stimulation. *Exp Neur, 25,* 295–330.

Goethe JW (1770) Poetry and truth from my own life. In RO Mood (trans.), *Goethe's autobiography* (1949). Public Affairs Press, Washington DC.

Goktepe EO, Young LB, & Bridges PK (1975). A further review of the results of stereotactic subcaudate tractotomy. *Br J Psychiat, 126,* 270–280.

Goldberg J, Yinon Y, Saffir M, Merbaum M (1977). Fear in periods of stress and calm among Israeli students. *J Beh Ther Exp Psychiat, 8,* 5–9.

Goldfried MR, Decentenceo ET, & Weinberg L (1974). Systematic rational restructuring as a self-control technique. *Beh Ther, 5,* 247–254.

Goldsmith HH & Gottesman II (1981). A longitudinal study of temperament in young twins. *Child Dev, 52,* 91–103.

Goldstein AJ & Chambless DL (1978). A re-analysis of agoraphobia. *Beh Ther, 9,* 47–59.

Good BJ & Kleinman AM (1985). Culture and anxiety. In Tuma H & Maser J (1985), *Anxiety and anxiety-related disorders* (Ch. 14, pp. 297–324). Erlbaum, Hillsdale, NJ.

Goodall J (1968). The behaviour of free-living chimpanzees in the Gombe Stream Reserve. *Animal Behaviour Monographs, 1,* Part 3.

Goodall J (1977). Infant killing and cannibalism in free-living chimpanzees. *Folia Primatol, 28,* 259–282.

Goodwin D (1983). *Phobias.* Oxford University Press, NY.

Goodwin D, Guze S & Robins E (1969). Follow-up studies in obsessional neurosis. *Arch Gen Psychiat, 20,* 182–187.

Goorney AB (1970). Treatment of aviation phobias by behaviour therapy. *Br J Psychiat, 117,* 535–544.

Goorney AB & O'Connor PJ (1971). Anxiety associated with flying: A survey of military aircrew psychiatric casualties. *Br J Psychiat, 119,* 159–166.

Gordon A & Baum M (1971). Increased efficacy of flooding (response prevention) in rats through intracranial stimulation. *J Comp Physiol Psychol, 75,* 68.

Gordon PK (1983). Switching attention from obsessional thoughts: Case study. *J Psychiat Treat Eval, 5,* 171–174.

Gorman JM, Fyer AF, Gliklich J et al. (1981a). Mitral valve prolapse and panic disorder: effect of imipramine. In Klein DF & Rabkin JG (Eds.), *Anxiety revisited* (pp. 317–326). Raven, NY.

Gorman JM, Fyer AF, Gliklich J et al. (1981b). Sodium lactate in panic disorder and mitral valve prolapse. *Am J Psychiat, 138,* 247–249.

Gorman JM, Levy, Liebowitz, McGrath P et al. (1983). Effect of acute beta-adrenergic blockade on lactate-induced panic. *Arch Gen Psychiat, 40,* 1079–1082.

Gorman JM, Martinez JM, Liebowitz MR et al. (1984). Hypoglycemia and panic attacks. *Amer J Psychiat, 141,* 101–102.

Gorman JM, Askanazi J, Liebowitz M et al. (1984a). Response to hyperventilation in panic disorder. *Am J Psychiat, 141,* 857–861.

Gottesman II (1963). Heritability of personality: A demonstration. *Psychology Monograph, 77,* no. 572.

Gottesman II, Carey GC, & Bouchard TJ (1982). MMPI personality scale similarity in 26 pairs of identical twins reared apart: A sensitive detector of genetic variance. Paper to Behavior Genetics Association, Fort Collins, CO, June.

Gould JL (1982). *Ethology.* Norton, NY.

Gournay K & Howells K (1985). The base for exposure treatment in agoraphobia: client's home or outpatient clinic? *Beh Psychother* (in press).

Goyer PF & Eddleman HC (1984). Same-sex rape of nonincarcerated men. *Am J Psychiat, 141,* 576–579.

Graeff FG (1981). Minor tranquilizers and brain defense systems. *Brazil J Med Biol Res, 14,* 239–265.

Graham DT (1961). Prediction of fainting in blood donors. *Circulation, 23,* 901–906.

Graham P (1964). Controlled trial behaviour therapy vs conventional therapy: A pilot study. Unpublished DPM dissertation, University of London.

Granell de Aldaz E, Vivas E, Gelfand DM, & Feldman L (1984). School refusal and school-related fears in a Venezuelan sample. *J Nerv Ment Dis, 172,* 722–729.

Grant QAFR (1958). Age and sex trends in the symptomatology of disturbed children. DPM dissertation, University of London.

Gray JA (1979). Anxiety and the brain: Not by neurochemistry alone. Editorial in *Psychol Med, 9,* 605–609.

Gray JA (1982). The neuropsychology of anxiety. An enquiry into the functions of the septo-hippocampal system. *Beh Brain Sci, 5,* 469–534.

Gray JA (1982a). The neuropsychology of anxiety: An enquiry into the functions of the septo-hippocampal system. Clarendon, Oxford.

Gray J (1985). Basic biological and psychological research approaches to anxiety. In Tuma H & Maser J (Eds.), *Anxiety and anxiety disorders* (ch. 1, pp. 5–26). Erlbaum, Hillsdale, NJ.

Grayson JB, Foa EB, & Steketee G (1982). Distraction v attention-focusing during exposure. *Beh Res Ther, 20,* 323–328.

Graziano AM & Mooney KC (1980). Family self-control instruction for children's nighttime fear reduction. *J Consult Clin Psychol, 48,* 201–213.

Graziano AM, DeGiovanni IS, & Garcia KA (1979). Behavioral treatment of children's fears: A review. *Psychol Bull, 86,* 804–830.

Green M & Carr WJ (1968). Hawk-goose phenomenon: Further confirmation and search for a releaser. *J Psychol, 69,* 271–276.

Green M, Green R, & Carr WJ (1966). Hawk-goose phenomenon: Replication and extension. *Psychonom Sci, 4,* 185–186.

Greenberg D (1984). Are religious compulsions religious or compulsive? A phenomenological study. *Am J Psychother, 38,* 524–532.

Greenberg D & Belmaker R (1985). DDAVP in obsessive-compulsive disorder as a possible method to enhance positive benefit of behaviour therapy. *Br J Psychiat, 147,* 713–715.

Greenberg D & Stravynski A (1985). Patients who complain of social dysfunction. *Canad J Psychiat, 30,* 206–216.

Greenberg ED (1981). Obsessive-compulsive neurosis and season of birth. *Biol Psychiat, 16,* 5, 513–516.

Greer HS & Cawley RH (1966). The natural history of neurotic illness. In *Mervyn Archdall Medical Monograph, No. 3.* Australian Medical Association.

Greist JH & Greist GL (1981). *Fearless flying: A passenger guide to modern airline travel.* Nelson Hall, Chicago.

Greist J, Marks IM, Berlin F, & Noshirvani H (1980). Avoidance versus confrontation of fear. *Beh Ther, 11,* 1–14.

Griez E & Van den Hout MA (1983). Treatment of phobophobia by exposure to CO_2 induced anxiety symptoms. *J Nerv Ment Dis, 175,* 506–508.

Griez E & Van den Hout MA (1984). Carbon dioxide and anxiety. Joint doctoral disertation, Riksuniversiteit Limburg, Maastricht, Netherlands.

Grimshaw L (1964). Obsessional disorder and neurological illness. *J Neurol Neurosurg Psychiat, 27,* 229–231.

Grinker RR & Spiegel JP (1945). *Men under stress.* Blakiston, Philadelphia.

Grosz HJ & Farmer BB (1972). Pitts & Mclure's lactate-anxiety study revisited. *Br J Psychiat, 120,* 415–418.

Grubb TC (1977). Discrimination of aerial predators by American coots in nature. *Animal Beh, 25,* 1065–1066.

Grunhaus L, Gloger S, Birmacher B et al. (1983). Prolactin response to cold pressor test in panic attacks. *Psychiatr Res, 8,* 171–177.

Guilani B (1972). Role of competing response and manner of presentation of the aversive stimulus in modifying avoidance behavior. Doctoral dissertation, UCLA.

Gurnani PD & Vaughan M (1981). Changes in frequency and distress during prolonged repetition of obsessional thoughts. *Br J Clin Psychol, 20,* 79–81.

Gurney C, Roth M, Kerr A, Schapira K (1970). Treatment and classification of anxiety disorders. *Br J Psychiat, 117, 251–255.*

Gurney C, Roth M, Garside RF, Kerr TA & Schapira K (1972). Studies in the classification of affective disorders: II. The relationship between anxiety states and depressive illness. *Br J Psychiat, 121,* 162–166.

Gurski JC, Davis K & Scott JP (1980). Interaction of separation discomfort with contact comfort and discomfort in dogs. *Dev Psychobiol, 13,* 463–467.

Gustavsson B, Jansson L, Jerremalm A, Öst LG (1985). Therapist behaviours during exposure treatment of agoraphobia. *Beh Mod, 9,* 491–504.

Guttmacher LB & Nelles C (1984). In vivo desensitization alteration of lactate-induced panic: A case study. *Beh Ther, 15,* 369–372.

Hackman A & McLean C (1975). Flooding v thought stopping in the treatment of obsessional neurosis. *Beh Res Ther, 13,* 263–269.

Haefely W (1983) The mechanism of action of benzodiazepines. *J Psychoact Drugs,* 1–32.

Haefely W (1985). Biochemistry of anxiety. *Ann Acad Med Singapore, 14,* 81–83.

Hafner RJ (1976). Fresh symptom emergence after intensive behaviour therapy. *Br J Psychiat, 129,* 378–383.

Hafner RJ (1977). The husbands of agoraphobic women and their influence on treatment outcome. *Br J Psychiat, 131,* 289–294.

Hafner RJ (1977a). The husbands of agoraphobic women: Assortative mating or pathogenic interaction? *Br J Psychiat, 130,* 233–239.

Hafner J (1978). Catharsis during prolonged exposure for snake phobia. *Am J Psychiat, 135,* 247–248.

Hafner RJ & Marks IM (1976). Exposure in vivo of agoraphobics: Contributions of diazepam, group exposure, and anxiety evocation. *Psychol Med, 6, 71–88.*

Hafner RJ & Milton F (1977). The influence of propanolol on the exposure in vivo of agoraphobics. *Psychol Med, 7,* 419–425.

Hafner RJ & Ross MW (1983). Predicting the outcome of behavior therapy for agoraphobia. *Beh Res Ther, 21,* 375–382.

Hagman E (1932). A study of fears of children of preschool age. *J Exp Educ, 1,* 110–130.

Hagnell O & Kreitman N (1974). Mental illness in married pairs in a psychiatric population. *Br J Psychiat,* 293–302.

Halcomb RA, Hegmann JP, DeFries JC (1975). Open-field behavior in mice: A diallel analysis of selected lines. *Beh Genet, 5,* 217–231.

Hall CS (1951). The genetics of behavior. In SS Stevens (Ed.), *Handbook of experimental psychology.* Wiley, NY.

Hall GS (1897). A study of fears. *Am J Psychol, 8,* 147–249.

Hall RA & Hinkle JE (1972). Vicarious desensitization of test anxiety. *Beh Res Ther, 10,* 407–410.

Hallam RS (1978). Agoraphobia: A critical review of the concept. *Br J Psychiat, 133,* 314–319.

Hallam RS (1983). Psychometric analyses. In Rachman S (Ed.), *Fear and courage among military bomb-disposal operators. Adv Beh Res Ther, 4,* 105–120.

Hallam RS (1985). *Anxiety: Psychological perspectives on panic and agoraphobia.* Academic, NY.

Hallam RS & Hafner RJ (1978). Fears of phobic patients: Factor analyses of self-report data. *Beh Res Ther, 16,* 1–6.

Hallstrom T & Halling A (1984), Prevalence of dentistry phobia in an urban community sample. *Act Psychiatr Scand, 70,* 438–446.

Halonen J & Denny MR (1980). *Comparative psychology. An evolutionary analysis of animal behaviour.*

Hammen CL, Jacobs M, Mayol A, Cochran SD (1980). Dysfunctional cognitions and the effectiveness of skills and cognitive-behavioral assertion training. *J Consult Clin Psychol, 48,* 685–695.

Hand I & Lamontagne Y (1976). Exacerbation of interpersonal problems after rapid phobia removal. *Psychother, Theory Res Practice, 13,* 405–411.

Hand I & Schröder (1980) Die vago-vasale Ohnmacht bei der Blut-Verletzungs-Katastrophen (BVK)-Phobie und ihre verhaltenstherapeutische Behandlung. *Therapiewoche 30,* 923–932.

Hand I & Tichatzky M (1979). Behavioral group therapy for OCD. In Sjöden P & Bates S (Eds.), *Trends in behavior therapy,* Academic, NY.

Hand I & Wittchen HU (1986). *Panic and phobias.* Springer, Verlag, NY.

Hand I, Lamontagne Y, & Marks IM (1974). Group exposure (flooding) in vivo for agoraphobics. *Br J Psychiat, 124,* 588–602.

Hand I, Spoehring B, & Stanik E (1977). Treatment of obsessions, compulsions and phobias as hidden couple-counseling. In Boulougouris JC & Rabavilas AD (Eds.), *Treatment of phobic and obsessive-compulsive disorders* (ch. 12, pp. 115–126) Pergamon, Oxford.

Handler L (1972). The amelioration of nightmares in children. *Psychother, Theory Res Practice, 9,* 54–56.

Harding TW, de Arango MV, Baltazer J et al (1980). Mental disorders in primary health care: their frequency and diagnosis in four developing countries. *Psychol Med, 10,* 231–241.

Hardy GE & Cotterill JA (1982). A study of depression and obsessionality in dysmorphophobia and psoriatic patients. *Br J Psychiat, 140,* 19–22.

Hare E, Price J, & Slater E (1972). Fertility in obsessional neurosis. *Br J Psychiat, 121,* 197–205.

Hare EH (1965). *Triennial Statistical Report, 1961–1963.* Bethlem Royal and Maudsley Hospital, London.

Hare RD (1972). Response requirements and directional fractionation of autonomic responses. *Psychophysiology, 9,* 419–427.

Harlow HF & Zimmermann RR (1959). Affectional Responses in the infant monkey. *Science, 130,* 421–432.

Harper M & Roth M (1962). Temporal lobe epilepsy and the phobia-anxiety-depersonalisation syndrome. *Compr Psychiat, 3,* 129–151.

Harper RM (1971). Frequency changes in hippocampal electrical activity during movement and tonic immobility. *Physiol Beh, 7,* 55–58.

Harris EL, Noyes R, Crowe RR, & Chaudry DR (1983). A family study of agoraphobia: A pilot study. *Arch Gen Psychiat, 40, 1061–1064.*

Harris GM & Johnson SB (1983). Coping imagery and relaxation instructions in covert modeling for test anxiety. *Beh Ther, 14,* 144–157.

Hartley PHT (1950). Experimental analysis of interspecific recognition. *Symp Soc Exp Biol, 4,* 313–336.

Hartman N, Kramer R, Brown T, & Devereux RB (1982). Panic disorder in patients with mitral valve prolapse. *Am J Psychiat, 139,* 669–670.

Harvey PH & Greenwood PJ (1978). Anti-predator defence strategies: Some evolutionary problems. In Krebs JR and Davies NB (Eds.), *Behavioral Ecology.* Sinauer Associates, Sunderland, MA.

Haslerud GM (1938). The effect of movement of stimulus objects upon avoidance reactions in chimpanzees. *J Comp Psychol, 25,* 507–528.

Hastings JH & Walker MJ (1975). Effects of level of fear and rate of approach and cardiac rate and avoidance of a phobic stimulus. *Beh Ther, 6,* 445.

Hatton DC, Woodruff ML, & Meyer ME (1978). Cholinergic modulation of tonic immobility in the rabbit. *J Comp Physiol Psychol, 89,* 1053–1060.

Hatzenbuehler LC & Schroeder HE (1978). Desensitization procedures in the treatment of childhood disorders. *Psychology 85, 831–844.*

Hausman MS (1984). Comparison of cognitive-behavioral and social skill approaches for loneliness. Doctoral dissertation, Southern Illinois University.

Havik O (1980). Patient information and education as an intervention in physical illness: Review of outcome research. In *Proceedings of Conference on Cost-Efficiency Analysis in Clinical Psychology,* Geilo, Norway.

Hawkins RD & Kandel ER (1984). Is there a cell biological alphabet for learning? *Psychol Rev, 91,* 375–391.

Hawkins RD, Abrams TW, Carew TJ, & Kandel ER (1983). Cellular mechanism of classical conditioning in *Aplysia:* Activity-dependent amplification of presynaptic facilitation. *Science, 219,* 400–405.

Hay GG (1970) Dysmorphophobia. *Br J Psychiat, 116,* 399–406.

Hay GG (1970a). Psychiatric aspects of cosmetic nasal operations. *Br J Psychiat, 116,* 85–97.

Hay GG (1983). Paranoia and dysmorphophobia. *Br J Psychiat, 142,* 309.

Hayes BJ & Marshall WL (1984). Generalization of treatment effects in training public speakers. *Beh Res Ther, 22,* 519–533.

Haynes S & Mooney D (1975). Nightmare: Etiological theoretical and behavioural treatment considerations. *Psychol Rec, 25,* 225–236.

Haynes-Clements LA & Avery AW (1984). A cognitive-behavioral approach to social skills training with shy persons. *J Clin Psychol, 40,* 710–713.

Headland K & McDonald R (1986). Audiotaped feedback for obsessions *Beh Psychother,* (in press).

Hebb DO (1946). On the nature of fear. *Psychol Rev, 53,* 250–275.

Hebb DO & Thompson WR (1954). The social significance of animal studies. In Lindzey G (Ed.), *Handbook of social psychology,* (vol. I, p. 554). Addison-Wesley, Cambridge.

Hecht HM, Fichter M, & Postpischil F (1983). Obsessive-compulsive neurosis and anorexia nervosa. *Int J Eating Disord, 2,* 69–77.

Hein A (1972). Acquiring components of visually guided behavior. In Pick A (Ed.), *Minnesota symposia on child psychology* (vol 6). University of Minnesota Press, Minneapolis.

Heinz G (1973). Responses of ring-necked pheasant chicks *(Phasianus colchicus)* to conspecific calls. *Animal Beh, 21,* 1–9.

Held R & Hein A (1972). Movement-produced stimulation in the development of visually guided behavior. *J Comp Physiol Psychol, 81,* 394–398.

Helgason T (1964). Epidemiology of mental disorders in Iceland. *Act Psychiat Scand, Supp. 173.*

Helgason T (1978). Prevalence and incidence of mental disorders from a health questionnaire and a case register. *Act Psychiatr Scand, 58,* 256–266.

Henauer SA, Gillespie HK, & Hollister LE (1984). Yohimbine and the model anxiety state. *J Clin Psychiat, 45,* 512–515.

Henderson RW (1978). Forgetting of conditioned fear inhibition. *Learn Motiv, 8,* 16–30.

Hennessy JW & Levine S (1979). Stress, arousal and the pituitary-adrenal system: A psychoendocrine hypothesis. In Sprague SM & Epstein AN (Eds.), *Progress in psychobiology and physiological Psychology* (pp. 134–178).

Hennig CW, Dunlap WP, & Gallup GG (1976). Effect of distance between predator and prey and the opportunity to escape on tonic immobility in *anolis carolinensis. Psychol Rec, 26,* 313–320.

Hepner A & Cauthen NR (1975). Effects of subject control and graduated exposure on snake phobias. *J Consult Clin Psychol, 43,* 297–304.

Hermann BP & Melyn M (1984). Effects of carbamazepine on interictal psychopathology in TLE with ictal fear. *J Clin Psychiat, 45,* 169–171.

Hershberg SGA, Carlson G, Cantwell DP, & Strober M (1982). Anxiety and depressive disorders in disturbed children. *J Clin Psychiat, 43,* 358–361.

Hersov L (1960a). Persistent non-attendance at school. *J Child Psychol Psychiat, 1,* 130–136.

Hersov L (1960b). Refusal to go to school. *J Child Psychol Psychiat, 1,* 137–142.

Hersov L & Berg I (Eds.) (1980). *Out of school: Modern perspectives on truancy and school refusal.* Wiley, Chichester.

Hesso R & Thorell LH (1969). Lithium treatment for obsessive-compulsive neurosis. *Nord Psykiat, 23,* 496–499.

Heyse H (1975). Paper to Society for Psychotherapy Research. London, July.

Hiatt SW, Campos JJ, & Emde RN (1979). Facial patterning and infant emotional expression: Happiness, surprise and fear. *Child Dev, 50,* 1020–1035.

Hickey AJ, Andrews G, & Wilcken DEL (1983). Independence of mitral valve prolapse and neurosis. *Br Heart J, 50, 333–336.*

Hillbom E (1960). After-effects of brain injuries. *Act Psychiat Neurol Scand,* (Supp. 142), 35, 125.

Hinde RA (1954). Factors governing the strength of the partially inborn mobbing response of the chaffinch *(Frinchilla coelebs):* I: Its nature and course. *Proc Roy Soc,* B, *142,* 306–331.

Hinde RA (1960). Factors governing the strength of the partially inborn mobbing response of the chaffinch (*Frinchilla coelebs*): III. Interaction of short- and long-term effects. *Proc Roy Soc,* B, *153,* 398–420.

Hinde RA (1970). *Animal behavior: A synthesis of ethology and comparative psychology* (2nd ed.). McGraw-Hill, New York.

Hinde RA (1981). Animal signals: Ethological and games theory approaches are not incompatible. *Animal Beh, 29,* 535–542.

Hinde RA (1982). *Ethology.* Fontana.

Hinde RA & McGinnis L (1977). Some factors influencing the effects of temporary mother-infant separation in rhesus monkeys. *Psychol Med, 7,* 197–212.

Hindus P, Bergström K, Levander SE et al. (1985). Gamma capsulotomy in anxiety and OCD. In *Abstracts of the World Congress of Biological Psychiatry* (Abstract 311.7). Philadelphia.

Hingston RWG (1933). The meaning of animal colour and adornment (pp. 54–59, 142–145). Edward Arnold, London.

Hinkle LE & Wolff HG (1957). Health and the social environment. In Leighton AH, Clausen JA, & Wilson JN (Eds.), *Explorations in social psychiatry* (p. 131). Tavistock, London.

Hirsch J, Lindley RH, & Tolman EC (1955). An experimental test of an alleged innate sign stimulus. *J Comp Physiol Psychol, 48,* 278–280.

Hoagland H (1928). On the mechanism of tonic immobility in vertebrates. *J Gen Physiol, 11,* 715–741.

Hobbs WR, Wilkinson C, Peterson GA et al. (1984). Psychophysiology of agoraphobia. In Ballenger JC (Ed.), *Biology of agoraphobia* (ch. 3, pp. 65–80). American Psychiatric Press, Washington, DC.

Hocking FH (1977). Migrants after massive stress experiences. In *Proceedings of VI World Congress in Psychiatry* (Abstract no. 33). Honolulu, September.

Hodgson RJ & Rachman S (1970). Experimental investigation of implosion. *Beh Res Ther, 8,* 21–27.

Hoehn-Saric R (1982). Neurotransmitters in anxiety. *Arch Gen Psychiat, 39,* 735–742.

Hoehn-Saric R & Barksdale VC (1983). Impulsiveness in obsessive-compulsive patients. *Br J Psychiat, 143,* 177–182.

Hoeper EW, Nycz GR, Cleary PD, et al. (1979). Estimated prevalence of RDC mental disorder in primary medical care. *Int J Ment Health, 8,* 6–15.

Hofer MA (1970). Cardiac and respiratory function during sudden prolonged immobility in wild rodents. *Psychosom Med, 32,* 633–647.

Hoffman HS (1974). Fear mediated processes in the context of imprinting. In Lewis M & Rosenblum LA (Eds.), *The origins of fear* (ch. 2, pp. 25–48). Wiley, NY.

Hohmann GW (1962). The effect of dysfunctions of the autonomic nervous system on experienced feelings and emotions. Paper to Conference on Emotions and Feelings at the New School for Social Research, New York, October.

Holden AE, O'Brien GT, Barlow DH et al. (1983). Self-help manual for agoraphobia: Preliminary report of effectiveness. *Beh Ther, 14,* 545–556.

Hollingsworth CE, Tanguay PE, Grossman L, & Pabst P (1980). Long-term outcome of OCD in childhood. *Am Acad Child Psychiat, 19,* 134–145.

Holmes FB (1936). An experimental investigation of a method of overcoming children's fears. *Child Dev, 7,* 6–30.

Holmes W (1940). Colour changes and colour patterns of Sepia officinalis L. *Proc Zool Soc Lond, 110,* 17–35.

Hoogduin K (1986). On the diagnosis of OCD. *Am J Psychother* (in press).

Hoogduin CAL (1985). Mislukking en success bij de ambulante behandeling van dwangneurose. Doctoral dissertation, University of Leiden, Netherlands.

Hoogduin CAL & Hoogduin WA (1983). Outpatient treatment of obsessive-compulsive disorder. *Beh Res Ther, 22*, 455–459.

Hoogland HL, Sherman PW (1981). Nepotism and cooperative breeding in the black-tailed prairie Dog *(Sciuridae: Cynomys ludovicianus)* In Alexander RD & Tinkle DW (Eds.), *Natural selection and social behavior* (pp. 283–310). Chiron Press, NY.

Hoover CF & Insel TR (1984). Families of origin in obsessive-compulsive disorder. *J Nerv Ment Dis, 172*, 207–215.

Horne DJ & King NJ (1986). Preparation for surgery and other invasive medical procedures. In King NJ & Remenyi AG (Eds.), *Behavioural health care: Guidelines for health professionals.* Harcourt Brace, Sydney.

Horne DJ deL & McCormack H (1984). Behavioural psychotherapy for a blood and needle phobic mastectomy patient receiving adjuvant chemotherapy. *Beh Psychother, 12*, 342–349.

Horner T (1980). Two methods of studying stranger reactivity in infants: A review. *J Child Psychol Psychiat, 21*, 203–219.

Horowitz MJ, Krupnick J, Kaltreider N et al. (1981). Initial psychological response to parental death. *Arch Gen Psychiat, 38*, 316–323.

Horowitz M (1976). *Stress response syndromes.* Jason Aronson, NY.

Horowitz MJ, Wilner N, Kaltreider N, & Alvarez W (1980). Signs and symptoms of posttraumatic stress disorder. *Arch Gen Psychiat, 37*, 85–92.

Howard WA, Murphy SA, & Clarke JC (1983). The nature and treatment of fear of flying: A controlled investigation. *Beh Ther, 14*, 557–567.

Howlin P (1984). The elimination of long-term sleeping problems in a 6-year old autistic boy. *Beh Psychother, 12*, 257–260.

Hrdy SB (1984). When the bough breaks: There may be method in the madness of infanticide. *The Sciences.*

Hrdy SB (1977). *The langurs of Abu.* Harvard University Press, Cambridge.

Hrdy SB (1981). *The woman that never evolved.* Harvard University Press, Cambridge.

Hruska K & Yonas A (1972). Developmental changes in cardiac responses to optical stimulus of impending collisions. *Psychophysiology, 9*, 272.

Hsu LK (1978). Novel symptom emergence after behavior therapy in a hypodermic injection phobic. *Am J Psychiat, 135*, 237–238.

Hudson B (1974). The families of agoraphobics treated by behaviour therapy. *Br J Soc Work, 4*, 51–59.

Hudson BB (1940). Avoidance behavior of rats at various age levels. *Psychol Bull, 37*, 431.

Hudson CJ & Perkins SH (1984). Panic disorder and alcohol misuse. *J Stud Alcohol, 45*, 462–464.

Hugdahl K & Kärker A-C (1981). Biological vs experiential factors in phobic conditioning. *Beh Res Ther, 19*, 109–115.

Hugdahl K & Öst L-G (1985). Subjective physiological and cognitive symptoms in six different clinical phobias. *Pers Indiv Diff, 6*, 175–188.

Hume WI (1973). Physiological measures in twins. In Claridge G, Canter S, & Hume WI (Eds.), *Personality differences and biological variations: A study of twins.* Pergamon, Oxford.

Humphries DA & Driver PM (1971). Protean defence by prey animals. *Oecologia, 5*, 285–302.

Hunt TJ (1970). Tachycardia & bradycardia associated with particular forms of stimuli. *J Physiol* (Land), *210*, 64.

Hunter RCA, Lohrenz MD, & Schwartzman AE (1964). Nosophobia and hypochondriasis in medical students. *J Nerv Mental Dis, 139*, 147–152.

Husain MZ (1971). Desensitization and flooding (implosion) in treatment of phobias. *Am J Psychiat, 127,* 1509–1514.

Hutt C & Ounsted C (1970), Gaze aversion and its significance in childhood autism. In Hutt SJ & Hutt C (Eds.), *Behaviour studies in psychiatry* (ch. 6, p. 103). Pergamon, Oxford.

Hymas N (1986). Obsessive-compulsive disorder and brain-dysfunction: A review. Unpublished manuscript.

Immelman K & Suomi SJ (1981). Sensitive phases in development. In Immelman K, Barlow G, Main M, & Petrinovich L (Eds.), *Issues in behavioral development.* Cambridge University Press, Cambridge.

Ingram IM (1961a). Obsessional illness in mental hospital patients. *J Mentl Sci, 107,* 382–402.

Ingram IM (1961b). The obsessional personality and obsessional illness. *Am J Psychiat, 117,* 1016–1019.

Ingram IM & McAdam WA (1960). The electroencephalogram, obsessional illness and obsessional personality. *J Ment Sci, 106,* 686.

Inouye R (1973). Electroencephalographic study in obsessive-compulsive states. *Clin Psychiat, 15,* 1071–1083.

Insel TR (1982). Obsessive-compulsive disorder—five clinical questions and a suggested approach. *Comp Psych, 23,* 241–251.

Inscl TR (1984). *New findings in OCD.* American Psychiatric Press, Washington, DC.

Insel TR & Pickar D (1983). Naloxone administration in obsessive-compulsive disorder: Report of two cases. *Am J Psychiat, 140,* 1219–1220.

Insel TR, Kalin NJ, Guttmacher LB et al. (1982a). The dexamethasone suppression test in OCD. *Psychiatr Res, 6,* 153–160.

Insel TR, Gillin JC, Moore A, Mendelson WB, Loewenstein RJ, & Murphy DL (1982b). The sleep of patients with OCD. *Arch Gen Psychiat, 39,* 1372–1377.

Insel TR, Alterman I, & Murphy DL (1982c). Antiobsessional and antidepressant effects of clomipramine in OCD. *Psychopharm Bull, 120,* 241–248.

Insel TR, Murphy DL, Cohen RM, Alterman I, Kilts C, & Linnoila M (1983). Clomipramine and clorgyline in OCD. *Arch Gen Psychiat, 40,* 605–612.

Insel TR, Donnelly EF, Lalakea ML, Alterman IS, & Murphy DL (1983a). Neurological and neuropsychological studies of OCD. *Biol Psychiat, 18,* 741–751.

Insel TR, Hamilton JA, Guttmacher LB, & Murphy DL (1983c). D-amphetamine in obsessive-compulsive disorder. *Psychopharmacology, 80,* 231–235.

Insel TR, Ninan PT, Aloi J, Jimerson D, Skolnick P, & Paul SM (1984). Bz receptors and anxiety in non-human primates. *Arch Gen Psychiat, 41,* 741–750.

Insel TR, Mueller EA III, Gillin C, Siever LJ, & Murphy DL (1984b). Biological markers in oc and affective disorders. *J Psychiat Res, 18,* 407–423.

Insel TR, Hoover C, & Murphy DL (1984c). Parents of patients with obsessive-compulsive disorder. *Psychol Med, 13,* 807–811.

Insel TR, Mueller EA, Alterman I et al. (1985). Obsessive-compulsive disorder and serotonin: Is there a connection? *Biol Psychiat, 20,* 1174–1188.

Isaacs B (1978). *Recent advances in geriatric medicine* (vol. 1). Churchill Livingstone, London.

Isaacson RL (1974). *The limbic system.* Plenum, N.Y.

Isom GE & Elshowihy M (1982). Interaction of acute and chronic stress with respiration: Modification by naloxone. *Biochem Beh, 16,* 599–603.

Iversen S (1985). Where in the central nervous system do benzodiazepines act? In *Psychopharmacology: Recent advances and future prospects.* Oxford University Press, NY.

Jablensky A (1985). Approaches to the definition classification of anxiety and related disorders in European psychiatry. In Tuma H & Maser J (Eds.), *Anxiety and anxiety-related disorders* (ch. 39, pp. 755–758). Erlbaum, Hillsdale, NJ.

Jablensky A, Sartorius N, Gulbinat W, & Ernberg G (1981). Depressives contacting psychiatric services in 4 cultures. *Act Psychiat Scand, 63,* 367–383.

Jacklin CN, Maccoby EE, & Doering CH (1983). Neonatal sex-steroid hormones and timidity in 6–18 month old boys and girls. *Dev Psychobiol, 16,* 163–168.

Jackson JH (1879). In Taylor J (Ed.) (1937), *Selected writings of John Hughling's Jackson. On Epilepsy and Epileptiform Convulsions.* (vol. I). Hodder & Stoughton, London.

Jacobi W (1923). *Grenzfr Nerv u Seelenleb, 114,* 1.

James IM, Burgoyne W, & Savage IT (1983). Pindolol for disturbed musical performance. *J Roy Soc Med, 76* 194–196.

James I & Savage I (1984). Nadolol, diazepam and placebo for anxiety in musicians. *Am Heart J, 108,* 1150–1155.

James IM, Pearson RM, Griffith DNW, & Newbury P (1977). Oxprenolol for stage fright in musicians. *Lancet, 2,* 952–957.

James JE, Hampton M, & Larsen SA (1983). Imaginal and in vivo desensitization in agoraphobia. *J Beh Ther Exp Psychiat, 14,* 203–207.

James W (1902). *Varieties of religious experience.* Republished 1961 by Collier, NY.

Janet P (1908). *Les obsessions et la psychasthénie* (2nd ed, 1908). Baillière, Paris.

Janet P (1925). *Psychological healing* (2nd ed.). Macmillan, NY.

Janis IL (1954). Problems of theory in the analysis of stress behaviour. *J Soc Issues, 10,* 12–25.

Jannoun L, Munby M, Catalan J, & Gelder M (1980). Home-based treatment for agoraphobia, replication and controlled evaluation. *Beh Ther, 11,* 294–305.

Jansson L, Jerremalm A, & Öst LG (1986). One-year followup of agoraphobics after exposure in vivo or applied relaxation. *Br J Psychiat* (in press).

Jardine JR, Martin NG, & Henderson AS (1984). Genetic covariation of neuroticism and the symptoms of anxiety and depression. *J Nerv Ment Dis, 1,* 89–107.

Jaremko ME (1982). Cognitive restructuring in the clinical extinction of fear and avoidance. *Scand J Beh Ther, 11,* 175–182.

Jasper HH & Douane B (1968). Neurophysiological mechanisms in learning. In Stellar E & Sprague M (Eds.), *Progress in physiological psychology.*

Jay SM, Elliot CH, Ozolins M et al. (1985). Behavioral management of children's distress during painful medical procedures. *Beh Res Ther, 23,* 513–520.

Jenike AJ & Brotman AW (1984). The EEG in obsessive-compulsive disorder. *J Clin Psychiat, 45,* 122–124.

Jenike MA (1985). Dysmorphophobia. Letter to *Br J Psychiat, 146,* 326.

Jenike MA, Baer L, Minichiello WE (1986). Obsessive-compulsive disorders: Theory and management. PSG, Littleton, Mass.

Jennings HS (1906). *Behavior of the lower organisms.* Columbia University Press, NY.

Jerremalm A, Jansson L, & Öst LG (1985). Individual response patterns in the treatment of dental phobia. Paper to EABT. Munich, August.

Jersild AT (1950). *Child psychology* (3rd ed., pp. 260–284). Staple Press, London.

Jersild AT & Holmes FB (1935). Children's fears. *Child Development Monograph no. 20.*

Jersild AT & Holmes FB (1935a). Methods of overcoming children's fears. *J Psychol, 1,* 75–104.

Jersild AT, Markey FU, & Jersild CL (1933). Children's fears, dreams, wishes, daydreams, likes, dislikes, pleasant and unpleasant memories. *Child Development Monograph* No. 12.

John E (1941). A study of the effects of evacuation and air raids on preschool children. *Br J Educ Psychol, 11,* 173–182.

Johnson A, Falsteen E, Szureck S, & Svendsen M (1941). School phobia. *Am J Orthopsychiat, 11,* 702–711.

Johnson LC (1970). A psychophysiology for all states. *Psychophysiology, 6,* 501–516.

Johnson LC & Lubin A (1967). The orienting reflex during waking and sleeping. *Electroenceph Clin Neurophysiol, 22,* 11–21.

Johnson SB & Melamed BG (1977). The assessment and treatment of children's fears. In Lahey BB & Kazdin AE (Eds.), *Advances in child psychol* (vol. 2, pp. 107–139). Plenum, NY.

Johnson WF, Emde RN, & Pannabecker BJ (1982). Maternal perception of infant emotion from birth through 18 months. *Infant Beh Dev, 5,* 313–322.

Johnston D & Gath D (1973). Arousal levels and attribution effects in diazepam-assisted flooding. *Br J Psychiat, 122,* 463–466.

Johnston DW, Lancashire M, Mathews AM et al. (1976). Imaginal flooding v real exposure in agoraphobics: Changes in treatment. *Br J Psychiat, 129,* 372–377.

Johnston M, Johnston DW, Wilkes H, Burnes LE & Thorpe GL (1984). Cumulative scales for the measurement of agoraphobia. *Br J Clin Psychol, 23,* 133–143.

Johnstone EC et al. (1980). Neurotic illness and its response to anxiolytic and antidepressant prescription. *Psychol Med, 10,* 321–328.

Jones E (1953). *Sigmund Freud: Life and work* (vol I). Hogarth, London.

Jones HG (1956). The application of conditioning and learning techniques to the treatment of a psychiatric patient. *J Abn Soc Psychol, 52,* 414–420.

Jones HE & MC (1928). Motivation and emotion: fear of snakes. *Childhood Educ, 5,* 136–143.

Jones I & Robinson I (1977). Severe illness and anxiety following a reported magical act on an Australian Aboriginal. *Med J Austr, 2,* 93–96.

Jones M (1948). Physiological and psychological responses to stress in neurotic patients. *J Ment Sci, 94,* 392–427.

Jones MC (1924). Elimination of children's fears. *J Exp Psychol, 7,* 382–390.

Jones RB, Sinnott A, & Fordham AS (1980). Group in vivo exposure plus counselling of significant others in agoraphobia. *Beh Psychother, 8,* 31–35.

Jones WH, Check JM, Briggs SR (1986). *Shyness.* Plenum, NY.

Jormakka L (1976). The behaviour of children during a first encounter. *Scand J Psychol, 17,* 15–22.

Juel-Nielsen N (1965). *Monozygotic twins reared apart.* International Universities Press, NY.

Julien RA, Riviere B & Note ID (1980). Traitement comportmentale et cognitif des obsessions et compulsions resultat et discussion. *Seance Due Lundi,* 27 Oct., 1123–1133.

Jungkunz G, Engel RR, King UG, & Kuss HJ (1983). Endogenous opiates increase pain tolerance after stress in humans. *Psychiatr Res, 8,* 13–18.

Jurgens V (1974). Hypothalamus and behavioral patterns. *Prog Brain Res, 41,* 445–464.

Kagan J (1979). Overview: Perspectives on human infancy. In Osofsky JD (Ed.), *The handbook of infant development* (pp. 1–25). Wiley, NY.

Kagan J (1981). *The second year.* Harvard University Press, Cambridge.

Kagan J (1982). The fearful child's hidden talents. *Psychol Today,* July, 50–59.

Kagan J & Moss HA (1962). *Birth to maturity.* Wiley, NY.

Kagan J, Kearsley RB & Zelazo PR (1975). The emergence of initial apprehension to unfamiliar peers. In Lewis M & Rosenblum LA (Eds.), *Friendship and peer relations* (ch. 7, pp. 187–206). Wiley, NY.

Kagan J, Kearsley RB, & Zelazo PR (1978). *Infancy: Its place in human development.* Harvard University Press, Cambridge.

Kagan J, Reznick JS, Clarke C, Snidman N, & Garcia-Coll C (1984). Behavioral inhibition to the unfamiliar. *Child Dev, 55,* 2212–2225.

Kahn JH & Nursten JP (1962). School refusal. *Am J Orthopsychiat, 32,* 707–718.

Kalin NH & Shelton SE (1984). Acute behavioral stress affects the dexamethasone suppression test in rhesus monkeys. *Biol Psychiat, 19,* 113–117.

Kalin NH, Shelton SE, McKinney WT et al. (1984). Stress alters the dexamethasone suppression test. *Psychopharm Bull* (in press).

Kamin LJ (1957). Retention of an incompletely learned avoidance response. *J Comp Physiol Psychol, 50,* 457–460.

Kamin LJ (1968). "Attention-like" processes in classical conditioning. In Jones MR (Ed.), *Miami symposium on the prediction of behavior: Aversive stimulation* (pp. 9–33). University of Miami Press, Miami.

Kandel ER (1976). *Cellular basis of behaviour.* Freeman, San Francisco.

Kandel ER (1979). Small systems of neurons. *Sci Am, 241,* 66–76.

Kandel ER (1983). From metapsychology to molecular biology: Explorations into the nature of anxiety. *Am J Psychiat, 140,* 1277–1293.

Kandel ER (1984). Steps toward a molecular grammar for learning: explorations into the nature of memory. Paper to Harvard/Bicentennial Symposium.

Kandel ER & Schwartz JH (1981). *Principles of neural science.* Arnold, London.

Kandel ER & Schwartz JH (1982). Molecular biology of learning: Modulation of transmitter release. *Science, 218,* 433–443.

Kanter NJ & Goldfried MR (1979). Rational restructuring vs self-control desensitization for interpersonal anxiety. *Beh Ther, 10,* 472–490.

Kantor JS, Zitrin CM, & Zeldis SM (1980). Mitral valve prolapse syndrome in agoraphobic patients. *Am J Psychiat, 137,* 467–469.

Karabanow O (1977). Double-blind controlled study in phobias and obsessions complicated by depression. *Int J Med Res, 5,* 42–48.

Kardiner A & Spiegel H (1947). *War stress and neurotic illness.* Paul Hoeber, NY.

Kasvikis GY, Tsakiris F, Marks IM, Basoglu M, & Noshirvani HR (1986). Women with OCD frequently had past anorexia nervosa. *Internat J Eating Dis* (in press).

Katzev R (1967). Extinguishing avoidance responses as a function of delayed warning signal termination. *J Exper Psychol, 75,* 339.

Katzev RD & Balch OK (1974). The restoration of extinguished avoidance responses. *Beh Res Ther, 12,* 77–87.

Katzev RD & Berman JS (1974). Effect of exposure to conditioned stimulus and control of its termination in the extinction of avoidance behavior. *J Comp Physiol Psychol, 2,* 347–353.

Katzev RD & Hendersen RW (1971). Effects of exteroceptive feedback stimuli on extinguishing avoidance responses in Fisher$_{344}$ rats. *J Comp Physiol Psychol, 74,* 66–74.

Kavanagh C (1983). Two psychological approaches for the severely burned child. *J Am Acad Child Psychiat, 22,* 145–156.

Kayton L & Borge C (1967). Birth order and the obsessive-compulsive character. *Arch Gen Psychiat, 17,* 751–55.

Kazarian SS & Evans DR (1977). Modification of obsessional ruminations: A comparitive study. *Can J Beh Sci, 9,* 91–100.

Keane TM & Kaloupek DG (1982). Imaginal flooding in the treatment of a posttraumatic stress disorder. *J Consult Clin Psychol, 50,* 138–140.

Kelleher MJ (1972). Cross-national (Anglo-Irish) differences in obsessional symptoms and traits of personality. *Psychol Med, 2,* 1, 33–41.

Kellogg, Rhoda (1959). *What children scribble and why*. National Press Publications, Palo Alto.

Kelly D (1966). Measurement of anxiety by forearm blood flow. *Br J Psychiat, 112*, 789–798.

Kelly D (1980). *Anxiety and emotions: Physiological basis and treatment*. Thomas, Springhill, NY.

Kelly D & Cobb JP (1985). Limbic leucotomy for severe OCD. In *Abstracts of the World Congress of Biological Psychiatry* (Abstract 311.6 p. 245). Philadelphia, September.

Kelly D & Walter CJS (1968). Diagnosis and anxiety assessed by forearm blood flow and other measurements. *Br J Psychiat, 114*, 611–626.

Kelly D, Guirguis W, Frommer E et al. (1970). Treatment of phobic states with anti-depressants. *Br J Psychiat, 116*, 387–398.

Kelly D, Mitchell-Heggs N, & Sherman D (1971). Anxiety and lactate effects assessed clinically and physiologically. *Br J Psychiat, 119*, 129–141.

Kendell RE (1974). Stability of psychiatric diagnoses. *Br J Psychiat, 124*, 352–356.

Kendell RE & Discipio WJ (1970). Obsessional symptoms and obsessional personality traits in depressive illness. *Psychol Med, 1*, 65–72.

Kendon, Adam (1965). Some functions of gaze-direction in social interaction. Unpublished manuscripts, Institute of Experimental Psychology, Oxford.

Kendrick MJ, Craig KD, Lawson DM, & Davidson PO (1982). Cognitive and behavioral therapy for musical performance anxiety. *J Consul Clin Psychol, 50*, 353–362.

Kennedy A (1960). Indications for psychological treatment. *Lancet, 1*, 1257.

Kennedy WA (1965). School phobia: Rapid treatment of 50 cases. *J Abn Psychol, 70*, 285–289.

Kenney M, Mason W, & Hill S (1979). Effects of age, objects, and visual experience on affective responses of rhesus monkeys to strangers. *Dev Psychol, 15*, 176–184.

Kenny FT, Mowbray RM, & Lalani S (1978). Faradic disruption of obsessive ideaion. *Beh Ther, 9*, 209–221.

Kent G (1984). Anxiety, pain and type of dental procedure. *Beh Res Ther, 22*, 465–469.

Kenward RE (1978). Hawks and doves: Attack success and selection in goshawk flights at wood-pigeons. *J Am Ecol, 47*, 449–460.

Kerr TA, Roth M, & Schapira K (1974). Prediction of outcome in anxiety states and depressive illnesses. *Br J Psychiat, 124*, 125–133.

Kerry RJ (1960). Phobia of outer space. *J Ment Sci, 106*, 1383–1387.

Ketterer MW (1982). Lateralized representation of affect, affect cognizance and the coronary-prone personality. *Biol Psychol, 15*, 171–189.

Kettl PA & Marks IM (1986). Neurologic factors in OCD. 2 case reports and a review of the literature. *Br J Psychiat* (in press).

Kilpatrick DG, Veronen LJ, Resick PA (1982). Psychological sequelae to rape: In Doleys DM, Meredith RL, & Ciminero AR (Eds.), *Behavioral medicine: Assessment and treatment strategies* (pp. 473–497). Plenum, NY.

Kilpatrick DG, Veronen LJ, & Best CL (1984). Factors predicting psychological distress among rape victims. In CR Figley (Ed.), *Trauma and its Wake*. Brunner/Mazel, NY.

Kilpatrick DG, Best CL & Veronen LJ (1984a). *Mental health after criminal victimization: A random community survey*. American Psychological Association, Toronto.

Kimble GA (1961). *Hilgard & Marquis' conditioning and learning*. Methuen, London.

Kindness K & Newton A (1984). Is social skills training enough? *Beh Psychother, 12*, 212–222.

King A (1962). Phenelzine treatment of Roth's calamity syndrome. *Med J Austr, 1,* 879–883.

King A & Little JC (1959). Thiopentone treatment of the phobic-anxiety-depersonalization syndrome. *Proc Roy Soc Med, 52,* 595–596.

King N & Hamilton NA (1986). *Children's phobias.* Wiley, Chichester.

Kinzie JD, Fredrickson RH, Ben R et al. (1984). PTSD among survivors of Cambodian concentration camps. *Am J Psychiat, 141,* 645–650.

Kipper DA (1977). Behavior therapy for fears brought on by war experiences. *J Consult Clin Psychol, 45,* 216–221.

Kirk JW (1983). Behavioural treatment of obsessive-compulsive patients in routine clinical practice. *Beh Res Ther, 21,* 57–62.

Kirsch I (1982). Efficacy expectations or response predictions. *J Pers Soc Psychol, 42,* 132–136.

Kirsch I (1985). Self-efficacy and expectancy: Old wine with new labels. *J Pers Soc Psychol, 49,* 824–830.

Kirsch I, Tennen H, Wickless C et al. (1983). Role of expectancy in fear-reduction. *Beh Ther, 4,* 520–533.

Kleck R (1966). Emotional arousal in interactions with stigmatized persons. *Psychol Rep, 19,* 1226.

Klein DF (1964). Delineation of two drug-responsive anxiety syndromes. *Psychopharmacologia, 5,* 397–408.

Klein DF (1967). Importance of psychiatric diagnosis in prediction of clinical drug effects. *Arch Gen Psychiat, 16,* 118–126.

Klein DF, Zitrin CM, Woerner MG, & Ross DC (1983). Treatment of phobias: II. Behavior therapy and supportive psychotherapy. *Arch Gen Psychiat, 40,* 139–145.

Klein SB & Spear NE (1970). Forgetting by rats after intermediate intervals ("Kamin Effect") as retrieval failure. *J Comp Physiol Psychol, 71,* 165–170.

Kleinknecht RA, Klepac RK, & Alexander LD (1973). Origin and characteristics of fear of dentistry. *J Am Dent Assoc, 86,* 842–847.

Klemm WR (1971). Neurophysiologic studies of the immobility reflex ("animal hypnosis"). In Ehrenpreis S & Solnitsky OC (Eds.), *Neurosciences research* (vol. 4, pp. 165–212). Academic, NY.

Klemm WR (1976). Identity of sensory and motor systems that are critical to the immobility reflex ("animal hypnosis"). *J Neurosci Res, 2,* 57–69.

Klepac RK, Lander EM, & Smith GR (1984). Graduated exposure and two forms of stress inoculation for dental fear. Paper to AABT. Washington, DC, November.

Klepac RK (1975). Treatment of dental avoidance by desensitisation or by increasing pain tolerance. *J Beh Ther Exper Psychiat, 6,* 307–310.

Klepac RK, McDonald M, Hang G, & Dowling J (1980). Reactions to pain among subjects high and low in dental fear. *J Beh Mod, 3,* 373–384.

Klepac RK, Dowling J, & Hauge G (1982). Reactions to pain in dental avoidance. *J Beh Ther Exp Psychiat, 13,* 293–300.

Klerman GL (1980). Anxiety and depression. In Burrows G & Davies B (Eds.), *Handbook of studies on anxiety* (ch. 9, pp. 145–164). Elsevier Biomedical Press, NY.

Klingman A, Melamed BG, Cuthbert MI, & Hermecz DA (1984). Effects of participant modeling on information acquisition. *J Consult Clin Psychol, 52,* 414–422.

Klinnert MD, Campos JJ, Sorce JF, Emde RN, & Svedja M (1983). Emotions as behavior regulators: social referencing in infancy. In Plutchik R & Kellerman H (Eds.) *The emotions. Emotions in early development* (vol. 2), Academic, NY.

Klorman R, Weissberg RD, & Wiesenfeld AR (1977). Individual differences in fear and response to affective stimuli. *Psychophysiology, 14,* 45–51.

Klorman R, Hilpert PL, Michael R et al. (1980). Coping and mastery modeling for experienced and inexperienced pedodontic patients. *Beh Ther, 11,* 156–168.

Klosko JS, Heimberg RG, Dodge CS, & Kennedy CR (1984). Depression, anxiety and outcome of treatment for social phobia. Paper to AABT. Philadelphia, November.

Knoll B (1972). Strain differences in escape responses of rats. *Activitas nervosa superior* (Praha) *14,* 4.

Knowles FW (1964). Hypnotherapy in chronic hysterical urinary retention: Report of a case. *NZ Med J, 63,* 38–40.

Ko GN, Elsworth JD, Roth PH, Rifkin BG, Leigh H, Hurzeler MA, & Redmond DE (1983). Panic-induced elevation of plasma MHPG in phobic-anxious patients: Effects of clonidine or imipramine. *Arch Gen Psychiat, 40,* 425–430.

Koff E, Borod JC & White B (1983). A left hemispace bias for visualizing emotional situations. *Neuropsychologia, 21,* 273–275.

Kohlenberg et al. (1972). Children's fears cited by King & Hamilton (1986).

Kohler W (1925). *The mentality of apes.* Routledge & Kegan Paul, London.

Kohts N (1935). Infant, ape, and human child (instincts, emotions, plays and habits). Russian with English Summary. *Sci Mem Mus Darwin* (Moscow), *3,* 1–596.

Kolvin I, Berney TP, & Bhate SR (1984). Classification and diagnosis of depression in school phobia. *Br J Psychiat, 145,* 347–357.

Koocher GP, O'Malley JE, Foster D, & Gogan JL (1976). Death anxiety in normal children and adolescents. *Psychiat Clin, 9,* 220–229.

Kora T (1968). A method of instruction in psychotherapy. *Jikeikai Med J 15,* 316–325.

Koskenvuo M, Langinvainio H, Kaprio J, & Sarna S (1983). Health related psychosocial correlates of neuroticism. In *Abstracts of the 4th International Congress on Twin Studies* (p. 32). London, June.

Koss MP (1983). The scope of rape: Implications for the clinical treatment of victims. *Clin Psychologist, 36,* 88–105.

Kothari LK, Bordia A, & Gupta OP (1973). The yogic claim of voluntary control over heart beat: An unusual demonstration. *Am Heart J, 86,* 282–284.

Kotila RR (1969). Education and 4 varieties of implosion in fear of snakes. Doctoral dissertation, Washington State University, Seattle.

Kozak MJ & Montgomery GK (1981). Multimodal behavioral treatment of recurrent injury-scene-elicited fainting. *Beh Psychother, 9,* 316–321.

Kraemer GW, Ebert MH, Lake CR, & McKinney WT (1984). Hypersensitivity to d-amphetamine several years after early social deprivation in rhesus. *Psychopharmacologia, 82,* 266–271.

Kraemer GW & McKinney W (1979). Interactions of pharmacological agents altering biogenic amine metabolism and depression. *J Affect Dis, 1,* 33–54.

Kraemer GW (1985). Effects of differences in early social experience on primate neurobiological-behavioral development. In Reite M & Field T (Eds.), *The psychobiology of attachment* (pp. 135–161). Academic, NY.

Kraepelin E (1913). *Lectures on Clinical Psychiatry,* Translation from 2nd ed., pp. 270–273.

Kraft T (1967). Treatment of the housebound housewife syndrome. *Psychother Psychom, 15,* 446–453.

Kramer SR (1975). Behavior rehearsal and practice dating for heterosexual social inhibition. Doctoral dissertation, University of Texas at Austin.

Krane RV & Wagner AR (1975). Taste aversion learning with a delayed shock US. *J Comp Physiol Psychol, 88,* 882–889.

Krapfl JE & Nawas MM (1970). Differential orderings of stimulus presentation in systematic desensitization. *J Abn Psychol, 75,* 333–337.

Krasne FB (1965). Branchiomma habituation. *J Exp Biol, 42,* 307–322.

Kraupl TF (1966). *Psychopathology: Its causes and symptoms* (pp. 156–169). Butterworths, London.

Krieckhaus EE (1966). Mammillothalamic tract in conditioned avoidance. In *Abstracts of VIII International Congress of Psychology* (vol. I, p. 312). Moscow, August.

Krieger DT & Martin JB (1982). Brain peptides. *N Eng J Med, 304,* 944–951.

Kringlen E (1965). Obsessional neurosis: A long term followup. *Br J Psychiat, 111,* 709–722.

Kruijt JP (1964). Ontogeny of social behavior in Burmese red jungle fowl *(gallus gallus spadiceus). Beh Supp, 12,* 1–201.

Krushinskii LV (1962). *Animal Behaviour. Its normal and abnormal development.* Consultants Bureau, NY.

Kruuk H (1972). *The spotted hyena: A study of predation and social behavior.* University of Chicago Press, Chicago.

Kullberg G (1977). Differences in effect of capsulotomy and cingulotomy. In Sweet WS, Obrador S, Martin-Rodriguez JG (Eds.), *Neurosurgical treatment in psychiatry, pain and epilepsy.* University Park Press, Baltimore.

Kunsebeck HW, Lempa W, & Freyberger H (1984). Prevalence of psychiatric disorders among nonpsychiatric inpatients. *Dtsch Med Wochenschr, 109,* 1438–1442.

Lacey JI (1967). Somatic response patterning and stress. In Appley MH & Trumbull R (Eds.). *Psychological stress.* Appleton, NY.

Ladee G (1966). Hypochondrische syndromen. Unpublished Ph.D dissertation, Leiden University.

Lader MH (1966). Predictive value of autonomic measures in patients with phobic states. DPM dissertation, University of London.

Lader MH (1975). *The psychophysiology of mental illness.* Routledge & Kegan Paul, London.

Lader MH (1976). Physiological research in anxiety. In HM van Praag (Ed.), *Research in neurosis.* Bohn, Scheltema, Utrecht.

Lader MH & Marks IM (1971). *Clinical anxiety.* Heinemann Medical, London.

Lader MH & Mathews AM (1970). Physiological changes during spontaneous panic attacks. *J Psychosom Res, 14,* 377–382.

Lader MH & Wing L (1966). Physiological measures, sedative drugs and morbid anxiety. *Maudsley Monograph No. 14.* Oxford University Press, London.

Lader MH, Gelder MG, & Marks IM (1967). Palmar skin-conductance measures as predictors of response to desensitisation. *J Psychosom Res, 11,* 283–290.

Ladouceur RL (1983). Participant modeling with or without cognitive treatment for phobias. *J Consult Clin Psychol, 51,* 942–944.

Lagler KF, Bardach JE, Miller RR, Passino DRM (1962). *Ichthyology* (p. 289). Wiley, NY.

Lamontagne Y & Marks IM (1973). Psychogenic urinary retention: Treatment by prolonged exposure. *Beh Ther, 4,* 581–585.

Lancet (1952). *Disabilities.* ("Anxiety Neurosis," pp. 79–83).

Landis C (1964). In *Varieties of psychopathological experience.* Mettler FA (Ed.), Holt, Rinehart, NY.

Lang PJ (1966). Fear reduction and fear behaviour. Problems in treating a construct. In *Third Conference in Research in Psychotherapy,* Chicago.

Lang P (1979). A bioinformational theory of emotional imagery. *Psychophysiology, 16,* 495–512.

Lang PJ (1983). Cognition in emotion. In Izard C, Kagan J, & Zajonc R (Eds.), *Emotion, cognition and behavior.* Cambridge University Press, NY.

Lang PJ (1985). The cognitive psychophysiology of emotion: Fear and anxiety. In Tuma AH & Maser JD (Eds.), *Anxiety and anxiety disorders* (ch. 7). Erlbaum, Hillsdale, NJ.

Lang P, Melamed BH, & Hart J (1970). Psychophysiological analysis of fear modification with automated desensitization. *J Abn Psychol, 76,* 220–234.

Langer WL (1974) Infanticide: A historical survey about parental infant only. *Hist Childhood Q, 1,* 353–366.

Laplane D, Baulac M, Widlöcher D, & Dubois B (1984). Psychic akinesia with bilateral lesions of basal ganglia. *J Neurol Neurosurg Psychiat, 47,* 377–385.

Lapouse R & Monk MA (1959). Fears and worries in a representative sample of children. *Am J Orthopsychiat, 29,* 803–818.

Laughlin HP (1956). *The neuroses in clinical practice* (p. 172). Saunders, London.

Laughlin HP (1967). *The neuroses.* Butterworth, Washington, DC.

Lautch H (1971). Dental phobia. *Br J Psychiat, 119,* 151–158.

Lazarus RS, Averill JR, Opton EM (1968). Towards a cognitive theory of emotion. Paper to Symposium on Feelings and Emotion. Chicago, October.

Leckman JF, Merikangas KR, Pauls DL et al. (1983). Anxiety disorders and depression: Contradictions between family study data and DSM-III conventions. *Am J Psychiat, 140,* 880–882.

Leckman JF, Weissman MM, Merikangas KR, Pauls DL, & Prusoff BA (1983). Increased risk of depression, alcoholism, panic and phobic disorders in families of depressed probands with panic disorder. *Arch Gen Psychiat, 40,* 1055–1060.

Lee I, Tyrer P, & Horn S (1983). Subliminal, supraliminal and faded phobic cine-films in the treatment of agoraphobia. *Br J Psychiat, 143,* 356–361.

Lefevre ER & West ML (1981). Assertiveness: Correlations with self-esteem locus of control, interpersonal anxiety, fear of disapproval, and depression. *Psychiat J Univ Ottawa, 6,* 247–251.

Leff J (1974). Speech to Royal College of Psychiatrists. London.

Leger LA (1978). Spurious and actual improvement in the treatment of preoccupying thoughts by thought-stopping. *Br J Soc Clin Psychol, 17,* 373–377.

Leibrecht BC & Askew HR (1980). Habituation from a comparative perspective. In Denny MR (Ed.), *Comparative Psychology: An evolutionary analysis of animal behavior.* J Henry Meyer.

Leitenberg H, Agras WS, Edwards JA et al. (1970). Practice as a psychotherapeutic variable: Experimental analysis within single cases. *J Psychiat Res, 7,* 215–225.

Lelliott P & Marks IM (1987). Behavioural therapy for oc rituals associated with delusions, hallucinations and depression (in press).

Lelliott P, Basoglu M, Marks IM, & Noshirvani H (1986). Psychophysiological aspects of obsessive-compulsive disorder (in press).

Lelliott P, Marks IM, Noshirvani H (1986a). 5-year followup of agoraphobics after imipramine and exposure (in press).

Lelliott P, Marks IM, Noshirvani H (1986b) Fixity of obsessive-compulsive beliefs. In preparation.

Lenington S (1981). Child abuse: The limits of sociobiology. *Ethol sociobiol, 2,* 17–29.

Leonard WE (1928). *The locomotive god.* Chapman and Hall.

Levenson EA (1961). The treatment of school phobias in the young adult. *Amer J Psychother, 15,* 539–552.

Leventhal H & Tomarken AJ (1985). Emotion: Today's problems. *Ann Rev Psychol* (in press).

Levi L (Ed.). (1972). Stress and distress in response to psychosocial stimuli. *Acta Med Scand, 191,* Supp. no. 528.

Levin AP, Liebowitz MR, Fyer AJ et al. (1984). Lactate induction of panic. In Ballenger JC (Ed.), *Biology of agoraphobia* (ch. 4, pp. 81–98). American Psychiatric Press, Washington, DC.

Levin RB & Gross AM (1985). Role of relaxation in systematic desensitization. *Beh Res Ther, 23,* 187–196.

Levine PH (1983). Platelet functions in panic attacks. Paper to Upjohn Conference on Biological Considerations in Panic Disorders. Boston, November.

Levine S (1982). Comparative and psychobiological perspectives on development. In Collins WA (Ed.), *Minnesota symposium on child psychology, 15,* Erlbaum, Hillsdale, NJ.

Levine S (1983). A psychobiological approach to the ontogeny of coping. In Garmezy N & Rutter M (Eds.), *Stress, coping, and development in children.* McGraw-Hill, NY.

Levine S & Coe C (1981). Normal responses to mother-infant separation in non-human primates. In Klein D & Rabkin J (Eds.), *Anxiety: Changing concepts.* Raven, NY.

Levine S, Goldman L, & Coover GD (1973). Expectancy and the pituitary-adrenal system. In *CIBA Symposium no. 8: Physiology, emotion and psychosomatic illness* (pp. 282–291). Elsevier, NY.

Levis DJ & Boyd TL (1979). Symptom maintenance by conservation of anxiety. *J Abn Psychol, 88,* 107–120.

Levis DJ & Boyd TL (1979). Symptom maintenance: Extension of the conservation of anxiety principle. *J Abn Psychol, 88,* 107–120.

Levy D (1951). Observations of attitudes and behavior in the child health center. *Am J Pub Health, 41,* 182–190.

Lewin W (1961). Observations on selective leucotomy. *J Neurol Neurosurg Psychiat, 24,* 37–44.

Lewin W (1973). Selective leucotomy: A review. In Laitinen LV & Livingston KE, (Eds.), *Surgical approaches in Psychiatry.* Medical and Technical Publishing.

Lewis AJ (1934). Melancholia: A clinical survey of depressive states. *J Ment Sci, 80,* 1–42.

Lewis AJ (1935). Problems of obsessional illness. *Proc Roy Soc Med, 29,* 325–336.

Lewis AJ (1967). The ambiguous word "anxiety" as used in psychopathology. *Israel Annals of Psychiatry and Related Disciplines, 5,* 105–121.

Lewis T (1917). Report on soldiers returned as cases of "Disordered Action of the Heart" (DAH) or "Valvular Disease of the Heart" (VDH). Medical Research Committee, Special Report Series No. 8, London.

Ley R (1985). Agoraphobia, the panic attack, and the hyperventilation syndrome. *Beh Res Ther* (in press).

Leyhausen P (1956). Das Verhalten der Katzen (Felidae). *Handbuch Zool Bd, VIII,* 10 (21), 1–34.

Liberthson RR (1983). MVP in patients with panic and other phobic anxiety. Paper to Upjohn Conference on Biological Considerations in Anxiety Disorders. Boston, December.

Liddell HS (1956). *Emotional hazards in animals and man.* Thomas, Springfield, IL.

Liddell A & Lyons M (1978). Thunderstorm phobias. *Beh Res Ther, 16,* 306–308.

Lieberman JA, Brenner R, Lesser M et al. (1983). Dexamethasone suppression tests in patients with panic disorder. *Am J Psychiat, 140,* 917–919.

Lieberman JA, Kane JM, Sarantakos S et al. (1985). Dexamethasone suppression tests in patients with obsessive-compulsive disorder. *Am J Psychiatry, 142,* 747–751.

Liebowitz M (1984). Paper to Conference on Anxiety Disorders. Vienna, November.

Liebowitz MR & Klein DF (1979). Assessment and treatment of phobic anxiety. *J Clin Psychiat, 40,* 486–492.

Liebowitz MR, Fyer AJ, Gorman JM et al. (1984). Lactate provocation of panics: I. Clinical and behavioral findings. *Arch Gen Psychiat, 41,* 764–770.

Liebowitz MR, Gorman JM, Fyer AJ & Klein DF (1985). Social phobia. *Arch Gen Psychiat, 42,* 729–736.

Lief HA (1955). Sensory association in the selection of phobic objects. *Psychiatry, 18,* 331–338.

Lifshitz K & Blair JH (1960). Polygraphic recording of repeated hypnotic abreaction. *J Nerv Ment Dis, 130,* 246–252.

Likierman H & Rachman S (1982). Thought stopping and habituation training for obsessions. *Beh Psychother, 10,* 324–338.

Lim ATW & Funder JW (1983). Stress-induced changes in plasma, pituitary and hypothalamic immunoreactive beta-endorphin. *Neuroendocrinology, 36,* 225–234.

Lin JTY, Ziegler DK, Lai CW et al. (1982). Convulsive syncope in blood donors. *Ann Neurol, 11,* 525–528.

Lindley P, Marks IM, Philpott R, & Snowden J (1977). Treatment of obs-compulsive neurosis with history of childhood autism. *Brit J Psychiat, 130,* 592–597.

Lindsay SJE (1983). Fear of dental treatment. In Rachman S (Ed.), *Contributions to Medical Psychology III.* Pergamon, Oxford.

Lindsay SJE & Busch CJ (1981). Behaviour modification in dentistry: A review. *Beh Psychother, 9,* 200–214.

Linehan M, Goldfried M, & Goldfried A (1979). Assertion therapy: Skills training or cognitive restructuring. *Beh Ther, 10,* 372–388.

Lipman RS, Covi L, Shapiro AK (1979). The Hopkins Symptom Checklist (HSCL). *J Affective Dis, 1,* 9–24.

Lipsedge MS (1974). Therapeutic approaches to compulsive neurosis. Unpublished M Phil dissertation. University of London.

Lipsedge MS & Prothero WBF (1986). A placebo-controlled trial of clonidine in obsessive ruminations (unpublished manuscript).

Lipsedge M, Hajioff J, Huggins P et al. (1973). Iproniazid and systematic desensitization for severe agoraphobia. *Psychopharmacologia, 32,* 67–80.

Lishman WA (1968). Brain damage in relation to psychiatric disability after head injury. *Br J Psychiat, 114,* 373–410.

Lloyd GG & Deakin HG (1975). Phobias complicating treatment of uterine carcinoma. *Br Med J,* Nov 22, 440–441.

Lo W (1967). A follow-up study of obsessional neurotics in Hong Kong Chinese. *Br J Psychiat, 113,* 823–32.

Locke J (1693). Some thoughts concerning education (pp. 481–482). Ward Lock & Co.

Loehlin JC & Nichols RC (1976). Heredity, environment and personality: A study of 850 sets of twins. University of Texas Press, Austin.

Logue PE, Gentry WD, Linnoila M, & Erwin CW (1978). Effect of alcohol consumption on state anxiety changes in nonalcoholics. *Am J Psychiat, 135,* 1079–1081.

Logue AW, Ophir I, & Strauss KE (1981). Acquisition of taste aversions in humans. *Beh Res Ther, 19,* 319–333.

LoPiccolo J (1969). Effective components of systematic desensitization. Doctoral dissertation, Yale University.

Lorenz K (1937). Uber die Bildung des Instinktbegriffes. *Naturwiss, 25,* 289–300, 307–318, 324–331.

Lorenz K (1981). *Foundations of ethology.* Springer Verlag, New York.

Lorenz R (1971). Goeldi's Monkey *Callimico goeldii* Thomas 1904 preying on snakes. *Folia Primatol, 15,* 133–142.

Lorr M et al. (1963). *Syndromes of psychoses.* Pergamon, NY.

Lowenstein LF (1983). Combined treatment of school phobia. *Br J Soc Clin Psychiat,* *2,* 32–38.

Lown B (1982). Mental stress, arrythmias and sudden death. *Am J Med, 72,* 177–180.

Lucas EA, Powell EW, & Murphree OD (1974). Hippocampal theta in nervous pointer dogs. *Physiol Beh, 12,* 609–613.

Lum LC (1981). Hyperventilation and anxiety state. *J Roy Soc Med, 74,* 1–4.

MacAlpine I (1957). Syphilophobia. *Br J Vener Dis, 33,* 92–99.

Maccoby EE & Feldman S (1972). Mother-attachment and stranger-reactions in the third year of life. *Monogr Soc Res Child Dev, 37* (1).

Maccoby EE & Jacklin CN (1974). *The psychology of sex differences.* Stanford University Press, Palo Alto.

Macfarlane JW, Allen L, & Honzik MP (1954). *Behaviour problems of normal children between 21 months and 14 years.* University of Calif Press, Berkeley.

Mackintosh NJ (1983). *Conditioning and associative learning.* Clarendon, Oxford.

Macrae D (1954). On the nature of fear with reference to its occurrence in epilepsy. *J Nerv Ment Dis, 120,* 385–393.

Magarian GJ (1982). Hyperventilation syndromes: Infrequently recognized common expressions of anxiety and stress. *Medicine* (Baltimore), *61,* 219–236.

Mahajer M & Mottaghi (1985). PTSD among Iranian veterans of the Iran-Iraq war. Paper to Annual Meeting of APA. Washington, DC, May.

Maier NRF (1949). *Frustration: The study of behavior with a goal.* McGraw-Hill, London.

Main M & Weston DR (1982). Avoidance of the attachment figure in infancy. In Parkes CM & Stevenson-Hinde J (Eds.), *The place of attachment in human behaviour* (pp. 31–59). Tavistock, London.

Malcuit B, Ducharme R, & Belanger D (1968). Cardiac activity in rats during bar-press avoidance and "freezing" responses. *Psychol Rep, 23,* 11–18.

Malloy PF, Fairbank JA, & Keane TM (1983). Validation of a multimethod assessment of PTSD in Vietnam veterans. *J Consult Clin Psychol, 51,* 488–494.

Malmo RB & Shagass C (1949). Physiologic study of symptom mechanisms in psychiatric patients under stress. *Psychosom Med, 11,* 25–29.

Malow RM (1981). Effects of induced anxiety on pain perception. *Pain, 11,* 397–405.

Maltzman I & Boyd G (1984). Stimulus significance and bilateral SCRs to potentially phobic picture. *J Abn Psychol, 93,* 41–46.

Maltzman I, Smith MJ, Kantor W, & Mandell MP (1971). Effects of stress on habituation of the orienting reflex. *J Exper Psychol, 87,* 207–214.

Manning A (1978). *Introduction to animal behaviour* (3rd ed.). Arnold, London.

Maple S, Bradshaw CM, & Szabadi E (1982). Drug responsiveness of sweat glands in anxious patients and healthy volunteers. *Br J Psychiat, 141,* 154–161.

Maranon G (1924). Contribution a l'etude de l'action emotive de l'adrenaline. *Revue Francaise d'Endocrinologie, 2,* 301–325.

Margalit C & Segal R (1983). Premorbid personality of soldiers with severe and chronic combat reactions. In *WPA Abstracts* (F247, p. 312), Vienna, July.

Margraf J, Ehlers A, Roth WT et al. (1985). Lactate panic provocation in panic patients and controls: Reactivity vs baseline differences? *Psychosom Med, 47,* 88–89 (abstract).

Margraf J, Ehlers A. Roth WT et al. (1985a). Panic induction in panic disorder and agoraphobic: Specific or nonspecific? Paper to EABT. Munich, August.

Margraf J, Ehlers A, & Roth WT (1985b). Sodium lactate infusions and panic attacks: A review and critique (in press).

Mark VH & Ervin RR (1970). *Violence and the brain.* Harper & Row, NY.

Marks IM (1965). *Patterns of meaning in psychiatric patients.* Oxford University Press, London.

Marks IM (1967). Components and correlates of psychiatric questionnaires in phobic patients. *Br J Med Psychol, 40,* 261–272.

Marks IM (1969). *Fears and phobias.* Academic, NY.

Marks IM (1970). The classification of phobic disorders. *Br J Psychiat, 116,* 377–386.

Marks IM (1970a). Agoraphobic syndrome (phobic anxiety state). *Arch Gen Psychiat, 23,* 538–553.

Marks IM (1971). Phobic disorders four years after treatment. *Br J Psychiat, 118,* 683–688.

Marks IM (1972). Phylogenesis and learning in the acquisition of fetishism. *Danish Med Bull, 19,* 307–310.

Marks IM (1972a). Symbolism and meaning in psychotherapy. *Int J Symbol, 3,* 27–34.

Marks IM (1972b). Flooding (implosion) and related treatments. In Agras WS (Ed.), *Behavior modification* (ch 6, pp. 151–214). Little, Brown, Boston.

Marks IM (1973). The reduction of fear: Towards a unifying theory. *J Can Psychiat Assoc, 18,* 9–12.

Marks IM (1975). Behavioral treatments of phobic and obsessive compulsive disorders: A critical appraisal. In Hersen R et al. (Eds.), *Progress in behavior modification* (pp. 65–158). Academic Press, NY.

Marks IM (1977). Phobias and obsessions: Clinical phenomena in search of a laboratory model. In J Maser and M Seligman (Eds.), *Psychopathology: Experimental models* (Ch. 5, pp. 174–213). Freeman, San Francisco.

Marks IM (1978). Exposure treatments. In Agras S (Ed.), *Behavior modification* (2nd ed.) (ch. 7 & 8, pp. 163–242). Little, Brown, Boston.

Marks IM (1978a). *Living with fear.* McGraw-Hill, NY.

Marks IM (1981). *Cure and care of neuroses.* Wiley, NY.

Marks IM (1981a). Space "phobia": A pseudoagoraphobic syndrome. *J Neurol Neurosurg Psychiat, 44,* 387–391.

Marks IM (1981c). Behavioral psychotherapy: Sexual disorders. *Am J Psychiat, 138*(5), 750–756.

Marks IM (1983). Are there anticompulsive or antiphobic drugs? Review of the evidence. *Br J Psychiat, 143,* 338–347.

Marks IM (1985a). *Psychiatric nurse therapists in primary care.* Research Series of Royal College of Nursing, Henrietta St., London WC1.

Marks IM (1985b). Behavioral treatment of social phobia. *Psychopharm Bull, 21,* 615–618.

Marks IM & Bebbington P (1976). Space phobia: Syndrome or agoraphobic variant. *Br Med J, 2,* 345–347.

Marks IM & Gelder MG (1965). A controlled retrospective study of behaviour therapy in phobic patients. *Br J Psychiat, 111,* 571–573.

Marks IM & Gelder MG (1966). Different onset ages in varieties of phobia. *Am J Psychiat, 123,* 218–221.

Marks IM & Herst ER (1970). A survey of 1200 agoraphobics in Britain. *Soc Psychiat, 5,* 16–24.

Marks IM & Huson J (1973). Physiological aspects of neutral and phobic imagery: Further observations. *Br J Psychiat, 122,* 567–72.

Marks IM & Lader MH (1973). Anxiety states (anxiety neurosis): A review. *J Nerv Ment Dis 156,* 3–18.

Marks IM & Mathews AM (1979). Brief standard self-rating for phobic patients. *Beh Res Ther, 17,* 263–267.

Marks IM & Tobeña A (1985). What do the neurosciences tell us about anxiety disorders? A comment. *Psychol Med 16*, 9–12.

Marks IM & Wilks CGW (1979). Treatment of a dentist's phobia of practising dentistry. *Br Dent J, 147*, 189–191.

Marks IM, Birley JLT, & Gelder MG (1966). Modified leucotomy in severe agoraphobia: A controlled serial enquiry. *Br J Psychiat, 112*, 757–769.

Marks IM, Gelder MG, & Edwards JG (1968). Hypnosis v desensitisation for phobias: A controlled prospective trial. *Br J Psychiat, 114*, 1263–1274.

Marks IM, Crowe M, Drewe E, Young J, & Dewhurst WG (1969). Obsessive-compulsive neurosis in identical twins. *Br J Psychiat, 115*, 991–8.

Marks IM, Boulougouris J, & Marset P (1971). Flooding v desensitization for phobic patients: A crossover study. *Br J Psychiat, 119*, 353–375.

Marks IM, Viswanathan R, Lipsedge MS, & Gardner R (1972). Enhanced relief of phobias by flooding during waning diazepam. *Br J Psychiat, 121*, 493–505.

Marks IM, Hodgson R, & Rachman S (1975). Treatment of chronic OCD 2 years after in vivo exposure. *Br J Psychiat, 127*, 349–64.

Marks IM, Connolly J, Hallam RS, & Philpott R (1977). *Nursing in behavioural psychotherapy.* Research Series of Royal College of Nursing, Henrietta St., London WC1.

Marks IM, Bird J, & Lindley P (1978). Psychiatric nurse therapy: Developments and implications. *Beh Psychother, 6*, 25–36.

Marks IM, Stern RS, Mawson D, Cobb J, & McDonald R (1980). Clomipramine and exposure for obs-compulsive rituals: I. *Br J Psychiat, 136*, 1–25.

Marks IM, Gray S, Cohen D, Hill R, Mawson D, Ramm E, & Stern R (1983). Imipramine and brief therapist-aided exposure in agoraphobics having self-exposure homework. *Arch Gen Psychiat, 40*, 153–162.

Marks IM, Waters H, & Lindley P (1985). Nurse therapy in primary care. *Br Med J, 290*, 1181–1194.

Marks IM, Basoglu M, Lelliott M et al. (1986). Clomipramine and exposure in OCD. A replication (in press).

Marks IM et al. (1986a). *Behavioural psychotherapy: Pocketbook of clinical management.* John Wright, Bristol.

Markus DF & Canavan AGM (1985). Effects of short exposures to phobic material upon subsequent phobic responses. *Beh Psychother, 13*, 218–229.

Marler P (1956). Behaviour of the chaffinch *Frinchilla coelebs. Behaviour* (Supp. 5), 1–184.

Marler P (1955). Characteristics of some animal calls. *Nature 176*, 6–7.

Marler P (1955b). Studies of fighting in chaffinches: (1) Behaviour in relation to the social hierarchy. *Br J Animal Beh, 3*, 111–117.

Marler P (1959). Animal Communication. In Bell PR (Ed.), *Darwin's biological work: Some aspects reconsidered* (pp. 150–202). Cambridge University Press, London.

Marler P (1975). On strategies of behavioural development. In Baerends G, Beer C, & Manning A (Eds.). *Function and evolution in behavior.* Oxford: Clarendon.

Marler P (1979). In Van Cranach M et al. (Eds.), *Human ethology.* Cambridge University Press, London.

Marler P & Hamilton WJ (1966). *Mechanisms of animal behavior.* Wiley, NY.

Marshall SLA (1963). *Battle at best.* Morrow, NY.

Marshall SLA (1947). *Men against fire.*

Marshall WL (1985). Variable exposure in flooding. *Beh Res Ther, 16*, 117–135.

Marshitz MH, Almarza MT, Barra E, & Medina AM (1973). Massed and spaced practice in systematic desensitization of test anxiety. Paper to EABT. Amsterdam, August.

Martin I, Marks IM & Gelder MG (1969). Conditioned eyelid responses in phobic patients. *Beh Res Ther, 7,* 115–124.

Martin RC & Melvin KB (1964). Fear responses of bobwhite quail *(Colinus virginianus)* to a model and a live red-tailed hawk *(Buteo jamaicensis). Pyschologische Forschung, 27,* 323–336.

Marzillier JS, Lambert C, & Kellett JA (1976). Desensitization and social skills training for socially inadequate patients. *Beh Res Ther, 14,* 225.

Mason WA (1978). Social experience and primate cognitive development. In Bekoff M & Burghardt (Eds.), *Ontogeny of behavior.* Garland, NY.

Mathew RJ, Ho BT, Francis DJ et al. (1982). Catecholamines and anxiety. *Act Psychiat Scand, 65,* 142–147.

Mathews AM (1971). Psychophysiological approaches to the investigation of desensitization and related procedures. *Psych Bull, 76,* 73–91.

Mathews AM & Shaw PM (1973). Continuous exposure and emotional arousal in flooding. *Beh Res Ther, 11,* 587–598.

Mathews AM & Rezin VA (1976). Imaginal exposure with dental phobics. *Beh Res Ther, 15,* 321–328.

Mathews AM, Johnston DW, Lancashire M et al. (1976). Imaginal flooding v real exposure in agoraphobics: Outcome. *Br J Psychiat, 129,* 362–371.

Mathews AM, Teasdale JD, Munby M et al. (1977). A home-based treatment program for agoraphobia. *Beh Ther, 8,* 915–924.

Mathews AM, Gelder MG, & Johnston DW (1981). *Agoraphobia: Nature and treatment.* Guilford Press, NY.

Matson JL (1982). Treating obsessive-compulsive behavior in mentally retarded adults. *Beh Mod, 6,* 551–567.

Maudsley H (1895). *The pathology of mind.* London.

Maurer A (1965). What children fear. *J Genet Psychol, 106,* 265–277.

Mavissakalian MR (1984). Agoraphobia: Behavioral therapy and pharmacotherapy. In Beitman BD & Klerman GL (Eds.), *Combining psychotherapy and drug therapy in clinical practice* (Ch. 10, pp. 187–211). Spectrum.

Mavissakalian M (Ed.) (1985). *Obsessive-compulsive disorders: Psychological and pharmacological treatments.* Plenum, NY.

Mavissakalian M & Barlow DH (1981). *Phobia: Psychological and pharmacological treatment.* Guildford, NY.

Mavissakalian M & Michelson L (1982). Agoraphobia: Behavioral and pharmacological treatments. *Psychopharm Bull, 18,* 91–103.

Mavissakalian M & Michelson (1983a). Self-directed in vivo exposure practice in behavioral and drug treatments of agoraphobia. *Beh Ther, 14,* 505–519.

Mavissakalian M & Michelson L (1983b). Tricyclic antidepressants in obsessive-compulsive disorder. *J Nerv Ment Dis, 171,* 301–306.

Mavissakalian M & Michelson L (1986). Agoraphobia: Therapist-assisted in vivo exposure and imipramine. *J Clin Psychiat, 47,* 117–122.

Mavissakalian M, Salerni R, Thompson ME, & Michelson L (1983). Mitral valve prolapse and agoraphobia. *Am J Psychiat, 140,* 1612–1614.

Mavissakalian M, Michelson L, Greenwald D et al. (1983a). Paradoxical intention vs self-statement training of agoraphobia. *Beh Res Ther, 21,* 75–80.

Mavissakalian M, Michelson L & Dealy RS (1983b). Imipramine versus imipramine with programmed practice for agoraphobia. *Br J Psychiat, 143,* 348–355.

Mavissakalian M, Turner SM, Michelson L & Jacob R (1985). Tricyclic antidepressants in obsessive-compulsive disorder: II. *Am J Psychiat, 142,* 572–576.

Mawson AN (1970). Methohexitone-assisted desensitization for phobias. *Lancet, 1,* 1084–1086.

Mawson D, Marks IM, Ramm E, & Stern RS (1981). Guided mourning for morbid grief: A controlled study. *Br J Psychiat, 138,* 185–193.

Mawson D, Marks IM, & Ramm E (1982). Clomipramine and exposure for chronic oc rituals: III. Two-year followup. *Br J Psychiat, 140,* 11–18.

May R (1950). *The meaning of anxiety.* Ronald, NY.

Mayes A (1979). The physiology of fear and anxiety. In Sluckin W (Ed.), *Fear in animals and man* (ch. 2, pp. 24–55). Van Nostrand, Berkshire, UK.

Maynard-Smith J (1978). The evolution of behavior. *Sci Am, 239,* 104.

McCaffrey RJ & Fairbank JA (1985). Behavioral assessment and treatment of accident-related PTSD: 2 case studies. *Beh Ther, 16,* 404–416.

McCarthy PR & Foa EB (1985). Cognitive influences on automatic and CNS activity in OCD. In *Abstracts of the World Congress of Biological Psychiatry,* (Abstract 119.3). Philadelphia, September.

McCormick WO (1972). Drug-assisted desensitisation of phobias. Paper to Conference on Behavioural Engineering, Wexford, Ireland.

McCowan PK & Cook LC (1928). The mental aspect of chronic epidemic encephalitis. *Lancet, 1,* 1316–1320.

McCutcheon BA & Adams HE (1975). The physiological basis of implosive therapy. *Beh Res Ther, 13,* 93–100.

McDonald R, Sartory G, Grey SJ et al. (1978). Effects of self-exposure instructions on agoraphobic outpatients. *Beh Res Ther, 17,* 83–85.

McDougall W (1920). The revival of emotional memories and its therapeutic value. *Br J Med Psychol, 1,* 23–33.

McFadyen M & Presly A (1977). Prolonged exposure for agoraphobia. Unpublished manuscript.

McGivern RF, Mousa S, Couri D, & Berntson GG (1983). Prolonged footshock stress decreases MET and LEU enkephalin levels in brain with concomitant decreases in pain threshold. *Life Sci, 33,* 47–54.

McGrath PJ, Liebowitz MD, & Klein DF (1985). Lactate infusion in depressed and anxious patients. Paper to APA. Dallas, May.

McGrath TA, Shalter MD, Schleidt WM, & Sarvella P (1972). Analysis of distress calls of chicken and pheasant hybrids. *Nature, 237,* 47–48.

McGraw CP & Klemm WR (1973). Genetic differences in susceptibility of rats to the immobility reflex ("animal hypnosis"). *Beh Genet, 3,* 155–161.

McGuffin P & Mawson D (1980). Obsessive-compulsive neurosis: Two identical twin pairs. *Br J Psychiat, 137,* 285–287.

McGuffin P & Reich T (1984). Psychopathology and genetics. In Adams HE & Sutker PB (Eds.), *Comprehensive handbook of psychopathology,* (ch. 3, pp. 47–75). Plenum, NY.

McGuffin P, Reveley A, & Holland A (1982). Identical triplets: Non-identical psychosis? *Br J Psychiat, 140,* 1–6.

McInnes RG (1937). Observations of heredity in neurosis. *Proc Roy Soc Med, 30,* 895–904.

McIntosh N (1983). *Learning.* Cambridge University Press, Cambridge.

McKeon JP (1983). Aetiological aspects of obsessive-compulsive neurosis. MD thesis, University College, Dublin.

McKeon P, Roa B, & Mann A (1984a). Life events and personality traits in obsessive-compulsive neurosis. *Br J Psychiat, 144,* 185–189.

McKeon P, McGuffin P & Robinson P (1984b). OCD following head injury: A report of four cases. *Br J Psychiat, 144,* 190–192.

McKinney WT (1985). Separation and depression: Biological markers. In Reite M & Field T (Eds.), *The psychobiology of attachment* (pp. 201–222). Academic, NY.

McKinney WT, Kraemer GW, Ebert MH, & Lake CR (1984). Separation and alcohol consumption in monkeys. Paper to APA. Dallas, May.

McLaughlin FL & Millar WM (1941). Employment of air-raid noises in psychotherapy. *Br Med J,* Aug 2, 158–159.

McNair DM & Kahn RJ (1981). Imipramine and chlordiazepoxide for agoraphobia. In Klein DF & Rabkin JG (Eds.), *Anxiety: New research and changing concepts* (pp. 169–180). Raven, NY.

McNair DM & Fisher S (1978). Separating anxiety from depression. In Lipton MA, DiMascio A & Killam KF (Eds.), *Psychopharmacology: A generation of progress.*

McNally RJ (1986). Pavlovian conditioning and preparedness: Effects of initial fear level (under review).

McNally RJ & Foa EB (1986). Preparedness and the resistance to extinction to fear-relevant stimuli: A failure to replicate. *Beh Res Ther* (in press).

McNally RJ & Reiss S (1984). The preparedness theory of phobias: The effects of initial fear level on safety-signal conditioning to fear-relevant stimuli. *Psychophysiology, 21,* 647–652.

McNally RJ & Steketee GS (1985). Etiology and maintenance of severe animal phobias. *Beh Res Ther, 23,* 431–435.

McPherson FM, Brougham L, & McLaren S (1980). Maintenance of improvement in agoraphobic patients treated by behavioural methods—a four-year followup. *Beh Res Ther, 18,* 150–152.

Mech LD (1970). *The wolf.* Natural History Press, Garden City, NY.

Mechanic D (1962). The concept of illness behaviour. *J Chron Dis 15,* 189–194.

Meichenbaum D (1977). *Cognitive behavior modification.* Plenum, NY.

Meikl S & Mitchell MC (1974). Factor analysis of the fear survey schedule with phobics. *J Clin Psychol, 40,* 44–46.

Melamed B (1982). Reduction of medical fears: Information processing and arousal level. In Boulougouris JC (Ed.), *Learning theory approaches to psychiatry* (ch. 19, pp. 205–218). Wiley, NY.

Melamed BG & Hermecz DA (1983). Considerations for surgery preparation: Age and previous experience. *Psychosom Med, 45,* 517–525.

Melamed BG, Weinstein D, Hawes R, & Katin-Borland M (1975a). Reduction of dental fear by filmed modeling. *J Am Dent Assoc, 90,* 822–826.

Melamed BG, Hawes RR, Heiby E, & Glick J (1975b). Filmed modeling to reduce childrens' unco-operative behavior during dental treatment. *J Dent Res,* Jul–Aug, 797–801.

Melamed BG, Yurcheson RY, Fleece L et al. (1978). Film modeling to reduce anxiety and varied experience of the stressor. *J Cons Clin Psychol, 46,* 1357–1367.

Melamed BG, Ross SL, Courts F et al. (1983). Dentists' behavior management as it affects compliance and fear in pediatric patients. *JADA, 106,* 324–330.

Melzack R (1952). Irrational fears in the dog. *Can J Psychol, 6,* 141–147.

Melzack R, Penick E, & Beckett A (1959). "Innate fear" of the hawk shape: An experimental study with Mallard ducks. *J Comp Physiol Psychol, 52,* 694–698.

Merz WA & Ballmer V (1983). Anxiety and depression in healthy volunteers and in general practice. In *Abstract P40,* (p. 458). Congress of Vienna, July.

Meyer G, McElhaney M, Martin W, & McGraw CP (1973). Cingulotomy: Acute stimulation and serial psychological testing. In Laitinen LV & Livingston KE (Eds.), *Surgical approaches in psychiatry.* Medical and Technical Publishing Co.

Meyer V, Levy T, & Schnurer AA (1974). Behavioral treatment of OCD. In Beech HR (Ed.), *Obsessional states* (ch. 10, pp. 233–258). Methuen, London.

Meyers DH & Grant GA (1972). Depersonalisation in students. *Br J Psychiat, 121,* 59–65.

Michaels JJ & Porter RT (1949). Psychiatric and social implications of contrasts between psychopathic personality and OCD. *J Nerv Ment Dis, 109,* 122–132.

Michelson L & Ascher LM (1984). Paradoxical intention for agoraphobia and other anxiety disorders. *J Beh Ther Exp Psychiat, 15,* 215–220.

Michelson L & Mavissakalian M (1985). Psychophysiological outcome of behavioral and drug treatments of agoraphobia. *J Consult Clin Psychol, 53,* 229–236.

Milan MA & Kolko DJ (1982). Paradoxical intention in the treatment of obsessional flatulence ruminations. *J Beh Ther Exp Psychiat, 13,* 167–172.

Millar DG (1983). Hostile emotion and obsessional neurosis. *Psychol Med, 13,* 813–819.

Miller D, Farmer R, & Green J (1984). Venereophobia. Letter to *Br J Hosp Med,* September.

Miller BV & Levis DJ (1971). The effects of varied short exposure times to a phobic test stimulus on subsequent avoidance. *Beh Res Ther, 9,* 17.

Miller JM (1983). The opiate receptor and its endogenous ligands. In Nandkumar et al. (Eds.), *Endorphins and opiate antagonists in psychiatric research.* Plenum, NY.

Miller L (1952). Auditory recognition of predators. *Condor, 54,* 89–92.

Miller LC, Hampe E, Barrett CL, & Noble H (1971). Children's deviant behavior within the general population. *J Cons Clin Psychol, 37,* 16–22.

Miller LC, Barrett CL, Hampe E, & Noble H (1972). Reciprocal inhibition, psychotherapy and waiting list for phobic children. *J Abn Psychol,* 269–279.

Miller LC, Barrett CL, & Hampe E (1974). Phobias of childhood. In Davids A (Ed.), *Child personality and psychopathology: Current topics* (vol. 1,). Wiley, NY.

Miller ML (1953). On street fear. *Int J Psychoan, 34,* 232–252.

Miller NE (1951). Learnable drives and rewards. In Stevens SS (Ed.), *Handbook of experimental psychology* (pp. 435–472). Wiley, Chichester.

Miller S, Mineka S, & Cook M (1982). Various flooding procedures to reduce fear and extinguish jump-up avoidance. *Animal Learn Beh, 10,* 390–400.

Mills GK & Solyom L (1974). Biofeedback of EEG alpha in the treatment of obsessive ruminations. *J Beh Ther Exper Psychiat, 5,* 37–41.

Milton F & Hafner J (1979). Outcome of behavior therapy for agoraphobia in relation to marital adjustment. *Arch Gen Psychiat, 36,* 807–811.

Mineka S (1976). Effects of flooding an irrelevant response on the extinction of avoidance responses. *J Exper Psychol, 2,* 142–153.

Mineka S (1979). The role of fear in theories of avoidance learning, flooding and extinction. *Psychol Bull, 86,* 985–1010.

Mineka S (1982). Depression and helplessness in primates. In Fitzgerald HE, Mullins JA, & Gaze P (Eds.), *Child nurturance* (vol. 3, pp. 197–242). Plenum, NY.

Mineka S (1985b). Animal models of anxiety-based disorders: their usefulness and limitations. In Tuma AH & Maser J (Eds.), *Anxiety and the Anxiety Disorders* (ch. 10, pp. 199–244). Erlbaum, Hillsdale, NJ.

Mineka S (1986). The frightful complexity of the origins of fears. In JB Overmier & FR Brush (Eds.), *Affect, conditioning and cognition: Essays on the Determinants of Behavior.* Erlbaum, Hillsdale, NJ.

Mineka S & Hendersen R (1985). Controllability and predictability in acquired motivation. *Ann Rev Psychol, 36,* 495–530.

Mineka S & Kihlstrom JF (1978). Unpredictable and uncontrollable aversive events and experimental neurosis. *J Abn Psychol, 87,* 256–271.

Mineka S & Suomi SJ (1976). Social separation in monkeys. *Psychol Bull, 85,* 1376–1400.

Mineka S, Seligman MEP, Hetrick M, & Zuelzer K (1972). Poisoning and conditioned drinking. *J Comp Physiol Psychol, 79,* 377–384.

Mineka S, Keir R, & Price V (1980). Fear of snakes in wild and lab-reared rhesus monkeys. *Animal Learn Beh, 8,* 653–663.

Mineka S, Miller S, Gino A, & Giencke L (1981). Dissociative effects of flooding on a multivariate assessment of fear reduction and on jump-up avoidance extinction. *Learning and Motivation, 12,* 435–461.

Mineka S, Suomi SJ, & Delizio R (1981a). Multiple peer separations in adolescent monkeys. *J Exper Psychol: Gen, 110,* 56–85.

Mineka S, Cook M, & Miller S (1984a). Fear conditioned with escapable and inescapable shock: Effects of a feedback stimulus. *J Exper Psychol: Animal Beh Processes, 10,* 307–323.

Mineka S, Davidson M, Cook M, Keir R, (1984b). Observational conditioning of snake fear in rhesus monkeys. *J Abn Psychol, 93,* 355–372.

Mineka S, Gunnar M, & Champoux M (1985). Effects of rearing infant rhesus monkeys in controllable and uncontrollable environments on emotional responsivity and social development. *Child Dev,* (in press).

Miniszek NA (1984). Flooding as a supplemental treatment for Vietnam veterans. Paper to Conference on PTSD, Baltimore, September.

Mitchell R (1982). *Phobias.* Penguin, London.

Mitchell S & Shepherd M (1967). The child who dislikes going to school. *Br J Educ Psychol, 37,* 32.

Mohr P (1980). Mass hysteria. *World Medicine,* Aug. 23, 17–19.

Mollard E, Cottraux J, & Defayolle M (1984). Changements positifs de MMPI chez 70 patients phobiques traités par therapie comportementale. *Psychologie Medicale, 16,* 2385–2394.

Monteiro W, Marks IM, & Ramm E (1985). Marital adjustment and treatment outcome in agoraphobia. *Br J Psychiat, 146,* 383–390.

Monteiro W, Marks IM, Noshirvani H, & Checkley S (1986). Normal dexamethasone suppression test in obsessive-compulsive disorder. *Br J Psychiat, 148,* 326–329.

Monteiro W et al. (1986a) Anorgasmia from clomipramine in OCD. *Br J Psychiat,* (in press).

Montgomery MA, Clayton PJ, & Friedhoff AJ (1982). Psychiatric illness in tourette syndrome patients and first-degree relatives. In Friedhoff AJ & Chase TN (Eds.), *Gilles de la Tourette syndrome.* Raven, NY.

Montgomery SA (1980). Clomipramine in obsessional neurosis: A placebo-controlled trial. *Pharm Med, 1,* 189–195.

Montgomery SA & DB, McAuley R, Rani SJ, & Braithwaite RA (1981). Clomipramine plasma levels in obsessional neurosis. In Perris C, Struwe G, & Jansson B (Eds.), *Biological psychiatry* (pp. 1118–1122).

Moody RL (1946). Bodily changes during abreaction. *Lancet, 2,* 934–935.

Moody RL (1948). In Harris NG (Ed.), *Modern trends in psychological medicine*, (pp. 286–288). Butterworths, London.

Moore N (1965). Behaviour therapy in bronchial asthma: A controlled study. *J Psychosom Res, 9,* 257–276.

Moran C & Andrews G (1985). The familial occurrence of agoraphobia. *Br J Psychiat, 146,* 262–267.

Moreau DL (1985). Physiological concomitants of anxiety. Paper to APA. Dallas, May.

Morgan GA & Ricciuti HM (1967). Infants' response to strangers during the first year. In Foss BM (Ed.) *Determinants of infants' behaviour.* Methuen, London.

Morley S (1977). Incubation of avoidance behavior: Strain differences in susceptibility. *Beh Res Ther, 15,* 365–367.

Morris R & D (1965), *Men and snakes.* Hutchinson, London.

Morris R & Suckerman K (1974). Therapist warmth in automated systematic desensitization. *J Consult Clin Psychol, 42,* 244–250.

Morris RJ & Magrath KH (1979). Therapist warmth in contact desensitization of acrophobia. *J Consult Clin Psychol, 47,* 786–788.

Morris RJ & Kratochwil TR (1983). *Treating children's fears and phobias: A behavioral approach.* Pergamon General Psychology Series, NY.

Morselli E (1886). Sulla dismorfofobia e sulla tafefobia. *Boll Acad Med* (Genova), *VI,* 110–19.

Mountjoy CQ & Roth M (1982a,b). The relationship between depressive disorders and anxiety states: I & II. *J Affect Dis, 4,* 127–147, 149–161.

Mountjoy CQ, Roth M, Garside RF, & Leitch IM (1977). Phenelzine in anxiety, depression and phobic neurosis. *Br J Psychiat, 13,* 486–492 and *Excerpta Medica,* Amsterdam (1974).

Moynihan M (1955). Reproductive behaviour in the black-headed gull *(Larus r. ridibundus)* and related species. *Behaviour* (Supp.), 4.

Moynihan M (1968). Social mimicry, character convergence versus character displacement. *Evolution* (Lancaster, PA), *22,* 315–331.

Moynihan M (1975). Conservatism of displays and comparable stereotyped patterns among cephalopods. In Baerends G, Beer C, & Manning A (Eds.), *Function and evolution in behavior.* Clarendon, Oxford.

MRC News (1984). March, p. 7.

Mullan MJ, Gurling HMD, Oppenheim BE, & Murray RM (1985). The relationship between alcoholism and neurosis: Evidence from a twin study. *Br J Psychiat, 148,* 435–441.

Mullaney JA (1984). Anxiety and depression: A review of some principal component analytic studies. *J Affect Dis, 7,* 139–148.

Mullaney JA & Trippett CJ (1979). Alcohol dependence and phobias: Clincial description and relevance. *Br J Psychiat, 135,* 565–573.

Müller C (1953). Der Übergang von Zwangsneurose in Schizophrenie im Lichte der Katamnese. *Schweiz Arch Neurol Psychiat, 72,* 218–25.

Munby M & Johnston DW (1980). Agoraphobia: The long-term followup of behavioural treatment. *Br J Psychiat, 137,* 418–427.

Munjack DJ (1984). Onset of driving phobias. *J Beh Ther Exp Psychiat, 15,* 305–308.

Munjack DJ & Moss HB (1981). Affective disorder and alcoholism in families of agoraphobics. *Arch Gen Psychiat, 38,* 869–871.

Munjack DJ, Rebal R, Shaner R et al. (1985). Imipramine vs propanolol for panic attacks: A pilot study. *Compr Psychiat, 26,* 80–89.

Murphree OD & Newton JE (1971). Crossbreeding and special handling of genetically nervous dogs. *Cond Reflex, 6,* 129–136.

Murphree OD, Dykman RA, & Peters JE (1966). Objective measures of behaviour in two strains of the pointer dog. Paper to Symposium on Higher Nervous Activity, IV World Psychiatry Congress. Madrid, September.

Murphy JM, Sobol AM, Neff RK et al. (1984). Stability of prevalence. Depression and anxiety disorders. *Arch Gen Psychiat, 41,* 990–997.

Murray E & Foote F (1979). The origins of fear of snakes. *Beh Res Ther, 17,* 489–493.

Murray RM & Reveley A (1981). The genetic contribution to the neuroses. *Br J Hosp Med,* Feb, 185–190.

Murray RM, Cooper JE, & Smith A (1979). The Leyton Obsessional Inventory: Responses of 73 obsessional patients. *Psychol Med, 9,* 305–311.

Murray RM, Clifford C, Fulker DW, & Smith A (1981). Does heredity contribute to obsessional traits and symptoms? In Tsuang MT (Ed.), *Genetics issue: The psychosocial epidemiology monograph series.* US NIMH. Neale Watson, NY.

Myers CS (1920). In *Symposium on the revival of emotional memories and its therapeutic significance. Br J Med Psychol, 1,* 20–22.

Myers JK, Weissman MM, Tischler GL et al. (1984). Six-month prevalence of psychiatric disorders in three communities. *Arch Gen Psych, 41,* 959–967.

Nadelson CC, Notman MT, Zackson H, & Gornick J (1982). A follow-up of rape victims. *Am J Psychiat, 139,* 1266–1270.

Nalven FB (1970). Manifest fears and worries of ghetto versus middle class suburban children. *Psychol Reports, 27,* 285–286.

Nash RF & Gallup GC (1976). Habituation and tonic immobility in domestic chickens. *J Comp Physiol Psychol, 90,* 870–876.

Nash RF, Gallup GC, & Czech DA (1976). Psychophysiological correlates of tonic immobility in the domestic chicken. *Psychol Beh, 17,* 413–418.

Naud J, Boisvert JM & Lamontagne Y (1973). Treatment of firearm phobia by flooding in vivo and motor activity. *J Beh Ther Exp Psychiat, 4,* 407–409.

Neale MC & Fulker DW (1984). A bivariate path analysis of fear data on twins and their parents. *Act Gen Med Gemell, 33,* 273–286.

Nee LE, Polinsky RJ, & Ebert MH (1982). Tourette syndrome. In Friedhoff AJ & Chase TN (Eds.), *Gilles de la Tourette syndrome.* Raven, NY.

Neftel KA, Adler RH, Kappeli L et al. (1982). Stage fright in musicians: Effect of beta blockers. *Psychosom Med, 44,* 461–469.

Neill SR & Cullen JW (1974). Does schooling by prey affect the hunting behaviour of cephalopod and fish predators. *J Zool London, 172,* 549–569.

Nelson C, Morse P, & Leavitt L (1979). Recognition of facial expressions by seven-month-old infants. *Child Dev, 50,* 1239–1242.

Nemeroff CB & Prange AJ (1978). Peptides and psychoneuroendocrinology. *Arch Gen Psychiat, 35,* 999–1010.

Nemiah (1975). Obsessive-compulsive neurosis. In Freedman AM & Kaplan HI (Eds.), *A comprehensive textbook of psychiatry.* Williams & Williams, Baltimore.

Nesse RM (1984). An evolutionary perspective on psychiatry. *Compr Psychiat, 25,* 575–580.

Nesse RM, Carli T, Curtis GC, & Kleinman PD (1980). Pretreatment nausea in cancer chemotherapy: A conditioned response? *Psychosom Med, 42,* 33–36.

Nesse RM, Curtis GC, & Brown GM (1982). Phobic anxiety does not affect plasma thyroid stimulating hormone in man. *Psychoneuroendocrinology, 7,* 69–74.

Nesse R, Cameron O, Curtis G, & McCann D (1983). Adrenergic mechanisms in panic disorder. Abstract in WPA Proceedings. Vienna, July.

Nesse RM, Curtis GC, Thyer BA, McCann DS et al. (1984). Endocrine and cardiovascular responses during phobic anxiety. *Psychosom Med, 47,* 320–332.

Nesse RM, Cameron OG, Curtis GC, McCann DS, & Huber-Smith MJ (1984a). Adrenergic function in panic anxiety. *Arch Gen Psychiat, 41,* 771–776.

Nesse RM, Curtis GC, Thyer BA et al. (1985). Endocrine and cardiovascular responses during phobic anxiety. *Psychosom Med, 47,* 320–332.

Nesse RM, Cameron OG, Buda AJ et al. (1985a). Urinary catecholamines and mitral valve prolapse in panic-anxiety patients. *Psychiat Res, 14,* 67–75.

Nestoros JN, Demers-Desrosiers LA, & Dalicandro LA (1982). Anxiety and depression in spinal cord-injured patients. *Psychosomatics, 23,* 823–827, 830.

Neuman F (1985). *Fighting fear: An eight-week guide to treating your own phobias.* Macmillan, NY.

Newman HH, Freeman FN, & Holzinger KJ (1937). *Twins: A study of heredity and environment.* University of Chicago Press, Chicago.

Newson J & Newson E (1968). *Four years old in an urban community.* Allen & Unwin, London.

Newsweek (1981). Oct 26 p. 59. Quote from *Breakthrough,* Moshe Dayan's book.

Newton G & Levine S (1968). *Early experience and behavior: The psychobiology of development.* Thomas, Springfield, IL.

Ngui PW (1969). The Koro epidemic in Singapore. *Austr NZ Psychiat, 3,* 263–266.

Nichols KA (1974). Severe social anxiety. *Br J Med Psychol, 47,* 301–306.

Nichols K & Berg I (1970). School phobia and self-evaluation. *J Child Psychol Psychiat, 11,* 133–141.

Nimmer WH & Kapp RA (1974). A multiple impact program for the treatment of injection phobias. *J Beh Ther Exp Psychiat, 5,* 257–258.

Ninan PT, Insel TR, Cohen RM et al. (1982). BZ receptor—mediated experimental "anxiety" in primates. *Science, 218,* 1332–1334.

Nishida T (1979). Predatory behavior among wild chimpanzees of the Mahale mountains. *Primates, 20* (1), 1–20.

Noreik K (1970). A follow-up examination of neuroses. *Act Psychiat Scand, 46,* 81–95.

Norton AS, Beran AV, & Misrahy GA (1964). Electroencephalograph during feigned sleep in the opossum. *Nature, 204,* 162–163.

Norton GR, Harrison B, Hauch J, & Rhodes L (1985). Characteristics of people with infrequent panic attacks. *J Abn Psychol, 94,* 216–221.

Noshirvani HF, Kasvikis YG, Tsakiris F, Basoglu M, & Marks IM (1986). Demographic characteristics of 280 cases of obsessive-compulsive disorder (in press).

Noyes R, Hoenk PP, Kuperman S, & Slyman DJ (1977). Depersonalisation in accident victims and psychiatric patients. *J Nerv Ment Dis, 164,* 401–407.

Noyes R Jr, Clancy J, Crowe R, Hoenk PR, & Slymen DJ (1978). The familial prevalence of anxiety neurosis. *Arch Gen Psychiat, 35,* 1057–1059.

Noyes R, Clancy J, Hoenk PR, & Slymen DJ (1980). Prognosis of anxiety neurosis. *Arch Gen Psychiat, 37,* 173–178.

Noyes R, Harris E, & Crowe RR (1982). Family study of panic disorder and agoraphobia. In *Abstracts,* (p. 68). APA, Toronto.

Noyes R, Anderson DJ, Clancy J et al. (1984). Diazepam and propranolol in panic disorder and agoraphobia. *Arch Gen Psychiat, 41,* 287–292.

Nunes J & Marks IM (1976). Feedback of true heart rate during exposure in vivo: Partial replication. *Arch Gen Psychiat, 33,* 1346–1350.

O'Brien GT, Barlow DH, & Last CG (1982). Changing marriage patterns of agoraphobics as a result of treatment. In Dupont R (Ed.), *Phobias* (ch. 15, pp. 140–152). Brunner/Mazel, NY.

O'Brien TP & Kelley JE (1980). Self-directed and therapist-directed practice for fear reduction. *Beh Res Ther, 18*, 573–579.

O'Connor M, Foch T, Sherry T, & Plomin R (1980). A twin study of problems of socialization as viewed by parents. *J Abn Psychol, 8*, 189–199.

O'Connor PJ (1970). Phobic reaction to flying: Historical background. *Proc Roy Soc Med, 63*, 877–878.

Oates JK & Gomez J (1984). Venereophobia. *Br J Hosp Med, 31*, 435–436.

Obler M & Terwilliger RF (1970). Desensitization with neurologically impaired children with phobic disorders. *J Consult Clin Psychol, 34*, 314–318.

Öhman A & Dimberg U (1984). An evolutionary perspective on human social behavior. In Waid WM (Ed.), *Sociopsychology*. Springer, NY.

Öhman A, Fredrikson M, Hugdahl K, & Rimmö P-A (1976). Equipotentiality in human classical conditioning: Conditioned electrodermal responses to potentially phobic stimuli. *J Exper Psychol: Gen, 105*, 313–337.

Öhman A, Fredrikson M, & Hugdahl K (1978). Towards an experimental model for simple phobic reactions. *Beh Anal Mod, 2*, 97–114.

Öhman A, Dimberg U, & Öst L-G (1984). Animal and social phobias: Biological constraints on learned fear responses. In Reiss S & Bootzin RR (Eds.), *Theoretical issues in behavior therapy*. Academic, NY.

Oler I & Baum M (1968). Facilitated extinction of an avoidance response through shortening of the inter-trial interval. *Psychol Sci, 11*, 323.

Oppenheimer BS & Rothschild MA (1918). The psychoneurotic factor in the irritable heart of soldiers. *J Am Med Assoc, 70*, 1919–1922, 1918.

Oppenheimer BS, Levine SA, Morison RA et al. (1918). Report on neurocirculatory asthenia and its management. *Military Surgeon, 42*, 409–426, 711–719.

Orchinik CW, Koch R, Wycis HT, Freed H, & Spiegel EA (1950). Thalamic lesions and emotional reactivity. In *Life stresses and bodily disease* (Research Publication of the Association for Research in Nervous and Mental Disorder, vol. 29). Williams & Williams, Baltimore.

Orley J & Wing JK (1979). Psychiatric disorders in two African villages. *Arch Gen Psychiat, 36*, 513–520.

Orr SP & Lanzetta JT (1980). Facial expressions of emotion as conditioned stimuli for human autonomic responses. *J Pers Soc Psychol, 38*, 278–282.

Orwin A, LeBoeuf A, Dovey J, & James S (1975). A comparative trial of exposure and respiratory relief therapies. *Beh Res Ther, 13*, 205–214.

Orwin W (1973). Augmented respiratory relief. *Br J Psychiat, 122*, 171–173.

Orwin W et al. (1975). Exposure v respiratory relief. *Beh Res Ther, 13*, 205–214.

Osgood CE (1953). *Method and theory in experimental psychology*. Oxford University Press, NY.

Öst LG (1978). Behavioral treatment of thunder and lightning phobias. *Beh Res Ther, 16*, 197–207.

Öst L-G (1986a). Age at onset in different phobias (submitted for review).

Öst L-G (1986b). Physiological reactions in blood phobic and non-phobic subjects in phobic and ordinary stress situations (submitted for review).

Öst L-G & Hugdahl K (1981). Acquisition of phobias and anxiety response patterns in clinical patients. *Beh Res Ther, 19*, 439–447.

Öst L-G & Hugdahl K (1983). Acquisition of agoraphobia, mode of onset and anxiety response patterns. *Beh Res Ther, 21*, 623–631.

Öst L-G & Hugdahl K (1985). Acquisition of blood and dental phobia and anxiety response patterns in clinical patients. *Beh Res Ther, 23*, 27–34.

Öst LG & Jannsson L (1986). Cognitive-behavioral treatments of anxiety disorders. In Michelson L & Ascher M (Eds.) Guilford, NY.

Öst L-G, Sterner U, & Lindahl I-L (1984). Physiological responses in blood phobics. *Beh Res Ther, 22,* 2, 109–117.

Öst LG, Jerremalm A, & Johansson J (1981). Individual response patterns and different behavioral treatments of social phobia. *Beh Res Ther, 19,* 1–16.

Öst LG, Johansson J, & Jerremalm A (1982). Individual response patterns and different behavioral treatments of claustrophobia. *Beh Res Ther, 20,* 445–460.

Öst L-G, Lindahl I-L, Sterner U, & Jerremalm A (1984a). Exposure in vivo vs applied relaxation for blood phobia. *Beh Res Ther, 22,* 205–216.

Öst LG, Jerremalm, & Jansson L (1984b). Individual response patterns and different behavioral treatments of agoraphobia. *Beh Res Ther, 22,* 697–707.

Owings DH, Borchert M & Virginia R (1977). Behaviour of California ground squirrels. *Animal Beh, 25,* 221–230.

Ozturk O (1980). Psychiatric disorders in Ankara. Unpublished manuscript.

Pacella BL, Polatin P, & Nagler SH (1944). Clinical and EEG studies in obsessive-compulsive states. *Am J Psychiat, 100,* 830–838.

Palmer HD & Jones MS (1939). Anorexia nervosa as a manifestation of compulsion neurosis. *Arch Neurol Psychiat, 41,* 856–858.

Palmer J (1966). School phobia. Paper to World Congress of Psychiatry. Madrid, July.

Paolino A (1984). *Agoraphobia (fear of fear).* Apollo, Fort Tilden, NY.

Papousek H & M (1979). Early ontogeny of human social interaction: Its biological roots and social dimensions. In Von Cranach M et al. (Eds.), *Human ethology* (ch. 7.2, pp. 452–478). Cambridge University Press, London.

Parker G (1979). Reported parental characteristics of agoraphobics and social phobics. *Br J Psychiat, 135,* 555–560.

Parker G (1983). *Parental overprotection: A risk factor in psychosocial development.* Grune & Stratton, NY.

Parkinson P & Rachman S (1980). Are intrusive thoughts subject to habituation? *Beh Res Ther, 18,* 409–418.

Parrino JJ (1971). Reduction of seizures by desensitization. *J Beh Ther Exp Psychiat, 2,* 215–218.

Pasnau R (Ed.) (1984). *Anxiety and the anxiety disorders.* American Psychiatric Press, Washington, DC.

Paul SM, Maranos PJ, Skolnick P, & Goodwin FK (1982). Biological substrates of anxiety: BZ receptors and endogenous ligands. *Encephale, 8,* 131–144.

Pauls DL, Noyes R, & Crowe RR (1979). The familial prevalence in second degree relatives in anxiety neurosis. *J Affect Dis, 1,* 279–285.

Pauls DL, Bucher KD, Crowe RR, & Noyes R (1980). A genetic study of panic disorder pedigrees. *Beh Genet, 32,* 639–644.

Paykel E, Klerman G, & Prusoff B (1976). Personality and symptom patterns in depression. *Br J Psychiat, 128,* 327–334.

Paykel ES, Parker RR, Rowan PR et al. (1983). Nosology of atypical depression. *Psychol Med, 13,* 131–139.

Pearce KA, Schauer AH, Garfield NJ et al. (1985). A study of PTSD in Vietnam veterans. *J Clin Psychol, 41,* 9–14.

Pecknold JC, McClure DJ, Appeltauer L et al. (1982). Does tryptophan potentiate clomipramine for agoraphobics and social phobics? *Br J Psychiat, 140,* 484–490.

Pepys S (1667). *The diary of Samuel Pepys* (Latham R & Mathews W, Eds. vol. 8). Reprinted by University of California Press, Los Angeles (1970).

Perini G & Mendius R (1984). Depression and anxiety in complex partial seizures. *J Nerv Ment Dis, 172*, 287–290.

Persons JB & Foa EB (1984). Processing of fearful and neutral information by obsessive-compulsives. *Beh Res Ther, 22*, 259–265.

Persson G & Nordlund CL (1985). Agoraphobics and social phobics: Differences in background factors, syndrome profiles and therapeutic response. *Act Psychiat Scand, 71*, 148–159.

Peterson M (1983). Carcinoids in panic disorder. Paper to Upjohn Conference on Biological Considerations in the Etiology and Treatment of Panic Disorders. Boston, November.

Petursson H & Lader MH (1981). Benzodiazepine dependence. *Br J Addict, 76*, 133–145.

Pfeiffer W (1963). Alarm substances. *Experientia, 19*, 13–123.

Pfeiffer W (1974). Pheromones in fish and amphibia. In Birch MC (Ed.), *Pheromones.* North Holland, London.

Philips HC (1985). Return of fear in the treatment of a fear of vomiting. *Beh Res Ther, 23*, 45–52.

Pinto R (1972). A case of movement epilepsy with agoraphobia treated successfully by flooding. *Br J Psychiat, 121*, 287–288.

Pittendrigh CS (1958). Adaptation, natural selection and behavior. In Roe A & Simpson GG (Eds.), *Behavior and Evolution*, (pp. 390–416). Yale University Press, New Haven.

Pitts FM & McClure JN (1967). Lactate metabolism in anxiety neurosis. *New Eng J Med, 277*, 1329.

Plimpton E, Swartz KB, & Rosenblum LA (1981). Foraging demand and social interactions in laboratory bonnet macaques. *Int J Primatol, 2*, 175–181.

Plomin R & Rowe DC (1977). A twin study of temperament in young children. *J Psychol, 97*, 107–113.

Plomin R & Rowe DC (1979). Genetic and environmental etiology of social behavior in infancy, *Dev Psychol, 15*, 62–72.

Plomin, R, De Fries JC, & McClearn GE (1980). *Behavioral genetics: A primer.* Freeman, San Francisco.

Pollard CA & Jensen B (1984). 3 coping strategies during in vivo exposure treatment of agoraphobia. Paper to AABT, Philadelphia.

Pollitt J (1957). Natural history of obsessional states. *Brit Med J, 1*, 195–198.

Pollitt JD (1960). Natural history. *J Mental Science, 106*, 93–113.

Poole AD & Yates AJ (1975). The modification of excessive frequency of urination: A case study. *Beh Ther, 6*, 78–86.

Pope C (1911). A note on tubercular phobia. *The Medical Fortnightly, 39*, 205–206.

Post F, Rees WL & Schurr PH (1968). An evaluation of bimedial leucotomy. *Br J Psychiat, 114*, 1223–1246.

Post RM (1980). Intermittent vs continuous stimulation: Effect of time interval on sensitization or tolerance. *Life Sciences, 26*, 1275–1282.

Post RM, Pickar D, Ballenger JC, Naber D & Rubinow DR (1984). Endogenous opiates in CSF: Relationship to mood and anxiety. In Post R & Ballenger JC (Eds.), *Neurobiology of mood disorders.* Williams & Wilkins, London.

Powell GVW (1974). The social value of flocking by starlings (Sturnus vulgaris) in relation to predation and foraging. *Animal Behav, 22*, 501–505.

Pratt KC (1945). The "fears" of rural children. *J Genet Psychol, 67*, 179–194.

Pratt RTC & McKenzie W (1958). Anxiety states following vestibular disorders. *Lancet, 2*, 347–9.

Prestrude AM (1977). Phylogenetic comparisons of tonic immobility with special reference to habituation and fear. *Psychol Rec, 1*, 21–39.

Prigatano CP & Johnston HJ (1974). Autonomic nervous system changes associated with a spider phobic reaction. *J Abn Psychol, 83*, 169.

Prince M & Putnam JJ (1912). Clinical study of a case of phobia: A symposium. *J Abn Soc Psychol, 7*, 259–303.

Procacci PM, Savran SV, Schreiter SL & Bryson AL (1976). Prevalence of clinical mitral valve prolapse in 1169 young women. *N Eng J Med, 294*, 1086–1088.

Pruitt WO (1965). A flight releaser in wolf-caribou relations. *J Mammal, 46*, 350–351.

Prusoff B & Klerman G (1978). Differentiating depressed from anxious neurotic outpatients. *Arch Gen Psychiat, 30*, 302–309.

Pujol R & Savy L (1968). *Le Devenir de l'obsédé*. Masson et Cie, Paris.

Pulst SM, Walshe TM, & Romero JA (1983). Carbon monoxide poisoning with features of Gilles de la Tourette syndrome. *Arch Neurol, 40*, 443–444.

Purchon RD (1968). *The biology of the mollusca*. Pergamon, Oxford.

Pynoos RS, Frederick C, Arroyo W et al. (1985). Post-traumatic stress in school age children. Paper to APA. Dallas, May.

Quinn WG & Dudai Y (1976). Memory phases in drosophila. *Nature, 262*, 576–577.

Quitkin FM, Rifkin A, Kaplan J, & Klein DF (1972). Phobic anxiety complicated by drug dependence and addiction. *Arch Gen Psychiat, 27*, 159–162.

Rabavilas AD, Boulougouris JC, & Stefanis C (1976). Duration of flooding sessions for obsessive-compulsive patients. *Beh Res Ther, 14*, 349–355.

Rabavilas AD, Boulougouris JC, Perissaki C, & Vaidakis N (1977). Superstition in obsessive-compulsive patients. Paper to WPA. Honolulu.

Rabavilas AD, Boulougouris J, & Stefanis C (1977b). Synchrony and concordance on subjective and psychophysiological measures after beta-blockade and flooding in obsessive-compulsive patients. In Boulougouris JC & Rabavilas AD (Eds.), *Treatment of phobic and obsessive-compulsive disorders* (ch. 14, pp. 115–126). Pergamon, Oxford.

Rabavilas A, Boulougouris JC, Perissaki C (1979). Therapist qualities related to outcome with exposure in vivo in neurotic patients. *J Beh Ther Exp Psychiat, 10*, 293–294.

Rachman SJ (1974). Primary obsessional slowness. *Beh Res Ther, 12*, 9–18.

Rachman SJ (1978). *Fear and courage*. Freeman, San Francisco.

Rachman SJ (1984) Fear and courage. *Beh Ther, 15*, 109–120.

Rachman S (1985) Letter to editor. *Beh Ther, 16*, 426–428.

Rachman SJ (1958a). An overview of clinical and research issues in OCD. In Mavissakalian M, Turner SM, & Michelson L (Eds.), *OCD* (ch. 1). Plenum, NY.

Rachman SJ & Hodgson R (1980). Obsessions and compulsions. Prentice-Hall, Englewood Cliffs, NJ.

Rachman S, Hodgson R, & Marks IM (1973). Treatment of OCD by modelling and flooding in vivo. *Beh Res Ther, 11*, 463–471.

Rachman S, de Silva P, Roper G (1976). Spontaneous decay of compulsive urges. *Beh Res Ther, 14*, 405–453.

Raguram R & Bhide A (1985). Patterns of phobic neurosis: A retrospective study. *Br J Psychiat, 147*, 557–560.

Raichle ME, Herscovitch P, Taylor J, Butler K, Robins E, & Guze S (1983). Local brain hemodynamics and metabolism in depression and sodium-lactate-induced anxiety. In WPA Conference (Abstract S524, p. 127) Vienna, July.

Rainey JM, Ettedgui E, Pohl B et al. (1984a). The B-receptor: Isoproterenol anxiety states. *Psychopathology, 17* (Supp. 3), 40–51.

Rainey JM, Pohl RB, Williams M, Knitter E et al. (1984b). A comparison of lactate and isoproterenol anxiety states. *Psychopathology, 17,* 74–82.

Rangell L (1952). The analysis of a doll phobia. *Internat J Psychoan, 33,* 43.

Rapoport J & Flament M (1985). Psychobiology of childhood OCD. In *Abstracts of the World Congress of Biological Psychiatry* (Abstract 119.1, p. 31). Philadelphia, September.

Rapoport J, Elkins R, & Mikkelsen E (1980). Chlorimipramine in adolescents with obsessive-compulsive disorder. *Psychopharm Bull, 16,* 61–63.

Rapoport J, Elkins R, Langer DH et al. (1981). Childhood obsessive compulsive disorder. *Am J Psychiat, 138,* 1545–1554.

Rapoport J, Berg CJ, Ismond DR et al. (1984). Dietary choice and the effects of caffeine challenge in children. *Arch Gen Psychiat, 41,* 1073–1079.

Raskin M, Peeke HVS, Dickman W, & Pinsker H (1982). Panic and generalized anxiety disorders. *Arch Gen Psychiat, 39,* 687–689.

Ratner SC (1967) Comparative aspects of hypnosis. In Gordon JE (Ed.), *Handbook of clinical experimental hypnosis.* Macmillan, NY.

Ratner SC (1976). Animal's defenses: Fighting in predator-prey relations. In Pliner P, Kramer L & Alloway T (Eds.), *Advances in the study of communication and affect. Nonverbal communication of aggression* (Vol. 2). Plenum, NY.

Ratner SC (1977). Immobility in invertebrates. *Psychol Rec, 27,* 1–13.

Ray I & Morphy J (1975). Metronome conditioned relaxation and urinary retention. *J Can Psychiatr Assoc, 20,* 139–141.

Ray S (1964). Obsessional states in New Delhi. *Br J Psychiat, 110,* 181–182.

Razani J (1974). Treatment of phobias by systematic desensitization. *Arch Gen Psychiat, 30,* 291–296.

Razran G (1961). Interoceptive conditioning, semantic conditioning, and the orienting reflex. *Psychol Rev, 68,* 81–147.

Redd WH & Andresen GV (1981). Conditioned aversion in cancer patients. *The Behavior Therapist, 4,* 3–4.

Redican WK (1975). Facial expressions in nonhuman primates. In Rosenblum L (Ed.) *Primate behavior* (ch. 4, pp. 103–194). Academic Press, NY.

Redmond DE Jr (1977). Alterations in the function of the nucleus locus coeruleus: possible model for studies of anxiety. In Usdin E & Hanin, I (Eds.), *Animal models in psychiatry and neurology* (pp. 293–305). Pergamon, NY.

Redmond DE Jr & Huang YH (1979). Current Concepts: II. New evidence for a locus coeruleus-norepinephrine connection with anxiety. *Life Sci, 25,* 2149–2162.

Redmond DE Jr & Huang YH (1982). The primate locus coeruleus and effects of clonidine on opiate withdrawal. *J Clin Psychiat, 43:6* (Sec. 2), 25–29.

Registrar-General (1953). *Statistical Review of England and Wales, 1949. Supplement on Mental Health, 1953.* HMSO, London.

Reich T, James JW, & Morris CA (1972). Multiple thresholds in the transmission of semi-continuous traits. *Ann Human Genet, 36,* 163–186.

Reichert H & Wine JJ (1982). Neural mechanisms for serial order in a stereotypical behavior sequence. *Nature, 296,* 86–87.

Reiman EM, Raichle ME, Butler FK, Herscovitch P, & Robins E (1984). PET focal brain abnormality in panic disorder. *Nature, 310,* 683–685.

Reinhardt JF, Bannon MJ, & Roth RH (1982). Diazepam antagonises dopamine synthesis and metabolism in prefrontal cortex. *Arch Pharm, 318,* 374–377.

Reinhardt RF (1970). The outstanding jet pilot. *Am J Psychiat, 127,* 732–736.

Reiss S, Gursky DM, Peterson RA, & McNally RJ (1986). Anxiety sensitivity, anxiety frequency and the prediction of fearfulness. *Beh Res Ther, 24,* 1–8.

Reite M, Short R, Seiler C, & Pauley JD (1981). Attachment, loss and depression. *J Child Psychol Psychiat, 22,* 141–169.

Rescorla RA (1967). Pavlovian conditioning and its proper control procedures. *Psychol Rev, 74,* 71–80.

Rescorla RA & Heth CD (1975). Reinstatement of fear to an extinguished conditioned stimulus. *J Exper Psychol: Animal Beh Proc, 104,* 88–96.

Revusky S & Taukulis H (1975). Effects of alcohol and lithium habituation on the development of alcohol aversions through contingent lithium injection. *Beh Res Ther, 13,* 163–166.

Reynierse JH & Wiff LI (1973). Temporal placement and response prevention of avoidance on extinction of avoidance in rats. *Beh Res Ther, 11,* 119.

Reynolds CF, Shaw DH, Newton TF, Coble PA, & Kupfer DJ (1983). EEG sleep in generalized anxiety and depression. *Psychiat Res, 8,* 81–89.

Reynolds EH & Trimble MR (Eds.) (1981). *Epilepsy and psychiatry.* Churchill Livingstone, NY.

Ricciuti HN (1974). Fear and social attachments in the first year of life. In Lewis M & Rosenblum LA (Eds.), *The origins of fear* (ch. 4, pp. 73–106). Wiley, NY.

Richter CP (1957). On the phenomenon of sudden death in animals and man. *Psychosom Med, 19,* 191–198.

Rifkin A, Klein DF, Dillon D, & Levitt M (1981). Blockade by imipramine or desimipramine of panic induced by sodium lactate. *Am J Psychiat, 138,* 676–677.

Rijksen HD (1981). Infant killing: A possible consequence of a disputed leader role. *Behaviour, 78,* 138–167.

Riley V (1981). Psychoneuroendocrine influences on immunocompetence and neoplasia. *Science, 212,* 1100–1109.

Rimm DC, Janda LH, Lancaster DW, Nahl M, & Dittmar K (1977). The origin and maintenance of phobias. *Beh Res Ther, 15,* 231–238.

Rimm D, Briddell D, Zimmerman M, & Caddy G (1981). The effects of alcohol and the expectancy of alcohol on snake fear. *Addict Beh, 6,* 47–51.

Rinieris P, Rabavilas A, Lykouras E, & Stefanis C (1983). Neuroses and ABO blood types. *Neuropsychobiology, 9,* 16–18.

Rippere V (1983). Dietary treatment of chronic obsessions. *Br J Clin Psychol, 22,* 314–316.

Rizley RC & Rescorla RA (1972). Associations in second-order conditioning and sensory preconditioning. *J Comp Physiol Psychol, 81,* 1–11.

Rizzo PA, Spadaro M, Albani G, & Morocutti C (1983). Contingent negative variation and phobic disorders. *Neuropsychobiology, 9,* 73–77.

Roberts AH (1964). Housebound housewives—a followup study of a phobic anxiety state. *Br J Psychiat, 110,* 191–197.

Robertson J (1979). A controlled investigation of the treatment of obsessive-compulsive disorders. MD dissertation, Middlesex Hospital, London.

Robertson J, Wendiggersen P, & Kaplan I (1983). Towards a comprehensive treatment for obsessional thoughts. *Beh Res Ther, 21,* 347–356.

Robertson HA, Martin IL, & Candy JM (1978). Differences in bz receptor binding in Maudsley reactive and non-reactive rats. *Eur J Pharm, 50,* 455–457.

Robertson JR (1975). Role of response prevention in treatment of OCD. Paper to Society for Psychotherapy Research. London, July.

Robins LN, Helzer JE, Weissman MM et al. (1984). Lifetime prevalence of specific psychiatric disorders in three sites. *Arch Gen Psychiat, 41,* 949–958.

Rockett FC (1955). Notes on "an experimental test" of an alleged innate sign stimulus by Hirsch, Lindley & Tolman. *Percep Motor Skills, 5,* 155–156.

Rockwell LF & Simons D (1947). The EEG and personality organization in the obsessive-compulsive reactions. *Arch Neurol Psychiat, 57,* 71–77.

Rodriguez A & Z, Eisenberg L (1959). Outcome of school phobias. *Am J Psychiat, 116,* 540–544.

Roeder KD (1965). Moths and ultrasound. *Sci Am, 212,* 94–102.

Rofé Y & Goldberg J (1983). Prolonged exposure to a war environment and the blood pressure of pregnant women. *Br J Med Psychol, 56,* 305–311.

Rogerson HL (1951). Venereophobia in the male. *Br J Vener Dis, 27,* 158–159.

Rohrbaugh M & Riccio DC (1970). Paradoxical enhancement of learned fear. *J Abn Psychol, 75,* 210–216.

Rohrbaugh M, Riccio DC, & Arthur A (1972). Paradoxical enhancement of conditioned suppression. *Beh Res Ther, 10,* 125–130.

Rohsenow DJ (1982a). Control over interpersonal evaluation and alcohol consumption in male social drinkers. *Addict Beh, 7,* 113–121.

Rohsenow DJ (1982b). Social anxiety, daily moods, and alcohol use over time among heavy social drinking men. *Addict Beh, 7,* 311–315.

Roper G, Rachman S, & Marks IM (1975). Passive and participant modelling in exposure treatment of OCD. *Beh Res Ther, 13,* 271-279.

Rose RJ & Ditto WB (1983). A developmental genetic analysis of common fears from early adolescence to early childhood. *Child Dev, 54,* 361–368.

Rose RJ, Miller JZ, Pogue-Geile MF, & Cardwell GF (1981). Twin-family studies of common fears and phobias. In *Twin research 3: Intelligence, personality and development* (pp. 169–174).

Rose RM (1980). Endocrine responses to stressful psychological events. *Psychiatric Clinics of North America, 3,* 251–276.

Rosen G (1976). *Don't be afraid.* Prentice-Hall, Englewood Cliffs, NJ.

Rosen H & Myers HJ (1947). Abreaction in the military setting. *Arch Neurol Psychiat, 54,* 161–172.

Rosenberg CM (1967). Familial aspects of OCD. *Br J Psychiat, 113,* 405–413.

Rosenberg CM (1968). Complications of OCD. *Br J Psychiat, 114,* 477–78.

Rosenblum LA & Alpert S (1974). Fear of strangers and specificity of attachment in monkeys. In Lewis M & Rosenblum LA (Eds.) *The origins of fear* (ch. 7, pp. 165–193). Wiley, NY.

Rosenblum LA & Cross HA (1963). Performance of neonatal monkeys in the visual cliff situation. *Am J Psychol, 76,* 318–320.

Ross J (1980). The use of former phobics in the treatment of phobias. *Am J Psychiat, 136,* 715–717.

Ross RR (1964). Positive and negative partial-reinforcement extinction effects carried through continuous reinforcement, changed motivation and changed response. *J Exper Psychol, 68,* 492–502.

Ross RR, Meichenbaum DH, & Humphrey (1971). Behavior modification of nocturnal headbanging: A case report. *Beh Res Ther, 9,* 151–154.

Ross SM & Proctor S (1973). Frequency and duration of hierarchy item exposure in a systematic desensitization analogue. *Beh Res Ther, 11,* 303.

Roth M (1959). The phobic-anxiety-depersonalisation syndrome. *Proc Roy Soc Med, 52,* 8, 587.

Roth M (1984). Agoraphobia, panic disorder and generalized anxiety disorder: Some implications of recent advances. *Psychiat Dev, 2,* 31–52.

Roth M & Argyle C (1985). Panic attacks in phobic and generalized anxiety and depression. In *Abstracts of the World Biological Psychiatry Congress* (Abstract 113.2). Philadelphia.

Roth M & Mountjoy CQ (1982). The distinction between anxiety states and depressive disorders. In Paykel E (Ed.), *Handbook of affective disorders.* Churchill Livingstone, Edinburgh.

Roth M, Garside RS, & Gurney C (1965). Classification of anxiety and depression. In *Proc Leeds Sym Beh Dis.* May & Baker.

Roth M, Garside RF, Gurney C, & Kerr TA (1972). Studies in the classification of affective disorders. *Br J Psychiat, 121,* 147–161.

Rottman SJ & Snowdon CT (1972). Demonstration and analysis of an alarm pheromone in mice. *J Comp Physiol Psychol, 81,* 483–490.

Routtenberg GA & Glickman SE (1964). Visual cliff behavior in undomesticated rodents, land and aquatic turtles and cats *(Panthera). J Comp Physiol Psychol, 58,* 143–146.

Roy A (1979). Obsessive-compulsive neurosis: Phenomenology, outcome and a comparison with hysterical neurosis. *Compr Psychiat, 20,* 528–531.

Roy-Byrne PP, Uhde TW, Geraci M, & Post RM (1985). Life events and onset of panic disorder. Paper to World Biological Psychiatry Congress. Philadelphia.

Roy-Byrne PP, Uhde TW, Post RM et al. (1985a). Normal pain sensitivity in patients with panic disorder. *Psychiat Res, 14,* 77–84.

Roy-Byrne PP, Uhde TW, Post RM, Mendelson WB, & Gillin JC (1985b). Sleep and sleep deprivation in panic patients. Paper to APA. Dallas, May.

Royce WS (1975). Practice and feedback as treatment for social isolation. Doctoral dissertation, University of Oregon, Portland.

Rozin P (1977). In Barker LM, Best MR & Domjan M (Eds.) *Learning mechanisms in food selection.* Baylor University Press, Waco, TX.

Rudin E (1953). Ein beitrag zur frage der zwangskrankheit insbesondere hereditaren beziehungen. *Arch Psychiatr Nervenkr, 191,* 14–54.

Rullier F (1948). Habituation in polychaetes. *Bull Lab Marit Dinard, 30,* 21–27.

Rush DK, Mineka S, & Suomi S (1983). Therapy for helpless monkeys. *Beh Res Ther, 21,* 297–301.

Russell PA (1979). Fear-evoking stimuli. In Sluckin W (ed.), *Fear in animals and man* (pp. 86–126). Van Nostrand, NY.

Rutner IT (1973). Effects of feedback and instructions on phobic behavior. *Beh Ther, 4,* 338–348.

Rutter M (1981). *Maternal deprivation reassessed.* Penquin, London.

Rutter M & Garmezy N (1983). Developmental psychopathology. In Mussen P (Ed.), *Handbook of child psychology* (4th ed., vol. IV).

Rutter M, Tizard J & Whitmore K (1980). In Rutter M et al. (Eds.), *Education, health and behaviour* (ch. 12). Longmans, London.

Ryan VL & Moses JA (1979). Therapist warmth and status in systematic desensitization of test anxiety. *Psychother: Theory Res Practice, 16,* 178–184.

Rychtarik RG, Silverman WK, VanLandingham WP, & Prue DM (1984). Treatment of an incest victim with implosive therapy. *Beh Ther, 15,* 410–420.

Ryle JA (1948). Nosophobia. *J Ment Sci, 94,* 1–17.

Sackett GP (1966). Monkeys reared in isolation with pictures as visual input. Evidence for an innate relearning mechanism. *Science, 154,* 1468–1472.

Saigh PA (1984). Pre- and postinvasion anxiety in Lebanon. *Beh Ther, 15,* 185–190.

Sainsbury P & Gibson JG (1954). Anxiety and tension and accompanying physiological muscular changes. *J Neurol Neurosurg Psychiat, 17,* 216–224.

Sakai T (1967). Clinico-genetic study on obsessive-compulsive neurosis. *Bull Osaka Med Sch-* (Supp. XII), 323–331.

Salkovskis PM (1983). Treatment of an obsessional patient using habituation to audiotaped ruminations. *Br J Clin Psychol, 22,* 311–313.

Salkovskis PM & Warwick HMC (1985). Cognitive therapy of obsessive-compulsive disorder. Treating treatment failures. *Beh Psychother, 13*, 243–255.

Salkovskis PM, Jones DRO, & Clark DM (1986). Respiratory control in the treatment of panic attacks: Replication. *Br J Psychiat, 148*, 526–532.

Salzen EA (1979). The ontogeny of fear in animals. In Sluckin W (Ed.), *Fear in animals and man* (ch. 5, pp. 125–128). Van Nostrand, London.

Salzen EA (1979b). Social attachment and a sense of security. In Von Cranach M et al. (Eds.), *Human ethology* (ch. 9, 1, 595–622. Cambridge University Press, London.

Samarasinghe DS, Tilley S, & Marks IM (1984). Alcohol and sedative drug use in neurotic outpatients. *Br J Psychiat, 145*, 45–48.

Samelson F (1980). JB Watson's Little Albert, Cyril Burt's twins, and the need for a critical science. *Am Psychol, 35*, 619–625.

Sandler J & Hazari A (1960). Obsessional character traits and symptoms. *Br J Med Psychol, 33*, 113–22.

Sandler M, Clow A, Elsworth JD, Glover V et al. (1983). Tribulin output in general anxiety disorder and lactate-induced panic. Paper to Conference on Biological Issues in the Etiology and Treatment of Panic Disorders. Boston, November.

Sanes JN, Ison JR, & Adelson AA (1978). Reflexogenic and Psychogenic reflex modulation: Differential effects according to polysynaptic and oligosynaptic pathways in humans. *Neurosci Abstr, 4*, 304.

Sapolsky RM (1984). Individual differences in cortisol secretion in the wild baboon: Role of negative feedback sensitivity. *Endocrinology, 113*, 2263–2267.

Sargant W (1948). Abreaction with drugs. *Digest Neurol Psychiat, 16*, 193–206.

Sargant W (1957). *Battle for the mind.* Pan, London.

Sargeant AB & Eberhardt LE (1975). Death feigning by ducks in response to predation by red foxes. *Am Naturalist, 94*, 108–119.

Sartory G (1977). The fearless avoiders: comparison of various strains of rats in an active avoidance task. *Beh Res Ther, 15*, 149–157.

Sartory G & Eysenck HJ (1976). Strain differences in the acquisition and extinction of fear responses in rats. *Psychol Rep. 38*, 163–187.

Sartory G, Rachman S, Grey S (1982). Return of fear: The role of rehearsal. *Beh Res Ther, 20*, 123–133.

Saul LJ, Rome H, & Leuser E (1946). Desensitization of combat fatigue patients. *Am J Psychiat, 102*, 476–478.

Savory TH (1928). *The biology of spiders* (pp. 207–208). Macmillan, NY.

Scaife M (1976). The response to eye-like shapes by birds: I & II. *Animal Beh, 24*, 195–206.

Scallet AC, Rush DR, Kalin NH et al. (1983). Shuttlebox avoidance in rhesus monkeys: Effect on plasma cortisol and beta-endorphin. *Peptides, 4*, 19–24.

Scarr S & Salapatek P (1970). Patterns of fear development during infancy. *Merrill-Palmer Quarterly, 16*, 53–90.

Schachter S (1957). Pain, fear and anger in hypertensives and normotensives. A psychophysiologic study. *Psychosom Med, 19*, 17–29.

Schachter S (1964). Interaction of cognitive and physiological determinants of emotional state. In PH Leiderman & D Shapiro (Eds.), *Psychobiological approaches to social behaviour* (pp. 138–173). Stanford University Press, Stanford.

Schachter S & Singer J (1962). Cognitive, social and physiological determinants of emotional state. *Psychol Rev, 69*, 379–399.

Schaffer HR (1974). Cognitive components of the infant's response to strangeness. In Lewis M & Rosenblum LA (Eds.), *Origins of fear* (ch. 1, pp. 10–24). Wiley, NY.

Schaller GB (1967). *The Deer and the tiger* (p. 269). University of Chicago Press, Chicago.

Schaller GB (1972). *The serengeti lion: A study of predator-prey relations.* University of Chicago Press, Chicago.

Schapira K, Kerr TA, & Roth M (1970). Phobias and affective illness. *Br J Psychiat, 117,* 25–32.

Schapira K, Roth M, Kerr TA, & Gurney C (1972). The prognosis of affective disorders: The differentiation of anxiety from depressive illness. *Br J Psychiat, 121,* 175–181.

Schatzberg AF, Rosenbaum A, & Sheehan D (1983). Biological Discrimination of Anxiety and Depressive Disorders. Paper to WPA. Vienna, July.

Schelver SR & Gutsch KU (1983). Effects of self-administered cognitive therapy on social-evaluative anxiety. *J Clin Psychol, 39,* 658–666.

Schenkel R (1947). Ausdruckstudien am Wolfen. *Behaviour, 1,* 81–129.

Schepank H (1976). Heredity and environmental factors in the development of psychogenic diseases. *Act Gen Med Gemellog, 25,* 237–239.

Scherer MW & Nakamura CY (1968). A fear survey schedule for children (FSS-FC). *Beh Res Ther, 6,* 173–182.

Schilder P (1938). The organic background of obsessions and compulsions. *Am J Psychiat, 94,* 1397–1414.

Schinder FE (1980). Treatment by systematic desensitization of a surviving nightmare of a real-life trauma. *J Beh Ther Exp Psychiat, 11,* 53–54.

Schleidt WM (1961). Reaktionen von Truthühnern auf Fliegende Raubvögel und versuche zur Analyse ihre AAMs. *Zeitschrift für Tier psychologie, 18,* 534–560.

Schleidt WM (1961a). Über die Auslösung Flucht von Raubvögel bei Trutühnern. *Naturwissenschaften, 48,* 141–142.

Schneirla TC (1965) Stimulation and organization in Approach/Withdrawal Processes in vertebrate behavioral development. In Lehrman DS, Hinde RA, & Shaw E (Eds.), *Advances in the study of behaviour* I (pp. 2–75). Academic, NY.

Schopf JW (1978). Evolution of the earliest cells. *Sci Am, 239,* 84–103.

Schraeder PL, Pontzer R, & Engel TR (1983). A case of being scared to death. *Arch Int Med, 143,* 1793–1794.

Schulberg HC, Saul M, McClelland M et al. (1985). Assessing depression in primary medical and psychiatric practices. *Arch Gen Psychiat, 42,* 1164–1170.

Schuyler D (1974). *The depression spectrum.* Aronson, NY.

Schwab JJ, Bell RA, Warheit GJ, & Schwab RB (1979). *Social order and mental health.* Brunner/Mazel, NY.

Schwab R, Chafetz ME, & Walker S (1954). Control of two simultaneous voluntary motor acts in normals and parkinsonians. *Arch Neurol Psychiat, 72,* 591–599.

Schwartz AN, Campos JJ, & Baisel EJ (1975). The visual cliff: Cardiac and behavioral responses on the deep and shallow sides at five and nine months of age. *J Exper Child Psychol, 15,* 85–99.

Schwartz GE, Weinberger DA, Singer JA (1981). Cardiovascular differentiation of happiness, sadness, anger and fear following imagery and exercise. *Psychosom Med, 43,* 343–364.

Schwartz LA (1945). Group psychotherapy in the war neuroses. *Am J Psychiat, 101,* 498–500.

Schwarz BE & Bickford RG (1956). EEG changes in animals under the influence of hypnosis. *J Nerv Ment Dis, 124,* 433–439.

Schwarz RM, Burkhart BR, & Green SB (1982). Sensation-seeking and anxiety as factors in social drinking by men. *J Stud Alcohol, 43,* 1108–1114.

Schweitzer L & Green L (1982). Acquisition and extended retention of conditioned taste aversion in preweanling rats. *J Comp Physiol Psychol, 96,* 791–806.

Scott A, Kelleher MJ, Smith A, & Murray RM (1982). Regional differences in obsessionality and obsessional neurosis. *Psychol Med, 12,* 131–134.

Scott JP & Fuller JL (1965). *Genetics and the social behavior of the dog.* University of Chicago Press, Chicago.

Scott LE & Clum GA (1984). Coping style and brief treatments for postsurgical pain. *Pain, 20,* 279–291.

Scrignar CB (1983). *Stress strategies.* Karger, Basel.

Segraves RT & Smith RC (1975). Treatment of neurotic outpatients by concurrent psychotherapy and behavior therapy. Paper to APA. Anaheim, May.

Seligman MEP (1970). On the generality of the laws of learning. *Psychol Rev, 77,* 406–418.

Seligman MEP (1975). *Helplessness.* WH Freeman, San Francisco.

Sepinwall J (1983). Neurochemical mechanisms of action of anxiolytics. In Malick JB, Enna SJ, & Yamamura HI (Eds.), *Anxiolytics: Neurochemical behavioral and clinical perspectives.* Raven, NY.

Sermet O (1974). Emotional and medical factors in child dental anxiety. *J Child Psychol Psychiat, 15,* 313–321.

Shafar S (1976). Aspects of phobic illness—a study of 90 personal cases. *Br J Med Psychol, 49,* 221–236.

Shagass C, Roemer RA, Straumanis JJ, & Josiassen RC (1984). Distinctive somatosensory evoked potentials in OCD. *Biol Psychiat, 19,* 1507–1524.

Shapiro AK, Shapiro E, Wayne H, & Carlkin J (1972). The psychopathology of Gilles de la Tourette syndrome. *Am J Psychiat, 129,* 427–434.

Shapiro MB, Marks IM, & Fox B (1963). Phobic and affective symptoms in an individual psychiatric patient. *Br J Soc Clin Psychol, 2,* 81–93.

Sharp JJ & Forman SG (1985). A comparison of two approaches to anxiety management for teachers. *Beh Ther, 16,* 370–383.

Shaw O (1975). Dental anxiety in children. *Br Dent J, 139,* 134–139.

Shaw P (1979). 3 behavior therapies for social phobia. *Br J Psychiat, 134,* 620–623.

Shear MK, Devereux RB, Kramer FR et al. (1984). Low prevalence of mitral valve prolapse in panic disorder. *Am J Psychiat, 141,* 302–303.

Shearman AR (1970). Response-contingent CS termination in the extinction of avoidance learning. *Beh Res Ther, 8,* 227.

Sheehan DV, Coleman JH, Greenblatt DJ, Jones KJ et al. (1984). Some biochemical correlates of panic attacks with agorphobia and their response to a new treatment. *J Clin Psychopharm, 4,* 66–75.

Sheehan D (1984). Paper to Upjohn Conference on Anxiety Disorders. Vienna, November.

Sheehan D (1984a). *The anxiety disease.* Scribner's, NY.

Sheehan DV & Sheehan KH (1982). The classification of phobic disorders. *Int J Psychiatr Med, 12,* 243–266.

Sheehan DV & Sheehan KH (1982). The classification of anxiety and hysterical states: I. Historical review and empirical delineation. *J Clin Psychopharm, 2,* 235–243.

Sheehan DV, Ballenger J, & Jacobsen G (1980). Treatment of endogenous anxiety. *Arch Gen Psychiat, 37,* 51–59.

Sheehan DV, Claycomb JB, Surman OS, Baer L et al. (1983). Panic attacks and the dexamethasone suppression test. *Am J. Psychiat, 140,* 1063–1064.

Shepherd MS, Oppenheim B, & Mitchell S (1971). *Childhood behaviour and mental health.* University of London Press, London.

Sher KJ, Frost JO, & Otto R (1983). Cognitive deficits in compulsive checkers. *Beh Res Ther, 21,* 357–363.

Sher KJ, Mann B, & Frost RO (1984). Cognitive dysfunction in compulsive checkers: Further explorations. *Beh Res Ther, 22,* 493–502.

Sherman AR (1972). Real life exposure as a primary therapeutic factor in desensitization treatment of fear. *J Abn Psychol, 79,* 19–28.

Sherman PW (1977). Nepotism and the evolution of alarm calls. *Science, 197,* 1246–1253.

Sherman PW (1981). Reproductive competition and infanticide in Belding's ground squirrels and other animals. In Alexander RD & Twinkle DW (Eds.), *Natural selection and social behavior* (pp. 311–331). Chiron Press, NY.

Shields J (1962). *Monozygotic twins brought up apart and brought up together.* Oxford University Press, London.

Shirley MM (1933). The first two years: A study of 25 babies. Vol 2 (In *Institute of Child Welfare Monograph Series, No. VII*). University of Minnesota Press, Minneapolis.

Shoben EJ & Borland L (1954). An empirical study of the etiology of dental fears. *J Clin Psychol, 10,* 171–174.

Shorkey C & Himley DP (1974). Systematic desensitisation treatment of a recurring nightmare and related insomnia. *J Beh Ther Exp Psych, 5,* 97–98.

Shorvon HG (1953). Discussion on abreaction. *Proc Roy Soc Med, 43,* 158–161.

Shukla GD & Katiyar BC (1980). Psychiatric disorders in temporal lobe epilepsy. *Br J Psychiat, 137,* 181–182.

Shukla GD & Mishra DN (1981). Koro-like syndrome: A case report. *Indian J Psychiat, 23,* 96–97.

Shute N (1956). *Slide rule.* Readers Union, William Heinemann, London.

Sieck MH, Baumbach HD, Gordon BL, & Turner JF (1974). Changes in spontaneous odor-modulated and shock-induced behavior patterns following discrete olfactory system lesions. *Physiol Beh, 13,* 427–439.

Siegeltuch M & Baum M (1971). Extinction of well established avoidance responses through response prevention (flooding). *Beh Res Ther, 9,* 103.

Silverman I & Geer JH (1968). The elimination of recurrent nightmare by desensitisation of a related phobia. *Beh Res Ther, 6,* 109–112.

Sim M & Houghton H (1966). Phobic anxiety and its treatment. *J Nerv Ment Dis, 143,* 484–491.

Simmons KEL (1952). Nature of the predator-reactions of breeding birds. *Behaviour, 4,* 161–172.

Simmons KEL (1955). Predator-reactions of waders towards humans with reference to aggressive, escape and brooding drives. *Behaviour, 8,* 130–173.

Singh AN (1983). Clomipramine in obsessive-compulsive disorder. Unpublished manuscript.

Singh PM, Gupta RC, Prasad GC, & Udupa KN (1980). Response of pineal gland in clinical cases of psychological stress. *Indian J Psychiat, 22,* 375–377.

Sinnott A, Jones B, & Fordham AS (1981). Agoraphobia: A situational analysis. *J Clin Psychol, 37,* 123–127.

Sireling L (1986). Prevalence of phobias in general practice. Awaiting publication.

Sisson LA, Van Hasselt VB, Hersen M, & Strain PS (1985). Peer interventions help social behaviors in multihandicapped children. *Beh Mod, 9,* 293–321.

Sitaram N, Dube S, Jones D et al. (1984). Separation of depression and anxiety. *Psychopath, 17,* (Supp. 3), 24–39.

Sjödén PO (1981). Biological boundaries and possibilities for learning. Paper to International Congress of Behavior Therapists. Trondheim, Norway, August.

Sjödén PO & Archer T (1983). Potentiation of a bottle aversion by taste in compound conditioning with rats. *J Experim Animal Beh.*

Skerritt PW (1983). Anxiety and the heart—a historical review. *Psychol Med, 13,* 17–25.

Skolnick P, Crawley JN, Glowa JR & Paul SM (1984). B-Carboline-induced anxiety states. *Psychopathology, 17,* (Supp. 3), 52–60.

Slater E (1939). Response to a nursery school situation of 40 children. *Soc Res Child Dev Monograph No. 4, 11,* 7.

Slater E & Shields J (1953). Psychotic and neurotic illness in twins. *Special Report Series of the Medical Research Council* (London), no. 278. HMSO, London.

Slater E & Shields J (1969). Genetical aspects of anxiety. In Lader MH (Ed.) *Studies of anxiety* (pp. 62–71). Royal Medico-Psychological Association, London.

Slough N, Kleinknecht RA, & Thorndike RM (1984). Relationship of the repression-sensitization scales to anxiety. *J Pers Assess, 48,* 378–379.

Sluckin W (1964). *Imprinting and early learning.* Methuen, London.

Sluckin W (Ed.) (1979). *Fear in animals and men.* Van Nostrand, NY.

Smail P, Stockwell T, Cantor S, & Hodgson R (1984) Alcohol dependence and phobic states: I. A prevalence study. *Br J Psychiat, 144,* 53–57.

Smirnov VM (1966). Neurophysiological study of human emotion. In *Symposium No. 3: Integrative forms of conditioned reflexes* (pp. 116–118). Presented to XVIII International Congress of Psychology. Moscow, August.

Smith FV (1969). *Attachment of the young: Imprinting and other developments.* Contemporary Science Paperbacks 38. Oliver & Boyd, Edinburgh.

Smith PK (1979). The ontogeny of fear in children. In Sluckin W (Ed.), *Fear in animals and man* (ch. 6, pp. 164–168). Van Nostrand, London.

Smith SL (1970). School refusal with anxiety: A review of 63 cases. *J Can Psychiat Assoc, 15,* 257–264.

Smith SM (1975). Innate recognition of coral snake pattern by a possible avian predator. *Science, 187,* 759–760.

Smith SM (1977). Coral-snake recognition and stimulus generalization by naive great kiskadees (Aves: *tyrranidae*). *Nature, 265,* 535–536.

Smith TW, Houston BK, & Zurawski RM (1984). Finger pulse volume as a measure of anxiety in response to evaluative threat. *Psychophysiology, 21,* 260–264.

Smotherman WP, Margolis A, & Levine S (1980). Flavor pre-exposures in conditioned taste aversion in rats: Dissociation of behavioral and endocrine effects. *J Comp Physiol Psychol, 94,* 25–35.

Smythe N (1970). On the existence of "pursuit invitation" signals in mammals. *Am Nat, 104,* 491–496.

Snaith RP (1968). A clinical investigation of phobias. *Br J Psychiat, 114,* 673–698.

Snowdon JA (1979). Family size and birth order in obsessional neurosis. *Act Psychiat Scandia, 60,* 121–128.

Snowdon T, Hainsworth FR, & Overmier JP (1966). Specific and permanent deficits in avoidance learning following forebrain ablation in the gold fish. Presented to *XVIII International Congress of Psychology* (vol. 1, p. 320). Moscow, August.

Snyder SH & Peroutka SJ (1984). Antidepressants and neurotransmitter receptors. In Post RM & Ballenger JC (Eds.), *Neurobiology of mood disorders* (Ch. 43, pp. 686–697). Williams & Wilkins, Baltimore.

Solantaus T, Rimpela M, & Taipale V (1984). The threat of war in the minds of 12–18-year-olds in Finland. *Lancet, 1/8380,* 784–785.

Solomon RL, Kamin LJ, & Wynne LC (1953). Traumatic avoidance learning: several extinction procedures with dogs. *J Abn Social Psychol, 48,* 291–302.

Solyom L & Sookman D (1977). Clomipramine and behavior therapy in obsessive neurosis. *J Int Med Res, 5,* 49–61.

Solyom L, Garze-Perez, Ledwidge BL, & Solyom C (1971). Aversion relief and desensitization for phobias. *Br J Psychiat, 119,* 299–303.

Solyom L, Heseltine GFD, McLure DJ, Heseltine et al. (1972b). Aversion relief therapy of phobics. *Beh Ther, 3,* 21–28.

Solyom L, Heseltine GFD, McLure DJ et al. (1973). Interaction of phenelzine and exposure in phobias. *J Can Psychiat Assoc, 18,* 25–32.

Solyom L & C, Shugar G, & Bryntnick (1973a). Treatment of fear of flying. *Am J Psychiat, 4,* 423.

Solyom L, Beck P, Solyom C, & Hugel R (1974). Some etiological factors in phobic neuroses. *J Can Psychiat Assoc, 19,* 69–78.

Solyom L, Silberfeld M, & Solyom C (1976). Maternal overprotection in the etiology of agoraphobia. *J Can Psychiatric Assoc, 21,* 109–113.

Solyom L & C, LaPierre Y, Pecknold J, & Morton L (1981). Phenelzine and exposure in the treatment of phobias. *Biol Psychiat, 16,* 239–247.

Solyom L, Ledwidge B, Solyom C (1986). Delineating social phobia. *Br J Psychiat, 149,* 464–470.

Sonnenberg SM, Blank AS, Talbott JA (1985). *The trauma of war stress and recovery in Vietnam veterans.* Am Psychiat Press, Washington, DC.

Sorce JF, Emde RN, Campos JJ, & Klinnert MD (1983). Maternal emotional signaling: Its effect on the visual cliff behavior of one-year-olds. *Dev Psychol.*

Sours JL (1965). The "break-off" phenomenon. *Arch Gen Psychiat, 13,* 447–456.

Spalding DA (1873). Instinct: In young animals. *MacMillans Magazine, 27,* 282–293. Reprinted in Gould SJ (1982), *Ethology.* Norton, NY.

Spetch ML, Wilkie DM, & Pinel JPJ (1981). Backward conditioning: A reevaluation of the empirical evidence. *Psychol Bull, 89,* 163–175.

Spiegler M & Liebert R (1970). Some correlates of self-reported fear. *Psychol Rep, 26,* 691–695.

Spitz RA & Wolff KM (1946). The smiling response: A contribution to the ontogenesis of social relations. *Genet Psychol Monogr, 34,* 57–125.

Spitzer RL & Williams JBW (1985). Proposed revisions in the DSM-III classification of anxiety disorders. In Tuma H & Maser J (Eds.), *Anxiety and the anxiety disorders* (ch. 40, pp. 759–774). Elbaum, Hillsdale, NJ.

Spitzer RL et al. (1967). Mental status schedule: Properties of factor analytically derived scales. *Arch Gen Psychiat, 16,* 479–491.

Sroufe LA (1974). Wariness of strangers and the study of infant development. *Child Dev, 48,* 731–746.

Sroufe LA, Fox NE, & Pancake VR (1983). Attachment and dependency in developmental perspective. *Child Dev, 54,* 1615–1627.

Stacey M, Dearden R, Pill R, & Robinson D (1970). *Hospitals, children and their families: A pilot study.* Routledge and Kegan Paul, London.

Starkman MN, Zelnik TC, Nesse RM, & Cameron OG (1985). Anxiety in patients with pheochromocytomas. *Arch Intern Med, 145,* 248–252.

Steinhausen CH & Glanville K (1983). Follow-up studies of anorexia nervosa: a review of research findings. *Psychol Med, 13,* 239–249.

Steketee GS & Foa EB (1986). Rape victims: Post-traumatic stress responses and their treatment. *J Anx Dis* (in press).

Steketee GS, Foa EB, & Grayson JB (1982). Recent advances in the behavioral treatment of obsessive-compulsives. *Arch Gen Psychiat, 39,* 1365–1371.

Steketee GS, Grayson JB, Foa EB (1985). OCD: Differences between washers and checkers. *Beh Res Ther, 23,* 197–201.

Steketee G, Foa EB, & Kozak MJ (1985a). Predictors of outcome in OCD. Paper to EABT. Munich.

Stengel E (1959). Classification of Mental Disorders. *Bull World Health Org, 21,* 601–663.

Steptoe A (1981). *Psychological factors in cardiovascular disorders.* Academic, NY.

Stern RS (1975). The medical student as behavioral psychotherapist. *Br Med J, 2,* 78–81.

Stern RS (1977). Letter to the editor. *Br J Psychiat, 130,* 418.

Stern RS (1978). Obsessive thoughts: The problem of therapy. *Br J Psychiat, 132,* 200–205.

Stern RS & Cobb JP (1978). Phenomenology of obsessive-compulsive neurosis. *Br J Psychiat, 132,* 233–239.

Stern RS & Marks IM (1973). Brief and prolonged flooding: A comparison in agoraphobic patients. *Arch Gen Psych, 28,* 270–276.

Stern RS & Marks IM (1973a). Contract marital therapy in obsessive-compulsive neurosis with marital discord. *Br J Psychiat, 123,* 681–684.

Stern RS, Lipsedge MS, & Marks IM (1975). Controlled trial of thought-stopping for obsessive ruminations. *Beh Res Ther, 11,* 659–662.

Stern RS, Marks IM, Mawson D, & Luscombe DK (1980). Clomipramine and exposure for compulsive rituals: II. Plasma levels, side effects and outcome. *Br J Psychiat, 136,* 161–166.

Stewart K (1969). Dream theory in Malaya. In Tart C (Ed.), *Altered states of consciousness* (ch. 9, pp. 159–168). Wiley, NY.

Stockwell T (1980). Relativity and the consequences of drinking alcohol. *Br J Addict, 75,* 214–216.

Stockwell T, Smail P, Hodgson R, & Canter S (1984). Alchohol dependence and phobic anxiety states: II. A retrospective study. *Br J Psychiat, 144,* 58–63.

Stokes E (1985). The neuroendocrinology of anxiety. In Tuma H & Maser J (Eds.), *Anxiety and anxiety disorders* (ch. 3, pp. 77–86). Erlbaum, Hillsdale, NJ.

Stone EA (1983). Problems with current catecholamine hypothesis of antidepressant agents. *Beh Brain Sci, 6,* 535–577.

Stone NM & Borkovec TD (1975). The paradoxical effect of brief CS exposure on analogue phobic subjects. *Beh Res Ther, 13,* 51.

Stonehill E & Crisp AH (1976). Anorexia nervosa before and after treatment and at follow-up 4–7 years later. *J Psychosom Res, 21,* 187–193.

Stouffer SA, Lumsdaine R, Williams M et al. (1949). *The American soldier: Combat and its aftermath.* Princeton University Press, Princeton.

Straker M (1951). Sickness fears: A manifestation of anxiety. *Treat Serv Bull, 6,* 197–199.

Stratton JG, Parker DA, & Snibbe JR (1984). Posttraumatic stress in police officers involved in shootings. *Psychol Rep, 55,* 127–131.

Stravynski A, Marks IM, & Yule W (1982). Social skills problems in neurotic outpatients. *Arch General Psychiat, 39,* 1378–1385.

Strom-Olsen R & Carlisle S (1971). Bi-frontal stereotactic tractotomy. *Br J Psychiat, 118,* 141–154.

Strong SR (1984). Experimental studies in paradoxical interventions. *J Beh Ther Exp Psychiat, 15,* 189–194.

Struhsaker TT (1967). Auditory communication among vervet monkeys *(Cercopithecus aethiops).* In Altman SA (Ed.), *Social communication among primates.* University of Chicago Press, Chicago.

Suarez SD & Gallup GG (1979). Tonic immobility as a response to rage in humans: A theoretical note. *Psychol Record, 29,* 315–320.

Sue D (1975). The effect of duration of exposure on systematic desensitization and extinction. *Beh Res Ther, 15,* 55.

Sugiyama T (1974). Clinico-electroencephalographic study on obsessive-compulsive neurosis. *Bull Osaka Med Sch, 20,* 95–114.

Suinn RM & Richardson F (1971). Anxiety-management training. *Beh Ther, 2,* 498–510.

Suinn RM, Edie CA, & Spinelli PR (1970). Accelerated massed desensitization. Innovation in short-term treatment. *Beh Ther, 1,* 303–311.

Suomi SJ (1982) Abnormal behavior and primate models of psychopathology. In Fobes J & King J (Eds.), *Primate behavior* (ch. 5, pp. 171–215). Academic, NY.

Suomi SJ (1983). The development of affect in rhesus monkeys. In Fox N & Davidson R (Eds.), *Affective development: A psychobiological perspective* (ch. 3, pp. 119–159). Erlbaum, Hillsdale, NJ.

Suomi SJ (1983b). Genetic, maternal and environmental influences on social development in rhesus monkeys. In Chiarelli AB & Corrullini RS (Eds.), *Primate behavior and sociobiology.* Springer, Verlag, Berlin.

Suomi SJ (1983c). Perception of contingency and social development. In Lamb ME & Sherrod L (Eds.), *Perception of social contingency* (ch. 8, pp. 177–203). Erlbaum, Hillsdale, NJ.

Suomi SJ (1984) Ethology: Animal models of psychopathology. In Saddock B (Ed.), *Comprehensive Textbook of Psychiatry.* Williams & Williams, Baltimore.

Suomi SJ & Harlow HF (1976). Production and alleviation of depressive behaviors in monkeys. In Maser JD & Seligman MEP (Eds.), *Psychopathology: Experimental models* (pp. 171–173). Freeman, San Francisco.

Suomi SJ, Harlow HF, & Novak MA (1974). Reversal of social deficits produced by isolation rearing in monkeys. *J Hum Evol, 3,* 527–534.

Suomi SJ, Kraemer GW, Baysinger CM, & DeLizio RD (1981). Inherited and experiential factors in anxiety of rhesus monkeys. In Klein DF & Rabkin JG (Eds.), *Anxiety: New research and changing concepts* (pp. 179–200). Raven, NY.

Suomi SJ, Mineka S, & Delizio RD (1983). Short- and long-term effects of repetitive mother-infant separations in social development in rhesus monkeys. *Dev Psychol, 19,* 770–786.

Svorad D (1957). Reticular activating system of brain stem and animal hypnosis. *Science, 125,* 156.

Surtees PG, Sashidharan SP & Dean C (1986). Affective disorder amongst women in the general population: A longitudinal study. *Br J Psychiat, 148,* 176–186.

Sweeney (1983). Speech to Institute of Psychiatry. London, May.

Sykes MK & Tredgold RF (1964). Restricted orbital undercutting. *Br J Psychiat, 110,* 609–640.

Symmes D (1959). Anxiety reduction and novelty as goals of visual exploration by monkeys. *J Genet Psychol, 94,* 181–198.

Talairach J, Bancaud J, Geier M, Bordas-Ferrer A, Bonis G, (1973). The cingulate gyrus and human behaviour. *Electroenceph Clin Neurophysiol, 34,* 45–52.

Talbert DG, Benson P, & Dewhurst J (1982). Fetal response to maternal anxiety: A factor in antepartum heart rate monitoring. *J Obstet Gynecol, 3,* 34–38.

Talbot M (1951). Panic in school phobia. *Am J Orthopsychiat, 27,* 286–295.

Tan E, Marks IM, & Marset P (1971). Bimedial leucotomy in obsessive-compulsive neurosis. A controlled serial enquiry. *Br J Psychiat, 118,* 155–164.

Taylor I (1986) Self-exposure instructions by telephone v face-to-face contact in agoraphobics. *Beh Psychother* (in press).

Taylor CB, Agras WS, Roth WT, King R, Dorian B, & Sheikh J (1985). Ambulatory heart rate changes in panic patients. Paper to APA. Dallas, May.

Taylor DP, Riblet LA, & Stanton HC (1983). Dopamine and anxiolytics. In JB Malick, SJ Enna, & HI Yamamura (Eds.), *Anxiolytics: Neurochemical, behavioral and clinical perspectives*. Raven, NY.

Tearnan BH, Telch MJ, & Keefe P (1984). Etiology and onset of agoraphobia: A critical review. *Comp Psychiat, 25,* 51–62.

Teasdale JD (1974). Learning models of obsessional-compulsive disorder. In Beech HR (Ed.) *Obsessional states* (ch. 9, pp. 197–232). Methuen, London.

Teasdale J, Walsh PA, Lancashire M, & Mathews AM (1974). Group exposure for agoraphobics: A replication. *Br J Psychiat, 130,* 186–193.

Telch M, Agras WS, Taylor CB et al. (1985). Imipramine and behavioral treatment for agoraphobia. *Beh Res Ther, 23,* 325–335.

Templer DI (1972). The obsessive-compulsive neurosis: Review of research findings. *Compr Psychiat, 13,* 375–383.

Tennant C et al. (1981). Demographic and clinical predictors of remission of neurotic disorders in the community. *Aust NZ J Psychiat, 15,* 111–116.

Tennant C, Hurry J, & Bebbington P (1982). Childhood separation experiences and adult depressive and anxiety states. *Br J Psychiat, 141,* 475–482.

Tennes K, Downey K, & Vernadakis A (1977). Urinary cortisol excretion rates and anxiety in normal one-year old infants. *Psychosom Med, 79,* 178–187.

Terhune WB (1949). The phobic syndrome. *Arch Neurol Psychiat, 62,* 162–172.

Terhune WB (1961). The phobic syndrome: Its nature and treatment. *J Arkan Med Soc, 58,* 23–236.

Terr LC (1983). Chowchilla revisited: The effects of psychic trauma four years after a school-bus kidnapping. *Am J Psychiat, 140,* 1543–1550.

Thomander LD (1975). Treatment of dating problems by practice dating and interaction group discussion. Doctoral dissertation, Michigan State University.

Thomas CS (1984). Dysmorphophobia: A question of definition. *Br J Psychiat, 144,* 513–516.

Thomas MR & Rapp S (1977). Physiological, behavioral and cognitive changes from flooding in a monosymptomatic phobia. *Beh Res Ther, 15,* 304–306.

Thompson GG (1962). *Child psychology: Growth trends in psychological adjustment* (2nd ed.). Houghton Mifflin, Boston.

Thompson RF (1983). Neuronal substrates of simple associative learning: Classical conditioning. *Trends in Neurosciences, 6,* 270–275.

Thompson RF & Spencer WA (1961). Habituation: A model phenomenon for the study of removed substrates of behavior. *Psych Rev, 73,* 16–43.

Thompson RKR, Foltin RW, Boylan RJ, Sweet A, Graves CA, & Lowitz CE (1981). Tonic immobility in Japanese quail can reduce the probability of sustained attack by cats. *Animal Learn Beh, 9,* 145–149.

Thorén P, Åsberg M, Cronholm B et al. (1980). Clomipramine treatment of obsessive-compulsive disorders: I. *Arch Gen Psychiat, 37,* 1281–1285.

Thorén P, Åsberg M, Bertilsson L, Mellström B, Sjoqvist F, & Traskman L (1980a). Clomipramine treatment of obsessive-compulsive disorders: II. Biochemical aspects. *Arch Gen Psychiat, 37,* 1289–1294.

Thoresen CE, Friedman M, Gill JK, & Ulmer DK (1982). The recurrent coronary prevention project. *Act Med Scand* (Supp.), *660,* 172–192.

Thorndike EL (1935). *The psychology of wants, interests and attitudes* (pp. 195–196). Appleton-Century, London.

Thorpe GK & Burns LE (1983). *The agoraphobic syndrome*. Wiley, NY.

Thorpe GL, Amatu HI, Blakey, & Burns LE (1976). Overt instructional rehearsal and specific insight with self-instruction. *Beh Ther, 7,* 504–511.

Thorpe GL, Barnes GS, Hunter JE, & Hines D (1983). Thoughts and feelings in 2 clinical and two nonclinical samples. *Cog Ther Res, 7,* 565–574.

Thorpe GL, Freedman EG, & McGailliard DW (1984). Components of rational-emotive imagery with nonassertive students. *J Rat Emot Ther, 2,* 11–19.

Thorpe GL, Freedman EG, & Lazar JD (1985). Assertiveness training and exposure in vivo for agoraphobics. *Beh Psychother, 13,* 132–141.

Thorpe GL (1975). Desensitization, behavior rehearsal, self-instructional training and placebo for assertion. *Beh Anal Modif, 1,* 30–44.

Thyer BA & Matthews J (1985). Phobic anxiety and plasma beta-endorphin in a single case. *Beh Res Ther, 24,* 237–341.

Thyer BA & Curtis GC (1984). The effects of ethanol intoxication on phobic anxiety. *Beh Res Ther, 22,* 599–610.

Thyer BA, Curtis GC, & Fechner SL (1984). Fear of criticism is not specific to obsessive-compulsive disorder. *Beh Res Ther* (in press).

Thyer BA, Papsdorf JD, & Wright P (1984a). Physiological and psychological effects of acute intentional hyperventilation. *Beh Res Ther, 22,* 587–590.

Thyer BA, Nesse RM, Cameron OG, & Curtis GC (1985). Agoraphobia: A test of the separation anxiety hypothesis. *Beh Res Ther, 23,* 75–78.

Thyer BA, Parrish RT, Curtis GC, Nesse RM, & Cameron OG (1985a). Ages of onset of DSM-III anxiety disorders. *Compr Psychiat, 26,* 113–122.

Timms MWH (1985). The treatment of urinary frequency by paradoxical intention. *Beh Psychother, 13,* 76–82.

Timpano P (1904). Clinical observation on a rare case of "phobia." *J Ment Path, 7,* 21–26.

Tinbergen N (1951). *The study of instinct* (p. 31). Oxford University Press, London.

Tinbergen N (1952). Derived activities: Causation, biological significance, origin and emancipation during evolution. *Q Rev Biol, 27,* 1–32.

Tinbergen N (1957). On antipredator responses in certain birds. *J Comp Physiol Psychol, 50,* 412–414.

Tomkins S (1963). *Affect, imagery, consciousness,* (vol. II, p. 157). Springer, NY.

Torgersen S (1978). The contribution of twin studies to psychiatric nosology. In Nance WE (Ed.), *Twin research* (Part A: Psychology and methodology, pp. 125–130). Liss, NY.

Torgersen S (1979). The nature and origin of common phobic fears. *Br J Psychiat, 134,* 343–351.

Torgersen S (1983). Genetics of neurosis: The effects of sampling variation upon the twin concordance ratio. *Br J Psychiat, 142,* 126–132.

Torgersen S (1983a). Genetic factors in anxiety disorders. *Arch Gen Psychiat, 40,* 1085–1089.

Torgersen S (1985). Hereditary differentiation of anxiety and affective neuroses. *Br J Psychiat, 146,* 530–534.

Torphy DM & Measey LG (1974). Marital interaction in agoraphobia. *J Clin Psychol, 30,* 351–354.

Trimble M (1981). *Neuropsychiatry* (p. 209). Wiley, NY.

Trimble M (1981a). *Post-traumatic neurosis.* Wiley, NY.

Tucker WI (1956). Diagnosis and treatment of the phobic reaction. *Am J Psychiat, 112,* 825–830.

Tuma AH & Maser JD (1985). *Anxiety and the anxiety disorders.* Erlbaum, Hillsdale, NJ.

Turner SM, Holtzman A, & Jacob RG (1983).Imaginal thought-stopping for compulsive looking. *Beh Modif, 7,* 576–582.

Turner RM, Steketee GS, & Foa EB (1979). Fear of criticism in washers, checkers and phobics. *Beh Res Ther, 17,* 79–81.

Turner RM, Meles D & DiTomasso R (1983). A controlled comparison among social phobics, obsessive-compulsives, agoraphobics, sexual disorders and simple phobics. *Beh Res Ther, 21,* 181–183.

Turner RM, Giles TR, & Marafiote R (1983a). Agoraphobics: A test of the repression hypothesis. *Br J Clin Psychol, 22,* 75–76.

Turner RM, Newman FI, & Foa EB (1983). Assessing the impact of cognitive differences in the treatment of obsessive-compulsives. *J Clin Psychol, 39,* 933–938.

Turner SM, Beidel DC, & Nathan RS (1985). Biological factors in obsessive-compulsive disorders. *Psychol Bull, 97,* 430–450.

Turner SM, Jacob RG, Beidel DC, & Himmelwoch J (1986). Fluoxetine treatment of obsessive-compulsive disorder. *J Clin Psychopharm* (in press).

Tyrer P, Candy J, & Kelly D (1973). Phenelzine in phobic anxiety: A controlled trial. *Psychopharmacologia, 32,* 237–254, and *Psychol Med, 3,* 120–124.

Tyrer P, Horn S, & Lee I (1976). Treatment of agoraphobia by subliminal and supraliminal exposure to phobic cine film. *Lancet, 1,* 358–360.

Tyrer P, Casey P, & Gall J (1983). Relationship between neurosis and personality disorder. *Br J Psychiat, 142,* 404–408.

Tyrer P & S (1974) School refusal, truancy and adult neurotic illness. *Psychol Med, 4,* 416–421.

Tyrer P & Steinberg D (1975). Symptomatic treatment of agoraphobia and social phobias: A followup. *Br J Pscyhiat, 127,* 163–168.

Uhde TW (1983). Caffeine/yohimbine challenge in panic disorder. Paper to Upjohn Conference on Biological Considerations in Etiology and Treatment of Panic Disorder. Boston, November.

Uhde TW, Boulenger JP, Post RM et al. (1984). Fear and anxiety: Relationship to noradrenergic function. *Psychopathology, 17,* (Supple 3), 8–23.

Uhde TW, Vittone BJ, & Post RM (1984a). Glucose tolerance testing in panic disorder. *Am J Psychiat, 141,* 1461–1463.

Uhde TW, Boulenger JP, Siever L et al. (1984b) Drug challenges in panic disorder. In *Abstracts of the Annual Meeting of APA* (Abstract 92D, p. 211). Los Angeles, May.

Uhde TW, Boulenger J-P, Roy-Byrne PP et al. (1985). Longitudinal course of panic disorder. *Prog Neuro-Psychopharm Biol Psychiat, 9,* 39–51.

Uhde TW, Roy-Byrne PP, Gold PW, Rubinow DR, Vittone BJ, & Post RM (1985a). Panic and depression: Biological relationships. Paper to APA. Dallas, May.

Uhlenhuth EH, Balter MB, Mellinger GD, Cisin IH, & Clinthorpe J (1983). Symptom checklist syndromes in the general population: Correlations with psychotherapeutic drug use. *Arch Gen Psychiat, 40,* 1167–1173.

Ullrich R & G, Crombach G, & Peikert V (1975). Three flooding procedures for agoraphobia. In Brengelmann JC (Ed.), *Progress in behaviour therapy* (pp. 59–67). Springer, NY.

Ultee CA, Griffioen D, & Schellekens J (1982). Systematic desensitization in vitro and in vivo for children's anxiety. *Beh Res Ther, 20,* 61–67.

Uno T, Greer SE, Groates SL (1973) Observational facilitation of response prevention. *Beh Res Ther, 11,* 207–212.

Ursin H (1969). The cingulate gyrus—a fear zone? *J Comp Physiol Psychol, 68,* 235–238.

Ursin H, Coover GD, Kohler C et al. (1975). Limbic structures and behavior: Endocrine correlates. In Gispen WH, van Wimersma TBG et al. (Eds.), *Progress in brain Research. Hormones, homeostasis and the brain* (vol 42, pp. 263–274).

Väisänen E (1975). Psychiatric disorders in Finland. In Anderson T, Astrup C, & Forsdahl A (Eds.), *Social, somatic and psychiatric studies of geographically defined populations. Act Psychiat Scand,* (Supp. 263), 27.

Valenta JG & Rigby MK (1968). Discrimination of the odor of stressed rats. *Science, 161,* 599–601.

Valentine CW (1930). The innate bases of fear. *J Genet Psychol, 37,* 394–419.

Valle FP (1970). Effects of strain, sex and domination on open-field behavior of rats. *Am J Psychol, 83,* 103–111.

Vandenberg SG, Clark PJ, & Samuels I (1965). Hereditability in twins' galvanic skin resistance, heartbeat and breathing rates. *Eugen Q, 12,* 7–10.

Vandenhout MA & Hessels K (1984). Deterioration of mood and elevation of anxiety in compulsive ritualising. *Can J Psychiat, 29,* 390–393.

Vandenhout MA, Vandermolen GM, Griez E, & Lousberg H (1986). Reducing vulnerability to anxiety provocation by exposure to CO_2 induced panic symptoms (in press).

Vandereycken W (1983). Agoraphobia and marital relationship: Theory, treatment and research. *Clin Psychol Rev, 3,* 317–338.

Van der Kolk BA (1984). *Post-traumatic stress disorder: Psychological and biological sequelae.* American Psychiatric Press, Washington, DC.

Van der Kolk BA et al. (1983). Traumatic and lifelong nightmares in veterans. In *Abstracts* (p. 233). Toronto.

Vandivert (1982). Scientific American.

Van Dyck R, Groeneveld-Ockhuysen AAW & Spinhoven P (1984). Hypnotizability and attitude to therapy in treating agoraphobia with hypnosis and exposure in vivo. Paper to Society of Clinical and Experimental Hypnosis. San Antonio.

Van Hasselt VB, Kazdin AE, Hersen M et al. (1985). Social skills in blind adolescents. *Beh Res Ther, 23,* 395–405.

Van Putten T & Emory WH (1973). Traumatic neuroses in Vietnam returnees. *Arch Gen Psychiat, 29,* 695–698.

Van Putten T & Yager J (1984). Post-traumatic stress disorder: Emerging from the rhetoric. *Arch Gen Psychiat, 41,* 411–413.

Van Valkenburg C, Akiskal HS, Puzantian V, & Rosenthal T (1984). Anxious Depressions: Comparisons with panic and major depressive disorders. *J Affect Dis, 6,* 67–82.

Vargo ME & Batsel WM (1984). Reduction of death anxiety: Comparison of didactic, experiential and non-conscious treatments. *Br J Med Psychol, 57,* 333–337.

Vaughan M (1976). The relationship between obsessional personality, obsessions in depression and symptoms of depression. *Br J Psychiat, 129,* 36–39.

Vermilyea JA, Boice R, & Barlow DH (1984). How do desynchronous response systems relate to the treatment of agoraphobia? *Beh Res Ther, 22,* 615–621.

Videbech T (1975). The psychopathology of anancastic endogenous depression. *Act Psychiatr Scand, 52,* 336–373.

Vincent (1919). Confessions of an agoraphobic victim. *Am J Psychol, 30,* 295–299.

Vittone BJ, Uhde TW, & Post RM (1985). Glucose intolerance and anxiety. Paper to APA. Dallas, May.

Vogel W, Peterson LE, & Broverman LK (1982). Habituation for treatment of obsessive-compulsive disorder. *Beh Res Ther, 20,* 101–104.

Volavka J, Neziroglu F, & Yaryura-Tobias JA (1985). Clomipramine and imipramine in obsessive-compulsive disorder. *Psychiat Res, 14,* 83–91.

Von Holst D (1972). Renal failure as cause of death in Tupaia belangeri exposed to persistent social stress. *J Comp Physiol, 78,* 236–273.

Wada JA (1961). Modification of cortically induced responses in brain stem of shift of attention in monkeys. *Science, 133,* 40–42.

Wahl CW & Golden JS (1963). Psychogenic urinary retention report of 6 cases. *Psychosom Med, 25,* 543–555.

Waldfogel S, Coolidge J, & Hahn P (1957). Development, meaning and management of school phobia. *Am J Orthopsychiat, 27,* 754–780.

Waldfogel S, Tessman E, & Hahn P (1969). Learning problems III: A programme for early intervention in school phobia. *Am J Orthopsychiat, 29,* 324–332.

Waldron S (1976). The significance of childhood neurosis for adult mental health: A follow-up study. *Am J Psychiat, 133,* 532.

Walk RD (1956). Self-ratings of fear in "fear-evoking" situations. *J Abn Psychol, 52,* 171–178.

Walk RD & Walters CP (1974). Importance of texture-density preferences and motion parallax for visual depth discrimination by rats and chicks. *J Comp Physiol Psychol, 86,* 309–315.

Wallen R (1945). Food aversions of normal and neurotic monkeys. *J Abn Soc Psychol, 40,* 77–81.

Wallis RS (1954). The overt fears of Dakota Indian children. *Child Dev, 25,* 185–192.

Wallnau LB & Gallup GG (1977). A serotonergic, midbrain-raphe model of tonic immobility. *Biobehav Rev, 1,* 35–43.

Wallnau LB & Gallup GG (1978). Morphine potentiation of tonic immobility. *Pharm Biochem Beh, 10,* 499–504.

Walters ET & Byrne JH (1983). Associative conditioning of single sensory neurons suggests a cellular mechanism for learning. *Science, 219,* 405–407.

Walters GC & Glazer RD (1971). Punishment of instinctive behavior in the Mongolian gerbil. *J Comp Physiol Psychol, 75,* 331–340.

Walther FR (1969). Flight behaviour and avoidance of predators in Thomson's gazelle. *Behaviour, 34,* 184–221.

Walton D & Mather MD (1963). The application of learning principles to the treatment of obsessive compulsive state in the acute and chronic phases of illness. *Beh Res Ther, 1,* 163–174.

Ward NG, Bloom VL, Fawcett J, & Friedel RO (1983). Urinary MHPG in the prediction of pain and depression relief with doxepin. *J Nerv Ment Dis, 171,* 55–58.

Wardle J (1982). Fear of dentistry. *Br J Med Psychol, 55,* 119–126.

Wardle J (1984). Dental pessimism: Negative cognitions in fearful dental patients. *Beh Res Ther, 22,* 553–556.

Wardle J & Jarvis M (1981). The paradoxical fear response to blood, injury and illness—a treatment report. *Beh Psychother, 9,* 13–24.

Warren W (1965). Adolescent psychiatric inpatients and outcome six or more years later: II. The follow-up study. *J Child Psychol Psychiat, 6,* 141–160.

Washburn SL & Devore I (1961). The social life of baboons. *Sci Am, 204,* 62–71.

Waters E, Matas L, & Sroufe LA (1975). Infants' wariness to an approaching stranger. *Child Dev, 46,* 348–356.

Watson JB & Morgan JJB (1917). Emotional reactions and psychological experimentation. *Am J Psychol, 28,* 163–174.

Watson JB & Rayner R (1920). Conditioned emotional reactions. *J Exper Psychol, 3,* 1–14.

Watson JP & Marks IM (1971). Relevant and irrelevant fear in flooding—a crossover study of phobic patients. *Beh Ther, 2,* 275–293.

Watson JP, Mullet GE, & Pillay H (1973). Prolonged group exposure for agoraphobic patients. *Beh Res Ther, 11,* 531–545.

Watson JP, Gaind R, & Marks IM (1972). Physiological habituation to continuous phobic stimulation. *Beh Res Ther, 10,* 269–278.

Watts FN (1971). Desensitization as an habituation phenomenon: I. Stimulus intensity as determinant of the effects of stimulus lengths. *Beh Res Ther, 9,* 209.

Watts FN (1973). Desensitization as an habituation phenomenon: II. Studies of interstimulus interval length. *Psychol Rep, 33,* 715.

Watts FN (1974). The control of spontaneous recovery of anxiety in imaginal desensitization. *Beh Res Ther, 12,* 57.

Waxman D (1975). Anafranil in phobic and obsessional disorders. *Scot Med J, 20,* 61–66.

Webster AS (1953). The development of phobias in married women. *Psychol Monog, 67,* whole no (367).

Weill AA (1959). Ictal emotions occurring in temporal lobe dysfunction. *Arch Neur, 1,* 87–97.

Weiss E (1964). *Agoraphobia in the light of ego psychology.* Grune and Stratton, London.

Weiss KJ & Rosenberg DJ (1985). Prevalence of anxiety disorder among alcoholics. *J Clin Psychiat, 46,* 3–5.

Weissman MM (1985). The epidemiology of anxiety disorders: Rates, risks and familial patterns. In Tuma H & Maser J (Eds.), *Anxiety and anxiety disorders* (ch 13, pp. 275–296). Erlbaum, Hillsdale, NJ.

Weissman MM, Myers JK, & Harding PS (1978). Psychiatric disorders in a US urban community. *Am J Psychiat, 135,* 459–462.

Weissman MM, Myers JK, Tischler GL, Leaf PJ, & Holzer CE (1983). Social risk factors for psychiatric disorders: Being young, poor and lonely. Paper presented to World Congress of Psychiatry. Vienna.

Weissman MM, Leckmann JF, Merikangas KR et al. (1984). Depression and anxiety disorders in parents and children. *Arch Gen Psychiat, 41,* 845–852.

Weissman MM, Leaf PJ, Holzer CE, & Merikangas KR (1985). Epidemiology of anxiety disorders. *Psychopharm Bull, 26,* 543–545.

Weizman A, Carmi M, Hermesh M et al. (1985). Decreased imipramine binding but not serotonin uptake in platelets of obsessive-compulsive adolescents and adults. In *Abstracts of the World Congress of Biological Psychiatry* (Abstract 238.3). Philadelphia.

Welch H J & Krapfl JE (1970). Order of stimulus presentation desensitization. Paper to Midwestern Psychological Association. Cincinnati, May.

Wells MJ (1968). *Lower animals.* Weidenfeld & Nicolson, London.

Welner A, Reich T, Robins I, Fishman R, & van Doren T (1976). Obsessive-compulsive neurosis: Record, follow-up, and family studies: I. Inpatient record study. *Compr Psychiat, 17,* 527–539.

Westphal C (1871–2). Die agoraphobie: eine neuropathische erscheinung. *Arch für Psychiatrie und Nervenkrankheiten, 3,* 138–171, 219–221.

Westphal C (1878) Dwangforstellungen. *Arch Psychiatr Nervenkrank, 8,* 734–750.

Whitehill MB & Hersen M (1980). *Beh Res Ther.*

Wickert F (ed.) (1947). Psychological research on problems on redistribution. Army Air Force Aviation Psychology Program Research Report No. 14. US Government Printing Office, Washington, DC.

Wheeler EO, White PD, Reed E, & Cohen ME (1948). Familial incidence of neurocirculatory asthenia ("Anxiety Neurosis," "Effort Syndrome"). *J Clin Invest, 27,* 562.

Wheeler EO et al. (1950). Neurocirculatory asthenia. 20 year followup study of 173 patients. *J Am Med Assoc, 142,* 878–889.

Whitehouse WG, Walker J, Margulies DL, & Bersh PJ (1983). Opiate antagonists overcome the learned helplessness effect but impair competent escape performance. *Physiol Beh, 30,* 731–734.

Whitfeld PI, Seeburg PH & Shine J (1982). The human pro-opiomelanocortin gene: Organization, sequence, and interspersion with repetitive DNA. *DNA, 1,* 133–143.

Wickler W (1968). *Mimicry in plants and animals.* Weidenfeld & Nicolson, London.

Wilde JF (1942). Narco-analysis for war neuroses. *Br Med J, 2,* 4.

Wilkinson CB (1983). Aftermath of a disaster: The collapse of the Hyatt Regency Hotel skywalks. *Am J Psychiat, 140,* 1134–1139.

Wilks CGW & Marks IM (1983). Reducing hypersensitive gagging. *Br Dent J, 155,* 263–265.

Williams SL & Kleifield E (1985). Transfer of behavioral change across phobias in multiply phobic clients. *Beh Modif, 9,* 22–31.

Williams CC (1981). A defense of monolithic sociobiology and genetic systicism. *Beh Brain Sci, 4,* 257.

Williams CD & Kuchta JC (1957). Exploratory behavior in two mazes with dissimilar alternatives. *J Comp Physiol Psychol, 50,* 509–513.

Williams D (1956). The structure of emotions reflected in epileptic experiences. *Brain, 79,* 29–67.

Williams GC (1966). *Adaptation and natural selection.* Princeton University Press, Princeton.

Williams GE & Johnson AM (1956). Recurrent urinary retention due to emotional factors: Report of a case. *Psychosom Med, 18,* 77–80.

Williams M, Pohl R, Rainey J, & Ettedgui E (1983). Dexamethasone test in panic disorder. In *Abstracts of the WPA Conference* (Abstract F41, p. 273). Vienna, July.

Williams SL (1984). On the nature and measurement of agoraphobia. In Hersen M et al. (Eds.), *Progress in behavior modification.* Academic, NY.

Williams SL & Rappoport A (1983). Cognitive treatment in the natural environment for agoraphobics. *Beh Ther, 14,* 299–313.

Williams SL, Dooseman G, & Kleifield (1984). Mastery and Exposure for intractable phobias. *J Consult Clin Psychol, 54,* 505–518.

Williams SL, Turner SM, & Peer DF (1985). Guided mastery and performance desensitization for severe acrophobia. *J Consult Clin Psychol, 53,* 237–247.

Willmuth R & Peters JE (1964). Recovery from traumatic experience in rats: specific "treatment" vs passage of time. *Beh Res Ther, 2,* 111–116.

Willows AOD (1971). Giant brain cells in mollusks. *Sci Am, 224,* 68–75.

Wilson GD (1966). An electrodermal technique for the study of phobias. *NZ Med J, 65,* 696–698.

Wilson GD (1967). GSR responses to fear related stimuli. *Percept Motor Skills, 24,* 401–402.

Wilson GT (1973). Innovations in the modification of phobic behaviors in two clinical cases. *Beh Ther, 4,* 426–430.

Wilson RL (1954). *The story of dentistry* (pp. 13–14). Unilever, Educational Booklet.

Windheuser HJ (1977). Anxious mothers as models for coping with anxiety. *Beh Anal Modif, 2*(1), 39–58.

Wine JJ & Krasne FB (1972). Organization of escape behavior in crayfish. *J Exp Biol,* *56,* 1–18.

Wine JJ & Krasne FB (1981). Cellular organization of crayfish escape behavior. In Bliss DE (Ed.), Vol. III: Atwood H & Sandeman D (Eds.), *Neural integration.* Academic, NY.

Wine JJ & Krasne FB (1982). *Cellular organization of crayfish escape behavior in the biology of crustacea* (vol 4). Academic, NY.

Wing L (1976). *Early childhood autism* (ch. 2, pp. 32–33). Pergamon, Oxford.

Winokur G & Holeman E (1963). Chronic anxiety neurosis: Clinical and sexual aspects. *Act Psychiat Scand, 39,* 384–412.

Winokur G & Leonard C (1963). Sexual life in patients with hysteria. *Dis Nerv Sys, 24,* 1–7.

Winokur G, Stewart M, Stern J, & Pfeiffer E (1962). A dynamic equilibrium in GSR habituation: Effect of interstimulus interval. *J Psychosom Res, 6,* 117–122.

Wittenborn JT & Holzberg JD (1951). The generality of psychiatric syndromes. *J Cons Clin Psychol, 15,* 372–380.

Wolfe JKL & Fodor IG (1977). Modifying assertive behavior in women: Comparison of three approaches. *Beh Ther, 8,* 567–574.

Wolff R (1977). Systematic desensitization and negative practice to alter the aftereffects of a rape attempt. *J Beh Ther Exp Psychiat, 8,* 423–425.

Wolff S & Wolff HG (1947). *Human gastric function.* Oxford University Press, NY.

Wolpe J (1958). *Psychotherapy by reciprocal inhibition.* Stanford University Press, Stanford.

Wood P (1941). Effort syndrome. *Br Med J, 1,* 767–772, 805–811, 845–851.

Woodruff ML & Lippincott WI (1976). Hyperemotionally and enhanced tonic immobility after rabbit septal lesions. *Brain Beh Evol, 13,* 22–33.

Woodruff ML (1977). Limbic modulation of contact defensive immobility ("animal hypnosis"). *Psychol Rec, 1,* 161–175.

Woodruff ML & Bailey SD (1979). Hippocampal lesions and immobility responses in the rat. *Physiol Psychol, 7,* 254–258.

Woodruff ML, Hatton DC, & Meyer ME (1975). Hippocampal ablation prolongs immobility response in rabbits. *J Comp Physiol Psychol, 88,* 329–334.

Woodruff ML, Baisden RH, & Douglas JR (1981). Effect of cingulate and fornix lesions on emotional behavior in rabbits *(Oryctolagus cuniculus). Exp Neurol, 74,* 379–395.

Woodruff RH, Guze SB, & Clayton PJ (1972). Anxiety neurosis among psychiatric outpatients. *Comp Psychiat, 13,* 165–170.

Woods DJ (1974). Paradoxical enhancement of learned anxiety responses. *Psychol Rep 35,* 295–304.

Woods SW, Charney DS, Loke J, Goodman WK, Redmond DE, & Heninger GR (1985). CO_2 chemoceptor sensitivity in panic patients. Paper to APA. Dallas, May.

Wooster EG (1963). Premorbid personality in depressive illness. DPM dissertation, University of London.

Wynne LC & Solomon RL (1955). Traumatic avoidance learning: Acquisition and extinction in dogs deprived of normal peripheral autonomic function. *Genet Psychol Monogr, 52,* 241–284.

Yarbus AL (1967). *Eye movements and vision.* Plenum, NY.

Yaryura-Tobias JA & Neziroglu FA (1983). *Obsessive-compulsive disorders: Pathogenesis—diagnosis—treatment.* Marcel Dekker, Basel.

Yaryura-Tobias JA, Neziroglu F, & Bergman L (1976). Chlorimipramine for obsessive-compulsive neurosis. *Curr Ther Res, 20,* 541–547.

Yerkes RM & Ada W (1936). Nature and conditions of avoidance (fear) response in chimpanzee. *J Comp Psychol, 21,* 53–66.

Yorkston N, Sergeant H, & Rachman S (1968). Methohexitone relaxation for desensitising agoraphobics. *Lancet, 2,* 651–653.

Young JPR (1971). An investigation of auditory evoked potentials in male twins. Unpublished MD thesis, Cambridge University.

Young LD, Lewis J, & McKinney WT (1975). Response to maternal separation: A reconsideration. In (Paper 105, pp. 100–101) APA, Anaheim, May.

Youssef I, Pohl R, Lycacki, & Rainey J (1985). Heart rate with isoproterenol and lactate infusions in panic disorder and controls. In *Abstracts of the World Congress of Biological Psychiatry* (Abstract 129.1). Philadelphia, September.

Yu PH, Bowen RC, Davis BA, & Boulton AA (1983). Catabolism of trace amines in agoraphobics with panics. *Can Prog Neuro-Psychopharm Biol Psychiat, 7,* 611–615.

Yuksel S, Marks IM, Ramm E, & Ghosh A (1984). Slow versus rapid exposure in vivo of phobics. *Beh Psychother, 12,* 249–256.

Yule W & Fernando P (1980). Case histories and shorter communications: Blood phobia—beware. *Beh Res Ther, 18,* 587–590.

Yule W, Sacks B, & Hersov L (1974). Successful flooding treatment of a noise phobia in an 11-year-old. *J Beh Ther Exp Psychiat, 5,* 209–211.

Zabin AM & Melamed BG (1980). Relationship between parental discipline and children's ability to cope with stress. *J Beh Assess, 2,* 17–38.

Zahn TP, Insel TR, & Murhpy DL (1984). Psychophysiologic changes during pharmacological treatment of OCD. *Br J Psychiat, 145,* 39–44.

Zanchetti A et al. (1972). Emotion and the cardiovascular system in the cat. In *CIBA Foundation Symposium 8: Physiology, emotion and psychosomatic illness.* Elsevier, NY.

Zane MD, Milt H (1984). *Your phobia.* Am Psychiat Press, Washington, DC.

Zborowski M (1952). Cultural components in response to pain. *J Soc Issues, 8,* 16–30.

Zikis P (1983). In vivo exposure and response prevention for rituals and tics in an 11-year-old girl. *Beh Psychother, 11,* 75–81.

Zitrin CM, Klein DF, & Woerner MG (1980). Treatment of agoraphobia with group exposure in vivo and imipramine. *Arch Gen Psychiat, 37,* 63–72.

Zitrin CM, Klein DF, Woerner MG, & Ross DC (1983). Treatment of phobias: I. Imipramine and placebo. *Arch Gen Psychiat, 40,* 125–138.

Zohar J, Insel T, Berman K et al. (1985). Xenon-localized cerebral blood flow during contamination of obsessive-compulsive washers. In *Abstracts of the World Congress of Biological Psychiatry* (Abstract 119.2, p. 31). Philadelphia, September.

Zohar J & Insel TR (1986). Drug treatment of OCD. *Psychiat Med,* (in press.)

Author Index

Subject Index

Continuous stimulation, ix. *See also* Massed stimulation
Controllability, 125, 134, 244, 277, 383, 510
Convergent evolution, 12, 49, 52, 58, 89–91
Cooperation as evolutionary strategy, x
Coping skills, 274–75, 478–91
Corneal reflex, 192–93, 196, 214, 289–90
Corpus callosium, 191
Cortex, cerebral, 162, 196–98, 200, 222, 224–25, 314–15, 449–50, 453
Corticosteroids, 4, 124, 126, 175, 196–97, 201, 204–5, 216–21, 223, 311
  in agoraphobia, 353–55
  in separation anxiety, 143–48, 152, 161, 164
Corticotropin-releasing hormone (CRH), 216, 223, 354
Cost-benefit analysis, 495, 520
Costs of adaptation, 15, 16
Counterconditioning, 274
Counterphobia, 6
Courage, 9, 18, 162, 243, 275, 278, 402, 407, 478. *See also* Delayed fear; Stoicism
Crawling and height fear, 129–31, 231. *See also* Delayed fear
Critical period. *See* Sensitive phases in development
Criticism, fear of, 439, 453
Crowds, fear of, 282. *See also* Agoraphobic cluster
  difference from social phobia, 363
Crypsis, 73
Cryptic immobility, 57
CS, 32, 183, 192–93, 231–78
  dissociation from US, 273, 278, 472
  duration, 250–51, 268–71
  intensity, 259–62, 266. *See also* Habituation, stimulus intensity
  termination, 246, 267, 269, 273–74, 470, 472, 493
CS-US interval and learning, 32, 34, 238–39
Culture, 33, 41, 72, 153, 165, 169, 229, 233–34, 241–43, 276, 297, 305, 363, 411, 421
  in blackbirds, 240–42
Curiosity, 29, 94, 97, 100, 163. *See also* Fascination
Cyanide, x
Cyclophosphamide, 220
Cyproheptadine, 201

Da Costa's syndrome, 166, 291
Dark, fear of, 28, 111, 128, 148–49, 151–52, 318, 328, 394, 400, 457, 491
Dating anxiety, 465, 488. *See also* Social dysfunction; Social phobia
DDAVP, 553
Death
  fear of, 150, 281, 410, 509. *See also* Cognitive fears, in agoraphobia; Illness fear
  feigning, 4. *See also* Tonic immobility
  from fear, 65, 69, 81, 215–16, 378
Defecation with fear, 4–5, 9, 28, 63, 69, 125, 153, 156–59, 201
Defecation fears. *See* Sphincteric phobias
Defense-activating system, 225
Defensive behavior. *See* Aggressive defense; Appeasement; Fear; Freezing; Withdrawal in fear
Defensive learning. *See* Aversion learning
Defensive reflexes, 177, 222
Definitions of fear, 5–7
Deflection of attack, 76–82, 93, 105, 224. *See also* Appeasement; Submission
Deimatic displays, 70–74, 259–63
DeLange syndrome, 451
Delayed fear, 4, 211, 249–51, 277, 402. *See also* Incubation

Delusion
  dysmorphophobic, 370
  illness, 413
  OCD, 430, 433, 446, 452–53
Demography, agoraphobia, 327–29. *See also* Gender; Onset age; Social class
Denial, 477. *See also* Dissociation
Dental/interposital nuclei, 192–93, 222
Dental phobia, 172, 198, 372, 381–85, 400
  physiology, 383
  prevalence, 382
  treatment, 382–85, 462, 475, 485, 491, 509–10
Dentistry, fear of doing, 385–87
Depersonalization, 291, 293, 332, 342–43, 360, 477
Depolarization, 180
Depression
  in agoraphobia, 338, 343, 345, 360, 527–59
  causing relapse, 496
  genetic aspects and fear, 168, 173–76
  neuroendocrine changes, 218
  noradrenergic effects in, 198
  in OCD, 424, 442–45, 450–53, 544–59
  relation to anxiety, 306–10
  relation to phobias and oc disorders, 247–48, 283, 287–96, 300–310, 321, 399, 410, 421–22
  in social dysfunction, 369
  in social phobia, 416
  and spontaneous panic, 339
  treatment of, 488–94
Derealization, 342, 477, 497–559. *See also* Depersonalization
Desensitization, 268, 389, 393, 395, 458–59, 461, 467, 473, 488–94, 530, 541. *See also* Exposure
  vs flooding, 473–75
Desimipramine, 544–45, 549, 552–53, 558
Despair. *See* Separation anxiety
Desynchrony. *See* Discordance of fear components
Detachment, 477. *See also* Dissociation; Separation anxiety
Development of fear, 109–53, 163, 177, 227, 231
Dexamethasone, 145, 204, 217–18, 220
Dexamethasone suppression test (DST), 218, 354, 361, 445
Diabetes insipidus and OCD, 448
Diarrhea, functional, 389
Diary, exposure homework, 461–66, 475, 488–94, 505–22, 528
Diazepam, 193, 196, 201, 480, 527, 534–37, 541, 544, 558
Diclotensine, 533
Diencephalon, 190
Differential conditioning. *See* Conditioning
Dilution of danger in groups, 85–88, 92
Diphenylhydantoin, 215
Dirt, fear of, 282, 290, 298, 424, 427–44, 515. *See also* Obsessive-compulsive disorder; Rituals
Disaster
  fear of, 395
  reaction to, 141–42, 401–3. *See also* Harming, fear of
Discomfort intolerance, 340–41, 358
Discordance of fear components, 8, 9, 24, 212–13, 217–19, 223, 227, 246, 269, 277, 312, 315–18, 514. *See also* Components of fear
Discrimination of emotions, 122, 237
Discriminative stimulus, 252
  for acquisition vs. extinction, 273–74, 278
Disease fear. *See* Illness fear; Obsessive-compulsive disorder
Dishabituation, 243, 257–60, 265–66. 278, 496
Displacement activity, 14, 245, 277

Taxon Index